Organizational Behaviour

PEARSON

At Pearson, we take learning personally. Our courses and resources are available as books, online and via multi-lingual packages, helping people learn whatever, wherever and however they choose.

We work with leading authors to develop the strongest learning experiences, bringing cutting-edge thinking and best learning practice to a global market. We craft our print and digital resources to do more to help learners not only understand their content, but to see it in action and apply what they learn, whether studying or at work.

Pearson is the world's leading learning company. Our portfolio includes Penguin, Dorling Kindersley, the Financial Times and our educational business, Pearson International. We are also a leading provider of electronic learning programmes and of test development, processing and scoring services to educational institutions, corporations and professional bodies around the world.

Every day our work helps learning flourish, and wherever learning flourishes, so do people.

To learn more please visit us at: **www.pearson.com/uk**

Andrzej A. **Huczynski**

David A. **Buchanan**

Organizational Behaviour

Eighth edition

PEARSON

Harlow, England • London • New York • Boston • San Francisco • Toronto • Sydney • Auckland • Singapore • Hong Kong
Tokyo • Seoul • Taipei • New Delhi • Cape Town • São Paulo • Mexico City • Madrid • Amsterdam • Munich • Paris • Milan

Pearson Education Limited
Edinburgh Gate
Harlow CM20 2JE
United Kingdom
Tel: +44 (0)1279 623623
Web: www.pearson.com/uk

First published by Prentice Hall International (UK) Ltd 1985 (print)
Second edition published by Prentice Hall International (UK) Ltd 1991 (print)
Third edition published by Prentice Hall Europe 1997 (print)
Fourth edition published by Pearson Education Ltd 2001 (print)
Fifth edition published 2004 (print)
Sixth edition published 2007 (print)
Seventh edition published 2010 (print)
Eighth edition published 2013 (print and electronic)

ISBN: 978-0-273-77481-5 (print)
978-1-292-00877-6 (PDF)
978-1-292-00878-3 (eText)

British Library Cataloguing-in-Publication Data
A catalogue record for the print edition is available from the British Library

Library of Congress Cataloging-in-Publication Data
Huczynski, Andrzej.
Organizational behaviour / Andrzej A. Huczynski, University of Glasgow School of Business, David A. Buchanan, Cranfield University School of Management. -- Eighth edition.
pages cm
ISBN 978-0-273-77481-5
1. Organizational behavior. I. Buchanan, David A. II. Title.
HD58.7.H83 2013
302.3'5--dc23

2013011950

10 9 8 7 6 5 4 3
17 16 15

Print edition typeset in 9/12pt Slimbach Std by 35
Print edition printed and bound by L.E.G.O. S.p.A., Italy

NOTE THAT ANY PAGE CROSS REFERENCES REFER TO THE PRINT EDITION.

From Andrzej

To Janet, Sophie, Gregory, Tom, Magnus, Freya, and Rosa

From David

To Lesley, Andrew, Mairi, Rachel, Séan, Charlie, Cíara, and Archie

Outline contents

Full contents

Guided tour

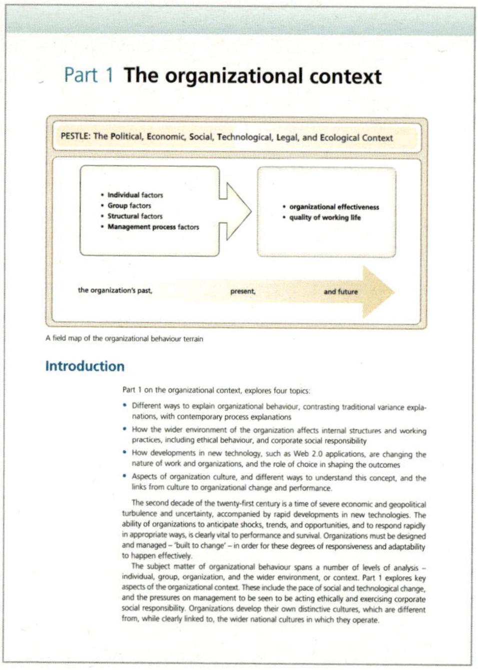

Part 1 The organizational context

PESTLE: The Political, Economic, Social, Technological, Legal, and Ecological Context

- Individual factors
- Group factors
- Structural factors
- Management process factors

- organizational effectiveness
- quality of working life

the organization's past, present, and future

A field map of the organizational behaviour terrain

Introduction

Part 1 on the organizational context, explores four topics:

- Different ways to explain organizational behaviour, contrasting traditional variance explanations, with contemporary process explanations
- How the wider environment of the organization affects internal structures and working practices, including ethical behaviour, and corporate social responsibility
- How developments in new technology, such as Web 2.0 applications, are changing the nature of work and organizations, and the role of choice in shaping the outcomes
- Aspects of organization culture, and different ways to understand this concept, and the links from culture to organizational change and performance.

The second decade of the twenty-first century is a time of severe economic and geopolitical turbulence and uncertainty, accompanied by rapid developments in new technologies. The ability of organizations to anticipate shocks, trends, and opportunities, and to respond rapidly in appropriate ways, is clearly vital to performance and survival. Organizations must be designed and managed – 'built to change' – in order for these degrees of responsiveness and adaptability to happen effectively.

The subject matter of organizational behaviour spans a number of levels of analysis – individual, group, organization, and the wider environment, or context. Part 1 explores key aspects of the organizational context. These include the pace of social and technological change, and the pressures on management to be seen to be acting ethically and exercising corporate social responsibility. Organizations develop their own distinctive cultures, which are different from, while clearly linked to, the wider national cultures in which they operate.

Invitation to see 3

A recurring theme in this text concerns the design of jobs, and the organization and experience of work. The organization of work reflects a number of influences, at different levels of analysis. We explain how the experience and organization of work is influenced by

- *contextual* factors, in Chapter 2;
- *technological* factors, in Chapter 3;
- *psychological* factors, in Chapter 9;
- *social psychological* factors, in Chapter 13;
- *historical* factors, in Chapter 15;
- *power and political* factors, in Chapter 22.

Invitation to see

Liang Xiaopeng/Color China Photo/PA Photos

This photograph, taken in a Chinese textiles manufacturing plant, appeared in The Sunday Times, 17 June 2012, p. 3

1. **Decoding**: Look at this image closely. Note in as much detail as possible what messages you feel that it is trying to convey. Does it tell a story, present a point of view, support an argument, perpetuate a myth, reinforce a stereotype, challenge a stereotype?
2. **Challenging**: To what extent do you agree with the messages, stories, points of view, arguments, myths, or stereotypes in this image? Is this image open to challenge, to criticism, or to interpretation and decoding in other ways, revealing other messages?
3. **Sharing**: Compare with colleagues your interpretation of this image. Explore explanations for differences in your respective decodings.

Part openers – the book is divided into five **parts**. Each part begins with a **part map** and a full **introduction**, making the structure of the book more transparent and easier to navigate

Invitation to see – explore how work and organizations are presented in the media through images. Learn how to analyse and 'decode' the messages within the image

4 Part 1 The organizational context

You're the employee: what would you do?

You are 25 years old, and a member of 'Generation Y'. How would you advise this manager to address his problem?

Help me generate results from Generation Y staff. I'm the Managing Director of a small firm operating in a high-pressure environment. Despite high attrition in our industry, our team prides itself on good management practice as well as getting results. However, with new starters now having an average age of 25, I am finding that since I was young (I'm now 40), a lot has changed. Attitudes have been transformed – but not for the better. Not only are we having to work harder to attract our recruits, but we are finding that in their first few months we have to 'counsel' them to see the bigger picture.

For example, we have always motivated our team by offering a modest basic salary, plus performance-related bonuses. But, increasingly, we are finding that our recruits are perfectly content to earn just the basic.

The younger generation now have higher expectations. This is great, but all too often they seem to expect too much, too soon – without putting in the necessary work. As someone who climbed to the top through hard graft, I find this bewildering. How can I motivate our new starters and channel their energies in the right direction?

From 'Troubleshooter', People Management, *15 May 2008, pp. 50–51.*

What would you do?: solve real-life problems to help you relate Organizational Behaviour theory to practice

Chapter contents – navigate each chapter easily using the contents list provided at the beginning of each chapter

Key terms – those mentioned in each chapter are listed for reference here, with definitions available in the margins and the **Glossary**

Learning outcomes – clear learning outcomes, which you should be able to achieve, are listed at the beginning of each chapter. A **Recap** feature at the end of the chapter can be used as a reminder and for revision

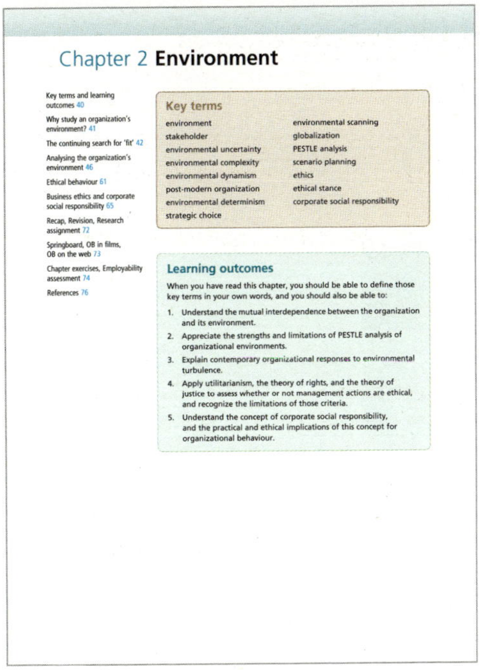
Chapter 2 **Environment**

Key terms

environment
stakeholder
environmental uncertainty
environmental complexity
environmental dynamism
post-modern organization
environmental determinism
strategic choice
environmental scanning
globalization
PESTLE analysis
scenario planning
ethics
ethical stance
corporate social responsibility

Learning outcomes

When you have read this chapter, you should be able to define those key terms in your own words, and you should also be able to:

1. Understand the mutual interdependence between the organization and its environment.
2. Appreciate the strengths and limitations of PESTLE analysis of organizational environments.
3. Explain contemporary organizational responses to environmental turbulence.
4. Apply utilitarianism, the theory of rights, and the theory of justice to assess whether or not management actions are ethical, and recognize the limitations of those criteria.
5. Understand the concept of corporate social responsibility, and the practical and ethical implications of this concept for organizational behaviour.

Why study . . . ? – each chapter begins with a discussion about why you should study the subject and what is important to understand

Key terms – those introduced at the start of the chapter are highlighted in the text where they first appear, with a brief explanation provided in the margin

Why study an organization's environment? 41

Why study an organization's environment?

Should that have happened?

Lee and Charlie

Lee is 61 and has been director of engineering for Burnside Semiconductors for fourteen years. Intelligent and with a reputation as a good manager, he has not kept up to date with technological developments. The manufacturing process produces toxic waste, and Lee's casual approach to disposal has culminated in two court cases which could cost the company considerable sums in damages. The company's executive vice president, Charlie, has tried for about three years to persuade Lee to prioritize the disposal problem, without success. Having decided that Lee should be removed from his position, Charlie is reluctant to fire him as that would demoralize other managers. He therefore tells colleagues, informally, that he is not satisfied with Lee's work, and exaggerates Lee's faults in these conversations. When Lee encounters a growing lack of support from colleagues, he decides to take early retirement.

Is Charlie's approach ethical?

Environment issues, trends, and events outside the boundaries of the organization, which influence internal decisions and behaviours.

Stakeholder anyone who is concerned with how an organization operates, and who will be affected by its decisions and actions.

An organization must interact with the outside world, with its **environment**. The operations of any organization – local café, city hospital, multinational car-producing company – can be described in terms of 'import-transformation-export' processes. The car plant imports materials, components, equipment, staff, and energy. It then transforms these resources into vehicles, which are exported to customers through online sales outlets or a dealer network. Organizations are involved in a constant series of exchanges with their suppliers, consumers, regulatory agencies, and other **stakeholders**, including their employees.

The environment for a car plant in the twenty-first century is complex. The costs of oil and petrol are high, and are sensitive to unpredictable geopolitical trends. The development of hybrid and electric-powered vehicles is starting to erode sales of petrol-driven cars. The industry consolidation of the late 1990s saw many smaller manufacturers (Saab, Rover, Rolls-Royce, Jaguar, Land Rover, Volvo) bought by larger companies (General Motors, BMW, Ford, the Tata Group). Competition encourages manufacturers to locate plants in low-wage countries (Hungary, Brazil, Romania) generating resentment in traditional manufacturing bases (America, Britain, Europe). In Japan, *gaiatsu*, or foreign pressure, led to restructuring at Toyota, Honda, and Nissan in the late 1990s.

Cost competition has encouraged the use of 'lean manufacturing' methods, with consequences for working practices and quality of working life. There is concern over the environmental pollution generated by internal combustion engines which burn petrol and diesel oil, encouraging the development of cleaner engines to reduce carbon emissions. The volume of traffic in many cities around the world has driven governments to consider road pricing, congestion charges, and taxes to encourage the use of public transport. These are just some of the factors in the external environment of a car plant. Such factors force constant adjustments to ways of thinking about the business of making cars. This means always thinking about the organization's business strategy, organization structure, use of resources, management decisions, job design, and working practices.

STOP AND THINK

What other factors, trends or developments in the external environment of a car plant have not been mentioned? How will these affect the company's behaviour?

What are the main factors in the environment of your college or university? How are those factors influencing management actions – and how are these affecting you?

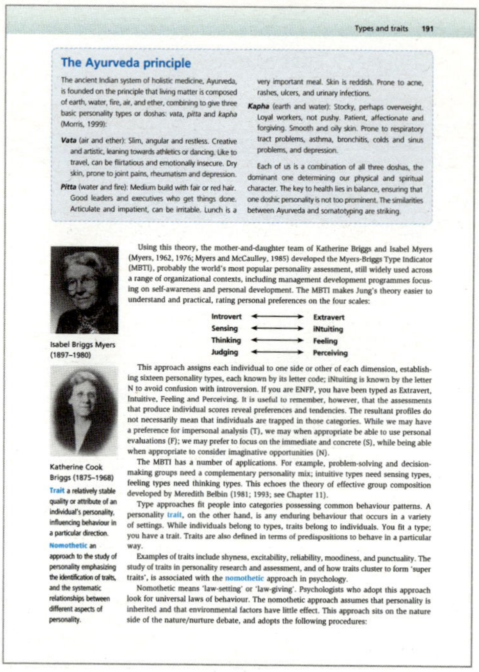

The Ayurveda principle

The ancient Indian system of holistic medicine, Ayurveda, is founded on the principle that living matter is composed of earth, water, fire, air, and ether, combining to give three basic personality types or doshas: *vata*, *pitta* and *kapha* (Morris, 1999):

Vata (air and ether): Slim, angular and restless. Creative and artistic, leaning towards athletics or dancing. Like to travel, can be flirtatious and emotionally insecure. Dry skin, prone to joint pains, rheumatism and depression.

Pitta (water and fire): Medium build with fair or red hair. Good leaders and executives who get things done. Articulate and impatient, can be irritable. Lunch is a very important meal. Skin is reddish. Prone to acne, rashes, ulcers, and urinary infections.

Kapha (earth and water): Stocky, perhaps overweight. Loyal workers, not pushy. Patient, affectionate and forgiving. Smooth and oily skin. Prone to respiratory tract problems, asthma, bronchitis, colds and sinus problems, and depression.

Each of us is a combination of all three doshas, the dominant one determining our physical and spiritual character. The key to health lies in balance, ensuring that one doshic personality is not too prominent. The similarities between Ayurveda and somatotyping are striking.

Isabel Briggs Myers (1897–1980)

Katherine Cook Briggs (1875–1968)

Trait a relatively stable quality or attribute of an individual's personality, influencing behaviour in a particular direction.

Nomothetic an approach to the study of personality emphasizing the identification of traits, and the systematic relationships between different aspects of personality.

Using this theory, the mother-and-daughter team of Katherine Briggs and Isabel Myers (Myers, 1962, 1976; Myers and McCaulley, 1985) developed the Myers-Briggs Type Indicator (MBTI), probably the world's most popular personality assessment, still widely used across a range of organizational contexts, including management development programmes focusing on self-awareness and personal development. The MBTI makes Jung's theory easier to understand and practical, rating personal preferences on the four scales:

Introvert ←→ **Extravert**
Sensing ←→ **iNtuiting**
Thinking ←→ **Feeling**
Judging ←→ **Perceiving**

This approach assigns each individual to one side or other of each dimension, establishing sixteen personality types, each known by its letter code; iNtuiting is known by the letter N to avoid confusion with introversion. If you are ENFP, you have been typed as Extravert, Intuitive, Feeling and Perceiving. It is useful to remember, however, that the assessments that produce individual scores reveal preferences and tendencies. The resultant profiles do not necessarily mean that individuals are trapped in those categories. While we may have a preference for impersonal analysis (T), we may when appropriate be able to use personal evaluations (F); we may prefer to focus on the immediate and concrete (S), while being able when appropriate to consider imaginative opportunities (N).

The MBTI has a number of applications. For example, problem-solving and decision-making groups need a complementary personality mix; intuitive types need sensing types, feeling types need thinking types. This echoes the theory of effective group composition developed by Meredith Belbin (1981; 1993; see Chapter 11).

Type approaches fit people into categories possessing common behaviour patterns. A personality trait, on the other hand, is any enduring behaviour that occurs in a variety of settings. While individuals belong to types, traits belong to individuals. You fit a type; you have a trait. Traits are also defined in terms of predispositions to behave in a particular way.

Examples of traits include shyness, excitability, reliability, moodiness, and punctuality. The study of traits in personality research and assessment, and of how traits cluster to form 'super traits', is associated with the nomothetic approach in psychology.

Nomothetic means 'law-setting' or 'law-giving'. Psychologists who adopt this approach look for universal laws of behaviour. The nomothetic approach assumes that personality is inherited and that environmental factors have little effect. This approach sits on the nature side of the nature/nurture debate, and adopts the following procedures:

Boxed features – **application** and **illustration** of concepts, theories and frameworks are discussed throughout the text. Boxed features highlight specific areas of interest, classic research, management applications, international examples and social commentary

Portraits – images of the leading scholars who have contributed to our understanding of the subject are included throughout

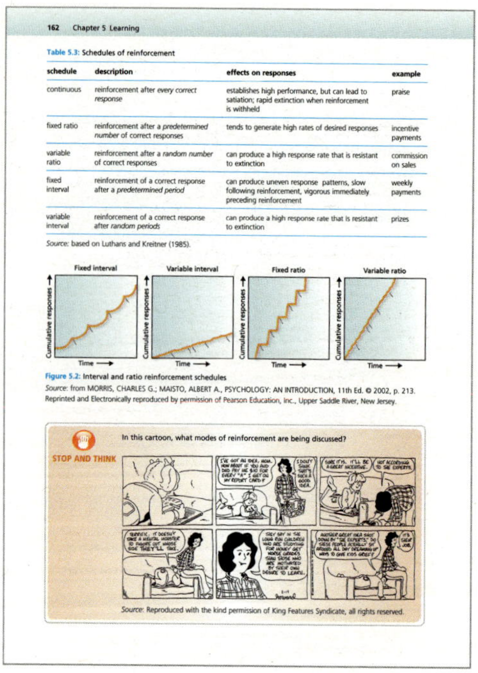

Table 5.3: Schedules of reinforcement

schedule	description	effects on responses	example
continuous	reinforcement after *every correct response*	establishes high performance, but can lead to satiation; rapid extinction when reinforcement is withheld	praise
fixed ratio	reinforcement after a *predetermined number* of correct responses	tends to generate high rates of desired responses	incentive payments
variable ratio	reinforcement after a *random number* of correct responses	can produce a high response rate that is resistant to extinction	commission on sales
fixed interval	reinforcement of a correct response after a *predetermined period*	can produce uneven response patterns, slow following reinforcement, vigorous immediately preceding reinforcement	weekly payments
variable interval	reinforcement of a correct response after *random periods*	can produce a high response rate that is resistant to extinction	prizes

Source: based on Luthans and Kreitner (1985).

Figure 5.2: Interval and ratio reinforcement schedules

Source: from MORRIS, CHARLES G.; MAISTO, ALBERT A., PSYCHOLOGY: AN INTRODUCTION, 11th Ed. © 2002, p. 213. Reprinted and Electronically reproduced by permission of Pearson Education, Inc., Upper Saddle River, New Jersey.

STOP AND THINK

In this cartoon, what modes of reinforcement are being discussed?

Source: Reproduced with the kind permission of King Features Syndicate, all rights reserved.

Highly illustrated and accessible – **cartoons**, **images**, **tables** and **diagrams** feature throughout the text to make the book more engaging and accessible

Stop and think – featuring frequently throughout the text, you are invited to consider contradictory and controversial points and arguments and encouraged to apply ideas and analysis to your own experience and challenge your own assumptions

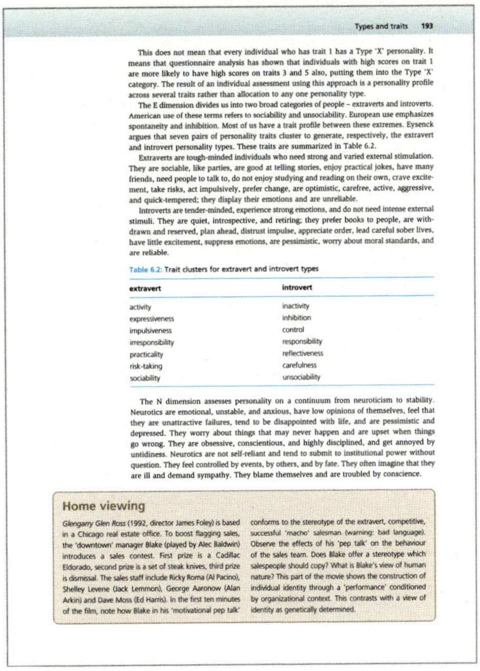

Types and traits 193

This does not mean that every individual who has trait 1 has a Type 'X' personality. It means that questionnaire analysis has shown that individuals with high scores on trait 1 are more likely to have high scores on traits 3 and 5 also, putting them into the Type 'X' category. The result of an individual assessment using this approach is a personality profile across several traits rather than allocation to any one personality type.

The E dimension divides us into two broad categories of people – extraverts and introverts. American use of these terms refers to sociability and unsociability. European use emphasizes spontaneity and inhibition. Most of us have a trait profile between these extremes. Eysenck argues that seven pairs of personality traits cluster to generate, respectively, the extravert and introvert personality types. These traits are summarized in Table 6.2.

Extraverts are tough-minded individuals who need strong and varied external stimulation. They are sociable, like parties, are good at telling stories, enjoy practical jokes, have many friends, need people to talk to, do not enjoy studying and reading on their own, crave excitement, take risks, act impulsively, prefer change, are optimistic, carefree, active, aggressive, and quick-tempered; they display their emotions and are unreliable.

Introverts are tender-minded, experience strong emotions, and do not need intense external stimuli. They are quiet, introspective, and retiring; they prefer books to people, are withdrawn and reserved, plan ahead, distrust impulse, appreciate order, lead careful sober lives, have little excitement, suppress emotions, are pessimistic, worry about moral standards, and are reliable.

Table 6.2: Trait clusters for extravert and introvert types

extravert	introvert
activity	inactivity
expressiveness	inhibition
impulsiveness	control
irresponsibility	responsibility
practicality	reflectiveness
risk-taking	carefulness
sociability	unsociability

The N dimension assesses personality on a continuum from neuroticism to stability. Neurotics are emotional, unstable, and anxious, have low opinions of themselves, feel that they are unattractive failures, tend to be disappointed with life, and are pessimistic and depressed. They worry about things that may never happen and are upset when things go wrong. They are obsessive, conscientious, and highly disciplined, and get annoyed by untidiness. Neurotics are not self-reliant and tend to submit to institutional power without question. They feel controlled by events, by others, and by fate. They often imagine that they are ill and demand sympathy. They blame themselves and are troubled by conscience.

Home viewing

Glengarry Glen Ross (1992, director James Foley) is based in a Chicago real estate office. To boost flagging sales, the 'downtown' manager Blake (played by Alec Baldwin) introduces a sales contest. First prize is a Cadillac Eldorado, second prize is a set of steak knives, third prize is dismissal. The sales staff include Ricky Roma (Al Pacino), Shelley Levene (Jack Lemmon), George Aaronow (Alan Arkin) and Dave Moss (Ed Harris). In the first ten minutes of the film, note how Blake in his 'motivational pep talk' conforms to the stereotype of the extravert, competitive, successful 'macho' salesman (warning: bad language). Observe the effects of his 'pep talk' on the behaviour of the sales team. Does Blake offer a stereotype which salespeople should copy? What is Blake's view of human nature? This part of the movie shows the construction of individual identity through a 'performance' conditioned by organizational context. This contrasts with a view of identity as genetically determined.

Home viewing – suggests films you can watch that illustrate particular points and topics in the text

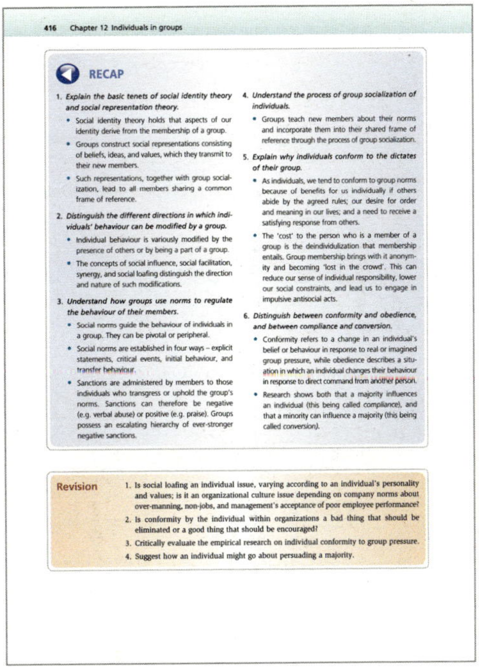

416 Chapter 12 Individuals in groups

RECAP

1. *Explain the basic tenets of social identity theory and social representation theory.*
   - Social identity theory holds that aspects of our identity derive from the membership of a group.
   - Groups construct social representations consisting of beliefs, ideas, and values, which they transmit to their new members.
   - Such representations, together with group socialization, lead to all members sharing a common frame of reference.
2. *Distinguish the different directions in which individuals' behaviour can be modified by a group.*
   - Individual behaviour is variously modified by the presence of others or by being a part of a group.
   - The concepts of social influence, social facilitation, synergy, and social loafing distinguish the direction and nature of such modifications.
3. *Understand how groups use norms to regulate the behaviour of their members.*
   - Social norms guide the behaviour of individuals in a group. They can be pivotal or peripheral.
   - Social norms are established in four ways – explicit statements, critical events, initial behaviour, and transfer behaviour.
   - Sanctions are administered by members to those individuals who transgress or uphold the group's norms. Sanctions can therefore be negative (e.g. verbal abuse) or positive (e.g. praise). Groups possess an escalating hierarchy of ever-stronger negative sanctions.
4. *Understand the process of group socialization of individuals.*
   - Groups teach new members about their norms and incorporate them into their shared frame of reference through the process of group socialization.
5. *Explain why individuals conform to the dictates of their group.*
   - As individuals, we tend to conform to group norms because of benefits for us individually if others abide by the agreed rules; our desire for order and meaning in our lives; and a need to receive a satisfying response from others.
   - The 'cost' to the person who is a member of a group is the deindividuation that membership entails. Group membership brings with it anonymity and becoming 'lost in the crowd'. This can reduce our sense of individual responsibility, lower our social constraints, and lead us to engage in impulsive antisocial acts.
6. *Distinguish between conformity and obedience, and between compliance and conversion.*
   - Conformity refers to a change in an individual's belief or behaviour in response to real or imagined group pressure, while obedience describes a situation in which an individual changes their behaviour in response to direct command from another person.
   - Research shows both that a majority influences an individual (this being called compliance), and that a minority can influence a majority (this being called conversion).

Revision

1. Is social loafing an individual issue, varying according to an individual's personality and values; is it an organizational culture issue depending on company norms about over-manning, non-jobs, and management's acceptance of poor employee performance?
2. Is conformity by the individual within organizations a bad thing that should be eliminated or a good thing that should be encouraged?
3. Critically evaluate the empirical research on individual conformity to group pressure.
4. Suggest how an individual might go about persuading a majority.

Recap – summaries the Learning outcomes listed at the beginning of the chapter. You can use these as a 'checklist' for your own learning

Revision – a series of typical essay questions, encapsulating the learning outcomes, which you can use for personal study or as tutorial revision aids

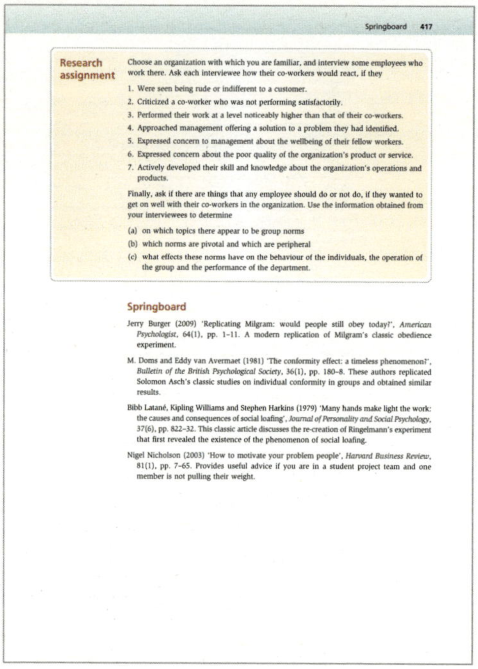

Springboard 417

Research assignment

Choose an organization with which you are familiar, and interview some employees who work there. Ask each interviewee how their co-workers would react, if they

1. Were seen being rude or indifferent to a customer.
2. Criticized a co-worker who was not performing satisfactorily.
3. Performed their work at a level noticeably higher than that of their co-workers.
4. Approached management offering a solution to a problem they had identified.
5. Expressed concern to management about the wellbeing of their fellow workers.
6. Expressed concern about the poor quality of the organization's product or service.
7. Actively developed their skill and knowledge about the organization's operations and products.

Finally, ask if there are things that any employee should do or not do, if they wanted to get on well with their co-workers in the organization. Use the information obtained from your interviewees to determine

(a) on which topics there appear to be group norms
(b) which norms are pivotal and which are peripheral
(c) what effects these norms have on the behaviour of the individuals, the operation of the group and the performance of the department.

Springboard

Jerry Burger (2009) 'Replicating Milgram: would people still obey today?', *American Psychologist*, 64(1), pp. 1-11. A modern replication of Milgram's classic obedience experiment.

M. Doms and Eddy van Avermaet (1981) 'The conformity effect: a timeless phenomenon?', *Bulletin of the British Psychological Society*, 36(1), pp. 180–8. These authors replicated Solomon Asch's classic studies on individual conformity in groups and obtained similar results.

Bibb Latané, Kipling Williams and Stephen Harkins (1979) 'Many hands make light the work: the causes and consequences of social loafing', *Journal of Personality and Social Psychology*, 37(6), pp. 822–32. This classic article discusses the re-creation of Ringelmann's experiment that first revealed the existence of the phenomenon of social loafing.

Nigel Nicholson (2003) 'How to motivate your problem people', *Harvard Business Review*, 81(1), pp. 7–65. Provides useful advice if you are in a student project team and one member is not pulling their weight.

Research assignment – provides an opportunity to test your knowledge and take your learning further

Springboard – a short annotated guide to some further reading and more advanced study

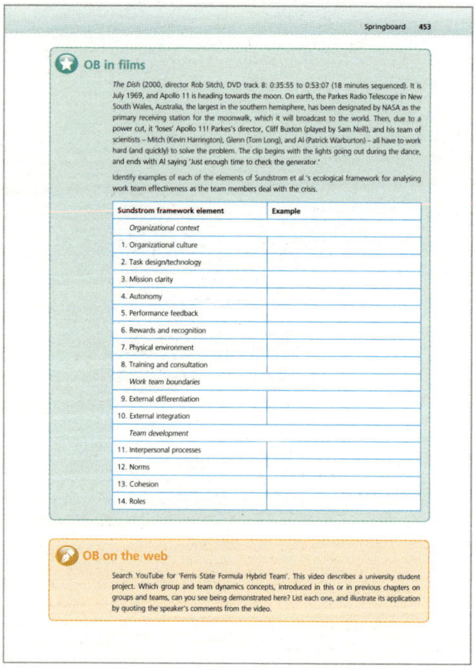

Springboard 453

OB in films

The Dish (2000, director Rob Sitch), DVD track 8: 0:35:55 to 0:53:07 (18 minutes sequenced). It is July 1969, and Apollo 11 is heading towards the moon. On earth, the Parkes Radio Telescope in New South Wales, Australia, the largest in the southern hemisphere, has been designated by NASA as the primary receiving station for the moonwalk, which it will broadcast to the world. Then, due to a power cut, it 'loses' Apollo 11! Parkes's director, Cliff Buxton (played by Sam Neill), and his team of scientists – Mitch (Kevin Harrington), Glenn (Tom Long), and Al (Patrick Warburton) – all have to work hard (and quickly) to solve the problem. The clip begins with the lights going out during the dance, and ends with Al saying 'Just enough time to check the generator.'

Identify examples of each of the elements of Sundstrom et al.'s ecological framework for analysing work team effectiveness as the team members deal with the crisis.

Sundstrom framework element	Example
Organizational context	
1. Organizational culture	
2. Task design/technology	
3. Mission clarity	
4. Autonomy	
5. Performance feedback	
6. Rewards and recognition	
7. Physical environment	
8. Training and consultation	
Work team boundaries	
9. External differentiation	
10. External integration	
Team development	
11. Interpersonal processes	
12. Norms	
13. Cohesion	
14. Roles	

OB on the web

Search YouTube for 'Ferris State Formula Hybrid Team'. This video describes a university student project. Which group and team dynamics concepts, introduced in this or in previous chapters on groups and teams, can you see being demonstrated here? List each one, and illustrate its application by quoting the speaker's comments from the video.

OB in films – identifies films or television programmes that illustrate the wider relevance and application of the issues and ideas introduced in the chapter

OB on the web – suggests internet sources that further illustrate particular concepts and themes from the chapter and suggest activities you can perform to test and apply the concepts and themes

Chapter exercises – each chapter contains two exercises, one designed for large classes and the other for smaller tutorial and seminar settings

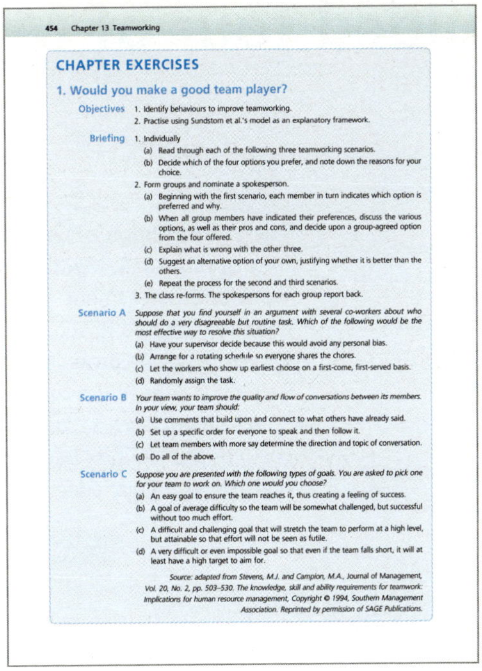

454 Chapter 13 Teamworking

CHAPTER EXERCISES

1. Would you make a good team player?

Objectives
1. Identify behaviours to improve teamworking.
2. Practise using Sundstom et al.'s model as an explanatory framework.

Briefing
1. Individually
   - (a) Read through each of the following three teamworking scenarios.
   - (b) Decide which of the four options you prefer, and note down the reasons for your choice.
2. Form groups and nominate a spokesperson.
   - (a) Beginning with the first scenario, each member in turn indicates which option is preferred and why.
   - (b) When all group members have indicated their preferences, discuss the various options, as well as their pros and cons, and decide upon a group-agreed option from the four offered.
   - (c) Explain what is wrong with the other three.
   - (d) Suggest an alternative option of your own, justifying whether it is better than the others.
   - (e) Repeat the process for the second and third scenarios.
3. The class re-forms. The spokespersons for each group report back.

Scenario A *Suppose that you find yourself in an argument with several co-workers about who should do a very disagreeable but routine task. Which of the following would be the most effective way to resolve this situation?*
- (a) Have your supervisor decide because this would avoid any personal bias.
- (b) Arrange for a rotating schedule so everyone shares the chores.
- (c) Let the workers who show up earliest choose on a first-come, first-served basis.
- (d) Randomly assign the task.

Scenario B *Your team wants to improve the quality and flow of conversations between its members. In your view, your team should:*
- (a) Use comments that build upon and connect to what others have already said.
- (b) Set up a specific order for everyone to speak and then follow it.
- (c) Let team members with more say determine the direction and topic of conversation.
- (d) Do all of the above.

Scenario C *Suppose you are presented with the following types of goals. You are asked to pick one for your team to work on. Which one would you choose?*
- (a) An easy goal to ensure the team reaches it, thus creating a feeling of success.
- (b) A goal of average difficulty so the team will be somewhat challenged, but successful without too much effort.
- (c) A difficult and challenging goal that will stretch the team to perform at a high level, but attainable so that effort will not be seen as futile.
- (d) A very difficult or even impossible goal so that even if the team falls short, it will at least have a high target to aim for.

Source: adapted from Stevens, M.J. and Campion, M.A., Journal of Management, Vol. 20, No. 2, pp. 503–530. The knowledge, skill and ability requirements for teamwork: Implications for human resource management, Copyright © 1994, Southern Management Association. Reprinted by permission of SAGE Publications.

Employability assessment – improve your employability by identifying significant issues from the chapter, relating them to employability competencies and deciding what actions you need to take in order to maintain and develop them

References – each chapter ends with a detailed list of references utilized in the chapter, covering the latest and classic research. Use these to take your study further

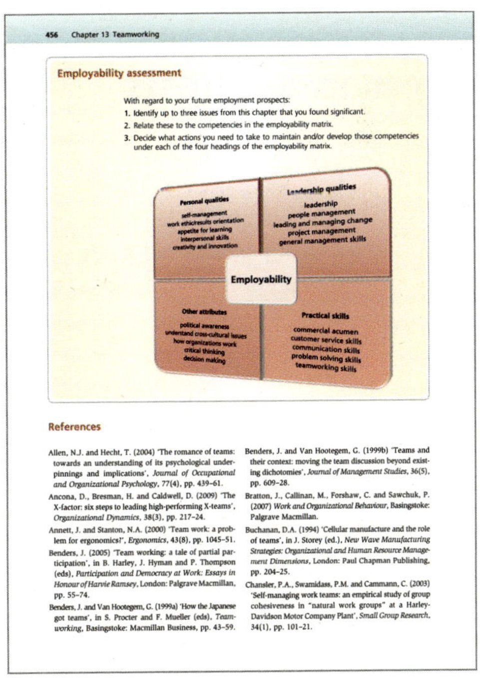

456 Chapter 13 Teamworking

Employability assessment

With regard to your future employment prospects:
1. Identify up to three issues from this chapter that you found significant.
2. Relate these to the competencies in the employability matrix.
3. Decide what actions you need to take to maintain and/or develop those competencies under each of the four headings of the employability matrix.

References

Allen, N.J. and Hecht, T. (2004) 'The romance of teams: towards an understanding of its psychological underpinnings and implications', *Journal of Occupational and Organizational Psychology*, 77(4), pp. 439–61.

Ancona, D., Bresman, H. and Caldwell, D. (2009) 'The X-factor: six steps to leading high-performing X-teams', *Organizational Dynamics*, 38(3), pp. 217–24.

Annett, J. and Stanton, N.A. (2000) 'Team work: a problem for ergonomics?', *Ergonomics*, 43(8), pp. 1045–51.

Benders, J. (2005) 'Team working: a tale of partial participation', in B. Harley, J. Hyman and P. Thompson (eds), *Participation and Democracy at Work: Essays in Honour of Harvie Ramsey*, London: Palgrave Macmillan, pp. 55–74.

Benders, J. and Van Hootegem, G. (1999a) 'How the Japanese got teams', in S. Procter and F. Mueller (eds), *Teamworking*, Basingstoke: Macmillan Business, pp. 43–59.

Benders, J. and Van Hootegem, G. (1999b) 'Teams and their context: moving the team discussion beyond existing dichotomies', *Journal of Management Studies*, 36(5), pp. 609–28.

Bratton, J., Callinan, M., Forshaw, C. and Sawchuk, P. (2007) *Work and Organizational Behaviour*, Basingstoke: Palgrave Macmillan.

Buchanan, D.A. (1994) 'Cellular manufacture and the role of teams', in J. Storey (ed.), *New Wave Manufacturing Strategies: Organizational and Human Resource Management Dimensions*, London: Paul Chapman Publishing, pp. 204–25.

Chansler, P.A., Swamidass, P.M. and Cammann, C. (2003) 'Self-managing work teams: an empirical study of group cohesiveness in "natural work groups" at a Harley-Davidson Motor Company Plant', *Small Group Research*, 34(1), pp. 101–21.

Guided tour of MyManagementLab

The eighth edition of *Organizational Behaviour* comes with **MyManagementLab**. Available from spring 2014, MyManagementLab is an online resource bank, offering a tutorial, homework and assessment system for Management and Organizational Behaviour courses. It enables lecturers to set assignments and use an online gradebook to track student progress. For students, it provides interactive, multimedia experiences that support your learning, helping you to revise and practise via a personalized study plan.

A student access code card may have been included with your textbook at a reduced cost. If you do not have an access code, you can buy access online. To buy access or register with your code, visit www.mymanagementlab.com.

Study plan and tests

MyManagementLab features a wealth of resources that help you to test your understanding of your course material and track your improvement over time. For every chapter, you can complete a *pre test* set of multiple-choice questions and, based on your performance, receive a personalized study plan tailored to help you in the areas where you most need to make improvements. Then, try the *post test* to see how much you've learned.

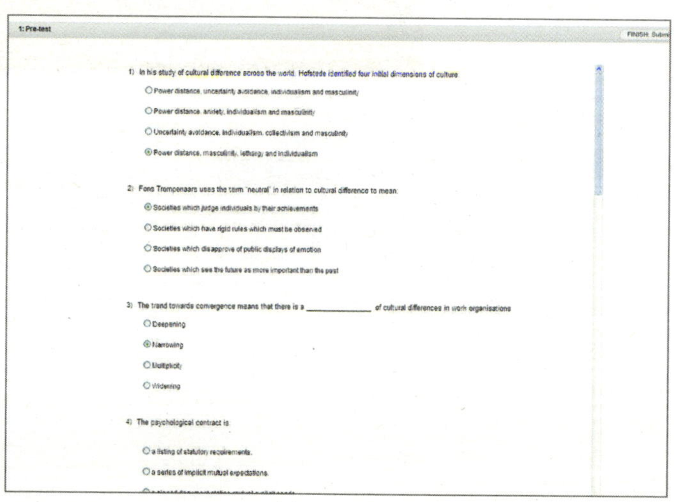

Case study videos

Watch interviews with managers from a range of firms discussing how their organizations function, and then answer questions designed to help you relate the video material to the book content. These organizations range from SMEs to well-known multinationals.

Mini-simulations

Mini-simulations are engaging interactive exercises that allow you to apply your knowledge to real-life situations and see the results of making certain decisions.

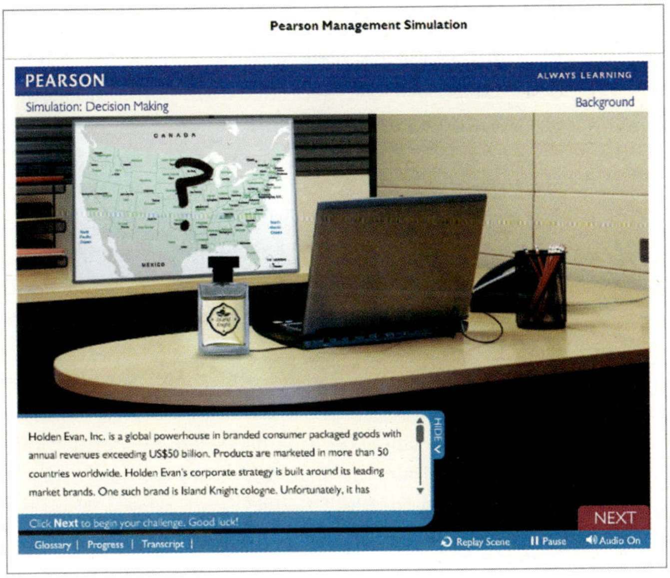

Acknowledgements

A large number of friends, colleagues and students have contributed their ideas, criticisms and advice to the development of this new edition of this text. Our special thanks in this regard are therefore extended to Lesley Buchanan, Nicola Chilvers, Margaret Christie, Janet Huczynska, Gabrielle James, Mary Lince, William McCulloch, Colin Stevenson, Rebecca Vickery and Lubica Asie Zemanova.

Publisher's acknowledgements

We are grateful to the following for permission to reproduce copyright material:

Cartoons

Figures

Figure 1.4 adapted from *Understanding the People and Performance Link: Unlocking the Black Box*, London: Chartered Institute of Personnel and Development (Purcell, J., Kinnie, N., Hutchinson, S., Rayton, B. and Stuart, J. 2003) p. 7, Reprinted by permission of the Chartered Institute of Personnel and Development; Figure on page 49 from Going native, why your products need to adapt to local conditions, *The Times Raconteur on Going Global Section*, 18/10/2011, pp. 6–7 (Clawson, T.), © Clawson/News International Trading Ltd, 18 October 2011; Figure 2.8 adapted from *Organizational Dynamics*, Vol. 12, No. 2, Velasquez, M., Moberg, D.J. and Cavanagh, G.F., Organizational statesmanship and dirty politics: ethical guidelines for the organizational politician, p. 72, Copyright 1983, with permission from Elsevier; Figure 2.9 after *Exploring Corporate Strategy: Text and Cases*, Johnson, G., Scholes, K. and Whittington, K. Pearson Education Limited, © Pearson Education Limited 2008; Figure 3.2 after *Web 2.0 and HR: A Discussion Paper*, Chartered Institute for Personnel and Development (Martin, G., Reddington, M. and Kneafsey, M.B. 2008) p. 7 with the permission of the publisher, the Chartered Institute of Personnel and Development, London (www.cipd.co.uk); Figure 4.1 adapted from *Organizational Behaviour and Analysis: An Integrated Approach*, Rollinson, D. Pearson Education Limited, © Pearson Education Limited 2008; Figure 4.2 from ROBBINS, STEPHEN P.; JUDGE, TIMOTHY A., ORGANIZATIONAL BEHAVIOR, 15th, © 2013. Printed and Electronically reproduced by permission of Pearson Education, Inc., Upper Saddle River, New Jersey; Figure 4.3 from Chao, G.T., O'Leary-Kelly, A.M., Wolf, S., Klein, H.J. & Gardner, P.D. Organizational socialization: Its content and consequences. *Journal of Applied Psychology*, Vol. 79 No. 5, pp. 730–743, 1994, American Psychological Association (APA), reprinted with permission; Figure 4.5 from Corporate culture; the last frontier of control? *Journal of Management Studies*, 23(3), pp. 287–97 (Ray, C.A. 1986) © Blackwell Publishing Ltd and Society for the Advancement of Management Studies 1986; Figure 4.7 from *Organizational Behaviour: Individuals, Groups and Organization*, Brooks, I. Pearson Education Limited © Pearson Education Limited 2003; Figure 4.8 from GRIFFIN, RICKY W; PUSTAY, MICHAEL W., INTERNATIONAL BUSINESS, 5th Edition, © 2007, p. 102. Reprinted and electronically reproduced by permission of Pearson Education, Inc., Upper Saddle River, New Jersey; Figure on page 161 © 2007 BJ Fogg; www.behaviormodel.org. For permissions contact BJ Fogg; Figure 5.2 from MORRIS, CHARLES G.; MAISTO, ALBERT A., PSYCHOLOGY: AN INTRODUCTION, 11th Ed. © 2002, p. 213. Reprinted and Electronically reproduced by permission of Pearson Education, Inc., Upper Saddle River, New Jersey; Figure 5.6 from http://selfleadership.com/blog/topic/leadership/reflecting-and-learning-2009-to-2010/; Figure 6.6 from I.T. Robertson, 'Personality and personnel selection', in C.L. Cooper and D.M. Rousseau (eds), *Trends in Organizational Behaviour*, 1994, p. 8 Copyright 1994 © John Wiley & Sons Limited. Reproduced with permission; Figure on page 228 from Charming the locals: A soldiers guide, *The Times*, 11/02/2008, p. 14 (Evans, M.), © Evans/News International Trading Ltd, 11 February 2008; Figure on page 238 from Toyota chief bows to pressure over pedal defect, *The Times*, 06/02/2010, p. 13 (Lewis, L. and Lea, R.), © Lewis and Lea/News International Trading Ltd, 6 February 2010; Figure 7.2 from *Gesture in Naples and Gesture in Classical Antiquity*, Indiana University Press (de Jourio, A., trans by Adam Kenton 2001) Cambridge University Press, Reprinted by the permission of the Syndics of Cambridge University Library; Figure 7.3 © *Making the Connections: Using Internal Communication to Turn Strategy into Action*, Quirke, B., 2008, Gower Publishing; Figure 8.3 from W.H. Hill (cartoonist), 1915, Artwork supplied by The Broadbent Partnership, London; Figure 9.3 reprinted by permission of *Harvard Business Review*. From 'Inner work life: understanding the subtext of business performance' by Amabile, T.M. and Kramer, S.J., 85(5) 2007. Copyright © 2007 by the Harvard Business School Publishing Corporation; all rights reserved; Figure 10.1 from *Group Dynamics*, Thomson Wadsworth (Forsyth, D.R. 2006) p. 14, adapted from MCGRATH, J.E. GROUPS: INTERACTION AND PERFORMANCE, 1st Ed., © 1984, p. 61. Reprinted and Electronically reproduced by permission of Pearson Education, Inc., Upper Saddle River, New Jersey; Figure 10.4 from GREENBERG, JERALD; BARON, ROBERT A., BEHAVIOR IN ORGANIZATIONS, 6th Ed. © 1997. Reprinted and

Electronically reproduced by permission of Pearson Education, Inc. Upper Saddle River, New Jersey; Figure 10.6 after *New Patterns of Management*, 1961, McGraw-Hill (Likert, R.) p. 105, 0070378509, © The McGraw Hill Companies, Inc.; Figure 10.7 from DAFT/MARCIC. *Management*, 6E. © 2009 South-Western, a part of Cengage Learning, Inc. Reproduced by permission. www.cengage.com/permissions; Figure on page 368 reprinted by permission of *Harvard Business Review*. Adapted from 'The new science of building teams' by Pentland, A., 90(4) 2012. Copyright © 2012 by the Harvard Business School Publishing Corporation, all rights reserved; Figure on page 375 and Figures 12.9 and 12.10 reproduced with permission from Hogg & Vaughan, *Social Psychology* © 2011 Pearson Australia, pages 55, 290 & 424; Figure 11.3 this article was published in *Group Processes* edited by L. Berkowitz, M.E. Shaw, Communications networks fourteen years later, pp. 351–61, Copyright Elsevier 1978; Figure 11.4 from GREENBERG, JERALD; BARON, ROBERT A., BEHAVIOR IN ORGANIZATIONS, 6th Ed. © 1997. Reprinted and Electronically reproduced by permission of Pearson Education, Inc. Upper Saddle River, New Jersey; Figure 11.5 adapted from WORK PSYCHOLOGY edited by Matthewman, Rose and Hetherington (2009) Fig. 7.3 'Key Team Roles' p. 150, adapted from Belbin 1981. By permission of Oxford University Press; Figure 11.6 reprinted from *Organizational Dynamics*, 40(3), Bushe, G.R. and Chu, A., Fluid teams: Solutions to the problems of unstable team membership, pp. 181–188 (p. 183, Figure 2 Problems and solutions for Fluid Teams) Copyright 2011, with permission from Elsevier; Figure 11.7 from *A Primer on Organizational Behaviour*, 5th ed., (Bowditch, J.L. and Buono, A.F. 2001) p. 170, Copyright © 2001 John Wiley & Sons, Inc. Reproduced with the permission of John Wiley & Sons, Inc; Figure on page 409 reprinted with the permission of Scribner, a Division of Simon & Schuster, Inc. from GROUPS, LEADERSHIP AND MEN edited by Harold Guetzkow. Copyright 1951 Carnegie Press; copyright © 1979 Harold Guetzkow (Russell & Russell, NY, 1963); Figure 12.2 from *Interactive Behaviour at Work*, Guirdham, M. Pearson Education Limited, © Pearson Education Limited 2002; Figures 12.3 and 12.4 reproduced by permission of SAGE Publications, London, Los Angeles, New Delhi and Singapore, adapted from Banyard, P.E., Davies, M.N.O., Norman, C. and Winder, B., Essential Psychology: A Concise Introduction, Copyright © Sage Publications, 2010; Figure 12.5 from GREENBERG, JERALD, MANAGING BEHAVIOR IN ORGANIZATIONS, 2nd Ed., © 1999, p. 158. Reprinted and Electronically reproduced by permission of Pearson Education, Inc., Upper Saddle River, New Jersey; Figure 12.7 from *Interactive Behaviour at Work*, Guirdham, M. Pearson Education Limited, © Pearson Education Limited 2002; Figure 12.9 adapted from *Advances in Experimental and Social Psychology*, Volume 15, L. Berkowicz (ed.), Socialization in small groups: temporal changes in individual-group relations by Moreland, R.L. and Levine, J.M., pp. 137–92. Copyright 1982, Academic Press, with permission from Elsevier; Figure 13.1 from Daft. *Organizational Behavior*, 1E. © 2001 South-Western, a part of Cengage Learning, Inc. Reproduced by permission. www.cengage.com/permissions; Figure 13.2 from Sundstrom, E., De Meuse, K.P. and Futrell, D., Work teams: applications and effectiveness, *American Psychologist*, 45(2), pp. 120–33 (Figure on p. 122) 1990 American Psychological Society, reprinted with permission; Figure 14.3 from Mike Noon and Paul Blyton, *The Realities of Work*, published 1997, Palgrave reproduced with permission of Palgrave Macmillan; Figure on page 506 from Appointments, *Daily Telegraph*, 31/12/1998, Reprinted by permission of Ward Executive Ltd; Figure on page 518 from http://www.dhs.gov/xabout/structure/editorial_0644.shtm, US Department of Homeland Security, Office of Multimedia, Washington, DC 20528, USA; Figure 15.4 from ROBBINS, STEPHEN P.; JUDGE, TIMOTHY A., ORGANIZATIONAL BEHAVIOR, 15th, © 2013. Printed and Electronically reproduced by permission of Pearson Education, Inc., Upper Saddle River, New Jersey; Figure 15.6 from *Management: An Introduction*, Boddy, D. Pearson Education Limited, © Pearson Education Limited 2011; Figure 15.7 from http://www.royalnavalmuseum.org/info_sheets_nav_rankings.htm, Trustees of the Royal Naval Museum; Figure 15.9 adapted from *Management: Theory and Practice*, Cole, G.A. and Kelley, P. © 2011 Cengage Learning EMEA. Reproduced by permission of Cengage Learning EMEA Ltd; Figure 15.11 from Organizational Analysis, Supplement to the, *British Journal of Administrative Management*, No. 18, March/April (Lysons, K. 1997); Figure on page 547 from http://media.popularmechanics.com/images/1206airbus_diagramTx.jpg; Figure 16.1

adapted from ROBBINS, STEPHEN P.; COULTER, MARY, MANAGEMENT, 10th Ed., © 2009, p. 45. Reprinted and Electronically adapted by permission of Pearson Education, Inc., Upper Saddle River, New Jersey; Figure 16.2 from *Creative Organization Theory*, Sage Publications, Inc. (Morgan, G. 1989) p. 66; Figure 16.3 from *Managing*, Financial Times Prentice Hall (Mintzberg, H. 2009) p. 48; Figure 16.4 from *Management and Technology*, HMSO (Woodward, J. 1958) p. 11, Contains public sector information licensed under the Open Government Licence (OGL) v1.0. http://www.nationalarchives.gov.uk/doc/open-government-licence/open-government; Figure 16.6 from Perrow, Charles. *Organizational Analysis*. 1E. © 1970 Wadsworth, a part of Cengage Learning, Inc. Reproduced by permission. www.cengage.com/permissions; Figure on page 581 from Boeing 787 Dreamliner Engineering Chief Describes Partners Organization, *Design News* (2007), http://www.designnews.com/article/2659-Boeing_787_Dreamliner_Engineering_Chief_Describes_Partners_Organization.php, Copyrighted 2013. UBM Electronics. 98714:313BC; Figure on page 589 from Boeing/AP/Press Association Images; Figure 17.15 reprinted by permission of *Harvard Business Review*. From 'The contribution revolution: Letting volunteers build your business' by Cook, S., 86(10) 2008. Copyright © 2008 by the Harvard Business School Publishing Corporation, all rights reserved; Figure 17.16 reprinted by permission of *Harvard Business Review*. From 'Which kind of collaboration is right for you?' by Pisano, G. and Verganti, R., 86(12) 2008. Copyright © 2008 by the Harvard Business School Publishing Corporation; all rights reserved; Figure 18.1 republished with permission of American Management Association from *Management Review*, 'Be a model leader of change', Schneider, D.M. and Goldwasser, C., 87(3), 1988; permission conveyed through Copyright Clearance Center, Inc.; Figure on page 669 reprinted by permission of *Harvard Business Review*. Adapted from 'When bossy is better for rookie managers' by Sauer, S.J., 90(5) 2012. Copyright © 2012 by the Harvard Business School Publishing Corporation; all rights reserved; Figure 19.2 reprinted by permission of *Harvard Business Review*. From 'How to choose a leadership pattern' by Tannenbaum, R. and Schmidt, W.H., Vol. 37, March–April 1958 reprinted in May–June, 1973. Copyright © 1958 by the Harvard Business School Publishing Corporation; all rights reserved; Figure 20.2 reprinted from *Organizational Dynamics*, 28(4), Vroom, V.H., Leadership and the decision making process, pp. 82–94, Copyright 2000, with permission from Elsevier; Figure 20.5 from Is decision-based evidence making necessarily bad?, *Sloan Management Review*, 51(4), pp. 71–76 (p. 73) (Tingling, P. and Brydon, M. 2010), © 2010 from MIT Sloan Management Review/Massachusetts Institute of Technology. All rights reserved. Distributed by Tribune Media Services; Figure 21.4 reprinted from *Organizational Behaviour and Human Performance*, Vol. 16 No. 1, T.H. Ruble and K. Thomas, Support for a two-dimensional model of conflict behaviour, p. 145, Copyright 1976, with permission from Elsevier; Figure 22.1 reuse of figure, p. 69 'Structural conditions producing the power . . .' from POWER IN ORGANIZATIONS by JEFFREY PFEFFER. Copyright © 1981 by Jeffery Pfeffer. Reprinted by permission of HarperCollins Publishers.

Tables

Table on page 32 adapted from 'Irish research throws light on HR's recession' in *People Management*, Roche, B. July 2011, reproduced from People Management Magazine (www.peoplemanagement.co.uk) with the permission of the publisher, the Chartered Institute of Personnel and Development, London (http://www.cipd.co.uk/); Table 1.1 adapted from The great mismatch: special report on the future of jobs, *The Economist*, 10/09/2011, pp. 1–18, Working the figures: Biggest employers (Bishop, M.), © The Economist Newspaper Limited, London 10/09/2011; Table on page 47 adapted from 'Restoring American Competitiveness' by Pisano, G.P. and Shih, W.C., *Harvard Business Review*, 87(7/8) 2009, p. 121; Table 2.1 from I. Ansoff, 'Measuring and managing for environmental tubulence: the Ansoff Associates approach', in Alexander Watson Haim (ed.), *The Portable Conference on Change Management*, HRSD Press Inc., 1997, pp. 67–83. Reprinted by permission of the Estate of H. Igor Ansoff; Table 2.6 Reprinted (with adaptation) from *Organizational Dynamics*, Vol. 12, No. 2, Velasquez, M., Moberg, D.J. and Cavanagh, G.F., Organizational statesmanship and dirty politics: ethical guidelines for the organizational politician, p. 72, Copyright 1983, with permission from Elsevier; Table on page 102 adapted from Work systems, quality of working life and attitudes of workers: an empirical study towards the effects of team and non-teamwork, *New Technology, Work and Employment* 16(3), pp. 191–203 (Steijn, B. 2001) © Blackwell Publishers Ltd. 2001; Table 4.3 from *Cultures in Organizations: Three Perspectives*, Oxford University Press (Martin, J. 1992) p. 13. Copyright © 1992 by Oxford University Press, Inc. www.oup.com (Adapted from Pondy et al. (1988), Martin and Meyerson (1987) and Martin and Frost ed. (1991)); Table 4.4 from *Organizational Behaviour: Improving Performance and Commitment in the Workplace* McGraw Hill (Colquitt, J.A., LePine, J.A. and Wesson, M.J. 2009) p. 557, 0073530085 © The McGraw-Hill Companies, Inc; Table on page 175 reprinted by permission of *Harvard Business Review*. Adapted from 'Is yours a learning organization' by Garvin, D.A., Edmondson, A. and Gino, F., 86(3) 2008. Copyright © 2008 by the Harvard Business School Publishing Corporation; all rights reserved; Table on page 189 reprinted by permission of *Harvard Business Review*. Adapted from 'The early bird really does catch the worm' by Randler, C., 88(7/8) 2010. Copyright © 2010 by the Harvard Business School Publishing Corporation; all rights reserved; Table on page 217 from Born to lose, *The Times*, 31/08/2006, Times 2 Supplement, pp. 4–5 (Ahuja, A.), © Ahuja/The Times/NI Syndication, 31 August 2006; Table 6.8 adapted from A survey of UK selection practices across different organization sizes and industry sectors, *Journal of Occupational and Organizational Psychology*, 83(2), pp. 499–511 (Table 3 on p. 506) (Zibarras, L.D. and Woods, S.A. 2010) © The British Psychological Society; Table 6.9 from *Human Resource Management at Work*, 3rd ed., Chartered Institute of Personnel and Development (Marchington, M. and Wilkinson, A. 2005) p. 177 (Originally adapted from Robertson, I. and Smith, M. Personnel selection, *Journal of Occupational and Organizational Psychology*, Vol. 74, No. 4, 2001, pp. 441–72) with the permission of the publisher, the Chartered Institute of Personnel and Development, London (http://www.cipd.co.uk); Table on page 236 from When 'no' means 'yes', *Marketing*, October pp. 7–9 (Kiely, M. 1993), reproduced from Marketing magazine with the permission of the copyright owner, Haymarket Business Publications Limited; Table on page 288 adapted from Too wet to work, *The Sunday Times*, 20/02/2011, p. 23 (Woods, R.), © Woods/The Sunday Times/NI Syndication, 20 February 2011; Table 10.1 from *Effective Behaviour in Organizations*. Homewood, IL: Irwin (sixth edn)., 6th ed., Irwin (Cohen, A.R., Fink, S.L., Gadon, H. and Willits, R.D. 1995) p. 142 © The McGraw-Hill Companies, Inc; Table on page 384 from Dodd-McCue, D., *Journal of Management Education*, 15(3), pp. 335–9, Copyright © 1991, OBTS Teaching Society for Management Educators. Reprinted by Permission of SAGE Publications; Table on page 385 from A WHACK ON THE SIDE OF THE HEAD by Roger von Oech. Copyright © 1983, 1990, 1998 by Roger von Oech. By permission of GRAND CENTRAL PUBLISHING. All rights reserved; Table on page 385 from Analytical or creative? A problem solving comparison, *The 1981 Annual Handbook for Group Facilitators*, pp. 24–6 (Pfeiffer), Copyright © 1981 Jossey-Bass Pfeiffer. Reproduced with permission of John Wiley & Sons, Inc.; Table 11.1 adapted from Stevens, M.J. and Campion, M.A., *Journal of Management*, Vol. 20, No. 2, pp. 503–530, The knowledge, skill and ability requirements for teamwork: Implications for human resource management, Copyright © 1994, Southern Management Association. Reprinted by permission of SAGE Publications; Table 11.5 from Nature of virtual teams: A summary of their advantages and disadvantages, *Management Research News*, 31(2), pp. 99–110, p. 107 Table 1: The advantages of using virtual teams (Bergiel, B.J., Bergiel, E.B. and Balsmeier, P.W. 2008) © Emerald Group Publishing Limited all rights reserved; Table 12.4 from *A Diagnostic Approach to Organizational Behaviour*, Allyn & Bacon (Gordon, J. 1993) p. 184, ISBN: 0205145205; Table 13.1 from Sundstrom, E., De Meuse, K.P. and Futrell, D., Work teams: applications and effectiveness, *American Psychologist*, 45(2), pp. 120–33 (Table on p. 125) 1990 American Psychological Society, reprinted with permission; Table 13.3 from 1996 Industry Report – 'What self-managing teams manage', *Training*, Vol. 33, No. 10, p. 69 (1996), Training Magazine Copyright 1996 by LAKEWOOD MEDIA GROUP LLC. Reproduced with permission of LAKEWOOD MEDIA GROUP LLC in the format Textbook via Copyright Clearance Center; Table 13.4 reproduced by permission of SAGE

Publications, London, Los Angeles, New Delhi and Singapore, from Clegg, S.R., Kornberger, M. and Pitsis, T., *Managing and Organizations*, Copyright Sage Publications 2011; Table 13.5 from The art of building a car: the Swedish experience re-examined, *New Technology, Work and Employment*, 6(2), pp. 85–90 (Table on p. 89) (Hammarstrom, O. and Lansbury, R.D. 1991), © Blackwell Publishing Ltd 1991; Table 14.2 from Paul S. Adler, The emancipatory significance of Taylorism, in, *Readings in Organizational Science – Organizational Change in a Changing Context*, p. 9 (Cunha, M.P.E. and Marques, C.A. (eds) 1999), Instituto Superior de Psicologia Aplicada, Lisbon; Table on page 511 from *Bosses in British Business*, Routledge and Kegan Paul (Jervis, F.R. 1974) p. 87; Table 15.3 after GRAY, J.L./STARKE, F.A., ORGANIZATIONAL BEHAVIOR CONCEPTS AND APPLICATION, 3rd Ed, © 1984, p. 412. Reprinted and Electronically adapted by permission of Pearson Education, Inc., Upper Saddle River, New Jersey; Table 16.4 after *The Analysis of Organization*, John Wiley, Inc. (Litterer, J.A. 1973) p. 339, Reproduced by permission of the estate of Joseph A. Litterer; Table 17.3 from *Strategy Synthesis: Text and Readings*, de Wit, B. and Meyer, R., Copyright 2005 International Thomson Business Press. Reproduced by permission of Cengage Learning EMEA Ltd; Table on page 631 adapted from THE FIFTH DISCIPLINE by Peter M. Senge, Copyright © 1990, 2006 by Peter M. Senge. Used by permission of Doubleday, a division of Random House, Inc. Any third party use of this material, outside of this publication is prohibited. Interested parties must apply directly to Random House, Inc. for permission; For UK and Commonwealth rights Table on page 631 adapted from *The Fifth Discipline: The Art and Practice of the Learning Organisation* by Peter Senge. Published by Random House Business Books. Reprinted by permission of the Random House Group Limited; Table 18.9 reprinted by permission of *Harvard Business Review*. Adapted from 'Strategies for learning from failure' by Edmondson, A.C., 89(4) 2011. Copyright © 2011 by the Harvard Business School Publishing Corporation; all rights reserved; Table on page 655 adapted and republished with permission of American Society for Training and Development, from It's time for a leadership (r)evolution, *Training & Development*, April, 52–8, Figure 3 Most critical skills needed in the future for leader effectiveness (Boatman, J. and Wellins, R. 2011); permission conveyed through Copyright Clearance Center, Inc; Table on page 679 from It's the fault that counts, *People Management*, 13(1), pp. 37–8 (Sonsino, S. 2007) original source: Moore, J. and Sonsino, S. (2007) *The Seven Failings of Really Useless Leaders*, MSL Publishing, London; Table 19.2 after *Managing*, Financial Times Prentice Hall (Mintzberg, H. 2009) Table 3.1 Roles of Managing; Table 19.4 adapted from *Woman Matter 2012: Making the Breakthrough*, McKinsey & Company (Devillard, S., Graven, W., Lawson, E., Paradise, R. and Sancier-Sultan, S. 2012) p. 9, Exhibit 4; Table 19.5 from Cast in a new light, *People Management*, 14(2), pp. 38–41 (Table on p. 41) (Alimo-Metcalfe, B. and Bradley, M. 2008); Table on page 709 reprinted by permission of *Harvard Business Review*. From 'What you don't know about making decisions' by Garvin, D.A. and Roberto, M.A., 79(8) 2001. Copyright © 2001 by the Harvard Business School Publishing Corporation; all rights reserved; Table 20.9 from *A Diagnostic Approach to Organizational Behaviour*, 4th ed., Prentice-Hall, Inc. (Gordon, J.R. 1993) p. 253; Table 21.1 reprinted by permission of *Harvard Business Review*. Adapted from 'Can marketing and manufacturing coexist?' by Shapiro, B.S., 55(September–October) 1977. Copyright © 1977 by the Harvard Business School Publishing Corporation; all rights reserved; Table 21.2 adapted from *Managing Through Organization*, Hales, C., Copyright 1993 Routledge, Reproduced by permission of Cengage Learning EMEA Ltd; Table 21.3 adapted from *Developing Management Skills for Europe*, Whetton, D., Cameron, K. and Woods, M. Pearson Education Ltd © Pearson Education Ltd. 2000, p. 345; Table 21.4 after JOHNSON & JOHNSON, JOINING TOGETHER: GROUP THEORY & GROUP SKILLS, 1st Ed., © 1975, pp. 182–183. Reprinted and Electronically adapted by permission of Pearson Education, Inc., Upper Saddle River, New Jersey; Table 21.6 from *The Psychology of People in Organizations*, Ashleigh, M. and Mansi, A. Pearson Education Limited © Pearson Education Limited 2012; Tables 22.3, 22.9 and 22.10 from Buchanan, D.A. and Badham, R.J., *Power, Politics, and Organizational Change: Winning the Turf Game*, Copyright (© Sage Publications 2008); Table 22.8 adapted from ROBBINS, STEPHEN P.; JUDGE, TIMOTHY A., ORGANIZATIONAL BEHAVIOR, 12th Ed., © 2007, p. 483. Reprinted and Electronically adapted by permission of Pearson Education, Inc., Upper Saddle River, New Jersey.

Text

Extract on page 4 from Troubleshooter, *People Management*, 15/05/2008, pp. 50–1; Box on page 83 from 'Special report: France: Insider and outsiders', *The Economist*, 28/10/2006, pp. 5–6, © The Economist Newspaper Limited, London (28/10/2006); Extract on page 152 from Troubleshooter, *People Management*, 24/01/2008, p. 72; Extract on page 321 from Troubleshooter, *People Management*, 04/09/2008, pp. 46–7; Extract on page 616 from Troubleshooter, *People Management*, 13/11/2008, p. 62; Box on page 10 from Has it damaged me?: probably, *The Times, Times 2*, 15/01/2009, pp. 7–8 (Mone, M.), © Mone/News International Trading Ltd, 15 January 2009; Extract on page 69 from Join the green shift, *People Management*, pp. 24–8, June 2011 (Smedley, T.); Box on page 87 from Workspaces: the new word for workplace?, *The Times, Raconteur on IT Supplement*, 06/10/2011, p. 17 (Twentyman, J.), © Twentyman/News International Trading Ltd, 6 October 2011; Exercise on pages 107–8 from MARCIC. *Organizational Behavior*, 4E. © 1995 South-Western, a part of Cengage Learning, Inc. Reproduced by permission. www.cengage.com/permissions; Quotes on page 129 and extract on page 408 from Schumpeter: Down with fun, *The Economist*, 18/09/2010, p. 84 © The Economist Newspaper Limited, London (18/09/2010); Exercise on pages 143–4 with thanks to Professor Phil Beaumont for his assistance in helping to develop this exercise; Exercise on pages 144–5 adapted from this article was published in *International Journal of Management Education*, 9(2), Sronce, R. and Li, L., Catching flies with honey: Using Chinese and American proverbs to teach cultural dimensions, pp. 1–11, Copyright Elsevier 2011; Box on page 176 from Carlsberg puts learning on tap, *People Management*, 30/10/2008, p. 8; Exercise on pages 215–17 after *The big five locator: a quick assessment tool for consultants and trainers*, The 1996 Annual: Volume 1 Training, pp. 107–22 (Howard, P.J., Medina, P.L. and Howard, J.K. 1996), Copyright 1996 Pfeffier & Company. Reproduced with permission of John Wiley & Sons, Inc; Extract on pages 223–4 from Leaders must act like they mean it, *The Sunday Times*, 10/10/2010, Appointments Section, p. 4 (Rea, K.), © Rea/News International Trading Ltd, 10 October 2010; Box on page 301 from We drive hard but we are loyal, *The Times*, 19/07/2011, p. 37 (Lea, R.), © Lea/News International Trading Ltd, 19 July 2011; Exercise on pages 385–7 adapted from *Management of Technology. The Technical Change Audit.*, Manpower Services Commission (Boddy, D. and Buchanan, D.A. 1987) Action for Results: 5: The Process Module pp. 32–5, Crown copyright, Contains public sector information licensed under the Open Government Licence (OGL) v1.0. http://www.nationalarchives.gov.uk/doc/open-government-licence/open-government; Exercise on page 419 from *Organizational Behaviour and Management*, 3rd ed., Martin, J., Copyright 2005 Thomson. Reproduced by permission of Cengage Learning EMEA Ltd; Exercise on pages 419–21 adapted from Griffin, R.W. (2007) *OB in Action: Cases and Exercises* (8th edn), Mason, OH: South Western Cengage Learning, with permission from Dr Steven B. Wolff (www.geipartners.com); Extract on page 438 from The case for multitasking, *Harvard Business Review*, October, p. 32 (Soultaris, V. and Marcello Maestro, B.M. 2011); Exercise on page 454 adapted from Stevens, M.J. and Campion, M.A., *Journal of Management*, Vol. 20, No. 2, pp. 503–530, The knowledge, skill and ability requirements for teamwork: Implications for human resource management, Copyright © 1994, Southern Management Association. Reprinted by permission of SAGE Publications; Exercise on page 455 from John Bratton, Peter Sawchuk, Carolyn Forshaw, Militza Callinan and Martin Corbett, *Work and Organizational Behaviour*, published 2007 Palgrave Macmillan reproduced with permission of Palgrave Macmillan; Exercise on pages 494–6 from *Organizational Behaviour and Management*, 3rd ed., Martin, J., Copyright 2005 Thomson. Reproduced by permission of Cengage Learning EMEA Ltd; Poetry on page 508 from *The Poetry of Business Life: An Anthology*, San Francisco, CA: Berrett-Koehler Publishers Inc. (Windle, R. 1994) pp. 80–82, Printed by permission of the author, Ralph Windle, creator of Bertie Ramsbottom in the pages of the Financial Times,

Harvard Business Review, BBC Radio and other media. He is also the Editor of 'The Poetry of Business Life and Anthology' (Berrett-Koehler Publishers, Inc, San Francisco 1994) in which 'The Job Description' appears pp. 24–6; Box on page 546 adapted from 'Banking against Doomsday', *The Economist*, 10/03/2012, p. 67, © The Economist Newspaper Limited, London (10/03/2012); Exercise on page 609 adapted and reproduced by permission of SAGE Publications, London, Los Angeles, New Delhi and Singapore, from Mullern, T., 'Integrating team-based structure in the business process', in Pettigrew, A.M. and Fenton, E.M. (eds), *The Innovating Organisation*, Copyright (© Sage Publications 2000); Extract on pages 639–40 from Max Headroom, *People Management*, 14(4), pp. 28–32 (McKeown, M. 2008), the article was developed from McKeown, M. (2008), *The Truth About Innovation*, London: Prentice Hall and ideas that were then included in his subsequent publications *The Strategy Book* (2012), London: FT Prentice Hall and *Adaptability* (2012), London: Kogan Page; Exercise on pages 684–6 after Marcic. *Organizational Behavior*, 3E. © 1992 South-Western, a part of Cengage Learning, Inc. Reproduced by permission. www.cengage.com/permissions; Box on page 701 adapted from 'Rogue hormones', *The Economist*, 24/09/2011, p. 98, © The Economist Newspaper Limited, London (24/09/2011); Exercise on pages 718–19 SASHKIN, MARSHALL; MORRIS, WILLIAM C.; HELLRIEGEL, DONALD, EXPERIMENTAL EXERCISES MANAGEMENT BOOK, 1st Ed., © 1987. Reprinted and Electronically reproduced by permission of Pearson Education, Inc., Upper Saddle River, New Jersey; Box on page 768 from 'The will to power', *The Economist*, 11/09/2010, p. 68, © The Economist Newspaper Limited, London (11/09/2010); Box on page 786 adapted from You can't be a good girl and get on in this world, *The Sunday Times News Review section*, 27/11/2011, p. 4 (Mills, E.), © Mills/News International Trading Ltd, 27 November 2011; Exercise on pages 789–90 adapted from Barbuto, J.E., Power and the changing environment, in *Journal of Management Education*, 24(2), pp. 288–96, Copyright © 2000, OBTS Teaching Society for Management Educators, reprinted by Permissions of SAGE Publications.

Photographs

The publisher would like to thank the following for their kind permission to reproduce their photographs:

(Key: b-bottom; c-centre; l-left; r-right; t-top)

Airbus Operations: M Chainey 321; **Alamy Images:** Bastian/Caro 138, Caroline Woodham 204, Chad Ehlers 87, Chad McDermott 305b, Chris Hennessy 116r, Craig Yates 69, CW Images 477, David Pearson 469, Everett Collection 159, 160, Ferenc Szelepcsenyi 596, H. Mark Weidman Photography 83, Helen Sessions 70, Interfoto 766, Jeremy Sutton-Hibbert 28, Paul Doyle 749, Peter Jordan 528, Robert Nicholas 305t, Roman Skyva 411, Travel Images 502, Vario Images GmbH & Co K.G. 32, Whitebox Media Ltd 72; © **Alan Bryman:** 51; **Archives of the History of American Psychology/The University of Akron:** 190t, 205t, 264, 270, 273t, 298t, 375l; **AT&T Archives and History Center:** 332b, 333, 334; **Bentley Historical Library/University of Michigan:** Charles Horton Cooley Collection 202t; **Bridgeman Art Library Ltd:** Detroit Institute of Arts 479; **Camera Press Ltd:** Fabian Bachrach 271t; **Center for the Study of Social Work Practice/Columbia University School of Social Work:** 173b; **Corbis:** Bettmann 770, Gareth Brown 56, © Jagadeesh/Reuters 342bl, Paul Nicklen/NGS 546, Ted Spiegel 242r, Toru Hanai 599, Underwood & Underwood 472; **Courtesy of Albert Bandura:** 167; **Courtesy of Alexandra Milgram:** From Obedience © 1965 Stanley Milgram 410r; **Courtesy of Barbara Tversky:** 698b; **Courtesy of Philip G Zimbardo, Ph.D.:** 526; **Courtesy of Steven Lukes:** 769; **Courtesy of the Ford Motor Company:** 475, 478; **Courtesy of Toyota (GB) Ltd:** 481; **Courtesy of University of Michigan:** 375r; **Dreamstime.com:** Martiens Bezuidenhout 401, Monkey Business Images 343, Pathathai Chungyam 751, Pressmaster 376, Xavier Marchant 361, Yuri Arcurs 139; **Gary P. Latham/University of Toronto:** 302b; **Georgetown University website:** photo by Stephen Voss 243; **Gerald Ferris:** 778; **Getty Images:** 47, 134, 157, 434t, 441, 449, 637, AFP 58, 151, 330, Bloomberg 126, 331, Justin Sullivan 335, Marwan Naamani/AFP 585b,

Mike Powell 748, Popperfoto 190b, VI 428; **Greg Oldham:** 307b; **Harvard Business School Archives:** Baker Library 341, 366, 563t, 563cl, 640; **Image courtesy of The Advertising Archives:** 523; **iStockphoto:** Portugal 2004 93; **Library of Congress:** 163; **Linn Products Limited:** 97; **Mary Evans Picture Library:** 189t, 780, 189t, 780; **Motorola:** 116l; **NASA:** 707, 727; **National Institute on Aging:** 195b; **nisyndication.com:** 554; **Press Association Images:** Albert S Llop 119, STR/AP xliv, Edmond Terakopian 118, Gregorio Borgia 187, Hanusa/AP 581, Larry MacDougal 476, Liang Xiaopeng/Color China Photo 3, Mark Lennihan 595, PA Archive 447, Richard Vogel/AP 585t, Yuin Schiling 287t, 741; **Reuters:** 12, Chip East 52, David Mercado 426, Sean Adair 762, Str Old 242l; **Rex Features:** 10, Action Press 488, Francis Dean 521, Geoff Moore 638, Image Source 342t, Jonathan Player 467; **S C Williams Library/Stevens Institute of Technology:** 474, Frederick Winslow Taylor Collection 465; **Science Photo Library Ltd:** ESA 326, James King-Holmes/Northern Foods 461, Ria Novosti 615; **Shutterstock.com:** Alexander Chalkin 301b, IQconcept 623, Pling 80, Pressmaster 374, Yuri Arcurs 258; **Smithsonian Institute:** National Museum of American History 473; **The Ohio State University:** 652; **University Archives, University of Pittsburgh:** 556; **William S Marras:** 464; **Yale Pictorial Records & Collections:** 705.

In some instances we have been unable to trace the owners of copyright material, and we would appreciate any information that would enable us to do so.

Student briefing

What are the aims of this book?

Introduce the subject We aim to bring the study of human behaviour in organizations to students, undergraduate and postgraduate, who have little or no previous social science background.

Link to practice We aim to show readers how to translate organizational behaviour concepts, theories, and techniques into practical work, organizational, and management settings.

Recognize diversity We aim to stimulate awareness of the diverse social and cultural factors that affect behaviour in organizations; social science can be culture bound, as laws, norms, and traditions vary from country to country, subculture to subculture.

Stimulate debate We aim to promote a challenging, critical perspective, observing that the 'correct' answers to organizational questions, and solutions to problems, rely on values, judgements, and ideology, as well as on evidence; 'authorities' and 'received ideas' must be questioned.

Who are our readers?

Our target readership includes students who are new to the social sciences, and to the study of organizational behaviour. This is a core subject on most business and management studies degree, diploma, and masters programmes. Accountants, architects, bankers, computer scientists, doctors, engineers, hoteliers, teachers, nurses, surveyors, and other subject specialists, who often have no background in social science, may all find themselves studying organizational behaviour as part of their professional examination schemes.

What approach do we adopt?

Social science perspective Our understanding of organizations derives from a broad range of social science disciplines. Most other texts adopt a managerial, psychological, or sociological perspective. However, many other occupations benefit from an understanding of organizational behaviour. Not all students are going to be managers, psychologists, or sociologists.

Self-contained chapters The understanding of one chapter does not rely on a prior reading of others. The material does not have to be read in the sequence in which it is presented. Ideas and theories are developed from the organizational context, to individual psychology, through social psychology, to organizational sociology, politics, and management topics. Chapters cover both theory and practice, classic and contemporary.

Challenging ideas Many of the issues covered in this book are controversial, and competing views are explained. The aim is not to identify 'correct answers' or 'best practices', which are often simplistic and misleading. The aim is to raise further questions, to trigger discussion and debate, and to stimulate your critical thinking.

Flexible design This book works with either a two-semester or three-term introductory-level programme. Short Springboard sections point to key sources for further project and assignment work. Organizational behaviour overlaps with other subjects such as human resource management, and this book is useful for those modules, too.

Comparative analysis One way to highlight the ways in which we behave in organizations is to compare our actions with those of others. Comparative studies have a long tradition in social science. As a student, you engage routinely in comparative analysis, on railways and aircraft, in buses, hotels, restaurants, and hospitals, through exposure to different organizational settings. Is that management behaviour appropriate? Is that employee response effective? Does our theory help us to understand those behaviours, or not?

What aids to learning are included?

Learning outcomes Clear learning outcomes are given for each chapter.

Key terms Chapters open with a list of the key terms that are to be explained, and these are combined in the Glossary.

Exercises Each chapter has two learning exercises for tutorial or seminar use, and these can be used in a flexible way.

What would you do? A problem or incident is described in the opening of each Part of the text, and you are asked to make, and to justify, your decision.

Learning resources The companion website for this textbook contains an additional set of resources related to each chapter.

Home viewing Each chapter lists at least one movie which illustrates the topic in a graphic, entertaining, and memorable way, for home viewing.

OB in films Movie clips are given for classroom use illustrating specific issues, concepts, or arguments for analysis.

OB on the web One or two websites have been carefully selected for each chapter for the manner in which they either illustrate or complement the chapter material.

"It sort of makes you stop and think, doesn't it."

Source: © Sam Gross/The New Yorker Collection/www.cartoonbank.com

Stop and think You are regularly invited to stop, to think through controversial and contradictory issues, to apply ideas and arguments to your own experience, to challenge your assumptions – individually or in class discussion.

Revision Each chapter includes sample examination questions, which can be used for personal study or as tutorial exercises.

Cartoons We want to make the subject interesting and memorable by introducing novel, varied, and unusual material, such as cartoons, illustrations, and research boxes, where appropriate, to change the pace, rhythm, and appearance of the text.

Recap Each chapter closes with a section summarizing the chapter content with respect to the learning outcomes.

Research assignment A short, focused information-gathering project involving either a website search, library exercise, or interviewing, or a combination of these methods, is given in each chapter.

Invitation to see The opening of each Part of the text includes a photograph showing how work and organizations are portrayed visually; visual images are rarely neutral, and you are invited to 'decode' these pictures, identifying the range of both obvious and more subtle meanings which they promote.

Employability Employability has been defined as 'a set of achievements, skills, understandings and personal attributes, that make graduates more likely to gain employment and be successful in their chosen occupations, which benefits themselves, the workforce, the community and the economy' (Yorke, 2006, p. 8).

While studying this subject and this text, you can improve your employability. What are employers looking for? A qualification on its own is usually not enough. Most organizations are also looking for other characteristics or 'competencies' – behaviours, skills and personal attributes that individuals must have, or must acquire, in order to perform effectively at work (Egan, 2011). Research by the Chartered Institute of Personnel and Development (2010) found that employers are looking in particular for the following competencies:

- leadership
- people management
- business skills/commercial acumen
- work ethic and results orientation
- customer service skills
- communication (oral and written)
- interpersonal skills
- project and programme management
- leading and managing change
- general management skills
- creativity and innovation
- teamworking skills
- problem-solving skills
- self-management.
- political and cultural awareness.

Components of critical thinking

Alan Thomas (2003) argues that critical thinking is one aspect of effective management, and identifies four components of the critical thinking process:

1. *Identifying and challenging assumptions about*
   - the nature of management, its tasks, skills, and purposes
   - the nature of people and why they behave as they do
   - the nature of organizations
   - learning, knowing, and acting
   - values, goals, and ends;
2. *Creating contextual awareness by understanding*
   - how management has developed historically
   - how management is conceived of in other societies
   - the implications of different industrial, organizational, economic, political, and cultural contexts for management
   - the interrelation between organizations and society;
3. *Identifying alternatives by*
   - becoming aware of the variety of ways in which managing and organizing can be undertaken
   - inventing and imagining new ways of managing and organizing
   - specifying new goals and priorities;
4. *Developing reflective scepticism by*
   - adopting a questioning, quizzical attitude
   - recognizing the limitations of much that passes for knowledge
   - knowing how to evaluate knowledge claims
   - developing a resistance to dogma and propaganda
   - being able to distinguish systematic argument and reasoned judgement from sloppy thinking, simplistic formulae, and sophistry.

Critical thinking can be contrasted with its opposite, uncritical thinking. Uncritical thinking is the kind in which we accept commonsense assumptions at face value without systematically checking their validity, deny or ignore the significance of context for influencing beliefs and practices, fail to seek out and evaluate alternatives, and cling rigidly and unquestioningly to dogmas and authoritative pronouncements. Critical thinking is, then, not so much a step-by-step process as an attitude of mind, one which places emphasis on the need to ask 'why?' (Thomas, 2003)

From an organizational behaviour perspective, we can add the following:

- knowledge of how organizations are managed
- critical thinking; research, analysis and synthesis
- prioritizing and decision-making
- appetite for learning; learning to learn
- understanding cross-cultural issues and differences.

What are your strengths and limitations as far as potential employers are concerned?

To help you to think about how to increase your value to employers, we have developed a simple *employability assessment* matrix. Each chapter asks you for an action plan to develop your profile in relation to the ideas, concepts, frameworks, behaviours, methods, and other issues that you have covered while studying that topic. This includes this text and wider reading, tutorial discussion, class presentations, assignment work (research and writing), and critical viewing (visual literacy). We hope that you will find this useful in developing your knowledge, skills, and behaviour repertoire beyond the text. This may be either working alone, or in association with your instructor, helping you to develop your employability.

The items on this list of competencies can overlap with each other, and this is not a rigid framework. Different commentators define and interpret these competencies in different ways, and different employers attach varying degrees of importance to them (Rothwell and

Arnold, 2007). What matters, however, is the importance that *you* attach to these competencies with respect to the development of *your* career.

The table shows how our chapters broadly map onto the twenty competencies, grouped for convenience under four main headings – personal qualities, leadership qualities, practical skills, and other attributes.

Competencies and chapters

Competencies that will improve your employability	Chapters containing relevant material
Personal qualities:	
self-management	6 Personality
work ethic/results orientation	2 Environment
appetite for learning	5 Learning
interpersonal skills	7 Communication; 8 Perception
creativity and innovation	18 Change
Leadership qualities:	
leadership	19 Leadership
people management	9 Motivation; 14 Work design
leading and managing change	3 Technology; 18 Change
project management	17 Organizational architecture; 18 Change
general management skills	all chapters relate to this area of competence
Practical skills:	
commercial/business acumen	2 Environment
customer service skills	1 Explaining organizational behaviour
communication skills	7 Communication
problem-solving skills	*What would you do?* features
teamworking skills	11 Group structure; 12 Individuals in groups; 13 Teamworking
Other attributes:	
political awareness	21 Conflict; 22 Power and politics
understanding cross-cultural issues	4 Culture
how organizations work	all chapters relate to this
critical thinking	Student briefing; 1 Explaining organizational behaviour
prioritizing, decision-making	20 Decision-making

Instructor briefing

What is our perspective?

Our aim is to provide you with a teaching resource, which includes a range of materials and ideas, that will enable you to design and to develop the courses that you want to deliver to the different student groups for which you are responsible. A single text and support materials cannot define the curriculum. We expect most instructors not to teach *to* this text, but *from* it, developing their own distinctive style and approach, incorporating their own topics and materials. This aim is accompanied by the goal of providing your students with a text that will also meet their needs in terms of content, interest, applicability, and readability.

Challenge

We use a number of text features to encourage *an active and questioning approach* to the subject. We want to challenge your students by inviting them to confront real, practical and theoretical problems and issues for themselves. Students are invited regularly to stop reading and to consider controversial points, individually or in group discussion. We want to alert students to the significance of organizational behaviour in everyday life. The study of this subject cannot be confined to the lecture theatre and library. Eating a pizza in a restaurant, joining a queue at a cinema, returning a faulty product to a store, purchasing a train ticket, arguing with a colleague at work, taking a holiday job in a factory, and reading a novel are all experiences related to aspects of organizational behaviour.

Perspective

Some organizational behaviour texts offer a managerial perspective, and give students little encouragement to question the material, or to consider other lines of reasoning and acting. In contrast, some texts offer a critical perspective, encouraging debate, but without always offering practical options. We aim to strike a balance. A perspective that encourages debate, challenge and criticism involves asking the following kinds of questions, when presented with a theory, an argument, evidence, or a recommendation for action:

- Does this make sense, do I understand it, or is it confused and confusing?
- Is the supporting evidence compelling, or is it weak?
- Does a claim to 'novelty' survive comparison with previous thinking?
- Is the argument logical and coherent, or are there gaps and flaws?
- What biases and prejudices are revealed in this line of argument?
- Is a claim to 'neutrality' realistic, or does it conceal a hidden agenda?
- Are the arguments and judgements based convincingly on the evidence?
- Whose interests are served by this argument, and whose are damaged?
- Is the language of this argument designed to make it more appealing?

Where appropriate, we explore competing perspectives, from commentators who base their approaches on different assumptions and values. This approach is reinforced in the *Stop and think* boxes, and in the exercises at the end of each chapter. For a fuller treatment of a critical approach to understanding and researching organizational behaviour, see Mats Alvesson and Karen Lee Ashcraft (2009). For a highly regarded text written from a critical stance, see Paul Thompson and David McHugh (2009).

Some instructors have criticized our use of cartoons in this text, presumably regarding them as frivolous and unnecessary. We disagree with that view. The selected cartoons always relate to the content, and as well as entertaining and engaging students who are new to this subject, are a potential memory aid. Elizabeth Doherty (2011) provides a more compelling rationale, viewing cartoons as providing insights into the deeper meanings of social situations and injustices, noting that 'the cartoon can indict human weakness and evil more incisively than columns of editorials' (p. 291). She analysed over 300 Dilbert comic strips published over a five-year period. With regard to how managers view employees, typical themes included: exploitable commodity, an expendable resource to be used, not important or having much worth or value, incompetent, invisible, needing close supervision, and at fault for management mistakes. With regard to how managers treat employees, recurring themes included: abuse, monitoring, constraining, depersonalizing, making life unpleasant, physical and/or mental threat, poor communication, overwork, problematic pay and recognition, lack of respect, indifference, behaving incompetently, and setting priorities that focus on the organization rather than the employee. Cartoon images depict feelings and emotions that readers can often relate to their own personal work experiences, particularly with regard to having one's dignity challenged. She concludes that

> Dilbert cartoons, much like aestheticism and comic art generally, provide a way to assess the feelings and emotions that exist between managers and their employees; they provide a mirror onto the culture in which we live and work. It appears that management does not always recognize employees as humans, an important contributor to the organization, or worth regarding with respect. Instead, some bosses view their subordinates as nonvalued, exploitable commodities and abuse them accordingly. (p. 298)

Comic art thus provides a novel and undervalued aesthetic perspective for understanding and challenging aspects of organizational behaviour that are not openly addressed in many textbooks in this area. This and future editions of our textbook will continue to incorporate cartoons.

Historical backdrop

Management theorists generate a constant stream of new ideas and techniques. Managers tend to be fashion-conscious, and are always interested in the latest thinking, which can create competitive advantage. Students (and textbook authors) also need to keep up with this flood of innovation. Armed with a knowledge of the history of the subject, however, one can often see, in 'new' thinking and methods, aspects of familiar 'old' ideas. What appears to be new is often less a 'paradigm shift' in thinking than a 'packaging shift'. Is the technique of 'job sculpting', invented in the late 1990s, really 'new' or just a reworking of 'job enrichment' from the 1960s? Is the 'McDonaldization' of work a contemporary trend, or the continuing expression of early-twentieth-century management thinking? Is the currently fashionable concept of emotional intelligence a startling fresh development of relevance to management in the twenty-first century, or simply a restatement of ideas from the 1940s about personal and interpersonal awareness and sensitivity? It is important to be aware of the findings and contributions of previous research.

Why recommend films?

The use of feature films and television programmes as teaching resources for organization and management studies is now well established (Billsberry et al., 2012). Voyeurism is a facet of our experience of cinema; we watch others dealing with their circumstances, their relationships, their problems. Film and television can influence attitudes and behaviours by telling us what is 'OK', desirable, acceptable, and what is not, by presenting role models which suggest, literally, how we should act. The people that we see on the screen are often people like us, or people we would want to be. We are also, therefore, cast in a judgemental role; was that behaviour effective, appropriate, and one that I could use in similar circumstances?

While watching a movie or a television programme appears to be a passive activity, this is also an opportunity for 'observational learning'. Hunt (2001) describes how he uses the often complex storylines and characters in popular television programmes to demonstrate, for example, aspects of motivation theory, perceptual bias, equity theory, and perceptions of justice. The possibilities in this respect are limited only by the imagination of the instructor.

As well as being entertaining, informative, and persuasive, film also offers the viewer a vicarious experience which can be used in a number of related ways. First, it is common for the audience to consider how the settings, strategies, and behaviours seen on the screen could be relevant to them. Second, vicarious experience is an invitation to explore unrealized possibilities safely: 'what would it be like to do this/to live like that?' Third, film can be inspirational: 'if I could do that'. Fictional narratives can contribute to our self-understanding and sense of identity. Feature films – and television programmes – can thus be an engaging way to illustrate aspects of organizational behaviour. The narratives on which films are based can also be valuable sources of theoretical insight, and may even be useful for testing theoretical ideas (Hassard and Buchanan, 2009).

Images of work, organization, and management are often seen in movies (Boozer, 2002; Zaniello, 2003, 2007; Bell, 2008; Billsberry et al., 2012). John Hassard and Ruth Holliday (1998) unkindly observe that textbooks like ours offer a *sanitized* picture of organizational behaviour. Stephen Ackroyd and Paul Thompson (1999) argue that orthodox texts overlook *mis*behaviour – 'soldiering', sabotage, pilfering, practical jokes. Gibson Burrell (1998, p. 52) is uncompromising in his view of what organization theory neglects: 'there is little mention of sex, yet organizations are redolent with it; little mention of violence, yet organizations are stinking with it; little mention of pain, yet organizations rely upon it; little mention of the will to power, yet organizations would not exist without it'. The use of film as a teaching and learning tool can help to address these criticisms.

Hassard and Holliday note that film (and television) 'plays out sex, violence, emotion, power struggle, the personal consequences of success and failure, and *dis*organization upon its stage'. The American Media Institute studied the portrayal of organizations in 200 episodes of 50 television programmes. Their analysis (Overell, 2002) showed that with fictional businesses portrayed on television

- only 3 per cent engage in socially or economically productive activity;
- 45 per cent of management behaviours are portrayed as illegal;
- 55 per cent of company bosses commit illegal acts, such as fraud and murder.

Is this view sensationalized or realistic? To what extent do film and television reinforce or challenge popular stereotypes of work, authority, power, status and organization structure? It can be argued that popular media are at least partly responsible for creating, embellishing, and maintaining those stereotypes. Nelson Phillips (1995) argues that the use of narrative fiction, in film and also in novels, short stories, plays, songs, and poems, is a way of strengthening the connection between organizational behaviour as an academic discipline, and the subjective experience of organizational membership. The advertising for some films suggests that stereotypes are challenged: *Philadelphia* for its portrayal of AIDS, *Disclosure* for the portrayal of female rape and sexual harassment at work. Hassard and Holliday argue, however, that the media reinforce conservative values in a stylized manner, rather than presenting challenges. Read their text and you will never again watch police and hospital television dramas without boring your companions with critical commentary on the conventional portrayal of hierarchy, group dynamics, sex role stereotyping, power relations, the role of authority figures, and dysfunctional bureaucratic rules. The action in popular movies often takes place in fictional organizations such as Tyrell Corporation (*Blade Runner*, 1982), Nakatomi Trading Company (*Die Hard*, 1988), Zap-Em (*Men in Black*,

1997), Ryan Entertainment (*Mulholland Drive*, 2001), Runway Magazine (*The Devil Wears Prada*, 2006), Donaldson's Supermarket (*The Promotion*, 2008), Career Transition Counselling (*Up in the Air*, 2009), Keller Zabel Investments (*Wall Street: Money Never Sleeps*, 2010), GTX Corporation (*The Company Men*, 2010), Comnidyne Industries (*Horrible Bosses*, 2011), and of course the non-fictional Ford (*Made in Dagenham*, 2009) and Facebook (*The Social Network*, 2010).

For further ideas on suitable movies, see Champoux (2005, 2006, 2007), and Huczynski and Buchanan (2004, 2005). Jon Billsberry and colleagues (2012) explore the rationale for and benefits from using film in management teaching, and provide many suggestions for conventional and innovative ways of using film in and beyond the classroom. They also assess the benefits and drawbacks of different film formats, and include a valuable discussion of copyright law.

Invitation to see: why analyse photographs?

Samantha Warren (2009) notes that visual research methods are well established in anthropology and sociology, but are rarely used in organization and management studies. But we live in a world saturated with visual imagery, from newspapers, magazines, street advertising, television, and the internet. We are also presented with a range of other visual information; the appearance and dress of the people we meet, the design, layout, colours, and decoration of their workplaces, the architecture of the buildings in which they work, the technology in use. Despite its volume, richness and complexity, we tend to take most of this visual information for granted, as part of the background tapestry in organizational and everyday life. While we may smile or grimace at the occasional photograph, we rarely pause for long to dissect, analyse, interpret, and debate the content of these visual images.

Why should we pay attention to these transient images? We see them once and rarely feel the need to refer back to them again. Street advertisements and internet banners are displayed for brief periods before being updated. The photographs in magazines and newspapers are just illustrations, contextualized with a brief caption, and it is the accompanying text that matters. The images in television and street advertising are clearly contrived to attract our attention, and they cannot mislead us in that respect.

However, visual images are rarely, if ever, neutral. They are not 'just' illustrations. They usually tell a story, present a point of view, support an argument, perpetuate a myth, or maybe create, reinforce or challenge a stereotype. Images carry messages, sometimes obvious, sometimes subtle, sometimes clear, sometimes confusing. Visual imagery is thus a valuable source of information which we often overlook. Visual research methods have been widely used in sociology and anthropology for many years (Bateson and Mead, 1942; Collier and Collier, 1986). There has been a recent growth of interest in the potential of visual methods in social science more generally, and in organizational behaviour specifically (Prosser, 1998; Emmison and Smith, 2000; Buchanan, 2001; Mitchell, 2009).

We would like to encourage students to adopt a more critical perspective on visual images of organizational behaviour. You will find at the beginning of each Part of the book a short section called *Invitation to see*, displaying photographs showing aspects of work and organizations. Visual information constitutes data, in the same way that interviews and survey questionnaires provide data, and also therefore requires interpretation.

The aims of *Invitation to see* are:

- to encourage students to look at the organizational world, and the actors who populate it, in an entirely different way;
- to demonstrate the value of visual data in offering insights into human and organizational behaviour; and
- to introduce and develop the concept of interpreting or 'decoding' visual images.

Photographs can be seen, read, interpreted, or decoded, in three main ways:

Reality captured — Images can be seen as captured fragments of reality, frozen in time, indisputably accurate renditions of scenes and actors. This was the way in which photography was regarded when it was invented. The conclusion which many commentators drew was that 'art is dead'. The artist could never hope to capture reality as accurately as a photograph, so why bother? This perspective is reflected in the saying 'the camera doesn't lie'.

Reality fabricated — Photographs can instead be regarded as social and technological constructs, which reveal as much about the photographer as they do about the image. The photographer selects the scene, a camera, a lens, which in combination determine properties of the image, such as sharpness, contrast, lighting, grain, and depth of field. More critically, the photographer selects the angle and framing of a shot, determining what is included, and also selects the moment to open the shutter and capture the image. Viewers see only what the photographer wants them to see. What is outside the frame, and the sequence of events before and after the shutter was fired, remain invisible. Digital photography allows many further possibilities to manipulate images after they have been captured. This perspective implies that 'the camera and the computer lie for the photographer'.

Multiple realities — How an image is interpreted by viewers, independent of the photographer's intent, is also significant. For the cover of this book, we wanted an image that had no direct association with organizations, factories, office buildings, managers, collaborative teams, aggressive animals, or any other typical organizational metaphor. There is a key question concerning whose interpretation of an image is correct, that of the photographer, or that of the viewer? Both points of view are equally valid, and are of equal interest. As discussed in Chapter 2, the idea that texts can have many valid interpretations also applies to visual images. The viewer does not have to know the photographer's intent, which may be inferred from the image and its caption. Photographers cannot predict the interpretations which viewers will place on their work, but it is those interpretations that condition the viewer's response. This perspective implies that 'what the camera produces is for us to determine'.

With *Invitation to see*, three questions are significant:

1. What are you being invited to see here? What did the *photographer* intend this image to convey? Does it tell a story, present a point of view, support an argument, perpetuate a myth, reinforce a stereotype, challenge a stereotype?
2. What does this image convey to *you*, personally? How do you interpret this? What do you think this means? Do you agree with what is being said here? Is the message inaccurate or misleading, perhaps insulting in some respect? Does this image carry meanings which the photographer may not have intended?
3. How do *others* interpret this image? Do they decode it in different ways? How can differences of interpretation of the same image be explained?

The photograph on the next page appeared in *The Times* (8 March 2003), with an article about 'Beauty in Epaulettes 2003', a Russian Army recruiting exercise in which contestants were assessed on their shooting as well as their appearance. The aim of the contest was to raise the profile of women in the Spetsnaz, the Russian equivalent of the British SAS. This

PA Photos

Russia's glamour brigade aims high

picture also appeared in *The Daily Telegraph* with the caption 'Guns and poses: Russian female soldiers with Kalashnikov rifles prepare to compete in a shooting match during one of the rounds of the Beauty in Epaulettes contest which aims to attract more women into the Russian army'.

Here is one decoding of this image:

> This photo shows two female Russian soldiers with guns. They are both laughing and smiling, clearly having fun. The male soldier in the background does not look quite so happy, but his comrade is standing too far back for us to see his expression. The ground around them is covered in snow. Perhaps the male soldier is cold, waiting for the photographer to finish? Perhaps it is his gun that one of the women is holding? Perhaps he is concerned that his role in the army – 'men's work' – is being invaded by women, posing a threat to his identity as a soldier? We are told that this photograph was taken at a shooting contest, in which these women were taking part, and is part of a campaign to attract more women into the Russian army. However, expecting to meet soldiers like these could attract more men into the army instead. Is this an attempt to shatter the stereotype of the Russian army as a male preserve?

What else does this image suggest?

> Unfortunately, the other stereotype shown here is the 'dizzy blonde'. Would female soldiers on duty, particularly working with assault rifles, be allowed to wear lipstick and have their hair down? The woman on the right has an earring, which would almost certainly be prohibited while on duty. The main clue to what is probably happening here, however, lies in the way in which the woman at the front of the image is holding her rifle. Her right hand is carefully wrapped around the magazine which holds the ammunition, and not the pistol grip behind the trigger. This is the grasp of someone who has never held a rifle before. Both rifles have muzzle guards, so they are not ready to fire, or ready to compete in a shooting match. Are these 'Russian female soldiers', or are they models hired specially for this publicity shoot? Is the male soldier unhappy, perhaps even suspicious, because he wants his gun back before one of the 'dizzy blondes' has an accident?

It is therefore possible to reach different interpretations of this image. The message lies, in part, in the photograph, but also depends on the perceptions of the viewers. It is therefore possible to see how this image can be seen as both contradicting and reinforcing a stereotype related to men's work and women's work, to blondes and soldiering. It is of course also possible to read too much into such an image. The key questions are, how do *you* read this image, what story does it tell *you*, what are *you* being invited to see here?

References

Ackroyd, S. and Thompson, P. (1999) *Organizational Misbehaviour*, London: Sage Publications.

Alvesson, M. and Ashcraft, K.L. (2009) 'Critical methodology in management and management and organization research', in D.A. Buchanan and A. Bryman (eds), *The Sage Handbook of Organizational Research Methods*, London: Sage Publications.

Bateson, G. and Mead, M. (1942) *Balinese Character: A Photographic Analysis*, New York: New York Academy of Sciences, Special Publications 2.

Bell, E. (2008) *Reading Management and Organization in Film*, London: Palgrave Macmillan.

Billsberry, J., Charlesworth, J. and Leonard, P. (eds) (2012) *Moving Images: Effective Teaching with Film and Television in Management*, Charlotte, NC: Information Age Publishing.

Boozer, J. (2002) *Career Movies: American Business and the Success Mystique*, Austin, TX: University of Texas Press.

Buchanan, D.A. (2001) 'The role of photography in organizational research: a re-engineering case illustration', *Journal of Management Inquiry*, 10(2), pp. 151–64.

Burrell, G. (1998) *Pandemonium: Towards a Retro-Theory of Organization*, London: Sage Publications.

Champoux, J.E. (2005) *Our Feature Presentation: Organizational Behaviour*, Mason, OH: Thomson South-Western.

Champoux, J.E. (2006) 'At the cinema: aspiring to a higher ethical standard', *Academy of Management Learning and Education*, 5(3), pp. 386–90.

Champoux, J.E. (2007) *Our Feature Presentation: Human Resource Management*, Mason, OH: Thomson South-Western.

Chartered Institute of Personnel and Development (2010) *Learning and Talent Development: Annual Survey Report 2010*, London: Chartered Institute of Personnel and Development.

Collier, J. and Collier, M. (1986) *Visual Anthropology: Photography as a Research Method*, Albuquerque: University of New Mexico Press.

Doherty, E.M. (2011) 'Joking aside, insights to employee dignity in "Dilbert" cartoons: the value of comic art in understanding the employer–employee relationship', *Journal of Management Inquiry*, 20(3), pp. 286–301.

Egan, J. (2011) *Competence and Competency Frameworks Factsheet*, London: Chartered Institute of Personnel and Development.

Emmison, M. and Smith, P. (2000) *Researching the Visual: Images, Objects, Contexts and Interactions in Social and Cultural Inquiry*, London: Sage Publications.

Hassard, J.S. and Buchanan, D.A. (2009) 'From *Modern Times* to *Syriana*: feature films as research data', in D.A. Buchanan and A. Bryman (eds), *The Sage Handbook of Organizational Research Methods*, London: Sage Publications.

Hassard, J. and Holliday, R. (eds) (1998) *Organization-Representation: Work and Organizations in Popular Culture*, London: Sage Publications.

Huczynski, A. and Buchanan, D. (2004) 'Theory from fiction: a narrative process perspective on the pedagogical use of feature film', *Journal of Management Education*, 28(6), pp. 707–26.

Huczynski, A. and Buchanan, D. (2005) 'Feature films in management education: beyond illustration and entertainment', *Journal of Organizational Behaviour Education*, 1(1), pp. 73–94.

Hunt, C.S. (2001) 'Must see TV: the timelessness of television as a teaching tool', *Journal of Management Education*, 25(6), pp. 631–47.

Mitchell, C. (2009) *Doing Visual Research*, London: Sage Publications.

Overell, S. (2002) 'The workplace story', *Personnel Today*, 30 April, p. 15.

Phillips, N. (1995) 'Telling organizational tales: on the role of narrative fiction in the study of organization', *Organization Studies*, 16(4), pp. 625–49.

Prosser, J. (ed.) (1998) *Image-Based Research: A Sourcebook for Qualitative Researchers*, London: Falmer Press.

Rothwell, A. and Arnold, J. (2007) 'Self-perceived employability: development and validation of a scale', *Personnel Review*, 36(1), pp. 23–41.

Thomas, A.B. (2003) *Controversies in Management* (2nd edn), London: Routledge.

Thompson, P. and McHugh, D. (2009) *Work Organization: A Critical Introduction* (4th edn), Basingstoke: Palgrave.

Warren, S. (2009) 'Visual methods in organizational research', in D.A. Buchanan and A. Bryman (eds), *The Sage Handbook of Organizational Research Methods*, London: Sage Publications.

Yorke, M. (2006) *Employability in Higher Education: What It Is – What It Is Not*, Heslington, York: The Higher Education Academy.

Zaniello, T. (2003) *Working Stiffs, Union Maids, Reds, and Riffraff: An Expanded Guide to Films About Labor*, Ithaca and London: ILR Press/Cornell University Press.

Zaniello, T. (2007) *The Cinema of Globalization: A Guide* to Films *About The New Economic Order*, Ithaca and London: ILR Press/Cornell University Press.

Part 1 The organizational context

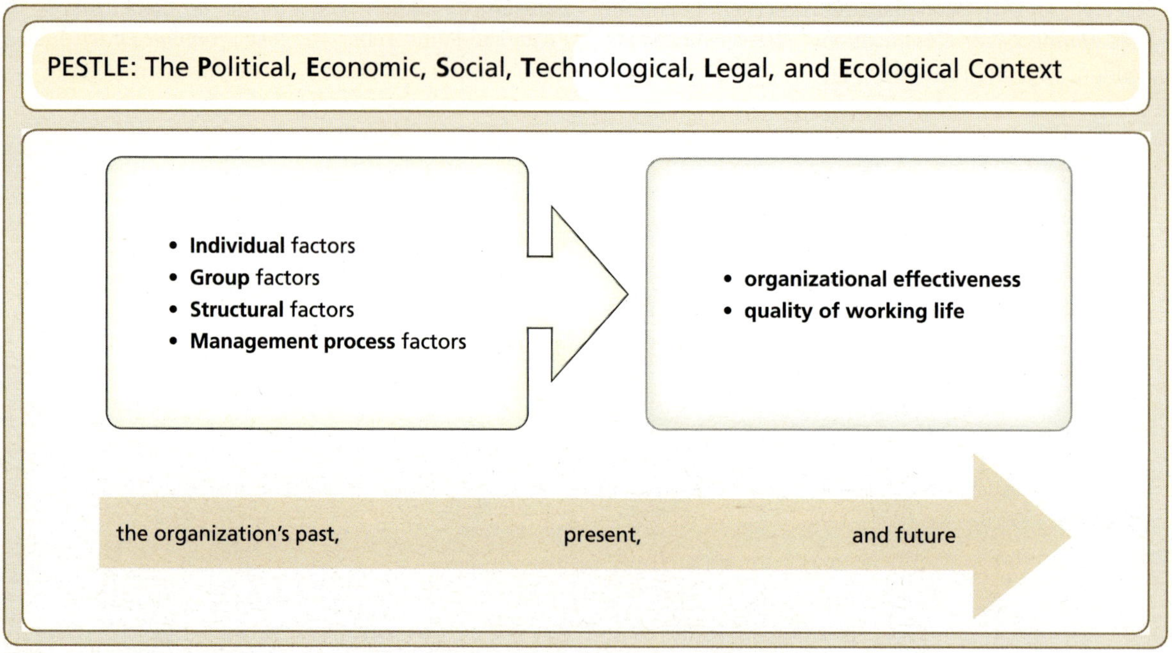

A field map of the organizational behaviour terrain

Introduction

Part 1 on the organizational context, explores four topics:

- Different ways to explain organizational behaviour, contrasting traditional variance explanations, with contemporary process explanations
- How the wider environment of the organization affects internal structures and working practices, including ethical behaviour, and corporate social responsibility
- How developments in new technology, such as Web 2.0 applications, are changing the nature of work and organizations, and the role of choice in shaping the outcomes
- Aspects of organization culture, and different ways to understand this concept, and the links from culture to organizational change and performance.

The second decade of the twenty-first century is a time of severe economic and geopolitical turbulence and uncertainty, accompanied by rapid developments in new technologies. The ability of organizations to anticipate shocks, trends, and opportunities, and to respond rapidly in appropriate ways, is clearly vital to performance and survival. Organizations must be designed and managed – 'built to change' – in order for these degrees of responsiveness and adaptability to happen effectively.

The subject matter of organizational behaviour spans a number of levels of analysis – individual, group, organization, and the wider environment, or context. Part 1 explores key aspects of the organizational context. These include the pace of social and technological change, and the pressures on management to be seen to be acting ethically and exercising corporate social responsibility. Organizations develop their own distinctive cultures, which are different from, while clearly linked to, the wider national cultures in which they operate.

A recurring theme in this text concerns the design of jobs, and the organization and experience of work. The organization of work reflects a number of influences, at different levels of analysis. We explain how the experience and organization of work is influenced by

- *contextual* factors, in Chapter 2;
- *technological* factors, in Chapter 3;
- *psychological* factors, in Chapter 9;
- *social psychological* factors, in Chapter 13;
- *historical* factors, in Chapter 15;
- *power and political* factors, in Chapter 22.

Invitation to see

Liang Xiaopeng/Color China Photo/PA Photos

This photograph, taken in a Chinese textiles manufacturing plant, appeared in *The Sunday Times*, 17 June 2012, p. 3

1. **Decoding**: Look at this image closely. Note in as much detail as possible what messages you feel that it is trying to convey. Does it tell a story, present a point of view, support an argument, perpetuate a myth, reinforce a stereotype, challenge a stereotype?
2. **Challenging**: To what extent do you agree with the messages, stories, points of view, arguments, myths, or stereotypes in this image? Is this image open to challenge, to criticism, or to interpretation and decoding in other ways, revealing other messages?
3. **Sharing**: Compare with colleagues your interpretation of this image. Explore explanations for differences in your respective decodings.

You're the employee: what would you do?

You are 25 years old, and a member of 'Generation Y'. How would you advise this manager to address his problem?

> Help me generate results from Generation Y staff. I'm the Managing Director of a small firm operating in a high-pressure environment. Despite high attrition in our industry, our team prides itself on good management practice as well as getting results. However, with new starters now having an average age of 25, I am finding that since I was young (I'm now 40), a lot has changed. Attitudes have been transformed – but not for the better. Not only are we having to work harder to attract our recruits, but we are finding that in their first few months we have to 'counsel' them to see the bigger picture.
>
> For example, we have always motivated our team by offering a modest basic salary, plus performance-related bonuses. But, increasingly, we are finding that our recruits are perfectly content to earn just the basic.
>
> The younger generation now have higher expectations. This is great, but all too often they seem to expect too much, too soon – without putting in the necessary work. As someone who climbed to the top through hard graft, I find this bewildering. How can I motivate our new starters and channel their energies in the right direction?

From 'Troubleshooter', People Management, *15 May 2008, pp. 50–51.*

Chapter 1 Explaining organizational behaviour

Key terms

organizational behaviour
organization
controlled performance
organizational dilemma
fundamental attribution error
organizational effectiveness
balanced scorecard
quality of working life
positivism
operational definition
variance theory
constructivism
process theory
evidence-based management
human resource management
employment cycle
discretionary behaviour

Learning outcomes

When you have read this chapter, you should be able to define those key terms in your own words, and you should also be able to:

1. Explain the importance of an understanding of organizational behaviour.
2. Explain and illustrate the central dilemma of organizational design.
3. Understand the need for explanations of behaviour in organizations that take account of relationships between factors at different levels of analysis.
4. Understand the difference between positivist and constructivist perspectives, and their implications for the study of organizational behaviour.
5. Understand the difference between variance and process theories and their uses in understanding organizational behaviour.
6. Explain the development and limitations of evidence-based management.
7. Recognize the breadth of applications of organizational behaviour theory, and in particular the contribution to human resource management practice.

What is organizational behaviour?

Why did that happen?

It was a bad experience. You just ordered a soft drink and a sandwich. The person who served you was abrupt and unpleasant, did not smile, ignored you, did not make eye contact, and continued their conversation with a colleague, instead of maybe asking if you wanted something else. They slapped your change on the counter rather than put it in your hand, and turned away. You have used this café many times, but you have never been treated so rudely. You leave feeling angry, deciding never to return.

How can you explain the unusual behaviour of the person who served you?

Organizational behaviour the study of the structure and management of organizations, their environments, and the actions and interactions of their individual members and groups.

Let's put it this way: if you have a limited understanding of organizational behaviour, then you have a limited understanding of one of the main sets of forces that affect you personally, that influence the society and culture in which you live, and which shape the world around you. Organizations affect everything that you do – sleeping, eating, travelling, working, relaxing, studying – everything. This chapter explores how we can explain the behaviour of people in organizations. First, let's define what **organizational behaviour** means.

The definition of a field of study defines the issues, questions, and problems that it explores. Organizational behaviour covers environmental (macro) issues and group and individual (micro) factors (Heath and Sitkin, 2001). We live in an organized world. Take a look at your clothes, food, computer – we are affected in many ways by organizations of different kinds.

Table 1.1: The top ten

organization	number of employees
US Department of Defense	3.2 million
Chinese Army	2.3 million
Walmart	2.1 million ('associates')
McDonald's	1.7 million (including franchise employees)
China National Petroleum Corporation	1.7 million
State Grid Corporation of China	1.6 million
National Health Service, England	1.4 million
Indian Railways	1.4 million
China Post Group	0.9 million
Hon Hai Group	0.8 million

Source: © The Economist Newspaper Limited, London 10/09/2011.

Table 1.1 lists the ten largest organizations in the world, in terms of number of employees (Bishop, 2011, p. 4). The study of organizational behaviour has direct practical implications for those who work in, manage, seek to subvert, or interact in other ways with organizations, whether they are small and local, or large and international.

You will see other similar labels: organization theory, industrial sociology, organizational psychology, organizational analysis, organization studies. Organization theory and industrial sociology tend to focus on macro-level studies of groups and organizations. Organizational psychology specializes in individual behaviour. Organizational analysis tends to emphasize practice rather than theory. Organization studies is a term which highlights the widening of the range of issues and perspectives that this field now embraces (Clegg et al., 2006). These labels indicate shifts in emphasis rather than clear boundaries. Organizational behaviour is widely recognized as the 'umbrella' term, but some would argue with that.

How can we explain your experience in the café? We can blame the personality and skills of the individual who served you. However, there are many other possible explanations such as:

- inadequate staff training;
- staff absences increasing working pressure;
- long hours, fatigue, poor work-life balance;
- equipment not working properly;
- anxiety about anticipated organizational changes;
- domestic difficulties – family feuds, ill-health;
- low motivation due to low pay;
- an autocratic supervisor;
- a dispute with colleagues creating an uncomfortable working atmosphere;
- timing – you came in at the wrong moment.

Your experience could be explained by contextual, individual, group, structural, and managerial process factors, in and beyond the workplace. The explanation could come from any one of those factors. In many cases, a combination of factors will explain the behaviour in question. The customer walks away. As a member of that organization, you have to live with these issues. As a manager, you may be responsible for solving the problem.

Organizational behaviour enjoys a controversial relationship with management practice. We will consider the practical applications of organizational behaviour theory. Most American and many British texts adopt a managerialist perspective. However, the focus on management is regarded by some commentators as unhelpful, for at least four reasons, concerning power inequalities, the subject agenda, multiple stakeholders, and fashion victims.

Power inequalities: Management is an elite occupational group, with access to information and resources beyond those available to mere employees. Organizations typically display inequalities of reward and power. Why should a field of academic study support the affluent and powerful? A managerialist perspective can encourage an uncritical, unchallenging approach to management practice.

The agenda: A managerialist perspective focuses on a narrow range of issues of importance to managers, concerning management control and organizational performance. This pushes other topics off the agenda, such as issues that are significant to particular individuals and groups, theoretical analyses that have limited practical application, and arguments critical of the managerial role.

Multiple stakeholders: Management is only one group with a stake in the behaviour of organizations and their members. An understanding of this subject is of value to employees, groups subjected to discrimination, trade unions, customers, suppliers, investors, and the wider community. Organizational behaviour is a subject of broad social and economic significance.

Fashion victims: Management is prone to pursue the latest in thinking and technique, in the interests of improving personal and organizational performance. A managerialist perspective, therefore, encourages a focus on fashion trends. Some fashions survive while others quickly fade. As some fads turn out to be old ideas freshly packaged, it is important to consider these developments in the context of the history of the subject, to reach an informed assessment.

In this text, we adopt a 'multiple-stakeholders-inclusive-agenda' view of organizational behaviour, developing a broad social science perspective. This does not mean that practical

Fritz Jules Roethlisberger (1898–1974)

applications are ignored, but readers are encouraged to adopt a challenging, critical approach to research, theory and practice, rather than to accept a managerial or a social scientific point of view without question. Even 'authorities' get it wrong sometimes.

The term organizational behaviour was first used by Fritz Roethlisberger in the late 1950s, because it suggested a wider scope than human relations (Wood, 1995). The term behavioural sciences was first used to describe a Ford Foundation research programme at Harvard in 1950, and in 1957 the Human Relations Group at Harvard (previously the Mayo Group) became the Organizational Behavior Group. Organizational behaviour was recognized as a subject at Harvard in 1962, with Roethlisberger as the first area head (Roethlisberger, 1977).

Organizational behaviour – a coherent subject area?

Management textbooks frequently state as fact that organizational behaviour is an inter-disciplinary field. It is not. It is in no way inter-disciplinary; multi-disciplinary perhaps, but not inter-disciplinary. OB is not a coherent field. It is a general area that encompasses thinking and research from numerous disciplines. It draws its material from psychology, sociology, anthropology, economics, the arts and humanities, law and medicine. Organizational behaviour is in reality a hodgepodge of various subjects; a collection of loosely related or even unrelated streams of scholarly and not-so-scholarly research. It is neither a discipline, nor is it a business function. And that makes it an anomalous area of management study.

From Wood (1995), p. 3.

Organizations do not 'behave'. Only people can be said to behave. Organizational behaviour is shorthand for the activities and interactions of people in organizations. Organizations populate our physical, social, cultural, political and economic environment, offering jobs, providing goods and services, creating our built environment, and contributing to the existence and fabric of communities. The products and services of McDonald's, Google, Apple, Microsoft, Ford, and Sony shape our existence and our daily experience. However, we tend to take organizations for granted precisely because they affect everything that we do. Familiarity can lead to an underestimation of their impact. With how many organizations have you interacted in some way *today*?

STOP AND THINK

Why should the term, 'organization', be difficult to define? Which of the following are organizations, and which are not? Explain your decision in each case.

- A chemicals processing company
- The Jamieson family next door
- King's College Hospital
- The local street corner gang
- Clan Buchanan
- Your local squash club
- A terrorist cell
- A famine relief charity
- The Azande tribe
- A primary school

The study of organizational behaviour has become a distinct discipline, with its own research traditions, journals, and international networks. This is a field where contributions from various social and behavioural sciences can be integrated. The extent of that integration, however, is weak. 'Multidisciplinary' means drawing from different subjects. 'Interdisciplinary' means that those subjects collaborate; interdisciplinary collaboration is rare.

Organization a social arrangement for achieving controlled performance in pursuit of collective goals.

What is an **organization**? Why are you uncomfortable about calling some of the items on that list 'organizations'? Perhaps you considered size as a deciding factor? Or the provision of goods and services for sale? Or the offer of paid employment? If we define a term too widely, it becomes meaningless. Our definition is *one* way to define an organization.

This definition should help to explain why you perhaps found it awkward to describe a street corner gang as an organization, but not a hospital, a company, or a club. Let us examine this definition more closely.

Social arrangements

To say that organizations are social arrangements is simply to observe that they are groups of people who interact with each other as a consequence of their membership. However, all of the items on our list are social arrangements. This is not a distinctive feature.

Collective goals

Common membership implies shared objectives. Organizations are more likely to exist where individuals acting alone cannot achieve goals that are considered worthwhile pursuing. Once again, all of the items on our list are social arrangements for the pursuit of collective goals, so this is not a distinctive feature either.

Controlled performance

Controlled performance setting standards, measuring performance, comparing actual with standard, and taking corrective action if necessary.

Organizations are concerned with **controlled performance** in the pursuit of goals. The performance of an organization as a whole determines its survival. The performance of a department determines the resources allocated to it. The performance of individuals determines pay and promotion prospects. Not just any level of performance will do, however. We live in a world in which the resources available to us are not sufficient to meet all of our desires. We have to make the most efficient use of those scarce resources. Levels of performance of individuals, departments, and organizations are therefore tied to standards which determine what counts as inadequate, satisfactory, or good.

Performance has to be controlled, to ensure that it is good enough, or that something is being done to improve it. An organization's members have to perform these control functions as well as the operating tasks required to fulfil their collective purpose. The need for controlled performance leads to a deliberate and ordered allocation of functions, or division of labour, between an organization's members.

Admission to membership of organizations is controlled, usually with reference to standards of performance – will the person be able to do the job? The price of failure to perform to standard is loss of membership. The need for controlled performance leads to the establishment of authority relationships. The controls only work where members comply with the orders of those responsible for performing the control functions.

To what extent are the Jamieson family, the Azande tribe, or the street gang preoccupied with determining and monitoring performance standards and correcting deviations? To what extent does their existence depend on their ability to meet predetermined targets? To what extent do they allocate control functions to their members, programme their activities, and control their relationships with other members? The way in which you answer these questions may explain your readiness or reluctance to describe them as organizations.

It can be argued, therefore, that it is the *preoccupation with performance* and the *need for control* which distinguish organizations from other social arrangements.

STOP AND THINK

In what ways could the Jamieson family be concerned with performance and control?

How is membership of a street gang determined? What do you have to do to become a member? What behaviours lead to exclusion from gang membership?

Are organizations different from other social arrangement in degree only, and not different in kind? Are *all* social groupings not concerned with setting, monitoring, and correcting standards of behaviour and performance, defined in different ways?

A family is not an organization?

Michelle Mone, founder of the lingerie company Ultimo, explains:

> I wouldn't say that I'm a natural mother in terms of wanting to stay at home and pick the kids up from school, and I don't feel guilty about that. I still leave instructions. In the utility room there's one whiteboard for each child, saying what they need to do and where they need to go, how much the fees are for the dancing, the rugby.
>
> My house is run like a business. My staff [nanny, gardener, housekeeper], the kids and my husband have key performance indicators and every Friday we get together with a flipchart and mark how the week has been. That sounds hard but it keeps everyone focused. Children love routine and this house is run like clockwork. I manage everything, but the kids and my husband aren't allowed to mark me.
>
> I have obsessive compulsive disorder and every night when I come in it takes me 17 minutes to go around the house and make sure everything is where it should be, all the white shirts together, the black shirts together. The kids come home, hang up their uniforms, put on their pyjamas, get their homework done, and when they've done their tasks they're free to do what they want and have their friends round. It sounds regimented but it's a happy home as well.

© *Mone* The Times *News International Trading Ltd 15 January 2009.*

Rex Features

The way in which one defines a phenomenon determines ways of looking at and studying it. The study of organizational behaviour is characterized by the view that organizations should be studied from a range of different perspectives. In other words, it is pointless to dispute which is the 'correct' definition. The American management guru Peter Drucker presented another viewpoint, arguing that organizations are like symphony orchestras. Information and computing technology, he argued, reduces the need for manual and clerical skills, and increases demand for 'knowledge workers'. Drucker sees knowledge workers as, like musicians, exploring outlets for their creative talent, seeking interesting challenges, enjoying the stimulation of working with other specialists (Golzen, 1989).

One author who has popularized the 'multiple perspectives' view of organizations is the Canadian academic Gareth Morgan. In *Images of Organization* (2006), he offers eight metaphors which invite us to see organizations through a series of different lenses, as

- machines;
- biological organisms;
- human brains;
- cultures, or subcultures;
- political systems;
- psychic prisons;
- systems of change and transformation; and
- instruments of domination.

Morgan presents these metaphors as ways of thinking about organizations, as approaches to the reading and evaluating organizations. The 'machine' metaphor suggests an analysis of component elements and their interaction. The 'psychic prison' metaphor suggests an analysis of how an organization shapes the thinking and intellectual growth of its members. He suggests that by using these different metaphors it is possible to identify new ways in which to design and manage organizations.

If we destroy this planet

If we eventually destroy this planet, the underlying cause will not be technology or weaponry. We will have destroyed it with ineffective organizations. The main limitation on human aspirations lies neither in intellect nor equipment, but in our ability to work together. The main cause of most man-made disasters (Bhopal, Three Mile Island, Challenger and Columbia, Deepwater Horizon) has been traced to organization and management factors.

The Macondo Well blowout

On 20 April 2010, when the blowout preventer failed, a mile under water, the explosion and fire on the 33,000-ton *Deepwater Horizon* drilling rig in the Gulf of Mexico killed 11 of the 126 crew members, and seriously injured 17 others. Oil poured from the well-head on the sea bed, drifting towards the Louisiana coast 50 miles away, threatening wildlife and local fishing and tourism industries. Around 5 million barrels of crude oil spilled into the Gulf before the flow stopped on 15 July. This was the biggest environmental disaster in the US since the Exxon Valdez spilled 750,000 barrels of crude oil in Prince William Sound in 1989.

Was this disaster the result of a technology failure? No. Two reports from a National Commission on the oil spill show that it was due to organization and management failures (*Deep Water*, and *Macondo: The Gulf Oil Disaster*, both published in 2011).

The rig's 'responsible operator' was BP, whose partners Anadarko Petroleum and MOEX Offshore were to share costs and profits. BP leased *Deepwater Horizon* from Transocean, whose staff operated the rig. Another company, Haliburton, was contracted to cement the pipe from the well to the rig. So the rig was manned by BP site leaders, Transocean managers, engineers, supervisors, drillers, and toolpushers, and Haliburton cementers and mudloggers. BP paid US$34 million in 2008 for the lease to drill in Mississippi Canyon Block 252. Macondo was its first well on the MC 252 lease, estimated to produce at least 50 million barrels of oil.

By April 2010, drilling at Macondo was six weeks behind schedule and $58 million over budget, costing BP $1 million a day to run; it was known as 'the well from hell'. Drilling for oil is risky. Since 2001, the Gulf workforce of 35,000 people, on 90 drilling rigs and 3,500 production platforms, had suffered 1,550 injuries, 60 deaths, and 948 fires and explosions.

The cement that Halliburton pumped to the bottom of the Macondo well did not seal it. Tests indicating

→

Reuters

problems with the cement formula were ignored. But as the cementing went smoothly, a planned evaluation was skipped. The following pressure test results were misinterpreted, and signs that the well had a major oil leak (or 'kick') were missed. Kicks must be detected and controlled in order to prevent blowouts. By the time the *Deepwater Horizon* crew realized that they were dealing with a kick, it was too late for the blowout preventer to stop an explosion. Oil was already in the riser pipe, and heading for the surface.

To create this disaster, eight factors had combined, all involving aspects of management.

1. Leadership

There was conflict between managers and confusion about responsibilities. After a BP reorganization in April 2010, engineering and operations had separate reporting structures. This replaced a project-based approach in which all well staff reported to the same manager.

2. Communication

Those making decisions about one aspect of the well did not always communicate critical information to others making related decisions. The different companies on the rig did not share information with each other. The BP engineering team was aware of the technical risks, but did not communicate these fully to their own employees or to contractor personnel.

3. Procedures

BP did not have clear procedures for handling the problems that arose. The last-minute redesign of procedures in response to events caused confusion on the rig. It would have been more appropriate to stop operations temporarily to catch up.

4. Training and supervision

BP and Transocean had inadequate personnel training, supervision and support. Some staff were posted to the rig without prior assessment of their capabilities. Individuals made critical decisions without supervisory checks. BP did not train staff to conduct and interpret pressure test results. Transocean did not train staff in kick monitoring and emergency response.

5. Contractor management

Subcontracting was common industry practice, but with the potential for miscommunication and misunderstanding. In this case, information about test results and technical analyses did not always find its way to the right person. BP's supervision of contractors was weak, and contractors did not feel able to challenge BP staff decisions, deferring to their expertise.

6. Use of technology

The blowout preventer may have failed, in part, due to poor maintenance. Drilling techniques were much more sophisticated than the technology required to guard against blowouts. Well-monitoring data displays relied on the right person looking at the right data at the right time.

7. Risk management

BP and Transocean did not have adequate risk assessment and management procedures. Decisions were biased towards saving costs and time. The Macondo well risk register focused on the impact of risks on time and cost, and did not consider safety.

8. Regulation

The Minerals Management Service was responsible for safety and environmental protection, and for maximizing revenues from leases and royalties – competing goals. MMS revenues for 2008 were $23 billion. Regulation had not kept pace with offshore drilling technology development. MMS lacked the power to counter resistance to regulatory oversight, and staff lacked the training and experience to evaluate the risks of a project like *Deepwater Horizon*.

Organization and management failures caused this disaster. This pattern can be seen in other cases of serious events, accidents, and catastrophes in different sectors.

Groups can achieve more than individuals acting alone. We human beings are social animals. We achieve psychological satisfaction and material gain from organized activity. Organizations, in their recruitment and publicity materials, like you to think that they are 'one big happy family'. Everyone is a team player, shooting at the same goals. Organizations, of course, do not have goals. People have goals. Collectively, the members of an organization may be making biscuits, treating patients, or educating students, but individual members also pursue personal goals. Senior managers may decide on objectives and try to get others to agree by calling them the 'organization's mission' or 'corporate strategy'; but they are still the goals of the people who determined them in the first place.

Organizations can mean different things to those who use them and who work in them, because they are significant personal and social sources of

- money, physical resources, other rewards;
- meaning, relevance, purpose, identity;
- order and stability;
- security, support, protection;
- status, prestige, self-esteem, self-confidence;
- power, authority, and control.

Organizational dilemma how to reconcile inconsistency between individual needs and aspirations on the one hand, and the collective purpose of the organization on the other.

The goals pursued by individual members of an organization can be quite different from the collective purpose of their organized activity. This creates an **organizational dilemma** – how to design organizations that are effective in achieving overall objectives, while also meeting the needs of those who work for them. An international study asked manufacturing workers whether or not they agreed that managers and employees shared the same interests in their businesses (Noon and Blyton, 2007). The percentages of workers who agreed to this were 24 per cent in the Netherlands, 36 per cent in Britain, and 42 per cent in Norway.

Organizations are social arrangements in which people control resources to produce goods and services efficiently. However, organizations are also political systems in which some individuals exert control over others. Power to define the collective purposes of organizations is not evenly distributed. One of the main mechanisms of organizational control is the hierarchy of authority. It is widely accepted (often with reluctance) that managers have the right to make the decisions while lower-level employees are obliged to comply, or leave.

How eighteenth-century pirates solved the organizational dilemma

Martin Parker (2012) notes that life on navy and merchant ships in the early eighteenth century was vicious and unsanitary. Sailors had poor food, their pay was low, and they enjoyed highly unequal shares of the treasure. Discipline was cruel, violent, and often sadistic. A voyage could be regarded as successful if half the crew survived.

Source: www.CartoonStock.com

Pirates, on the other hand, developed a radical alternative approach to work organization based on more democratic and egalitarian principles.

On pirate ships, written 'articles' gave each man a vote, and most had an equal share of the stores and the plunder, apart from senior officers. Crew members could earn extra rewards for joining boarding parties, and pirate vessels operated injury compensation schemes. There were clear rules, with graded punishments for theft, desertion and fighting on board: 'being set ashore somewhere where hardships would ensue, slitting the nose and ears, a slow death by marooning on an island or a quick death on board' (Parker, 2012, p. 42). Weapons were to be kept clean, and no boys or women were allowed on board. In addition, authority depended on consent. Pirate captains had to win a vote by their crew for their position, and only had absolute authority during a conflict. Contrary to the popular image, pirate ships often cooperated with each other in pursuit of a prize. For seafarers, therefore, piracy could be a more attractive alternative than the legitimate alternatives. While naval and merchant ships often had to 'press' their crew members into service by force, many pirates were ex-merchant seamen.

Parker thus argues that the boundaries between legitimate and illegal organizations and activities (including outlaws and the mafia) are not always as clear as they might appear to be. Eighteenth-century pirates seem to have solved the organizational dilemma, and could meet both individual and organizational needs more effectively than the 'legal' competition.

A concern with performance leads to rules and procedures, and to jobs that are simple and monotonous. These features simplify the tasks of planning, organizing and coordinating the efforts of large numbers of people. This efficiency drive, however, conflicts with the desire for freedom of expression, autonomy, creativity and self-development. It is difficult to design organizations that are efficient both in using resources and in developing human potential. Many of the 'human' problems of organizations arise from conflicts between individual needs and the constraints imposed in the interests of collective purpose. Attempts to control and coordinate human behaviour are thus often self-defeating.

That is a pessimistic view. Organizations are social arrangements, designed by people who can also change them. Organizations can be repressive and stifling, but they can also provide opportunities for self-fulfilment and expression. The individual and social consequences depend on how organizations are designed and run.

Happy cows give more milk

Clarence H. Eckles, in *Dairy Cattle and Milk Production* (Macmillan, New York, 1956) identifies methods for maximizing milk production (Gray and Starke, 1984, p. 14):

1. Cows become accustomed to a regular routine; interrupting this routine disturbs them and causes a decrease in milk production.
2. Attendants should come into close contact with the cows, and it is important that the best of relations exist between the cows and keepers.
3. The cows should not be afraid of the attendants.
4. Cows should never be hurried.
5. Chasing cows with dogs or driving them on the run should never be allowed.
6. In the barn, attendants must work quietly; loud shouting or quick movements upset cows and cause them to restrict production.

A field map of the organizational behaviour terrain

How can behaviour in organizations be explained? To answer this question systematically, we will first develop a 'field map' of the organizational behaviour terrain; see Figure 1.1. Organizations do not operate in a vacuum, but are influenced by their wider context, represented by the outer box on the map. One approach to understanding context influences is through 'PESTLE analysis', which explores the **P**olitical, **E**conomic, **S**ocial, **T**echnological, **L**egal and **E**cological issues affecting the organization and its members.

The map shows that we want to explain two sets of outcomes: organizational effectiveness, and quality of working life. There are four sets of factors which can explain those

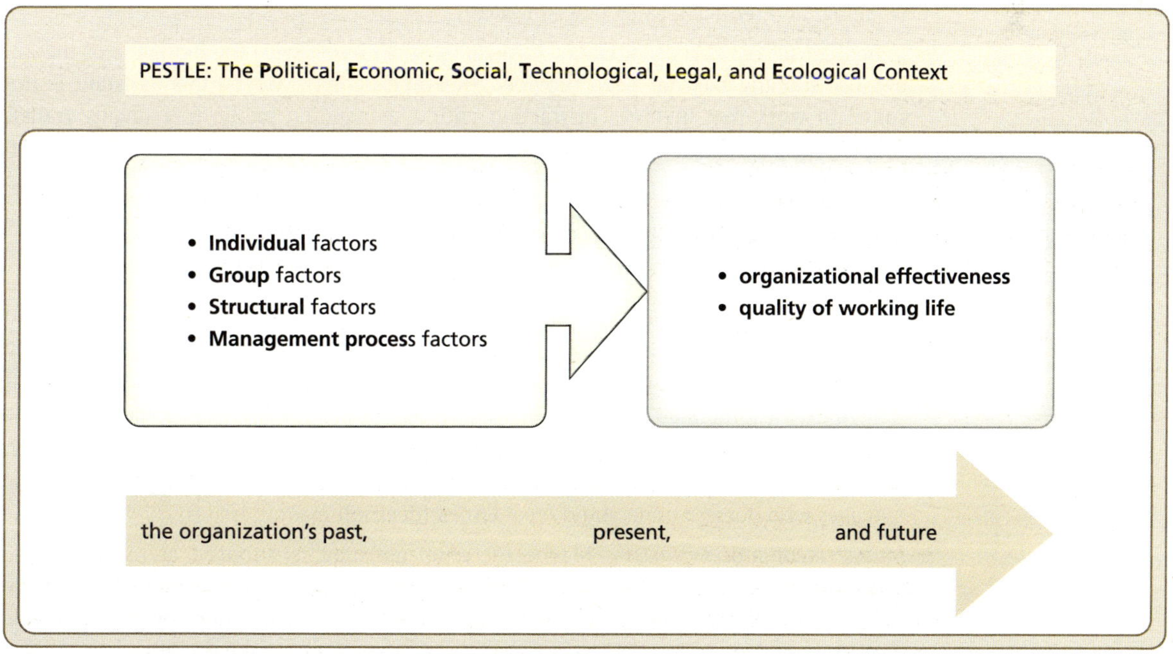

Figure 1.1: A field map of the organizational behaviour terrain

outcomes. These concern individual, group, structural, and management process factors. Finally, we cannot think of organizations as static. Organizations and their members have plans for the future which influence actions today. Past events shape current perceptions and actions. It is necessary to explain behaviours with reference to their location in time.

As well as helping to explain organizational behaviour, this model is an overview and a guide to the content of this book. You will find it reproduced at the beginning of each Part of the book, to help you to locate each topic in the context of the subject as a whole.

STOP AND THINK

The atmosphere just isn't the same any more, and the place is losing customers. Staff in the restaurant or bar that you use are less helpful and friendly than they used to be. The quality of service that you receive has declined sharply. Why?

Use the field map in Figure 1.1 as a source of possible explanations for this deterioration in performance. Can you blame the context, new technology, individuals, teamworking, organization structure, changes to the culture, or management style? Maybe the cause lies with a combination of these factors?

Fundamental attribution error the tendency to emphasize explanations of the behaviour of others based on their personality or disposition, and to overlook the influence of wider contextual influences.

Remember the rude and unhelpful person serving in your café? In these circumstances, we often assume that the person is to blame, and we overlook the context in which they find themselves. This tendency to blame the individual is known as the **fundamental attribution error**, a term first discussed by Lee Ross (1977).

In some circumstances, the individual may be to blame, but not always. If we are not careful, the fundamental attribution error leads to false explanations for the behaviour of others. We must also be aware of how aspects of the social and organizational situation can affect people's behaviour, and the influence of unseen and less obvious factors. To help overcome this attribution bias, Figure 1.1 includes individual factors, but also suggests a range of other possible explanations for the unhelpful behaviour of our shop assistant.

- *Context factors (PESTLE)*: Maybe the store is facing competition, sales have collapsed, the store is closing next month, and the loyal shop assistant is bitter about being made redundant (economic factors). Perhaps closure is threatened because the local population is falling, and reducing sales (social issues).
- *Individual factors*: Maybe the shop assistant is not coping with the demands of the job because training has not been provided (learning deficit). Maybe this assistant is not suited to work that involves interaction with a demanding public (personality traits). Or perhaps the shop assistant finds the job boring and lacks challenge (motivation problem).
- *Group factors*: Maybe the employees in this part of the organization have not formed a cohesive team (group formation issues). Maybe this shop assistant is excluded from the group for some reason (a newcomer, perhaps) and is unhappy (group structure problems). The informal norm for dealing with awkward customers like you is to be awkward in return, and this assistant is just 'playing by the rules' (group norms).
- *Structural factors*: Perhaps the organization is bureaucratic and slow, and our assistant is anxiously waiting for a long-standing issue to be resolved (hierarchy problems). Maybe there is concern about the way in which work is allocated (work design problems). Perhaps the unit manager cannot deal with problems without referring them to a regional manager who doesn't understand local issues (decision-making issues).
- *Management process factors*: Maybe the shop assistant is annoyed at the autocratic behaviour of the unit manager (inappropriate leadership style), or is suffering 'initiative fatigue' following organizational changes (change problems). Perhaps the assistant feels that management has made decisions without consulting employees who have useful information and ideas (management decision-making problems).

These are just some examples; maybe you can think of other contextual, individual, group, structural, and management process factors. This list of possible causes for your bad experience illustrates a number of features of explanations of organizational behaviour.

First, it is tempting to assume that the individual is at fault. However, this will often be incorrect. We need to look beyond the person, and consider factors at different levels of analysis: individual, group, organization, management, the wider context.

Second, it is tempting to look for the single main cause of behaviour. However, behaviour can be influenced by many factors which in combination, and over time, contribute to organizational effectiveness and the experience of work.

Third, while it is easy to address these factors separately, in practice they are often linked. Our employee's damaging behaviour could be the result of falling sales which jeopardize job security (context) and encourage an autocratic supervisory style (management), leading to changes in working practices (process), which affect existing jobs and lines of reporting (structure) and team memberships (group), resulting in increased anxiety and reduced job satisfaction (individual). These links are not shown in Figure 1.1 because they can become complex (and would make the diagram untidy).

Organizational effectiveness a multi-dimensional concept defined differently by different stakeholders, including a range of quantitative and qualitative measures.

Fourth, we need to consider the factors that we want to explain. The term **organizational effectiveness** is controversial, because different stakeholders have different ideas about what counts as 'effective'. A stakeholder is anyone with an interest, or stake, in the organization.

STOP AND THINK

Consider the institution in which you are currently studying. List the internal and external stakeholders. Identify how you think each stakeholder would define organizational effectiveness for this institution. Why the differences?

Organizational effectiveness can be defined in different ways. For commercial companies, effectiveness usually means 'profit', but this raises other issues. First, timescale is important, as improving short-term profits may damage future profitability. Second, some organizations forgo profit temporarily, in order to increase market share, which contributes to corporate survival and growth. Shareholders want a return on investment; customers want quality products or services at reasonable prices; managers want high-flying careers; most employees want decent pay, good working conditions, development and promotion opportunities, and job security. Environmental groups want organizations to protect wildlife, reduce carbon dioxide emissions and other forms of pollution, reduce traffic and noise levels, and so on.

Balanced scorecard an approach to defining organizational effectiveness using a combination of quantitative and qualitative measures to assess performance.

One approach to establishing organizational effectiveness is the **balanced scorecard**. This involves determining a range of quantitative and qualitative performance measures, such as shareholder value, internal efficiencies, employee development, and environmental concerns.

Quality of working life an individual's overall assessment of satisfaction with their job, working conditions, pay, colleagues, management style, organization culture, work-life balance, and training, development, and career opportunities.

The phrase **quality of working life** has similar problems, as we each have different needs and expectations. Quality of working life is linked to organizational effectiveness, and also to most of the other factors on the left-hand side of our map. It is difficult to talk about quality of working life without considering motivation, teamwork, organization design, development and change, human resource policies and practices, and management style.

What kind of model is this? The 'outputs' overlap with the 'inputs', and the causal arrow runs both ways. High motivation and group cohesiveness lead to organizational effectiveness, but good performance can increase motivation and teamwork. The 'outputs' can influence the 'inputs'. Can an 'effect' influence a 'cause'? Logically, this is the wrong way around.

The problem with social science

What can social science offer to organizational behaviour? The contribution of social science to the sum of human knowledge in general is often regarded with scepticism. The natural sciences do not have this problem. What is the problem with social science?

We can put people on the moon, deliver music and movies to your computer, send pictures to mobile telephones on which you can watch television, genetically engineer disease-resistant crops, perform 'keyhole' surgery, and so on. Natural science has also given us technologies with which we can do enormous damage, to each other and to the planet. Textbooks in electrical engineering, naval architecture, quantum mechanics and cardiovascular surgery tell the reader how things (including people) work, how to make things, and how to fix them. Students from these disciplines often find psychology, sociology, and organizational behaviour texts disappointing because they do not offer clear practical guidance. Social science often raises more questions than it answers, and draws attention to debates, conflicts, ambiguities, and paradoxes, which are left unresolved. Natural science gives us material technology. Social science has not given us a convincing social engineering, of the kind which, say, would reduce car theft, or eliminate football hooliganism. Nevertheless, managers expect organizational research to resolve organizational problems.

The goals of science include description, explanation, prediction, and control of events. These four goals represent increasing levels of sophistication. Social science, however, seems to struggle in all of these areas. Table 1.2 summarizes the problems.

Table 1.2: Goals of science and social science struggles

Goals of science	Practical implications	Social science struggles
description	measurement	invisible and ambiguous variables people change over time
explanation	identify the time order of events establish causal links between variables	timing of events not always clear cannot always see interactions
prediction	generalizing from one setting to another	uniqueness, complexity and lack of comparability between settings
control	manipulation	ethical and legal constraints

STOP AND THINK

You discover that one of your instructors has a novel way of enhancing student performance on her module. She always gives students poor grades for their first assignment, regardless of how good it is. This, she argues, stimulates higher levels of student performance in subsequent assignments.

This is an example of 'social engineering'. To what extent is this ethical?

These 'struggles' only arise if we expect social science to copy natural science practices. If the study of people and organizations is a different kind of enterprise, then we need different procedures. Social science is just a different kind of science.

Description

Natural and social science can differ in what they are each attempting to describe. Natural science is describing an objective reality. Social science, in contrast, is often describing (or documenting) the ways in which people understand and interpret their circumstances. Objective reality is stable. People's perceptions change with experience.

The first goal of science, however, is description, and to achieve this, social science has only three methods: observation, asking questions, and studying documents. Documents can include diaries, letters, company reports, committee minutes, or publications. Physicists and chemists, for example, use only one of these methods – observation. Metals, chemicals and interstellar objects do not respond well to interrogation, and do not publish autobiographies in the style that has become popular, for example, with corporate chief executives.

There are different modes of observation. The researcher can observe informal discussion in a cafeteria, join a selection interview panel, follow candidates through a training programme, or even take a job with an organization in order to experience what it is like to work there. Our understanding of the management role, for example, is based largely on observation, but this has obvious limitations. What can we know about someone's perceptions and motives merely by observing their behaviour? We could shadow somebody for a day or two, and make guesses. Eventually we will need to ask them some probing questions.

How do we study phenomena that cannot be observed directly, such as learning? We do this through inference. As you read this book, we would like to think that you are learning about organizational behaviour. However, if we could open your head as you read, we would struggle to find 'the learning process' – although neurophysiology has made breakthroughs in understanding memory processes. The term 'learning' is a label for an invisible (to a social scientist) activity whose existence we can assume or infer.

Home viewing

The 'behind the scenes' activities of consultants who manipulate trial outcomes are shown in the movie *Runaway Jury* (director Gary Fleder, 2003). Gene Hackman stars as Rankin Fitch, a ruthless jury consultant who observes that 'trials are too important to be left up to juries'. Identify the methods and tactics used in this movie to affect the trial outcome.

This may be fiction, but it reflects reality. Celebrity cases, like the one involving the late Michael Jackson for allegedly molesting a 13-year-old boy, are subject to intense study by specialists (Elsworth, 2005). Consultants are hired by both prosecution and defence to help choose jury members who are most likely to support their respective cases. In a case like Jackson's, consultants try to identify the 'stealth jurors' who want either to influence the outcome of the trial or to exploit media opportunities once the trial is over. Consultants construct psychological and social profiles of the jurors. They also observe each juror's reactions and gestures in the courtroom, in order to predict which presentation styles and arguments are most likely to influence them. So, 'each juror's current job, marital status, education, mannerisms, even their nervous tics, as observed in the courtroom, will be dissected by the army of pundits who will pontificate on the trial and its progress day after day on TV'. Michael Jackson was acquitted.

Some changes must take place inside your head if learning is to occur. Neurophysiology can help to track down the processes involved, but it is not clear how an improved understanding of the neurology and biochemistry of learning would help us to design better job training programmes. The procedures for studying learning by inference are straightforward. We can examine your knowledge of this subject before you read this book, and repeat the test afterwards. If the second set of results is better than the first, then we can infer that learning has taken place. Your ability to perform a particular task has changed, and we can use that change to help us identify the conditions that caused it. We can proceed in this manner to study the effects of varying inputs to the learning process – characteristics of the teachers, learners, physical facilities, and the time and other resources devoted to the process. We can study variations in the delivery and study processes, in terms of methods, materials, and timing. Our understanding of the learning process and what affects it can thus develop systematically. From this knowledge, we can begin to suggest improvements.

STOP AND THINK

A high street researcher asks you what you think caused the riots in London and other cities in England in the summer of 2011. How will you answer this question?

Questions can be asked in person in an interview, or through self-report questionnaires. The validity of responses, as a reflection of the 'truth', is questionable for at least three reasons.

First, our subjects may lie. People planning a bank robbery, or who resent the intrusion of a researcher, may give misleading replies. There are ways in which we can check the accuracy of what people tell us, but this is not always possible or convenient.

Second, our subjects may not know. The mental processes related to our motives typically operate without conscious effort. Few of us try to dig these processes out from our subconscious to examine them. Most of us struggle through life without constantly asking 'why am I here?' and 'what am I doing?'. The researcher gets the answers of which the person is aware, or which seem to be appropriate in the circumstances.

Source: Sidney Harris, www.ScienceCartoonsPlus.com

Third, our subjects may tell us what they think we want to hear. People rarely lie to researchers. They create problems by being too helpful. It can be easier to give a simple answer than a complex history of intrigue and heartbreak. The socially acceptable answer is better than no answer at all. This does *not* mean that the answers we get are wrong, but we must be aware of the social context in which information is collected.

Explanation

A second goal of science is explanation. It is often possible to infer that one event has caused another even when the variables are not observable. If your test score is higher after reading this book than before, and if you have not been studying other materials, then we can infer that reading this book has caused your score to improve. The timing of events is not always easy to establish. We might assume, for instance, that satisfaction leads to higher job performance. However, we also know that good performance makes people more satisfied in their work. Which comes first? Which way does the causal arrow run?

The laws that govern human behaviour seem to be different from those that govern the behaviour of natural phenomena. Consider, for instance, the meteorological law 'clouds mean rain'. This law holds good right around the planet. The cloud does not have to be told, either as a youngster or when it approaches hills, about the business of raining. Compare this situation with the social law 'red means stop'. A society can choose to change this law to 'blue means stop', because some people are red-green colourblind (and thus cause hideous accidents). The human driver can deliberately jump the red light, or have a lapse of concentration and pass the red light accidentally. Clouds cannot vote to change the laws that affect them, nor can they break these laws, or get them wrong by accident.

We are not born with pre-programmed behavioural guides, although it appears that we are equipped from birth to learn certain behaviours, such as language (Pinker, 2002). We have to learn the rules of our particular society at a given time. There are strikingly different cultural rules concerning relatively trivial matters, such as how close people should stand to each other in social settings. We also have rules about how and when to shake hands and for how long the shake should last, about the styles of dress and address appropriate to different social occasions, about relationships between superior and subordinate, between men and women, between elderly and young. Even across the related cultures of Europe, and of the Pacific rim, there are major differences in social rules, both between and within countries.

These observations have profound implications for the ways in which social science explains things, and we will explore the possibilities in more detail later in this chapter. It is important to recognize, however, that we cannot expect to discover laws governing human behaviour consistently across time and place. Social and cultural norms vary from country to country, and vary across subcultures in the same country. Our individual norms, attitudes, and values also vary over time and with experience, and we are likely to answer a researcher's questions differently if approached a second time, some months later.

Prediction

A third goal of science is prediction. Social science can often explain events without being able to make precise predictions (see Table 1.3). We may be able to predict the rate of suicide in a given society, or the incidence of stress-related disorders in an occupational group. However, we can rarely predict whether specific individuals will try to kill themselves, or suffer sleep and eating disorders. This limitation in our predictive ability is not necessarily critical. We are often more interested in the behaviour of groups than in that of individuals, and more interested in tendencies and probabilities than in individual predictions and certainties.

There is, however, a more fundamental problem. Researchers often communicate their findings to those who have been studied. Suppose you have never given much thought to the ultimate reality of human existence. One day, you read about an American psychologist, Abraham Maslow, who claims that we have a basic need for 'self-actualization', to develop our capabilities to their full potential. If this sounds like a good idea to you, and you act accordingly, then what he has said has become true, in your case. His claim has fulfilled itself. This may be because he has given you a new perspective on the human experience, or because he has given you a label to explain some aspect of your existing intellectual makeup.

Table 1.3: We can explain – but we cannot confidently predict

we can explain staff turnover in a supermarket in terms of the repetitive and boring nature of work	but we cannot predict which individual staff members will leave, or when they will choose to do so	**individual** factors
we can explain the factors that contribute to group cohesiveness in an organization	but we cannot predict the level of cohesion and performance of particular groups	**group** factors
we can explain why some types of organization structure are more adaptable in the face of external change than others	but we cannot predict the performance improvements that will follow an organizational structure change	**structure** factors
we can explain how different management styles encourage greater or lower levels of employee commitment and performance	but we cannot predict which managers will achieve the highest levels of commitment and performance in a given setting	**management** factors

Some predictions are thus self-fulfilling. The act of saying something will happen can either make that happen, or increase the likelihood of it happening. Predicting petrol shortages, for example, can trigger panic buying by motorists, thus creating petrol shortages. Equally, some predictions are intentionally self-defeating. Many of the disastrous predictions from economists, about budget deficits and interest rate movements, for example, are designed to trigger action to prevent their prophecies from coming true. In an organizational setting, one could predict that a particular management style will lead to the resignation of a number of valuable employees, in the hope that this will lead to a change in management style.

Control

A fourth goal of science is control, or the ability to change things. Social science findings can induce social change. Organizational research findings also prompt change. The natural scientist does not study the order of things in order to be critical, or to encourage that order to improve itself. It is hardly appropriate to evaluate, as good or bad, the observation that a gas expands when heated, or the number of components in a strand of DNA. Social scientists, on the other hand, are often motivated by a desire to change aspects of society and organizations. An understanding of how things currently work, and the strengths and weaknesses of those arrangements, is essential for that purpose. Such understanding, therefore, is not necessarily a useful end in itself. Social science can be deliberately critical of the social and organizational order that it uncovers, because that order is only one of many that we are capable of creating.

An agenda for inducing social and organizational change is not the same as controlling or manipulating human behaviour, which many regard as unethical. As already indicated, we do not have a social technology, comparable to material technology, enabling us to manipulate other people. Perhaps we should be grateful for this. However, Table 1.4 identifies a number of interventions that are designed to control aspects of employee behaviour.

Table 1.4: Interventions to control organizational behaviour

organizational intervention	attempts to control
staff training and development programmes (Chapter 5, Learning)	employee knowledge and skills
psychometric assessments (Chapter 6, Personality)	the types of people employed
employee communications (Chapter 7, Communication)	employee understanding of and compliance with management-inspired goals
job redesign (Chapter 9, Motivation)	employee motivation, commitment and performance
teambuilding (Part 3)	levels of team cohesion and performance
reorganization – structure change (Part 4)	ability of the organization to respond to external turbulence
organizational change (Chapter 18, Change)	speed of change and reduction of conflict and resistance
organization culture change (Chapter 4, Culture)	values, attitudes, beliefs and goals shared by management and employees
human resource management (Chapter 1, Explaining OB)	high employee performance
leadership style (Chapter 19, Leadership)	commitment to an overarching vision

It is important to recognize that our judgements and our recommendations are based not only on evidence, but also on values. Social science has been criticized as 'ideology in disguise'. However, if one studies organizations in order to change and improve them, then we cannot escape that criticism. Our improvement is not necessarily your improvement.

STOP AND THINK

You are a management consultant studying repetitive clerical work in an insurance company. The staff are bored, unhappy, and demotivated. Your study shows how work redesign can improve things by giving them variety and autonomy in their jobs. However, managers claim that their work system is cost-effective, and produces the service which customers want, while allowing them to keep their staff under control.

As the management consultant with the evidence, how would you resolve this disagreement, and persuade management to implement your recommendations? What do you think are your chances of being successful?

Explaining organizational behaviour

Positivism a perspective which assumes that the world can be understood in terms of causal relationships between observable and measurable variables, and that these relationships can be studied objectively using controlled experiments.

Operational definition the method used to measure the incidence of a variable in practice.

We need to revisit our discussion of how social science deals with the task of explanation. The natural sciences are based on an approach known as **positivism**. Indeed, the term 'scientific' is often used to mean a positivist approach that is objective and rigorous, using observations and experiments to establish universal relationships.

Heat a bar of metal, and it expands. Eat more salt, and your blood pressure rises. The factor that causes a change is the *independent* variable. The effect to which it leads is the *dependent* variable. These are also known as the *causal* and *outcome* variables. Salt is the independent (causal) variable; blood pressure is the dependent (outcome) variable. Those variables can be measured, and those causal relationships are universal and unchanging. To measure something, you need an **operational definition** – a method for quantifying the variable.

. . . and then he raises the issue of, 'how many angels can dance on the head of a pin?', and I say, you haven't operationalized the question sufficiently – are you talking about classical ballet, jazz, the two-step, country swing . . .

The operationalization of temperature and blood pressure involves thermometers and monitors. Questionnaires are often used as operational definitions of job satisfaction and management style. With those measures, we can answer questions about the effects of different management styles on employee satisfaction and job performance. That assumes that human behaviour can be explained with the methods used to study natural phenomena.

Our field map of the organizational behaviour terrain (Figure 1.1) can thus be read as a 'cause and effect' explanation. Manipulate the independent variables on the left, and you alter the values of the dependent variables – organizational effectiveness and quality of working life – on the right. This kind of explanation is known as a **variance theory** (Mohr, 1982). Do varying management styles lead to varying levels of job satisfaction? Do varying personality traits lead to varying levels of job performance?

Variance theory an approach to explaining organizational behaviour based on universal relationships between independent and dependent variables which can be defined and measured precisely.

Although positivism and variance theory have been successful in the natural sciences, many social scientists argue that this approach does not apply to social and organizational phenomena. Positivism assumes that there is an objective world 'out there' which can be observed, defined and measured. In contrast, **constructivism** argues that many aspects of that so-called objective reality are actually defined by us. In other words, 'reality' depends on how we perceive it, on how we *socially construct* it (Berger and Luckmann, 1966).

Constructivism a perspective which argues that our social and organizational worlds have no ultimate objective truth or reality, but are instead determined by our shared experiences, meanings, and interpretations.

What does it mean to say that 'reality is *socially constructed*'? Suppose you want to measure aggression at student functions. In positivist mode, you first have to decide what counts as 'aggression'. Your *operational definition* could be an 'aggressiveness index' which you use to count behaviours you observe that involve raised and angry voices, physical contact, pain and injury, and damage to property. This could reveal, for example, that some student functions are more aggressive than others, that aggressiveness is higher later in the evening, that female students are just as aggressive as male students, and so on.

Now, suppose you observe one male student shout at and punch another on the arm. The second student shouts angrily and pushes the first student away. A table is shaken, drinks are spilled, glasses are broken. Your 'aggressiveness index' just jumped by five or six points. In talking to the students, however, they describe their actions as friendly, fun, and playful. The other members of their group agree. This *socially constructed* version of events, for actors and observers, actually involves friendship. Your operational definition is misleading. What matters is how those involved interpret their own actions. Of course, in a different social or organizational setting, raised voices, physical violence, and damaged property will be understood as aggression. The interpretation of those behaviours is not consistent from one context to another. Temperatures of 45 degrees Celsius, or blood pressure readings of 180 over 90, will always be 'high', wherever you are.

Constructivism argues that we are *self-interpreting* beings. We attach meaning and purpose to what we do. Chemical substances and metal bars do not attach meaning to their behaviour, nor do they give interviews or fill out questionnaires. So, human behaviour cannot be studied using methods that apply to natural objects and events. In constructivist mode, our starting point must lie with how others understand, interpret, and define their own actions, and not with operational definitions that we create for them. The organizational behaviour variables in which we are interested are going to mean different things to different people, at different times, and in different places.

Variance theory, therefore, is not going to get us very far. To understand organizational issues, we have to use **process theory** (Mohr, 1982; Langley, 2009).

Process theory an approach to explaining organizational behaviour based on narratives which show how many factors, combining and interacting over time in a particular context, are likely to produce the outcomes of interest.

Process theory shows how a sequence of events, in a given context, leads to the outcomes in which we are interested. Those outcomes could concern individual satisfaction, the effectiveness of change, organizational performance, the resolution of conflict. The key point is that outcomes are often generated by *combinations* of factors *interacting* with each other over time. If salt raises your blood pressure, halving the amount of salt that you eat will reduce the pressure by a measurable amount. If leadership is necessary to the success of an organizational change initiative, it does not make sense to consider the implications of half that leadership.

The Macondo Well blowout described earlier is a good illustration of a process explanation. This disaster was caused by a combination of organization and management factors including confused leadership structures, poor communication, lack of procedures, mismanagement of contractors, poor maintenance and use of technology, inadequate risk management, and an ineffective regulatory system. No single factor was to blame; they all contributed to the sequence of disastrous events and to the outcomes.

Process theory is helpful when we want to understand complex and messy phenomena that are influenced by a number of factors which are difficult to define and measure, and which change with time and context; which combine and interact with each other; where the start and end points of the event sequence are not well defined; and where the outcomes are also difficult to define and measure.

Variance theory offers *definitive* explanations in which causes and outcomes are related in unchanging ways. The values of the causal variables always predict the values of the outcome variables (this temperature, that volume). Process theories offer *probabilistic* explanations. We can say that combinations of explanatory factors are more or less likely to generate the outcomes of interest, but not in every case.

STOP AND THINK

Hospital managers are concerned that some patients with serious conditions wait too long in the emergency department before they are diagnosed and treated.

How would a positivist approach this problem?

How would a constructivist approach this problem?

The positivist wants to observe and record emergency patient numbers, waiting and treatment times, staffing levels, bed numbers, and the availability of other resources. The constructivist, on the other hand, wants to talk to the doctors, nurses and ambulance crews, to find out how they feel about working here and where they believe the problems lie. Which approach do you think is more likely to resolve the waiting times problem, and why?

Positivism and *constructivism* are labels representing many shades of opinion (Deetz, 2009). While constructivism is now widely established, the study of organizational behaviour is still dominated by positivist methods and variance theories.

Table 1.5 summarizes the contrasting perspectives on which explanations for organizational behaviour can be based. What are the implications for our field map of organizational behaviour? Seen from a *positivist* perspective, that model prompts the search for consistent causal links: this organization structure will improve effectiveness and adaptability, that approach to job design will enhance performance and quality of working life. The positivist is looking for method, for technique, for universal solutions to organizational problems.

Seen from a *constructivist* perspective, the model prompts a range of other questions: how do we define and understand the term 'organization', and what does effectiveness mean to different stakeholder groups? What kind of work experiences are different individuals looking for, and how do they respond to their experience, and why? The constructivist argues that explanations may apply only to a small part of the social and organizational world, and that explanations may have to change as the context changes, with time. The constructivist thus seeks to trigger new ideas and change by stimulating self-critical awareness.

This field map, or model, therefore, does not in any straightforward sense lay out causal links across the organizational behaviour terrain. It is simply one way of displaying a complex subject quickly and simply. We hope that it also gives you an overview of the subject, and helps you to organize the material in this book. It also serves as a reminder to consider the range of interacting factors that may explain what we observe, that it is often helpful to look beyond what may appear to be the main and obvious explanations.

Table 1.5: Positivism versus constructivism

	Perspective	
	Positivism	**Constructivism**
Description	accepts mostly information that can be observed and quantified	accepts qualitative information, and relies on inference, studies meanings and interpretations
Explanation	uses variance theories relies mainly on observable quantitative data seeks universal laws based on links between independent and dependent variables	uses process theories relies mainly on qualitative data and self-interpretations develops explanatory narratives based on factors combining and interacting over time and in context
Prediction	based on knowledge of stable and consistent relationships between variables predictions are deterministic	based on shared understanding and awareness of multiple social and organizational realities predictions are probabilistic
Control	aims to shape behaviour and achieve desired outcomes by manipulating explanatory variables	aims at social and organizational change through stimulating critical self-awareness

Research and practice: evidence-based management

Do managers use organizational research to inform their plans and decision-making? Managers are more likely to be concerned with prediction and control than with description and explanation. Given the problems facing social science in the areas of prediction and control, do the kinds of evidence and explanation that social science produces help managers in their task? Is research useful when applied to real-world organizations and problems?

When the late Peter Drucker was asked why managers fall for bad advice and fail to use sound evidence, he didn't mince words. 'Thinking is very hard work. And management fashions are a wonderful substitute for thinking' (Pfeffer and Sutton, 2006, p. 219).

It is well known that there is a gap between academic research and organizational practice, and it is not difficult to explain why. Researchers publish their work in academic journals for other academics. Most managers do not read much, and few read academic journals. Many researchers follow lines of inquiry that do not focus on the problems that organizations and their managers are facing – so even if managers did turn to those journals, they would not necessarily find anything of use to them. Research and practice also work on different timescales. A manager with a problem wants to solve it today; a researcher with a project could take two to three years to come up with some answers.

Evidence, of course, is not the only ingredient that influences our decisions. Experience and judgement also play a role. Problems are likely to arise when decisions are based on habit, bias, and false assumptions. Jeffrey Pfeffer and Robert Sutton (2006) are particularly critical of 'pay for performance' schemes used to motivate people to higher levels of achievement.

Pay for performance is a popular political theme. For example, the UK government considered paying hospital surgeons according to their success in their operating theatres. These schemes assume that (a) job performance depends on motivation, (b) employees are motivated by financial incentives, (c) performance can be measured in a consistent and reliable way, and (d) employees work alone, and are not dependent on the contributions of others. These assumptions are all false. You may hate your job, but work harder in order to get a good reference. Performance in many jobs can have several different dimensions (consider a waiter in a restaurant, for example), and some of those are subjective (for example, courtesy to customers). The emphasis on financial rewards overlooks the importance that most of us attach to intrinsic rewards and doing a good job (the nature of the work). The surgeon in an operating theatre depends heavily on cooperation from many colleagues, all of whose efforts can affect the patient's wellbeing. Paying some members of staff more than others is divisive if the scheme is seen as unfair, and that will lower everyone's performance.

What does evidence-based management look like?

Here is what evidence-based management looks like. Let's call this example, a true story, 'Making Feedback People-Friendly'. The executive director of a healthcare system with twenty rural clinics notes that their performance differs tremendously across the array of metrics used. This variability has nothing to do with patient mix or employee characteristics. After interviewing clinic members who complain about the sheer number of metrics for which they are accountable (200+ indicators sent monthly, comparing each clinic to the 19 others), the director recalls a principle from a long-ago course in psychology: human decision-makers can only process a limited amount of information at any one time. With input from clinic staff, a redesigned feedback system takes shape. The new system uses three performance categories – care quality, cost, and employee satisfaction – and provides a summary measure for each of the three. Over the next year, through provision of feedback in a more interpretable form, the health system's performance improves across the board, with low-performing units showing the greatest improvement (Rousseau, 2006, p. 256).

In this example a *principle* (human beings can process only a limited amount of information) is translated into *practice* (provide feedback on a small set of critical performance indicators using terms people readily understand).

Pfeffer and Sutton note that, while pay-for-performance schemes are popular, there is no evidence that they work – except where those assumptions are correct – and there is evidence that these schemes actually lower performance. Managers aware of the evidence would avoid the costs of such schemes, and find better ways to motivate staff (see Chapter 9).

This line of reasoning, inspired by evidence-based medicine, has led to the growth of an **evidence-based management** movement. There is an Evidence-Based Management Collaborative, based at Carnegie Mellon University. Evidence-based management even has a Wikipedia entry.

Evidence-based management systematically using the best available research evidence to inform decisions about how to manage people and organizations.

The similarities between medicine and management have been exaggerated. While medicine may confidently advise 'take pill, cure headache', there are few if any such generic solutions to organizational problems. There is no such thing as 'best practice' because this depends on local circumstances. Management interventions thus vary widely according to the context. Usually, a number of initiatives or solutions are implemented simultaneously. It is rare to see a single intervention aimed at a single organizational problem. Medical and managerial decisions differ in other significant respects, too; doctors treating headaches do not have to consider the impact of their decisions on organization politics.

Organizational researchers cannot often say, 'if this is your problem, here is your solution', but can contribute to practice in five other ways (McGahan, 2007):

- generating counterintuitive insights;
- demonstrating that fundamental business practices are changing in an important business activity, routine, or practice;
- showing that a widely used management practice violates important principles;
- suggesting a specific theory to explain an interesting situation;
- identifying an iconic problem, phenomenon, or activity that opens new areas of academic inquiry and management practice.

Organizational research can shape practice by suggesting, in creative and positive ways, how problems are understood in the first place, and how they are approached. While we can rarely say 'here is the solution to your problem', we can often say 'here is a way to understand your problem, and to develop solutions that will work in this context'.

Great systems are more important than great people

Managers have become obsessed with 'talent management', identifying and retaining the best people, the top performers, the stars, the 'top graders'. The assumption behind this fashion is that great people will produce great organizational performance. However, there is no evidence to support this view of talent management (Pfeffer and Sutton, 2006, pp. 97–8). There is, however, good evidence that organizational systems are more important.

Over 15 years of research in the auto industry provides compelling evidence for the power of systems over individual talent in a business context. Wharton Business School's John Paul MacDuffie has combined quantitative studies of every automobile plant in the world with in-depth case studies to understand why some plants are more effective than others. MacDuffie has found that when lean or flexible production systems, with their emphasis on teams, training, and job rotation, and their de-emphasis of status differences between employees, are used, higher-quality cars can be built at a lower cost.

© jeremy sutton-hibbert/Alamy

The Toyota Tsutsumi car production line factory, near Nagoya, Japan

Toyota developed and still uses such practices, consistently achieving lower cost and higher quality than other companies – although some Honda plants give them a run for their money, and there are signs that General Motors is finally catching up. Toyota's success stems from its great system, not stunning individual talent. This starts at the top of the organization. One study showed that Toyota was the only major automobile company where a change in CEO had no effect on performance. The system is so robust that changing CEOs at Toyota is a lot like changing lightbulbs; there is little noticeable effect between the old one and the new one.

Human resource management: OB in action

Human resource management the function responsible for establishing integrated personnel policies to support organization strategy.

One area where organizational behaviour (OB) contributes to evidence-based practice is **human resource management** (HRM – or personnel management). These subjects are often taught separately, as they have their own specialized topics and methods, but there is overlap. OB is concerned with understanding micro- and macro-organizational issues, at individual, group, corporate, and contextual levels of analysis. HRM develops and implements policies which enhance the quality of working life and encourage commitment, engagement, flexibility, and high performance from employees in the context of corporate strategy. In designing

Employment cycle the sequence of stages through which all employees pass in each working position they hold, from recruitment and selection to termination.

those policies, HRM can be seen as 'organizational behaviour in practice', and this applies to all stages of the **employment cycle** (Figure 1.2) – stages that you will encounter at various points in your career. At the end of this cycle, 'termination' can mean that the employee has resigned, retired, been made redundant, or been fired.

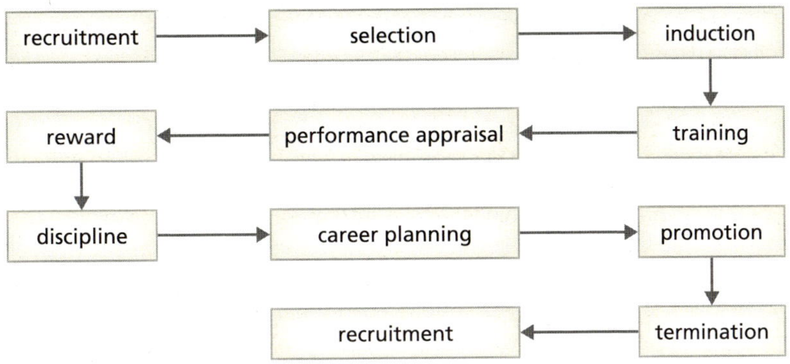

Figure 1.2: The employment cycle

To show the links between OB and HRM, Table 1.6 maps the OB topics covered in this text against areas of HRM practice. The basic model of HRM (Figure 1.3) says that, *if* you design your people policies in a particular way, *then* performance will improve. In terms of the concepts we introduced earlier, HRM policies are *independent variables*, and the quality of working life and organizational effectiveness are *dependent variables*. However, process theory may be more appropriate than variance theory for explaining the relationship between HR policies and organizational outcomes.

Table 1.6: Human resource management and organizational behaviour

HRM functions	issues and activities	OB topics
recruitment, selection, induction	getting the right employees into the right jobs; recruiting from an increasingly diverse population; sensitivity to employment of women, ethnic minorities, the disabled, the elderly	environmental turbulence; PESTLE analysis; personality assessment; communication; person perception; learning; new organizational forms
training and development	tension between individual and organizational responsibility; development as a recruitment and retention tool; coping with new technologies	technology and job design; new organizational forms; learning; the learning organization; motivation; organizational change
performance appraisal and reward	annual appraisal; pay policy; fringe benefits; need to attract and retain staff; impact of teamwork on individual pay	motivation; expectancy theory; equity theory; group influence on individual behaviour; teamworking
managing conduct and discipline	sexual harassment, racial abuse, drug abuse, alcohol abuse, health and safety; monitoring misconduct; using surveillance; formulation and communication of policies	surveillance technology; learning; socialization; behaviour modification; organizational culture; managing conflict; management style
participation and commitment	involvement in decisions increases commitment; design of communications and participation mechanisms; managing organizational culture; tap ideas, release talent, encourage loyalty	communication; motivation; organization structure; organization culture; new forms of flexible organization; organizational change; leadership style
organization development and change	the personnel/human resource management role in facilitating development and change; flexible working practices	organization development and change; motivation and job design; organization culture and structure; leadership

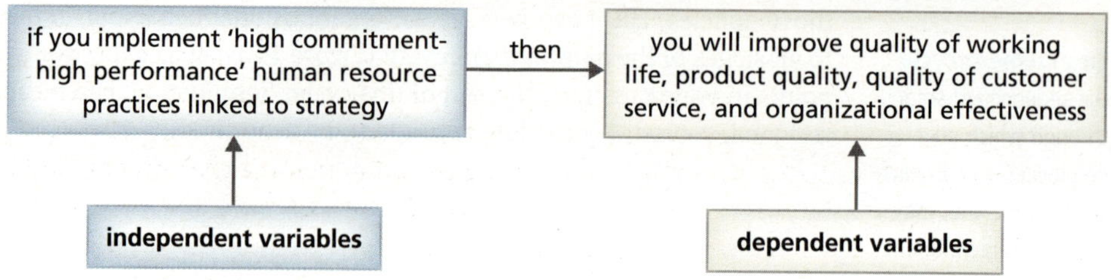

Figure 1.3: The basic model of HRM

The Bath model of HRM

This basic model needs further detail to make it work. The Bath People and Performance Model was developed at the University of Bath, UK (Purcell et al., 2003) and is shown in Figure 1.4. This approach focuses on the *processes* through which HR policies influence employee behaviour and performance. This model argues that, for people to perform beyond the minimum requirements of a job, three factors, Ability, Motivation and Opportunity (AMO) are necessary:

Factor	Employees must
Ability	have job skills and knowledge, including how to work well with others
Motivation	feel motivated to do the work, and to do it well
Opportunity	be able to use their skills, and contribute to team and organizational success

If one of these factors is weak or missing, then an individual's performance is likely to be poor. You may have the ability and the motivation, but if your supervisor prevents you from sharing ideas with colleagues and insists on 'standard procedure', then your performance is unlikely to excel. You will probably not 'go the extra mile'.

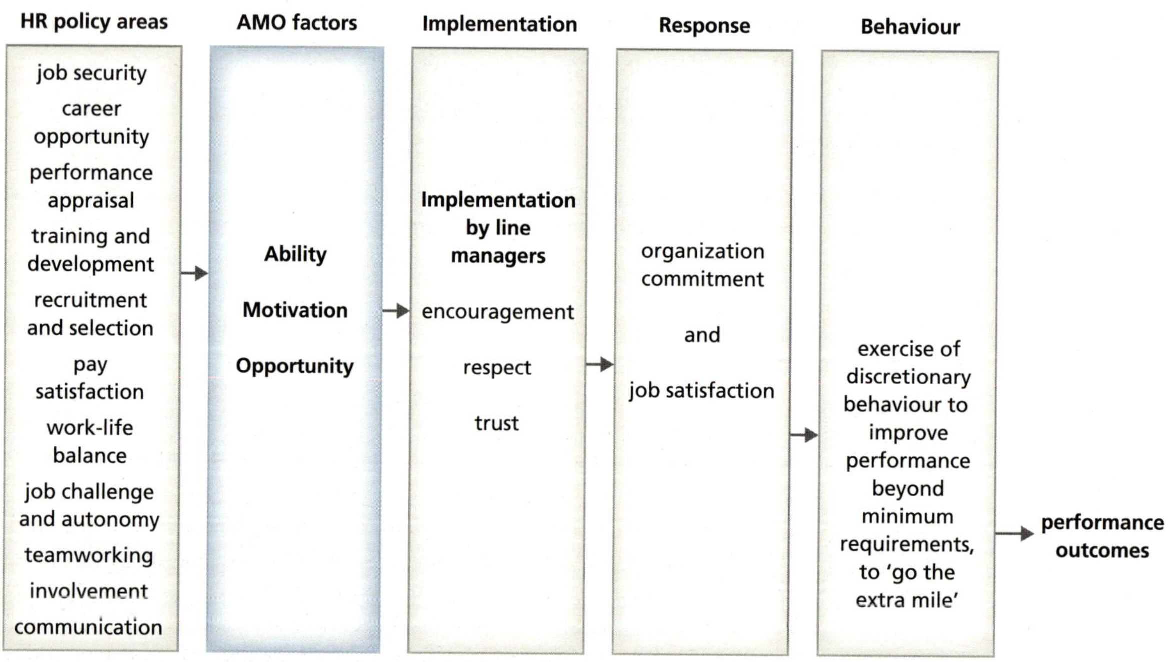

Figure 1.4: The Bath People and Performance Model

Source: Adapted from Purcell et al. (2003, p. 7). Reprinted by permission of the Chartered Institute of Personnel and Development.

Discretionary behaviour freedom to decide how work is going to be performed; discretionary behaviour can be positive, such as putting in extra time and effort, or it can be negative, such as withholding information and cooperation.

Most employees have some choice over how, and how well, they perform their jobs. This is known as **discretionary behaviour**. Sales assistants, for example, can decide to adopt a casual and unsympathetic tone, or they can make customers feel that their concerns have been handled in a competent and friendly way. Negative, uncaring behaviours are often a response to an employee's perception that the organization no longer cares about them. When one member of staff annoys a customer, and management finds out, then that employee has a problem. However, if staff collectively withdraw their positive discretionary behaviours, this affects the performance of the whole organization, and management have a problem.

What encourages employees to 'go the extra mile'? The answer lies in the model's *process theory*, which explains performance outcomes in terms of a combination of factors:

1. Basic HR policies are required to produce the Ability, Motivation and Opportunity central to any level of performance.
2. The line managers who 'bring these policies to life' have to communicate trust, respect and encouragement. This is achieved through the way that they give directions, and respond to suggestions.
3. The combination of HR policies with line management behaviours must lead to feelings of job satisfaction and employee commitment. Otherwise, the policies themselves will have little impact on behaviour and performance.
4. People tend to use positive discretionary behaviours when they experience pride in their organization, and want to stay there. Commitment and job satisfaction thus encourage employees to use discretionary behaviour to perform better.

While those policies must be in place, it is the *process* of implementing them that matters. The same policies, with inconsistent or half-hearted management, can lower commitment and satisfaction, leading to a withdrawal of positive discretionary behaviours. The policies central to this model are:

- *recruitment and selection* that is careful and sophisticated;
- *training and development* that equips employees for their job roles;
- *career opportunities* provided;
- *communication* that is two-way, and information-sharing;
- *involvement* of employees in management decision-making;
- *teamworking*;
- *performance appraisal* and development for individuals;
- *pay* that is regarded as equitable and motivating;
- *job security*;
- *challenge and autonomy* in jobs;
- *work-life balance*.

This suggests that a *positive bundle* of policies which reinforce each other will produce a greater impact than the sum of individual policies. On the other hand, a *deadly combination* of other policies can compete with and weaken each other; for example financial rewards based on individual contributions, with appraisal and promotion systems which encourage teamworking. Previous research showed that organizations using high performance work practices had higher levels of productivity and financial performance, and lower employee turnover, and that those work practices contributed US$18,500 per employee in shareholder value and around $4,000 per employee in additional profits (Huselid, 1995). Evidence also suggests that human resource practices can increase an organization's stock market value by US$20,000 to $40,000 per employee (Pfeffer, 1998).

Treat employees well, and your profits will rise. Comparative research by Malcolm Patterson and his colleagues (1997) at the Institute for Work Psychology at the University of Sheffield

HR – business partners and working the pumps

The human resource (HR) function is traditionally the 'employees' champion', but it is also responsible for ensuring that employment practices fit the company's commercial strategy. These roles involve the use of 'hard' and 'soft' HR practices. Hard HR aims to control or reduce costs. Soft HR aims to maintain motivation and commitment. In a recession, a company's need to control costs can conflict with its employees' desire for job security. So how does HR work in this situation? Research from Ireland suggests some answers.

hard HR	**soft HR**
cut pay and bonuses	improve communications
reduce headcount	engage and involve staff
cut working time	training, talent management, redeployment
control recruitment and promotion	larger pay cuts for higher paid staff
measure productivity	in-sourcing
reduce costs	*build motivation and commitment*

Source: adapted from 'Irish research throws light on HR's recession' in *People Management*, Roche, B. July 2011, reproduced from *People Management* Magazine (www.peoplemanagement.co.uk) with the permission of the publisher, the Chartered Institute of Personnel and Development, London (http://www.cipd.co.uk/).

Ireland has suffered the most serious economic crisis in its history, with a shrinking economy, rising unemployment, a high rate of company insolvencies, a fall in earnings in both private and public sectors, and the need for an internationally-financed rescue package. The traditionally good partnership relationships between Ireland's employers, trade unions, and government collapsed in 2009 when they failed to agree on pay and economic priorities.

A team from University College Dublin and Queen's University Belfast surveyed 450 managers and ran focus groups with a further 30 (Roche, 2011). They found that the influence of HR had grown, as companies relied more on the function's expertise. HR had developed a dual role, as 'business partners', helping senior managers with strategy, and 'working the pumps', helping line managers to implement changes.

Do hard times mean hard responses? Some companies, such as Dublin Airport Authority, introduced 'tiered' pay cuts that were deeper for staff on higher salaries, and seen to be fair. Most companies froze recruitment, wages, and salaries. But the recession also put a priority on communications, to make sure that everyone understood the commercial situation. Employee engagement was also important as a source of ideas for responding to the crisis.

In other words, the HR response to recession involved *bundles* of hard and soft practices. The hard part of the bundle dealt with the short-term business agenda. But companies were also aware of the need to maintain employee motivation and commitment beyond the recession.

Vario Images GmbH & Co K.G./Alamy

has shown that British manufacturing companies place less emphasis on empowering and capturing the ideas of employees than, for example, Australia, Japan, and Switzerland, whose managers make more use of HR practices. Britain's poor comparative productivity and innovation may thus lie with work organization and management processes.

Returning to our discussion of evidence-based management, there is compelling evidence for the link between 'high performance' human resource management and organizational performance. On commercial grounds alone, surely this evidence has made an impact on organizational practice? David Guest (2000) studied 18 HR practices, surveying more than 1,000 chief executives and HR directors in 237 companies. He found that only 25 per cent of those companies used more than half of those practices, and only 1 per cent used more than 12 of them. These 'best practices' are not as common out there as they are in textbooks.

STOP AND THINK There is compelling evidence to show that 'high performance' human resource management practices do work, and that they improve financial returns. They have been widely publicized in management journals. So why do you think these management practices are not more widely used?

While the concept of evidence-based management sounds appealing, the links between evidence and practice in organizational behaviour are complex. Management decisions are always going to be influenced by considerations other than research evidence: organization politics, for example, preserving personal power and reputation; and competitive advantage – why should we do what other companies are doing? Management is only one stakeholder group; why should evidence not be used to promote the interests of other groups?

With regard to the poor uptake of 'high performance' practices, there could be five main reasons (Guest and King, 2001):

- managers may not be aware of the research;
- managers may feel that research evidence does not apply to their organization;
- managers may believe that they already have appropriate practices;
- there may be constraints from more pressing priorities;
- implementation skills may be lacking.

RECAP

1. *Explain the importance of an understanding of organizational behaviour.*
   - Organizations influence almost every aspect of our daily lives in a multitude of ways.
   - If we eventually destroy this planet, the cause will not lie with technology or weaponry, but with ineffective organizations and management practices.
2. *Explain and illustrate the central dilemma of organizational design.*
   - The organizational dilemma concerns how to reconcile the inconsistency between individual needs and aspirations, and the collective purpose of the organization.
3. *Understand the need for explanations of behaviour in organizations that take account of relationships between factors at different levels of analysis.*
   - The study of organizational behaviour is multidisciplinary, drawing in particular from psychology, social psychology, sociology, economics and political science.
   - Organizational behaviour involves a multi-level study of the external environment, the internal

→

structure, functioning, and performance of organizations, and the behaviour of groups and individuals.

- Organizational effectiveness and quality of working life are explained by a combination of contextual, individual, group, structural, process, and managerial factors.
- In considering explanations of organizational behaviour, systemic thinking is required, avoiding explanations based on single causes, and considering a range of interrelated factors at different levels of analysis.

4. ***Understand the difference between positivist and constructivist perspectives, and their respective implications for the study of organizational behaviour.***
   - A positivist perspective uses the same research methods and modes of explanation found in the natural sciences to study and understand organizational behaviour.
   - It is difficult to apply conventional scientific research methods to people, because of the 'reactive effects' which come into play when people know they are being studied.
   - A constructivist perspective assumes that, as we are self-defining creatures who attach meanings to our behaviour, social science is different from natural science.
   - A constructivist perspective believes that reality is not objective and 'out there', but is socially constructed.
   - A constructivist approach means abandoning scientific neutrality in the interests of stimulating social and organizational change through providing critical feedback and encouraging self-awareness.
5. ***Understand the distinction between variance and process theories and their uses in understanding organizational behaviour.***
   - Variance theory explains organizational behaviour by identifying relationships between independent and dependent variables which can be defined and measured. Variance theories are often quantitative, and are based on a positivist perspective.
   - Process theory explains organizational behaviour using narratives which show how multiple factors produce outcomes by combining and interacting over time in a given context. Process theories can combine quantitative and qualitative dimensions, and can draw from positivist and constructivist traditions.
6. ***Explain the development and limitations of evidence-based management.***
   - The concept of evidence-based management is popular, but the links between evidence and practice are complex; evidence can help to shape the ways in which problems are understood and approached, rather than offering specific solutions.
7. ***Recognize the breadth of applications of organizational behaviour theory, and in particular the contribution to human resource management practice.***
   - The Bath model of human resource management argues that discretionary behaviour going beyond minimum requirements relies on having a combination of HR policies.
   - High performance work practices increase organizational profitability by decreasing employee turnover and improving productivity, but they are not widely adopted.

Revision

1. How is organizational behaviour defined? What topics does this subject cover? What is the practical relevance of organizational behaviour?
2. Describe an example of organizational *mis*behaviour, where you as customer were treated badly. Suggest possible explanations for your treatment.
3. Hospital managers are concerned that patients with medical emergencies wait too long in the casualty department before they are diagnosed and treated. Which approach, positivist or constructivist, is more likely to resolve this problem, and why?
4. How can evidence, concepts, theories, and models from organizational behaviour contribute effectively to organizational practice? Give examples.

Research assignment

Organizations affect all aspects of our lives. Buy a small notebook. Starting on Friday morning when you wake up, and ending on Sunday night when you go to bed, keep a list of all the organizations with which you have had contact over this period.

'Contact' includes, for example, a radio programme that you listen to at breakfast, a television station that you watch, the shops that you visit, the bank with whose card you make payments, the companies who run the buses, trains and taxis that you use. Also, which cinemas, bars, nightclubs, sports and social clubs did you visit? Religious and educational establishments? Medical facilities or emergency services that you have used (you never know)? Check your mail; which organizations have written to you? Do you have any utility or council tax bills to pay, and from which organizations do you get these services? Have you dealt with any charity requests? Have you checked your internet service provider and social networking organizations? What companies made your computer and mobile phone? Which companies designd the browser and other software that you are using? Whose advertisements have you watched?

Every time you do anything or go anywhere over these three days, stop and ask 'which organizations am I interacting with in some way?' – and write the names in your notebook. Then on Sunday night, or first thing Monday morning:

1. Total the number of organizations with which you have had contact on each of the three days – Friday, Saturday and Sunday.
2. Remove any duplicates and assign a number to each organization on your remaining list.
3. Devise a categorization scheme for your numbered organizations, including as many of them as possible – private/public, profit/charitable, goods/services, etc. Use as many categories as you need. Some organizations may not 'fit' your scheme, but this is not a problem. How many organizations were in each category?
4. Consider what this list of organizations reveals about you and your lifestyle. Be prepared to share your conclusions with colleagues.

Springboard

Alan Bryman and Emma Bell (2011) *Business Research Methods* (3rd edn), Oxford University Press, Oxford. Full account of methods in management and organizational research.

Chartered Institute of Personnel and Development (2010) *Sustainable Organizational Performance*, CIPD, London. Factsheet which explains the components of high performance working, and the role of the human resource function in sustaining performance.

Stella Cottrell (2011) *Critical Thinking Skills: Developing Effective Analysis and Argument* (2nd edn), Palgrave Macmillan, Basingstoke, Hants. The nature and application of critical thinking.

John Leopold and Lynette Harris (2009) *The Strategic Managing of Human Resources* (2nd edn), Financial Times Prentice Hall, Harlow, Essex. Comprehensive introductory text linking human resource policies and practices to corporate strategy, with case studies.

OB in films

Antz (1998, directors Eric Darnell and Tim Johnson). This clip (7 minutes) begins immediately after the opening credits with Z (played by Woody Allen) saying 'All my life I've lived and worked in the big city'; ends with General Mandible (Gene Hackman) saying, 'Our very next stop Cutter'. This is the story of a neurotic worker ant, Z 4195, who wants to escape from his insignificant job in an authoritarian organization – the ant colony.

1. Using the field map of the organizational behaviour terrain as a guide, identify as many examples as you can of how individual, group, structural and managerial process factors influence organizational effectiveness and quality of working life in an ant colony.
2. This is animated fiction with ants. What similar examples of factors affecting organizational effectiveness and quality of working life can you identify from organizations with which you are familiar?

OB on the web

Search YouTube for 'The Corporation (6/23): The Pathology of Commerce'. This short clip (47 seconds) from the movie *The Corporation* is presented by Dr Robert Hare, who is a consultant to the FBI on psychopaths. He argues that corporations, or organizations, have all the characteristics of psychopaths. Do you find his argument convincing? What are the implications of this viewpoint?

CHAPTER EXERCISES

1. Best job – worst job

Objectives

1. To help you to get to know each other.
2. To introduce you to the main sections of this organizational behaviour course.

Briefing

1. Pair up with another student. Interview each other to find out names, where you both come from, and what other courses you are currently taking.
2. In turn, introduce your partner to the other members of the class.
3. Two pairs now join up, and the group of four discuss:

   What was the worst job that you had? What made it so bad?
   What was the best job that you ever had? What made it so good?
4. Appoint a scribe, to record the recurring themes revealed in group members' stories about their best and worst jobs. Appoint also a group spokesperson.
5. The spokespersons then give presentations to the whole class, summarizing the recurring features of what made a job good or bad. As you listen, use this score sheet to record the frequency of occurrence of the various factors.

Factors affecting job experience

Factors	Examples	✓ if mentioned
Individual factors	Pay: reasonable or poor Job training: comprehensive or none Personality: clashes with other people Communication: frequent or little	
Group factors	Co-workers: helping or not contributing Conflict with co-workers Pressure to conform to group norms Staff not welded into a team	
Structural factors	Job tasks: boring or interesting Job responsibilities: clear or unclear Supervision: too close or little Rules: too many or insufficient guidance	
Management factors	Boss: considerate or autocratic Decisions imposed or opinions asked for Disagreements with managers: often or few Changes: well or poorly implemented	

2. Management versus workers

Rate each of the following issues on this five-point scale, in terms of whether you think managers and workers have shared, partially shared, or separate interests:

share identical interests 1 2 3 4 5 have completely separate interests

- health and safety standards
- basic pay
- introducing new technology
- levels of overtime working
- designing interesting jobs
- bonus payments
- flexible working hours
- equal opportunities
- company share price
- developing new products and/or services
- redundancy

Explain why you rated each of these issues in the way that you did.

(Based on Noon and Blyton, 2007, p. 305.)

Employability assessment

With regard to your future employment prospects:

1. Identify up to three issues from this chapter that you found significant.
2. Relate these to the competencies in the employability matrix.
3. Decide what actions you need to take to maintain and/or develop those competencies under each of the four headings of the employability matrix.

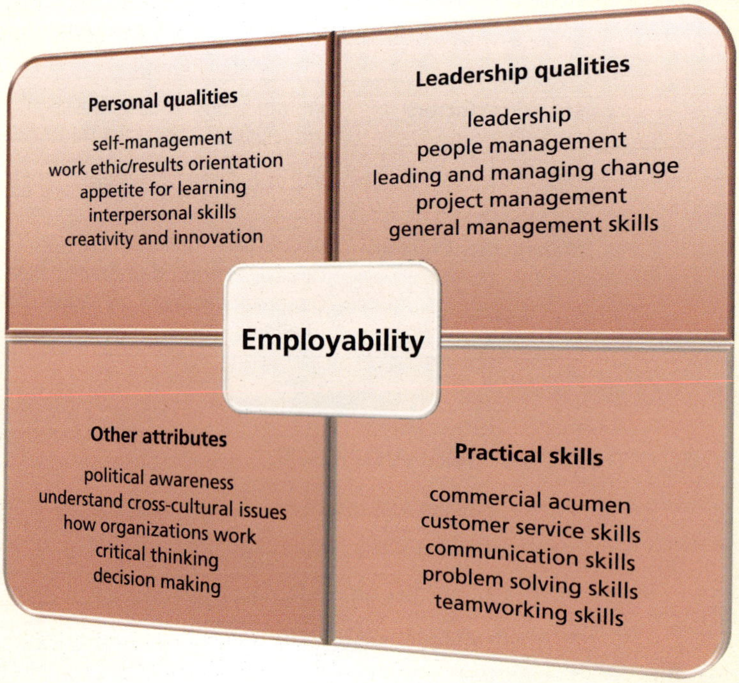

References

Berger, P. and Luckmann, T. (1966) *The Social Construction of Reality*, Harmondsworth: Penguin Books.

Bishop, M. (2011) 'The great mismatch: special report on the future of jobs', *The Economist*, 10 September, pp. 1–18.

Clegg, S.R., Hardy, C., Lawrence, T. and Nord, W.R. (eds) (2006) *The Sage Handbook of Organization Studies* (2nd edn), London: Sage Publications.

Deetz, S. (2009) 'Organizational research as alternative ways of attending to and talking about structures and activities', in D.A. Buchanan and A. Bryman (eds), *The Sage Handbook of Organizational Research Methods*, London: Sage Publications, pp. 21–38.

Elsworth, C. (2005) 'Jackson jurors face testing time as world tunes into courtroom', *The Daily Telegraph*, 29 January, p. 15.

Golzen, G. (1989) 'Maestro, learn the company score', *The Sunday Times*, appointments section, 25 June, p. 8.

Gray, J.L. and Starke, F.A. (1984) *Organizational Behaviour: Concepts and Applications* (3rd edn), Columbus, OH: Merrill Publishing.

Guest, D. (2000) 'Piece by piece', *People Management*, 6(15), pp. 26–31.

Guest, D. and King, Z. (2001) 'Personnel's paradox', *People Management*, 7(19), pp. 24–29.

Heath, C. and Sitkin, S.B. (2001) 'Big-B versus Big-O: what is *organizational* about organizational behavior?', *Journal of Organizational Behavior*, 22(1), pp. 43–58.

Huselid, M.A. (1995) 'The impact of human resource management practices on turnover, productivity, and corporate financial performance', *Academy of Management Journal*, 38(3), pp. 635–72.

Langley, A. (2009) 'Studying processes in and around organizations', in D.A. Buchanan and A. Bryman (eds), *The Sage Handbook of Organizational Research Methods*, London: Sage Publications, pp. 409–29.

McGahan, A.M. (2007) 'Academic research that matters to managers: on zebras, dogs, lemmings, hammers, and turnips', *Academy of Management Journal*, 50(4), pp. 748–53.

Mohr, L.B. (1982) *Explaining Organizational Behaviour: The Limits and Possibilities of Theory and Research*, San Francisco, CA: Jossey-Bass.

Mone, M. (2009) 'Has it damaged me?: probably', *The Times*, Times 2, 15 January, pp. 7–8.

Morgan, G. (2006) *Images of Organization* (3rd edn), London: Sage Publications.

National Commission on the BP Deepwater Horizon Oil Spill and Offshore Drilling (2011a) *Deep Water: The Gulf Oil Disaster and the Future of Offshore Drilling*, Washington, DC: National Commission.

National Commission on the BP Deepwater Horizon Oil Spill and Offshore Drilling (2011b) *Macondo: The Gulf Oil Disaster: Chief Counsel's Report*, Washington, DC: National Commission.

Noon, M. and Blyton, P. (2007) *The Realities of Work* (3rd edn), Basingstoke: Palgrave.

Parker, M. (2012) *Alternative Business: Outlaws, Crime and Culture*, London and New York: Routledge.

Patterson, M.G., West, M.A., Lawthom, R. and Nickell, S. (1997) *Impact of People Management Practices on Business Performance*, London: Institute of Personnel and Development.

Pfeffer, J. (1998) *The Human Equation: Building Profits by Putting People First*, Boston, MA: Harvard Business School Press.

Pfeffer, J. and Sutton, R.I. (2006) *Hard Facts, Dangerous Half-Truths, and Total Nonsense: Profiting from Evidence-Based Management*, Boston, MA: Harvard Business School Press.

Pinker, S. (2002) *The Blank Slate: The Modern Denial of Human Nature*, London: Allen Lane The Penguin Press.

Purcell, J., Kinnie, N., Hutchinson, S., Rayton, B. and Stuart, J. (2003) *Understanding the People and Performance Link: Unlocking the Black Box*, London: Chartered Institute of Personnel and Development.

Roche, B. (2011) 'HR's recession', *People Management*, July, pp. 32–5.

Roethlisberger, F.J. (1977) *The Elusive Phenomenon: An Autobiographical Account of My Work in the Field of Organizational Behaviour at the Harvard Business School*, Boston, MA: Harvard University Press.

Ross, L. (1977) 'The intuitive psychologist and his shortcomings: distortions in the attribution process', in L. Berkowitz (ed.), *Advances in Experimental Social Psychology*, New York: Academic Press, pp. 173–220.

Rousseau, D.M. (2006) 'Is there such a thing as "evidence-based management"?', *Academy of Management Review*, 31(2), pp. 256–69.

Wood, J. (1995) 'Mastering management: organizational behaviour', *Financial Times Mastering Management Supplement* (part 2 of 20).

Chapter 2 Environment

Key terms

environment
stakeholder
environmental uncertainty
environmental complexity
environmental dynamism
post-modern organization
environmental determinism
strategic choice
environmental scanning
globalization
PESTLE analysis
scenario planning
ethics
ethical stance
corporate social responsibility

Learning outcomes

When you have read this chapter, you should be able to define those key terms in your own words, and you should also be able to:

1. Understand the mutual interdependence between the organization and its environment.
2. Appreciate the strengths and limitations of PESTLE analysis of organizational environments.
3. Explain contemporary organizational responses to environmental turbulence.
4. Apply utilitarianism, the theory of rights, and the theory of justice to assess whether or not management actions are ethical, and recognize the limitations of those criteria.
5. Understand the concept of corporate social responsibility, and the practical and ethical implications of this concept for organizational behaviour.

Why study an organization's environment?

Should that have happened?

Lee and Charlie

Lee is 61 and has been director of engineering for Burnside Semiconductors for fourteen years. Intelligent and with a reputation as a good manager, he has not kept up to date with technological developments. The manufacturing process produces toxic waste, and Lee's casual approach to disposal has culminated in two court cases which could cost the company considerable sums in damages. The company's executive vice president, Charlie, has tried for about three years to persuade Lee to prioritize the disposal problem, without success. Having decided that Lee should be removed from his position, Charlie is reluctant to fire him as that would demoralize other managers. He therefore tells colleagues, informally, that he is not satisfied with Lee's work, and exaggerates Lee's faults in these conversations. When Lee encounters a growing lack of support from colleagues, he decides to take early retirement.

Is Charlie's approach ethical?

Environment issues, trends, and events outside the boundaries of the organization, which influence internal decisions and behaviours.

Stakeholder anyone who is concerned with how an organization operates, and who will be affected by its decisions and actions.

An organization must interact with the outside world, with its **environment**. The operations of any organization – local café, city hospital, multinational car-producing company – can be described in terms of 'import-transformation-export' processes. The car plant imports materials, components, equipment, staff, and energy. It then transforms these resources into vehicles, which are exported to customers through online sales outlets or a dealer network. Organizations are involved in a constant series of exchanges with their suppliers, consumers, regulatory agencies, and other **stakeholders**, including their employees.

The environment for a car plant in the twenty-first century is complex. The costs of oil and petrol are high, and are sensitive to unpredictable geopolitical trends. The development of hybrid and electric-powered vehicles is starting to erode sales of petrol-driven cars. The industry consolidation of the late 1990s saw many smaller manufacturers (Saab, Rover, Rolls-Royce, Jaguar, Land Rover, Volvo) bought by larger companies (General Motors, BMW, Ford, the Tata Group). Competition encourages manufacturers to locate plants in low-wage countries (Hungary, Brazil, Romania) generating resentment in traditional manufacturing bases (America, Britain, Europe). In Japan, *gaiatsu*, or foreign pressure, led to restructuring at Toyota, Honda, and Nissan in the late 1990s.

Cost competition has encouraged the use of 'lean manufacturing' methods, with consequences for working practices and quality of working life. There is concern over the environmental pollution generated by internal combustion engines which burn petrol and diesel oil, encouraging the development of cleaner engines to reduce carbon emissions. The volume of traffic in many cities around the world has driven governments to consider road pricing, congestion charges, and taxes to encourage the use of public transport. These are just some of the factors in the external environment of a car plant. Such factors force constant adjustments to ways of thinking about the business of making cars. This means always thinking about the organization's business strategy, organization structure, use of resources, management decisions, job design, and working practices.

STOP AND THINK

What other factors, trends or developments in the external environment of a car plant have not been mentioned? How will these affect the company's behaviour?

What are the main factors in the environment of your college or university? How are those factors influencing management actions – and how are these affecting you?

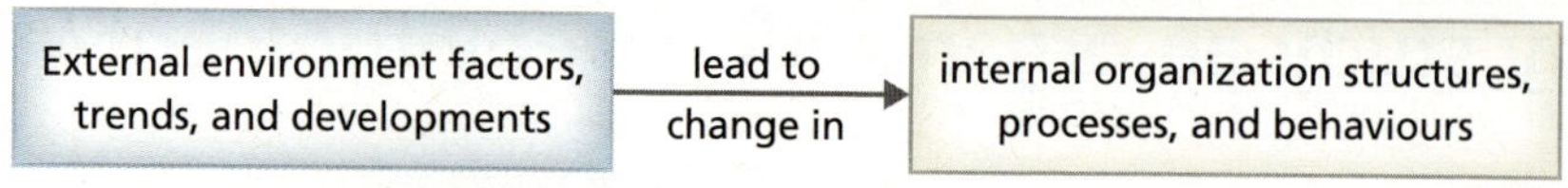

Figure 2.1: External environment–organization links

The argument of this chapter is illustrated in Figure 2.1, which argues that 'the world out there' influences 'the world in here'.

Social science texts annoy readers from other disciplines by first presenting a model, and then revealing that it is wrong. As this is the strategy adopted here, an explanation is needed. There are three reasons for using this 'build it up, knock it down' approach.

1. We have to start somewhere, so let us begin simple and work up to complex.
2. If we construct an argument using basic assumptions, then introduce more complex and realistic assumptions, the thinking behind the model is exposed more clearly.
3. Models like Figure 2.1 are just 'one point of view', and are not beyond dispute. The search for 'the one best way' or 'the correct answer' is usually inappropriate.

Environmental uncertainty the degree of unpredictable turbulence and change in the political, economic, social, technological, legal, and ecological context in which an organization operates.

An understanding of the dynamics of the external environment is central to organizational effectiveness. Organizations which are 'out of fit' have to change, or they may be forced out of business: still making CD players now that MP3 is here; still printing books now that e-book readers are commonplace. As the complexity and pace of environmental change seem to have increased, organizations that are able to adapt quickly to new pressures and opportunities are likely to be more successful than those which are slow to respond. However, the organization that makes a rapid jump in the wrong direction – making better CDs, for example – will still be in trouble. A key concern for organizational behaviour, therefore, has been the search for 'fit' between the internal properties of the organization, and features of the external environment.

The continuing search for 'fit'

Many commentators have argued that the internal structures and processes of an organization should reflect, or 'fit' with, the external environment. What does this mean? How can what happens outside an organization influence what happens inside?

One major factor that affects most organizations is **environmental uncertainty**. Most managers feel that the speed of events is increasing, and that they lack a clear view of the way ahead, the nature of the terrain, obstacles, or the final destination. How can organizations be adaptable enough to cope with continuous and unpredictable change?

Environmental complexity the range of external factors relevant to the activities of the organization; the more factors, the higher the complexity.

Robert Duncan defined uncertainty as the lack of adequate information to reach an unambiguous decision, and argued that environmental uncertainty has two dimensions (Duncan, 1972; 1973; 1974; 1979). One of these dimensions concerns the degree of *simplicity* or *complexity*, and the other concerns the degree of *stability* or *dynamism*. The **simplicity–complexity** dimension refers to issues such as the number of different issues faced, the number of different factors to consider, and the number of things to worry about. The **stability–dynamism** dimension refers to the extent to which those issues are changing or stable, and if they are subject to slow movement or to abrupt shifts.

Environmental dynamism the pace of change in relevant factors external to the organization; the greater the pace of change, the more dynamic the environment.

External factors can include customers, suppliers, regulatory agencies, competitors, and partners in joint ventures. Duncan argued that the 'stability–dynamism' dimension is more important in determining environmental uncertainty. **Environmental complexity** means that you just have a lot of variables to consider. **Environmental dynamism**, on the other hand, is more difficult to manage because you don't know what is going to happen next most of the time. Plotting these two dimensions against each other produces the typology of organizational environments in Figure 2.2. This typology can be applied to the organization, or to business units and departments.

		degree of complexity	
		low – simple	**high – complex**
degree of dynamism	**low – stable**	small number of similar external factors changing slowly: beer distributor florist	large number of different external factors changing slowly: insurance company university
	high – dynamic	small number of similar external factors changing frequently: fashion designer book publisher	large number of dissimilar external factors changing frequently: airline bank

Figure 2.2: Duncan's typology of organizational environments

Duncan argues that an organization's location in this typology is dependent on *management perception*, and not on an observer's classification. In other words, if you don't perceive that your environment is turbulent, then you will probably not respond to it as such. As our perception can change, so the location of an organization on this typology is unstable.

STOP AND THINK Which type of environment would you prefer to work in, stable/simple or dynamic/complex, and why? Share your choice with a colleague. You will have to consider this question every time you apply for a job.

Let's be clear: external environments do not *determine* internal structures and processes. Our perception is selective, paying attention to some factors, while filtering out others. The same environment may be perceived differently by different managers and organizations, even in the same sector. It is management perceptions which affect decisions about organization strategy, structures, and processes. In the language of Karl Weick (1979), managers *enact* rather than react to the external environment.

We have one perspective which claims that reality, the environment, is 'out there' waiting to be observed and analysed. The second perspective claims that 'the environment' is what we perceive and interpret it to be, and which therefore is enacted. This distinction between 'the truth is out there' and 'the truth is what we interpret it to be' takes us back to the discussion in Chapter 1 of positivist and constructivist perspectives on organizational behaviour.

Igor Ansoff (1997) has developed this argument, summarized in Table 2.1. He identifies five types of environment based on the turbulence being experienced, from 'repetitive' at one extreme, to 'surprising' at the other. Read the first two columns of his table *vertically*, working up and down this scale from 'repetitive' at one extreme to 'surprising' at the other:

1. repetitive
2. expanding
3. changing
4. discontinuous
5. surprising

Go to level 1, the repetitive environment, and read the table *horizontally*. Ansoff argues that we can identify the most appropriate strategy and management attitude for that environment. In a stable environment, strategy should be based on precedent. What made the organization successful in the past will work in the future. In a repetitive environment, the management attitude concerns stability. Change could ruin the business:

Table 2.1: Ansoff's typology of environments

Level	Environmental change	Organization strategy	Management attitude
1	**Repetitive** little or no change	**Stable** based on precedent	**Stability-seeking** rejects change
2	**Expanding** slow incremental change	**Reactive** incremental change based on experience	**Efficiency-driven** adapts to change
3	**Changing** fast incremental change	**Anticipatory** incremental change based on extrapolation	**Market-driven** seeks familiar change
4	**Discontinuous** discontinuous but predictable change	**Entrepreneurial** discontinuous new strategies based on observed opportunities	**Environment-driven** seeks new but related change
5	**Surprising** discontinuous and unpredictable change	**Creative** discontinuous new and creative strategies	**Environment-creating** seeks novel change

Source: Ansoff (2007).

environment is repetitive, with no change → strategy should be stable and based on precedent → management should seek stability and reject change.

Now go to level 5, to the surprising, discontinuous and unpredictable environment, and again read across the row. As you might expect, the recommended strategy is creative, based on new approaches, and not on what the organization has done in the past. The management attitude has to be novelty-seeking, helping to influence the environment in creative ways. Holding on to past precedents in this context will ruin the business:

surprising environment, unpredictable change → novel strategies should be based on creativity → management should embrace change, seek novelty

Now read the other three middle rows, again working *across* the table, noting the strategy and management implications for each of the other levels of change. Once that argument and the practical implications are clear, try reading the organization strategy column *vertically*. This can be read as a strategy scale, from stability (precedent-driven) at one extreme to creativity (novelty-driven) at the other. The final column works in the same way, with a management attitude scale, from stability (rejecting change) to creativity (embracing novelty).

Source: DILBERT © 1999 Scott Adams. Used by permission of UNIVERSAL UCLICK. All rights reserved.

Ansoff also distinguishes between *extrapolative* and *discontinuous* change, shown by the separation in Table 2.1 between levels 3 and 4. Where change is extrapolative, the future can be predicted, more or less, following (extrapolating from) current trends. When change is discontinuous, our ability to predict is limited. Ansoff claims that 80 per cent of managers say their organizations have level 4 or 5 environments.

Ansoff makes a number of cruel observations about managers who have been successful in organizations with extrapolative environments. He claims that they may lack the skills, knowledge, experience and attitudes to deal with discontinuous change. Success in a discontinuous environment requires entrepreneurial vision and creativity, anticipating change. He comments that 'Managers incapable of developing an entrepreneurial mindset must be replaced' (Ansoff, 1997, p. 76).

STOP AND THINK

Does your educational institution face extrapolative or discontinuous change?

To what extent is the institution's strategy and management attitude appropriate to that level of change?

Apply this analysis to yourself. What level of environmental change are you subject to, and how does this affect your behaviour?

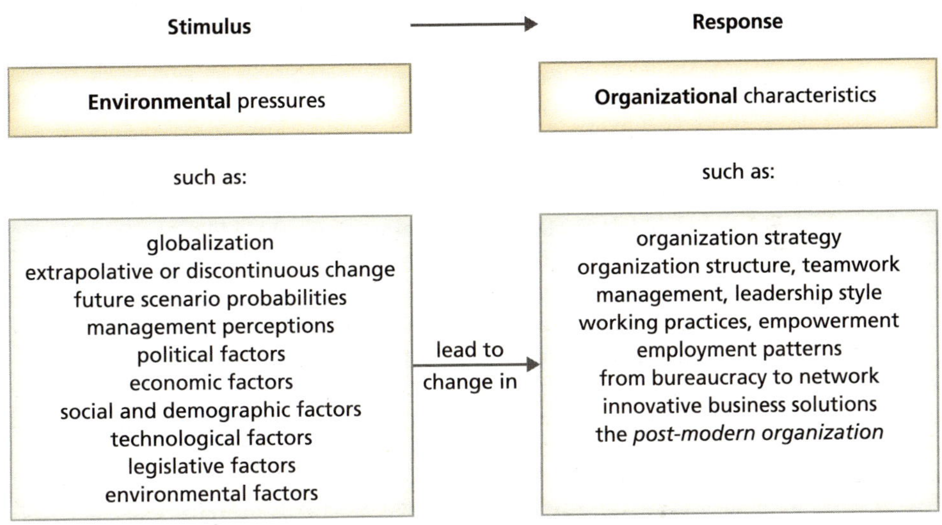

Figure 2.3: The search for environment–organization 'fit'

Post-modern organization a networked, information-rich, de-layered, downsized, boundaryless, high-commitment organization employing highly skilled, well-paid autonomous knowledge workers.

Our updated model is shown in Figure 2.3. This is a 'stimulus–response' model. The stimulus of external change prompts organizational responses. The scale, dynamism and complexity of environmental stimuli appear to encourage a new adaptive, environmentally responsive organizational 'paradigm', described as the **post-modern organization**.

Stewart Clegg (1990, p. 181) describes the post-modern organization:

> Where the modernist organization was rigid, post-modern organization is flexible. Where modernist consumption was premised on mass forms, post-modernist consumption is premised on niches. Where modernist organization and jobs were highly differentiated, demarcated and de-skilled, post-modernist organization and jobs are highly de-differentiated, de-demarcated and multiskilled.

So, it is claimed that bureaucracy, macho managers, and boring jobs are being replaced in the post-modern world by flexible organizations with participative, supportive managers and interesting, multiskilled jobs.

STOP AND THINK

Have you experienced, or observed, a flexible, boundaryless, post-modern organization with skilled and autonomous employees?

Have you experienced, or observed, the opposite – a bureaucratic organization with poorly paid, boring, and unskilled jobs that are controlled by autocratic managers?

Environmental determinism the argument that internal organizational responses are primarily determined by external environmental factors.

We promised that, having built a model, we would knock it down. There are four flaws in the reasoning in Figure 2.3. The first problem concerns **environmental determinism**. Duncan's argument about the role of perceptions is a powerful challenge to this perspective.

We know that internal organizational arrangements reflect the influence of a range of factors: the dynamics of the senior management team, their approach to decision-making, employee suggestions, past experience. We also know that, whatever the reality 'out there', what really matters is how the environment is understood and interpreted 'in here'. This means that the environmental 'stimulus' is just one stimulus among many, and that this stimulus is not always guaranteed either a response, or the expected response.

The second problem concerns assumptions about organizational boundaries. Can we say clearly what is 'out there' and what is 'in here'? The organization is involved in a constant process of exchange with the environment, importing staff and resources, exporting goods and services. Employees are members of the wider society, whose values and preferences are thus 'inside' the organization. Many organizations operate partnerships, with suppliers and competitors, to share the costs, for example, of developing new materials, processes, and products. Healthcare is delivered through networks of collaborating organizations. Some companies, such as gymnasiums and roadside motoring assistance providers, treat their customers as 'members'. The boundaries between organizations and their environments are often blurred.

Strategic choice the ability of an organization to decide on the environment, or environments – that is, sectors, and parts of the world – in which it will operate.

The third problem is one of interpretation. We are considering 'environment' and 'organization' as separate domains. However, an organization chooses and influences its environment; this is a matter of **strategic choice** (Child, 1997). European carmakers can choose whether or not to manufacture and market their cars in China. A restaurant changes its environment (customers, suppliers, competitors) when the owners choose to stop selling fast food and move into gourmet dining. In other words, the external environment of the organization is *enacted*: the organization creates and to some extent even becomes its own environment, rather than being 'given' or 'presented with' that environment.

The final problem concerns continuity. The model presents a picture of rapid and radical change. However, we know that is not the case. Looking back into the past, we can identify many continuities, environmental and organizational. The German Weihenstephan Brewery was founded in 1040, the Swedish company Stora in 1288, Oxford University Press in 1478, Beretta in 1530, Lloyd's in 1688, Sumitomo in 1690, Sotheby's in 1744, Guinness in 1759.

Analysing the organization's environment

Environmental scanning techniques for identifying and predicting the impact of external trends and developments on the internal functioning of an organization.

Identifying current and future factors 'out there' which could affect an organization usually generates a long list. The first problem, therefore, is to identify all of those factors. The next challenge is to predict their impact. The methods used to analyse the environment are known as **environmental scanning** techniques.

Environmental scanning involves collecting information from a range of sources: government statistics, newspapers and magazines, internet sites, specialist research and consulting agencies, demographic analysis, market research, focus groups. There are three major trends affecting most organizations: technology, globalization, and demographics.

Technology

Technology is probably the most tangible and visible aspect of environmental change. The pace of development appears to be unchecked. Since the previous edition of this text was published three years ago, we have seen the development of iPads and netbooks, and further developments in mobile telephony, e-books, and electric cars. Our previous edition cited social networking and cloud computing as 'new', but these are now established and 'old'.

Applications of computing affect most aspects of our lives, from entertainment to manufacturing, the provision of services, and how we communicate. These developments have increased the number of 'knowledge workers' whose value depends more on what they know than on what they can do. Software design and 'back office' support do not depend on location, and these kinds of knowledge work can be outsourced to countries where pay is lower. A focus on computing, however, overlooks developments in other fields, such as new materials, and in healthcare where the pace of development of new drugs, treatment regimes, and medical equipment seems to be as rapid as in computing, but attracts less attention.

STOP AND THINK

What new technologies, materials, medical treatments, services, processes, and so on, have affected your life and work recently?

In what ways? For better, or for worse?

The implications of technology for organizational behaviour are explored in more depth in Chapter 3. However, we must note that technology affects organizational behaviour in many ways, and on many levels. Technological developments influence the design and nature of products and services, corporate strategies, modes of communications and information exchange, and the day-to-day work of individuals. Expertise in making technologically sophisticated products has moved to developing countries with lower labour costs, raising concerns that the developed economies which invented those products have become unnecessarily dependent on their overseas manufacturers.

Not made in America: the Amazon Kindle

The Kindle 2 e-reader was designed by Amazon's Lab126 unit in California. However, most of its components are made in China, Taiwan, and South Korea, and the product is assembled in China (Pisano and Shih, 2009).

Component	Made in	Reason
Flex circuit connector	China	American supplier base eroded as the manufacture of consumer electronics and computers migrated to Asia.
Electrophoretic display	Taiwan	Manufacture requires expertise developed from producing flat-panel LCDs, which migrated to Asia with semiconductor manufacturing.
Highly polished injection-moulded case	China	US supplier base eroded as the manufacture of toys, consumer electronics, and computers migrated to Asia.
Wireless card	South Korea	South Korea used its infrastructure for designing and manufacturing consumer electronics to become a centre for making mobile phone components and handsets, especially products using CDMA technology, which is widely used in South Korea.
Lithium polymer battery	China	Battery development and manufacturing migrated from the US to Asia along with the development of consumer electronics and notebook computers.
Controller board	China	US companies long ago outsourced the manufacture of printed circuit boards to Asia, where there is now a huge supplier base.

Getty Images

Source: adapted from 'Restoring American competitiveness' by Pisano, G.P. and Shih, W.C., *Harvard Business Review*, 87(7/8) 2009, p. 121.

Why is it not made in America? Is this a problem?

Globalization

In the twenty-first century, developed Western economies see both threats and opportunities in the economic growth of countries such as Brazil, Russia, India and China – the so-called BRICs economies. Those economies have lower labour costs, and have become attractive locations for manufacturing operations and for customer service call centres. There is a widespread perception that 'outsourcing' manufacturing and service operations in this way is happening at the expense of jobs in Europe and North America. The term given to these trends and developments is **globalization** (Giddens, 1990).

Globalization the intensification of world-wide social and business relationships which link localities in such a way that local conditions are shaped by distant events.

One feature of globalization is 'the death of distance' (Cairncross, 2001), a term which means that geographical separation of countries and individuals is now unimportant. Globalization also means that the fate of a village in a developing country, dependent on export sales revenues from a single cash crop, is decided by price movements in exchanges in New York and Frankfurt. Globalization means that decisions taken in Tokyo in Japan affect employment in the English Midlands, where Toyota has an assembly plant. Globalization means that the collapse of the investment bank Lehman Brothers in 2008, due to high-risk lending practices, led to a financial crisis affecting banks and economies around the world.

BRICs and globality

Globalization used to mean 'Americanization'. Not any more. Everyone is now competing with everyone else, a new trend described as 'globality' by Harold Sirkin and colleagues (2008). Organizations in many developing economies are expanding into developed economies, buying up established businesses and brands. The famous American brewer Budweiser, for example, is now owned by a Brazilian–Belgian conglomerate. The traditional UK brands Jaguar, Land Rover, and Tetley Tea are owned by the Indian Tata Group. Chinese companies have invested heavily in Australian mining organizations. By 2008, there were over 60 companies based in 'emerging markets' on the Fortune 500 list of the world's biggest companies. Many of those were from the BRICs economies: Brazil, Russia, India, and China. The ten largest Fortune Global 500 emerging market companies in 2008 were:

Company	Country	Global rank	Revenue ($bn)
Sinopec	China	16	159.3
Stage Grid	China	24	132.9
China National Petroleum	China	25	129.8
Pemex	Mexico	42	104.0
Gazprom	Russia	47	98.6
Petrobras	Brazil	63	87.7
Lukoil	Russia	90	67.2
Petronas	Malaysia	95	66.2
Indian Oil	India	116	57.4
Industrial and Commercial Bank of China	China	133	51.5

Other global companies from emerging economies are Haier (China, white goods), Cemex (Mexico, cement), Embraer (Brazil, aircraft), Infosys and Ranbaxy (India, software and pharmaceuticals). Lenovo is a Chinese computer manufacturer which in 2005 bought the personal computer business of IBM for US$1.75 million, and now has annual revenues of around $17 billion. One of its products is a simple computer for farmers in rural markets, but with features (an 'express repair' key that recovers from a crash) that are used in products for sale elsewhere. The company's chairman Yang Yuanqing says 'We are proud of our Chinese roots', but 'we no longer want to be positioned as a Chinese company. We want to be a truly global company'. Lenovo has no headquarters; management meetings rotate through the company's locations around the world; development work is done by virtual teams in different countries; the global marketing department is in Bangalore. Virtual teams are teams which meet and collaborate using the internet and videoconferencing, but rarely meet in person. Mr Yang and his family moved to North Carolina to learn about American culture and to improve their English (Bishop, 2008).

Home viewing

Syriana (2006, director Stephen Gaghan) comes with the slogan 'everything is connected', and offers insights into the nature of globalization. The film is set in the fictional Gulf state of Syriana, and is based on relations between the global oil industry and national politics, illustrating the links between power and wealth, between political, organizational, and personal actions, between the decisions of corporate executives and the fate of workers. The action shifts between America, the Middle East, and Europe. Friends are enemies; colleagues are crooks. One character observes, 'Corruption ain't nothing more than government intrusion into market efficiencies in the form of regulation. We have laws against it *precisely* so we can get away with it. Corruption is our protection. Corruption is what keeps us safe and warm. Corruption is how we win'. George Clooney plays Bob Barnes, a CIA agent hunting Middle Eastern terrorists. His role is to prevent the ageing Emir and his idealistic son from finalizing a deal with China, and not America ('I want you to take him from his hotel, drug him, put him in the front of a car, and run a truck into it at fifty miles an hour'). *Syriana* attributes the radicalization of young immigrant Muslims from Pakistan, and their suicide terrorist attack on an oil tanker, to the casual manner in which a global oil company treats its employees. George Clooney won an Oscar for his part in this movie. As you watch this movie, identify positive and negative examples of globalization in action, and assess whether the advantages outweigh the disadvantages, from the viewpoint of this film.

STOP AND THINK

How does globalization affect you personally?

In what ways could globalization influence your working life and your career?

What are the personal benefits and disadvantages?

GLOBAL BUSINESS ETIQUETTE

It's not just your product which needs to go native. Refine your manners or risk irritating or insulting potential buyers.

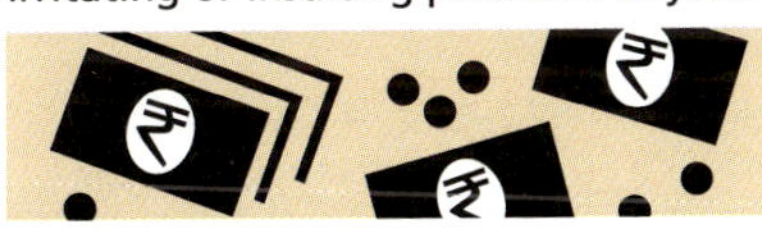

INDIA: Know your numbers: 1 Rupee is 100 Paise; 100,000 Rupees is 1 Lakh; 10 million Rupees is 1 Crore.

SOUTH KOREA: Gifts are expected at formal introductory meetings. Office products with your logo or British foods and drinks are acceptable.

JAPAN: Receive business cards, known as 'meishi', with both hands at once. Present yours Japanese side up.

LIBYA: Do not show the soles of your shoes. This is an insult across the Arab world.

IRAN: Learn the many public holidays. Business will close during two dozen festivals such as Nowruz, Eid ul-Fitr, and the Birth of Iman Mahdi.

SAUDI ARABIA: Meetings may be set by prayer times, rather than the precise hour. So 'between Maghrib and Isha' is preferable to stating 6.30 p.m.

Source: Clawson/*The Times*/News International Trading Ltd, 18 October 2011.

Consider your own experience of globalization. This may involve holiday plans, working abroad, the clothes that you wear, the food and drink that you consume, and the way in which you use the internet, phones, social networking sites, and different types of media technology. You probably have many direct and indirect encounters with other cultures, daily.

However, globalization is an uneven process. Many people around the world do not have access to the goods and technologies that contribute to the experience of globalization for affluent members of developed economies. Many societies and groups reject the dislocation that globalization can bring, and object to the spread of Western culture, signified most clearly by brand labels. Western organizations (from fast food outlets to national embassies) have become terrorist targets, as well as focal points for the (often violent) demonstration of anger over perceived attempts to impose Western values on other cultures.

This seems to be an age of 'disorganized capitalism', complex and rapidly changing, in which the boundaries of large organizations in particular are blurred, and in which the nature of work itself is in a state of flux. Figure 2.4, based on the work of John Kotter (1995), summarizes this argument. The arrows running down the figure set out a causal chain, from the technological, economic and geopolitical trends at the top, to the organizational changes at the bottom. Kotter argues that organizational changes in the direction of becoming faster, flatter, and more flexible are determined by external environmental pressures which are driving globalization, introducing new threats and problems, and opening up market opportunities. Change seems to be inevitable; 'adapt to survive'.

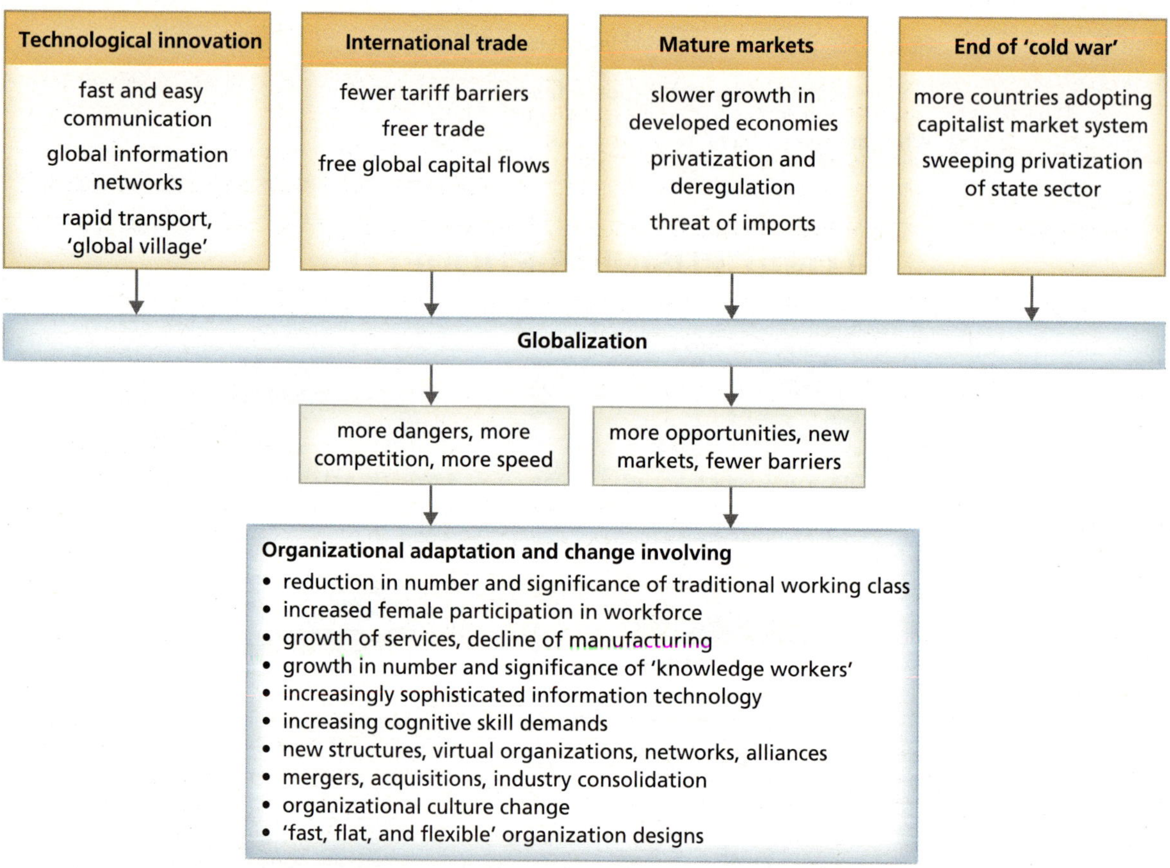

Figure 2.4: Globalization and organizational change

Are you future-proofed?

Lynda Gratton (2011) argues that developments in globalization, society, demography, technology, and energy use are reshaping the world of work. To make sure that you will be employable in this new world, Gratton suggests that you invest in your 'social capital'.

First, you need a 'posse' of around a dozen people to whom you can turn for advice and support when you run into difficulties.

Second, you need a 'big ideas crowd' of people with whom you can exchange creative ideas.

Third, you need a 'regenerative community', which is a fancy term for the family and friends with whom you can relax.

In order to 'future-proof' your career, she also suggests that you will have to develop fresh knowledge and skills every few years, so that you can change from one job and organization to another, to take advantage of new skill shortages. She calls this 'serial mastery', and notes that education systems do not currently develop the abilities that this requires. Do you have your posse, crowd, and community yet? How do you plan to develop serial mastery?

Disneyization

While most of us think of Disney as a company that makes animated and children's films, Alan Bryman (2004) argues that Disneyization is a global process infiltrating aspects of our social, cultural, and economic life. In short, our surroundings are becoming more like a Disney theme park. Disneyization has four main principles:

theming	settings and objects being presented and decorated in dramatic ways that are not directly related to their purpose, such as a restaurant with a Wild West theme
hybrid consumption	the blurring of boundaries between different types of products and services that are normally distinct and separate, such as with casinos that are also hotels including numerous restaurants
merchandising	the promotion of branded and licensed items, with copyright images and logos clearly on display, rather than just plain company products
performative labour	front line staff being hired to perform, smiling and helpful, joking and interacting with customers, to create atmosphere and mood

© Alan Bryman

The Hotel Luxor, in Las Vegas, with an 'Ancient Egypt' theme

If your restaurant or shopping mall has been Disneyized, it will look and sound different, and give the impression of providing a novel and dramatic experience. This process is being imitated because it increases the appeal of goods and services and the settings in which they are provided, and encourages you to buy things that you don't really need.

Barbie is a globalization icon

Chip East/Reuters

Barbie is one of the most profitable toys in history, selling at a rate of two per second, and generating over US$1 billion in annual revenues for the Mattell Corporation based in Los Angeles (Giddens and Sutton, 2009, p. 135). Sold in 140 countries, she is a global citizen, but she is global in another sense, too. Although she was designed in America, she has never been made there, and was first manufactured in 1959 in Japan (where wages were low at the time), and has since been made in other low-wage countries in Asia. The only components of Barbie which come from America are the cardboard packaging, and some paints. Her body and wardrobe come from elsewhere across the planet:

component/ manufacturing stage	source
designs, pigments, oils, moulds	United States
cardboard packaging	made in United States with pulp from Indonesia
oil for her plastic parts	Saudi Arabia
refined oil and PVC plastic pellets	Taiwan
injection moulding	China, Indonesia, Malaysia
nylon hair	Japan
cotton dresses	China
distribution	Hong Kong

The sign on the box may say 'made in China', or Indonesia, or Malaysia. But Barbie crosses many geographical boundaries on her journey from the designer's sketchpad to the customer.

Look at the products that you own and use. Where do they come from? Choose one of your favourite items and see if you can identify where in the world its components were made.

Demographics

Generations

Parry and Urwin (2011) identify the following generations:

- *Veterans*, born 1925 to 1942; also known as the silent generation, matures, or traditionalists;
- *Baby boomers*, born 1943 to 1960; also just called boomers;
- *Generation X*, born 1961 to 1981, also known as baby busters, the thirteenth, or the lost generation;
- *Generation Y*, born since 1982; also known as millennials, nexters, or echo boomers.

Other commentators recognize

- *Generation C*, born since 1990: Connected, Communicating, always Clicking.

These dates are approximate, and there is considerable disagreement about them. You will find different versions elsewhere.

Demographic changes pose some of the most significant challenges for management in the twenty-first century. The workforce in industrialized economies is ageing. The proportion of the population who have retired from employment is growing relative to the proportion of the population still in work. An ageing population is one consequence of people living longer and having fewer children. This is an accelerating global phenomenon. One measure is the percentage of the population aged 65 or over. In the UK, these percentages are as shown in Table 2.2.

Table 2.2: Percentage of UK population aged 65 or over

year	% of population aged 65 or over
1985	15
2010	17
2035*	23

*UK Office of National Statistics estimate: www.statistics.gov.uk.

In 2010, there were around 10 million people aged 65 or over in the UK. The percentage increase, from 15 to 17 per cent, between 1985 and 2010, added a further 1.7 million to that group. In addition, the average age of the UK population is also increasing, as shown in Table 2.3.

Table 2.3: Average age of UK population

year	average age
1985	35
2010	40
2035*	42

*UK Office of National Statistics estimate: www.statistics.gov.uk.

An ageing population has social consequences. The baby boomers who were born after the Second World War (which ended in 1945) started celebrating their 60th birthdays from around 2006. Boomers have also been called a 'silver tsunami' sweeping across affected countries (*The Economist*, 2010). *Boomsday* by Christopher Buckley (2007) is a fictional account of the anger of younger generations whose taxes pay for the pensions, health, and welfare of those boomers in their old age. Governments have been trying to raise retirement ages in order to reduce the drain on welfare budgets and pension systems.

The silver tsunami has organizational consequences. How will organizations fill the gaps as boomers retire, taking their knowledge and experience with them, while the proportion of skilled youngsters in the workforce is shrinking? Some older workers – 'nevertirees' – have decided to carry on working, and organizations will also have to learn how to manage them. Will older workers adapt to new technologies and working practices, and take management orders from youngsters? These are new problems, and there is little research or experience on which to draw. Some approaches to managing older workers include

- exit interviews to capture their wisdom
- mentoring systems in which boomers coach their replacements
- phased retirement rather than a sudden stop
- shorter working weeks with flexible hours
- pools of retired staff who can be called upon for special projects
- working during busy periods punctuated by 'Benidorm leave'.

A recent survey of over 1,000 managers found that most organizations had not yet developed their age management policies (Pickard, 2010). Younger managers find it difficult to manage older workers, who have different drives, and need flexibility (to care for elderly parents and grandchildren, for example). Management styles have to be consultative, drawing on the experience of older workers for whom money is probably not the main or only motivator.

Nevertirement and nevertirees

Barclays Wealth is a bank for 'high net worth' people (http://www.barclayswealth.com). To find out more about their customers' future plans, they surveyed 2,000 wealthy individuals, who had at least £1 million of assets to invest. They found that, rather than planning a conventional retirement, many planned to go on working (Leppard and Chittenden, 2010).

In Britain, 70 per cent of those under 45 said that they will always want to be involved in some form of commercial or professional work. In other words, 'nevertirement' could become more popular, and this may not apply just to the wealthy. Organizations will need to develop human resource policies and working practices to deal effectively with this trend. The number of people in Britain working beyond retirement age rose to over 800,000 in 2010. In that year, there were around 724,000 people aged 18 to 24 out of work. If the elderly don't retire, but carry on working, will this contribute to youth unemployment?

country	% planning to work beyond retirement age
Saudi Arabia	92
United Arab Emirates	91
Qatar	91
South Africa	88
Latin America	78
UK	60
Ireland	59
USA	54
Japan	46
Spain	44
Switzerland	34

Generation Y are the children of the boomers. Most of the student readers of this text will be Gen Ys. Do boomers and Gen Ys want different things from work? Sylvia Ann Hewlett and colleagues suggest that these groups actually share a number of attitudes, behaviours, and preferences (Hewlett et al., 2009). Their findings are based on surveys of around 4,000 college graduates, followed by focus groups and interviews.

They found that boomers and Gen Ys both want flexible work arrangements and opportunities to give something back to society. Both of those factors were more important than pay. The motives of boomers are summarized in Table 2.4.

Table 2.4: Portrait of baby boomers: what makes them 'tick'?

Staying in harness	*42% predict they will continue working after age 65* and 14% say they will never retire because they enjoy their work which is related to their identities.
Long runways	*47% see themselves as being in the middle of their careers:* global recession is also encouraging them to delay retirement.
From 'me' to 'we'	*55% are members of external volunteer networks.* The idealism of the 1960s lives on, and they volunteer time to environmental, cultural, educational, and other causes.
Familial obligations	*71% say they care for the elderly.* In addition to looking after elderly parents, they contribute financial support to their own children.
Yearning for flexibility	*87% say that flexible working is important:* they want to pursue other interests as well as work, and look for autonomy and flexibility in their jobs.

Source: based on Hewlett et al., 2009.

The rewards from work that boomers regard as important are:

1. high-quality colleagues
2. an intellectually stimulating workplace
3. autonomy regarding work tasks
4. flexible work arrangements
5. access to new experiences and challenges
6. giving back to the world through work
7. recognition from the company or the boss.

The motives of Gen Ys are summarized in Table 2.5. The rewards from work that Gen Ys regard as important are:

1. high-quality colleagues
2. flexible work arrangements
3. prospects for advancement
4. recognition from the company or the boss
5. steady rate of advancement and promotion
6. access to new experiences and challenges.

Both groups want to serve a wider purpose, want opportunities to explore their interests and passions, and say that flexible working and work-life balance are important to them. They also share a sense of obligation to the wider society and the environment. (Gen Xs are far less likely to find those obligations important.) It is also significant that both these groups say that financial gain is not their main reason for choosing an employer. They are interested in other forms of reward: teamwork, challenge, new experiences, recognition.

Human resource practices need to emphasize teamwork and collaboration, flexible working, phased retirement, project work, short-term assignments, opportunities to support external causes, and eco-friendly work environments. Another valuable practice is intergenerational mentoring; boomers welcome the chance to mentor and support Gen Ys, who can also share their potentially better understanding of social networking technologies.

Source: http://seldomlogical.com

Table 2.5: Portrait of Generation Y: what makes them 'tick'?

Loyalty versus quest	*45% expect to work for their current employer for their whole career.* They are faithful to a workplace, but most want new experiences and challenges and are likely to wander.
Networking by nature	*48% say having a network of friends at work is important.* Working in teams is a key motivator, connecting with others in open offices where bosses and others are readily accessible.
Multicultural ease	*78% are comfortable working with people from other cultures:* they are at ease with diversity (only 27% of boomers have this comfort level), and they network accordingly.
Ambition	*84% say they are very ambitious:* they are 'go-getters', willing 'to go the extra mile' for the company.
Healing the planet	*86% feel that it is important that their work make a positive impact on the world:* they want an employer who shares their eco-awareness and social consciousness, even down to details of office energy use.

Source: based on Hewlett et al., 2009.

On the grid 24/7: here comes Generation C

© Gareth Brown/Corbis

Generation C is the label being given to those born after 1990. The 'C' stands for connected, communicating, content-centric, computerized, community-oriented, and always clicking. This is the first generation to have grown up with the internet, social media, and mobile handheld computing, for whom 24/7 mobile and internet connectivity are taken for granted, and freedom of expression is the norm. These technologies encourage more flexible forms of working, and less hierarchical organizations, and they are blurring the boundaries between work and personal life. By 2020, Gen C will make up over 40 per cent of the population in America, Europe, and the BRICs countries (Friedrich et al., 2011).

Gen C will be 'on the grid' 24/7. Connected around the clock is normal for Gen C. Global mobile phone and internet use are predicted to increase as follows:

	2012	2020
mobile phone users	4.6 billion	6 billion
internet users	1.7 billion	4.7 billion

Gen C will be 'social animal 2.0', with a wide range of personal relationships driven by social networks, voice channels, online groups, blogs, and electronic messaging. This will create fast-moving business and political pressures as information and ideas spread more widely, more quickly.

There are organizational consequences. Most Gen C employees will bring their own computers to work rather than use corporate resources. There will probably be more work done by virtual project groups, with fewer face to face meetings, and less frequent travel.

Other demographic trends that will affect many organizations include global migration, triggered in part by wars, improved communications and transport, and in Europe new rules concerning harmonization and labour mobility. This contributes to a richer ethnic, cultural, and religious mix in a given workforce, and puts a premium on the ability to manage this diversity of values, needs, and preferences.

Further trends include the development of 'the hourglass economy', divided between educated and skilled knowledge workers, who are in demand, and poorly educated, untrained and poorly paid manual and clerical workers, for whom there are fewer job opportunities. Lifestyles and values are changing, affecting the formation and composition of households, patterns of living and consumption, trends in leisure and education, and preferences in working patterns. Social values also change. Environmental concern, expressed in punitive fines for organizations which create toxic waste, and in public protests, over new roads and airports, for example, were uncommon before the 1980s, but are now routine. These concerns contribute to the corporate social responsibility movement, explored later in this chapter.

STOP AND THINK

In what ways do your values differ from the values of your parents?

In what ways will your lifestyle differ from that of your parents?

In what ways will your experience of work differ from that of your parents?

How will your values and expectations as an employee make life easier or more difficult for the organizations that are likely to employ you?

PESTLE analysis

PESTLE analysis an environmental scanning tool identifying Political, Economic, Social, Technological, Legal, and Ecological factors that affect an organization.

One popular approach to environmental scanning is **PESTLE analysis**. This is a simple, structured tool which helps to organize the complexity of dealing with trends in technology, globalization, demographics, and other factors. Pestle analysis provides an audit of an organization's environment and is used to guide strategic decision-making and plan for possible future contingencies (Morrison and Daniels, 2010).

Figure 2.5 illustrates a typical range of PESTLE trends and pressures. The details under each heading are for illustration, and they are not comprehensive. The best way to approach environmental scanning is to do an analysis yourself. This will almost certainly reveal that

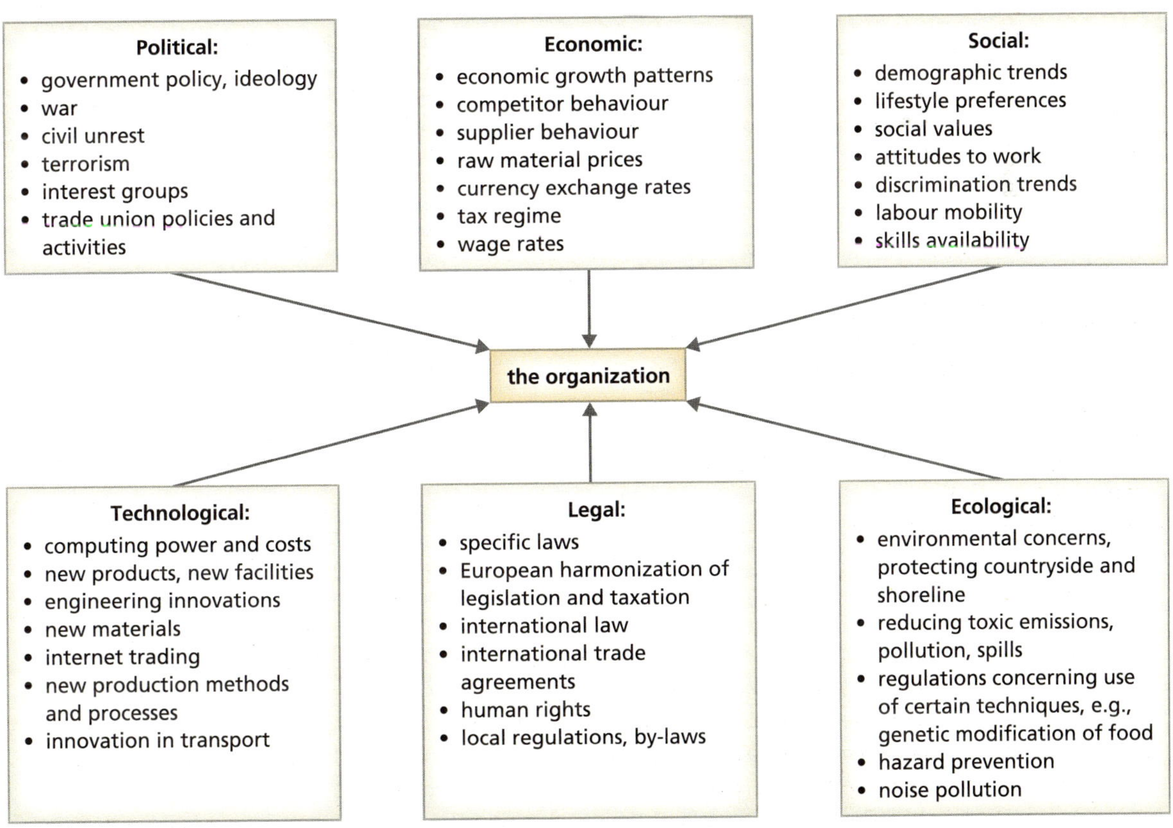

Figure 2.5: PESTLE factors affecting the organization

the neat categories in the model overlap in a rather untidy way in practice. Many legislative changes are politically motivated. Ecological concerns reflect changing social values and preferences. Some technological developments (electric cars) are encouraged by economic and ecological issues (the price of petrol and CO_2 emissions). However, the point of the analysis is to identify external environmental factors, their interrelationships, and their impact. It is less important to get them into the 'correct' boxes.

BMW's 2017 production line project

AFP/Getty Images

The BMW 7-series car is made at Dingolfing, in Lower Bavaria. Production managers were concerned about how to maintain the plant's productivity with an ageing workforce. Older workers tend to have longer sickness absences, and have to work harder to keep up their output. The average age of the plant's workers was expected to rise from 39 to 47 by 2017. So, management set up a pilot project, staffing one of the lines (making rear axle gearboxes) with a 'year-2017 mix' of 42 workers with an average age of 47. Could this '2017' group achieve the same productivity as lines with younger employees (Loch et al., 2010)?

The '2017 line' workers identified 70 changes. These were complemented by job rotation, to balance the workload on individuals, and strength and stretching exercises which were developed by a physiotherapist, then taken over by a volunteer from the group. Most changes concerned ways to reduce wear and tear on the workers, which also reduced sickness absence.

examples of changes	cost	benefits
wooden flooring	€5,000	reduce knee strain and static electric shocks
orthopaedic footwear	€2,000	reduce strain on feet
magnifying lenses	€1,000	reduce eyestrain, minimize errors
barbershop chairs	€1,000	enable short breaks; work while seated
manual hoisting cranes	€1,000	reduce back strain
angled monitors	no cost	reduce eyestrain
adjustable work tables	no cost	less physical effort; quick to adjust
large-handled tools	no cost	reduce strain on arms
stackable containers	no cost	less physical effort
larger typeface on screens	no cost	reduce eyestrain, minimize errors

Senior managers identified the problem; production managers set up the experiment; production line workers created the solution. This pilot was initially dismissed as 'the pensioners' line'. However, for a capital investment of €20,000, productivity rose 7 per cent in one year, to the same level as lines staffed by younger workers. The original line target was 440 gearboxes a shift. This was increased to 500 in 2008, then to 530 in 2009. With zero defects, and absenteeism below the plant average, the company now cites the line as a model of productivity, with similar projects in plants in Leipzig (Germany) and Steyr (Austria).

STOP AND THINK

Choose an organization with which you are familiar, such as a hospital, supermarket, university or college, or the place you worked last summer.

Make a list of the political, economic, social, technological, legislative, and ecological factors that affect that organization.

What practical advice would you give to the management of this organization?

How would you assess the practical value of this exercise to the organization?

Diet and airline costs

Why should airlines be concerned about their passengers' diets? The amount of fuel that an aircraft uses depends on the weight that it is carrying. The weight of the average American rose 10 pounds during the 1990s, resulting in an extra 350 million gallons of fuel being used by airlines in 2000, at a cost of £149 million. That extra fuel released 3.8 million tons of carbon dioxide into the environment. Airlines can reduce weight by using plastic cutlery and avoiding heavy magazines, but they cannot control passengers' weight. Southwest Airlines asks passengers who can't fit between the armrests to buy a second seat. A commuter plane crash in North Carolina in 2003, which killed 21 people, was blamed on passengers with above average weight (*The Daily Telegraph*, 2004; *The Economist*, 2006).

To cut costs, Ryanair and FlyBe are charging passengers for each bag they check in. As an incentive to carry less luggage, passengers with only cabin bags get discounted fares, and can avoid the check-in queues. Ryanair estimates that this will reduce airport handling and fuel costs, and cut turnaround times, saving the company €30 million a year.

PESTLE analysis raises a number of issues.

First, it is difficult to escape from the argument that the organization must pay attention to PESTLE trends and developments. The organization which fails to respond to those external factors will quickly run into difficulties.

Second, the long list of external factors, even under these neat headings, can be intimidating. Identifying which are most significant, and then predicting their impact, can be difficult.

Third, a full understanding of external factors can involve the analysis of a substantial amount of different kinds of data, and this takes time. How about analysing demographic trends in south-central Scotland, for example, or pan-European regulations affecting the food and drink industry, or forthcoming information technology software innovations, or collating the results of surveys concerning lifestyle changes and consumption patterns across South East Asia? The time spent on these analyses has to be balanced against the need for a rapid response.

Environmental complexity makes prediction hazardous. We can predict demographic trends with some accuracy, with respect to mortality, and gender and age profiles. We can normally predict economic trends with some confidence in the short to medium term, two to three years. Trends in social values and lifestyles, politics, technological innovation, or the impact of new technology, cannot be predicted with much confidence – although that does not stop journalists and others from making the attempt. Environmental scanning can mean a lot of informed guesswork and judgement.

PESTLE analysis has two strengths, and four weaknesses. The strengths are:

1. The analysis encourages consideration of the range of external factors affecting internal organizational arrangements and business planning.
2. The analysis is a convenient framework for ordering a complex and bewildering set of factors, helping an organization plan for future opportunities and threats.

The weaknesses are:

1. This analysis can identify many factors which may not be significant. It is difficult to strike a balance between identifying all factors and identifying those which are important.
2. It is difficult to anticipate 'defining events', such as wars, terrorist attacks, new discoveries, economic collapse, and major political or financial crises which shift country boundaries or radically change government policies.
3. This analysis can involve the time-consuming and expensive collection of data, some of which may be available, and some of which may have to be researched.
4. The time spent in information-gathering and analysis may inhibit a rapid and effective response to the very trends being analysed.

Scenario planning in a high-risk world – to 2019

Terrorism is not the only unexpected risk that might ruin a business. Outbreaks of infectious diseases such as the SARS epidemic can be equally damaging. Most companies are still well behind with contingency planning. In the past, according to a member of Bain's (a management consultancy firm), bosses were reluctant to draw up such plans in case they frightened employees and customers. Now, he says, 'it's a necessity'. The new concern with geopolitical risks has led to a revival of scenario planning. Pioneered in the 1970s by Pierre Wack at Royal Dutch/Shell (which includes three different forecasts of the global economy in its strategic planning), scenario planning became unfashionable because the geopolitical climate appeared to be benign. Now, however, it has become popular as a way to help managers to think about and plan for future uncertainties (Cave, 2008; *The Economist*, 2004).

At Microsoft, Brent Callinicos, the company's treasurer, keeps track of up to seven scenarios at a time. Microsoft calculates and discloses its 'value at risk' – an estimate of the greatest loss it is 95 per cent sure it will not exceed – for 20-day periods ahead. Scenarios are crucial in putting the value-at-risk calculations into context. The Economist Intelligence Unit surveyed 600 global executives in 2008 and asked them which risks were the most threatening to their business over the next decade, to 2019. The top 12 were:

- increase in protectionism
- major oil price shock
- collapse in asset prices
- emergence of a disruptive business model
- international terrorism
- unexpected regulatory change
- global recession
- instability in the Middle East
- increased competition from emerging market companies
- talent shortages
- climate change
- increased industrial pollution.

Only 26 per cent said that they used scenario planning regularly, 41 per cent used it on an ad hoc basis, and 29 per cent said that they would be using it in future.

Scenario planning the imaginative development of one or more likely pictures of the dimensions and characteristics of the future for an organization.

Environmental analysis with PESTLE is used for **scenario planning**, a technique developed by the oil company Royal Dutch/Shell in the 1970s, and also known as the 'Shell method'.

Scenario planning combines environmental scanning with creative thinking, to identify the most probable future scenario as a basis for planning and action. In the field of corporate strategy, scenario planning is used to explore 'best case, worst case' possibilities, and to encourage 'out of the-box' and creative 'blue skies' thinking. Environmental scanning is a useful predictive tool, particularly when allied with scenario planning and used as a guide to creative decision-making. This is also a useful framework which exposes the range of external environmental influences on internal organizational behaviour, and highlights the relationships between those external factors.

Work in 2020: colourful scenarios

The consultancy company PricewaterhouseCoopers used scenario planning to explore the future of work (Arkin, 2007). They developed three possible scenarios for 2020:

orange world Big companies have been replaced by networks of small specialized enterprises. People work on short-term contracts exploring job opportunities online through portals developed by craft guilds.

green world Demographic change, climate, and sustainability are key business drivers. Employment law, employee relations, and corporate responsibility are vital in this heavily regulated environment.

blue world Huge corporations are like mini-states providing staff with housing, health, education, and other welfare benefits. Human capital metrics are sophisticated, and people management is as powerful as finance.

What if none of these models turns out to be correct? Is this a waste of time? Sandy Pepper, the project leader, replies: 'You can respond more quickly to what does happen if you have trained yourself to think in a more innovative, lateral way about the future'.

We can now update our model. Figure 2.6 shows the links between external environmental pressures and internal organizational responses in more detail. This model relies on a number of basic assumptions:

- that all the relevant data can be identified, collected and analysed;
- that the analysis will lead to accurate forecasts, and to realistic future scenarios;
- that the analysis will be consistent, and not pull the organization in different directions at the same time;
- that the kinds of internal organizational responses indicated by the analysis can be implemented at an appropriate pace.

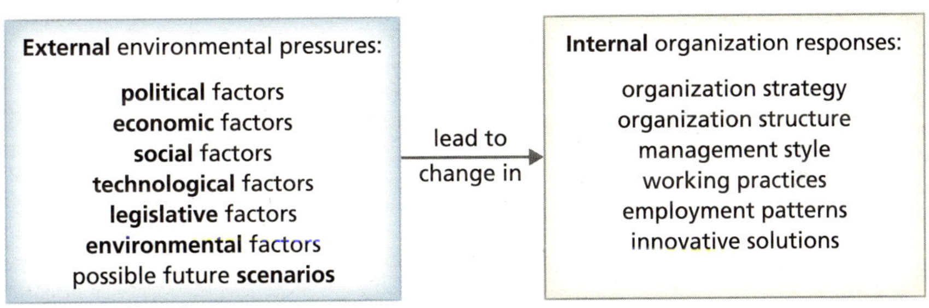

Figure 2.6: External environment–organization link detailed

Ethical behaviour

Organizations and managers are expected to behave ethically. The emphasis on this aspect of organizational behaviour has increased in the twenty-first century, for two reasons. The first concerns a number of high-profile corporate scandals (Enron, Worldcom). The second concerns increasing media scrutiny of organization and management practices, focusing on environmental issues and the use of low-cost labour. These concerns are of course not new, but they are seen as more important and attract more attention than they have done in the past.

Richard Daft (2008) distinguishes between the 'domain of codified law' and the 'domain of free choice'. In the domain of law, our behaviour – what we can and cannot do – is decided by legislation. Individuals are not allowed to murder or to steal, and organizations must conform with accounting, tax, health and safety, and employment legislation. If we do the wrong thing,

"When you say 'ethical' do you mean marginally ethical, semi-ethical, or appearing to be ethical?"

Source: © Randy Glasbergen, www.glasbergen.com

we end up in court, or in jail; organizations can be fined, and in some cases senior managers can be imprisoned. In the domain of choice, we can do what we like: smoke cigarettes, eat unhealthy food, take as little exercise as we choose. Organizations can decide which businesses to be in, where to locate their headquarters, which markets to expand.

Are we ever really 'free to choose' our behaviour? Daft (2008, p. 139) points out that, even where there are no laws to guide our behaviour, there are 'standards of conduct, based on shared principles and values about moral conduct that guide an individual or company'. We have to decide whether or not to comply with those norms. The domain of ethics thus sits between the domain of law and the domain of choice (see Figure 2.7). We may have to take responsibility for our actions in a courtroom (the domain of codified law), in the court of our own conscience (the domain of free choice), or in the court of social judgement (the domain of ethics).

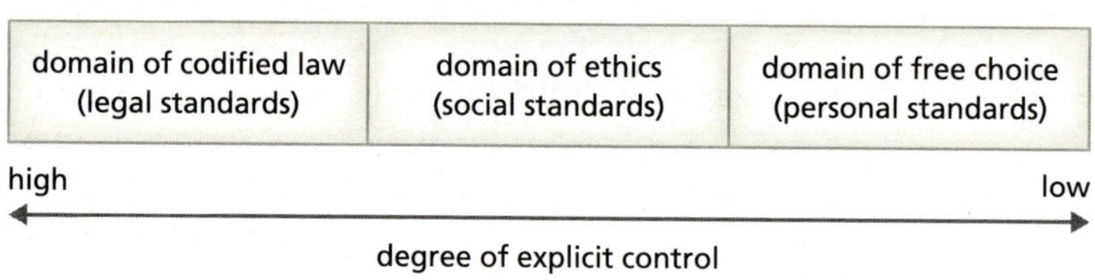

Figure 2.7: Three domains of action

We need to distinguish between *individual* ethics and *business* ethics. The behavioural choices facing individuals and organizations are different, and the criteria against which we judge those actions may also be different. Gerry Johnson, Kevan Scholes and Richard Whittington (2008) explore questions of individual and business ethics using a three-level framework which includes the ethics of the individual manager, the organization's ethical stance, and the organization's approach to corporate social responsibility.

- Level 1, *individual ethics*, concerns the decisions and actions of individual managers, and the ethical principles behind their behaviour;
- Level 2, *the organization's ethical stance*, concerns the extent to which the organization's minimum obligations to stakeholders and to society at large will be exceeded;
- Level 3, *corporate social responsibility*, focuses on how the organization puts its ethical stance into practice, by addressing different stakeholder interests.

Individual ethics

Ethics the moral principles, values, and rules that govern our decisions and actions with respect to what is right and wrong, good and bad.

Managers should surely act ethically. However, there is no consensus on what constitutes 'ethical' behaviour. Different commentators use different criteria with regard to decisions over what is right and what is wrong. Those differences leads to conflicting judgements about the same behaviour. As a result, **ethics** is a controversial subject.

Gerald Cavanagh, Dennis Moberg and Manuel Velasquez developed a template to distinguish ethical from unethical management actions (Cavanagh et al., 1981; Velasquez et al., 1983). Their perspective is based on three ethical frameworks: utilitarianism, individual rights, and natural justice (see Table 2.6). Instead of choosing one of these, they suggest that these criteria should be combined to reach ethical judgements.

Table 2.6: Ethical frameworks

	Strengths	Weaknesses
Utilitarianism	Encourages efficiency Parallels profit maximization Looks beyond the individual	Impossible to quantify variables Can lead to unjust resource allocation Individual rights may be violated
Rights	Protects the individual Establishes standards of behaviour independent of outcomes	May encourage selfish behaviour Individual rights may become obstacles to productivity and efficiency
Justice	Ensures fair allocation of resources Ensures democratic operation, independent of status or class Protects the interests of those under-represented in the organization	Can encourage a sense of entitlement that discourages risk and innovation Some individual rights may be violated to accommodate justice for majority

Source: adapted from *Organizational Dynamics*, Vol. 12, No. 2, Velasquez, M., Moberg, D.J. and Cavanagh, G.F., Organizational statesmanship and dirty politics: ethical guidelines for the organizational politician, p. 72, Copyright 1983, with permission from Elsevier.

- A *utilitarian* perspective judges behaviour in terms of outcomes; this is the classic 'ends justifies means' argument. This approach considers the 'balance sheet' of benefits and costs to those involved. Behaviour is ethical if it achieves 'the greatest good of the greatest number'. However, in even modestly complex settings, with several stakeholders, and actions with a range of consequences, calculating the costs and benefits can be challenging.
- The *rights* perspective judges behaviour on the extent to which fundamental individual rights are respected. These include the right of free consent, the right to privacy, the right to freedom of conscience, the right of free speech, and the right to due process in the form of an impartial hearing. The ethical decision depends on whether or not individual rights have been violated.
- The *justice* perspective judges behaviour on whether or not the benefits and costs flowing from an action are fairly, equitably, and impartially distributed. Distributive justice states that rules should be applied consistently, those in similar circumstances should be treated equally, and individuals should not be held responsible for matters beyond their control. As with the utilitarian view, these issues are awkward to resolve in practice, as judgements of consistency, similarity, and responsibility are subjective and vary from one setting to another.

These three perspectives produce a 'decision tree' for deciding whether an action is ethical or not (see Figure 2.8). First, 'gather the facts', then ask about benefits, rights, and justice. The framework also introduces circumstances which could justify unethical behaviour in some settings. 'Overwhelming factors' are issues that justify setting aside ethical criteria. Some actions may have 'dual effects', with positive and negative outcomes, and the negatives may be acceptable if they are outweighed by the positives. 'Incapacitating factors' may prevent the decision-maker from applying ethical criteria. For example, managers can be constrained by the views and actions of colleagues, and may be pressured into behaviour that they would not choose themselves. Individual managers may not have enough information on which to reach a judgement. Finally, the individual may doubt the relevance of one or more ethical criteria to a given setting. The right to free speech, for example, may not apply if this involves releasing information that would be damaging to others.

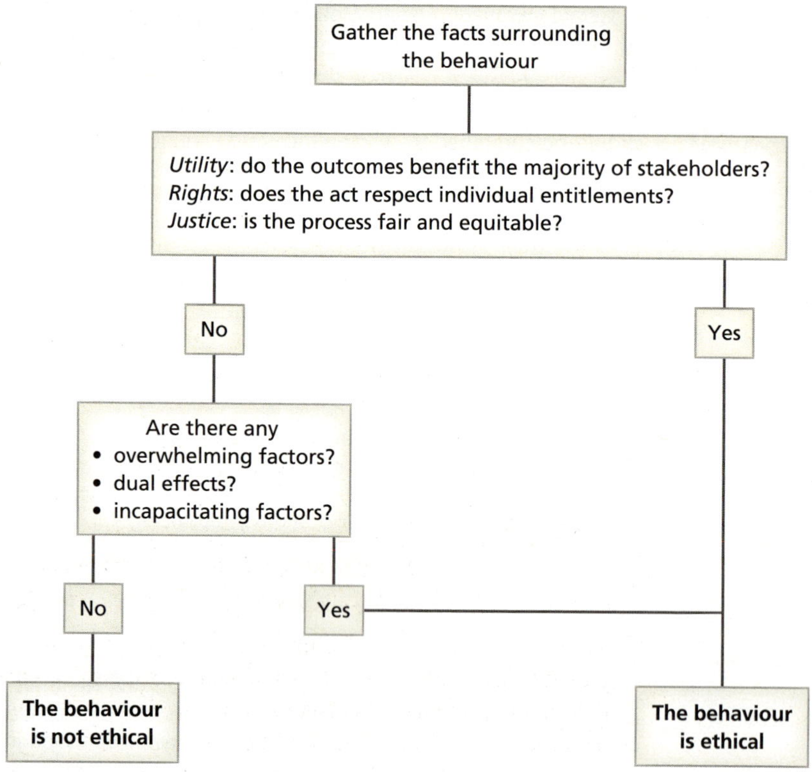

Figure 2.8: The ethical decision tree

Source: adapted from *Organizational Dynamics*, Vol. 12, No. 2, Velasquez, M., Moberg, D.J. and Cavanagh, G.F., Organizational statesmanship and dirty politics: ethical guidelines for the organizational politician, p. 72, Copyright 1983, with permission from Elsevier.

As a result, we have several escape routes which allow actions that would be prohibited by the three criteria. The urgency of the case, time pressures, resource constraints, penalties for inaction, and so on, can all be called upon as overwhelming, dual, or incapacitating factors.

STOP AND THINK

Sam and Bob are research scientists in the Greenhill Rubber Company product development laboratory. Sam, who is introverted, quiet, and serious, is more technically proficient; his patents have earned the company around $6 million over the past ten years. Bob does not have the same expertise, his output is 'solid though unimaginative', and he is extraverted and demonstrative. The rumour is that Bob will be moved into an administrative role. The lab offers a $300,000 fund each year for the best new product idea. Sam and Bob both submit proposals, which are assessed as having equal merit. Sam takes no further action, but Bob conducts a publicity campaign, about which he tells Sam in advance, promoting the advantages of his proposal to those who might influence the final decision. Informal pressure builds to decide in Bob's favour (Cavanagh et al., 1981).

Is Bob's behaviour ethical? Does the ethical decision tree help you to reach a decision?

Cavanagh and colleagues (1981) argue that Bob's actions are unethical. From a utilitarian perspective, the outcome is acceptable, as both proposals had equal merit. From a rights perspective, Sam had the same opportunities, and he knew about Bob's informal campaign. But by introducing 'irrelevant differences' between the proposals based on personal lobbying, Bob's behaviour breached the principles of justice, and was unethical.

How do you feel about this judgement? There is another view. Ideas in most organizations do not make progress on merit alone. Bob recognized that ideas benefit from good publicity. Should we praise Sam for his ethics and criticize Bob for his unfair practices? Or should we regard Sam as naive and lazy, and praise Bob for his enthusiasm and understanding of the context? Bob's actions were not secret, and he won the prize. For the company that wants to encourage innovation, Bob seems to be the better role model. This decision tree offers contradictory assessments, and can lead to judgements that are controversial.

This ethical decision framework seems to offer a structured approach for resolving difficult choices. However, it can produce outcomes which are confusing, and in some cases perverse. 'Ethical' in this example describes behaviour that is careless, amateurish and naive, while contextual awareness, astuteness, and professionalism are labelled unethical. This framework focuses on single incidents, but Bob and Sam have to continue working for that organization. The actions that they take, and the results they achieve, influence how they are regarded, which affects how colleagues feel about and respond to them. Whether they get results, or avoid the difficult issues, affects their career prospects and the degree of influence that they can exert in the organization in future. In other words, the way in which they handle these issues affects their reputation beyond the single incident. Maybe we should adopt a broader time horizon in reaching such decisions about ethical or unethical behaviour.

This framework can highlight the issues, but it cannot always make the decision for us. That is a matter of personal judgement. Velasquez et al. (1983, pp. 79–80) conclude:

> The manager who is unable to use ethical criteria because of these incapacitating factors may justifiably give them a lesser weight in making decisions about what to do. However, determining whether a manager's lack of freedom, lack of information, or lack of certitude is sufficient to abrogate moral responsibility requires one to make some very difficult judgements. In the end, these are hard questions that only the individuals involved can answer for themselves.

Let's return to our opening case, 'Should that have happened?'. Was Charlie acting ethically? In the utilitarian view, his actions are acceptable. However, Cavanagh and colleagues argue that Charlie violated Lee's right to be treated honestly by damaging his reputation behind his back, and that Charlie's actions were unethical. However, Lee had not responded to Charlie's request to alter his damaging behaviour; did Lee not ignore Charlie's rights, and also ignore the rights of shareholders and the community? Charlie's actions can be seen as personally sensitive and organizationally prudent, given Lee's behaviour, his proximity to retirement, his record, and the limited options open to Charlie to solve this problem quickly. To discipline or to fire Lee would be humiliating for him, and could damage his pension entitlement. Instead, Charlie informally creates the circumstances in which Lee reaches his own decision to quit.

Business ethics and corporate social responsibility

Business ethics has become a topic stimulating much interest and debate. Is is widely assumed that unethical behaviour, allowing financial institutions to take unacceptably high risks, contributed to the global financial crisis triggered by the collapse of Lehman Brothers in 2008 (Archer, 2010). There is a danger that the resultant recession, by creating harsh competitive conditions, could encourage higher levels of unethical behaviour. Some countries have particularly high rates of bribery and corruption, examples being China, India, and Russia. Companies which have been involved in corruption probes in emerging markets include BAE Systems, Daimler, Hewlett-Packard, Rio Tinto, and Siemens.

The previous section introduced a framework for exploring ethical questions, and considered the ethical dilemmas facing individual managers. The other two levels of the framework concern

Ethical stance the extent to which an organization exceeds its legal minimum obligations to its stakeholders and to society at large.

- the organization's **ethical stance**; and
- corporate social responsibility.

Ethical stance

Johnson et al. (2008, p. 189) suggest that organizations can take progressively more intense ethical stances (see Figure 2.9). Each stance incorporates an increasing range of stakeholder interests; includes a wider range of criteria; and involves a longer period over which outcomes are judged. At the start of this continuum is the minimum obligations position, focusing on the short-term financial interests of shareholders. This is not really an 'ethical' position. The organization works within the law, but does not engage in additional social or environmental activities such as charitable donations. Performance is measured in financial terms.

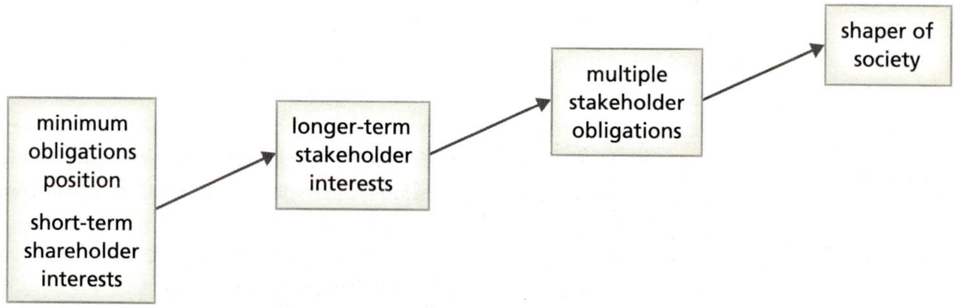

Figure 2.9: Intensity of ethical stance

Source: after *Exploring Corporate Strategy: Text and Cases*, Johnson, G., Scholes, K. and Whittington, K. Pearson Education Limited, © Pearson Education Limited 2008.

The next step in the continuum involves a shift in language as well as focus, from shareholders to stakeholders. There are many groups with a stake in an organization: employees, suppliers, customers, local community, government, society. This stance also focuses on shareholder interests, but recognizes that these can be enhanced by the positive management of relationships with other stakeholders. A company's engagement in, for example, charitable giving, while not producing shareholder gains in the short term, can enhance reputation and visibility, and contribute to long-term profits and share price. These actions can be regarded as promotional expenditure and investments in the future. Organizational performance is thus measured in financial terms over a longer period.

Moving two steps beyond minimum obligations addresses the interests and expectations of multiple stakeholders. The actions of organizations adopting this stance might include refusing to 'offshore' jobs to countries where wages are lower, contracting with 'fair trade' suppliers, keeping uneconomic units working to preserve employment, and not selling antisocial products. While these actions increase costs, and shareholder gains may not be maximized, other stakeholders benefit. The problem is balancing the interests of all the stakeholders. Organizational performance is therefore not measured solely in financial terms.

Moving three steps beyond the minimum position, organizations can be ideologically driven, aiming to reshape society. Google appears to be one example of an organization which takes this stance (although some of their actions and aspirations are controversial). While shareholders and financial constraints can limit the actions of organizations, private companies with no shareholders find it easier to adopt this ethical stance.

Corporate social responsibility

One of the problems facing companies operating in countries where corruption is high concerns the expectation that bribes will be involved if business deals are to be agreed. However, a new Bribery Act came into force in the UK in 2010, and the defence of 'normal business practice' no longer applies (Daniels, 2010). The Bribery Act creates:

- a general offence of offering or receiving bribes, inducing someone to perform a function or activity improperly;
- a specific offence of bribing an overseas public official with the intent to obtain or retain business;
- a corporate offence of failing to prevent people working on behalf of the organization (employees, agents, consultants) from being involved in bribery which results in obtaining or retaining business.

America has had a similar US Foreign Corrupt Practices Act since 1977, aimed at companies dealing with state and public sector contracts, but the UK legislation covers all business dealings. The penalties for corporate offences include unlimited fines for the organization and its directors, and a maximum ten-year jail sentence for individuals involved in bribery. An unresolved problem concerns corporate hospitality. Hospitality is an accepted element of business, but lavish hospitality could be seen as bribery; deciding what is lavish or not is, of course, a matter of interpretation. Corporate anti-bribery policies and procedures, including whistleblowing procedures, codes of conduct, and employee training, become important in this context, and this may be seen as a component of corporate social responsibility.

Should organizations adopt an ethical stance that supports social and environmental issues? This can be good for business, if it attracts socially responsible customers (Donaldson and Preston, 1995). The economist Milton Friedman (1970) once argued that 'The business of business is business'. His view is now unfashionable. The **corporate social responsibility** (CSR) movement expects organizations to promote social and environmental or 'green' issues. This has become a major environmental pressure, combining Political, Social, Technological, and Ecological aspects of PESTLE analysis. Many organizations are addressing these issues, to strengthen their reputation as 'responsible corporate citizens'.

Corporate social responsibility the view that organizations should act ethically, in ways that contribute to economic development, the environment, quality of working life, local communities, and the wider society.

The actions of large, wealthy, powerful organizations can have a major impact on local communities and national economies, world trade, the environment, employment, job security, and employee health and pensions. Surely organizations must behave 'responsibly', and promote social and environmental issues? Along with management ethics, the importance of corporate responsibility has been highlighted in the twenty-first century by corporate scandals at Enron, Worldcom, and the Japanese company livedoor, where executives were accused of fraudulent transactions which benefited them personally.

Table 2.7 lists typical CSR policies. While this all sounds desirable, CSR has its critics. The concept is vague, and can mean different things in different settings. Managers who pay for community projects and make charitable donations are giving away money that belongs to shareholders, and which could be reinvested in the business, or used to improve pay and working conditions. Another objection is that, if you are acting legally, then by definition you are acting morally, so what's the problem? It is hard to distinguish between 'responsible' actions that reflect a concern for society, and actions designed to enhance the reputation of the company. It is also important to recognize that business laws and customs vary between countries and cultures. What constitutes fair and just ethical conduct depends on where you are in the world. Finally, CSR seems to overlook the benefits of competition, which leads to better quality products and services, and to reduced costs for consumers. Critics of CSR also argue that furthering social and environmental issues is the job of governments.

Table 2.7: CSR policies and practices

General policies include signing up to national and international ethical codes, using ethical investment criteria, and taking part in surveys of sustainability. Specific policies include:

Environment
1. Pollution control
2. Product improvement
3. Repair of environment
4. Recycling waste materials
5. Energy saving

Equal opportunities
1. Minority employment
2. Advancement of minorities
3. Advancement of women
4. Support for minority businesses
5. Other disadvantaged groups

Personnel
1. Employee health and safety
2. Training
3. Personal counselling
4. Subcontractor code of behaviour
5. Providing medical care or insurance

Community involvement
1. Charitable donations
2. Promoting and supporting public health initiatives
3. Support for education and the arts
4. Community involvement projects

Products
1. Safety
2. Quality
3. Sustainability, percentage of materials that can be recycled

Suppliers
1. Fair terms of trade
2. Blacklisting unethical, irresponsible suppliers
3. Subcontractor code

STOP AND THINK

Look at the list of CSR policies and practices in Table 2.7. What behaviours would you like to add to that list, and what benefits would you expect those behaviours to produce?

The popularity of CSR

Interest in the social impact of business dates from the early nineteenth century, with Robert Owen, who managed New Lanark Mills, south of Glasgow, in Scotland, from 1800 to 1825. In contrast with other employers at the time, Owen wanted to give his employees good living and working conditions, education and healthcare. But it was not until the late 1960s that interest in corporate social responsibility and business ethics was taken more seriously. These themes are now well established in contemporary debate and organizational research, and CSR seems to have become popular for three main reasons:

Sustainability at Timberland

Craig Yates/Alamy

Liam Connelly is director, corporate culture, for Timberland Europe.

> Our idea of commerce and justice really got started in the late 1980s. We began providing each employee with work time to commit to doing community service, from 16 hours a year in 1992 to 40 hours a year today. That has resulted in large-scale projects across 27 different countries, such as the one million trees planted in the Horqin Desert in Mongolia. Our employees expect this element as part of the deal with working at Timberland and increasingly we are influencing business partners and customers.
>
> Having environmental and social change at the heart of everything has led to better, more responsible products being made and improved ways of doing business. We're being responsible and saving money at the same time.
>
> To engage employees in sustainability, the HR team has an approach to how it can help guide the core elements of the corporate culture. While our clothing and footwear makes a statement to consumers about sustainability, if our employees within one of the retail stores don't truly understand what we mean by sustainability, then we're only telling half the story. That's why learning and development, as well as a culture of community service, continues to be central to Timberland's growth. (Smedley, 2011)

If you were a Timberland customer or employee, how would you feel about the company planting trees in Mongolia instead of reducing product prices or increasing your wages?

- *CSR as self defence*: 'If we don't do it ourselves, we'll have it done to us.' While operating within the law, organizations are still self-regulating in many respects. However, there is always the danger that a high-profile corporate scandal will create demand for new regulation. The case of Enron and other similar fraud cases, for example, led to the introduction of new regulations affecting corporate governance in America (the infamous Sarbanes–Oxley Act, 2002). Expensive and cumbersome to implement, that legislation was designed to restore public confidence by improving corporate accounting controls. CSR can be seen as a strategy to demonstrate corporate concern with ethical behaviour and impact on the community.
- *CSR as a result of affluence*: 'If we don't do it, they'll stop buying from us.' Increased affluence encourages us to assess the behaviour of the companies from which we buy products and services. If we feel that a company is not behaving in a socially acceptable manner, then we can withdraw our custom. Patterns of customer demand can affect corporate actions, for example by focusing on healthy eating, the promotion of ethical investment, and concern for the environment. CSR can deflect criticism and maintain customer support.
- *CSR as impression management, or greenwashing*: 'If we tell people how responsible we are, our reputation will improve profits.' Every CSR initiative gets media attention, and free publicity. The company that frequently makes visible contributions to society may find that sales and market share increase. False or exaggerated claims, however, can damage reputation. CSR can be seen as a strategy to manage the impression that the consuming public has of the organization, and as a result to get good public relations and free advertising.

Corporate social responsibility at IKEA

Helen Sessions/Alamy

The Swedish home furnishings retailer IKEA has for over a decade been a 'corporate partner' working with UNICEF – the United Nations Children's Fund (www.unicef.org/corporate_partners). The IKEA Foundation, formed in 2005, has been UNICEF's largest corporate donor, committing over US$190 million. The Foundation's original aim was to address the use of child labour in the company's supply chain, focusing on South Asia and India, where IKEA has long business experience. Today, the aims of the Foundation are broader, to save and improve the lives of children and their families. IKEA also has partnership arrangements with the charity Save the Children and the World Wildlife Fund, to combat child labour and to influence forest companies to restrict trade in timber. The company also claims a history of conservation and environmental responsibility.

IKEA also involves its customers in children's issues through in-store advocacy campaigns in support of UNICEF. IKEA stores around the world have since 2003 generated $14 million through donations related to sales of soft toys. The Foundation has donated tables to schools and health centres in Liberia and Burundi; quilts to survivors of the 2004 tsunami that hit Indonesia and Sri Lanka; 45,000 baby blankets following the earthquake in Pakistan in 2005; and sheets, towels, sleeping bags, and bowls to survivors of the earthquake in China in 2008. The Foundation's support for UNICEF emergency programmes has been more than $10 million since 2005. The IKEA Foundation also has a programme in India where in partnership with UNICEF since 2000 it has focused on promoting the economic and social empowerment of women and children's rights to education, survival, and development.

IKEA is privately owned, and makes annual profits of around €2.5 billion on sales of €22 billion, making low-cost products in parts of the world where labour costs are low. This is not the only company to advertise how socially responsible it is.

It is often argued that successful companies should contribute in these kinds of ways to the development of the social and physical environments on which they depend.

It is also argued that such contributions are just inexpensive marketing tactics designed to improve the image of the company and its products in the eyes of customers.

Where do you stand on this argument? Should companies like IKEA donate funds to these kinds of programmes? Or should they focus instead on developing their businesses, and let local governments, aid agencies and charities do the work in which they have the expertise?

CSR, sustainability, and innovation

Many companies have linked CSR to product design and supply chain management, appointing chief sustainability officers to run sustainability units which employ sustainability consultants. Sustainability means making the most of scarce resources, reducing costs through lean production and 'tight' supply chains. Nike, which makes shoes, has a Materials Sustainability Index that tells designers about the environmental impact of products. The delivery company UPS uses a 'carbon calculator' to track the carbon footprint of individual packages. Strategies to improve sustainability can trigger innovation. Nike is making more clothes from polyester derived from recycled bottles, and has made a shoe with an 'upper' knitted from a single thread, replacing many wasteful components. Starbucks holds 'coffee cup summits' at the Massachusetts Institute of Technology to find ways to reduce the environmental impact of disposable cups. As companies become more frugal and imaginative, CSR contributes to profits as well as to reputation (*The Economist*, 2012).

Coca-Cola: thirsty for sustainability

Sensitive to accusations that it runs a wasteful, unethical, and polluting business that does not make a social contribution, Coca-Cola in Europe responded with a series of corporate responsibility initiatives (Wiggins, 2007):

- restricting the marketing of its products to children
- working with the World Wildlife Fund to find ways to cut back and to replenish the 290 billion litres of water that the company uses annually
- working with Greenpeace to develop environmentally friendly beverage coolers and vending machines to reduce the emission of hydrocarbon greenhouse gases
- monitoring the agricultural impact of the company into tea, coffee, and juice drinks which require it to purchase ingredients from around the globe.

Websites accuse the company of exaggerating the benefits of an unhealthy product, of management complicity in the deaths of union organizers in bottling plants in South America, and of reducing and polluting local water supplies in India: see www.killercoke.org and www.indiaresource.org/campaigns/coke/2004/risingstruggles.html.

Craigslist and Facebook

Craigslist is a classified ads website run by Craig Newark and Jim Buckmaster, who live in San Francisco. Theirs is one of the most successful internet companies ever, and their site is used by tens of millions of people daily, in more than 500 cities in over 50 countries. Craigslist dominates the online classified ads business. This is the eleventh-most-visited website in America, and is more popular than Amazon or CNN. The 'Craigslist community' uses the site to buy and sell just about anything, including stamps, houses, personal services, and dead moose ('a big issue in Alaska', according to Jim). Wall Street estimates the company value at US$5 billion. Craig and Jim live in rented accommodation, and drive old cars – not the stereotypes of Californian high-tech 'dot com' entrepreneurs. Despite its global reach, this is still a 'small' company which employs 25 staff, including the two bosses (eBay has around 15,000 staff).

Check the website (www.craigslist.org/about/sites) and you will find millions of personal ads, but no graphics, animation, pop-ups, or corporate banners. Craigslist charges no fees for posting most of those listings, and does not take a percentage of successful transactions (as other websites do, including eBay). The company makes its revenue from employers who post job vacancies, and from property agencies who post rentals (Goodwin, 2008).

Craig and Jim run the business based on what they themselves describe as their 'nerd value culture', which includes a refusal to maximize profits, and putting the needs of their users first. Their annual revenue is around US$100 million. Analysts estimate that they could earn five times that amount just by allowing banner advertising, like most other websites, and by charging for more listings (Harvey, 2008). Craig explains:

> I've seen companies with too much revenue. Having too much money, too many resources, means you don't have to work smart, so you work dumb. And then you lose your market position to smaller, hungrier competitors. Also, when you have too much cash and power, you tend to attract employees who are very good at organizational politics but who are really bad at everything else. We know a lot of these really rich guys and they are no happier than anyone else. Money has become a burden to them. That reinforces the values that Jim and I share, about living simply.

Facebook (en-gb.facebook.com) is one of the most-visited websites on the planet. This social network site was designed by Mark Zuckerberg and friends at Harvard in 2004, and has an estimated 845 million users. Like Craigslist, this is not a large company. Facebook had sales of $3.7 billion in 2011 from display advertising. Mark said that he was more concerned with helping people than with making money:

> The goal of the company is to help people to share more in order to make the world more open and to help promote understanding between people. If we can succeed in this mission then we will also be able to build a pretty good business and everyone can be financially rewarded.

In 2012, Mark turned Facebook into a public company and became a multi-billionaire.

STOP AND THINK

In 2008 Kenco Coffee introduced a new television advertising campaign. The old ads concentrated on the quality and taste of the product. The new ads for the Kenco Sustainable Development coffee range show the company helping coffee growers and their farming communities in developing countries with social, economic, and environmental projects.

Check their website:
www.kencocoffeecompany.co.uk.
Go to 'about us', and then 'our approach to sustainability'.

Is this a genuine contribution to economic growth and sustainability or a marketing tactic to persuade you to buy their coffee?

Whitebox Media Ltd/Alamy

RECAP

1. *Understand the mutual interdependence between the organization and its environment.*
   - To survive, organizations have to adapt their internal structures, processes and behaviours to cope with complexity and the pace of external change.
   - External pressures on organizations come from the globalization of business, developments in information technology, and social and demographic trends.
2. *Appreciate the strengths and limitations of PESTLE analysis of organizational environments.*
   - PESTLE analysis provides a comprehensive framework for identifying and planning responses to external factors that can affect an organization.
   - PESTLE analysis generates vast amounts of information, creating a time-consuming analysis problem, and making predictions based on this analysis can be difficult.
3. *Explain contemporary organizational responses to environmental turbulence.*
   - Ansoff argues that bureaucratic organizations are effective in stable environments, but that fluid structures are more effective in 'turbulent' environments.
   - Duncan and Weick argue that what counts is the management perception of environmental uncertainty; perception determines the management response.
4. *Apply utilitarianism, the theory of rights, and the theory of justice to assess whether or not management actions are ethical, and recognize the limitations of those criteria.*
   - The utilitarian perspective argues that behaviour is ethical if it achieves the greatest good for the greatest number.
   - The theory of rights judges behaviour on the extent to which individual rights are respected, including the right of free consent, the right to privacy, the right to freedom of conscience, the right of free speech, and the right to due process in an impartial hearing.
   - The theory of justice judges behaviour on whether or not the benefits and burdens flowing from an action are fairly, equitably, and impartially distributed.
   - These criteria produce different assessments of the same behaviour; and circumstances can include other factors which the application of these criteria make inappropriate.
5. *Understand the concept of corporate social responsibility, and the practical and ethical implications of this concept for organizational behaviour.*
   - Businesses and their managers are expected to act in responsible and ethical ways, contributing to social and environmental outcomes as well as making profit.
   - Responsible practices include, for example, the business contribution to the community, the sustainable use of resources, ethical behaviour in relationships with suppliers and customers, and the impact of the business on all stakeholders.
   - Critics argue that it is government's job to deal with social and environmental issues, that the role of business is to maximize profits while operating within the law, and that managers who donate company funds to 'good causes' give away shareholders' money.

Revision

1. Explain the concept of *organizational stakeholder*. Choose an organization that you are familiar with. List its main stakeholders, and suggest what expectations each may have of that organization.
2. What are the strengths and weaknesses of PESTLE analysis? Illustrate your answer with reference to issues and organizations with which you are familiar.
3. What are the dangers and the benefits of corporate social responsibility, for employees, management, organizations, society, the environment?
4. Why can it be difficult to decide whether a particular action is ethical or not?

Research assignment

Innocent Ltd started with fruit smoothies, and diversified into other drinks. Look at what the company says on its website – www.innocentdrinks.co.uk – about 'us' and about 'our ethics'. What ethical stance does this company take? In what ways do you think that this approach to 'sustainable business' will improve profitability? In what ways could this damage profitability? Are you more or less likely to buy their products, knowing what Innocent says about corporate social responsibility? In April 2009, Innocent sold a £30 million stake in the company to Coca-Cola, claiming that this would allow the company to 'do more of what Innocent is here to do'. How does this link with Coca-Cola change your assessment of Innocent's ethical stance? See Chapter 4 (Culture), where the influence of founders' values on company culture, including Innocent Ltd, is explored.

Springboard

Alison Beard and Richard Hornik (2011) 'It's hard to be good', *Harvard Business Review*, 89(11), pp. 88–96. Profiles five companies with exemplary approaches to responsible business practices: Royal DSM (Netherlands), Southwest Airlines (US), Broad Group (China), Potash Corporation (Canada), and Unilever (UK).

Lynda Gratton (2011) *The Shift: The Future of Work Is Already Here*, Collins, London. Explores how trends in globalization, society, demography, technology, and use of natural resources are reshaping work, and offers advice on how to 'future-proof' your career.

George F. Ritzer (2008) *The McDonaldization of Society*, Pine Forge Press, Thousand Oaks, CA. McDonaldization as an organizational paradigm is based on efficiency, predictability, calculability, and control. Ritzer asks if we are also seeing 'The Starbuckization of society' through 'the McDonaldization of the coffee shop business'.

Harold L. Sirkin, James W. Hemerling and Arindam K. Bhattacharya (2008) *Globality: Competing with Everyone from Everywhere for Everything*, Business Plus, New York and Boston. In the past, Western organizations expanded into poorer countries. With 'post-globalization', Eastern European and BRICs companies are investing in the West.

OB in films

Thank You for Smoking (2005, director Jason Reitman), DVD track 18: 1:13:39 to 1:20:26 (7 minutes). This is the story of a tobacco company spokesman and lobbyist for cigarettes. In this clip, Nick Naylor (played by Aaron Eckhart) testifies before a Senate hearing where issues of free choice and 'bad products' are discussed. As you watch this, identify:

1. Who are the cigarette companies' stakeholders?
2. What corporate social responsibility issues are raised here?
3. Where do you stand on the issue of freedom of choice for consumers?

OB on the web

Visit the websites of three different organizations. You could start with the American company Patagonia.com (click on their 'environmentalism' tab), or the German company Hessnatur.info (go to 'what we believe'). Compare and contrast these organizations in terms of what they say about corporate social responsibility and ethics. Write a brief report highlighting their similarities and differences. In what ways do you think their ethical stance could affect their profitability?

CHAPTER EXERCISES

1. Ethical conduct

Objectives

1. To explore the nature of ethical and unethical work behaviours.
2. To identify what makes some behaviour ethical, and some behaviour unethical.
3. To explore individual differences in reaching ethical judgements.

Briefing

The following table lists examples of behaviour at work (DeJong et al., 2008). Are these actions ethical? Tick your response in the column that best describes your opinion.

Share your answers with colleagues. Note the *differences* in your responses. Explore and explain *why* you hold different views on these issues. What makes some behaviours ethical and some behaviours unethical? Are differences between individuals linked to age, sex, experience, culture, religion, or to other factors? What are the implications of these differences for you personally and for your relationships with others? What are the implications for managing a diverse multicultural workforce?

Behaviour	Always ethical	Ethical in some contexts	Always unethical
1. Claim credit for the work of others	❐	❐	❐
2. Withhold information to slow others down	❐	❐	❐
3. Call in sick so that you can have the day off	❐	❐	❐
4. Make a false time report	❐	❐	❐
5. Pad your expenses claims	❐	❐	❐
6. Accept gifts for favours	❐	❐	❐
7. Use friends as sources of confidential information	❐	❐	❐
8. Deliberately make your boss look bad	❐	❐	❐
9. Use company materials for your own purposes	❐	❐	❐
10. Report colleagues who violate company rules	❐	❐	❐
11. Make friends with the power brokers	❐	❐	❐
12. Give others gifts or bribes in return for favours	❐	❐	❐
13. Deliberately make a colleague look bad	❐	❐	❐
14. Conduct personal business on company time	❐	❐	❐
15. Divulge confidential information to others	❐	❐	❐
16. Deliberately take your time to complete a task	❐	❐	❐
17. Drink alcohol during working hours	❐	❐	❐
18. Buy company products, not those of competitors	❐	❐	❐
19. Vote for issues because they support this company	❐	❐	❐
20. Work for more than one employer at a time	❐	❐	❐

2. Profits versus people

Objective To explore the nature and implications of management views of ethical issues.

Briefing In the late 'noughties' (2005–2010), a lot of companies and managers found themselves accused of making a lot of money through 'suspect' business practices. Observers and commentators always say that, if they had been in charge, this would not have happened.

Individual ranking (1): Consider the following business values, and rank them in order of importance according to your own beliefs and principles:

1. Career development of employees
2. Concern for employees as people
3. Concern for the environment
4. Customer orientation
5. Efficiency
6. High quality of products and services
7. Integrity
8. Managerial and organizational effectiveness
9. Profit-making
10. Social responsibility

Individual ranking (2): Now rank these items again, this time according to the values that you believe are actually given to them by practising managers.

Groupwork In groups of three:

1. Develop a consensus ranking (from top priority to bottom priority) of these business values based on the *personal sentiments and values* of your group's members.
2. Calculate the *practising managers*' rankings using the average of your group members' rankings (give 10 points to the top ranked item, 9 to the second, and so on).

Discussion How does your group's consensus ranking of personal values compare with the practising managers' ranking? Is there a difference? If so, why?

Based on Marcic (1995, pp. 367–8).

Employability assessment

With regard to your future employment prospects:

1. Identify up to three issues from this chapter that you found significant.
2. Relate these to the competencies in the employability matrix.
3. Decide what actions you need to take to maintain and/or develop those competencies under each of the four headings of the employability matrix.

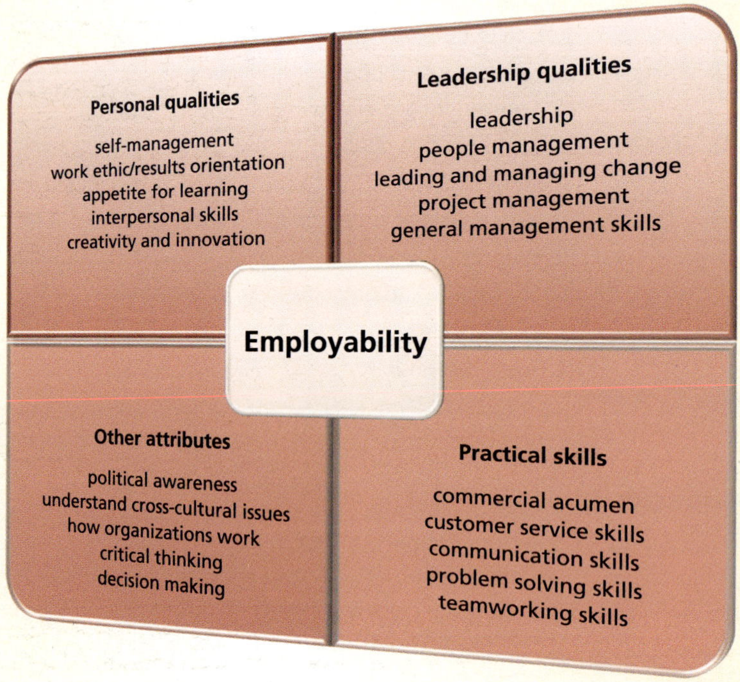

References

Ansoff, I. (1997) 'Measuring and managing for environmental turbulence: the Ansoff Associates approach', in A.W. Hiam (ed.), *The Portable Conference on Change Management*, Amherst, MA: HRD Press Inc., pp. 67–83.

Archer, P. (2010) 'Business ethics', *The Times*, 18 May, Raconteur supplement, p. 1.

Arkin, A. (2007) 'The generation game', *People Management*, 13(24), pp. 24–7.

Bishop, M. (2008) 'A bigger world: a special report on globalization', *The Economist* (supplement), 20 September.

Bryman, A. (2004) *The Disneyization of Society*, London: Sage Publications.

Buckley, C. (2007) *Boomsday*, London: Allison & Busby.

Cairncross, F. (2001) *The Death of Distance 2.0: How the Communications Revolution Will Change Our Lives*, Boston, MA: Harvard Business School Press.

Cavanagh, G.F., Moberg, D.J. and Velasquez, M. (1981) 'The ethics of organizational politics', *Academy of Management Review*, 6(3), pp. 363–74.

Cave, A. (2008) 'Build up your resilience to risk', *The Daily Telegraph*, 5 April, p. 30.

Child, J. (1997) 'Strategic choice in the analysis of action, structure, organizations and environments: retrospect and prospect', *Organization Studies*, 18(1), pp. 43–76.

Clawson, T. (2011) 'Going native: why your products need to adapt to local condition', *The Times*, 18 October, Raconteur on Going Global section, pp. 6–7.

Clegg, S.R. (1990) *Modern Organizations. Organization Studies in the Postmodern World*, London: Sage Publications.

Daft, R. (2008) *Management* (6th edn), Mason, OH: Thomson South-Western.

Daniels, K. (2010) *Bribery Act 2010*, London: Chartered Institute of Personnel and Development.

DeJong, P., Lancaster, J., Pelaez, P. and Munoz, J.S. (2008) 'Examination of correlates of ethical propensity and ethnical intentions in the United States, Australia, and the Philippines: a managerial perspective', *International Journal of Management*, 25(2), pp. 270–8.

Donaldson, T. and Preston, L. (1995) 'The stakeholder theory of the corporation: concepts, evidence, and implications', *Academy of Management Review*, 20(1), pp. 65–91.

Duncan, R.B. (1972) 'Characteristics of organizational environments and perceived environmental uncertainty', *Administrative Science Quarterly*, 17(3), pp. 313–27.

Duncan, R.B. (1973) 'Multiple decision making structures in adapting to environmental uncertainty: the impact on organizational effectiveness', *Human Relations*, 26(3), pp. 273–91.

Duncan, R.B. (1974) 'Modifications in decision making structures in adapting to the environment: some implications for organizational learning', *Decision Sciences*, 5(4), pp. 705–25.

Duncan, R.B. (1979) 'What is the right organization structure?: decision tree analysis provides the answer', *Organizational Dynamics*, 7(3), pp. 59–80.

Friedman, M. (1970) 'The social responsibility of business is to increase its profits', *New York Times Magazine*, 13 September.

Friedrich, R., Peterson, M. and Koster, A. (2011) 'The rise of Generation C', *Strategy+Business Magazine*, 62 (Spring), pp. 1–6.

Giddens, A. (1990) *The Consequences of Modernity*, Cambridge and Oxford: Polity Press and Blackwell.

Giddens, A. and Sutton, P.W. (2009) *Sociology*, Cambridge: Polity Press.

Goodwin, C. (2008) 'Shucks, we just can't help making billions', *The Sunday Times*, 7 September, Ingear Supplement, pp. 6–9.

Gratton, L. (2011) *The Shift: The Future of Work Is Already Here*, London: Collins.

Harvey, M. (2008) 'With friends like these – 110 million of them – making a profit should be easy, shouldn't it?', *The Times*, 20 October, pp. 44–5.

Hewlett, S.A., Sherbin, L. and Sumberg, K. (2009) 'How Gen Y and Boomers will reshape your agenda', *Harvard Business Review*, 87(7/8), pp. 71–6.

Johnson, G., Scholes, K. and Whittington, R. (2008) *Exploring Corporate Strategy: Text and Cases* (8th edn), Harlow, Essex: Financial Times Prentice Hall.

Kotter, J.P. (1995) *The New Rules: How to Succeed in Today's Post-Corporate World*, New York: Free Press.

Leppard, D. and Chittenden, M. (2010) 'Britain's "nevertirees" lead way in refusing to quit work', *The Sunday Times*, 26 September, p. 15.

Loch, C., Sting, F.J., Bauer, N. and Mauermann, H. (2010) 'How BMW is defusing the demographic time bomb', *Harvard Business Review*, 88(3), pp. 99–102.

Morrison, M. and Daniels, K. (2010) *Pestle Analysis Factsheet*, London: Chartered Institute for Personnel and Development.

Parry, E. and Urwin, P. (2011) 'Generational differences in work values: a review of theory and evidence', *International Journal of Management Reviews*, 13(1), pp. 79–96.

Pickard, J. (2010) 'Retirement age: grey matters', *People Management*, 16 September, p. 28.

Pisano, G.P. and Shih, W.C. (2009) 'Restoring American competitiveness', *Harvard Business Review*, 87(7/8), pp. 114–25.

Sirkin, H.L., Hemerling, J.W. and Bhattacharya, A.K. (2008) *Globality: Competing with Everyone from Everywhere for Everything*, New York and Boston: Business Plus.

Smedley, T. (2011) 'Join the green shift', *People Management*, June, pp. 24–8.

The Daily Telegraph (2004) 'Cost of fat air passengers takes off', 6 November, p. 10.

The Economist (2004) 'Be prepared', 24 January, *Supplement: Living Dangerously: A Survey of Risk*, p. 20.

The Economist (2006) 'Light up', 11 February, p. 72.

The Economist (2010) 'The silver tsunami', 6 February, p. 72.

The Economist (2012) 'Schumpeter: good business, nice beaches', 19 May, p. 66.

Velasquez, M., Moberg, D.J. and Cavanagh, G.F. (1983) 'Organizational statesmanship and dirty politics: ethical guidelines for the organizational politician', *Organizational Dynamics*, 12(2), pp. 65–80.

Weick, K.E. (1979) *The Social Psychology of Organizing*, Boston, MA: Addison-Wesley.

Wiggins, J. (2007) 'Coke develops thirst for sustainability', *Financial Times*, 2 July, p. 26.

Chapter 3 Technology

Key terms

material technology
social technology
replacement effects
compensatory effects
nonstandard work
Web 2.0 technologies
technological determinism
characteristics of mass production
job rotation
job enlargement
autonomous work group or team system
open system
socio-technical system
organizational choice
lean production

Learning outcomes

When you have read this chapter, you should be able to define those key terms in your own words, and you should also be able to:

1. Explain different uses of the term technology.
2. Explain why predictions about technology and unemployment are often exaggerated.
3. Give examples of how new technology is changing the nature of work.
4. Describe the potential of Web 2.0 to transform work and organizations, and explain why that transformation is currently slow.
5. Demonstrate how the consequences of technological innovation for skill requirements depend on the organization of work, and not just on technical capabilities.
6. Define the characteristics of mass production, and describe methods to combat them.
7. Apply the socio-technical system perspective to organizational analysis and design.
8. Contrast the Scandinavian and Japanese models of team-based work organization.

Why study technology?

Technological innovation is one of the key features of contemporary society. It affects:

how you communicate	email, mobile phone, smartphone, Twitter, Facebook, Skype
how you buy and use goods and services	cloud computing, smart cash cards, e-commerce, internet access to news, information, films and music
how you travel and find places	satellite navigation, iPhone location services
how you find and apply for jobs	LinkedIn; personality and skills assessment apps, online job applications through your iPhone
how you spend your leisure time	iPod, iPad, Xbox, YouTube, Kindle, surfing, blogging, interactive gaming, iPhone apps, social networking
how private you can be	CCTV, the GPS in your smartphone, web history recording, transaction logging, data mining

Technology also affects the organization of work and the design of jobs. However, while new technologies promise better personal and corporate performance, productivity gains are not always achieved. Technology can liberate and empower, but it can also increase workload and stress, and intensify surveillance and control. Many 'high-profile' computing projects have been costly disasters; examples in Britain include the computerization of the London Stock Exchange, the London Ambulance Service, the Passport Office, and the National Programme for IT in the National Health Service. The NHS programme which was cancelled in 2011 cost an estimated £11 billion, and did not come close to achieving its objectives. More than one commentator has noted that the bigger the project, the bigger the disaster. The problems usually lie not with the technology, but with organization and management issues.

In the popular media, new technology is often accused of creating unemployment while deskilling the jobs that are left. The impact of new technology is more complex than that. New technology has a mix of costs and benefits, depending on how it is used.

First, we will show that the impact of technology on employment is indeterminate. New technology creates new jobs while making 'old' jobs redundant, and has an overall skills upgrading effect while deskilling some tasks.

Second, we will consider how new technology can change the nature of work through teleworking, and through applications of Web 2.0 technologies.

Third, we will consider the argument that management motives for using new technology can explain the organizational consequences. Technology may have material benefits, but is also used to support social and political aims, affecting the status and power of particular groups.

Finally, we explore research into technology implications, and argue that classic studies are still relevant today. This applies in particular to socio-technical systems theory. We also consider the controversy around the merits of Swedish and Japanese approaches to work organization. Sweden is known for the use of autonomous teams; Japan has a reputation for 'lean' and 'build to order' manufacturing systems. Which is better?

The three-minute world in 2050

Drawing on the experience of a 'wise crowd' of 200 managers from 40 companies around the world, Lynda Gratton (2011) predicts how technology will shape our working lives:

1. Technological capability will increase exponentially: computing costs will continue to fall, putting complex technology in hand-held devices.

Pling/Shutterstock.com

2. Billions more people will become connected: this will be a global phenomenon, creating the possibility of 'global consciousness'.
3. The cloud will become ubiquitous: global infrastructure will make services available to anyone with a computer.
4. There will be continuous productivity gains, which depend on technology, and on organization cultures, cooperation, and teamwork.
5. Social participation will increase, with growth in user-generated content, with 'wise crowd' and open innovation methods.
6. The world's knowledge will become digitized, and available to anyone regardless of formal education links.
7. Mega-companies and micro-entrepreneurs will emerge: mega-companies will span the globe; many small entrepreneurial groups will emerge.
8. Avatars and virtual worlds will be ever-present: work will be performed virtually, through avatars.
9. The rise of cognitive assistants will help us to relate the ever-increasing content to the needs of our job roles.
10. Technology will replace jobs: robots will play more important roles, from manufacturing to caring for the elderly.

'Imagine it – no peace, no quiet, no reflection time. Constantly plugged in, hooked up, online.' Gratton (2011, p. 58) predicts that global connections and the norm of 24/7 working create a world 'where it seems that no activity lasts more than three minutes, and where those in employment are continuously competing with people across the globe to strive to serve the different stakeholders they work with. Do you think your world is already fragmented?'

Why technology predictions are often false

What is 'technology'? Langdon Winner (1977) argued that the way we use the term has changed as our concern with 'technological implications' has grown. In the eighteenth and nineteenth centuries, technology simply meant machines, tools, factories, industry, craft, and engineering. Today, 'technology' can refer to a whole range of tools, instruments, machines, organizations, methods, techniques, and supply chain and production systems.

STOP AND THINK

Which technologies affect your day-to-day experience?

How do you expect your life experiences to be different from those of your parents; and what part does technology play in creating those differences?

Rapid developments leave the language behind, and the word technology is simply a convenient umbrella term. Ambiguity in the language reflects the pace of innovation, and the concern over technology and its consequences – individual, organizational, and social. Winner also observes that we tend to oversimplify and polarize; technology is either a good thing or a bad thing; you are either for it or against it.

Material technology tools, machinery, and equipment that can be seen, touched, and heard.

Social technology the methods which order the behaviour and relationships of people in systematic, purposive ways through structures of coordination, control, motivation, and reward.

Alan Fox distinguished **material technology** from **social technology**. Material technology is the stuff we can see and touch. Social technology includes job definitions, payment systems, authority relationships, communications, control systems, disciplinary codes, and 'all the many other rules and decision-making procedures which seek to govern what work is done, how it is done, and the relationships that prevail between those doing it' (Fox, 1974, p. 1).

Research has studied the effects of technology on organizations, jobs, and society at large. Technology has often been regarded as the *independent variable*, the factor whose effects are to be studied. Economic growth, employment levels, organization structures, skill requirements, and quality of working life become the *dependent variables* that are likely to be affected by technology. This relationship is shown in Figure 3.1. However, some definitions of 'technology' go beyond the equipment itself (the machinery *and* the work system around it) and overlap with the dependent variables. Organization structures and the design of jobs are social technology. This makes it difficult to establish cause and effect.

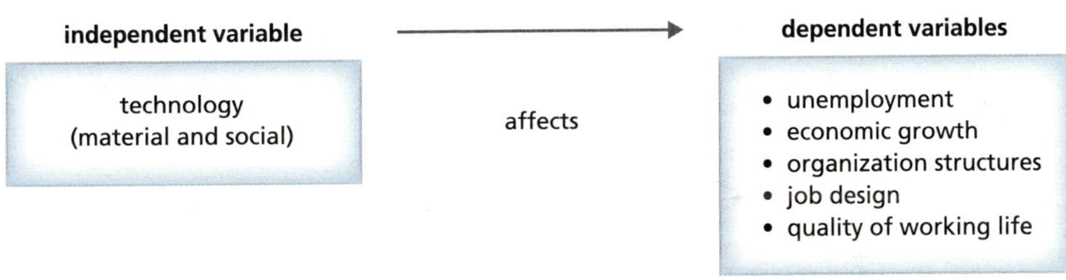

Figure 3.1: Technology as an independent variable

Advances in technology, and developments in computing and information technology in particular, often attract media predictions of doom. What does the evidence say?

STOP AND THINK

Which of the following media stories do you agree with?

- Robots are replacing people in factory jobs.
- The 'virtual organization' has arrived, based on mobile computing, so nobody needs to work in an office any more.
- The days of craft skill and worker autonomy are gone.

Compare your views with those of colleagues. Have the media got it wrong, or not?

Those media stories are partly correct. Some jobs have been eliminated and some work has been deskilled by technology. Some of us work wherever we happen to be at the time. Some traditional crafts are disappearing. Should we be concerned by these trends?

The myth of technological unemployment

Replacement effects processes through which intelligent machines substitute for people at work, leading to unemployment.

Compensatory effects processes that delay or deflect employment replacement effects, and which lead to the creation of new products and services, and new jobs.

New technology creates unemployment through **replacement effects**, which substitute equipment for people, while increasing productivity. For example, supermarkets use self-service checkout technology, reducing the number of checkout staff required.

It is natural to assume that, as machines do more, people do less. These fears date from the nineteenth century, when Luddites destroyed the mechanical looms that put them out of work. Why has technology since then not made the problem even worse? New technology is also consistent with economic growth. Unemployment is not higher today than in the nineteenth century; there has not been a technology-driven drop in job opportunities. The opposite is the case. The effects of new technology on employment also depend on **compensatory effects**.

There are six compensatory effects:

1. *New products and services mean job creation*:
   New products and services create demand which leads to investment in factories, offices, and other infrastructure, creating jobs in manufacturing, distribution, sales, and maintenance.
2. *Lower costs increase demand*:
   Technical innovation improves the productivity (same output, fewer resources) of existing operations. The consequent cost reduction leads to lower prices, and hence to increased demand. This also means that consumers have more money to spend on other goods and services, increasing demand and the creation of jobs elsewhere.
3. *Time lags delay the implications*:
   It takes time to build new technology into existing systems, products, and services. Technical and organizational problems need to be overcome. Organizations rarely adopt innovations as soon as they are available, as it is costly to scrap and replace existing facilities.
4. *Hedging risk delays the implications*:
   Organizations often approach experimental new technologies slowly. The 'learning curve' can be expensive and time-consuming. To hedge these risks, change is introduced gradually.
5. *Expectations of demand*:
   Organizations usually implement innovations only when their market is likely to expand. In that case, the organization has to retain, if not increase, the existing workforce.
6. *Technical limitations*:
   New technologies do not always live up to their promise. They may, in fact, not be able to do everything that the 'old' technology could do. Existing jobs, skills, and equipment are often found working alongside new devices. That is why, in a world of mobile phones, MP3 players, and e-books, many homes still have traditional landlines, and there is a market for compact discs, vinyl records, and printed books.

Technology does not necessarily increase unemployment. New technology can create as many jobs as it eliminates, if not more. The impact of technology depends on the interplay of replacement and compensatory effects, so that impact is indeterminate.

The myth of technological deskilling

If technology does not create unemployment, then surely the remaining jobs will be deskilled? The evidence suggests that 'technological implications' are not as one-dimensional as that. Technology can deskill, but it can also increase the demands on skill and understanding.

Studies of manufacturing show that sophisticated, flexible, expensive equipment often needs sophisticated, flexible, expensive people to operate and maintain it. It has been recognized since the 1980s that advanced technology increases

- interdependencies between functions
- skill requirements, and dependence on skilled people

Replacement effects in action?

This article appears to suggest that technology is to blame for the lack of job opportunities in this factory. Read carefully; there is another explanation.

On the banks of the sleepy river Loire, across the valley from Amboise's historic *château royal*, stands a model of modern high-tech French manufacturing. In a neatly landscaped business park, Pfizer, an American pharmaceutical giant, produces 80% of the world's Viagra, and the entire supply for the American market. Every bottle of Viagra bought in an American drugstore will have been filled, packaged, labelled, bar-coded and shipped from this site. The Amboise factory manufactures Viagra in 227 different guises, from pill jars to blister packs. In all, the site turns out nearly 70m packs or bottle of pills of various kinds each year, labelled in 44 different languages.

Employee on the production plant line

Pfizer's Amboise plant shows that, for foreign investors, France remains an attractive location. This particular site offers a mix of high productivity, technical expertise (it has a big research facility, and nearby Tours is home to a pharmaceutical college) and reliability in a market troubled by fakes. Yet a visit to the gleaming, ultra-clean production line prompts another, more unsettling observation: there are hardly any workers.

No human being drives forklift trucks around the factory floors, fills pill packets or loads them into boxes. Instead, unmanned laser-guided vehicles surge down the aisles, picking up packages that have been stuffed, wrapped and labelled by machine, and delivered to the robots along conveyor belts suspended from the ceiling. All this takes place in an eerie near-silence. The factory's director, Marie-Gabrielle Laborde-Rayna, says that even visitors from the pharmaceuticals industry familiar with high-tech production are impressed by the level of automation at Amboise.

A less comforting conclusion for the French, however, is that in France firms often invest in machines rather than hire people. This is not because French workers are inefficient. On the contrary, their productivity per hour worked is marginally higher than that of their American counterparts. It is, rather, because social-security contributions are high, the working week is short, the labour code is strict and shedding jobs is slow and difficult. Taking on an employee in France is a risk, so employers avoid it as best they can.

- capital investment per employee
- the speed, scope and costs of mistakes
- sensitivity of performance to changes in skill and attitudes.

Richard Walton and Gerald Susman (1987) argued that the response to these trends should include a skilled, flexible workforce, flat management structures, and these 'people policies':

- job enrichment, multiskilling, teamwork, 'pay for knowledge' reward systems;
- rethinking the organizational level at which decisions are taken;
- attention to selection and training, and to management development.

New digital manufacturing methods such as 3D printing (known as additive manufacturing) are likely to stimulate demand for customized products that were previously too expensive, and create more manufacturing jobs, which in turn will require high levels of skill, potentially developed in simulated production systems in a virtual environment (Markillie, 2012).

The development of nonstandard work

Nonstandard work employment that does not involve a fixed schedule at the same physical location for an extended time.

Technology encourages **nonstandard work**, which does not involve turning up at the same place and time every day to work under supervision with the mutual expectation that this arrangement will be permanent. Various labels are used for nonstandard work: alternative, contingent, contract, disposable, e-lance, freelance, telecommuting, workshifting. In a nonstandard job, your place of work is just as likely to be in your home or a coffee shop as in an office. Census data suggest that in America about 10 per cent of the working population have nonstandard jobs, and that these are more common for high-skilled, high-paid knowledge workers such as independent contractors, managers, and other professionals. The same trend applies in Japan, Britain, Australia, Canada, Europe, and parts of Asia (Ashford et al., 2007). The exercise of knowledge, creativity, and problem-solving skills requires more freedom and flexibility than traditional bureaucracy allows, and technology makes this possible.

STOP AND THINK

What for you are the benefits and disadvantages of nonstandard work?

If you know someone who has a nonstandard job, ask them how they feel about it. Would their experience encourage you to find nonstandard work?

The two main factors promoting growth in nonstandard work in the twenty-first century are technology and employee preferences. Relatively inexpensive mobile computing and telecommunications systems mean that many kinds of work (including researching and writing this textbook) can be carried out almost anywhere. The same technology can be used to monitor employees who are not on the premises, perhaps making managers comfortable with this style of working as they still have a degree of surveillance and control.

Generation Y

It is widely assumed that your attitudes and traits are influenced by the culture into which you are born. As social, economic, and political circumstances change, it is likely that different generations in the same culture will develop distinctly different characteristics. The so-called baby boomers were born between 1943 and 1960. Generation X includes those born between 1961 and 1980. Those born after 1980 are known as Generation Y.

Research evidence suggests that, if you belong to Gen Y:

- the society in which you live is more ethnically diverse and technologically sophisticated than previous generations have experienced;
- some people think of you as a 'digital native';
- about half of you were not brought up in a traditional 'nuclear family';
- you are a multi-tasker, comfortable working in groups or collaboratively;
- you value intelligence and education and have high self-esteem and confidence;
- you have a natural ability and are comfortable with technology;
- you prefer work that is defined by task, and not by time;
- you seek creative challenges and you want to make an impact;
- you like to work asynchronously, anywhere, any time;
- telecommuting, flexitime, and virtual working appeal to you, because this allows you freedom to 'have a life' and accommodate personal and family needs;
- you expect the organization to be concerned about your personal development;
- you do not expect to stay in the same job for long.

However, a recent survey showed that, although managers felt that Gen Y was distinctive in many ways, few organizations had developed management policies and practices to meet their needs and expectations (Birkinshaw and Pass, 2008).

Many of us prefer nonstandard work because it is more flexible and varied, is free from direct management supervision and organization politics, is often better paid, and gives us a lifestyle in which we can more easily combine work with personal and family interests. These preferences have been linked to the expectations of Generation Y – the Netgeneration – meaning those born since 1980 and who have grown up with today's technology. Generation Y does not have a monopoly on these preferences and lifestyles, which are also characteristic of many 'Gen Xers' and 'baby boomers'. One of the challenges created by these trends concerns managing a *blended workforce*, in which standard and nonstandard employees work side by side, with different working conditions and lifestyles.

Changing the nature of work: teleworking

Another example of how technology enables us to work in nonstandard ways, but without determining the nature of jobs, can be seen in teleworking. Communications with the far side of the planet, using email, mobile phones, instant messaging, videoconferencing, and Skype, are cheap and instantaneous. The world, for some, has become a virtual office.

If we define teleworking as using a computer and a broadband link to work from home, then less than 2 per cent of the workforce in Britain and America are teleworkers. However, the terms teleworking and telecommuting cover various kinds of employment, combining technology and location in different ways. For example, you do not need to have a computer to work from home. The distinction between homeworking and teleworking is blurred, and there seem to be six main categories (Haddon and Brynin, 2005):

net homeworkers	work from home using the internet
PC homeworkers	work from home using a PC
mobile users	rely on a mobile phone but are not net or PC homeworkers
day homeworkers	work at home but do not use the internet, a PC or a mobile phone
overtime workers	similar to day homeworkers but work evenings and weekends
standard workers	work at one or more workplaces excluding their home.

A survey of 1,750 households in Britain, Bulgaria, Germany, Israel, Italy and Norway showed that few employees work exclusively from home. Norway and Israel had the lowest proportions of standard workers, reflecting geographical and security issues respectively. About 20 per cent of all those surveyed said that they worked from home at least once a week, and most of those did this regularly. The average weekly working hours of net homeworkers varied from 8 in Norway to 19 in Germany. In Britain, about half of all net and PC homeworkers use a PC for their work at home at least half of the time.

Home viewing

Gattaca (1997, director Andrew Niccol) is based in a future society in which employment opportunities are determined by genetic profiling. People who are engineered to possess specific characteristics are called 'valids'. Those who are not engineered, the 'love children' who lack a genetic profile, are called 'invalids'. The invalids are restricted to low-skilled manual jobs. Vincent (played by Ethan Hawke) is an invalid who assumes the identity of a valid (Jude Law) so that he can get a job with the Gattaca Aerospace Corporation, in order to achieve his goal of going into space. As you watch this movie, gather evidence that would allow you to make a balanced assessment of the strengths and limitations – including the social benefits and drawbacks – of genetic engineering technology. In the end, what is your overall assessment: desirable, or not? And why?

The survey also showed that net and PC homeworkers are mostly male, except in Israel. Mobile users were also mostly male. In contrast, homeworkers who do not use computers are more likely to be female. This may be because teleworking is more common in managerial, professional, and technical jobs, and around 75 per cent of respondents were in those categories. Teleworking is clearly not a major option for those employed in more routine white-collar work. However, 20 per cent of net homeworkers in Germany, and 17 per cent in Britain and Italy, were employed in blue-collar work, and many of those were self-employed. Net homeworkers are thus more likely to be male, professional, and relatively well paid, in comparison with workplace-bound colleagues. PC homeworkers, in contrast, are more likely to be employed in lower-status jobs, with lower pay. In other words, teleworking and homeworking mirror traditional distinctions between jobs based on social and occupational status, and do not suggest some dramatic new shaping role for technology in the organization of work.

STOP AND THINK Your employer gives you a pc, helps you to set up a broadband internet connection and asks you to work at home. What are the advantages and disadvantages for the organization, and for you? Following this analysis, will you comply or complain?

Teleworking appeared in the 1970s, and developments in technology have made this option more available, and potentially more attractive. While the popularity of teleworking is technology-driven, there is no 'one best way' to do it. From a management perspective, there appear to be five main and five subsidiary reasons for introducing teleworking. The main reasons are:

1. in response to requests from employees;
2. to reduce costs;
3. to cope with maternity;
4. to help reduce office overcrowding;
5. following relocation of offices, where some staff were unable to move.

The subsidiary reasons are:

1. to cope with illness or disability;
2. to fit the kind of work being done;
3. because staff live some distance from the office;
4. because it allows more undisturbed working time;
5. database connections are faster out of main working hours.

There are many personal and organizational advantages. Teleworkers do not need expensive office space. There is no distracting office 'chit chat'. The time, costs, and frustrations of travel to work are cut. Many organizations report increased efficiency, productivity, work turnaround, accuracy, speed of response, and morale. Where location is not important, an organization can use people who they might not otherwise employ. For the teleworker, there is freedom to arrange the working day without supervision, and you become your own boss.

There are, however, several disadvantages:

- high set-up costs (though hardware costs have fallen);
- staff are not able to share equipment and other office facilities;
- lack of face to face social interaction, sharing of ideas, and team spirit;
- staff can lose touch with organization culture and goals;
- management cannot easily monitor and control activity;
- some customers expect to contact a 'conventional' office.

Workshifters

A *workshifter* is someone who works from coffee shops, hotels, airports, home, or indeed anywhere.

Workspace, not workplace: that's the new mantra of forward-thinking companies where business leaders know that it's not where their employees work, but how they work that makes the difference. Whether they are in an airport departure lounge, a conference centre, a client's offices or simply in the study or spare bedroom of their own home, a new breed of employee – a group sometimes referred to as 'workshifters' – is increasingly demanding access to corporate information from a huge variety of physical locations.

Chad Ehlers/Alamy

In fact, say workshifters, flexibility is key to their job satisfaction. In a recent survey of 3,100 mobile workers at over 1,100 enterprises worldwide, almost two-thirds (64 per cent) reported improved work/life balance and more than half (51 per cent) say that they feel more relaxed because of more flexible working arrangements.

At BT, for example, flexible workers are judged to be 20 per cent more productive than their office-based colleagues. At American Express, teleworkers handle 26 per cent more calls and produce 43 per cent more business. Bosses at Dow Chemicals, meanwhile, have calculated that average productivity has increased by around 38 per cent since the introduction of its flexible work programme. In all these cases, contributing factors seem to be fewer interruptions and more effective time management, because better connectivity means less time is wasted while sitting on a train, for example, or in the odd free hour between conference sessions.

© *Twentyman*/The Times/*News International Trading Ltd, 6 October 2011.*

To what extent does technology *determine* the consequences for teleworkers and the organizations which employ them? Technology makes some kinds of new working arrangements possible and more attractive. However, technology simply opens up a variety of different kinds of work and organizational options, some of which may simply be computer-based versions of what people did before. The consequences depend in part on the technology, and also on how we decide to use the technology in a given setting.

Teleworking at Lloyds

Michael Collins (2005) reports the results of an experiment in teleworking at the financial institution Lloyd's of London, looking at the impact on those involved, and at the business benefits. The experiment involved the Lloyd's Policy Signing Office (LPSO), which employed 300 full-time and 100 part-time staff providing support services to insurance syndicates, brokers, and managing agents. The work involved producing insurance policies, doing research, publishing information, providing accounting and regulatory services, and arranging cash settlements in multiple currencies. By 2001, LPSO had 52 teleworkers (47 women and 5 men), around 12.5 per cent of the department, working between 60 and 90 per cent of their time at home, using much the same technology, and performing the same tasks as colleagues in the conventional office. Detailed measurements were made of the costs involved in setting up and maintaining teleworking, and of staff performance.

→

The results showed that, while the quality of work was not affected, teleworkers were over 20 per cent more productive than their office-based colleagues. However, the financial benefits were almost equal to the set-up and running costs, and the experiment would not have been justified on this basis alone. The LPSO teleworkers expressed higher levels of satisfaction with work-life balance, and also had lower levels of absence, but felt that they had fewer training and career development opportunities than their office colleagues. Cut off from the office grapevine, an 'us and them' feeling developed between teleworkers and office staff. The teleworkers also had frustrating computing problems, particularly with slow response times, made worse by the lack of readily available technical support. Nevertheless, there was a queue of office staff asking to be allowed to become teleworkers.

Collins concludes that, although the business case for teleworking in this instance was not compelling, it is important to look at the broader range of issues and to consider non-financial benefits as well. It is also important to recognize that teleworking is not without problems and unintended consequences. The issues that arise will differ from one organization to another, and these must be recognized and addressed if the approach is to be effective.

Web 2.0: the impact

Web 2.0 technologies internet-based information systems that allow high levels of user interaction, such as blogs, wikis (collaborative databases), and social networking.

The internet has entered a new phase in the twenty-first century. Computing has become more 'social and sociable'.

Web 2.0 technologies involve a higher degree of participation and interaction between systems and users, and between users, than the old 'one-way' internet. This includes social networking, online coordination, blogs, podcasts, collaborative publishing, and RSS (really simple syndication) feeds. Julian Birkinshaw and Sarah Pass (2008) surveyed 488 senior managers to find out how they were responding to the challenges and opportunities of Web 2.0. The managers were asked to rate their agreement with the following statements:

- Web 2.0 enables the value of a service/activity to increase with the addition of each new user (network effect).
- Web 2.0 allows systems to evolve in an emergent or organic way; users derive value not only from the services themselves but also the overall shape that a service inherits from user behaviours.
- Web 2.0 allows experiences to be tailored to individual user needs by integrating the capabilities of multiple services from different places.
- Web 2.0 allows users to participate in the creation/delivery of new policies, services or offerings.
- Web 2.0 allows users to experience services on their own terms, not those of a centralized authority such as a corporation.

Most respondents did not have enough knowledge of Web 2.0, although it could radically change internal and external communication. IBM uses its corporate intranet for online 'jams' with up to 50,000 employees at a time. Comcast, AOL, and Dunkin Donuts, on the other hand, have suffered criticism of their poor service with video clips on YouTube. The next question concerned how managers were using these new capabilities. The most common uses involved communication and the recruitment and selection of staff, but the activity that received the most responses was 'I have read books and articles about Web 2.0'. Using online job advertisements, application forms, and tests is now common, but these are 'Web 1.0' methods. There was some evidence of wider experiments with Web 2.0 such as

- senior management communicating with staff through blogs, webcasts, and podcasts;
- management podcasts which staff could download and use outside work;
- using blogs for knowledge-sharing and problem-solving;
- live online forums allowing management to interact with thousands of employees.

Signs of the social networking times.

Web 2.0 applications

In 2011, the consulting company McKinsey held a contest to find companies using Web 2.0 tools and technologies in innovative ways, to improve management methods and engage front-line employees (McKinsey & Company, 2011). Here are some of the winners:

The Dutch Civil Service

Dutch government employees faced bureaucratic hurdles, such as having to book meeting rooms in their own buildings through an external agency, which took time and generated costs. Following a frustrated tweet from one member of staff, a group formed, and used open-source software to develop their own reservation system. This now covers over 50 offices and over 550 workplaces in government buildings across the country.

Essilor International

Essilor is a global manufacturer of ophthalmic lenses, and has a training programme with personal and Web 2.0 approaches to share best practices across 102 sites in 40 countries. It now takes one year to reach the level of skill that once took three years, and social networking allows coaching across different locations. A lens-processing centre in Thailand developed a game to teach new employees how to understand the shape of a particular type of lens, and this game is now also used in Brazil.

Best Buy

Best Buy is a consumer electronics retailer with 1,500 locations and 100,000 employees. To ensure that top management understood what front-line staff learned from customers, the company created an online feedback system which allowed everyone to see the customer information gathered in all the stores. This influenced a range of company practices, from improving shop signs to complex decisions about implementing a national promotion. This was a fast, flexible, and inexpensive way of responding to 'the voice of the customer'.

Cemex

Cemex is a large Mexico-based cement company, which developed an approach to employee collaboration called Shift. This helped to reduce the time taken to introduce new products and process improvements. Shift uses wikis, blogs, discussion boards, and web-conferencing to help employees around the world collaborate with each other. For example, 400 employees working on ready-mix products helped to identify which worked well, and which were obsolete, slimming the product line and updating the global catalogue. Now, with over 500 active communities, Shift is used to solve local problems, using global resources, as well as storing and sharing the knowledge that is generated.

Graeme Martin and colleagues (2008) argue that it is more useful to think of Web 2.0 as a system which includes inputs, transfer mechanisms, and outputs (see the discussion of open systems later in this chapter). Their view of this system is summarized in Figure 3.2. They note that traditional employee opinion surveys can *reduce* the sense of participation and engagement because they are designed and 'owned' by the organization, and constrain the responses that can be given. Addressing those limitations, in the UK, Her Majesty's Revenue and Customs (HMRC) uses an online discussion forum to capture employee contributions to the corporate suggestion scheme, known as 'Angels and Demons'. This attracts suggestions on how to improve work processes and organization culture. More than 12,000 HMRC employees had registered by October 2007, 8,000 had contributed to online discussions on specific themes, and 500 innovative business ideas had been logged.

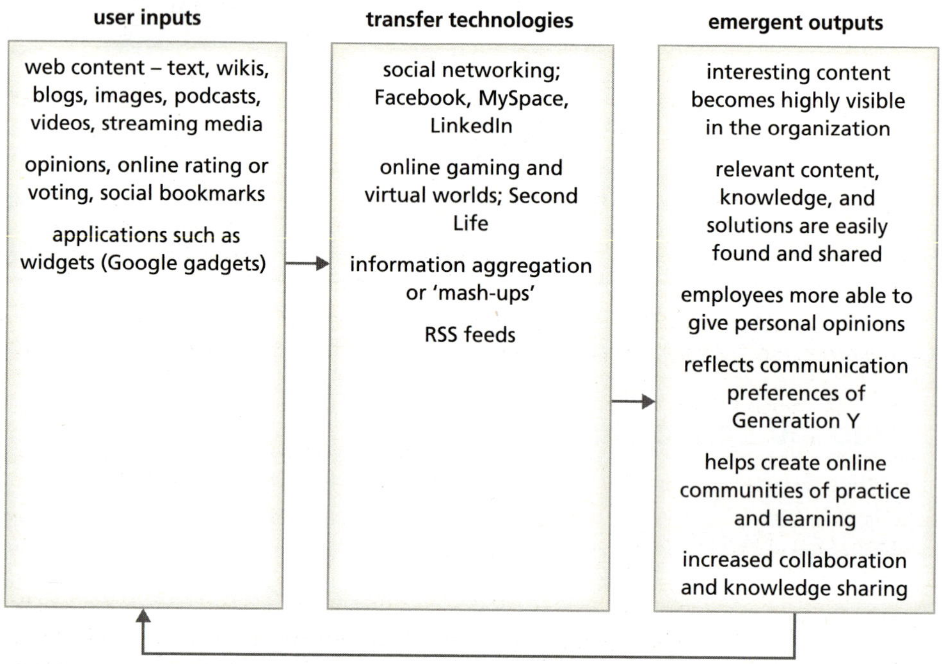

Figure 3.2: The Web 2.0 system

Source: after *Web 2.0 and HR: A Discussion Paper*, Chartered Institute for Personnel and Development (Martin, G., Reddington, M. and Kneafsey, M.B. 2008) p. 7, with the permission of the publisher, the Chartered Institute of Personnel and Development, London (www.cipd.co.uk).

Birkinshaw and Pass (2008, p. 15) argue that Web 2.0 could radically alter the nature of work, tapping knowledge from across the organization, encouraging informal coordination, and making the workplace more engaging. But most of the innovation is taking place in social networks whose members are often not traditional salaried employees. It seems that many organizations, despite researching these new technologies, have done little to exploit the organizational and business benefits. Barriers include lack of management expertise, uncertainty over costs and benefits, and fear of loss of control over information. Many organizations seem more concerned to prevent staff exploring Web 2.0; a survey of 1,765 British employers found that 80 per cent had disciplined employees for using social networking sites at work, and many had banned their use (Martin et al., 2008). Other reasons for management caution lie with perceptions of risk with regard to new technology, and with the uncertainty over how these technologies and their applications will develop.

How Web 2.0 creates Enterprise 2.0

Web 2.0	Enterprise 2.0
accessible from just about anywhere	companies can become more agile, modular and flexible
computers become 'virtual' machines as cloud computing resources are used only when and where they are needed	improved interpersonal collaboration and sharing – blogs, wikis, social networks, inside and outside the organization
software bought and used as an online service, when and where needed, flexible	organizational specialization; process networks of specialized firms
service-oriented architecture means using only the bit of the software relevant to you	capital expenditure becomes operational expenditure (easier and cheaper)
mash-ups; bits of software applications can be combined in creative ways	small companies can enjoy the same computing infrastructure as large competitors
wireless networks connect more devices; more products are designed with built-in radio connectivity; who needs a laptop?	cloud computing is the basis for whole new businesses (Animoto allows users to turn photos into music videos)
data centres become industrial-scale service factories	easier to outsource business processes to networks of small specialist companies
personal and corporate data storage and protection become major concerns	collaboration and openness – on a global scale generate security risks
some organizations block staff access to social networking sites through company computers	'digital natives' are impatient with the rules of traditional corporate IT, and build their own tailored applications

Based on Siegele (2008).

Determinism or choice?

Different technologies make different demands on those who work with them. The technology of an organization appears to determine the nature of work. When we compare a hospital with a call centre, or a retail store with a coal mine, the technology seems to determine the kinds of tasks that need to be done; the nature of jobs; the organization of work; the grouping of jobs; the hierarchy through which work is planned, coordinated and controlled; the knowledge and skills required; and the values and attitudes of employees.

But does technology really determine these factors? Can we predict the shape of an organization, and the nature and content of jobs in it, from a knowledge of its technology? As we have seen, while new technologies enable some new kinds of working arrangements, they do not uniquely determine the outcomes. The argument that technology does have predictable consequences for work and organization is known as **technological determinism**.

Technological determinism the argument that technology explains the nature of jobs, work groupings, hierarchy, skills, values, and attitudes in organizations.

Technological determinism assumes that work has to be organized to meet the requirements of the technology. Different technologies have different 'technological imperatives'. Arthur Turner and Paul Lawrence (1965) explained the background to their classic work on manufacturing jobs saying

> [T]his research started with the concept that every industrial job contained certain technologically determined task attributes which would influence the workers' response. By 'task attributes' we meant such characteristics of the job as the amount of variety, autonomy, responsibility, and interaction with others built into the design.

Technological determinism is an oversimplified perspective. Technology *suggests* and *enables*. The opposite perspective concerns the availability of organizational choice (defined later in this chapter). There are three areas of choice in the new technology implementation process, concerning choice of design, of goals, and of work organization.

First, there are choices in the design of tools, machinery, equipment and systems: for example, how much control is built into the machine, and how much is left to human intervention and discretion. There are settings where automation has been removed from aircraft cockpits, ships' bridges, and railway engine cabs following the discovery that pilots and drivers lose touch with the reality of their tasks when surrounded by sophisticated controls which function without their understanding or help.

Second, there are choices in the goals that technology is used to achieve. The needs to reduce costs, improve quality and customer service, and improve management information can be critical. However, managers also promote innovation for personal and political reasons, to strengthen power over resources and influence over decisions, to enhance status and prestige, and to exert closer surveillance and control over employees.

Third, there are choices in how work is organized. As we will see, car assembly work can be designed in several different ways, and it is not clear which of these approaches may be best.

These choices rely on the assumptions we make about human capabilities and organizational characteristics. They rely less on the capabilities of the equipment. These are called 'psychosocial assumptions', because they concern beliefs about individuals and groups. To consider the 'impact' of a technology, therefore, is to consider the wrong question. Technological innovations trigger a decision-making and negotiation process which is driven by the perceptions, goals, and assumptions of those involved. The choices that form in that process determine the 'impact'. Technology has a limited effect on work independent of the purposes of those who would use it and the responses of those who have to work with it.

Figure 3.3 summarizes this argument claiming that the consequences of technological change depend on the interaction between these implementation choices with regard to technical capabilities, objectives, and how work is organized.

Is this argument oversimplified? Technology must have *some* independent influence on the nature of work and organizations. One commentator who has challenged the 'organizational choice' argument, Ian McLoughlin, argues (McLoughlin, 1999) that information and computing technologies *do* create imperatives:

- reduction in tasks that require manual skills;
- creation of complex tasks requiring problem-solving skills;
- ability to combine knowledge of new and old technology;
- a relationship between technology and user that relies on informed intervention based on an understanding of system interdependencies.

In other words, cognitive skills become more valuable than 'action-centred' abilities. This is not to deny the role of organizational choice, or social shaping and negotiation, in affecting the outcomes for work experience that accompany technological innovations. Technology has 'enabling' properties; the technology of car production enables task fragmentation and supervisory control, but it also enables multiskilled, autonomous teamwork.

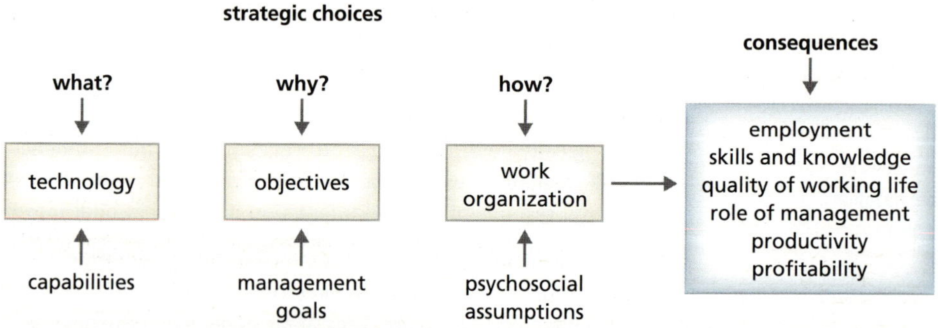

Figure 3.3: Technological indeterminism

Cyber crime, terror and warfare

Sophisticated international computer networks have enormous benefits, but they bring new threats and dangers. As with any technology, what counts is why and how it is used.

Kevin Townsend (2011) estimates that £12 billion was invested in IT security in 2010 in the UK, and that the annual cost of cyber crime to the economy is £27 billion, £17 billion of which is due to commercial espionage. Companies are experiencing Advanced Persistent Threats (APTs), or targeted attacks on systems and databases. APT is a term coined by the US air force, and attacks have been reported by Sony, Nintendo, RSA, Mitsubishi and Google. 'Operation Shady Rat', exposed in 2011 by the internet security company McAfee, is alleged to have stolen intellectual property from 70 government agencies and international companies in 14 countries over five years (Robertson, 2011).

Financial institutions and government agencies are susceptible to attacks with economic and political motives. The Stuxnet Worm which damaged uranium centrifuges in Iran in 2010 was an example of cyber warfare. Cyber bandits are suspected of causing the 'flash crash' that wiped US$860 billion off the stock values of several companies including General Electric and Procter & Gamble in May 2010. This could be due to bad data or technical faults, but cyber terrorism poses similar threats. Cyber attacks could disrupt communication systems, power and water distribution, and air traffic control systems, putting lives at risk. The US defense secretary Leon Panetta argued that a cyber attack on financial markets, power grids and government systems could be 'the next Pearl Harbor' (*The Economist*, 2011).

When computers and users were all in the same building, security was simple. Today, cloud computing and mobile devices mean that data and users can be anywhere. In addition, many of us want to use our own gadgets for personal and work purposes, rather than rely on clumsy corporate systems. Thus, establishing secure procedures and erecting barriers to crime and terrorism have become more difficult. Social networking, in particular, can provide access to personal information, which in turn can be used to get usernames, passwords, photographs, credit card details, and much more – which can then be used to bypass corporate security defences. This is known as 'phishing', or as 'spear phishing' and 'whaling', where attacks are targeted on key figures such as senior executives and other high-profile individuals.

Most countries have cyber warfare units to detect, deflect, and respond to such attacks. For organizations under threat, this means more sophisticated security systems, improved risk assessment, staff training, and heightened vigilance to detect intrusions (Frean, 2011). Another potential threat comes from unhappy employees who may seek revenge by deleting data and causing other systems damage (Glenny, 2011). People are the weakest links in security systems, putting human resource management policies in the front line against cyber attacks.

Portugal 2004/iStockphoto

The politics of technology

Commentators in the 1940s claimed that technological change increased task specialization, took skill and identity from work, and increased discipline in the workplace. This pessimistic view appeared in Harry Braverman's (1974) influential work which triggered a 'labour process debate' which still generates controversy today. Braverman argued that advances in technology give management progressive opportunities to reduce skill and discretion, and to tighten surveillance and control over workers. It is important to draw a distinction between what technology can achieve, and what management uses technology to achieve; Braverman's argument concerns the latter.

Humanization or intensification?

The problem as it presents itself to those managing industry, trade, and finance is very different from the problem as it appears in the academic or journalistic worlds. Management is habituated to carrying on labor processes in a setting of social antagonism and, in fact, has never known it to be otherwise. Corporate managers have neither the hope nor the expectation of altering this situation by a single stroke: rather, they are concerned to ameliorate it only when it interferes with the orderly functioning of their plants, offices, warehouses and stores.

For corporate management this is a problem in costs and controls, not in the 'humanization of work'. It compels their attention because it manifests itself in absenteeism, turnover, and productivity levels that do not conform to their calculations and expectations. The solutions they will accept are only those which provide improvements in their labour costs and in their competitive positions domestically and in the world market.

From Braverman (1974), p. 36.

This argument treats technology as a political tool, which managers use to maintain their position of power, and to manipulate employees and the conditions in which they work. This is an important observation because technology is often seen as politically neutral. However, if management can increase task specialization, and reduce the level of skill required in a job, lower wages can be offered, and the organization's dependence on those employees is reduced. If management can increase the discipline in work, improve surveillance and gain tighter control of employees, this can lead to reduced discretion and to work intensification.

Managers can manipulate employees by appealing to technological determinism: 'we have to do it this way because of the technology'. This argument can be used to justify and to protect from challenge unpopular decisions; those who argue just don't understand the technology. Improved control can lead to lower costs and higher profits, and also maintains management status and power, and control over employees. Technology's consequences are not the inescapable outcomes of the demands of machinery, but the result of management choices.

Chapter 14 explores *scientific management*, which is used today, although developed in the early twentieth century. Scientific management offers a rationale for task fragmentation, simplification, and tighter control. The typically negative response to repetitive work can confirm the management view that tight control of employees is necessary, to maintain discipline, and to produce goods and services effectively. Scientific management can become self-perpetuating through the 'vicious circle of control' (Clegg and Dunkerley, 1980) illustrated in Figure 3.4. This vicious circle can only be broken by a change in management perceptions, starting with higher trust in, and higher discretion for, employees. Technological determinism is thus replaced with an economic and political logic.

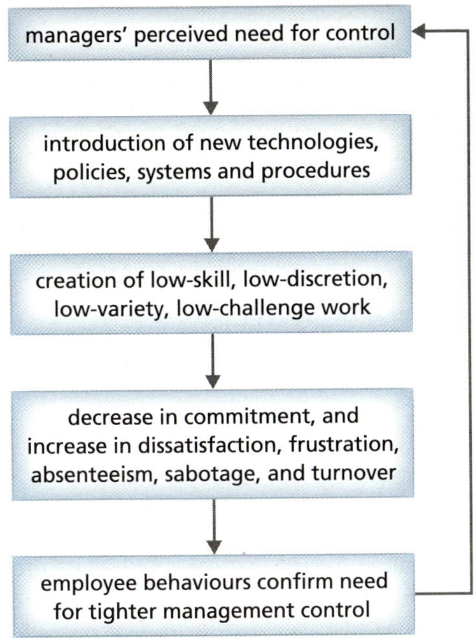

Figure 3.4: The vicious circle of control

Classic studies on work and technology

One of the first studies of the impact of technology on the nature of work was reported by Charles Walker and Robert Guest in 1952. They argued, in determinist mode, that some technologies prevent the formation of work groups and frustrate the social needs of employees. Their survey of 180 American automobile assembly workers identified six **characteristics of mass production**: mechanical pacing of work, no choice of tools or methods, repetitiveness, minute subdivision of product, minimum skill requirements, and surface mental attention. The assembly jobs were scored on these characteristics. Despite being content with their pay and conditions, employees in jobs with a high 'mass production score' disliked their work, and had a higher rate of absenteeism than those in low-scoring jobs. In other words, scientific management had taken task specialization too far. Monotony and boredom reduced work rate, output, and morale, and led to high levels of absenteeism and complaints. The solutions to boredom and monotony were **job rotation** and **job enlargement**.

Characteristics of mass production mechanical pacing of work, no choice of tools or methods, repetitiveness, minute subdivision of product, minimum skill requirements, and surface mental attention.

Job rotation a work design method in which employees are switched from task to task at regular intervals.

Job enlargement a work design method in which tasks are combined to widen the scope of a job.

Job enlargement was first used at IBM's Endicott plant (Walker, 1950). The jobs of machine operators were enlarged to include machine set-up and inspection of finished products. There was nothing in the technology to prevent operators doing these extra tasks. The benefits were improved product quality and a reduction in losses from scrap, less idle time for operators and machines, and a 95 per cent cut in set-up and inspection costs. Job enlargement reduced monotony and boredom, and increased variety, but in superficial ways. Job rotation and enlargement are still in use today.

Mass production characteristics also cause stress and illness. Arthur Kornhauser's (1965) study of car assembly workers in Detroit showed that factory work could lead to job dissatisfaction and poor mental health. The workers in his study had a list of grievances:

- low pay
- job insecurity
- poor working conditions
- low status
- restricted promotion opportunities

- simplicity of job operations
- repetitiveness and boredom
- lack of control over the work
- non-use of abilities
- feelings of futility
- the style of the supervisors

Workers in jobs with these characteristics had lower mental health, which meant that they

- were anxious and tense
- had negative self-concepts
- were hostile to others
- were less satisfied with life
- were socially withdrawn
- suffered from isolation and despair.

Kornhauser argued that work with mass production characteristics produces this pattern of psychological reactions. A later study showed that the most stressful jobs were those which combined high workload with low discretion (Karasek, 1979). Typical examples included assembly workers, garment stitchers, goods and materials handlers, nursing aides and orderlies, and telephone operators. The symptoms included exhaustion and depression, nervousness, anxiety, and sleeping difficulties.

These symptoms are not confined to the mid twentieth century and manual work. They are widespread today, across a range of occupations. A recent survey found that workload and management style are still the main sources of stress and mental health problems at work, and are the main causes of staff absence (Sinclair, 2011).

Technology and alienation

One classic study of the impact of technology on work was carried out by Robert Blauner (1964), who analysed working conditions in printing, dominated by craft work; cotton spinning, dominated by machine minding; car manufacture, dominated by mass production; and chemicals manufacture, dominated by process production.

Blauner identified four components of alienation, concerning feelings of

- *powerlessness*: loss of control over work processes, pace and methods;
- *meaninglessness*: loss of significance of work activities;
- *isolation*: loss of sense of community membership; and
- *self-estrangement*: loss of personal identity and of a sense of work as a central life interest.

Printing workers set their own pace, were free from management pressure, chose their own techniques and methods, had powerful unions, practised a complex skill, had good social contacts at work, had high status, identified closely with their work, and were not alienated.

Textile workers performed simple, rapid, and repetitive operations over which they had little control, worked under strict supervision, and had little social contact. Alienation, however, was low. Blauner argued that this was because textile workers lived in close rural communities whose values and way of life overcame feelings of alienation arising at work.

Car assembly workers had little control over work methods, saw little meaning in the tasks they performed, were socially isolated, and developed no meaningful skills.

Chemicals processing workers operated prosperous, technically advanced plants where manual work had been automated. They controlled their own work pace, and had freedom of movement, social contact and teamwork. They developed an understanding of the chemical reactions which they monitored, and also developed a sense of belonging, achievement, and responsibility. In addition they had close contact with educated, modern management.

Blauner concluded that advanced technology would eliminate alienation.

Based on Blauner (1964).

STOP AND THINK

What other jobs combine a high workload with low discretion?

Do employees in those jobs display symptoms of fatigue or depression?

What advice would you give to management to reduce workload and increase discretion in those jobs?

Swedish carmakers were the first to show that mass production characteristics can be avoided by creative work design. In 1970, Saab-Scania created production groups with 40 workers in the chassis shop of a new truck factory (Norstedt and Aguren, 1973). Group members decided how they would rotate between tasks, and took on maintenance and quality control jobs. These changes spread to about 600 manual workers, with the following results:

- productivity increased and product quality improved;
- unplanned stoppages of production were significantly reduced;
- costs were reduced to 5 per cent below budget;
- labour turnover was cut from 70 to 20 per cent;
- absenteeism was not affected;
- cooperation between management and workforce improved.

High performance hi-fi

Linn Products, based in Glasgow in Scotland, makes top of the range audio equipment. Despite the engineering sophistication and complexity, every product is assembled by hand, by a single employee. The company's founder and executive chairman, Ivor Tiefenbrun, explains why he abandoned the traditional assembly line in favour of 'single-stage build' (Morse, 2006):

> Early on, we did use an assembly line and tried to operate like a mini General Motors. But try as I might, I couldn't get all the manufacturing processes to synchronize efficiently. So, one day, I asked one of the women on the turntable assembly line to collect all the parts of the product, assemble it, and bring it to me. She looked at me a little strangely, went and gathered the components, and assembled the turntable in 17 and a half minutes – a process that took 22 and a half minutes on the line.
>
> That was an 'aha' moment for me. We reorganized the factory to accommodate a single-stage build model, using computer-controlled vehicles to distribute materials to work positions, and taught everyone in the plant how to build any product we made. That way, we could do real-time manufacturing, let customer orders pull, reconfigure the factory, and shift resources as needed to produce what customers wanted that day.
>
> When one person builds a product from start to finish, they feel responsible for it and can see the connection between what they do and how the product performs. And since the people who build the products are often responsible for servicing them later, those employees interact with customers and see how happy – or unhappy – they are. So, they're learning a lot more than just how to assemble a product. They start to spot connections that no engineer, service technician, or assembly-line worker ever would, and bring skills developed in one area to bear on what they do somewhere else. As a result, they can contribute to product quality with improvements and innovation.

Linn Products Limited

The Linn Artikulat speaker system

Autonomous work group or team a group or team allocated to a significant segment of the workflow, with discretion over how their work will be carried out.

System something that functions through the interdependence of its component parts.

Open system a system that interacts, in a purposive way, with its external environment in order to survive.

Saab's best-known experiment was at their engine factory at Södertälje. Here an oblong conveyor loop moved engine blocks to seven assembly groups, each with three members (Thomas, 1974). Each group had its own U-shaped guide track in the floor, to the side of the main conveyor. Engine blocks were taken from the main track, assembled by the group, and then returned to the conveyor. The engines arrived with their cylinder heads, and the groups handled the fitting of carburettors, distributors, spark plugs, camshafts, and other components.

Each assembly group decided for themselves how the work was allocated. The group had half an hour to build each engine, and they decided how that time would be spent. Individual jobs on the conventional assembly track had cycle times of less than two minutes. In 1974, Saab-Scania estimated that they saved around 65,000 Swedish kronor a year on recruitment and training costs alone with this approach. This form of work organization is known as the **autonomous work group**, (or self-regulating or self-managing group or team). Autonomous work groups make their own decisions about how tasks and responsibilities will be allocated, shared and rotated. This a feature of the 'high performance work systems' discussed in Chapter 9, and was the approach used by Sweden's other carmaker, Volvo. Volvo's plant at Kalmar pioneered the concept of 'dock assembly', in which teams completed whole stages of the car assembly in static bays to one side of the moving assembly track.

These early experiments with autonomous work groups have had a lasting impact on management practice in other sectors, an example being the manufacture of high performance hi-fi systems by Linn Products.

Socio-technical systems

Eric John Miller (1924–2002)

Albert Kenneth Rice (1908–1969)

Swedish managers did not invent the autonomous work group; it came from the work of British researchers at the Tavistock Institute in London. According to Martyn Sloman, advisor on learning at the Chartered Institute of Personnel and Development, one reason why technology often fails to deliver productivity gains is because the lessons of the Tavistock research are overlooked (Overell, 2005). The Tavistock group first developed the concept of the organization as a **system**. The term system can be applied to a range of phenomena: solar system, nervous system, traffic management system, telecommunications system, waste disposal system. Any system is defined by its boundaries, which in turn depend on what one wants to study, and why. In an organizational context, we may wish to analyse a performance measurement system, a product distribution system, a supply chain management system, or a production system.

Humans and organizations share one important property – their need to conduct exchanges with their environments. We breathe air, consume food and drink, and absorb sensory information. We convert these imports into energy and actions, dispose of waste products, and expend energy in our behaviour. The organization is also an **open system**. Open systems import resources such as people, materials, equipment, information, and money. Organizations transform those inputs by producing services and goods, which are then exported back into the environment. This view of organizations as living organisms is known as 'the organic analogy' (Miller and Rice, 1967).

Another property of open systems is their ability to reach an outcome from a variety of different starting points and through different routes. A chemical reaction is a closed system in which the end result depends on the concentrations and quantities of the items used to begin with. An autonomous work group at Saab, on the other hand, could assemble an engine in many different ways, with the same end results. This property is known as 'equifinality', and this means that it is not necessary to specify in detail the organization structure and the duties of every member. If an organization can develop its own mode of operating, and change as circumstances require, then it will only be necessary to detail the most significant aspects. This approach to organizational design is called 'minimum critical specification'.

Socio-technical system system which has both a material technology (machinery, equipment) and a social organization (job specifications, management structure).

Unlike closed systems which maintain or move towards states of homogeneity, organization structures become more elaborate and adaptable in attempts to cope with their environment (Emery and Trist, 1960). One Tavistock researcher and consultant, Eric Trist, developed the concept that an organization is also a **socio-technical system**.

The socio-technical system concept is illustrated in Figure 3.5. The goal of socio-technical system design is to find the best fit between the social and technical dimensions. Trist argued that effective socio-technical system design could never satisfy fully the needs of both subsystems. A system designed to meet social needs, ignoring the technical system, would run into problems. On the other hand, a system designed only to meet the demands of technology would raise social and organizational problems. 'Suboptimization' is a feature of socio-technical design, which aims at 'joint optimization' of social and technical needs. The resultant socio-technical system design is thus a matter of creative choice.

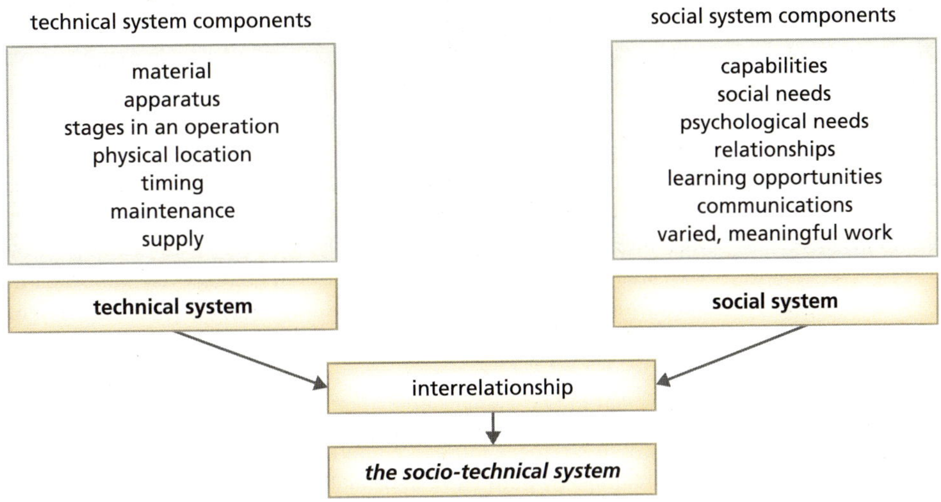

Figure 3.5: The organization as socio-technical system

Several new concepts have been introduced in this section:

system	anything that functions by virtue of the interdependence of its component parts
open system	a system that has to conduct regular exchanges with its environment in order to survive
the organic analogy	the organization as an open system has properties similar to a living organism
equifinality	the same end results can be achieved with different starting points and routes
minimum critical specification	it is not necessary to specify organization and task design in detail as open systems adapt themselves as necessary
socio-technical system	the organization combines a social system (people) with a technical system (plant and machinery)
joint optimization	the social and technical systems cannot be designed in isolation; trade-offs are necessary to design for 'best fit' between the two sub-systems.

Organizational choice the argument that work design is not determined by technology, and that the technical system does not determine the social system.

Tavistock researchers also introduced the concept of **organizational choice**, which we contrasted earlier in this chapter with the notion of technological determinism.

Eric Trist and Kenneth Bamforth developed the concept of the socio-technical system in their study of the social and psychological impact of longwall coal mining methods in the 1940s (Trist and Bamforth, 1951; Bamforth was a miner). Table 3.1 summarizes the developments in technology, work organization, and job characteristics which they studied.

Table 3.1: From single place to composite longwall coal mining

technology	work organization	job characteristics
1: hand and pneumatic picks	single place	composite autonomous miner
2: mechanized coal cutters and belt conveyors	conventional cutting longwall	task fragmentation, mechanization, mass production features
3: electric coal cutters and belt conveyors	composite longwall	composite autonomous, self-regulating teams

Their research contrasted the advantages of the traditional 'composite autonomous mining' method of single place working with the problems of highly mechanized coal getting (Trist et al., 1963). During their study, however, they found that some pits had developed a form of 'shortwall' working, with methods similar to those of traditional single place working.

One case, called 'The Manley Innovation' after the name of the pit, describes how miners developed a teamwork approach to shortwall mining, in response to underground conditions which made it dangerous to work long coal faces. When management tried to restore conventional longwall working, to reduce costs, the men resisted and negotiated an agreement to continue with their approach. This was based on composite, multiskilled, self-selecting groups, each with over 40 members, collectively responsible for the whole coal-getting cycle on any one shift. This contrasted sharply with conventional longwall working, in which each shift was restricted to one stage of the coal-getting cycle, and each miner was limited to one fragmented task, with limited opportunity to develop other underground skills. The Manley groups had no supervisors, but elected their own 'team captains' to liaise with management. They were paid on a common paynote, as all members made equivalent contributions.

This led to two conclusions:

1. Work in groups is more likely to be meaningful, to develop responsibility, and to satisfy human needs than work allocated to separately supervised individuals.
2. Work can be organized in this way regardless of the technology. Social system design is not determined by technical system characteristics and demands.

In other words, new technologies create implementation choices; technological change opens up *organizational choice*.

STOP AND THINK

Coal mining is hardly 'typical' work. To what extent can the concept of organizational choice be applied to other kinds of work and organizations?

Socio-technical systems thinking remains influential to this day, particularly in the Netherlands and Sweden, and Dutch researchers have developed a more elaborate socio-technical system design methodology (Benders et al., 2000):

1. an analysis of the environment to establish the main organizational design criteria, such as market objectives, but also quality of working life and labour relations;
2. an analysis of the product flow pattern;
3. design of the production structure, first approximate and then in detail, based on semi-autonomous production units operated by 'whole-task groups';
4. design of the control structure, allocating control tasks to the lowest possible level, which can be an individual workstation or an autonomous group;
5. the creation of 'operational groups' which combine support and line functions (such as maintenance and quality control) and which assist a number of whole-task groups.

Contemporary examples of autonomous teamworking are explored in Chapter 13.

Team versus lean: competing socio-technical paradigms

Until the early 1990s, the team-based plants of the Swedish car manufacturers Saab and Volvo were 'management tourist attractions'. The team-based approach was still popular in the 1990s, one study showing that over half of American manufacturing companies had scrapped their assembly lines in favour of 'cellular manufacturing' (*The Economist*, 1994).

Volvo built a new assembly plant at Uddevalla, on Sweden's West Coast, in the late 1980s. Instead of a traditional assembly line, teams of eight to ten car builders handled the final assembly on a static dock. The plant had a central store from which parts and sub-assemblies were delivered to teams by automatically guided vehicles. Each team managed its own recruitment, training, maintenance, and tooling. Teams elected their own spokespersons to plan and assign work, lead discussions, solve problems, and liaise with management.

In 1990 Saab sold its carmaking business to General Motors, and in 1991 closed its team-based plant at Malmo. In 1993, Volvo closed its plants at Kalmar and Uddevalla, and concentrated production at its traditional factory at Torslanda, outside Gothenburg. In January 1999, Volvo Car Corporation was sold to Ford Motor Company, which in turn sold Volvo to the Zhejiang Geely Group in 2010. As Swedish carmakers were closing and selling their facilities, Japanese companies such as Toyota, Honda, and Nissan were opening successful new plants in Europe and America based on traditional assembly line methods.

These developments helped to tarnish the image of team-based manufacturing. What went wrong? One explanation lies in the work of James Womack, Dan Jones and Daniel Roos (1990), who compared the production methods and productivity of car companies around the world. One of their measures was the number of hours of direct labour used to build, paint, and finally assemble a car. The main differences between the best and the worst companies, on the measure of labour assembly hours, were:

	Best	Worst
Japan	13.2	25.9
North America	18.6	30.7
Europe	22.8	55.7

These comparisons were damning, showing the advantages of Japanese methods, especially the approach developed by Toyota. At Uddevalla, the training time for team members was high, and the assembly time for each car was twice the European average. Womack and his colleagues argued that the productivity differences were due to production methods. The Japanese advantage was based on Toyota's **lean production** methods (Oliver et al., 1994).

Lean production a manufacturing method which combines machine-pacing, work standardization, just-in-time materials flow, continuous improvement, problem-solving teams, and powerful supervision.

Lean production, also known as the Toyota Production System (TPS), combines:

- machine-paced assembly, with task specialization, placing responsibility on workers to improve the 'one best way' for each task;
- 'just-in-time' delivery of materials to the point of assembly, replacing the need to hold costly inventories, reducing the need for storage space, and cutting the time that elapses between receipt of order and delivery to the customer;
- continuous improvement or *kaizen*. When the worker identifies an improvement, this is agreed with supervision and engineering, and the work procedure sheet is revised;
- aggressive problem-solving using 'quality circles', a team approach to kaizen;
- a ruthless approach to reducing equipment adjustment and retooling times, and eliminating defects. In a Japanese plant, one worker can bring the plant to a halt by pulling the 'andon cord' if a problem arises. This is a cord strung along the assembly track, and the line halts when the cord is tugged. The plant is not restarted until the problem is fixed;
- powerful first-line supervisors who monitor and encourage continuous improvement.

The Toyota Production System

The Toyota Production System (TPS) has become a global model for car manufacturing. TPS has two main principles. First, products are only made once they have been sold. Second, the manufacturing process is continuous and uninterrupted, using a 'just-in-time' flow of parts.

Traditionally, goods are made according to sales forecasts, and items are held in store until orders are placed. In TPS, manufacturing does not start until a customer has placed an order. This cuts the cost of storing goods in warehouses. Conventional production lines have separate stages, with 'buffers' where stocks of part-finished goods build up. In TPS, in-process stocks are seen as waste, or *muda*. Without buffers, a breakdown stops the whole assembly line. Breakdowns are addressed using kaizen, a problem-solving method in which employees continuously improve the process. While TPS is efficient, it is unpleasant for workers. The production schedule is tight, the work is repetitive, the pace is fast, the pressure is high, and the physical conditions are tough. Workers are expected to make a number of suggestions a year, and this requirement is linked to pay and promotion, leading to many unworkable suggestions.

In the late 1980s, Toyota had problems recruiting and retaining production staff, particularly in final assembly. The first response was to develop a more technically sophisticated production line, at the Tahara plant. However, the development and maintenance of this line were difficult, it used more space than the previous system, the reduction in staffing was marginal, there were frequent breakdowns, and workers did not like this system either. It was expensive to change equipment each time a new model was introduced, and the investment could only be recovered with high production volumes, which market conditions did not require. Toyota abandoned this approach in the late 1990s, and developed a 'worker friendly' system with four elements:

1. segmented lines built around production modules or *kumi* (for example, the whole exhaust system) separated by small buffers of approximately five cars, giving each employee a more meaningful task and contribution to the end product;
2. ergonomically improved working conditions, such as mobile component carts or 'dollies', and *raku-raku* ('comfort') seats, based on an employee's prize-winning suggestion, which allow easier access to the car body interiors;
3. automation of selected tasks, using only simple machinery, sometimes developed by assembly workers, to reduce heavy work such as tyre assembly;
4. a modified form of kaizen, with a broader emphasis on self-development, and with no link to pay, although good suggestions can still improve promotion chances.

TPS is often compared to Swedish autonomous groups, which are seen as less efficient. However, Volvo developed group working in the 1970s at the Kalmar plant because they could not recruit workers to conventional assembly lines (based on Benders and Morita, 2004).

Teamwork in Japan, therefore, is not the same as teamwork in most European or American companies (Buchanan, 2000). The closely supervised Japanese employee carries out a short-cycle repetitive task, and is under pressure to improve productivity. This is quite different from the experience of multiskilled autonomous team members, who decide how to allocate tasks, and who solve their own problems, at their own pace. Bram Steijn (2001) distinguishes four work systems in terms of their effects on employees:

	low autonomy	**high autonomy**
no teamwork	scientific management	professional work
teamwork	lean teams	autonomous teams

Source: adapted from Work systems, quality of working life and attitudes of workers: an empirical study towards the effects of team and non-teamwork, *New Technology, Work and Employment* 16(3), pp. 191–203 (Steijn, B. 2001) © Blackwell Publishers Ltd. 2001.

Is it safe to conclude that the Anglo-American-Scandinavian model of team-based manufacturing has been discredited, and that lean production is a more effective paradigm?

The evidence suggests that lean production can also be 'mean' production. The pace and intensity, the demands of kaizen, supervisory regulation of methods, and lack of discretion are stressful. A study of a plant run jointly by Toyota and General Motors in California – New United Motors Manufacturing Incorporated (NUMMI) – showed that this industry-standard approach to lean production was an example of 'management by stress'. Every worker motion and action was carefully timed to remove waste effort, reduce inventory, and continuously streamline production (Parker and Slaughter, 1988). Those pressures are often offset with job security and high wages, and Japanese 'transplant' factories are usually located in areas of traditionally high unemployment and low trade union membership. In addition, Japanese methods, based on traditional scientific management methods, appear to be 'natural' and 'safe' to many managers (Hammarstrom and Lansbury, 1991).

Source: DILBERT © 2011 Scott Adams. Used by permission of UNIVERSAL UCLICK. All rights reserved.

Swedish commentators defended their methods. Christian Berggren, at the Swedish Institute for Work Life Research in Stockholm, has been scathing of the narrow range of measures used in the American research, which focused on final assembly hours, and paid less attention to how the supply chain, from design to customer, was organized (Berggren, 1995). Berggren also argues that Volvo's decision to close Kalmar and Uddevalla was made despite analyses which showed that these plants were at least as productive as the conventional, but much larger and older, plant at Torslanda. The company had excess capacity in the early 1990s, and logistics and politics made it expedient to close the smaller, experimental plants located some distance from their main facilities.

The aim of lean manufacturing is to build products only when a customer order is received instead of making items to store in warehouses until they are sold. The ability to react instantly to business changes would create the 'real-time enterprise', and this is made possible with information technology. There is a growing demand in the motor manufacturing sector for vehicles tailored to individual requirements, and this is known as 'flexible mass customization'. Manufacturers thus aim for what is known as 'build to order', or BTO. With a conventional manufacturing system, the buyer might wait months for delivery. Many companies are now attempting to reduce this to fifteen days, or less, using the internet to integrate their supply chains. This improves customer service, and reduces supply chain and manufacturing costs. This approach also requires skills upgrading for assembly workers.

We are faced with a dispute between two socio-technical system paradigms, two different ways of organizing around production. The 'team versus lean' debate is far from resolution, although it appears that some lean approaches depend at least in part for their effectiveness on the use of small and relatively autonomous teams. While the arguments in car production may be unresolved, similar methods are being applied and developed in other manufacturing and service sector organizations. This debate is likely to run for some time.

Lean hospitals

The Toyota Production System was designed for assembling cars, but it may also now be saving the lives of patients in hospitals. 'Lean' methods can be used to improve efficiency, and to reduce waste and errors in hospitals as well as in factories. Anthony Manos et al. (2006) argue that 'the eight wastes' in manufacturing can arise in healthcare:

overproduction	doing more than necessary, extra tests and treatments, and paperwork
inventory	holding excess supplies, increasing storage space and clutter
motion	waste body movement, multiple trips, lots of walking around
transport	moving patients, materials, and information unnecessarily
overprocessing	doing more than the customer or patient wants
defects	unreadable labels, incomplete information, faulty items
waiting	patients waiting for a doctor or a bed; staff waiting for equipment
underusing staff	not using the knowledge and creativity of front-line staff.

These problems can be addressed with '5S workplace organization', a method developed by Hiroyuki Hirano, and based on Japanese terms which also start with 's'. The power of this method is based on its simplicity. To improve productivity and quality, those who work in a department or area are empowered to find and to implement ways to do these five things.

5S workplace organization

English	Japanese	meaning
sort	seiri	remove unnecessary items, equipment, tools, materials
set in order	seiton	simplify the workflow, reduce wasted movements
shine	seiso	clean, tidy, organized – part of daily routine
standardize	seiketsu	consistent working practices, identical workplaces
sustain	shitsuke	maintain the new standards and ways of operating

Sue Stanley and Mark Eaton (2011) describe how '5S' was used at Northampton Hospital in England to streamline pathology tests. This was important because 80 per cent of medical decisions are based on pathology data, and the speed at which results are generated affects the speed of patient treatment. In Northampton, the team in the pathology laboratory used '5S' to redesign the layout, streamline the flow of work, improve the visibility of priority samples, simplify decision-making, and pool unfinished work to prioritize it for the following day. These simple changes led to a 40 per cent reduction in turnaround times without increasing costs. For immunology tests, the turnaround time fell from two days to less than ten hours.

RECAP

1. *Explain different uses of the term technology.*
   - Material technology means equipment, machines, apparatus. Social technology refers to organization structures and processes of coordination and control.
2. *Explain why predictions about technology and unemployment are often exaggerated.*
   - The effects of technology on employment are indeterminate, because replacement effects (job losses) are offset by compensatory effects (job creation).
3. *Give examples of how new technology is changing the nature of work.*
   - Teleworkers and workshifters escape direct management control and have more freedom to organize themselves, but they can become socially isolated.
4. *Describe the potential of Web 2.0 to transform work and organizations, and explain why that transformation is currently slow.*
   - Web 2.0 has the potential radically to transform communications and information-sharing in organizations.
   - Some organizations have established Web 2.0 systems to make it easier for top management and staff to communicate with each other and to exchange knowledge.
   - Many organizations are reluctant to experiment because of the uncertainty and risk attached to these new technologies.
5. *Demonstrate how the consequences of technological innovation for skill requirements depend on the organization of work, and not just on technical capabilities.*
   - The impact of technology on work and skills depends on choices concerning equipment and system design, management objectives, and the organization of work.
   - New technology has reduced the need for manual labour, creating instead jobs which demand high levels of interpretative and problem-solving skills.
6. *Define the characteristics of mass production, and describe methods to combat them.*
   - Mass production characteristics include mechanical pacing, no choice of method, repetition, task fragmentation, and minimum use of skills and mental attention.
   - Psychological reactions to work with mass production characteristics include anxiety and tension, hostility, isolation and despair, and social withdrawal; these can be overcome to some extent by job enlargement and job rotation.
7. *Apply the socio-technical system perspective to organizational analysis and design.*
   - Socio-technical system design aims to find the best fit between social and technical subsystems, to achieve joint optimization through minimal critical specification.
8. *Contrast the Scandinavian and Japanese models of team-based work organization.*
   - Scandinavian companies use autonomous self-regulating work groups.
   - Japanese companies use 'off line' quality circles and problem-solving teams as part of a lean manufacturing approach which has mass production characteristics.

Revision

1. Why is technology such an important aspect of organizational behaviour?
2. Japanese and Scandinavian manufacturing companies use teams as part of their organizational design. What are the differences between the Japanese and Scandinavian approaches?
3. What is nonstandard work and what part does technology play in encouraging these types of jobs and employment?
4. What are the characteristics of Web 2.0 technologies, and in what ways can these new systems affect work and organizational behaviour?

Research assignment

Material technology influences social technology. What does that statement mean? How do different authors approach these issues? Interview two people who have been working in the same organization for a significant period. Ask one of them to explain how technology has changed their personal experience of work, at the level of the job role that they do. Ask the other to explain how technology has changed the organization as a whole. Has Web 2.0 technology started to have an effect, either on individual jobs or on the organization, and how? Relate their comments to your earlier review of the technology literature.

'Job role' refers to how work is done; tasks, procedures, skills, responsibilities eliminated, new ones acquired. Impact at the organization level could concern changes to structures, teams, systems, working practices, and external links with suppliers and customers. Any suitable employee will be able to answer questions about job role; a manager will be more knowledgeable about organizational changes.

Springboard

Susan J. Ashford, Elizabeth George and Ruth Blatt (2007) 'Old assumptions, new work: the opportunities and challenges of research on nonstandard employment', *The Academy of Management Annals*, 1(1), pp. 65–117. Comprehensive review of the nature, triggers, experience, and challenges of nonstandard work and the new questions which these developments raise.

Paul Boreham, Rachel Parker, Paul Thompson and Richard Hall (2007) *New Technology @ Work*, Routledge Business, London. Critical examination of the effects of information and communication technology on work and organizations, arguing that technology has no independent effects but is shaped by economic and political forces.

Lynda Gratton (2011) *The Shift: The Future of Work Is Already Here*, Collins, London. Also cited in the Springboard for Chapter 2, Gratton explores how trends and developments in technology are likely to reshape work and organizations in the coming decades.

Leslie A. Perlow (2012) *Sleeping with Your Smartphone: How to Break the 24/87 Habit and Change the Way You Work*, Harvard Business Review Press, Boston, MA. Explores individual and organizational benefits and problems of 'hyperconnectivity' and how to retain work-life balance and improve performance by collectively 'disconnecting'.

OB in films

Modern Times (1936, director Charles Chaplin), DVD track 2, 0:01:10 to 0:06.00 (5 minutes). Clip opens with flock of sheep and ends when the scene cuts from the assembly line to the manager's office. Despite the date, this sequence is still one of the most powerful movie illustrations of the human being treated as a machine, of the worker caught in the cogwheels of capitalist production.

1. Are employees still subjected to such treatment in organizations today? Give examples.
2. Can you identify instances where new technology has liberated workers from this kind of treatment?
3. Chaplin's movie was set in a factory; do office workers escape from the effects of technology?

DVD track 3: 00:06:07 to 00:12: 57 (6 minutes): clip begins in the manager's office as the salesmen bring in a piece of equipment; ends with the manager saying 'It's no good – it isn't practical' (caption). This is a disastrous demonstration of the Billows Feeding machine which is designed to feed employees while they work, thus improving productivity.

4. What does this scene reveal about management objectives in the use of technology?
5. What does this scene tell us about management values in relation to employees?

OB on the web

Search YouTube for 'What is a smartphone addiction?' Here you will find Leslie Perlow being interviewed about her book on the subject (see Springboard). Are you addicted to your phone and the other gadgets which mean that you are constantly available, to anyone, regardless of the time or your location? How can you achieve the benefits of these technologies while avoiding the negative consequences? How difficult would it be for you to turn them all off for 24 hours? Try it.

CHAPTER EXERCISES

1. The web we weave

Objectives

1. To encourage breadth of thinking about a topic, in this case Web 2.0 technology.
2. To develop skills in producing a wide-ranging and balanced assessment.
3. To consider the extent to which technology determines or facilitates the outcomes or impacts that it produces.

Briefing

The issue for debate is: What are the individual, organizational, and social benefits and dangers of Web 2.0 technology?

Divide into groups of three. Your group's task is to think of as many relevant points as you can concerning the issue for debate. List these points on a flipchart for presentation. Time allowed: 10 to 15 minutes.

Present your points in plenary. Your points will be awarded 'quality marks' for relevance, importance, plausibility, and creativity. If your argument for a point is particularly impressive or original, you can win more quality marks. The group with the highest quality marks will be declared the winner. Time allowed depends on number of groups: up to 45 minutes.

Consider two of the main benefits and two of the main dangers that you have identified. To what extent are these inevitable consequences of Web 2.0? To what extent do these consequences depend on how individuals and organizations decide to use the technology?

2. Old McDonald's Farm

Objective

To explore the integration of social and technical aspects of an organization.

Briefing

Organizations are socio-technical systems. This means that technology – equipment, machines, processes, materials, layout – has to work alongside people – structures, roles, role relationships, job design. You can't design an organization to suit the technology while ignoring the people, because that would be ineffective. Similarly, designing an organization just to suit the people, while ignoring the requirements of the technology, would be equally disastrous. The concept of socio-technical system design means that the social system and the technical system have to be designed so that they can work with each other.

Old McDonald's Farm

Let's consider Old McDonald's farm. On this farm, he had no pigs, cows, or chickens. He had only corn, planted in long rows that grew all year round. McDonald had a perfect environment for growing corn. The soil was rich, and the climate was perfect, twelve months every year.

→

McDonald's rows were so long that at one end of the row, the soil was being prepared for planting, while the next section on that row was being planted, the next section was growing, and the next was being harvested. McDonald had four of these long rows.

McDonald is a progressive and scientific farmer. He is concerned about both productivity and quality. He had an industrial engineer study the amount of effort required to complete the work in each function on each row. He found that two employees were required per section, on each row, fully employed in that function all year round. Therefore, he employed eight workers on each row.

Initially, Mr McDonald had only four rows, A, B, C and D, and a total of 32 people. But he decided to expand, adding two more rows. This added 16 more workers. Now he had 48 employees. Until this time, he had only one supervisor responsible for directing the work of all 32 employees on the initial four rows. Now he decided that there was too much work for one supervisor. He added another.

Mr McDonald now had to decide whether to reorganize the work of his managers and employees. He decided to talk to his two supervisors, Mr Jones and Mr Smith. He found that they had very different ideas.

Mr Jones insisted that the only intelligent way to organize was around the technical knowledge, the functional expertise. He argued that he should take responsibility for all employees working on the first two sections, soil preparation and planting, on all rows. Mr Smith, he acknowledged, had greater expertise in growing and harvesting, so he would take responsibility for all employees in the last two sections. They would each have an equal number of employees to supervise.

Mr Smith had a different idea. He argued that, while some specialized knowledge was needed, it was more important for the employees to take responsibility for the entire growing cycle. This way, they could move down the row, seeing the progress of the corn. He argued for organizing the employees into teams by row.

	soil prep	**planting**	**growing**	**harvesting**
row A				
row B				
row C				
row D				
row E				
row F				

Mr McDonald has hired you as a consultant to help him with his organization design. The questions that he wants you to answer are:

1. How will you organize employees on the farm, and how will you assign responsibility to Smith and Jones? You can recommend any assignment that you like, but the numbers of employees that are required will stay the same.
2. What socio-technical principles support your recommendations? Why is your approach better than the alternatives?

If you were one of Mr McDonald's employees, which approach to organization design would you prefer, and why?

Employability assessment

With regard to your future employment prospects:

1. Identify up to three issues from this chapter that you found significant.
2. Relate these to the competencies in the employability matrix.
3. Decide what actions you need to take to maintain and/or develop those competencies under each of the four headings of the employability matrix.

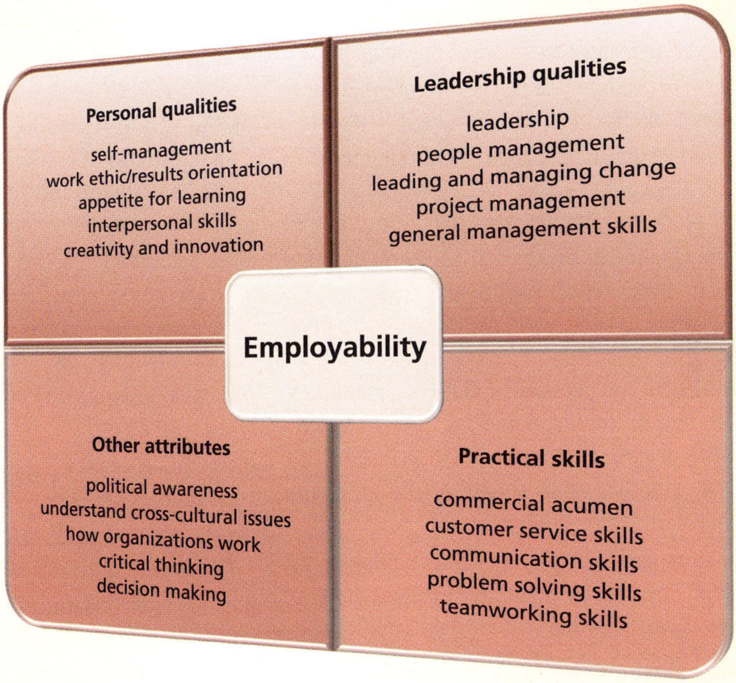

References

Ashford, S.J., George, E. and Blatt, R. (2007) 'Old assumptions, new work: the opportunities and challenges of research on nonstandard employment', *The Academy of Management Annals*, 1(1), pp. 65–117.

Benders, J. and Morita, M. (2004) 'Changes in Toyota Motors' operations management', *International Journal of Production Research*, 42(3), pp. 433–44.

Benders, J., Doorewaard, H. and Poutsma, E. (2000) 'Modern sociotechnology', in M. Beyerlin (ed.), *Work Teams: Past, Present and Future*, New York: Kluwer Academic Publishers.

Berggren, C. (1995) 'The fate of the branch plants – performance versus power', in Åke Sandberg (ed.), *Enriching Production: Perspectives on Volvo's Uddevalla Plant as an Alternative to Lean Production*, Aldershot: Avebury.

Birkinshaw, J. and Pass, S. (2008) *Innovation in the Workplace: How Are Organizations Responding to Generation Y and Web 2.0 Technologies?*, London: Chartered Institute for Personnel and Development.

Blauner, R. (1964) *Alienation and Freedom: The Factory Worker and His Industry*, Chicago, IL: The University of Chicago Press.

Braverman, H. (1974) *Labor and Monopoly Capital: The Degradation of Work in the Twentieth Century*, New York: Monthly Review Press.

Buchanan, D.A. (2000) 'An eager and enduring embrace: the ongoing rediscovery of teamworking as a management idea', in Stephen Procter and Frank Mueller (eds), *Teamworking*, Houndmills and London: Macmillan Business.

Clegg, S.R. and Dunkerley, D. (1980) *Organization, Class and Control*, London: Routledge & Kegan Paul.

Collins, M. (2005) 'The (not so simple) case for teleworking: a study at Lloyd's of London', *New Technology, Work and Employment*, 20(2), pp. 115–32.

Emery, R.E. and Trist, E.L. (1960) 'Socio-technical systems', in C.W. Churchman and M. Verhulst (eds), *Management Science, Models and Techniques*, Volume 2, London: Pergamon Press.

Fox, A. (1974) *Man Mismanagement*, London: Hutchinson.

Frean, A. (2011) 'Financial terrorists pose grave risk to US', *The Times*, 2 February, p. 9.

Glenny, M. (2011) 'The chink in the West's cyber-armour – you', *The Sunday Times News Review*, 30 October, p. 4.

Gratton, L. (2011) *The Shift: The Future of Work Is Already Here*, London: Collins.

Haddon, L. and Brynin, M. (2005) 'The character of telework and the characteristics of teleworkers', *New Technology, Work and Employment*, 20(1), pp. 34–46.

Hammarstrom, O. and Lansbury, R.D. (1991) 'The art of building a car: the Swedish experience re-examined', *New Technology, Work and Employment*, 6(2), pp. 85–90.

Karasek, R.A. (1979) 'Job demands, job decision latitudes, and mental strain: implications for job redesign', *Administrative Science Quarterly*, 24(2), pp. 285–308.

Kornhauser, A. (1965) *Mental Health of the Industrial Worker*, New York: John Wiley.

McKinsey & Company (2011) 'Social technologies on the front line: The Management2.0 M-Prize winners', *The McKinsey Quarterly*, September, pp. 1–4.

McLoughlin, I. (1999) *Creative Technological Change: The Shaping of Technology and Organizations*, London: Routledge.

Manos, A., Sattler, M. and Alukal, G. (2006) 'Make healthcare lean', *Quality Progress*, 39(7), pp. 24–30.

Marcic, D. (1995) *Organizational Behavior: Experiences and Cases* (4th edn), St Paul, MN: West Publishing.

Markillie, P. (2012) 'Manufacturing and innovation: special report', *The Economist* (supplement), 21 April.

Martin, G., Reddington, M. and Kneafsey, M.B. (2008) *Web 2.0 and HR: A Discussion Paper*, London: Chartered Institute for Personnel and Development.

Miller, E.J. and Rice, A.K. (1967) *Systems of Organization: The Control of Task and Sentient Boundaries*, London: Tavistock Publications.

Morse, G. (2006) 'High fidelity: Ivor Tiefenbrun on tapping talent', *Harvard Business Review*, 84(11), p. 28.

Norstedt, J.P. and Aguren, S. (1973) *Saab-Scania Report*. Stockholm: Swedish Employers' Confederation.

Oliver, N., Delbridge, R., Jones, D. and Lowe, J. (1994) 'World class manufacturing: further evidence in the lean production debate', *British Journal of Management*, 15(2), pp. 53–63.

Overell, S. (2005) 'Getting back to the coalface', *Personnel Today*, 15 March, p. 11.

Parker, M. and Slaughter, J. (1988) *Choosing Sides: Unions and the Team Concept*, Boston, MA: South End Press.

Robertson, D. (2011) 'Cyber bandits under suspicion for wiping billions off companies', *The Times*, 31 January, pp. 12–13.

Siegele, L. (2008) 'Let it rise: a special report on corporate IT', *The Economist*, 25 October, pp. 1–20.

Sinclair, A. (2011) *Absence Management*, London: Chartered Institute for Personnel and Development.

Stanley, S. and Eaton, M. (2011) 'Powerful change for pathology', *Health Service Journal*, 22 September, pp. 28–9.

Steijn, B. (2001) 'Work systems, quality of working life and attitudes of workers: an empirical study towards the effects of team and non-teamwork', *New Technology, Work and Employment*, 16(3), pp. 191–203.

The Economist (1994) 'The celling out of America', 17 December, pp. 71–2.

The Economist (2006) 'Special report: France: Insider and outsiders', 28 October, pp. 5–6.

The Economist (2011) 'The war on terabytes', 31 December, pp. 49–50.

Thomas, H. (1974) 'Finding a better way', *Guardian*, 17 January, p. 12.

Townsend, K. (2011) 'The evolving threat landscape', *The Times*, 6 October, Raconteur on IT Supplement, pp. 4–5.

Trist, E.L. and Bamforth, K.W. (1951) 'Some social and psychological consequences of the longwall method of coal-getting', *Human Relations*, 4(1), pp. 3–38.

Trist, E.L., Higgin, G.W., Murray, H. and Pollock, A.B. (1963) *Organizational Choice*, London: Tavistock Publications.

Turner, A.N. and Lawrence, P.R. (1965) *Industrial Jobs and the Worker: An Investigation of Response to Task Attributes*, Boston, MA: Division of Research, Harvard Business School.

Twentyman, J. (2011) 'Workspaces: the new word for workplace', *The Times*, 6 October, Raconteur on IT Supplement, p. 17.

Walker, C.R. (1950) 'The problem of the repetitive job', *Harvard Business Review*, 28(3), pp. 54–58.

Walker, C.R. and Guest, R.H. (1952) *The Man on the Assembly Line*, Cambridge, MA: Harvard University Press.

Walton, R.E. and Susman, G.I. (1987) 'People policies for the new machines', *Harvard Business Review*, 65(2), pp. 98–106.

Winner, L. (1977) *Autonomous Technology: Technics-Out-Of-Control as a Theme in Political Thought*, Cambridge, MA: MIT Press.

Womack, J.P., Jones, D.T. and Roos, D. (1990) *The Machine that Changed the World: The Triumph of Lean Production*, New York: Macmillan.

Chapter 4 **Culture**

Key terms

organizational culture

surface manifestations of organizational culture

organizational values

mechanistic organization structure

organic organization structure

basic assumptions

organizational socialization

pre-arrival stage of socialization

encounter stage of socialization

role modelling

metamorphosis stage of socialization

integration (or unitary) perspective on culture

differentiation perspective on culture

fragmentation (or conflict) perspective on culture

strong culture

weak culture

internal integration

external adaptation

social orientation

power orientation

uncertainty orientation

goal orientation

time orientation

Learning outcomes

When you have read this chapter, you should be able to define those key terms in your own words, and you should also be able to:

1. Account for the popularity of the concept of organizational culture among managers and academics.
2. List, describe, and give examples of Schein's three levels of organizational culture.
3. Distinguish the stages of organizational socialization.
4. Contrast managerial and social science perspectives on organizational culture.
5. Assess the link between organizational culture and organizational performance.
6. Distinguish between different types of organizational culture.
7. Distinguish different dimensions of national culture.

Why study organizational culture?

Culture can be thought of as the personality of an organization. It is also often referred to as corporate culture. It deals with how things are done in a company on a daily basis. It affects how employees perform their work, and how they relate to each other, to customers, and to their managers. Organizational culture affects not only task issues – how well or badly an organization performs – but also emotional issues – how workers feel about their work and their companies. Organizational culture has been a popular topic since the early 1980s. First adopted by senior executives and management consultants as a quick-fix solution to virtually every organization problem, it was later adopted by academics as an explanatory framework with which to understand behaviour in organizations (Deal and Kennedy, 2000; Alvesson, 2001).

Banking cultures of concern

Can you name a bank that has been reported as being involved in some financial irregularity in recent years? Perhaps it is easier to name one that has not. Banks have been accused of rash lending, financial mis-selling, attempts to manipulate the London Interbank Offer Rate (Libor), and even money laundering. Some have admitted their misdemeanours and been fined, sued, forced to make reparations, or all three. When challenged by the media or an investigating parliamentary committee, their senior managers claim that the problem was caused by a small group of staff or an isolated individual employee ('a bad apple') who has now resigned, has been dismissed or is being retrained. Many of these banks have had to be bailed out by governments using taxpayers' money, or had to pay fines which reduced the size of dividends available to pay their shareholders. The prevalence of such misconduct within the banking industry, not just in Britain, but also in continental Europe, the United States and elsewhere in the world, suggests that this form of organizational behaviour cannot be explained solely in terms of individual or group factors. Instead, it is necessary to ask questions about the values of the banking industry in general, and about the cultures of the individual banks in particular.

In his article entitled 'What's gone wrong with the banks?', Peter Day (2012) discusses the changed ethos of the City of London from the 1980s following the 'Big Bang'. This led to the abolition of the London Stock Exchange monopoly, and the demise of the partnership brokers and jobbers. He highlights the cultural gap between the natural caution of the old, trained bankers and the huge appetite for risk possessed by the new breed of traders created by the influx into investment banking. In the partnership world of the pre-1980s, profits were divided up at the end of the year between the partners. In good years, there were bonanzas, in bad years no payouts. The post-Big Bang City adopted this reward structure to motivate its adrenaline-fired staffers, but without the downside. They shared only in the putative profits. Day says that the most significant change in the City of London and its banks has been the nature of control within the industry. It has changed from employee self-control, based on cultural and ethical norms of the 1960s and 1970s, to a regulated environment after the Big Bang. Regulation defines those things that are regulated, creating enormous opportunities for those which are not (e.g. 'off-balance sheet entities' that gave US banks their sub-prime mortgage crisis). After regulators have drawn clear lines, the animal spirits of the bank's free market capitalist staff will lead them to operate outside the lines, and the banks will reward them hugely for doing so. The banking industry's culture thus changed from doing 'what is right' to doing what is OK by the lawyers and compliance officers or, as Day describes it, 'doing what you can get away with'. The old banking culture in Britain may have been snobby, introverted and uncompetitive, but it has been replaced by a far more disquieting one where short-term gains are king.

Ann Cunliffe (2008) states that organizational culture is important because it

- shapes the image that the public has of an organization;
- influences organizational effectiveness;
- provides direction for the company;
- helps to attract, retain and motivate staff.

STOP AND THINK

How would you define the culture of the organization that you currently work in, or the university at which you are studying?

Rise of organizational culture

Organizational culture the shared values, beliefs, and norms which influence the way employees think, feel, and act towards others inside and outside the organization.

Organizational culture remains a controversial concept. Some writers argue that just as one can talk about French culture, Arab culture, or Asian culture, so too it is possible to discuss the organizational culture of the British Civil Service, McDonald's, Microsoft, or Disney. Others reject this notion. In general, however, it is recognized that organizations have 'something' (a personality, philosophy, ideology, or climate) which goes beyond economic rationality, and which gives each of them a unique identity. Organizational culture has been variously described as 'the way we do things around here' (Deal and Kennedy, 1982); 'how people behave when no one is watching', and 'the collective programming of the mind' (Hofstede, 2001).

The current debates about culture are traceable to the early 1980s when two books catapulted the concept to the forefront of management attention: *In Search of Excellence*, written by Tom Peters and Robert Waterman (1982); and Terrence Deal and Allan Kennedy's (1982) *Corporate Cultures*. These publications suggested that a strong culture was a powerful lever for guiding workforce behaviour. Other factors also stimulated an interest in culture:

- Japan's industrial success during the 1970s and 1980s;
- increasing globalization, placing organizational culture into sharp focus alongside national culture;
- the assumption that organizational performance depends on employee values being aligned with company strategy;
- the contentious view that management can consciously manipulate culture to achieve organizational (change) objectives (Ogbonna and Harris, 2002);
- the belief that intangible (soft) factors such as values and beliefs impacted on financial (hard) ones and the conviction that managers were capable of changing cultures.

Although the idea was originally introduced to managers by consultants, it was not long before academics started to take an interest in organizational culture as well. Edgar Schein, a business school professor, was amongst the first to refine the concept, seeking to operationalize it for research purposes (Schein, 2004). Research attention turned to the meanings and beliefs that employees assigned to organizational behaviour, and how their assigned meanings influenced the ways in which they themselves behaved in companies (Schultz, 1995).

Tom J. Peters (b. 1942)

Robert H. Waterman

Terrence E. Deal

Allan A. Kennedy

Culture: surface manifestations, values and basic assumptions

Surface manifestations of organizational culture culture's most accessible forms, which are visible and audible behaviour patterns and objects.

Edgar Henry Schein (b. 1928)

Edgar Schein's (2004) model of culture is widely accepted and considers organizational culture in terms of three levels, each distinguished by its visibility to, and accessibility by, individuals (see Figure 4.1). Schein's first level is the **surface manifestations of organizational culture**, also called 'observable culture'. It refers to the visible things that a culture produces. It includes both physical objects and also behaviour patterns that can be seen, heard or felt – they all 'send a message' to an organization's employees, suppliers, and customers.

The surface level of culture is the most visible. Anyone coming into contact with it can observe it. Its constituent elements are defined below and illustrated in Table 4.1.

1. *Artefacts* are material objects created by human hands to facilitate culturally expressive activities. They include tools, furniture, appliances, and clothing.
2. *Ceremonials* are formally planned, elaborate, dramatic sets of activities of cultural expression, e.g. opening events, prize-givings, graduations, religious services.

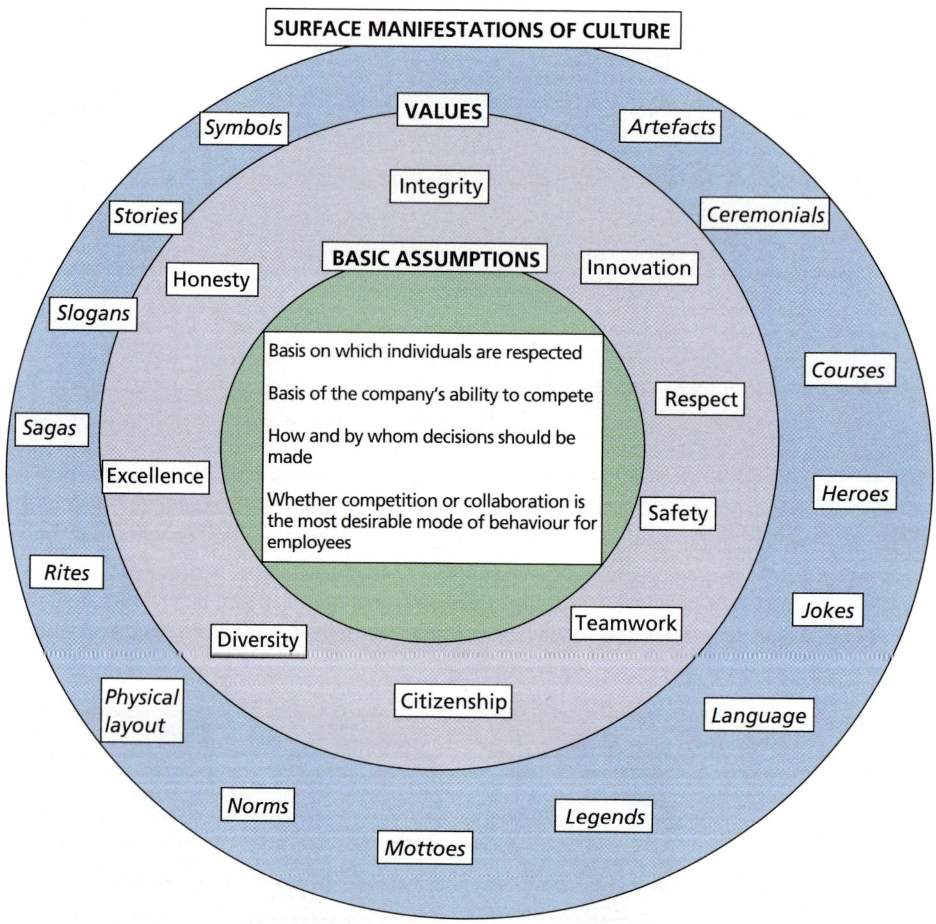

Figure 4.1: Schein's three levels of culture

Source: adapted from *Organizational Behaviour and Analysis: An Integrated Approach*, Rollinson, D. Pearson Education Limited, © Pearson Education Limited 2008.

Table 4.1: Examples of surface manifestations of organizational culture at Motorola and Rolls-Royce

Manifestation	Examples	
	Motorola	***Rolls-Royce***
1. Artefacts	Name badges, stationery, T-shirts, promotional items, celebratory publications	Name badges; standard work wear, issued to all staff levels in the organisation; each polo shirt is customised with the wearer's name
2. Ceremonials	Annual service dances, annual total customer satisfaction competition	Fun days, sporting events, commemorative shows
3. Courses	Basic health and safety course	Induction courses to orientate new starts to RR principles
4. Heroes	Paul Galvin, Joseph Galvin – founders	Henry Rolls, Charles Royce – founders
5. Jokes		'The Right Way, The Wrong Way and the Rolls-Royce Way' – humorous, self-deprecating comments about the evolution of certain ways of going about things, but also a reminder of the importance of individuality and identity
6. Language	Employees known as 'Motorolans'; role-naming conventions and communications remind everyone of their responsibilities as Motorolans	Divisional/departmental naming – job roles defined within particular naming structures
7. Legends	The first walkie-talkies; first words communicated from the moon via Motorola technology	Commemorative window in tribute to the Rolls-Royce Spitfire's contribution to World War II
8. Mottoes	Total Customer Satisfaction, Six Sigma Quality, Intelligence Everywhere, Engineering Intelligence with Style	Centre of Excellence; Trusted to Deliver Excellence
9. Norms	Ethics, Respect, Innovation	Code of Business Conduct – Quality, Excellence, Ethics, Respect
10. Physical layout	Semi-open plan – cubed group set up; junior managers have separate offices beside staff; senior managers have corporate offices distanced from most employees	Open plan layouts – applies to both offices and work cells where possible
11. Rites	Badges – initially the identity badge, but then the service badge, given at 5-year intervals, has a great deal of kudos	Length of Service Acknowledgement – rite of passage
12. Sagas	Motorola's time-lined history used repeatedly to demonstrate its influence on the world	The 1970s bankruptcy saga
13. Slogans	*Hello Moto* – modern re-invention of how the Motorola name came into being – a fusion of 'Motor' (representing a car) plus 'Hola' representing Hello in Spanish, to emphasise communications on the move	
14. Stories	About a particular vice-president who fell asleep at a very important customer meeting – a cautionary tale about what not to do	Impact of a particular shop-floor visit and how the feedback to quality managers changed thinking and processes: the tale is cautionary about how misunderstandings can generate unnecessary panics

Table 4.1: *continued*

Manifestation	**Examples**	
	Motorola	***Rolls-Royce***
15. Symbols	Motorola 'M' brand – known as the *emsignia*	The Rolls-Royce brand – RR

Source: Personal communications. Rolls-Royce logo © Chris Hennessy/Alamy.

3. *Courses* and workshops are used to instruct, induct, orient, and train new members in company practices.
4. *Heroes* are characters, living or dead, who personify the values and beliefs; who are referred to in company stories, legends, sagas, myths and jokes; and who represent role models that current employees should emulate.
5. *Jokes* are humorous stories intended to cause amusement, but their underlying themes carry a message for the behaviour or values expected of organizational members.
6. *Language* is the particular form or manner in which members use vocal sounds and written signs to convey meaning to each other. It includes specialist technical vocabulary related to the business (jargon) as well as general naming choices.
7. *Legends* are handed-down narratives about wonderful events based on company history, but embellished with fictional details. These fascinate employees and invite them to admire or deplore certain activities.
8. *Mottoes* are maxims adopted as rules of conduct. Unlike slogans, mottoes are rarely, if ever, changed.
9. *Norms* are expected modes of behaviour that are accepted as the company's way of doing things, thereby providing guidance for employee behaviour.
10. *Physical layout* concerns things that surround people, providing them with immediate sensory stimuli, as they carry out culturally expressive activities.
11. *Rites* are relatively elaborate, dramatic sets of activities that consolidate various forms of cultural expression into one event. They are formally planned, though not necessarily always officially sanctioned.
12. *Sagas* are historical narratives describing the unique accomplishments of a group and its leaders. They usually describe a series of events that are said to have unfolded over time and which constitute an important part of an organization's history.
13. *Slogans* are short, catchy phrases that are regularly changed. They are used both for customer advertising and to motivate employees.
14. *Stories* are narratives describing how individuals acted and the decisions they made that affected the company's future. Stories can include a mixture of both truth and fiction.
15. *Symbols* refer to any act, event, object, quality, or relationship that serves as a vehicle for conveying meaning.

STOP AND THINK

Think about the organizations of which you have had personal experience. Provide examples of as many of the 15 surface manifestations of organizational culture as you can.

Organizational values the accumulated beliefs held about how work should be done and situations dealt with, that guide employee behaviour.

Schein's second level of culture concerns **organizational values**. These

- represent something that is explicitly or implicitly desirable to an individual or group
- influence employees' choices from available means and ends of action
- reflect their beliefs as to what is right and wrong, or specify their general preferences.

Organizational values are the accumulated beliefs held about how work should be done and situations dealt with (Adler and Gundersen, 2008). They can be consciously or unconsciously held; are often unspoken, but guide employees behaviours. They can be encapsulated either in phrases or in single words such as

- Citizenship
- Diversity
- Excellence
- Honesty
- Integrity
- Innovation
- Respect
- Safety
- Teamwork

Values are said to provide a common direction for all employees, and to guide their behaviour. 'People way down the line know what they are supposed to do in most situations because the handful of guiding values is crystal clear' (Peters and Waterman, 1982, p. 76). Motorola has two 'key beliefs' – 'uncompromising integrity' and 'constant respect for people'. The Central Intelligence Agency's core values, shown on its website, state that 'quiet patriotism is our hallmark'; 'we pride ourselves on our extraordinary responsiveness to the needs of our customers'; staff 'embrace personal accountability', put 'country first and agency before self', and learn from their mistakes because they 'reflect on their performance'. Additionally, CIA employees 'seek and speak the truth', but, they add, only 'to our colleagues and our customers'. You can go to the website of any large, private, public or voluntary organization – for example Microsoft, the British National Health Service or Amnesty International – and locate their values in their vision or mission statement. Two well-known companies' values, Google's and IKEA's, are listed in Table 4.2.

Table 4.2: Corporate values

Google: ten things we've found to be true	IKEA's nine fundamental doctrines
1. Focus on the user and all else will follow.	1. The product range is our identity.
2. It's best to do one thing, really, really well.	2. The IKEA spirit – a strong and lively reality.
3. Fast is better than slow.	3. Profit gives us resources.
4. Democracy on the web works.	4. To reach good results with small means.
5. You don't need to be at your desk to need an answer.	5. Concentration of energy is important for our success.
6. You can make money without doing evil.	6. Simplicity is a virtue.
7. There's always more information out there.	7. The different way.
8. The need for information crosses all borders.	8. To behave responsibly is a privilege.
9. You don't need a suit to be serious.	9. Most things still remain to be done – a glorious future.
10. Great just isn't good enough.	

Based on Edwards (2011, pp. 272–3) and Stenebo (2010, p. 135).

Sources of values

Values distinguish one organization from another, but where do they come from? Some authors see them as representing organizational solutions to problems experienced in the past. Another source of values are the views of the original founder, as modified by the company's current senior management (Schein, 1983). Originally, a single person, or a group of people, has an idea for a new business, and brings in other key people to create a core group who share a common vision. This group creates an organization, brings in others, and begins to build a common history. Stephen Robbins and Timothy Judge (2013) suggest that a company's current top management acts as its 'culture carriers'. Thus 'organizational' values are really always the values of the current company elite (senior managers). This is similar to the way that 'organizational goals' actually represent the preferred aims of chief executives and their management teams (see Figure 4.2).

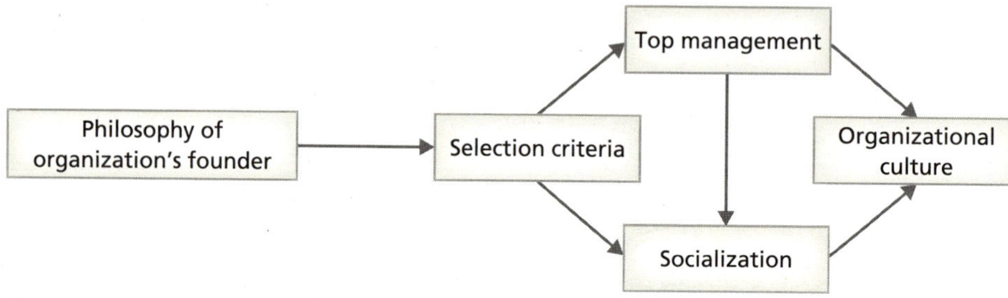

Figure 4.2: Where does organizational culture come from?

Source: ROBBINS, STEPHEN P.; JUDGE, TIMOTHY A., ORGANIZATIONAL BEHAVIOR, 15th, © 2013. Printed and electronically reproduced by permission of Pearson Education, Inc., Upper Saddle River, New Jersey.

These men are innocent

Richard Reed, Jon Wright and Adam Balon founded the Innocent Drinks Company with a very distinct philosophy and culture. The company guarantees 'that anything Innocent [produces] will always taste good and will do you good. We promise we'll never use concentrates, preservatives, stabilisers or any weird stuff in our drinks.' Its packaging is either recyclable or biodegradable. In 2010, Coca-Cola secured a 58% share of the firm (O'Hanlon, 2007; Lucas, 2011a). Reed stated that the existing directors would continue to control Innocent, and had the goal of bringing healthy drinks to a global market. He added, 'I genuinely believe that this is not a selling out but a continuation of our work. There will be no change in the commitment to natural healthy food, to sustainability and to giving 10% of our profits to charity.' While there is no evidence that Coca-Cola has changed the founders' goals, it will be intriguing to discover if and how the two respective cultures change, as they bump up against each other (Macalister and Teather, 2010).

Edmond Terakcpian/PA Photos

Barça corporate values

Albert S. Llop/PA Photos

As an organization, Barcelona Football Club ('Barça' to its fans) is the best club soccer team in the world at the present time. It has won the Spanish premier league and the European Championship, and has some of the best players in the world. As a cash-generating machine, the club is second only to Real Madrid. It had revenues of €398m ($488m) in 2009–10. The secret of long-term corporate performance lies in cultivating a distinct set of organizational values. Its website states that it is *Més que un club* – more than a club. In a sport populated by individual, international stars, Barça grows its own players. It is dominated by local players, and Catalan is often spoken in the dressing room. Eight of the team's leading players are products of its football school, La Masia, as is the team's coach Josep ('Pep') Guardiola. La Masia boarding school places as much emphasis on character-building as on footballing skills. The students are relentlessly instructed in the importance of team spirit, self-sacrifice and perseverance.

The players are taught that Barça is 'more than a club' – the embodiment of Catalan pride. Their fans regularly sport banners proclaiming that 'Catalonia is not Spain'. However, for people living elsewhere in Spain, the club is seen as 'a staunch defender of democratic rights and freedom'. Barça has used the 'more than a club' idea to cultivate a two-way relationship with its fans. It is owned by its 150,000 club members (called *socis*) rather than by shareholders or foreign tycoons. The club's management is answerable to an assembly of 2,500 randomly chosen *socis* and 600 senior members. The club also supports other sports and runs a popular museum. The club's history suggests that putting down deep roots and promoting from within contributes to corporate success. While soccer is an unpredictable business and the club has made mistakes in the past, having its Catalan soul at the centre of its operations has, for the moment at least, placed the club on top of the football world (based on *The Economist*, 2011a; FC Barcelona, 2012).

Mechanistic organization structure an organization structure that possesses a high degree of task specialization, many rules, tight specification of individual responsibility and authority, and centralized decision-making.

Organic organization structure an organization structure that possesses little task specialization, few rules, and a high degree of individual responsibility and authority, and in which decision-making is delegated.

Altering an organization's structure and its processes can also change its culture, by changing its values. For example, a structural change such as creating self-managing teams changes culture. Different structures give rise to different cultures (Handy, 1993). Change one and you change the other. For example, a **mechanistic organization structure** with a tall hierarchy, centralization, standardization, and little autonomy, encourages a culture which encourages caution, obeying authority, respecting tradition, predictability, and stability. In contrast, an **organic organization structure**, with its flat hierarchy and decentralization and reliance on mutual adjustment of staff, gives freedom to employees to choose and control their own activities, and creates a culture of creativity, risk-taking, and innovation.

In a sense, therefore, organizational values are always backward-looking, despite being developed to contribute to the future development of the company. For an organizational culture to form, a fairly stable collection of people, need to have shared a significant history, involving problems, which allows a social learning process to take place. Organizations that have such histories possess cultures that permeate most of their functions (Schein, 2004). Company values come in lists. They are to be found printed in company reports, framed on company walls, and published on organizational websites.

Lucy Kellaway (2011) reported that the chief executive of Philips emailed his company's 100,000 employees informing them of the company's newest set of values. The values change programme is called *Accelerate!* (with an exclamation mark), and he invited his company email recipients to 'Please join me and Accelerate! to win together'. Discussing the relationship between junior level employees and corporate values, Professor Chris Grey recounted the experience of an MBA student of his, a senior manager in a supermarket chain, a company known to be an exemplar of successful culture management. The staff had been subject to a multi-million-pound culture training initiative, and he wanted to discover the extent of their 'buy-in' to the company's culture values. To what extent did front-line staff subscribe to these corporate values? He found not only that staff did not believe in these values, but that three-quarters of them claimed never to have even *heard* of these values! (Grey, 2009, p. 74).

STOP AND THINK

Can you list any of the values of the organization that you work for currently or have done so in the past? Would knowing their values change your way of working?

Basic assumptions invisible, preconscious, unspoken, 'taken-for-granted' understandings held by individuals within an organization concerning human behaviour, the nature of reality, and the organization's relationship to its environment.

Finally, **basic assumptions** are the deepest level of culture, and are the most difficult to comprehend. They are the set of shared but unspoken assumptions about the best way to do things in the company and relate to the nature of reality and the organization's relationship to its environment. Because they are invisible, preconscious, and 'taken-for-granted', they are difficult to pin down (Notter and Grant, 2011). They begin with the founder's thinking; and then develop through a shared learning process. As employees act in accordance with company values and beliefs, these become 'baked' into the organization and embedded as basic assumptions. These too can be summarized briefly as:

- Quality
- Stability
- Morality
- Economy
- Excellence
- Profitability
- Predictability
- Responsibility
- Innovativeness.

Source: DILBERT © 2002 Scott Adams. Used by permission of UNIVERSAL UCLICK. All rights reserved.

Organizational socialization

Organizational socialization the process through which an employee's pattern of behaviour, values, attitudes, and motives is influenced to conform to that of the organization.

The ultimate strength of a company's culture depends on the similarity of its employees, and the length and intensity of their shared experiences within the firm. One learns about a company's culture through the process of **organizational socialization**. This is the process through which an employee's pattern of behaviour, values, attitudes, and motives is influenced to conform to those of the organization (see Figure 4.3). It includes the careful selection of new company members, their instruction in appropriate ways of thinking and behaving; and the reinforcement of desired behaviours by senior managers.

Socialization is important because, as John van Maanen and Edgar Schein (1979) argue, new organization recruits have to be taught to see the organizational world as their more

Figure 4.3: Dimensions addressed in most socialization efforts

Source: Colquitt et al. (2009, p. 558) from Chao, G.T., O'Leary-Kelly, A.M., Wolf, S., Klein, H.J. & Gardner, P.D. Organizational socialization: Its content and consequences. *Journal of Applied Psychology*, Vol. 79 No. 5, pp. 730–743, 1994, American Psychological Association (APA), reprinted with permission.

experienced colleagues do, if the culture of the organization is to endure. Socialization involves newcomers absorbing the values and behaviours required to survive and prosper in an organization. It reduces the variability of behaviour by instilling employees with an understanding of what is expected of them, and how they should do things. By providing an internal sense of how they should behave, plus a shared frame of reference, socialization standardizes employee behaviour, making it predictable for the benefit of senior management. Richard Pascale (1985) distinguished seven key steps in the process of organizational socialization process. These are shown in Figure 4.4.

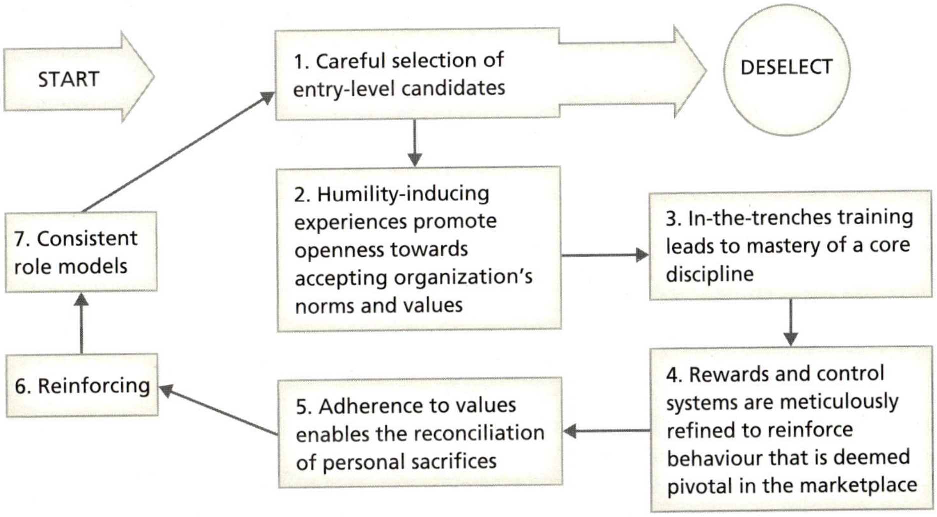

Figure 4.4: Seven steps of organizational socialization

Source: From Pascale (1985).

Pre-arrival stage of socialization the period of learning in the process that occurs before an applicant joins an organization.

Selection: Trained recruiters carefully select entry-level candidates seeking traits using standardized selection methods. The entrants are not 'oversold' on a particular position, because the companies rely on applicants 'deselecting' themselves, that is, withdrawing from the application process, if they find that the organization's values do not fit in with their own. This is also referred to as the **pre-arrival stage of socialization**.

Encounter stage of socialization the period during which the new recruit learns about organizational expectations.

Humility-inducing experiences: Once working, the organization encourages new entrants to question their past behaviour, beliefs and values. It does this by assigning them more work than they can possibly cope with, or giving them menial tasks to perform. The aim is to reduce their self-complacency, increase their self-examination, and prepare them to accept the organization's own norms and values. This represents the **encounter stage of socialization**.

How much guidance should a firm offer its employees as to how they dress in the workplace? How do new hires learn how they should behave so as to fit into the organization's culture? A number of learning methods (see Chapter 5) are used.

In-the-trenches training: The training received by recruits focuses on their achieving mastery of the core disciplines of the company's business. These extensive and carefully reinforced job experiences are intended to teach them the organization's way of doing things.

Rewards and control systems: New members' performances are carefully assessed and rewarded. The organization uses systems that are comprehensive and consistent, and which link to competitive success and company values.

Adherence to values: The employees identify with the common organizational values allowing them to reconcile the personal sacrifices that they have made in order to be a member of the organization. This creates the foundation of trust between them and their organization, and often involves linking company goals with significant higher level goals – not making profits from selling PCs but 'connecting humanity'!

Reinforcing folklore: New entrants are exposed to the organizational stories, myths, and symbols as they interact with their managers and colleagues within the workplace. These provide them with a code of conduct that clarifies 'how things are done around here' and, by implication, how they should do them as well.

Role modelling a form of socialization in which an individual learns by example, copying the behaviour of established organization members.

Consistent role models: Entrants also learn through **role modelling**. They are shown employees who are judged by the company to be 'winners', that is, who possess the traits, demonstrate the behaviours, and achieve the results that are recognized and valued by the firm. The learner observes these 'winners' and acquires a mental picture of the act and its consequences (rewards and punishments), and then copies them, acting out the acquired image. This marks the **metamorphosis stage of socialization** in which the new employee adjusts to their organization's values, attitudes, motives, norms and required behaviours.

Metamorphosis stage of socialization the period in which the new employee adjusts to their organization's values, attitudes, motives, norms, and required behaviours.

Beyond the induction period which, in some large companies, may last up to a year, performance-based appraisal systems and formal training programmes are also instituted by the company to visibly signal which goals new hires should be striving for and how. Finally, senior management's behaviour, in promoting, censoring and dismissing employees, also sends information to employees about company values, expectations about norms, risk-taking, acceptability of delegation, appropriate dress, topics of discussion, and so on.

Home viewing

Watch the opening 30 minutes of the film *The Firm* (1993, director Sidney Pollock) in which Harvard law graduate Mitch McDeere (played by Tom Cruise) joins a small Memphis law firm. McDeere first develops expectations about the organization during his job interview, and then experiences its reality. Which stages of the organizational socialization are being depicted here? What does he learn? Where does he learn it? How does he learn it? Have you experienced anything similar in your own work life?

Do you speak IKEA?

Founded by Ingvar Kamprad in 1943, IKEA is a private company which has about 250 stores around the world, 150,000 employees, and a turnover of 250 billion Swedish kronor (SEK). The print run of the IKEA catalogue is 198 million copies in 27 languages and 52 editions. Two decades ago, it was decided to make English the working language of the group. IKEA-Swenglish is a form of pidgin English that is a living and developing language, with a limited vocabulary and a fluid grammar. It has to be learned by anyone seeking to make a career within the company. In his presence, all IKEA staff, irrespective of their position in the hierarchy, should refer to Ingvar Kamprad as 'Ingvar', while in his absence he should be called 'IK' or 'the founder'; he should never be referred to as 'Kamprad' in the third person. The new IKEA employee also needs to become familiar with some other IKEA words and phrases which are explained below.

IKEA-speak	Translation
co-worker	IKEA employee
retailer	store
visitor	person visiting an IKEA store
customer	visitor who picks up an IKEA item
advantage	price difference below that of competitors
Swedish money	Swedish kronor (SEK)
'straight into the woodshed'	product achieving best-seller status
BTI – breath-taking item	product so cheap it makes customers gasp
PIJ – punch-in-the-jaw item	cheap alternative to a competitor's product
Ingvar's bag	blue bag with yellow lettering on the handles that customers carry around the shop
Ingvar-cakes	biscuits served at IKEA headquarters in Älmhult in Sweden
'open-the wallet' item	item so cheap that it is designed to be bought on impulse
'false nose'	taking an inefficient decision
'I have no confidence in you any longer'	'You will be dismissed'

Source: Based on Stenebo (2010).

Perspectives on culture contrasted

The debate about organizational culture takes place between two camps – managerial and social science. The managerial camp contains writers and consultants who believe that there is a relationship between a strong culture and organizational performance. They hold that 'A well-developed and business-specific culture in which management and staff are thoroughly socialized . . . can underpin stronger organizational commitment, higher morale, more efficient performance, and generally higher productivity' (Furnham and Gunter, 1993). Ranged against them is the social science camp containing those academics who believe that organizational culture is a term that is overused, over-inclusive and under-defined. The description of organizational culture on the preceding pages has taken a managerial perspective. Its distinguishing feature is that it is both prescriptive and normative, that is, it recommends what a company's culture *should* be. The managerial – social science debate about organizational culture can be considered under four headings:

Managerial		Social science
1. Culture *has*	versus	Culture *is*
2. Integration	versus	Differentiation/fragmentation
3. Culture managed	versus	Culture tolerated
4. Symbolic leadership	versus	Management control

1. Culture 'has' versus culture 'is'

The *has* view holds that every organization possesses a culture which, along with its strategy, structure, technology, and employees, is part of the organizational machine that can be controlled and managed. This is also known as the 'critical variable' view. It sees organizational culture as constituting an objective reality of artefacts, values, and meanings that can be quantified and measured. The culture is 'given' to new hires who have not participated in its formation. From this perspective, culture is acquired by employees. It is seen as capable of definition, intervention, and control, representing a 'tool for change' that can be used by managers. The writers most associated with this view, which is still current, are the management academics and consultants mentioned earlier in the chapter (Peters and Waterman, 1982; Deal and Kennedy, 1982; Pascale and Athos, 1982).

The alternative view sees organizational culture as something that the organization *is*. This is also known as the 'root metaphor' view. From this standpoint, individuals do things, and work together in certain ways. Thus, they create a culture which evolves spontaneously and is therefore not capable of being managed. It holds that culture cannot be easily quantified or measured, and that academics must study it the way that anthropologists study other societies. Culture is produced and reproduced continuously through the routine interactions between organization members. Hence organizational culture exists only in, and through, the social (inter)actions of employees. This approach seeks to understand social relations within organizations, and holds that a company's culture may not necessarily conform to what management wants. This critical perspective on organizational culture is still with us. Among researchers who take this position are Gagliardi (1986), Knights and Willmott (1987), Ogbonna (1993) and Smircich (1983).

Integration (or unitary) perspective on culture a perspective which regards culture as monolithic, characterized by consistency, organization-wide consensus, and clarity.

2. Integration versus differentiation/fragmentation

Joanne Martin (b. 1940)

Joanne Martin (1992) distinguished three perspectives on culture which she labelled integration, differentiation and fragmentation (see Table 4.3). These have formed the basis of research and writing on this topic. The managerial **integration (or unitary) perspective on culture** holds that an organization possesses a single, unified culture, consisting of shared values to which most employees subscribe. These integrating features lead to improved organization effectiveness through greater employee commitment and employee control, as measured by productivity and profitability. It includes the controversial notion of a 'strong' culture, which is defined by three characteristics: the existence of a clear set of values, norms and beliefs; the sharing of these by the majority of members; and the guidance of employees' behaviour by those same values, norms, and beliefs.

Table 4.3: Martin's contrasting perspectives on organizational culture

Features	*Cultural perspective*		
	Integration	**Differentiation**	**Fragmentation**
Orientation to consensus	Organization-wide consensus	Subcultural consensus	No consensus – multiplicity of views
Relations between different cultural elements	Consistent	Inconsistent	Complex
Orientation to ambiguity	Exclude it	Channel it outside subculture	Focus upon it

Source: from *Cultures in Organizations: Three Perspectives*, Oxford University Press (Martin, J. 1992) p. 13. Copyright © 1992 by Oxford University Press, Inc. www.oup.com (Adapted from Pondy et al. (1988), Martin and Meyerson (1987) and Martin and Frost ed. (1991)).

Differentiation perspective on culture a perspective which sees organizations as consisting of subcultures, each with its own characteristics, which differ from those of its neighbours.

In contrast, social science emphasizes two perspectives – differentiation and fragmentation. The **differentiation perspective on culture** regards a single organization as consisting of many groups, each with their own subcultures. Each of these has its own characteristics, which differ from those of its neighbours. This perspective therefore sees organizational culture as differentiated or as a plurality rather than as a unified whole. Within an organization, there are diverse interest groups who have their own objectives (e.g. management versus labour; staff versus line; marketing versus production). Thus, the differentiation perspective sees 'cultural pluralism' as a fundamental aspect of all organizations; seeks to understand the complexity and the interaction between frequently conflicting subcultures; and therefore stands in direct contrast to the managerial or integration (unitary) perspective on culture.

Martin Parker (2000) is one of several writers who, on the basis of a review of popular management works, concluded that rather than having a single, strong culture, organizations possess multiple (sub)cultures. These reflect the main ways in which employees distinguish themselves within companies – by their occupation or profession; by the function they perform; by their geographical location in the firm; and by their age (e.g. senior members of the engineering department in the research building). These subcultures overlap and contradict each other. Thus the neat typology of cultural types which is presented later in this chapter may understate the complexities of organizational life. These subcultures act to obstruct management attempts to develop a unified culture which might be used to control staff.

Fragmentation (or conflict) perspective on culture a perspective which regards culture as consisting of an incompletely shared set of elements that are loosely structured, constantly changing, and generally in conflict.

The other social science perspective – the **fragmentation (or conflict) perspective on culture** – assumes the absence of consensus; stresses the inevitability of conflict; focuses on the variety of interests and opinions between different groups; and focuses upon power differences in organizations. The fragmentation perspective sees organizations as collections of opposed groupings which are rarely reconciled. It is critical of managers and management consultants who underplay the differences that exist between individuals, groups, and departments within a company. It sees conflict rather than consensus as the norm within organizations; and it challenges the notion of the existence of a single organizational culture, and the value of the concept itself (Becker, 1982).

3. Culture managed versus culture tolerated

Since the managerialist perspective sees culture as something that an organization *has*, it further assumes that it is capable of being managed by corporate leaders. Some companies even have a 'Director of Corporate Culture'. This has sparked three debates: first, concerning how managers can change their company's culture from 'weak' to 'strong'; second, how culture can help a company innovate and adjust rapidly to environmental changes; third, the part played by leaders' visions and styles of management in managing their cultures. This view assumes that senior company executives can and should exercise cultural leadership. Cultural leadership is seen as maintaining, promoting and developing the company's culture (Trice and Beyer, 1984; 1993). The contrasting, social science view holds that culture is what an organization *is*, and hence that it is incapable of being managed. Instead, it is to be tolerated and its effects on its members studied. Some 'culture managed' writers, such as Fred Luthans (1995), argue that strong cultures can be created by management's use of rewards and punishments. In contrast, the 'culture tolerated' academics argue that employees' deeply held values and beliefs cannot be modified in the short term using such external stimuli.

Chris Grey was critical of culture management programmes. In his view, they had an ambitious desire to shape individuals' beliefs. This search for shared values (between the company's and the employees') entailed, in his view, an aggressive approach which focused primarily on employees rather than upon their work. He stated that 'Culture management aspires to intervene in and regulate [employee] being, so that there is no distance between individuals' purposes and those of the organization for which they work' (Grey, 2009, p. 69). Essentially, it attempts to eliminate the *organizational dilemma* (see Chapter 1).

Nampak Plastics' culture management programme

Bloomberg/Getty Images

Nampak Plastics is a South-African-owned company with eight manufacturing sites in the UK from Glasgow to Gloucestershire. It is a bottle and plastics manufacturer and is the country's leading producer of plastic milk bottles. Having driven efficiencies as far as it could by closing plants, reassessing working practices, and eliminating costs from within the business, the company's management decided to 'add value through people'. When he became the company's managing director in 2007, Eric Collins became aware of 'how bad the culture was at Nampak'. Symptoms of the problem included low morale, a tendency to blame others, people being treated badly, and a high rate of customer complaints. Within the organization, just a dozen people made the key decisions.

A survey of employees revealed that 80% of them would never recommend Nampak as a place to work to their friends and family. Their view was that 'there was everything wrong with this business that you can think of'. With his human resources manager, Collins introduced a change programme which aimed 'to turn the culture around'. He wanted 'an engaged culture in the business', that is, he wanted the involvement and engagement of the company's employees from the bottom of the organization to the top. It began with 'Challenge Collins' sessions at which employees at different sites vented their frustrations about the company. This was followed by focus group meetings where staff were asked to suggest what would make Nampak a better place to work. The three problem areas were found to be poor communication about the business; inadequate training, development, and career opportunities; and a lack of feedback on performance.

To change the culture, Collins implemented a company-wide performance management system that emphasized managers having conversations with their subordinates as well as several leadership courses as 'these people [company managers] mould the culture and are examples of the culture'. It introduced an undergraduate placement scheme, a graduate recruitment scheme, and a fast track career programme. Other staff were offered training courses leading to qualifications. New recruitment and selection methods replaced old ones. An induction course and a 'buddy scheme' were designed for new hires, a staff suggestion scheme and excellence awards were introduced. The company soon became aware of which employees were 'coming on the journey and who were not'. Having identified the cynics, Wright-Smith, the HR manager, 'performance-managed some people out of the business'. The final element of the culture change effort was the Corporate Social Responsibility programme which involved working with local schools. Commenting on the results, Eric Collins reported 'We've had a paradigm shift in culture'. Three years on, the employee satisfaction survey reversed the advocacy figure with 80% of staff now recommending Nampak as a good place to work, 90% of employees being happy with their jobs, and 98% believing that their managers listen to them. In terms of performance, there has been a 6.7% improvement in overhead costs per million bottles made, and a reduction in the annual figure for customer complaints from 1,110 to 255 (based on *Personnel Management*, 2011).

STOP AND THINK

Review the Nampak Plastics case study. How would you respond to the management's culture change programme if you were a shop-floor worker in the company?

In general, he felt that culture management programmes achieved this by selecting those staff amenable to organizational values; sacking employees who were less amenable; using training, and communication; exposing staff to organizational values through videos, mission statements, and having core values printed on pocket-sized cards and distributed to staff; and using company slogans, company songs, group exercises, and, in the case of one UK bank, having 'a parade of employees in animal costumes chanting the virtues of the bank as a fun place to be!' (Grey, 2009, p. 69).

4. Symbolic leadership versus management control

Symbolic leadership (or the management of organizational culture) is one way of encouraging employees to feel that they are working for something worthwhile, so that they will work harder and be more productive. Burman and Evans (2008) argue that it is only those managers who are also leaders who can impact culture in this way. This view treats leader-managers as heroes, who symbolize the organization both internally to their employees, and externally to customers, governments, and others (Smircich and Morgan, 1982). These leaders, said Carol Ray (1986, p. 294), 'possess direct ties to the values and goals of the dominant elites in order to activate the emotion and sentiment which may lead to devotion, loyalty and commitment to the company'.

The managerialist view holds that employees can be helped to internalize organizational values. In contrast, the social science perspective argues that symbolic leadership represents management's attempt to get employees to direct their behaviour themselves, towards organizational goals. People enter organizations with different motivations, experiences, and values. These natural individual differences tend to direct their behaviours in numerous, often divergent directions. Managers have always sought ways to control their employees, ensuring that they behave in relatively uniform and predictable ways. Carol Ray (1986) distinguished different types of management control through history (see Figure 4.5).

Bureaucratic control (F.W. Taylor)
manipulation of rewards → loyalty → increased productivity

Humanistic control (Elton Mayo)
'satisfying' task or work group → loyalty → increased productivity

Culture (symbolic) control (Deal and Kennedy, Schein)
manipulation of culture → love firm and its goals → increased productivity including myth and ritual

Figure 4.5: Contrasting forms of organizational control

Source: from Corporate culture; the last frontier of control? *Journal of Management Studies*, 23(3), pp. 287–97 (Ray, C.A. 1986) © Blackwell Publishing Ltd and Society for the Advancement of Management Studies 1986.

She noted the move away from *bureaucratic control* towards *humanistic control*. The former focuses on external, overt control of employees through rules, procedures, close supervision, appraisal, and rewards. Frederick Taylor, Henry Ford, Max Weber, and Henri Fayol all recommended this rationalist approach to direct the behaviour of employees towards organizational goals. It was expensive in terms of supervisory manpower required, frequently caused resentment, and elicited grudging compliance from the workers. In contrast, humanistic control sought to satisfy employees' needs by providing a satisfying work task, or a pleasant working group life to promote internal control. This was promoted originally by Mayo (1933, 1945), the hope being that individuals would willingly meet organizational goals by meeting their own personal goals and objectives (van Maanen and Barley, 1984).

From bureaucratic to culture control

Historically, Walmart employees' behaviour has been subjected to bureaucratic control through rules specifying a long list of things that they must do and not do. These cover every aspect of their work. However, given the challenges of globalization and technological change, the retailer has recently decided that this approach is too inflexible and is now attempting to instil a 'values-based' culture in which employees will be trusted 'to do the right thing', because they know what the firm stands for. Control by corporate cultural values has suddenly become a popular management approach. PepsiCo is preaching the value of 'performance with purpose' to its employees, while Chevron, an oil firm, affirms the value of, and sees itself as a purveyor of, 'human energy'.

The Boston Research Group's study, *The National Governance, Culture and Leadership Assessment*, surveyed thousands of American employees from all hierarchical levels. The largest category, 54%, saw their employer's culture as being top-down, but with skilled leadership, many rules, and a mixture of carrots and sticks – 'the informed acquiescence approach'. The second largest category, 43% of respondents, described their company's culture as being based on command-and-control, top-down management or leadership by coercion – the 'blind obedience approach'. The third group, consisting of only 3% of respondents, reported a culture where employees were guided by a set of core principles and values that inspired them to align their behaviour with their firm's mission – 'the self-governance approach'.

The differences are important in terms of whistleblowing and innovation. In blind-obedience companies, nearly half the employees said that they had observed unethical behaviour in the past year (compared to a quarter in the other two types of firm); and only a quarter of these respondents said that they were likely to blow the whistle on misconduct (compared to 90% in self-governing firms). With respect to innovation, over 90% of staff in self-governing firms, and 66% in informed-acquiescence firms, agreed that 'good ideas are readily adopted by my company'. In blind-obedience firms, the figure was under 20%. It seems that a lack of trust may inhibit innovation. The study found that bosses appeared to believe their own rhetoric, even if their subordinates did not. Bosses were more likely to believe that their company was self-governing (eight times more than average); that their employees were inspired by the firm (27 per cent compared to employees' 4 per cent); and that their firm rewarded performance based on values rather than merely financial results – 41 per cent compared to employees' 14 per cent (based on *The Economist*, 2011b).

The next change was from *humanistic control* to *culture control*. The latter involves shaping the internal worlds and identities of the employees in their workplaces. Carol Ray suggested that managers saw organizational culture as an effective control tool. It sought to affect what employees thought, believed, felt, and valued. She said that 'control by corporate culture views people as emotional, symbol-loving and needing to belong to a superior entity or collectivity' (Ray, 1986, p. 295). This form of control had previously only been attempted by religious organizations. A manager at a US high-tech company summarized the approach: 'Power plays don't work. You can't make 'em do anything. They have to want to. So you have to work through the culture. The idea is to educate people without [their] knowing it. Have the religion and not know how they got it' (quoted in Kunda, 1992, p. 5).

Work or play?

Peter Fleming and Andre Spicer researched what they termed the social geography of self and identity. They studied a call centre company that they named Sunray, which emphasised a culture of fun, epitomized in the slogan 'Remember the 3 Fs – Focus, Fun, Fulfilment'. Their study demonstrated how the company attempted to blur the traditional boundaries that typically divided work life and private life, in an effort to extend its control over employees. It disrupted and reorganized the traditional inside/outside boundary by holding team meetings before or after work at city centre cafés or nearby parks. Its teambuilding meetings involved participants bringing personal items from home to the workshop. Sunray used the private lives of workers as a training strategy to get them to invest more of themselves in their work. It also encouraged inside-the-organization activities that normally took place outside work, e.g. wearing pyjamas, drinking alcohol, bringing home-made food to share with colleagues, decorating a work area with personal items, and dressing casually – to be 'free to be themselves'. Additionally, it encouraged activities at home which were more appropriate inside the organization, such as the memorizing of the company slogan and workers attending company training sessions on Sundays. These actions challenged the social geography of work and non-work.

The researchers found that Sunray's cultural techniques evoked in employees feelings and identities not normally found inside work. The cultural message was that all the experiences that employees normally look forward to after work, such as having fun, partying, joy, fulfilment, exhilaration, and friendship, could be obtained inside the company. The aim of this conscious blurring of the boundary between private life and working life was to maximize the productive demands of the company. It was the 'whole' person that the company now desired, not just the uniform corporate self, since employee creativity and innovation were now linked to staff 'being themselves'. Sunray had a conscious recruitment strategy of employing young people whom they found 'can be themselves and know how to have fun'. The major corporations around the world seek to absorb the lifestyles, consumption patterns, and social activities of their employees by importing the positive experiences and emotions associated with non-work into the workplace (based on Fleming and Spicer, 2004; 2007).

The use of organizational culture to control and direct employees' behaviour involves the selective application of rites, ceremonials, myths, stories, symbols, and legends by company managers to direct the behaviour of their employees. It is called *symbolic management*. It involves encouraging employees to internalize desired company values and norms. External control is thus replaced by self-control, such as that used by professionals such as doctors, teachers, lawyers, and priests (Willmott, 1993; Rose, 1990). This approach appeals to managers because it is cheaper, avoids resentment, and builds employee commitment to the company and its goals. This theme of 'internalized control' is at the heart of the work of Michel Foucault (1979).

Cultures of fun

Expressions of individuality at work, particularly through employees expressing the fun side of their personalities, are based on the belief that when people are happy and have the freedom to be themselves, they are more likely to be productive and creative. Software firms in Silicon Valley have installed rock-climbing walls in their reception areas and put inflatable animals in their offices. Walmart wants its cashiers to smile at customers. Acclaris, an American IT company, has a 'chief fun officer'. TD Bank, the American arm of Canada's Toronto Dominion, has a 'Wow' department that despatches costume-clad teams to 'surprise and delight' successful workers. Red Bull, a drinks firm, has installed a slide in its London office. Creating this culture of fun is driven by three of the most popular management fads of the moment: empowerment, engagement, and creativity. Many companies pride themselves on devolving power to front-line workers. Managers hope that 'fun' will make workers more engaged and creative. However, when fun becomes part of the corporate strategy, does it cease to be fun and become the opposite? (© The Economist Newspaper Limited, London (18/09/2010); Bains, 2007)

STOP AND THINK

Consider the organizational approach to culture as described in the research on Sunray. Identify the costs and benefits to the following groups:

- Company management
- Employees
- Customers
- The wider community.

Culture strength and organizational performance

Strong culture
a culture in which an organization's core values are widely shared among employees and intensely held by them, and which guides their behaviour.

Weak culture
a culture in which there is little agreement among employees about their organization's core values, the way things are supposed to be, or what is expected of them.

A distinction has been made between **strong culture** and **weak culture** organizations (Gordon and DiTomaso, 1992), and a strong culture is defined by O'Reilly (1989) as one which possesses

- *intensity* – organization members have a strong emotional attachment to the core values of the organizations, and are willing to display approval or disapproval of fellow members who act in certain ways, and
- *sharedness* – there is widespread agreement among employees about these organization values.

In contrast, a weak culture is one in which there is little agreement among employees about their organization's core values.

Thus, the greater the number of employees who accept the organization's core values, the stronger their emotional attachment to those values is, and the more they 'walk their talk', then the stronger a company's culture will be, and vice versa. A strong culture is held to unite staff, and direct their attitudes and actions (Deal and Kennedy, 1982; Peters and Waterman, 1982). Currently, Apple, Google, Hewlett-Packard, McDonald's, and Disney are considered by many commentators to be 'strong culture' companies. Much of the managerial literature has assumed that companies with strong cultures perform better than those with weak ones.

Chris Grey (2009) reminds us that talking about a strong culture company with widely shared values says nothing about the values themselves or what that strength consists of. For example, employees may have a strong value which holds that they should drink tea and sit around rather than work. In fact, the shared values discussed in the culture change literature are senior management's values of increased productivity, reduced costs, rising company profits, improved customer service, flexibility, and innovation. They are not the employees' values of tea drinking and sitting around.

STOP AND THINK

Is a strong organizational culture likely to improve company performance and lead it to success?

What arguments can you make against this view?

Company success, measured in financial terms, depends on a great many factors other than culture (e.g. a technological lead; customer product appeal; low product price) and is therefore just as likely to be found in companies that have weak cultures. A firm's financial performance may itself affect the strength of its culture. That is, company success may *cause* its culture to become strong, rather than a strong culture being the cause of success. A strong culture may only be a good predictor of performance in the short term (Gordon and DiTomaso, 1992). Many of Peters and Waterman's strong culture companies subsequently failed. Finally, a strong culture only aids success if its values are appropriate ones, that is, if they are suitable for coping with the conditions faced by the organization at the time.

Strong cultures are slow to develop and difficult to change. Strong cultures may not necessarily be 'good' cultures if they result in employees holding inappropriate attitudes and managers making wrong decisions. A company's strong culture may impede its success if it encourages conformist attitudes. Miller (1994) suggested that it can cause inertia (clinging to past recipes); immoderation (foolish risk-taking); inattention (selective perception of signals); and insularity (failure to adapt to the environment). IBM, a corporation acknowledged for its strong culture, nearly collapsed in the 1990s when it failed to respond to Apple's challenge and initially failed to make the transition from mainframe to personal computers. Thus one can compare the advantages and disadvantages of strong cultures as shown in Table 4.4.

Table 4.4: Advantages and disadvantages of a strong culture

Advantages	Disadvantages
Differentiates the organization from others	Makes merging with another organization more difficult
Allows employees to identify themselves with the organization	Attracts and retains similar kinds of employees, thereby limiting the diversity of thought
Facilitates employees behaving in ways desired by management	Can be 'too much of a good thing' if it creates extreme behaviours among employees
Creates stability within the organization	Makes adapting to a changing environment more difficult

Source: from *Organizational Behaviour: Improving Performance and Commitment in the Workplace* McGraw Hill (Colquitt, J.A., LePine, J.A. and Wesson, M.J. 2009), p. 557, 0073530085 © The McGraw-Hill Companies, Inc.

John Kotter and James Heskett (1992) researched the relationship between organizational culture and a company's economic success. They empirically tested the cultural strength of 207 large firms from a variety of industries. They only found a moderate correlation, and discovered examples of successful weak culture companies and unsuccessful strong culture ones. They concluded that there was some evidence for a relationship between strong culture and success, but that it was insufficient as an explanation in itself.

Internal integration the process through which employees adjust to each other, work together, and perceive themselves as a collective entity.

External adaptation the process through which employees adjust to changing environmental circumstances to attain organizational goals.

Denison et al. (2004) noted that models linking organizational culture and organizational performance have to deal with the contradictions of companies attempting to achieve both **internal integration** (getting all their departments and staff to work in tandem) and **external adaptation** (responding quickly and effectively to environmental changes). They write that organizations that are market-focused and opportunistic have problems with internal integration. In contrast, those that are well integrated and over-controlled can have difficulties of external adaptation responding to their changing environments. Similarly, organizations with a top-down vision have to struggle with empowerment, in order to achieve the 'bottom-up' commitment and behaviour of employees who are needed to implement that vision. Meanwhile, those companies with a strong commitment to employee participation have problems deciding upon a strategic direction. The most effective companies, say Denison et al. (2004), are those that can resolve these contradictions without resorting to simple trade-offs.

This line of argument leads us away from a 'one best culture' viewpoint. Rob Goffee and Gareth Jones (2003) take this contingency approach to culture, which holds that 'it all depends'. These authors state that the most suitable culture for any organization is one that is 'environmentally appropriate' for it. This means that its culture should meet the environment challenges in which that particular company operates. Performance is likely to be better for companies possessing cultures that are both strong *and* able to adjust sufficiently well to their environments. Thus, a firm which operates in a volatile, competitive environment will need a strong culture that not only adapts quickly but even perhaps anticipates environmental changes. In contrast, if a company has a predictable and relatively static environment, it will need a strong but less adaptable culture. A study by Jose Garmendia

(2004) into companies in the health insurance industry confirmed that a strong culture had a positive impact on organizational performance (results), but only if that culture was adapted to the firm's environment and interacted proactively with it.

STOP AND THINK Organizational culture influences how employees dress for work. Think about what clothes your bosses and co-workers wear at your current or recent workplace. How do your university lecturers dress? What does it tell you about the culture of these organizations?

Types of organizational culture

Reflect on the mental process that you just went through in answering the last Stop and Think question. You had to assess the employee's clothing, and then consider the type of organizational culture into which it would best fit. In so doing, you had to differentiate between different types of organizational cultures. Writers have used this same mental process to categorize different company cultures to create organizational culture typologies – although they have not used employee dress as the basis of their classifications. Various writers have produced different culture typologies, all of which assume that, rather like different personality type classifications (e.g. introvert and extravert), an entire organization (like an individual) can be assigned to a single culture type category on the basis of its possession of certain unique cultural traits.

Perhaps the most popular organizational culture typology is Charles Handy's (Handy, 1993). His classification is based on the degree of centralization and formalization, and is shown in Figure 4.6. Centralization refers to how much power and authority is centralized at the top of the organization; and formalization concerns the extent to which rules, procedures, and policies govern organizational activities.

- *Power culture* organizations have a single, dominant individual who exerts their will; controlling by recruiting those of a similar viewpoint; and operating with the minimum of rules. Power culture is represented symbolically by a web. It works on precedent, anticipating desires of those at the centre. Decisions are based on a balance of power rather than logic, and there is little emphasis on discussion to reach consensus. Examples may be found in small companies run by their founder/owner.

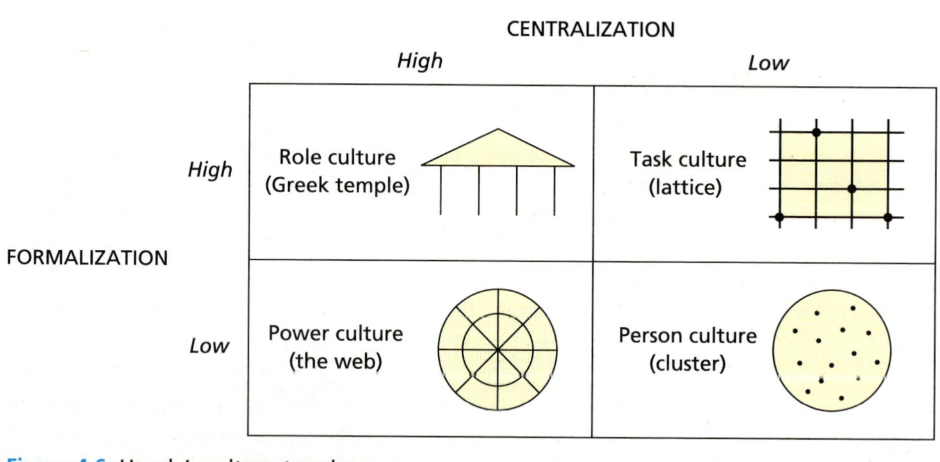

Figure 4.6: Handy's culture typology

Source: based on Handy (1993).

- *Role culture* organizations emphasize the importance of rules, procedures, role expectations, and job descriptions. Role culture is represented symbolically by a Greek temple. Managers within role culture organizations operate 'by the book', on the basis of their position in the hierarchy and their role, and in a depersonalized way. Role culture is based in functional departments and specialities, and its operations are driven by logic and rationality. This culture is characteristic of bureaucracies.
- *Person culture* organizations are focused on individuals. This culture is represented symbolically by a cluster. Such organizations exist for the benefit of their members, and may include a 'star performer'. Control is exercised only by mutual consent, and the organization is seen as subordinate to the individuals. This type of culture is typical of rock bands and classical chamber music groups, as well as small, start-up IT firms, architects' partnerships, and barristers' chambers.
- *Task cultures* are job or project oriented. This culture is represented symbolically by a lattice. The task is specified at the top, but then the emphasis shifts to finding the resources, and then getting the job done through using individuals' enthusiasm and commitment, working as a team. Influence within this culture is based on expertise, rather than position or personal power. Such cultures are found where sensitivity and flexibility to the organization's environment are important, for example, in client-focused agencies such as advertising companies or management consultancies.

Source: © 1996 Randy Glasbergen, www.glasbergen.com

Different as chocolate and cheese?

While the hostile £11.7 billion takeover of Cadbury's, a long-established British confectionary company, by Kraft, the US food conglomerate, in 2010 may have generated a great deal of controversy among the company's major stakeholders, it was also notable for stimulating much discussion about the question of clashing company cultures. Cadbury is rooted in Quaker attempts to build a socially benign business empire which practises 'principled capitalism'. Its CEO stated that the firm's performance-driven, values-led approach to business has built its unique corporate brand. Cadbury possessed an informal and egalitarian organizational culture. Its company managers were given the freedom to use their creativity and to act entrepreneurially, and the chief executive often left his office to talk to the shop-floor employees. Kraft is a conventional multinational, the world's second largest food company, which was created through mergers and demergers, and was once part of the tobacco and consumer goods conglomerate Philip Morris. Kraft is a much larger organization with a taller hierarchy, and commentators

→

Getty Images

report that it is more formal in its operations, with decisions requiring the approval of senior managers.

Writers have highlighted two areas of cultural difference between the two companies. Kraft's emphasis on multiculturalism contrasts with Cadbury's stress on heritage; following Kraft's acquisition of competitors, it presses them to adopt its culture, while Cadbury has historically remained unchanged; in terms of social atmosphere, Cadbury has more of a family feel while Kraft is more bureaucratic. Culture fit is crucial. The acquirer must first understand both its own and its target's cultural identity. It can do this by means of a cultural audit, using indicators such as company mission, strategic goals, management structures, leadership profiles, employee engagement, performance management, succession planning, and reward systems. Without such an understanding of culture, a merger or acquisition can lead to misunderstanding, confusion and conflict (Bowers, 2009; Hasenoehrl, 2010; Lucas, 2011b; Osborne et al., 2010; Strategicorner, 2011).

National cultures

The culture of a nation is affected by many variables. Laurent (1989) argues that the national culture is more powerful and stable than organizational culture. Brooks (2003) saw organizational culture being partly the outcome of societal factors, some of which are identified in Figure 4.7. National cultural stereotypes are well established: Scots are mean; Americans are brash; Germans are humourless; French are romantic; and Japanese are inscrutable. Researchers have studied how national cultures might affect organizational cultures in specific country settings. For example, there is much known about the processes and outcomes of multicultural teams (Stahl et al., 2010). There is much interest in how attempts to establish a common organizational culture in a multinational firm can be undermined by the strength of a national culture. An organization's culture, while having unique properties, is necessarily embedded within the wider norms and values of the country in which its office and facilities are located, and is affected by the personal values that employees bring with them to their jobs.

Vanhoegaerden (1999) felt that awareness and understanding of cultural differences was crucial for everybody in the organization. He suggested two reasons as to why these have

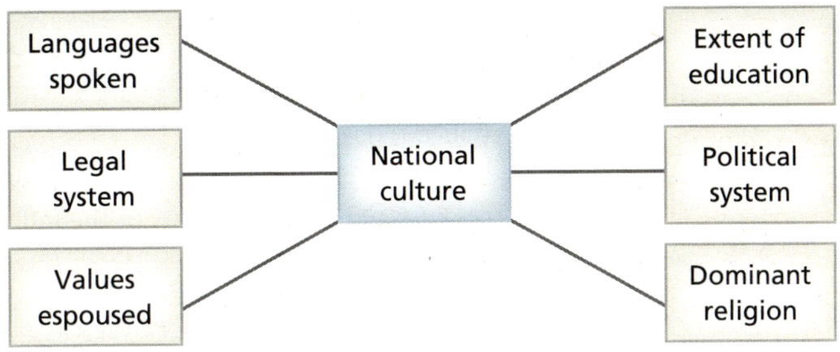

Figure 4.7: Factors affecting national culture

Source: from *Organizational Behaviour: Individuals, Groups and Organization*, Brooks, I. Pearson Education Limited © Pearson Education Limited 2003.

Social orientation the relative importance of the interests of the individual versus the interest of the group – individualism versus collectivism.

Power orientation the appropriateness of power/authority within organizations – respect versus tolerance.

Uncertainty orientation the emotional response to uncertainty and change – acceptance versus avoidance.

Goal orientation the motivation to achieve goals – aggressive masculinity versus passive femininity.

Time orientation the time outlook on work and life – short-term versus long-term.

Geert Hofstede (b. 1928)

been neglected. First, many people believed that, underneath, everybody was fundamentally the same. This belief is reinforced by the impression that cultures are merging. The success of global companies such as Disney, Coca-Cola and others can convince us that the world is becoming more alike. The convergence may exist, but only at a superficial level, and many cultural differences remain. The French philosopher Pascal noted that 'there are truths on this side of the Pyrenees which are falsehoods on the other'. Even the archetypal global brand McDonald's encounters cultural obstacles as it covers the world. When it opened in Japan, it found that Ronald McDonald's clown-like white face did not go down well. In Japan, white is associated with death and was unlikely to persuade people to eat Big Macs. The company also found that Japanese people had difficulty in pronouncing the 'R' in Ronald, so the character had to be renamed *Donald* McDonald.

At both the organizational and national levels of the cultural debate, one sees not only attempts to identify specific traits, but also attempts to classify organizations and countries into types. This creation of trait lists and typologies parallels work on individual personality. In the 1980s, Geert Hofstede (1986, 1991) carried out a cross-cultural study of 116,000 employees of the same multinational company located in forty countries. He distinguished national cultures in terms of five orientations – **social orientation**, **power orientation**, **uncertainty orientation**, **goal orientation**, and **time orientation** (Hofstede and Bond, 1988). Each cultural orientation affects the perceptions, attitudes, values, motivation, and behaviours of people who live in it. Like personality assessment, each of the orientations represents a separate cultural continuum (personality trait), so each national culture can be positioned somewhere along each dimension as shown in Figure 4.8.

Walmart's German exit

After eight years of never making a profit, Walmart said 'auf Wiedersehen' to Germany, announcing in 2006 that it was selling its 85 hypermarkets and pulling out of the country after incurring a £540 million pre-tax loss. It failed to understand how the American and German cultures differed. The use of 'greeters' in every American store (staff who were ordered to smile at every customer as they entered) was particularly unpopular among German customers. Neither did they like their purchases being bagged for them by store staff. At the same time, Walmart's employees resisted management demands which they felt were unjust, such as a ban on dating colleagues in positions of authority, a 'no flirting' rule between workers, being forced to work beyond contracted hours, video surveillance of workers, and a telephone hotline for employees to inform on their colleagues. Legal action by its German staff forced Walmart to amend its ethics manual concerning romantic attachments, and to ban video monitoring (Litterick, 2006; *Deutsche Welle*, 2006).

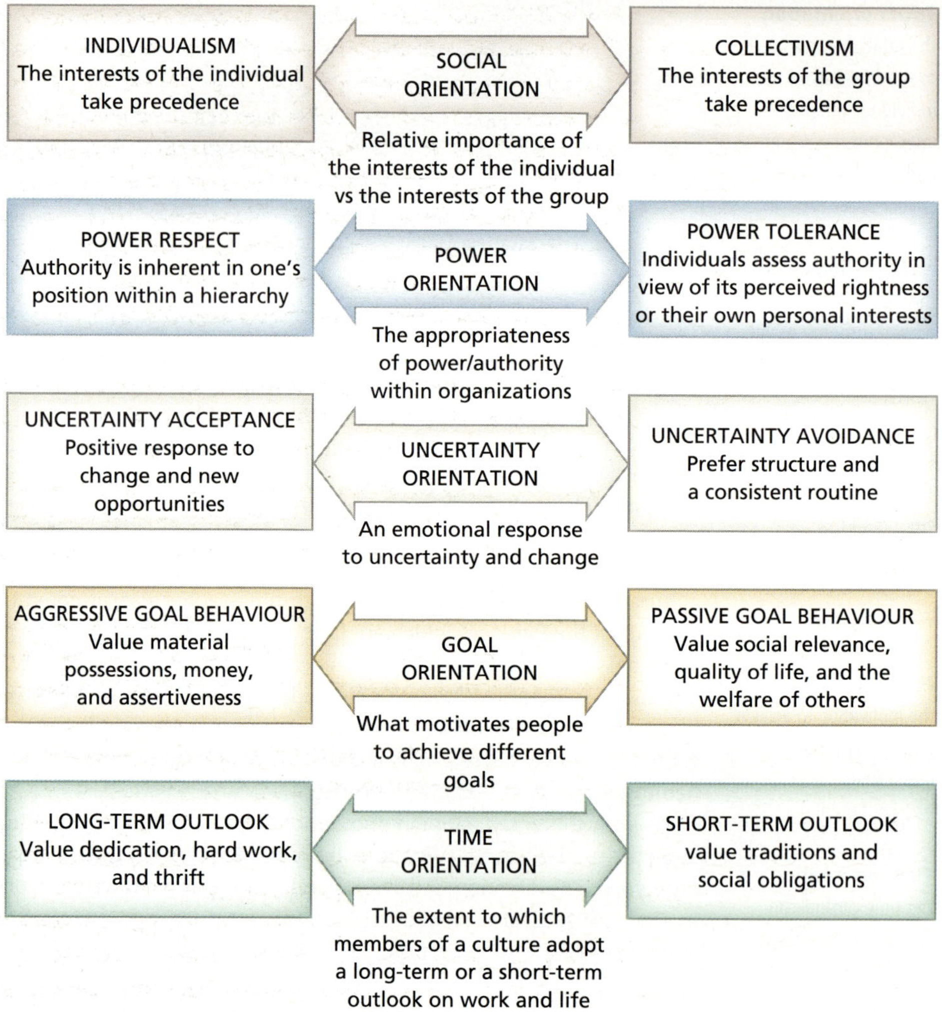

Figure 4.8: Hofstede's five dimensions of national culture

Source: from GRIFFIN, RICKY W; PUSTAY, MICHAEL W., INTERNATIONAL BUSINESS, 5th Edition, © 2007, pg. 102. Reprinted and electronically reproduced by permission of Pearson Education, Inc., Upper Saddle River, New Jersey.

Two groups of researchers have updated Hofstede's pioneering work. The first of these incorporated, updated, and extended it by means of the Global Leadership and Organizational Behaviour Effectiveness (GLOBE) programme. This is a longitudinal study of leadership and organizational culture of 825 organizations located in 62 countries (Javidan and House, 2001; House et al. 2004). Whereas Hofstede's was a one-off, snapshot survey, GLOBE is a longitudinal study reporting changes over time. GLOBE contrasts national cultures on nine dimensions, which include, but also go beyond, those proposed by Hofstede. The GLOBE researchers have summarized the findings of the first two decades of their research into leadership and national culture and these are shown in Table 4.5. This shows the three highest and lowest ranking countries on each of GLOBE's nine dimensions.

STOP AND THINK

If you were the host of an overseas business visitor (decide whether male or female) who was unaware of your country's culture, what two things would you advise that person to do and not do, so as to avoid embarrassing themselves and causing offence to others at work or at a social event?

Table 4.5: Cultural dimensions and GLOBE country rankings

Cultural dimension	Definition: the degree to which	Countries scoring high	Countries scoring low
Assertiveness	Individuals are bold, forceful, dominant, confrontational, or demanding in relationships with others	Spain USA Greece	Sweden New Zealand Switzerland
In-group collectivism	Individuals express pride, loyalty, and cohesiveness to their organizations or families	Egypt China Morocco	Denmark Sweden New Zealand
Institutional collectivism*	Organizational and government practices encourage and reward collective distribution of resources (as under socialism) and collective action	Greece Hungary Germany	Denmark Singapore Japan
Future orientation	Individuals engage in future-oriented behaviours such as planning, delaying gratification, and investing in the future	Denmark Canada Netherlands	Russia Argentina Poland
Gender differentiation	A collective minimizes different treatment of men and women, as through equal opportunities based on ability and performance	South Korea Egypt Morocco	Sweden Denmark Slovenia
Humane orientation	A society or organization encourages and rewards individuals for being fair, altruistic, generous, caring, and kind to others	Indonesia Egypt Malaysia	Germany Spain France
Performance orientation	A society encourages and rewards group members for performance improvements, excellence, high standards, and innovation	USA Taiwan New Zealand	Russia Argentina Greece
Power distance	Members of a collective expect power to be distributed equally	Russia Spain Thailand	Denmark Netherlands South Africa
Uncertainty avoidance	A society, organization, or group relies on social norms, rules, and procedures to alleviate unpredictability of future events	Austria Denmark Germany	Russia Hungary Bolivia

*A low score indicates collectivism.
Source: based on House et al. (2004) in Hellriegel and Slocum (2009); Javidan and House (2001) and Dorfman et al. (2012).

Taras et al. (2012) are the second group of researchers who have developed Hofstede's model. They argued that Hofstede's scores had been gradually eroded with the passing of each post-1980 decade. Their own research produced an updated set of national rankings based on his five dimensions of national culture. To do this, they conducted a meta-analysis (a study of studies), using a larger and more representative sample than Hofstede's. Theirs included 451 empirical studies, involving half a million individuals from 49 countries, and compared the scores over different decades. Their detailed rankings are contained in their research article. While the results obtained were generally consistent with those reported by Hofstede (1980), some nations were found to deviate from Hofstede's original rankings. For example, many East European and South American countries, described as being high on power distance and collectivism, scored lower scores on both dimensions. The researchers also found that the pace and direction of cultural change varied greatly between countries. This led to substantial changes in their *relative* rankings along the cultural dimensions.

National culture and car manufacture

© Caro/Alamy

Professor Lord Bhattacharyya, head of the Warwick Manufacturing Group, claimed that it was the arrogance of the Rover managers and the lack of a learning culture in the company that prevented it from obtaining the real benefits from its partnership with the Japanese group, Honda. In 1992, when BMW bought the Rover business, communication with the German managers was even worse (exacerbated by political in-fighting on the German side). Failure was the inevitable, bitter result. In a similar way, the collapse of the Daimler-Chrysler link indicates poor collaboration and internal strife, which stemmed, in part, from national cultural differences and traditions between German and US managers.

Two of Hofstede's five culture dimensions help to explain the difficulties faced by Honda, BMW, Daimler, and Chrysler managers. The first is *social orientation* – the relative importance of the interests of the individual versus those of the group. Out of 100, the US scored 91, close to extreme individualism; the UK was 89; and Germany was 67 (a little above the European average). In contrast, Japan's score was 46, well towards collectivism. The other dimension is *uncertainty orientation* – the emotional response to uncertainty and change. The Japanese scored 92 (very high indeed on the extreme uncertainty avoidance dimension); Germany was 65; the USA was 46; and Britain was 35. The last two scores are well towards the uncertainty acceptance end of the continuum. The lack of precise rules and procedures at Rover's Longbridge plant may have made the BMW team uncomfortable from the outset (based on Lester, 2007).

Home viewing

Outsourced (2007, director John Jeffcoat) tells the story of Todd Anderson (played by Josh Hamilton), a 32-year-old manager of a Seattle customer call centre whose entire order fulfilment department is outsourced to India. Despite facing unemployment, he accepts a temporary job to go there to train his replacements. What does he learn about Indian culture? As you watch, each time you notice a culture-specific practice, tradition, taboo, behaviour, attitude, assumption, or approach, pause the film and make a note of it. How many items do you end up with on your list? What issues does the film raise about the effect of cultural difference at work; the relationships between employees from different backgrounds; and the global economy's impact on national and personal identity?

Multicultural teamworking

Yuri Arcurs/Dreamstime.com

Multicultural teams are valued by companies because they provide them with benefits such as knowledge of different product markets; the teams can be culturally sensitive to customer service; and they offer the possibility of 24-hour working. Jeanne Brett and her colleagues studied the day-to-day working problems encountered by members of such multicultural teams (Brett et al., 2006). The team members studied came from a variety of countries including the United States, India, Japan, Korea, Brazil, Mexico, the UK, Poland, and Greece. The authors identified four main barriers to team success:

- *Direct/indirect communication*: In Western cultures, communication is generally direct and explicit. The meaning is on the surface, and is not dependent on a listener's knowledge of the speaker or the context for its interpretation. In cultures using indirect communication, however, the meaning is embedded in the message's presentation. For example, a negotiator's preferences and priorities have to be inferred, rather than asked about directly. Uncovering and discussing the real problems may have to be done hypothetically – by asking what would happen if some system part failed – even though the failure being discussed is real and immediate. Such communication challenges reduce information-sharing and create interpersonal conflict.
- *Trouble with accents and fluency*: Despite English being the international business language, misunderstandings and frustrations occur as a result of non-native speaker accents, their lack of fluency, and translation and usage problems, all of which create misunderstandings and influence team members' perceptions of each other's status and competence. Non-fluency prevents the team benefiting from members' expertise; it demotivates individuals; and it can be another cause of interpersonal conflict.
- *Differing attitudes to hierarchy and authority*: Multicultural teams necessarily have a flat (non-hierarchical) structure which can be uncomfortable for those members who come from cultures in which people are treated according to their organizational status. For example, deferring to higher-status members is appropriate when most of the team come from a hierarchical culture, but can be damaging to status and credibility, and even humiliating, if most of the team come from an egalitarian culture. A project can fail if members feel that they have been treated disrespectfully.
- *Conflicting norms for decision-making*: Cultures differ in terms of degree of prior analysis required and speed of decision-making. For example, US managers like to make a quick decision with little analysis compared to their Brazilian counterparts.

The most successful teams and their managers use four strategies to deal with these challenges:

- *adaptation* – acknowledging the culture gaps openly and working around them;
- *structural intervention* – changing the shape of the team (size, membership);
- *managerial intervention* – establishing team norms early;
- *exit* – removing a team member when other options have failed.

Despite company preferences for multicultural teams, more recent research by Stahl et al. (2010) and Zander et al. (2012) has found no direct link between cultural diversity and team performance. Performance was affected by contextual factors like team tenure, team dispersion, team size, and task complexity. Culturally diverse teams demonstrated higher levels of creativity, conflict, and satisfaction, but lower integration between members, than homogeneous teams.

Corporate culture versus national culture

Does organizational culture diminish the influence of national culture? Research by Lubatkin et al. (1998) suggests not. Both company managers and employees bring their cultural background and ethnicity to the workplace. In Hofstede's (2001) study, national culture explained more of the differences than did role, age, gender, or race. Laurent (1983) also found more pronounced cultural differences among employees from around the world working within the same multinational company than among those working for companies in their native lands. The company's culture did not replace or eliminate national differences. Various researchers have reported that pressure to conform to the culture of a foreign-owned company brought out employees' resistance, causing them to cling on, even more strongly, to their own national identities. The unambiguous conclusion, they say, is that employees maintain or enhance their culture-specific ways of working when employed by multinational organizations (Adler and Gundersen, 2008; Adler and Jelinek, 1986; Schneider, 1988).

RECAP

1. *Account for the popularity of organizational culture among managers and and academics.*
    - Culture management offers managers a route to economic success.
    - For consultants, the concept provides an appealing, easy-to-grasp quick-fix solution to sell to managers wishing to improve their organization's performance.
    - For academics, it offers an alternative perspective with which to research and theorize about organizations and provided a new context within which to explore postmodernist ideas.
2. *List, describe, and give examples of Schein's three levels of organizational culture.*
    - Schein distinguished surface manifestations of culture at level one (e.g., artefacts, rites, ceremonials); organizational values at level two (e.g. customer obsession); and basic assumptions at level three which actually was the culture (e.g. nature of reality and truth).
3. *Distinguish the stages of organizational socialization.*
    - The stages of organizational socialization are pre-arrival, encounter and metamorphosis.
4. *Contrast managerial and social science perspectives on organizational culture.*
    - Organizational culture is either something that a company *has*, or what a company *is*.
    - Organizational culture is a single, integrated unit or a differentiated entity consisting of multiple, different subcultures, fragmented with conflicting interests.
    - An organization's culture can be managed by its leaders or it is beyond their direct control and has to be tolerated by them.
    - Culture signals a new era of symbolic leadership which relies on internalized forms of employee direction, or it is an old style management control under a new guise.
5. *Assess the link between organizational culture and organizational performance.*
    - Few research studies have been conducted which explicitly test a causal link between an organization's culture and its economic performance.
    - Those that have been conducted do not illustrate any direct causal relationship between a 'strong' culture and high economic performance suggesting, at a minimum, that other mediating variables may be more significant.
    - There is anecdotal data, as well as a logical argument, to suggest that organizations possessing a strong culture at a time of required change may be less flexible, less able to change, and hence less likely to perform well economically.
6. *Distinguish between different types of organizational culture.*
    - Handy categorized the cultures of organization using a four-type framework: role, power, task, and person.
7. *Distinguish different dimensions of national culture.*
    - Hofstede suggested that national culture could be differentiated along five dimensions: power distance; uncertainty avoidance; individualism–collectivism; masculinity–femininity; and short-term–long-term perspective.
    - The GLOBE framework for assessing national culture incorporates and extends Hofstede's dimensions and includes assertiveness, future orientation, gender differentiation, uncertainty avoidance, power distance, individualism/collectivism, in-group collectivism, performance orientation, and humane orientation.

Revision

1. Is organizational culture capable of being managed or do chief executive officers have to tolerate the culture that they inherit?
2. How can culture help or hinder an organization's effectiveness?
3. What guidance does the research into national culture offer managers working around the world for global corporations?
4. To what extent, and in what ways, might a national culture affect an organization's own culture?

Research assignment

First, familiarize yourself with the list of Schein's 15 surface manifestations of culture (as shown on pp. 114–16). Use this list to (a) interview a manager and obtain examples of as many of the surface manifestations of culture as they are able to provide you with. (b) For each manifestation, ask your manager what purpose it serves within their organization. (c) Ask them what external and internal factors have moulded the organization's culture into what it is today. (d) Fit your organization into Handy's organizational culture typology, justifying your choice with examples from the company concerned.

Springboard

Doug Edwards (2011) *I'm Feeling Lucky: The Confessions of Google Employee Number 59*, London, Allan Lane. The author describes the evolution and impact of the company's culture over a five-year period from the company's foundation to its becoming quoted on the stock exchange.

Michael Kramer (2010) *Organizational Socialization*, Cambridge, Polity Press. The author describes individuals' experiences of joining and leaving organizations. It explores the entire process from anticipatory socialization onwards to the voluntary or involuntary exiting from those same organizations.

Vas Taras, Piers Steel and Bradley Kirkman (2011) 'Three decades of research on national culture in the workplace: do the differences still make a difference?', *Organizational Dynamics*, 40(3), pp. 89–198. This article discusses the effect of national culture on employee attitudes and behaviour.

Hugh Willmott (1993) 'Strength is ignorance, slavery is freedom: managing culture in modern organizations', *Journal of Management Studies*, 30(5), pp. 515–52. A classic article in which the author proposes that culture is a particular form of control which operates, not by external regulation, but by shaping the identity (internal world) of an organization's employees.

OB in films

Dead Poets Society (1989, director Peter Weir), DVD track 1: 0:00:53 to 0:04:44 (4 minutes). To establish context, many films begin with shots of an organization to communicate its culture. The clip begins with the opening credits of the film, and ends after Mr Keating has been introduced and sits down and there is a shot of an outside scene.

1. Which surface manifestations of Welton Academy's culture are being communicated here?
2. What values can you infer about Welton Academy's organizational culture from viewing this clip?

	Welton Academy culture
1. *Artefacts* are material objects created to facilitate culturally expressive activities. They include tools, furniture, appliances and clothing.	
2. *Ceremonials* are formally planned, elaborate, dramatic sets of activities of cultural expression.	
3. *Courses* and workshops are used to instruct, induct, orient, and train new members, and to recognize the contributions of existing ones.	
4. *Heroes* are characters, living or dead, who personify the values and beliefs; who are referred to in company stories.	
5. *Jokes* are humorous stories intended to cause amusement but whose underlying themes may carry a message for the behaviour or values.	
6. *Language* is the particular form or manner in which members use vocal sounds and written signs to convey meaning to each other.	
7. *Legends* are handed-down narratives about wonderful events based on history, but embellished with fictional details.	
8. *Mottoes* are maxims adopted as rules of conduct which are rarely, if ever, changed.	
9. *Norms* are expected modes of behaviour that are accepted as the company's way of doing things.	
10. *Physical layout* concerns things that surround people, providing them with sensory stimuli.	
11. *Rites* are relatively elaborate, dramatic sets of activities that consolidate various forms of cultural expression into one event.	
12. *Sagas* are historical narratives describing the unique accomplishments of a group and its leaders.	
13. *Slogans* are short, catchy phrases that are regularly changed.	
14. *Stories* are narratives describing how individuals acted and the decisions they made that affected the company's future	
15. *Symbols* refer to any act, event, object, quality or relation that serves as a vehicle for conveying meaning.	

OB on the web

How do cultural differences get in the way of communicating? Search YouTube for 'Cultural differences video.wmv' which discusses differences in verbal communications. Two other videos, 'Gestures around the world' and 'Cultural gaffes beyond your borders', focus on aspects of non-verbal communication. Prepare a briefing report for a visitor coming to your country, highlighting the most important aspects of your culture, so as to prevent them embarrassing, shocking, confusing, or offending the locals. You should discuss both appropriate and inappropriate verbal and non-verbal behaviours including dress, discussion topics, manners, etiquette and so on.

CHAPTER EXERCISES

1. Surface manifestations

Objectives

1. Understand how organizational structure and processes affect organizational culture.
2. Speculate how the organizational culture might affect your views and behaviours as an employee.

Briefing

Examine the four clusters of descriptions as directed by your instructor. For each one:

1. Decide what 'message' each one sends to employees about the organization's culture.
2. Speculate on the views and behaviours it might encourage or discourage among employees.

Descriptions

1. Companies value high-performing employees.
   (a) Company A conducts annual staff appraisals between an employee and their manager. Those performing below standard are asked to explain their poor performance.
   (b) Company B conducts quarterly reviews between an employee and their manager. If employees exceed their annual performance target, they are given a substantial bonus in that year.
   (c) Company C conducts regular team appraisals in which team members comment on each other's strengths and weaknesses. All receive extensive preparatory training and each person promptly gets a summarized, anonymized report of these comments about them, and this is used when promotion decisions are made.
2. Companies want their employees to have creative ideas.
   (a) Company A hires only the smartest people and then, immediately after appointment, sends them on creativity workshops.
   (b) Company B has a rigorous selection procedure. Its expensive and elaborate three-day assessment centre selection approach focuses on determining each applicant's level of creativity.
   (c) Company C has a staff restaurant with only six-seater tables to allow different staff to meet; its rest areas have whiteboards on the walls; and there are suggestion boxes in every main corridor.

→

3. Companies have different approaches to employees' work spaces.
   (a) Company A encourages staff to personalize their work spaces by decorating them with photos, toys, and other items brought from home. Staff are free to come to work dressed as they like.
   (b) Company B has open space work areas for all staff. They wear business dress and address each other by their first names. Managers do not have their own offices or secretaries. The conference suite is used for department meetings to which secretarial and support staff are invited. Recycling boxes are located throughout the building.
   (c) Company C believes messy desks demonstrates a lack of personal organization; it operates a paperless office system and requires managers to enforce a 'clear surface' policy. Non-business-related items in work spaces are considered unprofessional and are banned. 'Dress-down Fridays' were introduced by senior management after much discussion, some time ago.
4. Companies have different approaches to employees' errors.
   (a) In Company A, an employee's mistake is discussed at a team meeting, and recorded on the employee's file, and senior management is informed for possible disciplinary action.
   (b) In Company B, the manager identifies errors made by subordinates and talks to the individuals, showing them where they went wrong and what they should do in the future.
   (c) In Company C, employees discuss their mistakes with their managers. The manager assists the subordinate to analyse their error, helps them learn from it, and agrees an action plan for future improvements.

Exercise developed in association with Professor Phillip Beaumont, University of Glasgow.

2. National cultures through proverbs

Objectives

1. To recognize the similar ways in which national cultural values are shared.
2. To understand three differences between two national cultures.
3. To master the technique of understanding national cultures through their expressions in proverbs.

Briefing

1. Students form into small groups.
2. The table below shows three six proverb groups. Compare Group 1 and 2, and answer the following questions:
   (a) Which of Hofstede's orientations does each proverb group promote?
   (b) Explain the message in the proverbs related to that dimension.
   (c) What countries do you think these proverbs describe? What is your reasoning?

GROUP 1	GROUP 2
• one palm makes no applause • a single tree makes no forest; one string makes no music • giving convenience to others is to give it to yourself • the nail that sticks up gets pounded • rafters that jut out rot first	• too many cooks spoil the broth • two's company, but three's a crowd • a squeaking wheel gets the grease • lend your money and lose your friend • familiarity breeds contempt • don't hide your light under a bushel
GROUP 3	GROUP 4
• a turnip cooked hastily may still have soil residue • honing the hatchet will not delay woodcutting • an oak is not felled at one stroke • when drawing water from a well, never forget the well diggers • a constant drip wears away a stone • a flower deliberately grown may not bloom; but a sapling planted accidentally may grow into a tree	• a bird in the hand is worth two in the bush • don't put off for tomorrow what you can do today • no news is good news • easy come, easy go • a new broom sweeps clean • eat, drink, and be merry, for tomorrow you may die
GROUP 5	GROUP 6
• a teacher for a day is a father for a lifetime. • honour the teacher and revere his teaching • be at other's beck and call • rather be the head of a chicken than a tail of a phoenix • a golden hammer breaks an iron door let the emperor be an emperor, the minister a minister, the father a father, and the son a son	• a wise man admits his ignorance; an ignorant man admits his wisdom • from little acorns mighty oaks do grow • do unto others as you would have them do unto you • what is good for the goose is good for the gander • those you pass on the way up the ladder will be the same ones you pass on the way down

3. Repeat the process for Group 3 and 4; and then for Group 5 and 6.
4. Can you think of another proverb from your own country that seems to reflect an aspect of its national culture?
5. If you were to offer a foreign visitor to your own country one piece of cultural advice as to what to do or avoid doing when interacting with a resident (in their home, in an office, or on the street) what would that advice be?

This article was published in International Journal of Management Education, *9(2), Sronce, R. and Li, L., Catching flies with honey: Using Chinese and American proverbs to teach cultural dimensions, pp. 1–11, Copyright Elsevier 2011.*

Employability assessment

With regard to your future employment prospects:

1. Identify up to three issues from this chapter that you found significant.
2. Relate these to the competencies in the employability matrix.
3. Decide what actions you need to take to maintain and/or develop those competencies under each of the four headings of the employability matrix.

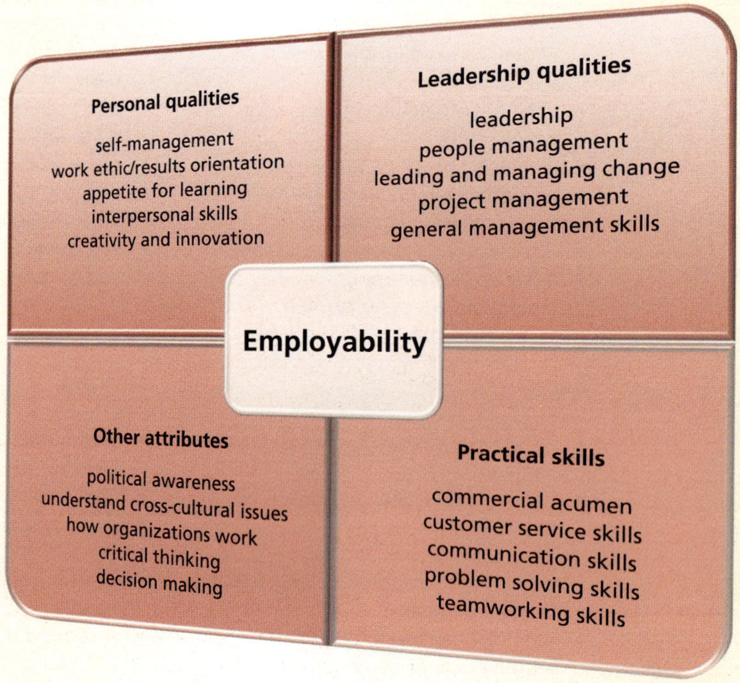

References

Adler, N.J. and A. Gundersen (2008) *International Dimensions of Organizational Behaviour* (5th edn), London: International Thomson.

Adler, N.J. and Jelinek, M. (1986), 'Is "organization culture" culture bound?', *Human Resource Management*, 25(1), pp. 73–90.

Alvesson, M. (2001) *Understanding Organizational Culture*, London: Sage Publications.

Bains, G. (2007) *Meaning Inc.: The Blueprint for Business Success in the 21st Century*, London: Profile Books.

Becker, H. (1982) 'Culture: a sociological view', *Yale Review*, 71, pp. 513–27.

Bowers, S. (2009) 'Cadbury warns of culture clash under craft', *The Guardian Online*, 21 October, http://www.guardian.co.uk/business/2009/oct/21/cadbury-kraft-sales-profits-job-losses, accessed 8 August 2012.

Brett, J., Behfar, K. and Kern, M.C. (2006) 'Managing multicultural teams', *Harvard Business Review*, 84(11), pp. 84–91.

Brooks, I. (2003) *Organizational Behaviour: Individuals, Groups and Organization* (2nd edn), Harlow, Essex: Financial Times Prentice Hall.

Burman, R. and Evans, A. (2008) 'Target zero: a culture of safety', in R. Oddy (ed.) *Defence Aviation Safety Centre Journal*, RAF Bentley Priory, Stanmore: MoD Aviation Regulatory and Safety Group, pp. 22–7.

Chao, G.T., O'Leary-Kelly, A.M., Wolf, S., Klein, H.J. and Gardner, P.D. (1994) 'Organizational socialization: its content and consequences', *Journal of Applied Psychology*, 79(5), pp. 730–43, di: 10.1037/0021-9010.79.5.730.

Colquitt, J.A., LePine, J.A. and Wesson, M.J. (2009) *Organizational Behaviour: Improving Performance and Commitment in the Workplace*, London: McGraw-Hill.

Cunliffe, A.L. (2008) *Organization Theory*, London: Sage Publications.

Day, P. (2012) 'What's gone wrong with the banks?', *BBC News Online*, 24 July, http://www.bbc.co.uk/news/business-18915060?print=true.

Deal, T.E. and Kennedy, A.A. (1982), *Corporate Cultures: The Rites and Rituals of Organization Life*, Reading, MA: Addison Wesley.

Deal, T.E. and Kennedy, A.A. (2000) *The New Corporate Cultures*, New York and London: Texere Publishing.

Denison, D.R., Haaland, S. and Goelzner, P. (2004) 'Corporate culture and organizational reflectiveness: is Asia different from the rest of the world?', *Organizational Dynamics*, 33(1), pp. 98–109.

Deutsche Welle (2006) 'World's biggest retailer Wal-Mart closes up shop in Germany', from http://www.dw-world.de/dw/article/0,,2112746,00.html.

Dorfman, P., Javidan, M., Hanges, P., Dastmalchian, A. and House, R. (2012) 'GLOBE: A twenty year journey into the intriguing world of culture and leadership', *Journal of World Business*, 47(4), pp. 504–518.

Edwards, D. (2011) *I'm Feeling Lucky: The Confessions of Google Employee Number 59*, London: Allan Lane.

FC Barcelona (2012) http://www.fcbarcelona.com/club/identity, accessed 24 May 2012.

Fleming, P. and Spicer, A. (2004) 'You can checkout anytime, but you can never leave: spatial boundaries in a high commitment organization', *Human Relations*, 57(1), pp. 75–94.

Fleming, P. and Spicer, A. (2007) *Contesting the Corporation: Struggle, Power and Resistance in Organizations*, Cambridge: Cambridge University Press.

Foucault, M. (1979) *Discipline and Punish*, Harmondsworth, Middlesex: Penguin Books.

Furnham, A. and Gunter, B. (1993) 'Corporate culture: definition, diagnosis and change', in Cary L. Cooper and Ivan T. Robertson (eds) *International Review of Industrial and Organizational Psychology*, vol. 8, Chichester: John Wiley, pp. 233–61.

Gagliardi, P. (1986) 'The creation and change of organizational cultures: a conceptual framework', *Organization Studies*, 7(2), pp. 117–34.

Garmendia, J.A. (2004) 'The impact of company culture on company performance', *Current Sociology*, 52(6), pp. 1021–38.

Goffee, R. and Jones, G. (2003) *The Character of a Corporation: How Your Company's Culture Can Make or Break Your Business*, London: Profile Business.

Gordon, G.G. and DiTomaso, N. (1992) 'Predicting corporate performance from organizational culture', *Journal of Management Studies*, 29(6), pp. 783–98.

Grey, C. (2009) *A Very Short, Fairly Interesting and Reasonably Cheap Book about Studying Organizations*, London: Sage.

Griffin, R. and Putsay, M.W. (2007) *International Business: A Managerial Perspective*, Upper Saddle River, NJ: Pearson Prentice Hall.

Handy, C. (1993) *Understanding Organization* (4th edn), Harmondsworth, Middlesex: Penguin Books.

Hasenoehrl, C. (2010) 'Employee engagement: Kraft's intentions for Cadbury could leave a bitter taste for both consumers and employees', *HR Magazine*, www.hrmagazine.co.uk/hro/features/1017450/employee-engagement-kraft-inte, accessed 8 August 2012.

Hellriegel, D. and Slocum, J.W. (2009) *Organizational Behavior* (13th edn), Mason, OH: South-Western Cengage Learning.

Hofstede, G. (1980) *Culture's Consequences: International Differences in Work-Related Values*, Beverley Hills, CA: Sage Publications.

Hofstede, G. (1986) 'Editorial: the usefulness of the concept of organization culture', *Journal of Management Studies*, 23(3), pp. 253–57.

Hofstede, G. (1991) *Cultures and Organizations*, London: McGraw-Hill.

Hofstede, G. (2001) *Culture's Consequences: International Differences in Work-Related Values* (2nd edn), London: Sage Publications.

Hofstede, G. and Bond, M. (1988) 'The Confucian connection: from cultural roots to economic growth', *Organizational Dynamics*, 16(4), pp. 4–21.

House, R.J., Hanges, P.J., Javidan, M., Dorfman, M. and Gupta, V. (eds) (2004) *Culture, Leadership and Organizations: The GLOBE Study of 62 Societies*, Thousand Oaks, CA: Sage Publications.

Javidan, M. and House, R.J. (2001) 'Cultural acumen for the global manager: lessons from the Project GLOBE', *Organizational Dynamics*, 29(4), pp. 289–305.

Kellaway, L. (2011) 'A contract not worth the email it is written on', *Financial Times*, 6 June, p. 14.

Knights, D. and Willmott, H. (1987) 'Organizational culture as management strategy: a critique and illustration from the financial services industry', *International Studies of Management and Organization*, 17(3), 40–63.

Kotter, J.P. and Heskett, J.L. (1992) *Corporate Culture and Performance*, New York: Free Press.

Kunda, G. (1992) *Engineering Culture: Control and Commitment in a High Tech Corporation*, Philadelphia, PA: Temple University Press.

Laurent, A. (1983) 'The cultural diversity of Western conceptions of management', *International Studies of Management and Organization*, 13(1–2) (whole issue).

Laurent, A. (1989) 'A cultural view of organizational change', in P. Evans, Y. Doz and A. Laurent (eds) *Human Resource Management in International Firms*, London: Macmillan, pp. 83–94.

Lester, T. (2007) 'Masters of collaboration', *Financial Times*, 29 June, Understanding the Culture of Collaboration supplement, p. 8.

Litterick, D. (2006) 'Wal-Mart quits Germany but insists Asda is safe', *The Daily Telegraph*, 29 July, p. 31.

Lubatkin, M., Calori, R., Very, P. and Veiga, J. (1998) 'Managing mergers across borders: a two nation explanation of a nationally bound administrative heritage', *Organizational Science*, 9(6), pp. 670–84.

Lucas, L. (2011a) 'Preserve your unique flavour', *Financial Times*, 8 February, p. 14.

Lucas, L. (2011b) 'Cadbury people still chewing on Kraft culture', *Financial Times*, 14 January, p. 13, http://www.ft.com/cms/s/0/71a34530-2019-11e0-a6fb-00144feab49a.html.

Luthans, F. (1995) *Organizational Behaviour* (7th edn), New York: McGraw-Hill.

Macalister, T. and Teather, D. (2010) 'Innocent smoothie denies sell-out after Coca-Cola gets majority stake', *The Guardian*, 9 April.

Martin, J. (1992) *Cultures in Organizations: Three Perspectives*, Oxford: Oxford University Press.

Mayo, E. (1933) *The Human Problems of an Industrial Civilization*, New York: Macmillan.

Mayo, E. (1945) *The Social Problems of an Industrial Civilization*, Cambridge, MA: Harvard University Press.

Miller, D. (1994) 'What happens after success: the perils of excellence', *Journal of Management Studies*, 31(3), pp. 325–58.

Notter, J. and Grant, M. (2011) *Humanize: How People-Centric Organizations Succeed in a Social World*, Indianapolis: Indiana: Que Publishing.

Ogbonna, E. (1993) 'Managing organizational culture: fantasy or reality?', *Human Resource Management Journal*, 3(2), pp. 42–54.

Ogbonna, E. and Harris, L.C. (2002) 'Organizational culture: a ten year, two-phase study of change in the UK food retailing sector', *Journal of Management Studies*, 39(5), pp. 673–706.

O'Hanlon, J. (2007) 'Innocent Drinks', *ExecDigital*, http://www.execdigital.co.uk/Innocent-Drinks_3545.aspx.

O'Reilly, C.A. (1989) 'Corporations, culture and commitment: motivation and social control in organizations', *California Management Review*, 31(4), pp. 9–25.

Osborne, A., Songonuga, V. and Chibwana, M. (2010) 'The implications of Kraft-Cadbury takeover: Culture change – presentation transcript', http://www.slideshare.net/hyperalz/the implications of kraftcadbury-takeover-culture-change, accessed 8 August 2012.

Parker, M. (2000) *Organizational Culture and Identity: Unity and Division at Work*, London: Sage Publications.

Pascale, R.T. (1985) 'The paradox of organization culture: reconciling ourselves to socialization', *California Management Review*, 27(2), pp. 26–41.

Pascale, R.T. and Athos, A.G. (1982) *The Art of Japanese Management*, Harmondsworth, Middlesex: Penguin Books.

Personnel Management (2011) 'Business Case: Nampak', April, pp. 38–41.

Peters, T.J. and Waterman, R.H. (1982) *In Search of Excellence: Lessons from America's Best Run Companies*, New York: Harper and Row.

Ray, C.A. (1986) 'Corporate culture; the last frontier of control?', *Journal of Management Studies*, 23(3), pp. 287–97.

Robbins, S.P. and Judge, T.A. (2013) *Organizational Behaviour* (15th edn), Harlow, Essex: Pearson Education.

Rollinson, D. (2008) *Organizational Behaviour and Analysis: An Integrated Approach* (4th edn), Harlow, Essex: Financial Times Prentice Hall.

Rose, N. (1990) *Governing the Soul: The Shaping of the Private Self*, London: Routledge.

Schein, E.H. (1983) 'The role of the founder in creating organization culture', *Organization Dynamics*, 12(1), pp. 13–28.

Schein, E.H. (2004) *Organizational Culture and Leadership* (3rd edn), San Francisco, CA: Jossey-Bass.

Schneider, S. (1988) 'National vs. corporate culture: implications for human resource management', *Human Resource Management*, 27(2), pp. 231–46.

Schultz, M. (1995) *Studying Organizational Cultures: Diagnosis and Understanding*, Berlin: De Gruyter.

Smircich, L. (1983) 'Concepts of culture and organizational analysis', *Administrative Science Quarterly*, 28(3), pp. 339–58.

Smircich, L. and Morgan, G. (1982) 'Leadership: the management of meaning', *Journal of Applied Behavioural Science*, 18(2), pp. 257–73.

Sronce, R. and Li, L. (2011) 'Catching flies with honey: using Chinese and American proverbs to teach cultural dimensions', *International Journal of Management Education*, 9(2), pp. 1–11.

Stahl, G.K., Maznevski, M.L., Voigt, A. and Jonsen, K. (2010) 'Unravelling the effects of cultural diversity in teams: a meta-analysis of research on multi-cultural workgroups', *Journal of International Business Studies*, 41(4), pp. 690–709.

Stenebo, J. (2010) *The Truth about IKEA*, London: Gibson Square Books.

Strategicorner (2011) 'Kraft's acquisition over Cadbury: Cultural root issue', 18 September, http://www.slideshare.net/strategicorner/kraft-cadbury-cultural-issue, accessed 8 August 2012.

Taras, V., Steel, P. and Kirkman, B.L. (2012) 'Improving national cultural indices using a longitudinal meta-analysis of Hofstede's dimensions', *Journal of World Business*, 47(3), pp. 329–41.

The Economist (2010) 'Schumpeter: down with fun', 18 September, p. 84.

The Economist (2011a) 'Schumpeter: the Catalan kings', 21 May, p. 78.

The Economist (2011b) 'The view from the top and bottom', 24 September, p. 86.

Trice, H.M. and Beyer, J.M. (1984) 'Studying organization cultures through rites and ceremonials', *Academy of Management Review*, 9(4), pp. 653–69.

Trice, H.M. and Beyer, J.M. (1993) *The Cultures of Work Organizations*, Englewood Cliffs, NJ: Prentice Hall.

van Maanen, J. and Barley, S. (1984) 'Occupational communities: culture and control in organizations', in B. Staw and L.L. Cummings (eds) *Research in Organizational Behaviour*, Vol. 6, Greenwich, CT: JAI Press, pp. 287–366.

van Maanen, J. and Schein, E.H. (1979) 'Toward a theory of organization socialization', *Research in Organization Behaviour*, 1, pp. 209–64.

Vanhoegaerden, J. (1999) 'Sense and sensitivity', *Directions: The Ashridge Journal* (Ashridge corporate website, August).

Willmott, H. (1993) 'Strength is ignorance, slavery is freedom: managing culture in modern organizations', *Journal of Management Studies*, 30(5), pp. 515–52.

Zander, L., Mockaitis, A.I. and Butler, C.L. (2012), 'Leading global teams', *Journal of World Business*, 47(2), pp. 592–603.

Part 2 Individuals in the organization

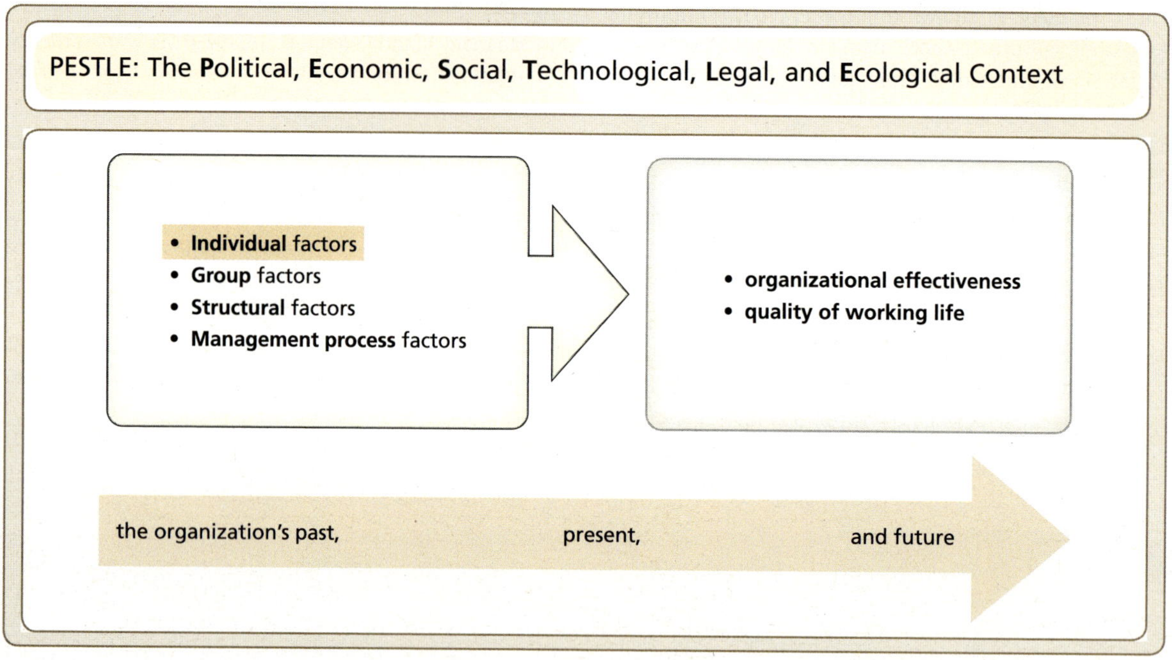

A field map of the organizational behaviour terrain

Introduction

Part 2, on individuals in the organization, explores five topics from psychology:

- *Learning*, in Chapter 5
- *Personality*, in Chapter 6
- *Communication*, in Chapter 7
- *Perception*, in Chapter 8
- *Motivation*, in Chapter 9.

These topics are of enduring significance to management and organizational behaviour. However, in an economic downturn, such as the second decade of the twenty-first century has produced, maintaining a capable, informed, motivated, and engaged workforce becomes more, not less, important. Achieving those outcomes in a period of uncertainty is difficult, as training budgets are cut, work becomes more intensified, and nobody has the time for communications. We know that, as a general rule, giving people at all levels of an organization more autonomy, and more freedom to experiment and to solve their own problems, can increase individual and organizational performance. However, the management tendency in times of crisis is to tighten controls on employee behaviour and to centralize decision-making – actions which can have the opposite effect on motivation and performance. In a difficult and uncertain economic climate, it may be necessary to pay even more attention to employee psychology than when times are good – remembering that managers are employees, too.

These aspects of psychology are closely related, and contribute in different ways to our understanding of behaviour in general, to our understanding of behaviour in organizations in particular, and to our analysis of performance at work and quality of working life. The coverage of these topics is clearly more limited than you will find in a psychology textbook, because we are focusing on issues that help us to understand organizational behaviour, and on techniques and approaches that have shaped organization and management practice.

Invitation to see

AFP/Getty Images

Traders at the New York Stock Exchange

1. **Decoding**: Look at this image closely. Note in as much detail as possible what messages you feel that it is trying to convey. Does it tell a story, present a point of view, support an argument, perpetuate a myth, reinforce a stereotype, challenge a stereotype?
2. **Challenging**: To what extent do you agree with the messages, stories, points of view, arguments, myths, or stereotypes in this image? Is this image open to challenge, to criticism, or to interpretation and decoding in other ways, revealing other messages?
3. **Sharing**: Compare with colleagues your interpretation of this image. Explore explanations for differences in your respective decodings.

You're the employee: what would you do?

What advice can you give to management to help solve this problem? Base your advice on your own experience and views, as well as on the information provided.

> Our company prides itself on attracting the best talent and for many years has run a successful training scheme for both graduate entrants and non-graduates. Competition for places on our schemes is always fierce and we believe that the breadth of training we provide is recognized as something of a gold standard in our industry. Newly qualified trainees invariably settle in well and make an impact in whatever area of the business they join.
>
> However, a recent analysis of our retention rate for these trainees has made uncomfortable reading. It seems that a large number are benefiting from the training and then departing for higher salaries or prospects elsewhere. Despite being afforded every opportunity to progress within the firm, the reality is that too few of them see us as a 'job for life', or even a job for a decade – it looks like for many, we are merely the first rung on their personal career ladder.
>
> Our schemes are a serious investment and it goes without saying that we need to retain entrants to make the expense worthwhile. Although it could be argued that we are boosting skills in the industry as a whole, we aren't in the business of altruism and are not prepared to act as a training ground for our competitors to come along and poach the best of the talent we have developed.
>
> Of course, our employees cannot be blamed for listening to offers from our rivals, especially if they are being approached by headhunters – but our pay and benefits are more than competitive, so we do not believe that throwing money at the problem will solve anything.
>
> What can we do to foster greater loyalty among the talent we have developed and ensure that all our good work in the recruitment field is not going to waste?

From 'Troubleshooter', People Management, *24 January 2008, p. 72.*

Chapter 5 **Learning**

Key terms

learning
behaviourist psychology
cognitive psychology
feedback
positive reinforcement
negative reinforcement
punishment
extinction
Pavlovian conditioning
Skinnerian conditioning
shaping
intermittent reinforcement
schedule of reinforcement
cybernetic analogy
intrinsic feedback
extrinsic feedback
concurrent feedback
delayed feedback
behaviour modification
socialization
behavioural modelling
provisional selves
behavioural self-management
learning organization
single-loop learning
double-loop learning
tacit knowledge
explicit knowledge
knowledge management

Learning outcomes

When you have read this chapter, you should be able to define those key terms in your own words, and you should also be able to:

1. Explain the characteristics of the behaviourist and cognitive approaches to learning.
2. Explain and evaluate the technique of behaviour modification.
3. Explain the socialization process, and assess the practical relevance of this concept.
4. Explain and evaluate the technique of behavioural self-management.
5. Describe features of knowledge management and the learning organization.

Why study learning?

In an economy dominated by knowledge work and rapid, unpredictable change, the ability to learn, and to continue learning, for individuals and organizations, is crucial. The Web 2.0 technologies discussed in Chapter 3 have led to the growing use of electronic simulations or 'sims' for training and management development (Syedain, 2008). As a general rule, the higher the level of your education, the more employable you are likely to be, and the higher your salary. In contributing to organizational effectiveness, employees have to know what to do, how to do it, and how well they are expected to perform. Learning theories thus affect many management practices including

- induction of new recruits;
- the design and delivery of job training;
- design of payment systems;
- how supervisors evaluate performance and provide feedback;
- methods for modifying employee behaviour;
- creation of learning organizations;
- design and operation of knowledge management systems.

One of the learning mechanisms explored in this chapter is *positive reinforcement*. In practice, this means praising employees for good performance. Timothy Hinkin and Chester Schriesheim (2009) argue that, at a time of economic crisis, when financial rewards are scarce, positive reinforcement becomes a valuable management resource.

Thinking for a living in the twenty-first century

Central to much thinking about how organizations should be restructured for the twenty-first century is the idea that innovation and growth will depend more and more on so-called knowledge workers, the sort of people who, to quote the title of a recent book by Thomas Davenport of Babson College, Massachusetts, find themselves 'thinking for a living'.

Lowell Bryan and Claudia Joyce at McKinsey reckon that knowledge workers 'represent a large and growing percentage of the employees of the world's biggest corporations'. In some industries, such as financial services, media, and pharmaceuticals, they think the share may already be as high as 25 per cent.

Others would put it much higher. One of the secrets of Toyota's success, says Takis Athanasopoulos, the chief executive of the Japanese carmaker's European operations, is that the company encourages every worker, no matter how far down the production line, to consider himself a knowledge worker and to think creatively about improving his particular corner of the organization (Hindle, 2006, p. 9).

Learning is one of the most fundamental and controversial topics in psychology. The extremes of this controversy lie in behaviourist and cognitive theories of learning. The concept of the learning organization has also been popular for some time. The learning organization is a combination of structures and policies which encourage learning, with individual and corporate benefits. Some larger companies regard learning as so important that they have established their own corporate universities. Some commentators argue that organizations, as well as individuals, are able to learn, but this is a controversial view.

Knowledge has thus become an asset more important than equipment and materials for many organizations, where understanding of processes – the 'how to' of making products and providing services – is critical. Competitive advantage means knowing *how to* make products, *how to* innovate more rapidly, *how to* bring new products and services more quickly to the marketplace, *how to* meet changing customer needs. The capacity to develop new knowledge affects the organization's ability to grow and to survive, as technologies, customer requirements, government policies, and economic conditions change.

What is learning all about?

1. Learning is a part of work and work involves learning; these are not separate functions but intertwined; the separation we have made of them is artificial and often does not serve us well.
2. Learning is not only or even primarily about obtaining correct information or answers from knowledgeable others; it is fundamentally about making meaning out of the experience that we and others have in the world.
3. Organizational learning results from intentional and planned efforts to learn. Although it can and does occur accidentally, organizations cannot afford to rely on learning through chance.
4. As a collective, we are capable of learning our way to the answers we need to address our difficult problems. It is ourselves we must rely on for these answers rather than experts, who can, at best, only provide us with answers that have worked in the past (Dixon, 1999, p. xiv).

The learning process

How do we learn? How do we come to know what we know, and to do what we are able to do? These questions lie at the heart of psychology, and it is not surprising that we are faced with different approaches to the topic. This variety maintains controversy, excitement, and interest in the subject, and also helps to generate new thinking.

Psychology is associated with the study of rats in mazes. Rats, and other animals, have contributed much to our understanding of human behaviour, and have been widely used by psychologists concerned with the development of learning theories. Rat biochemistry is similar to ours. We have to accept that humans are animals in many respects, and that we can learn much about ourselves by studying other creatures.

The ability to learn is not unique to human beings. Animals also learn, as dog owners and circus fans can confirm. One feature that seems to distinguish us from animals is our ability to learn about, adapt to, survive in, and manipulate our environment for purposes that we ourselves define. Animals can adapt to changes in their circumstances, but their ability to manipulate their environment is limited, and they appear to have little choice over their goals. In addition, animals have developed no science, technology, or engineering – or social science.

We hope that when you have finished reading this book you will be able to say that you have learned something. The test is whether or not you will be able to do things that you could not do before. You should know what the study of organizational behaviour involves, and you should be able to tell others what you know and think about it. You should be able to write essays and answer examination questions that previously you could not tackle. We can describe this process as **learning**, and the result as knowledge.

Learning the process of acquiring knowledge through experience which leads to a lasting change in behaviour.

It is important to note the limits on what counts as learning defined in terms of durability and experience. Behaviour can be changed temporarily by many factors, in ways which are not described as learning. Factors other than experience which alter our behaviour temporarily include maturation (in children), ageing (in adults), drugs, alcohol, and fatigue.

From neurological research, we now know which areas of the brain are involved in learning and memory processes, although our understanding of these processes is incomplete. The study of learning, however, is not confined to brain surgery. We can *infer* that learning has taken place by examining changes in your behaviour. If we assume that behaviour does not alter spontaneously, for no reason, then we can look for experiences that may be causes of behaviour change. These experiences may be derived from inside the body, or they may be sensory, arising outside. The task of inferring whether or not learning has taken place may be an obvious one, but observable behaviour may not always reveal learning.

It is helpful to distinguish between two types of learning. Procedural learning, or 'knowing how', concerns your ability to carry out skilled actions, such as riding a horse or painting a picture. Declarative learning, or 'knowing that', concerns your store of factual knowledge, such as an understanding of the history of our use of the horse, or of the contribution of the European Futurist movement to contemporary art.

Changes in behaviour can be measured using a 'learning curve', one example of which is shown in Figure 5.1, concerning the development of manual skills.

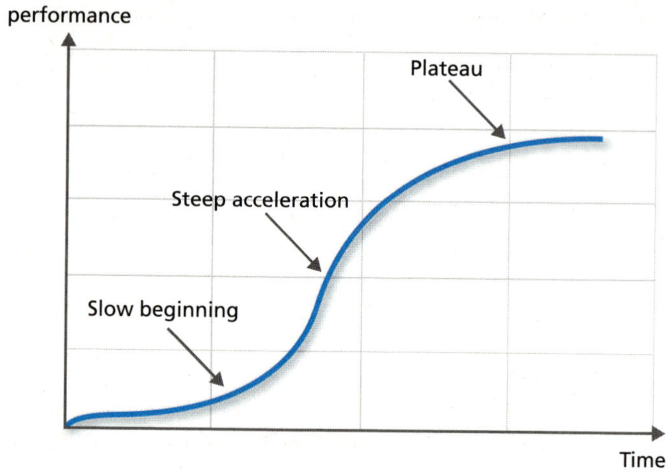

Figure 5.1: The typical manual skills learning curve

The learning can be plotted for one person, for a group of trainees, or even for a whole organization. The learning curve illustrated in Figure 5.1 shows that

1. Learning is not a smooth process, but changes in pace over time, until a stable peak performance is eventually reached.
2. The learner's ability develops slowly at first, then accelerates and develops more quickly, before finally reaching a plateau.

Learning curves for manual skills often follow this profile, but cognitive skills can develop in the same way. The shape of a learning curve depends on the characteristics of the task and of the learner. It is often possible to measure learning in this way, to compare individuals with each other, and to establish what constitutes good performance. If we understand the factors influencing the shape of the curve, we can develop ways to make learning more effective.

STOP AND THINK

Draw your own learning curve for this organizational behaviour course.

Why is it that shape? What would be your ideal learning curve look like?

How could you change the shape of this learning curve?

The experiences that lead to changes in behaviour have a number of important features. First, the human mind is not a passive recorder of information picked up through the senses. We can often recall the plot of a novel, for example, but remember very few of the author's words. This suggests that we do not record experiences in a straightforward way.

Second, we are usually able to recall events in which we have participated as if we were another actor in the drama. We are able to reflect, to see ourselves 'from outside', as objects in our own experience. At the time when we experienced the events, those cannot have been the sense impressions that we picked up. Reflection is a valuable capability.

Third, new experiences do not always lead to behaviour change. Declarative learning, for example, may not be evident until we are asked the right questions. Our experiences must be processed in some way if they are to influence our behaviour in future.

Behaviourist psychology a perspective which argues that what we learn are chains of muscle movements, and that mental processes are not observable, and are not valid issues for study.

Cognitive psychology a perspective which argues that what we learn are mental structures, and that mental processes can be studied by inference, although they cannot be observed directly.

Fourth, the way in which we express our drives depends on a mix of genetics and experience. We have innate drives, which are expressed in behaviour in different ways, depending on a combination of factors. Our innate makeup biases our behaviour in certain directions, but these biases can be modified by experience.

This chapter explains two influential approaches to learning, based on **behaviourist psychology** (or 'stimulus–response' psychology) and **cognitive psychology** (or 'information-processing' psychology). These perspectives are in many respects contradictory, but they can also be seen as complementary. Summarized in Table 5.1, these theoretical standpoints have different implications for organization and management practice.

Table 5.1: Behaviourist and cognitive perspectives

Behaviourist/stimulus–response	Cognitive/information-processing
studies observable behaviour	studies mental processes
behaviour is determined by learned sequences of muscle movements	behaviour is determined by memory, mental processes and expectations
we learn habits	we learn cognitive structures
we solve problems by trial and error	we solve problems with insight and understanding
routine, mechanistic, open to direct research	rich, complex, studied using indirect methods

The behaviourist approach to learning

John Broadus Watson (1878–1958)

The American psychologist John B. Watson (1878–1958) introduced the term *behaviourism* in 1913. He was critical of the technique of introspection, a popular psychological technique at that time, in which subjects were asked to talk about their experiences and thought processes, to explore their minds, and to describe what they found there. Instead, Watson wanted objective, 'scientific' handles on human behaviour, its causes and its consequences. This took him, and many other psychologists, away from the intangible contents of the mind to study relationships between visible stimuli and visible responses. That is why behaviourist psychology is also referred to as 'stimulus–response psychology'.

Behaviourism assumes that what lies between the stimulus and the response is a mechanism that will be revealed as our knowledge of the biochemistry and neurophysiology of the brain develops. This mechanism must relate stimuli to responses in a way that governs behaviour. We can therefore continue to study how stimuli and responses are related without a detailed understanding of the nature of that mechanism. Behaviourism thus argues that nothing of *psychological* importance happens between stimulus and response. Cognitive psychology argues that something of considerable psychological importance happens here.

Feedback information about the outcomes of our behaviour.

Positive reinforcement the attempt to encourage desirable behaviours by introducing positive consequences when the desired behaviour occurs.

The oldest theory of learning states that actions that are experienced together tend to be associated with each other (touching a flame, pain). We use knowledge of the outcomes of past behaviour to do better in future (don't touch flames). You learn to get higher assignment grades by finding out how well you did last time and why. We cannot learn without **feedback**. Behaviourists and cognitive psychologists agree that experience affects behaviour, but disagree over how this happens.

Feedback can be rewarding or punishing. If a particular behaviour is rewarded, then it is more likely to be repeated. If it is punished or ignored, it is likely to be avoided in future. This is known as the 'law of effect', which states that we learn to repeat behaviours that have favourable consequences, and avoid those that have neutral or undesirable outcomes. Rats can be trained to run through mazes with a combination of food pellets and electric shocks.

Behaviourism makes subtle distinctions relating to reward and punishment, illustrated in Table 5.2. With **positive reinforcement**, desired behaviours lead to positive consequences.

Table 5.2: Reinforcement regimes

	behaviour	reinforcement	result	illustration
positive reinforcement	desired behaviour occurs	positive consequences are introduced	desired behaviour is repeated	confess, and stick to your story, and you will get a shorter prison sentence
negative reinforcement	desired behaviour occurs	negative consequences are withdrawn	desired behaviour is repeated	the torture will continue until you confess
punishment	undesired behaviour occurs	a single act of punishment is introduced	undesired behaviour is not repeated	fail to meet your scoring target and we kick you off the team
extinction	undesired behaviour occurs	day's work not counted towards bonus	undesired behaviour is not repeated	ignore an individual's practical jokes used to gain attention

Negative reinforcement the attempt to encourage desirable behaviours by withdrawing negative consequences when the desired behaviour occurs.

Punishment the attempt to discourage undesirable behaviours through the application of negative consequences, or by withholding a positive consequence, following the undesirable behaviour.

Extinction the attempt to eliminate undesirable behaviours by attaching no consequences, positive or negative, such as indifference and silence.

With **negative reinforcement**, the undesirable outcomes continue until the desired behaviour occurs. As one-off **punishment** follows undesirable behaviour, this is different from negative reinforcement. Where behaviour has no positive or negative outcomes, this can lead to the **extinction** of that behaviour, as it comes to be seen as unimportant.

Source: © Doug Savage.

STOP AND THINK

Some airlines, concerned about the cost of fuel, want to encourage passengers to carry less luggage (a lighter plane uses less fuel). One approach is to allow passengers with hand luggage only to skip the check-in queues. Another is to charge passengers extra for each item of luggage that they check in.

Which reinforcement regimes are being used to teach passengers to travel light?

Behaviour modification in practice

David Boddy (2010, p. 458) reports the following communication from a call centre manager:

> In our call centre, staff are rewarded when behaviour delivers results in line with business requirements. Each month, staff performance is reviewed against a number of objectives, such as average call length, sales of each product, and attention to detail. This is known as Effective Level Review and agents can move through levels of effectiveness ranging from 1 to 4, and gain an increase in salary after six months of successful reviews. Moving through effective levels means that they have performed well and can mean being given other tasks instead of answering the phone. The role can become mundane and repetitive so the opportunity to do other tasks is seen as a reward for good performance. Thus it reinforces acceptable behaviour.
>
> Conversely, staff who display behaviour that is not desirable cannot move through these levels, and repeated failure to do so can lead to disciplinary action. This can be seen as punishment rather than behaviour modification. People can become resentful at having their performance graded every month, particularly in those areas where it is their line manager's perception of whether or not they have achieved the desired results.

Which reinforcement regimes does this call centre manager describe?

Ivan Petrovich Pavlov (1849–1936)

Pavlovian conditioning a technique for associating an established response or behaviour with a new stimulus.

The development of associations between stimuli and responses occurs in two different ways, known as **Pavlovian conditioning** and Skinnerian conditioning. Pavlovian conditioning, also known as classical conditioning and respondent conditioning, was developed by the Russian physiologist Ivan Petrovich Pavlov (1849–1936).

The best-known response which Pavlov studied concerned a dog salivating at the sight of food. Pavlov demonstrated how this could be associated with a completely different stimulus, such as the sound of a bell. Dog owners are trained today in classical conditioning methods. If you show meat to a dog, it will produce saliva. The meat is the stimulus, the saliva is the response. The meat is an *unconditioned* stimulus; the dog salivates naturally, and the saliva is an *unconditioned* response. Unconditioned responses are also called reflexes. Your lower leg jerks when you are struck just below the kneecap; your pupils contract when light is shone into your eyes. These are typical human reflexes. Humans also salivate, another unconditioned response, at the sight and smell of food.

Source: PEANUTS © 1989 Peanuts Worldwide LLC. Dist by UNIVERSAL UCLICK. Reprinted with permission. All rights reserved.

Suppose we ring a bell before we show the meat to the dog. Do this often enough, and the dog will associate the bell with the meat. Soon, it will salivate at the sound of the bell, without food being present. The bell has become a *conditioned* stimulus, and the saliva is now a conditioned response. The dog has learned from experience to salivate at the sound of a bell as well as at the sight of food. It does not have to be a bell. All manner of stimuli can be conditioned in this way. Pavlov discovered this form of conditioning by accident. His research was initially concerned with salivation, but he observed that his dogs salivated at the sight and sound of his laboratory assistants, before they were given their meat. He found this more interesting, and changed the focus of his research.

STOP AND THINK

Can you recognize conditioned responses in your own behaviour?

Is there a particular song, or a smell (perfume or after shave, or food cooking), that makes you think of another person, another place, another time, another experience?

Home viewing

Pavlov has influenced Hollywood. In *The Truman Show* (1998, director Peter Weir), Truman Burbank (played by Jim Carrey) is adopted as a child by a television network. He believes that he is living a normal life, but he is actually a prisoner in an immense domed city-sized soundstage, simulating the town of Seahaven, where he is surrounded by actors who play members of his family, teachers, and employers. As in the *Big Brother* television series, his every action is broadcast to viewers around the world, twenty-four hours a day, and has created a multi-million-dollar franchise for the network. If Truman were to quit, network profits would collapse. To stop him from leaving, the production team devise a plan based on Pavlovian conditioning. As you watch this movie, note how Truman's original conditioning is achieved. How does this conditioning affect Truman's daily life? How does he overcome his conditioning in his attempt to escape from Seahaven?

Burrhus Frederic Skinner (1904–1990)

Skinnerian conditioning a technique for associating a response or a behaviour with its consequence.

Suppose we now stop giving the meat to the dog after the bell. The dog will continue to salivate at the sound of the bell alone, expecting the bell to signal the arrival of food. If we continue to do this, however, the volume of saliva produced falls, and the association between the conditioned stimulus and conditioned response eventually suffers *extinction*.

Skinnerian conditioning is also known as instrumental conditioning and as operant conditioning. It is the discovery of the American psychologist Burrhus Frederic Skinner (1904–1990). Instrumental conditioning demonstrates how new behaviours or responses become established through association with particular stimuli.

Where the consequence of a behaviour is desirable to the individual, then the frequency of that behaviour is likely to increase. Given a particular context, any behaviour that is rewarded or reinforced will tend to be repeated in that context. Skinner put a rat into a box (known as a 'Skinner box') with a lever which, when pressed, gave the animal food. The rat is not taught to press the lever in the box. However, wandering around the box, the rat eventually moves the lever. It may sit on it, knock it with its head, or push it with a paw. That random behaviour is reinforced with food, and so it is likely to happen again.

Skinnerian conditioning is also called instrumental conditioning because it concerns behaviours that are a means to getting some material reward. Skinner's rat has to be under the influence of some drive before it can be conditioned in this way. His rats were hungry when they went into his box, and their behaviour thus led to a desired reward.

Where do the terms respondent and operant conditioning come from? Respondent conditioning comes from Watson's stimulus–response psychology which stated that there was no behaviour, or no response, without a stimulus to set it in motion. One could thus condition a known response to a given stimulus. Such responses are called respondents. Knee jerks, pupil contractions, and salivation are well known and clearly identified responses that are amenable to conditioning.

Shaping the selective reinforcement of chosen behaviours in a manner that progressively establishes a desired behaviour pattern.

Skinner, on the other hand, observed that animals and humans do behave in the absence of specific stimuli, as with a rat wandering around in his Skinner box. He argued that most human behaviour is of this kind. Behaviours that do not have identifiable stimuli are called operants. Operant conditioning thus explains how new behaviours, such as pressing that lever to get food, are established. Respondent conditioning does not alter the animal's behaviour (the dog always did salivate when it thought that food was coming), only the behaviour's timing. Skinner also developed the technique of **shaping**, or the selective reinforcement of desired behaviours. He was able to get pigeons to play ping-pong and to walk in figures of eight

Intermittent reinforcement a procedure in which a reward is provided only occasionally following correct responses, and not for every correct response.

– demonstrating how how spontaneous behaviours can be shaped by operant conditioning. You can see a demonstration at www.youtube.com/watch?v=vGazyH6fQQ4.

Skinner studied numerous variations on the operant conditioning theme. One important variation concerns the occasional reward of desired behaviour rather than delivering rewards in a continuous and regular manner. This mirrors real life more closely than the laboratory experiment. Why, for example, do gamblers keep playing when they lose most of the time? Why do anglers continue to fish when they catch nothing for hours at a time? There are many such examples of the power of **intermittent reinforcement**. Behaviour can be maintained without regular and consistent reinforcement every time that it occurs.

Automating behaviour modification

B.J. Fogg (2009) argues that technology can be used to modify people's behaviour, by 'automating persuasion'. One persuasive technology is the fuel gauge in a Toyota Prius. This measures engine efficiency, and encourages owners to change driving behaviour to get more miles per gallon. The games that come with the Nintendo Wii tell families to 'get off the couch and start moving'. Fogg's five rules for designing automated persuasion are:

1. *Target a simple behaviour.* 'Reduce stress levels' is a complex and ambitious goal; persuading people to stop and stretch for 20 seconds when prompted is more realistic, anyone can do it, and the success rate is measurable.
2. *Understand what is preventing the target behaviour.* The reason always concerns lack of motivation, lack of ability, or lack of a trigger to perform the behaviour. In other words, **B**ehaviour change depends on **M**otivation, **A**bility, and a **T**rigger:

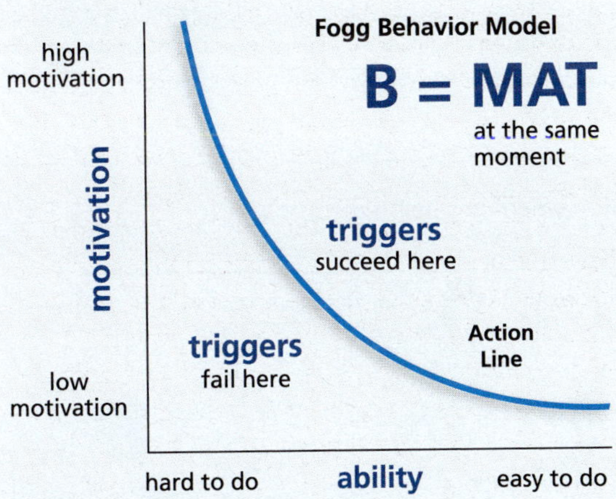

Source: © 2007 BJ Fogg; www.behaviormodel.org. For permissions contact BJ Fogg.

3. *Choose the right technology channel.* Email, online video, e-commerce websites, social networks, text messages – these are simple and direct. Installed software and specialist devices can make target behaviours simpler and increase ability.
4. *Start small and fast.* Sophisticated ideas take time to design, and users may reject the complexity. Creating a simple, focused persuasive experience with a clear goal is inexpensive, can be implemented quickly, and is easy to change if it doesn't work.
5. *Build on small successes*: Getting people to stretch for 20 seconds is not a sexy project. However, Fogg's trial had a 70 per cent compliance rate, and the prompt was expanded to include relaxation techniques – again with high compliance.

The trigger, therefore, lies in the technology. Once a simple approach is working, it can be expanded. Get people to repeat the behaviour routinely, on a fixed schedule. Increase the difficulty of the behaviour. Reach more people. Target other simple behaviours. Target less persuadable groups. Automating behaviour modification is inexpensive, and it works.

Schedule of reinforcement the pattern and frequency of rewards contingent on the display of desirable behaviour.

The pattern and timing of rewards for desired behaviour is known as the **schedule of reinforcement**. The possible variation in schedules of reinforcement is limitless, and Skinner investigated the effects of a number of these (Ferster and Skinner, 1957). However, there are two main classes of intermittent reinforcement, concerning interval schedules and ratio schedules, which are described in Table 5.3, contrasted with continuous reinforcement. Figure 5.2 illustrates these different schedules.

Table 5.3: Schedules of reinforcement

schedule	description	effects on responses	example
continuous	reinforcement after *every correct response*	establishes high performance, but can lead to satiation; rapid extinction when reinforcement is withheld	praise
fixed ratio	reinforcement after a *predetermined number* of correct responses	tends to generate high rates of desired responses	incentive payments
variable ratio	reinforcement after a *random number* of correct responses	can produce a high response rate that is resistant to extinction	commission on sales
fixed interval	reinforcement of a correct response after a *predetermined period*	can produce uneven response patterns, slow following reinforcement, vigorous immediately preceding reinforcement	weekly payments
variable interval	reinforcement of a correct response after *random periods*	can produce a high response rate that is resistant to extinction	prizes

Source: based on Luthans and Kreitner (1985).

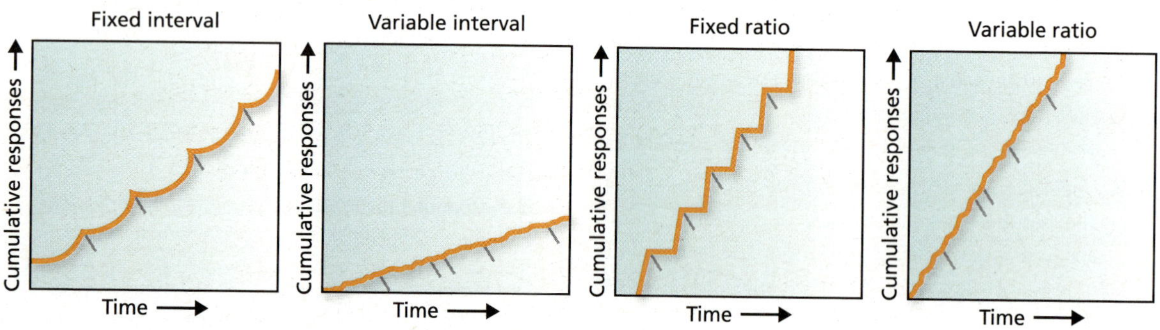

Figure 5.2: Interval and ratio reinforcement schedules

Source: from MORRIS, CHARLES G.; MAISTO, ALBERT A., PSYCHOLOGY: AN INTRODUCTION, 11th Ed. © 2002, p. 213. Reprinted and Electronically reproduced by permission of Pearson Education, Inc., Upper Saddle River, New Jersey.

STOP AND THINK

In this cartoon, what modes of reinforcement are being discussed?

Source: Reproduced with the kind permission of King Features Syndicate, all rights reserved.

Skinner claimed to be able to explain the development of complex patterns of behaviour with the theory of operant conditioning. This shows how our behaviour is shaped by our environment, by our experiences in that environment, and by the selective rewards and punishments that we receive. Thinking, problem-solving, and the acquisition of language, he argued, are dependent on these simple conditioning processes. Skinner rejected the use of 'mentalistic' concepts and 'inner psychic forces' in explanations of human behaviour because these were not observable, were not researchable, and were therefore not necessary to the science of human psychology. Why use complicated and unobservable concepts when simple and observable phenomena seem to provide adequate explanations?

Skinner's ambitious and influential project led to the development of programmed learning, a technique of instruction designed to reinforce correct responses in the learner and to let people learn at their own pace. The *behaviour modification* techniques described later are also based on his ideas. As the behaviour of a conditioned animal is consistent and predictable, this can be used to test the effects of drugs.

Reinforcing desired behaviour is generally more effective than punishing undesirable behaviour. However, Walters and Grusek (1977), from a review of research, suggest that punishment can be effective if it meets the following conditions:

- the punishment should be quick and short;
- it should be administered immediately after the undesirable behaviour;
- it should be limited in its intensity;
- it should be specifically related to behaviour, and not to character traits;
- it should be restricted to the context in which the undesirable behaviour occurs;
- it should not send 'mixed messages' about what is acceptable behaviour;
- penalties should take the form of withdrawal of rewards, not physical pain.

STOP AND THINK

To what extent should the criteria for effective punishment be used by managers when disciplining employees in an organizational context?

The cognitive approach to learning

Why should we look only at observable stimuli and responses in the study of psychology? Is it not possible to study the internal workings of the mind in indirect ways, by inference? Behaviourism seems to be unnecessarily restrictive, excluding those characteristics that make us interesting, different and, above all, human.

How do we select from all the stimuli that bombard our senses those to which we are going to respond? Why are some outcomes seen as rewarding and others as punishments? This may appear obvious where the reward is survival or food and the punishment is pain or death. However, with intrinsic or symbolic rewards this is not always clear. To answer these questions, we have to consider states of mind concerning perception and motivation.

Norbert Wiener (1894–1964)

The rewards and punishments that behaviourists call reinforcement work in more complex ways than conditioning theories suggest. Reinforcement is always knowledge, or *feedback*, about the success of past behaviour. Feedback is information that can be used to modify or maintain previous behaviours. This information has to be perceived, interpreted, given meaning, and used in decisions about future behaviours. The feedback has to be processed. This is why cognitive learning theories are called information-processing theories.

This approach draws concepts from the field of cybernetics which was established by the American mathematician Norbert Wiener (1954). He defined cybernetics as 'the science of

Cybernetic analogy an explanation of the learning process based on the components and operation of a feedback control system.

communication in the animal and in the machine'. One central idea of cybernetics is the notion of the control of system performance through feedback. Information-processing theories of learning are based on what is called the **cybernetic analogy**.

The elements of a cybernetic feedback control system are outlined in Figure 5.3.

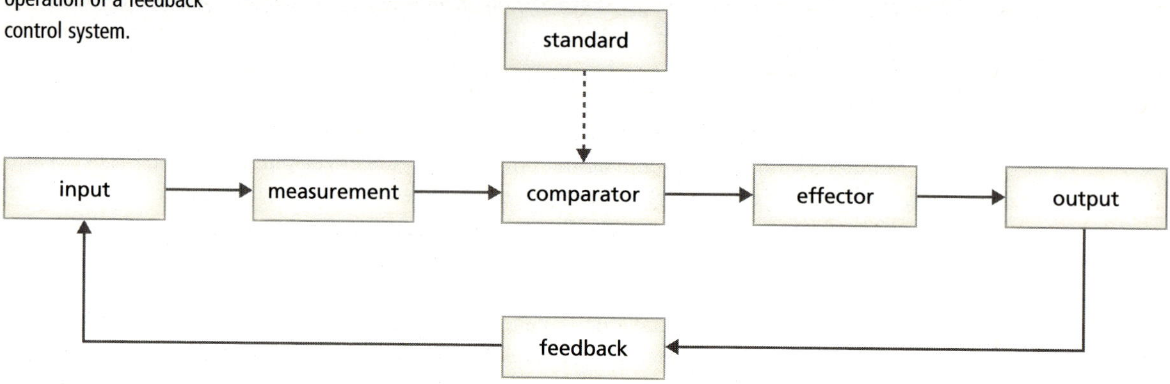

Figure 5.3: Elements of cybernetic feedback control

Consider a domestic heating control system. The temperature standard is set on a thermostat, and a heater (effector) starts to warm up the room. The output of the system is heated air. Changes in temperature are measured by a thermometer. The temperature of the room is continually compared with the standard. When the room reaches the required temperature, the effector is switched off, and when the room cools, it is switched on again.

The cybernetic analogy says that this control loop is a model of what goes on inside the mind. For standard, read motive, purpose, intent, or goals. The output is behaviour. The senses are our measuring devices. Our perceptual process is the comparator which organizes and imposes meaning on the sensory data which control behaviour in pursuit of our goals. We have some kind of internal representation or 'schema' of ourselves and our environment. This internal representation is used in a purposive way to determine our behaviour, and is also known as the individual's *perceptual world* (see Chapter 8).

We formulate plans to achieve our purposes. These plans are sets of mental instructions for guiding the required behaviour. Within the master plan (get an educational qualification) there are likely to be a number of subplans (submit essays on time; pass examinations; make new friends). The organization of our behaviour is hierarchical – a concept which is also seen in computer programs where routines and subroutines are 'nested' within each other.

World of Warcraft, world of learning

If your boss tells you to stop playing that computer game and get back to work or you're fired, you now have a good answer. It's not just a game. It's a training programme, and you are learning valuable business skills that will improve your performance at work. David Edery and Ethan Mollick (2008) argue that the skills required to succeed in computer games such as *World of Warcraft* or *The Sims* are also useful organizational and managerial capabilities. These include mental, social, and creative problem-solving skills. As well as developing persistence and competition, gaming promotes community-building, as users exchange ideas and game modifications ('mods').

Games are used by companies for product placement and advertising (advergames, adverworlds), and are now also used in corporate training programmes. Medical schools use game-like simulations to train surgeons, reducing their error rate. Google uses video games to turn visitors into voluntary employees, asking them to label the millions of images on the web which Google cannot identify on its own. Games are also used to reach new customers, build brands, recruit and develop new staff, and encourage creativity and experimentation.

Games are fun and motivational. Before it releases a new operating system, Microsoft asks staff to help debug it. The Microsoftees find this boring, and project managers spend a lot of time persuading them to do it. For Windows Vista, participation in debugging quadrupled when Microsoft created a game that awarded points for bug-testing and prizes for achieving goals. Now that you have read this, is it back to work, or back to the keyboard?

Intrinsic feedback information which comes from within, from the muscles, joints, skin, and other mechanisms such as that which controls balance.

Extrinsic feedback information which comes from our environment, such as the visual and aural information needed to drive a car.

We can also use information on how we are doing – feedback – to update our internal representation and to refine and adapt our plans. Feedback can either be self-generated or come from an external source: it can be either **intrinsic feedback** or **extrinsic feedback**.

Independent of the source and nature of the feedback, timing is also important. Feedback can arrive during, or after the behaviour in which we are interested in learning: it can be either **concurrent feedback** or **delayed feedback**.

STOP AND THINK From your own experience, identify an example of each of the four varieties of feedback. What changes in that feedback would be required for you to be able to improve your performance (on this course, at sport, whatever)?

Concurrent feedback information which arrives during our behaviour and which can be used to control behaviour as it unfolds.

Delayed feedback information which is received after a task is completed, and which can be used to influence future performance.

Intrinsic feedback is invariably concurrent. When you throw rings over pegs at the fair to win a soft toy, the intrinsic concurrent visual feedback means that you know immediately how well (or how badly) you are performing. Some extrinsic feedback is also concurrent: from a driving instructor, for example. However, for your next course assignment, feedback from your lecturer is going to be delayed. Instructors cannot provide concurrent feedback on your essay or project, but the longer the delay, the less effective the feedback is likely to be.

Feedback, rewards and punishments, and knowledge of results also have a *motivating* effect on behaviour, as well as a reinforcing effect. Several researchers argue that opportunities to learn new skills and knowledge, to understand more, to develop more effective ways of coping with our environment, are intrinsically motivating. The American psychologist Robert W. White (1959) suggests that we have a motive to develop 'competence' and that this gives us satisfaction. As the later section on the *learning organization* demonstrates, the 'urge towards discovery' and the 'will to understand' has triggered a search for novel organizational forms in which individual and organizational learning are encouraged.

Behaviourism in practice

Behaviourism led to the development of **behaviour modification** techniques, first used to treat mental and learning disorders, and phobias, and for psychiatric rehabilitation and accident and trauma recovery. These methods are now used in many organizational settings.

Fred Luthans (b.1939)

Behaviour modification a technique for encouraging desired behaviours and discouraging unwanted behaviours using operant conditioning.

As developed by Fred Luthans (Luthans and Kreitner, 1985; Luthans et al., 1998), organizational behaviour modification, or OBMod, has five steps:

1. *Identify* the critical, observable, and measurable behaviours to be encouraged.
2. *Measure* the current frequency of those behaviours, to provide a baseline against which to measure improvement.
3. *Establish* the triggers or antecedents for those behaviours, and also establish the consequences – positive, neutral, and negative – that follow from those behaviours.
4. *Develop* a strategy to strengthen desired behaviours and weaken dysfunctional behaviours through positive reinforcement (money, recognition) and feedback; punishment may be necessary in some cases, for example to inhibit unsafe behaviour.
5. *Evaluate* systematically the effectiveness of the approach in changing behaviour and improving performance compared with the original baseline measurement.

Behaviour modification is attractive to managers who can manipulate the reinforcement of employee behaviours, and the approach focuses on behaviour rather than on internal mental states and processes. Desirable behaviours include speaking politely to customers, attending training, helping colleagues, or, in a hospital, washing hands regularly to reduce infections. Undesirable behaviours include lateness, making poor-quality items, and being rude to customers. OBMod uses reinforcement to eliminate undesired behaviour and to encourage desired behaviour. Suppose a manager wants more work assignments completed on time, and fewer submitted beyond the deadline. The OBMod options are summarized in Table 5.4.

Table 5.4: Behaviour modification options

Procedure	Operationalization	Behavioural effect
Positive reinforcement	manager praises employee each time work is completed on schedule	increases desired work behaviour
Negative reinforcement	unpaid overtime continues to be mandatory until work is completed on schedule, then overtime is rewarded	increases desired work behaviour
Punishment	manager asks employee to stay late when work is not handed in on time	eliminates or decreases undesired behaviour
Extinction	manager ignores the employee when work is handed in late	eliminates or decreases undesired behaviour

Fred Luthans and colleagues (1998) describe how OBMod improved productivity in a Russian textile mill. For performance improvements, workers were given extrinsic rewards including American products such as adults' and children's clothing, jeans, T-shirts with popular logos, music tapes, and food that was difficult to get in Russia. They were also given 'social rewards' (attention, recognition, feedback) for specific actions, such as checking looms, undertaking

OBMod, MRSA and ICUs

Adverse events cost the UK health service £2 billion a year, and hospital-acquired infections cost a further £1 billion. Human error seems to be the main cause, but research shows that organization culture and management systems can encourage undesirable behaviour. Could behaviour modification techniques be used to improve patient safety?

Dominic Cooper and colleagues (2005) describe a hospital OBMod programme which aimed to reduce infections such as MRSA (methicillin-resistant *staphylococcus aureus*). The usual methods include screening, isolation, cleaning, monitoring, training, awareness-raising, and improved policies and protocols, but that wasn't enough to solve the problem. Two intensive care units (ICUs) were involved, employing 140 doctors, nurses, healthcare assistants, and administrative staff. The units had many visitors, including physicians, other hospital staff, and family members and friends. The programme focused on two behaviours. The first was hand-washing, to reduce the spread of infection; research shows that doctors wash their hands on less than 10 per cent of appropriate occasions. The second concerned the accuracy and completeness of nursing documents which record patient' conditions.

Staff were briefed on the aims and conduct of the programme, to engage them in problem-solving and in generating ideas (such as installing a sink at the entrance where visitors could wash before coming in). Staff were asked to identify their main concerns, and what they saw as the most common undesired behaviours. A project coordinator and eight observers were trained in behaviour modification methods: how to observe, how to give feedback, how to set improvement goals. A checklist of 36 desired behaviours was developed, so that observers could record compliance, which they did by standing at the central nursing station for 20 minutes at a randomly chosen time each day. Observation data were analysed weekly, posted on a feedback chart, and discussed in group feedback meetings.

The results showed significant changes in behaviour which along with other methods reduced MRSA infections by 70 per cent. With fewer MRSA patients, there was extra ICU capacity, reduced laboratory costs, less overtime and temporary staff costs, and reduced costs of complaints. These outcomes were attributed to motivation to provide quality care (goals), and to the weekly performance data (feedback) which let staff know that they were doing a good job. Apart from the time that staff spent training, observing, and in meetings, the programme costs came to only a few hundred pounds for clerical materials and cleaning items.

repairs, monitoring fabric quality, and helping others. This approach had a 'very positive impact' leading to 'highly significant increases in performance' (Luthans et al., 1998, p. 471). Asking the workers for ideas on how to improve performance got no response; the culture and political climate prevented them from making suggestions which would criticize methods and colleagues. Luthans concludes that OBMod 'fits' Eastern European organizational cultures where it has wide applicability.

OBMod has the following characteristics:

- It applies to clearly identifiable and observable behaviours, such as timekeeping, absenteeism, carrying out checks and repairs, and the use of particular work methods.
- Rewards are contingent on the performance of the desirable behaviours.
- Positive reinforcement can take a number of forms, from the praise of a superior to cash prizes, food, or clothing.
- Behaviour change and performance improvements can be dramatic.
- The desired modification in behaviour may only be sustained if positive reinforcement is continued (although this may be intermittent).

STOP AND THINK

How do you feel about being given food, T-shirts, and praise for working harder?

Do you regard this approach as practical, or as demeaning – and why?

Cognitive perspectives in practice

Socialization the process through which individual behaviours, values, attitudes, and motives are influenced to conform with those seen as desirable in a given social or organizational setting.

Albert Bandura (b.1925)

Behavioural modelling learning how to act by observing and copying the behaviour of others.

When people join an organization, they give up some personal freedom of action. That is part of the price of membership. Employees thus accept that an organization can make demands on their time and effort, as long as these demands are perceived to be legitimate. Other members of the organization have to teach new recruits what is expected of them. The process through which recruits are 'shown the ropes' is called **socialization**. Cognitive psychologists regard behaviour modification as simplistic, and turn to more complex social explanations and methods for organizational behaviour change.

This perspective draws on social learning theory which is based on assumptions about human psychology different from those behind OBMod techniques. One of the most influential advocates of social learning theory has been Albert Bandura (1977; 1986), who showed that we learn new behaviours by observing and copying others, through **behavioural modelling**. We copy the behaviour of others without the need for rewards or punishments to encourage us to do this. However, if the behaviours that we copy are successful (in other words, rewarded or reinforced by positive results), then we are more likely to continue to act in that way. Our capabilities for reflection and self-determination are central in this perspective. We construct, through observation and experience, internal models of our environment, and plan courses of action accordingly. The ways in which we model ourselves on others is particularly apparent in children, and we continue to copy or imitate others as adults.

Bandura's argument that we learn through social experience, through observation and modelling, does not deny the importance of reinforcement. Behavioural modelling involves the four processes of attention, retention, production, and reinforcement outlined in Figure 5.4. Suppose we choose to base some of our behaviours (how to handle a job interview, how to make new friends) on modelling ourselves on someone who is successful in those areas. Suppose that our new approach does not lead to the desired results – we don't get the job, we fail to establish relationships. Without reinforcement, we abandon those new behaviours and look for other models. If our new methods are successful, however, we will use them again.

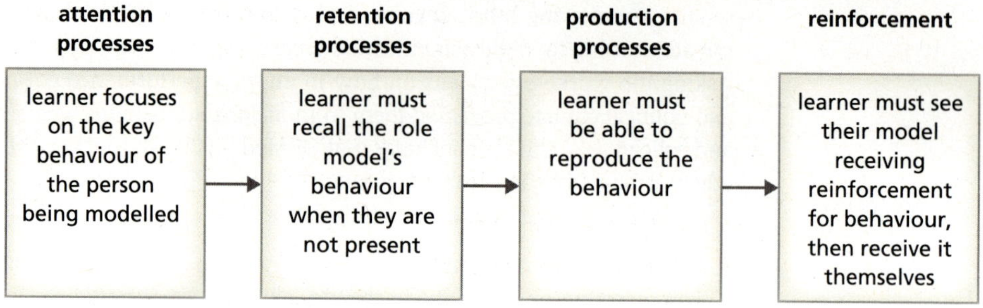

Figure 5.4: The behavioural modelling process
Source: Based on Weiss (1990).

Provisional selves from observing others, the experiments that we make with the ways in which we act and interact in new organizational roles.

When we get a new job, we have to learn how to 'fit in', and this means following the norms and rules that are considered to be appropriate in the organization and work group. From her study of financial analysts and consultants, Herminia Ibarra (1999; Ibarra and Barbulescu, 2010) shows how we adapt to new roles by experimenting with **provisional selves**, which are based on the role models that we see around us. This process, she found, has three stages:

observing we watch other people to see how they behave and respond

experimenting we try out some of those behaviours to see how they work for us

evaluating we use our own assessment and feedback from others to decide which behaviours to keep, and which to discard.

Our observations of role models in a new organizational setting can cover a wide range of issues; physical appearance, personal style, ways of interacting, displays of skill. This does not simply mean that we copy others. We choose the behaviours that we feel are credible, and consistent with how we see ourselves, and consistent with how we want others to see us; for example, as competent, creative, enthusiastic, trustworthy. We do this by experimenting, keeping those actions that we like, and discarding those that do not work, or which are inconsistent with our self-image. Comments from Ibarra's interviewees illustrate this:

> There are a good half dozen to a dozen senior people I'd view as mentors. I think up until director, you're building your skills, you're trying on different styles, like different clothes, almost. You try and figure out what styles fit your personality and fit what you're good at. And then that's how you should try to go after business. (p. 777)

> I've been out with X and watched him in action. He's very aggressive in new business – one of the best in the firm. He has a very charismatic personality, which is something you can't teach. I don't think I could really replicate his style. I'm not as outgoing, but I think the attitude and persistence are things that I have. (p. 775)

> I don't have an aggressive personality. I have been told I need to improve. I have adjusted to it by becoming more assertive over time. Just watching P was good. She is very vocal, asks lots of questions, always makes sure she has a point to make, is very assertive. Now I do like she does. (p. 780)

STOP AND THINK

Think of two people who you have observed recently – one a real person, the other a character in a movie or a television programme. How have they influenced you? Which of their behaviours have you adopted? How did that work out? What behaviours have you decided not to adopt, and why? For whom are you a role model in this way?

How does social learning theory apply to organizational settings? Organizations encourage different standards concerning

- what counts as good work performance;
- familiarity in social interactions at work;
- the amount of deference to show to superiors;
- dress and appearance;
- social activities after work;
- attitudes to work, colleagues, managers, unions, customers.

You have to learn these standards and the ways of behaving and related attitudes that they involve, to become an effective and accepted member of the organization. You do not have to believe that the organization's standards are appropriate. In order to 'fit in', what matters is that you behave *as if* you believe in those norms.

Home viewing

In the first half of *Full Metal Jacket* (1987, director Stanley Kubrick), unquestioning obedience from new recruits is demanded for membership of the US marines. In *Fight Club* (1999, director Peter Fincher), a similar level of compliance is required in order to join 'Project Mayhem'. As you watch these films, identify the different rules of membership in the two organizations. What learning processes are used to elicit conformity from members? What is the purpose of the oral intimidation to which they are exposed? How do these learning processes affect individuals' identities?

The socialization process can thus be informal. Often, newcomers learn the ropes just by watching their new colleagues. Socialization is thus achieved without planned intervention, by giving rewards such as praise, encouragement, and promotion for 'correct' behaviour. It is supported by negative reinforcements and punishments, like being ignored, ridiculed or fined for behaviour that is 'out of line'. We quickly learn what attitudes to take, what style of language to use, what 'dress code' to obey, where to take lunch and with whom, and so on. Some organizations have formal induction courses, but these are often brief, and focus on routine issues like organization structures and policies, and health and safety regulations.

STOP AND THINK

Remember when you first joined this college or university; how did you feel about the formal socialization or induction process? To what informal, unplanned socialization were you exposed? Which had the greater impact on your behaviour, the formal or the informal processes?

Note that some of the rewards are material: these include not just money, but also desirable working conditions such as bigger offices and desks, subsidized meals, access to free sports and leisure facilities, or a space in a car park. Other rewards, such as prestige, status, recognition and public praise, are symbolic and social.

Of course, organizations do not rely on socialization alone in order to equip employees with appropriate knowledge and skills. Most use a combination of other formal and informal learning and development methods. The Chartered Institute of Personnel and Development (2011, p. 7) surveyed employers to find out which methods were considered effective. The results are shown in Figure 5.5.

Managed socialization in action

Social learning theory argues that we learn correct behaviours through experience and through the examples or role models that other people provide. While this can happen naturally, some companies prefer not to leave it to chance, and to manage the process instead. For example, some companies use a 'buddy system', pairing new recruits with established employees. However, if you get a job with the American computer software company Trilogy, based in Austin, Texas, you will not be given a buddy, or a one-day induction by your new boss. Instead, you will be sent to Trilogy University (TU) for three months, to join an orientation programme modelled on Marine Corps basic training (Tichy, 2001). This is a 'boot camp', intense and intimidating, designed to challenge new recruits, most of whom are university graduates with an average age of 22. Trilogy wants to familiarize them with appropriate knowledge and job skills, and also with the company's 'vision and values'. Run twice a year, over twelve weeks, for between 60 and 200 recruits at a time, the boot camp has three stages.

Month one

New recruits are assigned to a section, of about 20 people, and to an instruction track. The section leader is an experienced Trilogy employee, and the tracks resemble work in the company. Along with functional training, the recruits are assessed on a series of increasingly challenging assignments, which mirror real customer problems, but with reduced timescales. Students are stretched beyond the point of failure in order to introduce company values including humility, creativity, innovation, teamwork, customer problem-solving, and risk-taking. Another goal is to develop lasting, trusting relationships with colleagues.

Month two

This is project month, and recruits are told that 'in order for the company to survive, they have to come up with a frame-breaking great new business idea'. Teams of three to five have to generate an idea, create a business model, build the product, develop a marketing plan, and present the results to the Chief Executive. These projects are real, and around 15 per cent are funded. Recruits are expected to learn about the need to set priorities, evaluate probabilities, and measure results. Failure to generate a successful idea is not punished.

Month three

Most recruits move on to business-related 'graduation projects', and leave TU as they find sponsors willing to take them on. Graduation involves a meeting with the recruit, the new manager, and the section leader, at which the recruit's abilities are reviewed, their personal career objectives are examined, and the manager's three- to five-year goals for the recruit (including further skill development) are agreed. Most graduates find a home in the company, but those few who cannot find a sponsor have to leave.

Since 1995, when TU was founded, projects developed by recruits have generated revenues of $25 million, and have formed the basis for $100 million in new business for the company. These innovative ideas include internet-based car retailing, and a website which allows shoppers to put products from several different internet retailers into a single purchase. In addition, the section leaders assigned for three months to inspire, motivate, mentor, and develop the new recruits develop their leadership and change agency skills.

	Learning and development methods
most effective ↑	in-house development programmes
	coaching by line managers
	on-the-job training
	job rotation, secondment, and shadowing
	coaching by external practitioners
	instructor-led training off the job
	action learning sets
	mentoring and buddying schemes
	internal knowledge-sharing events
	formal education courses
	external conferences, workshops, and events
	e-learning
least effective ↓	audio tapes, videos, and learning resources

Figure 5.5: Effectiveness of learning and development methods

It is interesting to note that organizations consider that their own internal methods are best: in-house development, management coaching, on-the-job training, and so on. Formal education is close to the bottom of this list. Also interesting is the position of what might be considered modern technology-based methods. Audio, video, e-learning and other resources are considered to be the least effective learning and development methods.

Behaviour modification versus socialization

Is behaviour modification a useful approach to learning at work and the development of appropriate behaviours? The evidence suggests a qualified 'yes'; there are two qualifications.

First, behaviour modification needs careful planning to identify specific behavioural goals, and procedures for reinforcing the behaviours that will achieve those goals. The method can be effective when behaviour and reinforcement are clearly identified and linked (e.g., wear your seat belt and we'll give you cash). The method is less effective when this relationship is vague (e.g., demonstrate your commitment and we will consider you for promotion).

Second, the 'rewards for good behaviour' method appears broadly consistent with American (and perhaps Eastern European) cultural values and aspirations. The transfer of this approach to other cultures is questionable. The most often cited practical examples are American.

STOP AND THINK You are responsible for training the new shelf-stacker in your local supermarket. What combination of behaviour modification and socialization techniques will you use, and how will you apply these?

Behaviour modification is manipulative, often ignores internal needs and intrinsic rewards, and can be a threat to individual dignity and autonomy. It can be seen as a simplistic and transparent attempt to manipulate, prompting cynicism rather than behaviour change. The technique thus has limitations. However, OBMod requires the communication of goals and expectations in unambiguous terms. Many would argue that such clarity is desirable. Fred Luthans and Robert Kreitner (1985) summarize the problems with behaviour modification:

1. Appropriate reinforcers may not always be available (for example, in limited and boring work settings).
2. We do not all respond in the same way to the same reinforcers; what one person finds rewarding may be of little consequence to someone else.
3. Once started, a behaviour modification programme has to be sustained.
4. There may not be enough extrinsic motivators (money and luncheon vouchers, for example) available.

They also argue, however, that the technique has made significant contributions:

1. Behaviour modification techniques put the focus on observable employee behaviour and not on hypothetical internal states.
2. The method shows how performance is influenced by outcomes that depend in turn on the individual's behaviour.
3. It supports the view that positive reinforcement is more effective in changing employee behaviour than punishment.
4. It is possible to show a clear causal link to performance, which is often hard to establish with other behaviour change methods such as job enrichment.

Social learning is dependent on the cultural context, and is a process rather than a specific technique. Socialization, in contrast is more flexibile. American socialization techniques, for example, may be quite different from Swedish, Belgian, Nigerian, Malaysian, or Spanish ones.

Socialization is a process that takes place anyway, planned or not. The issue concerns appropriate socialization, with respect to existing organization culture and behavioural preferences. Because it is a 'natural' process, with no clear financial or other material benefit from investing in its operation, it may be difficult to persuade management to give socialization the attention and resource that some commentators suggest. Table 5.5 summarizes the contrasts between behaviour modification and socialization.

Table 5.5: Behaviour modification versus socialization

Behaviour modification	Socialization
feedback needed in both approaches for behaviour to change	
planned procedure	naturally occurring, even if also planned
stimulus determines responses	individual needs determine responses
externally generated reinforcements	internally generated reinforcements
focuses on observable behaviour	focuses on unobservable internal states
focus on tangible rewards and punishments (money, other material rewards)	focus on intangible rewards and punishments (social inclusion, self-esteem)
clear links between desired behaviour and consequences	intangible links between desired behaviour and consequences
compliance required by external agent	conformity encouraged by social grouping

However, some organizations have introduced the methods of the learning organization, which we discuss below. This is an attempt to socialize an organization's members with respect to attitudes and behaviours related to the acquisition and development of new knowledge, creativity, innovation, flexibility and readiness for change.

Behavioural self-management

Behavioural self-management a technique for changing one's own behaviour by systematically manipulating cues, cognitive processes, and contingent consequences.

Management attempts to modify the behaviour of others raise ethical questions. Self-improvement, however, is acceptable and fashionable. Fred Luthans and Tim Davis (1979) developed the technique of **behavioural self-management** (BSM) for individual use.

BSM combines the behavioural focus of OBMod with the cognitive processes central to social learning theory. It is not merely a form of self-imposed behaviour modification. Social learning theory argues that we actively process stimuli and consequences, in a self-monitoring fashion, whereas behaviourism sees our behaviour shaped by rewards and punishments.

BSM involves the following steps (Kreitner et al., 1999):

1. *Identify the undesirable behaviour* that you want to change, develop, or improve.
2. *Manage the situational cues* which trigger desired behaviour. Avoid situations which trigger the target behaviour, and seek situations which encourage desired behaviour instead. Use 'reminders and attention focusers' such as notes stuck in prominent places, and 'self-observation data' recording success and lapses. Set personal contracts, establish behavioural goals, and post records of these in prominent places.
3. *Provide cognitive support* for the new behaviour. There are three ways to do this: first, through *symbolic coding*, using visual images and acronyms to support the desired

Learning organization an organizational form that enables individual learning to create valued outcomes, such as innovation, efficiency, environmental alignment, and competitive advantage.

behaviour (KISS, MBWA); second, through *mental rehearsal* of the desired behaviour (a technique used by many successful sports people); third, through *self-talk* which is positive and supportive of the desired behaviour change.

4. *Develop self-reinforcement* which is within your control and which is delivered only on condition that the desired behaviour change is achieved. This can be strengthened by arranging also for positive reinforcement from supportive friends and colleagues.

This web of situational cues, cognitive support, and self-reinforcement can be a powerful combination in helping to eliminate target behaviours and establish desired behaviours in their place. Using this technique, Rakos and Grodek (1984) report how American college students successfully modified behaviour problems concerning smoking, lack of assertiveness, poor study habits, overeating, sloppy housekeeping, lack of exercise, and moodiness. Luthans and Davis (1979) describe how the technique was used to deal with management behaviour problems such as overdependence on the boss, ignoring paperwork, leaving the office without notifying anybody, and failing to fill out expense reports.

Apply behavioural self-management

Apply behavioural self-management to yourself. Target a behaviour of current personal significance, such as drinking, smoking, overeating, excessive clubbing, or inappropriate study habits. Establish a pattern of situational cues, cognitive support, and self-reinforcement. Set a timescale, and use your experience to assess the power and relevance of this technique.

The learning organization

Chris Argyris (b.1923)

Donald Schön (1930–1997)

The concept of the learning organization is based on the work of Chris Argyris and Donald Schön (Argyris and Schön, 1974 and 1978; Argyris, 1982). This is an organization that helps individuals to learn and to perform more effectively.

The learning organization concept has become significant for several reasons:

- the production of goods and services increasingly involves sophisticated knowledge;
- knowledge is, therefore, as valuable a resource as raw materials;
- many organizations have lost knowledgeable staff through retirements and de-layering;
- information technologies are knowledge-intensive;
- some knowledge can have a short lifespan, and be made obsolete by innovation;
- flexibility, creativity, and responsiveness are now prized capabilities;
- knowledge can thus be a source of competitive advantage for an organization.

Ikujiro Nonaka and Hirotaka Takeuchi (1995) argue that the ability to create knowledge and solve problems is a 'core competence' for most organizations. For them, everyone is a knowledge worker. Anyone dealing with customers is a source of intelligence on customer perceptions of products, services, and pricing. These 'boundary workers' are often poorly paid (receptionists, porters, sales staff), and their customer intelligence is overlooked as their positions are distant, in terms of physical location and organization structure, from management.

Karl Weick and Frances Westley (1996, p. 440) argue that the concepts of 'organization' and 'learning' are contradictory. Organization implies structure, order, stability. Learning implies change, variety, disorganization. Management is concerned with best practice and consulting tools. The book by Peter Senge et al. (1999) includes an 'owner registration form', to return after indicating in tick boxes your interest in speakers, seminars, further materials, or hiring the authors as consultants.

Learning is the new sex (or should be)

When Barclays Bank set up its corporate university, it wanted to develop something different (Persaud, 2004). Paul Rudd, director of Barclays University (known as 'BU'), said 'Corporate universities are pretty ill-defined and many organizations just re-branded their training departments to make them sound sexier.' The company focus groups showed that employees were not 'engaged' either by attending training courses or by sitting at computer screens.

The bank set up leading edge 'metro centres' in existing bank buildings, but with a radically different environment. Each metro centre cost £1 million to establish, and typical features include

- background music
- café area
- high-tech training rooms
- Zen room in which to relax
- library
- 48-hour free ordering service for books, videos and CDs.

The libraries have books not on banking, but on subjects such as teaching children to read, t'ai chi, and anger management. The centres are open in the evenings, and also at weekends, when families are allowed to visit. Each of the bank's 65,000 staff has a £150 allowance to spend on anything that is related to learning. During the summer, the centres run courses, and there is a BU summer school for employees' children. Paul Rudd argues that

> We're trying to develop Barclays into an employer of choice. It's something more than working in a great environment. It's something you can involve your wife, husband, partner or children in, and it's a reason for not just coming to work but to develop through your work and through the opportunities at Barclays University.

He also says that 'learning is something we want people to see as sexy and something they want to do as opposed to being forced to do'. In other words, if learning isn't the new sex, then it should be.

STOP AND THINK

An organization doesn't exist without its members. How can an organization 'learn'?

Peter Senge (b.1947)

The idea of the learning organization was popularized by Peter Senge, whose book *The Fifth Discipline* (1990) was an international best-seller. Senge argues (1990, p. 4) that work at all levels must become more 'learningful', by applying the five 'learning disciplines' shown in Table 5.6.

Table 5.6: Five learning disciplines

Learning discipline	Explanation
1. Personal mastery	*aspiration*, concerning what you as an individual want to achieve
2. Mental models	*reflection and inquiry*, concerning the constant refinement of thinking and development of awareness
3. Shared vision	*collective commitment* to a common sense of purpose and actions to achieve that purpose
4. Team learning	*group interaction*, concerning collective thinking and action to achieve common goals
5. Systems thinking	*understanding interdependency and complexity* and the role of feedback in system development

Senge's argument is – have realistic goals, challenge your assumptions, commit to a shared vision, teamworking is good. The application of these 'disciplines', however, is problematic, and is linked to our discussion of socialization, to encouraging the 'correct' attitudes, values, and beliefs among employees at all levels. The most important learning discipline is 'the fifth discipline', systems thinking, which means understanding how complex organizations function, and how they can be changed to work more effectively. The theory is:

Organizational learning in Ireland

A survey of over 260 senior human resource managers in multinational companies in Ireland showed that over half had a formal policy to facilitate organizational learning across their global operations (Gunnigle et al., 2007). The most common learning methods were

- international informal networks
- international project groups
- expatriate assignments
- international formal committees
- international secondments to external organizations.

Over 60 per cent of multinational companies used more than three of these organizational learning methods, and only 15 per cent used none. American-owned multinationals, however, spent more on organizational learning than their British, European, or Irish competitors.

> [T]he practice of organizational learning involves developing tangible activities: new governing ideas, innovations in infrastructure, and new management methods and tools for changing the way people conduct their work. Given the opportunity to take part in these new activities, people will develop an enduring capability for change. The process will pay back the organization with far greater levels of diversity, commitment, innovation and talent. (Senge et al., 1999, p. 33)

In other words, the manager who wants commitment, flexibility and creativity from employees must provide them with lots of learning opportunities.

Is yours a learning organization?

A survey tool for deciding if you have a learning organization has been developed by David Garvin and colleagues (2008). They felt that while others had provided a compelling vision of the learning organization, they had not developed a practical approach to implementing the idea. The effective learning organization, they argue, has three building blocks. Here are the three blocks and their components, with a sample of the survey questions which employees are asked to rate in order to measure how well the learning organization functions.

Block 1: Supportive learning environment

psychological safety	'In this unit, it is easy to speak up about what is on your mind.'
appreciation of differences	'Differences in opinion are welcome in this unit.'
openness to new ideas	'In this unit, people are interested in better ways of doing things.'
time for reflection	'Despite the workload, people in this unit find time to review how the work is going.'

Block 2: Concrete learning processes and practices

experimentation:	'This unit experiments frequently with new ways of working.'
information collection	'This unit frequently compares its performance with that of competitors and best-in-class organizations.'
analysis	'This unit engages in productive conflict and debate during discussions.'
education and training	'In this unit, time is made available for education and training activities.'
information transfer	'This unit regularly shares information with networks of experts within and outside the organization.'

Block 3: Leadership that reinforces learning

'My managers invite input from others in discussion.'
'Managers acknowledge their limitations with respect to knowledge, information, or expertise.'
'My managers listen attentively.'

Source: Reprinted by permission of Harvard Business Review. *Adapted from 'Is yours a learning organization' by Garvin, D.A., Edmondson, A. and Gino, F., 86(3) 2008.*

These three blocks overlap with and reinforce each other, but measuring an organization's performance in each area identifies areas of excellence and opportunities for improvement.

Some commentators argue that a learning organization helps its members to learn. Others claim that the organization itself learns. How can this be? Silvia Gherardi (1997, p. 542) treats the term learning organization as a metaphor which regards an organization as a biological entity, as 'a subject which learns, which processes information, which reflects on experiences, which is endowed with a stock of knowledge, skills and expertise'.

Gherardi supports the view that organizations learn with experience, the proof lying with visible changes in an organization's behaviour. For example, in the development of manufacturing processes, the staff hours required to produce a unit of output decrease with accumulated experience, even though the staff change. Another example concerns the ways in which organizations evolve and adapt to 'fit' their environment, introducing internal structural changes in response to environmental opportunities and pressures.

Carlsberg puts learning on tap

Carlsberg shut its entire Leeds brewery for one day for staff to be given additional training. The move was designed to give health and safety advice to 170 staff at the Danish lager firm, update them on new technology and hold wellness and personal development sessions. Such a large-scale initiative marks a change of thinking for Carlsberg.

Natalie Steed, change manager, HR, told *People Management* (30 October 2008, p. 8) that 'Stopping production for training is rare in manufacturing, if not unprecedented. But feedback from staff told us it was what they wanted, and having all the trainers on site on a single day meant we could spend our training budget in the most effective way.'

Usually, training at the company is conducted in groups of eight people, which is as many as can be spared at any one time. Shutting the plant gave them time to go beyond the bare essentials, explained Steed. 'It's given us the time to carry out things we've always wanted to do – particularly around health and well-being – rather than just doing what we have to do', she said.

The day was a boost for learning at all levels. Engineers, who typically have high-level degrees, were given the chance to carry out a 'skills gap analysis' to identify areas to improve. It was also an opportunity to promote Carlsberg's new learning centre, where staff can pursue courses in numeracy, literacy, and basic IT skills. The learning day idea is now set to be repeated in Carlsberg's other UK brewery, in Northampton.

From People Management, *30 October 2008, p. 8.*

Organizations also have available to them several different types of knowledge, not all of which are dependent on individual expertise (Gherardi, 1997, p. 547). This includes learning from past experience through assessment and evaluation, and learning from the experience of other organizations. There is also knowledge 'built in' to equipment and raw materials, with formulae, ingredients, recipes, known properties, and so on. Standard operating procedures can usually be found in instruction manuals, forms, and job descriptions – all ways of codifying knowledge. Many organizations also possess patents and property rights.

Single-loop learning the ability to use feedback to make continuous adjustments and adaptations, to maintain performance at a predetermined standard.

Karl Weick and Frances Westley (1996) argue that organizational learning is best understood in terms of *organization culture*. Culture includes values, beliefs, feelings, artefacts, myths, symbols, metaphors, and rituals, which taken together distinguish one organization or group from others. Organizations are thus 'repositories of knowledge' independent of their members (Schön, 1983, p. 242). Organizations which accumulate stocks of codified, documented knowledge, independent of their members, can thus be said to learn.

Double-loop learning the ability to challenge and to redefine the assumptions underlying performance standards and to improve performance.

Weick and Westley (1996) note how different organizational forms are better equipped for learning. The post-modern organization described in Chapter 2 adapts to change in its environment in an innovative, creative, responsive manner. This is an organizational form associated with creative thinking and rapid learning, and has also been described as 'adhocracy'. Bureaucracy, on the other hand, is concerned with efficiency, division of labour, rigid chains of command, and clear distinctions and rationality.

How can 'organizational learning' be understood? Argyris and Schön (1974) developed the distinction between **single-loop learning** and **double-loop learning** (see Figure 5.6).

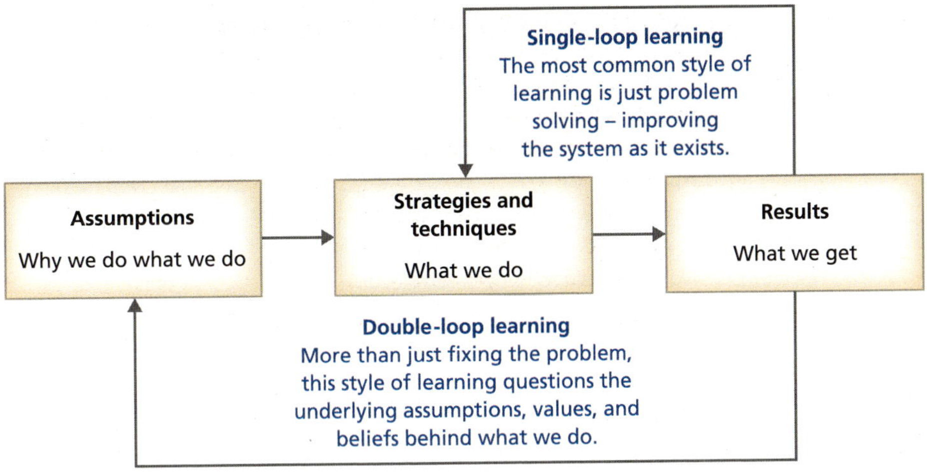

Figure 5.6: Single- and double-loop learning

Source: http://selfleadership.com/blog/topic/leadership/reflecting-and-learning-2009-to-2010/

The concept of single-loop learning comes from cybernetics, where control systems are designed around norms, standards, procedures, routines, and feedback. As previously discussed, the classic example of cybernetic control is the thermostat which, by detecting temperature variations, takes action to correct deviations from a set norm. In single-loop learning, the system maintains performance at that norm, and is unable to 'learn' that the norm is too high or too low. It cannot 'learn how to learn', to challenge and rethink its assumptions and values. Limited to making small-scale changes, single-loop learning is not really learning at all.

STOP AND THINK Let us assume that you are learning during your organizational behaviour course. Is this single-loop learning, or double-loop learning? Which of these two types of learning should you be engaged in?

Learning how to learn involves double-loop learning. This means challenging assumptions, beliefs, norms, routines, and decisions, rather than accepting them and working within those limitations. In single-loop learning, the question is, how can we better achieve that standard of performance? With double-loop learning, in contrast, the question becomes, is that an appropriate target in the first place? Mary Jo Hatch (1997, p. 372) observes:

> Double-loop learning, once strictly the domain of strategists and top managers, is increasingly being seen as taking place, or needing to take place, throughout organizations as they hire professionals and skilled technicians to help them adapt to the increasing rates of change they perceive as necessary to their survival. As double-loop learning diffuses, organizational stability is replaced by chaos and new organizational orders emerge from the internal dynamics of the organization rather than at the behest of top management.

Tacit knowledge knowledge and understanding specific to the individual, derived from experience, and difficult to codify and to communicate to others.

Explicit knowledge knowledge and understanding which is codified, clearly articulated, and available to anyone.

When we learn, we acquire knowledge – of organizational behaviour, gardening, guitar playing, accountancy, electrical engineering, and so on. Knowledge, however, is a difficult term to define clearly. For Nonaka and Takeuchi (1995), there are two types of knowledge, **tacit knowledge** and **explicit knowledge**.

Tacit knowledge includes insights, intuition, hunches, and judgements, and concerns the individual's unarticulated mental models and skills. Tacit knowledge tends to be personal, specific to particular contexts, and difficult to communicate. For example, if you are able to drive a car with a manual gear shift, then you will know where to position your foot to 'slip the clutch' and prevent the car from rolling on a slope. You will be able to move your foot

Oiling the wheels of knowledge management

Shell International Exploration and Production is a knowledge-intensive global oil company. A problem arising in Nigeria may have already been solved in the North Sea off the coast of Scotland. To put the people with the answers in touch with the people with problems, the company developed a knowledge management system (Carrington, 2002). 'New Ways of Working' has three web-based global networks dealing with sub-surface, surface, and wells knowledge. Each business group allows members to share their knowledge with 3,000 to 4,000 other members.

- When Shell Brazil wanted help to retrieve broken tools from a borehole, engineers asked colleagues in other countries for help. This exchange of ideas saved the well, and saved the company US$7 million.
- A manager in Shell Malaysia had problems shutting down a gas turbine. Searching for ideas in the archived material on the global network, he found that teams in Australia and America had already posted solutions.
- The Shell sales company in Singapore beat bigger rivals to a contract by using the global network to gain insights into the work which they and competitors had done with that client in the past.

This idea was expanded to eleven knowledge communities covering support functions, human resources, information technology, finance, and procurement. Each community has a coordinator responsible for controlling content and traffic flow, and encouraging people to contribute. If a particular question receives no answers, the coordinator attempts to find an expert in the area. Each community has developed a massive archive of knowledge which is used for personal development, problem-solving, and contacting those with specialist information and expertise. Total savings from this initiative were estimated in 2002 to be US$200 million, considering only those instances where savings could be quantified.

to that position, accurately and consistently, without much conscious thought. However, expect to run into difficulties when you try to explain this tacit skill to a learner driver.

Explicit knowledge on the other hand is articulated, codified, expressed, and available to anyone. Nonaka and Takeuchi argue that the Japanese emphasize tacit knowledge, while Westerners emphasize explicit, formal, codified knowledge. In Western cultures, tacit knowledge is undervalued because it is intangible and difficult to measure. However, tacit and explicit knowledge are complementary. Nonaka and Takeuchi are thus concerned with 'knowledge conversion' in which tacit knowledge is made available to the organization, on the one hand, and organizational knowledge becomes the individual's tacit knowledge, on the other (Nonaka, Umemoto and Sasaki, 1999).

Table 5.7 summarizes the main positive and negative aspects of the learning organization, and its related concepts of intellectual capital and knowledge management. Organizational learning is related to, but is different from, knowledge management (Rajan et al., 1999).

Knowledge management the conversion of individual tacit knowledge into explicit knowledge so that it can be shared with others in the organization.

Knowledge management concerns turning individual learning into organizational learning. Amin Rajan and colleagues (1999) describe how some organizations have developed 'intelligent search engines'. These are technology-based systems which facilitate access to expertise by creating a catalogue of specialists, each with their own web site on the company intranet. The number of times somebody's expertise is used can be monitored and used to influence pay and promotion decisions (Rajan et al., 1999, p. 6).

Knowledge management tends to be distinguished from the learning organization concept by the focus on information technology and on the development of online databases. Company buyers and their suppliers have much better information and forecasts on which to base purchasing and delivery decisions. Zeneca Pharmaceuticals has developed a system called Concert, to bring together information on new drug discoveries and licences in a highly competitive sector. Managers around the company are responsible for identifying relevant knowledge, and for putting it into the system (Coles, 1998). Harry Scarbrough (1999), however, is critical of the emphasis on technological solutions, which overlook the ways in which people develop, use, and communicate knowledge as part of their working activity.

The concepts of the learning organization and knowledge management are still fashionable. This popularity has been reinforced by the growth of knowledge work, by the realization

Table 5.7: Learning organization positives and negatives

learning organization positives	learning organization negatives
a rich, multi-dimensional concept affecting many aspects of organizational behaviour	a complex and diffuse set of practices, difficult to implement systematically
an innovative approach to learning, to knowledge management, and to investing in intellectual capital	an attempt to use dated concepts from change management and learning theory, repackaged as a management consulting project
a new set of challenging concepts focusing attention on the acquisition and development of individual and corporate knowledge	a new approach for encouraging employee compliance with management directives in the guise of 'self-development'
an innovative approach to organization, management, and employee development	an innovative approach to strengthening management control over employee behaviour
innovative use of technology to manage organizational knowledge through databases and the internet or intranets	a technology-dependent approach which ignores how people actually develop and use knowledge in organizations

that ideas generate competitive advantage, and by technological developments. However, there are barriers to the implementation of these ideals, and it will be interesting to observe whether they remain fashionable in the second decade of the twenty-first century.

RECAP

1. *Explain the characteristics of the behaviourist and cognitive approaches to learning.*
   - Behaviourism argues that we learn chains of muscle movements. As mental processes are not observable, they are not considered valid issues for study.
   - Cognitive psychology argues that we learn mental structures. Mental processes are important, and they are amenable to study although they cannot be observed.
   - In behaviourist theory, feedback contributes to learning by providing reinforcement; in cognitive theory, feedback provides information and is motivational.
2. *Explain and evaluate the technique of behaviour modification.*
   - Respondent (or Pavlovian, or classical) conditioning is a method by which an established response (good work performance) is associated with a new stimulus (supervisory encouragement).
   - Operant (or Skinnerian, or instrumental) conditioning is a method by which a behaviour (good work performance) is associated with a new consequence (bonus payment).
   - Positive reinforcement, negative reinforcement, punishment, and extinction condition the target by manipulating the consequences of desirable and undesirable behaviours.
   - Behaviour modification works well when rewards are linked clearly to specific behaviours, but does not work well when these links are ambiguous and vague; this manipulative approach may not be acceptable in some cultures.
3. *Explain the socialization process, and assess the practical relevance of this concept.*
   - Social learning theory argues that we learn values, beliefs, and behaviour patterns through experience, observation, and modelling.
   - Socialization can be informal – this happens anyway – or it can be formally organized through induction and training programmes.
4. *Explain and evaluate the technique of behavioural self-management.*
   - Behavioural self-management involves identifying the behaviour you want to change, altering the situational cues which trigger that behaviour, and establishing support and reinforcement for your new behaviour.

→

5. *Describe features of knowledge management and the learning organization.*
   - A learning organization is characterized by its approach to strategy, to environmental scanning, to the use of information, to the creation of learning opportunities, and to the creation of structures that are flexible and enable employee learning, in contrast to rigid bureaucratic organizations in which learning is the employee's responsibility.
   - The learning organization concept became popular as managers recognized the strategic need for more highly skilled and trained, flexible, and creative workforces.
   - Knowledge management is a technology-based technique for making tacit knowledge available more widely, typically through individual and corporate databases which can be accessed through the organization's intranet.

Revision

1. What part do feedback and reinforcement play in the cognitive and behaviourist approaches to learning?
2. Describe and illustrate the technique of organizational behaviour modification, and identify the advantages and disadvantages of this technique.
3. Why are positive and negative reinforcement more effective than punishment? In what circumstances can punishment be effective in changing behaviour?
4. What are the advantages and disadvantages of the learning organization in practice, first from a management perspective, and then from an employee perspective? Why should there be any difference between these viewpoints?

Research assignment

Review your understanding of social learning theory, behaviour modelling, and the concept of provisional selves. How do these approaches explain the ways in which new employees learn about the organization and their job? Interview a manager, a supervisor or team leader, and a front-line employee in an organization of your choice. Find out how each of those three individuals learned about the organization and their work when they first joined (and/or when they moved to a new job in another part of the organization). Collect examples of behaviour modelling, and of their experiments with provisional selves. How effective were those methods in helping the new employee to 'fit in'? What other methods and sources of information did those individuals use in order to help them to 'fit in'? From this evidence, what are the strengths and limitations of behaviour modelling and provisional selves as an explanation of how new employees are socialized by organizations?

Springboard

Chris Argyris (1982) *Reasoning, Learning, and Action*, Jossey-Bass, San Francisco. Classic text on the nature of individual and organizational learning.

Thomas H. Davenport (2005) *Thinking for a Living: How to Get Better Performance and Results from Knowledge Workers*, Harvard Business School Press, Boston, MA. Argues that knowledge workers have motives, attitudes, and needs for autonomy that require a new management style if their high performance is to be achieved and maintained.

David Edery and Ethan Mollick (2008) *Changing the Game: How Video Games Are Transforming the Business World*. Financial Times Prentice Hall, Harlow, Essex. Explores multiple business applications of computer games, and allows you to justify playing games at work.

Amy C. Edmondson (2010) *Teaming: How Organizations Learn, Innovate, and Compete in the Knowledge Economy*, Jossey-Bass, San Francisco. Argues that team learning is the key to organizational learning. Factors preventing team learning include fear of failure, groupthink, power structures, and information hoarding. Leaders can help by encouraging reflection, psychological safety, and encouraging the sharing of ideas. Illustrated with case studies from Bank of America, Children's Hospital, and Verizon.

OB in films

A Clockwork Orange (1971 and 2000, director Stanley Kubrick), DVD track (scene) 19: 1:06:57 to 1:11.40 (5 minutes). Clip begins with doctor introducing herself: 'Good morning. My name is Dr Branom.' Clip ends with Dr Branom (played by Madge Ryan) saying 'Dr Brodski is pleased with you. You've made a very positive response.'

This movie is based in a future a totalitarian state in which the Droog (thug) Alex (played by Malcolm McDowell) is subjected to aversion therapy to cure him of his addiction to violence, rape, drugs, and classical music. Fiction? Aversion therapy was used to 'treat' homosexuals in the 1960s. It was an extremely violent film for its time, and Kubrick removed it from circulation in 1974 when it was accused of triggering copycat crimes. The film was re-released on the anniversary of Kubrick's death, in 2000. In this clip (which contains violence and nudity):

1. To what conditioning and reinforcement regime is Alex subjected?
2. How effective is this in changing his behaviour?
3. Does society have a moral right to interfere with individual behaviour in this way?

OB on the web

To see how reflexes can be conditioned, and to find out how easy or how difficult this can be, play the game of *Pavlov's Dog* at http://www.nobelprize.org/educational/medicine/pavlov/about.html.

Can you identify examples of ways in which your own behaviour has been conditioned by this kind of approach? Can you identify how the behaviour of other people whom you know may have been conditioned in this way?

CHAPTER EXERCISES

1. Reinforcement and behaviour

Objective To examine the effects of positive and negative reinforcement on behaviour change.

This exercise takes about half an hour, and although it can be used with any size of group, it works particularly well with large classes (Marcic, 1995, pp. 61–3 and 122–3).

Exercise overview Two or three volunteers will receive reinforcement from the rest of the class while performing a simple task. The volunteers leave the room while the class is being briefed.

→

The instructor identifies an object which the student volunteers must find when they return to the room. This object should be unobtrusive, but it should be clearly visible to the class: a piece of paper stuck to the wall, a briefcase or bag in the corner, a mark on the wall.

The instructor specifies the reinforcement regime that will apply when each of the volunteers comes back into the room.

Negative reinforcement regime: the class will hiss, boo, make sarcastic comments, and throw harmless items at the first volunteer when they are moving away from the chosen object, and sit silently when they are moving towards it.

Positive reinforcement regime: the class will smile, cheer, applaud, and make encouraging comments with compliments when the second volunteer is moving towards the chosen object, and sit silently when they move away.

Combined reinforcement regime: the class will cheer when the third volunteer approaches the object, and boo when they move away from it.

Nominate one student to record the time that it takes each of the volunteers to find the object.

Exercise sequence

1. The first volunteer is brought back into the room, and instructed: Your task is to find and touch a particular object in the room. The class will help you, but you cannot ask questions, and they cannot speak to you. The first volunteer continues to look for the object until it is found, with the class giving negative reinforcement.
2. The second volunteer is brought back into the room, and is given the same instruction, to look for the object, with the class giving positive reinforcement.
3. The third volunteer is brought back into the room, and is instructed to find the object with the class giving a combination of negative and positive reinforcement.

Class discussion

- Ask the volunteers how they each felt during this exercise. What were their emotional responses to the different kinds of reinforcement they received?
- What effects did the different reinforcement regimes have on the behaviour of the volunteers?
- Which reinforcement regime do you think is most common in today's organizations? What are the likely effects on motivation and productivity?

2. Branto Bakery

Branto Bakery is a large company producing a range of bakery products for the major supermarkets. Analysis by the human resources department has revealed that the sales and administration departments have the highest rates of absenteeism and latecoming. Interestingly, each of these departments also has individuals with the best absence and timekeeping records. The managing director has asked the two department heads to address these absence and timekeeping problems. Alan Anderson, head of sales, has decided to adopt a behaviour modification approach. Barbara Brown, head of administration, has chosen to develop a socialization approach with current and new staff. You have been asked to advise one of them, as an external management consultant:

1. Design either a behaviour modification programme for Anderson, or a socialization plan for Brown, that will reduce absenteeism and improve timekeeping in their departments.
2. Explain the elements of your plan, how it will address these problems, and how it will be implemented.
3. Assess the strengths and weaknesses of your plan in the short term, and in the long term.

Employability assessment

With regard to your future employment prospects:

1. Identify up to three issues from this chapter that you found significant.
2. Relate these to the competencies in the employability matrix.
3. Decide what actions you need to take to maintain and/or develop those competencies under each of the four headings of the employability matrix.

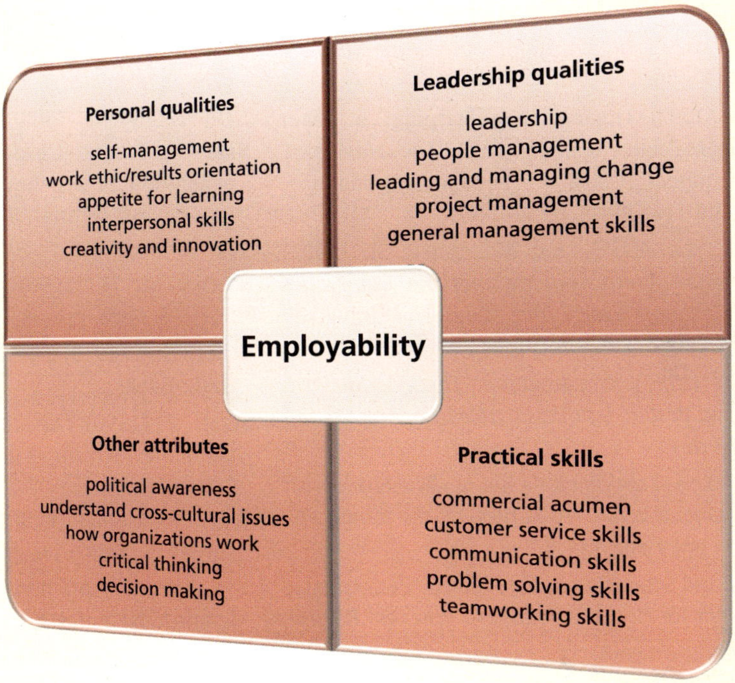

References

Argyris, C. (1982) *Reasoning, Learning, and Action*, San Francisco: Jossey-Bass.

Argyris, C. and Schön, D. (1974) *Theory in Practice*, San Francisco: Jossey-Bass.

Argyris, C. and Schön, D. (eds) (1978) *Organizational Learning: A Theory of Action Perspective*, Cambridge, MA: Addison-Wesley.

Bandura, A. (1977) *Social Learning Theory*, Englewood Cliffs, NJ: Prentice Hall.

Bandura, A. (1986) *Social Foundations of Thought and Action: A Social Cognitive Theory*, Englewood Cliffs, NJ: Prentice Hall.

Boddy, D. (2010) *Management: An Introduction* (5th edn), Harlow, Essex: Financial Times Prentice Hall.

Carrington, L. (2002) 'Oiling the wheels', *People Management*, 8(13), pp. 31–4.

Chartered Institute of Personnel and Development (2011) *Learning and Talent Development: Annual Survey Report 2010*, London: Chartered Institute of Personnel and Development.

Coles, M. (1998) 'Unlock the power of knowledge', *The Sunday Times*, 20 September, section 7, p. 28.

Cooper, D., Farmery, K., Johnson, M., Harper, C., Clarke, F.L., Holton, P., Wilson, S., Rayson, P. and Bence, H. (2005) 'Changing personnel behavior to promote quality care practices in an intensive care unit', *Therapeutics and Clinical Risk Management*, 1(4), pp. 321–32.

Davenport, T.H. (2005) *Thinking for a Living: How to Get Better Performance and Results from Knowledge Workers*, Boston, MA: Harvard Business School Press.

Dixon, N.M. (1999) *The Organizational Learning Cycle: How We Can Learn Collectively* (2nd edn), Aldershot: Gower.

Edery, D. and Mollick, E. (2008) *Changing the Game: How Video Games Are Transforming the Business World*, Harlow, Essex: Financial Times Prentice Hall.

Ferster, C.S. and Skinner, B.F. (1957) *Schedules of Reinforcement*, New York: Appleton-Century-Crofts.

Fogg, B.J. (2009) 'The new rules of persuasion', *RSA Journal*, Spring, pp. 24–8.

Garvin, D.A., Edmondson, A. and Gino, F. (2008) 'Is yours a learning organization?', *Harvard Business Review*, 86(3), pp. 109–16.

Gherardi, S. (1997) 'Organizational learning', in Arndt Sorge and Malcolm Warner (eds), *The Handbook of Organizational Behaviour*, London: International Thomson Business Press, pp. 542–47.

Gunnigle, P., Lavelle, J. and McDonnell, A. (2007) *Human Resource Practices in Multinational Companies in Ireland: A Large-Scale Survey*, Limerick: University of Limerick Employment Relations Research Unit.

Hatch, M.J. (1997) *Organization Theory: Modern, Symbolic and Postmodern Perspectives*, Oxford: Oxford University Press.

Hindle, T. (2006) 'Thinking for a living', *The Economist, The New Organization: A Survey of the Company*, 21 January, pp. 9 and 12–14.

Hinkin, T.R. and Schriesheim, C.A. (2009) 'Performance incentives for tough times', *Harvard Business Review*, 87(3), p. 26.

Ibarra, H. (1999) 'Provisional selves: experimenting with image and identity in professional adaptation', *Administrative Science Quarterly*, 44(4), pp. 764–91.

Ibarra, H. and Barbulescu, R. (2010) 'Identity as narrative: prevalence, effectiveness, and consequences of narrative identity work in macro work role transitions', *Academy of Management Review*, 35(1), pp. 135–54.

Kreitner, R., Kinicki, A. and Buelens, M. (1999) *Organizational Behaviour*, London: McGraw-Hill.

Luthans, F. and Davis, T.R.V. (1979) 'Behavioural self-management: the missing link in managerial effectiveness', *Organizational Dynamics*, 8(1), pp. 42–60.

Luthans, F. and Kreitner, R. (1985) *Organizational Behaviour Modification and Beyond* (2nd edn), Glenview, IL: Scott, Foresman.

Luthans, F., Stajkovic, A., Luthans, B.C. and Luthans, K.W. (1998) 'Applying behavioural management in Eastern Europe', *European Management Journal*, 16(4), pp. 466–74.

Marcic, D. (1995) *Organizational Behavior: Experiences and Cases* (4th edn), St Paul, MN: West Publishing.

Nonaka, I. and Takeuchi, H. (1995) *The Knowledge Creating Company*, New York: Oxford University Press.

Nonaka, I., Umemoto, K. and Sasaki, K. (1999) 'Three tales of knowledge-creating companies', in Georg von Krogh, Johan Roos and Dirk Kleine (eds), *Knowing in Firms: Understanding, Managing and Measuring Knowledge*, London: Sage Publications, pp. 146–72.

Persaud, J. (2004) 'Higher return', *People Management*, 10(7), pp. 40–1.

Rajan, A., Lank, E. and Chapple, K. (1999) *Good Practices in Knowledge Creation and Exchange*, London: Focus/London Training and Enterprise Council.

Rakos, R.F. and Grodek, M.V. (1984) 'An empirical evaluation of a behavioural self-management course in a college setting', *Teaching of Psychology*, October, pp. 157–62.

Scarbrough, H. (1999) 'System error', *People Management*, 8 April, pp. 68–74.

Schön, D.A. (1983) *The Reflective Practitioner*, New York: Basic Books.

Senge, P. (1990) *The Fifth Discipline: The Art and Practice of the Learning Organization*, New York: Doubleday Currency.

Senge, P., Kleiner, A., Roberts, C., Ross, R., Roth, G. and Smith, B. (1999) *The Dance of Change: The Challenges of Sustaining Momentum in Learning Organizations*, London: Nicholas Brealey.

Syedain, H. (2008) 'Keyboard directors', *People Management*, 14(12), pp. 34–6.

Tichy, N.M. (2001) 'No ordinary boot camp', *Harvard Business Review*, 79(1), pp. 63–70.

Walters, C.C. and Grusek, J.E. (1977) *Punishment*, San Francisco, CA: Freeman.

Weick, K.E. and Westley, F. (1996) 'Organizational learning: affirming an oxymoron', in S.R. Clegg, C. Hardy and W.R. Nord (eds), *Handbook of Organization Studies*, London: Sage Publications, pp. 440–58.

Weiss, H.M. (1990) 'Learning theory and industrial and organizational psychology', in M.D. Dunnette and L.M. Hough (eds), *Handbook of Industrial and Organizational Psychology*, Palo Alto, CA: Consulting Psychologists Press, pp. 75–169.

White, R.W. (1959) 'Motivation reconsidered: the concept of competence', *Psychological Review*, 66(5), pp. 297–333.

Wiener, N. (1954) *The Human Use of Human Beings: Cybernetics and Society*, New York: Avon Books.

Chapter 6 **Personality**

Key terms

personality
psychometrics
chronotype
type
trait
nomothetic
big five
Type A personality
Type B personality
idiographic
self-concept
generalized other
unconditional positive regard
thematic apperception test
need for achievement
projective test
reliability
predictive validity

Learning outcomes

When you have read this chapter, you should be able to define those key terms in your own words, and you should also be able to:

1. Distinguish between type, trait, and self theories of personality.
2. Identify the strengths and limitations of formal methods of personality assessment.
3. Explain the uses and limitations of objective questionnaires and projective tests as measures of personality.
4. Explain the relationship between personality and stress, and identify appropriate individual and organizational stress management strategies.
5. Evaluate the benefits and problems of psychometric assessment as a tool to assist management decision-making, particularly in selection.
6. Assess realistically the main characteristics of your own personality.

Why study personality?

Latin roots

per sonare	to speak through
persona	an actor's mask; a character in a play
persona grata	an acceptable person
persona non grata	an unacceptable person

Personality the psychological qualities that influence an individual's characteristic behaviour patterns, in a stable and distinctive manner.

Psychometrics the systematic testing, measurement, and assessment of intelligence, aptitudes, and personality.

Who are you? How do you describe yourself? How do you differ from others? How can we define and measure those characteristics and differences? Psychology answers these questions using the concept of **personality**. It is widely believed that personality is related to job performance and career success, so personality assessment is a widely used selection tool. Most of us believe that we are 'a good judge of character'. Even without a formal personality assessment, you are unlikely to get that job unless 'your face fits'. What are the foundations of personality assessments, or **psychometrics**, and what value are they?

The use of online testing, particularly for graduates, is now widespread, and an internet search for 'psychometrics' will take you to numerous sites. In this chapter, we explain two approaches to personality assessment: *nomothetic* and *idiographic*. Nomothetic approaches form the basis for most contemporary psychometrics. These are usually based on 'tick box' questionnaires, which are easy to administer and to score. The open-ended questions used by idiographic methods to capture an individual's unique characteristics take up more time, and are more difficult to score and to interpret. Nomothetic techniques appear to be more objective and quantitative. However, idiographic techniques rely on different assumptions about human psychology. It is on the validity of these assumptions that our judgements of different methods should be based, and not simply on matters of operational convenience.

The term psychometrics covers a range of assessments and measurements of aptitude, intelligence, integrity, and personality. An entire industry has developed, devoted to designing and supplying personality assessments which many organizations now use as part of their staff selection, development, and promotion procedures.

When measuring aspects of aptitude or intelligence, we can use the term 'test', because for those characteristics, a high score is usually better than a low score. When measuring personality, however, it is more appropriate to use the term 'assessment'. There are no 'correct' answers in a personality assessment, and so a high score on one factor (extraversion, for example) cannot be said to be better or worse than a low score. In addition to selecting job applicants, psychometric assessment has several other applications:

- assessment of suitability for promotion;
- assessment for redeployment purposes;
- evaluation of training potential;
- team and leadership development;
- career counselling and development;
- graduate recruitment, for applicants with limited work experience;
- vocational guidance;
- redundancy counselling.

Psychometrics often complement less formal and more subjective methods, to help managers reach better informed and objective judgements about people. However, psychometrics have been criticized for being unfair and misleading in gender and cultural terms, as well as being poor predictors of performance. Should you wish to improve your scores, or even to 'cheat' on a forthcoming assessment, you will find several 'how to' websites and popular psychology books on psychometrics and personality assessment to help you do that.

Oops!: is there an 'accident-prone' personality?

The luxury cruise liner *Costa Concordia* ran aground off the Tuscany coast in January 2012. Discussing incidents like this, Adrian Furnham (2012) identifies six personality factors that can make some people (such as a ship's captain) more prone to accidents than others:

defiant (rather than compliant)	defiant individuals have problems with authority, they don't like being told what to do, which makes them accident-prone
panicky (rather than strong)	in a crisis, the person who is cool and confident can prevent others from panicking and making mistakes
irritable (rather than cheerful)	people who are easily upset, get depressed and lose their tempers can annoy those around them and become indecisive
distractible (rather than vigilant)	people who get bored quickly are inattentive, and more likely to make mistakes; vigilance is needed to avoid accidents
reckless (rather than cautious)	some people just don't listen to warnings
arrogant (rather than self-confident)	arrogant individuals are less willing to learn and more likely to make bad decisions – but overconfident people don't listen to others either.

You may want to avoid working (and sailing) with people who are defiant, panicky, irritable, easily distracted, reckless, and arrogant. Watch the news for stories about people involved in 'high-profile' accidents. The press often describe their characters; do they fit this profile?

Gregorio Borgia/PA Photos

Costa Concordia cruise liner aground off the Tuscany coast, January 2012

Defining personality

The concept of personality underpins psychology's attempt to identify our unique characters and to measure and understand differences between individuals. Personality describes aspects of behaviour which are stable and enduring, and which distinguish the individual from others. Using the term personality in this way assumes that behaviour does have stable features, and does not change frequently, and that those distinctive properties can somehow be measured.

Personality theory deals with behaviour patterns that are consistent in different contexts, and over time. We are less interested in behaviours that are occasional and transient. Mood swings and related behaviours caused by illness, or the consumption of drugs, are not stable and are thus not regarded as personality characteristics, unless they become permanent. However, there is a problem here. Personality does appear to be flexible. The manager who is loud and autocratic in the office can be a caring and supporting parent at home. The 'stable' behaviours which we exhibit depend, in part, on social context. Some personality features (as with allergies) may only appear in specific social and physical conditions.

Personality theory is concerned with the pattern of dispositions and behaviours unique to the individual, and is less concerned with properties that all or most other people share. You may be aggressive towards waiters, friendly with librarians, deferential to professors, and terrified of mice. You may share some of these dispositions with a friend who breeds mice.

Some psychologists argue that personality is largely inherited, determined by genetics and the biochemistry and physiology of the brain. Evidence suggests, for example, that because measures of job satisfaction are fairly stable over time and across jobs, a predisposition to be content or frustrated at work may have a genetic component. From this perspective, your personality is fixed at birth, if not before, and life's experiences do little to alter it.

Others argue that our characters are shaped by environmental, cultural and social factors, that our feelings and behaviour patterns are learned. Social learning theory argues that we acquire new behaviours by observing and imitating others. Motivation theory demonstrates how job satisfaction can be influenced by changes in supervisory style and the design of jobs. Every society has distinctive ways of doing things. We cannot possibly be born with this local knowledge. In this perspective, your personality is flexible, changing with experience. Psychological wellbeing may indeed depend on such adaptability.

Source: www.CartoonStock.com

The controversy over the relative effects of heredity and environment on personality is known as the 'nature/nurture' debate. Few psychologists if any now hold the extreme positions set out here. Both genetic *and* situational factors influence behaviour. Theorists disagree over the emphases to be given to these factors, how they should be measured, and how they interact. During the 1960s and 1970s, 'nurture' was the position in vogue. Since the 1990s, biological and genetic evidence have moved thinking in the direction of 'nature'. Steven Pinker (2002) offers a scathing criticism of the view that the mind is a 'blank slate' inscribed by our environment and our experiences, arguing for an innate human nature, based on evidence from evolutionary biology, genetics, and neurophysiology.

Chronotype a cluster of personality traits that can affect whether someone is more active and performs better in the morning or in the evening.

These debates have implications for organizational behaviour. There are many situations in which we want to be able to *explain* behaviour, and personality can give us clues. However, there are also settings where it is important to be able not just to explain, but also to *predict* behaviour. Prediction is particularly important with job selection and promotion. Can personality assessment help us to make better predictions about someone's job performance?

Types and traits

Are you a morning person or a night owl – and does it matter?

Christoph Randler (2010) argues that those who are most energetic and proactive in the morning (and who get up early) are more likely to have successful careers than those who are at their best in the evening. You might be able to adjust your **chronotype** with training, but Randler argues that it is difficult to make major changes. His research on university students showed that morning people, on average, tend to

- get better grades in school and go to better colleges
- have better job opportunities
- anticipate and try to minimize problems
- perform better at work
- have greater career success and higher wages.

The typical personality traits associated with these chronotypes are:

morning people	evening people
agreeable	creative
optimistic	intelligent
stable	humorous
proactive	extraverted
conscientious	pessimistic
satisfied with life	neurotic and depressed

Source: Reprinted by permission of Harvard Business Review. Adapted from 'The early bird really does catch the worm' by Randler, C., 88(7/8) 2010.

Evening people can be smart, creative, funny, and outgoing, but Randler notes that 'they're out of sync with the typical corporate schedule'. Most organizational timetables are tailored to morning types. The evidence suggests that the population is evenly split between morning and evening types, but after age 50, most become morning types.

Is your chronotype geared for career success? If not, what can you do about that?

Type a descriptive label for a distinct pattern of personality characteristics, such as introvert, extravert, or neurotic.

Descriptions of the components and structure of personality have focused on the concepts of **type** and **trait**. One of the most straightforward ways of describing and analysing personality concerns the categorization of people into personality **types**.

One of the first personality theorists was Hippocrates ('the father of medicine'), who lived in Greece around 400 BC. He claimed that personality type or 'temperament' was determined by bodily 'humours', generating the different behaviour patterns shown in Table 6.1.

Table 6.1: Hippocrates' type theory of personality

body humour	temperament or type	behaviours
blood	sanguine	confident, cheerful, optimistic, hopeful, active
phlegm	phlegmatic	sluggish, apathetic
black bile	melancholic	depressed, sad, brooding, prone to ill-founded fears
yellow bile	choleric	aggressive, excitable, irritable

Hippocrates (450–370 BC)

These temperament labels are still in use today, with the same meanings. Hippocrates' theory, however, is unsound for two reasons. First, evidence concerning the relationships between body chemistry and behaviour does not confirm the theory. Second, our personal experience suggests that there are more than four types of people in the world.

William H. Sheldon (1898–1970)

William Sheldon (1942) argued that temperament was related to physique, which he called *somatotype*. Your personality type thus depends on your 'biological individuality', your body size and shape (and perhaps on how many hamburgers you eat). His typology is shown in Figure 6.1.

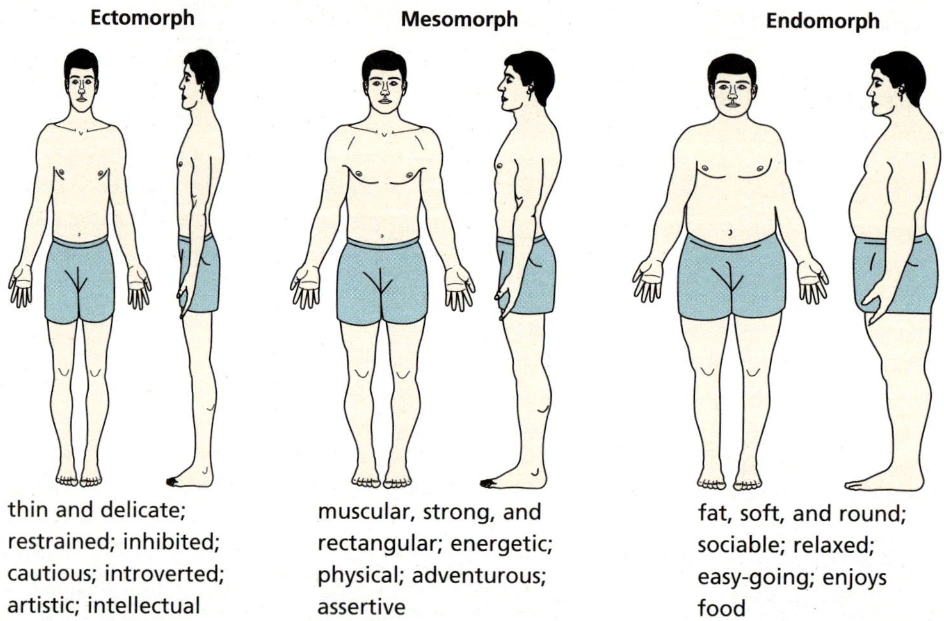

Figure 6.1: Somatotypes

Carl Gustav Jung (1875–1961)

This typology has intuitive appeal, but it may not be a good model for predicting behaviour. Can you think of an endomorph who is introverted and intellectual? Are you friendly with a mesomorph who is a relaxed gourmet – or with an ectomorph who is sociable and assertive?

Type theory owes a debt to the Swiss psychologist Carl Gustav Jung (1875–1961), whose approach is based on *psychological preferences* for extraversion or introversion, for sensation or intuition, for thinking or feeling, and for judging or perceiving (Jung, 1953; 1971). At the heart of this complex theory lie four personality types, plotted across the sensation–intuition and thinking–feeling dimensions, illustrated in Figure 6.2.

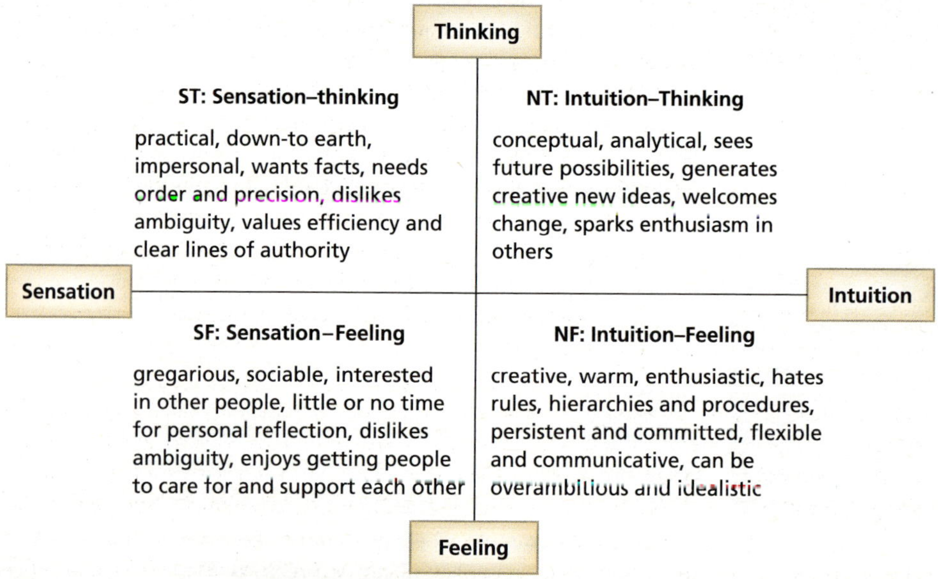

Figure 6.2: Jung's personality type matrix

The Ayurveda principle

The ancient Indian system of holistic medicine, Ayurveda, is founded on the principle that living matter is composed of earth, water, fire, air, and ether, combining to give three basic personality types or doshas: *vata*, *pitta* and *kapha* (Morris, 1999):

Vata (air and ether): Slim, angular and restless. Creative and artistic, leaning towards athletics or dancing. Like to travel, can be flirtatious and emotionally insecure. Dry skin, prone to joint pains, rheumatism and depression.

Pitta (water and fire): Medium build with fair or red hair. Good leaders and executives who get things done. Articulate and impatient, can be irritable. Lunch is a very important meal. Skin is reddish. Prone to acne, rashes, ulcers, and urinary infections.

Kapha (earth and water): Stocky, perhaps overweight. Loyal workers, not pushy. Patient, affectionate and forgiving. Smooth and oily skin. Prone to respiratory tract problems, asthma, bronchitis, colds and sinus problems, and depression.

Each of us is a combination of all three doshas, the dominant one determining our physical and spiritual character. The key to health lies in balance, ensuring that one doshic personality is not too prominent. The similarities between Ayurveda and somatotyping are striking.

Isabel Briggs Myers (1897–1980)

Katherine Cook Briggs (1875–1968)

Trait a relatively stable quality or attribute of an individual's personality, influencing behaviour in a particular direction.

Nomothetic an approach to the study of personality emphasizing the identification of traits, and the systematic relationships between different aspects of personality.

Using this theory, the mother-and-daughter team of Katherine Briggs and Isabel Myers (Myers, 1962, 1976; Myers and McCaulley, 1985) developed the Myers-Briggs Type Indicator (MBTI), probably the world's most popular personality assessment, still widely used across a range of organizational contexts, including management development programmes focusing on self-awareness and personal development. The MBTI makes Jung's theory easier to understand and practical, rating personal preferences on the four scales:

Introvert	⟷	**Extravert**
Sensing	⟷	**iNtuiting**
Thinking	⟷	**Feeling**
Judging	⟷	**Perceiving**

This approach assigns each individual to one side or other of each dimension, establishing sixteen personality types, each known by its letter code; iNtuiting is known by the letter N to avoid confusion with introversion. If you are ENFP, you have been typed as Extravert, Intuitive, Feeling and Perceiving. It is useful to remember, however, that the assessments that produce individual scores reveal preferences and tendencies. The resultant profiles do not necessarily mean that individuals are trapped in those categories. While we may have a preference for impersonal analysis (T), we may when appropriate be able to use personal evaluations (F); we may prefer to focus on the immediate and concrete (S), while being able when appropriate to consider imaginative opportunities (N).

The MBTI has a number of applications. For example, problem-solving and decision-making groups need a complementary personality mix; intuitive types need sensing types, feeling types need thinking types. This echoes the theory of effective group composition developed by Meredith Belbin (1981; 1993; see Chapter 11).

Type approaches fit people into categories possessing common behaviour patterns. A personality **trait**, on the other hand, is any enduring behaviour that occurs in a variety of settings. While individuals belong to types, traits belong to individuals. You fit a type; you have a trait. Traits are also defined in terms of predispositions to behave in a particular way.

Examples of traits include shyness, excitability, reliability, moodiness, and punctuality. The study of traits in personality research and assessment, and of how traits cluster to form 'super traits', is associated with the **nomothetic** approach in psychology.

Nomothetic means 'law-setting' or 'law-giving'. Psychologists who adopt this approach look for universal laws of behaviour. The nomothetic approach assumes that personality is inherited and that environmental factors have little effect. This approach sits on the nature side of the nature/nurture debate, and adopts the following procedures:

- First, it is necessary to identify the main dimensions on which personality can vary. Trait approaches assume that there is a common set of dimensions – temperament, character, predispositions – on which we can be compared. This approach assumes that your unique personality can be measured and compared with others on the same dimensions.
- Second, the personalities of groups of people are assessed, usually with self-report questionnaires based on 'forced-choice' questions: 'true' or 'false', 'yes' or 'no', or 'strongly agree' to 'strongly disagree'.
- Third, your personality profile is constructed across the traits measured. Your score on each dimension is compared with the average and the distribution of scores for the whole group. This enables the assessor to identify individuals around the norm, and those with pronounced characteristics that deviate from the norm. Your personal score has little meaning outside the scores of the population with which you are being compared. You cannot have a 'high' or 'low' score; you can only have scores that are high or low when compared with others.
- Fourth, the group may be split into subgroups, say by age, sex, or occupation. This produces other reference points, or norms, against which individual scores can be compared. Patterns of similarities and differences among and between subgroups enable general laws about personality to be formulated. One may find, for example, that successful Scottish male managers tend to be introverted, or that women under the age of 30 employed in purchasing have unusually low scores on shyness. This approach is impersonal, and it is difficult to use the results to predict individual behaviour, even with 'extreme' scores. It may be possible, however, to make probabilistic predictions about groups, in terms of behaviour tendencies.

It may seem odd that one approach to individual personality assessment relies on studies of large groups. However, through this method, it is possible to find out what is normal or average (in the statistical sense) and then compare individuals with that. Individuals who 'deviate from the norm' are not social outcasts. However, assessments based on this method are often used as a guide to the profile of individuals, especially in employment selection.

Hans Jürgen Eysenck (1916–1997)

One of the most influential trait theories of personality is that of Hans Jürgen Eysenck (1970; 1990), who was born in Germany in 1916, and who worked in Britain until his death in 1997. Following Jung, his research explored the key dimensions on which personality varies, including the extraversion–introversion or 'E' dimension, and the neuroticism–stability or 'N' dimension. However, unlike Jung, Eysenck sought to identify trait clusters.

Eysenck's approach is nomothetic. His sympathies lie with behaviourist psychologists who seek a scientific, experimental, mathematical psychology. Behaviourists claim, however, that behaviour is shaped by environmental influences. Eysenck's explanations of personality, on the other hand, are based on genetics and biology.

Eysenck's model offers a way of linking types, traits, and behaviour. He argues that personality structure is hierarchical. Each individual possesses more or less of a number of identifiable traits – trait 1, trait 2, trait 3, and so on. Research shows how individuals who have a particular trait, say trait 1, are more likely to possess another, say trait 3, than people who do not have trait 1. In other words traits tend to 'cluster' in systematic patterns. These clusters identify a 'higher order' of personality description, which Eysenck refers to as personality types, as Figure 6.3 illustrates.

Figure 6.3: A hierarchical model of personality types and traits

This does not mean that every individual who has trait 1 has a Type 'X' personality. It means that questionnaire analysis has shown that individuals with high scores on trait 1 are more likely to have high scores on traits 3 and 5 also, putting them into the Type 'X' category. The result of an individual assessment using this approach is a personality profile across several traits rather than allocation to any one personality type.

The E dimension divides us into two broad categories of people – extraverts and introverts. American use of these terms refers to sociability and unsociability. European use emphasizes spontaneity and inhibition. Most of us have a trait profile between these extremes. Eysenck argues that seven pairs of personality traits cluster to generate, respectively, the extravert and introvert personality types. These traits are summarized in Table 6.2.

Extraverts are tough-minded individuals who need strong and varied external stimulation. They are sociable, like parties, are good at telling stories, enjoy practical jokes, have many friends, need people to talk to, do not enjoy studying and reading on their own, crave excitement, take risks, act impulsively, prefer change, are optimistic, carefree, active, aggressive, and quick-tempered; they display their emotions and are unreliable.

Introverts are tender-minded, experience strong emotions, and do not need intense external stimuli. They are quiet, introspective, and retiring; they prefer books to people, are withdrawn and reserved, plan ahead, distrust impulse, appreciate order, lead careful sober lives, have little excitement, suppress emotions, are pessimistic, worry about moral standards, and are reliable.

Table 6.2: Trait clusters for extravert and introvert types

extravert	**introvert**
activity	inactivity
expressiveness	inhibition
impulsiveness	control
irresponsibility	responsibility
practicality	reflectiveness
risk-taking	carefulness
sociability	unsociability

The N dimension assesses personality on a continuum from neuroticism to stability. Neurotics are emotional, unstable, and anxious, have low opinions of themselves, feel that they are unattractive failures, tend to be disappointed with life, and are pessimistic and depressed. They worry about things that may never happen and are upset when things go wrong. They are obsessive, conscientious, and highly disciplined, and get annoyed by untidiness. Neurotics are not self-reliant and tend to submit to institutional power without question. They feel controlled by events, by others, and by fate. They often imagine that they are ill and demand sympathy. They blame themselves and are troubled by conscience.

Home viewing

Glengarry Glen Ross (1992, director James Foley) is based in a Chicago real estate office. To boost flagging sales, the 'downtown' manager Blake (played by Alec Baldwin) introduces a sales contest. First prize is a Cadillac Eldorado, second prize is a set of steak knives, third prize is dismissal. The sales staff include Ricky Roma (Al Pacino), Shelley Levene (Jack Lemmon), George Aaronow (Alan Arkin) and Dave Moss (Ed Harris). In the first ten minutes of the film, note how Blake in his 'motivational pep talk' conforms to the stereotype of the extravert, competitive, successful 'macho' salesman (warning: bad language). Observe the effects of his 'pep talk' on the behaviour of the sales team. Does Blake offer a stereotype which salespeople should copy? What is Blake's view of human nature? This part of the movie shows the construction of individual identity through a 'performance' conditioned by organizational context. This contrasts with a view of identity as genetically determined.

Stable people are 'adjusted', self-confident, and optimistic; they resist irrational fears, are easygoing and realistic, solve their own problems, have few health worries, and have few regrets about their past. The trait clusters for emotionally unstable and stable types are summarized in Table 6.3.

Table 6.3: Trait clusters for emotionally unstable and stable types

emotionally unstable	emotionally stable
anxiety	calm
guilt	freedom from guilt
hypochondriasis	sense of health
lack of autonomy	autonomy
low self-esteem	self-esteem
obsessiveness	casualness
unhappiness	happiness

The questionnaire that Eysenck used to measure the E and N dimensions has 96 questions, 40 for each dimension and 16 'lie detector' questions. The questions are mainly in the 'yes/no' format. The E and N dimensions are not correlated; if you are extraverted, you could be either stable or neurotic. If you are stable, you could be either extravert or introvert.

Is one personality type more desirable than another? The extravert may be sociable, friendly, cheerful, active, and lively. However, extraverts are unreliable, fickle in friendships, and easily bored with uninteresting or time-consuming tasks. There are positive and negative sides to the extravert personality, as with the introvert. Those with extreme scores have what Eysenck calls an 'ambiguous gift'. It is thus important to be aware of your personality, and to be aware of the characteristics that could be seen by others as strengths and weaknesses. To understand others, you must begin with an understanding of your own personality and emotions, and the effect that you have on others.

Would you pass an integrity test?

Employers want staff who are conscientious, dependable, and honest. Many companies now use integrity tests to identify candidates who could pose risks, such as dishonesty, cheating, lying, stealing, drug abuse, racism, sexism, and violent and criminal behaviour. After using integrity testing in 600 of its 1,900 stores, one American retailer reported a 35 per cent drop in the loss (or theft) of stock in its stores, while losses rose by over 10 per cent in stores that did not use integrity testing (Arnold and Jones, 2006). Paul Whitely (2012) at the University of Essex Centre for the Study of Integrity has developed a test that asks you to rate the following ten items using these scores and ratings:

1. never justified 2. rarely justified
3. sometimes justified 4. always justified

a. avoiding paying the fare on public transport
b. cheating on taxes if you have a chance
c. driving faster than the speed limit
d. keeping money you found in the street
e. lying in your own interests
f. not reporting accidental damage you've done to a parked car
g. throwing away litter in a public place
h. driving under the influence of alcohol
i. making up things on a job application
j. buying something you know is stolen.

If your score is	this means
up to 15	you are very honest and really want to do the right thing
15 up to 19	your integrity is above average but you don't mind bending the rules
20 up to 24	you are relaxed about breaking the rules when it suits you
25 and above	you don't believe in rules and it's easy to break them when it suits you.

A survey in 2011 found that just under 50 per cent of UK respondents scored up to 15, and only 5 per cent scored over 25. The average was 16. There was high tolerance for keeping money found in the street, exceeding the speed limit, and lying in one's own interests. Faking job applications, dropping litter, buying stolen goods, and drunk driving were universally condemned. There were no differences depending on affluence, education, or occupational status. Women had slightly higher scores than men, but the difference was small.

Younger people were more relaxed about 'low-level' dishonesty. For example, while 75 per cent of those over 65 regarded making false statements on a job application as never justified, only 33 per cent of those under 25 took that view, with similar views about telling lies. Comparison with a survey from 2000 showed that the percentage of respondents saying that a behaviour is never justified had fallen for eight out of the ten indicators. Attitudes to dropping litter have not changed much, but on the whole we appear to be more tolerant now of low-level dishonesty than we were ten years ago.

Declining integrity is a problem for employers. Societies in which trust and integrity are strong have better economic performance. This effect may apply to organizations in a world increasingly sensitive to corporate responsibility (see Chapter 2). And it is easy to cheat on these tests, to give yourself a higher integrity score, especially if you are low in integrity.

The big five

Big five trait clusters that appear consistently to capture main personality traits: Openness, Conscientiousness, Extraversion, Agreeableness, and Neuroticism.

Paul T. Costa (b.1943)

Robert McCrae (b.1949)

The search for trait clusters has culminated in what is known as the **big five**. The most influential advocates of this approach are Paul Costa and Robert McCrae (1992). This approach has achieved broad acceptance as a common descriptive system. Research has consistently reproduced these dimensions in different social settings and cultures, with different populations, with different forms of data collection, and in different languages. However, the labelling and interpretation of the factors and sub-traits remains controversial.

The big five (which spell OCEAN) are not personality types. They are sets of factors, 'super traits', which describe common elements among the sub-factors or traits which cluster together. Costa and McCrae (1992) identify six traits under each of the five headings, giving 30 traits in total. Table 6.4 summarizes the big five trait clusters. You can profile your own personality at the end of this chapter using this approach.

Table 6.4: The big five personality trait clusters

High ⟵		⟶ Low
explorer (O+) creative, curious, open-minded, intellectual	**Openness** rigidity of beliefs and range of interests	*preserver* (O–) conventional, unimaginative, narrow-minded
focused (C+) organized, self-disciplined, achievement-oriented	**Conscientiousness** desire to impose order and precision	*flexible* (C–) disorganized, careless, frivolous, irresponsible
extravert (E+) outgoing, sociable, talkative, assertive	**Extraversion** level of comfort with relationships	*introvert* (E–) reserved, quiet, introverted
adapter (A+) good-natured, trusting, compliant, soft-hearted	**Agreeableness** the ability to get along with others	*challenger* (A–) rude, quarrelsome, uncaring, irritable, uncooperative
reactive (N+) anxious, depressed, self-conscious	**Neuroticism** tendency to maintain a balanced emotional state	*resilient* (N–) calm, contented, self-assured
High ⟵		⟶ Low

The six traits relating to **Openness** (fantasy, aesthetics, feelings, actions, ideas, values) run on a continuum from 'explorer', at one extreme, to 'preserver' at the other. Explorer (O+) traits are useful for entrepreneurs, architects, change agents, artists, and theoretical scientists. Preserver (O–) traits are useful for finance managers, stage performers, project managers, and applied scientists. Those in the middle of this spectrum (O) are labelled 'moderates' who are interested in novelty when necessity commands, but not for too long.

The traits relating to **Conscientiousness** (competence, order, dutifulness, achievement-striving, self-discipline, deliberation) run from 'focused' to 'flexible'. Focused (C+) traits are useful for leaders, senior executives, and other high achievers. Flexible (C–) traits are useful for researchers, detectives, and management consultants. Those in the middle (C) are 'balanced', and find it easy to move from focus to being flexible, from production to research.

The traits relating to **Extraversion** (warmth, gregariousness, assertiveness, activity, excitement-seeking, positive emotions) run from 'extravert' to 'introvert' (surprise, surprise). Extravert (E+) traits are useful in sales, politics, and the arts. Introvert (E–) traits are useful for production management, and in the physical and natural sciences. Those in the middle of this spectrum (E) are 'ambiverts' who move easily from isolation to social settings.

The traits relating to **Agreeableness** (trust, straightforwardness, altruism, compliance, modesty, tender-mindedness) run from 'adapter' to 'challenger'. Adapter (A+) traits are useful in teaching, social work, and psychology. Challenger (A–) traits are useful in advertising, management, and military leadership. Those in the middle of this spectrum (A) are 'negotiators' who move from leadership to followership as the situation demands.

The traits relating to **Neuroticism**, or 'negative emotionality' (worry, anger, discouragement, self-consciousness, impulsiveness, vulnerability), run from 'reactive' to 'resilient'. Reactive (emotional) or 'N+' traits are useful for social scientists, academics, and customer service professionals, but extreme reactivity interferes with intellectual performance. Resilient (unflappable) or 'N–' traits are useful for air traffic controllers, airline pilots, military snipers, finance managers, and engineers. Those in the middle of this spectrum (N) are 'responsives', able to use levels of emotionality appropriate to the circumstances.

This analysis implies that certain traits will lead to success in particular occupations. Reviewing the research, Ivan Robertson (2001) argues that the relationship between personality and performance is not straightforward. In particular, findings suggest that

- only two of the big five personality factors, conscientiousness and emotional stability, are consistently associated with better performance, in most occupations;
- conscientiousness is a better predictor of work performance than emotional stability;
- although openness, agreeableness, and extraversion are not universally important, any of the big five personality factors could be significant in certain occupations;
- the correlations that have been found between personality factors and job performance are not strong, as performance is also affected by a range of other factors.

High conscientiousness is not always a reliable predictor of someone's suitability for a job. One study showed that employees who scored low in conscientiousness were rated by supervisors as innovative and promotable (Robertson, 2001, p. 43). Organizations facing high levels of competition and change want staff with good interpersonal skills, motivation, flexibility, and adaptability, and high conscientiousness may be less relevant.

The big five and your management career

Does success in your chosen career depend on your personality? Research has shown that *conscientiousness* is positively related to salary, promotions, and job status in most occupations. However, *neuroticism* is negatively related to performance, salary, and status. The findings for *extraversion* are inconsistent, linked to performance, salary, and job level in some studies, but not in others. These differences may depend on the type of work being studied; introverts may be better at handling routine, for example. *Openness* and *agreeableness* do not correlate consistently with job performance; these attributes could contribute to lower performance in some jobs; openness has been shown to reduce the performance of rugby referees, and agreeableness interferes with management potential.

Using the Big 5 personality assessment (you will find a short version at the end of this chapter), Joanna Moutafi, Adrian Furnham and John Crump (2007) studied 900 British managers, from ten organizations, in retailing, telecoms, manufacturing, consultancy, accounting, and legal services. They reached three main conclusions:

- *Conscientiousness* was positively related to management level. This suggests that you are more likely to be promoted if you are capable, sensitive, effective, well-organized, thorough, dependable, reliable, ambitious, and hard-working. However, it may also be the case that high-level jobs encourage the development of those characteristics.
- *Neuroticism* was negatively related to management level. This means that you are less likely to be promoted if you appear nervous, tense, anxious, stress-prone, unhappy, depressed, shy, and unable to cope. People with those characteristics may avoid management jobs with high levels of responsibility, but the stress of those jobs may increase neuroticism.
- *Extraversion* was positively related to management level. This implies that you are more likely to be promoted if you are dominant, socially ascendant, confident, assertive, energetic, determined, outgoing, and sociable. The researchers note that 'Management is an extraverted activity. Managers attend meetings, give talks and socially interact all day long, which are activities more easily handled by extraverts than introverts' (p. 277).

Psychometric tests of mental ability tend to be good predictors of job performance, while measures of personality traits are poorer predictors. This study suggests, however, that personality assessment could be useful in selecting people for management roles.

Personality Types A and B

Meyer Friedman (1910–2001)

Type A personality a combination of emotions and behaviours characterized by ambition, hostility, impatience, and a sense of constant time pressure.

Type B personality a combination of emotions and behaviours characterized by relaxation, low focus on achievement, and ability to take time to enjoy leisure.

Personality and health seem to be linked in a way particularly relevant to organizational behaviour. Meyer Friedman and Ray Rosenman (1974) identified two extreme 'behaviour syndromes' which explained differences in stress levels. They claim to have identified a 'stress-prone' personality. Much subsequent research has focused on what they called **Type A personality** and its opposite, **Type B personality**, summarized in Table 6.5.

Friedman and Rosenman found that Type A personalities were three times more likely to suffer heart disease than Type Bs. The typical Type A thrives on long hours, large amounts of work, and tight deadlines. These are socially and organizationally desirable characteristics, as are competitiveness and a high need for achievement. However, those who are extreme Type A may not be able to relax long enough to stand back from a complex problem to make an effective and comprehensive analysis, and may lack the patience and relaxed style required in some management positions. A further problem lies in the fact that their impatience and

Table 6.5: Type A and Type B personality characteristics

Type A personality characteristics	Type B personality characteristics
competitive	able to take time out to enjoy leisure
high need for achievement	not preoccupied with achievement
aggressive	easygoing
works fast	works at a steady pace
impatient	seldom impatient
restless	not easily frustrated
extremely alert	relaxed
tense facial muscles	moves and speaks slowly
constant feeling of time pressure	seldom lacks enough time
more likely to suffer stress-related illness	**less likely to suffer stress-related illness**

hostility can increase the stress levels in those who have to work with them. Like the extravert, a Type A personality can appear to have many admirable facets, but this behaviour syndrome can be dysfunctional for the individual, and for others.

STOP AND THINK

Are you a Type A or a Type B?

Do you suffer from: alcohol abuse, excessive smoking, dizziness, upset stomach, headaches, fatigue, sweating, bad breath? If 'yes', these could be stress responses to your Type A behaviour pattern. Expect your first heart attack before you are 45.

If you don't suffer stress-related symptoms, perhaps you are a Type B. Do you think that your relaxed, casual behaviour will damage your career prospects?

Whichever your response, what are you going to do about it?

Friedman and Rosenman argue that a Type A can change into a Type B, with awareness and training, and suggest a number of personal 're-engineering strategies':

- keep reminding yourself that life is always full of unfinished business;
- you only 'finish' when you die;
- learn how to delegate responsibility to others;
- limit your weekly working hours;
- schedule time for leisure and exercise;
- take a course in time management skills.

The problem, of course, is that the extreme Type A personality – the person most at risk – can never find time to implement these strategies.

Stress management: individual and organization

The work of Friedman and Rosenman reveals a relationship between personality and health. Negative emotional states such as depression, hostility, and anxiety can be linked to heart disease, respiratory disorders such as asthma, headaches, and ulcers. Health risks are greater where negative states are chronic, particularly when they are part of personality. Stress is also caused by individual factors: difficulty in coping with change, lack of confidence, poor time management, poor stress management skills. Noreen Tehrani and Lisa Ayling (2008) summarize recent research findings which show that

- stress may become the most dangerous business risk in the twenty-first century;
- three-quarters of executives say that stress adversely affects their health, home life, and performance at work;
- one in five workers (5 million in Britain) report feeling extremely stressed at work;
- work-related stress, anxiety, or depression accounts for around 10.5 million lost working days a year in Britain.

Stress has many causes other than personality. The pace of life and constant change generate stress by increasing the range and intensity of the demands on our time. Any condition that requires an adaptive response from the individual is known as a stressor. Typical stressors that arise in organizational contexts are:

- *inadequate physical working environment*: noise, bad lighting, inadequate ventilation, lack of privacy, extremes of heat and cold, old and unreliable equipment;

- *inappropriate job design*: poor coordination, inadequate training, lack of information, rigid procedures, inadequate staffing, excessive workloads, no challenge, little use of skills, no responsibility or participation in decision-making, role ambiguity;
- *poor management style*: inconsistent, competitive, crisis management, autocratic management, excessive time pressures placed on employees;
- *poor relationships*: with superiors, with colleagues, and with particular individuals; lack of feedback, little social contact, racial and sexual harassment;
- *uncertain future*: job insecurity, fear of unemployment or redeployment, few promotion opportunities, low-status job;
- *divided loyalties*: conflicts between personal aspirations and organizational requirements, conflict between job and family and social responsibilities.

Stress – or pressure – can also be arousing and exciting, and can enhance our sense of satisfaction and accomplishment and improve our performance. The term *eustress* describes this positive aspect of stress. The prefix 'eu' is Greek for 'good'. This contrasts with *distress*, which means the unpleasant, debilitating, and unhealthy side of stress.

Stress can be episodic. When dealing with life's problems, we get anxious, cope with the problem, and then relax again. Some events, such as the death of a relative, or a prison sentence, can be extremely stressful. Other experiences, such as getting a poor exam grade, being fined for speeding, or arguing with a friend, can be stressful, but trigger a less extreme response. Each of these episodes on its own is unlikely to cause lasting damage. However, when several of these episodes occur around the same time, the health risk is increased.

Stress can be chronic. This happens when we face constant stress, with no escape, and can lead to exhaustion and 'burnout'. This may be due to the unfortunate coincidence of several unrelated episodes. However, chronic stress also arises from the enduring features of our personal, social, and organizational circumstances. If we are always under pressure, always facing multiple and unrealistic demands, always having difficulties with our work, our colleagues, and our relationships, then the health risk from stress is likely to increase.

Stress can be a personal response to life's challenges. What you brush aside may be a problem for others. In addition to whether stress is episodic or chronic, there are three factors moderating the impact of stress factors:

Condition You are better able to cope with stress if you are in good health.

Cognitive appraisal If you believe that you are not going to cope with a particular event, this belief can become a 'self-fulfilling prophecy'.

Hardiness Hardiness is an outlook on life characterized by a welcoming approach to change, commitment to purposeful activity, and a sense of being in control. This combination increases resilience to stress.

Stress has many symptoms which, taken on their own, do not appear significant and are not particularly threatening if they are temporary. An occasional headache is seldom cause for concern. Many of these symptoms have other causes, so they can be overlooked, and stress passes unrecognized and untreated. Table 6.6 identifies typical symptoms of stress.

Table 6.6: Typical stress symptoms

excessive alcohol intake	heavy cigarette smoking	dependence on tranquillisers
tiredness	low energy	dizziness
headaches	stomach upsets and ulcers	bad breath
high blood pressure	sleep problems	hyperventilation
temper tantrums	irritability	moodiness
loss of concentration	aggression	overeating
excess worrying	anxiety	inability to relax
pounding heart	feelings of inadequacy	memory loss

Stress can have emotional consequences such as anxiety, fatigue, depression, frustration, nervousness, and low self-esteem. At the extreme, stress can contribute to mental breakdown and suicide. Stress also influences behaviour in many other ways, from 'comfort tricks' involving alcohol and other drugs and excessive eating, to accident-proneness and emotional outbursts. Stress affects our ability to think, and interferes with concentration, decision-making, attention span, and reaction to criticism. There are several physiological responses, such as increased heart rate and blood pressure, sweating, and 'hot and cold flushes'.

The organizational consequences of stress can be damaging. The performance of stressed employees can be poor, and stress causes absenteeism, staff turnover, accidents, and wilful sabotage. Stress can also damage relationships (although poor relationships may cause stress in the first place), and commitment to work and to the organization are also likely to fall.

There are two broad strategies for reducing stress: *individual* emotion-focused strategies, and *organizational* problem-focused strategies.

Individual emotion-focused strategies improve resilience and coping skills and include

- consciousness-raising to improve self-awareness;
- exercise and fitness programmes;
- self-help training in biofeedback, meditation, relaxation, and coping strategies;
- time management training;
- development of other social and job interests.

Organizational problem-focused strategies deal directly with the stressors and include

- improved selection and training mechanisms;
- staff counselling programmes;
- improved organizational communications;
- job redesign and enrichment strategies;
- development of teamworking systems.

Built to rush: pressure and stress are good for you

In his book *Rush: Why You Need and Love the Rat Race*, Todd Buchholz (2011a) argues that speed, stress and competition at work are good for us, and make us healthier and happier. Taking it easy, on the other hand, can make us unhealthy, depressed, and miserable. Buchholz is a Harvard economics professor and a former White House economic advisor. Contrary to popular opinion, he has no time for 'work-life balance', lazy vacations, or yoga retreats. Instead, he emphasizes the benefits of activity. As we are 'built to rush', pressure and stress drive us to perform better, and competition encourages creativity and innovation.

Friedman and Rosenman (1974) argued that people with Type A personalities have problems with their health and with making good decisions. In contrast, Buchholz cites an Australian study, involving 9,000 people, which found that those with a passive lifestyle, who spent four or more hours a day 'de-stressing' in front of the television, had an 80 per cent higher chance of developing heart disease than those who spent less than two hours a day channel-hopping:

> In your bloodstream is an enzyme called lipoprotein lipase. It's a friendly enzyme because it draws fat to your muscles, where it can be burned as fuel. But sitting on your bum leaves fat in your bloodstream, where it might as well clog into formations that spell out 999.
>
> We want to feel that rush of dopamine when we face a new challenge at work. We need that push of forward momentum in order to be creative. And we need it much more than we need mantras, deep breathing or the murmur that comes when we try to snooze through life. (Buchholz, 2011b, p. 21)

Research has also shown that cognitive abilities – speed and clarity of thought – decay in people after they retire from work.

Competition in an organization is beneficial. At Apple, teams of designers and engineers were encouraged to compete with each other to persuade Steve Jobs which features to include in new iPhones and iPads. Buchholz is critical of the 'Edenists' who argue for a simpler, happier lifestyle. What would you rather do when you have finished reading this book chapter: relax, or rush on to the next task?

Idiographic an approach to the study of personality emphasizing the uniqueness of the individual, rejecting the assumption that we can all be measured on the same dimensions.

It is not always appropriate to 'blame' the individual for their experience of and response to stress, despite the known link to personality. Stress is also caused by organizational factors. While individual resilience can be improved, the need for problem-focused organizational solutions is inescapable.

Figure 6.4 summarizes the argument of this section, with respect to the causes of stress, factors that moderate the experience of stress, stress symptoms, and coping strategies.

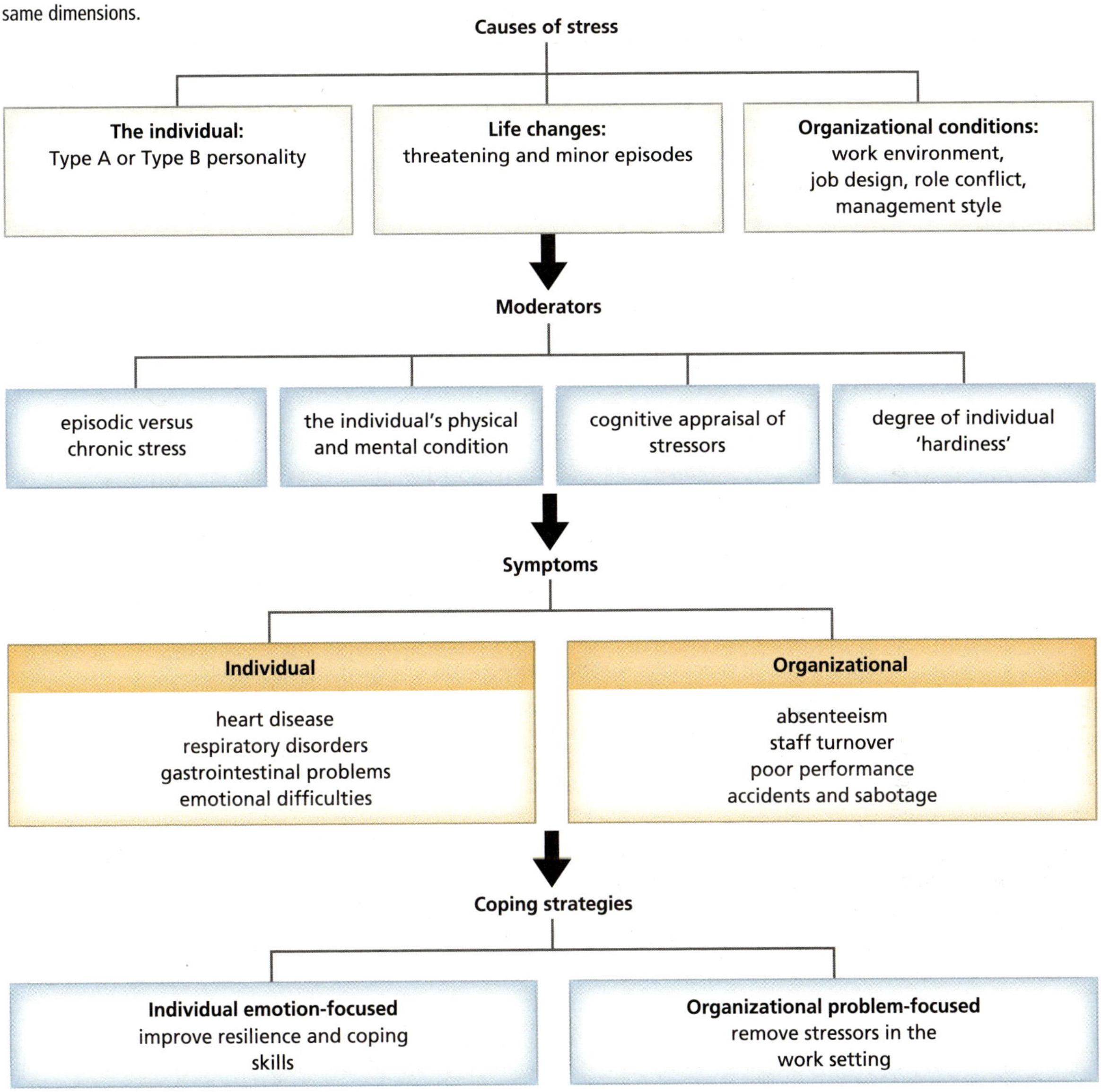

Figure 6.4: Stress causes, moderators, symptoms, and coping strategies

The development of the self

The nomothetic approach to the study of personality has been criticized by those who advocate an **idiographic** approach, which contrasts sharply in perspective and implications.

Idiographic means 'writing about individuals'. Psychologists who adopt this perspective begin with a detailed picture of one person, aiming to capture the uniqueness, richness, and complexity of the individual. It is a valuable way of deepening our understanding, but does not readily produce universal laws of behaviour.

The idiographic approach makes the following assumptions:

- First, each individual has unique traits that are not comparable with the traits of others. Your sensitivity and aggression are not necessarily comparable with my sensitivity and aggression. Idiographic research produces in-depth studies of normal and abnormal individuals, with information from interviews, letters, diaries, and biographies. The data include what people say and write about themselves, and are not restricted to scores on paper-and-pencil tests.
- Second, we are not just biological machines powered by heredity. We are also socially self-conscious. Our behaviour patterns are influenced by experience, and by conscious reflection and reasoning, not just by instinct and habit.
- Third, we behave in accordance with the image that we have of ourselves – our self, or **self-concept**. We learn about ourselves through our interactions with others. We take the attitudes and behaviours of others and use those to adjust our self-concept and behaviour.

Self-concept the set of perceptions that we have about ourselves.

- Fourth, as the development of the self-concept is a social process, it follows that personality can change through social experiences. The development of personality is therefore not the inevitable result of genetic inheritance. It is through interaction with others that we learn to understand ourselves as individuals. We cannot develop self-understanding without the (tacit) help of others. In this view, there is no such thing as 'human nature'. Our character is shaped through social interactions and relationships. Remember, this contrasts starkly with the argument that human nature is largely influenced by biology and genetics (Pinker, 2002). This perspective, therefore, is on the nurture side of the nature/nurture debate.

Your self-understanding thus determines your behaviour. For example, confidence in your ability to do something is related to the successful demonstration of that ability. Ability combined with lack of confidence usually leads to failure or poor performance.

The mind's ability to reflect on its own functions is an important capability. We experience a world 'out there' and we are capable of experiencing ourselves in that world, as objects that live and behave in it. We can observe, evaluate, and criticize ourselves in the same conscious, objective, impersonal way that we observe, evaluate, and criticize other people and events, and we experience shame, anxiety, or pride in our own behaviour. Our capacity for reflective thought enables us to evaluate past and future actions and their consequences.

Charles Horton Cooley (1864–1929)

The American psychologist Charles Horton Cooley introduced the concept of the 'looking glass self' (Cooley, 1902). Our mirror is the other people with whom we interact. If others respond warmly and favourably towards us, we develop a 'positive' self-concept. If others respond with criticism, ridicule and aggression, we develop a 'negative' self-image. The personality of the individual is thus the result of a process in which the individual learns to be the person they are. Most of us learn, accept, and use most of the attitudes, values, beliefs, and expectations of the society in which we are brought up.

In other words, we learn the stock of knowledge peculiar to our society. Red means stop. Cars drive on the left hand side of the road (in Australia and Britain). An extended hand is a symbol of respect and friendship, not of hostility or aggression. These examples, on their own, are trivial. Taken together, these make up our 'recipe knowledge' of how society works. The taken-for-granted 'rules' that govern our behaviour are created, re-created and reinforced through our ongoing interactions with others based on shared definitions of our reality. We interact with each other successfully because we share this understanding. How could we develop such a shared understanding on our own? What we inherit from our parents cannot possibly tell us how to behave in a specific culture. We have to learn how to become *persona grata* through social interaction.

George Herbert Mead (1863–1931)

If we all share the same ideas and behaviours, we have a recipe for a society of conformists. This is not consistent with the evidence, and the theory does not imply this. George Herbert Mead (1934) argued that the self has two components:

I The unique, individual, conscious and impulsive aspects of the individual

Me The norms and values of society that the individual learns and accepts, or 'internalizes'.

Generalized other what we think other people expect of us, in terms of our attitudes, values, beliefs, and behaviour.

Mead used the term **generalized other** to refer to the set of expectations one believes others have of one. 'Me' is the part of self where these generalized attitudes are organized. The 'Me' cannot be physically located. It refers rather to the mental process that enables us to reflect on our own conduct. The 'Me' is the self as an object to itself.

The 'I' is the active, impulsive component of the self. Other people encourage us to conform to current values and beliefs. Reflective individuals adjust their part in the social process. We can initiate change by introducing new social values. Patterns of socially acceptable conduct are specified in broad and general ways. There is plenty of scope for flexibility, modification, originality, creativity, individuality, variety, and significant change.

STOP AND THINK

List the ten words or phrases that best describe the most important features of your individual identity.

These features could concern your social roles, physical characteristics, intellectual qualities, social style, beliefs, and particular skills.

Then make a second list, putting what you regard as the most important feature at the top, and ranking all ten items with the least important at the bottom.

Starting at the bottom of your list, imagine that these items are removed from your personality one by one. Visualize how you would be different without each personality feature. What difference does its absence make to you?

This is the start of the process of establishing your **self-concept**. How much more or less valid is this approach than one based on forced-choice questionnaires – and why?

Carl Ransom Rogers (1902–1987)

Figure 6.5 illustrates what Carl Rogers (1947) called the 'two-sided self'.

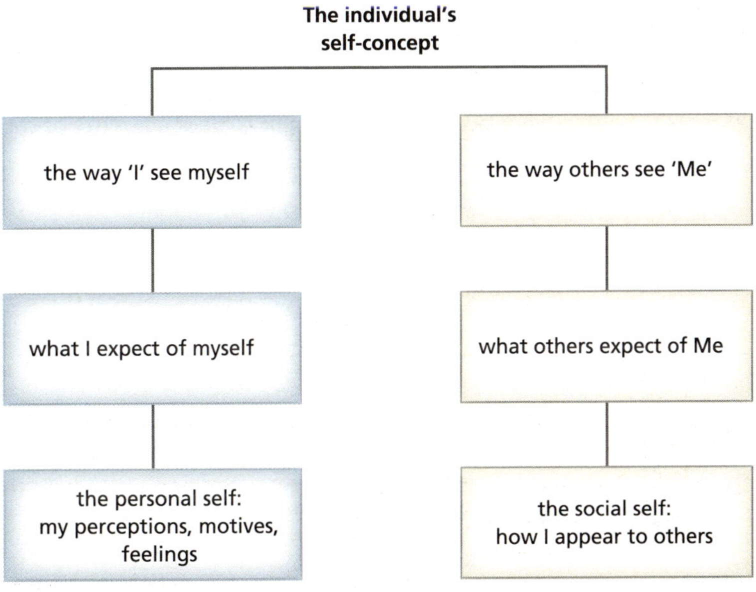

Figure 6.5: The two-sided self

Our self-concept gives us a sense of meaning and consistency. But as our perceptions and motives change through new experiences and learning, our self-concept and our behaviour change. Personality in this perspective, therefore, is not stable, as the self-concept can be reorganized. We have perceptions of our qualities, abilities, attitudes, impulses, and so on. If these perceptions are accurate, conscious, organized, and accepted, then we can regard our self-concept as successful in that it will lead to feelings of comfort, freedom from tension, and psychological adjustment. Well-adjusted individuals thus have flexible images of themselves, which are open to change through new experiences.

Personality disorders can be caused by a failure to bring together experiences, motives, and feelings into a consistent self-concept. We usually behave in ways consistent with our self-images, and when we have new experiences or feelings that are inconsistent we either recognize the inconsistency and try to integrate the two sets of understanding – the healthy response – or deny or distort one of the experiences, perhaps by putting the blame onto someone or something else – an unhealthy defence mechanism.

Unconditional positive regard unqualified, non-judgemental approval and respect for the traits and behaviours of the other person (a term used in counselling).

Rogers argued that at the core of human personality is the desire to realize fully one's potential. To achieve this, the right social environment is required, one in which we are treated with **unconditional positive regard**. This means that one is accepted for whatever one is; one is valued, trusted, and respected, even in the face of characteristics which others dislike. In this environment, the individual is likely to become trusting, spontaneous, and flexible, with a rich and meaningful life and a harmonious self-concept. However, this is far from the type of social environment in many contemporary organizations. Most of us face highly conditional regard, in which a narrow range of thoughts and behaviours is accepted.

Thematic apperception test an assessment in which the individual is shown ambiguous pictures and is asked to create stories of what may be happening in them.

Compared with nomothetic methods, an idiographic approach appears to be a complex, untidy view of personality and its development. It has been influential in research, but is conspicuous by its absence in contemporary psychometrics. How can the individual's self-understanding be studied? An approach based on questions worded by a researcher is not going to work; you may reject that wording as inappropriate to *your* self-concept.

We need another route into the individual's mind. Well, we can ask people to write and to speak freely about themselves. These and similar techniques, including free association, interpretation of dreams, and the analysis of fantasies, are in common use. Here the individual has freedom of expression and responses are not tied to predetermined categories. The researcher's job is to identify the themes that reveal the individual's preoccupations, interests, and personality. One technique is the **thematic apperception test**, or TAT.

Need for achievement a concern with meeting standards of excellence, the desire to be successful in competition, and the motivation to excel.

This concept breaks our rule about not describing personality assessments as 'tests'. However, we have to be consistent with the literature. This is how the TAT works. First, you are told that you are about to take a test of your creative writing skills. Then you are shown photographs or drawings, typically including people, and asked to write an imaginative story suggested by what you see. The images do not imply any particular story. The contents of your imaginative accounts are then assessed in various ways. One of these concerns your **need for achievement**. This is not a test of your imaginative writing at all.

STOP AND THINK

Write an imaginative story (100 words) about what is happening in this picture:

Caroline Woodham/Alamy

Henry Alexander Murray (1893–1988)

David Clarence McClelland (1917–1998)

Projective test an assessment based on abstract or ambiguous images, which the subject is asked to interpret by projecting their feelings, preoccupations, and motives into their responses.

The assessment procedure first involves determining whether any of the characters in your story have an achievement goal. In other words, does somebody in your story want to perform better? This could involve doing something better than someone else, meeting or exceeding a self-imposed standard of excellence, doing something unique, or being involved in doing something well. Points are scored for the presence of these features in your story. The more achievement imagery, the higher your score.

The TAT is widely used today in psychological research, occupational choice, psychiatric evaluation, and screening candidates for high-stress jobs. The test was invented by Henry Murray and Christiana Morgan in the 1930s, and was later developed by David McClelland (1961; McClelland et al., 1976) as a means of measuring the strength of need for achievement. The TAT is also used to measure the needs for power and affiliation, using similar scoring procedures, but looking for different imagery. In the original full test, you are asked to write stories about 31 pictures.

What can short, creative stories about ambiguous pictures tell us about your distinctive and stable personality characteristics? The thematic apperception test is a **projective test**. The label 'projective' is used because subjects project their personalities into the stories they write. The Rorschach test is a form of projective assessment which uses random inkblots instead of pictures or photographs. McClelland argues that it is reasonable to assume that the person with a strong concern with achievement is likely to write stories with lots of achievement imagery and themes. The evidence seems to support this view.

Need for achievement is important in an organizational context. People with low need for achievement are concerned more with security and status than with personal fulfilment, are preoccupied with their own ideas and feelings, worry more about their self-presentation than their performance, and prefer bright Scottish tartans. People with high need for achievement tend to have the following characteristics:

- They prefer tasks in which they have to achieve a standard of excellence rather than simply carrying out routine activities.
- They prefer jobs in which they get frequent and clear feedback on how well they are doing, to help them perform better.
- They prefer activities that involve moderate risks of failure; high-risk activities lead to failure, low-risk activities do not provide opportunities to demonstrate ability.
- They have a good memory for unfinished tasks and do not like to leave things incomplete.
- They can be unfriendly and unsociable when they do not want others to get in the way of their performance.
- They have a sense of urgency, appear to be in a hurry and to be working against time, and have an inability to relax.
- They prefer sombre Scottish tartans with lots of blues and greens (Buchanan tartan has lots of red and yellow); unobtrusive backgrounds allow them to stand out better.

Organizations want employees with drive, ambition and self-motivation. Can the TAT be used to identify them? Unfortunately, it is not a good assessment for this purpose. Although the detailed scoring is not obvious to the untrained, the definition of achievement imagery is close to popular understanding. So, when you know what the 'test' is all about, it is easy to fake your score. We have here the same problem as with objective questionnaires. Personality assessment scores are not necessarily good predictors of job performance.

The TAT faces other problems as an organizational selection tool. The output of the assessment is hard for the untrained eye to regard as 'objective data'. The scoring procedure involves subjective interpretation. Expensive training is required in the full technical procedure to produce judges who can reach reliable assessments. With an objective questionnaire, anyone with the scoring key can calculate the results quickly and accurately.

McClelland argues that need for achievement can be increased by teaching you the scoring system, and by helping you to write high-scoring stories. This increases your need for achievement by encouraging you to see and to understand daily life more vividly in achievement terms. McClelland and colleagues used this approach in many different settings, for example with senior managers, entrepreneurs, police officers, and social workers, and the first application outside America was with Indian businessmen in 1963. In other words, the TAT can be used both as a personality assessment, and also to change personality.

Nomothetic versus idiographic

The contrast between the nomothetic and idiographic perspectives on personality is summarized in Table 6.7.

Table 6.7: Nomothetic versus idiographic

The nomothetic approach	The idiographic approach
positivist bias	constructivist bias
generalizing; emphasizes the discovery of laws of human behaviour	individualizing; emphasizes the richness and complexity of the unique individual
based on statistical study of large groups	based on intensive study of individuals
uses objective questionnaires	uses projective assessments (tests) and other written and spoken materials
describes personality in terms of the individual's possession of traits, and trait clusters or personality types	describes personality in terms of the individual's own understanding and interpretation of their identity
personality is composed of discrete and identifiable elements	personality has to be understood as an indivisible, intelligible whole
personality is primarily determined by heredity, biology, genetics	personality is primarily determined by social and cultural processes
personality is given and cannot be altered	personality is adaptable, open to change through experience

How can we choose between these perspectives? We can examine the logic of the arguments, consider how the evidence supports the theories, and consider the comprehensiveness of the explanations. We can resort to practical considerations and assess the methods used to treat personality disorders, and to analyse and predict behaviour. These forms of judgement miss the point that these approaches are based on very different views of human nature. The evidence is such as to leave us debating for a considerable time without satisfactory resolution. We thus have to resort to criteria such as:

- Which theory is more aesthetically pleasing?
- Which approach 'feels' right?
- How does each approach fit with my world view?

A better approach is to regard these perspectives as complementary. They offer two broad research strategies, each of which is capable of telling us about different aspects of human psychology. What each alone reveals is interesting, but partial. Perhaps we should use both approaches and not concentrate on one alone. However, contemporary employee assessment and selection methods ignore this advice, and use predominantly nomothetic methods.

Selection methods

Choosing the right candidate for a job, or for promotion, is a critical decision. Incorrect decisions lead to frustrated employees and poor performance. Selection procedures are costly and time-consuming, and it is expensive to repeat them to recover from errors.

A selection (or a promotion) decision is a prediction about the ability of a candidate to perform well in the particular job. Predictions are based on an understanding of the demands of the position to be filled, and on information about the candidates. Traditionally, candidate information has come from application forms, the testimony of referees, and interviews. The application form provides background, but is impersonal. Referees notoriously reveal only good things about candidates. Research suggests that interviews can also be unreliable, and are not suitable for all occupations (what would you think of the football team captain who selected players on the basis of how well they performed in their interview?).

Psychometrics

Psychometrics, the systematic testing, measurement, and assessment of intelligence, aptitudes, and personality, promise to improve the objectivity of selection and promotion decisions, by systematically collecting information that has predictive power. Psychometric applications developed rapidly in the last two decades of the twentieth century, and there are now over 5,000 such tests and assessments in use.

When choosing a psychometric assessment for any purpose, two criteria are particularly important: **reliability** and **predictive validity**.

Reliability the degree to which an assessment delivers consistent results when repeated.

Predictive validity the extent to which assessment scores accurately predict behaviours such as job performance.

If the same group of people is given the same assessment on two or more occasions, and the results are the same or similar, then the assessment can be described as reliable. This is known as 'test-retest reliability'.

The validity of an assessment concerns the extent to which it actually measures what it sets out to measure. There are different types of validity:

face validity	does it look right?
construct validity	does it relate to other similar measures?
predictive validity	will it tell us how well someone will perform on the job?

In employee selection, predictive validity is particularly important. One key question for this chapter, therefore, is – can we predict job performance from personality assessments? We can answer this question using the following method. First, assess a large applicant group. Second, hire them all regardless of their scores. Third, wait for an appropriate period (say, three to five years). Finally, assess their performance, to see whether those with 'good' scores became high performers, or not. If they are, then you have a valid test.

No single selection method can accurately predict how well an individual will perform in a particular role. Most employers use several methods for gathering information about candidates. To find out how popular different methods are, Lara Zibarras and Stephen Woods (2010) surveyed around 600 organizations in the UK, of different sizes and across different sectors. Their findings are summarized in Table 6.8.

This survey showed that asking for a CV, along with the 'traditional triad' of application form, interview, and references, was still the most commonly used approach. Informal methods, such as unstructured interviews and trial periods, were more popular than formal methods, such as aptitude and numeracy testing and assessment centres. This is despite research which shows that formal methods have higher levels of validity. Large organizations were just as likely to use formal methods as small and medium size enterprises, but public sector organizations were more likely than private sector ones to use formal methods. This may be because the public sector is more strictly monitored, with more formal decision-making and bureaucratic structures, which encourage the use of formal approaches.

Table 6.8: The popularity of different selection methods

selection method	Percentage of organizations using method
CV	85
references	72
structured interview	69
application form	60
trial period on the job	58
unstructured interview	42
aptitude/ability test	39
numeracy/literacy test	28
biodata	27
criminal check	27
personality questionnaire	26
work sample	19
assessment centre	17
drug test/medical check	16
group exercise	15

Source: adapted from A survey of UK selection practices across different organization sizes and industry sectors, *Journal of Occupational and Organizational Psychology*, 83(2), pp. 499–511 (Table 3 on p. 506) (Zibarras, L.D. and Woods, S.A. 2010) © The British Psychological Society.

Approaches to selection vary from country to country. Employers in Britain and America rely on interviews, but graphology (handwriting analysis) is more widely used in France. Assessment centres are popular in Britain, Germany, and the Netherlands. Blood group is a selection criterion in Japan. The validity, or accuracy, of different selection methods in predicting job performance is shown in Table 6.9 (Marchington and Wilkinson, 2005). The 'perfect' selection method would be right every time, and so would score '1'. Choosing candidates at random with a pin would score '0'.

Table 6.9: Validity coefficients for a range of selection methods

method(s)	validity coefficient
perfect selection	1.0
intelligence and integrity tests	0.65
intelligence tests and structured interviews	0.63
intelligence tests and work sampling	0.60
work sampling	0.54
intelligence tests	0.51
structured interviews	0.51
integrity tests	0.41
personality assessments	0.40
assessment centres	0.37
biodata	0.35
references	0.26
years of job experience	0.18
years of education	0.10
graphology (handwriting analysis)	0.02
selection with a pin	0.0

Source: from *Human Resource Management at Work*, 3rd ed., Chartered Institute of Personnel and Development (Marchington, M. and Wilkinson, A. 2005) p. 177 (Originally adapted from Robertson, I. and Smith, M. Personnel selection, *Journal of Occupational and Organizational Psychology*, Vol 74, No 4, 2001, pp. 441–72) with the permission of the publisher, the Chartered Institute of Personnel and Development, London (http://www.cipd.co.uk).

There are two points to note from these figures. First, any method with a validity coefficient of less than 0.5 is going to be wrong more often than it is right. Second, personality assessments have relatively low predictive validity. The average cost of filling a vacancy is around £7,500 for senior managers and directors, and £2,500 for other employees, so selection errors can be expensive, and these figures do not consider errors that the wrong person could make (Chartered Institute of Personnel and Development, 2011).

prometheuscomic.wordpress.com © Mark Weinstein

STOP AND THINK At your next job interview, you are asked 'Why should we employ you?'. The first part of your answer concerns your knowledge and skills. The second part of your answer concerns your personality. What are you going to say? Will this help you to get the job?

The results of personality assessments are rarely used as the sole basis of a selection decision. While they may be useful complements to other methods, personality assessments are usually poor performance predictors because

- people are flexible and multifaceted, able to develop new skills and behaviours and to adapt to new circumstances; personality assessment captures a fragment of the whole;
- most jobs are multifaceted in their demands on skill and knowledge, and traits which enhance competence in one task may not improve overall job performance;
- job performance usually depends on many factors unrelated to personality such as luck, training, payment systems, physical facilities, supervisory style, organization structure, company policies and procedures, and organization culture and norms;
- most jobs change over time, so predictions based on current measures are unreliable;
- nomothetic methods work with populations and large samples, against which individual profiles can be compared; these methods were not designed to make predictions about individuals, although that is how they are often used;
- in clinical and research settings, most people give honest answers about personality, but these assessments are easy to falsify when job or promotion is at stake.

New, improved interview techniques

It can be difficult to predict the future job performance of candidates using traditional interviews. Interviewees prepare, and good social skills can influence interviewers who do not have time to gather more information. Interviews can be improved by training interviewers in questioning techniques, effective probing of candidates' responses, taking notes (many interviewers do not do this), using structured rating scales, and not making any decisions until after the interviews are over. However, there are four other types of interview technique which can improve the process (Brittain, 2012). These are shown in Table 6.10.

Table 6.10: Features and drawbacks of interview techniques

interview technique	features (and drawback)
structured competency interview	interviewer asks questions focusing on key competencies and behaviours, answers are matched with desired criteria, questions are tailored to each individual candidate (may be seen as unfair)
career history interview	interviewer guides candidate through the key events in their career, what they achieved and how, what failures they have experienced and what they learned, reveals behaviour patterns leading to success (takes a lot of time)
pseudo-clinical psychology interview	interviewer asks candidate to describe earliest memories and childhood experiences, on the basis that these have an impact on work behaviour when extrapolated into adult life (may be seen by candidates as not relevant to the job)
conversational interview	similar to structured competency technique, interviewer adopts the style of a peer who is taking an interest in the candidate's role and aspirations, and allows conversation to flow naturally (needs a highly trained interviewer)

Source: based on Brittain (2012)

Interviews provide valuable, but partial, information about candidates. It is helpful to draw on information from other sources as well, such as aptitude tests and business simulation methods. Structured, competency-based, or situational interviewing has relatively high predictive validity (Chartered Institute of Personnel and Development, 2011). Candidates may also be given a series of work-based problems, and asked how they would respond. Imagine that you have applied for a job as an emergency telephone operator. Your interviewer asks you this question (Schmitt and Chan, 1998):

> Suppose a friend calls you and is very upset. Apparently, her child has been injured. She begins to tell you, in a hysterical manner, all about her difficulty in getting baby-sitters, what the child is wearing, what words the child can speak, and so on. What would you do?

How would you answer this question? Your response will be rated for communication skills, emotional control and judgement, and will be compared against the actual behaviour of high-level performers in this occupation. It is difficult for you to cheat or to practise your responses to a structured interview such as this, because you do not know what behaviours are being sought by assessors. Companies using these methods report a high success rate.

Table 6.11: Dimensions of successful intelligence

analytical	analysing, evaluating, making judgements on abstract data removed from day-to-day practicalities
creative	finding novel, high-quality solutions, going 'beyond the given', 'making do in a rapidly changing world'
practical	the solution of real problems, application of common sense, not dependent on educational qualifications

Robert Sternberg (1988, 1999) designed measures of *successful intelligence*, that is, the ability to operate effectively in a given environment. Sternberg claims that successfully intelligent people have the three kinds of abilities shown in Table 6.11. The techniques used to assess this concept in practice are similar to those used in structured or situational interviewing. Sternberg (1999, p. 31) reports this example:

> I have developed a test in which a candidate for a sales job would make a phone call and try to sell a product to an examiner. During the call, the candidate has to reply to standardized objections to the sale. Responses to test items are compared against the responses of designated experts in each field, and scoring is done by comparative profile analysis [comparing the profile of the candidate with that of the expert].

Assessment centres

Assessment centres, which use a wide range of methods, were first used during the Second World War by British War Office Selection Boards. Groups of around 6 to 10 candidates are brought together for one to three days. They are presented, individually and as a group, with a variety of exercises, tests of ability, personality assessments, interviews, work samples, team problem-solving, and written tasks. Their activities are observed and scored. This is useful for selection and promotion, staff development, talent-spotting, and career guidance and counselling. The evidence suggests that this combination of techniques can improve the probability of selecting and promoting appropriate candidates.

Critics of assessment centres point to the investment in time and money they require to design and operate. Qualified assessors are necessary, and a lack of senior management commitment to the process can give both assessors and candidates inappropriate signals. Methods must be specifically tailored to each organization's needs. The focus on observable and measurable aspects of behaviour overlooks less apparent and less easily assessed skills.

Advocates argue that the information collected is comprehensive and comparable, and candidates have opportunities to demonstrate capabilities unlikely to appear in interviews. The self-knowledge gained can also be valuable to candidates. It is claimed that a well-designed assessment centre using a variety of methods can achieve a predictive validity of 0.8 with respect to job performance (Chartered Institute of Personnel and Development, 2001).

On the horizon

Psychometrics, interviews, and simulation exercises are still used to assess the suitability of job applicants, but new approaches are on the horizon, and some are already here:

- *smartphone apps*, so that you can complete tests and fill in job applications;
- *neurological assessment*, based on the experience of Alcoholics Anonymous and WeightWatchers, exploring what causes major shifts in behaviour, and how this can be applied to the behaviours that organizations want in employees;
- *online-enabled full behavioural assessments*, based on business simulations which explore behaviour in critical leadership skills areas.

Many organizations look for more than competency and job skills. *Future potential* and *change management skills* are now vital. Anna Scott (2011) notes that

> Focusing on cultural fit has meant that organizations are incorporating their employer brand values into bespoke assessment. The Chemistry Group has taken this approach in its work with the mobile phone company O2 to create a bespoke online game that an applicant completes for an in-store 'guru' position. The game – *O2 Village* – involves candidates pretending to be a guru, with their responses to questions assessed. This is followed by a behavioural telephone assessment and then an in-store interview. In its first week, the programme saved O2 125 working days, and the quality of applicants increased.
>
> Cubiks took a similar approach in the online game it created for L'Oreal's recruitment portal, which allowed candidates to visit a number of rooms in a virtual office at the cosmetics company, and take online tests involving situational judgement questions and problem solving.

Organizations also want methods tailored to their needs and jobs. Social media such as LinkedIn, Facebook, and Twitter have also become popular ways to attract candidates. And if you find yourself being asked to play a video game such as *Happy Hour*, *Words of Wisdom*, or *Balloon Brigade*, you need to know that these have been designed to test your cognitive skills such as pattern recognition, emotional intelligence, appetite for risk, and adaptability to changing situations. In other words, selection is being 'gamified' (*The Economist*, 2012).

Does personality assessment have a future as part of the selection process? The relationships between personality constructs and job performance are modelled by Ivan Robertson (1994; see Figure 6.6). Robertson argues that the links between personality, performance, and career success must be weak. There are too many factors to allow us to make reliable predictions.

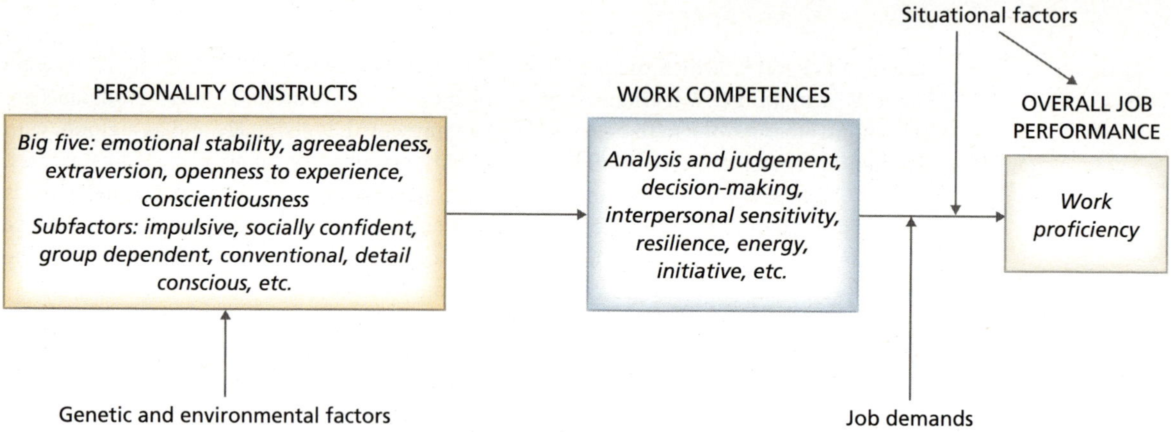

Figure 6.6: Personality and job performance

Source: from I.T. Robertson, 'Personality and personnel selection', in C.L. Cooper and D.M. Rousseau (eds), *Trends in Organizational Behaviour*, 1994, p. 8 Copyright 1994 © John Wiley & Sons Limited. Reproduced with permission.

His model identifies the demands of the job, and factors in the organizational context that can influence behaviour at work independently of, or in interaction with, personality. Robertson argues, however, that personality measures can be related to specific competencies, such as judgement, resilience, sensitivity, and energy. This is an appealing argument, and perhaps explains the popularity of psychometric assessment in the twenty-first century. He claims that the evidence supports this view, and that this is where future research should focus. He concludes that 'When the personality constructs involved are clear and thought is given to the expected link between these constructs and work behaviour, it is likely that worthwhile information may be derived from personality measurement' (Robertson, 1994, p. 85).

RECAP

1. ***Distinguish between type, trait, and self theories of personality.***
   - Type theories (Hippocrates; Sheldon; Jung) *classify* individuals using a limited number of personality categories.
   - Trait theories, based on a nomothetic perspective (Eysenck; Costa and McCrae), *profile* the individual's personality across a number of different facets.
   - Self theories, based on an idiographic perspective (Cooley; Mead), *describe* unique individual personalities.
2. ***Identify the strengths and limitations of formal methods of personality assessment.***
   - Formal methods offer objective and comprehensive assessments of personality. But they are impersonal, are based on group norms, and don't capture individual uniqueness.
   - Formal methods provide objective information about job candidates, but the links between personality assessment scores and job performance are often weak.
3. ***Explain the uses and limitations of objective questionnaires and projective tests as measures of personality.***
   - Objective questionnaires are easy to score and offer quantitative rigour. But they can only be interpreted using group norms; individual scores are meaningless.
   - Projective tests capture the richness and uniqueness of the individual. But they have complex scoring, they are subjective, and individual results cannot easily be compared.
4. ***Explain the relationship between personality and stress, and identify appropriate individual and organizational stress management strategies.***
   - Type A personalities (competitive, impatient) are more stress-prone than Type B personalities (easygoing, relaxed).

- Individuals can develop physical and psychological resilience and coping skills.
- Management has to reduce or remove work-related stressors (job design, management style, adverse working conditions, excessive workload).

5. *Evaluate the benefits and problems of psychometric assessment as a tool to assist management decision-making, particularly in selection.*
   - Psychometrics offer objective, systematic, comprehensive and quantitative information. They are also useful in career guidance, counselling and development.
   - Individual scores are meaningless outside the context of group norms.
   - It is difficult to predict job performance from a personality profile.
   - Personality assessment can identify strengths in specific areas of competence.

6. *Assess realistically the main characteristics of your own personality.*
   - Current thinking profiles personality on 'the big five' trait clusters of Openness, Conscientiousness, Extraversion, Agreeableness and Neuroticism (OCEAN). Self theories argue that the self-concept is what is important, not your test scores.

Revision

1. What is psychometrics, and what are the main applications? What are the benefits and drawbacks of psychometric assessment in organizational contexts?
2. What is 'personality' and why is this term difficult to define clearly?
3. What is the difference between 'type' and 'trait' theories of personality? Using at least one example of a trait theory, explain the benefits and problems associated with this approach to personality assessment.
4. Explain the distinction between nomothetic and idiographic views of personality. How do idiographic methods assess personality, and what are the advantages and drawbacks of these methods?

Research assignment

Interview two managers who are involved in recruiting and selecting candidates for jobs in their organizations. Choose two different types of organization for this assignment: for example, large and small, public and private sector, or manufacturing and retailing. First ask them (a) what selection methods are used by their organizations, (b) why they use those methods, and (c) what in their experience are the strengths and weaknesses of their chosen methods. Then ask them for their judgement concerning the relative importance of personality as a predictor of a candidate's future job performance. If they use psychometrics to assess personality, find out the extent to which the scores influence selection decisions. Your report will cover the following issues:

1. Describe the range of selection methods used by these organizations.
2. If the two managers reported using different methods, how can this be explained? Was this due to personal preferences, to the nature of the work for which candidates were being chosen, or to the differing nature of the organizations?
3. Summarize the strengths and weaknesses of the methods which they mentioned. Is their experience-based assessment consistent with the research evidence presented in this chapter? From what the evidence tells us about the value of different selection methods, what practical advice would you give to these two managers?
4. Prepare a brief assessment of the importance placed on personality factors by those two managers in their selection processes, compared with what the evidence says about our ability to predict job performance using personality assessment scores.

Springboard

Kathy Daniels and Lisa Ayling (2011) *Stress and Mental Health at Work*, Chartered Institute of Personnel and Development, London. Explains the nature and significance of stress, identifies the symptoms, and outlines strategies for managing stress along with legal issues. An excellent summary, available from the CIPD website.

John Toplis, Victor Dulewicz and Clive Fletcher (2005) *Psychological Testing: A Manager's Guide* (4th edn), Chartered Institute of Personnel and Development, London. Practical guide to evaluating, choosing, and using tests, including computer-administered testing.

Ashley Weinberg, Valerie J. Sutherland and Cary Cooper (2010) *Organizational Stress Management: A Strategic Approach*, Palgrave Macmillan, Houndmills, Basingstoke. Practical approaches to stress management with individual and organizational benefits, based on a thorough review of research evidence.

Moshe Zeidner, Richard D. Roberts and Gerald Matthews (2008) 'The science of emotional intelligence: current concerns and controversies', *The European Psychologist*, 13(1), pp. 64–78. Reviews the evidence on how emotional intelligence has been defined, assessed, and applied in practice, revealing the confusion and disagreement surrounding this concept.

OB in films

Who Framed Roger Rabbit (1988, director Robert Zemeckis), DVD track (scene) 7: 0:35:20 to 0:39:36 (5 minutes). Scroll into the scene to the point where Eddie enters his office; clip ends with Eddie saying to Roger, 'What's all this "we" stuff. They just want the Rabbit', when the door is shattered by gunfire and the weasels enter (from a suggestion by Champoux, 2001).

This Oscar-award-winning movie is a murder mystery involving a man, a woman, and a rabbit, in a world populated by cartoon characters ('toons') and ordinary people. Roger (a toon played by Charles Fleischer) has been framed for a murder, and asks detective Eddie Valiant (Bob Hoskins) to find his wife, and to clear his name. Eddie is an alcoholic who hates toons. During investigation, Eddie uncovers a plot to destroy all the toons.

1. Describe Roger's personality on the 'big five' dimensions.
2. Is Roger a Type A or a Type B personality? How do you know?

OB on the web

SHL is one of the leading companies developing and selling psychometric tests. Their product range includes tests of verbal, numerical, inductive, deductive, and spatial reasoning, as well as reading comprehension, situational judgement, motivation, and personality. As well as becoming familiar with what to expect when you are subjected to such tests by potential employers, it is possible to improve your performance with practice. SHL provides a number of practice tests on its website; www.shldirect.com/practice_tests.html.

Choose one or more of these tests and follow the instructions through to your score. Is this assessment accurate, in your opinion? How do you think that a potential employer would view your results? Do you think that you could get better scores with more practice?

CHAPTER EXERCISES

1. The Big Five locator

Objectives

1. To assess your personality profile on the 'big five' personality trait clusters.
2. To assess the value of this kind of personality assessment in career counselling and employment selection.

Briefing

The Big Five Locator is an easy-to-use instrument for assessing an individual's personality profile (Howard and Howard, 1993). The short version shown here for demonstration should be seen as providing only an approximate measure of traits and individual differences.

Scoring

Calculate your **openness** score by adding the numbers you circled on the third row of each five-line grouping: row 3 + row 8 + row 13 + row 18 + row 23: score = ____________

Calculate your **conscientiousness** score by adding the numbers you circled on the last row of each five-line grouping: row 5 + row 10 + row 15 + row 20 + row 25: score = ____________

Calculate your **extraversion** score by adding the numbers you circled on the second row of each five-line grouping: row 2 + row 7 + row 12 + row 17 + row 22: score = ____________

Calculate your **agreeableness** score by adding the numbers you circled on the fourth row of each five-line grouping: row 4 + row 9 + row 14 + row 19 + row 24: score = ____________

Calculate your **negative emotionality** score by adding the numbers you circled on the first row of each five-line grouping: row 1 + row 6 + row 11 + row 16 + row 21: score = ____________

Enter your five scores in this table (in OCEAN order):

Trait	Score
Openness	
Conscientiousness	
Extraversion	
Agreeableness	
Negative emotionality	

On the centre scale, circle the point which most accurately describes you between each of the two terms presented. If the two terms are equally accurate in their description, then mark the middle point.

→

1	Eager	5	4	3	2	1	Calm
2	Prefer being with others	5	4	3	2	1	Prefer being alone
3	A dreamer	5	4	3	2	1	No-nonsense
4	Courteous	5	4	3	2	1	Abrupt
5	Neat	5	4	3	2	1	Messy
6	Cautious	5	4	3	2	1	Confident
7	Optimistic	5	4	3	2	1	Pessimistic
8	Theoretical	5	4	3	2	1	Practical
9	Generous	5	4	3	2	1	Selfish
10	Decisive	5	4	3	2	1	Open-ended
11	Discouraged	5	4	3	2	1	Upbeat
12	Exhibitionist	5	4	3	2	1	Private
13	Follow imagination	5	4	3	2	1	Follow authority
14	Warm	5	4	3	2	1	Cold
15	Stay focused	5	4	3	2	1	Easily distracted
16	Easily embarrassed	5	4	3	2	1	Don't give a damn
17	Outgoing	5	4	3	2	1	Cool
18	Seek novelty	5	4	3	2	1	Seek routine
19	Team player	5	4	3	2	1	Independent
20	A preference for order	5	4	3	2	1	Comfortable with chaos
21	Distractible	5	4	3	2	1	Unflappable
22	Conversational	5	4	3	2	1	Thoughtful
23	Comfortable with ambiguity	5	4	3	2	1	Prefer things clear-cut
24	Trusting	5	4	3	2	1	Sceptical
25	On time	5	4	3	2	1	Procrastinate

When you have calculated your five scores, transfer them to this interpretation sheet by putting a cross at the approximate point on each scale:

Big five locator score interpretation

low openness: practical, conservative, efficient, expert	preserver 10	moderator 15	explorer 20	**high openness**: curious, liberal, impractical, likes novelty
low conscientiousness: spontaneous, fun-loving, experimental, unorganized	flexible 10	balanced 15	focused 20	**high conscientiousness**: dependable, organized, disciplined, cautious, stubborn
low extraversion: private, independent, works alone, reserved	introvert 10	ambivert 15	extravert 20	**high extraversion**: assertive, sociable, warm, optimistic
low agreeableness: sceptical, tough, aggressive, self-interested	challenger 10	negotiator 15	adapter 20	**high agreeableness**: trusting, humble, altruistic, team player
low negative emotionality: secure, unflappable, unresponsive, guilt-free	resilient 10	responsive 15	reactive 20	**high negative emotionality**: excitable, worrying, reactive, alert

Syndicate groups

1. How accurate do you find your personality profile from this assessment? If it was inaccurate, why do you think that was the case?

2. How helpful is this personality assessment to job interviewers who need to make predictions about a candidate's future job performance? What aspects of the assessment make it valuable in this respect? What aspects make it unhelpful?
3. What actions can be taken to maximize the contribution of personality assessments in selecting candidates for jobs?

Plenary

- Why do you think we as individuals are interested in understanding more about our personalities?
- Why do you think organizations are interested in the personalities of job applicants?

This exercise is based on Howard et al. (1996).

2. Biters and bleaters

It may be obvious that we all like to win and hate to lose, but it seems that some of us actually find winning stressful. To assess your own views, take the following test. Rate how you feel you would respond – strongly disagree to strongly agree – to each of these situations:

	strongly disagree	**disagree**	**agree**	**strongly agree**
You get really wound up when your sports team loses.	1	2	3	4
You really hate it when you go to a meeting to seek approval for a decision and approval is not forthcoming.	1	2	3	4
If you were in charge of a budget, and it was cut, you would willingly accept it.	4	3	2	1
You choose a fixed-rate mortgage and a month later interest rates are cut. This doesn't bother you.	4	3	2	1
You are interviewed for a job and fail to make the final shortlist. You are gutted for weeks.	1	2	3	4
You compete with a colleague for promotion. You hear on the grapevine that your competitor has got it. It doesn't bother you.	4	3	2	1
When you're in social situations and others are dominating the conversation, this frustrates you.	1	2	3	4
At the office party, your partner makes a lighthearted remark about your lack of competence at domestic chores. You are hurt.	1	2	3	4

Oliver Schultheiss at the University of Michigan suggests that we are divided between wolves, who want to win, and sheep, who are distressed by beating others (Ahuja, 2006). The research first used a projective test, asking subjects to describe what they saw in photographs of people competing. The stories were scored for 'implicit power motivation' with high scorers designated wolves, and low scorers as sheep. They were then paired and asked to compete on a task requiring speed and accuracy, but the results were fixed in advance.

Saliva samples were used to measure the level of a stress hormone. When the wolves lost, they became stressed. But when the sheep *won*, they became stressed. If you know the category to which you belong, you can adjust your work environment accordingly. Typical

→

wolf occupations are: politician, teacher, stand-up comedian. Typical sheep occupations are: office worker, researcher, accountant. While some of us are competitive and find positions of power satisfying, others are less comfortable dominating others.

Which are you? To calculate your score, just add the numbers in the boxes that you ticked:

Score 8–15: Sheep. You don't hate winning, but when you lose, it doesn't baa-ther you.

Score 16–24: Wolf in sheep's clothing. Winning is more important in some aspects of life (work) than in others (relationships).

Score 25–32: Wolf. You have a howl-at-the-moon obsession with winning at everything.

Syndicate groups

1. Who are the sheep and who are the wolves in your group? Are the sheep happy about their scores, or do they want to be wolves instead? Are the wolves happy, or would they prefer to be sheep? Is it possible for people to change from one to the other?
2. Find out whether the wolves and sheep in your group have already chosen occupations and careers that are typical for people with those profiles. Do you think that sheep in wolves' occupations will be less comfortable and less effective – and vice versa?

Plenary

- How useful are the results of this assessment to potential employers?

Employability assessment

With regard to your future employment prospects:

1. Identify up to three issues from this chapter that you found significant.
2. Relate these to the competencies in the employability matrix.
3. Decide what actions you need to take to maintain and/or develop those competencies under each of the four headings of the employability matrix.

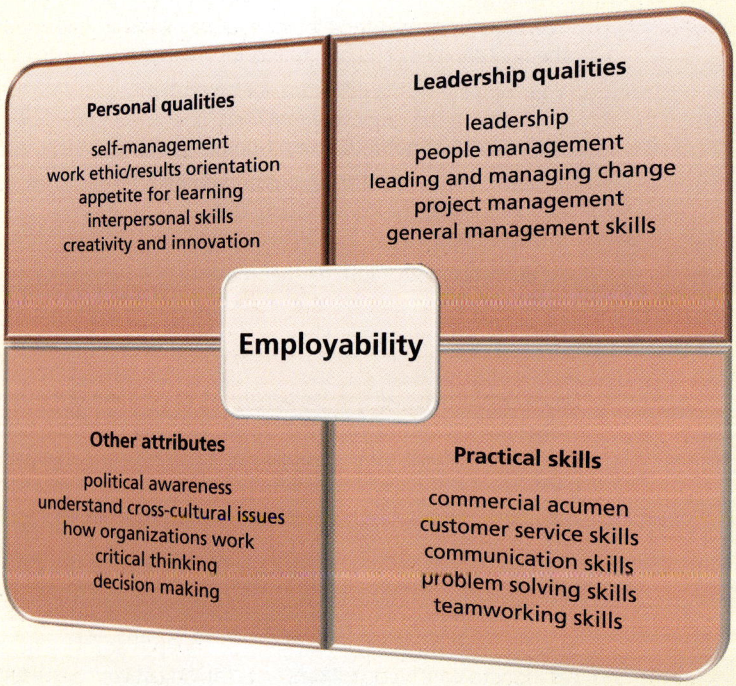

References

Ahuja, A. (2006) 'Born to lose?', *The Times*, Times 2, 31 August, pp. 4–5.

Arnold, D.W. and Jones, J.W. (2006) 'Who the devil's applying now?', from www.crimcheck.com/employment_testing.htm.

Belbin, R.M. (1981) *Management Teams: Why They Succeed or Fail*, London: Butterworth Heinemann.

Belbin, R.M. (1993) *Team Roles at Work*, Oxford: Butterworth Heinemann.

Brittain, S. (2012) 'Interviewing skills: building a solid structure', *People Management*, April, pp. 30–3.

Buchholz, T.G. (2011a) *Rush: Why You Need and Love the Rat Race*, New York: Hudson Street Press.

Buchholz, T.G. (2011b) 'Stressing the benefits', *RSA Journal*, Autumn, pp. 20–1.

Champoux, J.E. (2001) *Organizational Behavior: Using film to Visualize Principles and Practices*, Cincinnati, OH: South-Western College Publishing.

Chartered Institute of Personnel and Development (2001) *Quick Facts: Assessment Centres for Recruitment and Selection*, London: Chartered Institute of Personnel and Development.

Chartered Institute of Personnel and Development (2011) *Resourcing and Talent Planning: Annual Survey Report*, London: Chartered Institute of Personnel and Development.

Cooley, Charles Horton (1902) *Human Nature and the Social Order*, New York: Scribner's.

Costa, P. and McCrae, R.R. (1992) *NEO PI-R: Professional Manual*, Odessa, Florida: Psychological Assessment Resources.

Eysenck, H.J. (1970) *The Structure of Human Personality* (3rd edn), London: Methuen.

Eysenck, H.J. (1990) 'Biological dimensions of personality', in L.A. Pervin (ed.), *Handbook of Personality, Theory and Research*, New York: Guilford Press, pp. 244–76.

Friedman, M. and Rosenman, R.F. (1974) *Type A Behaviour and Your Heart*, New York: Knopf.

Furnham, A. (2012) 'Signs that you are sailing with Captain Catastrophe', *The Sunday Times*, Appointments section, 29 January, p. 3.

Howard, P.J. and Howard, J.M. (1993) *The Big Five Workbook: A Roadmap for Individual and Team Interpretation of Scores on the Five-Factor Model of Personality*, Charlotte, NC: Center for Applied Cognitive Studies.

Howard, P.J., Medina, P.L. and Howard, J.M. (1996) 'The big five locator: a quick assessment tool for consultants and trainers', in *The 1996 Annual: Volume 1, Training*, San Diego, CA: Pfeiffer & Company, pp. 107–22.

Jung, C.G. (1953) *Collected Works*, New York: Bollingen Series/Pantheon.

Jung, C.G. (1971) *Psychological Types (The Collected Works of C.G. Jung, Volume 6)*, Princeton, NJ: Princeton University Press (first published 1923).

McClelland, D.C. (1961) *The Achieving Society*, Princeton, NJ: Van Nostrand Reinhold.

McClelland, D.C., Atkinson, J.W., Clark, R.A. and Lowell, E.L. (1976) *The Achievement Motive* (2nd edn), New York: Irvington.

Marchington, M. and Wilkinson, A. (2005) *Human Resource Management at Work* (3rd edn), London: Chartered Institute of Personnel and Development.

Mead, G.H. (1934) *Mind, Self and Society*, Chicago, IL: University of Chicago Press.

Morris, S. (1999) 'An Eastern art of healing that is heading West', *The Times*, 26 October, p. 47.

Moutafi, J., Furnham, A. and Crump, J. (2007) 'Is managerial level related to personality?', *British Journal of Management*, 18(3), pp. 272–80.

Myers, I.B. (1962) *The Myers-Briggs Type Indicator Manual*, Princeton, NJ: Educational Testing Service.

Myers, I.B. (1976) *Introduction to Type* (2nd edn), Gainesville, FL: Centre for Applications of Psychological Type.

Myers, I.B. and McCaulley, M.H. (1985) *Manual: A Guide to the Development and Use of the Myers-Briggs Type Indicator*, Palo Alto, CA: Consulting Psychologists Press.

Pinker, S. (2002) *The Blank Slate: The Modern Denial of Human Nature*, London: Allen Lane The Penguin Press.

Randler, C. (2010) 'The early bird really does get the worm', *Harvard Business Review*, 88(7/8), pp. 30–1.

Robertson, I.T. (1994) 'Personality and personnel selection', in C.L. Cooper and D.M. Rousseau (eds), *Trends in Organizational Behaviour*, London: John Wiley.

Robertson, I. (2001) 'Undue diligence', *People Management*, 7(23), pp. 42–3.

Rogers, C.R. (1947) 'Some observations on the organization of personality', *American Psychologist*, 2(9), pp. 358–68.

Schmitt, N. and Chan, D. (1998) *Personnel Selection: A Theoretical Approach*, Thousand Oaks, CA: Sage Publications.

Scott, A. (2011) 'Assessment: promise land', *People Management*, 31 August, pp. 49–52.

Sheldon, W. (1942) *The Varieties of Temperament: A Psychology of Constitutional Differences*, New York: Harper and Row.

Sternberg, R.J. (1988) *The Triarchic Mind: A New Theory of Human Intelligence*, New York: Viking.

Sternberg, R.J. (1999) 'Survival of the fit test', *People Management*, 4(24), pp. 29–31.

Tehrani, N. and Ayling, L. (2008) *Stress at Work*, London: Chartered Institute of Personnel and Development.

The Economist (2012) 'Work and play: the gamification of hiring', 26 May, p. 65.

Whitely, P. (2012) 'Are Britons getting more dishonest?', *University of Essex Centre for the Study of Integrity Working Paper*, Essex, January.

Zibarras, L.D. and Woods, Stephen A. (2010) 'A survey of UK selection practices across different organization sizes and industry sectors', *Journal of Occupational and Organizational Psychology*, 83(2), pp. 499–511.

Chapter 7 **Communication**

Key terms

social intelligence
communication process
coding
decoding
perceptual filters
noise
feedback
non-verbal communication
power tells
high context culture
low context culture
impression management
emotional intelligence
communication climate

Learning outcomes

When you have read this chapter, you should be able to define those key terms in your own words, and you should also be able to:

1. Describe the dimensions of social intelligence, and explain the importance of these capabilities, especially for managers.
2. Understand the main components of the interpersonal communication process.
3. Identify the main barriers to effective interpersonal communication.
4. Understand the effective use of different questioning techniques, conversation controls, and listening skills.
5. Explain the nature and significance of non-verbal communication.
6. Understand the nature and mechanisms of impression management skills and techniques.
7. Be able to explain the concept of emotional intelligence and its practical significance.
8. Understand the ways in which corporate communication can be used to manipulate understanding and encourage compliance with management directions.

Why study communication?

Communication is central to understanding organizational behaviour for several reasons:

- communication affects organizational performance and individual career prospects;
- very few people work alone, and the job of most managers involves interacting with other people, often for more than 90 per cent of their time;
- communication is seen as a problem in many organizations;
- in an increasingly diverse multicultural society, sensitivity to the norms and expectations of other cultures is vital to effective cross-cultural communication;
- new technology is radically changing our patterns of communication.

Organizational communication is a discipline in its own right, with its own research traditions and specialist journals. Everything significant that happens in an organization involves communication: hiring and training staff, providing feedback, purchasing supplies, solving problems, dealing with customers, deciding strategy. However, communication is often interrupted by hierarchical structures, power and status differences, the design of jobs, the nature of (part-time, temporary) employment, physical layouts, and rules.

Most managers spend a lot of time in meetings and in conversation, talking and listening, networking and influencing, gathering information and negotiating. Henry Mintzberg (2009) emphasizes the need for managers to have 'information competencies', or a range of communication skills. John Kotter (1999) found that general managers spend most of their time talking to others, often on topics not related to the business, but central to maintaining networks and relationships, and to developing goals and action plans.

Social intelligence the ability to understand the thoughts and feelings of others and to manage our relationships accordingly.

Are you able to 'feel' what others are feeling? Can you 'read' what's happening in complex social settings? Do you use that understanding to manage your relationships? If so, then you have **social intelligence**. Despite modern communications technology, personal interactions including one-to-one, face-to-face, 'F2F', or 'face time' are still important, perhaps even more so. Our ability to interact effectively with others was first described as social intelligence in 1920 by Edward Thorndike, but the idea was seen then as just another aspect of general intelligence. (We will explore the related concept of *emotional intelligence* later in this chapter.)

Daniel Goleman (2006) argues that social intelligence is a special set of capabilities, including social awareness (what we sense about others) and social facility (how we act on that awareness). Each of these dimensions has four ingredients, shown in Table 7.1. He argues that you can improve your social intelligence with training and experience, and that these capabilities lead to personal and management effectiveness. Globalization and international mobility mean that we often find ourselves working with people from other countries and cultures. Different cultures have differing norms concerning how conversations should be handled, including appropriate greetings, degree of formality, the use of eye contact, suitable topics for discussion, physical distance between speakers, and the interpretation of gestures. Social intelligence in a culturally diverse context has become increasingly important. Goldman Sachs, the US bank, has a programme designed to help its Japanese staff to interact more comfortably and effectively with colleagues from other countries. Social norms in Japan encourage holding back in meetings, acting with modesty, and avoiding 'behind the scenes' lobbying – the opposite of expectations in Western companies (Nakamoto, 2012).

Modern communications technologies have not yet overcome the need for people to meet in person. Where information is easily codified (a booking, a bank statement), and transactions are simple (pay a bill, buy a ticket), an exchange can be completed online. However, where transactions are complex and based on judgements ('what is your opinion?', 'could we do it this way?'), where emotions and feelings are as significant as facts and figures, the social and geographical context, the quality of relationships, and interpersonal trust are all crucial.

Table 7.1: Social intelligence

social awareness	*primal empathy*	'reading' others' emotions intuitively from small clues (such as a brief facial expression)
	attunement	understanding the other person through complete and sustained attention and careful listening
	empathic accuracy	explicit understanding, through observation and inference, of what someone feels and thinks
	social cognition	knowing how the social world works and what is expected; reading the social signals
social facility	*synchrony*	harmoniously orchestrating our interactions with the right gestures (smiles, nods, posture, timing)
	self-preservation	ability in interactions to trigger desired emotional responses in others; charisma
	influence	shaping the outcomes of interactions with tact and control, tuning actions to fit the circumstances
	concern	capacity for compassion, sharing others' emotions of elation or distress

Source: based on Coleman (2006).

Can social intelligence really be improved with training? Ken Rea (2010), who teaches acting at the Guildhall School of Music and Drama in London, tells this story:

> Recently, when I was coaching a senior manager of a multinational, he confided, 'When I speak in a meeting people cut me off. They don't seem to listen to my ideas. Then another person in the meeting will have the same idea and they will all listen to her. If I could fix that, I'd be happy.' We did a role play where he had to ask his chief executive for more resources. I sat in as the chief executive. He sat hunched.

Medical diagnoses

Most professions develop their own 'jargon' which can confuse outsiders. Although their use is declining, Roland White (2011) collected the following medical terms:

medical diagnosis	**meaning**
FLK	funny-looking kid
NFN	normal for Norfolk
JPROOG	just plain ran out of gas (old age eventually took its course)
LOBNH	lights on but nobody home (patient of limited intelligence)
TTFO	told to shove off
PRATTFO	patient reassured and told to shove off
GOK	God only knows (no specific diagnosis as yet)
PFO	pissed, fell over (patient has minor alcohol-related injury)
UBI	unexplained beer injury (possibly PFO)
Mrs Brown is waiting	there is a cup of tea ready for you
Hasselhof	patient with an unusual injury, after the actor David Hasselhof who severed a tendon in his arm on a chandelier while shaving

Now, when you sit like that, you are not going to be breathing properly and it will affect your voice, which will sound monotonous. It will also affect how you feel. He soon had a scowl on his face. I asked him to sit up, then to send out a more friendly energy. When we looked at the video recording afterwards, he was amazed. He never realized what negative signals he had been sending out. Suddenly he could see why people were cutting him off: there was absolutely no commitment to his message. He could see it in his body and hear it in his voice. But by sitting up straight and projecting a friendly energy, suddenly the voice brightened and became more powerful. The eyes came alive, and there on the screen was the commitment to what he was saying. Nobody would cut off this person. He walked out of the room a different man.

Interpersonal communication

> *Conversation*: a competitive sport in which the first person to draw breath is declared the listener.

Communication process the transmission of information, and the exchange of meaning, between at least two people.

In most cultures, conversation is a social imperative in which silences are discouraged (Finland is different). Normally, as soon as one person stops talking, another takes their turn. The currency of conversation is information. We ask you the time. You tell us the time. Information has been transmitted. Interpersonal communication has been achieved. However, the **communication process** is often more subtle and interesting.

We will first focus on interpersonal communication. A more detailed study would recognize the importance of other aspects of communication, including the use of different media, networks, and inter-organizational communication. The principles that we will explore, however, have wide application. For the moment, let us focus on 'one-on-one' or 'F2F' communication, and examine our definition of the communication process.

STOP AND THINK

We all have experience of ineffective communication. Either the other person misunderstood what you had to say, or you misunderstood them. Remember the last time this happened. What went wrong? What caused that communication to fail? Share your analysis with colleagues to see whether there are common causes.

We do not receive communication passively. We have to interpret or decode the message. To the extent that we interpret communication from others in the manner they intended, and they in turn interpret our messages correctly, then communication is effective. However, communication is an error-prone process.

Interpersonal communication typically involves much more than the simple transmission of information. Pay close attention to the next person who asks you what time it is. You will often be able to tell how they are feeling, and about why they need to know, if they are in a hurry, perhaps, or if they are anxious or nervous, or bored with waiting. In other words, their question has a purpose or a meaning. Although it is not always stated directly, we can often infer that meaning from the context and from their behaviour.

Communication is an error-prone process

I rang the bell of a small bed-and-breakfast place, whereupon a lady appeared at an upstairs window. 'What do you want?', she asked. 'I want to stay here', I replied. 'Well, stay there then', she said and banged the window shut.

Chick Murray, Scottish comedian

The same considerations apply to your response. Your reply suggests, at least, a willingness to be helpful, may imply friendship, and may also indicate that you share the same concern as the person asking the question (we are going to be late; when will this film start?). However, your reply can also indicate frustration and annoyance; 'five minutes since the last time you asked me!'. Communication thus involves the transmission of both information and meaning.

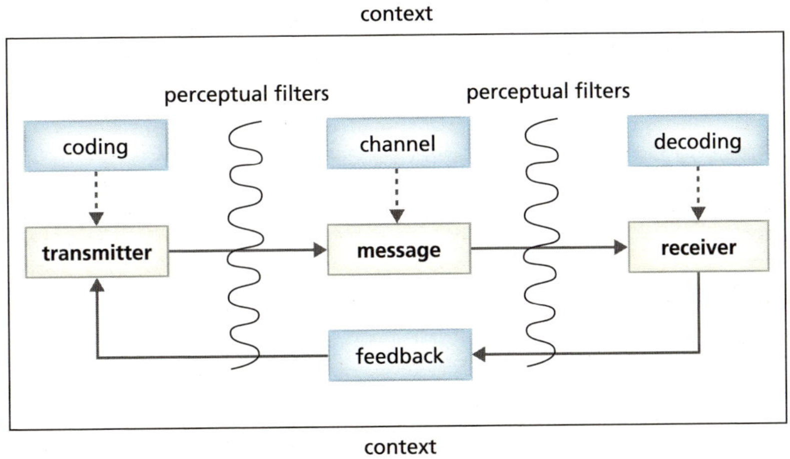

Figure 7.1: Exchanging meaning: a model of the communication process

Coding the stage in the interpersonal communication process in which the transmitter chooses how to express a message for transmission to someone else.

Decoding the stage in the interpersonal communication process in which the recipient interprets a message transmitted to them by someone else.

Perceptual filters individual characteristics, predispositions, and preoccupations that interfere with the effective transmission and receipt of messages.

This process of exchange is illustrated in Figure 7.1, which shows the main elements of interpersonal communication. This model is based on the work of Claude Shannon and Warren Weaver (1949), who were concerned with signal processing in electronic systems, rather than with organizational communication.

At the heart of this model, we have a transmitter sending a message to a receiver. We will assume that the channel is face-to-face, rather than over a telephone, or through a letter, or a videoconference, or email. It is useful to think of the way in which the transmitter phrases and expresses the message as a **coding** process; the transmitter chooses words, and also how the message will be expressed (loud and with exasperation, or quiet and in a friendly manner, for example). The success of our communication depends on the accuracy of the receiver's **decoding**; did they understand the language used, and appreciate the exasperation or friendship? We each have our own **perceptual filters** which can interfere with accurate decoding, such as predispositions to hear, or not to hear, particular types of information, and preoccupations which divert our attention elsewhere.

This model highlights the problems that arise in communication, and suggests solutions. There are many ways in which coding and decoding can go wrong; some common terms can lead to misunderstandings:

term	popular use	dictionary definition
decimate	devastate	cut by ten per cent
exotic	colourful, glamorous	from another country
aggravate	to annoy, to irritate	to make worse
clinical	cold, impersonal	caring, at the bedside of the sick
avid	enthusiastic	greedy

The branch manager who receives from head office an instruction to 'decimate' her or his salesforce would thus be advised to check the original coding of the message before taking action. Using the dictionary definition of the word exotic implies that Hyundai, Kia, Volvo, and Skoda sell exotic motor cars in Britain. To be successful, transmitters and receivers need to share a common 'codebook'.

STOP AND THINK

What other expressions create coding and decoding problems? Identify examples – which can be humorous, as with the man who asked for wild duck in a restaurant and was told by the waiter 'I don't have wild duck, sir, but I can annoy one for you.'

Eurocommunications fog

With the growth in membership of the European Union, the problems of translating communications, both written and spoken, have multiplied (*The Economist*, 2004). So we need guides to what, for example, English and French speakers actually mean.

English speaker	French interpreter	Actual meaning
I hear what you say	He accepts my point of view	I disagree and do not want to discuss it further
With the greatest respect	He is complimenting me	I think you are wrong or foolish
By the way	This is not important	The main aim of this discussion
I'll bear that in mind	I will act on that	I will do nothing about that
Correct me if I'm wrong	Correct him if he's wrong	I'm correct, please don't contradict me

French speaker	Literal English	Actual meaning
Je serai clair	I will be clear	I will be rude
Il faut la visibilité Européenne	We need European visibility	The EU must indulge in some pointless international grand-standing
Il faut trouver une solution pragmatique	We must find a pragmatic solution	I am about to propose a highly complex, theoretical, legalistic, and unworkable way forward

Language is also used to 'soften' or to disguise unpleasant events. Employees being made redundant, for example, may be 'given the pink slip', 'downsized', 'rightsized', 'delayered', or invited to 'take gardening leave', to 'spend more time with the family', or to 'put their careers on hold'. They may also be 'counselled on', 'repositioned', or urged to 'develop their careers elsewhere' or to 'explore other opportunities for their talents', but are rarely 'fired' or 'given the chop'. In some organizations, there are no 'problems and difficulties', only 'challenges and opportunities'. The fictional character Martin Lukes is advised not to compare his strengths with his weaknesses, but with his 'less strong strengths' (Kellaway, 2005). This is similar to the student who does not 'fail' exams, but experiences 'deferred success'.

The communication process is further complicated by the perceptual filters which affect what we say, and which in turn affect what we hear and how we hear it. When you asked what time it was, did you 'hear' the frustration or friendship in the response? Or did you simply focus on the time issue, because that was more important to you? The transmitter of a message has motives, objectives, personality traits, values, biases, and prejudices, which colour the content and expression of communication. We decide the information we wish to reveal, and which to withhold or conceal from others. We do not always perform this filtering consciously. Similarly, at the receiving end, perceptual filtering can affect what is heard, what is decoded, what is not decoded, and the way in which the message is understood.

There is a further complicating factor: the physical, social, and cultural context. The casual remark by a colleague across a restaurant table ('we could all be redundant by Christmas') may be dismissed. The same casual remark by a colleague across an office desk can be a source of considerable alarm. An innocent gesture in one culture can cause offence in another. The style and content of our conversation depends often on our relationships with others. Status differences colour our communication. We do not reveal to the boss what we discuss with colleagues. The style and content of communication can change in a striking manner when normal organizational relationships are 'suspended', such as during an office party.

Noise factors outside the communication process which interfere with or distract attention from the transmission and reception of the intended meaning.

Anything that interferes with a communication signal is called **noise** by electronics experts. Communication suffers from noise, a term which covers more than just the sound of machinery and other people talking. Noise includes coding and decoding problems and errors, perceptual filters, and any other factors that damage the integrity of our chosen channel, including issues arising from our relationships with others. Our motives, emotions and health can constitute noise; coding and decoding are affected by anxiety, pressure, stress, and our levels of enthusiasm and excitement.

Source: www.CartoonStock.com

Our past experiences also affect the way in which we see things today, and lead us to filter what we transmit and what we receive. Communication stumbles when transmitter and receiver have different frames of reference, and do not share experience and understanding, even where they share a common language. We make judgements about the honesty, integrity, trustworthiness, and credibility of others, and decode their messages and act on them (or not) accordingly. People in an organizational setting may have time to reflect, or they may be under time pressure or 'communication overload'.

Feedback processes through which the transmitter of a message detects whether and how that message has been received and decoded.

There is a final aspect of our communication model which we have to consider: **feedback**. When we communicate face-to-face, we can usually tell if the other person likes us, if they agree with us, and if they are interested in what we have to say – or not. How do we know this? Well, they may say 'that's interesting', or 'I disagree', or 'I have to catch my flight'. We can also tell from cues such as the tone of their replies, their facial expression, body posture, and limb gestures. We will explore the coding and decoding of *non-verbal communication* (body language) later in the chapter.

When we communicate face-to-face, we get instant feedback from what others say and how they say it. This rich feedback loop helps us to exchange information more effectively. Our communication can be awkward where feedback is delayed or absent. Feedback allows us to check the accuracy of the coding and decoding processes. We ask a question, see the other person look annoyed or puzzled, realize that we have not worded our question appropriately, and 'recode' the message. Face-to-face, if we pay attention, this works well. With more formal and distant forms of communication, feedback can be partial (as over the phone), delayed or nonexistent, and we need to be more careful about our coding.

Charm offensive

British soldiers in Iraq and Afghanistan were given a guide to social interaction, with advice on conversation topics, responding to hospitality, and how to read gestures (Evans, 2008).

The Arab world: an introduction to cultural appreciation

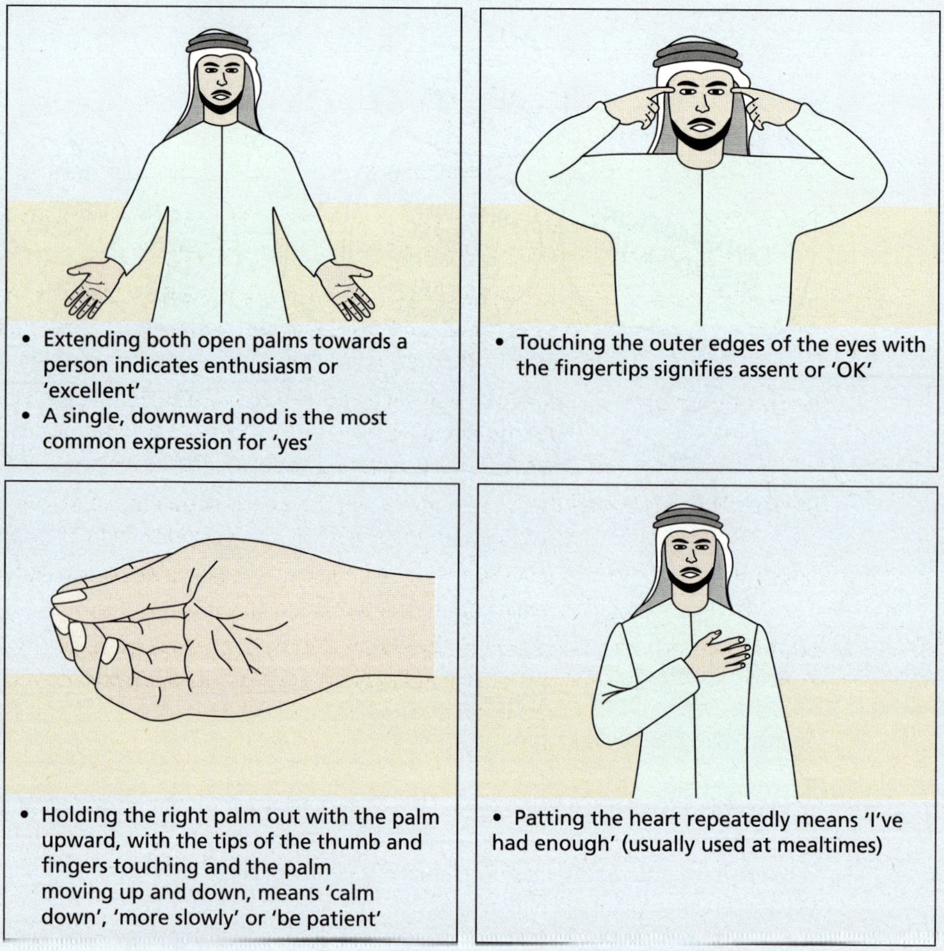

© Evans/*The Times*/News International Trading Ltd, 11 February 2008.

Troops were given the following advice to avoid causing offence in the Arab world:

gestures	Avoid the 'OK' sign which widely means the 'evil eye'.
shaking hands	It is disrespectful for a man to offer his hand to a woman.
social interaction	There is no 'personal space'; Arab culture stresses the need to 'share the breath' of a companion.
conversation	Men should not question other men about the women in their family.

In Afghanistan, men should not have any physical contact with women in public; food is served in communal dishes and eaten with the right hand; legs should be crossed when sitting; women's legs, ankles, and feet must be covered; and it is offensive to point the soles of your shoes towards someone.

STOP AND THINK

With whom do you communicate often? What prevents effective communication in your experience? How can you improve the effectiveness of your communication?

We can be careless coders and lazy listeners. The communication process appears to be simple, but it is prone to errors arising on both sides of the exchange. We cannot confidently assume that receivers will always decode our messages in a way that gives them the meaning that we intended to transmit. Communication is central to organizational effectiveness, but this claim has practical implications. We assume that organizations function better where

- communications are open,
- relationships are based on mutual understanding and trust,
- interactions are based on cooperation rather than competition,
- people work together in teams, and
- decisions are reached in a participative way.

These features, however, are not universal, and do not feature in all countries or cultures.

The main barriers to effective organizational communication are:

power differences	Research consistently shows that employees distort upward communication, and that superiors often have a limited understanding of subordinates' roles, experiences and problems.
gender differences	Men and women use different conversational styles which can lead to misunderstanding; men tend to talk more and give information while women tend to listen and reflect more.
physical surroundings	Room size and layout influence our ability to see others and our readiness to participate in conversations and discussions.
language	Even within one country, variations in accent and dialect can make communication difficult.
cultural diversity	Different cultures have different norms and expectations concerning formal and informal conversations; lack of awareness of those norms creates misunderstanding.

Skype skills

Computer screens, like television, exaggerate small movements such as stroking your hair, picking your nose, or biting your lip. With the growing use of Skype and videoconferencing, your online behaviour can influence your reputation and your career. Here is some advice on online communication style (Lublin, 2006):

Choose your clothes carefully

Dress as you would for the office, and avoid 'busy' patterns. Do not wear casual shorts under the smart top, as you may have to stand up to get something.

Pay attention

Do not stare at the screen, or you will appear 'stiff'. Maintain eye contact with viewers and with those in the room. When selling an idea, lean slightly towards the camera. Do not shift your gaze frequently or appear detached. Do not frown, slouch, cup your chin in your hands, or bounce around in your chair. Do not leave the room, and do not lean back in your chair. Women appear more effective if they perch on the edge of their seat throughout the session.

Remember the camera's reach

If you roll your eyes or make some other dismissive gesture while somebody else is speaking, your viewers may see that, even if colleagues in the room do not. Do not fall asleep, and if you do, don't snore. Remember that those at the other end may be able to see and to hear you before the meeting begins formally, and will hear what you say about them in advance.

→

Avoid culturally insensitive gestures
For example, Asian viewers are often uncomfortable with large demonstrative hand and body movements. This is particularly important for international videoconferencing.

Calm your nerves by practising
Rehearse, role-play, sharpen your delivery, practice boldness. Make a video of yourself, and replay with the sound off to monitor your body language. Then replay without watching to monitor your vocal delivery; avoid 'squeak speak' – sounding like a mouse.

Maureen Guirdham (2002) offers this advice for improving our communications:

face-to-face When we are able to speak with someone directly, we can use the feedback constantly to check the coding and decoding processes, and to correct mistakes and misunderstanding.

reality checks We should not assume that others will necessarily decode our messages in the way we intended, and we should check the way in which our messages have been interpreted.

place and time The right message delivered in the wrong place or at the wrong time is more likely to be decoded incorrectly, or even ignored, so choose the time and place with sensitivity and care.

empathetic listening See things from the other person's point of view, consider the thinking that may have led to their behaviour, decode the message the way they might decode it, listen attentively to feedback.

Verbal communication

The word 'verbal' also causes decoding problems. Verbal means 'in words', which can be either spoken or written. 'Verbal agreement' and 'verbal warning' can thus refer either to oral or to written communication, and both are contrasted with non-verbal communication.

Most conversations involve exchanges of information or meaning. How do we get the information we want? We achieve this through a range of questioning techniques. The main types of question are shown in Table 7.2. By using these labels, it becomes easier to analyse the questioning techniques used by others, and it is easier for us to make conscious choices about how to conduct our own side of a conversation more effectively.

The first basic distinction in questioning strategy is between closed and open questions. Closed questions invite a factual statement in reply, or a simple yes or no response. Open questions, in contrast, invite the person responding to disclose further information. Predict the differences in response to these two questions:

Will you have dinner with me this evening?

What are you doing this evening?

It seems as though closed questions are limited while open questions are more effective. If the purpose is to get the other person to divulge lots of information, then this assessment is correct. However, closed questions are particularly useful in two settings. First, where all that is required is simple factual information, for example 'Are you coming to the meeting?'. Open questions invite the discussion of irrelevant information, for which there may be no time. Second, interviewers often begin with a short series of closed questions in order to establish the conversation pattern. We have all had experience of conversations where the other person took control, giving us information which we did not want. Closed questioning can avoid this. Consider the following questioning sequence used at the beginning of an interview:

Table 7.2: Questioning techniques

question type	illustration	uses
closed	Did you enjoy the movie?	to get a 'yes' or 'no' answer; to obtain factual information; to establish conversation control
open	What did you think of that movie?	to introduce a subject; to encourage further discussion; to keep the other person talking
probe	Can you tell me more about that?	to follow up an open question; to get more information; to demonstrate interest
reflective	You thought the acting was poor?	to show interest and concern; to encourage further disclosure of feelings and emotions
multiple	What did you think of the movie, and wasn't the star excellent in that role, and didn't you think that the ending was predictable?	confuses the listener; gives them a choice of question to which to respond
leading	You didn't see anyone leaving the house?	to get the answer that you expect to hear (so, why ask?)
hypothetical	What would happen if. . . .?	to encourage creative thinking

What is your current job title?

How long have you been in your present position?

What was your previous position?

This can help to establish the conversation pattern by signalling to the other person 'I ask the questions, you give the answers'. Usually, by the time the third or fourth closed question has been answered, the person being interviewed will wait for the interviewer to ask their next question, and will not begin talking about some other issue.

Probes are simply another type of open question, and indicate that the listener is interested. In most cases, that indication of interest encourages the disclosure of further information.

The reflective statement is a powerful technique for maintaining rapport and encouraging the disclosure of information, particularly concerning feelings and emotions. All that you have to do is to mirror or reflect back to the person an emotion that they have 'given' to you. The emotion expressed can be spoken ('you didn't enjoy your holiday then') or it can reflect a non-verbal expression ('you look happy this morning'). As with probes, reflective statements signal interest and concern and encourage the other person to continue disclosing information.

STOP AND THINK

Record a television police drama, a magazine programme, or a news broadcast. Watch somebody being interviewed: for example, police interviewing suspect, host interviewing celebrity, or news reader interviewing politician. Identify the questioning techniques used. What advice can you give the interviewer to help improve their questioning?

Replay this interview with the sound off. Can you identify any barriers which made this communication less effective – physical layout, posture, timing, non-verbal behaviours? What further advice can you give to the interviewer?

Multiple questions and leading questions are rarely used by trained interviewers. Multiples are often heard on radio and television, particularly when politicians are being asked about their positions and views on topical subjects. Leading questions are especially ineffective when fresh information is required. Watch a police drama on television, and identify how many times witnesses and suspects are confronted with questions such as:

So you didn't see anyone else leave the house after five o'clock?

You're saying that the stolen televisions were put in your garage by somebody else?

Hypothetical questions can be useful in stimulating creative and innovative 'blue skies' thinking. Used in selection interviewing, this technique only tells us how well the candidate handles hypothetical questions, and reveals little about their future job performance.

We also control our conversations through a range of conscious and unconscious verbal and non-verbal signals which tell the parties to a conversation, for example, when one has finished an utterance and when it is somebody else's turn to speak. These signals reveal agreement, friendship, dispute, and dislike – emotions which in turn shape the further response of the listener. The four main conversation control signals are explained in Table 7.3. Note that the different uses and implications of pauses in conversation depend on the context.

Table 7.3: Conversation control signals

signal	example	meaning
lubricators	'uh huh'; 'mmm, mmm' and other grunts and groans	I'm listening, keep talking, I'm interested
inhibitors	'what !'; 'really', 'oh', and similar loud interjections	I'm surprised, I don't agree, I've heard enough of this
bridges	'I'd like to leave that and move on to ask you about . . .'	I'd like to make a clean link to the next conversation topic
pauses (1)	about two seconds silence	in normal conversation: same as lubricators
pauses (2)	silence of three seconds or longer	in a threat context: I'm going to wait until I get an answer
pauses (3)	silence of three seconds or longer	in a counselling context: I'll give you time to think

When bosses lie

People speak differently when they lie. By analysing thousands of transcripts of quarterly conference calls of American chief executives and chief financial officers, David Larker and Anastasia Zakolyukina (2012) found that they could tell when bosses were being truthful about their earnings and profits, and when they were not. The bosses whose profits were later 'materially restated' chose different words. The language that gave the deceptive bosses away included:

- making more references to general knowledge – 'you know' – and referring less to shareholder value, to reduce the risk of lawsuits;
- using stronger positive-emotion terms such as 'fantastic' instead of 'good' in order to sound more persuasive;
- using fewer anxiety words, such as 'worried', 'fearful', 'nervous';
- using the third person ('It seems as if'), and avoiding the first person ('I think that');
- using fewer hesitation cues such as 'um' and 'er';
- making more frequent use of swear words.

This means that we can now tell when bosses are being deceitful, at least until they have taken the training course which advises them to hesitate more, swear less, sound reassuring, and avoid excessive emotional terms. No more fantastic profit forecasts after that, then.

When conversing normally, we use these signals habitually. However, awareness of the methods being used can allow us to bring these under conscious control. Therapists and counsellors, for example, use a range of methods to shape conversations in ways that allow their clients to articulate their difficulties and to work towards identifying appropriate solutions. Managers holding selection, appraisal, or promotion interviews need to understand conversation control techniques in order to handle these interactions effectively.

Non-verbal communication

Which part of the human anatomy is capable of expanding up to ten times in size when we are emotionally aroused? The answer, of course, is the pupil of your eye. When we look at something we find interesting – an image, a scene, a person – our pupils dilate. When we lose interest, our pupils contract. There is a physiological basis in non-verbal communication for the 'dark limpid pools' to which romantic novelists refer.

When we interact with others face-to-face, we are constantly sending and receiving messages through our signs, expressions, gestures, postures, and vocal mannerisms. In other words, **non-verbal communication** accompanies our verbal communication. We code and transmit factual information primarily through verbal communication. We also code and transmit feelings and emotions, and the strength of those feelings, through non-verbal communication.

Non-verbal communication the process of coding meaning through behaviours such as facial expressions, limb gestures, and body postures.

Non-verbal communication is popularly known as *body language*. We will use the technical term for two reasons. First, non-verbal communication is rich and varied; the term body language suggests that we are only concerned with body movements and postures. Second, the term body language implies that gestures have specific meanings, that we can produce a dictionary. That is not the case, as the meaning of non-verbal communication also depends on context. The technical term has the advantage of including a range of behaviours, and signals our concern with how these behaviours are embedded in the communication process.

Non-verbal hints for the job interview

When you sit down, lean forward slightly; this shows interest. Use open-handed gestures – palm upwards – to convey sincerity. Keep regular eye contact, but not for more than 60 per cent of the time, or you'll look mad. However, do it for less than 30 per cent of the time and you may seem shifty or bored.

Don't sit defensively – hands across the body, knees pressed together, hand over your mouth – it can look neurotic or unstable. Equally, don't fidget or play with your hair, or grin maniacally. Above all, don't slouch back in the chair, arms behind your head, with a challenging stare. It threatens the interviewer and makes you look arrogant and difficult (Burne and Aldridge, 1996).

Allan Pease (1997; Pease and Pease, 2005) implies in the titles of his popular books that one can 'read' somebody else's attitudes and emotions from their non-verbal communication. Is this possible? If we are careful, yes, sometimes. This 'body and mind reading' claim deserves cautious support. We can exchange meaning with non-verbal codes, as long as we evaluate the verbal and non-verbal components together, and pay close attention also to the context.

The first study of gesture was conducted by the Italian cleric Andrea de Jorio, born in 1769. To help him to decipher the Greek figures excavated by archaeologists at Herculaneum, Pozzuoli, and Pompeii in the early nineteenth century, he studied the facial and bodily gestures of the people of Naples, a city founded by the ancient Greeks. His book *Gesture in Naples and Gesture in Classical Antiquity* is available in translation (de Jorio, 2001), and some of his explanations of gestures are shown in Figure 7.2.

The main dimensions of non-verbal behaviour are summarized in Table 7.4. Maureen Guirdham (2002, p. 165) lists 136 non-verbal communication behaviours, in nine categories:

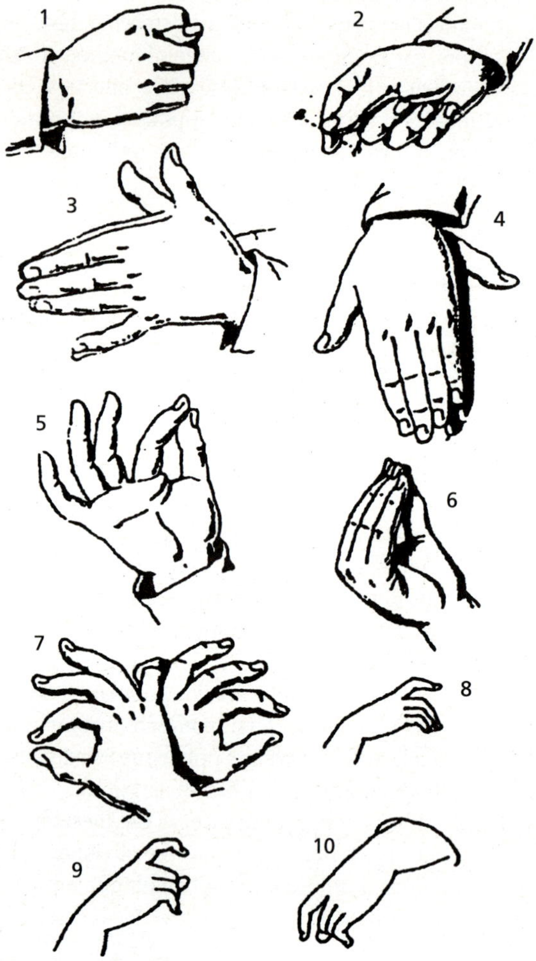

1. *Mano in fica* (sexual insult)
2. *Danaro* (money)
3 & 4. *Stupido* (stupid)
5. *Amore* (love)
6. *Chiedere* (asking)
7. *Condotta versipelle* (deceitful conduct)
8. *Schiopetto* (finger–snap)
9 & 10. *Disprezzo* (scorn)

Figure 7.2: Early Italian hand gestures (from de Jorio)

Source: Reprinted by the permission of the Syndics of Cambridge University Library.

Table 7.4: Dimensions of non-verbal communication

occulesics: eye behaviour
kinesics: body and limb movements
proxemics: the use of space
paralanguage: tone and pitch of voice
facial expressions
posture
chromatics: the use of colour
chronemics: the use of time
haptics: bodily contacts

what we do with our mouths, eyebrows, eyelids and eyes, gaze, facial expressions, head movements, hands and arms, lower limbs, and trunk movements. The subheading 'mouth region' lists 40 behaviours, such as tongue out, open grin, yawn, wry smile, sneer, tight lips, lower lip tremble – and so on. The subheading 'hands and arms' lists 40 behaviours, including scratch, sit on hands, hand flutter, digit suck, palms up, caress, and hand on neck.

Non-verbal courtship

According to Allan Pease (1997), typical male courtship gestures involving non-verbal communication include: preening (straightening tie, smoothing hair), thumbs-in-belt (pointing towards genitals), turning his body to face a female, pointing his foot towards her, holding her gaze, hands on his hips, dilated pupils, and the 'leg spread' (crotch display). Women, on the other hand, have a much richer repertoire of non-verbal courtship behaviour which includes:

- preening gestures such as touching hair, smoothing clothing;
- one or both hands on hips;
- foot and body pointing towards the male;
- extended eye contact or 'intimate gaze';
- thumbs-in-belt, but often only one, or thumb protruding from pocket or handbag;
- pupil dilation;
- flushed appearance;
- the head toss, to flick hair away from face (used even by women with short hair);
- exposing the soft smooth skin on the wrists to the male;
- exposing the palms of the hands;
- the sideways glance with drooped eyelids ('you caught me looking at you');
- wet lips, mouth slightly open;
- fondling cylindrical objects (stem of wine glass, a finger);
- the knee point, one leg tucked under the other, pointing to the male, thighs exposed;
- the shoe fondle, pushing the foot in and out of a half-on-half-off shoe;
- crossing and uncrossing the legs slowly in front of the man;
- gently stroking the thighs (indicating a desire to be touched).

How many of these non-verbal courtship gestures, male and female, are illustrated here?

Colin McDougall.

Courtship gestures

Another important aspect of non-verbal communication is 'paralanguage'. This concerns the rate of speech, and pitch and loudness of our voice, regardless of the words we are using. There are many different ways of saying the same sequence of words; it's not what you say, but the way that you say it. Paralanguage demonstrates some of the overriding power of non-verbal communication. Consider the simple statement 'That was a really great lecture.' Think of the many ways in which you can say this, the differences in gaze and posture as you say it, and particularly the differences in the tone and pitch of your voice. For some of these expressions, listeners will hear you say that you really *did* enjoy the lecture. However, there are other ways in which you can 'code' these same words, non-verbally, in such a way that listeners will be left in no doubt that you thought the lecture poor. When verbal and non-verbal messages contradict each other, it is the non-verbal message which is believed.

STOP AND THINK

Say out loud exactly the same sentence, 'This is a really interesting textbook', in two different ways, with opposite meanings.

Meaning 1	Why don't I take **YOU** to dinner tonight?	I was going to take someone else.
Meaning 2	Why don't **I** take you to dinner tonight?	Instead of the guy you were going with.
Meaning 3	Why **DON'T** I take you to dinner tonight?	I'm trying to find a reason why I shouldn't take you.
Meaning 4	**WHY** don't I take you to dinner tonight?	Do you have a problem with me?
Meaning 5	Why don't I **TAKE** you to dinner tonight?	Instead of going on your own.
Meaning 6	Why don't I take you to **DINNER** tonight?	Instead of lunch tomorrow.
Meaning 7	Why don't I take you to dinner **TONIGHT**?	Not tomorrow night.

From Kiely (1993) Reproduced from Marketing *magazine with the permission of the copyright owner, Haymarket Business Publications Limited.*

Another aspect of non-verbal communication concerns the way in which we use distance in relationships. The study of this aspect of behaviour is known as 'proxemics'. British culture requires a 'social distance' of about half a metre or more between people in normal conversation. If you cross this invisible boundary and step into someone's 'personal space' they usually move backwards to maintain the distance; a failure to 'retreat' implies intimacy. The comfortable distance in Arab and Latin (American and European) countries is smaller, and you are likely to be regarded as arrogant and distant by trying to maintain your personal space when interacting with members of those cultures.

It is possible to test the theory of personal space. At a social gathering, a party perhaps, move gradually and tactfully into someone else's space, by pretending to reach for a drink, moving aside to let someone else past, leaning forward to be heard better, and so on. You can move someone across a room in this way. The same result can be achieved while seated, if the chairs are easy to move. However, if your target does not retreat as predicted, and you are now in their intimate space, you have a decoding problem, and this textbook can't help you.

When we are lying, we may unconsciously send non-verbal 'deceit cues', which include rapid shifts in gaze, fidgeting in our seats, long pauses and frequent speech corrections. When lying, it is important to control these cues, ensuring that verbal and non-verbal messages are consistent. Similarly, when we want to emphasize the sincerity or strength of our feelings, it is important that the non-verbal signals we send are consistent with the verbal message.

Maureen Guirdham (2002, p. 184) describes non-verbal communication as a 'relationship language'. This is how we communicate trust, boredom, submission, dislike and friendship without stating our feelings directly. When decoding non-verbal communication, it is important to pay attention to context, and to the pattern or cluster of behaviours on display. For example, when someone wishes to indicate liking or friendship, they are likely to turn their body towards you, look you straight in the face, establish regular eye contact and look away infrequently, and to nod and smile a lot, keeping their hands and arms by their sides or in front of them. This cluster conveys friendship, or positive non-verbal communication.

We can often identify disagreement or dislike by negative non-verbal communication. This cluster includes turning the body away, folding the arms tightly, crossing the legs such that they point away from the other person, loss of eye contact, wandering gaze, looking

Lie detectors

Can we use non-verbal communication to detect when someone is lying? Adrian Furnham (2005) identifies several (UK) verbal and non-verbal 'lie detectors'. However, in other cultures, these cues may constitute normal interpersonal behaviour and may *not* signal deceit.

Verbal cues	
Response latency	The time between the end of a question and the start of a reply. Liars take longer, hesitate more.
Linguistic distance	Not saying 'I', but talking in the abstract: for example, 'one might believe that . . .'
Slow, uneven speech	As an individual tries to think through their lies. They might also suddenly talk quickly, attempting to make a sensitive subject appear less significant.
Too eager to fill gaps in conversation	Liars keep talking when it is unnecessary, as if a silence signifies that the other person does not believe them.
Too many pitch raises	Instead of the pitch dropping at the end of a reply, it is lifted in the same way as asking a question.

Non-verbal cues	
Too much squirming	Someone shifting around in their seat is signalling their desire not to be there.
Too much eye contact, rather than too little	Liars tend to overcompensate. They need to look at you to monitor how successful they are being.
Micro-expressions	Flickers of surprise, hurt or anger that are difficult to detect. Sudden facial expressions of pain are often giveaways.
An increase in comfort gestures	These often take the form of self-touching, particularly around the nose and mouth.
An increase in stuttering and slurring	Including what are known as 'Freudian slips'.
A loss of resonance in the voice	It tends to become flatter and more monotonous.

at someone else or at the door (suggesting a desire to leave), and a lack of nods and smiles. The cluster of behaviours producing this 'closed posture' often mean that we know that someone does not like what we are saying before they state their disagreement in words. Some interpretations of gesture clusters are shown in Table 7.5.

Table 7.5: Interpreting gesture clusters

cluster signals	indicating
flexible open posture, open hands, display of palms and wrists, removing jacket, moving closer to other person, leaning forward in chair, uncrossed arms and legs, smiling, nodding, eye contact	openness
rigid, closed posture, arms and legs tightly crossed, eyes glancing sideways, minimal eye contact, frowning, no smiling, pursed lips, clenched fists, head down, flat tone of voice	defensiveness
drumming fingers, head cupped in palm of hand, foot swinging, brushing or picking lint from clothing, body pointing towards exit, repeatedly looking at a watch or the exit or a book	boredom, impatience
small inward smile, erect body posture, hands open and arms extended outwards, eyes wide and alert, lively walk, expressive and well-modulated voice	enthusiasm
knitted forehead, deadpan expression, tentative nodding or smiling, one slightly raised eyebrow, strained voice, saying 'I understand' while looking away	lack of understanding
blank expression, phoney smile, tight posture, arms stiff at side, sudden eye shifts, nervous apping, sudden mood shifts, speech toneless and soft or too loud and animated	stress

However, awareness of the context is critical to this decoding or 'mind reading'. People also engage in negative non-verbal communication when they are unwell, or when they are anxious about something that is perhaps unrelated to your conversation and relationship. People also 'close up' and fold their arms when they are cold and uncomfortable.

The dilation and contraction of our pupils is beyond our direct control, unlike our hand movements, but our eyes also send non-verbal information. Our pupils dilate in low light, and when we see something or someone interesting. Dilation conveys honesty, openness, and sexual attraction. Our pupils also dilate when we are relaxed, and with the consumption

Saying 'sorry' without saying anything

In Japan, the way in which bosses bow indicate how sorry the company is for mistakes, such as Toyota's recall of 8 million cars in 2010 due to faulty accelerator pedals.

A slight bow from the waist, not held for very long, indicates a mild apology.

Scarcely bothered
25-degree bend, no hold.
Connotes 'Sorry, that was clumsy of me'.

A deeper bow, at an angle of about 45 degrees, and lasting for about one and a half seconds, suggests contrition, without accepting personal responsibility.

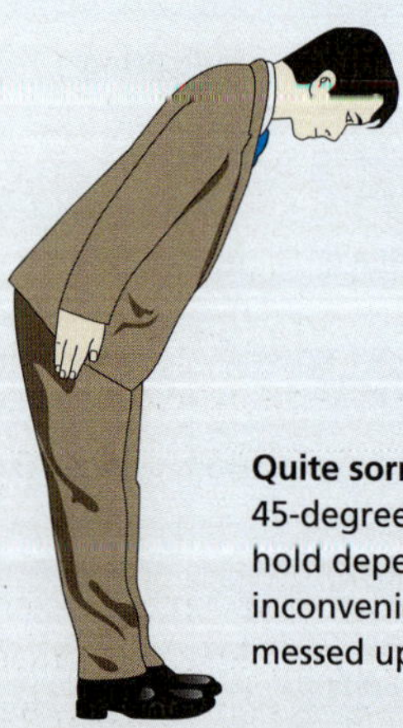

Quite sorry
45-degree bend, 1- to 3-second hold depending on extent of inconvenience. Connotes 'Yes, we messed up, won't happen again'.

A full 90-degree bow, held for up to seven seconds, indicates personal and/or official responsibility for an incident that has caused significant damage, and for which the person is asking forgiveness.

Actually or officially sorry
90 degrees, held for 3–7 seconds depending on total loss of money/life/reputation. Connotes 'We have done something pretty awful. We need you to forgive us'.

The most extreme form of bow involves kneeling with one's head on the floor for perhaps 30 seconds. This indicates that, 'The law may punish me, but that does not cover how sorry I am'.

Really spectacularly sorry
The *dogeza* (rare) kneeling, head on floor, could last for up to 30 seconds. Connotes 'The law may punish me, but that does not cover how sorry I am'.

When Toyota announced the accelerator defect and recalled its cars, the company president Akio Toyoda performed a 25-degree bow. This suggested that he was only 'quite sorry': 'In bowling terms, it holds the same apology value as you might get from a waiter who had forgotten your order' (© Lewis and Lea, 2010, *The Times*/News International Trading Ltd, 6 February 2010).

of alcohol and other drugs. Context is thus critical to accurate decoding. Contracted pupils can signify low lighting conditions, or lack of interest, distrust, hatred, hostility, fatigue, stress, sorrow, or perhaps a hangover. It is only possible to decode pupil dilation or contraction with reference to other non-verbal clues, and to the context in which this behaviour appears.

Someone who is anxious usually displays 'self manipulation': playing with an ear lobe, stroking lips, playing with hair. Anxiety can also be signalled by shifting direction of gaze. Friendship is conveyed by an open non-verbal behaviour cluster. Other friendship signals can be amusing to use and to identify. When we meet someone to whom we are attracted, we often use 'preening gestures': smoothing our clothes, stroking our hair, straightening our posture. Observe a group of friends together and you will often see them standing, sitting, and even holding cups or glasses in an almost identical manner. This is known as 'posture mirroring'. You can often identify the 'outsider' as the one not adopting the posture. Friendship groups also copy each others' gestures; this is known as 'gesture mirroring'.

Power tells non-verbal signals that indicate to others how important and dominant someone is, or how powerful they would like us to *think* they are.

We also use non-verbal communication to show how important we are with **power tells** we discuss power further in (Chapter 22). The power tells that dominant people display include using open postures and invasive hand gestures, smiling less, looking away while speaking, speaking first and dominating the conversation, and interrupting others.

Signals which suggest a submissive attitude include modifying your speech to sound like the other person, hesitations (lots of 'um's and 'er's), close postures, and self-comfort gestures such as clasping your hands and touching your face and hair (Collett, 2004).

Cultural differences in communication style

The use and interpretation of non-verbal communication differ from culture to culture. In Japan, smiling and nodding implies understanding, but not necessarily agreement. In Australia, raising the pitch of your voice at the end of a sentence signifies openness to challenge or question, not a lie. In some Asian cultures, it is impolite to give superiors direct and prolonged eye contact; a bowed head signifies deference and not defensiveness or lack of self-confidence. People from northern European cultures prefer a lot of personal space and rarely touch each other. French, Italians, and Latin Americans, in contrast, stand closer together and touch more often to indicate agreement and friendship.

Simple gestures must also be used with care. Make a circle with your thumb and forefinger, extending the other three fingers. How will this be interpreted? In America, and to scuba divers, it means 'OK'. In Japan, it means money. In France, it means zero or nothing. In some Arab countries, it signifies a curse. In Germany and Brazil, it is obscene.

High context culture a culture whose members rely heavily on a range of social and non-verbal clues when communicating with others and interpreting their messages.

Low context culture a culture whose members focus on the written and spoken word when communicating with others and interpreting their messages.

Edward Hall (1976; 1989) distinguished between **high context culture** and **low context culture**, as shown in Table 7.6.

Table 7.6: High context culture and low context culture

high context culture	low context culture
establish relationship first	get down to business first
value personal relations and goodwill	value expertise and performance
agreement based on trust	agreement based on legal contract
slow and ritualistic negotiations	fast and efficient negotiations

China, Korea, Japan and Vietnam are high context cultures, where people tend to take a greater interest in your position, business card, dress, material possessions, and other signs of status and relationships. Written and spoken communications are not ignored, but they are secondary. Agreements can be made on a handshake, on someone's word.

North America, Scandinavia, Switzerland, and Germany are low context cultures, where people pay secondary attention to non-verbal messages. People in German organizations tend to be preoccupied with detailed written rules, and Americans like to have precise legal documents. Agreements are not made until the contract is in writing, signed.

These categorizations reflect tendencies and are not absolutes. Most countries have subcultures with very different norms. In addition, men tend to be more high context than women, but this observation does not apply to all men or to all women. Nevertheless, it is easy to see how misunderstanding can arise when high and low context cultures meet, unless those communicating are sensitive to their respective differences. You can reduce these misunderstandings with the following four rules (Robbins et al., 2010, p. 307):

1. *assume that others are different*, unless you can establish otherwise; we tend to assume that others are more like us than they often are, so you are less likely to make a mistake if you assume difference until you can prove similarity;
2. *use description and avoid evaluation*, until you have had time to observe and understand the perspectives of the other culture, or cultures, as interpretations and evaluations are based on cultural background rather than on what you observe;
3. *practice empathy*, putting yourself in the other person's position, understanding their values, background and experience, and frames of reference;
4. *treat interpretations as working hypotheses*, and keep testing and questioning your conclusions and explanations, using feedback and checking with colleagues.

Aboriginal culture and communication

Australian Aboriginal culture uses verbal and non-verbal communication in ways that are different from European and North American communication styles (Nelson-Jones, 2000):

- Aborigines value brevity in verbal communication rather than detailed elaboration, and simple 'yes' and 'no' replies are common.
- There is no word for 'thank you' in Aboriginal languages. People do things for you as an obligation.
- In some Aboriginal tribes, it is unlawful to use the name of a dead person.
- The terms 'full-blood', 'half-caste', 'quarter-caste', 'native' and 'part-Aborigine' are regarded as offensive by Aborigines.
- Long silences in Aboriginal conversation are common and are not regarded as awkward.
- To some Aboriginal people, it is not acceptable to look another straight in the eye.
- Some Aboriginal groups do not allow men and women to mix freely.
- Aborigines feel that it is not necessary to look at the person who is speaking to them.
- Aborigines do not feel that it is necessary to attend meetings (an interview, for example) at specific times.

How do these norms and preferences compare with the communication style of your culture?

Erving Goffman (1922–1982)

Impression management

We usually send and receive non-verbal messages unconsciously. However, it is possible to control the non-verbal signals that we send, and to be aware of and to read the cues that others are giving to us. This level of attention and control can be difficult to sustain, but it can be important in organizational settings, especially where we want to control the image or impression that others have of us. We can do this through **impression management** techniques, based originally on the work of Erving Goffman (1959).

Impression management the processes through which we control the image or impression that others have of us.

Paul Rosenfeld and colleagues (2001) observe that our impression management methods are rich and varied, including

- what we do and how we do it
- what we say and how we say it
- the furnishings and arrangement of our offices
- our physical appearance including clothes and make-up
- non-verbal communication such as facial expressions or postures.

Effective impression management means being consciously aware and in control of the cues that we send to others through verbal and non-verbal channels. This suggests that we consciously seek to manipulate the impression or perceptions that others have of us.

STOP AND THINK

Is impression management simply a form of deceit? What in your view are the ethical problems raised by the advice that we should consciously manipulate the impression that others have of us through verbal and non-verbal communication?

Do you use, or do you avoid, impression management methods when you are deciding what to wear to go to parties, clubs, job interviews?

As with conversation controls, we can use impression management to manipulate the behaviour of others. We do this, for example, by 'giving off' the impression that we are friendly, submissive, apologetic, angry, defensive, confident, intimidating, and so on. The more effectively we manage our impression, the greater the control we can achieve in social interaction, and the greater our power to pursue our preferred outcomes over others.

Some people regard impression management as acting. However, we manage our impression all the time. It is hardly possible to avoid sending signals through, for example, our dress, posture, facial expressions, gestures, tone and pitch of voice, and even location in a room. We can distinguish between conscious (by implication more effective) and unconscious (by implication less effective, or misleading) impression management. Conscious impression management has many advantages. Interactions run more smoothly when we provide the correct signals to others who in turn accurately decode these signals of our attitudes and intents. Impression management is a critical skill in many organizational contexts, such as counselling, and in selection, appraisal, and disciplinary interviews.

Home viewing

Catch Me If You Can (2003, directed by Steven Spielberg) is a comedy drama based on the true story of the forger and confidence trickster Frank Abagnale Jr (played by Leonardo Di Caprio) and the FBI agent Carl Hanratty (Tom Hanks) who finally apprehends him, but not before Frank has committed millions of dollars' worth of fraud. Frank is a master of the art of impression management, effortlessly convincing others that he is, at various stages in his 'career', a newspaper journalist, high school teacher, airline pilot, doctor, and lawyer. He is so convincing that, when he does at one point decide to reveal the truth, his fiancé's father (Martin Sheen) does not believe him. Note examples of how Frank uses a combination of non-verbal communication, courtship techniques, avoidance of lie detection cues, paralanguage, and gesture clusters, to manage the impression that he wants to convey.

Daniel Feldman and Nancy Klich (1991) offer advice on how to manage your impression to enhance your career, suggesting six methods for creating a favourable self-image (Table 7.7).

The ethics of impression management

At first, Richard Nixon vowed he would not debate John Kennedy. He had little to gain from such an encounter, and much to lose. As vice-president, he was better known than the young senator and universally considered a heavyweight. But in the end his fear of appearing fearful overcame his caution. It was a mistake. The camera is unkind to men who look shifty.

At the first debate in 1960, Nixon was not feeling well. After hearing Kennedy turn down the offer of make-up, he turned it down too, although it might have covered his five o'clock shadow. Kennedy got his aides to apply make-up when Nixon wasn't looking, and presented a tanned and handsome face to the nation. Nixon looked like a sweaty corpse. Radio listeners thought he did well. But on television, Kennedy won by a mile (*The Economist*, 2008).

© Ted Spiegel/CORBIS

John F. Kennedy

Reuters/Str Old

Richard M. Nixon

In your judgement, was John F. Kennedy's behaviour ethical at that debate in 1960?

Table 7.7: Creating a favourable self-image

Ingratiation	Use flattery, agree with the opinions of others, do favours to encourage people with power and influence to befriend you.
Intimidation	Convey the image of potential danger to those who could stand in the way of your advancement. Use veiled threats of exposure.
Self-promotion	Win respect and admiration of superiors through embellishing your accomplishments, overstating your abilities, displaying awards.
Exemplification	Create an impression of selfless dedication and self-sacrifice, so those in positions of influence will feel guilty and offer reward or promotion.
Accounting	Distance yourself from negative events, deny personal responsibility for problems, diminish the seriousness of difficulties.
Supplication	Get those in positions of influence to be sympathetic and nurturing, for example, through requests for 'mentoring' and other support.

Will you get that job?

Summarizing research on communication in selection interviews, Fredric Jablin (2001, pp. 749–50) concludes that

- Interviewers report that applicants' communication skills including fluency of speech, composure, appropriate content, and ability to express ideas in an organized manner, are critical to selection decisions.
- Interviewers rate more favourably interviewees who display appropriate levels of non-verbal immediacy, including eye contact, smiling, open posture, interpersonal distance, and direct body orientation.
- Interviewers rate more highly and are more satisfied with interviewees who talk more of the time in interview, who elaborate on their answers, and whose discussion of topics closely matches the interviewer's expectations.
- Interviewers rate more favourably interviewees who display assertive impression management techniques, such as agreeing with the interviewer, emphasizing positive traits, asking positive-closed questions, claiming that they 'fit' the organization, and telling personal stories to confirm that they are competent, hardworking, goal-oriented, confident, adaptable, interpersonally skilled, and effective leaders.
- Where the interviewer is seen as trustworthy, competent, composed, empathic, enthusiastic, and well-organized, the applicant is more likely to accept the job offer.

Deborah Tannen (b.1945)

Do men and women use impression management tactics in different ways? Deborah Tannen (1990; 1995) argued that girls and boys learn different linguistic styles – characteristic speaking patterns – which create communication barriers, and affect career prospects. Her research found that, while girls learn to develop rapport, boys learn that the status dimension of relationships is more important. Girls focus on a small group of friends, emphasizing similarities, and playing down ways in which someone could be better than others. Girls tend to be modest and less self-assured, and ostracize those who claim superiority. Boys play in large groups, emphasize status and leadership, display their knowledge and abilities, challenge others, take 'centre stage' by telling jokes and stories, and try to acquire status in their group by giving orders. This childhood learning follows girls and boys into adult life.

More recently, Andrew DuBrin (2011, pp. 49–50) has summarized research contrasting how women and men *typically* (note this term) use impression management tactics and communication styles:

women	**men**
use conversation to build rapport, emphasize similarities, listen carefully, be supportive	use talk mainly to preserve independence and status by showing knowledge and skill
are more likely to praise the work of colleagues	are more likely to be critical
emphasize politeness, say 'I'm sorry' and 'thank you', even when unnecessary	are more direct, attempt to build a positive impression by being decisive
become conciliatory when facing differences, to maintain relationships	become intimidating when facing differences, to make sure they come out in front
willing to share success and recognition	call attention to their own accomplishments
speak less then men in meetings, create positive impression by being reflective and nodding	dominate discussion in meetings, create positive impression by being dominant

Source: based on DuBrin (2011).

Remember that these are only *stereotypes* – generalizations based on averages. These stereotypes will not apply to everyone – women or men – but they may be useful benchmarks against which to test our experience and assessments of others.

DuBrin (2011, pp. 76–7) also identifies tactics for creating a *negative* impression of yourself. Here is a selection of the tactics that you should avoid:

- mumbling, putting your hand over your mouth, not using facts to persuade someone;
- writing business email messages in the style that teenagers use when communicating with each other, and by adults when sending 'tweets';
- appearing immature, unprofessional, and uninterested;
- ignoring colleagues while they are talking, for example by looking at your watch, taking a mobile phone call, or checking your email;
- making immature excuses for being late – 'my alarm clock broke', 'the traffic was bad', 'my laptop crashed';
- denying rather than apologizing for your own mistakes;
- appearing unenthusiastic and bored when others talk about their problems;
- when asked a job-related question, replying 'I don't know, I haven't googled it yet'.

Emotional intelligence

Non-verbal communication is one way in which we display emotion. While often embarrassing, an open show of emotion can sometimes be desirable. Emotions are a key source of motivation. Inability to display and share feelings can be a handicap. Sharing feelings of frustration and anger can be as important in an organizational setting as showing positive feelings of, for example, praise, satisfaction and friendship. The ability to handle emotions can be regarded as a mental skill, which can be developed with training, but some commentators regard this skill as a personality dimension (see Chapter 6).

Emotional intelligence the ability to identify, integrate, understand, and reflectively manage one's own and other people's feelings.

The concept of **emotional intelligence** was developed by Peter Salovey and John D. Mayer (1990) who argued that the concept of 'rational' intelligence ignores emotional competencies. The concept was popularized by Daniel Goleman (1998, 2005), who argues that emotional intelligence is more important to career success than technical skills or rational intelligence. Goleman's dimensions of emotional intelligence are summarized in Table 7.8.

Table 7.8: The five dimensions of emotional intelligence

Dimension	Definition	Hallmarks
1. Self-awareness	the ability to recognize and understand your moods, emotions, and drives as well as the effect you have on others	self-confidence, realistic self-assessment, self-deprecating sense of humour
2. Regulating feelings	the ability to control your disruptive moods and impulses; the propensity to suspend judgement, to think before acting	trustworthiness and integrity; comfort with ambiguity; openness to change
3. Motivation	a passion to work for reasons beyond status and money; a propensity to pursue goals with energy and persistence	high achievement need, optimism even in the face of failure, organizational commitment
4. Empathy	the ability to recognize and understand the emotional makeup of others; skill in dealing with the emotional responses of others	expertise in building and retaining talent; cross-cultural sensitivity; service to clients and customers
5. Social skills	effectiveness in managing relationships and building networks; ability to find common ground, to build rapport	effectiveness in leading change; persuasiveness; expertise in building and leading teams

Goleman claims that emotional intelligence gives us an advantage, at work and in social relationships, but that it is particularly important for top management, where conventional notions of intelligence are taken for granted. At senior levels, high emotional intelligence is a mark of the 'star performer'. There are several assessments for measuring emotional intelligence (sometimes confusingly called EQ), and some commentators argue that emotional intelligence can be learned and developed through experience and training.

Woodruffe (2001) notes a paradox concerning tests which measure emotional intelligence. A typical test question is 'I can easily express emotions over the phone'. What is the 'correct' answer? Only an emotionally intelligent person, he points out, could recognize whether or not they can do this. He then asks 'Is it emotionally intelligent to express the emotion or to be aware that you don't express it?'. Woodruffe argues that emotional intelligence is not a useful concept and that its impact on job performance is exaggerated.

Source: © Grantland Enterprises; www.grantland.net

Organizational communication

Communication is central to individual and organizational performance, but many managers regard communication as a problem, and many employees feel that they are not fully informed about management plans. Employee communication has become more important, partly due to the volume of other information available through the internet, and because of an increase in employee expectations, to be kept informed, and to contribute ideas.

A survey of 100 UK employers in 2010 (Wolff, 2010) found that only 40 per cent had formal communication strategies. Companies with formal strategies were four times more likely to agree that this contributed to their success. The main goals of internal communications were keeping staff informed of changes and strategies, staff engagement, and providing information about policies and procedures. Only one organization was mentioned for using communications to encourage new ideas and innovation. The most popular communication methods were department meetings, one-on-one meetings with line managers, team meetings, letters and memos, and email. Social media were unpopular: online video, instant messaging, internal blogging, wikis, Skype, and podcasts were used by very few organizations.

There was no one best method. Face-to-face was seen as more successful than print or computer-based methods. Intranet sites were useful for providing information on policies, procedures, and legal requirements. Top management briefings were considered best in terms of employee engagement, opinion surveys the best way to encourage feedback, and meetings with line managers the best way to improve individual performance.

One key management problem is to persuade employees to work in the interests of the organization as a whole. However, the interests of individuals and organizations do not always coincide. How can employee behaviour be channelled in the desired directions? In their seminal contribution to organizational behaviour, James March and Herbert Simon (1958) argued that management cannot change individual behaviour directly, or by attempting to alter people's personalities. It is more effective and practical, they argued, to influence the premises on which people make their own decisions about how they will behave.

Thirteen points for an effective communication strategy are suggested by Cannell (2010):

1. Convince top management that communication is important.
2. Build alliances across the organization to support initiatives.
3. Recognize that no one method will be effective.
4. Use a mix of approaches and use all available channels where relevant.
5. Target communication to the audience; use different methods for shop floor and managers.
6. Respect cultural diversity and vary approaches accordingly.
7. Make sure that messages are consistent, over time and between audiences.
8. Ensure clarity of message and keep things simple.
9. Train managers in communication skills.
10. Develop and sustain two-way communication, dialogue and feedback.
11. Ensure that employees feel that they can say what they think without discomfort.
12. Ensure that communication is built into the planning stages of all activities.
13. Review communication initiatives to check what has worked, what hasn't, and why.

How can management influence the premises – the underlying assumptions – which affect the decisions of employees? For example, pay can be based on attendance, timekeeping, and work rate (through piece rates and bonuses). Company rules, how these are enforced, and the terms in which they are expressed, are also ways of 'signalling' or 'coding' desirable and undesirable behaviours. Desirable behaviours can be reinforced through the appraisal system which, in a retail store for example, can evaluate employee behaviours such as 'expresses ideas clearly, keeps others informed, shares knowledge, provides timely communication, listens and responds to customers'.

STOP AND THINK

How does your educational institution use rewards and sanctions to influence the decisions that you make about the nature and direction of your studies? What 'signals' do teaching staff send in order to communicate to students how they expect them to behave?

These 'signalling systems' are saying 'behave this way and you will be rewarded and/or promoted, but behave that way and you will be overlooked for promotion – or fired'. These systems are often complemented by organization vision and mission statements, and by statements of corporate values.

Better communication is often advocated by management consultants as a cure for many organizational problems such as low morale, high absenteeism and turnover, labour unrest and conflict, low productivity, and resistance to change. This advice is based on the theory that, if people understand what is going on, then they will be more likely to follow management directions. A well-presented argument supported with compelling evidence should result in consensus and compliance. Is that always the case?

Organizations use a range of mechanisms for communicating with employees, such as

- the management chain of command;
- regular meetings with senior and/or middle managers;
- in-house newspapers and magazines;
- company intranet;
- noticeboards;
- videos and in-house television;
- conferences and seminars;
- employee reports;
- team briefings;
- email, intranet, blogs, podcasts.

Those are traditionally one-way-top-down modes of communication. Two-way exchanges are more effectively achieved through methods such as

- Web 2.0 interactive systems (see Chapter 2)
- 'speak out' programmes in which problems are taken to counsellors;
- suggestion or 'bright ideas' schemes;
- open door policies;
- the appraisal system;
- quality circles;
- attitude surveys;
- interactive email (where managers guarantee to reply).

Bill Quirke (2008, p. 236) argues that communications depend on change. The more significant the change, the more employees need to be involved. He uses the 'communication escalator' (Figure 7.3) as a guide to designing communications strategy. Levels of involvement can go from awareness, through understanding, support, and involvement, to commitment. The escalator indicates the communications appropriate to each level. For commitment, the organization should consider using all of those approaches. At the awareness level, the focus is on information. However, for involvement and commitment, communication needs to concentrate on improving the quality of interactions and relationships.

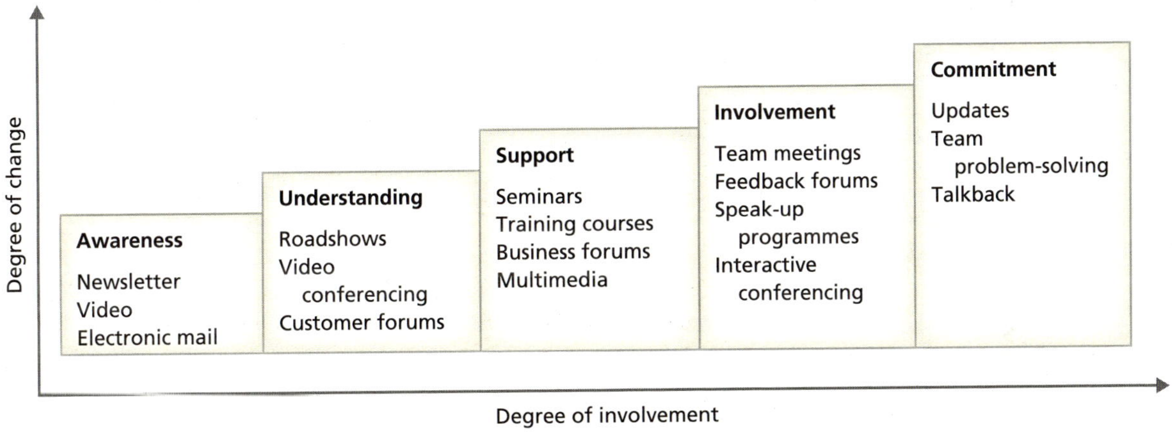

Figure 7.3: The communication escalator

Source: Quirke (2008) © *Making the Connections: Using Internal Communication to Turn Strategy into Action*, Quirke, B., 2008, Gower Publishing.

Culture differences in organizational communication

In the 'North' [of Europe] the policy is that everyone knows. 'Southern' management discourages an open, critical attitude of younger and 'inexperienced' employees, whereas in the North such an attitude is welcomed. On the corporate information front, five years ago Unilever started 'Cascade', a system to acquaint all employees yearly with information about how the Corporation was doing financially. For this, corporate HQ prepares a big packet full of information, complete with overhead sheets and even videos. All business groups receive the same information and are expected to pass it on to their companies and eventually to all employees. Random checks among employees after the Cascade exercise have shown that in Eastern Europe all employees are very interested in corporate information and that 'coverage' is near 100%; in Western Europe coverage is 'average', some 80%, but in Latin countries coverage is 'difficult', at around 65%, because local management seems to decide that not all information is 'necessary' or fit for their employees (Fourboul and Bournois, 1999).

Communication climate the prevailing atmosphere in an organization – *open* or *closed* – in which ideas and information are exchanged.

Jack Gibb (1961) developed the concept of **communication climate**. An open communication climate promotes collaborative working; people develop self-worth, feel that they can contribute freely without reprisal, know that their suggestions will be welcomed and that mistakes will be seen as learning opportunities, and feel trusted, secure, and confident in their job. In a closed communication climate, information is withheld unless it is to the advantage of the sender, and recrimination, secrecy, and distrust can make working life unpleasant. This distinction is summarized in Table 7.9. These extremes are not absolutes; most organizations are likely to have a climate which lies on the continuum between open and closed, and the climate may vary between sections or departments.

Table 7.9: Open and closed communication climates

Open, supportive communication climate	Closed, defensive communication climate
Descriptive: informative rather than evaluative communication	**Judgemental**: emphasis on apportioning blame, making people feel incompetent
Solution-oriented: focus on problem-solving rather than on what is not possible	**Controlling**: conformity expected, inconsistency and change inhibited
Open and honest: no hidden messages	**Deceptive**: hidden meanings, insincerity, manipulative communication
Caring: emphasis on empathy and understanding	**Non-caring**: detached and impersonal, little concern for others
Egalitarian: everyone valued regardless of role or status	**Superior**: status and skill differences emphasized in communication
Forgiving: errors and mistakes recognized as inevitable, focus on minimizing	**Dogmatic**: little discussion, unwillingness to accept views of others or compromise
Feedback: positive, essential to maintaining performance and relationships	**Hostile**: needs of others given little importance

STOP AND THINK

How would you describe the communication climate of your educational institution? Of an organization where you have recently worked? Of your current employer?

The theory that 'people will comply if they understand' suggests that communication has an educational component. Employees who are better informed about 'economic realities' are more likely to have realistic expectations, and make reasonable demands. However, this argument equates communication with propaganda which attempts to shape attitudes and behaviours in particular directions, to generate consensus by giving the logic of managerial decision-making a greater legitimacy. With the growing use of Web 2.0-based interactive communications, alongside traditional methods such as team briefings and teamworking, management can bypass trade unions by working through team leaders instead.

Communication in an organization is not a neutral process. Organizational communication is constructed from a perspective which represents management interests. Organizational power inequalities require management to direct and dominate workforce behaviour. Information is not simply a commodity to be transmitted. Communication mechanisms are tools for manipulating employee attitudes and behaviours. The 'context' in our model of the communication process (Figure 7.1) must consider not just physical and interpersonal factors, but also the wider social and political context of organizational communication.

RECAP

1. *Describe the dimensions of social intelligence, and explain the importance of these capabilities, especially for managers.*
   - The capabilities that make up social intelligence involve a combination of awareness – what we sense about others – and facility – how we act on that awareness.
   - Managers spend a lot of time interacting with others, and it becomes more important to understand the thoughts and feelings of others in a more culturally diverse population.
2. *Understand the main components of the interpersonal communication process.*
   - Communication involves an exchange of meaning, achieved through the processes of coding, transmission, decoding, and feedback.
   - Face-to-face communication allows instant feedback; coding and decoding problems arise with other forms of communication where feedback is delayed or absent.
3. *Identify the main barriers to effective interpersonal communication.*
   - The main barriers to effective communication include power and gender differences, physical surroundings, language variations, and cultural diversity.
   - Barriers can be overcome through face-to-face communication, by checking decoding, by paying attention to context, and by seeing things the way the other person does.
4. *Understand the effective use of different questioning techniques, conversation controls, and listening skills.*
   - Getting appropriate information from someone else involves the effective use of different questioning methods: open, closed, probe, hypothetical, and reflective.
   - Effective communication involves the use of a range of simple conversation controls: lubricators, inhibitors, bridges, and pauses.
   - Active listening involves a range of verbal and non-verbal skills.
   - Communication methods differ between high context and low context cultures.
5. *Explain the nature and significance of non-verbal communication.*
   - Non-verbal communication includes facial expressions, eye behaviour, gesture and posture, distance between ourselves and others, and paralanguage.
   - If the verbal and non-verbal messages which we are sending are inconsistent, the verbal will be discounted and the non-verbal accepted.
   - Lies can be detected in non-verbal communication, but many clues are culture-specific.
6. *Understand the nature and mechanisms of impression management skills and techniques.*
   - We influence the image that others have of us through verbal and non-verbal signals.
   - We use impression management to create a favourable image through ingratiation, intimidation, self-promotion, exemplification, accounting, and supplication.
   - Impression management can be seen as natural and unconscious, or as a deliberate attempt at deceit.
7. *Be able to explain the concept of emotional intelligence and its practical significance.*
   - Emotional intelligence concerns the ability to identify, integrate, understand, and reflectively manage one's own feelings and the feelings of other people.
   - As with social intelligence, understanding your own emotions and the emotions of others is a key skill for all of us, particularly for managers, and its importance is heightened in culturally diverse organizational settings.
8. *Understand the ways in which corporate communication can be used to manipulate understanding and encourage compliance with management directions.*
   - Organizations use a range of media for communicating with employees.
   - The communication climate in an organization can be classed as open and supportive, or closed and defensive.
   - Organizational communication is not neutral, but is constructed from a management perspective in an attempt to manipulate the attitudes and behaviour of recipients.

Revision

1. What is social intelligence, and why are these capabilities now seen as ranking in importance with general intelligence, especially for managers?
2. What are the main problems affecting the communication process, and how can these problems be solved?
3. Explain, with appropriate examples, the questioning techniques which we use to obtain information from others, and the conversation control methods that we use to ensure that our interactions run smoothly, and in our favour.
4. What is non-verbal communication, and what part does it play in human interaction in general and in organizational settings in particular?

Research assignment

Choose two different television programmes which include interviews: news, political commentary, magazine programmes, chat shows. It does not matter whether the interview is about news information, or simply audience entertainment. In each case observe one interviewer or host or commentator interviewing someone, and make notes on:

1. what questioning techniques are used, and their effectiveness
2. what questioning techniques are not used
3. the interviewer's use of body language
4. whether the interviewer displays social intelligence, and what evidence you can cite
5. whether the interviewer displays emotional intelligence, and what evidence you can cite
6. who controls the flow of conversation – interviewer or interviewee.

Write a report comparing the similarities and differences in these two interviews. Assess the skill and effectiveness of the interviewer in each case. Where appropriate, determine from your assessment what practical advice you would give to these interviewers to help them to improve their technique. What general conclusions can you reach concerning interviewing skills in general, and television interviewing in particular?

Springboard

Daniel Goleman (2005) *Emotional Intelligence: Why It Can Matter More than IQ*, Bloomsbury, London. This book turned emotional intelligence into a management fad. Argues that, if you are not committed to the organization, to team working, and to high performance, then you lack emotional intelligence.

Maureen Guirdham (2002 and 2011) *Interactive Behaviour at Work* (3rd edn), Financial Times Prentice Hall, Harlow (3rd edn); and *Communicating Across Cultures at Work* (3rd edn), Palgrave Macmillan, London. Guides to research, theory and practice in interpersonal skills, and cross-cultural and technology-mediated communication, with self-assessments and advice.

Andrzej Huczynski (2004) *Influencing within Organizations*, Routledge, London. Practical guide to the realities of influence, arguing that job skills alone are not enough to ensure career advancement. Chapters on verbal and non-verbal influencing and impression management.

Helen Rosethorn and Annette Frem (2010) *Harnessing the Power of Employee Communication*, Chartered Institute of Personnel and Development, London. Emphasizing importance of internal communication, develops a strategic approach, linking communication with motivation and personal contribution, illustrated with organizational examples.

OB in films

Burn After Reading (2008, directors Joel and Ethan Cohen), DVD track 6: 0:27:13 to 0:29:08 (2 minutes). Clip opens with Linda asking for 'just a tea'; clip ends with Linda saying, 'Haven't you heard of the power of positive thinking?'.

Gym employee Linda Litzke (played by Frances McDormand) is talking to the gym manager, Ted Treffon (Richard Jenkins).

1. What does Linda want to achieve in this conversation?
2. What tactics does she use?
3. Why does she not achieve her goal?
4. What advice can you give to Linda about managing this conversation more effectively?
5. What does Ted want to achieve in this conversation?
6. What tactics does he use?
7. Why does he not achieve his goal?
8. What advice can you give to Ted about managing this conversation more effectively?

OB on the web

Search YouTube for video clips concerning 'body language' and 'impression management'. There are many to choose from. They mostly offer tips and techniques, and 'do's and don'ts' for leaders and for job interviewees in particular. Select two videos on each topic, based on how interesting and relevant they appear to you. As you watch, make notes on how you can improve your impression management and body language, particularly with regard to improving your employability. Note the behaviours that you could use, but also what to avoid.

Do a deal with a friend or colleague. Agree to monitor each other's impression management and body language for a week. Provide each other with regular, honest, critical, and constructive feedback on impression management and body language strengths and weaknesses.

CHAPTER EXERCISES

1. Impression management check

Objective To assess aspects of the way in which you deal with other people.

Briefing As you read each of the following 18 statements (based on Snyder, 1987, p. 179), ask yourself whether or not it applies to you, and answer (tick) 'yes' or 'no' accordingly. You will of course occasionally feel that you want to answer 'sometimes'. But try in each case to decide where your personal preferences, strengths, and priorities really lie, and answer 'yes' or 'no' accordingly. You don't always get to sit on the fence. This is not a test with right or wrong answers. It is designed for personal reflection and group discussion.

→

	Yes	No
1. I find it hard to imitate the behaviour of other people.		
2. At parties and gatherings, I do not attempt to do or say things that others will like.		
3. I can only argue for ideas which I already believe.		
4. I can make impromptu speeches even on topics about which I have almost no information.		
5. I guess I put on a show to impress or entertain others.		
6. I would probably make a good actor.		
7. In a group of people, I am rarely the centre of attention.		
8. In different situations and with different people, I often act like very different persons.		
9. I am not particularly good at making other people like me.		
10. I'm not always the person I appear to be.		
11. I would not change my opinions or the way I do things in order to please someone or win their favour.		
12. I have considered being an entertainer.		
13. I have never been good at games like charades, or acting.		
14. I have trouble changing my behaviour to suit different people and different situations.		
15. At a party I let others keep the jokes and stories going.		
16. I feel a bit awkward in company and do not show up quite as well as I should.		
17. I can look anyone in the eye and tell a lie with a straight face, if for an appropriate reason.		
18. I may deceive people by being friendly when I really dislike them.		

Scoring

You get either one point or zero, depending on how you responded to each statement. Simply add up the number of points you got.

	Score		
Statement	**Yes**	**No**	**Your score**
1	0	1	
2	0	1	
3	0	1	
4	1	0	
5	1	0	
6	1	0	
7	0	1	
8	1	0	
9	0	1	
10	1	0	
11	0	1	
12	1	0	
13	0	1	
14	0	1	
15	0	1	
16	0	1	
17	1	0	
18	1	0	
	Total:		

Interpretation A score of 13 or more implies strong impression management skills:

Awareness: you are consciously aware of your own and other people's feelings and behaviour, and of how you affect others.

Flexibility: you are able to adjust what you say and do to match other people's expectations, and to achieve your goals.

Control: you are able consciously to control your behaviour, and thus to control other people; you probably enjoy this.

A score of 7 or less implies weak impression management skills:

Awareness: you are not always aware of your own or other people's feelings and behaviour, or of how you affect others.

Flexibility: you are unable to adjust what you say and do to match other people's expectations, and to achieve your goals.

Control: you are unable consciously to control your behaviour, and may feel uncomfortably manipulated at times.

A score between 8 and 12 implies moderate impression management skills. Read over the interpretations above, and judge your strengths for yourself. Which way would you now like to go – up or down?

Analysis Whatever your own score, consider the following key issues:

1. To what extent are impression management skills learnable and to what extent are we born with them?
2. Is it immoral or unethical to adjust one's behaviour in order to modify the feelings and behaviours of others?
3. Regardless of your own impression management score, would it benefit you to be more aware of how other people use these skills? Give specific examples.
4. In what ways would it benefit you personally to improve your own impression management skills, or to enhance your awareness of how you use them? Give specific examples.

2. How would you respond?

Objectives

1. To analyse the practical uses of questioning techniques and conversation controls.
2. To explore appropriate management options in dealing with employee grievances.

Briefing

1. Individual analysis: Read these sets of statements on your own, without discussing them with colleagues. In each case decide, as the supervisor:
   - which of the four statements is the best, and why?
   - what objective(s) you would have for this interaction – that is, what you would like to have achieved by the end?
   - what are the key issues relevant to the individual, team, and organization in this context?
   - what is your behavioural plan for the meeting – that is, beyond the stated comment, what else will you say and do?
   - a fifth response that you think is better than those suggested.
2. Syndicate discussion: Following your instructor's advice on size of syndicate and timing, share your assessments, selections and, where appropriate, alternative responses, and attempt to reach a group consensus.
3. Plenary: Each group presents and explains its conclusions to the group as a whole.
4. Debriefing: Your instructor will lead a discussion of the implications of the different responses in each case, and of the key learning points from this exercise.

Here are three statements from employees, directed at you, their immediate supervisor.

→

Situation A: Assistant Supervisor, age 30, computer manufacturing plant

'Yes, I do have a problem. I'd like to know more about what happened with the promotions last month. Charlie got the supervisor's job in motherboard assembly and I didn't even know he was interested. Why did you give the job to him? I would like to know more about what you think of my promotion prospects here. I've been doing this job for about three years now, and I've been with the company for almost five years. I haven't had any complaints about my work. Seems to me I've been doing a pretty good job, but I don't see any recognition for that. What do I have to do to get promoted round here?'

1. You'll make a great supervisor, Bill, but give it time. I'll do what I can to make your case. Don't be discouraged, OK? I'm sure you'll get there soon, you'll see.
2. So, you're not sure about how the company regards your work here?
3. I understand how you feel, but I have to admit it took me five years to make supervisor myself. And I guess I must have felt much the same way you do today. But we just have to be patient. Things don't always happen when we'd like them to, do they?
4. Come on, you've been here long enough to know the answer to that one. Nobody got promoted just by waiting for it to happen. Get with it, you've got to put yourself forward, make people stand up and take notice of your capabilities.

Situation B: Secretary, age 45, insurance company headquarters

'Can I ask you to do something about the calendars that Mr Johnson and Mr Hargreaves insist on displaying in their offices? They are degrading to women and I find them offensive. I know that some of the other secretaries who work on their floor feel exactly the same way as I do. I have to work with these men and I can't stay out of their offices. Don't we have a company policy or something? I'm surprised you've allowed it to go on this long as it is.'

1. You and some of the other secretaries find these calendars insulting?
2. Look, you're taking this all too seriously. Boys' toys, that's all it is, executive perks. Doesn't mean anything, and there's nothing personal behind it at all. You've no cause for concern.
3. You're right, I don't like that either, but we're talking about their own offices here, and I think that they have the right, within reason, to make their own decisions about what pictures to put on the walls, same as you and I do.
4. I'll see if I can't get a chance to have a quiet word with them some time next week, maybe try to persuade them to move their calendars out of sight, OK? I'm sure they don't mean anything by it.

Situation C: Personnel Officer, age 26, local authority

'I've just about had it. I can't put up with this kind of pressure for much longer. We just don't have the staff to service the level of requests that we're getting and still do a good job. And some of the people we have to deal with! If that old witch in administration calls me one more time about those files that went missing last week, she's going to get a real mouthful in return. How come you let your department get pushed around like this?'

1. You're not alone. Pressure is something that we've all had to endure at some time. I understand that, it comes with the territory. I think it's about developing the right skills and attitudes to cope.
2. You're right, this is a difficult patch, but I'm sure that it will pass. This can't go on for much longer, and I expect you'll see things start to come right at the end of the month.
3. Well, if you can't stand the heat, I suppose you just have to get out of the kitchen. And please don't refer to people who are senior to you in this organization in that manner ever again.
4. Let me check – this is not about Mrs Smith in admin is it? You're saying the strain is such that you're thinking of leaving us?

Employability assessment

With regard to your future employment prospects:

1. Identify up to three issues from this chapter that you found significant.
2. Relate these to the competencies in the employability matrix.
3. Decide what actions you need to take to maintain and/or develop those competencies under each of the four headings of the employability matrix.

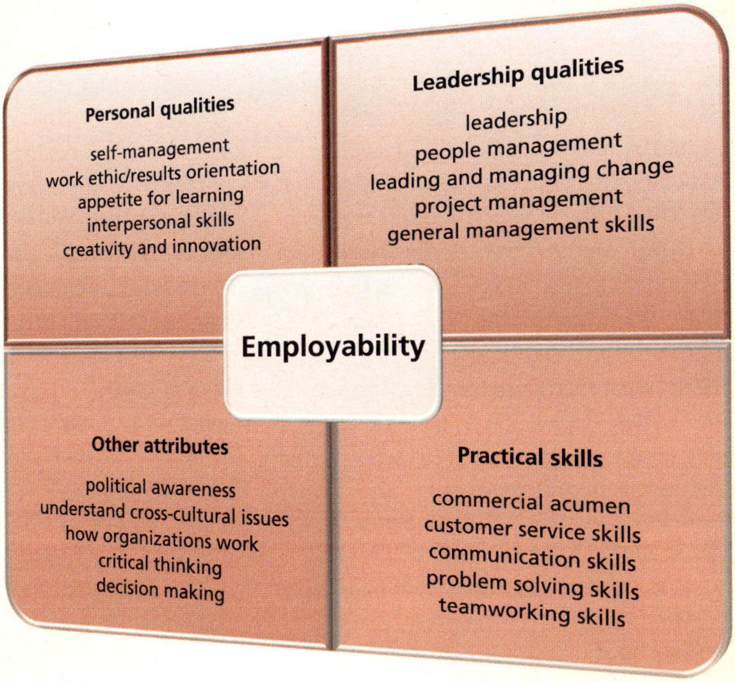

References

Burne, J. and Aldridge, S. (1996) 'Who do you think you are?', *Focus Extra*, pp. 1–8.

Cannell, M. (2010) *Employee Communication Factsheet*, London: Chartered Institute of Personnel and Development.

Collett, P. (2004) 'Show and tell', *People Management*, 10(8), pp. 34–5.

DuBrin, A.J. (2011) *Impression Management in the Workplace: Research, Theory, and Practice*, New York and London: Routledge.

Evans, M. (2008) 'Charming the locals: a soldier's guide', *The Times*, 11 February, p. 14.

Feldman, D.C. and Klich, N.R. (1991) 'Impression management and career strategies', in K. Giacalone and P. Rosenfeld (eds), *Applied Impression Management: How Image Making Affects Managerial Decisions*, London: Sage Publications, pp. 67–80.

Fourboul, C.V. and Bournois, F. (1999) 'Strategic communication with employees in large European companies: a typology', *European Management Journal*, 17(2), pp. 204–17.

Furnham, A. (2005) *The Psychology of Behaviour at Work* (2nd edn), Hove, Sussex: Psychology Press/Taylor & Francis.

Gibb, J.R. (1961) 'Defensive communication', *Journal of Communication*, 11(3), pp. 141–8.

Goffman, E. (1959) *The Presentation of Self in Everyday Life*, New York: Doubleday Anchor.

Goleman, D. (1998) *Working with Emotional Intelligence*, London: Bloomsbury Publishing.

Goleman, D. (2005) *Emotional Intelligence: Why It Can Matter More than IQ*, London: Bloomsbury (first published 1995).

Goleman, D. (2006) *Social Intelligence: The New Science of Human Relationships*, London: Hutchinson.

Guirdham, M. (2002) *Interactive Behaviour at Work* (3rd edn), Harlow, Essex: Financial Times Prentice Hall.

Hall, E.T. (1976) *Beyond Culture*, New York: Doubleday/Currency.

Hall, E.T. (1989) *Understanding Cultural Differences*, Yarmouth, ME: Intercultural Press.

Jablin, F.M. (2001) 'Organizational entry, assimilation, and disengagement/exit', in Fredric M. Jablin and Linda L. Putnam (eds), *The New Handbook of Organizational Communication: Advances in Theory, Research, and Methods*, Thousand Oaks, CA: Sage Publications, pp. 732–818.

de Jorio, A. (2001) *Gesture in Naples and Gesture in Classical Antiquity* (trans. Adam Kenton), Indiana: Indiana University Press.

Kellaway, L. (2005) *Martin Lukes: Who Moved My BlackBerry?*, London: Viking Books.

Kiely, M. (1993) 'When "no" means "yes" ', *Marketing*, October, pp. 7–9.

Kotter, J.P. (1999) 'What effective general managers really do', *Harvard Business Review*, 77(2), pp. 145–59.

Larker, David F. and Zakolyukina, A.A. (2012) 'Detecting deceptive discussions in conference calls', *Rock Center for Corporate Governance, Working Paper Series No. 83*, Stanford, CA: Stanford University.

Lewis, L. and Lea, R. (2010) 'Toyota chief bows to pressure over pedal defect', *The Times*, 6 February, p. 13.

Lublin, J.S. (2006) 'Some do's and don'ts to help you hone videoconference skills', *The Wall Street Journal (Marketplace Supplement)*, 7 February, p. B1.

March, J. and Simon, H.A. (1958) *Organizations*, New York: Wiley.

Mintzberg, H. (2009) *Managing*, Harlow, Essex: Financial Times Prentice Hall.

Nakamoto, M. (2012) 'Cross-cultural conversations', *Financial Times*, 12 January, p. 16.

Nelson-Jones, R. (2000) *Introduction to Counselling Skills: Text and Activities*, London: Sage Publications.

Pease, A. (1997) *Body Language: How to Read Others' Thoughts by Their Gestures* (3rd edn), London: Sheldon Press.

Pease, A. and Pease, B. (2005) *The Definitive Book of Body Language: How to Read Others' Attitudes by Their Gestures*, New York: Bantam.

Quirke, B. (2008) *Making the Connections: Using Internal Communication to Turn Strategy into Action*, Aldershot: Gower Publishing.

Rea, K. (2010) 'Leaders must act like they mean it', *The Sunday Times, Appointments Section*, 10 October, p. 4.

Robbins, S.P., Judge, T.A. and Campbell, T.T. (2010) *Organizational Behaviour*, Harlow, Essex: Financial Times Prentice Hall.

Rosenfeld, P., Giacalone, R.A. and Riordan, C.A. (2001) *Impression Management: Building and Enhancing Reputations at Work*, London: Thomson Learning.

Salovey, P. and Mayer, J.D. (1990) 'Emotional intelligence', *Imagination, Cognition and Personality*, 9, pp. 185–211.

Shannon, C.E. and Weaver, W. (1949) *The Mathematical Theory of Communication*, Urbana, IL: University of Illinois Press.

Snyder, M. (1987) *Public Appearance and Private Realities: The Psychology of Self-Monitoring*, New York: W.H. Freeman.

Tannen, D. (1990) *You Just Don't Understand: Women and Men in Conversation*, New York: William Morrow.

Tannen, D. (1995) 'The power of talk: who gets heard and why', *Harvard Business Review*, 73(5), pp. 138–48.

The Economist (2004) 'I understand, up to a point', 4 September, p. 44.

The Economist (2008) 'Debating the debates', Lexington, 11 October, p. 62.

White, R. (2011) 'Help doctor, I've got Aims – acute interest in medical slang', *The Sunday Times, News Review Section*, 13 March, p. 4.

Wolff, C. (2010) 'IRS internal communications survey 2012: employer practice', *IRS Employment Review*, June.

Woodruffe, C. (2001) 'Promotional intelligence', *People Management*, 7(1), pp. 26–9.

Chapter 8 Perception

Key terms

perception

perceptual world

selective attention

perceptual threshold

habituation

perceptual organization

perceptual set

halo effect

stereotype

self-fulfilling prophecy

attribution

Learning outcomes

When you have read this chapter, you should be able to define those key terms in your own words, and you should also be able to:

1. Identify the main features of the process of perception.
2. Distinguish between the bottom-up processing of sensory information and the top-down interpretation of that information.
3. Understand the nature and implications of selective attention and perceptual organization.
4. Give examples of how behaviour is influenced by our perceptions.
5. Explain and illustrate the main processes and problems in perception, including false attributions, halo effects, and stereotyping.
6. Explain some less widely appreciated sources of discrimination at work arising from characteristics of the person perception and attribution processes.
7. Suggest techniques for improving perceptual accuracy and avoiding errors.

Why study perception?

Of all the topics covered in this text, perception is perhaps the one which most clearly sets social science apart from natural science. We attach meanings, interpretations, values, and aims to our actions. Our actions are influenced by how we perceive ourselves, and on how we perceive our social and physical environment. We explain our behaviour with terms like reason, motive, intention, purpose, and desire. Astronomers, chemists, engineers, and physicists do not face this complication in coming to grips with their subject matter. For a natural scientist, there is a reality 'out there' to observe and study. For a social scientist, 'reality' is often what people perceive it to be.

Alphas

Yuri Arcurs/Shutterstock

Perception is key. How other people see you counts just as much as who you think you are. Andrew DuBrin (2011) cites research which found that three-quarters of senior executives and half of all middle managers are *alphas* – people who are ambitious, self-confident, competitive, and brash. Non-alphas who want to make it to the executive suite will not get there unless they are seen to have alpha traits. To be an alpha – female or male – you have to be seen by others to:

- be self-confident and opinionated
- be highly intelligent
- be action oriented
- have high performance expectations, of self and others
- have a direct communication style
- be highly disciplined.
- be unemotional.

Alpha females and alpha males are usually perceived positively by others, who in turn respond positively to them. However, alphas have to be careful not to exaggerate their attributes. For example, if an alpha is so self-confident that they ignore others, or focuses on results at the expense of others' feelings, then the perceptions of others may be extremely negative.

Source: © Chris Medden.

Perception the dynamic psychological process responsible for attending to, organizing, and interpreting sensory data.

It is our **perception** of reality which shapes and directs our behaviour, not some objective understanding of it. We each perceive the world around us in different ways. If one person on a hillside perceives that it is cold, they will reach for a sweater. If the person standing next to them perceives that it is warm, they will remove their sweater. These contrasting behaviours can occur simultaneously, regardless of the ambient temperature. Human behaviour is a function of the way in which we perceive the world around us, and how we perceive other people and events in that world.

STOP AND THINK

Choose a film that you have seen recently, and which you particularly enjoyed. Now find a friend or colleague who has seen the same film, and who hated it.

Share your views of that film. What factors (age, sex, background, education, interests, values and beliefs, political views, past experience) can you identify that explain the differences in perception between you and your friend or colleague?

We often find ourselves unable to understand other people's behaviour. People can say and do surprising things in settings where it is obvious to us that some other behaviour would have been more appropriate. If we are to understand why you behaved in that way in that context, we first need to discover how you perceive that context and your place in it. When we are able to 'see it the way you see it', to put ourselves in your position, what initially took us by surprise is likely to become readily understandable. To understand each other's behaviour, we need to be able to understand each other's perceptions. We need to be able to understand why we perceive things differently in the first place.

Perceptions of empowerment

How do employees perceive management attempts at empowerment? Empowerment implies flexibility and freedom to make decisions about how work is carried out. The construction industry tends to rely on collaborating teams, which work on-site at a distance from company management, and high levels of employee empowerment might be expected under these conditions. When problems are solved by those who are closest to the work, decision-making is quicker, and job satisfaction and performance can increase. Kay Greasley and colleagues interviewed sixteen workers, on four large construction projects, to find out how they perceived empowerment in practice. Four themes emerged (Greasley et al., 2005):

The role of supervision: The style of the first line supervisor is crucial, as this is often the only manager with whom construction workers come into contact regularly. Some trusted their workers to get on with the job, but others monitored the work closely.

The employee view: Employees felt more competent, trusted, and empowered when supervisory monitoring was low. However, while some workers wanted extensive decision-making powers, others were more comfortable with routine decisions.

Consequences: Feeling valued, and implementing one's own ideas, prompted a positive emotional response, increasing self-esteem, job satisfaction, and pride in the work.

Barriers: Supervisory style and health and safety regulations are barriers to empowerment in the construction industry. Senior management are too distant to encourage supervisors to adopt a more empowering approach, and the many safety regulations are stringent (although managers do not always seem to follow the same rules).

The temporary project-based nature of construction work, with distant senior managers, makes it difficult to develop a consistent approach to employee empowerment, even where this is management policy. However, if employees perceive that they are not trusted, and have little or no control over their work, they can withdraw goodwill and delay the construction process.

Selectivity and organization

We do not passively register sense impressions picked up from the world around us. We process and interpret the incoming raw data in the light of our past experiences, in terms of our current needs and interests, in terms of our knowledge, expectations, beliefs and motives.

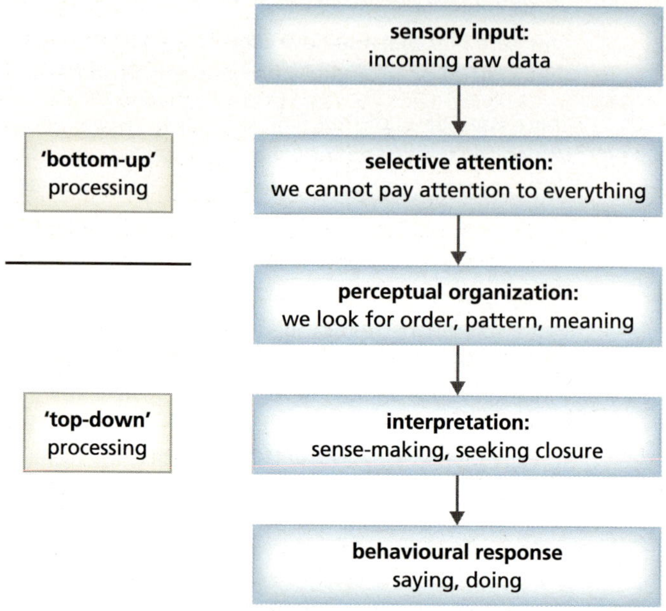

Figure 8.1: Elements in the process of perception

The main elements in the perceptual process are shown in Figure 8.1. From a psychological point of view, the processes of sensation, on the one hand, and perception, on the other, work together through what are termed *bottom-up* and *top-down* processing. The bottom-up phase concerns the way in which we process the raw data received by our sensory apparatus. One of the key characteristics of bottom-up processing concerns the need for selectivity. We are simply not able to attend to all of the sensory information available to us at any given time. Bottom-up processing screens or filters out redundant and less relevant information so that we can focus on what is important.

The top-down phase, in contrast, concerns the mental processing that allows us to order, interpret, and make sense of the world around us. One of the key characteristics of top-down processing concerns our need to make sense of our environment, and our search for meaning.

This distinction between sensation (bottom-up) and perception (top-down) can be illustrated in our ability to make sense of incomplete, or even incorrect, sensory information. The missing letter or comma or the incorrectly spelled term does not interfere with comprehension, as you will know from text messaging:

This sent nce us incorr ct, bit U wull stell B abl to udersta d it.

Our top-down conceptual processing ability means that we are able to fill in the gaps and correct the mistakes, and make sense of 'imperfect' raw data.

We each have a similar nervous system and share more or less common sensory equipment. However, we have different social and physical backgrounds which give us different values, interests, and expectations, and therefore different perceptions. We do not behave in, or respond to, the world 'as it really is'. This idea of the 'real world' is somewhat arbitrary. The 'real world' as a concept is not a useful starting point for developing an understanding of human behaviour in general, or organizational behaviour in particular. We behave in, and in response to, the world as we perceive it. We each live in our own **perceptual world**.

Perceptual world the individual's personal internal image, map, or picture of their social, physical, and organizational environment.

Successful interpersonal relationships depend on some overlap between our perceptual worlds, or we would never be able to understand each other. Our perceptual worlds, however, are in a detailed analysis unique, which makes life interesting, but also gives us problems.

Our perceptual processing is normally carried out without much conscious deliberation or effort. In fact, we often have no effective control over the process, and, fortunately, control is not always necessary. We can, however, control some aspects of the process simply by being consciously aware of what is happening. There are many settings where such control is desirable and can help us to avoid dangerous and expensive errors. Understanding the characteristics of perception can be useful in a variety of organizational settings: for example, with the design of aircraft instruments and displays for pilots, in the conduct of selection interviews for new employees, and in handling disputes and employee grievances.

Perception is a dynamic process because it involves ordering and attaching meaning to raw sensory data. Our sensory apparatus is bombarded with vast amounts of information. Some of this information, such as sensations of hunger, lust, pain, and fatigue, comes from inside our bodies. Some of this information comes from people, objects, and events in the world around us. We do not passively record these sensory data. We are constantly sifting and ordering this stream of information, making sense of it and interpreting it.

Perception, therefore, is an information-processing activity which concerns the phenomenon of **selective attention**.

Selective attention the ability, often exercised unconsciously, to choose from the stream of sensory data, to concentrate on particular elements, and to ignore others.

Our senses – sight, hearing, touch, taste, smell, and the sensing of internal bodily signals or 'kinaesthesia' – each consist of specialist nerves that respond to specific forms of energy, such as light, sound, pressure, and temperature changes. There are some forms of energy that our senses cannot detect unaided, such as radio waves, sounds at very low and very high pitch, and infrared radiation. Our sensory apparatus has limitations that we cannot overcome without the aid of special equipment. We are unable to hear sound frequencies above 10,000 hertz, but many animals, including dogs and dolphins, can. We are unable to hear sounds below 30 hertz, but whales can. Owls have much better eyesight than we do.

Home viewing

The Sixth Sense (1999, director M. Night Shyamalan) concerns the attempts by a disillusioned child psychologist, Malcolm Crowe (played by Bruce Willis), to cure a young boy, Cole (Haley Joel Osment), who is tormented because he sees dead people. Crowe's depression, and his eagerness to help Cole, are explained at the beginning of the film, when he is attacked at home by an ex-patient who had the same problem, but whom Crowe was unable to help. Crowe spends so much time with Cole that he ignores his wife Anna (Olivia Williams). However, this film cleverly manipulates the perceptions and assumptions of the audience. Once you have watched the film to the end, either reflect on the action, or watch it again. Notice which clues you 'saw', but either ignored or misinterpreted the first time around. Notice how your interpretation of events relied on the assumptions that you made, or rather the assumptions that you were expected to make. It is only when you know the full plot of the film that you can begin to make 'correct' assumptions and interpretations, based on exactly the same evidence you were presented with the first time around. What does this movie tell you about the ease with which your perceptions, assumptions, and understanding can be manipulated?

The constraints imposed by our sensory apparatus can be modified in certain ways by experience. The boundary, or **perceptual threshold**, between what we can and cannot detect can be established by experiment. We can explore individual differences in thresholds across the senses, and these thresholds can sometimes be altered by training and experience.

Perceptual threshold a boundary point, either side of which our senses respectively will or will not be able to detect stimuli such as sound, light, or touch.

If there is a clock ticking in the room where you study, you will almost certainly not be aware of the sound, until somebody mentions it, or the clock stops. Next time you visit a library, close your eyes for a few seconds and pay attention to the background noise that you do not usually hear. But surely, you must have heard it, as you must have heard the clock ticking, if your ears were working properly?

Our sensory apparatus responds, not simply to energy, but to changes in energy levels. Having detected a stimulus, such as a clock or the hum of air conditioning, the nerves concerned become tired of transmitting the same information indefinitely and give up, until the stimulus changes. This explains our surprise at the sudden silence which follows when machinery stops.

Habituation the decrease in our perceptual response to stimuli once they have become familiar.

Once stimuli become familiar, they stop being sensed. This phenomenon, in which the perceptual threshold is raised, is known as **habituation**.

Our sensory apparatus has design limitations which filter out some information, such as x-rays and dog whistles. Perception involves other filtering processes, as the phenomenon of habituation suggests. In particular, information that is familiar, non-threatening, and unnecessary to the task in hand is screened out of our conscious awareness.

Stand on the pavement of a busy street and pay attention to as much of the available information as you can: the noise of the traffic, the make and colour and condition of passing vehicles, the smell of rubber tyres and exhaust fumes, the pressure of the pavement on the soles of your feet, the breeze across your face, the smell of the perfume of a passing woman, the clothes of the man across the street and the type of dog he is walking, an overheard mobile telephone conversation. When you think you are taking it all in, start to cross the road. If you get across safely, you will find that your heightened awareness has lapsed, dramatically. You would be mown down fairly quickly if this were not the case. Selective attention allows us to concentrate on the important and significant, and to ignore the insignificant and trivial.

Nancy Adler (2002) offers an excellent example of habituation in our use of language. Read the following sentence, and then quickly count the number of Fs:

FINISHED FILES ARE THE RESULT OF YEARS OF SCIENTIFIC STUDY
COMBINED WITH THE EXPERIENCE OF YEARS

Most people who speak English as a second language see all six Fs. Native English speakers usually pick up only three or four, because they tend to miss out the Fs in 'of'. Native English speakers have been conditioned – habituated – to skip the 'of' because it does not contribute to the meaning of the sentence.

Adler's explanation is that, once we stop seeing the 'ofs', we do not see them again, even as in this example when we are looking for them. There is simply too much information available at any one time for us to pay attention to all of it, so we screen out that which is apparently of little or no value. The image of the world that we carry around inside our heads can only ever be a partial representation of what is 'really out there'. This leads to the conclusion that our behavioural choices are determined not by reality, but by what we perceive that reality to be. Our perception is influenced by what are called *perceptual filters* (individual characteristics, predispositions, and preoccupations that interfere with the effective transmission and receipt of messages), which we met in Chapter 7.

The internal and external factors which affect selective attention are illustrated in Figure 8.2. The external factors affecting selective attention include stimulus factors and

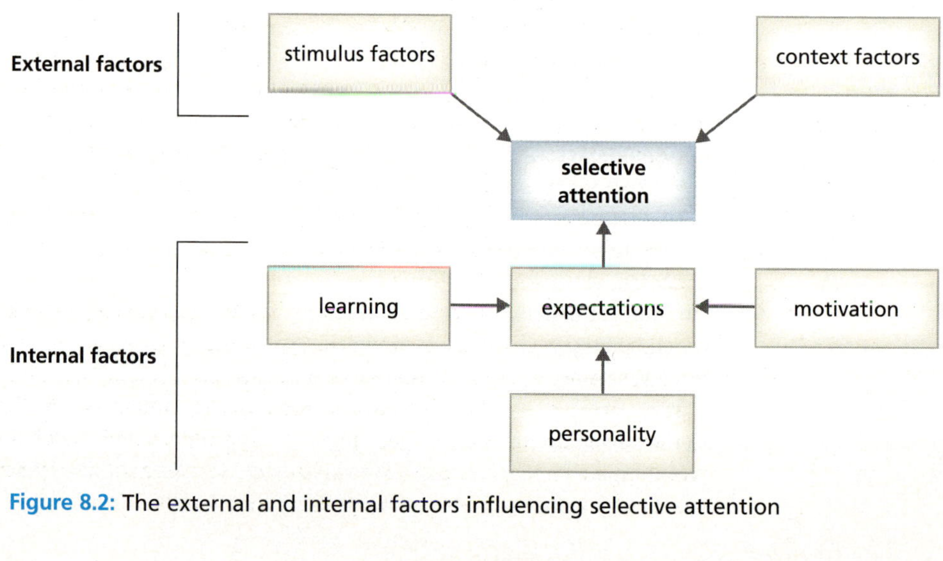

Figure 8.2: The external and internal factors influencing selective attention

context factors. With respect to the stimulus factors, our attention is drawn more readily to stimuli that are:

large	rather than	small
bright		dull
loud		quiet
strong		weak
unfamiliar		familiar
different from surroundings		similar to surroundings
moving		stationary
repeated (but not repetitive)		one-off

Note, however, that we do not merely respond to single features, as this list might imply; we respond to the pattern of stimuli available to us.

STOP AND THINK **Identify examples of the ways in which advertisements creatively use stimulus factors to attract our attention in newspapers and magazines and on billboards and television.**

Our attention is also influenced by context factors. The naval commander on the ship's bridge and the cook in the kitchen may both have occasion to shout 'fire', but these identical statements mean quite different things to those within earshot, and will lead to radically different forms of behaviour (the taking and saving of lives, respectively). We do not need any help to make this crucial distinction, beyond our knowledge of the context.

The internal factors affecting perception include:

- *Learning*. You've heard that argument before (the pre-flight safety briefing), so are you going to listen carefully to it again? Our past experience leads to the development of expectations or *perceptual sets*, which predispose us to pay attention to some stimuli, and to ignore others.
- *Personality*. How come you (gregarious, sociable) saw the advertisement for the party, but your friend (reserved, shy) did not? Our personality traits predispose us to pay attention to some issues and events and human characteristics and not others.
- *Motivation*. Do you get out of the shower to take a phone call, perhaps expecting a party invitation or a job offer? We are more likely to respond to stimuli that we perceive as important and motivating.

Much of perception can be described as classification or categorization. We categorize people as male or female, lazy or energetic, extrovert or shy. In fact our classification schemes are usually more sophisticated than that. We classify objects as cars, buildings, furniture, crockery, and so on, and we refine our classification schemes further under these headings. However, we are not born with a neat classification scheme 'wired in' with the brain. These categories are learned. They are social constructs. What we learn is often culture bound, or culture specific. The British revulsion at the thought of eating dog (classified as pet), the Hindu revulsion at the thought of eating beef (classified as sacred), and the Islamic aversion to alcohol (classified as proscribed by the Koran) are all culturally transmitted emotions based on learned values.

Problems arise when we and others act as if our culture had a monopoly on 'right thinking' on such issues. Different does not imply wrong. Different people within the same culture have different experiences and develop different expectations. The internal factors – our past experience and what we have learned, our personalities, our motivations – contribute to the development of our expectations of the world around us, what we want from it, what will happen in it, and what should happen. We tend to select information that fits our expectations, and pay less attention to information that does not.

Perceptual organization the process through which incoming stimuli are organized or patterned in systematic and meaningful ways.

Our categorization processes, and the search for meaning and pattern, are key characteristics of perception. This perceptual work is captured by the concept of **perceptual organization**. The principles by which the process of perceptual organization operates were first identified by Max Wertheimer (1880–1943) in 1923. The 'proximity principle' notes that we tend to group together or to classify stimuli that are physically close to each other and which thus appear to 'belong' together. Note how you 'see' three sets of pairs rather than six blobs here:

Max Wertheimer (1880–1943)

The 'similarity principle' notes that we classify or group together stimuli that resemble each other in appearance in some respect. Note how you 'see' four pairs here, not eight objects:

The fact that we are able to make use of incomplete and ambiguous information, by 'filling in the gaps' from our own knowledge and past experience, is known as the 'principle of closure'. These principles of perceptual organization apply to simple visual stimuli. Of more interest here, however, is the way in which these principles apply to person perception. How often do we assume that people are similar just because they live in the same neighbourhood, or work in the same section of the factory or office building (proximity principle), or just because they wear the same clothes or have similar ethnic origins (similarity principle)? How often do we take incomplete information about someone (e.g. he's Scottish) and draw inferences from this (closure principle)? This can cause the spread of false rumours in organizations through what is sometimes called 'the grapevine'.

Change blindness: just how selective can we get?

Picture the following, and prepare to be amazed. You're walking across a college campus when a stranger asks you for directions. While you're talking to him, two men pass between you carrying a wooden door. You feel a moment's irritation, but they move on and you carry on describing the route. When you're finished, the stranger informs you that you've just taken part in a psychology experiment. 'Did you notice anything change after the two men passed with the door?' he asks. 'No', you reply uneasily. He then explains that the man who initially approached you walked off behind the door, leaving him in his place. The first man now comes up to join you. Looking at them standing side by side, you notice that the two are of different height and build, and dressed differently, have different haircuts, and different voices.

It sounds impossible, but when Daniel Simons, a psychologist at Harvard University, and his colleague Daniel Levin of Kent State University in Ohio actually did this experiment, they found that fully 50 per cent of those who took part failed to notice the substitution. The subjects had succumbed to what is called 'change blindness'. Rather than logging every detail of the visual scene, says Simons, we are actually highly selective about what we take in. Our impression of seeing everything is just that – an impression. In fact we extract a few details and rely on memory, or perhaps even our imagination, for the rest (Spinney, 2000).

Perceptual sets and perceptual worlds

We have shown how the perceptual process selects incoming stimuli and organizes them into meaningful patterns. We have also argued that this processing is influenced by learning, motivation, and personality – factors which give rise to expectations, which in turn make us more ready to respond to certain stimuli in certain ways and less ready to respond to others. This readiness to respond is called the individual's **perceptual set**.

Perceptual set an individual's predisposition to respond to people and events in a particular manner.

Look at Figure 8.3, a reproduction of a drawing made in 1915 by the cartoonist W.H. Hill. What do you see? Is she an old woman, or a young woman? The drawing is ambiguous; you

Source: Artwork supplied by *The Broadbent Partnership*, London

Figure 8.3: Old woman or young woman?

Is it ethical?

Sally Power and Lorman Lundsten (2005) studied employee perceptions of ethical behaviour in the workplace. They asked 280 white-collar and managerial staff to identify three ethical challenges they experienced at work. 'Ethical' was not defined, as the researchers wanted to find out how employees interpreted the term. The 764 ethical challenges that were reported fell into six categories:

category	examples
honesty	misreporting financial figures; over-billing; hiding information; not telling the whole truth; stealing through expense reports
personal issues	stealing time from employer; lack of integrity; self-interest; acting contrary to company policy
complex business issues	concern about excess corporate profit; environmental issues; competitive practices; sexual harassment; insider trading
relationships	taking credit for others' work; favouritism; stealing ideas; inappropriate relationships; backstabbing; threat of job loss
fairness	discrimination; taking advantage of customers
other	disloyalty; bribes or rebates

These respondents had no difficulties in identifying situations in which ethical or moral principles had been violated. Much of the academic commentary on this issue, however, is less confident about categorizing these behaviours. For example, it is often necessary to balance competing interests, and behaviour perceived as unethical in one context could be appropriate in another setting. The two settings most often described as ethical challenges by respondents in this study involved the treatment of employees by employers, and the treatment of customers by the company and its employees.

should be able to 'see' two different people. Your answer may be influenced by what you are predisposed to see, at the time you are reading this. The reactions of different individuals will not be consistent, and it does not make sense to argue over which perception is correct. We must accept that two people can observe the same thing, but perceive it in quite different ways.

Another issue where perceptual variations can cause problems concerns bullying. At what point does dynamic hands-on management become harassment and bullying? There is limited agreement on the behaviours that constitute bullying, which can easily be perceived as autocratic management (Hoel et al., 2001; Woodman and Kumar, 2008).

Failure to appreciate the importance of differences in individual perception creates many organizational problems, particularly with communication. Employees may perceive that they face chronic problems, while management perceive that such complaints are trivial and transient. It makes little sense to ask whose perceptions are correct. The starting point for resolving such issues must lie with the recognition that different people hold different, but equally legitimate, views of the same set of circumstances. Chapter 1 identified two views of human behaviour. The positivist perspective sets out to discover an objective world out there, as it really is. The constructivist perspective sets out to discover how our world is socially constructed, and how we experience and interpret that world. The argument in this chapter suggests that 'the world out there' is not a good starting point for developing an understanding of human behaviour. We each have a unique version of what is out there and of our own place in it. We each live in our own *perceptual world*.

We each have a perceptual world that is selective and partial, and which concentrates on features of particular interest and importance to us. Through the processes of learning, motivation, and personality development, we each have different expectations and different degrees of readiness to respond to objects, people, and events in different ways. We impose meaning on received patterns of information; the meanings that we attach to objects, people, and events are not intrinsic to these things, but are learned through social experience and are coloured by our current needs and objectives.

Our perceptions, that is, the meanings that we attach to the information available to us, shape our actions. Behaviour in an organization context can usually be understood once we understand the way in which the individual perceives that context. Figure 8.4 (based on Dixon, 1999) illustrates the links between available information based on observation and experience, the perception based on that information, and outcomes in terms of decisions with respect to actions. This example explains why employees would ignore apparently reasonable management requests to become 'team players'.

Figure 8.4: The information–perception–actions link

STOP AND THINK

Source: R. Beau Lotto

Look carefully at this picture. The green and red tables appear to be different in size. The green table seems to be longer and thinner. But their dimensions are almost identical, as the second picture shows (note the yellow and blue lines).

Source: R. Beau Lotto

How can we get this so wrong? The designer of this illusion, Dr Beau Lotto, argues that we take into account the visual cues that we have learned in the past. We estimate size by the way in which objects appear to us in space, rather than using precise measurements. This involves the effects of light, shadow, and perspective. The 'real' world, however, is three-dimensional, and we can be tricked when objects are presented in two dimensions, as in these pictures. As this chapter argues, perception always depends on context.

From Beau Lotto, TimesOnline, *2 May 2008,*
http://www.timesonline.co.uk/tol/life_and_style/health/article3861639.ece

Cultural factors play a significant role in determining how we interpret available information and experience. You order a meal in a restaurant. Was the service fast or slow? Research into cultural differences in the perception of time suggest that your answer to this question depends to some extent on where in the world you come from. One study (Levine, 1990) compared the pace of life in six countries (Britain, Italy, Indonesia, Japan, Taiwan, and the United States) by measuring

- the accuracy of clocks in city bank branches;
- the speed at which city pedestrians walked;
- the length of time it took to buy a postage stamp.

The research revealed that Japanese cities had the most accurate clocks, the fastest pedestrians, and the most efficient post office clerks. Indonesian cities, in contrast, had the least accurate clocks, and the slowest pedestrians. Italy, however, had the slowest post office clerks. The overall results of this study were as follows:

fast pace of life ↑	Japan
	United States
	Britain
	Taiwan
	Italy
↓ **slow pace of life**	Indonesia

To understand an individual's behaviour, therefore, we need to know something of the elements in their perceptual world, and the pattern of information and other cultural influences that have shaped that world. To change an individual's behaviour, therefore, we first have to consider changing their perceptions, through the information and experiences available to them. In the example in Figure 8.4, this would involve radical, visible, and sustained changes in company performance review, and in promotion policies and practice.

Developing an understanding of our own perceptual world is difficult because there are so many influences of which we are not fully aware. Information about the perceptual worlds of others is even more elusive. Although we can in principle find out how others perceive things, a lack of mutual understanding creates barriers to interpersonal communications. Unfortunately, we often forget that our own perceptual world is not the only possible or correct one.

STOP AND THINK

Here is a story from the computer company IBM (Carroll, 1994). How would an understanding of the concept of perceptual world have helped the manager Reiswig?

> The IBM programmers still found things heavy-handed at times, despite Reiswig's attempts to lighten up. For instance, Reiswig at one point made fifty-hour weeks mandatory. Some of the programmers, who had been working eighty- to ninety-hour weeks, took that as an insult. They said that if IBM wanted to play those sorts of penny-ante games, then they'd work exactly fifty hours a week. Progress on OS/2 actually *slowed* after extra hours became required. An apocryphal memo began circulating among the IBM programmers about a rowing race that had supposedly taken place between IBM and Microsoft. Microsoft had one coxswain shouting orders while eight people rowed, the memo said. IBM had eight coxswains shouting orders while one rowed. Microsoft won big. So IBM launched several task forces to do some coxswain/oarsman analyses and decided after several weeks that the problem was that the oarsman wasn't rowing hard enough. When the race was rerun and Microsoft won big again, the oarsman was fired.
>
> After a month or so, though, Reiswig figured out what was going on and removed the requirement. Hours soared, and the OS/2 project became one of the most engaging in the history of IBM.

Do we see to know or know to see?

Fortunately, we as individuals are not as isolated from each other as the argument so far suggests. We do not live in a social and organizational world of constant misunderstanding and failed communication. A high proportion of our interactions are effective, or tolerably so. Why? We are, of course, not wholly unique as individuals, and our personal perceptual worlds overlap. We share the same, or similar, sensory apparatus. We share the same basic needs. We share much of the same background social environment. Within the same society, although there are vast differences in experience, we share some of the same problems and environmental features. All this common ground makes the tasks of mutual understanding and interpersonal communication possible.

We have defined the process of perception in terms of making sense of the information available to us. We are active processors of that information, not passive recipients. However, much of that information is already processed for us. We are bombarded with sensory information, from other people, from books and newspapers and magazines, from street advertising, from radio and television, from the internet, and from various internal organizational sources – annual reports, team briefings, newsletters.

In the contemporary organizational context, employees at all levels have experienced major upheavals in recent years as organizations have introduced initiatives to improve performance. These changes, which have often led to stress, burnout, initiative fatigue and work intensification as well as to improved organizational performance, have typically been communicated using arguments like this:

> In order to survive in a rapidly changing, turbulent, and highly competitive environment, we need to become more efficient, more cost-conscious, more flexible and adaptable, and more customer-focused. Therefore, we need to implement the following radical changes to organization structures, procedures, and jobs.

There are two ways to read this turbulent world argument.

First, this is a taken-for-granted expression of contemporary organizational reality. There is nothing unusual in this argument about the need for organizational flexibility to deal with external change. People have been saying that for years. It's obvious, isn't it? This is a widely accepted view.

Second, this is an attempt to promote a particular perception of organizational reality, based on management values. After all, change is stressful and employees are likely to resist. If we can present a case that is difficult to challenge, then resistance can be avoided and the changes can go ahead more smoothly.

The key to this second reading lies with our use of language. One view of language is that we use it as a tool to communicate observations and understanding. An alternative view is that language, particularly the concepts that we use, constructs that understanding. You cannot 'see' twenty different types of snow until you know what they are called and can link those labels to different visual stimuli. In other words, one view of language simply says that we 'see in order to know'. The alternative view is that we need to know first, before we can 'see'. The implication of this second view of language, that 'we know to see', is that perceptions can potentially be influenced, that is can be managed, through language.

Consider the 'turbulent world so we must change' argument. What language typically accompanies this exhortation? Looking through job advertisements and other forms of organizational literature, note how many times the following kinds of statements appear:

- We need to become more *customer orientated*.
- Our mission is *excellence*.
- We believe in employee *empowerment*.
- Our survival depends on *efficiency* and *cost-effectiveness*.
- *Initiative* and *creativity* are key competencies.
- *Flexibility* is the key to competitive success.

- We must strive for *continuous improvement*.
- We are a *total quality* organization.

The 'turbulent world' argument is hard to challenge. Communications of this kind have the potential to lead employees to internalize management values as their own, without question. It is difficult to argue that 'there is so little change in the business environment that we should be developing a rigid bureaucracy', or that 'customers don't matter, let's pay attention to our own staff'. However, rapid change can be personally and socially damaging: factory and office closures and relocation, loss of jobs, loss of community. An organization that ignores the wellbeing of its staff may find that it loses customers who feel that they have been given inadequate or discourteous service.

Language promotes a particular set of perceptions related to a specific set of values. An organization can have 'difficulties and problems' (negative), or 'challenges and opportunities' (positive). The term 'turbulent world' creates an impression of 'the way things are', of 'it makes sense doesn't it?', of 'that's obvious'. Why experience 'failure' when you can enjoy 'deferred success'? If you can get people to accept this kind of language and these arguments, then language becomes a tool for manipulating perceptions. If we can manipulate perceptions, we can control behaviour because, as argued already, our behaviour depends not on some 'external reality' but on our perception of reality.

This 'second reading' of the 'turbulent world' argument, viewing it as an attempt to manage perception, reflects a change in our understanding of the use of language, not simply to represent the world, but also to create it. This perspective argues that 'reality out there' is not simply waiting to be discovered, but is created in social exchange through language. We don't go out and discover reality. Multiple realities are presented to us through our interactions. What matters is the version of reality in which most people come to believe. The management of perception is thus a tool for 'keeping people in their place' by inhibiting criticism. You cannot easily criticize something that appears to be, and is widely accepted as, natural, obvious, or inevitable without appearing deviant or eccentric.

Halo effect a judgement based on a single striking characteristic, such as an aspect of dress, speech, posture, or nationality.

This argument highlights the existence and value of differences in perception, of multiple perspectives, arguing that no single perspective should be given the privilege of being correct. This also invites us to question the obvious and the taken-for-granted.

STOP AND THINK

It seems that we are 'fed' information in language which reinforces the management definition of reality and justifies decisions in order to make employees compliant.

Find examples of managers or politicians using language in order to make what they have to say more acceptable to their audience.

Perceptual sets and assumptions

Edward Lee Thorndike (1874–1949)

The concept of perceptual set, or perceptual expectation, applies to the ways in which we see other people, events, and objects. To understand the nature of perception is to understand, at least in part, the sources and nature of many organizational problems. There are two related and prominent features of the process of people perception: the **halo effect** and stereotyping.

The term 'halo effect' was first used by the psychologist Edward Thorndike in 1920. It is a natural human response, on meeting a stranger, to 'size them up', to make judgements about the kind of person they are, and whether we will like them or not. We do this to others on a first encounter; they do this to us. It seems as if first impressions really do count, after all.

However, faced with so much new information about someone – the physical and social setting, their appearance, what they say, how they say it, their posture, their non-verbal behaviour, how they respond to us – we must be selective. In terms of the model of the perceptual process shown in Figure 8.1, the halo effect is an error at the selective attention stage. Our judgements can rely on a single striking characteristic: a familiar accent, a perfume, dress or tie, hairstyle. If our judgement is favourable, we give the other person a positive halo. We may then overlook other information that could lead us to a different, more balanced, evaluation. If our judgement, on the other hand, is not favourable, we give the other person a negative halo (or horn). The halo effect can work in both directions.

The halo effect can thus act as an early screen that filters out later information which is not consistent with our earlier judgement. The problem, of course, is that what we notice first about another person is often not relevant to the judgement that we want to make. A confounding factor is that we tend to give more favourable judgements to people who have characteristics similar to ours. However, since when did somebody's voice, hairstyle, deodorant, or clothes enable us to predict, say, their ability to design bridges, or manage a department in a hotel? Some people feel that they can make predictions from such limited evidence, based presumably on their own past experiences. The halo effect can apply to things as well as to people. How many examples can you think of where country of origin leads you automatically to believe that the product quality will be good or bad (Australian wine, Belgian chocolates, French perfume, German cars, Italian clothes, Scottish whisky)?

Stereotype a category or personality type to which we allocate people on the basis of their membership of some known group.

Walter Lippmann (1889–1974)

The term **stereotyping** was first used by typographers to made-up blocks of type, and was used to describe bias in person perception by Walter Lippmann in 1922. The concept refers to the way in which we group together people who seem to share similar characteristics. Lippmann saw stereotypes as 'pictures in the head', as simple mental images of groups and their behaviour. So, when we meet, say, an accountant, a nurse, an engineer, a poet, or an engineering student, we attribute certain personality traits to them because they belong in one of those groups. Everybody knows, for example, that Scots are mean, and blondes have more fun. In terms of the model in Figure 8.1, therefore, stereotyping is an error at the perceptual organization stage in the process of perception.

Dress to impress

'We call it "the button of uncertainty", says Claire Niven, a former trader at Lehman Brothers who now works for a private investment firm. "On women's shirts, three undone buttons show too much, and yet two seems a bit dowdy. So there's a lot of confusion as to which way to go at work."' (Soames, 2010)

This uncertainty extends to hemlines, collars, jacket choices, and shoes. It is not unusual for candidates for promotion or pay rises to be overlooked because of how they dress. Niven was once sent home because she wore red polka dot shoes to a meeting. To resolve the confusion, the Swiss Bank UBS developed a 43-page dress code for its 65,000 employees. Rules in the code included:

- Men's jackets should have only two buttons, done up when standing and unbuttoned when sitting, and pockets should not be bulging.
- Shirt pockets must be empty, except for a pen or a badge, and no cartoon motifs on socks.
- Women should wear flesh-coloured underwear, and blazers which cover their posterior.
- The heels on women's shoes must not exceed 7 centimetres.

Men were also told to use skin moisturizer, to get their hair cut in a simple style every month, never to dye their hair, not to grow their nails more than 1.5 millimetres, and never to tuck their ties into their trousers. Women were advised to wear light make-up including foundation, mascara, and a discreet lipstick, to ask themselves whether their hairstyle corresponded with their age, and not to paint their nails. All staff were advised not to wear strong scents or perfumes at work. Other companies have dress codes, but UBS was widely criticized for this extreme micromanagement. The code was withdrawn in 2011, and UBS circulated 'general guidance' instead.

Self-fulfilling prophecy a prediction that becomes true simply because someone expects it to happen.

Another shortcut that we make when we meet people is the **self-fulfilling prophecy**. For example, if you predict an avalanche in a loud voice under a large and loose overhang of snow, your prediction is likely to be self-fulfilling. The UK government discovered in 2012 that the quickest way to create a fuel crisis was to announce that 'motorists are advised not to start panic-buying petrol'. In other words, we create what we expected to find in the first place. This phenomenon also applies to human behaviour. For example, if we expect people at work to be lazy, apathetic, and careless, and treat them accordingly, we are likely to find that they respond to our treatment of them by displaying the behaviours that we expected. The reverse can also be true; if we treat people as though we expect them to be motivated, enthusiastic, and competent, then they are likely to respond accordingly. We will meet this phenomenon again in Chapter 9 in our discussion of motivation, and Douglas McGregor's contrast between Theory X and Theory Y.

STOP AND THINK

Explore your own stereotypes by completing each of the following sentences with three terms that you think describe most or all members of the category concerned:

University lecturers are . . .

Artists are . . .

Computer scientists are . . .

Trainee nurses are . . .

Airline pilots are . . .

You may find it interesting to share your stereotypes with those of colleagues, particularly if some of them have friends or close relatives who are pilots, nurses, computer scientists . . .

If we know, or assume, somebody's apparent group membership, our quick categorization allows us to attribute a range of qualities to them. Stereotypes are overgeneralizations, and are bound to be radically inaccurate on occasion. But they can be convenient. By adopting a stereotyped perspective, we may be able to shortcut our evaluation process, and make quicker and more reliable predictions of behaviour. We can have problems, however, with those who fall into more than one category with conflicting stereotypes: the mechanical engineer who writes poetry, for instance.

Stereotyping also works at an international level. See if you can match these stereotyped (not necessarily accurate) images with the right countries:

Culture	Stereotyped image
1 **American**	A Demonstrative, talkative, emotional, romantic, bold, artistic
2 **English**	B Mañana attitude, macho, music lovers, touchers
3 **French**	C Inscrutable, intelligent, xenophobic, golfers, group-oriented, polite, soft-spoken
4 **Italian**	D Conservative, reserved, polite, proper, formal
5 **Latin American**	E Arrogant, loud, friendly, impatient, generous, hardworking, monolingual
6 **Japanese**	F Arrogant, rude, chauvinistic, romantics, gourmets, cultural, artistic

Clearly, while some members of each of these cultures may possess some of the attributes of their stereotype, it would be false to claim that every member of a culture shared the same attributes to the same degree. Not all Japanese are keen golfers; not all English people are reserved and polite; not all Americans are arrogant and hardworking.

Sex, appearance, attractiveness, and discrimination

Height of success

Taller women earn more money than their shorter female colleagues because they are perceived as more authoritative, a survey has found. Those standing taller than 5ft 8in are twice as likely to earn more than £30,000 a year, and make an average of £5,000 more annually, according to a poll of over 1,400 women carried out by Opinion Matters and commissioned by retailer Long Tall Sally.

'Research shows that tall people are consistently more successful in the workplace – not only do they earn more but they're also more likely to be in leadership positions', said Arianne Cohen, author of *The Tall Book*. 'As taller people look down when speaking to shorter colleagues, they are instinctively perceived to have confidence – which means they are respected by their colleagues and bosses' (*People Management*, 22 April 2010, p. 15).

Attribution the process by which we make sense of our environment through our perceptions of causality.

Fritz Heider (1896–1988)

Harold H. Kelley (1921–2003)

We emphasized earlier that the perceptual process is concerned with making sense of and explaining the world around us, and the people and events in it. Our need for explanation and understanding is reflected in the way in which we search for the causes of people's actions. Our perceptions of causality are known as attributions. An **attribution** is a belief about the cause or causes of an event or an action. Attribution theory was developed in the 1950s and 1960s by Fritz Heider (1958) and Harold Kelley (1971). They argue that our understanding of our social world is based on our continual attempts at causal analysis based on how we interpret experience.

Why is that person so successful? Why did that project fail? Why are those people still arguing? If we understand the causes of success, failure, and conflict, we may be able to adjust our behaviour and other factors accordingly. Attribution is simply the process of attaching causes or reasons to the actions and events we see. We tend to look for causes either in people's abilities and personalities, or in aspects of the setting or circumstances in which they find themselves. This distinction is usually described in terms of internal causality and external causality. We may explain a particular individual's success, or promotion, with reference to their superior skills and knowledge (internal causality), or with reference to luck, friends in high places, and coincidence (external causality).

Research has revealed patterns in our attributions. When we explain our personal achievements (exam success), we point to our capabilities, but when we are explaining our lack of success, we blame our circumstances (poor teaching). This is known as *projection*. We project blame onto external causes that are beyond our control. However, we tend to attribute the behaviour of others to their disposition, that is, to aspects of their personality. We met the *fundamental attribution error* in Chapter 1. This refers to the tendency to exaggerate the disposition and personality of the individual rather than the context in which they find themselves (explaining company success in terms of the chief executive's leadership, rather than the buoyant economy).

Attribution theory can explain aspects of discrimination in organizational settings. For example, sex and appearance affect how we are paid and promoted. In Britain, Barry Harper (2000) studied over 11,000 people (belonging to the long-term National Child Development Study) aged 33 to determine the effects of looks, height, and obesity on pay. This study confirmed that attractive people, men and women, earn more, and that tall men earn substantially more. Height is slightly less important for women. Tall men earn 10 per cent more than men of average height, but tall women earn only 5 per cent more. Unattractive men earn 15 per cent less than colleagues with average looks, while unattractive women earn 11 per cent less. Obese women earn 5 per cent less than those of average weight, but obese men are not affected. While widespread, the benefits of height and the costs of being unattractive were more common in 'white-collar' occupations. For women, a 15 per cent penalty for being unattractive was most common in secretarial and clerical jobs. Attractive men in

Short changed in China

In 2002, Jiang Tao brought a court case against the Chengdu branch of The People's Bank of China in Sichuan province for discrimination on the basis of his height. The Bank advertised a job in a local newspaper stating that male applicants should be at least 1.68 metres tall, and that female applications should be at least 1.55 metres. Mr Jiang was three centimetres too short, and this criterion excluded around 40 per cent of the male population of Sichuan.

Height requirements are common in China. The East China University of Politics and Law in Shanghai requires male and female students to be at least 1.70 and 1.60 metres tall respectively, thereby excluding around half of the otherwise eligible students from rural areas where average heights are lower. A teacher in Fujian province was fired because he was found to be four centimetres shorter than the required 1.60 metres.

Height in China is considered to be an important attribute for those in jobs which carry authority, in catering and leisure industries where tall is considered beautiful, and in jobs that involve contact with foreigners. This is because it is undignified to have to look up to others. Height may not be important in politics. Deng Xiaoping, who ruled China for over a decade, was only 1.50 metres tall (based on *The Economist*, 2002).

customer-facing sales roles earned 13 per cent more, while tall men in 'high touch' positions earned 25 per cent more. Some commentators are critical of 'beauty bias', putting appearance before capability, and see this as another form of unfair discrimination at work.

Why should appearance affect career progression? Our attributions are related to our stereotypes. We seem to attribute explanations of people's behaviour to aspects of their appearance. Discrimination against particular groups and individuals, on the basis of sex, sexual orientation, age, or ethnic background, is now widely recognized. Legislation seeks to address sexual and racial discrimination, and social attitudes towards homosexuals and the elderly in organizational settings do appear, slowly, to be changing. However, attribution research suggests that discrimination based on our perceptions of causal links between sex, appearance, and job performance is more subtle, and less public.

With respect to attractiveness, sex, height, and weight, we are dealing with factors which cannot have any meaningful impact on performance for most jobs or occupations. The tall, attractive female computer programmer of average weight may be more effective in her job than the short, overweight male programmer with the unremarkable features. A moment's consideration, however, would probably lead us to reject height, weight, and attractiveness as causal factors in this equation, and lead us to look for differences in education, experience, and ability instead. The problem seems to be, however, that we make attribution errors by jumping quickly and unconsciously to judgements of this kind, particularly when we have little information about the other person on which to base a more careful assessment.

Hot dogs, old dogs, new tricks

Fast food outlets traditionally employ younger and less experienced staff and managers. With an ageing workforce, the supply of young employees is declining. In America, less than 8 per cent of employees and managers working in food service are over 55, and the main age group for employees is 18–24. As the sector expands, however, and the proportion of the workforce in the 55–64 range grows, the industry will have to recruit increasing numbers of older staff. But there is a problem. While younger workers are often regarded as less reliable and more accident-prone than their older colleagues, research shows that stereotyped perceptions of older workers are more often negative: difficult to train, lacking in creativity, too cautious, resistant to new technology, inflexible. In the hospitality industry, some managers keep older workers out of front-line positions in service areas, believing that they have a negative impact on customer perceptions of the business. Hiring more elderly staff could of course help to overcome that negative stereotype.

Robin Depietro and Merwyn Strate (2007) studied the perceptions that American managers in this sector had of older workers. They also asked these managers about the numbers of older workers they expected to employ in future. The 20 managers in this study perceived older workers to

"I was hoping by this age to have outlived my usefulness."

Source: © Barbara Smaller/The New Yorker Collection/ www.cartoonbank.com

be self-motivated, disciplined, loyal, and dependable, with good communication skills, lower levels of absenteeism, respect for authority, and credibility with customers.

Despite these positive perceptions, only 25 per cent of the managers said that they would prefer to have older workers in their restaurants. Only 10 per cent said that they expected to employ more older workers in future, and 15 per cent said that they expected to employ fewer. Management perceptions, it seems, are not consistent with management actions in this sector. Dipietro and Strate argue that fast food organizations need to rethink their human resource and organization development policies, to match management perceptions with recruitment practices, adding that there are sound business reasons for doing this:

> There needs to be some thought and planning for how older workers can add some dependability and maturity into restaurants, and can possibly change part of the image of quick service restaurants. Working to actively recruit and hire older employees could add a new dimension and some new markets for quick service restaurants.

Any aspect of our appearance is a form of non-verbal communication. We cannot control our age or height, but these factors, combined with behaviour that is under our control, send signals that others decode in the light of their experiences (age is related to reliability), expectations (tall and handsome means self-confident and knowledgeable) and prejudices (short and overweight women will deter customers). This also applies to choice of clothing. This is an aspect which is, of course, within our control. Dress can indicate organizational culture, and can contribute significantly to the individual's impression management. The way in which we dress can tell others how we want to be seen (as formal, relaxed, creative, businesslike) rather than what we are really like. However, we may not always be aware how others perceive our attempts to manage our impression through our dress style.

Should you put your photograph in your job application?

If you include a photograph with your job application, will this give you an advantage, or not? Researchers at Ben-Gurion University in Israel have the answers. They sent fictional applications for 2,500 real job vacancies. For each job, they sent two similar applications, one with a photo, and one without. The photos had been graded for attractiveness. Attractive men were more likely to be given an interview if they included a photo, and advice for unattractive men is – ditch the photo. The results were different for women, however. Attractive women were less likely to be interviewed if they included a photo. On average, an attractive woman would have to apply for eleven jobs to get an interview, but an equally qualified and less attractive woman would only have to apply for seven.

Is this due to 'the dumb blonde hypothesis' – people assume that beautiful women are less intelligent? The photos had been graded for intelligence, so that explanation was ruled out. The researchers noted that human resources departments are staffed mainly by women who decide who to invite for interview. They conclude that pretty women suffer discrimination in recruitment due to old-fashioned jealousy. So, should attractive women just use less attractive photographs of themselves? The researchers argue that the practice of including photos should be discouraged, noting that in the public sector in Belgium, even candidates' names are not allowed (based on *The Economist*, 2012).

Perceptual errors and how to avoid them

The main sources of errors in person perception seem to include:

- not collecting enough information about other people;
- basing our judgements on information that is irrelevant or insignificant;
- seeing what we expect to see and what we want to see, and not investigating further;
- allowing early information about someone to colour our judgement, despite later and contradictory information;
- allowing our own characteristics to influence our judgements of others;
- accepting stereotypes uncritically;
- attempting to decode non-verbal behaviour outwith the context in which it appears;
- basing attributions on flimsy and potentially irrelevant evidence.

The remedies, therefore, include:

1. Take more time and avoid instant or 'snap' judgements about others.
2. Collect and consciously use more information about other people.
3. Develop self-awareness, and an understanding of how our personal biases and preferences affect our perceptions and judgements of other people.
4. Check our attributions – the assumptions we make about the causes of behaviour, particularly the links we make between aspects of personality and appearance on the one hand and behaviour on the other.

Adrian Furnham's unlucky thirteen

Adrian Furnham (2005) argues that the process of making evaluations, judgements, or ratings of the performance of employees is subject to a number of systematic perception errors. This is particularly problematic in a performance appraisal context:

1. *Central tendency*: Appraising everyone at the middle of the rating scale.
2. *Contrast error*: Basing an appraisal on comparison with other employees (who may have received undeserved high or low ratings) rather than on established performance criteria.
3. *Different from me*: Giving a poor appraisal because the person has qualities or characteristics not possessed by the appraiser.
4. *Halo effect*: Appraising an employee undeservedly well on one quality (performance, for example) because they are perceived highly by the appraiser on another quality (attractiveness, perhaps).
5. *Horn effect*: The opposite of the halo effect. Giving someone a poor appraisal on one quality (attractiveness) influences poor rating on other qualities (performance).
6. *Initial impression*: Basing an appraisal on first impressions rather than on how the person has behaved throughout the period to which the appraisal relates.
7. *Latest behaviour*: Basing an appraisal on the person's recent behaviour, rather than on how they have behaved throughout the appraisal period.
8. *Lenient or generous rating*: Perhaps the most common error, being consistently generous in appraisal, mostly to avoid conflict.
9. *Performance dimension error*: Giving someone a similar appraisal on two distinct but similar qualities, because they happen to follow each other on the appraisal form.
10. *Same as me*: Giving a good appraisal because the person has qualities or characteristics possessed by the appraiser.
11. *Spillover effect*: Basing this appraisal, good or bad, on the results of the previous appraisal, rather than on how the person has behaved during the appraisal period.
12. *Status effect*: Giving those in higher-level positions consistently better appraisals than those in lower-level jobs.
13. *Strict rating*: Being consistently harsh in appraising performance.

If we are to improve our understanding of others, we must first have a well-developed knowledge of ourselves – our strengths, our preferences, our flaws, and our biases. The development of self-knowledge can be an uncomfortable process. In organizational settings, we are often constrained in the expression of our feelings (positive and negative) about other people, due to social or cultural norms and to the communication barriers erected by status and power differentials. This may in part explain the enduring appeal of training courses in social and interpersonal skills, self-awareness, and personal growth designed to help us overcome these problems, to 'get in touch' with other people, and to 'get in touch with ourselves'. Training in interpersonal communication skills typically emphasizes openness and honesty in relationships, active listening skills, sensitivity to non-verbal behaviour, and how to give and receive both critical and non-evaluative feedback.

The accuracy of management perception

How accurate are the perceptions of managers? Inaccurate perceptions could lead to inappropriate decisions and ineffective organizational practices. John Mezias and William Starbuck (2003) found that management perceptions are often wrong. Decisions are of course based on information from a range of sources: company documents, rumours overheard at the water cooler, committee meetings, articles in journals, speeches by the chief executive. Mezias and Starbuck identify ten factors that influence management perceptions of all that information, and which can lead to distortions:

1. *Subject matter*	Managers are more likely to notice recent incidents, larger changes, and dramatic events, but may have more accurate perceptions of older and smaller changes and routine events. People are better at perceiving sounds, symbols, and objects than abstract concepts and unobservable processes.
2. *Individual differences*	Our perceptual systems vary. Some of us have better sight, hearing, and recall than others.
3. *Experience*	Experience predisposes us to notice some stimuli and not others.
4. *Training and job role*	If you work in marketing, you learn more about customers and competitors and less about materials and production processes.
5. *Memory*	We find it easier to recall some experiences than others.
6. *Interpersonal skills*	A manager's style can either encourage colleagues to share or to conceal information.
7. *Information systems*	Organization information systems are selective in capturing and disseminating information, usually emphasizing factors that have been relevant in the past while overlooking new and emerging trends.
8. *Culture*	Social and organization cultures focus attention on particular phenomena and de-emphasize others, sometimes making it difficult to share experiences.
9. *Seniority*	Managers at the top of the hierarchy see things differently from those at the bottom, often perceiving fewer and milder problems.
10. *Environment*	Some business environments are more volatile than others, so data quickly become obsolete.

Mezias and Starbuck asked managers about their companies and their business environments, including number of employees, communication practices, processes for evaluating strategies, sales growth, industry concentration, sector growth, and fluctuations in sales. These were areas where 'objective' answers could be found in documented sources, and the researchers expected that managers' perceptions would be more accurate than previous studies suggested. Instead, they found a number of perceptual errors. These concerned inaccurate perceptions of sales levels (overestimates and underestimates), with some errors exceeding 1,000 per cent, with the highest being 5,000 per cent beyond the 'correct' answer. Only a third of the managers questioned had 'very accurate' perceptions, reporting errors of less than 11 per cent. Many managers also appear to underestimate the rate of change over time, reporting much smaller changes than had actually occurred.

In one of their studies, they asked senior managers questions about their company's quality improvement programme. This is what they found:

> [F]our respondents gave numerical answers having six significant digits. Obviously, these managers looked up the numbers in the quality performance reports that they were then receiving monthly. Three of these four respondents were quality specialists, and two of these specialists gave the correct numbers. The other quality specialist and a finance manager gave the same extremely precise incorrect number. They had both pulled this number from the wrong section of the quality-performance report. Thus, even having written documents in front of them and having relevant training does not assure that managers will give accurate information. (Mezias and Starbuck, 2003, p. 14)

These findings are not as disastrous as they appear. We don't always have to perceive problems accurately in order to solve them; 'people can act effectively without having accurate perceptions: they need only pursue general, long-term goals' (Mezias and Starbuck, 2003, p. 15). John Maule and Gerard Hodgkinson (2003) agree that incorrect judgements may not be damaging if they are refined, with feedback, over time. That is how management perception affects most decisions, and this is not necessarily a problem. While perceptual accuracy is important in some instances, perception that is 'good enough' and can be corrected as better information is gathered is adequate for most situations.

Mezias and Starbuck suggest three strategies to improve the accuracy of management perception and reduce the cost of mistakes:

1. Anticipate perceptual inaccuracy, and focus on key factors, using extra resources and backup systems where serious errors are most likely to occur.
2. Arrange multifaceted feedback about performance outcomes, so that mistakes and unpredicted outcomes can be quickly detected.
3. Concentrate on incremental steps and avoid drastic changes, as small innovations are less risky.

RECAP

1. ***Identify the main features of the process of perception.***
   - People behave according to how they perceive the world, not in response to 'reality'.
   - The perceptual process involves the interpretation of sensory input in the light of past experience, and our store of knowledge, beliefs, expectations, and motives.
2. ***Distinguish between the bottom-up processing of sensory information and the top-down interpretation of that information.***
   - Sensation, or bottom-up processing, determines the data to which we pay attention.
   - Perception, or top-down processing, determines the way in which we organize and interpret perceived information in order to make behavioural choices.
3. ***Understand the nature and implications of selective attention and perceptual organization.***
   - Selective attention is influenced by external factors relating to the stimulus and the context, and by internal factors such as learning, personality, and motivation.
   - The way in which we organize and interpret sensory data in meaningful ways, even when it is incomplete or ambiguous, is known as perceptual organization.

4. *Give examples of how behaviour is influenced by our perceptions.*
   - We each have our own perceptual world, an internal mental image of our environment.
   - Different cultures lead to differences in perception and consequently in behaviour.

5. *Explain and illustrate the main processes and problems in perception, including false attributions, halo effects, and stereotyping.*
   - An attribution is a belief about cause and effect. When speaking about ourselves, we tend to attribute success to personal factors and failure to external factors. When speaking about others, we tend to attribute success and failure to personality features.
   - Making a favourable judgement of someone on the basis of a single positive characteristic is known as the halo effect; making an unfavourable judgement on the basis of one negative perception is called the horn effect.
   - Assuming that someone possesses a set of personality traits because they belong to a particular social group is known as stereotyping.

6. *Explain some less widely appreciated sources of discrimination at work arising from characteristics of the person perception and attribution processes.*
   - Aspects of behaviour are attributed to appearance, leading to discrimination. You are likely to be paid less at work if you are an overweight or underweight female, a short man, or are perceived to be unattractive.
   - The fundamental attribution error leads us to emphasize individual personality and ignore social and organizational context when explaining behaviour.

7. *Suggest techniques for improving perceptual accuracy and avoiding errors.*
   - To avoid mistakes, avoid rapid judgements, take more time, collect more information, be aware of your own prejudices and biases, and develop increased self-awareness.
   - To improve accuracy, expect errors to occur, use as much feedback as you can get, and take small steps rather than radical ones to reduce risks.

Revision

1. Explain the distinction between sensation and perception. What is the significance of this distinction?
2. What is the individual's perceptual world? What factors influence this construct, and how does an understanding of someone's perceptual world help us to understand their behaviour?
3. What is the difference between selective attention and perceptual organization? What factors influence the latter process?
4. What are the factors influencing selective attention? How can a knowledge of these factors be exploited in commercial settings?

Research assignment

Look carefully at the style of dress and appearance of the instructors in your educational institution, across all the subjects that you are studying. How does their appearance affect your perceptions of their

- approachability
- subject knowledge
- professionalism
- understanding of the world beyond the academic 'ivory tower'?

Write a report that first identifies specific aspects of your instructors' dress and appearance that lead you to make judgements on those criteria. Conclude your report with advice to instructors on how they could change their dress and appearance to improve the ways in which they are perceived by students on those criteria – to make them appear more approachable, more professional, and so on.

Springboard

E. Bruce Goldstein (2009) *Sensation and Perception* (8th edn), Wadsworth Publishing, Belmont, CA. Introduction to the psychology and physiology of sensation and perception. Describes with fascinating illustrations how the senses function, exposing the complexity of perceptual processes.

Daniel S. Hamermesh (2011) *Beauty Pays: Why Attractive People Are More Successful*, Princeton University Press. Handsome men earn 4 per cent more than average-looking men, and unattractive men earn up to 13 per cent less. The laws of 'pulchronomics' also apply to women. Attractive workers may attract more customers, so perhaps they should be paid more, but Hamermesh argues that those who are unattractive should have legal protection.

Phil Rosenzweig (2007) *The Halo Effect: And the Eight Other Business Delusions that Deceive Managers*, Free Press, Glencoe, IL. Does an organization's culture determine its success, as many researchers have argued? Or does good performance lead employees and others to rate a company highly? The latter is an example of the halo effect. Rosenzweig is critical of research that argues differently because it has muddled up cause and effect.

OB in films

Legally Blonde (2001, director Robert Luketic) DVD track (scene) 8: 0:21:17 to 0:22:46 (2 minutes). Clip begins with the tutor saying 'OK, welcome to law school'; clip ends with Elle saying 'Whoever said that orange was the new pink was seriously disturbed'.

Legally Blonde is the story of a blonde sorority queen, Elle Woods (played by Reece Witherspoon), whose boyfriend leaves her to go to Harvard Law School. To get him back, she goes to Harvard, too. Every character in this movie plays a stereotyped role. In this clip, on the law school lawn, Elle and three of her classmates are asked by a tutor to introduce themselves. As you watch the clip, observe the five characters carefully and:

1. Decide on an appropriate stereotype label (e.g. 'absent-minded professor') for each character.
2. Explain why you have chosen that label, based on the evidence that each character provides (what they say, how they say it, appearance, non-verbal behaviour).
3. For each character identify two adjectives that you think would describe how they would be likely to interact socially with others.
4. Thinking of each of those characters in an organizational context, assess what you feel would be their strengths and their weaknesses.

OB on the web

This YouTube clip is part of the documentary *The Corporation* (2006, directors Jennifer Abbott and Mark Achbar). You can find it by searching YouTube for 'The Corporation perception management' or at http://www.youtube.com/watch?v=kQTkczvE17U.

Watch the first two minutes and ten seconds. The commentators argue that large corporations are not just selling products and services. They are also advertising a way of life, a way of thinking. They are 'manufacturing consent' for their actions and for business norms and values. Is this a form of propaganda? One of the interviewees, the chief executive of a public relations company, explains his profession in terms of 'perception management', arguing that this is a valuable contribution to business and to society.

After you have watched this, identify the ways in which your own perceptions are managed in this way by large organizations. What is your conclusion: is corporate perception management necessary and valuable, or an unacceptable form of manipulation?

CHAPTER EXERCISES

1. Person perception

Objective To explore factors influencing our perception of other people. Research has shown, for example, that we assess others' characters from their faces. These assessments include how friendly, aggressive, trustworthy, and creditworthy another person is. The judgements that we reach based on such apparently limited information often turn out to be correct.

Briefing

1. Break into groups of three.
2. Your instructor will give you five or six photographs of people, taken from recent newspapers and magazines. You have 5 minutes to work out as much as you can about each of these people, using only what you can see in the picture. Consider characteristics such as their
   - conscientiousness,
   - sense of humour and fun,
   - intelligence,
   - aggressiveness,
   - approachability,
   - reliability, and
   - other characteristics suggested by the photographs.
3. Prepare a presentation based on your photographs and your assumptions. Explain clearly which items of evidence from the photographs led you to make those assessments.

2. You're the interviewee: what would you do?

You are about to go for a job interview, but first you will be kept waiting in the interviewer's office. During that time, you can observe clues about your interviewer and perhaps about the organization. What clues do you think are significant and revealing? What personal experiences in your own past affect how you observe and make judgements in this setting?

This exercise can be completed in class time, but is more effective if steps 1 to 3 are completed in advance. For a one-hour tutorial, time will be tight without preparation.

Step 1 Read the manager's room description, to get a feel for the setting in which you find yourself.

Step 2 Complete the analysis sheet.

- In the *data* column, record those observations that you find significant and revealing about the kind of person who occupies this room.
- In the *inferences* column, note the perceptions or conclusions that you reach from your data.
- In the *experiences* column, record past incidents or events, recent or distant, that you think influence your inferences.

→

data I observe in the room	the inferences that I make	based on past experience

Step 3 Using that analysis, construct a profile of your interviewer.

Step 4 Finally, record your answers to the following questions:

1. What is the sex, marital status, and ethnic background of the managing director? Identify the data in the room that lead you to your inferences.
2. How would you describe the managing director's character? What are this person's interests? What would you expect this person's management style to be like? Once again, identify the data on which you base these judgements.
3. Given your own personality, do you think that you would be happy working for this person?
4. Explain how your analysis illustrates the concepts of selective attention, perceptual organization, perceptual world, halo effect, and stereotyping.

Step 5 Present your findings, according to your instructor's directions.

The manager's room description

You are now in the company offices, top floor, for your job interview. It sounds like your ideal position. As personal assistant, you will be working for the managing director who has asked to interview you. You have arrived on time, but the managing director's secretary apologizes and tells you there will be a delay. The managing director has been called to an important meeting which will take up to fifteen minutes. The secretary tells you that you are welcome to wait in the managing director's private office, and shows you in.

You know that you will be alone here for fifteen minutes. You look around the room, curious about the person with whom you may be working. The shallow pile carpet is a warm pink, with no pattern. You choose one of six high-backed chairs, upholstered in a darker fabric that matches well with the carpet and curtains, and with polished wooden arms. In the centre of the ring of chairs is a low glass-topped coffee table. On the wall behind you is a large photograph of a vintage motor car, accompanied by its driver in leather helmet, goggles, scarf, and long leather coat; you can't make out the driver's face. The window ledge holds four plants arranged equal distances apart; two look like small exotic ferns and the others are a begonia and a geranium in flower.

On the other side of the room sits a large wooden executive desk, with a black leather chair. A framed copy of the company's mission statement hangs on the wall behind the desk, and below that sits a black leather briefcase with combination locks. The plain grey wastepaper basket by the wall beside the desk is full of papers. At the front of the desk sits a pen-stand with a letter opener. To the side is a 'state of the art' laptop computer and a desk lamp. In front of the lamp sits a metal photograph frame holding two pictures. One is of an attractive woman in her thirties with a young boy around eight years old. The other photograph is of a retriever dog in a field to the side of some farm buildings. In front of the framed photographs is a stack of file folders. Immediately in front of the chair, on the desk, is a small pile of papers, and a Mont Blanc pen with the company logo on the barrel.

On the other side of the desk is a delicate china mug. In front of it lies what looks like a leather-covered address book or perhaps a diary, a passport, and a pad of yellow paper. Beside the pad there is a pile of unopened mail with envelopes of differing sizes. On top of the mail and behind are some half-folded newspapers: *The Guardian*, *The Independent*, and *The Financial Times*. You note that there is no telephone on the desk. Behind the desk is a small glass-fronted display case. There are some books lined up on top of the case: *Plugged In: The Generation Y Guide to Thriving at Work*, *The Oxford Concise Dictionary of Quotations*, *Managing Difficult Interactions*, and *Shattering the Glass Ceiling*. Also on top of the case sits a small bronze statue, of a man sitting with his legs crossed in a yoga position. There is a cheese plant on the far side of the display case. Inside the case, there are computing systems manuals and books and pamphlets on employment law, many of which deal with race and sex discrimination issues.

You decide to get up and look out the window. There is a three-seater settee under the window, covered in the same fabric as the armchairs with matching scatter cushions in the corners. From the window you can easily see people shopping and children playing in the nearby park. You turn to another table beside the settee. Several magazines sit in front of a burgundy ceramic lamp with a beige shade. There are two recent copies of *The Economist*, and a copy each of *Asia Today*, *Classic CD*, and *Fortune*. As you head back to your chair, you notice that the papers on the desk in front of the chair are your application papers and curriculum vitae. Your first name, obviously indicating your sex, has been boldly circled with the Mont Blanc pen. As the managing director may return at any moment, you go back and sit in your chair to wait.

Employability assessment

With regard to your future employment prospects:

1. Identify up to three issues from this chapter that you found significant.
2. Relate these to the competencies in the employability matrix.
3. Decide what actions you need to take to maintain and/or develop those competencies under each of the four headings of the employability matrix.

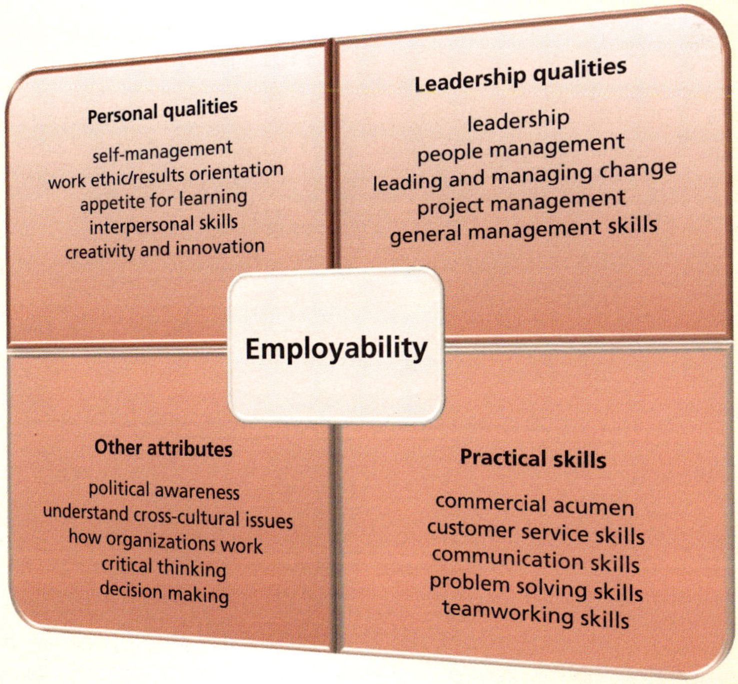

References

Adler, N.J. (2002) *International Dimensions of Organizational Behaviour* (4th edn), London: International Thomson.

Carroll, P. (1994) *Big Blues: The Unmaking of IBM*, London: Orion Books.

Depietro, R.B. and Strate, M.L. (2007) 'Management perceptions of older employees in the US quick service restaurant industry', *Journal of Foodservice Business Research*, 9(2), pp. 169–85.

Dixon, N.M. (1999) *The Organizational Learning Cycle: How We Can Learn Collectively* (2nd edn), Aldershot: Gower.

DuBrin, A.J. (2011) *Impression Management in the Workplace: Research, Theory, and Practice*, New York and Abingdon, Oxon: Routledge.

Furnham, A. (2005) *The Psychology of Behaviour at Work*, Hove, Sussex: Psychology Press.

Greasley, K., Bryman, A., Dainty, A., Price, A., Soetanto, R. and King, N. (2005) 'Employee perceptions of empowerment', *Employee Relations*, 27(4), pp. 354–68.

Harper, B. (2000) 'Beauty, stature and the labour market: a British cohort study', *Oxford Bulletin of Economics and Statistics*, 62(S1), pp. 771–800.

Heider, F. (1958) *The Psychology of Interpersonal Relationships*, New York: John Wiley.

Hoel, H., Cooper, C.L. and Faragher, B. (2001) 'The experience of bullying in Great Britain: the impact of organizational status', *European Journal of Work and Organizational Psychology*, 10(4), pp. 443–65.

Kelley, H.H. (1971) *Attribution: Perceiving the Causes of Behaviour*, New York: General Learning Press.

Levine, R.V. (1990) 'The pace of life', *American Scientist*, 78(5), pp. 43–53.

Maule, J.A. and Hodgkinson, G.P. (2003) 'Re-appraising managers' perceptual errors: a behavioural decision-making perspective', *British Journal of Management*, 14(1), pp. 33–7.

Mezias, J.M. and Starbuck, W.H. (2003) 'Studying the accuracy of managers' perceptions: a research odyssey', *British Journal of Management*, 14(1), pp. 3–17.

Power, S.J. and Lundsten, L.L. (2005) 'Managerial and other white-collar employees' perceptions of ethical issues in their workplace', *Journal of Business Ethics*, 60(2), pp. 185–93.

Soames, G. (2010) 'Which button says I get promoted?', *The Sunday Times*, 19 October, p. 16.

Spinney, L. (2000) 'Blind to change', *New Scientist*, 18 November, pp. 27–32.

The Economist (2002) 'No small matter', 2 March, pp. 68–9.

The Economist (2012) 'Don't hate me because I'm beautiful', 31 March, p. 74.

Woodman, P. and Kumar, V. (2008) *Bullying at Work: The Experience of Managers*, London: Chartered Management Institute.

Chapter 9 **Motivation**

Key terms

extreme job
boreout
drive
motive
motivation
self-actualization
equity theory
expectancy theory
valence
instrumentality
expectancy
total rewards
goal-setting theory
inner work life theory
job enrichment
motivator factors
hygiene factors
vertical loading factors
intrinsic rewards
extrinsic rewards
growth need strength
job diagnostic survey
motivating potential score
empowerment
engagement
high performance work system

Learning outcomes

When you have read this chapter, you should be able to define those key terms in your own words, and you should also be able to:

1. Understand different ways in which the term motivation is used.
2. Understand the nature of motives and motivation processes as influences on behaviour.
3. Use expectancy theory and job enrichment to diagnose organizational problems and to recommend solutions.
4. Explain the continuing contemporary interest in this field, with respect to extreme jobs, boreout, and high performance work systems.

Why study motivation?

The why guy

Interviewed about his new book on motivation and why people work, David Ulrich said:

> Meaning is finding a 'why' for work. Employees are more productive when they have a compelling reason to work. In the talent domain, we have seen a focus on competencies, commitment or engagement, and now we see an emerging focus on contribution or finding meaning from doing the work. . . . The general principles we identify can be adapted to all jobs. This point comes across in the US television show Undercover Boss, where the CEO of a company disguises himself or herself and goes 'undercover' to discover what motivates employees. In every the case the CEOs doing routine and menial jobs are amazed at the passion and energy of their employees. These people may be sweeping streets or cleaning toilets, serving coffee or working on an assembly line, but they find meaning through work where they have an identity built on awareness of their own strengths, a clear purpose, relationships based on trust, a positive environment, interesting tasks, opportunities to learn or develop – and, of course, fun. (Arkin, 2010)

A motivated workforce can be a sign of a successful organization. How is that achieved? Each of us has a different reason for getting out of bed in the morning. Our motives – from the Latin *movere*, to move – are key determinants of our behaviour. If we understand your motives (desire for more leisure), we can influence your behaviour (take a day's holiday if you finish that assignment). What motivates you? A recent survey suggested (Twentyman, 2010) that the top career goals for UK university students were:

1. to have work-life balance
2. to be competitively or intellectually challenged
3. to be secure or stable in my job
4. to be dedicated to a cause or to feel that I am serving a greater good
5. to have an international career
6. to be entrepreneurial or creative and innovative
7. to be a leader or manager of people
8. to be a technical or functional expert
9. to be autonomous or independent.

Employers concerned with attracting, motivating, and retaining college and university graduates should therefore try to provide jobs that lead to these kinds of work and career experiences and opportunities. This pattern is apparently seen in many other countries, too. In other words, look for the job advertisements which suggest that 'we don't pay much, but it's fun'.

A demotivated workforce, on the other hand, can be disastrous. When Apple released the iPad in May 2010, pictures of iPhones were burned in Hong Kong and protesters called for a global boycott of Apple products. This followed a series of employee suicides at Foxconn, a contract manufacturer which makes products for Apple and other electronics companies at Foxconn City, an industrial park in Shenzen. Foxconn City has 15 multi-storey manufacturing buildings where there were twelve suicides in one year. These deaths raised questions about 'sweatshop' working conditions. Although Foxconn paid the Shenzen minimum wage, employees compared the company facilities to a prison, said that they were forced to work illegal overtime and night shifts, were exposed to hazardous materials, and had their privacy invaded by management. In response to the suicides, the company put nets around its buildings, hired counsellors, and brought in Buddhist monks to pray. The chief executive denied that he was running a 'sweatshop', but Apple, Foxconn, and other companies had already suffered 'bad press' (*The Economist*, 2010).

Yuin Schilling/PA Photos

Inside Foxconn City

Douglas Murray McGregor (1906–64)

The question of work motivation is particularly significant in a global economic recession. Most companies and public sector organizations try to cut costs in a downturn. This means findings ways to motivate employees other than offering more money. However, is more money really more motivating? Douglas McGregor (1960) set out two sets of motivational propositions, which he called 'Theory X' and 'Theory Y'. To find out which propositions apply to you, complete the questionnaire in Table 9.1. Read each pair of statements, and circle the number that reflects your view.

Table 9.1: Theory X/Theory Y scoring questionnaire

the average person inherently dislikes work	1 2 3 4 5	work is as natural as rest to people
people must be directed to work	1 2 3 4 5	people will exercise self-discretion and self-control
people wish to avoid responsibility	1 2 3 4 5	people enjoy real responsibility
people feel that achievement at work is irrelevant	1 2 3 4 5	achievement is highly valued by people
most people are dull and uncreative	1 2 3 4 5	most people have imagination and creativity
money is the only real reason for working	1 2 3 4 5	money is only one benefit from work
people lack the desire to improve their quality of life	1 2 3 4 5	people have needs to improve their quality of life
having an objective is a form of imprisonment	1 2 3 4 5	objectives are welcomed as an aid to effectiveness

Add up the numbers that you circled to give you a score between 8 and 40. If you scored 16 or less, then you subscribe to Theory X. If you scored 32 or more, then you subscribe to Theory Y. Managers who subscribe to Theory X believe in giving orders and direct supervision, and in the motivating power of money. Managers who subscribe to Theory Y believe in giving autonomy and responsibility, and in the motivating power of interesting jobs. As an employee, which management theory would you like to have applied to you at work?

McGregor argued that Theory Y was a more accurate description of most people's attitudes to work, and that Theory X in practice demotivated people. In other words, non-financial rewards can be as powerful, if not more powerful, motivators than money, as we also value recognition, jobs with a worthwhile purpose, flexible working, and personal development. McGregor died in 1964, but his terminology has entered the language, and his ideas remain influential (Heil et al., 2000).

As discussed in Chapter 2 (Environment), there has been much debate concerning the different approaches to work of the different generations – Gen X, Gen Y, Gen C. Are there really differences in attitude between generations, or are individual differences more important? The celebrity chef and restaurant manager Jamie Oliver has criticized in public the low work motivation of his Gen C employees in particular. If his observations are correct, this provides managers with a significant motivation challenge for the foreseeable future.

The youth of today

The celebrity chef Jamie Oliver has accused British youth of being lazy and workshy. To find out what the general public thought, a British newspaper commissioned a YouGov survey of 2,500 adults who were asked in 2011 whether or not they agreed with Jamie Oliver's views (Woods, 2011). These were the responses:

The wet generation question:

	agree	disagree	don't know
Jamie Oliver has criticized young people in Britain today, saying he has 'never experienced such a wet generation' as the 16- to 20-year-olds he has employed.	65%	18%	17%

The European comparisons question:

	less hard-working	more hard-working	about the same	don't know
Are young people in Britain less hard-working than their counterparts in other European countries?	55%	4%	24%	17%

The long hours question:

	agree	disagree	don't know
Jamie Oliver said that young people should be prepared to put in 'seven 18-hour days' a week in the current economic climate.	24%	68%	8%

Source: © Woods/*The Sunday Times*/News International Trading Ltd, 20 February 2011.

What is your response to Jamie Oliver's criticisms? Are students workshy and lazy? How should educational organizations be doing more to prepare their graduates for the world of work?

Extreme jobs and boreout: how work is changing

Once a popular topic, research into work motivation declined in the 1990s. The ideas developed in the mid to late twentieth century, however, are still 'current'. Managers still use the terms and the tools which those earlier researchers introduced. Richard Steers and colleagues (2004), however, argue that work today is more short-term in outlook, uses time as a measure of performance, emphasizes teamwork, and produces more conflicts of motives and values: my company versus the environment, work versus my family. The idea of a 'job for life' has also become a rarity in some sectors. Two other trends suggest that motivation remains a core issue. One concerns the development of *extreme jobs*, and the other concerns the phenomenon of *boreout*.

Extreme jobs

Extreme job a job that involves a working week of 60 hours or more, with high earnings, combined with additional performance pressures.

Some of us are motivated by the **extreme job** which involves long hours, frequent travel across different time zones, and multiple other pressures. The characteristics of extreme jobs include

- physical presence in the office of at least 10 hours a day
- tight deadlines and fast working pace
- unpredictable workflow
- inordinate scope of responsibility
- frequent travel
- after-hours work events
- availability to clients 24/7
- responsibility for profit and loss
- responsibility for mentoring and recruiting.

Sylvia Ann Hewlett and Carolyn Buck Luce (2006) found that people in extreme jobs enjoy their work and are fulfilled by it. Answers to the question 'why do you do it?' included adrenaline rush, great colleagues, high pay, recognition, status, and power. They cite this example (p. 49):

> A financial analyst we'll call Sudhir emigrated five years ago from Mumbai, India. He works at a major commercial bank in New York. Summertime, when he puts in 90 hours a week, is his 'light' season. The rest of the year, he works upwards of 120 hours a week – leaving only 48 hours for sleeping, eating, entertaining, and (he smiles) bathing. Sudhir stays late in the office even when he has nothing particularly pressing to do. His get-a-life existence is a hazard of the profession – but worth it: As a 23-year-old with a first job, he is in the top 6 per cent of earners in America.

There are more men than women in extreme jobs; only 20 per cent of 'extreme jobbers' are female. Long hours and intense pressure are also exhausting, and have implications for family life. Women in extreme jobs are concerned that their children are less disciplined, eat more junk food, and watch too much television as a result of their frequent absence. Hewlett and Luce also found that

- 53 per cent of women in extreme jobs say that their job interferes with their sex life;
- 65 per cent of men say their extreme jobs damage relationships with their children.

Working constantly at this pace may not be sustainable (Pfeffer, 2010). Research has shown that extreme jobs with long hours are associated with higher satisfaction, better career prospects, and higher salary, but with also with higher levels of stress, more psychosomatic symptoms, lower family satisfaction, and poorer emotional health (Burke and Fiksenbaum, 2009a and 2009b). Companies are dealing with 'extremists' in different ways. American Express gives high performers time to work on their own projects. Other companies encourage key managers to work from home and to take career breaks. ProLogis, a distribution company with offices in America and China, uses short-term global assignments to reduce the pressures of relocation (Millard, 2006). The motivational impact of extreme jobs needs to be balanced with ways to reduce the long term personal and domestic costs.

Boreout

Boreout boredom, demotivation, and lack of energy and enthusiasm caused by uninteresting, unchallenging, and monotonous work.

According to Philippe Rothlin and Peter Werder (2008), demotivation is common, especially among office workers, and is caused by repetitive, uninteresting, unchallenging work, leading to **boreout**. They estimate that 15 per cent of office workers are affected. Boreout leads to high levels of sick leave and reduces company loyalty. If you suffer boreout, you turn up for work lacking energy and enthusiasm, and spend your time surfing the internet, chatting to colleagues, and trying to look busy. The journalist Roger Boyes (2007) describes one of his tactics:

> I remember while working for the *Financial Times* in the 1970s that colleagues developed an 'Italian Jacket' system. A spare jacket, kept in the office, would be spread over the back of your chair, a half-drunk cup of coffee would be placed next to the phone – and you could disappear for a couple of hours. The editor would assume that you were briefly somewhere else in the building.

Other tactics include the fake stomach upset which creates time to read magazines in the toilet, and 'fake smokers' who use their 'addiction' as an excuse to escape from their desk. The employee who answers 'yes' to four or more of these questions may be suffering boreout:

1. Do you complete private tasks at work?
2. Do you feel under-challenged or bored?
3. Do you sometimes pretend to be busy?
4. Are you tired and apathetic after work even if you experienced no stress in the office?
5. Are you unhappy with your work?
6. Do you find your work meaningless?
7. Could you complete your work quicker than you are doing?
8. Are you afraid of changing your job because you might take a salary cut?
9. Do you send private emails to colleagues during working hours?
10. Do you have little or no interest in your work?

Today's theories about work motivation, and the techniques that influence management practice, were developed some time ago. Are they relevant to current trends involving extreme jobs and boreout? Those theories and techniques are used today in companies as diverse as Linn Products (audio equipment) and Morgan Motor Company (cars). We will also see how one 'new' theory of motivation is similar to a popular 'old' theory.

Drives, motives, and motivation

Motivation can be explored from three distinct but related perspectives.

1. *Goals*. What are the main motives for our behaviour? Wealth, status, and power trigger behaviours directed towards their achievement. This perspective views motivation in terms of our desired outcomes or goals. This question is addressed by *content* theories of motivation.
2. *Decisions*. Why do we choose to pursue certain goals? Why do you study hard to earn distinctions while a friend has a full social life and is happy with pass grades? This perspective views motivation in terms of the cognitive decision-making processes influencing an individual's choice of goals. This question is addressed by *process* theories of motivation.
3. *Influence*. How can we get you to work harder? Managers want to motivate employees to turn up on time and be helpful to customers. This perspective views motivation as a social influence process and is addressed by *job enrichment* theories.

Drive an innate, biological determinant of behaviour, activated by deprivation.

Do we inherit our goals, or are they acquired through experience? If our motives are innate, then it would be pointless to attempt to change them. If they are acquired, then they can be altered. Our behaviour is influenced by our biological equipment. We appear to have an innate need for survival. Our needs for oxygen, water, food, shelter, warmth, and sex can be overpowering. These needs are triggered by deprivation and are known as **drives**.

Home viewing

American Beauty (1999, director Sam Mendes) is a story of 'the perfect family' falling apart. Lester Burnham (played by Kevin Spacey) quits his dead-end management job to work serving burgers in Mr Smiley's, while his wife Carolyn (Annette Bening) has an affair with her local competitor in the real estate business. The story displays the corrosive effects of dissatisfying, demotivating work on family, personal identity, and relationships. Also of interest is the way in which the main characters define 'success' in life.

Our drives may not be restricted to basic biological needs. Some psychologists claim that we are active sensation-seekers who have the innate cognitive drives listed in Table 9.2.

Table 9.2: Innate cognitive drives

curiosity	the need to explore, to play, to learn more
sense-making	the need to understand the nature of the world around us
order and meaning	the need for order, certainty, equity, consistency, predictability
effectance or competency	the need to exert mastery and control over the world around us
self-understanding	the need to know who and what we are

The drives come with the body. We do not have to learn to be cold, thirsty, or hungry. However, we can *override* these drives. Some religious orders inflict celibacy on willing members. Altruism can overcome personal safety needs in extraordinary circumstances. The idea that our behaviour is pre-programmed is too simple. Psychologists once thought that human behaviour could be explained in terms of instincts, but that turns out to be unhelpful. Animal behaviour, in contrast, is triggered largely by instincts. Birds and squirrels cannot override their programming, and remain locked into their niches in nature. The ways in which we, on the other hand, seek to satisfy our drives are innumerable, and vary between individuals and across cultures. Consider differences in eating habits around the world, and the range of things that individuals do to satisfy their sex drives. **Motives**, in contrast, appear to be acquired through experience.

Motive a socially acquired need activated by a desire for fulfilment.

Polygamy is a crime in most Western cultures, but is a sign of male achievement, wealth, and status in parts of the Arab world. In some Muslim societies, the consumption of alcohol is punished, while gifts of alcohol are the norm in many Western cultures. Our choice of goals and behaviours is influenced by the norms of our society. Those who choose not to conform are often shunned, ridiculed, and sometimes imprisoned. Table 9.3 outlines the distinction between drives and motives.

Table 9.3: Drives versus motives

drives	**motives**
are innate	are learned
have a physiological basis	have a social basis
are activated by deprivation	are activated by environment
are aimed at satiation	are aimed at stimulation

This distinction between innate drives and acquired motives is not clear. The terms 'needs' and 'goals' are also used to refer to both drives and motives. We try to satisfy our biological drives in ways acceptable to our society. The innate drives for competency, sense-making, and curiosity are socially prized in most cultures. The constructivist perspective (see Chapter 1) argues that human behaviour is purposive; we attach reasons to our goals and behaviours. To understand your motives, and to influence your behaviour, we need to understand why you choose particular outcomes and how you decide to pursue them.

Motivation the cognitive decision-making process through which goal-directed behaviour is initiated, energized, directed, and maintained.

Motivation is a broad concept which includes preferences for particular outcomes, strength of effort (half-hearted or enthusiastic), and persistence (in the face of problems and barriers). These are the factors that we have to understand in order to explain your motivation and behaviour. These are the factors which a manager has to appreciate in order to motivate employees to behave in organizationally desirable ways.

Content theories

Theories of motivation based on drives and needs are known as content theories, because drives and needs are seen as part of our common 'mental luggage'. The most recent content theory of work motivation was developed by Nitin Nohria, Boris Groysberg and Linda-Eling Lee (2008). Their 'emotional needs' theory claims that we are driven by four basic and innate ('hardwired') drives:

- the drive to *acquire* (obtain scarce goods, develop social status);
- the drive to *bond* (form connections with other individuals and groups);
- the drive to *comprehend* (satisfy our curiosity, master our environment);
- the drive to *defend* (protect against threats, promote justice).

From a survey of around 700 employees of large companies, they found that an organization's ability to meet the four drives contributes to employee motivation by influencing feelings of involvement, energy and initiative, satisfaction, commitment, and intention to quit (or stay). Fulfilling employees' drive to bond has the greatest impact on commitment, while meeting the drive to comprehend is closely linked to involvement, energy and initiative. However, the best way to improve motivation is to meet all four drives; 'a poor showing on one drive substantially diminishes the impact of high scores on the other three'. How can this framework be used in practice? There is a 'primary lever' linked to each of the drives. These are the organization's reward system, its culture, the way that jobs are designed, and performance management and resource allocation processes. Organizational policies and practices in each of those areas can enhance motivation, as shown in Table 9.4.

Abraham Harold Maslow (1908–1970)

This emphasis on organizational factors does not mean that management behaviour is not important. On the contrary, because managers have some control over the way in which company policies are implemented, they can help to meet their employees' drives. For example, a line manager or supervisor can link performance and reward through the use of praise, recognition, favoured assignments, the allocation of bonuses, encouraging teamwork, and making jobs interesting and meaningful. Once again, employees expect their managers to address all four drives, within the constraints of the organization. Managers who fail to fulfil just one drive are rated poorly.

This new theory is similar to the framework developed several decades ago by the American psychologist Abraham Maslow (1943; 1954; 1971). Maslow also argued that we have innate needs (including drives and goals), and identified nine of these, shown in Figure 9.1.

Self-actualization the desire for personal fulfilment, to develop one's potential, to become everything that one is capable of becoming.

If our biological and safety needs are not satisfied, we die. If our needs for love and esteem are not satisfied, we can feel inferior and helpless, but if these needs are satisfied, we feel self-confident. **Self-actualization**, Maslow argued, is our ultimate goal, and freedom of inquiry and expression is a prerequisite for this. Aesthetics and the metaphysical concept of transcendence have been largely ignored by management writers and researchers who have focused

Table 9.4: Emotional needs theory and implications for practice

drive	primary lever	management actions
acquire	reward system	differentiate good from average and poor performers tie rewards clearly to performance pay as well as your competitors
bond	culture	foster mutual reliance and friendship among co-workers value collaboration and teamwork encourage sharing of best practices
comprehend	job design	design jobs that have distinct and important roles in the organization design jobs that are meaningful and foster a sense of contribution to the organization
defend	performance management	increase the transparency of all processes emphasize their fairness build trust by being just and transparent in granting rewards, assignments, and other forms of recognition

1 *self-actualization*	need to develop our full potential
2 *freedom of inquiry and expression*	need that is a prerequisite for the satisfaction of other needs
3 *transcendence*	a spiritual need, 'to be at one with the universe'
4 *aesthetics*	need for order and beauty
5 *to know and to understand*	need to gain and to systematize knowledge, the need for curiosity, learning, philosophizing, experimenting, and exploring
6 *esteem*	need for strength, confidence, achievement, self-esteem, independence, reputation, prestige, recognition, attention and appreciation, and the respect of others
7 *affiliation*	need for attachment, belongingness, affection, love, relationships
8 *safety*	need for security, comfort, tranquillity, freedom from fear and threat from the environment, shelter, order, predictability, and an organized world
9 *biological*	need for sunlight, sexual expression, food, water, rest, and oxygen – needs basic to our survival

Figure 9.1: Abraham Maslow's needs hierarchy

instead on self-actualization. Maslow argued that self-actualized people are rare, and that creating the conditions for us to develop our capabilities to this extent was a challenging task. He also argued that these needs are organized in a hierarchy, with lower-order biological and safety needs at the bottom, and higher-order self-actualization and transcendence needs at the top, as in Figure 9.1.

STOP AND THINK Most textbooks ignore needs 2 to 5 in Maslow's framework, and concentrate instead on the other five needs. One explanation is that freedom of inquiry, transcendence, aesthetics, and the need to know are not relevant to work, organizations, or management. How valid is that explanation? How else can we explain why those needs are rarely discussed?

This hierarchy, Maslow argued, has the following properties.

1. A need is not an effective motivator until those lower in the hierarchy are more or less satisfied. You are unlikely to be concerned about the sharks (threat to safety) if you are drowning (biological deprivation).
2. A satisfied need is not a motivator. If you are well fed and safe, we would have difficulty energizing and directing your behaviour with offers of food and shelter.
3. Lack of need satisfaction can affect mental health. Consider the frustration, anxiety, and depression that can arise from lack of self-esteem, loss of the respect of others, an inability to sustain relationships, and an inability to develop one's capabilities.
4. We have an innate desire to work our way up the hierarchy, pursuing the satisfaction of our higher-order needs once our lower-order needs are more or less satisfied.
5. The experience of self-actualization stimulates desire for more. Maslow claimed that self-actualizers have 'peak experiences'. When you have had one of these, you want another. Self-actualization cannot be satisfied in the same way as the other needs.

Maslow did not intend this hierarchy to be regarded as rigid, but as a typical picture of how human motivation is likely to develop under ideal conditions.

Maslow's theory has been criticized as a statement of white American middle-class values in the mid twentieth century. The idea that human needs are universal is not consistent with the view that our needs are shaped by the society into which we are born. However, Louis Tay and Ed Diener (2011) have found that subjective wellbeing is associated with need fulfilment around the world. They analysed data from the Gallup World Poll which asks about subjective wellbeing, and about six needs related to those identified by Maslow: food and shelter, safety and security, social support, respect and pride, mastery, and self-direction. This poll covers over 60,000 people in 123 countries in eight regions: Africa, East and South Asia, Former Soviet Union, Latin America, Middle East, Northern Europe, South East Asia, and Southern Europe. Need fulfilment was found to be an important basis for wellbeing in 80 per cent of those surveyed. There was also support for Maslow's concept of a hierarchy of needs which we seek to fulfil in sequence, starting with the most basic, although we sometimes seek to meet our social needs even when basic needs are not fully met. In other words, human needs do appear to be universal, and are independent of culture. However, it also turns out that one person's wellbeing is influenced by the wellbeing of others. Maslow focused on the individual, but need fulfilment must also be achieved across a society.

Maslow's ideas are still influential, particularly in recognizing that behaviour depends on a range of needs, drives, and motives (even if his theory does not allow us to predict individual behaviour). His ideas still influence management practice concerning rewards, management style, and work design. Many techniques such as job enrichment, total quality management, process re-engineering, self-managing teams, 'new leadership', empowerment, and engagement have been influenced by his thinking. We also find the emotional needs identified by Nohria and colleagues in Maslow's framework (see Table 9.5), and the latter still appears to be the more useful of the two.

Table 9.5: Nohria and Maslow compared

Nohria's needs	Maslow's needs
acquire	biological, esteem
bond	affiliation, esteem
comprehend	knowing and understanding, freedom of inquiry
defend	safety

China and the West: diverging or converging?

Do Western motivation theories apply to other countries, such as China? Western management thinking traditionally emphasizes the role of individual tasks, performance, and rewards. Since the 1980s, however, the importance of teamwork and information-sharing has been more widely recognized. In contrast, Chinese attitudes to work have been influenced by the collectivist philosophy of Confucianism which stresses benevolence, right conduct, loyalty, and good manners. Selfishness and materialism are shunned, and sharing is valued.

Are these cultural differences being strengthened, or eroded, by current economic trends and developments? In other words, are the work cultures of China and the West diverging or converging? Maria Rotundo and Jia Lin Xie (2008) compared Chinese and Western management attitudes to misconduct at work, to identify the differences.

While both cultures felt that stealing from the organization was wrong, Chinese managers rated more highly the importance of task completion, challenging work, and opportunity for advancement – which are all individual aspects of work. Chinese and Western managers rated cooperative working equally. Over the last 20 years, the centralized and planned economy of China has become more decentralized and market-driven. In this more competitive context, managers need to pay more attention to task completion, and Chinese workers may have become more individualistic as a result. The researchers conclude, therefore, that Western and Chinese attitudes to work behaviour and performance seem to be converging.

Source: DILBERT © 2011 Scott Adams. Used by permission of UNIVERSAL UCLICK. All rights reserved.

Process theories

Theories of motivation that focus on how we make choices with respect to goals are known as process theories. Unlike content theories, process theories give us a decision-making role in choosing our goals and how to pursue them. Individuals are motivated by different outcomes. Cultures encourage different patterns of motivation. We thus appear to have some choice of motives, and the means to achieve them. The theories of Nohria and colleagues, and of Maslow, are universalist – they apply to everyone, and cannot readily explain differences between individuals and cultures. We will explore four process theories of work motivation, *equity theory*, *expectancy theory*, *goal-setting theory*, and *inner work life theory*.

Equity theory

Equity theory
a process theory of motivation which argues that perception of unfairness leads to tension, which motivates the individual to resolve that unfairness.

Several theorists have argued that we look for a just or equitable return for our efforts. The calculation of what is just or equitable depends on the comparisons we make with others. **Equity theory** is thus based on our perceptions of fair treatment. Stacy Adams (1963, 1965) argued that we are motivated to act in situations which we perceive to be inequitable or unfair. Inequity occurs when you get either more or less than you think you deserve. The theory is based on perceptions of *in*equity, but is traditionally called *equity* theory.

This theory explains behaviour using perceptions of social comparisons. Equity theory argues that, the more intense the perceived inequity, the higher the tension, and the stronger the motivation to act. Adams argues that we respond differently to 'over-reward' and 'under-reward'. We tend to perceive a modest amount of over-reward as 'good luck', and do nothing, while a modest under-reward is not so readily tolerated.

J. Stacy Adams

How do you calculate inequity? Adams proposed that we compare our rewards (pay, recognition) and contributions (time, effort, ideas) with the outputs and inputs of others. Equity thus exists when these ratios are equal:

$$\frac{\text{my rewards (minus my costs)}}{\text{my efforts and contributions}} = \frac{\text{your rewards (minus your costs)}}{\text{your efforts and contributions}}$$

Rewards can include a range of tangible and intangible factors: pay, status symbols, fringe benefits, promotion prospects, satisfaction, job security. Inputs similarly relate to any factor that you believe you bring to the situation, including age, experience, skill, education, effort, loyalty, and commitment. The relative priority or weighting of these various factors depends on the individual's perception.

How do you resolve inequity? Let's imagine that you are working in a restaurant in Gamla Stan (the Old Town) in Stockholm and you discover that Annika is earning 25 Swedish kronor (about US$3.0) an hour more than you, for the same work (about US$100 a week more than you). Table 9.6 shows Adams's seven strategies for reducing this inequity.

Table 9.6: Strategies for reducing inequity

strategy	example
1. alter your outcomes	persuade the manager to increase my pay
2. adjust your inputs	I won't work as hard as Annika
3. alter the comparison person's outcomes	persuade the manager to cut Annika's pay
4. alter the comparison person's inputs	leave the difficult tasks to Annika
5. compare with someone else	Per gets the same as I get
6. rationalize the inequity	Annika has worked here for much longer
7. leave	get another job

Choice of strategy is a sensitive issue, and equity theory does not predict which strategy an individual will choose. Each option has different short-term and long-term consequences. Arguing with your manager, reducing your input, or making Annika do the hard work may reduce inequity in the short term, but could have long-term consequences for your relationships and employment at this location.

The theory's predictions of behaviour for over- and under-reward are shown in Figure 9.2.

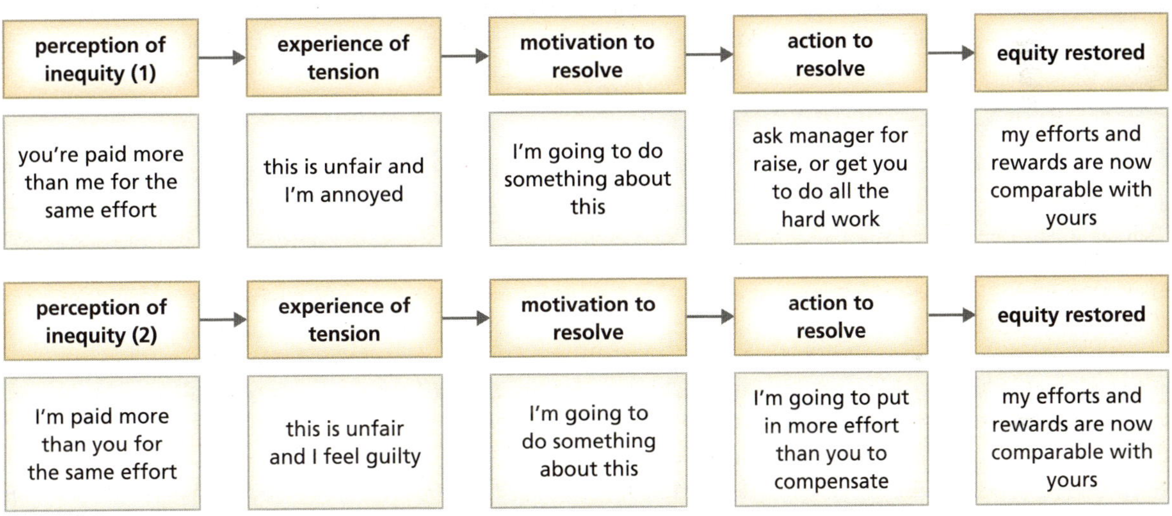

Figure 9.2: Equity theory – causal chains

Evidence from laboratory research supports the theory, and confirms that people who are overpaid reduce their perceived inequity by working harder. Studies in real settings also broadly confirm equity theory predictions. Interestingly from a management perspective, perceived equity seems to lead to greater job satisfaction and organizational commitment (Sweeney et al., 1990).

Equity theory has some problems. A number of quantitative and qualitative variables have to be considered when calculating an equity ratio. These variables depend on individual perception, and are difficult to measure. Different people use different timescales when calculating fairness; short-term calculations may be different from long-term implications. There are individual differences in tolerance levels, and not everyone will respond in the same way to a particular level of inequity. Whether or not you believe there is a valid explanation for inequity will also moderate your response.

Equity theory also overlooks the wider organizational context in two ways. The first concerns the basis of our social comparisons, which can be extremely varied. Some of us compare our situations with immediate colleagues, while others make comparisons with people in other organizations, sectors, and countries. There is no rationale for preferring one basis of comparison to another. The second way in which equity theory ignores context concerns the systemic inequities in capitalist economies. Colleagues may receive the same treatment from their employing organization (perception of equity) while being exploited by more senior individuals in positions of wealth, influence, and power (perception of inequity). However, this inequity is a 'normal' feature of capitalist society, and is thus difficult to challenge.

STOP AND THINK

What actions would you take if you were earning just a little more than Annika in our example from the Stockholm restaurant?

What actions would you take if you were earning very much more than Annika?

To what extent do you think equity theory can make accurate predictions of your behaviour in inequitable situations like these?

Edward Chace Tolman (1886–1959)

Expectancy theory a process theory which argues that individual motivation depends on the *valence* of outcomes, the *expectancy* that effort will lead to good performance, and the *instrumentality* of performance in producing valued outcomes.

Victor Harold Vroom (b.1932)

Equity theory has implications for management practice. Employees compare pay (even in organizations that insist on pay secrecy) and perceived inequity quickly generates resentment. Comparisons are often subjective and imprecise, particularly where information is lacking and employees rely on rumour. It is important to recognize that perceptions of inequity generate tension, even where there is actually little inequity. The circulation of accurate information about rewards, and the links between effort and rewards, is thus crucial.

Expectancy theory

A motive is an outcome that has become desirable. The process through which outcomes become desirable is explained by the **expectancy theory** of motivation.

Cognitive theories in psychology assume that we are purposive, and that we are aware of our goals and actions. Expectancy theory is a cognitive theory, and was developed by the American psychologist Edward C. Tolman in the 1930s as a challenge to the behaviourist views of his contemporaries. Tolman argued that behaviour is directed by the expectations that we have about our behaviour leading to the achievement of desired outcomes.

For work motivation to be high, productive work has to be seen as a path to valued goals. If you need more money, and if you expect to get more money for working hard, then we can predict that you will work hard. If you still need more money, but if you expect that hard work will only result in happy smiles from the boss, then we can predict that you will decide not to work hard (unless you value happy smiles). This theory thus assumes that we behave in ways that are instrumental (that is, will lead us) to the achievement of our valued goals.

The American psychologist Victor H. Vroom (1964) developed the first expectancy theory of work motivation, based on three concepts: **valence**, **instrumentality**, and **expectancy**. This is known as *valence-instrumentality-expectancy theory* – expectancy theory for short.

Instrumentality and expectancy are both *subjective probabilities*. What is important is what the individual estimates to be the likelihood of good performance leading to valued rewards, and of effort leading to good performance, respectively.

The force (F) of your motivation to work hard is the result of the product (multiplication) of these three variables and not their sum (addition). This is because, if one of the variables is zero, then, despite the value of the other two, the product, F, will be zero, and that is what we would expect. This cumbersome explanation is expressed in *the expectancy equation*:

$$F = V \times I \times E$$

What is the effect of a low 'V' value? If you do not care what grade you get for your next assignment, then you will not be motivated to work hard for it.

What is the effect of a low 'E' value? If you believe that long hard hours in the library will not get you a high assignment grade, then you will not be motivated to work hard.

Valence the perceived value or preference that an individual has for a particular outcome; can be positive, negative, or neutral.

Instrumentality the perceived probability that good performance will lead to valued rewards; measured on a scale from 0 (no chance) to 1 (certainty).

What is the effect of a low 'I' value? If you believe that a good grade will not lead to a chosen qualification, or to your preferred career, then you will not be motivated to work hard.

Only when all three of the terms in the expectancy equation are positive and high will the motivating force be positive and strong. However, behaviour typically has a number of outcomes. Working hard affects our work performance, levels of fatigue, social life, today's pay, and tomorrow's promotion prospects. The expectancy equation thus has to be summed for all possible outcomes. The full expectancy equation is:

$$F = \Sigma(V \times I \times E)$$

The sign Σ is the Greek letter sigma, which means 'add up all the values of the calculation in the brackets'. Note that there will be only a single E value, concerning the probability that high effort will lead to high performance. However, there will be several different I values, one for each rated outcome, concerning the probability that these will be obtained.

STOP AND THINK

Measure the force (F) of your motivation to get a high grade in organizational behaviour:

What are your V values? Identify the range of outcomes from working hard for this subject. Rate the value of each of these to you, as 1 (positive), 0 (ambivalent) or –1 (negative).

What are your I values? For each outcome, estimate the subjective probability of that occurring (you could get a high grade, you could ruin your social life).

What is your E value? Estimate the subjective probability that high effort will produce a high grade in this subject. This probability will be between 0 (little or no chance) and 1 (certainty of high grade).

Sum the calculation across all your outcomes, and compare your score with colleagues. If the theory is correct, those with higher F scores are more highly motivated to get a good grade for the organizational behaviour course.

Consider the process through which you have just worked. To what extent is this a realistic picture of the cognitive decision-making process that we undertake when deciding on aspects of our behaviour?

Expectancy the perceived probability that effort will result in good performance; measured on a scale from 0 (no chance) to 1 (certainty).

In summary:

- Expectancy theory states that behaviour results from a conscious decision-making process based on expectations, or subjective probabilities, that the individual has about the results of different behaviours leading to performance and to rewards.
- Expectancy theory can explain individual differences in motivation and behaviour.
- Expectancy theory measures the strength or force of the individual's motivation to behave in particular ways.
- Expectancy theory assumes that behaviour is rational, and that we are aware of our motives.

Expectancy theory has a number of management consequences:

- The link between effort and performance must be supported with adequate training, instruction and resources.
- The link between performance and rewards must be clear if rewards are to have the desired motivational effect.
- If employees are instructed to do one thing but rewarded for doing another, they will focus on the behaviours which are rewarded and ignore other instructions.
- Money is only one of several extrinsic rewards, and to be motivating it must be linked clearly to performance and be seen as equitable.

- Performance standards must be clear, otherwise employees will not know how best to direct their efforts.
- There is no point in offering rewards which employees do not value, or which are not valued highly enough to influence behaviour.
- If different employees value different kinds of rewards, it may help to introduce a 'cafeteria benefits' scheme, offering choices of medical insurance, health club memberships, car breakdown cover, bus passes, shopping vouchers, cinema tickets, bicycle allowances, financial planning advice, and travel insurance, for example.
- The value of different rewards may change with time and has to be monitored.

Total rewards All aspects of work that are valued by employees, including recognition, development opportunities, organization culture, and attractive work environment, as well as pay and other financial benefits.

In other words, to ensure low motivation and poor performance,

1. Keep performance goals vague and ambiguous.
2. Provide inadequate advice and resources for goal achievement.
3. Reward behaviour other than good job performance.
4. Offer rewards which employees do not value.
5. Concentrate on financial rewards and ignore other intrinsic and extrinsic rewards.
6. Make sure performance ratings are subjective and inconsistent.

These arguments have led many organizations to think in terms of **total rewards**, which takes into account all of the extrinsic and intrinsic rewards that can be used to attract, motivate, and retain employees. This involves developing a comprehensive approach that covers pay and fringe benefits, the design of jobs and experience of work (recognition, autonomy, work-life balance, personal development), as well as the organization culture and physical work environment – everything that is of potential value to employees. An annual survey in the UK by the Chartered Institute of Personnel and Development (2012) found that around one-third of employers had a total reward strategy.

Managerial motivational spillover

Does your manager's motivation affect you? Jean-Francois Coget (2011) reports research in a travel agency call centre involving over a thousand customer service representatives (CSRs), with 400 managers. The call centre had just adopted a new service technology. Were the CSRs motivated to adopt this new technology? The study found that managers' own motivations influenced their CSRs. When managers adopted the new technology themselves, CSRs were more likely to do so, and as managers' motivation to adopt the technology increased, so did that of their CSRs.

Source: www.CartoonStock.com

Motivation was measured using Vroom's expectancy theory, which argues in this case that the motivation to adopt the new technology depends on (1) *expectancy*: the belief that this will increase performance, (2) *instrumentality*: the judgement that increasing performance will result in positive outcomes such as more pay, and (3) *valence*: the extent to which those outcomes are desired. The expectancy and instrumentality (but not the valence) of the managers appeared to be mirrored by their CSRs, probably as a result of social learning, as CSRs modelled the attitudes and behaviours of their managers. However, this motivational effect was stronger for charismatic managers, who also affected the valence (desirability of outcomes) of their CSRs. Non-charismatic managers who supported the new technology actually reduced the extent to which their CSRs valued the new tool.

Managers wishing to encourage specific behaviours in subordinates should thus be motivated to engage in those behaviours themselves, and being a charismatic leader also helps.

STOP AND THINK

Think about the job that is ideal for you, in your ideal organization. Apart from pay, what other benefits and rewards do you want that job and that organization to give you? Realistically, what does your personal 'total rewards' package contain?

Goal-setting theory a process theory of motivation which argues that work motivation is influenced by goal difficulty, goal specificity, and knowledge of results.

Edwin Locke (b.1938)

Goal-setting theory

Goal-setting theory is another process theory of motivation, based on a series of propositions which predict and explain work behaviour. However, the main advocate of this approach, Edwin Locke (1968) once argued that 'goal-setting is more appropriately viewed as a motivational technique rather than a formal theory' (Locke, 1975, p. 465). It seems to be both a theory and a technique.

Goal-setting theory has established four propositions which are well-supported by research:

1. *Challenging goals* lead to higher levels of performance than simple and unchallenging goals. Difficult goals are also called 'stretch' goals because they encourage us to try harder (unless the goal is beyond our level of ability).
2. *Specific goals* lead to higher levels of performance than vague goals such as 'try harder' or 'do your best'. It is easier to adjust our behaviour when we know precisely what is required of us, and goal specificity avoids confusion. Goals should thus be SMART: specific, measurable, attainable, realistic and time-related.
3. *Participation* in goal-setting, particularly when this is expected, can improve performance by increasing commitment to those goals, but managerially assigned goals that are adequately explained and justified can also lead to high performance.
4. *Knowledge of results* of past performance – feedback – is necessary for effective goal achievement. Feedback contains information and is also motivational.

Driving people hard

The secret to a happy workforce, says Charles Morgan, the third-generation head of The Morgan Motor Company, is not so much that they work for a family company but that there is a long-term plan and a product of which they can be proud. Morgan, founded in 1910, employs 190 staff in Malvern, Worcestershire, producing 1,000 of its trademark cars a year, which speak of a different age when British automotive design and engineering were at their height.

The relaunch in 2011 of the Morgan three-wheeler, the model that originally made the 101-year-old company's name, should take production up to 1,500 a year. 'We can think in the long term and are very loyal to our staff', Mr Morgan said. 'We drive people hard but this is because we know they enjoy the pressure. We work to task not to the clock but are flexible so people can build up time off. We also have an open-door policy, which means the customer can come and see their car made. That is fairly powerful for staff and increases their satisfaction in a product in which they can be proud. We have made a commitment to launching a new model every year and that brings its own incentives for people, it puts people on their toes and they can see what they are doing next', he said. 'It also helps that when Aston Martin and Bentley were laying off people during the recession, we did not let anyone go. It helps here that people feel they are not working for a company which might make arbitrary decisions based on moves in exchange rates and labour costs', Mr Morgan said (© Lea, 2011, *The Times*/News International Trading Ltd, 19 July 2011).

Alexander Chalkin/Shutterstock

This theory has been tested mainly in situations where short-term targets can be expressed in clear and quantifiable terms. It is unclear if the theory applies to longer-term goals, say over a period of years, as targets are likely to be more qualitative and to change as circumstances alter. It is also uncertain whether this applies where goals are difficult to measure, such as in most types of professional work. Another limitation is the focus on individual goals and performance rather than on teamwork.

Gary Philip Latham (b.1945)

The main positive feature of goal-setting theory concerns the clarity of the practical implications (Locke and Latham, 1990):

- *Goal difficulty*: set goals for performance at levels which will stretch employees, but which are not beyond their ability levels.
- *Goal specificity*: express goals in clear and precise language, if possible in quantifiable terms, and avoid setting vague and ambiguous goals.
- *Participation*: allow employees to take part in the goal-setting process to increase the acceptability of and their commitment to goals.
- *Acceptance*: if goals are set by management, ensure that they are adequately explained and justified, so that those concerned understand and accept them.
- *Feedback*: provide information on the results of past performance to allow employees to adjust their behaviour, if necessary, to improve future performance.

Inner work life theory

Inner work life theory a process theory of motivation which argues that our behaviour and performance at work are influenced by the interplay of our perceptions, emotions, and motives.

Equity, expectancy, and goal-setting theories of motivation allow us to make choices, implying a rational, logical, reasoned approach to the decisions that shape our behaviour. They do not allow for the influence of emotions. The **inner work life theory** developed by Teresa Amabile and Steven Kramer (2007) argues that our behaviour and work performance are influenced by the way in which our perceptions, motives, and emotions interact with each other, triggered by everyday events.

Our private thoughts and feelings may not be visible to others, but we do not leave them at home when we go to work. To find out how the dynamics of our 'inner work life' can affect performance, Amabile and Kramer asked 238 professionals from 26 project teams to complete a personal diary, in a standard format, every day for the duration of their projects. The researcher sent daily emails to each professional, asking for a description of an event that stood out in their mind that day and how that made them feel (similar to the critical incident method used by Herzberg, described below). This gave the researchers around 12,000 diary entries to analyse, revealing the richness and intensity of people's inner work lives, what they call 'the reality management never sees'.

Figure 9.3 summarizes the 'inner work life' model of work performance. One of the most important implications of this perspective concerns the role of emotions. Neuroscience has shown that cognition (including perception) and emotion are closely linked. Events at work trigger a combination of perceptual, emotional, and motivational processes. The way in which these processes interact shapes our behaviour and our performance at work.

The researchers conclude that we perform better when our experiences at work include more positive emotions, stronger intrinsic motivation, and favourable perceptions of the work, the team, management, and the organization. Positive emotions, perceptions, and motivation were also linked to higher levels of creativity. Productivity, commitment, and collegiality are also improved when we 'are in a good mood'.

The practical management implications of this research differ from those of other motivation theories, which emphasize the 'daily pat on the back' and attempts to make work fun. This research suggests that the two most important management behaviours involve 'enabling people to move forward in their work' and 'treating them decently as human beings'.

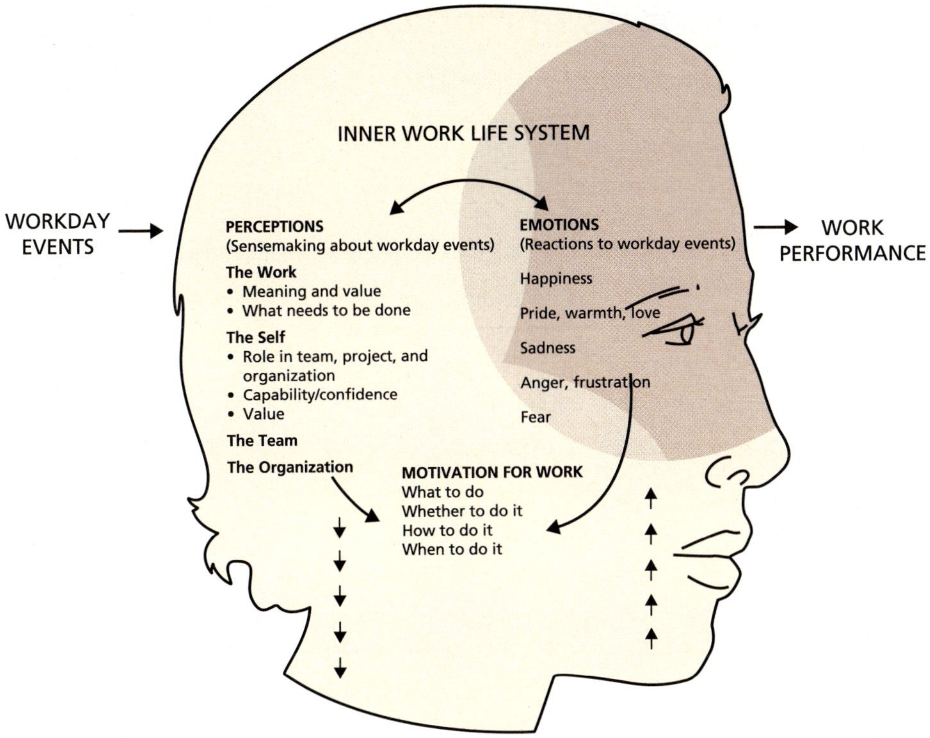

Figure 9.3: Inner working life theory

Source: Reprinted by permission of *Harvard Business Review*. From 'Inner work life: understanding the subtext of business performance' by Amabile, T.M. and Kramer, S.J., 85(5) 2007. Copyright © 2007 by the Harvard Business School Publishing Corporation; all rights reserved.

1. Enable progress

The factor that made the difference between 'good days' and 'bad days' for the respondents in this study was a sense of being able to make progress. This could mean achieving a goal, accomplishing a task, or solving a problem. The worst days – frustrating, sad, fearful – were characterized by setbacks, and even small delays could have this impact. Managers should

- provide direct help and not get in the way;
- make sure that time and other resources are adequate;
- react to successes and failures with a learning orientation;
- set clear and unambiguous goals (as goal-setting theory suggests).

2. Manage with a human touch

Interpersonal relationships are also important, treating people fairly and with respect. These events had almost as much impact as 'enabling progress' on the distinction between good and bad days. Praise in the absence of real progress has little positive impact, and can arouse cynicism. Good progress without recognition leads to anger and sadness.

The researchers conclude that

> Managers' day-to-day (and moment-to-moment) behaviours matter not just because they directly facilitate or impede the work of the organization. They're also important because they affect people's inner work lives, creating ripple effects on organizational performance. When people are blocked from doing good, constructive work day by day, they form negative impressions of the organization, their coworkers, their managers, their work, and themselves; they feel frustrated and unhappy; and they become demotivated in their work. But when managers facilitate progress, every aspect of people's inner work lives are enhanced, which leads to even greater progress. This positive spiral benefits individual workers – and the entire organization. (Amabile and Kramer, 2007, p. 83)

The social process of motivating others

Motivation can also be seen as a social influence process. The advice in the previous section about enabling progress and 'managing with a human touch' illustrates this. The general question is, how do we motivate others to do what we want them to do? The question for management is, how do we motivate employees to perform well? Many jobs are still designed using the methods of the American engineer Frederick Winslow Taylor (1911). Taylor's *scientific management* approach to designing jobs (see Chapter 14) is as follows:

1. Decide on the optimum degree of *task fragmentation*, breaking down a complex job into a sequence of simple steps.
2. Decide the *one best way* to perform the work, through studies to discover the most effective method for doing each step, including workplace layout and design of tools.
3. *Train* employees to carry out these simple fragmented tasks in the manner specified.
4. *Reward* employees financially for meeting performance targets.

STOP AND THINK

You are employed on a job in which you repeat the same simple task every fifteen seconds, perhaps wiring plugs for lamps, 9.00 a.m. until 5.30 p.m., every day (with a lunch break), five days a week. Describe your emotional response to this work.

Is it inevitable that some jobs just have to be like this, given the nature of work and technology, and the need to keep quality high and costs low?

Job enrichment a technique for broadening the experience of work to enhance employee need satisfaction and to improve motivation and performance.

Motivator factors aspects of work which lead to high levels of satisfaction, motivation, and performance, including achievement, recognition, responsibility, advancement, growth, and the work itself.

Task fragmentation has advantages:

- employees do not need expensive and time-consuming training;
- repeating one small specialized task makes employees very proficient;
- unskilled work gets lower pay; and
- some of the problems of achieving controlled performance are simplified.

The disadvantages include:

- repetitive work is very boring;
- the individual's contribution to the organization is meaningless and insignificant;
- monotony leads to apathy, dissatisfaction, and carelessness; and
- the employee does not develop skills that might lead to promotion.

Taylor's approach to job design appears logical and efficient, but it creates jobs that do not stimulate motivation or improve performance. Taylor had a simplified view of human motivation, regarding 'lower level' employees as 'coin operated' and arguing that the rewards for working as instructed should be financial. Taylor's methods are more likely to encourage absenteeism and sabotage than commitment and flexibility. Managers are thus interested in theories of motivation as sources of alternative methods for encouraging motivation and high performance. During the 1960s and 1970s, these concerns created the Quality of Working Life (QWL) movement; its language and methods are still influential today. One QWL technique is **job enrichment**.

Frederick Herzberg (1923–2000)

The concept of job enrichment was first developed by the American psychologist Frederick Herzberg (1966, 1968). While this work is about half a century old, recent research suggests that many employees still respond in ways that Herzberg's theory predicts (Bassett Jones and Lloyd, 2005). To discover what factors affected job satisfaction and dissatisfaction, 203 Pittsburgh engineers and accountants were asked two 'critical incident' questions. They were asked to recall events which had made them feel good about their work, and events which had made them feel bad about it.

Hygiene factors aspects of work which remove dissatisfaction, but do not contribute to motivation and performance, including pay, company policy, supervision, status, security, and physical working conditions.

Analysis of these critical incident narratives showed that the factors which led to job satisfaction were different from those which led to job dissatisfaction. Herzberg called this a 'two factor theory of motivation', the two sets of factors being **motivator factors** and **hygiene factors**, summarized in Table 9.7. Motivators are also known as (job) content factors, while hygiene factors are known as (organizational) context factors.

Table 9.7: Motivator and hygiene factors

Motivator (job content) factors	Hygiene (organizational context) factors
achievement	pay
advancement	company policy
growth	supervisory style
recognition	status
responsibility	security
the work itself	working conditions

High performance office space

The pharmaceutical company Lilly had a traditional 'cube farm' office space, with 3,300 employees in 470,000 square feet. This layout puts staff in the same department close to each other, but a lot of activities involve inter-department coordination. Studies of traditional cube farms suggest that it can take a knowledge worker almost five hours, on average, to get a response from a colleague, and ten hours to get a response from a manager. People working in these conditions can lose over an hour a day to inefficiencies, hassles, and distractions, and spend only about one-third of their time at their desks. Productivity is lower, and decisions take longer.

Chad McDermott/Alamy

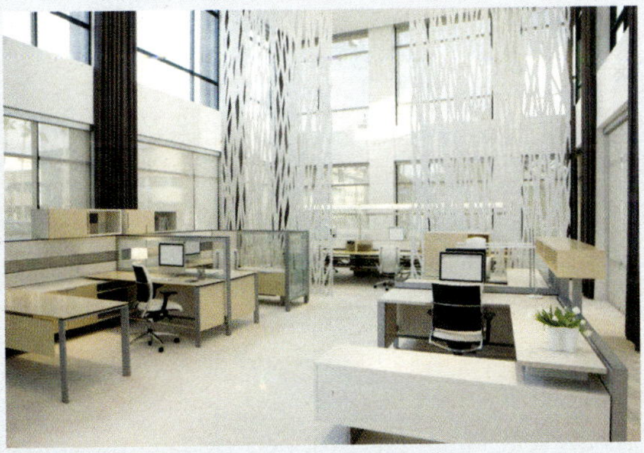
Robert Nicholas/Alamy

To deal with these problems, Lilly reduced the amount of assigned space, and increased the amount of shared, temporary, unassigned space. Staff could use the unassigned space when they were not at their own desks. The new spaces were designed for different types of work: quiet focus rooms for concentration, cafés for collaboration, enclaves for private conversations. This encouraged ad hoc communication, and stimulated creativity. Job satisfaction doubled, furniture costs halved, and the time lost to distractions such as looking for meeting rooms fell by 16 per cent (Laing and Craig, 2011).

When asked how they felt about this office redesign, here is how Lilly's employees replied:

	before (cube farm)	after (shared space)
workspace was an attractive aspect of the job	21%	58%
workspace created a stimulating atmosphere	18%	45%
satisfied overall with workspace	34%	64%

In other words, office layout may be a hygiene factor, in Herzberg's theory, but it can have a significant impact on job satisfaction, stimulation, creativity, and employee motivation.

Vertical loading factors methods for enriching work and improving motivation, by removing controls and increasing accountability, and by providing feedback, new tasks, natural work units, special assignments, and additional authority.

Intrinsic rewards valued outcomes or benefits which come from the individual, such as feelings of satisfaction, competence, self-esteem, and accomplishment.

Extrinsic rewards valued outcomes or benefits provided by others, such as promotion, pay increases, a bigger office desk, praise, and recognition.

Herzberg (1987) claimed that this pattern of motivation had been identified in Finland, Hungary, Italy, Israel, Japan, and Zambia. In South Africa, however, while managers and skilled workers, black and white, produced the expected results, unskilled workers' satisfaction appeared to be dependent on hygiene. Herzberg claims that 'the impoverished nature of the unskilled workers' jobs has not afforded these workers with motivators – thus the abnormal profile'. He also cites a study of unskilled Indian workers who were 'operating on a dependent hygiene continuum that leads to addiction to hygiene, or strikes and revolution'.

According to this theory, the redesign of jobs to increase motivation and performance should thus focus on motivator or content factors. Improvement in the hygiene or context factors, Herzberg (1968) argued, will remove dissatisfaction, but will not increase motivation and performance. He suggested using **vertical loading factors** to achieve job enrichment.

The way in which a job is designed determines the rewards available, and what the individual has to do to get those rewards. It helps to distinguish between **intrinsic rewards** and **extrinsic rewards**. Intrinsic rewards are valued outcomes within the control of the individual, such as feelings of satisfaction and accomplishment. For some of us, and for some actions, the outcome is its own (intrinsic) reward. Mountaineers, poets, athletes, authors, painters, and musicians are usually familiar with the concept of intrinsic reward. Few people ever get paid for climbing hills, and there are few wealthy poets on this planet. Extrinsic rewards are valued outcomes that are controlled by others, such as recognition, promotion, or pay increases.

The relationships between performance and intrinsic reward are more immediate than those between performance and extrinsic reward. Intrinsic rewards are thus more important influences on our motivation to work. It has long been argued that 'eat what you kill' incentive reward schemes do not work well (Kohn, 1993). Money is not an overriding

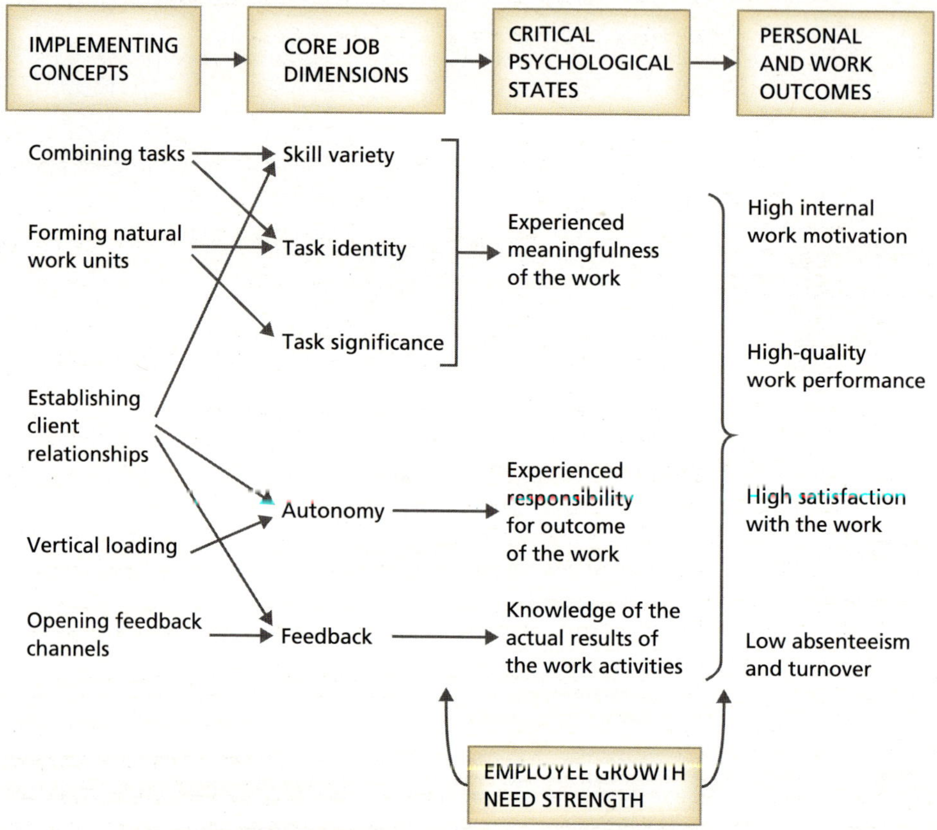

Figure 9.4: The Job Characteristics Model

Source: Hackman et al. (1975).

Richard Hackman (1940–2013)

Greg Oldham

concern for most people, and 'bribing' people to perform better with cash incentives can be seen as manipulative and controlling. Incentive pay schemes also discourage risk-taking and creativity, and undermine interest in the job itself. Extrinsic rewards might buy compliance, but they do not encourage commitment.

The Job Characteristics Model (Figure 9.4) describes the job enrichment strategy of the expectancy theorists Richard Hackman and Greg Oldham (1974; Hackman et al., 1975). This model sets out the links between the features of jobs, the individual's experience, and outcomes in terms of motivation, satisfaction and performance. The model suggests that jobs can be analysed in terms of five *core dimensions*:

- *skill variety*: the extent to which a job makes use of different skills and abilities;
- *task identity*: the extent to which a job involves a 'whole' and meaningful piece of work;
- *task significance*: the extent to which a job affects the work of others;
- *autonomy*: the extent to which a job provides independence and discretion;
- *feedback*: the extent to which performance information is related back to the individual.

This model also takes into account individual differences in **growth need strength**, a concept based on Maslow's concept of self-actualization. Growth need strength (GNS) is an indicator of your willingness to welcome personal development through job enrichment. The causal chain, from job design, through individual experience, to performance outcomes, depends on GNS. With employees whose GNS is low, an enriched job is unlikely to improve their performance.

STOP AND THINK

Your instructor offers to enrich your educational experience of studying organizational behaviour, with additional classes and tutorials, further reading, and extra feedback and revision sessions. There is no guarantee, however, that this will increase your course grades. How do you feel about this offer?

Jobs can be assessed on these core dimensions. Richard Hackman and colleagues developed an opinion questionnaire called the **job diagnostic survey** (JDS) for this purpose. Skill variety and autonomy are measured in the JDS by questions such as:

> How much *variety* is there in your job? That is, to what extent does the job require you to do many different things at work, using a variety of your skills and talents?
>
> How much *autonomy* is there in your job? That is, to what extent does your job permit you to decide *on your own* how to go about doing the work?

Respondents rate their answers to these questions on a seven-point scale. The JDS thus provides *operational definitions* (see Chapter 1) of the variables in the Job Characteristics Model. The core job dimensions are *independent variables*, and critical psychological states and performance outcomes are *dependent variables*. Growth need strength is a mediating variable in this causal chain. The JDS can be used to establish how motivating a job is, by calculating the **motivating potential score** (MPS) from answers across groups of employees doing the same job.

The MPS is calculated using the values of the variables measured by the JDS:

$$\text{MPS} = \frac{(\text{skill variety} + \text{task identity} + \text{task significance})}{3} \times \text{autonomy} \times \text{feedback}$$

The first part of this equation concerns aspects of the job. The second part concerns how the work is managed. Autonomy and feedback are more important than the other dimensions. The equation reflects this by treating them as two separate components. Only the arithmetic mean of the ratings for skill variety, task identity, and task significance is used. If one of the three main components – job aspects, autonomy, feedback – is low, then the

Growth need strength a measure of the readiness and capability of an individual to respond positively to job enrichment.

Job diagnostic survey a questionnaire which assesses the degree of skill variety, task identity, task significance, autonomy, and feedback in jobs.

Motivating potential score an indicator of how motivating a job is likely to be for an individual, considering skill variety, task identity, task significance, autonomy, and feedback.

MPS will be low. A near-zero rating on either autonomy or feedback, for example, would pull the score down disproportionately (five times zero equals zero). A near-zero rating on task variety, identity, or significance would not have much impact on the overall score. The five core dimensions stimulate three psychological states critical to high work motivation, job satisfaction, and performance. These critical psychological states are:

- *experienced meaningfulness*: the extent to which the individual considers the work to be meaningful, valuable, and worthwhile;
- *experienced responsibility*: the extent to which the individual feels accountable for their work output;
- *knowledge of results*: the extent to which the individual knows and understands how well they are performing.

Jobs with high MPS are more likely to lead to the experience of critical psychological states than jobs with low scores. Expectancy theorists argue that all three critical states must be present if the personal and work outcomes on the right-hand side of the model are to be achieved. One or two is not good enough. The MPS is only a guide to how motivating a job will be because different employees can have different perceptions of the same job. Those who put a low value on personal growth (revealed by a low GNS score) will not respond as the model suggests. No point, then, in offering them enriched jobs, unless one believes that the experience of personal development can in itself stimulate future growth need.

The model also shows how the motivating potential of jobs can be improved by applying five *implementing concepts*. These (including vertical loading, from Herzberg) are:

1. *Combine tasks*. Give employees more than one part of the work to do. This increases variety, and allows the individual to make a greater contribution to the product or service. For example, train call centre staff to handle a range of customer problems rather than specializing in a few areas.
2. *Form natural work units*. Give employees meaningful patterns of work. This increases individual contribution and task significance. For example, create teams which build the whole motor car engine, rather than assigning individual assembly workers to fragmented and repetitive tasks.
3. *Establish client relationships*. Give employees responsibility for personal contacts. This increases variety, gives the person freedom in performing the work, and also increases feedback. For example, staff working in a hospital pharmacy can deal directly with staff and patients on nominated wards, rather than responding on the basis of 'first come first served by whoever is free at the time'.
4. *Vertical loading*. Give employees responsibilities normally allocated to supervisors:

work scheduling	work methods	problem-solving
quality checks	training others	cost control
work times and breaks	deciding priorities	recruitment decisions

   This gives individuals more autonomy, by removing the supervisory role, or redesigning it to involve other activities, such as training, coaching, and liaising with other departments.
5. *Open feedback channels*. Give employees performance summaries and corporate information, as well as establishing client relationships. This improves opportunities for feedback of results. Feedback tells people how well they are doing, and provides a basis for improvement.

Can the theory and practice of job enrichment be abandoned by organizations today? No. The language and the method have become a taken-for-granted aspect of management practice. Applications are no longer novel; they pass unreported. However, their significance is if anything heightened in a global economic downturn when costs are being cut and jobs are being lost, but employee motivation remains an imperative.

Job enrichment was traditionally applied to groups of employees. However, recognizing that individuals have different motivational profiles, attention has also focused on designing and enriching individual jobs, through three routes: 'job sculpting', 'job crafting', and 'i-deals'.

Job sculpting first identifies what interests and challenges employees: new technology, developing theories, mentoring others, negotiating, and persuading. Jobs, special assignments, and career paths can then be 'sculpted' to match those interests, enhance motivation and performance, and discourage people from leaving. Timothy Butler and James Waldroop (1999) describe a bank lending officer who was good at customer services but was interested in theory and conceptual thinking. He was about to leave the company until it gave him a role in competitive analysis and strategy formulation.

Job crafting involves individuals adapting jobs to fit more closely their skills and interests by making adjustments to activities, time commitment, and work intensity, and 'task trading' with colleagues. Amy Wrzesniewski and Jane Dutton (2001) argue that most employees do this naturally.

I-deals are personally negotiated – idiosyncratic – work arrangements that differ from those of co-workers, and can include pay and other benefits, work-at-home arrangements, flexible hours, special projects, and training and development opportunities. Traditionally this approach may have been limited to 'superstars' who had the power to negotiate their own special packages (top musicians and movie stars, for example). Denise Rousseau and colleagues (2006) conclude that these deals are now widespread in many organizations, in response to increasing complexity and the pace of change.

Empowerment, engagement, and high performance

Practice in many organizations has gone beyond the enrichment of individual jobs, to focus on teamworking, organizational culture change, and other forms of employee empowerment. In the 1960s, an executive of American Telephone and Telegraph, concerned about low levels of staff commitment to the company, complained that 'we have lost too many people who are still with us' (Ford, 1969). AT&T employees expected interesting, meaningful work, which was not on offer, and performance suffered. Those expectations do not appear to have changed. A well-educated, media-informed, information-rich, knowledge-based workforce, conscious of individual rights and social comparisons, is much less willing to tolerate bureaucratic control, and is more ready to challenge management decisions and actions.

Empowerment organizational arrangements that give employees more autonomy, discretion, and decision-making responsibility.

Engagement the extent to which people enjoy and believe in what they do, and feel valued for doing it.

High performance work system a form of organization that operates at levels of excellence far beyond those of comparable systems.

As a result, many organizations during the 1990s reconsidered job enrichment and other approaches to improve quality of working life, through employee **empowerment**. In the twenty-first century, this has been linked with the related concept of employee **engagement**.

Techniques for improving motivation and performance through empowerment and engagement fall into two broad categories: individual job enrichment, and self-managing or autonomous teamwork. This chapter focuses on individual motivation and jobs. Chapter 13 explores teamwork. These approaches converge in the **high performance work system**.

The features of high performance work systems were first explored by Peter Vaill (1982, p. 25). Organizations, or groups, are a high performance system if they

- perform excellently against a known external standard;
- perform beyond what is assumed to be their potential best;
- perform excellently in relation to what they did before;
- are judged by observers to be substantially better than comparable groups;
- are achieving levels of performance with fewer resources than necessary;
- are seen to be exemplars, as a source of ideas and inspiration;
- are seen to achieve the ideals of the culture;
- are the only organizations that have been able to do what they do at all, even though it might seem that what they do is not so difficult or mysterious.

Do we need more empowerment?

Toby Wall and Stephen Wood (2002) argue that empowerment can be an effective management tool. Their study of 80 manufacturing companies found that empowerment had a more significant impact on organizational performance than new technology or research and development. Empowerment works best where there is uncertainty in the production process, and employees have to deal with variable demands and ambiguity. (Where jobs are routine, output is unaffected by empowerment.) Empowerment improves individual performance by encouraging new ideas, and by allowing employees to work more effectively. Empowerment itself is not motivating. The research also revealed international differences:

	management preferences (per cent)			
	Britain	**Japan**	**Australia**	**Switzerland**
empowerment	23	21	34	47
teamworking	35	22	45	50
total quality management	42	61	55	54
just in time methods	41	40	39	61

Based on Wall and Wood (2002).

Engagement

Employers clearly want employees who are motivated and committed, who identify with their employing organization, and who are prepared to 'go the extra mile' at work. The term for this combination of attributes is *engagement*, which means more than just motivation or job satisfaction. However, this may have become a problem, with increasing work intensity, longer working hours, and a growing concern for work-life balance. Can engagement be measured, and what steps can management take to enhance engagement? Commitment and 'organizational citizenship' can be measured with attitude surveys, and the results can become the basis for appropriate action to strengthen engagement and employee performance.

Lucy McGee of the consultancy organization DDI argues that it is just as important to select employees who are more likely to become engaged, as it is to increase the engagement of existing staff (Emmott, 2006; McGee, 2006). From cross-sectoral research involving around 4,000 employees, six characteristics are believed to predict the probability of individual applicants becoming engaged employees. The characteristics that identify 'engagement readiness' are

- *adaptability*: openness to new ideas, willingness to change approach;
- *passion for work*: maintaining positive view despite stress and frustration;
- *emotional maturity*: customer focus under fire, results before ego;
- *positive disposition*: eagerness to help others, outstanding teamwork;
- *self-efficacy*: confidence in one's ability;
- *achievement orientation*: the need to succeed and to excel.

It is important to establish 'job fit', with work that the candidate enjoys. Ability to do a job does not necessarily mean that the person will be committed to that work for any length of time. By using a combination of 'career battery' psychometric questionnaires and situational interviews (asking candidates how they would handle typical work problems), an organization can increase the probability of employing engaged employees who not only are high performers, but also are more likely to be good coaches, effective salespeople, and strong team players.

Are the claims for high performance work systems justified? Research suggests that organizations adopting high performance practices perform better than those which do not (CIPD, 2008). Work redesign methods have remained the same, and theories of motivation have seen little development since the 1980s. However, the organizational context to which these theories and techniques are applied has changed dramatically. The distinctions between the quality of working life (QWL) approach and the high performance work systems (HPWS) approach are summarized in Table 9.8.

Table 9.8: QWL versus HPWS

QWL in the 1970s	HPWS today
aimed to reduce costs of absenteeism and labour turnover and increase productivity	aims to improve organizational flexibility and product quality for competitive advantage
autonomy improves quality of work experience and job satisfaction	empowerment and engagement improve skill, decision-making, and adaptability
focused on repetitive manual and office work	focuses on challenging knowledge work
had little impact on management roles	redefinition of management roles
'quick fix' applied to problematic groups	takes time to change attitudes and behaviour
most employees broadly want the same kinds of things from work	need to cater for a wide range of individual differences in interests and expectations

Empowerment has become a broad term applied to any arrangements which pass decision-making responsibilities from managers to lower-level employees. Anna Psoinos and Steve Smithson (2002) surveyed the human resource managers of the top 450 manufacturing companies in Britain. The findings suggest that empowerment is widely developed. Of the 103 companies which replied,

- 91 (88 per cent) had introduced changes that could lead to empowerment, such as de-layering, downsizing, total quality management, and process re-engineering;
- of those 91 companies, 79 (87 per cent) delegated to lower-level staff decisions such as quality responsibility, problem-solving, job and shift allocations, quality control, production and maintenance scheduling, and plant modifications and improvements;
- of those 79 companies, 25 per cent said that empowerment had been unsuccessful, while 18 per cent said information was not available, or that it was too soon to tell;
- empowerment was successful in 60 per cent of companies where it had been used.

One manager said (p. 139)

> I think empowerment to [this company] is actually giving employees flexibility and the room to manoeuvre, to actually do their job and to do their job to a high standard. It's about providing them with the right training, providing them with the right skills and the right tools to actually look at their job and see how they're doing their job, and are they doing their job in the best way. And giving them scope to actually make decisions and have some impact on what they're doing.

However, another manager argued

> That doesn't mean to say that everybody can do what they like. You've got to have a process to say yes, this is a good idea, and you put it in, in a way that enables you to control the changes.

The main reasons for introducing empowerment concerned quality, productivity, flexibility, and cost reduction, not concern for quality of working life. The main constraints on empowerment were traditional job and status demarcations, hierarchical structures, organization culture, middle management resistance, and complex production systems.

McFlexible working

Research has shown that many employees rate flexible working as a highly prized benefit. In America, the fast food chain McDonald's allows friends and family members employed in the same outlet to cover each other's shifts without advance notice. In Europe, employees can apply for a 'McPassport' which allows them to work for the company anywhere on the continent. Shift allocations can be changed through 'McTime', a scheme that lets employees manage their own schedules. These flexible policies have allowed McDonald's to improve the diversity of their workforce, and have made staff prouder to work for the company.

The German government allocated €5.1 billion (US2.2 billion) in 2009 to support *Kurzarbeit* or 'short time' working. A study estimated that this saved 500,000 jobs. KPMG introduced its own Kurzarbeit programme in the UK in 2009. Over three-quarters of their staff volunteered to work a four-day week, or to take a sabbatical, saving the company €4 million, equivalent to 100 full-time jobs.

Flexible working not only helps to save jobs in an economic downturn, but can contribute to engagement, motivation, work-life balance, and productivity (Marsh, 2011).

The argument of this chapter is summarized in Figure 9.5. This begins with the need for involvement and autonomy in work, and with the challenge and personal development that we desire. These needs seek fulfilment in contexts facing multiple socio-economic pressures. Addressing these needs and pressures involves job enrichment, self-managing teamwork, and other approaches to empowerment. The emphasis on personal development and continuous improvement helps to promote adaptability, product quality, and customer care, increasing organizational effectiveness and quality of working life.

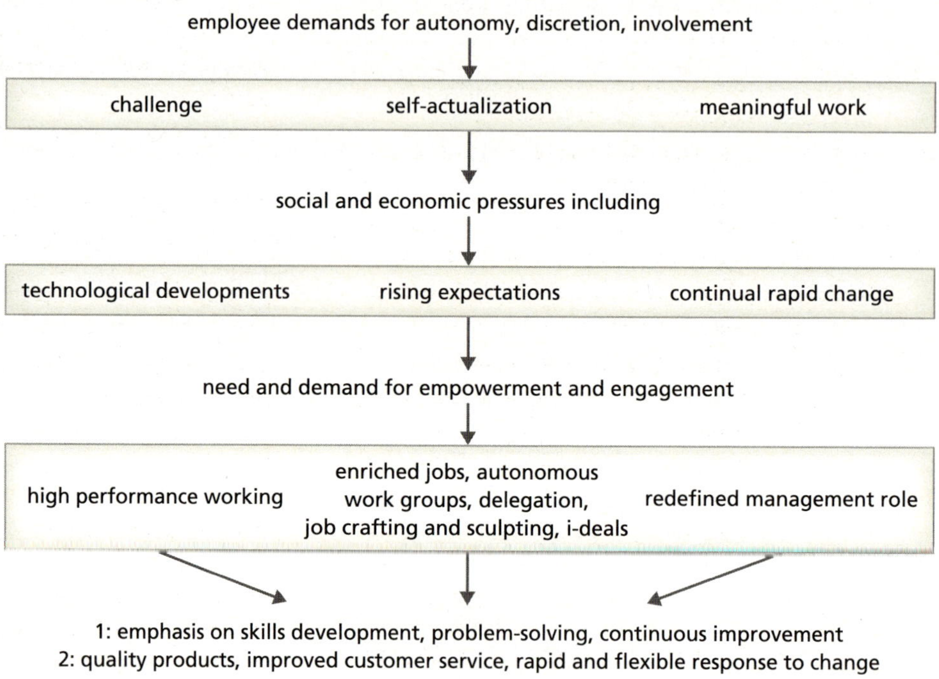

Figure 9.5: The case for high performance work systems

STOP AND THINK Some commentators argue that high performance work systems and empowerment are radical changes to organization design and management–employee relationships. Others argue that these are cosmetic, and have no effect on the power and reward inequalities and exploitation in contemporary organizations. Given your own experience of work, which view do you support?

Employee engagement at Marks and Spencer

'Engagement' is usually defined as the willingness of employees 'to go the extra mile' on behalf of the organization, colleagues, or customers. But does employee engagement actually improve business performance? The retail chain Marks and Spencer conducts an annual survey of its 80,000 employees, including questions about engagement. Stores with the highest levels of engagement perform better than those that have low engagement, on volume of sales, the scores of mystery shoppers, and staff absenteeism. The company's human resources director argues that factors contributing to their employees' engagement include their passion for the brand, pride in working for a company committed to sustainability, and knowing that the company cares about their wellbeing, even during difficult economic and trading conditions (based on Arkin, 2011).

RECAP

1. ***Understand different ways in which the term motivation is used.***
   - Motivation can refer to desired goals which we as individuals have or acquire.
   - Motivation can refer to the individual decision-making process through which goals are chosen and pursued.
   - Motivation can refer to social influence attempts to change the behaviour of others.
2. ***Understand the nature of motives and motivation processes as influences on behaviour.***
   - Motives as desirable goals can be innate (drives) or acquired (socially learned).
   - Content theories of motivation explain behaviour in terms of innate drives and acquired motives.
   - Equity theory explains motivation in terms of perceived injustice or unfairness.
   - Expectancy theory explains motivation in terms of valued outcomes and the subjective probability of achieving those outcomes.
   - Goal-setting theory explains behaviour in terms of goal difficulty and goal specificity.
   - Inner work life theory explains behaviour in terms of the interactions between perceptions, motives, and emotions.
3. ***Use expectancy theory and job enrichment to diagnose organizational problems and to recommend solutions.***
   - A job will only be motivating if it leads to rewards which the individual values.
   - Rewards motivate high performance when the link between effort and reward is clear.
   - Hygiene factors can overcome dissatisfaction but do not lead to motivation.
   - Content factors lead to job satisfaction, motivation, and high performance.
   - Jobs can be enriched by applying vertical job loading factors.
   - The motivating potential of a job can be increased by improving skill variety, task identity, task significance, autonomy, and feedback.
   - Job enrichment will not improve the performance of individuals with low Growth Need Strength.
   - As we each have different motivational profiles, personalized approaches to job redesign have become popular, including job sculpting, job crafting, and the negotiation of personal 'i-deals'.
4. ***Explain the continuing contemporary interest in this field, with respect to extreme jobs, boreout, and high performance work systems.***
   - Some people are motivated by extreme jobs, working long hours under pressure, for the adrenalin rush, high pay, status, and power, but with personal and social problems.
   - For some office workers, their jobs are so uninteresting and lacking in challenge that they suffer boreout, becoming drained and unenthusiastic, devoting their time to the appearance of working hard, while surfing the internet and chatting to colleagues.
   - An educated, informed, knowledge-based workforce expects more participation in management decisions, and opportunities for self-development.
   - In a rapidly changing competitive business environment, organizations need to motivate employees to be flexible, adaptable, committed, and creative, not just to turn up on time and follow instructions.
   - High performance work systems use combinations of individual job enrichment, autonomous teamworking, facilitative supervisory style, and other forms of delegation to empower lower-level employees.

Revision

1. What is an extreme job? Why would anyone want to live and work like this? What are the benefits and costs of holding an extreme job?
2. What are the causes and implications of boreout? What steps can management take to reduce or prevent boreout among office staff?
3. Explain the distinction between content and process theories of motivation. Give an example of a content theory of motivation and describe the implications for organizational practice. What are the limitations of this approach in practice?
4. How does equity theory explain motivation and behaviour, and how can equity theory be used to diagnose and improve employee motivation?

Research assignment

Linn Products (see also Chapter 3) is mentioned in this chapter as a company that uses job enrichment successfully in the manufacture of its hi-fi products. Their website is www.LinnProducts.net. Linn also has its own record label: www.LinnRecords.com. Check out the company's websites. How does Linn describe the kinds of work that they provide? What about the working conditions, and their terms and conditions of employment? What can you find out about personal development and career opportunities?

What does this tell you about the company's approach to employee motivation? What is the balance between intrinsic and extrinsic motivation? Is this what you expected to find?

Repeat this assessment with another organization of your own choice. Prepare a report describing the similarities and differences in approach to employee motivation in these two organizations, concluding with an assessment of which one you would choose on the basis of this information if both were to offer you employment.

Springboard

Nigel Bassett-Jones and Geoffrey C. Lloyd (2005) 'Does Herzberg's motivation theory have staying power?', *Journal of Management Development*, 24(10), pp. 929–43. Presents the results of a survey of employee attitudes, finding that money and recognition are not primary sources of motivation. Intrinsic satisfaction was found to be more important. This is consistent with Herzberg's predictions, and the researchers conclude that his theory still has utility half a century after it was developed.

Craig C. Pinder (2008) *Work Motivation in Organizational Behaviour* (2nd edn), Psychology Press/Taylor & Francis, Hove, East Sussex. Comprehensive overview of the development of motivation theories. Emphasizes how behaviour at work is shaped by a range of factors including frustration and violence, love and sex, and power – topics which most treatments of motivation ignore. Just the text for that module assignment.

David Ulrich and Wendy Ulrich (2010) *The Why of Work*, New York: McGraw-Hill. Argues that as work organizations take up a lot of our time, they are the settings in which most of us meet our needs, including the need for meaning. Organizations that can help their employees find meaning through work are therefore potentially more successful in motivating employees to higher productivity.

OB in films

Tough culture

Enron: The Smartest Guys in the Room (2005, director Alex Gibney), DVD track 4, 0:17:00 to 0:23:00 (6 minutes). Clip begins at the start of this track; clip ends when the trader says 'Well I'll stomp on the guy's throat'.

The collapse of Enron is one of the largest corporate scandals in twenty-first-century America. We are introduced in this clip to senior executive Jeff Skilling, hired by company president Kenneth Lay because he saw Skilling as a visionary, as 'a man with a big idea'.

1. How would you describe Jeff Skilling's management style?
2. What effect does he have on employee motivation?
3. Jeff's view of human motivation is based on competition, greed, and 'survival of the fittest'. He introduces the Performance Review Committee system which applies a 'rank and yank' approach to staff appraisals. What are the advantages and disadvantages of this system, for managers, and for employees?

OB on the web

Look at http://www.mindtools.com/pages/ar and http://www.time.com/time/business/article/0,8599,1944101,00.html.

These websites offer practical advice on how to reshape or 'craft' your job, to make it more interesting, meaningful, and personally satisfying. This means being creative in making some subtle and not-so-subtle changes, perhaps simply restructuring how time is spent during the day, or 'task trading' with colleagues. These changes may not have to be approved by management.

Thinking of the jobs that you have held, how practical is the advice on offer here? Could you have put this into practice, and would this have enabled you to craft a more satisfying role, or not?

CHAPTER EXERCISES

1. Chris and Pat compare salaries

Objectives

1. To identify factors affecting pay decisions.
2. To understand the complexity of pay determination.
3. To distinguish between legal and illegal bases for pay decisions.
4. To distinguish between wise and unwise pay decisions.

Briefing

1. Form groups of four or five.
2. Read *Chris and Pat compare salaries* (based on Renard, 2008).
3. Individually, list all the reasons you can think of why Chris and Pat earn different salaries. You can include reasons that may be legal or illegal, wise or unwise.
4. As a group, combine your reasons, where possible adding to them, so that your group list contains 20 items.

→

Chris and Pat compare salaries Chris Clements and Pat Palmer are both computer programmers. One day, they find out that Chris earns £31,750 a year while Pat earns £40,100. Chris is surprised and says 'I can't think of any reasons why we should be paid so differently'. Pat replies 'I can think of at least 20 reasons.'

2. Job characteristics model and job redesign

Objectives

1. To assess the motivating potential score (MPS) of a particular job or jobs.
2. To determine which core job characteristics would need to change to improve the MPS of that job or those jobs.

Briefing To measure the MPS for a given job, researchers developed the Job Diagnostic Survey (JDS). For this exercise, we will use a short version of the JDS, which allows job design problems to be diagnosed, and generates ideas for job redesign.

Complete this analysis for a job in which you are currently employed (full or part time); or for a job that you have performed recently. (If you have never been employed, analyse the 'job' of a student.) The JDS is designed to be completed by the job holder, and not by an observer. For each of the twelve statements, decide whether this is an accurate or an inaccurate description of the chosen job, and rate it using this scale:

1 = very inaccurate

2 = mostly inaccurate

3 = somewhat inaccurate

4 = uncertain

5 = somewhat accurate

6 = mostly accurate

7 = very accurate.

The job chosen for analysis is: ______________________

Item	Rating	
1	__________	Supervisors often let me know how well they think I am performing.
2	__________	The job requires me to use a number of complex high-level skills.
3	__________	The job is arranged so that I have the chance to do a complete piece of work from beginning to end.
4	__________	Just doing the work required by the job provides many chances for me to work out how well I am doing.
5	__________	The job is not simple and repetitive.
6	__________	This job is one where a lot of other people can be affected by how well the work is done.
7	__________	The job does not deny me the chance to use my personal initiative or judgement in carrying out the work.
8	__________	The job gives me the chance to completely finish the pieces of work I begin.
9	__________	The job itself provides plenty of clues about whether or not I am performing well.
10	__________	The job gives me considerable opportunity for independence and freedom in how I do the work.
11	__________	The job itself is very significant and important in the broader scheme of things.
12	__________	The supervisors and co-workers on this job almost always give me feedback on how well I am doing in my work.

Scoring Work out the average of the two items that measure each job characteristic:

job characteristic	item numbers	average score
skill variety	2 + 5 ÷ 2 =	________
task identity	3 + 8 ÷ 2 =	________
task significance	6 + 11 ÷ 2 =	________
autonomy	7 + 10 ÷ 2 =	________
feedback		
from the job itself	4 + 9 ÷ 2	
+		
from others	1 + 12 ÷ 2	
	= __ ÷ 2 =	________

To calculate the MPS for this job, first add your scores for the two feedback items, and divide the total by two, to give a single, average, feedback score. Then put all of the scores into the MPS formula:

$$\text{MPS} = \frac{(\text{skill variety} + \text{task identity} + \text{task significance})}{3} \times \text{autonomy} \times \text{feedback}$$

Reminder: the core job dimensions in this model are:

1. *Skill variety*: does the job make use of different skills and abilities?
2. *Task identity*: does the job involve a 'whole' and meaningful piece of work?
3. *Task significance*: does the job affect the work of others?
4. *Autonomy*: does the job provide independence and discretion?
5. *Feedback*: is performance information related back to the individual?

If you have completed this analysis *alone*:

- assess the strengths and weaknesses of this job in terms of its motivating potential;
- identify recommendations for redesigning this job to improve the MPS;
- assess the difficulties in implementing these recommendations, given the nature of the work and the organizational context in which it is performed.

If you have completed this analysis *with colleagues*:

- share the results of your analysis with colleagues and pick the job with the lowest MPS;
- identify redesign options for improving the job's MPS (you will first need to ask the job holder for a detailed description of the job);
- assess the difficulties in implementing these recommendations, given the nature of the work and the organizational context in which it is performed.

Employability assessment

With regard to your future employment prospects:

1. Identify up to three issues from this chapter that you found significant.
2. Relate these to the competencies in the employability matrix.
3. Decide what actions you need to take to maintain and/or develop those competencies under each of the four headings of the employability matrix.

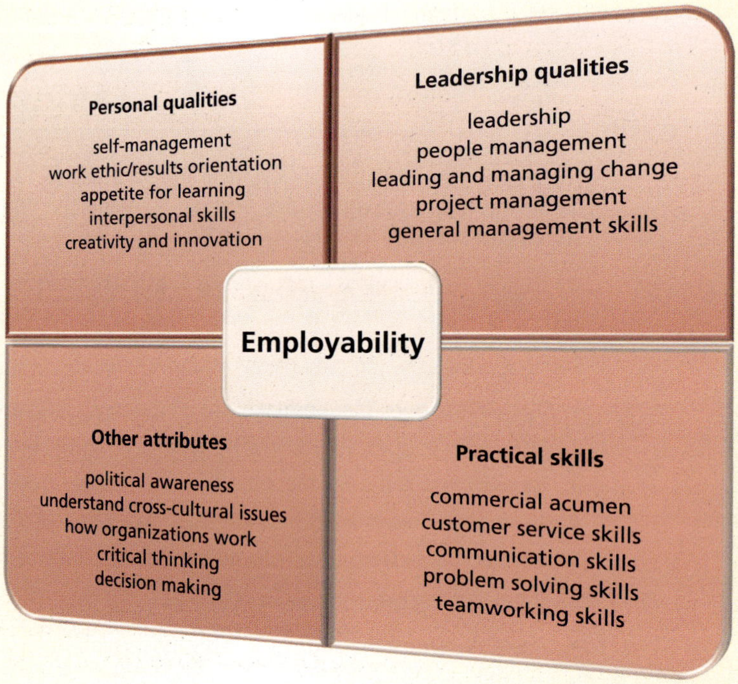

References

Adams, J.S. (1963) 'Toward an understanding of inequity', *Journal of Abnormal and Social Psychology*, 67(4), pp. 422–36.

Adams, J.S. (1965) 'Inequity in social exchange', in L. Berkowitz (ed.), *Advances in Experimental Social Psychology*, New York: Academic Press, pp. 267–99.

Amabile, T.M. and Kramer, S.J. (2007) 'Inner work life: understanding the subtext of business performance', *Harvard Business Review*, 85(5), pp. 72–83.

Arkin, A. (2010) 'The why guy', *People Management*, June, pp. 28–9.

Arkin, A. (2011) 'Is engagement working?', *People Management*, November, pp. 23–7.

Bassett-Jones, N. and Lloyd, G.C. (2005) 'Does Herzberg's motivation theory have staying power?', *Journal of Management Development*, 24(10), pp. 929–43.

Boyes, R. (2007) 'Forget burnout, now it's boreout', *The Times*, 15 September, p. 3.

Burke, R.J. and Fiksenbaum, L. (2009a) 'Managerial and professional women in "extreme jobs": benefits and costs', *Equal Opportunities International*, 28(5), pp. 432–42.

Burke, R.J. and Fiksenbaum, L. (2009b) 'Are managerial women in "extreme jobs" disadvantaged?', *Gender in Management*, 24(1), pp. 5–13.

Butler, T. and Waldroop, J. (1999) 'Job sculpting: the art of retaining your best people', *Harvard Business Review*, 77(5), pp. 144–52.

Chartered Institute of Personnel and Development (2008) 'High Performance Working Factsheet', London: Chartered Institute for Personnel and Development.

Chartered Institute of Personnel and Development (2012) *Strategic Reward and Total Reward Factsheet*, London: Chartered Institute of Personnel and Development.

Coget, J-F. (2011) 'Does managerial motivation spill over to subordinates?', *Academy of Management Perspectives*, 25(4), pp. 84–5.

Emmott, M. (2006) 'What drives employee engagement?', *Impact: Quarterly Update on CIPD Policy and Research*, 16 (August), pp. 4–5.

Ford, R.N. (1969) *Motivation through the Work Itself*, New York: American Management Association.

Hackman, J.R. and Oldham, G.R. (1974) *The Job Diagnostic Survey: An Instrument for the Diagnosis of Jobs and the Evaluation of Job Redesign Projects, Technical Report no. 4*, Department of Administrative Sciences, Yale University.

Hackman, J.R., Oldham, G., Janson, R. and Purdy, K. (1975) 'A new strategy for job enrichment', *California Management Review*, 17(4), pp. 57–71.

Heil, G., Bennis, W. and Stephens, D.C. (2000) *Douglas McGregor Revisited*, New York: John Wiley.

Herzberg, F. (1966) *Work and the Nature of Man*, New York: Staples Press.

Herzberg, F. (1968) 'One more time: how do you motivate employees?', *Harvard Business Review*, 46(1), pp. 53–62.

Herzberg, F. (1987) 'Workers' needs the same around the world', *Industry Week*, 21 September, pp. 29–32.

Hewlett, S.A. and Luce, C.B. (2006) 'Extreme jobs: the dangerous allure of the 70-hour workweek', *Harvard Business Review*, 84(12), pp. 49–59.

Kohn, A. (1993) 'Why incentive plans cannot work', *Harvard Business Review*, 71(5), pp. 54–63.

Laing, A. and Craig, D. (2011) 'High-performance office space', *Harvard Business Review*, 89(9), pp. 32–4.

Lea, R. (2011) 'We drive hard but are loyal', *The Times*, 19 July, p. 37.

Locke, E.A. (1968) 'Towards a theory of task performance and incentives', *Organizational Behaviour and Human Performance*, 3(2), pp. 157–89.

Locke, E.A. (1975) 'Personnel attitudes and motivation', *Annual Review of Psychology*, 26, pp. 457–80.

Locke, E.A. and Latham, G.P. (1990) *A Theory of Goal Setting and Task Performance*, Englewood Cliffs, NJ: Prentice Hall.

McGee, L. (2006) 'Interview for engagement', *People Management*, 12(15), pp. 40–1.

McGregor, D.M. (1960) *The Human Side of Enterprise*, New York: McGraw-Hill.

Marsh, V. (2011) 'Flexible working', *Financial Times*, 18 May, p. 8.

Maslow, A. (1943) 'A theory of human motivation', *Psychological Review*, 50(4), pp. 370–96.

Maslow, A. (1954) *Motivation and Personality*, New York: Harper and Row.

Maslow, A. (1971) *The Farther Reaches of Human Nature*, Harmondsworth, Middlesex: Penguin Books.

Millard, R. (2006) 'Drawing back from extreme jobs', *The Sunday Times*, 3 December, News Review, p. 9.

Nohria, N., Groysberg, B. and Lee, L.-E. (2008) 'Employee motivation: a powerful new model', *Harvard Business Review*, 86(7/8), pp. 78–84.

Pfeffer, J. (2010) 'Building sustainable organizations: the human factor', *Academy of Management Perspectives*, 24(1), pp. 34–45.

Psoinos, A. and Smithson, S. (2002) 'Employee empowerment in manufacturing: a study of organizations in the UK', *New Technology, Work and Employment*, 17(2), pp. 132–48.

Renard, M.K. (2008) 'It's all about money: Chris and Pat compare salaries', *Journal of Management Education*, 32(2), pp. 248–61.

Rothlin, P. and Werder, P.R. (2008) *Boreout!: Overcoming Workplace Demotivation*, London: Kogan Page.

Rotundo, M. and Xie, J.L. (2008) 'Understanding the domain of counterproductive work behaviour in China', *International Journal of Human Resource Management*, 19(5), pp. 856–77.

Rousseau, D.M., Ho, V.T. and Greenberg, J. (2006) 'I-deals: idiosyncratic terms in employment relationships', *Academy of Management Review*, 31(4), pp. 977–94.

Steers, R.M., Mowday, R.T. and Shapiro, D.L. (2004) 'The future of work motivation theory', *Academy of Management Review*, 29(3), pp. 379–87.

Sweeney, P.D., McFarlin, D.B. and Inderrieden, E.J. (1990) 'Using relative deprivation theory to explain satisfaction with income and pay level: a multistudy examination', *Academy of Management Journal*, 33(2), pp. 423–36.

Tay, L. and Diener, E. (2011) 'Needs and subjective well-being around the world', *Journal of Personality and Social Psychology*, 101(2), pp. 354–65.

Taylor, F.W. (1911) *Principles of Scientific Management*, New York: Harper.

The Economist (2010) 'Light and death', 29 May, p. 72.

Twentyman, J. (2010) 'Working together for ethical business', *The Times*, 18 May 2010, Raconteur supplement, pp. 4–5.

Vaill, P.B. (1982) 'The purposing of high-performing systems', *Organizational Dynamics*, 11(2), pp. 23–39.

Vroom, V.H. (1964) *Work and Motivation*, New York: John Wiley.

Wall, T. and Wood, S. (2002) 'Delegation's a powerful tool', *Professional Manager*, 11(6), p. 37.

Woods, R. (2011) 'Too wet to work', *The Sunday Times*, 20 February, p. 23.

Wrzesniewski, A. and Dutton, J.E. (2001) 'Crafting a job: revisioning employees as active crafters of their work', *Academy of Management Review*, 26(2), pp. 179–201.

Part 3 Groups and teams in the organization

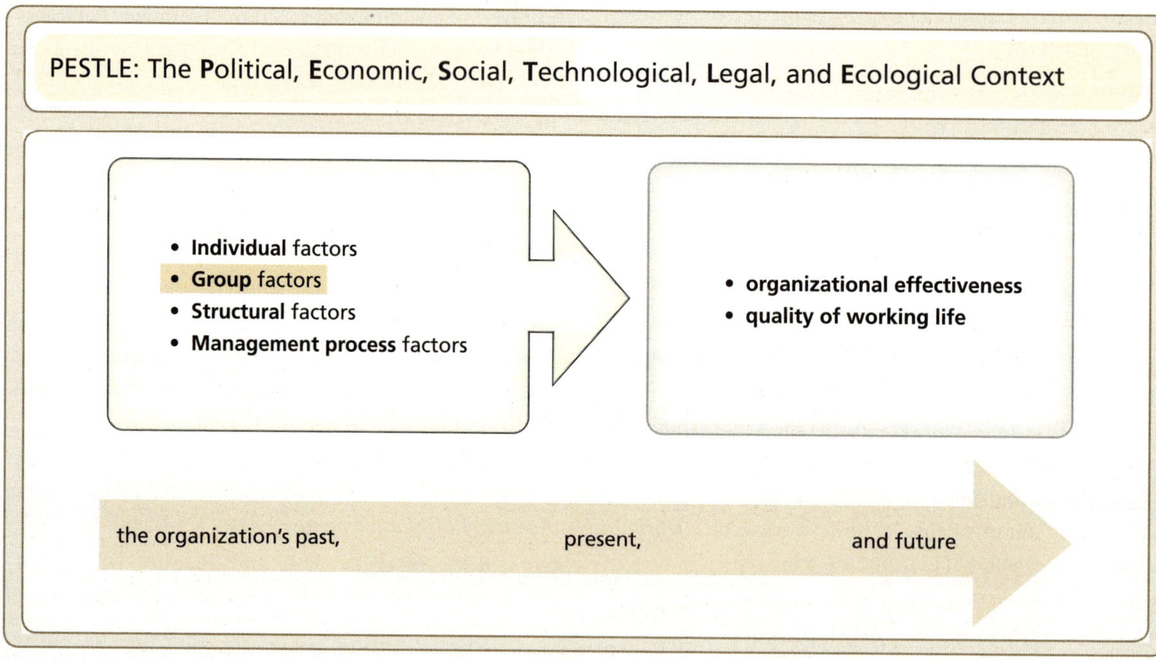

A field map of the organizational behaviour terrain

Introduction

Part 3, on groups and teams in the organization, explores the following four topics:

- *Group formation*, in Chapter 10
- *Group structure*, in Chapter 11
- *Individuals in groups*, in Chapter 12
- *Teamworking*, in Chapter 13.

Many organizations claim to be organized around teams. It seems to be widely accepted that teamwork is both natural and essential. In your next job interview, you may well be asked if you are 'a team player', and if you can provide examples to support your (positive) answer. Teams and groups have been the subject of research for many years. Studies have explored how teams are created and structured. Teams influence individual behaviour, and are in turn influenced by their individual members. Much is also known about the factors and conditions contributing to team performance. These topics thus reflect the progress of collections of people over time in different organizational settings. A number of individuals may informally develop into a group, or a team can be formally set up by management. Groups and teams often develop their own internal structures, which allow members to work together more effectively. Management's aim is to get individuals working together as a single, cohesive, productive unit. Groups and teams offer a distinct but related level of analysis, between the individual and the organization structure and its processes.

Invitation to see

Airbus Operations/M. Chainey

Airbus factory in North Wales, *The Times*, 14 October 2011, p. 54.

1. **Decoding**: Look at this image closely. Note in as much detail as possible what messages you feel that it is trying to convey. Does it tell a story, present a point of view, support an argument, perpetuate a myth, reinforce a stereotype, challenge a stereotype?
2. **Challenging**: To what extent do you agree with the messages, stories, points of view, arguments, myths, or stereotypes in this image? Is this image open to challenge, to criticism, or to interpretation and decoding in other ways, revealing other messages?
3. **Sharing**: Compare with colleagues your interpretation of this image. Explore explanations for differences in your respective decodings.

You're the adviser: what would you do?

Obesity has become a social problem, and not only in developed economies. Here is an example of how this can affect the workplace.

> I am the human resources manager for a nationwide furniture manufacturer. Recently, an employee on our delivery team gained a lot of weight. We've received reports from his colleagues that he is having difficulty carrying furniture from the van into customers' properties. He is willing to do the work and is normally very hard-working. But we're concerned that his lack of fitness is adding to the risk of injury for his colleagues. One member of staff recently spent three weeks off work with a back injury, which colleagues say was caused partly by working with this person and his inability to carry our products.
>
> His line manager has raised the issue but he has denied any problem. The manager argues that he is not capable of performing his duties but we are not in a position to offer him another role. Are there grounds for dismissal or a requirement for him to improve his fitness? How can we be fair to him without exposing other members of the delivery team to health and safety risks?

As an external adviser, how would you advise the manager to deal with this problem, taking into account the needs of the individual, his colleagues, and the organization as a whole?

From 'Troubleshooter', People Management, *4 September 2008, pp. 46–7.*

Chapter 10 **Group formation**

Key terms

group
group dynamics
aggregate
additive task
conjunctive task
disjunctive task
Hawthorne effect
human relations approach
formal group
informal group
group self-organization
activities
interactions
sentiments

Learning outcomes

When you have read this chapter, you should be able to define those key terms in your own words, and you should also be able to:

1. List the key characteristics of a group.
2. Distinguish between different types of group tasks.
3. Name the four research phases of the Hawthorne studies.
4. Distinguish between a formal and an informal group
5. Outline Homans's theory of group formation.
6. Enumerate the five stages of Tuckman and Jensen's model of group development.
7. Summarize Katzenbach and Santamaria's distinction between a team and a single-leader working group.

Why study groups?

Work groups and teams have become a nearly ubiquitous part of contemporary management practice in the majority of prominent organizations in the world (Manz et al., 2009). Diane Coutu (2009, p. 99) observed that

> Over the last couple of decades, a cult has grown up around teams. Even in a society as fiercely independent as America, teams are considered almost sacrosanct. The belief that working in teams makes us more creative and productive is so widespread that when faced with challenging new tasks, leaders quickly assume that teams are the best way to get the job done.

However, Richard Hackman, reflecting on his many years of research into groups and teams, concluded:

> I have no question that when you have a team, the possibility exists that it will generate magic, producing something extraordinary, a collective creation of previously unimagined quality or beauty. But don't count on it. Research consistently shows that teams underperform despite the extra resources that they have. That's because problems with coordination and motivation typically chip away at the benefits of collaboration. And even when you have a strong and cohesive team, it's often in competition with other teams, and that dynamic can also get in the way of real progress. (in Coutu, 2009, p. 100)

While the practical aspects of groups may be significant, as Marion Hampton (1999, p. 113) explains, the symbolic ones may be even more important:

> Groups embody many important cultural values of Western society: teamwork, co-operation, a collective that is greater than the sum of its parts, informality, egalitarianism and even the indispensability of the individual member. Groups are seen as having a motivating, inspiring influence on the individual, drawing the best out of him or her, enabling him or her to perform feats that would be beyond him or herself as a detached individual. Groups can have a healing effect on individuals, bolstering their self-esteem and filling their lives with meaning.

According to Vašková, (2007) and the European Foundation (2007),

- 60 per cent of EU workers perform all or part of their work in teams;
- most teamworking is to be found in the UK and Estonia (81 per cent) and the least in Lithuania (38 per cent) and Italy (41 per cent);
- most teamwork occurs in industrial rather than service industries;
- teamwork is most often found in larger organizations.

McGrath's circumplex model shown in Figure 10.1 reflects the four major activities performed by groups, and classifies eight different group tasks (Arrow and McGrath, 1995). Groups generate plans and ideas (e.g. solutions, strategies); they execute tasks (e.g. surgical operations, military missions); they engage in negotiations (e.g. in labour–management conflicts and company–government disputes); and they choose between options (e.g. appointment decisions, investment decisions).

Group performance thus affects the success of the organization as a whole. Being able to work productively with others is so important that companies place an emphasis on their recruits being good 'team players'. To ensure this, they invest in team development activities to develop their teamworking abilities. Hayes (1997, p. 1) noted that,

> To an ever-increasing extent, modern management has become focused on the idea of the team. Management consultants propose organizational restructuring to facilitate teamwork; directors make policy statements about the importance of the team to the organization; and senior managers exhort their junior staff to encourage team working in their departments.

Headhunters are increasingly being asked to assemble teams of top executives, and the bosses themselves are expected to be good at putting together teams (Nadler et al., 2006).

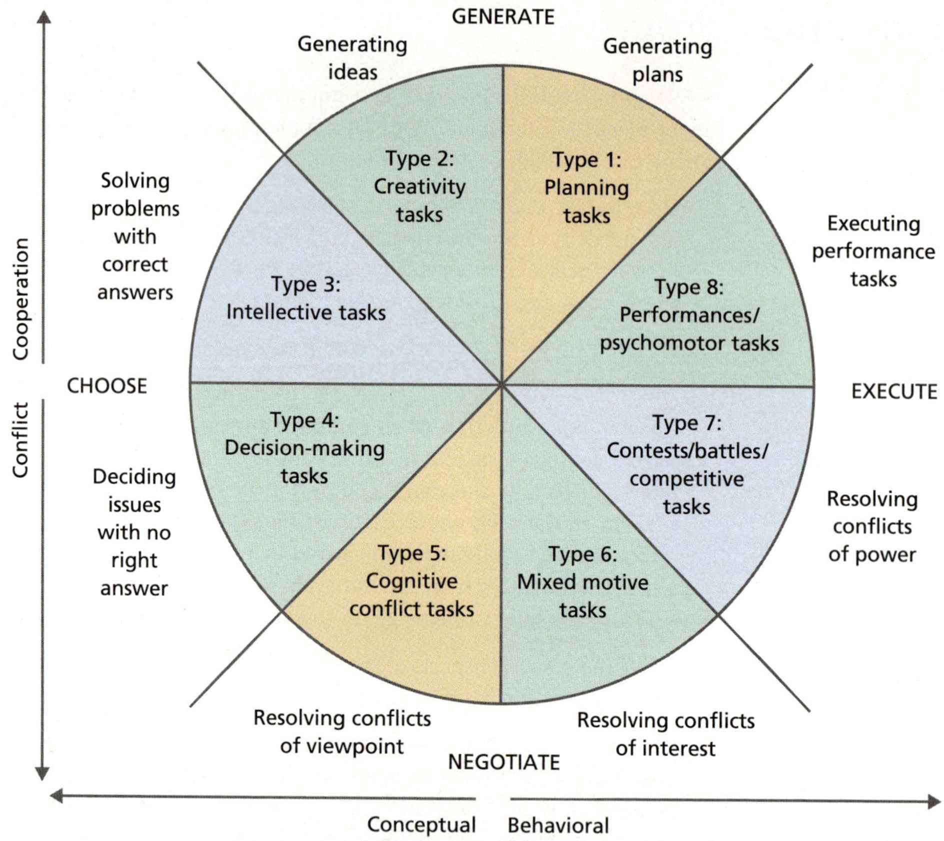

Figure 10.1: McGrath's circumplex model of group tasks

Source: from *Group Dynamics*, Thomson Wadsworth (Forsyth, D.R. 2006) p. 14, 0495007293/978-0495007296 adapted from MCGRATH, J.E. GROUPS: INTERACTION AND PERFORMANCE, 1st Ed., © 1984, p. 61. Reprinted and Electronically reproduced by permission of Pearson Education, Inc., Upper Saddle River, New Jersey.

Teams and knowledge production

A study that investigated 19.9 million research papers published over five decades and 2.1 million patents showed that teams increasingly outperform solo authors in the production of knowledge. Research is increasingly done in teams across nearly all fields. Teams typically produce more frequently cited research than individuals do, a trend that has been increasing over time. Teams now also produce the exceptionally high-impact research, even where that distinction was once the domain of solo authors. These findings apply to sciences and engineering, social sciences, arts and humanities, and patents, suggesting that the process of knowledge creation has fundamentally changed (Wuchty et al., 2007).

It has been argued that the modern organization is no longer a collection of individuals, but rather a network of interconnected teams (Kozlowski and Bell, 2003). Group working and teamworking has been an aspect of organizational life for a long time, yet remains controversial. The management literature promotes the benefits of group working, and stresses the commonality of interests between individual workers, organized by management into teams, and the goals of the 'organization as a whole', that is, those of senior management. Critics, in contrast, contend that the extent of group-management conflict has been misinterpreted, underplayed, or simply ignored. Employees also have been less convinced about teamworking. David Knights and Darren McCabe (2000) reported team members' uncertainties and highlighted three main issues. Team members

- disliked the intrusion it had into their personal lives, causing them to distrust management;
- claimed they did not understand the norms of teamworking and its protocols; and
- resented the move away from traditional, individual working.

Loners do the best work

Susan Cain observed that the modern workplace is all about teams, open plan offices, and collective brainstorming. Schools are increasing arranged in teaching 'hubs' rather than individual desks to encourage group learning. However, she suggests that teamwork might actually be stifling the creativity it is intended to encourage. The lone wolf, who likes to sit in an office with the door closed in order to think, has become an endangered species. Lone geniuses are out, collaboration is in. However, research suggests that people are more creative when they have privacy and freedom from interruption. Seventy per cent of American employees inhabit open plan offices. People are in each other's faces all the time, listening to each other's conversations. This constant interaction is exhausting and unproductive according to Cain. Studies show that workers who are constantly interrupted make 50% more mistakes and typically take twice as long to complete tasks. In contrast, some of the most spectacularly creative people in many fields are introverts, who see themselves as individualistic, independent non-joiners. Perhaps it is time to review our approach to people working together in organizations (Cain, 2012, Driscoll, 2012).

"Individuals can and do make a difference, but it takes teamwork to really mess things up."

Source: www.CartoonStock.com

STOP AND THINK

Suggest reasons why group working has become so popular in organizations.

In what ways does it benefit individual employees? How does it improve organizational performance?

To boldly go . . . in groups

Perhaps the most fictional aspect of the classic science fiction TV and film series *Star Trek* was how well the crew members got on with each other despite being in such close proximity in the spaceship for years. Here on Earth, Anatoly Perminov, the head of the Russian space agency, Roskosmos, revealed Russia's intention of building an inhabited space station on the moon by 2032, as a prelude to launching a manned mission to Mars. The estimated duration of a round trip to Mars, including a stay on the surface, is 520 days. This would be as much of a psychological as a technical challenge.

In preparation for this, in June 2010, a Frenchman and a Columbian-Italian, together with three Russians and one Chinese, entered a set of four steel containers which they would occupy together. This was a 17-month simulated mission to Mars designed by Roskosmos and the European Space Agency (ESA) to test the physical and mental requirements of an ultra-long-duration spaceflight. The cramped metal construction (see photo), which has no windows, and in which the volunteers lived, was the Mars 500 'spaceship'. It was located in Russia's Institute of Biomedical Problems (IBP). Like the contestants on the TV's show *Big Brother*, the subjects were required to complete tasks, and were monitored to determine the effects of separation and close proximity living. During a similar experiment in IBP's *Mars Flyer* isolation chamber in 1999, two Russian cosmonauts broke into a fist fight, spluttering blood on the module walls. One of them then pressed unwelcome kisses on a Canadian crew member.

Russian psychologists claim that cosmonauts can develop 'space dementia'; become clinically depressed; and suffer from 'asthenization', which causes irritability and low energy and leads crew members to get on badly with each other. Nick Kanas of the University of California investigated interactions between space crew and their mission controllers on the ground of Mir (the Soviet Union's first space station), Skylab (NASA's first station), and the current International Space Station. He found that the way crew coped with stress was to blame the ground staff. They converted tensions on board into feelings that the people on Earth did not care. One Skylab crew became so annoyed with mission control during its 84 days in space that they sulked, mutinied, and turned off all communications. Psychologists are unsure whether a Mars mission should be crewed entirely by women (they are less likely to commit suicide or murder each other when irritable); be mixed (the sexes would support each other); or consist of psychologically robust and less libidinous robots. At the start of November 2011, the Mars 500 volunteers emerged after their 17-month, 70-million-mile virtual journey complaining of boredom. These studies tell us that group dynamics within a confined space are problematic and need to be better understood (based on Amos, 2010, 2011; Wood, 2001).

ESA/Science Photo Library

Definitions of groups

Group two or more people, in face-to-face interaction, each aware of their group membership and interdependence, as they strive to achieve their goals.

Group dynamics the forces operating within groups that affect their performance and their members' satisfaction.

Interpersonal behaviour builds up into group behaviour that in turn sustains and structures future interpersonal relations. The term **group** is thus reserved for people who consider themselves to be part of an identifiable unit, who relate to each other in a meaningful fashion, and who share dispositions through their shared sense of collective identity. Researchers often refer to these as *psychological groups* (Johnson and Johnson, 2012). Groups affect the behaviour of the individuals who compose them. For this reason, social psychologists study internal **group dynamics**. They ask how members of a group communicate with each other and coordinate their activities; how they influence each other; what roles they play in the group; what kind of relationships they have; which members lead, and which follow; how they balance a focus on their task with social issues; and how they resolve conflicts (see Figure 10.2).

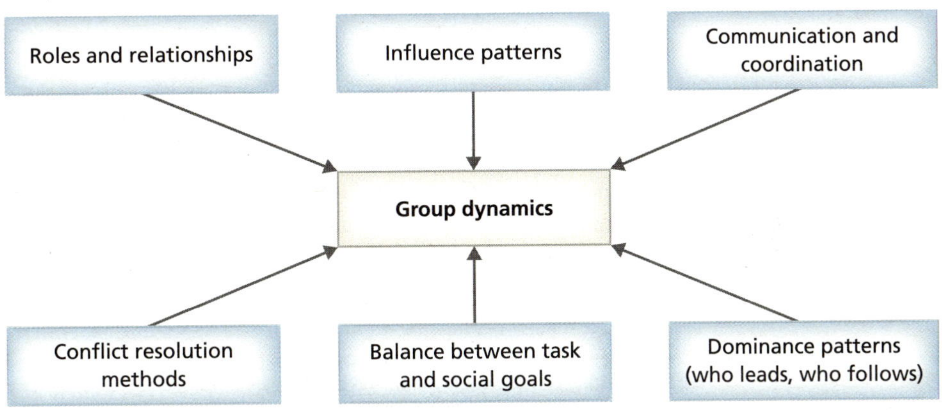

Figure 10.2: Group dynamics

STOP AND THINK

Why would only *one* of the following be considered to be a group? In what circumstances could one of the other aggregates become a group?

(a) people riding on a bus
(b) blonde women between 20 and 30 years of age
(c) members of a football team
(d) audience in a theatre
(e) people sheltering in a shop doorway from the rain

Aggregate a collection of unrelated people who happen to be in close physical proximity for a short period of time.

It is important to maintain a distinction between mere aggregates of individuals and what are called groups. The latter are so called because they exist not only through the (often visible) interactions of members, but also in the (not observable) perceptions of their members. In the Stop and think example, only the football team would fulfil our criteria for a group, and we can usefully distinguish it from an **aggregate**. Aggregates are collections of individuals who happen to be together at any particular time. The bus travellers, theatre audience, and rain shelterers are examples: they do not relate to one another in any meaningful fashion, nor consider themselves a part of any identifiable unit, despite their temporary physical proximity. By the same token, the definition allows one to exclude classes of people who may be defined by physical attributes, geographical location, economic status, or age. Even though a trade union in an organization may like to believe it is a group, it will fail to meet our definition if all of its members do not interact with each other, and if they are not aware of each other. This need for all members to interact has led to the suggestion that in practice, a psychological group is unlikely to exceed twelve or so persons. Beyond that number, the opportunity for frequent interaction between members, and hence group awareness, is considerably reduced.

It is possible for small aggregates of people to be transformed into a group through outside circumstances. This is the plot of many 'disaster movies' in which people fight for their lives on board sinking ships, hijacked aeroplanes, and burning skyscrapers. The story typically involves aggregates of people setting out at the start of the film. The danger causes them to interact with one another, and this increases their awareness of one another and leads them to see themselves as having common problems. By the end of the film, the survivors demonstrate all the characteristics of the group as defined here. The disaster movie example helps us to understand some of the characteristics of a group. Groups differ in the degree to which they possess the five characteristics listed below. The more of them that they possess, the more a group will be recognized as such, and the more power it will have with which to influence its members.

1. *A minimum membership of two people.* Groups can range from two people to over 30. However, the greater the number of group members, the higher the number of possible relationships between them, the greater the level of communication that is required, and the more complex the structure needed to operate the group successfully.
2. *A communication network.* Each group member must be capable of communicating with every other member. In this communication process, the aims and purposes of the group are exchanged. The mere process of interaction satisfies some of our social needs, and it is used to set and enforce standards of group behaviour.
3. *A shared sense of collective identity.* Each member must identify with the other members of their group, and not see themselves as an individual acting independently. They must all believe themselves to be participants in the group which itself is distinct from other groups.
4. *Complementary goals.* Members have individual objectives which can only be met through membership of and participation in the group. Their goals may differ but are sufficiently complementary that members feel able to achieve them through participation in the group. They recognize the need to work collectively and not as individuals.
5. *Group structure.* Individuals in the group will have different roles, e.g. initiator/ideas person, suggestion-provider, compromiser. These roles, which tend to become fixed, indicate what members expect of each other. Norms or rules exist which indicate which behaviours are acceptable in the group and which are not (e.g. smoking, swearing, late arrival).

Size matters

Technological developments have enabled organizations to create ever larger teams to tackle ever larger challenges. The problem is how to motivate and direct their members. Google has 30,000 employees, but tasks are still divided up into projects that can be handled by groups of between five and ten people. At Amazon, founder and chief executive Jeff Bezos limits team size numbers to those small enough to be fed with two pizzas. Limited numbers improve accountability and goal clarity. In a small group no one can avoid pulling their weight, or claim that they do not know what their goal is. Research by Peter Klimek, a physicist from the Medical University in Vienna, confirmed that the more people there are at a meeting, the harder it is to get consensus. He used a program that simulated decision-making by different sized committees. Once they exceed 20 members, it is difficult for it to reach consensus because too many subgroups are formed. However, small can also be a problem. A meeting of eight people is the worst total for decision-making. It produces neither a consensus nor a majority view, and has the highest probability of becoming deadlocked (based on Hill, 2012; Taher, 2009).

Once formed, all groups face a number of challenges, irrespective of whether they are government ministers or university students completing a group project. Eleven of these challenges, which have a direct affect on the group's success or failure, are listed in Table 10.1.

Table 10.1: Issues facing any work group

Issue	Questions
1. Atmosphere and relationships	What kinds of relationships should there be among members? How close and friendly, formal or informal?
2. Member participation	How much participation should be required of members? Some more than others? All equally? Are some members more needed than others?
3. Goal understanding and acceptance	How much do members need to *understand* group goals? How much do they need to *accept* to be *committed* to the goals? Everyone equally? Some more than others?
4. Listening and information-sharing	How is information to be shared? Who needs to know what? Who should listen most to whom?
5. Handling disagreements and conflict	How should disagreements or conflicts be handled? To what extent should they be resolved? Brushed aside? Handled by diktat?
6. Decision-making	How should decisions be made? Consensus? Voting? One-person rule? Secret ballot?
7. Evaluation of member performance	How is evaluation to be managed? Everyone appraises everyone else? A few take the responsibility? Is it to be avoided?
8. Expressing feelings	How should feelings be expressed? Only about the task? Openly and directly?
9. Division of labour	How are task assignments to be made? Voluntarily? By discussion? By leaders?
10. Leadership	Who should lead? How should leadership *functions* be exercised? Shared? Elected? Appointed from outside?
11. Attention to process	How should the group monitor and improve its own process? Ongoing feedback from members? Formal procedures? Avoiding direct discussion?

Source: from *Effective Behaviour in Organizations*. 6th ed., Irwin (Cohen, A.R., Fink, S.L., Gadon, H. and Willits, R.D. 1995) p. 142 © The McGraw-Hill Companies, Inc.

STOP AND THINK

The groups to which you belong provide you with shared goals and a sense of identity, and meet your social needs. However, they can also constrain your thinking, stifle your freedom of expression, limit your behaviour, and restrict your freedom of expression. What is your opinion?

As the size and complexity of modern organizations has increased, the need to integrate the work of different groups within organizations has also grown. McLaren Racing is well known in Formula 1 competition. The company is divided into four groups – those who conceive the car, those who engineer it, those who manufacture it, and those who race it (Blitz, 2007). There are many benefits of group working:

- Groups allow organizations to develop and deliver products and services quickly and cost-effectively while maintaining quality.
- They enable organizations to learn, and to retain learning, more effectively.
- Cross-functional groups promote improved quality management.
- Cross-functional design groups can undertake effective process re-engineering.
- Production time can be reduced if tasks currently performed consecutively by individuals are performed concurrently by people in groups.

- Group-based organization promotes innovation because of the cross-fertilization of ideas.
- Organizations with flat structures can be monitored, coordinated and directed more effectively if the functional unit is the group rather than the individual.
- Groups can better handle the rise in organizational information-processing requirements caused by increasing complexity than individuals (Mohrman et al., 1995).

Types of group tasks

Borrill and West (2005) reported research estimating that 88% of the variation in a group's performance could be explained with reference to the task that it was asked to perform. As McGrath's circumplex model shows, group tasks vary in terms of intrinsic interest; need for member cooperation; whether they are unitary or divisible, and whether they are conceptual or behavioural; and level of difficulty. Ivan Steiner (1972) classified group tasks on the basis of the type of interdependence that they required between their members.

Additive tasks

Additive task a task whose accomplishment depends on the sum of all group members' efforts.

With an **additive task**, all group members do basically the same job, and the final group product or outcome (group performance) is the sum of all their individual contributions. The final outcome is roughly proportional to the number of individuals contributing. There is low interdependency between these people. A group working together will normally perform better than the same number of individuals working alone, provided that all group members make their contribution. Social loafing can, however, reduce performance on an additive task. Examples of additive tasks are tug-of-war contests and pedestrians giving a stalled car a push-start (Littlepage, 1991).

Conjunctive tasks

Conjunctive task a task whose accomplishment depends on the performance of the group's least talented member.

In a **conjunctive task**, one member's performance depends on another's. There is high interdependency. Thus, a group's *least* capable member determines performance. A successful group project at university depends on one member finding the information, a second writing it up, and a third presenting it. All three elements are required for success, and hence coordination is essential in conjunctive tasks. Groups perform less well on conjunctive tasks than lone individuals. Examples of conjunctive tasks include climbing a mountain, running a relay race, and playing chamber music (Steiner and Rajaratnam, 1961).

The handover

AFP/Getty

Yves Morieux of the Boston Consulting Group observed that relay races were often won by teams whose members did not necessarily have the fastest individual times. Members of the medal-winning French women's Olympic relay team explained that, at some point, each had to decide whether to run their guts out, and literally be unable to see straight when they passed the baton, or whether they held something back, to make a better baton change, and thus enable their team mate to run a faster time. The value of this sort of decision making, and each individual's contribution to the team, was beyond measure (Hindle, 2006).

Disjunctive tasks

Disjunctive task a task whose accomplishment depends on the performance of the group's most talented member.

In a **disjunctive task**, once again, one member's performance depends on another's. Again there is high interdependency. However, this time, the group's *most* capable member determines its performance. Groups perform better than their average member on disjunctive tasks, since even the best performer will not know all the answers, and working with others helps to improve overall group performance. Diagnostic and problem-solving activities performed by a group would come into this category. Coordination is important here as well, but in the sense of stopping the others impeding the top performers (Diehl and Stroebe, 1991). Examples of disjunctive task performers are quiz teams (*University Challenge*, pub quiz) and a maintenance team in a nuclear power generating plant.

Groups are more likely to outperform the same number of individuals working separately when working on disjunctive tasks than on additive or conjunctive tasks. This is provided that the most talented member can convince the others of the correctness of their answer. The attitudes, feelings, and conflicts in a group setting might prevent this from happening.

World of Warcraft group dynamics

Bloomberg/Getty

MMORPGs (massively multiplayer online role-playing games) such as Hazzard Fntertainment's *World of Warcraft* have become some of the most popular computer games in recent times. Typically, 40 to 200 players combine into groups (or guilds), getting to know each other and forming their relationships within the game world. Members adopt different roles and responsibilities on behalf of their group, which has to undertake some incredibly difficult task. Guild membership often changes as players/members become fed up with their colleagues, or seek more attractive opportunities elsewhere. Researchers have become interested in studying the group dynamics that emerge in these games. Irrespective of how strong an individual game character may be, the challenges require that the person works with others who possess complementary skills and competences (as well as weaknesses).

Leading a raiding party of 25 group (guild) members on a six-hour raid on Illidan the Betrayer's temple fortress poses many organizational challenges. These include recruiting, training, assessing, motivating, rewarding, and retaining a talented and culturally diverse number of team members, and coordinating their efforts. Decision-making has to be done quickly but collectively, using limited information, and has long-term implications. The organization must be built and sustained with a volunteer workforce and a digitally-mediated environment. That environment features a fluid workforce; self-organized and collaborative work activities; and decentralized, non-hierarchical, rotating leadership, which is changed when conditions alter. It is therefore not surprising that companies and management consultants are exploring the potential of online 'group management simulators' to develop managers' group leadership skills (Reeves et al., 2008).

The Hawthorne studies

The famous Hawthorne studies consisted of a series of experiments conducted during the 1920s and 1930s. Although they are approaching their centenary anniversary, they are still of interest to us today. This is because they formed the basis of the Human Relations School of Management, which in turn became the basis of organizational behaviour – the subject

George Elton Mayo (1880–1949)

Fritz Jules Roethlisberger (1898–1974)

William J. Dickson (1904–1973)

of this textbook. The studies revolutionalized social science research methods and provided a vocabulary with which to discuss social relations in the workplace which continues to be used today.

The studies were conducted at the Hawthorne plant of the Western Electric Company, located in Cicero, Illinois, which manufactured telephones. They resulted in the creation of the human relations approach to management. At that time, factories used natural daylight or candles to illuminate workspaces. In an attempt to promote the sales of light bulbs, the company paid for a series of experiments to try to demonstrate a positive correlation between the amount of light and worker productivity. The original experiments therefore examined the effect of physical changes – originally illumination – on worker productivity (Gillespie, 1991).

Later, Professor George Elton Mayo of the Harvard Business School was invited to bring an academic research team into the factory. Team members included Fritz Jules Roethlisberger, who later became the first Professor of Organizational Behaviour, holding his post in the Harvard Business School, and William J. Dickson. It was through their 1939 book, *Management and the Worker*, that the results of the Hawthorne studies were communicated to the world (Roethlisberger and Dickson, 1939). The Hawthorne research revolutionized social science thinking.

The illumination experiments (1924–1927)

These explored the relationship between the quality of illumination and efficiency. No correlation was found between production output obtained and the lighting provided. Production sometimes even increased when the light intensity was reduced. The conclusion was that lighting was only one of several factors affecting production, and perhaps a minor one. A different study, with fewer workers, was needed to control for the effect of any single variable.

Relay Assembly Test Room experiments (1927–1933)

These experiments focused on the effects of rest pauses and the length of the working day on employees and their attitudes to their work and the company. Six self-selected female workers, drawn from the regular workforce of the Relay Assembly Department, were placed in a separate room for closer observation (see Figure 10.3). They had been working a 48-hour week including Saturdays with no tea breaks. A researcher was placed in the room with them, kept a note of what happened, maintained a friendly atmosphere by listening to their complaints, and told them what was going on. A total of thirteen time periods were studied during which changes were made to the women's rest pauses, hours of work, and refreshment breaks. The results (see Figure 10.4) showed a nearly continuous increase in output over those thirteen periods. This increase began when employee benefits such as rest periods, served lunches, and early finishes were added, but was maintained even when these privileges were withdrawn and the women returned to their normal 48-hour week. The six reasons offered for the increases in output included:

- the motivating effect of acquiring a special status through their selection for and involvement in the experiment;
- the effect of participation as the women were consulted and informed by the experimenter;
- the effect of observer friendliness which improved their morale;
- a different and less intensive form of supervision which reduced their stress while increasing their productivity;
- the self-selected nature of the group creating higher levels of mutual dependence and support appropriate for group working.

Hawthorne effect the tendency of people being observed to behave differently than they otherwise would.

The increase in output due to the increased attention paid to employees in this study is now referred to as the **Hawthorne effect**. It is defined as the tendency of people being observed as part of a research effort to behave differently than they otherwise would. Mayo

AT&T Archives and History Center

Figure 10.3: Relay Assembly Test Room, c. 1929

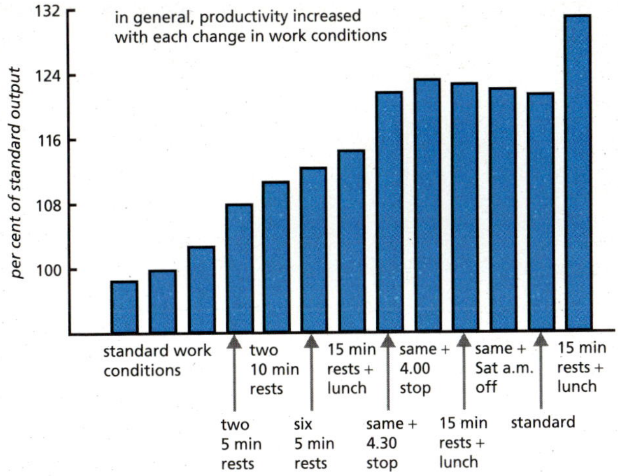

Figure 10.4: Productivity and work conditions

Source: based on data from Roethlisberger and Dickson (1939). From GREENBERG, JERALD; BARON, ROBERT A., BEHAVIOR IN ORGANIZATIONS, 6th Ed. © 1997. Reprinted and Electronically reproduced by permission of Pearson Education, Inc. Upper Saddle River, New Jersey.

and his colleagues became convinced that the women were not solely motivated by money or by improvements in their working conditions. Their attitudes towards and achievement of increased output seemed to be affected by the group to which they belonged. These results led management to study employee attitudes using an interviewing programme.

Interviewing programme (1928–1930)

To find out more about how employees felt about their supervisors and working conditions and how these related to morale, management instituted an interviewing programme involving over 20,000 interviews, which extended to family and social issues. These interviews also revealed the existence of many informal, gang-like groups within the formal working groups. Each had its own leaders and 'sidekicks' who controlled production output. Examining this became the focus of the next experiment.

Bank Wiring Observation Room experiments (1931–1932)

The interviews had revealed that groups exercised a great deal of control over the behaviour of their members. To find out more, a group of men were observed in another part of the company. The Bank Wiring Observation Room (see Figure 10.5) housed fourteen men who were formally organized into three subgroups, each of which contained three wirers and one supervisor, and two inspectors who moved between the three groups.

There were two major findings. First, the detailed observation of interactions between the men revealed the existence of two informal groups or 'cliques' within the three formal groups. The membership of these crossed the formal group boundaries. Second, it was found that these cliques developed informal rules of behaviour or 'norms', as well as mechanisms to enforce these. The total figure for the week's production would tally with the total week's output, but the daily reports showed a steady, level output regardless of actual daily production. This group was operating below its capability, and individual group members were not earning as much as they could. The norms under which the group operated were found to be the following (Roethlisberger and Dickson, 1939, p. 522):

- You should not turn out too much work. If you do, you are a *rate-buster*.
- You should not turn out too little work. If you do, you are a *chisler*.
- You should not tell a supervisor anything that might get a colleague into trouble. If you do, you are a *squealer*.

Figure 10.5: Men in the Bank Wiring Observation Room, c. 1932

- You should not attempt to maintain social distance or act officiously. If you are an inspector, for example, you should not act like one.

The researchers discovered that the Bank Wiring Observation Room men were afraid that if they significantly increased their output, the piece rate would be cut and the daily output expected by management would increase. The men could be reprimanded, and lay-offs might occur. To avoid this, the group members agreed between themselves what was a fair day's output (neither too high nor too low). They enforced this informal output norm through a system of negative sanctions or punishments. These included

- ridicule, as when a group member was referred to as The Slave or Speed King;
- 'binging', which involved striking a norm-violator painfully on the upper arm;
- total rejection or exclusion of the individual by the group as a whole.

Roethlisberger and Dickson wrote:

> The social organization of the bankwiremen performed a twofold function (1) to protect the group from internal indiscretions and (2) to protect it from outside interference . . . nearly all the activities of this group can be looked upon as methods of controlling the behaviour of its members. (1939, pp. 523–4)

These results showed that workers were more responsive to the social forces of their peer group than to the controls and incentives of management. Mayo concluded that

- work is a group activity and not just an individual activity;
- the social world of the adult is primarily patterned around work activities;
- at work, within their social group, people fulfil their needs for belonging and recognition, which enhances their productivity;
- a worker's complaint is a manifestation of a more basic, often psychological problem;
- informal groups at work exercise strong social controls over the work habits and attitudes of individual workers;
- managers need to collaborate with these informal groups to increase cohesion for the company's benefit.

human relations approach a school of management thought which emphasizes the importance of social processes at work.

Those conclusions led to the **human relations approach** to management which held that work should be a source of social relationships for individuals, a way of meeting their need for belonging and for group membership, and even a focus for their personal identity. As Rose (1988, p. 104) noted,

Within work-based social relationships or groups . . . behaviour, particularly productivity or cooperativeness with management, was thought to be shaped and constrained by the worker's role and status in a group. Other informal sets of relationships might spring up within the formal organization as a whole, modifying or overriding the official social structure of the factory which was based on purely technical criteria such as division of labour.

STOP AND THINK Employees in the Bank Wiring Observation Room were subject to group-devised norms which its members policed and enforced. Think of a group that you have known, e.g. at school, work, college or socially. What norms did that group have; and how were they policed and enforced?

Group-oriented view of organizations

In his book *The Social Problems of an Industrial Civilization* (1945), Elton Mayo went on to propose a social philosophy which placed groups at the centre of our understanding of human behaviour in organizations. He stressed the importance of informal groups, and encouraged managers to 'grow' them. He discussed *natural groups* of 3–6 workers and *family groups* of between 8 and 30 members. These would develop into one large *organized group*, consisting of a plant-wide network of family groups, each with its own natural groups. Mayo's vision was of a community organization, in which all or most employees were members of well-knit, natural groups, which were linked together in common purpose. These were not the formal groups discussed earlier. Mayo invited managers to act somewhat like gardeners rather than engineers, and to use their skills, intelligence, and experience to deliberately integrate individuals within groups.

Back to the future: work as the new community?

Justin Sullivan/Getty Images

Eighty years on from Mayo, the idea of the workplace taking on the functions of the community is back in vogue. For example, the workers at the internet search engine company Google are not offered a job but 'the chance to be part of a community of people doing meaningful work. It is not the role so much as belonging that is the key; employees are consumers of a collective experience.' Doug Edwards, the 59th employee to be hired by Google, wrote about his time at the company. He explained that his colleagues in their twenties, who had joined the company, had no friends or relatives living in the area. This vacuum was filled by the company which provided them with all the essential services that they required such as on-site haircuts, car washes, dental and medical services, free massages, food, film nights, wine clubs and guest speakers. There were few distractions, he said, and thus hardly anyone ever needed to leave the office.

Work, it appears, can give us friends, lovers, identity, childcare, and dry cleaning. Researchers have documented a renewed appetite for community and belonging in Western democracies, and 'corporate communities' and 'company families' are developing to fill the gap. Many social issues are currently being tackled through the suffix 'at work' – bullying, racism, stress, drugs. Some employers are acting as quasi-national states, offering healthcare, eye tests and playgroups (Ignattius, 2006; *The Economist*, 2007; Cook, 2008; Edwards, 2011).

The work-as-community theory reflects the observation that many employees now spend more time at work than was the case in previous generations. For many staff, it is the most important thing in their lives. Arlie Hochschild (1997) suggests that individuals are working longer not because of employers' demands but because they find greater satisfaction at work than where they live. Work gives them order; a degree of stability; and involvement in teamwork, which replaces family relationships. In contrast, life at home is dysfunctional and uncertain, making work a place to which to escape. Critics respond by saying that in addition to applying only to a tiny section of the professional middle class, the work-as-community view merely betrays a desire to put a positive gloss on the long hours culture. It's a nice motherhood notion that makes work seem worthwhile.

Rebuilding companies as communities

In an article with the above title, Henry Mintzberg argued that one of the causes of the current financial crisis is that company employees no longer possess a sense of community – a feeling of belonging to, or caring for, anything other than themselves. This has been the result of the increase in the importance ascribed to the individual leadership of chief executive officers (CEOs) and an equivalent reduction in importance placed on everyone else in the firm who has been treated as a 'human resource' to be 'downsized' (fired) when the share price falls. The result in the banks, he feels, has been the mindless, reckless behaviour that maximized employees' own bonuses, but which ignored the ultimate consequences, and which has brought major organizations and giant economies to their knees.

He argued that the veneration of CEO leadership undermines a sense of community in organizations. Companies had to re-engage their employees, and remake themselves into places where people were committed to one another and to their enterprises. Individualism cannot promote leadership and development on its own because humans are social animals, and cannot function effectively without 'community' – a social system that is larger than themselves. Community provides the social glue that binds us together for the greater good. Community means caring about our work, our colleagues, and our communities. Some of the most admired companies, such as Toyota, Semco, Mondragon, and Pixar, all possess a strong sense of community. The president of Pixar attributed his company's success to 'its vibrant community where talented people are loyal to one another and their collective work, everyone feels that they are part of something extraordinary, and their passion and accomplishments make their community a magnet for talented people'. In our hectic, individualistic world, this sense of community has been lost in many organizations.

Mintzberg suggested that 'communityship' (as he called it) should stand between individual leadership on one side and collective citizenship on the other. Perhaps we should wean ourselves off idolizing heroic leaders and realize that we need just enough leadership to encourage employees to get on with things together. To allow a sense of community to bloom requires a compelling culture. Employees must know what the place is all about, and a mission statement like Google's 'to organize the world's information and make it universally accessible and useful' allows committed people to work in cooperative relationships based on mutual respect. Mintzberg concludes that the ultimate test of whether a company has become a true community is whether its employees see themselves as responsible citizens of a wider community (Mintzberg, 2009; Catmull, 2008).

STOP AND THINK Do you agree or disagree with Henry Mintzberg's view on rebuilding companies as communities? Are not heroic leaders like the late Steve Jobs more critical to company success than those followers who work in those companies?

Another famous psychologist, Rensis Likert, echoed the idea that organizations should be viewed and managed as a collection of groups rather than individuals (Likert, 1961). He felt that group forces were important in influencing the behaviour of individual work groups with regard to productivity, waste, absence, and so on, and thus affected the performance of the entire organization. In his book chapter entitled 'The principle of supportive

Rensis Likert (1903–1981)

relationships', Likert, like Mayo, attempted to derive a theory of organizational design with the group as the basic building block. He argued that

- work groups are important sources of individuals' need satisfaction;
- groups in organizations that fulfil this psychological function are also more productive;
- management's task is therefore to create effective work groups by developing 'supportive relationships';
- an effective organizational structure consists of democratic-participative work groups, each linked to the organization as a whole through overlapping memberships;
- coordination is achieved by individuals who carry out 'linking functions'.

"We like to bring together people from radically different fields and wait for the friction to produce heat, light and magic. Sometimes it takes a while."

Source: www.CartoonStock.com

Likert is also remembered for proposing the concept of the overlapping group membership structure. This he termed a 'linking pin' process. The overlapping works vertically by having the leaders of related subordinate groups as members of the next higher group, with their common superior as leader, and so on up the hierarchy. The organization is therefore conceived as consisting of many overlapping groups. This is shown in Figure 10.6. In his view, an organizational design based around groups rather than individuals

- improves communications;
- increases co-operation;
- provides more team member commitment; and
- produces faster decision-making.

While Likert's 'linking pin' concept focused on *vertical* coordination, today the stress is placed upon *horizontal* integration in the form of cross-functional teams. Nevertheless, most people in an organization are now members of several teams. This overlap of groups in organizations, due to matrix structures and cross-functional teamworking, means that an individual can be a member of a project team and a geographical group, both at the same time. This will hinder their ability to identify with any one particular group.

Following Likert, a succession of academics and consultants have followed Mayo in promoting the cause of organizations built around groups, rather than just including them. In the 1970s, Leavitt (1975) asked management to use small groups as the basic building

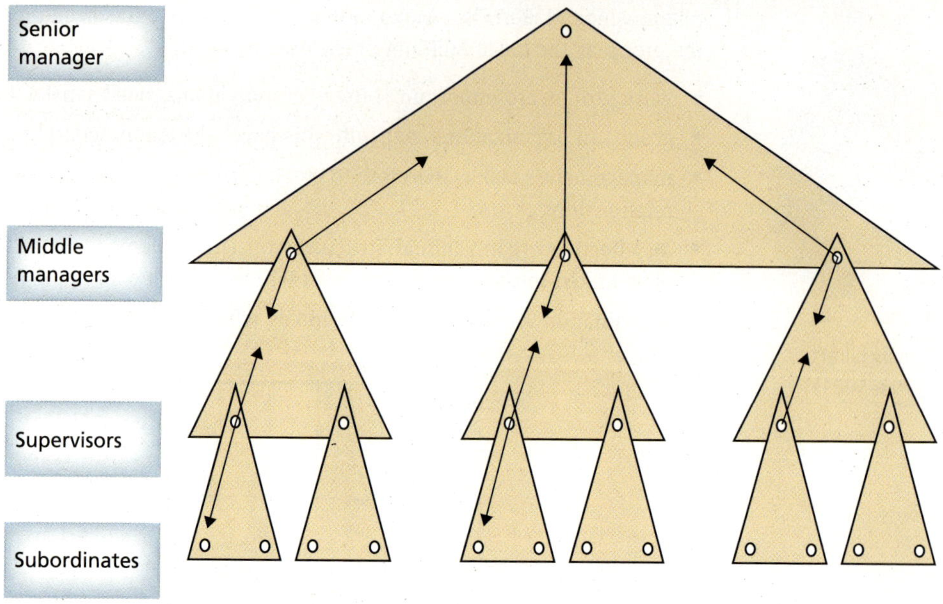

Figure 10.6: Rensis Likert's linking pin model

Source: after New Patterns of Management, 1961, McGraw-Hill (Likert, R.) p. 105, 0070378509, © The McGraw Hill Companies, Inc.

blocks for an organization. Ouchi and Johnson (1978) echoed Mayo's thesis that people in society lacked social support anchors which made life tolerable, and they recommended that large organizations should be organized around 'clans' (similar to Mayo's natural groups) which could provide the associational ties and cohesion for their employees. In the 1980s, Tom Peters (1987, p. 296) said that 'The modest-sized, task-oriented, semi-autonomous, mainly self-managing team should be the basic organization building block'. Finally, in the 1990s, team-based organizational models were proposed (see Chapter 17).

STOP AND THINK

You have accepted a job and your new employer tells you that you will become 'part of the team', and a 'member of one big happy family here'.

- How do you feel about the organization as your 'psychological home' in this respect?
- When managers say that they want you 'to belong' what do they *really* mean?
- Why do you think teamworking has been so consistently popular with managers interested in improving employees' performance?

Formal and informal groups

Workplace behaviour can be considered as varying along a continuum from formally to informally organized. At one extreme, formal behaviour is organized to achieve the collective purpose of an organization. This may be to make washing machines, provide a repair service, earn £200,000 profit a year, or achieve a 5 per cent return on investment. To achieve such collective purposes, the organization is structured in such a way so as to use the limited resources it has at its disposal as efficiently and effectively as possible. It does this by creating what is called a formal organization. The overall collective purpose or aim is broken down into sub-goals and sub-tasks. These are assigned to different sub-units in the organization. The tasks may be grouped together and departments thus formed. Job requirements in terms of job descriptions may be written. The subdivision continues to take place until a small group of people is given one such sub-goal and divides it between its members. When this occurs, there exists the basis for forming the group along functional lines. This process of identifying the purpose, dividing up tasks, and so on is referred to as the creation of the formal organization. A group formed through this division of labour is called a **formal group**.

Formal group a group that has been consciously created by management to accomplish a defined task that contributes to the organization's goal.

Managers make choices as to how technology and organization will be combined to create task-oriented (formal) groups. The purpose of the groups in the production department may be to manufacture 100 cars a day, while that of the group in the design department may be to draw up a set of construction plans. Whatever type of formal group we are interested in, they all have certain common characteristics:

- They are task-orientated.
- They tend to be permanent.
- They have a formal structure.
- They are consciously organized by management to achieve organizational goals.
- Their activities contribute directly to the organization's collective purpose.

Informal group a collection of individuals who become a group when they develop interdependencies, influence one another's behaviour, and contribute to mutual need satisfaction.

Alongside these formal groups, and consisting of the same employees, albeit arranged differently, will be a number of informal groups. These emerge in an organization and are neither anticipated nor intended by those who create the formal organization. They emerge from the informal interaction of the members of the formal organization. These unplanned-for groups share many of the characteristics of small social leisure groups. These function alongside the formal groups. An **informal group** develops during the spontaneous interaction of people in the group as they talk, joke, and associate with one another.

Why do informal groups exist and what purpose do they serve? In the Bank Wiring Observation Room in the Hawthorne studies, workers' interests centred upon restricting their output. In so doing, they gained a degree of personal control, that is, they increased their autonomy in relation to management. Two cliques emerged, and each developed its own, separate identity. Self-interest and self-identity interact and reciprocate. These processes have implications for the behaviour of the groups concerned. This phenomenon is termed **group self-organization**.

Group self-organization the tendency of groups to form interests, develop autonomy, and establish identities.

Ackroyd and Thompson (1999) introduced the concept of group self-organization to help our understanding of the nature of formal and informal groups. Group self-organization refers to the tendency of groups to

- form interests,
- develop autonomy, and
- establish identities.

Home viewing

Office Space (1998, director Mike Judge) follows the progress of Peter Gibbons (played by Ron Livingston), an employee of the computer company Initech. His behaviour is driven by the nature of his work and imminent loss of his job due to downsizing. Peter shows signs of alienation (see Chapter 3), particularly feelings of *powerlessness*, *meaninglessness* and *self-estrangement*. As you watch, look for the symptoms of his alienation being expressed. The fourth alienation symptom, *isolation*, is not present because he is a member of an informal group which provides each member with a sense of community and membership, and helps Peter cope with the futility of his work life. How does this informal group operate? What are its goals? What do its members talk about? Also, how does the film depict the idea that modern organizations deny white-collar male employees their essential masculinity? How does Peter resolve this issue?

Social networks of informal groups

The term *social network* now most commonly refers to internet-based groups like Facebook and LinkedIn. However, the same term is also used to refer to the 'informal organization' (in contrast to the 'formal organization'), which is considered by management to be unobservable and ungovernable, and thus often treated as an 'invisible enemy'. In consequence, managers frequently try to work around or ignore them. Even where a network's existence is acknowledged and valued, managers tend to rely on intuition to nurture this social capital, but commonly misunderstand the links between their network's members. Cross and Prusak (2002; Cross and Parker, 2004) studied the social networks that existed within 50 large organizations, and argued that it was possible for managers to develop informal networks systematically in order enhance their company's effectiveness. The first step was for them to identify and map the many different informal networks of people within a company, which could be done using a graphical tool called *social network analysis.* The next step was for the managers to focus their attention on just a few role-players in the network whose performance was critical to the entire organization. Their research revealed four such key roles:

- *Central connectors* link most of the people within an informal network to one another. Despite not being formal leaders, they know who possesses the critical information or expertise required to get the work done.
- *Boundary spanners* connect the informal organization with other parts of the company or with similar networks in other organizations. They consult and advise individuals from many different company departments, regardless of their own functional affiliations.
- *Information brokers* keep different subgroups in an informal network together. Failure to communicate across subgroups would lead to their splintering into smaller, less effective segments.
- *Peripheral specialists* are those members within an informal network to whom anyone can turn to for specialized expertise.

The diagram in Figure 10.7 depicts a social network. It shows three different departments (formal organization) in a company, and the informal links between individuals within each one. Some individuals are more interacted with than others. It also demonstrates the informal linkages between individuals in each of the different departments.

A study by Allen and his colleagues of the staff of ICI's research and development (R&D) department (Allen et al., 2007) confirms the earlier work. Network researchers recommend that managers transform an ineffective informal network into a productive one by focusing on these key individuals, and determining whether these people are performing their roles effectively or are being prevented from doing so. Are the central connectors hoarding information? Are boundary spanners talking to the right people outside the group? Do the peripheral specialists need to be drawn more closely into the network? Additionally, managers should actively encourage social contacts by installing coffee rooms and water-coolers, where staff can meet; identify individuals who are the 'knowledge nodes' in the network and train and coach them; map the social networks to reveal any gaps; and be aware that a loss of personnel means not only a loss of formal know-how but also the collapse of their associated social network (based on Cross and Parker, 2004; Allen et al., 2007).

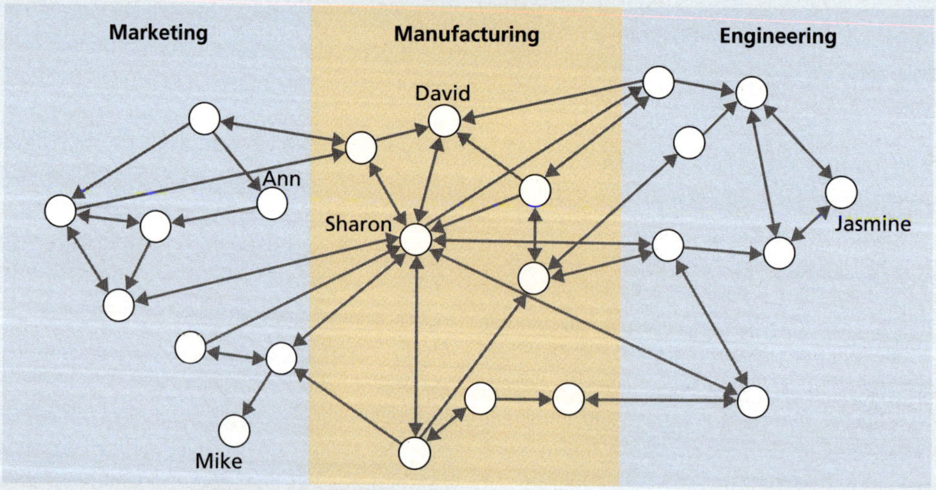

Figure 10.7: A social network in an organization

Source: from DAFT/MARCIC. *Management*, 6E. © 2009 South-Western, a part of Cengage Learning, Inc. Reproduced by permission. www.cengage.com/permissions

Motivation theory suggests that humans have a need for love, esteem, and safety (see Chapter 9). Love needs are concerned with belongingness and relationships; esteem needs focus on recognition, attention, and appreciation; safety needs concern security of employment. The failure to satisfy these needs may result in our inability to feel confident or capable, or that we are necessary or useful members of society. These needs concern our relationships with others. The time that we do spend at work remains considerable, and we frequently seek to satisfy these needs through our relationships with work colleagues. The difficulty is that the organizations are not primarily designed to allow individuals to meet such needs at work.

A formal organization is ostensibly designed on rational principles and is aimed at achieving the collective purpose of the organization. It thus limits employees' behaviour in order to be able to control and predict it. Individuals bring their hopes, needs, desires, and personal goals to their job. While the company may not be interested in these, the employee will, nevertheless, attempt to achieve their personal ambitions while at work by manipulating the situation to fulfil their unmet needs. Most other staff will generally be seeking to do the same so it will not be difficult to set up series of satisfying relationships. These relationships in turn will lead to the formation of informal groups. Because of our social nature, we have a tendency to form informal groups. The task-oriented, formal groups rarely consider the social needs of their members. Indeed these needs are frequently considered to be dispensable and counterproductive to the achievement of the formal purpose of the organization.

STOP AND THINK

Consider how your educational institution contributes to the satisfaction of your social needs while studying through your membership of social groups (class, tutorial groups, self-help and study groups, clubs and societies, sports teams).

Conversely, how are other aspects of your institution's structure, rules, procedures, and policies blocking your satisfaction?

How could your institution meet your social needs and those of your fellow students more effectively through different forms of group arrangement? Would these be consistent with good teaching and learning practice?

Group formation

George Caspar Homans (1910–1989)

Groups do not suddenly appear out of nowhere. Before being able and willing to contribute as part of a collective, individuals who were previously strangers have to become acquainted with each other in order to establish how best to work together to achieve the common task. George Homans addressed this question of how groups formed (Homans, 1951). His three-part model is summarized in Figure 10.8, and we shall examine it in relation to management and workers in organizations.

Environment of group		External system		Internal system		
Physical Technological Social	➡	Required activities Required interactions Required sentiments	➡	Emergent activities Emergent interactions Emergent sentiments	➡	Formation of a group

Figure 10.8: Homans's model of group formation

Group environment

Homans proposed that every group (or *social system* in his model) exists within an environment which affects it physically, technologically, and socially. This environment is created by management's decisions in three areas:

- *Physical*. These are the actual surroundings within which a group functions. It includes the spatial arrangement of physical objects and location of human activities, e.g. office architecture and work furniture; placement of workers on an assembly line.
- *Technological*. This includes both material technology (the tools, machinery, and equipment that can be seen, touched, and heard) that group members use to do their jobs, and social technology (the methods which order their behaviour and relationships).
- *Social*. This encompasses the norms and values of the group itself; of its managers (e.g. employees as motivated solely by money) and of the organization culture (stressing mutual support and collaboration or competition, distrust and backstabbing).

Homans's group environments

Image Source/Rex Features

Physically, the context of a group in a call centre differs depending on management's choice of work furniture. Each arrangement limits the form and nature of operators' interactions with each other, and requires them to behave in certain ways. Managers can select work furniture to isolate operators, discourage them from interacting with colleagues and thus prevent informal groups from forming. Alison Barnes's study of Australian call centres reported a manager saying 'It's not the sort of place where you can talk to the person beside you or behind you if you're not taking calls . . . it's not a job where there is a lot of interaction during the day'. Barnes noted that the lack of spaces at work where staff members could meet privately hindered their collective organization. A company policy of 'hot desking' also prevented an operator working with the same group of people.

Technologically, the context of their work consists of the material technology that requires staff to interact with customers using the telephone and computer. In addition, there are the wallboards, with their 6 inch high LED numbers, which show the number of calls waiting to be answered. This flashes faster as the length of the queue increases. Computers monitor how many calls each operator deals with, and how quickly, keeping figures on all staff. The social technology consists of the script and prompt software held in the computer that directs their conversations in certain required ways. Socially, the norms, values, and goals that make up the shared understanding within which the group will function are specific to each group and are influenced by the culture of the call centre organization in which it operates. Barnes concluded:

© Jagadeesh/Reuters/Corbis

> The design of work in the call centres – the technology such as the automatic call distribution or the focus on statistics – inhibited worker interaction. Designing an office space in order to facilitate employee communication would have been inconsistent with company objectives (based on Barnes, 2008).

Homans argued that a group's environment was created by the organization's management through its design of the physical workplace; its purchase of equipment and choices in job design; and its choice of strategy, structure, and culture.

External system

Activities in Homans's theory, the physical movements and verbal and non-verbal behaviours engaged in by group members.

Interactions in Homans's theory, the two-way communications between group members.

Sentiments in Homans's theory, the feelings, attitudes, and beliefs held by group members towards others.

Homans's external system broadly equates to the concept of the formal organization introduced earlier. Managers have certain requirements or expectations of employees which, from the employees' perspective, are the 'givens' of their jobs. They require individuals to perform certain **activities**; to have certain **interactions** with others; and to have certain **sentiments** or feelings towards their work.

For example, in a supermarket, the physical/technological/social environment is represented by the design and positioning of the checkout stations, the choice of scanning equipment, and the company's 'the customer is always right' policy. The supermarket management wants its checkout operators to scan customers' purchases (activities); greet them, offer to pack their bags, and say goodbye to them (interactions). They are also expected to have positive attitudes and feelings towards their customers and their employer (sentiments). Homans prefaced each of these elements with the term 'required' (*required activities*, *required interactions*, and *required sentiments*) and referred to them collectively as the *external system*.

Each of these three elements reinforces each other. The more activities employees share, the more frequent will be their interactions, and the stronger will be their shared activities and sentiments (how much the other persons are liked or disliked). The greater the number of interactions between persons, the more will be their shared activities and the stronger their sentiments towards each other. The stronger the sentiments people have for one another, the greater will be the number of their shared activities and interactions. Persons in a group interact with one another, not just because of spatial or geographical proximity (called propinquity), but also to accomplish goals such as cooperation and problem-solving.

Homans's required activities and interactions

Monkey Business Images/www.dreamstime.com

At most supermarkets, checkout operators are expected to conform to particular patterns of non-verbal behaviour even when not serving. For example, one checkout operator, Denise (name changed) commented in an interview with the authors that, at her store, not only were the checkouts constantly monitored by closed-circuit television but supervisors regularly patrolled behind the checkouts, preventing any of the operators turning around to talk to fellow operators, by whispering the command 'FF', which meant 'Face the Front'. Denise and her colleagues were required not only to 'FF', but also to sit straight at all times; they were strictly forbidden, for example, from putting their elbows on the counter in front of them to relax their backs'. (Noon and Blyton, 2007, p. 189)

Internal system

Homans's internal system broadly equates to the concept of the informal organization introduced earlier. It consists of another, different set of group members' activities, interactions, and sentiments that emerge from the physical/technological/social environment, and as a result of the required activities, required interactions, and required sentiments themselves. Homans prefaced each of these elements with the term 'emergent' (*emergent activities, emergent interactions*, and *emergent sentiments*) and referred to them collectively as the *internal system*. These represent the creation of informal groups within the organization.

These can occur in addition to, or in place of, the latter, and are not asked for by the organization's management. For example, if the job is repetitive (technological context), operators might see how quickly they can perform it (emergent activity), so as to give their work more challenge. If employees are in close proximity to each other (physical context), they might relieve their boredom by talking to each other (emergent interaction) even though company rules forbid it. Group members may come to view customers as a nuisance and develop anti-customer feelings (emergent sentiments). For Homans, the relationship between the external and internal systems was crucial.

- *The internal and the external systems are interdependent.* A change in one system will produce a change in the other. For example, the replacement of a management-selected team leader (external system) can impact on the activities between the group members (internal system). Similarly, the sentiments of group members (internal system) can affect the way they do their work (external system).
- *The environment and the internal and external systems are interdependent.* Changes in the environment produce changes in the external (formal) and internal (informal) work organization. Individuals and groups will modify what they do and how they do it, to respond to the changes they perceive.

Diversity or homogeneity in groups?

When managers choose members to form a working group, should those selected be different from, or similar to, one another in terms of their sex, ages, status, ethnicity, personality, skills, and status? The argument for diversity is that it provides a group with a greater pool of information from which to draw, thereby increasing its chances of improved decision-making, problem-solving, and creativity. Diversity therefore can improve group performance. The argument against diversity is that, if group members distinguish between those who are 'like them' and those who are not, it creates a 'them and us' bias. This reduced liking for, trust in, and cooperation with those group members perceived to be 'different' can increase suspicion and misunderstandings, and creates conflict within the group. Diversity therefore can reduce group performance.

The research evidence suggests that, compared to homogeneous groups, when they begin, groups with a diverse membership experience more difficulties in clarifying their objectives, agreeing group roles, communicating with each other, and reviewing their performance. Such groups appear never to recover from such initial setbacks. Their members' own beliefs as to the value of diversity itself – whether they see it as a source of strength to the group or as a weakness – play a critical role. If they see diversity as a strength, then it is likely to have a positive impact on their group's performance. The leader of the group can play a vital role in helping to engender positive attitudes towards diversity among the group's members, and in encouraging collaboration between them (Van Knippenburg and Schippers, 2007; Edmondson and Roloff, 2009).

Homans's model of group formation established the basis for our understanding of group behaviour. First, it highlights how the environment within which a group functions (the physical dispersion of staff, the technology that they use, and their social context) helps or hinders the process of group formation. Second, it highlights how this management-created environment imposes the required activities, required interactions, and required sentiments on individuals, and groups in an organization, and then how these in turn stimulate the emergent activities, emergent interactions, and emergent sentiments that are not required by the external system.

Group development

Bruce Wayne Tuckman (b.1938)

Groups of whatever type do not come into existence fully formed. Bruce Tuckman and Mary Ann Jensen suggested that groups pass through five clearly defined stages of development which they labelled forming, storming, norming, performing, and adjourning (Tuckman and Jensen, 1977; see Figure 10.9). Of course not all groups develop through all the stages and some get stuck in the middle and remain inefficient and ineffective. Progress through the stages may be slow, but appears to be necessary and inescapable.

1. *Forming*. This is the orientation stage, at which the set of individuals has not yet gelled. The individual asks 'How do I fit in?' and the group asks 'Why are we here?'. Everyone is busy finding out about each other's attitudes and backgrounds, and establishing ground rules. Members are also keen to fix their personal identities in the group and make a personal impression on the others. In the personal relations area, members are *dependent* on some leader to provide them with structure in the form of ground rules and

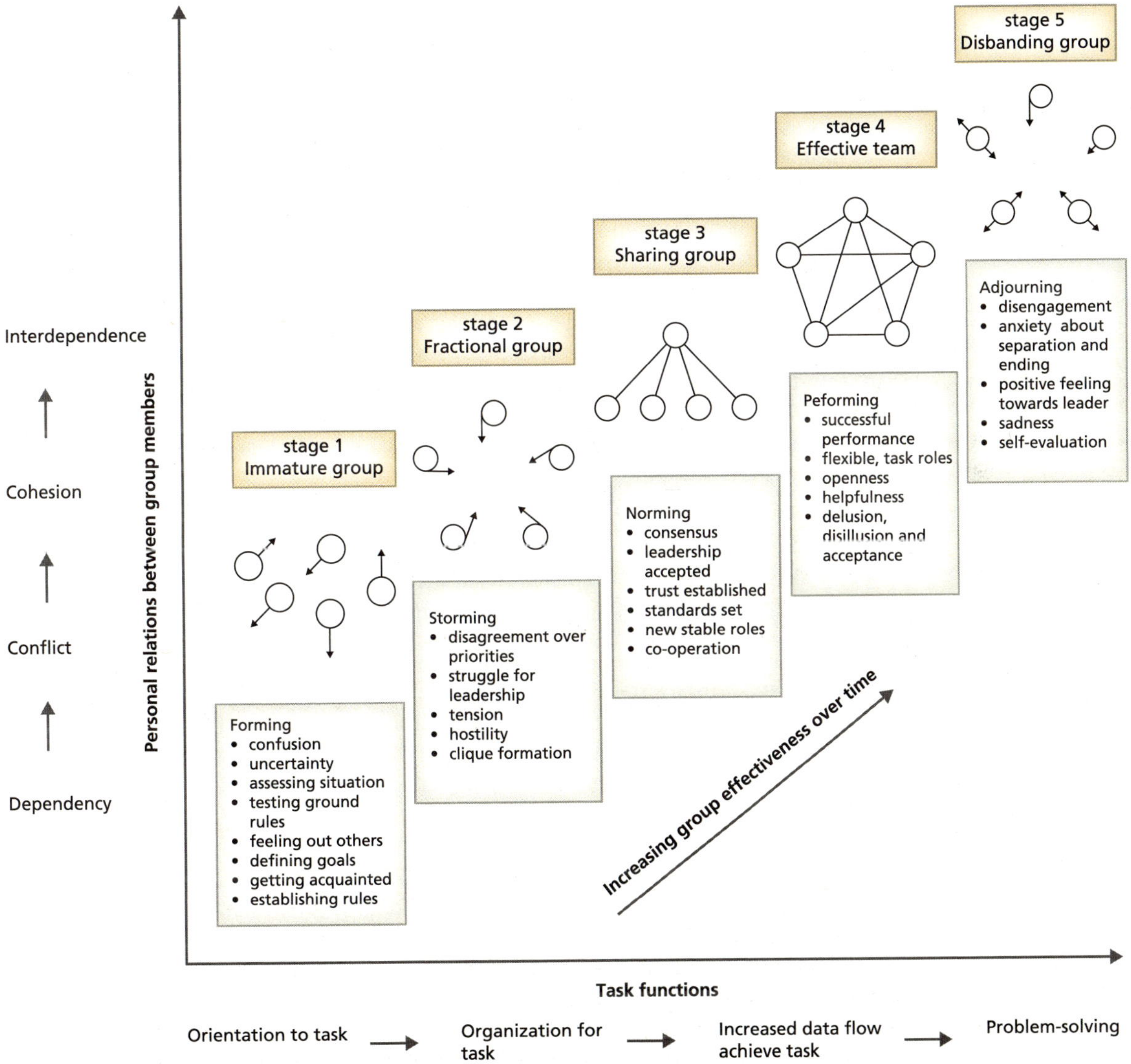

Figure 10.9: Stages of group development

Source: based on Tuckman and Jensen (1977); Jones (1973).

an agenda for action. Task-wise, they seek *orientation* as to what they are being asked to do, what the issues are, and whether everyone understands the task.

2. *Storming*. This is a conflict stage in the group's life and can be an uncomfortable period. The individual asks 'What's my role here?' and the group asks 'Why are we fighting over who's in charge and who does what?'. Members bargain with each other as they try to sort out what each of them individually, and what they as a group, want out of the group process. Individuals reveal their personal goals and it is likely that interpersonal hostility is generated when differences in these goals are revealed. Members may resist the control of other group members and may show hostility. The early relationships established in the forming stage may be disrupted. The key personal relations issue in this stage is the management of *conflict*, while the task function question is *organization* – how best to organize to achieve the group objective.
3. *Norming*. In this cohesion stage, the members of the group develop ways of working to develop closer relationships and camaraderie. The individual asks 'What do others expect me to do?' and the group asks 'Can we agree on roles and work as a team?'. The questions of who will do what and how it will be done are addressed. Working rules are established in terms of norms of behaviour (e.g. do not smoke) and role allocation (e.g. Jill will be the spokesperson). A framework is therefore created in which each group member can relate to the others and the questions of agreeing expectations and dealing with a failure to meet members' expectations are addressed. The personal relations within the group stress *cohesion*. Members feel that they have overcome conflict and have 'gelled', and experience a sense of 'groupiness'. On the task side, there is an *increase in data-flow* as members become more prepared to be more open about their goals.
4. *Performing*. By this stage the group has developed an effective structure, and it is concerned with actually getting on with the job in hand and accomplishing objectives. The individual asks 'How can I best perform my role?' and the group asks 'Can we do the job properly?'. The fully mature group has now been created and can get on with its work. Not all groups develop to this stage; some may become bogged down in an earlier and less productive stage. In personal relations, interdependence becomes a feature. Members are equally happy working alone, in sub-groupings, or as a single unit. Collaboration and functional competition occur between them. On the task side, there is a high commitment to the objective, jobs are well defined, and problem-solving activity ensues.
5. *Adjourning*. In this final stage, the group may disband, either because the task has been achieved or because the members have left. The individual asks 'What's next?' and the group asks 'Can we help members make the transition to their next task or group?'. Before they do so, they may reflect on their time together, and ready themselves to go their own ways.

Tuckman and Jensen's stages need not occur in sequence. While groups do pass through these different stages, they have been found to go through more of an iterative process. They cycle back and forth between the different stages. They may pass through one stage several times, or become frozen in a certain stage for a period of time. Some groups pass through certain stages more quickly than others. Moreover, progress through to any given stage is not inevitable (Gersick, 1988, 1989).

The value of the Tuckman and Jensen framework shown in Figure 10.9 is that it can help us to explain some of the problems of group working. A group may be operating at half power because it may have failed to work through some of the issues at the earlier stages. For example, the efficiency of a project team may be impaired because it had not resolved the issue of leadership. Alternatively, people may be pulling in different directions because the purpose of the group has not been clarified, nor its objectives agreed. Members might be using the group to achieve their personal and unstated aims (so-called hidden agendas). For all these reasons, effective group functioning may be hindered.

Home viewing

Two films illustrate the different stages of group formation. In *The Breakfast Club* (1984, director John Hughes) five American high school students spend a whole Saturday in detention, under a teacher's less than watchful eye. Over the day, the individuals form into a group. In *Remember the Titans* (2000, director Boaz Yakin), a different set of students are welded into a successful American football team under the leadership of their coach played by Denzil Washington. In both cases, identify the transition between the forming, storming, norming, performing, and adjourning stages of group formation (based on Reimers and Parsons, 2003, and Smith, 2009).

STOP AND THINK

Identify a group to which you currently belong – sports club, drama society, tutorial group, project group, etc.

- Identify which stage of development it has reached.
- What advice would you give to this group based on your analysis of its development?

Groups and teams

In the literature, the terms *group* and *team* are used interchangeably, with the choice of word being guided by the personal preference of writers and tradition, rather than conceptual distinction. For example, the 'how-to-do-it' books aimed at a management audience tend to refer to teams in organizations, while, for historical reasons, discussions about shop-floor working arrangements refer to autonomous work groups. Management consultants frequently use the term team metaphorically, that is, they apply this label to a collection of employees to which it is imaginatively, but not literally, appropriate. Hayes (1997) noted that the idea of team must be one of the most widely used metaphors in organizational life. These same writers also use the term normatively, that is, to describe a collection of people as what they *should* be, or what they would *prefer* them to be, rather than as they actually are.

In their examination of the managerial practices used by the U.S. Marine Corps to engage the hearts and minds of their front line troops, Jon Katzenbach and Jason Santamaria (1999) contrasted the characteristics of a team with that of a single-leader work group. These are summarized in Table 10.2. The authors describe the training of marines, and note that the highly cohesive groups produced by this process learn when and how to function as a real team, and when to rely on a single leader.

Most commonly, writers focus on the transformation of a group into a team. They see the difference between the two as being in terms of a group being 'stuck' in the forming, storming, or norming stage of Tuckman and Jensen's model, while a team is a group that has successfully arrived at the performing stage. From the point of view of management, a team is a group which possesses extra, positive features. As a group comes to acquire these positive characteristics, it is seen as progressing towards the team end of the continuum. These positive 'team traits' include cooperation, coordination, cohesion, and so on. From this perspective, a group turns into a team once it has organized itself to fulfil a purpose. This implies a process of conscious self-management by the group's members during which they assign tasks, develop communication channels, and establish decision-making processes. Thus, the transition from a group to a team is the result of a learning process.

Table 10.2: Teams and work groups

	Teams	**Work groups**
Leadership	rotating among capable members	one assigned senior individual
Goals	agreed by team discussion	set by formal leader
Work organization	decided by team members	determined by leader
Outputs	collective results achieved by members' close collaboration	individual results achieved by people working on their own
Performance	low at first as team learns how to work together, then same rate as work group	at first faster than a team, as members do not have to learn how to work with each other
Performance evaluation	by team members themselves and senior management	by formal leader and senior management
Accountability	team members hold each other accountable	group members held individually accountable by leader
Works well with	complex, challenging tasks requiring collaboration and a mix of interdependent skills	time pressured tasks requiring leader's knowledge to integrate various contributions

Source: based on Katzenbach and Santamaria (1999).

STOP AND THINK

Management has just told you that you are not a 'real team' and that you are certainly not a 'high performance team'. How do you feel about that, and what are you doing to do about it?

Mayo's 'human relations approach' and Katzenbach and Santamaria's managerial practices to create teams are separated by over seventy years, but have remarkable similarities. Both

- are directed at managers who design jobs and structure organizations
- promote the virtues of teams and groups over individuals
- assume that teams and the individuals share common goals and interests
- ignore or explain away areas of conflict or dissent
- seek to use the power of the team in management's interest.

RECAP

1. *List the key characteristics of a group.*
   - A group consists of two or more people, in face-to-face interaction, each aware of his or her membership in the group, each aware of the others who belong to the group, and each aware of their positive interdependence as they strive to achieve mutual goals.
2. *Distinguish between different types of group tasks.*
   - Groups can be assigned many different tasks, many of which can be categorized under the headings of additive, conjunctive, and disjunctive.
3. *Name the four research phases of the Hawthorne studies.*
   - The Hawthorne studies consisted of four major phases – illumination experiments, Relay Assembly Test Room experiments, an interviewing programme, and the Bank Wiring Observation Room experiments.
4. *Distinguish between a formal and an informal group.*
   - Formal groups can be distinguished from informal groups in terms of who creates them and the purposes that they serve.
5. *Outline Homans's theory of group formation.*
   - George Homans's theory of group formation distinguishes between background factors and required and emergent activities, interactions, and sentiments, to explain how individuals come to form groups.
6. *Enumerate the five stages of Tuckman and Jensen's model of group development.*
   - Tuckman and Jensen distinguish five stages through which groups typically proceed, which they name forming, storming, norming, performing, and adjourning.
7. *Summarize Katzenbach and Santamaria's distinction between a team and a single-leader working group.*
   - Katzenbach and Santamaria contrast a team with a single-leader working group on the dimensions of: who runs it; who sets the goals; performance evaluation; work style; business context; speed and efficiency; primary end products; and accountability.

Revision

1. Why have the results of the Hawthorne studies remained so important to this day? Of what value are they to those working in groups and those managing groups, today?
2. How do informal groups within an organization differ from formal ones? What function do informal groups perform and which members' needs do they meet?
3. Choose a group with which you are familiar, and analyse it using the four elements of Homans' model of group formation.
4. Under what circumstances should management form a group or a team to perform a task, and when should it arrange for individuals to work individually on their own?

Research assignment

Select either a group featured in a television series or one which you know well (e.g. sports team; scout/guide group; social club).

(a) Is this a formal or informal group?

(b) What stage is this group at, in terms of Tuckman and Jensen's model of group development?

(c) What is your group's size, composition, function, and status?

(d) How do these factors affect its operation and outcomes?

(e) What roles do group members play in the group, and what are their relationships with one another?

(f) What expectations, rights and responsibilities are attached to each of the group member roles?

(g) What formal rules and informal norms does the group use to control its members' behaviour?

(h) How does the group react if a member breaks its rules or norms?

Springboard

Timothy Franz (2012) *Group Dynamics and Team Interventions*, Wiley. Links academic research findings on group behaviour with real life workplace practices.

Henry Mintzberg (2009) 'Rebuilding companies as communities', *Harvard Business Review*, 76(7/8), pp. 140–3. Mintzberg's discussion of 'communityship' updates Mayo's original idea placing it into a contemporary context.

Bernard Nijstad (2009) *Group Performance*, Psychology Press, Hove, East Sussex. The author provides a summary of classic and contemporary research on group behaviour and performance.

Amanda Sinclair (1992) 'The tyranny of a team ideology', *Organization Studies*, 13(4), pp. 611–26. This classic article provides a critical review of the concept of team in managerial and organizational writings.

OB in films

The Magnificent Seven (1960, director John Sturges), DVD track 6: 0:18:35, to track 12: 0:39:48 (21 minutes – sequenced). In this American western film, a group of Mexican farmers cross the border, initially with a view to buying guns in order to defend their village against bandits. Eventually, they end up hiring gunmen. The clip begins as the three villagers enter Chris's (played by Yul Brynner) hotel room. As you watch the clip of the selection process, speculate on which of the needs identified by Maslow (see Chapter 9) each of the gunmen appears to want to meet by joining the group. (Each may have more than one need.)

	Needs				
Character (actor)	**biological**	**safety**	**affiliational**	**esteem (self and others)**	**self-actualization**
Chris (Yul Brynner)					
Harry (Brad Dexter)					
Vin (Steve McQueen)					
O'Reilly (Charles Bronson)					
Britt (James Coburn)					
Lee (Robert Vaughn)					
Chico (Horst Buchholz)					

OB on the web

Search YouTube for 'AT&T Archives: The year they discovered people (bonus edition)'. This summarizes the findings of the Hawthorne studies. It includes original film of the company and the experiments. These studies, now nearly ninety years old, continue to be taught and feature in all management and organizational behaviour textbooks. Were the Hawthorne studies mainly about productivity or about employee participation? Answer this question and write a report summarizing the continuing relevance of the Hawthorne studies to today's organizations.

CHAPTER EXERCISES

1. Group experiences

Objective Demonstrate how groups affect your work and social life.

Briefing

1. Individually,
   (a) Make a list of all the different groups to which you belong at the present time.
   (b) Distinguish work groups from non-work groups, and formal from informal groups.
2. Form groups.
   (a) Share the number of groups that you each belong to. What does this tell you about yourself and the way the world is organized?
   (b) Identify which types of groups all or most of you belong to. Why is this?
   (c) Using examples, explain how being in a group affects your behaviour. Do you behave differently when in a group than when alone? Do you behave differently in different groups?
3. In your groups,
   (a) Each person shares a *positive* experience that they have had while being a member of a group.
   (b) Each person shares a *negative* experience that they have had while being a member of a group.
   (c) Identify any common factors in your positive experiences, and any in your negative experiences.
   (d) What conclusions do you draw about the way that groups should be designed and managed?

2. Work group arrangements

Objectives

1. Analyse a group's behaviour using a theoretical framework.
2. Assess the situation from a management perspective.

Briefing

1. Form into groups.
2. Analyse the *Factory paint shop case* below using Homans's model: environment of group (physical, technological, social); external system (required activities, required interactions, required sentiments): internal system (emergent activities, emergent interactions, emergent sentiments).
3. Make the case for and against management intervention. Give your reasons and state your recommendations.

Factory paint shop case

Factory work can be boring and monotonous. Employees must work at the pace of the assembly line or machine, with output levels closely prescribed and monitored by management. It is not surprising that factory workers will try anything to break the boredom and relentless grind of the controlled activity in a factory. In a particular factory a large paint-spraying machine was approximately 100 metres long and required a team of 24 people to keep it running. There were only 18 workstations on the machine, but the staffing plan was that six people would float between jobs, thereby allowing everyone to take a break whilst keeping the machine running. In practice four people would be in the mess room for their entire shift running a card syndicate. Everyone else in the work team would take shorter breaks and simply drop in and out of the card game as their breaks allowed. A different team of four people would be informally 'rostered'

→

each day so that over a period everyone had the total break time allowed by the company. The team achieved their allowed breaks in a way not intended (or approved) by management. Gambling was not allowed by the company either, but this did not bother the workers. Supervisors also turned a blind eye to the process as long as the work was completed and productivity was at acceptable levels.

Employability assessment

With regard to your future employment prospects:

1. Identify up to three issues from this chapter that you found significant.
2. Relate these to the competencies in the employability matrix.
3. Decide what actions you need to take to maintain and/or develop those competencies under each of the four headings of the employability matrix.

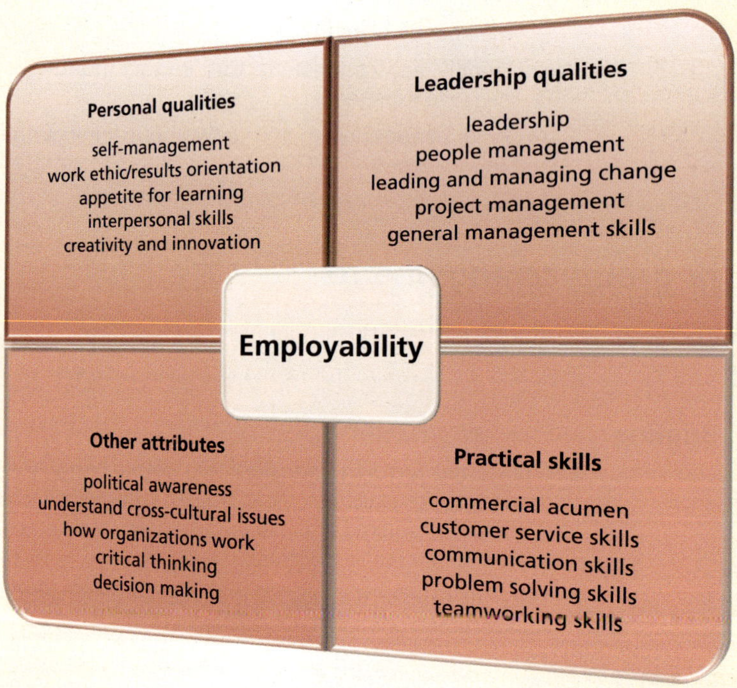

References

Ackroyd, S. and Thompson, P. (1999) *Organizational Misbehaviour*, London: Sage Publications.

Allen, J., James, A.D. and Gamlen, P. (2007) 'Formal versus informal knowledge networks in R&D: a case study using social network analysis', *R&D Management*, 37(3), pp. 179–96.

Amos, J. (2010) 'Cosmonauts chosen for Mars test', *BBC News*, 10 May.

Amos, J. (2011) 'Simulated Mars mission "lands" back on Earth', *BBC News*, 4 November.

Arrow, H. and McGrath, J.E. (1995) 'Membership dynamics in groups at work: a theoretical framework', *Research in Organizational Behaviour*, 17, pp. 373–411.

Barnes, A. (2008) 'The construction of control: the physical environment and the development of resistance and accommodation within call centres', *New Technology, Work and Employment*, 22(3), pp. 246–59.

Blitz, R. (2007) 'Winning formula', *Financial Times Magazine*, 11 August, pp. 22–3.

Borrill, C. and West, M. (2005) 'The psychology of effective teamworking', in N. Gold (ed.), *Teamwork*, London: Palgrave Macmillan, pp. 136–60.

Cain, S. (2012) *Quiet: The Power of Introverts in a World that Can't Stop Talking*, New York: Crown Publishing.

Catmull, E. (2008) 'How Pixar fosters collective creativity', *Harvard Business Review*, 86(9), pp. 64–72.

Cohen, A.R., Fink, S.L., Gadon, H. and Willits, R.D. (1995) *Effective Behaviour in Organizations* (6th edn), Homewood, IL: Irwin.

Cook, J. (2008) 'Perks make Google office hardly feel like work', from http://www.seattlepi.com/business/347434_google16.html, accessed 18 January 2009.

Coutu, D. (2009) 'Why teams don't work', *Harvard Business Review*, 87(5), pp. 99–105.

Cross, R. and Parker, A. (2004) *The Hidden Power of Social Networks*, Cambridge, MA: Harvard Business School Press.

Cross, R. and Prusak, L. (2002) 'The people who make organizations go – or stop', *Harvard Business Review*, 80(6), pp. 104–12.

Daft, R. and Marcic, D. (2009) *Management: The New Workplace* (6th edn), London: South-Western Cengage Learning.

Diehl, M. and Stroebe, W. (1991) 'Productivity loss in idea generating groups: tracking down the blocking effect', *Journal of Personality and Social Psychology*, 61(3), pp. 392–403.

Driscoll, M. (2012) 'Do not disturb: Loners do the best work', *The Sunday Times*, 22 January, p. 8.

Edmondson, A.C. and Roloff, K.S. (2009) 'Overcoming barriers in collaboration: Psychological safety in diverse teams' in Salas, E., Goodwin, G.F. and Burke, C.S. (eds), *Team Effectiveness in Complex Organizations: Cross Disciplinary Perspectives and Approaches*, London: Routledge.

Edwards, D. (2011) *I'm Feeling Lucky: The Confessions of Google Employee Number 59*, London: Allen Lane.

European Foundation for the Improvement of Living and Working Conditions (2007) *Fourth European Working Conditions Survey*, http://eurofound.europa.eu.

Forsyth, D.R. (2006) *Group Dynamics*, London: Thomson Wadsworth.

Gersick, C.J. (1988) 'Time and transition in work teams', *Academy of Management Journal*, 31(1), pp. 9–41.

Gersick, C.J. (1989) 'Marking time: predictable transitions in task group', *Academy of Management Journal*, 32(2), pp. 274–309.

Gillespie, R. (1991) *Manufacturing Knowledge: A History of the Hawthorne Experiments*, Cambridge: Cambridge University Press.

Greenberg, J. and Baron, R.A. (1997) *Behaviour in Organizations* (6th edn), Englewood Cliffs, NJ: Pearson/Prentice Hall.

Hampton, M.M. (1999) 'Work groups', in Yiannis Gabriel (ed.), *Organizations in Depth*, London: Sage Publications, pp. 112–38.

Hayes, N. (1997) *Successful Team Management*, London: International Thomson Business Press.

Hill, A. (2012) 'We should stop trying to change the world', *Financial Times*, 27 March, p. 14.

Hindle, T. (2006) 'Take a deep breath', *The Economist, The New Organization: A Survey of the Company*, 21 January, pp. 5, 6 and 8.

Hochschild, A.R. (1997) *The Time Bind: When Home Becomes Work and Work Becomes Home*, New York: Owl Books.

Homans, G.C. (1951) *The Human Group*, London: Routledge and Kegan Paul.

Ignattius, A. (2006) 'In search of the real Google', *Time*, 20 February, pp. 32–42.

Johnson, D.W. and Johnson, F.P. (2012) *Joining Together: Group Theory and Group Skills* (11th edn), Harlow: Pearson.

Jones, J.E. (1973) 'Model of group development', in, *The 1973 Annual Handbook for Group Facilitators*, San Francisco, CA: Jossey-Bass, pp. 127–9.

Katzenbach, J.R. and Santamaria, J.A. (1999) 'Firing up the front line', *Harvard Business Review*, 77(3), pp. 107–17.

Knights, D. and McCabe, D. (2000) 'Bewitched, bothered and bewildered: the meaning and experience of teamworking for employees in an automobile plant', *Human Relations*, 53(11), pp. 1481–1518.

Kozlowski, S.W.J. and Bell, B. (2003) 'Work groups and teams in organizations', in W.C. Boreman, D.R. Ilgen and I.B. Weiner (eds), *Handbook of Industrial and Organizational Psychology*, Vol. 12, New York: Wiley, pp. 333–76.

Leavitt, H.J. (1975) 'Suppose we took groups seriously', in E.L. Cass and F.G. Zimmer (eds), *Man and Work in Society*, London: Van Nostrand Reinhold, pp. 67–77.

Likert, R. (1961) *New Patterns of Management*, New York: McGraw-Hill.

Littlepage, G.E. (1991) 'Effects of group size and task characteristics on group performance: a test of Steiner's model', *Personality and Social Psychology Bulletin*, 17(4), pp. 449–56.

McGrath, J.E. (1984) *Groups: Interaction and Performance*, Upper Saddle River, NJ: Prentice Hall.

Manz, C.C., Pearce, C.L. and Sims, H.P. (2009) 'The ins and outs of leading teams', *Organizational Dynamics*, 38(3), pp. 179–82.

Mayo, E. (1945) *The Social Problems of an Industrial Civilization*, Cambridge, MA: Harvard University Press.

Mintzberg, H. (2009) 'Rebuilding companies as communities', *Harvard Business Review*, 76(7/8), pp. 140–3.

Mohrman, S.A., Cohen, S.G. and Mohrman, A.M. (1995) *Designing Team-Based Organizations*, San Francisco, CA: Jossey-Bass.

Nadler, D., Behan, M.A. and Nadler, B.A. (2006) *Building Better Boards*, San Francisco, CA: Jossey-Bass.

Noon, M. and Blyton, P. (2007) *The Realities of Work* (3rd edn), Basingstoke: Palgrave.

Ouchi, W.G. and Johnson, A.M. (1978) 'Type Z organizations: stability in the midst of mobility', *Academy of Management Review*, 3(2), pp. 305–14.

Peters, T. (1987) *Thriving on Chaos: Handbook for a Management Revolution*, London: Macmillan.

Reeves, B., Malone, T.W. and O'Driscoll, T. (2008) 'Leadership online labs', *Harvard Business Review*, 86(5), pp. 58–66.

Reimers, J.M. and Parsons, G. (2003) 'Case study: *Remember the Titans* (2000) to examine power, servant leadership, transformational leadership, followership and change', *Journal of Behavioural and Applied Management*, 5(2), pp. 152–65.

Roethlisberger, F.J. and Dickson, W.J. (1939) *Management and the Worker*, Cambridge, MA: Harvard University Press.

Rose, M. (1988) *Industrial Behaviour and Control*, Harmondsworth, Middlesex: Penguin Books.

Smith, G.W. (2009) 'Using feature films as the primary instructional medium to teach organizational behaviour', *Journal of Management Education*, 33(4), pp. 462–89.

Steiner, I. (1972) *Group Process and Productivity*, New York: Academic Press.

Steiner, I. and Rajaratnam, N.A. (1961) 'A model for the comparison of individual and group performance scores', *Behavioural Science*, 6(2), pp. 142–7.

Taher, A. (2009) 'Number's up for "unlucky" eight', *The Sunday Times*, 11 January, p. 7.

The Economist (2007) 'Inside the Googleplex', 1 September, pp. 52–4.

Tuckman, B.W. and Jensen, M.A.C. (1977) 'Stages of small group development revisited', *Group and Organizational Studies*, 2(4), pp. 419–27.

Van Knippenburg, D. and Schippers, M.C. (2007) 'Work group diversity', *Annual Review of Psychology*, 58, pp. 515–41.

Vašková, R. (2007) *Teamwork and High Performance Team Organization* European Foundation for the Improvement of Living and Working Conditions, http://eurofound.europa.eu.

Wood, W.S. (2001) 'Can we go to Mars without going crazy?', *Discover Magazine*, 5 May, from http://discovermagazine.com/2001/may/cover, accessed May 2009.

Wuchty, S., Jones, B.F. and Uzzi, B. (2007) 'The increasing dominance of teams in production of knowledge', *Science*, 316 (5827), pp. 1036–8.

Chapter 11 **Group structure**

Key terms

team player
group structure
group process
power
formal status
social status
sociometry
sociogram
communication network analysis
communigram
communication pattern analysis
communication pattern chart
Interaction Process Analysis
task activity
maintenance activity
social role
team role
virtual team
global virtual team
synchronous communication
asynchronous communication

Learning outcomes

When you have read this chapter, you should be able to define those key terms in your own words, and you should also be able to:

1. List the six dimensions of group structure.
2. Identify the sources of power within the group.
3. Distinguish between two common uses of the concept of status.
4. Understand how emotional relationships within a group can be represented symbolically.
5. Distinguish between communication network analysis, communication pattern analysis, and Interaction Process Analysis.
6. Distinguish between task, socio-emotional, and individual classes of roles within a group.
7. Distinguish Belbin's team roles.
8. Give examples of three leadership styles identified by White and Lippitt.
9. Distinguish between a task and a socio-emotional group leader.
10. List the four key dimensions of a virtual team.

Why study group structure?

Organizations are keen to employ people who work well together. Nicky Binning, a senior manager at KPMG, says that

> There is now such a pace of change that it almost doesn't matter what you have done in the past . . . It is the ability to understand what is in front of you, and work collaboratively that counts. You have to work together as a team because it is likely that you are facing something that you have never faced before. (Tieman, 2012)

An individual from a function like marketing may be delegated to participate in various teams which can be face-to-face, project, ad hoc, virtual, cross-cultural, or a combination of these. Increasingly, members of one firm may be required to create a joint team with those of another company, in order to meet a client's needs. A study by Pam Jones of teamworking in 600 organizations around the world revealed that 75 per cent of them were dispersed geographically; 30 per cent were spread across time zones; and half were 'virtual' and rarely met (Tieman, 2012). Companies' need for collaboration skills among employees has heightened the search for the **team player**. This is the person who is humble, does not pursue personal glory, values the performance of the group over individual recognition, and is committed to a common goal and to achieving it selflessly.

Team player a person who works willingly in cooperation with others for the benefit of the whole team.

Robert Jackall (1988) concluded that the language of team playing derived from American football and was used to discipline individuals into conforming. From his research, he argued that advancement in large organizations relied on being seen as a 'team player' and on not standing out from the team by displaying strong convictions or distinctive characteristics. However, how the group or team as a whole performs depends very much on the behaviour and contribution of its individual members. Because so much work in organizations is now done in groups and teams, companies invest a great deal of time and effort during the selection process to find applicants who are good 'team players'. Michael Stevens and Michael Campion (1994, 1999) listed the knowledge, skills, and attitudes (KSAs) needed by team members for team success. As Table 11.1 shows, these are divided into interpersonal and self-management clusters, each with its own sets of particular KSAs.

Table 11.1: Knowledge, skills, and abilities possessed by team players

Interpersonal KSAs
1. Conflict resolution Recognizing the types and sources of conflict; encouraging functional and discouraging dysfunctional conflict; employing win-win negotiation strategies.
2. Collaborative problem-solving Identifying situations in which participative group problem-solving is appropriate; judging the appropriate degree of participation; overcoming obstacles to ensure it happens.
3. Communication Understanding and using decentralized communication networks; achieving consistency in verbal and non-verbal communication; correctly interpreting others' non-verbal communication.
Self-management KSAs
4. Goal-setting and performance management Establishing specific, challenging, and accepted team goals; evaluating progress towards them; providing feedback to members on their own and overall team performance.
5. Planning and task coordination Coordinating team members' activities and tasks; assisting them to establish individual tasks and role assignments, thereby balancing the workload between members.

Source: adapted from Stevens, M.J. and Campion, M.A., *Journal of Management*, Vol. 20, No. 2, pp. 503–530, The knowledge, skill and ability requirements for teamwork: Implications for human resource management, Copyright © 1994, Southern Management Association. Reprinted by permission of SAGE Publications.

STOP AND THINK

'Companies want to hire applicants who are good team players.'

What does that mean to you in practice? Do you think that you are a good or poor team player?

Having selected and trained new employees to work in groups, management monitors how well they perform in order to pinpoint any problems and rectify them so as to raise team effectiveness. Group structure is an important aspect of 'engineering the group'. When a group or team is performing poorly, a management consultant may be brought in to observe its operation and to evaluate its outputs. The consultant will initially focus on the group's individual members, assessing their performance of their roles, and ensuring that everyone is working well together. Individuals who are not contributing or who do not 'fit in' may be replaced by others. The consultant checks that communication between team members is timely and effective, that group members are clear about the goals, that leadership within the group is contributing towards the achievement of those goals, and that the way decisions are reached secures the commitment of members.

Team problem

There were four team members named Everybody, Somebody, Anybody, and Nobody.

There was an important job to do and Everybody was asked to do it.

Everybody was sure Somebody would do it.

Anybody could have done it, but Nobody did.

Everybody was angry about that, because it was Somebody's job.

Everybody thought Anybody could do it, but Nobody realized that Everybody wouldn't.

In the end, Everybody blamed Somebody when Nobody did what Anybody could have done.

Source unknown.

Group structure and process

Group structure the relatively stable pattern of relationships among different group members.

A central idea in helping us to examine the nature and functioning of groups is that of structure. **Group structure** refers to the way in which members of a group relate to one another. The formation of group structure is one of the basic aspects of group development. When people come together and interact, differences between individuals begin to appear. Some talk while others listen; some make decisions, while others accept them; some ask for information, while others provide it. These differences between group members serve as the basis for the establishment of group structure. As differentiation occurs, relations are established between members. Group structure is the label given to this patterning of relationships.

Group structure carries with it the connotation of something fixed and unchanging. While there is an element of permanency in terms of the relationships between members, these do continue to change and modify. Group members continually interact with each other, and in consequence their relationships are tested and transformed. As we describe the structure of any group, it is useful to view it as a snapshot, correct at the time the shutter was pressed, but to acknowledge that things were different the moments before and after the photo was taken.

Differences between the members of a group begin to occur as soon as it is formed. This differentiation within a group occurs not along one dimension, but along several. The most important of these are

- power;
- status;

- liking;
- communication;
- role;
- leadership.

There are as many structures in a group as there are dimensions along which a group can be differentiated. Although in common usage we talk about the structure of a group, in reality a group will differentiate simultaneously along a number of dimensions. Group members will be accorded different amounts of status and hence a group will have a status hierarchy. Members will be able to exert differing amounts of power and thus a power structure will emerge. While it is possible to examine each structural dimension of the group in turn, we need to remember that all are closely related and operate simultaneously in a group setting. A group's structure is determined by

- the requirements for efficient group performance;
- the abilities and motivations of group members;
- the psychological and social environment of the group.

Why does a group have structure?

Why does a patterning of relationships between individuals in a group occur and what purpose does it serve? Robert Bales (1950a) offered a psychological explanation based on the individual's desire for stability, 'need for order', and 'low tolerance of ambiguity'. He argued that meeting and dealing with other people within a group can cause an individual stress. It is the potential uncertainty and unpredictability in the actions of others that causes this. If the behaviour between group members can be made predictable, this can reduce the tension for all concerned. This, he explained, is what group structure does.

A sociological explanation would point to structure as a manifestation of power, with structure 'imposed' on groups (as a natural aspect of efficient functioning, of course) to maintain the power position of key players in the organization. All groups are overlaid with the power and cultural patterns of the organization within which they exist. Whether a group's structure results from its members' basic need for predictability, or is imposed by powerful outsiders, the effect in either case is to create differences between the individuals within the group along several dimensions at the same time (e.g. status, role, power). One person will therefore simultaneously have high status and power since each person stands at the intersection of several dimensions. The combination of all of these for each group member is referred to as their position in the group structure. A group's structure will be affected by **group process**, which refers to the group activity which occurs over time, specifically to the oral and non-verbal contributions of group members. Examples of a group's process include

Group process the patterns of interactions between the members of a group.

- direction of communication (who talks to whom);
- quantity of communication (number of times each group member speaks);
- content of communication (type of oral utterance made);
- decision-making style (how decisions are made in the group);
- problem-solving style (how problems are approached and solved).

The structure of a group can affect its process. For example, when an individual is appointed the leader of a formal group, they will tend to speak more often, and will be listened to more closely. Being group leader will therefore determine the direction, frequency, and content of their communication with others in the group. Conversely, group process can determine group structure. In an informal group, the individual who speaks most often to all fellow members may come to be liked the most. Their status will rise in the eyes of the other members, and they may be given permission to take on a leadership role within the group. If a group can become aware of its processes, and manage them better, then it is likely to achieve improved outcomes.

Power structure

Power the capacity of individuals to overcome resistance on the part of others, to exert their will, and to produce results consistent with their interests and objectives.

Individual members of a group differ in terms of how much **power** they each possess, and hence in their ability to direct the behaviour of other members. For this reason, it becomes necessary for the group to have established control relations between members. This means clarifying and accepting which types of power are possessed by different members of the group. By having a power structure, the group avoids continued power struggles, which can disrupt its functioning. It can also link activities intended to achieve its goals to a system of authority which is seen as legitimate by all members (Dahl, 1957).

Various writers have defined power in terms of influence. Power is an aspect not only in relationships between individuals within a group, but also in leadership relations and political issues. We shall therefore re-visit the work of these authors in other chapters. For now, we can draw upon the classic work of John French and Bertram Raven (1958), who saw power as a property not of the individual, but of the relationship. These authors distinguished five types of power:

- **reward power**: the ability to exert influence based on the other's belief that the influencer has access to valued rewards which will be dispensed in return for compliance;
- **coercive power**: the ability to exert influence based on the other's belief that the influencer can administer unwelcome penalties or sanctions;
- **referent power**: the ability to exert influence based on the other's belief that the influencer has desirable abilities and personality traits that can and should be copied;
- **legitimate power**: the ability to exert influence based on the other's belief that the influencer has authority to issue orders which they in turn have an obligation to accept;
- **expert power**: the ability to exert influence based on the other's belief that the influencer has superior knowledge relevant to the situation and the task.

Saying that power is a property of the relationship and not of the individual means that, for example, what matters is not whether or not you actually have rewards to distribute, but rather the fact that others *perceive* you to have that ability. So you have reward power when others believe that you have rewards up your sleeve, even if you do not.

Home viewing

Aliens (1986, director James Cameron) is a science fiction thriller set in the distant future on the planet LV-426. The characters in this group include Lieutenant Gorman (the senior officer of the space marines), Sergeant Apone, and Corporal Hicks. In addition to these military personnel, there is Burke, who represents the Weyland-Yutani Corporation that owns the facilities on the planet and employs Ripley. Watch the first part of the film from the scene where Burke and Gorman visit Ripley's quarters to persuade her to join the expedition to the point where, having escaped the creature's attack, they decide to 'nuke the planet'. Use French and Raven's five types of power, introduced in this chapter, to decide which of the characters possesses which type(s) within the group. Also assess who gains and who loses which type of power. How does this happen? What does this tell us about the power structure of a group?

STOP AND THINK

- Who gains from having stable power in a group, and why?
- Who loses, how, and why?
- Make the argument for having an *unstable* power structure in a group.

Status structure

Status is a prestige ranking within a group that is independent of formal status or position. It is closely related to leadership, because if an individual's higher status is accepted by others within the group, they can influence, control, or command those around them. Status ranking indicates the group's 'pecking order'. Some writers argue that status is important because it motivates people and has consequences for their behaviour. This is particularly the case when individuals perceive a disparity between their own perception of themselves and how others perceive them to be. Each position in a group has a value placed upon it. Within the organization, a value is ascribed by the formal organization to a position such as chief executive officer, vice-president, or supervisor, and this can be labelled formal status. **Formal status** is best thought of as being synonymous with rank as in the police or the armed forces and reflects a person's position on the 'organizational ladder'.

Formal status the collection of rights and obligations associated with a position, as distinct from the person who may occupy that position.

Social status the relative ranking that a person holds and the value of that person as measured by a group.

A second way in which value is placed on a position is the social honour or prestige that is accorded an individual in a group by the other group members. In this second sense, the word status is prefixed by the word 'social', indicating the degree of informally established value accorded to that position, as compared with other positions, as perceived by both the formal and the informal group. While one can view **social status** as a sort of badge of honour awarded for meritorious group conduct, it can also be viewed as a set of unwritten rules about the kind of behaviour that people in a group are expected to exhibit with regard to one another. It can indicate the degree of respect, familiarity, or reserve that is appropriate in a given situation.

One of the powers possessed by an informal group is its ability to confer status on those of its members who meet the expectations of the group. These members are looked up to by their peers, not because of any formal position they may hold in the organization, but because of their position in the social group. Many people actively seek status in order to fulfil their need for self-esteem. The granting of it by the group provides them with personal satisfaction. Similarly, the withholding of status can act as a group control mechanism to bring a deviant group member into line. The status accorded by the group to a member is immediate in terms of face-to-face feedback. The recognition and esteem given to group members reinforces their identification with the group and increases their dependence upon it. A group member's informal status may be due to their ability to contribute to a group's goals – those whose contributions are critical to group success are accorded higher status – or to their possession of personal characteristics valued by the group (e.g. intelligence, money, good looks, friendly personality).

Within a formal group or team, individual members will be accorded formal status, based on hierarchical position and task ability. The organization is made up of a number of defined positions arranged in order of their increasing authority. The formal status hierarchy reflects the potential ability of the holders of positions to contribute to the overall goals of the organization. It differentiates the amounts of respect deserved and simultaneously ranks them on a status scale. The outward symbols associated with formal status (e.g. size of office, quality of carpet) are there to inform other members in the organization of where exactly that person stands on the 'organizational ladder'. This topic leads ultimately to the issue of organization structure, which will be considered later.

STOP AND THINK Consider a group of which you are currently a member. What action could you take to change your status in this group and what impact would this have on your relationships and friendships?

What effect does the status structure have on group behaviour? Research shows that, as one would expect, people with higher status in a group have more power and tend to be more influential than those with lower status (Greenberg, 1976). Knowing this, individual members may take steps to enhance their status in the eyes of their colleagues, and thereby be able to get the group to make the decisions that they want.

Status, authority and problem-solving in an aeroplane cockpit

Xavier Marchant/Dreamstime.com

Commercial aeroplanes are piloted by groups, not individuals. The actions needed when taxiing, taking off, flying, making the final approach, and landing all require the cockpit crew to work together. However, smooth group working can be impeded by status differences and group dynamics. Larger aircraft consist of a pilot, a co-pilot and a flight engineer. To indicate the relative social status and authority of each position, these roles are labelled captain, flight engineer, and second officer. By law, the final authority on board rests with the captains, who exert their authority and power in various ways. The US National Transportation Safety Board attributed the causes of many fatal crashes to two factors – the captain's refusal to comply with the suggestions of other crew members, and the crew's excessive obedience to the captain's authority. A near miss occurred when a captain ignored his co-pilot's warning to reduce airspeed. In the case of a DC-8 running out of fuel and crashing in Portland, Oregon, the flight recorder revealed that the captain had ignored the flight engineer's repeated reminders of their dwindling fuel. A Northwest Express Airlines co-pilot failed to correct the captain's errors on an approach, leading to a crash. Aviation authorities have now recognized the abuse of power by captains and the negative impact of excessive obedience by flight crews. Rather than attempt to change the group structure in terms of the norms of hierarchy and cockpit deference, they have sought to improve communication between all members of the flight crew. To fly safely, team members need to engage in the behaviours of *inquiring* why one member is taking certain actions; *advocating* alternative options; and *asserting* their views on matters. The accident literature is full of examples where this had not been done (Foushee, 1984; Milanovich et al., 1998; National Transportation Safety Board, 1994; Tarnow, 2000).

Interaction with others perceived as lower in status can be threatening because of the potential identification of the person with the group or individual being associated with. Status is abstract and ascribed through the perceptions of others. One's status is therefore always tenuous. It may be withdrawn or downgraded at any time. The reference group with which one identifies, and whose values and behaviour one adopts, plays an important part in establishing and maintaining one's status. To preserve that status, one cannot leave the reference group for a lower-status reference group.

Sociometry the study of interpersonal feelings and relationships within groups.

Liking structure

Jacob Levy Moreno (1889–1974)

Within any group, individual members will like, dislike, or be indifferent to other members, in varying degrees. Their combined feelings towards each other represent their group's liking structure. This can be studied using the technique of **sociometry**. The term derives from the Latin *socius* (companion) and the Greek *metron* (measure). Sociometry was devised by Jacob Moreno, who coined the term in his book *Who Shall Survive?* (Moreno, 1953). Moreno and his colleagues originally used the technique in their research in the New York Training School for Girls in the 1930s. They mapped the friendship choices among girls in a reformatory.

Sociometry diagrammatically maps the emotional relationships between individual members in a group on the basis of their personal choices of selection and rejection of other group members using a few standard symbols. This network of a group's interpersonal feelings is exposed by the use of sociometric tests. These reveal the spontaneous feelings and choices that individuals in a group have and make towards each other. Moreno asked individuals to complete the test. This revealed that spontaneous feelings within a person are divided into three classes – attraction (liking), rejection (disliking), and indifference (neutral feeling). A sociometric assessment is made using a preference questionnaire through which group members are asked with whom they would prefer (or not prefer) to work, study, play, or live. After analysing the answers, Moreno calculated how many times an individual had been chosen as a comrade by the other members of the group for the activity in question. This feeling (the sociometric term for which is *tele)*, may be one of attraction (positive *tele*) or repulsion (negative *tele*); alternatively there may merely be indifference. As shown in Figure 11.1, the members' choices are depicted on a **sociogram**, which reveals the group's liking structure by showing all the different members' positions. A sociometric assessment can reveal 'stars', 'isolates', 'neglectees', 'rejectees', 'mutual pairs', and 'mutual trios' in a group (see Table 11.2).

Sociogram a chart which shows the liking (social attraction) relationships between individual members of a group.

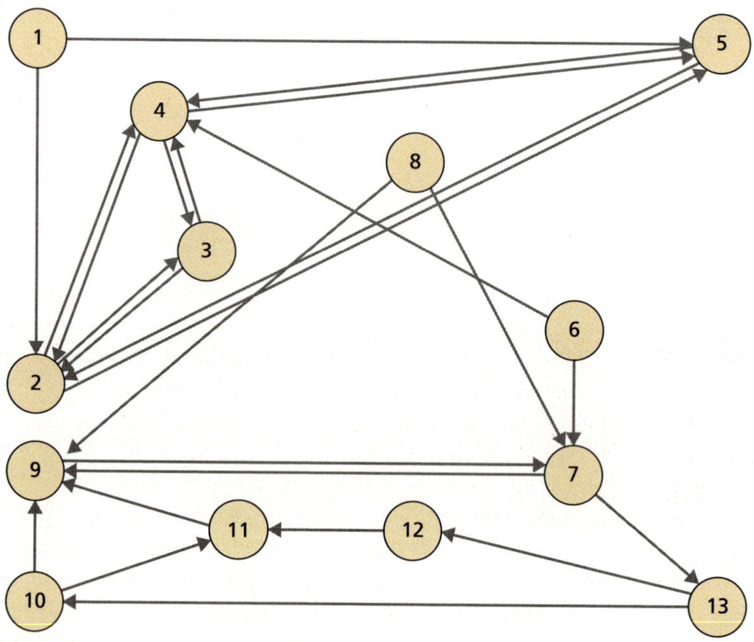

Figure 11.1: Sociogram

Table 11.2: Sociometric positions within a group

Star	Recipient of a large number of choices, sometimes described as 'over-chosen'
Isolate	Person who makes no choices at all and receives none, i.e., a relationship of mutual indifference to the remainder of the group
Neglectee	Person who, although he or she makes choices, receives none at all
Rejectee	Person who is not chosen by anyone and who is rejected by one or more persons
Mutual pair or mutual trio	Individuals who choose one another

STOP AND THINK

Look at the sociogram in Figure 11.1. Identify a 'star', an 'isolate', a 'neglectee', a 'rejectee', a 'mutual pair', and a 'mutual trio'.

Sociometry continues to be applied in organizations today under its newer label of *social network analysis* (Kilduff and Krackhardt, 2008). A company's formal organization structure is depicted on its organizational chart, but its informal organization can only be revealed through a sociometric assessment. Sociograms can be used to avoid personality clashes, raise group cohesion, and increase a group's performance (for example, it may be used with flight crews). The method can also be used to reveal the feelings of unhappy pupil isolates who may not have adjusted to their school class group, or isolate employees who have not fitted into work teams. Comparative sociograms of productive and unproductive teams can highlight areas where aspects of group structure require modification. Sociograms have also been used in the selection and training of group leaders to increase cooperation, productivity, and morale amongst employees, and to anticipate turnover and conflict problems.

Communication network analysis a technique that uses direct observation to determine the source, direction, and quantity of oral communication between congregated members of a group.

STOP AND THINK Think of an organization with which you are familiar. Identify two individuals with whom you would *not* like to work in a group. List the reasons for your reluctance.

Communication structure

To understand the communication structure of a group, it is necessary to know the pattern of positions, that is, the role and status of every member, and the duration and direction of communication from position to position. Each group member depends on information provided by others. Solving a problem, making a decision, or reaching agreement all require information exchange between individuals. The members of a group may work closely together, interacting frequently, and attending regular meetings. Alternatively, they may be physically dispersed within a building or located in different buildings, and therefore only able to come together occasionally, to attend a meeting. Increasingly, different members of the same group may be located in different countries (globally dispersed groups) and interact through videoconferencing. Whatever the situation, there are different ways to determine a group's communication structure.

Communigram a chart that indicates the source, direction, and quantity of oral communication between the members during a group meeting.

Communication network analysis

When group members come physically together, meet face-to-face, and participate in a meeting around a table, they are said to be *co-located*. In such circumstances, a **communication network analysis** of their meeting can be conducted. This approach was pioneered by Noel Tichy and Charles Fombrun (1979). The observer makes a note of each participant's oral utterance and to whom they direct their comment. The outcome is a **communigram**. In some ways this resembles a sociogram, but, instead of detailing mutual liking, it answers the questions of who spoke to whom and how often. An example is shown in Figure 11.2.

Communication pattern analysis a technique that uses analysis of documents, data, and voicemail transmission to determine the source, direction, and quantity of oral and written communication between the dispersed members of a group.

Communication pattern analysis

When members of a group are physically dispersed around the same building, around different buildings, or even in different countries, it is still possible to determine the source, frequency, and direction of their communication with each other by using **communication pattern analysis**. Instead of observing the interactions between individuals, which is impossible, the researcher would note the initiation and direction of telephone conversations, memos, texts, and emails between the group's members. This information is documented in a **communication pattern chart**.

Communication pattern chart indicates the source, direction, and quantity of oral and written communication between the dispersed members of a group.

For example, the information flow between the members of a group can take the form of a chain. A tells B, B tells C, and so on. In his classic study, William Foote Whyte (1948) described

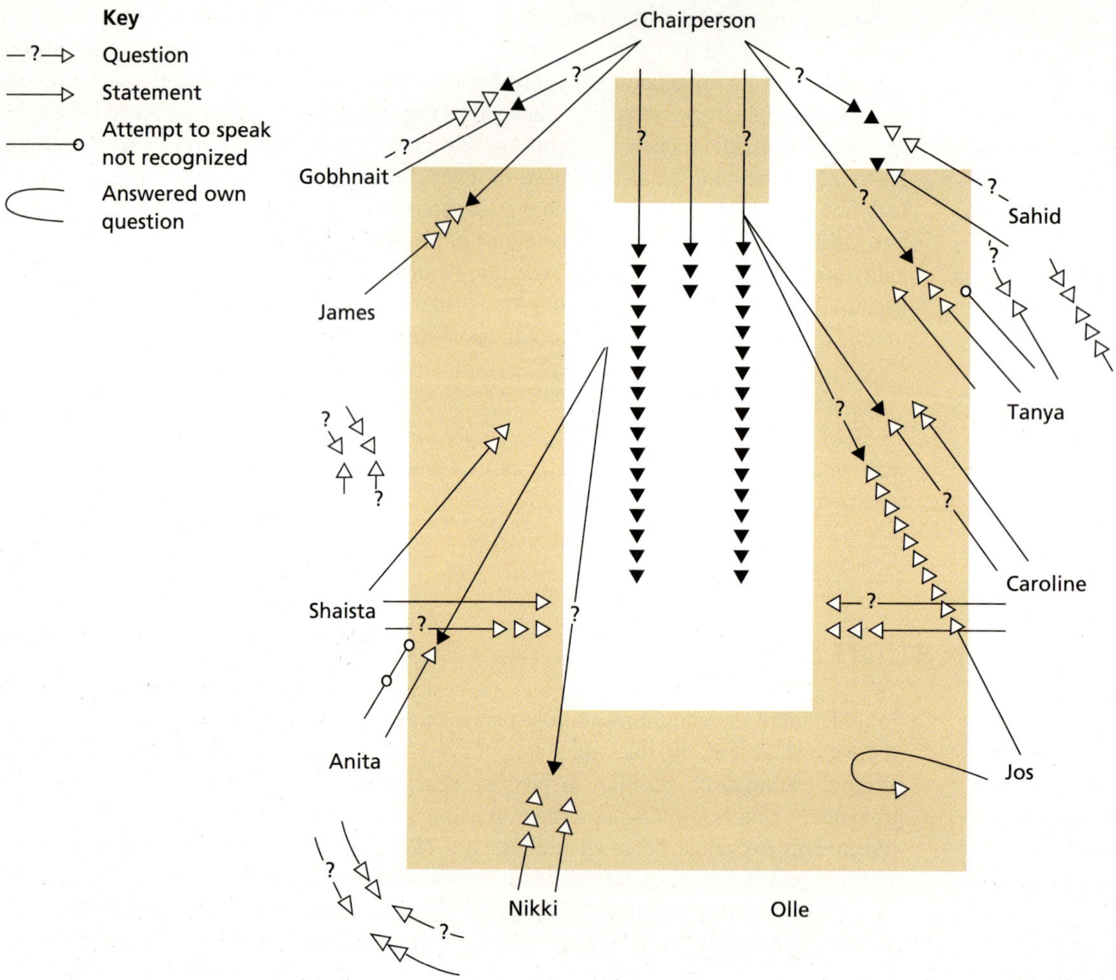

Figure 11.2: Communigram showing participation at a meeting

one such chain pattern in a restaurant in which customers gave their orders to a waitress, who passed it to a runner, who passed it to a pantry worker, before it was finally delivered to the cook. This communication network could produce a distortion in the message. When information arrived through this route, the cook was unable to check it; had no opportunity to negotiate with the customer; and hence was unable to discuss any problems.

The aforementioned 'chain' is only one of several communication networks used by groups. To discover the full range, and the effectiveness of each, Marvin Shaw (1978) conducted a laboratory experiment to test if certain group communication networks impeded or facilitated the performance of a task. While all the communication networks studied were adequate for the group to do the task, he discovered that some were superior in terms of standing up to disruption and encouraging the emergence of leadership. Shaw studied the effects of five group communication networks on task performance and member satisfaction, and these are shown in Figure 11.3.

The way in which different communication networks affect group functioning in terms of group performance, structure, and member satisfaction continues to be a subject of interest. Robert Baron and Jerald Greenberg (1990) studied the differences in performance between centralized and decentralized networks. The focus of their study was upon the type of task that a group was required to complete. The previous chapter distinguished between additive, conjunctive, and disjunctive tasks. Baron and Greenberg distinguished between 'simple' and 'complex' tasks. They concluded that centralized networks are superior on simple tasks (top), and decentralized networks are superior on complex tasks (bottom). These are summarized in Figure 11.4.

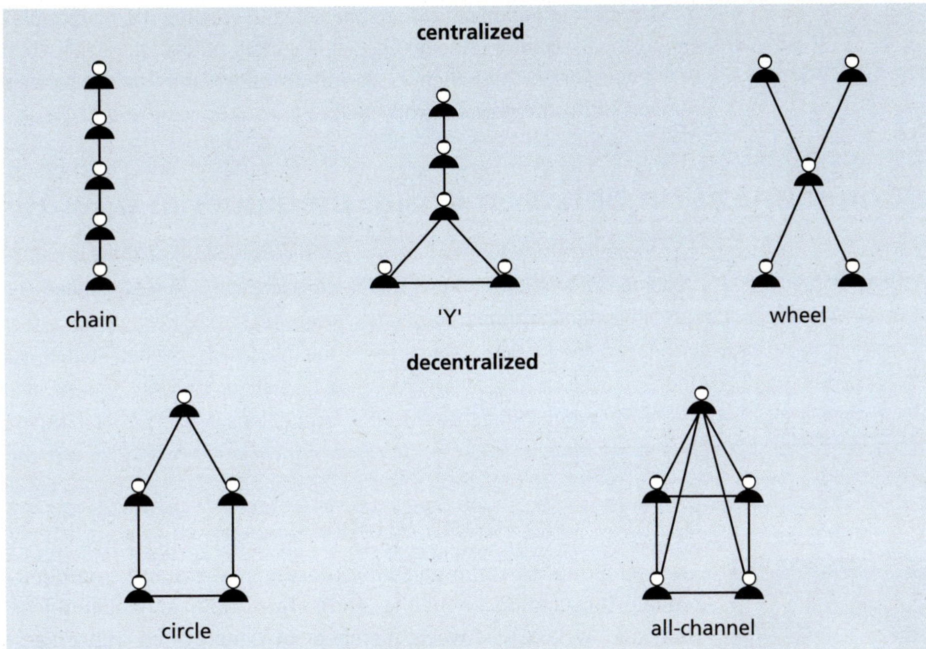

Figure 11.3: Centralized and decentralized communication patterns in groups

Source: this article was published in *Group Processes* edited by L. Berkowitz, M.E. Shaw, Communications networks fourteen years later, pp. 351–61, Copyright Elsevier 1978.

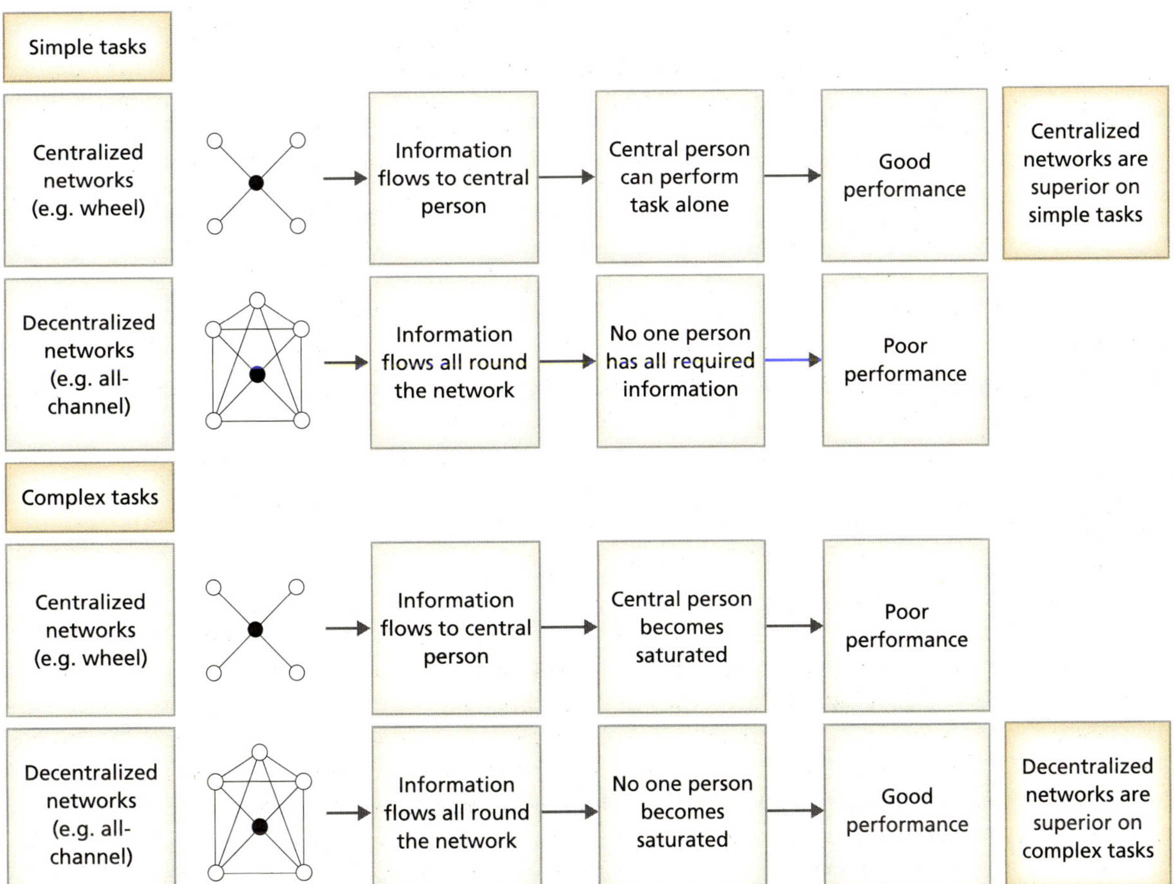

Figure 11.4: Task type and communication network performance

Source: from GREENBERG, JERALD; BARON, ROBERT A., BEHAVIOR IN ORGANIZATIONS, 6th Ed. © 1997. Reprinted and Electronically reproduced by permission of Pearson Education, Inc. Upper Saddle River, New Jersey.

Managers in organizations are interested in ensuring that a group's communication network supports rather than impedes the achievement of its task. Hence, by first identifying the type of network used, and then assessing its effect, they can take steps to match the type of network with the type of group task.

Communication between group members in operating theatres

Martin Makary and his colleagues from Johns Hopkins University surveyed 2,100 surgeons, anaesthesiologists, and nurses about operating room communications. Surgeons received the lowest, and nurses the highest, ratings for teamwork. Another study of 60 hospitals investigated surgical mistakes (e.g. leaving a sponge inside the patient) and concluded that these could be avoided with 'better collaboration'. Nurses defined 'better collaboration' as meaning having their input respected by physicians, while the physicians defined 'better collaboration' as nurses anticipating surgeons' needs and following surgeons' instructions (Makary et al., 2005, 2006).

Interaction Process Analysis

Robert Freed Bales (1916–2004)

Interaction Process Analysis a technique used to categorize the content of speech.

Task activity an oral input, made by a group member, that contributes directly to the group's work task.

Maintenance activity an oral input, made by a group member, that reduces conflict, maximizes cohesion, and maintains relationships within a group.

The techniques of communication process analysis and communications network analysis provide information about the source, direction, and quantity of verbal communication (oral and written) between members of congregated and dispersed teams respectively. However, neither of them considers the content of the communications between the individuals involved. When we observe a congregated group in action, for example, rugby players discussing their strategy for the second half, or a group of students discussing their tutorial system, what we observe are individuals saying certain things. If we want to study the content of their oral behaviour within that group, we need a precise and reliable way of categorizing it. Robert Freed Bales (1950b) and his colleagues at Harvard University's Laboratory of Social Relations went beyond their original research on who talked to whom and how often. He developed a technique for categorizing the *content* of group member's oral behaviours (utterances) that he called **Interaction Process Analysis** (IPA).

Bales discovered that every group engaged in two types of oral activities – **task activities** (getting the job done) and **maintenance activities** (keeping the group working together). He found that when work groups were assigned a task, such as solving a problem or making a recommendation, their members inevitably engaged in twelve different types of oral interactions which are shown in Table 11.3.

Table 11.3: Bales's categories of oral interaction in small groups

Task

Questions
1. Asks for orientation; direction; implying autonomy for others.
2. Asks for opinion, evaluation, analysis, expression of feeling.
3. Asks for orientation, information, repeats, clarifies, confirms.

Answers
4. Gives suggestion, direction, implying autonomy in others.
5. Gives opinion, evaluation, analysis, expresses feelings, wishes.
6. Gives orientation, information, repeats, clarifies, confirms.

Maintenance

Positive reactions
7. Shows solidarity, raises others' status, gives help, reward.
8. Releases tension; asks for help; withdraws from field.
9. Shows antagonism; deflates others' status, defends or asserts self.

Negative reactions
10. Disagrees, shows passive rejection, formality, withholds help.
11. Shows tension release; asks for help; withdraws out of field.
12. Shows antagonism; deflates others' status; defends or asserts self.

Based on Bales (1959).

One can classify or 'code' each person's oral utterance during a group discussion, into these twelve categories. For example, Category 7 is 'shows solidarity, raises others' status, gives help, reward'. So, if one group member said 'That's an excellent idea from Lucy', that would be an example of a category 7 utterance. In contrast, Category 12 is 'shows antagonism; deflates other's status; defends or asserts self'. If another member said 'Jill's report was pathetic! I could do one that was twice as good in half the time', that would be an example of a category 12 utterance. Bales felt that with his twelve categories, one could classify most utterances that were likely to be made by individuals in a group when they engaged in oral interaction. In his original experiments, his researchers acted as observers, and watched groups from behind a one-way mirror.

Analysing oral interactions in a group

Below is a simplified version of Bales's Interaction Process Analysis (IPA) oral behaviour classification scheme. It consists of six oral behaviour categories, and each has an explanation alongside. Also provided is a chart for categorizing group members' oral contributions. There is a space for their initials along the top row. Next time you are present at a group discussion, listen to what each individual says. Every time they speak, decide in which oral category their utterance belongs, and place a tick or dot beside that category, under their name. Continue to do this, building up a record of the whole discussion.

After you have finished observing your discussion, total up your ticks or dots in the columns (horizontally) and for each group member (vertically). Your horizontal scores total gives you an indication of the behaviour of the group as a whole. For example, is this a group whose members are cooperating or competing with each other? Your vertical scores contrast the contributions of the individual group members, and can provide a clue to the roles that they are playing in the group.

Proposing	Any behaviour that puts forward a new suggestion, idea or course of action.
Building	Any behaviour that develops or extends an idea or suggestion made by someone else.
Supporting	Any behaviour that declares agreement or support with any individual or idea.
Disagreeing	Any behaviour that states a criticism of another person's statement.
Giving information/opinions/suggestions	Any behaviour that gives facts, ideas, or opinions or clarifies these.
Seeking information/opinions/suggestions	Any behaviour that asks for facts, ideas, or opinions from others.

Oral interaction score sheet

Oral category	**Members' names**				
					TOTAL
Proposing					
Building					
Supporting					
Disagreeing					
Giving • information • opinions • suggestions					
Seeking • information • opinions • suggestions					
TOTAL					

Bales's IPA is the most refined and exhaustive (empirically usable) method yet developed which can be used to study the content of the oral communication between individuals in groups. He provided the first rounded picture of what happens in face-to-face groups, by developing a theory of group functioning. He argued that group behaviour could be explained by showing how groups dealt with certain recurring problems such as orientation, evaluation, control, decision-making, tension management, and integration (Bales, 1953). His theory of group functioning thus pre-dates the Tuckman and Jenson model discussed previously.

STOP AND THINK You have been assigned to a group and given a task to perform. You hate your job and the management, and intend to resign shortly. What steps would you take to sabotage the work of your new group, while leaving you blameless in your boss's eyes, and confident of obtaining a good reference?

Badging up for effective teamwork

Sandy Pentland (2012) and his research team at the MIT's Human Dynamics Laboratory discovered that the pattern of communication – the manner in which members communicated – was the most important predictor of a team's success. It was more important than all the other factors – individual intelligence, personality, skill, and content of discussions – put together. The researchers equipped team members with electronic badges that collected data on their individual communication behaviour. This included whom they talked to; how much they talked, listened, gestured, and interrupted; their tone of voice; whether they faced each other; and even their levels of extraversion and empathy. These badges produce *sociometrics* – measures of how people interacted.

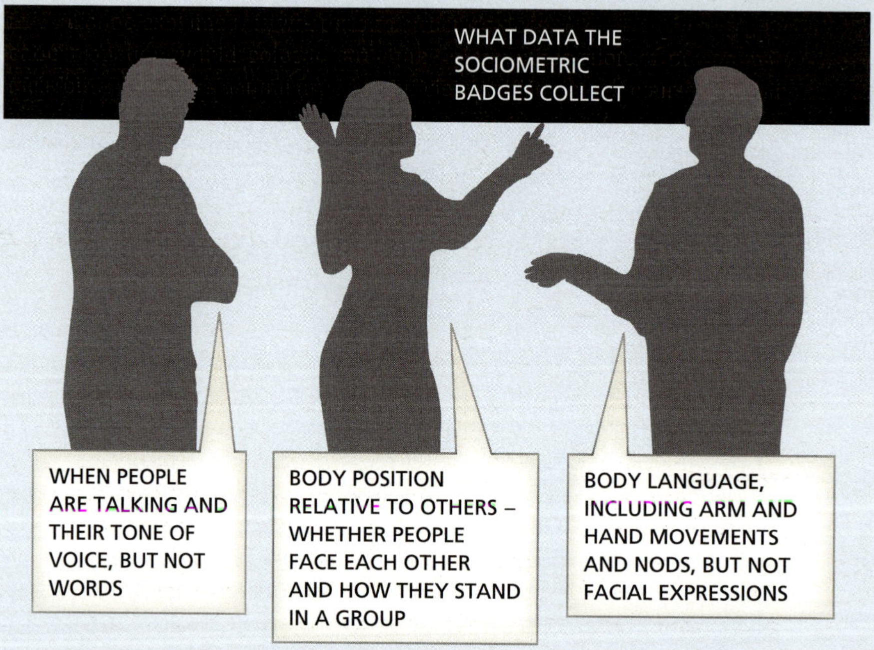

Source: Reprinted by permission of *Harvard Business Review*. Adapted from 'The new science of building teams' by Pentland, A., 90(4) 2012. Copyright © 2012 by the Harvard Business School Publishing Corporation, all rights reserved.

These data were then compared with team performance, and used to identify which communication patterns contributed to successful teamwork. The same communication patterns were found in different teams, irrespective of their type or their goals. Successful call centre teams and successful senior management teams shared certain 'data signatures' allowing the researchers to predict team success without actually having to meet team members. The three aspects of communication found to affect team performance were energy, engagement, and exploration.

Energy was measured by the number and nature of exchanges between team members. An exchange was represented by a comment followed by an acknowledgement. The most valuable form of communication was judged to be face-to-face, followed by the phone/videoconference. The least valuable forms were email and texting. Counting the number of exchanges and weighting them by communication value gives each team member an energy score which is averaged with others, to give a team score. At a meeting, as members start talking to one another, the energy rockets.

Engagement reflects the distribution of energy between team members. If all team members have a relatively equal and reasonably high energy with one another, engagement will be strong. Members in widely dispersed teams that talked mostly by telephone demonstrated weak engagement.

Exploration involves the communication that members engage in outside their team. It is the energy between a team and the other teams it interacts with. High-performing teams, especially those responsible for innovation, seek out a lot of outside connections. Exploration and engagement, while both good, do not easily coexist as both require the energy of team members. Devoting energy to one means that it cannot be used for the other. Successful, creative teams oscillate between 'exploration for discovery' and 'engagement for integration' of ideas gathered from outside.

The authors concluded that 35 per cent of variation in a team performance could be accounted for by the number of face-to-face exchanges; that the ideal number of exchanges in a team was two dozen per working hour; that members should be listening or speaking to the whole group for only half the time; and that each member's oral contribution should be limited and use to-the-point statements. The remainder of the time should be devoted to short, one-to-one conversations. Since social time accounted for 50 per cent of positive changes in communication patterns, the researchers persuaded a call centre management to schedule coffee breaks to allow all staff to take a break simultaneously, allowing them to socialize with their teammates away from their workstations. This resulted in a fall of over 20 per cent in average handling time among the low-performing teams.

Based on Pentland 2012

Role structure

Social role the set of expectations that others hold of an occupant of a position.

It is a short step from identifying the main class of oral contributions that an individual makes in their group to determining their team member role. The occupants of every position in the group are expected to carry out certain functions when the members of the group interact with one another. The expected behaviours associated with a position within the group constitute the social role of the occupant of that position. **Social role** is the concept which relates the individual to the prescriptive dictates of the group. People's behaviour within the organization is structured and patterned in various ways. An understanding of role helps us to see and explain how this happens.

Social role is the set of expectations that others hold of an occupant of a position in an organization structure, e.g. shop manager, bishop, head of the production department, etc. These expectations presume attitudes, relationships, and behaviours. A role is similar to a script that actors are given. The same actor changes roles, and can act out different parts in front of different audiences. The topic of role within the context of organizational structure will be discussed later. Here, our concern is with the different roles that are played out by various members of a group or team. Totalling each individual's oral contributions reveals that group members contribute in different ways to discussion. Bales found that individuals played different roles (role differentiation) within their groups, and that this was a universal feature of face-to-face interaction in groups. As the group deals with its problems, individual members begin to 'specialize' in certain types of behaviours, thereby taking on different 'roles' within the group.

Group member roles

Within a group activity, such as a staff meeting or a tutorial discussion, some people will show a consistent preference for certain oral behaviours and not for others. The particular oral

Kenneth Dean Benne (1908–1992)

behaviour or set of behaviours that a person engages in within a group can lead them to be seen to be playing a particular role within that group. Kenneth Benne and Paul Sheats (1948) distinguished the roles that were played by the members of a group and developed three main headings. The names of their roles, under each heading, are shown in Table 11.4.

Table 11.4: Benne and Sheats's roles commonly played by members of a group

Task	Building and maintenance	Individual (self-interested)
Initiator-contributor	Encourager	Aggressor
Information seeker	Harmonizer	Blocker
Opinion seeker	Compromiser	Recognition seeker
Information giver	Gatekeeper and expeditor	Self-confessor
Opinion giver	Standard-setter	Playboy
Evaluator-critic	Observer and commentator	Dominator
Energizer	Follower	Help seeker
Procedural technician		Special interest pleader
Recorder		

Source: based on Benne and Sheats (1948).

The first of these are *task roles*, which are principally directed towards achieving the group's task. The second heading, *building and maintenance roles*, is concerned primarily with establishing and sustaining good relations between individual members so as to ensure that the group as a whole can work together. Both of these categories of roles help the group to achieve its objective. In contrast, the third category, *individual roles*, impedes the group's efforts to achieve its aims. They have also been called 'self-interested roles' because they advance the interests of the individual member, rather than those of the group as a whole.

Team role an individual's tendency to behave in preferred ways which contribute to, and interrelate with, other members within a team.

This distinction between behaviour that is orientated towards achieving the task and behaviour that is focused upon individuals was originally made in the 1940s and 1950s. It has become the foundation for many subsequent teamwork theories and much teamwork training, and has also laid the foundation for many theories of leadership. Following Benne and Sheats's original list of roles, many writers offered their own lists of team roles or team-player roles, which vary in number from four to fifteen (e.g. Davis et al., 1992; Margerison and McCann, 1990).

Raymond Meredith Belbin (b.1926)

Belbin's team role theory

A popular and widely used framework for understanding roles within a group or team was developed by Meredith Belbin and was based on research conducted at the Administrative Staff College, Henley (Belbin, 1993, 1996, 2003). He distinguished nine team roles. Each **team role** makes its own distinctive contribution to the performance of the team.

Researchers have grouped these nine roles into three categories labelled *action roles* (shaper, implementer, and completer-finisher); *social roles* (coordinator, teamworker, and resource investigator); and *thinking roles* (plant, monitor-evaluator, and specialist). These are shown in Figure 11.5.

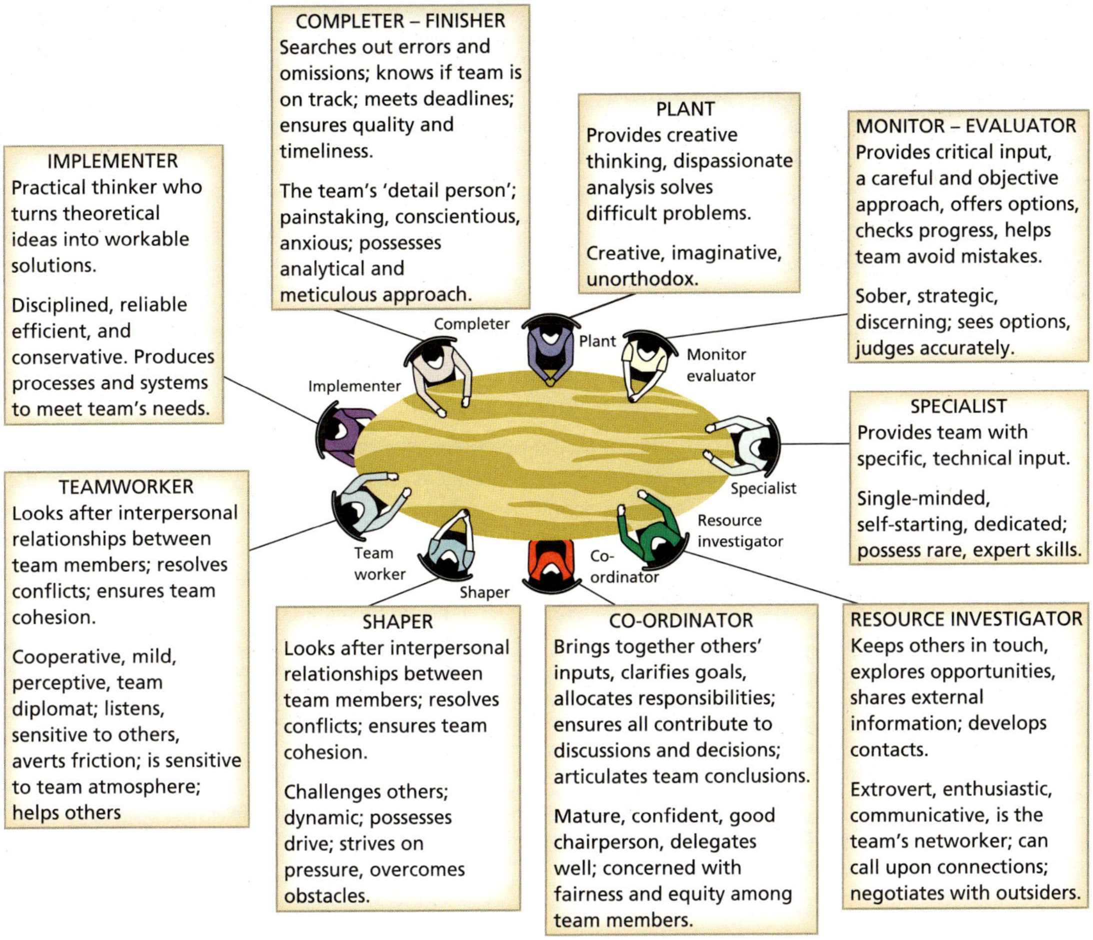

Figure 11.5: Belbin's team roles

Source: adapted from Matthewman, et al. (2009); based on Belbin, (1981).

Belbin (1996) argued that

1. Within an organization people are generally appointed to a functional role on the basis of their ability or experience, e.g. marketing. They are rarely selected for personal characteristics that would fit them to perform additional tasks within a team. In an ideal world, a person's functional role and their team role would coincide.
2. The personal characteristics of an individual fit them for some roles within a team, while limiting the likelihood that they will be successful in other roles. For Belbin, therefore, team roles are *individual preferences* based on personality, and not the *expectations of others*, as discussed earlier in this chapter with respect to social role.
3. Individuals tend to adopt one or two team roles fairly consistently.
4. The roles that individuals are naturally inclined towards can be predicted through personality assessments, and the team role questionnaire.
5. In an ideal ('dream') team, all the necessary roles are represented, and the preferred roles of members complement each other, thereby avoiding 'gaps'. This does not mean that every team has to consist of nine people. A single member can 'double up' and play several roles, thereby enabling the overall size of the team to be reduced.
6. The assessment, selection, placement, and guidance of individual employees by management is the way to improve team effectiveness. Once management knows employees' team role preferences, it can use them to compose teams in which all the required role preferences are represented.

STOP AND THINK Belbin argued that a successful team was one in which all nine of his roles were represented. What factors, inside or outside the organization, other than team role preferences, are likely to affect the success or failure of a team within an organization?

Critique of team role theory

Because of its widespread popularity, Belbin's theory has been extensively researched, and it continues to receive a great deal of critical assessment, which has been summarized by Aitor Aritzeta et al. (2007). The main criticisms of the theory are:

- There is little empirical evidence to support his theory and it is difficult to devise measures of team success that can be objectively related to team composition. It is difficult to say that a given team succeeded because it possessed all nine roles or failed because it lacked some of them.
- The questionnaire is based on respondents' self-reporting. Self-perceptions are a poor basis upon which to select team members. A more objective measure might be obtained through the use of peer ratings and an established personality assessment questionnaire.
- How individuals see their team roles is influenced as much by the roles that they habitually play, and what is expected of them in such roles. Thus the questionnaire scores reflect not only an individual's personality traits, but also their social learning of roles.
- The theory takes an excessively psychological perspective on role, neglecting the sociological dimension of the social position they habitually adopt, and what is expected of them in such positions by others.
- The theory does not sufficiently take into account differences in the type of task that the team is being asked to perform. Additive, conjunctive, and disjunctive tasks may require different combinations of team roles to achieve success.
- Team performance is affected by a variety of different factors such as strategy and leadership, structure and management style, interpersonal skills, and company resources. Focusing exclusively on team composition leads to ignoring these other critical factors.

- The concepts of team role and personality have become intertwined, being treated as interchangeable, rather than as separate but interrelated. Team roles and individual personality differences have been insufficiently related.

Gervase Bushe and Alexandra Chu (2011) noted that unstable team membership greatly impedes team performance. A fluid team is defined as a collection of individuals made responsible for an outcome by their organization, but whose membership changes. Fluid teams have been widespread in healthcare and in aviation (flight crews), and are increasingly common in engineering, product development, and sales and customer support. Among the reasons for team membership changes are upsizing and downsizing; different skill requirements at different times; the desire for flexible personnel allocation; and staff career development opportunities. The authors identified four problems and suggested solutions to each of these, as summarized in Figure 11.6.

Unstable membership creates barriers to effective team functioning because of . . .	Solutions	For increased
Loss of individual knowledge	• Create generalized roles and prescribed processes for teams. • Use standardization of skills for coordination. • Create a few stable roles which act as knowledge resources for others.	Efficacy
Lack of shared mental models	• Reduce task interdependence. • Substitute simple structures and knowledge management. • Increase understanding of coordination needs of other roles.	
Low individual commitment to group success	• Design motivating roles. • Design peer transparency into work.	Belonging
Lack of cohesion	• Build identification and cohesion through the pools of expertise that form more stable groups. • Build loyalty to higher level groups and the organization as a whole.	

Figure 11.6: Problems and solutions for fluid teams

Source: Reprinted from *Organizational Dynamics*, 40(3), Bushe, G.R. and Chu, A., Fluid teams: Solutions to the problems of unstable team membership, pp.181–188 (p. 183, Figure 2 Problems and solutions for Fluid Teams) Copyright 2011, with permission from Elsevier.

Home viewing

The Flight of the Phoenix (1965, director Robert Aldrich) tells the story of the aftermath of the crash of an oil company aeroplane in the Sahara desert (do not view the 2004 version which is very different). It is also the story of the formation of a project team that has to deal with the inevitable interpersonal issues of group process, conflict, team roles, and differences in members' values and power, as it attempts to rebuild the plane to escape. There were thirteen people on the plane but the story focuses on six main characters – Towns, Moran, Harris, Watson, Renaud, and Dorfmann. Using French and Raven's five types of power, decide which person possessed which type. How would you motivate each of these characters to do what you wanted? There are two types of conflict demonstrated in the film. What are these, and what triggers them? Identify the values held by Towns, Harris, and Dorfmann, and assess which ones are the most important for each man. Using either Belbin's team roles model or Benne and Sheats's group member roles model, decide what each of the characters contributed to the rebuilding of the aeroplane. Until the crash, the passengers were a collection of individuals. Identify the point at which the group enters each of the five stages of group development of Tuckman and Jensen's group development theory.

Based on Huffman and Kilian, 2012.

What makes a team smarter – more women?

Pressmaster/Shutterstock

Anita Woolley and Thomas Malone (2011) gave subjects aged 18 to 60 standard individual intelligence tests and assigned them randomly to teams. Teams were asked to complete brainstorming, decision-making, visual puzzle, and problem-solving tasks, and were then given a collective (team) intelligence score based on their performances. It was found that there was little correlation between a group's collective intelligence and the IQs of its collective members. However, if a group included more women, its collective intelligence rose. This collective group intelligence was not found to correlate with group satisfaction, group cohesion, group motivation, or individual intelligence. The teams that had members with higher IQs did not achieve higher team scores, but those which had more women did. So, are brainy people overrated and are women the true key to team success?

The researchers' concluded that gender did make a difference. The traditional argument is that diversity is good and that you should have a mixture of men and women on your team. However, this research suggests that the more women the better. Why? The explanation runs as follows. Studies of excellently performing groups report that members listen to each other, share constructive criticism, have open minds, and are not autocratic. These are all aspects of what is called *social sensitivity*, and women in general score higher in tests of social sensitivity than do men. So what is important is to have people high in social sensitivity whether they are men or women. If you don't know the sensitivity of an individual, then choose a female, as she is likely to have more of it. This study showed that intelligence tests used to predict individuals' performances on a range of tasks could also predict group performance. A group's collective intelligence can be increased by changing its membership or increasing incentives for collaboration.

Leadership structure

There are many jobs to be done in a group if it is to be both productive and satisfying for its members. The emergence of a leader within any group is a function of its structure. Usually, a group makes a leader of the person who has some special capacity for coping with the group's particular problems. They may possess physical strength, shrewdness, or some other relevant attribute. The leader and the members all play roles in the group. Through them, a group atmosphere is created which enables communication, influence, and decision-making to occur. In much of the management literature, leadership is considered exclusively as a management prerogative.

Leadership styles in groups

Kurt Zadek Lewin
(1890–1947)

Ronald O. Lippitt
(1914–1986)

A classic study of leadership of groups was conducted by Kurt Lewin, Ralph White, and Ronald Lippitt in the 1930s. It involved four groups of ten-year-old boys, each of whom attended an after-school hobby club. Each group's members had been matched on characteristics such as age, personality, IQ, physical characteristics, and socio-economic status, to be as similar as possible. The adult leaders were trained in three leadership styles:

Authoritarian leadership: The primary focus was upon achievement. The leader gave orders, and praised or criticized the boys without giving reasons. He behaved in a distant and impersonal way, discouraging communication between the boys themselves.

Democratic leadership: The primary focus was on the boys' choices. When the leader made comments, he explained them. He used discussions to help the boys plan their projects; allowed them to choose their own work mates; and permitted them to communicate freely with each other. He also participated in the group activities himself.

Laissez-faire leadership: The primary emphasis was minimal involvement. The leader left the boys to themselves; only gave advice and help when directly asked; and provided no praise, blame, or any other comments.

Leadership style	Effects: Liking for leader	Group atmosphere	Productivity
Autocratic	Liked less	Aggressive, dependent, self-oriented	High (leader present) Low (leader absent)
Democratic	Liked more	Friendly, group-centred, task-oriented	Relatively high (unaffected by presence or absence of leader)
Laissez-faire	Liked less	Friendly, group-centred, play-oriented	Low (increased in absence of leader)

The three leadership styles had different effects on group atmosphere and productivity and on liking for the leader. The researchers found that the autocratic leadership style led to high productivity, but only in the presence of the leader. It also created an aggressive but dependent atmosphere among the boys. The democratic leadership style led to relatively high productivity; to the boys liking their leaders most; to the creation of a friendly atmosphere; and to the boys proceeding with their work, irrespective of the presence or absence of the leader. The laissez-faire leadership style led to low productivity that only increased when the leader was present. It created a friendly but play-oriented atmosphere.

Based on White and Lippitt, 1960; diagram reproduced with permission from Hogg and Vaughan, Social Psychology *© 2011 Pearson Australia, page 555.*

It has been found that the type of leadership exercised affects group performance and member satisfaction. Activities are performed and actions are taken by the leader. There has been an increasing interest in *distributed leadership* within a group as opposed to individual leadership (see Chapter 19). One can distinguish between a leader and acts of leadership. If we accept Raymond Cattell's (1951) view that the leader is any group member who is capable of modifying the properties of the group by their presence, then we can acknowledge that any member of the group can perform acts of leadership, and not just a single, designated individual. The group leadership approach considers the characteristics of small groups, seeking to understand the organizational context in which they exist, and the objectives that they seek to achieve. It seems therefore more useful to view leadership as a set of behaviours that change their nature depending on circumstances, and which switch or rotate between group members as circumstances change, rather than a static status associated with a single individual.

Distributed or centralized leadership?

Pressmaster/Dreamstime.com

Jennifer Berdahl and Cameron Anderson (2005) considered the performance of groups, and found that quality suffered when leadership was highly centralized, and when a majority of group members did not perform leadership tasks, or contribute to the group's efforts. Previous research had shown that generally, centralized leadership reduced performance in tasks such as brainstorming, judgement, and decision-making. However, situations that require planning and coordinating, such as large groups doing complex tasks, may benefit from the more hierarchical male model. Further research is needed as centralized leadership is also associated with high levels of staff late arrival, absenteeism, and turnover, and low levels of cohesion and satisfaction in the workplace.

The relationship between the group's leader, at a given point in time, and the followers may be thought of as one of social exchange. The leader provides rewards for the group by helping its members to achieve their own and the group's goals. They in turn reward the leader by giving the individual heightened status and increased influence. However, members can rescind that influence at any time if they feel that the leader is no longer worthy of their respect. This may be viewed as a social exchange process: the leader has power in terms of their ability to influence the behaviour of those around them; nevertheless, it is the group members who give the leader the power to influence them.

Research by Robert Bales and Philip Slater (1956) into newly constituted groups found that two leaders regularly emerged. One was the *task leader* who specialized in making suggestions, giving information, expressing opinions, and generally contributing to helping the group achieve its objective. The other was the *socio-emotional leader* who helped maintain relationships between group members, allowing them to express their ideas and positive feelings (compare the distinction made earlier between task and maintenance activities in groups). This person made jokes, and released tensions in the group, and helped to maintain the group as a functioning entity. Although there was some rivalry, the two group leaders, *task* and *socio-emotional*, typically cooperated and worked together well. Lynda Gratton and her colleagues (Gratton et al., 2007) confirmed this distinction fifty years later when investigating teams which demonstrated high levels of collaboration. They found that the flexible behaviour of their team leaders, both task and relationship-oriented, was crucial. Successful group leaders changed their style. Initially, they emphasized task leadership – clarifying goals, committing members, and defining individual responsibilities. Later, they switched to a relationship orientation, once the tensions around sharing knowledge emerged. Ambidextrous team leaders, possessing both task and relationship skills, appeared to be essential.

Virtual teams

Virtual team
a team that relies on technology-mediated communication, while crossing boundaries of geography, time, culture, and organization, to accomplish an interdependent task.

Global virtual team
a team that is nationally, geographically, and culturally diverse and which communicates almost exclusively through electronic media.

Synchronous communication
communication that occurs when people are online at the same time, engaging in a real-time conversation with others, somewhat similar to normal face-to-face discussions.

Asynchronous communication
communication that occurs when participants start a discussion topic (or thread) and post replies to each other, and when, after delays, individuals read to catch up with the discussion. It is similar to a dialogue conducted by post.

Increasing competition and globalization is forcing organizations to speed up their development and production of new products and services. Simultaneously, advancing communications hardware is allowing individuals to interact with others anywhere in the world, on the move, via laptop or mobile phone. Additionally, project-management software ('groupware') links the members of a team electronically, allowing them instantly to share and analyse project information. This combination of market-push and technology-pull has led companies to explore new types of working arrangements and organizational forms. One such development is the **virtual team**.

Virtual teams give companies access to the most qualified individuals to do a particular job irrespective of their geographical location; allow them to respond faster to competition; and give individuals greater flexibility in working from home. The virtual team has disrupted many aspects of traditional group structures – power, status, liking, communication, role, and leadership. Much current social science research is devoted to describing and explaining the changes involved. According to Yuhyung Shin, virtual teams can be distinguished on four dimensions (Shin, 2005):

Spatial dispersion:	the extent to which team members work in different geographical locations
Cultural dispersion:	the extent to which a team consists of employees from different countries or cultures
Temporal dispersion:	the extent to which team members work at different times
Organizational dispersion:	the degree to which team members work across organizational boundaries.

A virtual team can be of the single-country or multi-country type. If the latter, it is called a **global virtual team** and is defined as a nationally, geographically, and culturally diverse group that communicates almost exclusively through electronic media (Jarvenpaa and Leidner, 1999). Team members therefore work across temporal and spatial boundaries, usually without face-to-face interaction, to coordinate their activities to attain common goals from different locations around the globe (Zander et al., 2012). This new organization form has surfaced so quickly that few researchers have so far studied either such teams themselves (Kirkman et al., 2004) or the leadership of them (Davis and Bryant, 2003; Malhotra et al., 2007; Zigurs, 2002). Considering a continuum of groups and teams based on their degree of face-to-face interaction, global virtual teams are at one pole of the continuum, and collocated groups (members facing each other over a table in a room) would be on the other.

Virtual teams can choose from a range of communication technologies to supplement or replace face-to-face interaction (Bell and Kozlowski, 2002; Griffith et al., 2003). Their choice is affected by spatial dispersion, i.e. the spread of team members at different geographical locations or different workplaces at the same geographic location; and by temporal dispersion, i.e. the timing of members' communications (synchronicity) with each other, as they seek to accomplish their team's task. These can take the form of either synchronous or asynchronous communications. **Synchronous communication** is when you get an immediate answer to your question (e.g. telephone). **Asynchronous communication** is when you send a message and wait for an answer (e.g. email). If a virtual team member is dealing with a colleague in another country who speaks a different first language, asynchronous communication gives them more time to think and react. It is a disadvantage to them if they have to think in real time.

Source: Copyright Grantland Enterprises; www.grantland.net

On the positive side, the virtual context allows these teams to complete tasks more quickly and efficiently than before, and gives them access to the best people and resources in locations around the world. On the negative side, members' different cultural backgrounds, the fact that they are not 'in synch' because of different time zones, and the technological interface all make the task of leading these global virtual teams very challenging.

Cultural dispersion refers to the fact that a virtual team is composed of individuals from diverse cultural backgrounds, while organizational dispersion relates to the fact that the members of a virtual team may be members of more than one company, and could include suppliers, retailers, and even consumers. It is therefore not uncommon for differences to exist in members' assumptions, motivations, knowledge bases, and working styles (Shapiro et al., 2002). The differences in time and place associated with different forms of information exchange possibilities were summarized by James Bowditch and Anthony Buono (2001) and are shown in Figure 11.7. It shows that the members of a team may be present in the same place (co-located) or in different places (distributed), when receiving or giving information. Similarly, their communication may be synchronous or asynchronous. Successful collaboration within virtual teams requires participants to establish contact with each other, agree lines of communication, and build trust. This is done more easily face-to-face. Psychologists recommend that virtual team members who typically interact through email, telephone, and videoconference should occasionally meet physically to become aware of each other's personal and cultural contexts (Newing, 2007).

		PLACE	
		Same	**Different**
TIME	**Same**	**Co-located/Synchronous** • Face-to-face meetings • Technography • Decision-support rooms I	**Distributed/Synchronous** • Audio (telephone) • Videoconferencing • Distance whiteboarding II
	Different	III **Co-located/Asynchronous** • Resource centre • Team rooms • 'War' room	IV **Distributed/Asynchronous** • Voicemail, email • Computer conferencing • Groupware, intranets

Figure 11.7: Time and place dimensions of team information exchange
Source: From Bowditch and Buono (2001, p. 170).

Problems experienced by virtual teams include:

- less social support and less interaction between members;
- their inability to duplicate normal face-to-face discussions;
- greater task-orientation, because members have not previously met;

- less exchange of social-emotional information between members;
- lower satisfaction with the group process compared to face-to-face teams.

Current thinking about virtual teams is moving away from viewing them as a special type of team that exists in contrast to 'traditional' face-to-face teams, and focuses instead on the concept of *virtualness* as a potential characteristic of all teams. The phrase 'virtual team' immediately conjures up images of Skype, a proprietary Voice Over Internet Protocol service and software application. A great number of both long-distance and local communications are today conducted over Skype. It has been promoted as a suitable vehicle for communication in doctor-patient exchanges, in an effort to reduce unnecessary hospital visits and to save doctors' time. Skype represents a low-cost or free virtual team tool.

However, the members of every team, when communicating with each other, are likely to use other ('lower') technology such as telephones, email, real-time calendar/scheduling systems, electronic bulletin boards, websites, and so on. That is why Shin (2005) argues that the more any team possesses the four characteristics of spatial, temporal, cultural, and organizational dispersion, the more virtual it becomes. In consequence, discussion is conceived of as a continuum, with face-to-face teams at one end, and virtual teams on the other, and real teams being placed somewhere along that continuum, depending on their characteristics (Griffith and Neale, 2001).

Virtual teams are now an established feature in the organizational landscape. Often, they consist of cross-functional members working on highly interdependent tasks and sharing responsibility for team outcomes. Information and communication technologies can potentially increase the effectiveness of teamworking by removing barriers of place, and enabling individual team members to work together across organizational and geographical boundaries. Using a literature review and reported findings from interviews with experts and practitioners in the field, Blaise Bergiel and colleagues (2008) identified the advantages and problems of virtual teams so that organizations could establish and manage such teams. Their findings are summarized in Table 11.5.

Table 11.5: Benefits and problems of using virtual teams

Benefits	Problems
Reduces travel and cost	Sometimes requires complex technological applications
Enables recruitment of talented employees	Lack of knowledge among employees about virtual teams; need for human resource development interventions
Promotes different areas	Lack of knowledge among senior managers concerning advanced technological applications
Builds diverse teams	Not suitable for all employees due to their psychological makeup and predispositions
Assists in promoting proactive employment practices for disadvantaged individuals and groups; reduces discrimination	Not an option for all companies because of their operational environment

Source: Nature of virtual teams: A summary of their advantages and disadvantages, *Management Research News*, 31(2), pp. 99–110, p. 107 Table 1: The advantages of using virtual teams (Bergiel, B.J., Bergiel, E.B. and Balsmeier, P.W. 2008)

Given the problems of virtual teams, it is more difficult for them to be successful since there is a greater potential for misunderstandings to arise and for more things to go wrong. Bowditch and Buono (2001) explain that while team leaders are skilled in dealing with Quadrant I interactions – same time/same place (see Figure 11.7) – they generally lack the experience and expertise to guide and facilitate interactions in the other three quadrants. Using observations, interviews, and survey data, Arvind Malhotra and his colleagues (2007) studied 54 virtual teams from 33 different companies in 14 different industries. They identified six leadership practices of effective leaders of virtual teams, which are summarized in Table 11.6.

Table 11.6: Practices of effective virtual team leaders

Leadership practices of virtual team leaders	How do virtual team leaders do it?
1 Establish and maintain trust through the use of communication technology	• Focusing the norms on how information is communicated • Revisiting and adjusting the communication norms as the team evolves ('virtual get-togethers') • Making progress explicit through use of team virtual work space • Equal 'suffering' in the geographically distributed world
2 Ensure diversity in the team is understood, appreciated, and leveraged	• Prominent team expertise directory and skills matrix in the virtual work space • Virtual sub-teaming to pair diverse members and rotate sub-team members • Allowing diverse opinions to be expressed through use of asynchronous electronic means (e.g. electronic discussion threads)
3 Manage virtual work-cycle and meetings	• All idea divergence between meetings (asynchronous idea generation) and idea convergence and conflict resolution during virtual meetings (synchronous idea convergence) • Use the start of virtual meeting (each time) for social relationship building • During meeting – ensure through 'check-ins' that everyone is engaged and heard from • End of meeting – ensure that the minutes and future work plan are posted to team repository
4 Monitor team progress through the use of technology	• Closely scrutinize asynchronous (electronic threaded discussion and document postings in the knowledge repository) and synchronous (virtual meeting participation and instant messaging) communications patterns • Make progress explicit through balanced scorecard measurements posted in the team's virtual work space
5 Enhance external visibility of the team and its members	• Frequent report-outs to a virtual steering committee (comprised of local bosses of team members)
6 Ensure individuals benefit from participating in virtual teams	• Virtual reward ceremonies • Individual recognition at the start of each virtual meeting • Making each team member's 'real location' boss aware of the member's contribution

Source: adapted from Malhotra *et al.* (2007, p. 62) used with permission.

RECAP

1. *List the six dimensions of group structure.*
   - The six main dimensions along which the members of a group differ are power, status, liking, communication, role, and leadership. A person may be placed high on one dimension and simultaneously low on another.
   - The group's structure acts to increase the predictability of behaviour between the group's members.
2. *Identify the sources of power within the group.*
   - There are five bases or types of power – reward, coercive, referent, legitimate, and expert.
3. *Distinguish between two common uses of the concept of status.*
   - The status structure of a group is determined by how much status an individual member possesses. There is formal status and social status.
4. *Understand how emotional relationships within a group can be represented symbolically.*
   - The liking (emotional) structure of a group is revealed through the use of sociometry, a technique developed by Jacob Moreno.
5. *Distinguish between communication network analysis, communication pattern analysis, and Interaction Process Analysis.*
   - A communication network analysis maps the direction and quantity of oral communication in a group. It is depicted on a communigram.
   - A communication pattern analysis analyses documents, data, and voicemail transmission, to determine the source, direction, and quantity of both oral and written communication between the dispersed members of a group. It is depicted on a communication pattern chart as a 'chain', 'Y', 'wheel', 'circle' or 'all channel'.
   - Interaction Process Analysis (IPA) classifies the content of oral communications between group members. It was developed by Robert Bales.
6. *Distinguish between task, socio-emotional, and individual classes of roles within a group.*
   - The role structure of a group can differentiate those members who perform task-focused roles, relations-oriented roles, and self-oriented roles. This distinction was made by Benne and Sheats.
7. *Distinguish Belbin's team roles.*
   - Meredith Belbin's team role theory distinguishes the roles played by the members of a team. They are plant, resource investigator, coordinator, shaper, monitor-evaluator, teamworker, implementer, completer-finisher, and specialist.
8. *Give examples of three leadership styles identified by White and Lippitt.*
   - White and Lippitt distinguished three leadership styles which they labelled authoritarian, democratic, and laissez-faire.
9. *Distinguish between a task and a socio-emotional group leader.*
   - Bales and Slater suggested that a group often had both a task leader and a socio-emotional leader. The first drove the group towards task achievement, while the second maintained the group as a co-operative working unit.
10. *List the four key dimensions of a virtual team.*
    - The four key dimensions of a virtual team are: spatial dispersion – the extent to which team members work in different geographical locations; cultural dispersion – the extent to which a team consists of employees from different countries or cultures; temporal dispersion – the extent to which team members work at different times; and organizational dispersion – the degree to which team members work across organizational boundaries.

Revision

1. Select any two groups with which you are familiar. Contrast them in terms of any group structure dimensions that are relevant – e.g. power, communication, liking, roles, leadership. Suggest possible reasons for the similarities and differences that you have highlighted.
2. Describe situations in which (a) a team role analysis and (b) a sociogram would be relevant to improve a group's functioning. How would you apply these two techniques? How would you use the results?
3. Critically assess the strengths and weaknesses of Belbin's team role theory as a guide for the manager wishing to construct a team that will be effective.
4. Identify some of the problems of virtual teamworking for (a) the companies which establish them, and (b) the individuals who work in them. How might these problems be overcome?

Research assignment

Studies suggest that employees spend many hours each week in meetings. Get invited to a real meeting that takes place in an organization which is likely to last at least 30 minutes. Consult the box 'Analysing oral interactions in a group' (on page 367) making several copies of the oral interaction score sheet that you will find there. Read and follow the instructions detailed in the box. After 30 minutes of silently observing and scoring, excuse yourself and leave the meeting quietly. After you have added up your scores, write a brief report which comments on (a) the way this group as a whole was working, (b) the roles played by its individual members, and (c) the adequacy of your scoring sheet and its underlying assumptions. Make recommendations as to how your group's members' interactions could be improved.

Springboard

Blaise Bergiel, Erich Bergiel and Philip Balsmeier (2008) 'Nature of virtual teams: a summary of their advantages and disadvantages', *Management Research News*, 31(2), pp. 99–110. Based on a literature review and interviews with practitioners, the article discusses the creation and managing of virtual teams.

Keith Dixon and Niki Panteli (2010) 'From virtual teams to virtuality in teams', *Human Relations*, 63(8), pp. 1177–1197. The authors consider the dynamics of virtuality in teams by means of an in-depth case study of an inter-organizational virtual centre of excellence.

John Mathieu, Maynard M. Travis, Tammy Rapp and Lucy Gilson (2010) 'Team effectiveness 1997–2007', in J.A. Wagner and J.R. Hollenbeck (eds) *Readings in Organizational Behaviour*, London: Routledge, pp. 321–80. The authors review contemporary team research highlighting the difference between different types of teams.

Bernard Nijstad (2009) *Group Performance*, Psychology Press, Hove, East Sussex. The author outlines the current state of social psychological theories concerning the performance of groups, focusing on group interaction, development, and how groups affect their members.

OB in films

Network (1976, director Sidney Lumet), DVD track 16: 1:48:00 to 1:53:00 (5 minutes). This film is set in the US television industry. Because of his falling ratings, the Union Broadcasting System (UBS) fires its leading news anchorman Howard Beale (played by Peter Finch). Beale's on-air behaviour then becomes increasingly bizarre, after he promises to kill himself on television. Initially, his ratings skyrocket as he becomes the 'Mad Prophet of the Airways', but they then decline, affecting UBS's other programmes and its revenue. The clip begins as network executives assemble for a meeting, and ends with Diana saying 'let's kill the son-of-a-bitch'. Hackett (played by Robert Duvall) sits at the desk and begins the meeting by describing the problem.

Listen to the discussion between the six individuals in the room. Each time one of them speaks, decide into which of the six oral categories it fits, and indicate this by putting a tick or dot, under their name. Continue until the clip has finished.

B Joe | C Man in chair | D Man in armchair | E Herb (standing) | F Diana

A Hackett

Oral Interaction score sheet

Oral category	**Meeting participants**						
	A Hackett	**B Joe**	**C Main in chair**	**D Man in armchair**	**E Herb (standing)**	**F Diana**	**TOTAL**
Proposing							
Building							
Supporting							
Disagreeing							
Giving • information • opinions • suggestions							
Seeking • information • opinions • suggestions							
TOTAL							

OB on the web

Watch and compare two business school trailers on virtual team courses, the first entitled 'Managing global virtual teams' (www.youtube.com/watch?v=Y1YokiumAkQ) and the second 'Create effective virtual teams: Short focused programs' (www.youtube.com/watch?v=tgWgplaPnSU). What do they see as the main challenges for those managing virtual teams? Make a list of these based on the content of the two videos. Then, search the internet to find possible solutions to these problems. How do you create, build, develop, and manage virtual teams?

CHAPTER EXERCISES

1. Tasks and groups

Objectives

1. To distinguish between the different types of tasks that a group may perform.
2. To examine group processes including member roles, decision-making, and leadership.

Briefing

(a) Form groups.

(b) Nominate a group observer to sit silently near the group and make a note of how the group went about its task; which people played which roles; how decisions were made; and how leadership was exercised.

(c) You have 15–20 minutes to complete four tasks which vary in their nature.

(d) The tasks are:

Task 1 – Rhyming words

Task 2 – Word equations

Task 3 – Whose job?

Task 4 – Motoring advice.

(e) Group observers provide feedback to their groups.

(f) Instructor explains the difference between different tasks and supplies solutions.

(g) Groups compare their answers and are provided with the correct answers.

(h) All the groups then

- identify the unique characteristics of each type of task they performed
- provide other examples of each type of task in social or work life
- consider the effect of task type on group aspects such as choice of members, ways of working, and methods of decision-making.

Group tasks

Task 1 – Rhyming words. Generate words that rhyme with the 15 words listed below.

feast	beard	battle	flowers	hissed
hurried	profit	world	orange	load
sorrow	song	accounting	great	smiles

Source: Dodd-McCue, D., *Journal of Management Education*, 15(3), pp. 335–9, Copyright © 1991, OBTS Teaching Society for Management Educators. Reprinted by Permission of SAGE Publications.

Task 2 – Word equations. Solve each of the word equations below by substituting the appropriate words for the letters e.g. 3F = 1Y (3 feet = 1 yard)

1. '1B in the H = 2 in the B'	7. 23Y – 3Y = 2D
2. 8D – 24H = 1W	8. 3P = 6
3. E – 8 = Z	9. C + 6D = NYE
4. HH & MH at 12 = N or M	10. A & E were in the G of E
5. 4J + 4Q + 4K = CC	11. 29 = D in F in a LY
6. S & M & T & W & T & F & S are D of W	12. 'NN = GN'

Source: A WHACK ON THE SIDE OF THE HEAD by Roger von Oech. Copyright © 1983, 1990, 1998 by Roger von Oech. By permission of GRAND CENTRAL PUBLISHING. All rights reserved.

Task 3 – Whose job? Discover which person has which job.

Betty, Tom, Edward, Sid, and Dave comprise the employees of the firm and fill the jobs of clerk, administrator, manager, accountant, and surveyor, but not in that order. Read the information below to determine which person holds which job. Use the grid below as a bingo card, eliminating individuals, as you go.

The administrator bandaged the surveyor's finger when he cut it.

While the manager and the surveyor were away from the office, the accountant docked their subordinates – Dave and Sid – a half day's pay each, for taking the afternoon off.

The accountant is a fine bridge player, and Tom admires his ability.

Dave invited the administrator for lunch but his invitation was not accepted.

Betty	clerk	administrator	manager	accountant	surveyor
Tom	clerk	administrator	manager	accountant	surveyor
Edward	clerk	administrator	manager	accountant	surveyor
Sid	clerk	administrator	manager	accountant	surveyor
Dave	clerk	administrator	manager	accountant	surveyor

Task 4 – Motoring advice. Suggest the best route between your educational establishment and the nearest coastal town or city.

Exercise idea and task 1 from Diane Dodd-McCue (1991) 'Led like sheep: an exercise for linking group decision making to different types of tasks', Journal of Management Education *15(3), pp. 335–9; Task 2 items taken from Roger Von Oech (1998)* A Whack on the Side of the Head, *Warner Books; Task 3 adapted from 'Analytical or creative? A problem solving comparison',* The 1981 Annual Handbook for Group Facilitators, *Jossey-Bass, pp. 24–6.*

2. Team roles questionnaire

Objectives

1. To introduce team role theory.
2. To identify your preferred team roles.

→

Instructions Listed below are statements that describe behaviours that members use when they are participating in a team. As a student, you may demonstrate these behaviours at work, in team projects, in student organizations and societies, or in interactions with your flatmates.

Use the 1–5 scale below to indicate how frequently you engage in these behaviours when part of a team. Place a number from 1 to 5 in the space to the left of each statement.

Very infrequently 1 2 3 4 5 Very frequently

____ 1. I organize and use other people's abilities and talents productively.
____ 2. I react strongly when meetings look like losing track of the objective.
____ 3. I start to look around for possible ideas and openings.
____ 4. I often produce a new approach to a long-continuing problem.
____ 5. I analyse other people's ideas objectively for their merits and flaws.
____ 6. I can be relied on to see that the work we need to do is organized.
____ 7. I am always ready to support good suggestions that help us resolve a problem.
____ 8. I notice omissions and have an eye for getting the details right.
____ 9. I like to employ my experience, training, and qualifications.
____ 10. I often draw out contributions from other team members.
____ 11. I am ready to make my personal views known in a forceful way if necessary.
____ 12. A broad range of personal contacts is important to my style of working.
____ 13. I like to use my imagination to suggest completely new approaches.
____ 14. I like to weigh up several alternatives thoroughly before choosing, which may take time.
____ 15. I am interested more in practicalities than in new ideas.
____ 16. I am concerned to help others with their problems.
____ 17. I keep a watchful eye on areas where difficulties may arise.
____ 18. I usually only contribute when I really know what I'm talking about.
____ 19. I am happy to take the lead when action is needed.
____ 20. It is worth incurring some temporary unpopularity to get my views across.
____ 21. I like to discover the latest ideas and developments as I easily get bored.
____ 22. I can quickly see how ideas and techniques can be used in new relationships.
____ 23. I approach the topic in a carefully analytical way.
____ 24. Given an objective, I can sort out the concrete steps to achieve it.
____ 25. I get on well with others and work hard for the team.
____ 26. I like to finish my current work before I start something new.
____ 27. My technical knowledge and experience are usually my major contributions.

Transfer the points from each of the 27 statements into the table below, placing them next to the statement number. Then add up the points in each of the nine columns. Enter these in the 'Total' row. This indicates the roles that you most frequently play in a team. The higher the score, the more you see yourself taking that role.

Coordinator	Shaper	Resource investigator	Plant	Monitor-evaluator	Implementer	Teamworker	Completer-finisher	Specialist
1.	2.	3.	4.	5.	6.	7.	8.	9.
10.	11.	12.	13.	14.	15.	16.	17.	18.
19.	20.	21.	22.	23.	24.	25.	26.	27.
TOTAL								

Briefing

1. Divide into groups.
2. Remind yourself of each of the nine team roles.
3. In your groups:
   (a) Compare your top two team role scores with those of the other members of your group. Give an example of behaviours that demonstrate your performance of that role.
   (b) Identify which roles are preferred among students in this group (high-scoring roles). Identify which roles are avoided or rejected, or are missing (low-scoring roles).
   (c) If this was a real management or project team, what could be done to cover the missing roles?
   (d) Decide whether certain roles are more important in certain phases of a team's operation? For example, which two team roles are likely to be crucial in the getting-started phase of a team's work; the generating-ideas phase; the developing-the-ideas phase; and the implementing-the-decision phase?
   (e) Decide to what extent your preferred team roles are a reflection of your personality.

This questionnaire was adapted from one developed by Nancy Foy, building on the work of Meredith Belbin. It appeared in Boddy, D. and Buchanan, D.A. (1987) Management of Technology. The Technical Change Audit. Action for Results: 5: The Process Module, *pp. 32–5, Manpower Services Commission, Moorfoot, Sheffield, Crown Copyright.*

Employability assessment

With regard to your future employment prospects:

1. Identify up to three issues from this chapter that you found significant.
2. Relate these to the competencies in the employability matrix
3. Decide what actions you need to take to maintain and/or develop those competencies under each of the four headings of the employability matrix.

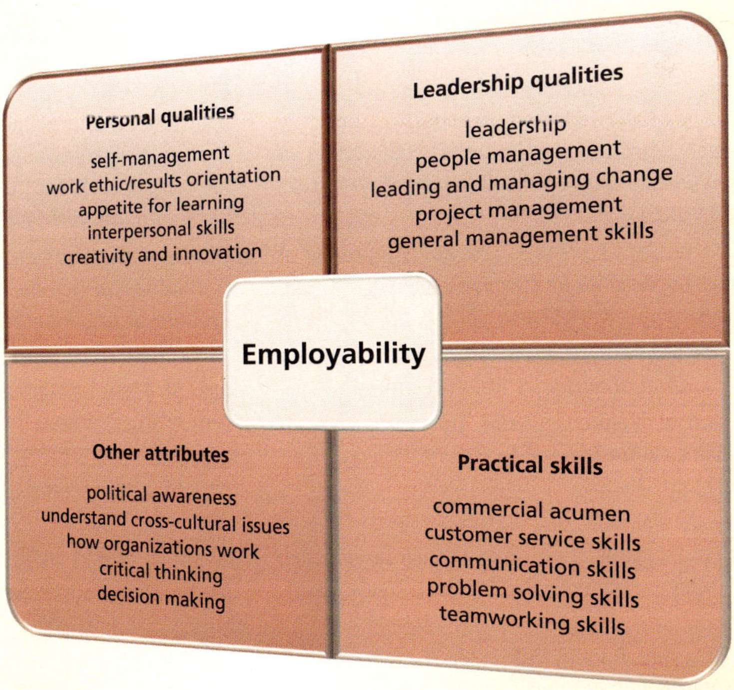

References

Aritzeta, A., Swailes, S. and Seniuor, B. (2007) 'Belbin's team role model: development, validity and applications for teambuilding', *Journal of Management Studies*, 44(1), pp. 96–118.

Bales, R.F. (1950a) *Interaction Process Analysis*, Reading, MA: Addison-Wesley.

Bales, R.F. (1950b) 'A set of categories for the analysis of small group interaction', *American Sociological Review*, 15(2), pp. 257–63.

Bales, R.F. (1953) 'The equilibrium problem in small groups', in T. Parsons, R.F. Bales and E.A. Shils (eds), *Working Papers in the Theory of Action*, New York: The Free Press, pp. 111–61.

Bales, R.F. (1959) 'Task roles and social roles in problem solving groups', in E.E. Maccoby, M. Newcomb and E.L. Hartley (eds), *Readings in Social Psychology* (3rd edn), New York: Holt, Rinehart and Winston.

Bales, R.F. and Slater, P.E. (1956) 'Role differentiation in small decision-making groups', in T. Parsons and R.F. Bales (eds), *Family, Socialization and Interaction*, London: Routledge, pp. 259–306.

Baron, R.A. and Greenberg, J. (1990) *Behaviour in Organizations* (3rd edn), Upper Saddle River, NJ: Allyn and Bacon.

Belbin, R.M. (1993) *Team Roles at Work*, Oxford: Butterworth Heinemann.

Belbin, R.M. (1996) *The Coming Shape of Organizations*, London: Butterworth Heinemann.

Belbin, R.M. (2003) *Management Teams: Why They Succeed or Fail* (2nd edn), Oxford: Butterworth Heinemann.

Belbin Associates (2009) *Method, Reliability & Validity, Statistics and Research: A Comprehensive Review of Belbin Team Roles*, http://www.belbin.com/downloads/BELBIN-MRVSR2009.pdf.

Bell, B.S. and Kozlowski, S.W.J. (2002) 'A typology of virtual teams: implications for effective leadership', *Group and Organizational Management*, 27(1), pp. 14–49.

Benne, K.D. and Sheats, P. (1948) 'Functional roles of group members', *Journal of Social Issues*, 4(2), pp. 41–9.

Berdahl, J., and Anderson, C. (2005) 'Do groups need an alpha animal?', *Group Dynamics: Theory, Research and Practice*, 9(1) pp. 45–57.

Bergiel, B.J., Bergiel, E.B. and Balsmeier, P.W. (2008) 'Nature of virtual teams: a summary of their advantages and disadvantages', *Management Research News*, 31(2), pp. 99–110.

Bowditch, J.L., and Buono, A.F. (2001) *A Primer on Organizational Behavior*, New York: Wiley.

Bushe, G.R. and Chu, A. (2011) 'Fluid teams: solutions to the problems of unstable team membership', *Organizational Dynamics*, 40(3), pp. 181–8.

Cattell, R. (1951) 'New concepts for measuring leadership in terms of group syntality', *Human Relations*, 4(2), pp. 161–8.

Dahl, R.A. (1957) 'The concept of power', *Behavioural Science*, 2(3), pp. 201–15.

Davis, D.D. and Bryant, J.L. (2003) 'Influence at a distance: leadership in global virtual teams', *Advances in Global Leadership*, 3, pp. 303–40.

Davis, J., Millburn, P., Murphy, T. and Woodhouse, M. (1992) *Successful Team Building: How to Create Teams that Really Work*, London: Kogan Page.

French, J.R.P. and Raven, B.H. (1958) 'The bases of social power', in D. Cartwright (ed.), *Studies in Social Power*, Ann Arbor, Michigan: Institute for Social Research, University of Michigan Press, pp. 150–67.

Foushee, H.C. (1984) 'Dyads and triads at 35,000 feet: factors affecting group process and air crew performance', *American Psychologist*, 39(8), pp. 885–93.

Gratton, L., Voight, A. and Erickson, T. (2007) 'Bridging fault lines in diverse teams', *Sloan Management Review*, 48(4), pp. 22–9.

Greenberg, J. (1976) 'The role of seating position in group interaction: a review with applications for group trainers', *Group and Organizational Studies*, 1(3), pp. 310–27.

Greenberg, J. and Baron, R.A. (1997) *Behaviour in Organizations* (6th edn), Englewood Cliffs, NJ: Prentice Hall.

Griffith, T.L., and Neale, M.A. (2001) 'Information processing in traditional, hybrid and virtual teams: from nascent knowledge to transactive memory', *Research in Organizational Behaviour*, 23, pp. 379–421.

Griffith, T.L., Sawyer, J.E. and Neale, M.A. (2003) 'Virtualness and knowledge in teams: managing the love triangle of organizations, individuals and information technology', *MIS Quarterly*, 27(2), pp. 265–87.

Hogg, M.A. and Vaughan, G.M. (2008) *Social Psychology* (5th edn), Pearson/Prentice Hall.

Huffman, B.J. and Kilian, C.M. (2012) 'The Flight of the Phoenix: interpersonal aspects of project management', *Journal of Management Education*, 36(4), pp. 568–600.

Jackall, R. (1988) *Moral Mazes: The World of Corporate Managers*, London: Sage Publications.

Jarvenpaa, S.L. and Leidner, D.E. (1999) 'Communication and trust in global virtual teams', *Organization Science*, 10(6), pp. 791–815.

Kilduff, M. and Krackhardt, D. (2008) *Interpersonal Networks in Organizations*, Cambridge: Cambridge University Press.

Kirkman, B.L., Rosen, B., Tesluk, P.E. and Gibson, C.B. (2004) 'The impact of team empowerment on virtual team performance: the moderating role of face-to-face interaction', *Academy of Management Journal*, 47(2), pp. 175–92.

Makary, M.A., Sexton, J.B., Freischlag, J.A., Holzmueller, C.G., Millman, E.A., Rowen, L. and Pronovost, P.J. (2005) 'Operating room teamwork among physicians and nurses: teamwork in the eye of the beholder', *Journal of the American College of Surgeons*, 202(5), pp. 746–52.

Makary, M.A., Sexton, J.B., Freischlag, J.A., Millman, E.A., Pryor, D., Holzmueller, C. and Pronovost, P.J. (2006) 'Patient safety in surgery', *Annals of Surgery*, 243(5), pp. 628–35.

Malhotra, A., Majchrzak, A. and Rosen, B. (2007) 'Leading virtual teams', *Academy of Management Perspectives*, 21(1), pp. 60–70.

Margerison, C. and McCann, D. (1990) *Team Management*, London: W.H. Allen.

Matthewman, L., Rose, A. and Hetherington, A. (eds) (2009) *Work Psychology*, Oxford, Oxford University Press.

Milanovich, D.M., Driskell, J.E., Stout, R.J. and Salas, E. (1998) 'Status and cockpit dynamics: a review and empirical study', *Group Dynamics*, 2(3), pp. 155–67.

Moreno, J.L. (1953) *Who Shall Survive?* (2nd edn), New York: Beacon Press.

National Transportation Safety Board (1994) *A Review of Flightcrew-Involved Major Accidents of US Air Carriers, 1978 through 1990*, Safety Study NTSB/SS-94/01, Washington, DC.

Newing, R. (2007) 'The great enabler: trust', *Financial Times*, 29 June, Understanding the Culture of Collaboration Supplement, pp. 18–19.

Pentland, A. (2012) 'The new science of building teams', *Harvard Business Review*, 90(4), pp. 60–70.

Shapiro, D.L., Furst, S.A., Speitzer, G.M. and Von Glinow, M.A. (2002) 'Transnational teams in the electronic age: are teams' identity and high performance at risk', *Journal of Organizational Behaviour*, 23(4), pp. 455–67.

Shaw, M.E. (1978) 'Communication networks fourteen years later', in L. Berkowitz (ed.), *Group Processes*, New York: Academic Press, pp. 351–61.

Shin, Y. (2005) 'Conflict resolution in virtual teams', *Organizational Dynamics*, 34(4), pp. 331–45.

Stevens, M.J. and Campion, M.A. (1994) 'The knowledge, skill and ability requirements for teamwork: implications for human research management', *Journal of Management*, 20(2), pp. 503–30.

Stevens, M.J. and Campion, M.A. (1999) 'Staffing work teams: development of a selection test for teamwork settings', *Journal of Management*, 25(2), pp. 207–28.

Tarnow, E. (2000) 'Self-destructive obedience in the airplane cockpit and the concept of obedience optimization', in T. Blass (ed.), *Obedience to Authority: Current Perspectives on the Milgram Paradigm*, Mahwah, NJ: Erlbaum.

Tichy, N. and Fombrun, C. (1979) 'Network analysis on organizational settings', *Human Relations*, 32(11), pp. 923–65.

Tieman, R. (2012) 'From teamwork to collaboration', *Financial Times*, 15 March, Executive Appointments, p. 1.

White, R. and Lippitt, R. (1960) *Autocracy and Democracy*, New York: Harper and Row.

Whyte, W.F. (1948) *Human Relations in the Restaurant Industry*, New York: McGraw-Hill.

Woolley, A. and Malone, T. (2011) 'What makes a team smarter? More women', *Harvard Business Review*, 89(6), pp. 32–3.

Zander, L., Mockaitis, A.I. and Butler, C.L. (2012) 'Leading global teams', *Journal of World Business*, 47(2), pp. 592–603.

Zigurs, I. (2002) 'Leadership in virtual teams: oxymoron or opportunity?', *Organizational Dynamics*, 31(4), pp. 339–51.

Chapter 12 **Individuals in groups**

Key terms

social identity
social categorization
self-categorization
self-esteem
social representations
shared frame of reference
social influence
social facilitation
social inhibition
synergy
social compensation
social loafing
free rider
group norm
pivotal norms
peripheral norms
group sanction
conformity
obedience
group cohesion
group socialization
deindividuation
compliance
conversion

Learning outcomes

When you have read this chapter, you should be able to define those key terms in your own words, and you should also be able to:

1. Explain the basic tenets of social identity theory and social representation theory.
2. Distinguish the different directions in which individuals' behaviour can be modified by a group.
3. Understand how groups use norms to regulate the behaviour of their members.
4. Understand the process of group socialization of individuals.
5. Explain why individuals conform to the dictates of their group.
6. Distinguish between conformity and obedience, and between compliance and conversion.

Why study individuals in groups?

The enthusiasm of management for groups and teams in the workplace is tempered by the research of social scientists who see them possessing a darker side, one which becomes evident when manifested in the behaviour of some mobs and crowds on the street. They are seen as taking over the individual's mind, depressing intelligence, eliminating moral responsibility, and forcing conformity. A group can cause its members a great deal of suffering and despair and can perpetuate acts of great cruelty. The man and woman in the street, observing the collapse of the Royal Bank of Scotland, Halifax Bank of Scotland (HBOS) and Northern Rock, and experiencing the ongoing financial crisis which began in 2008, will have wondered 'How could this have happened?'. How were decisions made to lend ever larger amounts of money to borrowers who were unable to repay them? Discussing HBOS and its staff, Ellis and Taylor (2010) reported that 'many had their doubts about the strategy' (p. 806). What part did groups play in this process? Did group pressure silence those who felt that such lending might be a bad idea?

There is now extensive research evidence which demonstrates the power of groups to affect the behaviour of their members. This was originally conducted by Elton Mayo at the Hawthorne plant in the 1920s. Since that time, managements have harnessed this power by creating groups and teams which police and discipline their own members, keeping their behaviour in line with organizational (management) objectives. This chapter introduces the basic concepts of group norms, socialization, and sanctions. While the power of the group to affect the perceptions, performance, and attitudes of its individual members is well established, there has also been a growing body of research that shows how a lone individual can have an influence on a majority. The two concepts of compliance and conversion have generated a great deal of interest in this field.

STOP AND THINK

Are you a team player? What evidence would you provide an employer at a selection interview to demonstrate whether or not you are a 'team player'? Use an example from school, university, social life, or work life.

The individual and the group

Henri Tajfel and John Turner (1986) argued that as long as individuals see themselves as more important than their group, then the latter cannot function effectively. Participants have to stop seeing themselves as individuals, and instead identify themselves as group members, treating the group's values as their own. Such an attitudinal 'switch' and commitment, facilitates the long-term existence and success of their group. This question of how much an individual should be part of the group (for their own well being, for that of their group, and for the organization) and how much separate from it (to remain creative, critical and for their own mental health), is a continuing debate in the literature.

Let us first consider some theories which seek to explain the relationship between the individual and their group. Tajfel and Turner (1986) developed a *social identity theory* which holds that a person's self-concept is based not only on their individual characteristics or personal identity (*I am reserved, I am interested in music, I have blond hair*), but also on their group membership (*I am French, I work for ABC corporation, I am a member of the accounting profession*). They then compare themselves to other individuals and groups. Group formation can be seen as an adaptive process as one moves from feeling and thinking as an individual (personal identity) to feeling and thinking as a representative of a group (social identity). Group identity holds that group membership affects people's sense of who they are. The groups or social categories to which we belong (e.g. student course member; management

Social identity that part of the self-concept which comes from our membership of groups and which contributes to our self-esteem.

Social categorization classifying the people we meet on the basis of how similar to or different from the way that we see ourselves they are.

Self-categorization perceiving ourselves as sharing the same social identity as other category members, and behaving in ways consistent with that category stereotype.

team member; parent or sports club secretary) are an integral part of our *self-concept*. Our own self-concept (a term we met in Chapter 6) is the way in which we see ourselves, the set of perceptions that we have about ourselves. It affects both how we feel about ourselves and how we act within a group. This is because joining a group lowers our self-awareness and raises our group awareness. The roles that we play within different groups, especially those that are important to us, influence and shape our attitudes and behaviours.

The part of an individual's self-concept that comes from their membership of a group is called **social identity** and fulfils two functions. First, it defines and evaluates a person (e.g. 'she's a member of the design team'). Such definition and evaluation is done both by others and by the person themselves. Second, it prescribes appropriate behaviour for them. They think and behave in characteristically 'design team' ways. How this happens is through social comparison. According to Tajfel, in order to evaluate your own opinions and abilities, you not only compare yourself with other individuals with whom you interact, but you also compare your own group with similar, but distinct, out-groups. This comparison process is called **social categorization**. It involves classifying the people we meet on the basis of how similar or different they are from the way that we see ourselves. If I see myself as motivated, I will categorize other people as more, equally, or less motivated. We also *self-categorize*, which means that we perceive ourselves as having the same social identity as other category members. It leads us to behave in ways that are consistent with the stereotypes of the categories to which we believe that we belong. The **self-categorization** process transforms a number of individuals into a group (see Figure 12.1).

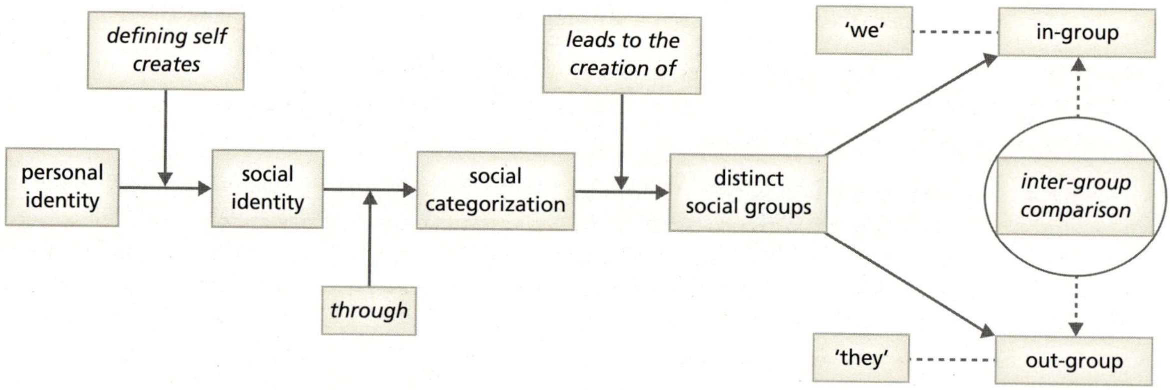

Figure 12.1: Social identity theory (based on Tajfel and Turner, 1986)

Social categorization and self-categorization lead to assumptions of similarity among those who are categorized together. They minimize the perceived differences between members of the in-group, and maximize the differences between the in-group and out-groups. When this happens, the individuals who are part of the in-group will have assumed a social identity, and will view other people from this standpoint (see Figure 12.2).

We all see ourselves as members of various social groupings, which are distinguishable and hence different from other social groupings. The consequence is that by identifying with certain groupings but not others, we come to see the world in terms of 'us-and-them'. There are two benefits for us from this. First, our understanding of the world is enhanced by classifying everybody this way. Second, our **self-esteem** can be maintained or even enhanced. Membership of a high-status group gives us prestige, which in turn raises our self-esteem. We are highly motivated to feel proud to belong to the group of which we are members. If we cannot achieve this feeling of pride, we will try either to change the group's perceived status or to detach ourselves from it. Although such social identification can potentially lead to conflict between different groups within an organization, it can also be effectively managed in a way that improves the performance of both groups.

Self-esteem that part of the self which is concerned with how we evaluate ourselves.

Categorizing people into groups and identifying with some of these groups appears to be a fundamental human characteristic which derives from the fact that human beings are

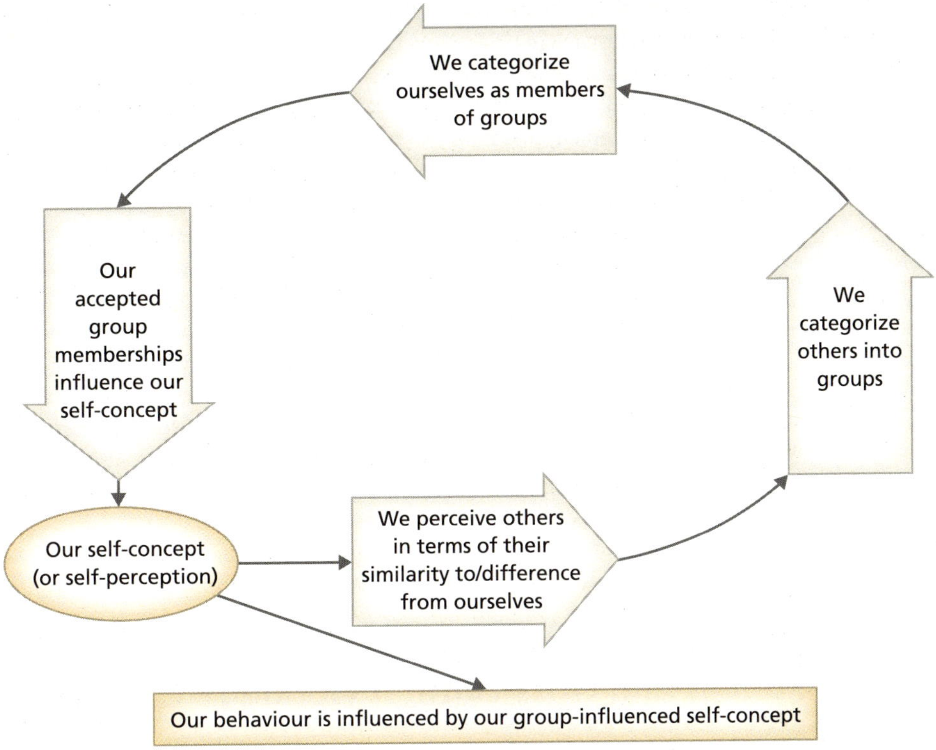

Figure 12.2: Processes of social and self-categorization

Source: from *Interactive Behaviour at Work*, Guirdham, M. Pearson Education Limited, © Pearson Education Limited 2002.

social animals. Because of these two basic needs for differentiating themselves from others and for belonging, individuals expose themselves to the control of others. Within the organizational context, we offer control to fellow group members who wish to direct our attitudes, thoughts, and ideas in line with what the group considers appropriate; and also to managers who seek both to motivate and control us, through instituting various team working arrangements.

STOP AND THINK Which group memberships do you cite when you introduce yourself to others? From the 'us-and-them' perspective, who are 'us' and who are 'them' for you? Has this helped your own group improve its performance? Has it raised your own self-esteem? Has the management in your organization used this distinction to motivate or control your group? How?

Group influences on individuals' perceptions

How does a group affect the perceptions of its individual members? One explanation was offered at the start of this text with the *constructivist* perspective (see Chapter 1). This argued that our social and organizational surroundings possess no ultimate truth or reality, but are determined instead by the way in which we experience and understand those worlds which we construct and reconstruct for ourselves, in interaction with others. In short, we don't see things as they are – we see things as *we* are. Among these important 'others' with whom we interact, and with whom we experience and understand the world, are the members of the groups to which we belong.

Social representations the beliefs, ideas, and values about objects, people, and events that are constructed by current group members, and which are transmitted to its new members.

Another explanation is provided by *social representation theory* which was formulated by Serge Moscovici (1984). This refers to the finding that when individuals join a new group, its members will construct and transmit complex and unfamiliar ideas to them, in straightforward and familiar ways. This process creates what are termed **social representations**, which come to be accepted, in a modified form, by the new members of a group, and these help the new recruits to make sense of what is going on around them within the group and the organization. The explanation of some occurrence is simplified, distorted, and ritualized by the group, and becomes a 'common-sense explanation' which is accepted as orthodoxy among its members, and is then communicated to new members. Social representations are a group's theories about how the world works and are used to justify actions. The prefix 'social' reminds us about the collective way in which reality is jointly manufactured, accepted, and shared.

As a new company recruit, you discuss your role in the group with existing members. During these interactions, representations are presented, developed, adapted, and negotiated before being incorporated into your own existing belief framework. This happens during the period of socialization, shortly after you join the group. It is not a matter of you, as a new recruit, being given and accepting a bundle of existing group assumptions, ideas, beliefs, and opinions to absorb. Rather, Moscovici's theory emphasizes the interactive nature of the process between you, as an individual, and the other group members. Once incorporated, the group representations are revealed in all group members' talk and actions.

Global teams and cross-cultural working

Organizations that operate in a global business environment create teams whose members are culturally diverse and can have difficulty understanding, communicating, and working with each other. For example, the International Air Transport Association (IATA) represents 230 airlines, employs 1,600 staff from 140 nationalities, operates in 74 countries, and has its headquarters in Geneva (Switzerland) and Montreal (Canada). Companies have traditionally used either the 'colonial' approach, using skilled expatriates from the base country, or a 'cultural translators' approach, using staff who have working experience in more than one cultural setting. Western companies operating in mainland China, for example, often fill management roles with Chinese staff from Taiwan, Singapore, and Hong Kong. However, cultural differences can limit the effectiveness of expatriates, and cultural translators are in high demand, which makes them expensive. Chinese, Indian, and many Asian cultures are 'collectivist' and are acutely aware of status differences; they are known as cultures high in power distance (see Chapter 4). In contrast, Western European and North American cultures are more individualist, with low power distance. Junior team members from cultures with lower power distance share their ideas and challenge others, including more senior members of the team. In contrast, Chinese staff are cautious about making such interventions and defer to senior team members.

IATA developed a special training programme for twenty of their change agents, ten from East Asia and ten from European and American cultures. This programme was launched in Beijing by IATA's chief executive Giovanni Bisignani and his top team. This group was then paired to co-lead ten teams whose members were high-potential junior employees in different locations. This meant that each member of the co-management pair had to learn about and adjust their approaches to each other, as well as to their team members. The teams worked on defined projects, in addition to their routine jobs, for a couple of months. The change agents also had to provide skills training to another ten-person team on issues such as teamwork, project management, and cross-cultural awareness. This programme had powerful learning effects. For example, one participant said 'Being Chinese, it was surprising how much I learnt about Chinese culture from the programme – but it was from the perspective of my Western colleagues, so my insight now has a stereo effect.' The experience led to this plan for integrating different cultures:

- Identify two cultures that need to collaborate.
- Nominate leaders from each culture.
- Allocate appropriate pairs of co-leaders.
- Use real projects as the basis for teamworking.
- Establish a realistic time frame.
- Share practices, both good and bad.
- Adapt for the next cross-cultural challenge.

The IATA chief executive concluded that this programme was 'helping me and my senior management team to accelerate the process of building a leadership pool within our Asian employee ranks. And it has exposed our current high-potential leaders to other cultures and sensitized them to doing business with Asian cultures' (based on Jonsen and Bryant, 2008).

Shared frame of reference assumptions held in common by group members, which shape their thinking, decisions, actions, and interactions, while being constantly defined and reinforced through those interactions.

Through these social representations, group members gain a **shared frame of reference**. Over time, new group members learn about the different assumptions, ideas, beliefs, and opinions held by their fellow group members about their common work situation. Some agreement on perception and meaning is essential among the members of a group if they are to interact, communicate, agree on goals, and generally act in concert on a common task. Such a shared view is essential for a group to continue and to develop. Moreover, as we work in a group, we find that our views begin to coalesce with those of other members. A shared frame of reference and social representations suggest the existence of a group-level process equivalent of organizational culture forming – a 'group culture' (see Chapter 4). Together, the shared frame of reference and social representations processes determine the meanings that group members come to attach to events and to other people's behaviour around them.

STOP AND THINK What challenges have you found when working in tutorial or project groups at university with fellow students coming from different parts of the world? In your view, does their ethnic or national background affect their behaviour within your group? In what ways?

Group influences on individuals' performance

Social influence, social facilitation, and social inhibition

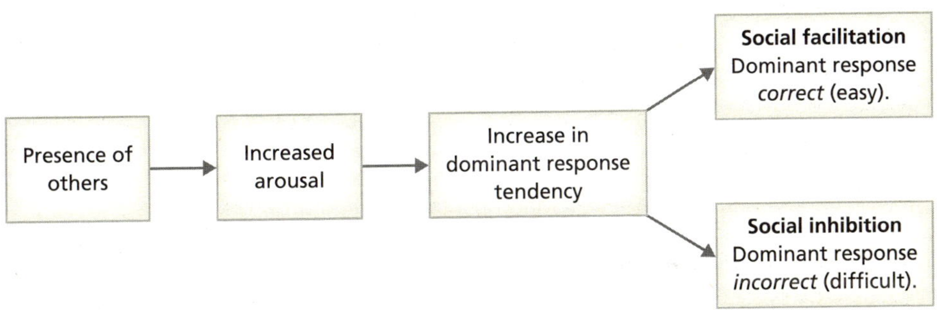

Figure 12.3: Social facilitation and social inhibition

Source: reproduced by permission of SAGE Publications, London, Los Angeles, New Delhi and Singapore, adapted from Banyard, P.E., Davies, M.N.O., Norman, C. and Winder, B., *Essential Psychology: A Concise Introduction*, Copyright © Sage Publications, 2010.

Social influence the process whereby attitudes and behaviours are changed by the real or implied presence of others.

Social facilitation the effect of the presence of other people enhancing an individual's performance.

Social inhibition the effect of the presence of other people reducing an individual's performance.

Social influence refers to the process whereby our attitudes and behaviour are influenced by the presence of others. The presence of others can either improve or reduce our performance. These are termed **social facilitation** and **social inhibition**. Figure 12.3 indicates that having other people around you increases your arousal, and that, plus the complexity of the task that you perform (easy or difficult), determines how well you do.

Early research investigated individuals performing various physical tasks. Norman Triplett (1898) studied children winding fishing reels and cyclists racing. The children were found to turn the reels faster when other children were present, and the cyclists performed 20 per cent faster when accompanied by a pacemaker than when alone, even in a non-racing situation. Later studies focused on non-physical tasks. Floyd Allport (1920) discovered that students completed mathematical calculations faster in the company of other students than when alone, and coined the term *social facilitation*. However, research also revealed that the presence of others can also reduce task performance, a process that is labelled *social inhibition*.

The explanation is that the presence of others increases arousal which acts to enhance whatever a person's 'dominant response' is. If the task is easy to complete successfully; has been frequently performed in the past; or is already well learned; then there will be an increase in the person's performance in the presence of others. In contrast, if a task is difficult to

Synergy the positive or negative result of the interaction of two or more components, producing an outcome that is different from the sum of the individual components.

complete successfully; has rarely been performed in the past; or has been poorly learned; then the increased arousal caused by the presence of others will reduce performance. Also relevant here is the concept of **synergy**, which refers to the positive or negative result of the interaction of two or more individuals which produces an outcome (which can be positive or negative) that is different from the sum of the individuals operating separately.

Positive synergy is a concept which underpins all kinds of groups working in organizations. In particular, it supports the use of cross-functional teams. Positive synergy means that the final output produced by a group of individuals working together, rather than separately, will equal more than the sum of the individual members' abilities and efforts. A popular shorthand term for this is 2 + 2 = 5. It has been argued that the designated purpose of group tasks should necessarily *require* more than its members are able to offer working as individuals, so as to benefit from the positive aspects of synergy.

Social compensation and social loafing

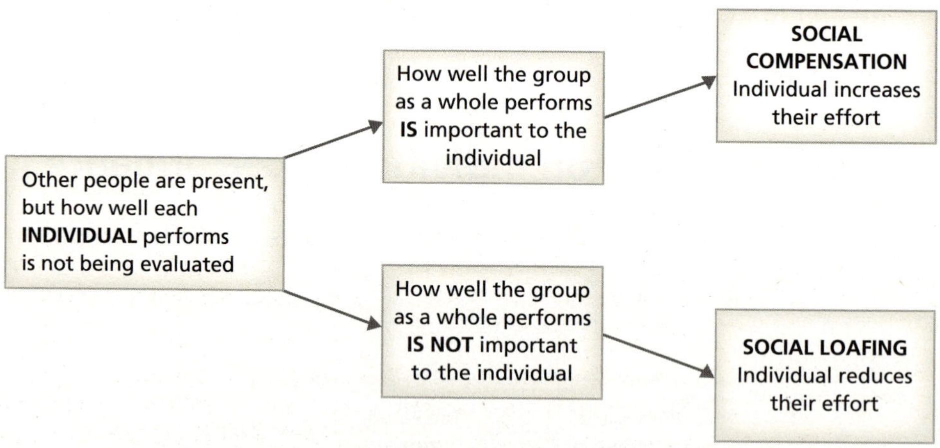

Figure 12.4: Social compensation and social loafing

Source: reproduced by permission of SAGE Publications, London, Los Angeles, New Delhi and Singapore, adapted from Banyard, P.E., Davies, M.N.O., Norman, C. and Winder, B., *Essential Psychology: A Concise Introduction*, Copyright © Sage Publications, 2010.

Social compensation persons increasing their effort, and working harder, when in a group.

Social loafing the tendency for individuals to exert less effort when working as part of a group than when working alone.

Sometimes, when people work together as a group, they perform better than if they worked alone. At other times, when working in a group, they will expend less effort because their input, within the group, is therefore more hidden. The term **social compensation** refers to persons increasing their effort, and working harder, when in a group than when alone (Williams and Karau, 1991; Zaccaro, 1984). This happens when individuals place greater value upon the group rather than on the individual, or when group members are expected to achieve goals that are important both to the individuals and to the group (Guzzo and Dickson, 1996). Much of management's enthusiasm for teamworking (see Chapter 13) is based on its belief (or hope) that social compensation will be triggered among employees when they are organized to work in a group rather than on their own (see Figure 12.4).

STOP AND THINK

Think of a time when you put a lot of effort into a group of which you were a part – work group, sports team or social group. Was the performance or well being of that group important to you? Did you contribute far more than would normally have been expected of you?

Social loafing is the tendency of individuals to exert less effort when working as part of a group than when working alone. Jos Benders (2005) traced management's concern with employees working less hard than they theoretically could to the start of the twentieth century. In Europe, the famous German sociologist Max Weber wrote about what he called 'braking'

(Weber, 1924). At the same time in America, Frederick Taylor, a management consultant, was concerned with 'systematic soldiering' among the workers (see Chapter 14). This shirking or withholding of individual effort can explain why teamworking can reduce productivity.

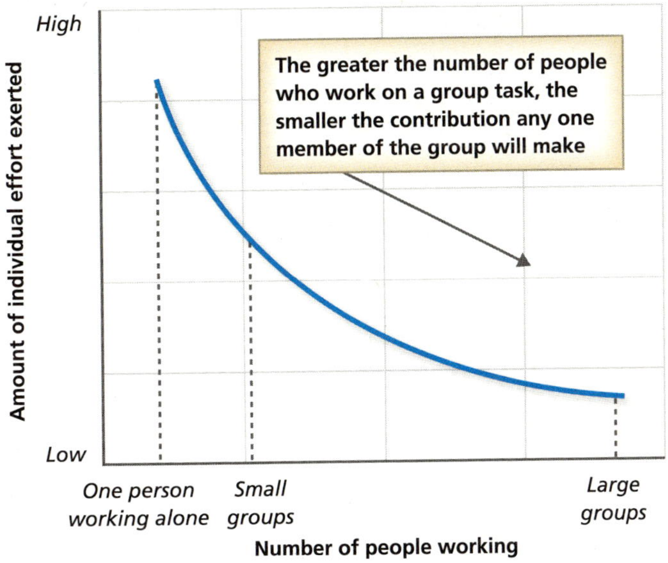

Figure 12:5: The social loafing effect

Source: GREENBERG, JERALD, MANAGING BEHAVIOR IN ORGANIZATIONS, 2nd Ed., © 1999, p. 158. Reprinted and Electronically reproduced by permission of Pearson Education, Inc., Upper Saddle River, New Jersey.

Max Ringelmann, a French professor of agricultural engineering, conducted the original research in the late 1920s on subjects, arranged in a row, pulling a rope, as in a 'tug-of-war' contest (Kravitz and Martin, 1986). People in the first position on the rope pulled less hard when they thought that people behind them were also pulling. Research suggests that individual effort tends to decrease as the size of the group increases. Ringelmann found that three people pulling together only achieved two and a half times the average individual rate, while eight 'pullers' achieved less than a quarter of the average individual rate. Ingham et al. (1974) later repeated these experiments and reported that subjects expended 18 per cent more effort when pulling alone than when pulling as part of a group (see Figure 12.5). The 'Ringelmann effect' was renamed social loafing in the 1970s by Bibb Latane following investigations at Ohio University to confirm Ringelmann's original work (Latane et al., 1979).

Social loafing is an example of negative synergy. Teamwork of all kinds is fraught with tensions, conflicts, obstacles, and problems. If these are not managed effectively, rather than surpassing the best member's capabilities, the total group output may actually equal *less* than the weakest members' efforts. This is caused by various 'process losses' which can hinder effective group functioning (Steiner, 1972). If group process losses exceed group process gains, then one will have a situation of negative synergy. The mathematical analogy would be 2 + 2 = 3. Suggestions have been offered at both the individual and the social levels to account for social loafing (George, 1992; Karau and Williams, 1993; Latane and Nida, 1980). These 'group process losses', as they are known, have been ascribed to various causes listed in Table 12.1.

Table 12.1: Causes of social loafing with illustrative statements

Cause	What people say
Inequity of effort	'Others are not contributing, why should I?'
Diffusion of responsibility	'I'm not personally responsible for the outcome.'
Negative effect of group reward	'Everyone will get the same, why should I work harder?'
Problems of coordination	'People are getting in each other's way.'
Anonymity	'I'm hidden in the crowd, no one will notice me.'

Social loafing has been found to occur most often when

- the task was perceived as unimportant, simple, or boring;
- group members thought their individual output was not identifiable;
- the nature of each person's contribution was similar to that of the others;
- group members expected their colleagues to loaf.

The solutions offered to managers to overcome social loafing assume that it is our natural state, and that something has to be added to a situation to avoid it (Greenberg and Baron, 1997; Baron and Byrne, 2000). Suggestions include:

Make work more involving:	Raise commitment to successful task performance, and encourage members to perform at a high level.
Upgrade task:	Increase the perceived importance of the task in the group members' eyes.
Increase group significance:	Increase the significance that the group has for its individual members.
Strengthen group cohesion:	Make the group size small, with membership attractive and stable, with common goals; facilitate member interaction.
Identify workers:	Point out each member's individual contribution in order to prevent their getting away with a 'free ride'.
Reward contributions to the group:	Reward members for helping others achieve the common goal, and not just for their individual contributions.
Threaten punishment:	Fear of punishment prevents loafing and gets members to 'pull their weight' in the group.

How many pickles could a pickle packer pack if pickle packers were only paid for properly packed pickles?

What are the problems facing production line workers in a pickle factory? A key job is stuffing dill pickle halves into jars. Only dill halves of a certain length can be used. Those that are too long will not fit, those that are too short will float and dance inside and look cheap and crummy. The dill halves and jars are carried on separate high speed conveyor belts past the contingent of pickle stuffers. If the stuffers don't stuff quickly enough, the jars pile up at the workers' stations while they look for pickles of the appropriate length, so stuffers have a great temptation to stuff whichever pickles come to hand. The individual outputs of the stuffers are unidentifiable, since all jars go into a common hopper before they reach the quality control section. Responsibility for the output cannot be focused on one worker. This combination of factors leads to poor performance and improper packing. This research suggests making individual production identifiable and raises the question 'How many pickles could a pickle packer pack if pickle packers were only paid for properly packed pickles?' (based on Williams et al., 1981).

Free rider a member who obtains benefits from team membership without bearing a proportional share of the costs for generating that benefit.

Social loafing is related to free riding (Frohlich and Oppenheimer, 1970; Kerr, 1983). A **free rider** obtains benefits from team membership without bearing a proportional share of the costs for generating the benefit. Hogg and Vaughan (2008) give the example of a tax evader who uses the healthcare service, the education system, and the roads. The main difference between social loafing and free riding is that although loafers reduce their individual effort on team tasks, they still contribute something to the group's goal. In contrast, free riders exploit the group product, as in the case of a team project, where a student gets the same grade as all the others, without having contributed anything whatsoever to the team's final report.

Free riding dooms a team to ineffectiveness and is abhorrent to team members for three reasons. It violates an equity standard – members who have contributed baulk at others who receive the same benefits despite having contributed nothing. It violates a social responsibility standard – everyone should contribute their fair share. Finally, it violates a reciprocity standard – members should exchange their contributions with each other. The basic strategy for management to counteract free riding is to broaden the individual's concept of self-interest and arrange matters so that an individual's personal goals are attained by the achievement of the group's collective goal (Albanese and Van Fleet, 1985).

Source: www.phdcomics.com

STOP AND THINK

Have you had experience of social loafing or free riding in your educational or work context? What advice would you give to your instructor or manager to remove it?

Group influences on individuals' behaviour

Muzafer Sherif (1906–1988)

Elton Mayo originally noted the existence of **group norms**, and their enforcement through sanctions, during the Bank Wiring Observation Room studies at the Hawthorne works. The men there restricted their output to conform to a group-agreed norm or standard. In another study which has now become a classic in experimental social psychology, Muzafer Sherif (1936) showed how group norms emerged.

Sherif placed a group of three subjects in a darkened room and presented them with a small spot of light on a wall to view. He then asked them to track the apparent movement of the spot, and to say, aloud, each in turn, the direction in which they thought that the light was moving. The apparent movement is an optical illusion known as the 'autokinetic effect'. The light does not move. Sherif's subjects made three series of 100 estimates on successive days. Initially, there were quite wide individual differences in the response to this situation. Some subjects saw little movement while others saw a lot. However, Sherif discovered that they started to agree on the amount of apparent movement quite quickly. Having exchanged information on their judgements, their behaviour changed. They began seeing the light moving in the same direction as those who had spoken earlier.

Group norm an expected mode of behaviour or belief that is established either formally or informally by a group.

Gradually, all the members came to see the light as moving in the same direction at the same time. There was of course no 'real' movement of the light. Each individual began to see the light in the same way as the group saw it. The results Sherif obtained with two-person and three-person groups are shown in Figure 12.6. When a group norm emerged it was found that it became the basis for subsequent judgement when subjects were re-tested independently. The group norm therefore became a relatively permanent frame of reference for individual behaviour (Sherif, 1936).

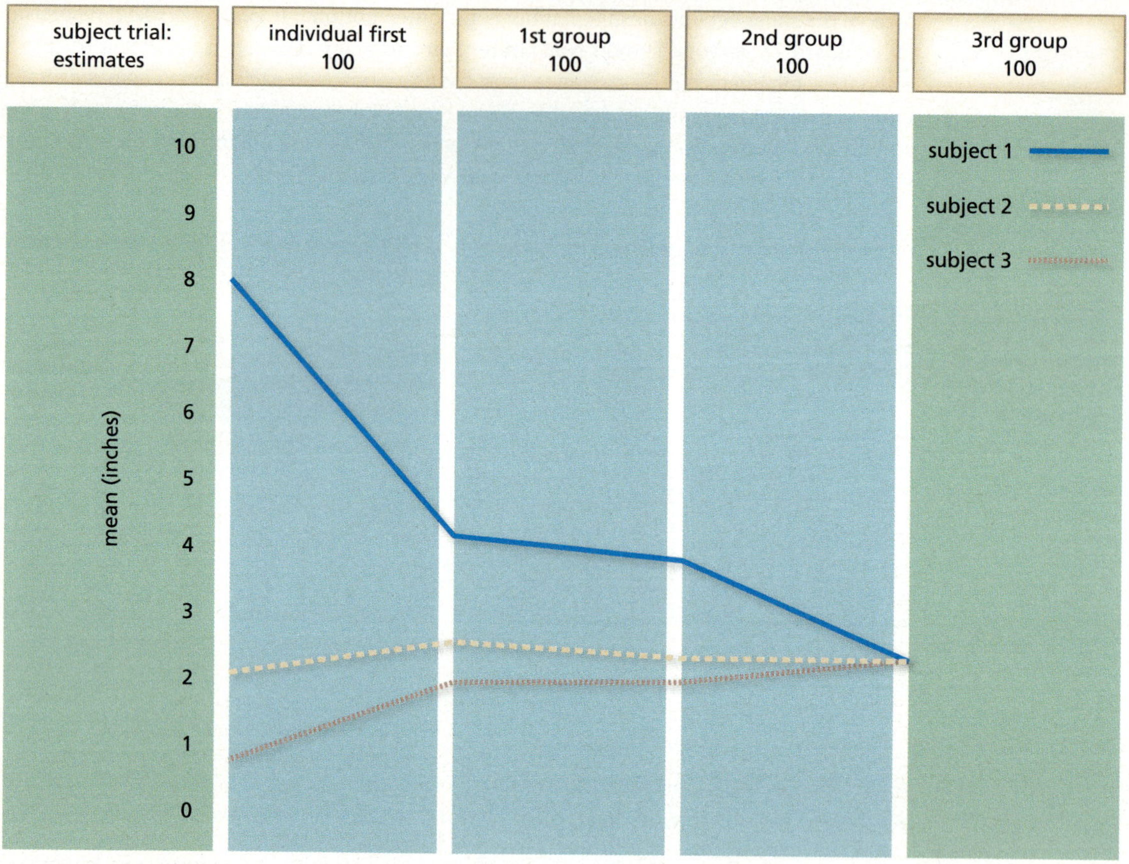

Figure 12.6: Emergence of group norms

Sherif's work showed that in a situation where doubt and uncertainty exist and where first-hand information is lacking, a person's viewpoint will shift to come into line with those of other group members. In essence this situation leads to the creation of a group norm. This occurs quickly amongst group members who have had little previous experience of the group's work, but it also occurs amongst those who have had experience, although more slowly. Few of the subjects who took part in Sherif's experiments felt conscious that others had influenced their judgements. Sherif's work suggested that in order to organize and manage itself, every group develops a system of norms. Norms are behavioural expectations and they serve to define the nature of the group. They express the values of the members of the group and provide guidelines to help the group achieve its goals. A group may develop its norms both consciously and unconsciously.

Pivotal norms socially defined standards relating to behaviour and beliefs that are central to a group's objective and survival.

Peripheral norms socially defined standards relating to behaviour and beliefs that are important but not crucial to a group's objective and survival.

Norms guide behaviour and facilitate interaction by specifying the kinds of reactions expected or acceptable in a particular situation. Not all group norms have equal importance. **Pivotal norms** guide behaviour which is central to the group, for example, the level of output or the amount of work preparation done. In contrast, **peripheral norms** guide behaviour that is important but not essential, for example, choice of clothing or break-time activities. Group members who violate pivotal norms can impede group objectives or endanger the group's survival. Therefore, the consequences for such transgressing individuals are severe. In contrast, violation of peripheral norms, although frowned upon, has fewer negative consequences for the offender

Bloody beefers and hanging beef tongues

Martiens Bezuidenhout/Dreamstime.com

William Thompson, a university researcher, worked as an assembly line worker in a beef-processing plant in the American Midwest. In the role of participant observer, he studied the day-to-day activities of his fellow workers. He reported that working in the beef plant was 'dirty' work, not only in the literal sense of being drenched with perspiration and beef blood, but also in the figurative sense of performing a low-status, routine, and demeaning job. Thompson and his co-workers had to hang, brand, and bag between 1,350 and 1,500 beef tongues during an eight-hour shift. The work was monotonous and routine.

Thompson described the camaraderie between the 'beefers', as they called themselves. Because of the noise, the need for earplugs, and the isolation of certain work areas, it was virtually impossible for the men on the assembly line to speak to each other. Instead, they communicated using an elaborate system of symbols. These included exaggerated gestures, shrill whistles, 'thumbs up' and 'thumbs down', and the clanging of knives against stainless steel tables and tubs. Thompson observed that in a setting which apparently eliminated social interaction, the workers' desire for it won out and interaction flourished.

To reduce the feeling of alienation and retain a sense of humanity, the beefers developed certain coping mechanisms. They replaced the formal, managerially imposed norms of the workplace with their own informal ones. At certain times, instead of working at a steady speed which matched the line speed, they would work at a frantic pace, and get ahead of the line. While such behaviour added only a few precious minutes to their scheduled break time, its importance was primarily symbolic, in that it challenged the company's dictates concerning the speed of the line, and it gave the men a small measure of control over the work process. The informal group norms also encouraged certain types of rule-breaking. The workers made a game out of doing forbidden things, simply to see if they could get away with them. For example, despite strict rules to the contrary, workers covered in beef blood washed their hands, arms, and knives in a tub of water reserved for cleaning tongues. In addition, workers often cut out pieces of meat, and threw them at other employees. If not noticed by the supervisor, the thrown meat chunks might be picked up off the floor, and put back onto the line – a blatant violation of hygiene rules. Thompson concluded that such 'artful sabotage served as a symbolic way in which workers could express a sense of individuality, and hence self-worth' (based on Thompson, 1983).

STOP AND THINK

It is important to feel that you fit in with your peers (others in your group, school, or neighbourhood). However, sometimes you may find yourself doing something because others are doing it, and that makes you feel uncomfortable or unsafe. Sometimes it is hard to say no to your friends. Can you think of an occasion when you experienced such a situation? How did you feel?

Why do group norms develop? David Feldman (1984) argued that their purpose was to

- *facilitate group task achievement or group survival* – groups develop norms which increase their chances of being successful and protect themselves from outsiders;

- *increase the predictability of group members' behaviours* – predictability means that internally, members can anticipate and prepare for the actions of colleagues, thereby smoothing social interaction, while externally, it allows them to relate appropriately to outsiders;
- *reduce embarrassing interpersonal problems for group members* – knowing what to do and say in a group (and what not to) increases an individual member's comfort;
- *express the group's core values and define their distinctiveness* – norms allow members to gain a sense of the essence of the group.

Discovering the norm

In a classic study, Donald Roy, a researcher who acted as a participant observer in a factory, described the pressures that were placed on an individual to adhere to the group norm. Roy's earnings, and those of others, were based on a piece-rate system. The more he produced, the more he earned.

> From my first to my last day at the plant I was subject to warnings and predictions concerning price cuts. Pressure was the heaviest from Joe Mucha, who shared my job repertoire and kept a close eye on my production. On November 14, the day after my first attained quota, Joe Mucha advised: Don't let it go over $1.25 an hour, or the time-study man will be right down here! And they don't waste time, either! They watch the records like a hawk! I got ahead, so I took it easy for a couple of hours. Joe told me that I had made $10.01 yesterday and warned me not to go over $1.25 an hour. Jack Starkey spoke to me after Joe left. 'What's the matter? Are you trying to upset the applecart?' Jack explained in a friendly manner that $10.50 was too much to turn in, even on an old job. 'The turret-lathe men can turn in $1.35', said Jack, 'but their rate is 90 cents and ours is 85 cents.' Jack warned me that the Methods Department could lower their prices on any job, old or new, by changing the fixture slightly or changing the size of the drill. According to Jack, a couple of operators . . . got to competing with each other to see how much they could turn in. They got up to $1.65 an hour, and the price was cut in half. And from then on they had to run that job themselves, as none of the other operators would accept that job. According to Jack, it would be all right for us to turn in $1.28 or $1.29 an hour, when it figured out that way, but it was not all right to turn in $1.30 an hour. Well now I know where the maximum is – $1.29 an hour. (Roy, 1960)

How do group norms develop? Feldman (1984) reported that they did so in four ways:

- *Initial pattern of behaviour* – the first behaviour pattern that emerges in a group can establish group expectations. For example, if the first speaker shares his feelings and anxieties with the other group members, the discussion of emotions in a group can become a norm.
- *Explicit statement by a supervisor or co-worker* – this person may explicitly state certain expectations. The project leader may tell the newcomer that the group meetings start promptly on the hour, when all members are expected to be present.
- *Critical events in the group's history* – a shop-floor employee makes a suggestion for an improvement to his supervisor who criticizes and ridicules him. Group members ensure that in the future, none of them offer any more suggestions.
- *Transfer behaviours from past situations* – when individuals carry over behaviours from past situations, they can increase the predictability of group members' behaviours in new settings. For example, instructors and students transfer constant expectations from class to class.

Research carried out into teams in 27 widely differing organizations has shown that the things that happen the first time a new group meets strongly affect how that group will operate throughout its entire future life. The first few minutes at the start of the first group meeting are crucial as they establish not only where the group is going but also what the relationship will be between the team leader and the group, and what basic norms of conduct will be expected and enforced. Richard Hackman quoted a distinguished orchestra conductor who reported that he pays the greatest attention to the first few minutes of his first rehearsal with any new orchestra as, in his view, its members will very quickly make an assessment about whether or not he and they are going to make great music together (Coutu, 2009, p. 103).

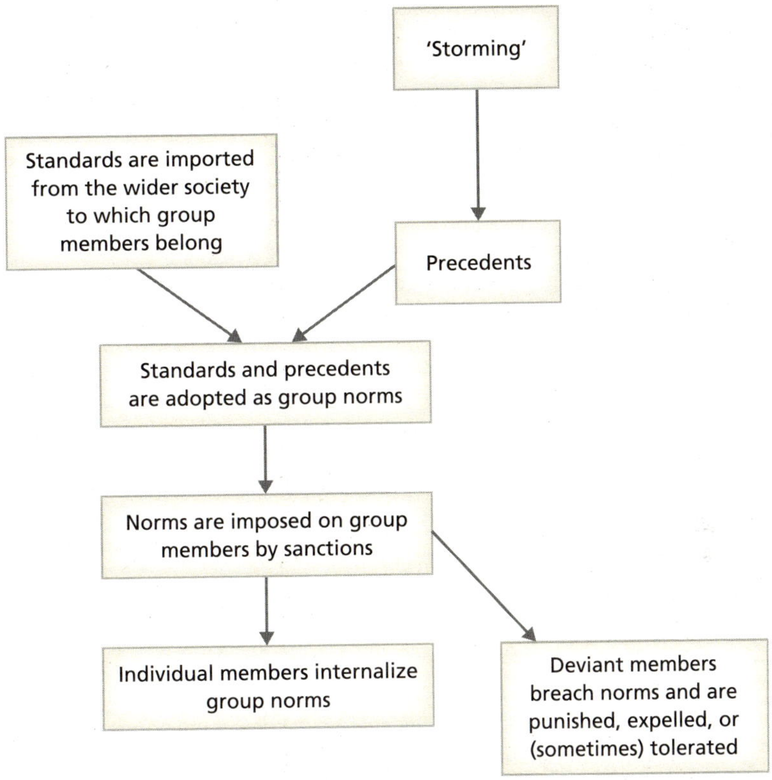

Figure 12.7: The formation and operation of group norms

Source: *Interactive Behaviour at Work*, Guirdham, M. Pearson Education Limited, © Pearson Education Limited 2002.

Group sanction a punishment or a reward given by members to others in the group in the process of enforcing group norms.

Figure 12.7 shows the process of the formation and operation of group norms. It appears that once established, group norms are difficult to change. Since the group members originally created the norms, it is they who ultimately change them. Members will tend to resist any attempts by managers or any other outsiders, to modify their group's norms. Some examples of norms and the reasons for their enforcement are shown in Table 12.2. To enforce its norms, a group develops a set of sanctions with which to police them. The term **group sanction** refers to the punishments and rewards that are given by a group to its members, in the process of enforcing group norms. Punishment is a negative sanction and a reward is a positive sanction.

The earliest examples of negative sanctions exercised in groups studied by researchers were revealed in the Bank Wiring Observation Room phase of the Hawthorne studies. The researchers discovered that persons who broke the group norm, for example, producing either over or under the group norm, were 'binged'. This involved a group member flicking the ear of the norm transgressor or tapping him painfully on the upper part of his arm. Both actions were intended to indicate physically to the man that his behaviour was unacceptable to the other group members. Other negative sanctions can also be used by the group, and can be placed in ascending order of severity as shown in Figure 12.8. If negative sanctions represent the 'stick' to enforce group norm compliance, then the positive sanctions represent the 'carrot'. Such carrots for the conforming individual include accolades from other members, emotional support, increase in social status, and acceptance of their ideas by others (Doms and van Avermaet, 1981).

Table 12.2: Norms and sanctions

Norm	Enforcement reason	Examples of sanctions to enforce the norm
Members attend all group meetings regularly and arrive on time.	Group survival	Absentees or latecomers are first teased or ridiculed, and then criticized.
All members are required to prepare written work before the group meetings to avoid delay at meeting.	Group task achievement	Group members compliment individuals whose preparation has been particularly thorough.
Members listen to each other's ideas without interrupting, allowing them to fully present their thoughts and opinions.	Clarification of behavioural expectations	A member who interrupts is taken aside after the meeting, and asked, in future, to let the person finish speaking.
Members do not discuss their private lives with colleagues at work.	Avoidance of embarrassment	Members who insist on discussing such matters are ostracized until they stop doing so.

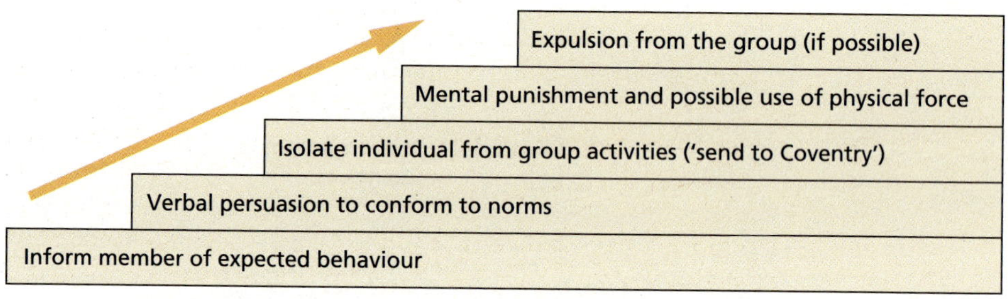

Figure 12.8: Escalating group pressure to secure individual conformity to group norms

Sent to Coventry

Being 'sent to Coventry' means becoming a social outcast. Individuals in a group can be punished in this way by their colleagues, who ignore them, refuse to speak to them, and isolate them from group activities. During the English Civil War (1642–1651) fought between the Royalists and the Parliamentarians, the city of Coventry was a strong outpost of parliamentary support. Royalist prisoners who were captured in the Midlands were frequently sent to the city of Coventry, where the local population would have nothing to do with them.

Conformity a change in an individual's belief or behaviour in response to real or imagined group pressure.

Obedience a situation in which an individual changes their behaviour in response to direct command from another.

Conformity with norms tends to increase under certain conditions. An increase in conformity is associated with a decrease in the size of the group; and also with an increase in the group's homogeneity, visibility and a stable experience. Members who perceive themselves to be of low status in the group will tend to conform more, and feel that they have to 'earn' the right to be deviant. High conformers are also those who feel that they are not fully accepted by the others. Diagnosing a team's norms and its members' conformity to them can help to explain group behaviour (Rothwell, 1992). Conformity can be contrasted with **obedience**, a situation in which individuals change their behaviour in response to a direction from others.

Source: © Lee Lorenz/The New Yorker Collection/www.cartoonbank.com

If you want to deviate from a group norm you have several options. You can attempt to persuade others to your viewpoint, and thus alter the group norm. Of course, the other members may respond by persuading you to conform to the existing norm. The higher your status, the more power you will have in the group and the more you will be able to change the behaviours and beliefs of the other members (and the less likely they will be to change your own). What other options are there? If the group is of little importance to you, and if you are free to leave the group, you will do so. Conversely, if you are of little importance to the group, you may be forced either to conform to its norms or else be rejected by its members. If, however, your presence is important to your group (e.g. because you possess high status, power, popularity, or special skills), then the group may tolerate your deviant behaviour and beliefs in order to avoid the threat of losing you as a valued member. Hence, the power that a group has to influence its members towards conformity to its norms depends on three main factors:

- the positive and negative sanctions (rewards and punishments) that the group has at its disposal;
- the member's desire to avoid negative sanctions such as social and physical punishments or expulsion from the group;
- the degree of attraction that the group has for an individual member and the attraction that group members have for each other.

Home viewing

The film *Big* (1988, director Penny Marshall) is a fantasy-comedy about a boy, Josh Baskin (played first by David Moscow, and then by Tom Hanks) whose wish to become 'big' is granted, and his 13-year-old mind comes to occupy the body of a 35-year-old man. Josh joins the Macmillan Toy Company, and is promoted to product testing because of his unique childlike insights into the business. During his time at the company, he is a member of several groups. As you watch the film, consider how his behaviour affects the other group members, and also how they affect what he does.

Group cohesion the number and strength of mutual positive attitudes between individual group members.

The last factor in the list above is called **group cohesion**. It refers to the number and strength of mutual positive attitudes towards group members. As Table 12.3 shows, how cohesive a group is can have a major impact on how it functions and what it achieves (Pearce et al., 2002).

Table 12.3: Group cohesion – contributors and consequences

Contributors to group cohesion	Consequences of group cohesion
Small size	
External threat	
Stable membership	Group success
Past success of group	Member satisfaction
Difficulty of entry to group	Productivity high or low
Members sharing common goals	Greater conformity by members
Opportunity to interact with others	Members' evaluations become distorted
Attractiveness of group to individuals	Increased interaction between members
Fairness of rewards between members	Increased group influence over members
Members' agreement about their statuses	More cooperative behaviour between individuals

STOP AND THINK

Consider a group of which you are a member, and its norms and sanctions. Reflect on a situation in which a member (perhaps yourself) broke a norm and received a sanction.

Assess the positive and negative outcomes of this occurrence for the individual group member concerned and for the group as a whole.

Having established a set of norms and the sanctions to enforce them, a group has to communicate these to new members. The new group member 'learns the ropes', and is shown how to get things done, how to interact with others and how to achieve a high social status within the group. An important aspect of achieving such status is to adhere to the group's rules or norms. Initial transgressions will be pointed out to the new member gently. However, the continued violation of norms by a group member puts at risk the cohesion of the group. When there is disagreement on a matter of importance to the group, the preservation of group effectiveness, harmony, and cohesion requires a resolution of the conflict. Hence pressure is exerted on the deviating individual through persuasive communication to conform. The name given to this 'educational' process which the new member undergoes is **group socialization** and it occurs within most groups in all types of organizations (see Figure 12.9).

Group socialization the process whereby members learn the values, symbols, and expected behaviours of the group to which they belong.

If new recruits are thoroughly socialized, they are less likely to transgress group norms and require sanctions to be administered. However, while such pressure to go along with the majority of other members may be beneficial in many respects for the group, it also carries costs. If conformity is allowed to dominate, and individuals are given little opportunity to present different views, there is the danger of the group collectively making errors of judgement, leading them to take unwise actions. Chapter 20 will consider the concept of groupthink which, through internal conformity and external group pressure, leads individual members collectively to make poor decisions. It is important to remember that while a work group will be attempting to get its new member to adopt its own values, symbols, and expected behaviours, the organization which recruited the person will be endeavouring to do the same (see Table 12.4).

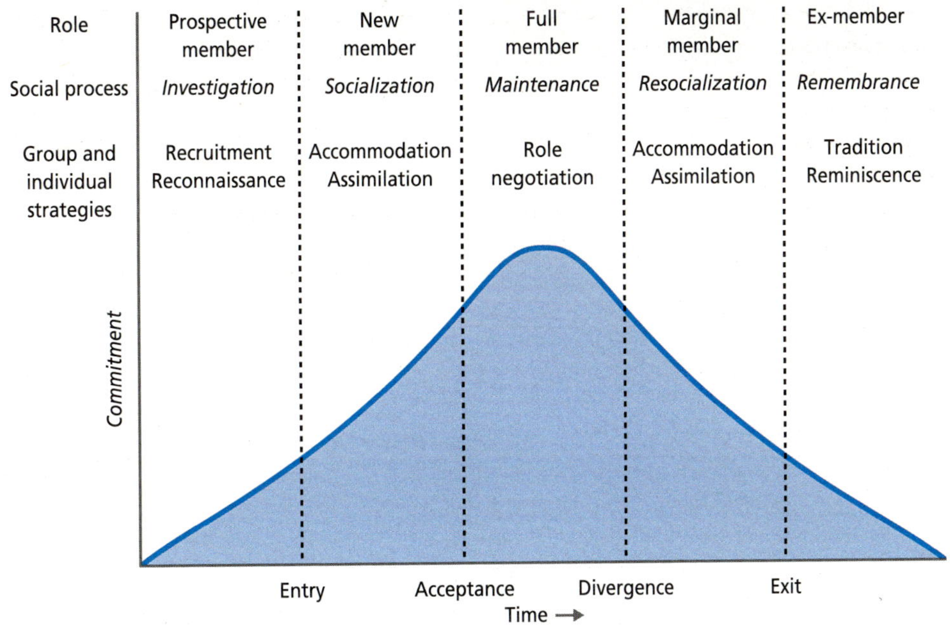

Figure 12.9: A model of the process of group socialization

Source: adapted from *Advances in Experimental and Social Psychology*, Volume 15, L. Berkowicz (ed.), Socialization in small groups: temporal changes in individual-group relations by Moreland, R.L. and Levine, J.M., pp. 137–92. Copyright 1982, Academic Press, with permission from Elsevier. Reproduced with permission from Hogg & Vaughan, *Social Psychology* © 2011 Pearson Australia, Page 290.

Table 12.4: Comparison of stages of group development to stages of socialization

	Group development	Organizational socialization
Stage 1: Orientation	1. Forming • Establish interpersonal relationships • Conform to organizational traditions and standards • Boundary testing in relationships and task behaviours	1. Getting in (anticipatory socialization) • Setting of realistic expectations • Determining match with the newcomer
Stage 2: Redefinition	2. Storming • Conflict arising because of interpersonal behaviours • Resistance to group influence and task requirements	2. Breaking in • Initiation to the job • Establishing interpersonal relationships • Congruence between self and organizational performance appraisal
Stage 3: Coordination	3. Norming • Single leader emerges • Group cohesion established • New group standards and roles formed for members	3. Settling in (role management) • The degree of fit between one's life interests outside work and the demands of the organization • Resolution of conflicts at the workplace itself
Stage 4: Formalization	4. Performing • Members perform tasks together • Establishing role clarity • Teamwork is the norm	

From Gordon (1993, p. 184).

Some companies, such as Disney, are famous for, and put much time, money and effort into, getting their new employees to adopt the 'company way' of doing things. This equivalent process is called *organizational socialization* (see Chapter 4). If the picture of organizational life that the newcomer is presented with by the organization is congruent with the picture held by the workforce, they will accept it. If not, the newcomer is more likely to adopt the picture held by their own work group, as these are the people with whom they will spend most of their time.

Teamworking? – *do* make me laugh!

American firms such as Southwest Airlines, Ben & Jerry's, Sun Microsystems, Facebook, and eBay invest a lot of time and resources in play and humour and in making their workplaces fun for their employees. Kingston, a technology company, lists among its six values '"Having fun" – working in the company of friends'. Today's young workers (18–25), known as Generation C (Connected, Communicating, always Clicking) want to play and have fun at work. Google, Microsoft, and other firms have created campus-style work environments which address employee demands for play, fun, and a relaxed workplace. In addition, increasing numbers of people, especially in knowledge-intensive industries, are employed in jobs which require successful cooperation, collaboration, and creativity. Such groups are a source of value to the company and are hard to duplicate. In order to motivate, resolve conflicts, and inspire group members (and stop them from leaving), companies have increasingly used play, fun, and humour as management motivational tools.

Some business journals such as *The Economist* (2010), take a negative view of fun in organizations. It writes that: 'These days many companies are obsessed with fun. Software firms in Silicon Valley have installed rock-climbing walls in their reception areas and put inflatable animals in their offices . . . The cult of fun has spread like some disgusting haemorrhagic disease. Acclaris, an American IT company, has a "chief fun officer". TD Bank, the American arm of Canada's Toronto Dominion, has a "Wow" department that dispatches costume-clad teams to "surprise and delight" successful workers. Red Bull, a drinks firm, has installed a slide in its London office'. Mangers hope that 'fun' will make workers more engaged and creative.

Researchers disagree with the negative view of play and fun. Sørensen and Spoelstra contrast 'serious play', as an engine of business, with the view that work and play are indistinguishable in post-industrial organizations. They conclude that 'It pays to play'. Studies also show that humour, defined as amusing communications that produce positive emotions and cognitions in the individual, group, or organization, does create a positive mental state that acts as a social lubricant. When humour is used in groups, their members experience positive emotions that make interactions between them more effective and efficient, leading the group to bond faster. Humour is thus an important contributor to group effectiveness because it positively affects group cohesiveness, communication, and creativity; it reduces stress; and it fosters *esprit de corps*.

Humour produces an increase in physical and psychological energy, leading workers to expend more effort in challenging tasks, and it ensures good communication by inducing positive feelings. It reduces listener resistance, making the listener more receptive to the message that management sends. This more persuasive message also tends to be more interesting to its recipients, requiring less need for repetition and explanation by management. It also reduces social distance between supervisors and subordinates. From a group's point of view, joking and teasing serve as a foundation of group culture, and are used to communicate group values, beliefs, and expectations to its new members. Humour reaffirms the reason for the formation of a group, emphasizes shared values, indicates appropriate behaviour, and aids the development of group norms. Thus while critics may laugh at what may seem to be a management fad, the research suggests that play, fun, and humour appear to be effective in building high morale and cohesion, good communication patterns, and strong social bonds, especially among groups of young employees. It may therefore be management which has the last laugh! (based on © The Economist Newspaper Limited, London (18/09/2010); Romero and Pescosolido, 2008; Sørensen and Spoelstra, 2011; www.kingston.com/ukroot/company/values.asp).

Solomon Asch (1907–1996)

Why do members conform to group pressure? Group norms increase the predictability of the behaviour of others, and reduce the chances of individuals embarrassing each other when interacting, for example, when speaking at social events. Complying with group norms may be of such personal benefit to us that we are willing to abide by them. In so doing, we suppress our own personal desires and reduce our individual freedoms. Moreover, we also punish those who violate the group's norms and reward those who do not. Additionally, we have a desire for order and meaning in our lives. We view uncertainty as disturbing and as something that should be reduced to the absolute minimum. Norms, and the adherence to norms, help us 'make sense' of seemingly unconnected facts and events, provide us with explanations of 'what's going on', and allow us to feel in control of the situations in which we find ourselves. The earliest experimental studies into conformity to group norms were carried out by Solomon Asch (1951, 1952, 1956). He found that those subjects who yielded to group pressure did so for different reasons. He distinguished three types of yielding:

1. *Distortion of perception*. These subjects seem to have convinced themselves that they actually did see the lines the way the other group members stated their judgements. Yielding at the perceptual level was rare, and occurred primarily among those who displayed a lack of trust in themselves. They were unaware that their estimates had been displaced or distorted by the majority.
2. *Distortion of judgement*. These subjects yielded either because they were unsure that they understood the task set for them, or because they did not want to 'spoil the experiment'. They suffered from primary doubt and lack of confidence. The factor of greatest importance was their decision that their perceptions were inaccurate, and that those of the majority were correct. Distortion of judgement occurred frequently.
3. *Distortion of action*. The subjects did not suffer a modification of perception, nor did they conclude that they were wrong. They yielded because they feared being excluded, ostracized, or considered eccentric. These subjects suppressed their observations, and voiced the majority position with a full awareness of what they were doing.

Asch's study of conformity

In the early 1950s, Solomon E. Asch constructed a laboratory experiment into individual conformity in groups.

The task was an easy one: to judge which of three lines was equal in length to one they had seen earlier.

The situation

Seven men sat around a table supposedly to participate in a study on visual perception.

The subject

Only number 6 (second from the right) was a real subject. The remainder were Asch's paid accomplices.

The task

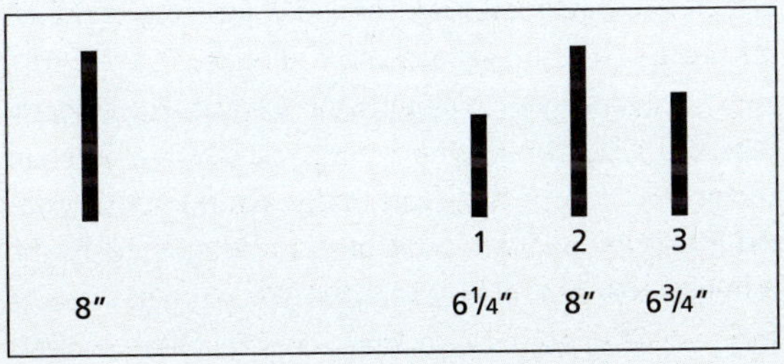

The problem

In experimental conditions, the accomplices had been instructed to lie about which line was correct. Under pressure, the subject (no. 6) shows signs of conflict, of whether to conform to the group judgement or give the response he judges to be correct.

The results

Members making at least one error	76%
Times average member conformed	37%
Members who never conformed	24%
Members who conformed over 10 times	11%
Members who made at least one error when tested alone	5%

Based on Asch (1951).

Source: reprinted with the permission of Scribner, a Division of Simon & Schuster, Inc. from GROUPS, LEADERSHIP AND MEN edited by Harold Guetzkow. Copyright 1951 Carnegie Press; copyright © 1979 Harold Guetzkow (Russell & Russell, NY, 1963).

Asch's experiment was replicated more than thirty years later, this time with five individuals using PCs who were told that they had been linked together (Doms and van Avermaet, 1981). Whereas Asch had found that the number who refused to conform to the group to any trial was just 25 per cent, in a repeat study 69 per cent of the subjects made no errors. Maybe a computer-mediated communication environment reduces our tendency to conform to a unanimous group position.

STOP AND THINK

Think of an occasion when you have given an opinion or supported a decision contrary to your own feelings and judgement, but consistent with those around you at the time.

How can you live with yourself for acting in such a socially compliant and submissive manner? What is your pathetic excuse for having done so?

Milgram's 'electric shock' experiments

Stanley Milgram (1933–1984)

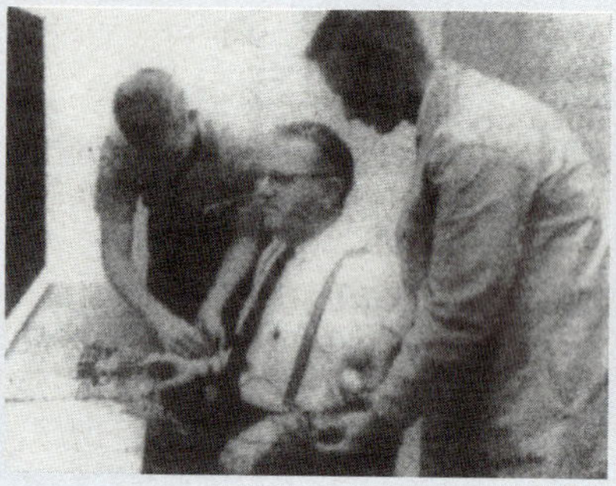

Courtesy of Alexandra Milgram

Volunteer subject, accomplice 'learner' and accomplice experimenter

A study by Stanley Milgram showed that a group can pressure an individual to defy authority. Would you torture another person simply because you were told to do so by someone in authority? Of course not, you would probably reply with little hesitation. In a series of now famous and highly controversial experiments, Stanley Milgram examined people's level of obedience to authority. The research involved ordinary people of different ages, sexes, races, and occupations. First, groups of psychiatrists, postgraduate students, and social science lecturers were asked by Milgram to predict how many of the research subjects would actually obey the experimenter's order. There was a high agreement that virtually all subjects would refuse to obey. Only one in a hundred would do it, said the psychiatrists, and that person would be a psychopath.

Milgram's experiment involved volunteer subjects participating in a learning experiment. They were to act as teachers of people who were trying to learn a series of simple word pairs. As teachers they were told to punish the student when he failed to learn by giving him an electric shock. At the start the shocks were small in intensity but every time the learner made a mistake, the teacher was told to increase the size of the shock. In carrying out the experiments Milgram found that two out of every three subjects tested administered the electric shocks up to a level which was clearly marked 'fatal' simply because an authority figure told them to do so. In fact, no electric shocks were ever actually given although the volunteer 'teachers' believed that the learners were really receiving the shocks they administered. An earlier experiment by Asch had shown that it only needed one other person to agree with a deviant for the conformity effect to be counteracted. In one variation of his experiment, Milgram placed two of his accomplices alongside the subject, so that the testing of the wired-up learner would be done by a group and not by a single subject. This experimental situation was thus similar to Asch's.

The experiment began with one of the accomplices administering the shocks. The first accomplice then refused to continue, argued with the experimenter, and withdrew sitting in the corner of the room. The second accomplice then took over, continued for a bit, and then refused just as the previous one had done. The real subject now remained to administer the shocks. Milgram repeated this procedure forty times, each with a different subject. In thirty of these forty cases, he found that once the subjects had seen their group colleagues defy the experimenter, they also defied him. When group pressure for such defiance was lacking, only fourteen subjects defied the authority figure. Milgram concluded that peer rebellion is a very powerful force in undercutting the experimenter's authority. A replication of Milgram's experiment by Jerry Burger revealed that things had not changed greatly in the intervening 45 years. A total of 70 per cent of his participants (compared to Milgram's 82.5 per cent) were prepared to continue delivering shocks after the learner had cried out in pain at 150 volts. Contrary to expectations, participants who saw a confederate refuse the experimenter's instructions obeyed the instructor as often as those who did not see such behaviour modelled in front of them. Men and women did not differ in their rates of obedience (Milgram, 1973; Burger, 2009; Blass, 2007).

Deindividuation

Deindividuation an increased state of anonymity that loosens normal constraints on individuals' behaviour, reducing their sense of responsibility, and leading to an increase in impulsive and antisocial acts.

Social facilitation explains how groups can arouse individuals and stimulate their performance, while social loafing shows that groups can diffuse and hence diminish individual responsibility. Together, arousal and diffused responsibility combine to decrease normal, social inhibitions, and create deindividuation. **Deindividuation** refers to a person's loss of self-awareness and self-monitoring. It involves some loss of personal identity and greater identification with the group.

The influence of the crowd

Roman Skyva/Alamy

Gustave LeBon stated that the crowd is 'always intellectually inferior to the isolated individual . . . mob man is fickle, credulous, and intolerant showing the violence and ferocity of primitive beings'. He added, 'by the mere fact that he forms part of an organized crowd, a man descends several rungs in the ladder of civilization. Isolated he may be a cultivated individual, in a crowd he is a barbarian – that is a creature acting by instinct' (LeBon, 1908, p. 12). The street rioting that started in the Tottenham neighbourhood of London in 2011 quickly spread across the capital, and then to other English cities – Manchester, Birmingham, Liverpool, and Nottingham – on the following four nights. The police were pitted against mocking, mobile, and mostly young gangs of violent looters.

In his book *The Crowd*, originally published in 1895, LeBon hypothesized that humans had a two-part personality. The upper half was conscious and unique to each individual, and contained dignity and virtue. The lower half, in contrast, was unconscious, was shared with everyone else, and contained bad desires and instincts. *The Economist* (2011a, 2011b) reported 'As long as rioters are part of a street mob they feel strong and invulnerable. Once individuals are arrested in large numbers . . . powerful peer pressure and the groupthink that goes with them are broken'. LeBon attributed this primitive behaviour to three things:

Anonymity Individuals cannot be easily identified in a crowd.

Contagion Ideas and emotions spread rapidly and unpredictably.

Suggestability The savagery that is just below the surface is released by suggestion.

The writings of Gustave Le Bon led to the theory of deindividuation, which was first proposed by Leon Festinger, Albert Pepitone and Theodore Newcomb (1952). However, it is Marion Hampton (1999, p. 112) who neatly captures the experience of deindividuation when she writes:

> There are moments when we can observe ourselves behaving irrationally as members of crowds or audiences, yet we are swept by the emotion, unable to check it. In smaller groups too, like committees or teams, we may experience powerful feelings of loyalty, anxiety or anger. The moods and emotions of those around us seem to have an exaggerated effect on our own moods and emotions.

Edward Diener (1980) considered self-awareness (i.e. awareness of oneself as an object of attention) to be the crucial element in the deindividuation process. The environmental conditions which reduce self-awareness and thereby trigger deindividuation, and the consequences of deindividuation, are summarized in Figure 12.10.

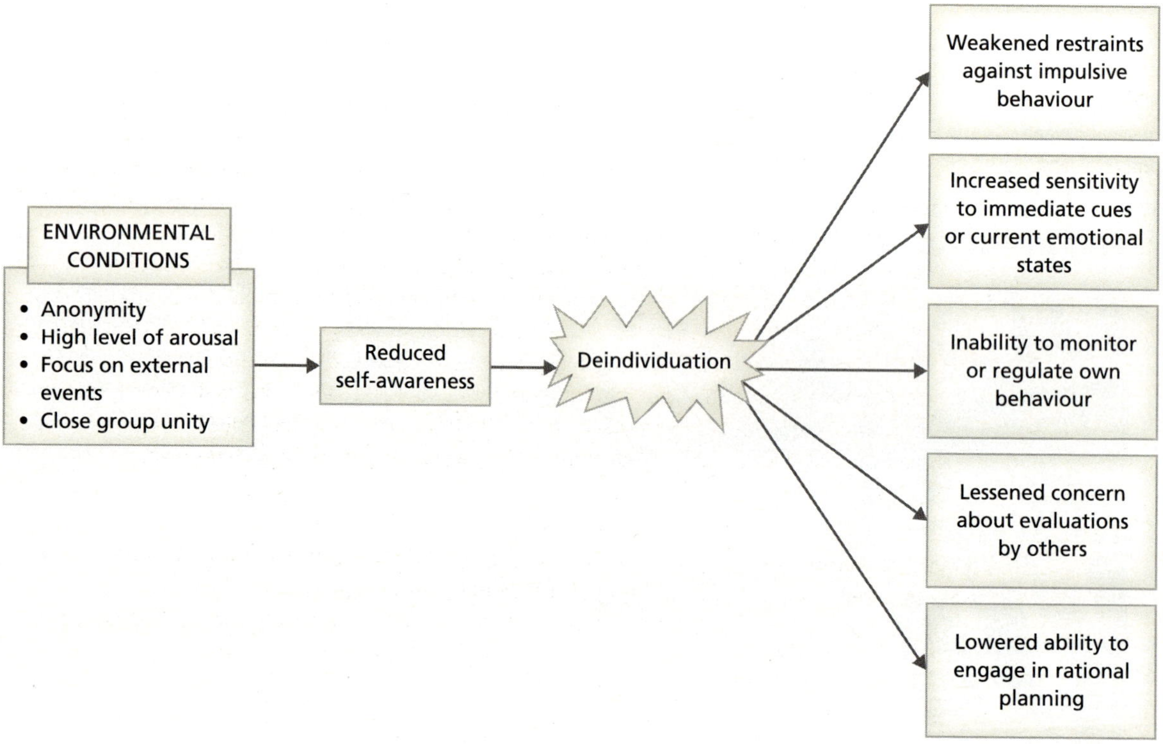

Figure 12.10: Self-awareness and deindividuation

Source: reproduced with permission from Hogg & Vaughan, *Social Psychology* © 2011 Pearson Australia, page 424.

Anonymity within a crowd or large group lessens inhibitions. Warriors in a tribe paint their faces and wear masks. In his novel *Lord of the Flies* (later made into a film), William Golding (1954) describes how a group of boys marooned on a desert island, through their shouting, clapping, and face painting, 'hype themselves up' and reduce their self-consciousness, turning themselves into a single organism, within which the individual members lose their identity. The unrestrained behaviours are provoked by the power of the group. When attention is drawn away from the individuals in crowd and group situations, their anonymity is increased, and they are more likely to abandon their normal restraints and to lose their sense of individual responsibility. This can lead to antisocial behaviour, such as attacking a policeman during protest demonstrations. In military organizations, members have always worn uniforms; but increasingly companies are requiring their staff to dress in corporate clothing. While this may get them to identify more closely with their organizations, it can also increase their anonymity.

STOP AND THINK What deindividuating tendencies can you identify in the organizations with which you are familiar? Are these being created consciously or unconsciously? What effect are they having on organizational employees and clients?

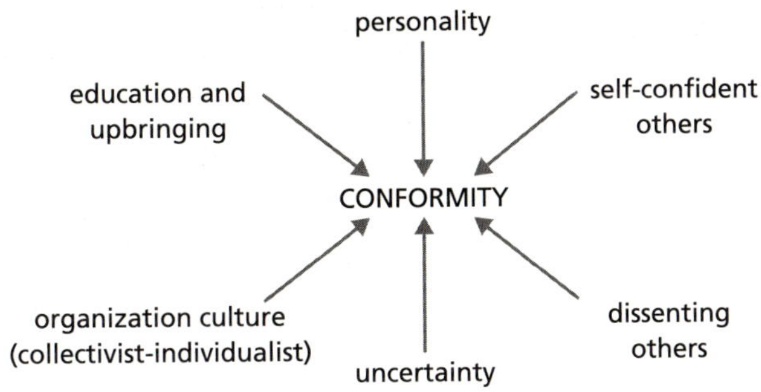

Figure 12.11: Factors influencing conformity to group norms

A great number of different factors influence conformity to norms (see Figure 12.11). The personality characteristics of individuals play a part in predisposing them to conform to group norms. The kind of stimuli eliciting conformist behaviour are also important. That people conform to norms when they are uncertain about a situation was demonstrated by the Sherif experiments. He also discovered that a person with a high degree of self-confidence could affect the opinions and estimates of other group members. Asch found that if even only one confederate in his experiment broke the unanimity with his dissenting voice, then the dramatic effects of conformity were erased, and the experimental subject felt free to give the correct answer that seemed obvious all along. Upbringing (including formal education) also plays an important part. Bond and Smith's (1996) analysis showed a steady decline in conformity since the original Asch studies. Countries with a collectivist culture show higher levels of conformity than those with an individualist culture (see Chapter 4).

STOP AND THINK Is conformity by the individual within organizations a bad thing that should be eliminated; or is it a good thing that should be encouraged?

Monkey see, monkey do

Sandra Robinson and Anne O'Leary-Kelly (1998) studied antisocial actions in organizations. These were defined as behaviours which could potentially harm individuals or the organization. Such actions included sexual harassment, stealing, insubordination, sabotage, rumour spreading, withholding effort, and absenteeism. The researchers studied 187 employees from 35 groups in 20 organizations. They examined the extent to which individual employees' antisocial actions were shaped by the group in which they worked.

They found that as the richness of the group experience increased, members became more likely to match their individual level of antisocial behaviour to that of the group in general. The stronger the group's antisocial behaviour climate, the more it affected an individual's actions. Where individuals in the group relied on each other to complete a task, their behaviour was more strongly related to the level of antisocial behaviour exhibited by the group. Where an individual exhibited less antisocial behaviour than the group in general, he or she was less satisfied with their co-workers. Groups can display high levels of either antisocial or prosocial behaviour, and can encourage similar behaviour from their members. The group thus provides a social context to an individual's interpretation of organization-level systems, and this context has a significant effect on the individual's antisocial behaviour in the organization.

→

The authors also point to the group-induced *contagion effect* that explains the spread or clustering of aggressive acts in particular organizations or industries. They conclude that antisocial groups encourage antisocial individual behaviour, and that isolating or ignoring them is unlikely to change them. They found that the likelihood of punishment was more effective than closeness of supervision in weakening the group–individual behaviour link. Antisocial behaviour was thus not solely an individual-level phenomenon. Although individual characteristics such as personality, prior learning of aggressive behaviour, family background, and upbringing all played a part, they argued that the social context of the work group exerted a major influence on whether individuals behaved in an antisocial way at work. Managers had both the ability and the responsibility to influence antisocial behaviour by shaping work group dynamics.

Individual influences on group attitudes and behaviour

Compliance a majority's influence over a minority.

Conversion a minority's influence over a majority.

So far, the focus has been on the group influencing its members. Does this mean that an individual can never influence their group? Clearly not, since history recounts numerous instances of individuals – revolutionaries, rebels, radical thinkers, religious zealots – who created minority groupings, and as minorities successfully persuaded majorities. Indeed, leadership can be considered an example of minority influence. The theoretical underpinning to the process of a minority's influence on a majority is provided by Serge Moscovici's (1980) social influence theory. He used the term **compliance** to describe what happens when a majority influences a minority, through its possession of various kinds of power and its ability to implement positive and negative sanctions. He applied the term **conversion** to describe a minority's persuasion of a majority. The concept of conversion is illustrated every time an employee persuades their company to adopt a new product or create a new division.

In their review of 143 studies of minority influence, Wood et al. (1994) found that minorities had the ability to change the opinions of those who listened to them, especially if the listeners were not required to publicly acknowledge such a change. Moscovici (1980) stressed the importance of consistency in the conversion process. The individual persuading the group had to stick unswervingly to his or her point of view. Moscovici's research provides us with an understanding of how a minority can influence a majority (Nemeth, 1986). These different writings have been summarized by Huczynski (2004) who listed what the minority influencer of a majority has to do:

Become viable	Take a position that others are aware of; make yourself heard; get yourself noticed, and generally overcome the illusion of unanimity.
Create tension	Motivate those in the majority to try to deal with your ideas.
Be consistent	Stick unswervingly to the same position. Do not take a variety of positions that disagree with the majority.
Be persistent	Restate your consistent position in the face of others' opposition to you.
Be unyielding	Being firm and unyielding involves digging your heels in and not compromising.
Be self-confident	This is conveyed by one's consistency and persistence. It raises self-doubts among the majority, leading them to reconsider their position.
Seek defectors	Defections from the majority increase the self-doubt of the remaining majority and free its doubters who may have self-censored themselves to speak out, perhaps encouraging more converts.

Before the 1980s, the idea that a minority could influence a majority was not a widely held view among social psychologists. However, through their research and publications, Moscovici and his colleagues presented an alternative view that possessed all the above characteristics. Minority influencing has now become a recognized phenomenon which regularly features in social psychology texts.

Home viewing

In the film *Twelve Angry Men* (1957, director Sidney Lumet) a jury retires to deliberate and to decide on the guilt or innocence of a youth from a slum background. At the outset, eleven of the twelve jurors are convinced of the boy's guilt and are keen to find him guilty without further discussion. Only one member of the jury, played by Henry Fonda, has reservations and persuades the other members to take the time to review the evidence. Fonda manages to change the guilty votes of the other eleven jurors, and persuades them to acquit the young defendant. The film illustrates the concept of *conversion*. Watch Fonda's behaviour carefully. At first sight it appears that it is random. But then, you'll see a pattern. What behaviours do you see him repeating? What influencing tactics does he use? Which types of power are possessed by which characters in the film?

Teamwork takes longer, and there are many occasions when collaboration is a hindrance rather than a help. Companies therefore need to balance individual autonomy with collective action. We are aware of the downside of individualism in organizations, but teams can be just as destructive, by being strong and controlling, thereby ignoring individuals' voices, learning, and contributions. Would the crisis in the financial world have been quite so catastrophic if more people had spoken out in their team meetings about what they knew to be wrongful practices?

Reality TV torture

Reality television often ends in humiliation and ridicule for those taking part – but who would be prepared to take part in a game show that featured torture or death? The answer is most of us, judging by the results of a French TV experiment. Entitled *Zone Xtrême*, this controversial 'game of death' programme was broadcast on the terrestrial channel France 2 on 24 March 2010. The show sought to criticize reality shows in general and to warn viewers of the dangers of obeying authority unquestioningly. Eighty volunteers were told that they were taking part in a pilot for a new game show which involved memorizing words and punishing mistakes. As it was only a trial, no prizes were awarded; only a small fee was paid to participants but they had to sign a contract agreeing to inflict electric shocks on other contestants. After being placed in a game show type studio, they were told to give electric shocks of up to 450 volts to (supposedly) another contestant whenever he failed to answer a question correctly.

Tania Young, a television presenter who hosted the mock game show, insisted that even the most reticent volunteers should continue – and almost all did. Participants were seen struggling between revulsion at the pain they were causing and their ability to confront the authority of the television star, Ms Young, but most ended up obeying her. Almost half were delighted by the concept. 'It's violent, yeah, I love it', said one, while 28 appeared indifferent and 14 were puzzled. Eighty per cent of the participants ignored the victim's shrieks of pain and pleas to stop and continued increasing the voltage in response to wrong answers, dramatic music, and cries of 'go on' from the audience. 'Is he dead?' asked one contestant when the voltage reached 400, and the victim fell silent, having apparently either lost consciousness or died. In fact, Laurent Le Doyen, the supposed fellow contestant and torture victim, was an actor who simulated experiencing pain, as no electric shocks were given. This TV experiment was a variant of a celebrated experiment conducted by Stanley Milgram in the 1960s. How far did 2010's contestants go? While 20 per cent of the eighty stopped before administering the maximum voltage, the other 80 per cent went all the way to 450 volts. Unlike in the Milgram study, group pressure, in the form of a large studio audience, audibly encouraged the contestants to give ever larger shocks (based on Sage, 2010).

RECAP

1. ***Explain the basic tenets of social identity theory and social representation theory.***
   - Social identity theory holds that aspects of our identity derive from the membership of a group.
   - Groups construct social representations consisting of beliefs, ideas, and values, which they transmit to their new members.
   - Such representations, together with group socialization, lead to all members sharing a common frame of reference.
2. ***Distinguish the different directions in which individuals' behaviour can be modified by a group.***
   - Individual behaviour is variously modified by the presence of others or by being a part of a group.
   - The concepts of social influence, social facilitation, synergy, and social loafing distinguish the direction and nature of such modifications.
3. ***Understand how groups use norms to regulate the behaviour of their members.***
   - Social norms guide the behaviour of individuals in a group. They can be pivotal or peripheral.
   - Social norms are established in four ways – explicit statements, critical events, initial behaviour, and transfer behaviour.
   - Sanctions are administered by members to those individuals who transgress or uphold the group's norms. Sanctions can therefore be negative (e.g. verbal abuse) or positive (e.g. praise). Groups possess an escalating hierarchy of ever-stronger negative sanctions.
4. ***Understand the process of group socialization of individuals.***
   - Groups teach new members about their norms and incorporate them into their shared frame of reference through the process of group socialization.
5. ***Explain why individuals conform to the dictates of their group.***
   - As individuals, we tend to conform to group norms because of benefits for us individually if others abide by the agreed rules; our desire for order and meaning in our lives; and a need to receive a satisfying response from others.
   - The 'cost' to the person who is a member of a group is the deindividulization that membership entails. Group membership brings with it anonymity and becoming 'lost in the crowd'. This can reduce our sense of individual responsibility, lower our social constraints, and lead us to engage in impulsive antisocial acts.
6. ***Distinguish between conformity and obedience, and between compliance and conversion.***
   - Conformity refers to a change in an individual's belief or behaviour in response to real or imagined group pressure, while obedience describes a situation in which an individual changes their behaviour in response to direct command from another person.
   - Research shows both that a majority influences an individual (this being called *compliance*), and that a minority can influence a majority (this being called *conversion)*.

Revision

1. Is social loafing an individual issue, varying according to an individual's personality and values; is it an organizational culture issue depending on company norms about over-manning, non-jobs, and management's acceptance of poor employee performance?
2. Is conformity by the individual within organizations a bad thing that should be eliminated or a good thing that should be encouraged?
3. Critically evaluate the empirical research on individual conformity to group pressure.
4. Suggest how an individual might go about persuading a majority.

Research assignment

Choose an organization with which you are familiar, and interview some employees who work there. Ask each interviewee how their co-workers would react, if they

1. Were seen being rude or indifferent to a customer.
2. Criticized a co-worker who was not performing satisfactorily.
3. Performed their work at a level noticeably higher than that of their co-workers.
4. Approached management offering a solution to a problem they had identified.
5. Expressed concern to management about the wellbeing of their fellow workers.
6. Expressed concern about the poor quality of the organization's product or service.
7. Actively developed their skill and knowledge about the organization's operations and products.

Finally, ask if there are things that any employee should do or not do, if they wanted to get on well with their co-workers in the organization. Use the information obtained from your interviewees to determine

(a) on which topics there appear to be group norms

(b) which norms are pivotal and which are peripheral

(c) what effects these norms have on the behaviour of the individuals, the operation of the group and the performance of the department.

Springboard

Jerry Burger (2009) 'Replicating Milgram: would people still obey today?', *American Psychologist*, 64(1), pp. 1–11. A modern replication of Milgram's classic obedience experiment.

M. Doms and Eddy van Avermaet (1981) 'The conformity effect: a timeless phenomenon?', *Bulletin of the British Psychological Society*, 36(1), pp. 180–8. These authors replicated Solomon Asch's classic studies on individual conformity in groups and obtained similar results.

Bibb Latané, Kipling Williams and Stephen Harkins (1979) 'Many hands make light the work: the causes and consequences of social loafing', *Journal of Personality and Social Psychology*, 37(6), pp. 822–32. This classic article discusses the re-creation of Ringelmann's experiment that first revealed the existence of the phenomenon of social loafing.

Nigel Nicholson (2003) 'How to motivate your problem people', *Harvard Business Review*, 81(1), pp. 7–65. Provides useful advice if you are in a student project team and one member is not pulling their weight.

OB in films

The Secret of My Success (1987, director Herbert Ross), DVD track 4: 0:17:00 to 0:20:00 (3 minutes). In this film, Brantley Foster (played by Michael J. Fox) leaves his home in Kansas to make his career as an executive in New York City. However, the only job he can get is in the mailroom of the Penrose Corporation. The clip begins with the mailroom manager saying 'You can't come in here bozo, take your crap to the mail slot', and ends with Melrose saying 'you put these things away'. On his first day, Brantley learns a great deal about the organization.

1. What are the sources of his information?
2. What does he learn from each?
3. In your current or last job, what did you learn? How?

OB on the web

Search YouTube for 'Asch conformity experiment' which is a reconstruction of Asch's famous line experiment. Then find 'Psychology Experiment – Conformity'. This is a student replication of that experiment using soft drinks instead of lines. Try this experiment yourself (or think of something similar) and write a report summarizing your findings.

CHAPTER EXERCISES

1. Group controls work

Objectives

1. Analyse a group's behaviour using a theoretical framework.
2. Assess the situation from a management perspective.

Briefing

1. Individually, read the *Factory paint shop case*, which we already met in Chapter 10, and answer the questions below:
   (a) As an existing employee, imagine that you had been transferred to a job on the machine described. Would you be happy to go along with the break system described? What would you do if you were not a card player?
   (b) What would you do if you were a new employee to the company who had been allocated to work on that machine?
   (c) If you were an existing group member, and a new member had been transferred into your unit, and was reluctant to participate in the group's informal work arrangements described in the case, how might your group persuade them?
   (d) Should management ignore such adjustments to official policy and intentions? What are the advantages and disadvantages of doing so?
   (e) Have you ever been in a job when something similar has occurred?
2. Form into groups of 3 to 5 members and nominate a spokesperson.
3. Discuss your individual answers to the questions and prepare a group response.
4. Your spokesperson will report back to the class as a whole, as directed by your instructor.

Factory paint shop case

Factory work can be boring and monotonous. Employees must work at the pace of the assembly line or machine, with output levels closely prescribed and monitored by management. It is not surprising that factory workers will try anything to break the boredom and relentless grind of the controlled activity in a factory. In a particular factory a large paint-spraying machine was approximately 100 metres long and required a team of 24 people to keep it running. There were only 18 workstations on the machine, but the staffing plan was that six people would float between jobs, thereby allowing everyone to take a break whilst keeping the machine running. In practice four people would be in the mess room for their entire shift running a card syndicate. Everyone else in the work team would take shorter breaks and simply drop in and out of the card game as their breaks allowed. A different team of four people would be informally 'rostered' each day so that over a period everyone had the total break time allowed by the company. The team achieved their allowed breaks in a way not intended (or approved) by management. Gambling was not allowed by the company either, but this did not bother the workers. Supervisors also turned a blind eye to the process as long as the work was completed and productivity was at acceptable levels.

2. Team member from hell

Objective

To evaluate a student group's attempt to change the behaviour of one its members.

Briefing

1. Form groups. Read the *Team member from hell* scenario.
2. Each group considers the questions specified by their instructor.

Discussion questions

1. What motivates John?
2. What mistakes did the group make in trying to motivate John?
3. How did the team contribute to John's motivational problem?
4. Given what you know about effective group performance, how well did the group handle its problem with John?
5. What suggestions would you make to help the group both achieve its goal and to motivate John?

Team member from hell

Let me tell you about my team member from hell. Someone with no desire to succeed is the worst kind of person to have as a member in your student project group because it is nearly impossible to induce him to do the work and perform it well. It was apparent from the beginning that John had no motivation. After our group had already been created by the course lecturer, a latecomer came to class, and the lecturer assigned him to our group. His name was John. Already I was a little wary. Students who turn up to a class a couple of days after it has started are the slackers; they have either skipped the first few days of class, or haven't got their schedule of courses organized.

At our first meeting my expectations were confirmed. I found out that John was a member of the university drinking club, and he did nothing but talk about his social life. I must say though, John was entertaining. He could make us laugh, mainly because he didn't seem to know what he was talking about. Unfortunately, John could also be loud and obnoxious and often his jokes were simply not funny. He just didn't understand the difference between social time and work life. Although John planned to work in his family's business when he graduated, he was working 20 to 30 hours a week to earn money to pay for his tuition fees and cover his living expenses. I don't think he wanted to be at university really, and he might have dropped out if it wasn't for all his friends. John seemed like someone you would always have to push a little harder in order to get anything done. He made no attempt to discuss anything

→

about our team project or about the courses he was taking. All he ever talked about was partying.

In our team, we began by discussing what we would prepare for our next meeting. John did not volunteer his services for any of the tasks and when we assigned him one, he seemed very annoyed and dissatisfied. At the next meeting, John showed up late and was unprepared. I was disappointed, but not surprised. It wasn't the end of the world, but I couldn't help but look ahead at the complex project we had to complete. If this was the attitude and work ethic that John brought to only our second meeting, how were we ever going to get a reasonable project finished? I intend to make something of myself when I graduate, so I am concerned with my grades and don't want to be dragged down by someone who doesn't care. I would almost rather do things on my own.

We decided to distribute the workload evenly among all the members of the group. Each person chose a certain task, and we all began working to complete it. Things seemed to be going quite well until another group member and I realized that John was not completing his part of the work. He had a bad attitude about university that was not very positive, and was not doing well in classes. We tried to motivate him by explaining that if we completed the project successfully, he would complete the course and get a good grade. This seemed to work initially, but we soon learned he was still not completing the work. We discussed the situation and offered to help him if he was having difficulties. Again this worked temporarily but he fell back into his same old pattern.

It wasn't as though the group didn't make an effort to get him involved. Two of us kept reminding him to do his part of the project. However, John would just smile, give a little chuckle, and reply 'I don't really care about this stupid course. I don't know why we have to do this anyway.' We also sent him numerous emails, practically begging him to attend our meetings, so that we could have his input as well as to save his grade. He never responded to any of the messages. At the meetings that he did show up to, we confronted him, and asked him to make more of an effort to attend regularly. He was really laid back and would always just tell us that he was busy, and that he would do what he could.

Eventually one of the members exploded with anger at him. She told him that he was being extremely disrespectful, and that if he didn't want to do any work, he shouldn't show up at the meetings at all! After that, the only thing that changed was that he began coming to our meetings, but he didn't contribute and still did almost no work. He just walked in, sat there while we did the work, and then took credit for work that he had not done.

As time went on, we noticed that John was trying to make small attempts to slowly work his way back into the group. I think he began to notice what a good time we were having working together to complete the project. Although he became more vocal and offered some opinions, we really didn't want to listen to what he had to say. We were well advanced with the project and didn't need his input by this time. Also, we no longer trusted him and did not feel that we could rely on him. I didn't take anything that John said seriously any more, and when he offered to do something, I didn't expect him to do it. He continued to derail our meetings with stories of his weekend parties. He began to complain and make sarcastic comments such as 'Oh, I guess nobody hears me.'

As the project deadline approached, the group agreed to meet at the start and end of the week and then again, over the weekend, for one final time. However, after thinking about the plans just made, John realized that his club's formal dance was scheduled for the same weekend, and he claimed there was no time to work on the project. His statement really annoyed me. Did he expect the rest of us to finish the project for him? Did he really have the nerve to change our plans, just so that he could get drunk all weekend? What were his priorities – university or partying? Suddenly, after this occurred to me, I felt a tremendous pressure. Not only did I and my other team members have to organize everything to finish the project, but we were also the only ones who cared about the quality of the work we produced. We could have talked to John again about his performance, but we never did. We just wanted to get the work done and go home as soon as we could. We decided to speak to the course lecturer to see if we could get John removed from our group. We told John of our intentions and he realized that he would not be able to successfully complete the project on his own, which he would have had to do if he was removed from our group. John agreed to fulfil his duties and, although we had done a large part of the required work that had been assigned to him, he did successfully complete the rest himself.

Adapted from Griffin, R.W. (2007), pp. 218–19; with permission from Dr Steven B. Wolff (www.geipartners.com).

Employability assessment

With regard to your future employment prospects:

1. Identify up to three issues from this chapter that you found significant.
2. Relate these to the competencies in the employability matrix.
3. Decide what actions you need to take to maintain and/or develop those competencies under each of the four headings of the employability matrix.

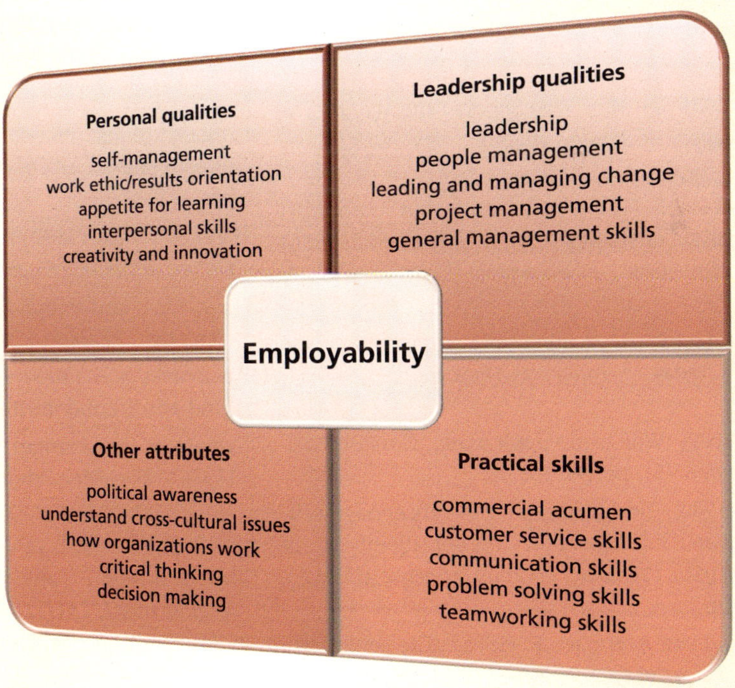

References

Albanese, R. and Van Fleet, D.D. (1985) 'Rational behaviour in groups: the free rider tendency', *Academy of Management Review*, 10(2), pp. 244–55.

Allport, F.H. (1920) 'The influences of the group upon association and thought', *Journal of Experimental Psychology*, 3(3), pp. 159–82.

Asch, S.E. (1951) 'Effects of group pressure upon the modification and distortion of judgements', in H. Guetzkow (ed.), *Groups, Leadership and Men*, Pittsburgh, PA: Carnegie Press, pp. 177–90.

Asch, S.E. (1952) *Social Psychology*, Englewood Cliffs, NJ: Prentice Hall.

Asch, S.E. (1956) Studies of independence and submission to group pressure: a minority of one against a unanimous majority, *Psychological Monograph: General and Applied*, 9(416), pp. 1–70.

Banyard, P.E., Davies, M.N.O., Norman, C. and Winder, B. (2010) *Essential Psychology: A Concise Instruction*, London: Sage.

Baron, R. and Byrne, D. (2000) *Social Psychology* (9th edn), London: Allyn and Bacon.

Benders, J. (2005) 'Team working: a tale of partial participation', in B. Harley, J. Hyman and P. Thompson (eds), *Participation and Democracy at Work: Essays in Honour of Harvie Ramsey*, London: Palgrave Macmillan, pp. 55–74.

Blass, T. (2007) *The Man Who Shocked the World: The Life and Legacy of Stanley Milgram*, New York: Basic Books.

Bond, R. and Smith, P.B. (1996) 'Culture and conformity: a meta-analysis of studies using Asch's (1952b, 1956) line judgment task', *Psychological Bulletin*, 119(1), pp. 111–37.

Burger, J.M. (2009) 'Replicating Milgram: would people still obey today?', *American Psychologist*, 64(1), pp. 1–11.

Coutu, D. (2009) 'Why teams don't work', *Harvard Business Review*, 87(5), pp. 99–105.

Diener, E. (1980) 'Deindividuation: the absence of self-awareness and self-regulation in group members', in P.B. Paulus (ed.), *Psychology of Group Influence*, Hillsdale, NJ: Erlbaum.

Doms, M. and van Avermaet, E. (1981) 'The conformity effect: a timeless phenomenon?', *Bulletin of the British Psychological Society*, 36(1), pp. 180–8.

Ellis, V. and Taylor, M. (2010) 'Banks, bailouts and bonuses: a personal account of working in Halifax Bank of Scotland during the financial crisis', *Work, Employment and Society*, 24(4), pp. 803–12.

Feldman, D.C. (1984) 'The development and enforcement of group norms', *Academy of Management Review*, 9(1), pp. 47–53.

Festinger, L., Pepitone, A. and Newcomb, T. (1952) 'Some consequences of deindividuation in a group', *Journal of Abnormal and Social Psychology*, 47(2 supplement), pp. 382–9.

Frohlich, N. and Oppenheimer, J. (1970) 'I get by with a little help from my friends', *World Politics*, 23(1), pp. 104–20.

George, J.M. (1992) 'Extrinsic and intrinsic origins of perceived social loafing in organizations', *Academy of Management Journal*, 35(1), pp. 191–202.

Golding, W. (1954) *Lord of the Flies*, London: Faber and Faber.

Gordon, J. (1993) *A Diagnostic Approach to Organizational Behavior*, Boston, MA: Allyn and Bacon.

Greenberg, J. (1999) *Managing Behaviour in Organizations* (2nd edn), Upper Saddle River, NJ: Prentice Hall.

Greenberg, J. and Baron, R.A. (1997) *Behaviour in Organizations* (6th edn), Englewood Cliffs, NJ: Prentice Hall.

Griffin, R.W. (2007) *OB in Action: Cases and Exercises* (8th edn), Mason, Ohio: South-Western Cengage Learning.

Guirdham, M. (2002) *Interactive Behaviour at Work*, Harlow, Essex: Financial Times Prentice Hall.

Guzzo, R.A. and Dickson, M.W. (1996) 'Teams in organizations: recent research on performance and effectiveness', *Annual Review of Psychology*, 47, pp. 307–38.

Hampton, M.M. (1999) 'Work groups', in Y. Gabriel (ed.), *Organizations in Depth*, London: Sage, pp. 112–38.

Hogg, M.A. and Vaughan, G.M. (2008) *Social Psychology* (5th edn), Pearson Education.

Huczynski, A.A. (2004) *Influencing within Organizations* (2nd edn), London: Routledge.

Ingham, A.G., Levinger, G., Graves, J. and Peckham, V. (1974) 'The Ringelmann effect: studies of group size and group performance', *Journal of Experimental Social Psychology*, 10(4), pp. 371–84.

Jonsen, K. and Bryant, B. (2008) 'Stretch target', *People Management*, 14(7), pp. 28–31.

Karau, S.J. and Williams, K.D. (1993) 'Social loafing: meta-analytic review and theoretical integration', *Journal of Personality and Social Psychology*, 65(4), pp. 681–706.

Kerr, N.L. (1983) 'Motivation losses in small groups: a social dilemma analysis', *Journal of Personality and Social Psychology*, 45(4), pp. 819–28.

Kravitz, D.A. and Martin, B. (1986) 'Ringelmann rediscovered: the original article', *Journal of Personality and Social Psychology*, 50(5), pp. 936–41.

Latane, B. and Nida, S. (1980) 'Social impact theory and group influence: a social engineering perspective', in P.B. Paulus (ed.), *Psychology of Group Influence*, Hillsdale, NJ: Lawrence Erlbaum Associates, pp. 3–34.

Latané, B., Williams, K. and Harkins, S. (1979) 'Many hands make light the work: the causes and consequences of social loafing', *Journal of Personality and Social Psychology*, 37(6), pp. 822–32.

LeBon, G. (1908; first published 1895 by Ernest Benn) *The Crowd: A Study of the Popular Mind*, London: Unwin.

Martin, J. (2005) *Organizational Behaviour and Management* (3rd edn), London: Thomson.

Milgram, S. (1973) *Obedience to Authority*, London: Tavistock Publications.

Moreland, R.L. and Levine, J.M. (1982) 'Socialization in small groups: temporal changes in individual-group relations', in L. Berkowicz (ed.), *Advances in Experimental and Social Psychology*, New York: Academic Press, Volume 15, pp. 137–92.

Moscovici, S. (1980) 'Towards a theory of conversion behaviour', in L. Berkowitz (ed.), *Advances in Experimental Social Psychology*, New York: Academic Press, Volume 13, pp. 209–39.

Moscovici, S. (1984) 'The phenomenon of social representations', in R.M. Farr and S. Moscovici (eds), *Social Representations*, Cambridge: Cambridge University Press, pp. 3–69.

Nemeth, C. (1986) 'Differential contributions of majority and minority influences', *Psychological Review*, 93(1), pp. 23–32.

Pearce, C.L., Gallagher, C.A. and Ensley, M.D. (2002) 'Confidence at the group level of analysis: a longitudinal investigation of the relationship between potency and team effectiveness', *Journal of Occupational and Organizational Psychology*, 75(1), pp. 115–20.

Robinson, S.L. and O'Leary-Kelly, A.M. (1998) Monkey see, monkey do: the influence of work groups on the antisocial behaviour of employees', *Academy of Management Journal*, 41(6), pp. 658–72.

Romero, E. and Pescosolido, A. (2008) 'Humour and group effectiveness', *Human Relations*, 61(3), pp. 395–418.

Rothwell, J.D. (1992) *In Mixed Company: Small Group Communication*, Fort Worth, Texas: Harcourt Brace Jovanovich.

Roy, D. (1960) 'Banana time: job satisfaction and informal interaction', *Human Organization*, 18(1), pp. 158–61.

Sage, A. (2010) 'Contestants have power to make reality TV torture', *The Times*, 26 February, p. 43.

Sherif, M. (1936) *The Psychology of Social Norms*, New York: Harper and Row.

Sørensen, B.M. and Spoelstra, S. (2011) 'Play at work: continuation, intervention and usurpation', *Organization*, 19(1), pp. 81–97.

Steiner, I. (1972) *Group Process and Productivity*, New York: Academic Press.

Tajfel, H. and Turner, J.C. (1986) 'The social identity theory of inter-group behaviour', in S. Worchel and W.G. Austin (eds), *Psychology of Inter-Group Relations* (2nd edn), Chicago, IL: Nelson-Hall, pp. 7–24.

The Economist (2010) 'Schumpeter: down with fun', 18 September, p. 84.

The Economist (2011a) 'Under fire', 13 August, p. 23.

The Economist (2011b) 'The fire this time', 13 August, pp. 21–3.

Thompson, W.E. (1983) 'Hanging tongues: a sociological encounter with the assembly line', *Qualitative Sociology*, 6(3), pp. 215–37.

Triplett, N. (1898) 'The dynamogenic factors in pacemaking and competition', *American Journal of Psychology*, 9(4), pp. 507–33.

Weber, M. (1924) 'Zur Psychophysik der industriellen Arbeit' (first written in 1908/1909), in M. Weber (ed.), *Gesammelte Aussatze zur Sociologie und Sozialpolitik von Max Weber*, Tubingen: J.C.B. Mohr, pp. 61–255.

Williams, K.D. and Karau, S.J. (1991) 'Social loafing and social compensation: the effect of expectations of co-worker performance', *Journal of Personality and Social Psychology*, 61(4), pp. 570–81.

Williams, K., Harkins, S. and Latane, L. (1981) 'Identifiability and social loafing: two cheering experiments', *Journal of Personality and Social Psychology*, 40(2), pp. 303–11.

Wood, W., Lundgren, S., Ouellette, J.A., Busceme, S. and Blackstone, T. (1994) 'Minority influence: a meta-analytical review of social influence processes', *Psychological Bulletin*, 115(3), pp. 323–45.

Zaccaro, S.J. (1984) 'Social loafing: the role of task attractiveness', *Personality and Social Psychology Bulletin*, 10(1), pp. 99–106.

Chapter 13 Teamworking

Key terms

team

team autonomy

advice team

quality circle

action team

project team

cross-functional team

production team

Japanese teamworking

total quality management

just-in-time system

kaizen

external work team differentiation

internal work team differentiation

external work team integration

team performance

team viability

Learning outcomes

When you have read this chapter, you should be able to define those key terms in your own words, and you should also be able to:

1. Understand why 'team' is a contested concept in the organizational literature.
2. List the nine dimensions of team autonomy.
3. Differentiate between four major types of teams and give an example of each.
4. Discuss the types of obstacles to effectiveness experienced by each type of team.
5. Contrast Western with Japanese concepts of teamworking.
6. List the four main variables in the ecological framework for analysing work team effectiveness.
7. Understand the continuing importance of teamworking.

Why study teamworking?

The modern concept of teamworking goes back to Eric Trist and Kenneth Bamforth (1951), who analysed coal miners' psychological and emotional responses to underground working. Their socio-technical paradigm was developed during the 1960s, but became more widely known through applications in the late 1960s and 1970s. As twenty-first-century companies experience increasing challenges, and organizations become more diverse, groups of staff are being increasingly formed into teams to achieve organizational goals (Glassop, 2002). Teamworking provides a mechanism to bring together different employee expertise and skills that are required to complete increasingly complex work tasks in ever shorter time frames. There has therefore been a worldwide trend among firms to introduce newer forms of teamworking. These include

- *global teams*, possessing national, cultural, and linguistic heterogeneity and operating within multinational organizations, often virtually (Zander et al., 2012);
- *parallel global virtual teams*, which operate outside the formal organization structure (Cordery et al., 2009);
- *X-teams*, whose members reach across company boundaries to forge networks of connection (Ancona et al., 2009);
- *hot groups*, self-forming teams seeking to achieve groundbreaking and significant tasks (Lipman-Blumen and Leavitt, 2009).

Teams are popular in organizations and are positively perceived by their members, by managers, and by society at large. Companies appear to believe that teams are an effective way of

- improving performance;
- reducing production costs;
- speeding up innovations;
- improving product quality;
- increasing work flexibility;
- introducing new technologies;
- increasing employee participation;
- achieving better industrial relations;
- meeting the challenge of global competition; and
- identifying and solving work-related problems.

Delarue et al. (2008) reviewed the empirical research on the relationship between teamworking and organizational performance and concluded that the evidence suggested that companies which adopted teamworking obtained both positive operational outcomes (increased productivity, quality, flexibility) and improved worker outcomes in the form of positive worker attitudes (job satisfaction, motivation, commitment) and worker behaviours (lower turnover and absenteeism). The researchers found that while, in general, teams appeared to have had a positive impact on company performance, the link between the two was moderated by organizational factors. For example, company compensation schemes which gave employees a 'team reward' (rather than compensating them individually) were more likely to have an impact on effectiveness by creating interdependencies between team members. A company strategy emphasizing value (rather than cost), which used semi-autonomous teamworking, achieved higher levels of financial performance. Companies which were unionized (rather than non-unionized) were found to tap the benefits of employee participation in teams more, perhaps by providing employees with reassurance about continued employment.

Teams at Google

In Douglas Edwards's (2011) account of the early days of Google, he described Urs Hölzle as a key person on the engineering side ('Saint Urs, Keeper of the Blessed Code'):

> Urs's most significant accomplishment, however, was building the team that built Google. 'Your greatest impact as an engineer comes through hiring someone who is as good as you or better' he exhorted everybody who would listen, 'because over the next year, they double your productivity. There's nothing else that you can do to double your productivity. Even if you are a genius, that's extremely unlikely to happen'. . . 'If you have very good people it gives you a safety net' he believed. 'If there's something wrong, they self-correct. You don't have to tell them "Hey, pay attention to this." They feel ownership and fix it before you even knew it was broken.' (p. 36)

Allen and Hecht (2004) discussed the 'romance of teams' which they defined as a faith in the effectiveness and even superiority of team-based work. The reason that teams are increasingly used, they claim, is because they fulfil not only economic needs but also certain psychological, social, and political ones. Teams make people more satisfied and bolster their confidence; they promote the idea that everyone is unique and has something different to contribute to a task, and that individuals should pull together. Teamworking seems to fit in with currently attractive ideas of empowerment, participation, and democracy. Thus, despite being inappropriate or ineffective in certain circumstances, teams continue to be used uncritically within organizations (Naquin and Tynan, 2003; Sinclair, 1992). Thus, a reason for studying teamworking is to determine whether or not teams are superior to individuals working alone, and, if so, in which circumstances.

Teamworking at Copiapó

On 14 October 2010, the last of the 33 Chilean miners who had been trapped for 69 days at the San José gold and copper mine in Copiapó in the Atacama Desert, 2,300 feet below the Earth's surface, was pulled to safety with the help of an unlikely source – the United States's National Aeronautics and Space Administration (NASA). It was a dire situation. While developing their rescue plans, the Chilean government also sought advice and information from other governments and organizations as to how to assist the trapped miners. One of the organizations that responded to the call for assistance was NASA. It quickly formed a team consisting of two medical doctors, a psychologist, and an engineer. The team spent three days at the rescue site in Chile assessing the similarities between the miners' plight and life in space.

They gave advice to the rescue team at the mine site. This ranged from warning rescuers not to give the starving men too much food too quickly (which could prove fatal) to suggesting they wear sunglasses when surfacing after two months underground. Most importantly, the NASA team also provided the design for the innovative rescue capsule (nicknamed Phoenix) that was used to pull the miners to the surface, and ultimately saved their lives. The four-person NASA team consulted with twenty of their colleagues, and came up with fifty design

David Mercado/Reuters

recommendations: for example, that exterior rollers would cushion the capsule's ride up, reducing both the friction with the tunnel walls, and the possibility of it getting stuck halfway. On the day, with remarkable speed – and flawless execution – miner after miner climbed into the capsule, and was hoisted through the rock and saw precious sunlight after the longest underground entrapment in history. Dr Michael Duncan, NASA's deputy chief medical officer, stated: 'We were able to bring the knowledge we learned in space to the surface, and under the surface, to help people here on Earth.' The Copiapó incident involved not only very unusual team composition (these occupations, professions, and cultures do not normally collaborate in this way), but also a very unusual team context – rescuing trapped miners is not something that is done routinely (adapted from National Aeronautics and Space Administration, 2011).

The T-word and team work design

Team a group whose members share a common goal that they pursue collaboratively and who can only succeed or fail collectively.

The word **team** derives from the old English, Frisian, and Norse word for a bridle and thence came to refer to a set of draught animals harnessed together and, by analogy, to a number of persons involved in joint action (Annett and Stanton, 2000). It refers to a group whose members share a common goal that they pursue collaboratively; the group can only succeed or fail collectively.

Nicky Hayes saw teams as a sporting metaphor used frequently by managers and consultants. Sainsbury's, a large British supermarket chain, used the employee job title of 'checkout *captain*'. The metaphor stresses inclusiveness and similarity – members sharing common values and cooperating to achieve common goals – while also emphasizing differences, as various individuals play distinct, albeit equally valuable, roles, and have different responsibilities. She wrote that

> The idea of 'team' at work must be one of the most widely used metaphors in organizational life. A group of workers or managers is generally described as a 'team', in much the same way that a company or department is so often described as 'one big family'. But often, the new employee receiving these assertions quickly discovers that what was described as a 'team' is actually anything but. The mental image of cohesion, co-ordination and common goals which was conjured up by the metaphor of the team was entirely different from the everyday reality of working life. (Hayes, 1997, p. 27)

Source: DILBERT © 1995 Scott Adams. Used by permission of UNIVERSAL UCLICK. All rights reserved.

Jos Benders and Geert Van Hootegem (1999a; 1999b) felt that after decades of experimentation, teams had finally achieved the status of 'good management practice' in Western organizations. The terms 'group' and 'team' are words which are frequently used interchangeably in the management literature. Katzenbach and Smith (1993) suggest that the key distinction between a work group and a team relates to performance results. They wrote:

> A working group's performance is a function of what its members do as individuals. A team's performance includes both individual results and what we call 'collective work products'. A collective work product is what two or more members work on together . . . [it] reflects the joint, real contribution of team members. (1993, p. 112)

Paul Paulus and Karen van der Zee (2004) explained how, historically, research into groups and that into teams had followed distinct and separate paths, with the literature on groups appearing in psychology textbooks, and that on teams in management textbooks, journals, and magazines. They also wrote that 'team is a word for managers' – an appealing word used as a rhetorical strategy through which managers hope to achieve their goals. It conveys the view that we are 'all in it together' and the interests of workers and top management are the same. Other critics have argued that management's promotion of the *team* concept was a union-busting device – a way of threatening the existence of unions as independent institutions promoting workers' interests, and of increasing employees' personal insecurity. They imply that, in contrast, *group* (which we defined in Chapter 10 as meaning two or more people, in face-to-face interaction, each aware of their group membership and interdependence, as they strive to achieve common group goals), is a word that is used by those academics who study human behaviour in organizations.

Football teams

VI/Getty

The golden years of the Ajax Amsterdam football team were the 1970s, when the team included the legendary Johan Cruyff and Piet Keizer. The players enjoyed unparalleled freedom at the highest level of the modern game. There has been nothing since to compare with the giddy, unintended experiment in football democracy. It was probably as close as anyone has ever come to running a major football club like a workers' cooperative. Not only did the team practically pick itself, but the players also determined most of their own tactics and decided which friendly matches they would play. It was the custom every year for the Ajax team captain to be chosen by the players without the presence of the coach. Teamwork in Dutch football was based on the fact that the team had to be the star, not its players.

Confirming this view, John Kay argued that in the 2006 World Cup, while the conquering Italian team was more than the sum of its individual parts, the Brazilian team (the final losers) was not. What distinguishes a great team from a group of great players? Kay highlights two factors. The first is the quality of a club's 'organizational learning', particularly its post-match debriefings, and its pre-match communication with players about other players, other clubs, and pitches. His second factor has to do with personal benefit. Kay says 'A player can choose to kick for goal or pass to a better situated player. His choice of behaviour will depend on the degree to which his incentives relate to the performance of the team rather than his performance as an individual, and on his expectations about whether the next player will shoot or pass in turn. Because an individual's behaviour depends on the expectations of the behaviour of others, teams will become locked into particular states.' Italy's success was testimony to the fact that outstanding teams can defeat groups of outstanding individual players – 'A team of champions can be beaten by a champion team' (based on Winner, 2001; Kay, 2006).

Types of teams

Eric Sundstrom, Kenneth De Meuse and David Futrell (1990) distinguished four types of teams – advice, action, project and production teams (see Table 13.1). Advice teams (e.g. quality circles) provide information to management to be used in its own decision-making. Action teams (e.g. football teams) execute brief performances that are repeated under new conditions. Project teams bring together employees from different departments to accomplish a specific task, such as new product development. Production teams consist

Table 13.1: Types of teams and their outputs

Types and examples	Differentiation	Coordination	Specialization	Work cycles	Typical outputs
ADVICE Committees Review panels and boards Quality control circles Employee involvement groups Advisory councils	Low	Low	Low	Work cycles can be brief or long; one cycle can be a team lifespan	Decisions Selections Suggestions Proposals Recommendations
ACTION Sports teams Entertainment groups Expeditions Negotiating teams Surgery teams Cockpit crews Military platoons and squads	High	High	High	Work cycles brief, repeated under new conditions	Competitive events Expeditions Contracts Lawsuits Concerts Surgical operations Flights Combat missions
PROJECT Research groups Planning teams Architect teams Engineering teams Development teams Task forces	High	Low (for traditional units) or high (for cross-functional teams)	High	Work cycles typically differ for each new project; one cycle can be a team's lifespan	Plans Designs Investigations Presentations Prototypes Reports Findings
PRODUCTION Assembly line teams Manufacturing cells Mining teams Hospital reception teams Data processing groups Maintenance crews	Low	High	High	Work cycles typically repeated or continuous process; cycles often briefer than team lifespan	Food Chemicals Components Assemblies Retail sales Customer service Equipment repairs

Source: from Sundstrom, E., De Meuse, K.P. and Futrell, D., Work teams: applications and effectiveness, *American Psychologist*, 45(2), pp. 120–33 (Table on p. 125) 1990 American Psychological Society, reprinted with permission.

of individuals who share a production goal. Each team type can be further differentiated along five dimensions:

1. *Degree of differentiation from other units*. How similar (low differentiation) or different (high differentiation) is this team from others within the department or organization?
2. *Degree of coordination*. Is its work closely related to and intertwined with that of other work units within the organization (high coordination), or does it operate relatively independently (low coordination)?
3. *Degree of technical specialization*. Are members required to apply special technical skills acquired through higher education or extensive training (high specialization); or do they draw upon their general experience and innate problem-solving ability (low specialization)?
4. *Work cycles*. How much time does the team need to achieve its aims? Does it perform short, repetitive work cycles, or a single, long one?
5. *Typical outputs*. What does the team produce as its output?

Sundstrom et al.'s team typology allows you to categorize existing teams in organizations, and compare and contrast their processes, analyse their outputs, and suggest ways of making improvements.

Team autonomy the extent to which a team experiences freedom, independence, and discretion in decisions relating to the performance of its tasks.

Team autonomy refers to the extent to which a team experiences freedom, independence, and discretion in decisions related to the performance of its tasks. However, providing an operational definition of a team with high or low autonomy is difficult (Nijholt and Benders, 2010). Benders noted the taken-for-granted assumption that the word 'team' was inherently associated with a high level of autonomy. The adjectives that frequently precede the word 'team' in the organizational literature are *autonomous*, *semi-autonomous*, *self-managing*, *self-regulating*, and *self-directing*. However, there are many types of teams, for example, those in the archetypal Japanese system of lean production, which are not necessarily participative, let alone self-managing (Procter and Currie, 2004). Teams differ in terms of how much autonomy management grants them.

When encountering an example of a supposed 'autonomous team' within a company, it is necessary to ask: who decides about what, and to what extent? Jan Gulowsen (1979), a Norwegian researcher, provided a framework which enabled more specific assessments to be made about team autonomy, shown in Table 13.2. He distinguished nine 'task areas' or dimensions in a team's working which offered the potential for autonomy. Within each area, he specified four possible levels of team input. This allows different teams to be distinguished in terms of the level of autonomy that they possess, and allows them to be compared and contrasted.

Table 13.2: Team task areas, levels of team input, and team autonomy levels

Team task area / dimensions

1. Selection of the team leader
2. Acceptance of a new member into the team
3. Distribution of work
4. Time flexibility
5. Acceptance of additional work
6. Representation outside the team
7. Production methods (choice of)
8. Production goals (output determination)
9. Production goals (quality determination)

Team input levels

1. *None* – No team participation and total management control. Managers make all the decisions and the team implements them. Team members have no input into the decision-making process; there is no element of participation, not even in the form of suggestions or requests.
2. *Some* – The team has some input into decisions concerned with its immediate working environment. It can make suggestions and requests, and has discussions with management who may adopt its ideas.
3. *Joint* – A situation of co-decision-making, in which a team shares decision-making power with management, and plays an equal role in the taking and implementing of decisions.
4. *Autonomy* – The team is fully trusted by management, and is truly autonomous. It reaches its decisions with no input from management whatsoever. Management accepts the team as a full and equal partner.

Team autonomy level

low autonomy teams	moderate autonomy teams	high autonomy teams
assembly line workers	quality circles	autonomous work groups
supermarket checkouts	semi-autonomous groups	high performance teams
		self-directed team

Source: based on Gulowsen (1979).

Home viewing

The film *Rumours – Classic Albums DVD* (2008) chronicles the making of one of rock music's biggest selling albums by Fleetwood Mac. The film describes the internal struggles of band members who stayed together for several years. As you watch the video, consider the following questions which draw from the various group and team chapters. Which group members performed task roles and which played maintenance roles? How did the band's experience of making the album balance between team performance and team viability? How did the interpersonal turmoil within the group help or hinder their work product? Identify the different types of conflict within the band. What were the effects of this conflict and how were they resolved? How did the compatibility of group members, and a common goal, contribute to group cohesiveness? How was the group able to stay together during the making of the album? What common norms guided their behaviour?

Based on Comer and Holbrook (2012).

Researchers use four specific criteria to distinguish autonomous from semi-autonomous teams:

1. Members work together as a team.
2. Team members are responsible for specific products or services.
3. Team members jointly decide how work is done.
4. The team appoints its own leader.

To be classed as 'semi-autonomous', a team must fulfil the first three criteria, while a fully autonomous team meets all four requirements (Procter and Burridge, 2008). Table 13.3 lists the types of tasks that self-managing teams are most likely to perform for themselves.

Table 13.3: Tasks performed by self-managing teams themselves

A survey conducted of 1,456 organizations in the United States with over 100 employees found the following:

Task	Percentage of teams performing tasks
Set own work schedules	67
Deal directly with external customers	67
Conduct own member training	59
Setting own production quotas / performance targets	56
Deal with suppliers / vendors	44
Purchase equipment / services	43
Develop budgets	39
Do their own performance reviews on members	36
Hire co-workers	33
Fire co-workers	14

Source: from *Training*, 1996, p. 69.

According to Druskat and Wheeler (2004), 79 per cent of Fortune 1000 companies, and 81 per cent of Fortune 1000 manufacturing companies, had self-managing teams. Reviewing previous studies, Park (2012) reported that it appeared that such teams had a positive effect on productivity and customer satisfaction at company level, while at the individual employee level they increased job satisfaction, organizational commitment, and organizational citizenship behaviour. However, some contradictory research led him to speculate that the effects of self-managing teams may depend on the organizational context in which they operate.

His own research suggested that these teams are more effective in capital-intensive industries than in labour-intensive ones, in increasing employees' commitment to the organization and reducing staff turnover.

STOP AND THINK

If you are a member of a team (work, sports, musical, religious, social), what level of decision input do you and your fellow team members have on which tasks, in relation to your supervisor, coach, choirmaster or conductor, priest or minister, club president?

Make a list of tasks relevant to your team and then identify those which your team performs itself.

Collaboration conundrums

Major corporations rely on large, diverse teams of highly educated specialists to implement major changes or launch initiatives. Examples include the BBC teams covering the World Cup or the Olympics, and the Marriott Hotels developing an enhanced IT system. Research by Lynda Gratton and Tamara Erickson (Gratton and Erickson, 2007; Gratton, 2007) into team behaviour in fifteen multinational companies discovered the paradox that the four qualities required for team success were the same ones that undermined that success. These were large size, diversity, virtual participation, and high educational levels.

- *Size* – past teams of 20 now typically consist of 100 or more members. The increase is due to new technologies, wider stakeholder involvement, coordination of diverse activities, and harnessing of multiple skills. Negatively, they found that beyond 20 members, the natural level of cooperation between members decreases.
- *Diversity* – tasks require the rapid assembly of people from different backgrounds and perspectives, few of whom have ever previously met. Dissimilar views and knowledge can trigger innovation. Negatively, the greater the diversity and the number of strangers in a team, the less likely they are to share their knowledge.
- *Virtual participation* – complex tasks require insights and knowledge from people from many locations, so virtual teamworking is common. Negatively, as teams become more virtual, then collaboration declines.
- *Higher education levels* – teams draw on members who possess highly specialized skills and knowledge. Negatively, the greater the proportion of highly educated specialists on a team, the more likely it is to disintegrate into unproductive conflicts.

Advice teams

Advice team a team created by management to provide the latter with information for its own decision-making.

Quality circle shop-floor employees from the same department, who meet for a few hours each week to discuss ways of improving their work environment.

An **advice team** is created primarily to provide a flow of information to management for use in its own decision-making. Advice teams require little in the way of coordination with other work units in the company. Following a major accident or disaster, governments often set up committees of experts and eminent people to advise on future action. The committee reviews the events that occurred, and makes recommendations about improvements.

In organizations, the **quality circle** (also known as a kaizen team) is the best known and most publicized advice team of recent times. The original concept was of a team of six to twelve employees from the shop floor of the same manufacturing department, meeting regularly to discuss quality problems, investigating their causes, and recommending solutions to management. In practice, a wide range of different arrangements was established under this label. Quality circles varied in terms of the number of members; were applied in service as well as manufacturing contexts; included supervisory staff; discussed non-quality issues;

and some had authority to implement their suggestions. All these matters depended on how the quality circle was established by management in the particular organization.

Quality circles are a Japanese export, and have been used all over the world. They were introduced into the West during the 1980s in an effort to emulate Japanese successes. The first quality circle in the United States is claimed to have been at the Lockheed Missile and Space Company at Sunnyvale in California in 1974. The first one in Britain appeared at Rolls-Royce in Derby in 1978. Although originally used in manufacturing, quality circles have been applied extensively in service industries, government agencies, the voluntary sector, the British National Health Service, and many other types of organizations. Despite their differences, which were mentioned earlier, quality circles do possess some common features:

- Membership is voluntary, and members are drawn from a particular department.
- No financial rewards are given for team suggestions.
- Members receive training in problem-solving, statistical quality control, and team processes.
- Their problem-solving domain is defined by management (often, but not always quality, productivity and cost reduction).
- Meetings are held weekly, usually in company time, often with trained facilitators helping members with training issues and helping them to manage the meetings.
- The decision to install quality circles is made at the top of the organization, and the circles are created at the bottom.

Management's objectives for introducing quality circles vary greatly, including, for example, quality improvement, quality enhancement, and employee involvement. Although an organization may claim to have introduced quality circles, even at the height of their popularity only a small proportion of the employees ever took part (Marchington, 1992). Quality circles represent one of the largest experiments in the use of advice teams to improve organizational performance during the 1980s. From the 1990s, quality circles begun to be superseded by the 'total quality movement' (Hill, 1991).

Action teams

Action team a team that executes brief performances that are repeated under new conditions. Its members are technically specialized, and need to coordinate their individual contributions with each other.

The members of an **action team** are specialized in terms of their knowledge, skill, and contribution to the team's objective. The 'performance' of an action team is brief, and is repeated under new conditions each time. Additionally, both the specialized inputs of the various team members and the need for individuals to coordinate with other team members is high.

If a football player sustains an injury on the field, an action team consisting of the club physiotherapists will work on him. If the injury is serious, he may be taken to hospital, where another action team – a surgeon and his co-workers – operate on him. Finally, when recuperating in his private room, he may watch TV, and see a Formula 1 race where an action team change the tyres of racing cars and refuel it. In all these situations, action team members have to exhibit peak performance on demand.

One example of an action team is a *crew*. This term is frequently used to refer to employees who work on aircraft, boats, spacecraft, and film sets. A distinguishing feature of a crew is that it is equipment- or technology-driven. That is why perhaps McDonald's refers to its restaurant employees as 'crew members'. If the technology changes, then so too does the nature of the crew. A crew depends on its technology, which transforms difficult cognitive tasks into easy ones. The crew's 'tools' affect the division of labour among its members; and crew members use various techniques to coordinate their activities (Hare, 1992; Hutchins, 1990).

The five-second tyre change

Getty Images

When the Grand Prix racing car flicks into the pits to collect fresh tyres, it is time for the pit crew to take their brief place in the sun under the eyes of the packed grandstands and TV cameras. A pit crew can change all four tyres of a racing car in under five seconds. Pit stops are a critical time, as they can make the difference between victory and defeat. The speed of the mechanics practically defeats the eye. Have you seen a tyre change on a Formula 1 car? How many mechanics are involved?

The answer is at least thirteen. There are three men at each corner of the car: one with the wheel gun, another to remove the wheel, and a third to put on the replacement; and the last man operates the car jack. In fact, the fourteenth member of the team is the driver himself who has to streak down the pit lane and stop 6 to 12 inches in front of where the mechanics are positioned. Moving equipment wastes valuable tenths of a second. The tyre change is fraught with danger. One slip-up, one sticking wheel nut, one man unable to fling his arms up in the all-clear signal, and the race can be lost. To achieve a consistent, high level of team performance requires military precision, movement programmes (like ballet), and practised rehearsals which go on throughout the year.

Ginnett (1993) reported how, on a Boeing 727 aircraft, the crew members' roles were determined by the location of their seats in the cockpit. The captain sat in the left seat, from which he tested all the emergency warning devices. He was the only one who could taxi the aircraft, since the nose wheel gear steering was located on that side of the cockpit. The first officer, who started the engines and who communicated with the control tower, occupied the right-hand seat. The flight engineer sat sideways, facing a panel that allowed him to monitor and control the various subsystems in the aircraft. He was the only one able to reach the auxiliary power unit. In other transportation craft, the relationship of roles to equipment would be different. Aeroplane personnel consist of those in the cockpit – flight crew (pilot, co-pilot, flight engineers) – and those outside it – the cabin crew (flight attendants). Between 1959 and 1989, 70 per cent of all severe aircraft accidents were at least partly attributable to flight crew behaviour (Weiner et al., 1993). Thus, it is a more common cause than either pilot error or mechanical failure.

Mending a broken heart

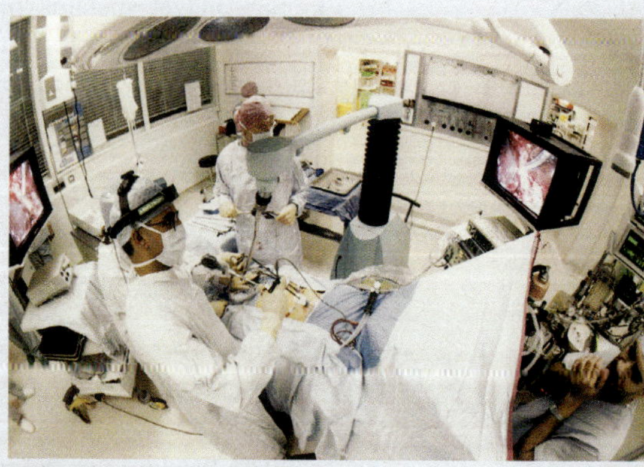

Armstrong Healthcare Ltd

Operating theatre

During cardiac surgery, a patient is rendered functionally dead – the heart stops beating, the lungs stop pumping air – while a surgical team repairs or replaces damaged arteries or valves. A week later, the patient walks out of the hospital. The team that performs this task is as important as the technology that allows them to do it. It consists of different specialists – a surgeon, an anaesthetist, a perfusionist (a technician who runs the bypass machine that takes over the functions of the heart and lungs), and a scrub nurse – working closely and cooperatively together. It exemplifies an *action team* where a single error, miscommunication, or slow response by any member can result in failure. Individuals are in *reciprocal interdependence* with each other, *mutually adjusting* their actions to match those of fellow members.

Edmondson and her colleagues (2001) found that since this type of team performed hundreds of cardiac operations annually, it established a sequence of individual tasks that became very well-defined and routine. Indeed, team members often needed only to look at, rather than speak to, one another, to signal the initiation of the next stage of the procedure. The change from traditional, open-heart surgery procedures to minimally invasive ones involved several changes. The new procedure not only required individual team members to learn new, unfamiliar tasks, but also required a number of familiar tasks to be performed in a different order. Thus, team members had to unlearn old routines before learning new ones. Additionally, the new technology required a greater degree of interdependence and communication between team members. For example, the surgeon had to rely more on team members for essential information (obtained from ultrasound images and digital readouts) than before. This not only disrupted the team's routine but also changed the surgeon's traditional role as order-giver in the operating team's tightly structured hierarchy. Improvements in team performance were found partly to depend on 'the ability of the surgeon to allow himself to become a partner, not a dictator' (Edmondson et al., 2001, p. 128). Through trying out things that might not work, making mistakes, and pointing out problems, learning was accelerated. Such a climate was fostered by the words and actions of surgeons acting as team leaders.

Project teams

Project team a collection of employees from different work areas in an organization brought together to accomplish a specific task within a finite time.

A **project team** consists of individuals who have been brought together for a limited period of time, from different parts of the organization, to contribute towards a management-specified task. The task may be, for example, developing a product, refining a service, or commissioning a new plant. Once this has been completed, either the team is disbanded, or its members are given new assignments. Project teams are created when

- creative problem-solving is required involving the application of different types of specialized knowledge;
- there is a need to closely coordinate the work on a specific project, e.g. design and development, or the production and testing of a new product.

Every university has hundreds of project teams who are conducting research. Most of their members are on two-to-three-year contracts which span the period of the research project. Team members are recruited on the basis of their specialist knowledge, and their output consists of research reports, books, and journal articles.

Cross-functional team employees from different functional departments who meet as a team to complete a particular task.

Within the organizational context, the best known and most common types of project team is the **cross-functional team**. This is a collection of employees who are brought together from different departments (functions) of the company to accomplish a specific task within a finite time. Jack Gordon (1992) reported that in the United States, in organizations with more than 100 employees, 82 per cent had staff working in teams, of which 18 per cent were in cross-functional teams. Another survey, by the Hay Group, revealed that approximately 25 per cent of US companies had implemented cross-functional teamworking (Leshner and Brown, 1993). Emmerson, an electronics company based in St. Louis, Missouri, established cross-functional teams in the 1990s to deal with large customers who bought products and services from several of its divisions. Cross-functional teams cut across the company's long-standing boundaries and allowed customers to see Emmerson as a single, integrated supplier rather than a collection of independent divisions (Hindle, 2006; Knight, 2005).

Traditionally, organizations have been divided into functional departments. These have been dubbed 'boxes', 'silos', or 'chimneys' to stress their insularity. By forming teams consisting of people from these different boxes, organizations can break down the boundaries between their functions (e.g. accounting, marketing, research, product design, human resources), improve coordination and integration, release the creative thought of their employees, and increase the speed and flexibility of their responses to customers. Cross-functional teams are established in order to combine a wide range of employee expertise to achieve a more informed and rounded outcome than would otherwise be possible.

Cross-functional teams comprise employees who traditionally work in different departments or work areas. Sometimes, such teams also include customers, suppliers, and external consultants. They are supported by their organization's structures, systems, and skills which enable the teams to operate successfully as a more independent unit (less bound by functional ties) towards goals which transcend the combined abilities of individual members. Advocates of cross-functional teams claim that they are beneficial to their customers, to employees, and to the organization as a whole. Customers obtain more attractive and customized products, and have their needs met more rapidly. Team members benefit through

- having more challenging and rewarding jobs with broader responsibilities;
- greater opportunities for gaining visibility in front of senior management;
- an increased understanding of entire processes across their organizations;
- a 'fun' working environment and
- closer relationships with colleagues.

The organization gains through

- increased productivity;
- improved coordination and integration;
- significantly reducing processing times;
- improving market and customer focus;
- reducing the time needed to develop new products; and
- improving communications by having boundaries between functions spanned.

Cross-functional management teams at Nissan

Following the strategic alliance between Renault and Nissan in 1999, Carlos Ghosn went to Tokyo to lead Nissan back to profitability. He wanted to introduce changes that went against both the company's long-standing operating practices and some of the behavioural norms of Japanese society. Rather than imposing these changes from the top, he used cross-functional teams (CFTs) comprising Nissan's middle management, and made these the centrepiece of his turnaround plan. While executives preferred working in teams consisting of similarly oriented colleagues, Ghosn wanted them to look beyond the functional or regional boundaries that defined their direct responsibilities, and to ask difficult questions. Cross-functional teamworking would, in his view, encourage his managers to think in new ways and to challenge existing practices. In this organizational context, the teams would also provide a means for explaining the need for change, and for communicating difficult messages across the whole company. Ghosn quickly established nine CFTs, each with its own area of responsibility.

Together, the CFTs addressed all the key drivers which determined Nissan's performance. Each team consisted of about ten middle managers, and created its own sub-teams to investigate some issues in greater depth. To give each CFT authority within the company, two 'leaders' from the executive committee were appointed to it (to prevent a single function's perspective predominating). They served as that team's sponsors, helping to smooth its path, and removing institutional obstacles to its work. To avoid charges of top-down, imposed change, these leaders took a back seat, and rarely attended team meetings, leaving the real work to the team's 'pilot', who took the lead in discussions and progressed the team's work. All the CFTs were given three months, and asked to review the company's operations, and recommend ways of returning Nissan to profitability and uncovering opportunities for future growth. None of them had any decision-making responsibility. The outcome was a detailed blueprint for the Nissan Revival Plan developed by Nissan's own executives. They proposed major changes to some Nissan business practices (e.g. in engineering specifications and reducing some quality standards); and 'harsh medicine' in the form of plant closures and headcount reductions, which challenged Japanese business traditions (based on Ghosn, 2002).

Cross-functional teams differ from other types of teams in three important respects:

- They are *representative* in that their individual members usually retain their position back in their 'home' functional department.
- They are *temporary*: they have a finite life, even if their end is years in the future.
- They are *innovative*: they are established to solve non-conventional problems and meet challenging performance standards.

The most common applications of cross-functional teams have been in new product development, innovation, and research and development (R&D). However, they have also been used whenever an organization requires an input of diverse, specialist skills and knowledge – for example, in manufacturing and production; in IT development, automation, and support; to implement quality, cost, speed improvements, and process re-engineering initiatives; to facilitate customer service improvements; and to streamline purchasing and procurement. Recent years have seen the evolution of global virtual (project) teams. These now permeate all levels of most large organizations, often supplementing traditional, face-to-face teams (Cordery et al., 2009).

Since team members are departmental representatives, they owe their true allegiance to their home, functional department. These members are therefore likely to experience a high degree of pressure and divided loyalties. Their temporary nature also places strains on members who have quickly to develop stable and effective working group processes. Cross-functional teams can therefore have a negative effect on their participants. Organizations and managers need to clearly define cross-functional team assignments in order to maintain order and accountability.

STOP AND THINK

You are a middle manager at Nissan who has been a member of one of their nine cross-functional teams. Do you feel pleased to have been given the responsibility to participate in setting the company's future direction, or resentful that the senior management seems to have manipulated you and your colleagues, through the means of cross-functional teams, into proposing unpalatable solutions that they lack the courage to recommend themselves?

Production teams

Production team a stable number of individuals who share production goals, and who perform specific roles which are supported by a set of incentives and sanctions.

Typically, a **production team** consists of individuals who are responsible for performing day-to-day, core operations. These may be product-oriented teams such as those assembling a computer on a factory floor; construction workers placing a bridge in position across a motorway; or teams assembling sound and light systems for a rock concert. The degree of technical specialization required of the team members varies from medium to low, depending on the nature of the duties performed. However, the required degree of coordination, both between the members of each team and between the team and other work units, is high. It is these other units that are responsible either for providing support activities such as quality control and maintenance, or for providing the inputs to, or receiving the outputs of, that team.

The focus of 1970s experiments into employee participation and industrial democracy sought to raise productivity by providing employees with more interesting and varied work. In contrast, team-based working innovations of the 1990s represent a greater concern with efficiency and effectiveness. They were stimulated by the need for companies to remain competitive in a fiercely aggressive global environment. The rationale is that in the race to improve service quality or reduce new product cycle times, technology only gives an organization a short-term advantage, and one which can be copied anyway. It is the way that human resources are organized and developed that is more critical.

Is yours a polychronic or a monochronic team?

Using questionnaires and interviews, Souitaris and Maestro (2011) studied senior executive teams in 200 new technology ventures listed on the London Stock Exchange. They measured each team's 'polychronicity' – its tendency to multi-task – and the firm's financial performance. A polychronic team member interviewed said 'This team prides itself on being able to oversee several ongoing projects at the same time quite easily. We enjoy the variety, that constant switching, the challenge of needing to concentrate harder.' In contrast, a monochronic team member stated 'Hopping from one project to another? Is that really wise? I mean, there is no time to really think things through, right? I believe it would only ruin our concentration and disrupt our thought processes.'

Technical ventures are dynamic, and the executive teams which manage them often consist of self-selected members who share similar outlooks. The researchers found that the performance of the companies with highly polychronic teams was significantly better than that of companies with average or monochronic teams. Why? The authors wrote:

> The polychronic teams proved to be superior information-brokers, absorbing and disseminating more-insightful information than their average and monochronic counterparts. As a result, they were much less apt than the other teams to bog down. They could make strategic decisions faster, placing less emphasis on analyzing large quantities of data. Their expedited decision-making process, we believe, boosted their companies' performance. (p. 32)

Source: from The case for multitasking, Harvard Business Review, *October, p. 32 (Soultaris, V. and Marcello Maestro, B.M. 2011).*

Management's interest in production teams has always been in finding ways of improving employee motivation and performance. Employee participation in decision-making can take the form of increasing their autonomy. Bram Steijn distinguished between *individual* autonomy for the employee who was not part of a team, for example, in the form of job enrichment (see chapter 9) and team autonomy which was 'the (*collective*) autonomy for the workers *as a team* to do a task' (Steijn, 2001, p. 193). It is the latter that is considered in this chapter. In practice, the individual and the teamworking approaches have converged in what has come to be known as the *high performance work system*, which we discussed in Chapter 9. Studies have attempted to evaluate its success (Ramsey et al., 2000). The contrast between traditional hierarchical management and team management is summarized in Table 13.4.

Table 13.4: Hierarchical and team management compared

Hierarchical management: hierarchically ordered supervision	**Team management: shift to self-management**
The supervisor has precise supervisory responsibilities.	The supervisor is replaced by a team of 10 to 15 people, who take over the responsibilities of their former supervisor.
The supervisor gives instructions.	Self-managing employees gather and synthesize information, act on it, and take collective responsibility for their actions.
Management relies on formal rules and authority expressed in terms of disciplines that seek to reinforce this authority.	Management provides a value-based corporate vision that guides day-to-day actions by being a reference point from which employees infer appropriate action.
The supervisor checks that instructions have been followed.	The self-managing team guides its own work and coordinates with other areas of the company.
The supervisor ensures that each employee fulfils his or her job description.	The self-managing team is responsible for completing a specific, well-defined job function for which all members are cross trained. All members of the team have the authority and responsibility to make essential decisions, set work schedules, order materials, and coordinate with other teams.

Source: reproduced by permission of SAGE Publications, London, Los Angeles, New Delhi and Singapore, from Clegg, S.R., Kornberger, M. and Pitsis, T., *Managing and Organizations*, Copyright Sage Publications 2011.

Authors have noted the social and historic processes that have led to the emergence of the *autonomous work team*. This is a team (confusingly often labelled 'group' in the research literature) that is allocated to a significant segment of the workflow, with discretion over how their work will be carried out. It is argued that such teams reduce costs by eliminating the need for having supervisors, and their members produce more, because they are more motivated and committed to their jobs (Langfried, 2000; Kirkman et al., 2001; Chansler et al., 2003). Alan Jenkins (1994) argued that management had become preoccupied with autonomous teamworking, and that such teams had come to be seen as the basis for effective organizational designs.

A self-managing orchestra

Larry Fink/studio 55

Orpheus Chamber Orchestra

In the dictatorial world of orchestras, it is the conductors who choose the repertoire, organize rehearsals, and tell musicians how to play. In contrast, the Orpheus Chamber Orchestra in New York shares and rotates leadership roles on a weekly basis. The orchestra chooses a concertmaster and the principal players for each section. These represent the core group who decide on the initial interpretation of the piece, and work with the whole ensemble, shaping the rehearsal process. Initially, this chaotic democracy led to inefficient rehearsals and bruised egos, but the process has improved despite remaining a long process, requiring twice as many rehearsals as with a conductor. Musicians rely on being able to see and hear each other and so limit their number to 40 players. Playing without a conductor is risky, but triggers spontaneity. If a great conductor makes all the important decisions, musicians start to play in a more passive way. One clarinettist said 'Sometimes, I'm tired and don't feel like thinking and just want someone to guide me. On the other hand, conductors aren't inspiring and just get in the way' (based on *The Economist*, 2006; Levine and Levine, 1996).

Suitable autonomous work team settings

There are different kinds of teams, work tasks, and work settings. Some are suitable for autonomous teamworking, while others are not. Louis Davis and George Wacker (1987) listed the situational factors which they believed most suited autonomous group working.

1. The work is not entirely unskilled.
2. The work group can be identified as a meaningful unit of the organization; inputs and outputs are definable and clearly identifiable; and different groups can be separated by stable buffer areas.
3. Turnover in the group can be kept to a minimum.
4. There are definite criteria for performance evaluation of the group and group members.
5. Timely feedback is possible.
6. The group has resources for measuring and controlling its own critical variances in workflow.
7. The tasks are highly interdependent, so that group members must work together.
8. Cross-training is desired by management.
9. Jobs can be structured to balance group and individual tasks.

Self-steering teams at Volvo Cars

In 1965, Volvo Cars established a manufacturing plant in Ghent, Belgium. In 1987, the work organization of the plant was redesigned. Originally, operators had been located at their own, fixed workstations on the assembly line, performing only online tasks. Highly paid specialists were responsible for maintenance and quality control; an inspector provided training; and a multiskilled relief man supported the operators. One supervisor controlled an assembly line comprising eighty operators.

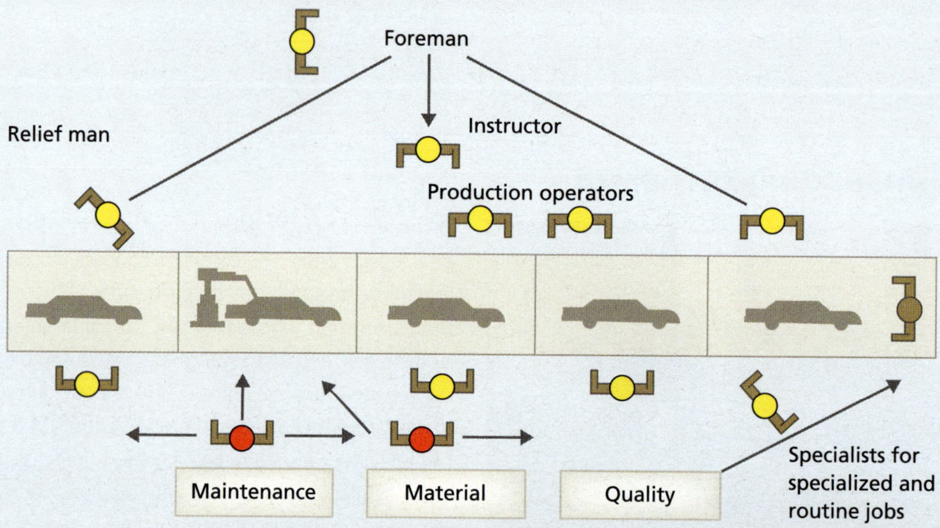

Source: European Foundation for the Improvement of Living and Working Conditions (2005).

The inherent inefficiencies led to the introduction of the self-steering (self-managing) teamwork organization. The company strictly adhered to short-cycle line production, so the new work system was operated within the limitations imposed by this assembly line technology. Groups of 12 to 20 operators were formed including a team leader. Each team was assigned a corner of the factory to meet, exchange information, and communicate team results. The teams were delegated the responsibility for quality, maintenance, and repair tasks. These tasks were no longer performed by the specialist, but were integrated within general production, and allocated to all team members, not just the team leader. Job rotation and job enlargement were also introduced.

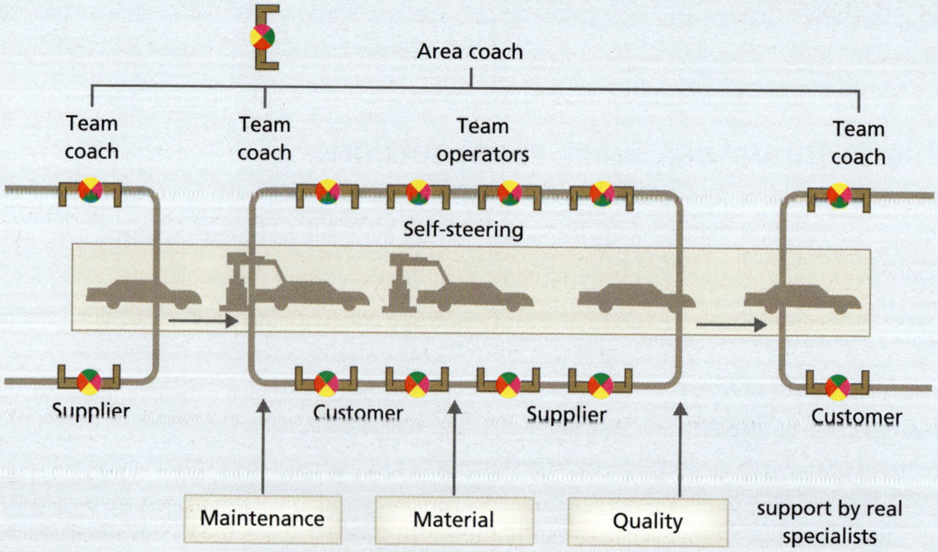

Source: European Foundation for the Improvement of Living and Working Conditions (2005).

Over time, this form of teamwork organization at Volvo Cars has been adapted to increase employee self-management. A seven-point star-shaped model is used to critically evaluate the tasks that relate to cost, delivery, environment, quality, and safety. Within each team, individual members volunteer to take responsibility for each of these seven tasks, thereby creating a greater sense of team ownership. Team members are given feedback with respect to their specialized task, and the team leader's role becomes more of a coach and less that of a supervisor.

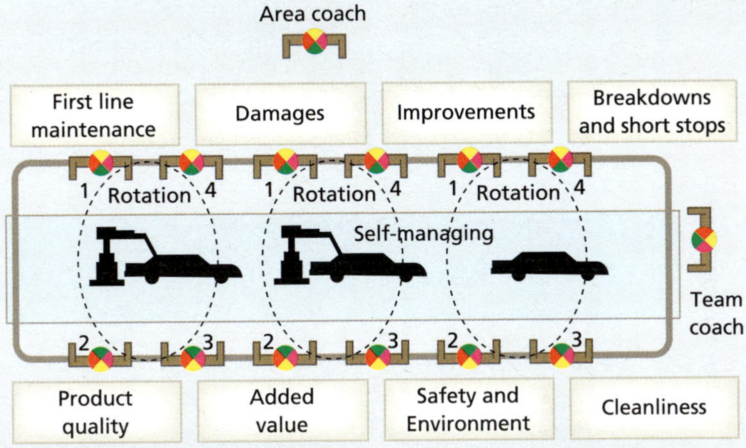

Source: European Foundation for the Improvement of Living and Working Conditions (2005).

Getty Images

A huge expansion of the Ghent plant occurred between 2001 and 2004 when two new Volvo car models were introduced. The plant's production capacity was doubled and 1,400 new employees were hired. This rapid expansion has created problems for the continued application of this distinctive work organization model at Volvo Cars Ghent. The costs of manufacturing in Europe mean that the Ghent plant will always face challenges. It will be interesting to see if their self-managing teams approach will be able to survive in the future, in an increasingly unpredictable automobile manufacturing environment (European Foundation for the Improvement of Living and Working Conditions, 2005). The plant currently employs 5,000 staff who build the Volvo S60 model.

There has been confusion about the use of the concept of teamworking in different countries and in different companies. Western teamworking emphasizes enhanced employee control and job satisfaction through participation, and represents an example of worker *empowerment*. This refers to organizational arrangements that give employees more autonomy, discretion, and decision-making responsibility. Grey (2009) reminds us that employee empowerment in organizations is only allowed by management if it is exercised in ways that are beneficial to the organization.

Van den Broek et al. (2002) distinguished between 'teams' and 'teamworking'. A number of organizations use team structures, yet design work to be done individually. Call centre companies offer a good example of this. Individuals who work within these so-called 'teams' are unable to influence the activities of their fellow workers or control the nature of their work, yet can still 'look after their mates'. Asking why management would want to introduce a team structure that did not empower the employees, Townsend (2005) concluded that it was a way of exercising control over employees through group norms and company culture. To recap, in companies, teamworking is not necessarily synonymous with employee empowerment. Daft and Noe (2001) described a range of empowerment possibilities for individuals and teams, indicating the number and range of skills needed by the employees involved (see Figure 13.1).

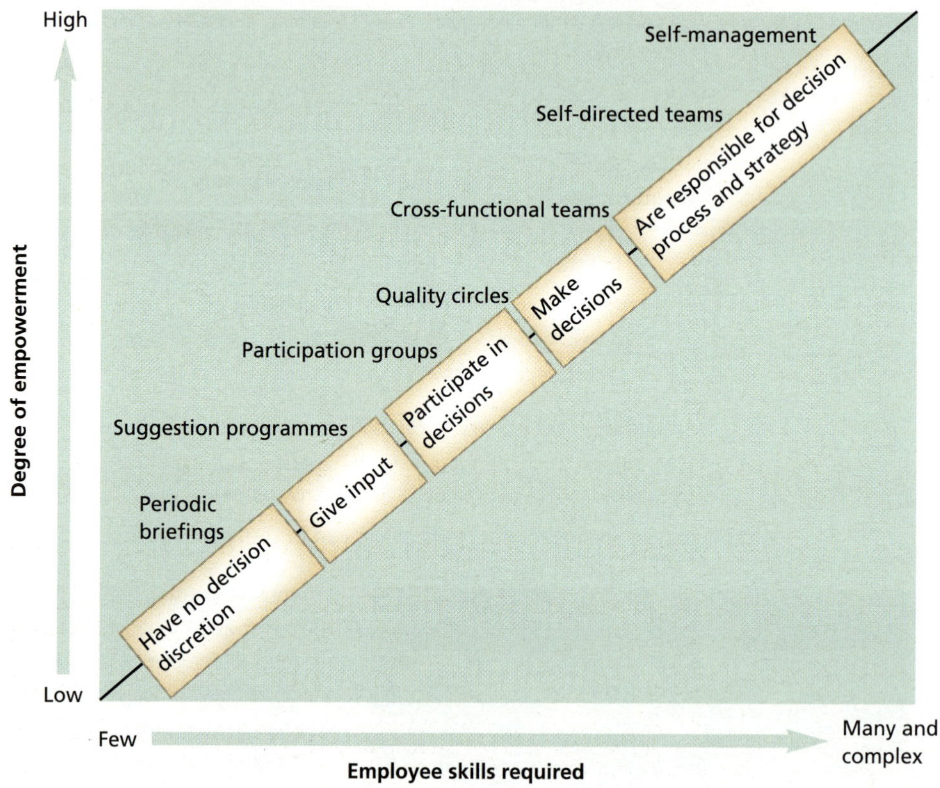

Figure 13.1: A continuum of empowerment

Source: from Daft. *Organizational Behavior*, 1E. © 2001 South-Western, a part of Cengage Learning, Inc. Reproduced by permission. www.cengage.com/permissions

Japanese teamworking use of scientific management principles of minimum manning, multi-tasking, multi-machine operation, pre-defined work operations, repetitive short-cycle work, powerful first line supervisors, and a conventional managerial hierarchy.

Total quality management a philosophy of management that is driven by customer needs and expectations, and which is committed to continuous improvement.

Just-in-time system a system of managing inventory (stock) in which items are delivered when they are needed in the production process, instead of being stored by the manufacturer.

Japanese teamworking, in contrast, operates at the other end of the autonomous teamwork continuum. It uses the scientific management principles of 'minimum manning, multi-tasking, multi-machine operation, pre-defined work operations, repetitive short cycle work, powerful first line supervisors, and a conventional managerial hierarchy' (Buchanan, 1994, p. 219). Japanese work teams tend to be advice teams mistaken for production teams. They meet and function as teams 'off line' (outside the production context) in contrast to autonomous work teams which function as teams 'on line' (inside the production context).

This is also called lean production (or *Toyotaism*) because, compared to other mass production plants, Toyota's achieve higher labour flexibility by using multiskilled employees who operate different machines; fewer workers not directly involved in product manufacture; a minimum of unfinished products (work in progress/process); and requires very little rectification of work already carried out. In a Toyota production system, work operations are highly standardized. After three days, new workers are able to perform any particular job specified on a standard operation sheet. Each highly standardized job is combined with other, similarly standardized ones, so as to extract the maximum amount of effort from employees with minimum labour input. **Japanese teamworking** also incorporates **total quality management** (TQM) and the **just-in-time system** (JIT).

With respect to shop-floor production teams, Marchington and Wilkinson (2005, pp. 78–9) suggest that there may be limits to the possibility of introducing autonomous forms of teamworking. They point to situations in which workers are unable to enlarge their jobs to embrace higher level skills or where there are legal or technical reasons that prevent workers from making certain types of decision. Moreover, the prospect of teamworking is limited where the rotation of a large range of low-level jobs means that one boring job is merely swapped for another boring job on a regular basis. In situations such as these, teamworking may only serve to make work more stressful and intrusive, and adds nothing to the skills or initiative that workers are able to deploy.

As previously mentioned, teamworking does not necessarily empower workers. How work is structured and the context in which teamworking takes place both make a great difference. Japanese teamworking is not the same as the teamworking that came to prominence in Scandinavian and American companies during the 1960s and 1970s (MacDuffie, 1988). Some types of teamworking, such as that used in lean production settings can actually disempower and deskill workers. Thus teamworking may differ little from Fordism with its emphasis on direct management control, repetitive tasks, and labour discipline (Danford, 1998). In contrast, other types of teamworking allow employees to perform a variety of tasks, to make decisions, to engage in problem-solving, and to have a sense of shared responsibility. The differences are summarized in Table 13.5.

Table 13.5: A comparison of Japanese and Swedish approaches to the organization of production and work

Variables	Japan: Toyota	Sweden: Volvo
production flow design	trimmed lines; JIT techniques	socio-technical design; job enrichment
relations between groups	high degree of sequential dependence; elimination of buffers	group control of boundaries; independence through buffers
supervision	high-density production; emphasis on the authority and role of the supervisor	low-density production; emphasis on planning and coordination by supervisors
administrative control	leading hands appointed by management; suggestions encouraged but decisions hierarchically determined to ensure standardization	leading hands appointed by the group; job rotation
workload and performance	intensive peer and supervisory pressure for maximum job performance and low absenteeism	regulated by union–management agreements
role of unions	management exclusively decides about work organization and wage systems; weak union influence	job content and wage system regulated by agreement; union involvement in production design and development

Source: from The art of building a car: the Swedish experience re-examined, *New Technology, Work and Employment*, 6(2), pp. 85–90 (Table on p. 89) (Hammarstrom, O. and Lansbury, R.D. 1991) © Blackwell Publishing Ltd 1991.

Kaizen Japanese term for 'continuous improvement' which refers to an element within total quality management in which employees are given responsibility, within limits, to suggest incremental changes to their work practices.

Within total quality management, continuous improvement (or **kaizen**) is achieved by using standardized operating procedures (Benders, 2005). Taiichi Ohno, the engineer responsible for the Toyota Production System, who devised detailed descriptions which specified how tasks were to be performed, wrote:

> The first thing I did was standardization of jobs. The shop floor of those days was controlled by foremen-craftsmen. Division managers and section managers could not control the shop floor, and they were always making excuses for production delays. So we first made manuals of standard operating procedures, and posted them above the work station so that supervisors could see if the workers were following the standard operations at a glance. Also, I told the shop floor operators to revise the standard operating procedures continuously. (Fujimoto, 1999, p. 64)

Ohno's account echoes the approach adopted by Frederick Taylor, who developed his scientific management approach to work design at the start of the twentieth century (see Chapter 14). Yet the last sentence, referring to continuous revisions, introduces the kaizen principle. Conti and Warner (1993, p. 39) noted this contradiction in labour process with 'employees working four hours a month in a very non-Taylorian manner to make their work for the rest of the month even more Taylor-like'. The participation of employees in teams, in this non-routine task of suggesting improvements, takes up a small percentage of their total working time, but has the effect of making the remaining bulk of their work time even more routine. Other key aspects of the Toyota production system are the minimization of inventory (stockholding) and the elimination of wasted effort.

Martin Parker and Jane Slaughter (1988) were critical of Japanese teamworking, describing it as part of an overall management package which they labelled 'management-by-stress'. In their view, what appeared to be participation was in fact a new form of exploitation. Innovations like the Japanese 'team concept' increased the pace and pressure of work, despite the rhetoric of worker empowerment. This innovation expands management's control by getting workers to 'participate' in the intensification of their own exploitation. The outcome is a low-skill and repetitive ('lean and mean') mass production system. Japanese teamworking contains the following elements (Garrahan and Stewart, 1992, p. 88):

- interchangeability, meaning the workers are required or induced (through pay-for-knowledge) to be capable of doing several jobs;
- drastic reduction of job classifications, giving management increased control to assign workers as it sees fit;
- detailed definition of every job step, increasing management control over the way jobs are done;
- workers' participation in increasing their own workload;
- more worker responsibility, without more authority, for jobs previously performed by supervisors;
- a management attempt to make workers aware of the interrelatedness of the plant's departments and the place of the individual in the whole;
- an ideological atmosphere that stresses competition between plants and workers' responsibility for winning work away from other plants.

Benders (2005) noted that some companies had allowed their employees to participate in the design of their work. He suggested several reasons for this. The daily immersion of workers in the detail of their work made these shop-floor/front-line employees the experts in what they were doing. Using the workers' own knowledge was likely to increase their willingness to use the system that they themselves had developed, and they were more likely to accept the working conditions that they had helped to create. Ruth Milkman (1997) and Karen Legge (2005) suggest reasons why there has not been more overt opposition from production-line workers, who appear to be colluding in their own subjugation:

1. *Careful selection of employees.* On greenfield sites, new staff are chosen on the basis of their behavioural traits (rather than relevant skills), that is, having the 'right attitude' towards teamworking and flexibility.

2. *Team leader's role*. The role of the trade (labour) union representative on the shop floor has been marginalized through developing the role of the team leader. This individual is responsible both for achieving production targets and for the social organization of the work team.
3. *Innate appeal*. The appealing aspects of this teamworking approach - mutual support, limited participation, collective endeavour, emphasis on consensus, coupled with the company's 'family orientation' and the potential to enhance job satisfaction and to save jobs - all make it appealing to new recruits.
4. *Contrast with past*. Workers who have experienced both the traditional, authoritarian management system and the new, participatory initiatives tend to prefer the latter, despite its shortcomings.

During 2009–2010, the reputation of Toyota Motor Corporation's legendary production system took a hammering. It had to initiate three vehicle recalls related to problems with floor mats, foot pedals, acceleration and anti-lock brake software. A total of more than 9.2 million Camry and Corolla models were involved. Additional recalls continued into 2011. Toyota had had several warnings about its deteriorating quality which it had ignored. Before the massive recalls in 2009, it had disbanded a high-level task force team set up four years earlier to deal with quality issues. It believed that quality had become part of the company's culture and no longer needed to be enforced. Robert Cole (2011) identified two causes of Toyota's quality problems. The first was that rapid growth (measured in percentage of market share) had taken priority over the company's traditional focus on quality. The second was product complexity - cars had become more sophisticated in how they were designed and manufactured. Cole argued that incoming, new senior management teams needed to recognize that systems and values which had historically underpinned company success could not be sustained without renewed commitment.

Ecological framework for analysing work team effectiveness

Eric Sundstrom, Kenneth De Meuse and David Futrell's (1990) ecological framework for analysing work teamwork effectiveness provides a perspective which looks at teams as embedded within their organization (see Figure 13.2). It holds that the effectiveness of any work team is facilitated or impeded by the team's own internal processes and by the features of the organization within which it operates. The framework emphasizes the interactions between a team and the different aspects of its environment. The framework is intentionally vague about causation and timing. The spiked circular symbols in the figure stress that team effectiveness is *dynamically interrelated* with organizational context, boundaries, and team development - being more of an ongoing process than a fixed end-state.

The framework also makes extensive use of the concept of boundary. Boundaries act to

- distinguish (differentiate) one team from another;
- present real or symbolic barriers to the access to, or transfer of, information, goods, or people;
- serve as points of external exchange with other teams, customers, peers, competitors, or other entities;
- define what constitutes effectiveness for the team within its particular organizational context.

The framework suggests that, at any time, a team's effectiveness is the outcome of team development and the organizational context, mediated by the team's boundaries. Each of these four sets of variables will be described in turn.

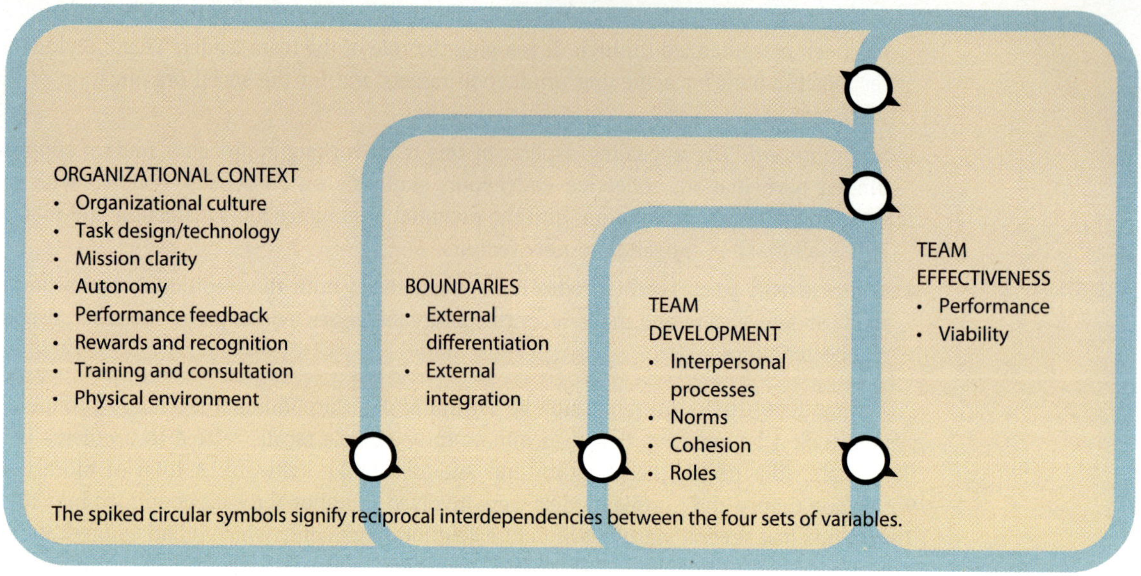

Figure 13.2: Ecological framework for analysing work team effectiveness

Source: from Sundstrom, E., De Meuse, K.P. and Futrell, D., Work teams: applications and effectiveness, *American Psychologist*, 45(2), pp. 120–33 (Figure on p. 122) 1990 American Psychological Society, reprinted with permission.

Organizational context

The first major variable in Sundstrom et al.'s framework is the organizational context of the work team. This refers to those features of an organization which are external to the work team, but which are relevant to the way it operates. The framework lists eight such features.

1. Organizational culture

Every team operates within an organization that has its own corporate culture set in a wider national culture. How do these values and beliefs impact on team effectiveness? Certain countries (e.g. Germany) have a multi-stakeholder culture, where teamworking is more likely to succeed than in a shareholder culture (such as the USA or Britain).

2. Task design and technology

Every team works to complete its given task in a particular way. The way that management defines the team task, and specifies the technologies it will use to achieve it, both social and material technologies (see Chapter 3), will affect the arrangement of individual team roles.

3. Mission clarity

If a team has a clearly defined mission or purpose within the organization, it can assist those teams which are closely related to or synchronized with its work. How clear is the team's mission and how clearly has it been communicated to others?

4. Autonomy

Externally, management will determine a team's autonomy. Internally, it will depend on the role of the leader and how they delegate their authority within the team. Every effective team has to coordinate and integrate the contributions of its individual members. Which type of team leadership best achieves this?

5. Performance feedback

Does the team receive accurate, timely feedback on its performance from dependable measurement systems?

6. Rewards and recognition

These can range from financial rewards to oral praise. Are rewards sufficiently connected to performance in a way that contributes to team effectiveness?

7. Training and consultation

Training and consultation in technical skills and interpersonal processes are seen as key elements in achieving team effectiveness. Cross-training in technical skills is very often a prerequisite for job rotation, which itself can be an aspect of autonomous teamworking.

8. Physical environment

The proximity of team members to one another affects both their ability to communicate and their level of team cohesion. Whether communicating across a table during a meeting, or between workstations on a factory shop floor, territories can reinforce team boundaries and encourage or inhibit exchanges. Physical environments are therefore central to group boundaries (Sundstrom and Altman, 1989).

Tenerife air disaster

PA PHOTOS/Press Association Images

At 5.01 p.m. on 27 March 1977 at Tenerife airport in the Canary Islands, two 747–100 jets began taxiing along the runways, their captains in communication with the airport's traffic controllers. Four minutes later, Pan Am 1736 and KLM 4805 collided on the tarmac when the Dutch aircraft took off without permission. The collision led to the death of 583 people, to this day the biggest air fatality in history. A number of contextual variables came together, interrupting the routines of the cockpit and air-traffic control crews, and generating stress. These included Dutch law (pilots' work hours), difficult manoeuvres, and unpredictable weather. In this stressful setting, KLM cockpit crew interaction broke down. More stress improves team performance but reduces individual performance by lowering task complexity. Hence the importance of cockpit crew members coalescing into a team with a distinctive identity, rather than falling apart and acting more like individuals.

Karl Weick (1990) stated that it was unclear whether the KLM crew experienced negative synergy, defined as a form of interaction between team members which caused a failure of coordination within the team so severe that nobody knew what they were supposed to be doing. It might have been that the three individuals in the cockpit acted independently and in parallel, falling back on their most familiar and well-rehearsed response routines, rather than behaving as a team, The interruption of their normal operating procedures induced a high level of arousal in the crew members which reduced their cognitive information-processing abilities, and led them to ignore important cues. As a result, both the flight cockpit crew and the air-traffic control team made the wrong responses which resulted in the deadly crash. This was an example of the context influencing individuals and teams, who responded in a way that changed the context as the events unfolded. A well-functioning, highly integrated cockpit crew might have responded to the increased stress with increased performance.

Work team boundaries

The second major variable in Sundstrom et al.'s framework is the set of work team boundaries. The boundary for a team is like the fence around a piece of property. It allows its members to know who is a member and who is not. It defines both physically and psychologically on whom group members can rely, and thereby indicates when it may be necessary for them to go beyond their own team for assistance and resources. For example, the boundary for an aircraft cockpit crew is physically defined by the design of the aircraft. A Boeing 727 has seats for three cockpit members and hence there is an expected boundary of three for the crew of that aeroplane.

Who's in and who's out?

In their study of 120 senior management teams, Ruth Wageman and her colleagues (2007) found that nearly every top team thought that it had set ambiguous boundaries. When asked to list their team members, fewer than 10 per cent agreed as to who was on their team – and these were senior executives! It appears that chief executives, fearful of appearing exclusionary or determined to include a member for political reasons, are responsible for the fuzziness of team boundaries.

While working to complete an assigned task (e.g. improving a procedure, designing a new product, or winning a match), a team has to meet the needs of the larger organization within which it is embedded (external integration). At the same time, it has to secure enough independence to allow it to get on with its own work (external differentiation). These two features define every team's boundary, and boundary management refers to the process by which teams manage their interactions with other parts of their organization. How successfully a team manages its boundaries will affect its performance.

External work team differentiation the degree to which a work team stands out from its organizational context, in terms of its membership, temporal scope, and territory.

External work team differentiation refers to the team as a whole in relation to the rest of the organization (team-organization focus). For example, a temporary team may be assembled by management and given resources to deal with a crisis. This team thus stands out, and hence *differs* from, other work units within the company by virtue of containing an identifiable collection of people (membership) working in a specific place (territory) over a set period of time (temporal scope) on a unique task.

Four features define the team's boundary, distinguishing it from other teams within the organization:

Team membership The identity of the individuals treated as members by both the team and the organization is crucial. Who decides the composition and size of a work team?

Team territory A work team has to have its 'own turf' to establish its identity and manage its external relations, especially in teams whose missions demand both external integration and differentiation.

Temporal scope The longer a work team exists and the more time its members spend cooperating, the greater will be its temporal scope and its differentiation as a distinct team.

Team task The task given to the team may be *additive* (accomplishment depends on the sum of all members' efforts); *conjunctive* (depends on the performance of the least talented member); or *disjunctive* (depends on the performance of the most talented member).

Internal work team differentiation the degree to which a team's members possess different skills and knowledge that contributes towards the achievement of the team's objective.

Internal work team differentiation refers to the degree to which a team's members possess different skills and knowledge that contribute towards the achievement of the team's objective. A team may have high differentiation with its members having special, perhaps unique skills, as with the cockpit crew in an aircraft; or it may have low differentiation, when the knowledge and contributions of members tend to be similar, as in a quality circle team.

Check before you board

Nearly all commercial airlines now rotate members of their flight crews. Senior pilots on large planes often fly with a different co-pilot on every trip during a month. Airlines do not stick to the same crews because financially, the airline gets most from its capital equipment and labour by treating each aeroplane and each pilot and every other crew member as an individual unit, and then uses an algorithm to maximize their utilization. In consequence, pilots dash through the airports just like passengers, since they have to fly two or three different aircraft, each with a different crew, in a single day. If you look at the research, this is not particularly encouraging. The US National Transportation Safety Board found that 73 per cent of accident incidents occurred on a crew's first day of flying together, before individuals had a chance to learn, through experience, how best to operate as a team. A NASA study found that fatigued crews who had a history of working together made about half as many errors as crews composed of rested pilots who had not flown together before. Asked how long it would take for two crew members to work together well on a flight, an airlines operations staff member estimated 5 to 6 years. Clearly this is not good news from a passenger point of view. Next time you board a plane, ask if this crew has ever flown together before (Coutu, 2009).

Differentiation within the peloton

Getty Images

The Tour de France cycle race was first run in 1903 and now involves about 150 top cyclists. The racers cover over 2,700 miles during their 23-day journey, and the winner receives a €400,000 prize. The competitors ride together in the *peloton* – the picturesque mob of competing teams that fly, like birds in formation, across the French countryside every summer. Despite the focus on individual riders, the Tour is a sport structured around the teams sponsored by different organizations. In the past, there has been Lance Armstrong's Team Discovery and Jan Ulrich's T-Mobile team. There are twenty different teams in the race. During each 125-mile, 5-hour stage, team members fight to put their leader in a position to win. What appears to be a random mass of bicycles is really an orderly, complex web of shifting alliances, crossed with brutal competition, designed to keep or acquire the market's most valuable currency – energy. A cycling team consists of nine riders, each of whom is a specialist. The *rouleurs* are fast riders who create draughts for their team's leader over flat terrain. Riding close behind a rouleur can reduce drag by 40 per cent. *Grimpeurs* are hill specialists who create a slipstream (a field of low wind resistance) for their leader as he goes up mountains; and *domestiques* are riders who carry supplies. Towards the end of the race, team members will bunch together ahead of their sprinter, shielding him from the wind for as long as possible, while leaving a space to let him break out near the finish line (based on Hochman, 2006).

External work team integration the degree to which a work team is linked with the larger organization of which it is a part.

External work team integration refers to the degree to which a work team is linked with the larger organization of which it is a part. It is measured in terms of how its goals and activities are coordinated and synchronized with those of other managers, peers, customers, and suppliers inside and outside the company. The degree to which these need to be coordinated and synchronized with those of other teams will depend on the type of team and its task.

"Every detail of the proposal must be perfect! Get Davidson to write the vowels, Mulroy to write the consonants, Schwartz to write the punctuation and Lewis to put the spaces between the words."

Source: © 2003 by Randy Glasbergen, www.glasbergen.com

Team development

The third major variable in Sundstrom et al.'s framework concerns the internal development of the team. Four factors are relevant here – interpersonal processes, roles, norms, and cohesion.

1. *Interpersonal processes*

A group of individuals passes through a series of stages before achieving effective performance at the performing stage. Tuckman and Jensen's (1977) model describes the characteristics of each preceding stage – forming, storming, and norming.

2. *Roles*

Roles in general are a defining feature of a team, and the role of a leader is much studied. Are the required member roles being performed given the group's tasks, and are the task and interpersonal aspects of the leadership role being fulfilled?

3. *Norms*

Are the norms and rules of behaviour which are agreed on by the team members supportive or in conflict with effective performance? Can organizational culture be used to modify team norms?

4. *Cohesion*

Team cohesion can engender mutual cooperation, generosity, and helping behaviour, motivating team members to contribute fully. However, it can also stifle creative thinking as individuals seek to 'fit in' and not 'rock the boat'. Small group size, similar attitudes, and physical proximity of work spaces have all been found to encourage cohesion. Does the level of cohesion aid or impede the team's effectiveness?

Team performance a measure of how well a team achieves its task, and meets the needs and expectations of management, customers, and shareholders.

Team effectiveness

Team effectiveness is the dependent variable in the Sundstrom et al. framework, and is measured using two criteria – performance and viability. **Team performance** is externally focused and concerns meeting the needs and expectations of outsiders such as customers, company colleagues, or fans. It is assessed using measures such as quantity, quality, and

Team viability a measure of how well a team meets the needs and expectations of its members.

time. Meanwhile, **team viability** is the social dimension, which is internally focused and concerns the enhancement of the team's capability to perform effectively in the future. Team viability indicators include its degree of cohesion, shared purpose, and the level of team member commitment. The two are closely related since there is a possibility that a team may get a job done but self-destruct in the process.

Teams in the NHS

West et al. (2011) investigated staff management and health service quality within the British National Health Service (NHS) – the third largest organization (by employee numbers) in the world. A survey of staff in 390 hospital trusts, conducted between 2006 and 2009, which used data from 155,000 respondents, found that positive staff engagement, achieved by good management of NHS staff, led to higher-quality care, more satisfied patients, lower patient mortality and significant financial savings. One important predictor of patient mortality rates in hospital trusts was the percentage of staff working in well-structured teams that had clear objectives, met regularly to review performance and how to improve it, and had members who worked closely and effectively together. An engaged and supportive culture for staff reduced absenteeism and staff turnover. NHS staff are absent, on average, 10.7 days a year, costing £1.75 billion.

RECAP

1. *Understand why 'team' is a contested concept in the organizational literature.*
   - Teamworking is being increasingly adopted as a favoured form of work organization in different companies and industries around the world.
   - The different purposes for which, and ways in which, managers have introduced this innovation have meant that the term 'team' is used to describe a wide range of radically different working arrangements.
2. *List the nine dimensions of team autonomy.*
   - Gulowsen's nine dimensions of team autonomy are selection of the team leader; acceptance of a new member into the team; distribution of work; time flexibility; acceptance of additional work; representation outside the team; production methods (choice of); production goals (output determination); and production goals (quality determination).
3. *Differentiate between four major types of teams and give an example of each.*
   - Teams in organizations can be classified as advice teams (e.g. quality circles; action teams (e.g. surgery teams); project teams (e.g. cross-functional teams) or production teams (e.g. autonomous work teams).
4. *Discuss the types of obstacles to effectiveness experienced by each type of team.*
   - Advice teams frequently lack authority to implement their recommendations. Action teams can fail to integrate their members' contributions sufficiently closely. Project team members can suffer 'divided loyalties' between their team and their home department. Production teams may lack autonomy for job satisfaction.
5. *Contrast Western with Japanese concepts of teamworking.*
   - The Western concept is based upon principles of empowerment and on-line teamworking, while the Japanese concept is based upon management principles of individual working on-line, and teams advising off-line.
6. *List the four main variables in the ecological framework for analysing work team effectiveness.*
   - Team development, work team boundaries, and organizational context affect team effectiveness.
7. *Understand the continuing importance of teamworking.*
   - Japanese forms of teamworking (Toyotaism) have influenced the production processes used in both manufacturing and service industries all around the world.
   - As a concept, teamworking has an appeal in a management philosophy that stresses egalitarianism, non-hierarchy, and inclusiveness within organizations.

Revision

1. Self-managing or autonomous work teams are heavily promoted in the literature. What are the costs and benefits of these to (a) the management that establishes them and (b) the individuals who are members of such teams?
2. What impact can technology have on the behaviour and performance of teams. Discuss positive and negative effects, illustrating your answer with examples.
3. 'Autonomous team is a relative term'. Discuss the concept of team autonomy explaining why similarly labelled teams may, in practice, operate very differently, and consider why management might have difficulty in increasing the autonomy that it gives to a team.
4. Highlight briefly the main differences between West European and Japanese-style teamworking. Then, using references to the literature, consider the positive and negative aspects of both systems for EITHER shop-floor workers OR management.

Research assignment

Using your library and the internet, locate any relevant research and management literature on effective teamworking and devise a list of best practice 'do's' and 'don'ts', and use it to develop a list of questions. Select two organizations and, in each of them, interview a team member, a team leader, or a manager responsible for a team. Begin by determining the team's purpose, method of working, and performance, and the challenges that it faces. Write a brief report comparing these two teams, and assessing them against your best practice list items from the research literature.

Springboard

Alan Jenkins (1994) 'Teams: from "ideology" to analysis', *Organization Studies*, 15(6), pp. 849–60. This is an article defending management's interest in teams.

Journal of Occupational and Organizational Psychology (2004), 77(4). There continues to be a strong belief in the superiority of teams over individuals among managers, employees, and the general public. The first five articles in this issue all discuss the phenomenon of the 'romance of teams'.

Andreas Richter, Jeremy Dawson and Michael West (2011) 'The effectiveness of teams in organizations: a meta-analysis', *The International Journal of Human Resource Management*, 22(13), pp. 2749–2769. Reviews and summarizes past research studies into whether teamworking in organizations is related to organizational effectiveness.

Michael West (2012) *Effective Teamwork: Practical Lessons from Organizational Research* (3rd edn), Blackwell, Oxford. Reviews the academic research literature on groups and teams to highlight what affects their performance.

OB in films

The Dish (2000, director Rob Sitch), DVD track 8: 0:35:55 to 0:53:07 (18 minutes sequenced). It is July 1969, and Apollo 11 is heading towards the moon. On earth, the Parkes Radio Telescope in New South Wales, Australia, the largest in the southern hemisphere, has been designated by NASA as the primary receiving station for the moonwalk, which it will broadcast to the world. Then, due to a power cut, it 'loses' Apollo 11! Parkes's director, Cliff Buxton (played by Sam Neill), and his team of scientists – Mitch (Kevin Harrington), Glenn (Tom Long), and Al (Patrick Warburton) – all have to work hard (and quickly) to solve the problem. The clip begins with the lights going out during the dance, and ends with Al saying 'Just enough time to check the generator.'

Identify examples of each of the elements of Sundstrom et al.'s ecological framework for analysing work team effectiveness as the team members deal with the crisis.

Sundstrom framework element	Example
Organizational context	
1. Organizational culture	
2. Task design/technology	
3. Mission clarity	
4. Autonomy	
5. Performance feedback	
6. Rewards and recognition	
7. Physical environment	
8. Training and consultation	
Work team boundaries	
9. External differentiation	
10. External integration	
Team development	
11. Interpersonal processes	
12. Norms	
13. Cohesion	
14. Roles	

OB on the web

Search YouTube for 'Ferris State Formula Hybrid Team'. This video describes a university student project. Which group and team dynamics concepts, introduced in this or in previous chapters on groups and teams, can you see being demonstrated here? List each one, and illustrate its application by quoting the speaker's comments from the video.

CHAPTER EXERCISES

1. Would you make a good team player?

Objectives

1. Identify behaviours to improve teamworking.
2. Practise using Sundstom et al.'s model as an explanatory framework.

Briefing

1. Individually
   (a) Read through each of the following three teamworking scenarios.
   (b) Decide which of the four options you prefer, and note down the reasons for your choice.
2. Form groups and nominate a spokesperson.
   (a) Beginning with the first scenario, each member in turn indicates which option is preferred and why.
   (b) When all group members have indicated their preferences, discuss the various options, as well as their pros and cons, and decide upon a group-agreed option from the four offered.
   (c) Explain what is wrong with the other three.
   (d) Suggest an alternative option of your own, justifying whether it is better than the others.
   (e) Repeat the process for the second and third scenarios.
3. The class re-forms. The spokespersons for each group report back.

Scenario A

Suppose that you find yourself in an argument with several co-workers about who should do a very disagreeable but routine task. Which of the following would be the most effective way to resolve this situation?

(a) Have your supervisor decide because this would avoid any personal bias.
(b) Arrange for a rotating schedule so everyone shares the chores.
(c) Let the workers who show up earliest choose on a first-come, first-served basis.
(d) Randomly assign the task.

Scenario B

Your team wants to improve the quality and flow of conversations between its members. In your view, your team should:

(a) Use comments that build upon and connect to what others have already said.
(b) Set up a specific order for everyone to speak and then follow it.
(c) Let team members with more say determine the direction and topic of conversation.
(d) Do all of the above.

Scenario C

Suppose you are presented with the following types of goals. You are asked to pick one for your team to work on. Which one would you choose?

(a) An easy goal to ensure the team reaches it, thus creating a feeling of success.
(b) A goal of average difficulty so the team will be somewhat challenged, but successful without too much effort.
(c) A difficult and challenging goal that will stretch the team to perform at a high level, but attainable so that effort will not be seen as futile.
(d) A very difficult or even impossible goal so that even if the team falls short, it will at least have a high target to aim for.

Source: adapted from Stevens, M.J. and Campion, M.A., Journal of Management, Vol. 20, No. 2, pp. 503–530. The knowledge, skill and ability requirements for teamwork: Implications for human resource management, Copyright © 1994, Southern Management Association. Reprinted by permission of SAGE Publications.

2. Land Rock Alliance Insurance

Objective To assess the suitability of tasks for teamworking.

Briefing

1. Read the case study below.
2. Working individually or in teams, provide a written recommendation for or against introducing teamworking at the Edinburgh office.
3. Group spokespersons should be ready to report their group's decision and the reasoning behind it.

Background Since the 1940s, the use of asbestos in building materials and other products has led to many claims for damages as a result of personal injury or wrongful death. The procedure for those making claims is complicated and time-consuming. Insurance companies employ groups of employees trained to process the claims from each particular industry. The employees are given information on the history, use, and current medical research results on the product. The processing of each individual claim application form is tedious but very important: any mistakes may affect the total amount paid to the claimant. Land Rock Alliance Insurance has successfully bid for the contract to process the claims for over 213,000 asbestosis-related chest impaired cases (ACD) and vibration white finger (VWF) victims, their partners or descendants.

The company Land Rock Alliance Insurance's main office is based in Sheffield, England. The company has decided to open a branch office in Edinburgh to manage the new contract. It will be dedicated to processing the asbestosis and VWF claims. The plan is to hire 60 new employees including supervisors and line managers. Senior managers at head office, however, disagree on how the work should be organized at the new office.

Planning meeting At the meeting to review how the work will be organized at the Edinburgh office, Eleanor Brennan, the HR director, suggested it would be more effective and efficient to create four teams of around 15 employees, with each team processing the claims according to geographical area: Scotland, Wales, northern England and southern England. She explained that each application form would be processed by team members, to enable each member to complete the whole processing task and to contribute to the recommendation of the final settlement. Presenting some of the advantages of teamworking, Eleanor commented, 'The synergy generated by teamworking and communication will enhance efficiency and motivate employees to actively participate in reaching a decision in optimum time.' She argued that there was a direct link between job enrichment and high performance.

However, the director of facilities, Thomas Campion, strongly disagreed. He informed the assembled management team that in his opinion, 'self-regulated teams were b*** s***!' Besides, work teams required a much longer training period for employees. Moreover, it was his belief that increased communication impeded decision-making rather than enhanced it. Campion, continuing to dominate the meeting, outlined an alternative work arrangement for the processing of claimants' forms. The work, he said, was to be divided into three major steps:

Step 1: Scrutinize and verify biographical details, date of birth, gender.

Step 2: Scrutinize and verify employment details, start/end/job description.

Step 3: Scrutinize and verify medical history including lifestyle (such as smoker or non-smoker, or whether there was evidence of exposure to second-hand smoke).

Of the 60 new employees, 20 would be trained to complete Step 1, 20 to complete Step 2, and 20 to complete Step 3. Each major step in the claim process would also have a supervisor, a technical advisor, and a section manager. Organizing the work this way, Campion insisted, would optimize training time, and enable the easy replacement of any employee resigning from the company. Individual employees would be assigned a target to achieve each month, which would determine an annual bonus payment. Every six months, their section manager would appraise each employee based on how quickly he or she successfully processed the application forms.

Source: from John Bratton, Peter Sawchuk, Carolyn Forshaw, Militza Callinan and Martin Corbett, Work and Organizational Behaviour, *published 2007 Palgrave Macmillan reproduced with permission of Palgrave Macmillan.*

Employability assessment

With regard to your future employment prospects:

1. Identify up to three issues from this chapter that you found significant.
2. Relate these to the competencies in the employability matrix.
3. Decide what actions you need to take to maintain and/or develop those competencies under each of the four headings of the employability matrix.

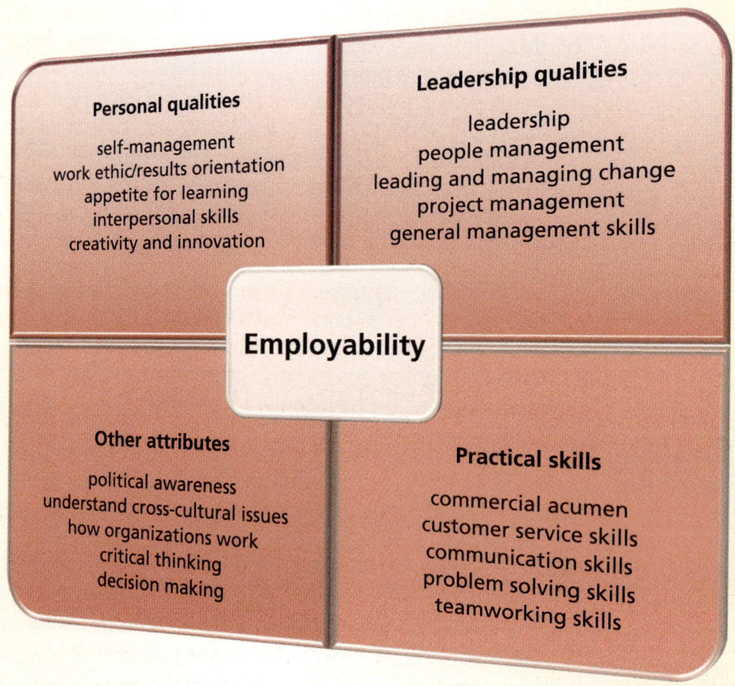

References

Allen, N.J. and Hecht, T. (2004) 'The romance of teams: towards an understanding of its psychological underpinnings and implications', *Journal of Occupational and Organizational Psychology*, 77(4), pp. 439–61.

Ancona, D., Bresman, H. and Caldwell, D. (2009) 'The X-factor: six steps to leading high-performing X-teams', *Organizational Dynamics*, 38(3), pp. 217–24.

Annett, J. and Stanton, N.A. (2000) 'Team work: a problem for ergonomics?', *Ergonomics*, 43(8), pp. 1045–51.

Benders, J. (2005) 'Team working: a tale of partial participation', in B. Harley, J. Hyman and P. Thompson (eds), *Participation and Democracy at Work: Essays in Honour of Harvie Ramsey*, London: Palgrave Macmillan, pp. 55–74.

Benders, J. and Van Hootegem, G. (1999a) 'How the Japanese got teams', in S. Procter and F. Mueller (eds), *Teamworking*, Basingstoke: Macmillan Business, pp. 43–59.

Benders, J. and Van Hootegem, G. (1999b) 'Teams and their context: moving the team discussion beyond existing dichotomies', *Journal of Management Studies*, 36(5), pp. 609–28.

Bratton, J., Callinan, M., Forshaw, C. and Sawchuk, P. (2007) *Work and Organizational Behaviour*, Basingstoke: Palgrave Macmillan.

Buchanan, D.A. (1994) 'Cellular manufacture and the role of teams', in J. Storey (ed.), *New Wave Manufacturing Strategies: Organizational and Human Resource Manage-*

ment Dimensions, London: Paul Chapman Publishing, pp. 204–25.

Chansler, P.A., Swamidass, P.M. and Cammann, C. (2003) 'Self-managing work teams: an empirical study of group cohesiveness in "natural work groups" at a Harley-Davidson Motor Company Plant', *Small Group Research*, 34(1), pp. 101–21.

Clegg, S.R., Kornberger, M. and Pitsis, T. (2011) *Managing and Organizations* (3rd edn), London: Sage Publications.

Cole, R.E. (2011) 'What really happened to Toyota?', *Sloan Management Review*, 52(4), pp. 29–35

Comer, D.R. and Holbrook, R.L. (2012) 'Setting behind the scenes of Fleetwood Mac's Rumours: using a documentary on making a music album to learn about task groups', *Journal of Management*, 36(4), pp. 544–67

Conti, R.E. and Warner, M. (1993) 'Taylorism, new technology and just-in-time systems in Japanese manufacturing', *New Technology, Work and Employment*, 8(1), pp. 31–42.

Cordery, J., Soo, C., Kirkman, B., Rosen, B. and Mathieu, J. (2009) 'Leading parallel global virtual teams: lessons from Alcoa', *Organizational Dynamics*, 38(3), pp. 204–16.

Coutu, D. (2009) 'Why teams don't work', *Harvard Business Review*, 87(5), pp. 99–105.

Daft, R.L. and Noe, R.A. (2001) *Organizational Behaviour*, San Diego, CA: Harcourt Inc.

Danford, A. (1998) 'Teamworking and labour relations in the autocomponents industry', *Work, Employment and Society*, 12(3), pp. 409–31.

Davis, L.E. and Wacker, G.J. (1987) 'Job design', in Salvendy, G. (ed.), *Handbook of Human Factors*, New York: Wiley.

Delarue, A., Van Hootegem, G., Procter, S. and Burridge, M. (2008) 'Teamworking and organizational performance: a review of survey-based research', *The International Journal of Management Reviews*, 10(2), pp. 127–48.

Druskat, V.U. and Wheeler, J.V. (2004) 'How to lead a self-managing team', *MIT Sloan Management Review*, 45(4), pp. 65–71.

Edmondson, A., Bohmer, R. and Pisano, G. (2001) 'Speeding up team learning', *Harvard Business Review*, 79(9), pp. 125–32.

Edwards, D. (2011) *I'm Feeling Lucky: The Confessions of Google Employee Number 59*, London: Allen Lane.

European Foundation for the Improvement of Living and Working Conditions (2005) 'Volvo Cars Ghent: a self-managing team model', Box 1: Overview, *Workplace Innovation: Four Case Examples*, EMCC Company Network, http://www.eurofound.europa.eu/emcc/publications/2005/ef055enC.pdf.

Fujimoto, T. (1999) *The Evolution of the Toyota Production System*, New York: Oxford University Press.

Garrahan, P. and Stewart, P. (1992) *The Nissan Enigma: Flexibility at Work in a Local Economy*, London: Mansell Publishing.

Ghosn, C. (2002) 'Saving the business without losing the company'. *Harvard Business Review*, 80(1), pp. 37–45.

Ginnett, R.C. (1993) 'Crews as groups: their formation and leadership', In E.L. Wiener, B.G. Kanki and R.L. Helmreich (eds), *Cockpit Resource Management*, San Diego, CA: Academic Press, pp. 71–98.

Glassop, L.I. (2002) 'The organizational benefits of teams', *Human Relations*, 55(2), pp. 225–49.

Gordon, J. (1992) 'Work teams – how far have they come?', *Training*, 29(10), pp. 59–65.

Gratton, L. (2007) *Hot Spots: Why Some Teams, Workplaces, and Organizations Buzz with Energy – and Others Don't*, San Francisco, CA: Berrett-Koehler.

Gratton, L. and Erickson, T.J. (2007) 'Ways to build collaborative teams', *Harvard Business Review*, 85(11), pp. 101–9.

Grey, C. (2009) *A Very Short, Fairly Interesting and Reasonably Cheap Book about Studying Organizations* (2nd edn), London: Sage.

Gulowsen, J. (1979) 'A measure of work-group autonomy', In L.E. Davis and J.C. Taylor (eds), *Design of Jobs* (2nd edn), Santa Monica: Goodyear, pp. 206–18.

Hammarstrom, O. and Lansbury, R.D. (1991) 'The art of building a car: the Swedish experience re-examined', *New Technology, Work and Employment*, 6(2), pp. 85–90.

Hare, A.P. (1992) *Groups, Teams and Social Interactions*, New York: Praeger.

Hayes, N. (1997) *Successful Team Management*, London: International Thompson Business Press.

Hill, G.W. (1991) 'Why quality circles failed but total quality management might succeed', *British Journal of Industrial Relations*, 29(4), pp. 517–39.

Hindle, T. (2006) 'The new organization: a survey of the company', *The Economist*, 21 January, pp. 3–5.

Hochman, P. (2006) 'Pack mentality', *Fortune*, 1 June.

Hutchins, E. (1990) 'The technology of team navigation', in J. Galegher, R.E. Kraut and C. Egido (eds), *Intellectual Teamwork: Social and Technological Foundations of Co-operative Work*, Hillsdale, NJ: Lawrence Erlbaum Associates, pp. 191–220.

Jenkins, A. (1994) 'Teams: from "ideology" to analysis', *Organization Studies*, 15(6), pp. 849–60.

Katzenbach, J.R. and Smith, D.K. (1993) *The Wisdom of Teams: Creating the High Performance Organization*, Boston, MA: Harvard Business School Press.

Kay, J. (2006) 'Football's example can help companies score', *Financial Times*, 10 July.

Kirkman, B.L., Gibson, C.B. and Shapiro, B.L. (2001) 'Exporting teams: enhancing the implementation and effectiveness of work teams in global affiliates', *Organizational Dynamics*, 30(1), pp. 12–29.

Knight, C. (2005) *Performance Without Compromise*, Cambridge, MA: Harvard Business School Press.

Langfried, C.W. (2000) 'Work group design and autonomy', *Small Group Research*, 31(1), pp. 54–70.

Legge, K. (2005) *Human Resource Management: Rhetorics and Realities (Anniversary Edition)*, Houndmills, Basingstoke: Macmillan Business.

Leshner, M. and Brown, A. (1993) 'Increasing efficiency through cross-training', *Bet's Review*, 95(8), pp. 39–40.

Levine, S. and Levine, R. (1996) 'Why they're not smiling: stress and discontent in the orchestra workplace', *Harmony*, 2(April), pp. 15–25.

Lipman-Blumen, J. and Leavitt, H.J. (2009) 'Beyond typical teams: hot groups and connective leaders', *Organizational Dynamics*, 38(3), pp. 225–33.

MacDuffie, J.P. (1988) 'The Japanese auto transplants: challenges to conventional wisdom', *ILR Report*, 26(1), pp. 12–18.

Marchington, M. (1992) *Managing the Team: A Guide to Successful Employee Involvement*, Oxford: Blackwell.

Marchington, M. and Wilkinson, A. (2005) *Human Resource Management at Work* (3rd edn), London: Chartered Institute of Personnel and Development.

Milkman, R. (1997) *Farewell to the Factory: Autoworkers in the Late Twentieth Century*, Berkeley, CA: University of California Press.

Naquin, C.E. and Tynan, R.O. (2003) 'The team halo effect: why teams are not blamed for their failures', *Journal of Applied Psychology*, 88(2), pp. 332–40.

National Aeronautics and Space Administration (2011) 'NASA's response to mine disaster remembered', 14 October. http://www.nasa.gov/news/chile_assistance.html, accessed 24 January 2012.

Nijholt, J.J. and Benders, J. (2010) 'Measuring the prevalence of self-managing teams: taking account of defining characteristics', *Work, Employment and Society*, 24(2), pp. 375–85.

Park, R. (2012) 'Self-managing teams and employee attitudes: the moderating role of capital intensity', *The International Journal of Human Resource Management*, 23(4), pp. 714–30.

Parker, M. and Slaughter, J. (1988) *Choosing Sides: Unions and the Team Concept*, Boston, MA: South End Press.

Paulus, P.B. and van der Zee, K. (2004) 'Should there be romance between teams and groups?', *Journal of Occupational and Organizational Psychology*, 77(4), pp. 474–80.

Procter, S. and Burridge, M. (2008) 'Teamworking and performance: the extent and intensity of teamworking in the 1998 UK Workplace Employee Relations Survey (WERS98)', *The International Journal of Human Resource Management*, 19(1), pp. 153–68.

Procter, S. and Currie, G. (2004) 'Target-based teamworking: groups, work and interdependence in the UK civil service'. *Human Relations*, 57(2), pp. 1547–1572.

Ramsey, H., Scholaris, D. and Harley, B. (2000) 'Employees and high performance work systems', *British Journal of Industrial Relations*, 38(4), pp. 501–31.

Sinclair, A. (1992) 'The tyranny of team ideology', *Organization Studies*, 13(4), pp. 611–26.

Souitaris, V. and Maestro, B.M.M. (2011) 'The case for multitasking', *Harvard Business Review*, 89(10), p. 32.

Steijn, B. (2001) 'Work systems, quality of working life and attitudes of workers: an empirical study towards the effects of team and non-teamwork', *New Technology, Work and Employment*, 16(3), pp. 191–203.

Sundstrom, E. and Altman, I. (1989) 'Physical environments and work group effectiveness', in L.L. Cummings and B. Staw (eds), *Research in Organizational Behaviour, Volume 11*, Greenwich, CT: JAI Press, pp. 175–209.

Sundstrom, E., De Meuse, K.P. and Futrell, D. (1990) 'Work teams: applications and effectiveness', *American Psychologist*, 45(2), pp. 120–33.

The Economist (2006) 'Headless', 5 October, p. 76.

Townsend, K. (2005) 'Electronic surveillance and cohesive teams: room for resistance in an Australian call centre?', *New Technology, Work and Employment*, 20(1), pp. 47–59.

Training (1996) 'What self-managing teams manage', 1996 Industry report, 33(10).

Trist, E.L. and Bamforth, K.W. (1951) 'Some social and psychological consequences of the longwall method of coal-getting', *Human Relations*, 4(1), pp. 3–38.

Tuckman, B.W. and Jensen, M.A.C. (1977) 'Stages of small group development revisited', *Group and Organizational Studies*, 2(4), pp. 419–27.

Van den Broek, D., Callaghan, G. and Thompson, P. (2002) 'Teams without teamwork: explaining the call centre paradox', paper presented at the Sixth International Workshop on Teambuilding, Malmo University, Sweden.

Wageman, R., Nunes, D.A., Burruss, J.A. and Hackman, J.R. (2007) *Senior Leadership Teams*, Boston, MA: Harvard Business School Press.

Weick, K.E. (1990) 'The vulnerable system: an analysis of the Tenerife air disaster', *Journal of Management*, 16(3), pp. 571–93.

Weiner, E.L., Kanki, B.G. and Helmreich, R.L. (eds) (1993) *Cockpit Resource Management*, New York: Academic Press.

West, M., Dawson, J., Admasachew, L. and Topakas, A. (2011) *NHS Staff Management and Health Service Quality*, London: Department of Health.

Winner, D. (2001) *Brilliant Orange: The Neurotic Genius of Dutch Football*, London: Bloomsbury Press.

Zander, L., Mockaitis, A.I. and Butler, C.L. (2012) 'Leading global teams', *Journal of World Business*, 47(2), pp. 592–603.

Part 4 **Organization structures**

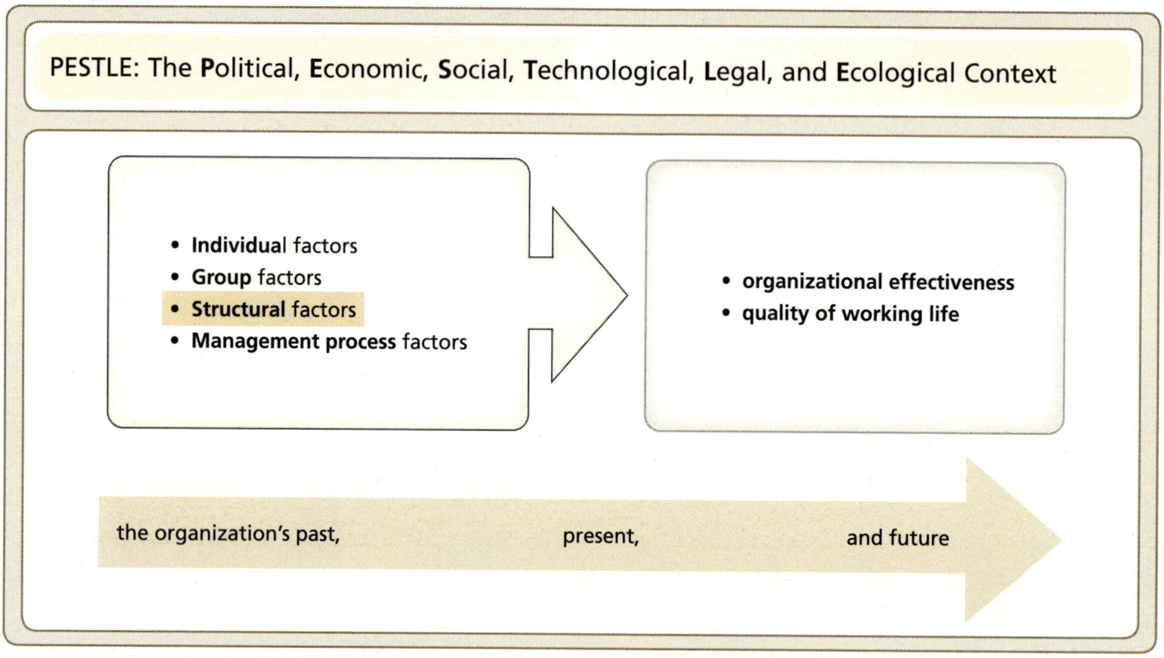

A field map of the organizational behaviour terrain

Introduction

Part 4, on organization structures, explores four related topics:

- *The roots of contemporary work design*, in Chapter 14
- *Elements of structure*, in Chapter 15
- *Early organization design*, in Chapter 16
- *Organizational architecture*, in Chapter 17.

These topics relate to how the way in which work is defined and designed affects employee behaviour. Chapter 14 on the roots of contemporary work design provides a backdrop to the earlier Chapter 3 on technology. It links technology to structure by highlighting how choices about the former have an impact on design decisions concerning the latter. Chapter 15 on elements of structure provides an introduction to the key concepts, theories, models, and authors in this field. This 'vocabulary' is then used to understand early organization design, particularly in the work of Max Weber, Henri Fayol, Tom Burns and George Stalker, and Henry Mintzberg. The final chapter in Part 4 explains how contemporary thinking about structures in the field of organizational behaviour has merged with debates about corporate strategy and strategic management. It also brings the consideration of structural forms up to date by exploring hollow, modular, virtual, collaborative, and network structures. The structural perspective offers a separate but related level of analysis after individuals and groups.

Invitation to see

James King-Holmes/Northern Foods/Science Photo Library

Northern Foods pizza factory

1. **Decoding**: Look at this image closely. Note in as much detail as possible what messages you feel that it is trying to convey. Does it tell a story, present a point of view, support an argument, perpetuate a myth, reinforce a stereotype, challenge a stereotype?
2. **Challenging**: To what extent do you agree with the messages, stories, points of view, arguments, myths, or stereotypes in this image? Is this image open to challenge, to criticism, or to interpretation and decoding in other ways, revealing other messages?
3. **Sharing**: Compare with colleagues your interpretation of this image. Explore explanations for differences in your respective decodings.

You're the team leader: what would you do?

You are the research team leader in this situation. Focus on the objective. Using your knowledge of the concepts, theories, authors, models, and frameworks acquired so far from course lectures and reading, as well as your personal experience, evaluate the advantages and limitations of each of the four options, which are the only options available to you at this time. Decide which one you would choose, and why.

Your problem

Lynette joined your research team six months ago, making five members, including yourself. Her knowledge of the topic (organizational change) is limited, but she has superb references and an excellent theoretical and practical grounding in social research. There is no problem in transferring her expertise to this project. She starts work with enthusiasm. You and colleagues brief her on the project aims, and provide background reading. Two months into her appointment, she has produced none of the outputs that you have been expecting – review of wider literature, details of research methods, appropriate first contacts, and so on. In an informal meeting, it emerges that her understanding of the research aims and scope are still unclear, so you go over these issues again. You are reassured by this discussion. Four months into the project, she has still to produce any useful output. In another informal meeting, she indicates that the support she expected from colleagues is lacking. You promise to speak to the team, and remind her of the research aims and timescale. Six months into the project, Lynette has still not produced any material that will help to make progress towards the research aims. Before meeting with her again, a reliable senior colleague tells you in confidence that he has been told by a trustworthy friend that Lynette has been setting up a management development and consulting business, specializing in organization development and change; you check this for yourself, and you have now seen her website. Academic research projects have deadlines, and you are not going to meet this one unless you can solve this problem. Failure to meet the project aims on time jeopardizes future research funding, and threatens the jobs of other members of the research team.

Your objective

Your overarching objective is to meet the research project deadline, now eighteen months away, while dealing with Lynette's failure to contribute to the work.

Your options

1. Hold another meeting with Lynette, to establish why her contribution has been so limited, to clarify misunderstandings, and to agree new performance objectives.
2. Confront Lynette with the knowledge that she has not been contributing to this project because she has been setting up her own business. If she does not have a convincing response to this allegation, terminate her employment immediately.
3. The lack of subject knowledge is more of a problem than you first thought. Pair Lynette with an experienced researcher, who will mentor her closely for the next six months, with regard to both the research topic and the proposed methods.
4. The UK Standing Conference on Organizational Change at University of Loamshire runs a highly-regarded research methods training programme which runs for four days in May. Send Lynette on this course, all expenses paid, to familiarize her in depth with the research topic and appropriate methods.

Chapter 14 **Work design**

Key terms

rationalism

scientific management

systematic soldiering

initiative and incentive system

time-and-motion studies

Fordism

mass production

McDonaldization

instrumental orientation

introjection

identification

concertive control

chimerial control

Learning outcomes

When you have read this chapter, you should be able to define those key terms in your own words, and you should also be able to:

1. Understand how scientific management met the needs of its historical context.
2. Describe the main objectives and principles of the scientific management approach.
3. Enumerate the contributions of the Gilbreths and Gantt to scientific management.
4. Understand how Fordism developed out of Taylorism.
5. Understand the deskilling debate, and the contributions of Braverman and Ritzer.
6. Provide examples of scientific management in contemporary society.

Why study work design?

This chapter examines the roots of the design of jobs that we see in today's organizations. Only a handful of theories can claim to be truly revolutionary, and to have had an enduring and worldwide impact on organizational thought and management practice. Those of Frederick Winslow Taylor and Henry Ford are two of them. Contrary to other textbooks which argue that their ideas are no longer relevant to our modern, high-tech organizational lives, we contend that both are having a more pervasive impact on society today than they did a hundred years ago. You need only to visit a call centre or a fast food restaurant, attend a university course, or think about how the car you are sitting in today was manufactured, to see how the provision of goods and services has been affected by Taylor's and Ford's ideas.

Developments in information technology have increased rather than reduced their relevance. For example, one current debate focuses on whether the virtual organization is a new organizational arrangement or a refinement of scientific management thinking. Taylorism and Fordism are alive and well, still thriving at the start of the twenty-first century (Sewell et al., 2012; Carter et al., 2011; Russell, 2009; Stewart et al., 2009). Their ideas continue to affect all our lives as students, employees, consumers and citizens, even though we may not be aware of it.

Study of work today

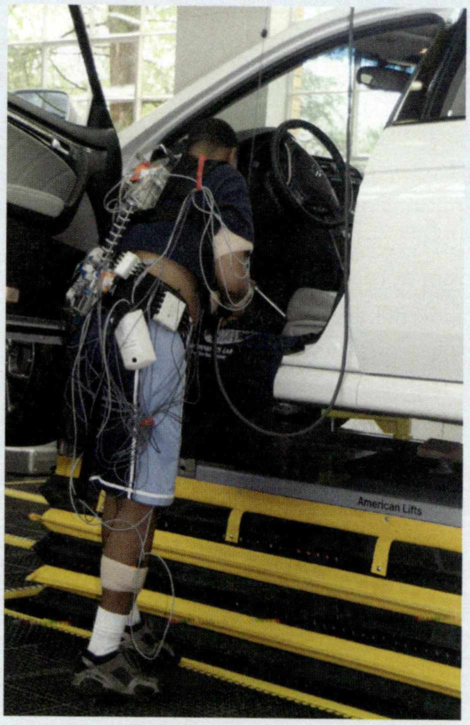

William S. Marras

Looking like an industrial version of Robocop, the motor car assembly line worker of 2012 displays protruding transmitters, wires, and electrodes. He approaches the vehicle in order to fit a part, and his every movement is being recorded by researchers at the Centre for Occupational Health and Automobile Manufacturing (COHAM) at Ohio State University. Engineers apply the latest biomechanical technology and test new production technologies such as overhead car carriers and adjustable skillet systems which orient the vehicle to the worker, so as to reduce employees' musculoskeletal stress. The centre works in partnership with various car manufacturers and suppliers to design assembly tasks, processes, and tools which minimize occupational risks and enhance product quality and worker productivity. One such partner is Honda. Through its Honda-OSU Partnership, it is seeking to reduce illness-based absences among its employees. The company has achieved a 70 per cent reduction in accidents by changing the way employees are required to move and lift. This is modern-day work study, and its roots go back over a hundred years (based on http:coham.osu.edu; http://elearn.eng.ohio-state.edu/honda/research.htm).

Birth of scientific management

Between 1880 and 1910, the United States underwent major and rapid industrialization, including the creation of its first large corporations. Many of today's well-known organizations, such as the Standard Oil Trust (Esso), United States Steel, General Motors, and Ford, were created at that time. These firms used new technologies of production and employed large workforces. The workers in these new factories came from agricultural regions of America, or were immigrants from Europe. Directing the efforts of workers with little knowledge of the English language, few job skills, and no experience of the disciplined work of a factory was a major organizational problem. Scientific management offered a solution, and represented one of the first organizational practices capable of being applied to different companies. It introduced a formal system of industrial discipline.

At this time, most products were hand-made by skilled operators who handcrafted items using general-purpose machine tools such as lathes. It took these craftsmen years of training to acquire the necessary skills and experience. They could read a blueprint and visualize the final product, and they possessed a level of hand–eye coordination and gentleness of touch that allowed them to manufacture the required item (Littler, 1982). However, there were insufficient numbers of them to permit mass production. It was against this background that Frederick Taylor and Henry Ford developed and implemented their ideas. Both shared a belief in **rationalism**, which is the theory that reason is the foundation of certainty in knowledge. They believed that if one understands something, one should be able both to state it explicitly, and to write a law or a rule for it. The consequence of developing and applying rules, laws and procedures, is to replace uncertainty with predictability, both in the human and non-human spheres.

Rationalism the theory that reason is the foundation of certainty in knowledge.

Scientific management a form of job design which stresses short, repetitive work cycles; detailed, prescribed task sequences; a separation of task conception from task execution; and motivation based on economic rewards.

All manufacturing (e.g. turning a piece of wood into a chair leg) involves three separate activities: (1) the transformation of work pieces, (2) the transfer of work pieces between workers and operations, and (3) the coordination and control of these two processes, ensuring that sufficient raw material is available to operators to work on and that finished pieces flow smoothly through assembly. Originally, each of these three processes was performed manually, and the history of work transformation has involved the mechanization of each one. Scientific management or Taylorism – the first major approach to work rationalization – focused on the first of these three stages – the transformation of the work piece (Gill, 1985). Taylor's approach is known by two names. **Scientific management** is also known as *Taylorism* and in this chapter the two terms are used interchangeably.

Taylorism

Frederick Winslow Taylor (1856–1915)

Frederick Winslow Taylor was the world's first efficiency expert. He was born into a wealthy Philadelphia Quaker family in 1856. The city was the industrial heart of 1800s America. It contained many manufacturers who had ready access to the Pennsylvanian coal and iron mines. Taylor became an apprentice machinist in a firm of engineers before joining the Midvale Steel Company in 1878 where he developed his ideas. The company manufactured locomotive wheels and axles, and it was here that he rose to the position of shop superintendent by 1887. In this role, he observed that workers used different and mostly inefficient work methods. He also noticed that few machinists ever worked at the speed of which they were capable. He contrasted natural soldiering (i.e. the inclination to take it easy), with what he labelled **systematic soldiering**. Taylor attributed systematic soldiering to a number of factors:

- the view among the workers that an increase in output would result in redundancies;
- poor management controls which enabled them to work slowly, in order to protect their own best interests;
- the choice of methods of work which were left entirely to the discretion of the workers who wasted a large part of their efforts using inefficient and untested rules-of-thumb.

Systematic soldiering the conscious and deliberate restriction of output by operators.

Appalled by what he regarded as the inefficiency of industrial practices, Taylor took steps to increase production by reducing the variety of work methods used by the workers. He set out to show how management and workforce could both benefit from adopting his more efficient work arrangements. His objectives were to achieve

Soldiering

Robert Kanigel (1997) explained that the word 'soldiering' had nautical roots. It related to soldiers who, when transported by ship, acted as privileged passengers. They were exempt from the work on board that the seamen had to perform. To the sailors, such work avoidance came to be known as 'soldiering'. Frederick Taylor identified, on the one hand, the tendency of workers to take it easy. This he labelled 'natural soldiering'. He considered it unfortunate, but almost excusable. On the other hand, and more insidious in his view, was 'systematic soldiering' which was the organized, collective behaviour of workers in the whole workshop, who restricted their production, prevented their employers knowing how fast they could work, and thus allowed them to pursue their own narrow self-interest.

"It has come to my attention gentlemen, that you've been doing the work of two men."

Source: www.CartoonStock.com

- *efficiency*, by increasing the output per worker and reducing deliberate 'underworking' by employees,
- *predictability*, of job performance by standarizing tasks by dividing up tasks into small, standardized, closely specified sub-tasks, and
- *control*, by establishing discipline through hierarchical authority and introducing a system whereby all management's policy decisions could be implemented.

Taylor's approach involved studying each work task. He chose routine, repetitive tasks performed by numerous operatives where study could save time and increase production. Many variables were measured including size of tools, location of tools, height of workers, and type of material worked. His studies tried to answer the question 'How long should it take to do any particular job in the machine shop?' He wanted to replace rules-of-thumb with scientifically designed working methods. Taylor experimented with different combinations of movement and method to discover the 'one best way' of performing any task.

One best way of assembling a Pret a Manger sandwich

Jonathan Player/Rex Features

A senior Pret a Manger manager explained how to make a sandwich:

> It is very important to make sure the same standards are adhered to in every single shop, whether you're in Crown Passage in London, Sauchiehall Street in Glasgow, or in New York. The way we do that is by very, very detailed training. So, for example, how to make an egg mayonnaise sandwich is all written down on a card that has to be followed, and that is absolutely non-negotiable. When somebody joins Pret, they have a 10-day training plan, and on every single day there is a list of things that they have to be shown, from how to spread the filling of a sandwich right to the edges (that is key to us), how to cut a sandwich from corner to corner, how to make sure that the sandwiches look great in the box and on the shelves. So every single detail is covered on a 10-day training plan. At the end of that 10-days the new team member has to pass a quiz, it's called the big scary quiz, it is quite big and it is quite scary, and they have to achieve 90 per cent on that in order to progress. (Boddy, 2011, p. 46)

In 1898, Taylor was hired by the Bethlehem Iron Company to improve work methods. For many years, the output of the company's blast furnaces had been moved by 75 pig iron handlers who loaded an average of twelve and a half tons per man per day. Taylor estimated that a first class pig iron handler ought to handle between 47 and 48 tons per day. Taylor introduced his experimental changes, raised productivity by a factor of four, and increased workers' wages by 60 per cent. The savings achieved with his improved work plan were between $75,000 and $80,000 per annum at 1911 prices. The cost of handling pig iron dropped substantially, and the employed men did the work previously done by many more. Taylor specified what tools workers were to use and how to do their jobs. His 'deal' with his workers was as follows:

> You do it my way, by my standards, at the speed I mandate, and in so doing achieve a level of output I ordain, and I'll pay you handsomely for it, beyond anything you might have imagined. All you do is take orders, give up your way of doing the job for mine. (Kanigel, 1997, p. 214)

Taylor attempted to align the goals of the workers with those of management.

Bethlehem Steel Corporation

Machine Shop No. 2 at Bethlehem Steel Works in Bethlehem, Pennsylvania, USA

Bethlehem Steel Corporation

Pig iron handlers at the Bethlehem Steel Works

Initiative and incentive system a form of job design in which management gives workers a task to perform and provides them with the financial incentive to complete it, but then leaves them to use their own initiative as to how they will perform it.

Taylor's scientific management was a powerful and largely successful attempt to wrest the organization of production from the workers, and place it under the control of management. Before Taylor, the use of the **initiative and incentive system** within the company involved management specifying production requirements, providing workers with incentives in the form of a piece-rate bonus, and leaving them to use their own initiative in deciding how best to organize their work. In Taylor's view, not only did this result in wasted effort but also, and more importantly, workers kept their craft secrets to themselves, and worked at a collectively agreed rate that was below their ability. Taylor argued that managers should exercise full responsibility for the planning, coordinating, and controlling of work, including selecting the tools to be used (management work), thereby leaving workers free to execute the specified tasks (shop floor work). His five principles of scientific management were:

1. A clear division of tasks and responsibilities between management and workers.
2. Use of scientific methods to determine the best way of doing a job.
3. Scientific selection of the person to do the newly designed job.

4. The training of the selected worker to perform the job in the way specified.
5. Surveillance of workers through the use of hierarchies of authority and close supervision.

Management–worker relations, in Taylor's eyes, should be cooperative rather than adversarial. He saw the two pulling together to produce as much product as possible for their mutual benefit. His techniques were meant to improve the efficiency and social harmony of industrial life, and they required, in his phrase, a 'Mental Revolution' by both parties. By this he meant the application of the principles of science to determine the best way to perform any given task and the acceptance of the results obtained thereby, by both workers and management. He also believed that his 'scientific' approach would end arbitrary management decisions. Management would plan and organize the work, and labour would execute it, all in accordance with the dictates of science.

Once his methods had been introduced within a company, trade unions and collective bargaining would, in his view, become redundant. Scientific assessment would eliminate all ambiguity and argument. This and all his other ideas were detailed in his book *The Principles of Scientific Management* (Taylor, 1911). Workers were concerned that scientific management just meant 'work speed-up' – that is, more work for less pay. Taylor was adamant that after the implementation of his methods, workers would be rewarded by large pay increases and managers would secure higher productivity and profits. Sometimes workers complained about the inequality of pay increases as when a 300 per cent productivity increase resulted in a 30 per cent pay increase. Taylor argued that his approach enabled people to do more work, in less time, using less effort because of the more efficient physical movements. Since they were expending less effort, this had to be taken into account when calculating their wage increases. The efficiency savings also led to the requirement for fewer workers. Would existing workers be redeployed or made redundant? In later years the unions became reconciled with work-study, and accepted it, especially if financial benefits followed.

Call centres

Call centres have been extensively studied because they possess many features of Taylorist work design. Generalizing the findings of numerous studies, researchers have found work in call centres to be pressurized and highly paced, stoked by management's preoccupation

David Pearson/Alamy

with cost minimization and productivity. Most of the jobs were narrowly defined and closely monitored. The time duration of each call taken, the content of the conversation with each customer, and the advice to be given, were all closely prescribed. There was a high level of task fragmentation, scripting, and call streaming. Most operators were trained to deal with just one aspect of incoming phone inquiries. Staff were force-fed a diet of standardized calls by automatic systems that were allocated to match the appropriate employee's 'skill set'. By packaging knowledge for rapid assimilation during training, call-centre firms could train new recruits and plug them into the system in the shortest possible time. Bureaucratic support systems operated to police adherence to the scripts and work targets. Teams within call centres resemble manufacturing industry lean production teams (Taylor and Bain, 2007; Taylor et al., 2002; Ellis and Taylor, 2006).

Sometimes task fragmentation just doesn't work

Google's 'translation console' was a 'break-it-into-tiny-pieces solution' for translating the company's sites into different languages using volunteers. It split all the text on Google's pages into single sentences, phrases, and even words, to make it easy for volunteers to translate the interface one bit at a time. If the system worked, it would make Google's site available in hundreds of different languages. To manage this alone was a long and arduous task. Some fun languages were used to test the system including Pig Latin, Klingon, and Bork, Bork, Bork (the language of the Swedish chef in the *Muppet Show*). A Google employee who used the console to render the interface into Korean found that it lacked context. Translators using the console saw only one word or one phrase at a time, without any information about its context. The word 'Bulgarian' might refer to the Bulgarian language or to a Bulgarian woman. Each piece of text went to a different translator so there was no continuity in the flow. Once reassembled it often read awkwardly or even nonsensically. The problem was identified as being the translators, not the technology. Industry standard management software was bought and people were hired who were good translators and who were able to work with the translation console. They would do the top eight languages and the remaining ones would be done by the volunteers. The first new interfaces to launch were Afrikaans, Bulgarian, and Catalan. Within five months, volunteers had translated Google's interface into sixty-four languages (based on Edwards, 2011, pp. 259–62).

Criticisms of Taylorism

Critics of Taylorism have argued that

1. It assumed that the motivation of the employee was to secure the maximum earnings for the effort expended. It neglected the importance of other rewards from work (achievement, job satisfaction, recognition) which later research has found to be important.
2. It neglected the subjective side of work – the personal and interactional aspects of performance, the meanings that employees give to work, and the significance to them of their social relationships at work.
3. It failed to appreciate the meanings that workers would put on new procedures and their reactions to being timed and closely supervised.
4. It had an inadequate understanding of the relation of the individual incentive to interaction with, and dependence on, the immediate work group. Taylor did attribute 'underworking' to group pressures but misunderstood the way in which these worked. He failed to see that these might just as easily keep production and morale up.
5. It ignored the psychological needs and capabilities of workers. The one best way of doing a job was chosen with the mechanistic criteria of speed and output. The imposition of a uniform manner of work can both destroy individuality and cause other psychological disturbances.
6. It had too simple an approach to the question of productivity and morale. It sought to keep both of these up exclusively by economic rewards and punishments. However, the

fatigue studies of the Gilbreths during the 1920s did signal the beginnings of a wider appreciation of the relevant factors than had initially been recognized by Taylor. Incentive approaches under the scientific approach tended to focus on workers as individuals and ignored their social context.

Taylorism in today's HMRC

Much research has been conducted into customer-facing 'front-office' work in call centres. In contrast, Bob Carter and his colleagues investigated clerical work in the 'back offices' of Her Majesty's Revenue and Customs (HMRC) tax-processing centres in the UK. They studied 840 front-line staff who had experienced the virtually untrammelled application of Taylorism, in the form of lean production (Toyotaism). This impacted on their organization and control of their work; discretion over their task performance; their degree of skill utilization; and the intensity of their work effort. The HMRC had redesigned the work to be completed more efficiently with fewer staff. Work-study techniques were used to appropriate and codify workers' tacit knowledge into written operating procedures and to generate optimum work cycle time targets for individuals and teams. Lean advisors and line managers, armed with clipboards and stopwatches, performed detailed time-and-motion studies.

Originally, staff had operated a system of 'whole-case working' where an administrative officer would deal with all aspects of a tax return – answer phone calls related to it; deal with all its correspondence; ensure compliance with regulations and standards; and complete the job to its conclusion. The targets for work output were the norms of how much work would be completed daily or weekly. Staff enjoyed sufficient autonomy to manage their own workloads within broad parameters. Subsequently, HMRC management introduced a process of work rationalization to increase labour utilization and productivity rates. This involved task fragmentation with core responsibilities being separated out and assigned to specialist offices. Thus some offices become solely responsible for particular parts of the work process, e.g. for corresponding with taxpayers or for dealing with phone calls. They dealt with nothing else.

The previously relaxed and relatively high-trust form of work organization was abandoned in the interests of work discipline and flow line efficiency. The lean-management concept of 'value-streaming', in which each worker was assigned responsibility for a single fragmented task which had been strictly defined by standard operating procedures, was implemented. The job itself (processing a tax return) was expected to flow efficiently from worker to worker, in a Taylorized (indeed, Toyotaized) assembly line fashion. These changes to work organization were accompanied by the introduction of Taylorist management control techniques which set hourly output targets and systematically monitored employees' performance. These targets varied from six items an hour for tax letters, to 80 items an hour for opening tax cases. The targets were announced at the start of each shift by line managers, who then patrolled the offices, monitoring individual worker performance, and updating the targets and staff performances on whiteboards on an hourly basis. Staff who failed to meet minimum standards were disciplined. Most staff found this new control system degrading and repressive.

A survey indicated that, prior to the lean initiative, 75 per cent of staff had set their own work pace, decided when to take breaks, and planned how to carry out their work themselves. After the change, most felt that the reverse was the case. They reported that the all-round skill and accumulated experience needed to complete their work had become superfluous to requirements; their control over their working hours had declined; monotony of work had increased; and their capacity to use their own personal judgement and initiative had fallen significantly. Workers reported being driven to the limit, and were unable to control the pace and quantity of their work. Carter et al. concluded that the imposition of lean-management methods by an increasingly authoritarian HMRC management regime had resulted in a significant degradation of the tax staff's quality of working life. The findings of their study at these HMRC offices bore very close similarities to the cases of clerical labour rationalization and degradation under scientific management which had been identified by Harry Braverman (1974) four decades earlier (based on Carter et al., 2011).

STOP AND THINK You have travelled back through time and are able to meet Taylor. What three things would you congratulate him for, and what three things would you criticize him for?

Taylorism in the orchestra

Here is the way in which a Taylorist industrial engineer might report an orchestral concert:

> For considerable periods the four oboe players had nothing to do. The number should be reduced and the work spread more evenly over the whole concert, thus eliminating peaks and valleys of activity. All the twelve violins were playing identical notes, this seems unnecessary duplication. The staff of this section should be drastically cut. If a larger volume of sound is required, it could be obtained by means of electronic apparatus. Much effort was absorbed in the playing of demi-semi-quavers; this seems to be an unnecessary refinement. It is recommended that all notes be rounded up to the nearest semi-quaver. If this were done, it would be possible to use trainees and lower grade operatives more extensively.
>
> There seems to too much repetition of some musical passages. Scores should be drastically pruned. No useful purpose is served by repeating on the horns something which has already been handled by the strings. It is estimated that if all redundant passages were eliminated the whole concert time of 2 hours could be reduced to 20 minutes and there would be no need for an intermission. In many cases the operators were using one hand for holding the instrument, whereas the introduction of a fixture would have tendered the idle hand available for other work. Also, it was noted that excessive effort was being used occasionally by the players of wind instruments, whereas one compressor could supply adequate air for all instruments under more accurately controlled conditions. Finally, obsolescence of equipment is another matter into which it is suggested further investigation could be made, as it was reported in the programme that the leading violinist's instrument was already several hundred years old. If normal depreciation schedules had been applied, the value of this instrument would have been reduced to zero and purchase of more modern equipment could then have been considered. (Fulmer and Herbert, 1974, p. 27)

Development of Taylorism

The Gilbreths' contributions

Frank Bunker Gilbreth's background resembled Taylor's in that both were practising engineers and managers. Gilbreth's experience was in the construction industry, and his most famous experiments involved bricklayers. He refined the techniques for measuring work, while his wife Lillian, a trained psychologist, focused on the human aspects of work. Together they contributed in three main areas:

Lillian Moller Gilbreth (1878–1972) and Frank Bunker Gilbreth (1868–1924)

Time-and-motion studies measurement and recording techniques used to make work operations more efficient.

- *Motion study*: This refers to the investigation and classification of the basic motions of the body. Gilbreth developed motion study. Taylor had looked mainly at time, and had not focused as closely on motions. Gilbreth rectified this omission, and his ideas were published in his book *Motion Study* in 1911. To study and improve workers' body movements, Gilbreth attached small electric lamps to workers' hands and left the camera lens open to track their changing positions, creating *chronocyclegraphic* photographs showing their motion paths. He also used *motion picture cameras* to record workers' motions and times simultaneously.
- *Therbligs*: In his experiments, the elementary movement was considered to be the building block of every work activity. Gilbreth developed a system for noting such movements, each with its own symbol and colour. These he called 'therbligs' – a term based on his name spelt backwards. Like dance, all the movements of the worker's body performing a particular task were noted down using the therblig notation (see Figure 14.1). In addition, Gilbreth developed a standard time for each job element, thereby combining time study with motion study. **Time-and-motion studies** are conducted to this day, and are used for improving occupational health, increasing productivity, and designing wage payment systems, whose universal application Gilbreth advocated.

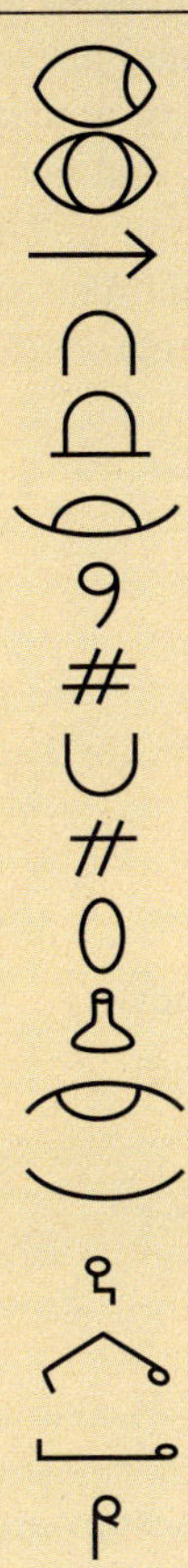

symbol	name	colour
	search	black
	find	grey
	select	light grey
	group	red
	bold	gold ochre
	transport loaded	green
	position	blue
	assemble	violet
	use	purple
	disassemble	light violet
	inspect	burnt ochre
	preposition	pale blue
	release load	carmine red
	transport empty	olive green
	rest for overcoming fatigue	orange
	unavoidable delay	yellow
	avoidable delay	lemon yellow
	plan	brown

Figure 14.1: Therblig symbols and colours

Source: *Developments in Management Thought*, Heinemann (Pollard, H.R. 1974) ISBN 10: 0434915750/ISBN 13: 9780434915750.

Smithsonian Institution, National Museum of American History

Micro-motion studies and chronocyclegraphic models

- *Fatigue study*: Lillian Gilbreth's work complemented her husband's. She studied motions to eliminate unnecessary and wasteful actions, so as to reduce the fatigue experienced by workers. Since all work produced fatigue, for which the remedy was rest, her aim was to find the best mixture of work and rest to maximize productivity. To do this, she focused on the total working environment, and not just on selecting first-class workers as Taylor had done. They studied jobs to eliminate fatigue-producing elements. Together, the Gilbreths shortened the working day; introduced rest periods and chairs; and instituted holidays with pay (Gilbreth and Gilbreth, 1916).

STOP AND DRINK

Go up to the bar and order a pint of beer.

Start position: standing at bar

Movement 1: Hand to glass (2 seconds)

Movement 2: Grip glass (0.5 seconds)

Movement 3: Lift to horizontal (1 second)

Movement 4: Lift to lips (1 second)

Movement 5: Swallow 0.05 litres beer (2 seconds)

Movement 6: Move arm to horizontal (1 second)

Movement 7: Move glass to bar (1 second)

Movement 8: Release grip on glass (0.5 seconds)

Movement 9: Belch (1 second)

End position: standing at bar

Total time for operation: 10 seconds.

Go to your local pub or bar with a friend and a stopwatch, and check the above timings.

(Grey, 2009, pp. 37–8)

Gantt's contributions

Henry Laurence Gantt (1861–1924)

In 1887, Henry Laurence Gantt joined the Midvale Steel Company and became an assistant to the company's chief engineer, F.W. Taylor. Gantt supported Taylor's approach, but humanized scientific management to make it more acceptable (Gantt, 1919). He tempered Taylor's work with greater insight into human psychology, and stressed method over measurement. He believed that Taylor's use of incentives was too punitive and lacked sensitivity to the psychological needs of the workers. He believed in consideration for, and fair dealings with, employees, and felt that scientific management was being used as an oppressive instrument by the unscrupulous. He made three major contributions:

- *Best-known-way-at-present*: Gantt's system was based on detailed instruction cards in the best scientific management tradition. However, he replaced Taylor's 'one best way' with his own 'best known way at present'. This involved a much less detailed analysis of jobs than Taylor had suggested.
- *Task-and-bonus payment scheme*: He replaced Taylor's differential piece-rate wage system with his own task-and-bonus scheme. Each worker was set a task and received a set day rate and an additional 20 to 50 per cent bonus.
- *'Gantt Chart'*: He developed a bar chart used for scheduling (i.e. planning) and coordinating the work of different departments or plants. His chart depicted quantities ordered, work progress, and quantities issued from store. Although he never patented it, it is still in use today, and bears his name; an example is shown in Figure 14.2.

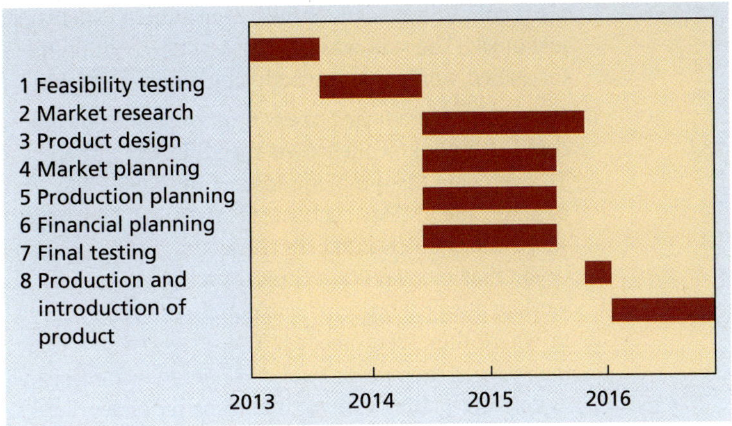

Figure 14.2: Gantt chart for new product development plan beginning 2013

Fordism

Henry Ford (1863–1947)

Fordism a form of work design that applies scientific management principles to workers' jobs; the installation of single-purpose machine tools to manufacture standardized parts; and the introduction of the mechanized assembly line.

By 1920, the name of Henry Ford had become synonymous not only with his Model T motor car, but also with his revolutionary techniques of mass producing it. In terms of the three separate manufacturing activities distinguished by Gill (1985) which we discussed earlier, Ford developed the last two – the transfer of work pieces between workers and operations; and the coordination and control of these processes, ensuring that sufficient raw material was available to operators and that finished pieces flowed smoothly through assembly. Thus he moved on from the mechanization and rationalization of work on the individual work piece or object pioneered by Taylor, to mechanizing the flow of objects between operatives. The process by which this was done is known as **Fordism**. In this sense, Fordism is distinguishable from Taylorism in that it represents a form of work organization designed for efficient mass production.

Ford established his company in 1903. In the 1890s, it was skilled craftsmen who built motor cars. Ford claimed that there were not enough of them to meet the level of car production that he wanted, and that was why, in his view, the deskilling of work was necessary. Others argue that deskilling made labour easier to control and replace. Ford's goal was 'continuous improvement' rather than the 'one best way'. His objective was to increase his control by reducing or eliminating uncertainty (Ford, 1924). Among his major innovations were analysis of jobs using time-and-motion techniques; installation of single-purpose machine tools to manufacture standardized parts; and the introduction of the mechanized assembly line.

Analysing jobs: Ford applied the principles of scientific management to remove waste and inefficiency. He established a Motion Picture Department that filmed work methods in different industries, so as to learn from them. He applied the principles of work rationalization. Employees were allocated simple tasks, all of which had been carefully designed to ensure maximum efficiency. Ford's approach was entirely experimental, very pragmatic, and always open to improvements – try it, modify it, try it again, keep on until it's right. The Ford mechanic, originally a skilled craftsman, became an assembler who tended his machine, only performing low-grade tasks. For example, the wheelwright's job was divided into almost a hundred operations, each performed by a different man using specialized equipment.

Installation of single-purpose machine tools to produce standardized parts: Ford used rigid and heavy machine tools, carbon alloy tool steels, and universal grinding machines. This ensured that each part was exactly like the next, and hence interchangeable. This facilitated the division of labour and increased certainty. The single-purpose machines that he designed for his factory were called 'farmer machines' because farm boys, coming off the land, could be quickly trained to use them. Their operators did not have to be skilled, just quick. The skill was now incorporated within the machine. This eliminated the need for skilled workers as anybody could now assemble an automobile.

Creation of the mechanized assembly line: Despite the aforementioned innovations, employees could still work at their own speed. In 1913, it still took 90 minutes to assemble a car. To overcome this problem, instead of moving the men past the car, the car was moved past the men. The mechanized assembly line imposed upon employees the working speed that Ford wanted. By 1914, the plant had installed a continuous automatic conveyor that met Ford's technical and philosophical objectives. The engineers arranged work in a logical order. The materials and semi-completed parts passed through the plant to where they were needed. The conveyor belt took radiator parts to assemblers, and then carried their work away to solderers, who finished off the product (Gartman, 1979).

After integrating various production processes, Ford's engineers produced a continuously moving line which was fed by overhead conveyors. Each worker was feeding, and being fed by, the assembly line. In 1908, when the Model T was introduced, production ran at 27 cars per day. By 1923, when the River Rouge plant had been completed, daily production had reached 2,000 cars. The credit for the original concept of the assembly line concept is disputed. Some stories tell of Henry Ford getting the idea at an abattoir where beef carcasses, suspended from moving hooks, were being disassembled. Other accounts have him visiting a watch plant, and seeing the staged assembly process of timepieces (Collier and Horowitz, 1987).

Assembly line aircraft and paintings

At its Renton factory near Seattle, Boeing uses lean manufacturing techniques and resembles a Toyota car plant. Aircraft fuselages come in at one end and are hooked onto a moving assembly line. Nose-to-tail, they move along at a rate of two inches a minute through the final assembly process. Out at the other end roll off complete aircraft with wings, tails, cockpits, toilets, galleys, and seats. There are other features of the Toyota

Larry MacDougal/Press Association Images

Boeing factory

CW Images/Alamy

system – the visual displays of work in progress, and alarms to stop production if a quality problem emerges. By using two assembly lines, the current version of its 737 is being manufactured at a record rate of 37 a month. The first plane on the line is destined for flydubai; the second for Ryanair; and the third for Korean Air. The plan is to increase production to 42 planes a month by 2014 by squeezing a third assembly line into the giant hangar. Elizabeth Lund, a director of manufacturing, stated that 'A moving line is the most powerful tool available to identify and eliminate waste in a production system . . . [it] drives efficiency throughout the system because it makes problems visible and creates a sense of urgency to fix the root causes of those problems' (*The Economist*, 2012).

There are about 300 officially licensed artists working in the Place du Tertre in the Paris quarter of Montmartre, selling their works to French and foreign visitors. It is big business, over 10 million tourists pass through annually, and many buy paintings of Parisian landmarks to take home as souvenirs. Although perhaps not great artists, their creators are skilled painters. However, their livelihoods are being threatened because local souvenir shops are selling cheap, mass produced paintings from China and Eastern Europe. Costing a fraction of those sold by the Montmartre artists, these oil paintings are produced on mass assembly lines, where one person paints the sky, a different person does a tree, another inserts figures, and so on. One of the street artists comments 'It isn't art, it's decoration' (Chazon, 2009).

Taylor's ambition had always been to wrest control of the production process from the workers, and place it into the hands of management. Under Fordism, this was broadly achieved. Ford's objective was to allow unsophisticated workers to make a sophisticated product in volume. He sought to make his workforce as uniform and interchangeable as the parts that they handled. He created an authoritarian work regime with closely monitored, machine-paced, short-cycle, unremitting tasks. In the 1930s, Walt Disney applied the techniques of mass production to the task of making cartoons in his Hollywood film studio (Watts, 2001).

Control over the worker was exerted through task specialization and assembly line working. Such control was both invisible and non-confrontational. It was the system, not the supervisor, that told the employee to work faster. It de-personalized the authority relationship to such a degree that workers were no longer aware that they were being directed. Control over the environment was achieved through purchase of vital raw materials. Ford experienced production hold-ups when his suppliers had strikes. To avoid this he sought to

Source: www.CartoonStock.com

First moving assembly line

The photograph below shows men working on the first moving assembly line at Ford's Highland Park factory, 1913.

Ford Motor Company: *Collection of Henry Ford Museum and Greenfield Village*

control all aspects of the production process. In the Brazilian rain forest, he carved out rubber plantations the size of Connecticut which he called 'Fordlandia'. He bought coal mines in Kentucky and iron mines in Michigan, as well as glassworks, shipping lines, and railways. He even owned the land on which the sheep whose wool went into his cars' seat covers grazed! Ford was determined to control every element of the manufacturing process, both inside and outside his company. By 1920, one Ford car rolled off the line every minute, and by 1925, the figure was one every ten seconds. In 1935, Ford's River Rouge plant in Dearborn on the outskirts of Detroit, spread over 1,096 acres, had 7.25 million square feet of floor space, possessed 235 acres of glass windows and 90 miles of railway track; it employed 100,000 men, and built 2 million cars each year. Little wonder that it was called the *Cathedral of Industry*.

Cathedral of Industry

In the 1930s, the Mexican artist Diego Rivera (1886–1957) was commissioned by the Detroit Institute of Art to paint frescos devoted to the city's motor car industry. His panels feature Ford's River Rouge plant. Rivera was an independent artist with a Marxist perspective. He painted the factory workers and the machines that they used. The ethnic mix of the workforce is depicted. The panels show various stages in the production of the automobile. The men in the murals are depicted as sullen and angry, working amid the clamour and din of the machinery around them. The strength shown in their faces was perceived as intimidating by some observers who accused Rivera of producing left-wing propaganda.

Bridgeman Art Library Ltd/Detroit Institute of Arts

Detroit Industry (South Wall), Diego Rivera, 1932–1933

Mass production
a form of work design that includes mechanical pacing of work, no choice of tools or methods, repetitiveness, minute subdivision of product, minimum skill requirements, and surface mental attention.

Ford's legacy was twofold. First, he created what came to be defined as the characteristics of **mass production** work:

- mechanical pacing of work;
- no choice of tools or methods;
- repetitiveness;
- minute subdivision of product;
- minimum skill requirements;
- surface mental attention.

Second, he raised people's standard of living. Having shown that something as complicated as a motor car could be built using the techniques of mass production, it was recognized that the manufacture of other, simpler products was also possible – radios, washing machines, refrigerators, vacuum cleaners, personal computers, mobile phones. Mass production led to mass consumption, giving more people more access to more goods than ever in human history. In the fifty years to 1970, the standard of living of Americans skyrocketed. Other countries that adopted Ford's system of manufacturing production also benefited. While Taylorism and Fordism had many similarities, they also had some differences, as Table 14.1 shows.

Table 14.1: Differences between Taylorism and Fordism

	Taylorism	Fordism
Approach to machinery	Organized labour around existing machinery	Eliminated labour with new machinery
Technology and the work design	Took production process as given and sought to reorganize work and labour processes	Used technology to mechanize the work process; workers fed and tended machines
Pace of work	Set by his workers or the supervisor	Set by machinery – the speed of the assembly line

Critics have argued that Ford destroyed craftsmanship and deskilled jobs. He did indeed change the work process by introducing greater amounts of rigidity and regulation, thereby affecting the skill content of jobs. Others argue that since there were insufficient numbers of skilled workers available to do the original jobs, Ford had to redesign the tasks so that the existing, pre-industrial labour force could cope with them. In their view, it was less a question of forcing a highly-skilled, high-priced employee to accept a cheapened, dead-end job, and more an issue of identifying tasks appropriate for unskilled people who would otherwise have performed even less enjoyable, more tedious work.

The same critics also assert that short-cycle repetitive jobs have caused worker alienation and stress, and have subjugated human beings to the machine. The assembly line is vilified for exerting an invidious, invisible control over the workers. Other commentators observe how Fordism has shaped reforms within the British National Health Service. 'Fordism monitors the time doctors and nurses spend with each patient; a medical treatment system based on dealing with auto parts, it tends to treat cancerous livers or broken backs rather than patients in the rounds' (Sennett, 2008, p. 47). The debate over the balance of costs and benefits of Fordism and its precursor, Taylorism, continue to this day, as the next section illustrates.

Fordism in the orchestra

What do assembly line workers in car plants and musicians in professional orchestras have in common? Both have limited autonomy in their jobs. Research has found that orchestra musicians have high internal motivation but lower levels of job satisfaction than their counterparts playing in string quartets and small chamber ensembles. The reason is that the members of prestigious orchestras, with their sought-after positions, have little freedom to perform their jobs as they personally want. Historically, orchestra musicians have been under the strict direction of the often dictatorial maestros with their batons on the podium. The conductor is in charge, and makes all the decisions, down to exactly how a particular note is to be played. At the other end of the musical continuum are the players in jazz bands who are not only allowed, but encouraged to improvise. In between are the smaller musical groups whose members have autonomy to interpret their pieces and use more of their talents which increases their involvement in the performance, and hence their job satisfaction (based on Levine and Levine, 1996: Allmendinger et al., 1994).

Today, Henry Ford's legacy in motor manufacturing is discussed in terms of the development and application of the Toyota Production System (TPS) or *Toyotaism*. As Tommaso Pardi (2007) noted, that critics' claim that TPS's aim of constant improvement, reduction in costs through the systematic elimination of waste using the assembly line system, represents a continuity with the classic Fordist approach, and uses the 'management by stress' approach (Durand and Hatzfeld, 2003; Parker and Slaughter, 1988). He observed:

> The work tasks in the TPS are completely standardized, to the point that each standard worksheet does not only state the whole sequence of the operations, but also the exact positions and movements that the worker must perform. The capability of executing the standard task according to the standard task sheet is evaluated every month by the team leader. (Pardi, 2007, pp. 9–10)

In contrast, other writers see TPS as different from the Fordist approach in that the Taylorist principle separates the design of work from its execution (jobs designed upstairs, by industrial engineers in the shop office, are performed downstairs, by the workers on the assembly line). By involving industrial workers in the process of constant improvement through teamwork organization, the system increases their participation in, and satisfaction from, work (Womack et al., 1990).

STOP AND THINK

Courtesy of Toyota (GB) Ltd

Toyota Motor Company's advertisement in *The Economist* magazine is entitled 'Your Toyota is My Toyota'. It shows a photograph of a female production team member on the assembly line at the company's Burnaston plant in the UK with a thick yellow and black rope above her head. The text reads as follows:

> 'If I suspect a problem, I pull the Andon cord and the whole production line stops immediately, and it doesn't start again until the issue has been resolved. I've pulled it thousands of times and it's good because it makes everyone personally responsible for producing the highest quality car.'

The advertising copy implies that this is an example of employee empowerment. Do you agree? (*The Economist*, 2010)

Home viewing

Modern Times (1936, directed by Charlie Chaplin) is a satire of the automated age. It stars Chaplin himself and Paulette Goddard. In the opening sequence, Chaplin is a comic victim of the assembly line in a huge manufacturing plant in the 1930s. Watch the first fifteen minutes of the film. How many different aspects of Taylorism and Fordism can you identify?

After Ford: the deskilling debate

The idea of fragmenting work tasks and simplifying jobs was begun by Taylor and developed by Ford. Since that time, has this process of deskilling work continued and been extended to other occupations and types of workers? Or, on the contrary, has work become more complicated, employees been better trained and educated, and jobs made more skilled? Taylor and Ford placed the issue of job skill at the centre of all subsequent discussions about work design. The deskilling debate provides a useful perspective from which to consider the plethora of theoretical, empirical, and prescriptive writings produced by academics, managers, and consultants.

Two seemingly contradictory trends in work design occurred in the second half of the twentieth century. From the 1950s, both in the United States and Europe, there was a reaction against Taylorism, and a steady and consistent interest in more 'people-oriented' approaches. Labels like human relations, socio-technical systems, quality of working life, organization development, and human-centred manufacturing reflected this inclination. Then, during the 1970s, Japanization, and in particular the success of Japanese 'lean production' manufacturing techniques and Japanese teamworking, became prominent. The contradiction was very apparent. On the one hand, lean production involved many features of Taylorist and Fordist work designs, while on the other, it appeared to incorporate numerous people-oriented features like teamworking. This paradox generated much research and debate.

At the same time, the information technology revolution signalled the increasing importance of knowledge-based jobs, and of the need for so-called 'knowledge workers' to fill them. The necessity of having a well-educated and trained workforce to perform these more technically complex jobs was widely discussed. Commentators asked if a fundamental change was taking place in the nature of work, and if so, whether it was resulting in people being deskilled and their work degraded, or upskilled and their work and working lives enriched. This is the 'deskilling debate'. Although the deskilling and upskilling positions stand in opposition to one another, the former has, to date, generated the greatest amount of research and literature.

Harry Braverman (1920–1976)

The deskilling position

Crudely summarized, the deskilling thesis holds that the principles and practices of Taylorism and Fordism continue to be ever more widely applied within modern organizations. The thesis first appeared in 1974 in the book *Labor and Monopoly Capital: The Degradation of Work in the Twentieth Century* by Harry Braverman (1920–1976), an American theorist, who had originally been trained as a craftsman coppersmith, and who had worked in naval shipyards, railway repair shops, and steel plants, before becoming a journalist and sociologist. Braverman died shortly after his book was published, and he was not around to enjoy the reputation that his book brought him, or to contribute to the debate – the labour process debate – that his work triggered (Littler and Salaman, 1982).

The Braverman deskilling thesis

'There is a long-run tendency through fragmentation, rationalization and mechanization for workers and their jobs to become deskilled, both in an absolute sense (they lose craft and traditional abilities) and in a relative one (scientific knowledge progressively accumulates in the production process). Even when the individual worker retains certain traditional skills, the degraded job that he or she performs does not demand the exercise of these abilities. Thus, a worker, regardless of his or her personal talents, may be more easily and cheaply substituted in the production process. (Zimbalist, 1979, p. xv)

McDonaldization a form of work design aimed at achieving efficiency, calculability, predictability, and control through non-human technology, to enhance organizational objectives by limiting employee discretion and creativity.

Writing in the 1970s, Braverman rejected the then popular view that Taylorism had been superseded by human relations and other, more sophisticated managerial approaches, and that it no longer determined work design or work organization methods. On the contrary, he argued, far from having been replaced, Taylorism in his view had become institutionalized, and now formed the basis of production control within modern organizations of all kinds. The 'Braverman thesis', as it came to be known, stimulated a wide-ranging debate among labour process theorists. It was based on Marxist economic theory and the crisis of capitalism in industrial societies. Braverman saw scientific management as a method of allowing managers to directly control their employees. They did so by reducing the autonomy and discretion exercised by workers in how they performed their jobs, thereby deskilling their work.

Banks, bailouts, and bonuses

Vaughan Ellis and Margaret Taylor (a bank worker at The Lloyds Banking Group) explained how technology in banking had contributed to the financial collapse of many institutions:

> Technology facilitated a deskilling of the work force because people no longer needed to know much about lending practice to make good lending decisions. It is a strategy that has facilitated the cutting of jobs and seen people [being] paid less. You now don't really know many people who know that much about banking and insurance. And that has been critical to some of the issues that we are now seeing, people that work in the industry don't know much about what it actually needs to do because they've taken that skill away and replaced it with IT systems. (Ellis and Taylor, 2010, p. 806)

Braverman contrasted two types of deskilling. The first, *organizational deskilling*, involved Taylor's separation of task conception from task execution. Workers no longer planned their work or solved their problems since these were now dealt with by managerial or technical staff. The second type, *technological deskilling*, involved the use of material technology (such as tools, machinery, and equipment) and social technology (work arrangements that co-ordinated, controlled and rewarded workers) to do the same thing (see Chapter 3 on technology). He felt that this trend was growing in all forms of capitalist enterprises, and was being extended to clerical, administrative and increasingly even professional occupations (Braverman, 1974). The Braverman deskilling thesis was proposed in 1974, but since the 1990s has been discussed as the McDonaldization thesis. This followed the publication in 1993 of a book by George Ritzer, *The McDonaldization of Society* (Ritzer, 2011).

George Ritzer (b.1940)

In his book, Ritzer argued that the process of **McDonaldization** was affecting many areas of our social and organizational lives. He used the term to refer to the process by which the principles of fast food restaurants were coming to dominate more and more sectors of American society as well as the rest of the world. Ritzer had no particular complaint against McDonald's restaurants; he merely used this fast food chain as an illustration of the wider process which was the real focus of his attention. For him, the new model of rationality, with its routinization and standardization of product and service, as represented by McDonald's, had replaced the bureaucratic structures of the past, as described by Max Weber. He saw the McDonald's approach as possessing four key elements:

1. *Efficiency*: every aspect of the organization being geared towards the minimization of time. The optimal production method is the fastest production method. For McDonald's customers, it is the fastest way to get from hungry to full.
2. *Calculability*: an emphasis on things being measurable. The company quantifies its sales, while its customers calculate how much they are getting for their money. McDonaldization promotes the notion that quantity is equivalent to quality, e.g. that a large amount of product delivered quickly represents a quality product.
3. *Predictability*: the provision of standardized, uniform products and services, irrespective of time or location. It is the promise that, irrespective of whichever McDonald's outlet you visit in the world, you will receive the same product in the same manner.
4. *Control*: Standardized and uniform employees performing a limited range of tasks in a precise, detailed manner complemented by non-human technology which is used to replace them whenever possible.

Ritzer's argument is that the process of McDonaldization is spreading and that, while it yields a number of benefits, the associated costs and risks are, in his view, considerable (Ritzer, 2010). His own view is that this trend is undesirable. He looks at the issue primarily from the point of view of what the consumer, client, or citizen is receiving – a uniform, standardized product or service. However, he recognizes that to achieve this, the jobs of producers have to be deskilled. In addition to the simplified jobs that McDonald's employees perform, their work is also limited by the sophisticated technology of fast food preparation which gives them little or no discretion in how they prepare and deliver food to customers. Given our definition of action teams, it is perhaps appropriate that McDonald's restaurant employees are referred to by the company as 'crew members'. Crews are a form of team which are equipment- or technology-driven, and if that technology changes, then so too does the nature of the crew.

Hamburger grilling instructions are precise and detailed, covering the exact positioning of burgers on the grill, cooking times, and the sequence in which burgers are to be turned. Drinks dispensers, french-fry machines, programmed cash registers – all limit the time required to carry out a task and leave little or no room for discretion, creativity, or innovation on the part of the employee. Such discretion and creativity would of course subvert the aims of efficiency, calculability, predictability, and control.

The McJob debate

The term 'McJob' was coined by the eminent sociologist Amitai Etzioni in his 1986 article in the *Washington Post* newspaper entitled 'McJobs are bad for kids' and first entered major dictionaries in 2001. Anthony Gould noted that the scholarly literature on the jobs of crew members (non-management employees) depicted the jobs as non-stimulating, low-waged with few benefits, factory-like, requiring little skill, intellectually unchallenging, and often temporary. He added that academics had argued that such work occurred in an exploitative context with companies seeking to manipulate employees into believing that they had coveted jobs with great opportunities. In contrast, other commentators, mainly although not exclusively industry advocates, took a positive perspective, arguing that such jobs offered teenage employees training, the chance to develop effective work habits and attitudes, and an opportunity to observe cutting-edge management practices; that it helped groups from minority backgrounds who might otherwise experience labour market disadvantages, and that it gave junior employees career progression to the company's managerial and executive positions. The contrasting negative and positive opinions arise partly as a result of commentators emphasizing different aspects of these McJobs – the former focusing primarily on work organization, and the latter on human resource management.

From an employee perspective, this implies that while the jobs are routinized and simplistic, the organization itself may operate helpful and supportive human resource management practices. This view allows for the possibility of a job's attractiveness being multifaceted, possessing both positive and negative characteristics simultaneously. Gould's research attempted to reconcile these two aforementioned perspectives on fast food jobs. He used structured surveys, statistical analysis of data sets, and a broad focus on crews' and managers' perceptions of different aspects of company work organization and human resource management. His findings with regard to fast food work organization were that

- crew work was organized according to Taylorist principles;
- crew members overwhelmingly perceived their duties as comprising a limited range of non-complex tasks to be performed in prescribed ways;
- repeatedly doing the same task did not burn out or indoctrinate crew members;
- many crew members adapted to the way the work was organized, or at least did not view the job negatively;
- a large minority of crew appeared to like the way McDonald's work was organized and were satisfied with their job.

Gould's findings with regard to human resource management were that

- fast food jobs offered crew members job security and the possibility of careers;
- McDonald's' strategy was compatible with the needs and aspirations of industry-suitable crew;
- managers adopted a benign developmental view of their workforce, believing that good work performance should result in promotion and advancement opportunities and continuity of employment tenure.

This researcher concluded that fast food work was a more complex phenomenon than had previously been suggested. Despite being low-paid and, in this respect, unambiguously negative, crew jobs were best understood in terms of their compatibility with individual employee lifestyles (human resource management/employment characteristics) and in terms of a match between individuals' personalities and the company's work organization characteristics (based on Gould, 2010).

STOP AND THINK

Anthony Gould's research (see box) revealed that many McDonald's workers were satisfied with their jobs. Do you find this surprising?

The significance of this development is that much of the current literature about the nature of work and workplace organization is discussed in terms of Ritzer and his McDonaldization thesis, rather than in terms of Braverman and his deskilling and work degradation thesis. The key point is that both writers address broadly the same issues. Academics such as Bryman (2011) and Gould (2010) criticized the shortcomings of commentators and researchers who had written about and studied McDonaldization:

- reliance on polemic rather than empirical research data;
- imposition of their own views on others' experiences, not taking the perspective of users into account;
- dependence on qualitative and ethnographic research methods that identified only the problems but not the advantages of fast food jobs;
- promulgation of a simplistic view of the globalization process that ignores local adaptations to the global spread of McDonaldization principles;
- minimization of the role and significance of countervailing trends such as customers' desire for variety and mass customization;
- a focus on a narrow range of aspects of fast food jobs, e.g., work organization, HRM policies.

There have been many criticisms of Braverman and his deskilling thesis. These include the following (Noon and Blyton, 2007; Fincham and Rhodes, 2005):

- *It ignores alternative management strategies*. It ignores management's ability to choose between using Taylorism to deskill a job or empowering workers to create responsible autonomy. Leaving employees with some discretion can be to management's advantage. Thus, employee empowerment facilitates greater worker interchangeability, thereby allowing better assembly line balancing. These employees are not deskilled, but management nevertheless continues to control the labour process. This suggests that deskilling is neither inevitable nor necessarily always desirable.

- *It overstates management's objective of controlling labour*. The thesis underestimates the diversity and complexity of management objectives and plurality of interests, many of which may be competing (Buchanan and Boddy, 1983; Child, 1985). Marketing, technological, financial, and political considerations may have as much, if not more, impact on work organization. The cost of direct labour is, in many cases, only a small proportion of the total cost of a product, and its control today may not be as significant a factor as it was in the past.
- *It treats workers as passive*. The thesis treats workers as passive and compliant, yet there is evidence of collective, union, and individual resistance to deskilling. The manifestations of such resistance have been extensively documented, although not widely discussed (Ackroyd and Thompson, 1999; Wilson, 2004). Historically, management's shift from direct Taylorist forms of control to technological and bureaucratic control and now to a cultural type of control is a testimony to the existence and effect of such resistance (Ray, 1986).
- *It underestimates employee consent and accommodation*. There is contrary evidence of workers welcoming rather than resisting the opportunity to Taylorize their own jobs. This phenomenon was originally proposed by Burawoy (1979), and has been observed by managers. 'They [workers] understood the technique because it had been done *to* them for years, and they liked the idea because now they had the chance to do it for themselves' (quoted both in Adler, 1993a, p. 106, and in Boje and Winsor, 1993, p. 62).
- *It ignores gender*. Braverman's concept of skill ignores gender dimensions. Acting as a social group, men have in the past socially constructed their notion of skill to benefit themselves and to disadvantage women. Research by Suchman (1996) in a law firm employing lawyers (mainly men) and support staff (female) illustrated this. The use of image-processing technology called 'litigation support' required skilled coding and retrieval of documents by the women. The males described this work as 'mindless labour' which could be automated, thereby rendering this form of knowledge work invisible by their gendered definition of skill.
- *It overlooks skill transfer possibilities*. Deskilling in one area may be balanced by upskilling in another. The 'areas' may be different national economies, different jobs within the same plant, or perhaps even different aspects of one person's job. Observers of Japanese just-in-time (JIT) production systems note that one facet of a production worker's job can be upskilled (e.g. when they participate as a group in a job's design), while another aspect of it can be deskilled (e.g. when they have to perform the job that they themselves have 'Taylorized' (Conti and Warner, 1993)).

STOP AND THINK

The obvious way to resolve the deskilling debate is to ask individual employees whether they think that their job now possesses a higher or lower level of skill requirement and responsibility compared to five years ago. Alternatively, if they have a new job, ask whether that requires more skill to perform it than their previous job. Why is this approach unlikely to provide a reliable answer?

The upskilling position

Mike Noon and Paul Blyton (2007) provide a clear exposition of the deskilling/upskilling debate, and this section draws heavily upon their explanatory structure. They argue that deskilling theory has failed to provide a satisfactory explanation of the diverse empirical evidence obtained by researchers. Instead, these authors offer an exploratory framework, and we shall see how they reached their conclusion. These authors traced the genesis of the upskilling position back to the 1960s with the economics of human capital theory (Becker, 1964; Fuchs, 1968). The theory held that 'human capital' (i.e. employees) was more important than physical assets such as machinery or buildings in accumulating profits. Companies, it was claimed, would invest in their workforce through the provision of education and training, to help them cope with the greater complexity of work tasks. The upskilling position holds that the general tendency to greater technical sophistication of work requires higher levels of skill among employees, with flexible specialization being one such trend.

This original view has now been developed and expanded by both popular business writers and academic writers. It has been incorporated into what Warhurst and Thompson (1998, p. 3) describe as 'claims of an emerging knowledge economy . . . third waves, information societies and computopia'. Upskilling is now most commonly discussed in terms of whether or not there is a growth in 'knowledge workers'. Proponents of the upskilling thesis draw upon the features of the post-industrialist economy (Bell, 1999) to support their claims that

- success depends more on 'brains than brawn' (Barley, 1996);
- the information age has replaced the machine age (Hamel and Prahalad, 1996);
- locating vital information and using it to help understand what is happening in a turbulent environment has become a major determinant of organizational success (Quah, 1997);
- providing services is more important than making tangible products;
- a small group of core workers with steady jobs and fixed salaries will be outnumbered by a growing number of 'portfolio workers' offering their skills to clients (Handy, 1984);
- the work of symbolic analysts who trade and manipulate symbols is too complex, domain-specific, and esoteric to be capable of being controlled by management (Reich, 1993).

Writers have highlighted the steep rise in recent years of intangible but talent-intensive assets (Wooldridge, 2006). These include everything from a skilled workforce to patents to know-how. It is claimed that these now account for half the market capitalization of America's public companies. Accenture, a management consultancy, has estimated that the value of the intangible assets of leading companies has risen from 20 per cent to 70 per cent of their assets in the 1980–2007 period. McKinsey, another management consultancy, divided American jobs into three classes: *transformational* jobs (extracting raw materials or converting them into finished products); *transactional* jobs (interactions that can be easily scripted or automated); and *tacit* jobs (complex interactions requiring a high level of judgement). In the 2000–2006 period, it estimated, tacit knowledge jobs had grown two and a half times as fast as employment in general. They constituted 40 per cent of the American labour market in 2006, accounting for 70 per cent of all jobs created there since 1998. It is expected that this trend will affect other countries too. Noon and Blyton (2007, pp. 164–7) listed five criticisms of the upskilling thesis, saying that it

- falsely assumes that the growth of the service sector will create skilled jobs;
- overstates the extent to which advanced technology requires higher-level skills from employees;
- overstates the extent of change;
- oversimplifies the skill-enhancing impact of new working methods;
- needs to be put into a global perspective.

What is needed is a conceptual framework to analyse and then map the actual cases of job design. Noon and Blyton (2007, pp. 172–3) offer just such a conceptual framework that is capable of being developed into an analytical tool. These authors conceptualize the work performed by employees as varying along two dimensions – *range of work* and *discretion in work*. These are shown in Figure 14.3.

The vertical *range of work* dimension distinguishes at one extreme those workers who repeatedly perform a single task, for example, factory workers attaching a wheel on a car

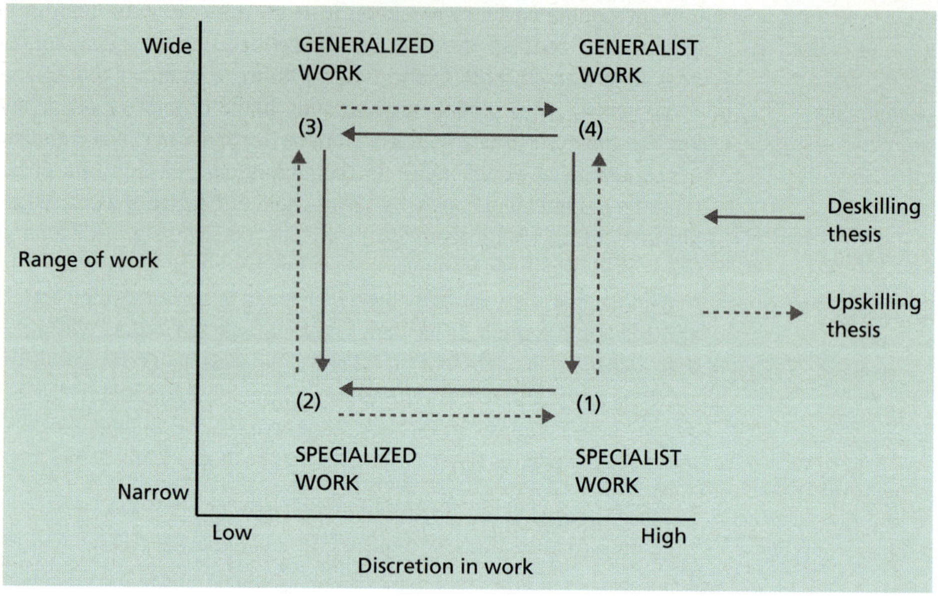

Figure 14.3: Work categorization framework and trends in skill change
Source: From Noon and Blyton, 2007, p. 173.

on an assembly line. Their work range would be narrow. At the other end of this dimension, there might be a shop assistant serving staff, re-stocking shelves, stocktaking, and changing window displays. Since she performed many different tasks, her range of work would be wide.

Specialist work – playing three-dimensional chess

Action Press/Rex Features

German Air Traffic Control's (Deutsche Flugsicherung GmbH's) four centres direct over three million flights each year within Germany's airspace. One of these is at Langen, south of Frankfurt. The staff there work in a large, windowless room, a 1,700-square-metre space, with over 100 workstations. Its walls are covered in soundproof panels at a temperature of 22.2 degrees Celsius. They are seated in large chairs with headsets, in front of long consoles equipped with computer monitors, display screens, switches, buttons, and microphones. Their eyes are fixed on small yellow squares set against a black background; each has its own letter and number. These indicate the position of each aircraft, its call number, height, sink and climb rates, and velocity. The data constantly change as the coordinates change. The job is complicated. Although there are airways and pre-defined routes in the sky, in order to manage the airspace according to traffic volume, the controllers have to improvise. At peak times, up to 600 aircraft are in German airspace. Each needs to be guided safely, precisely, and as fast as possible to its destination. It is like playing chess in three dimensions. Each staff member has to think several steps ahead. The work is exceptionally strenuous, requiring extreme concentration and precision; and errors are not acceptable. Ulrike Münzer, a long-serving controller, says that you have to keep calm in stressful situations, react quickly, and be able to process all kinds of information simultaneously. Such skills tend to deteriorate with the ticking of the biological clock. Each controller is only allowed to work two consecutive hours, after which they are required to take a prescribed half-hour break. The job is so hard on the nerves that controllers are sent on compulsory regeneration courses every four years. None of the controllers is over 55 (based on Bielefeld, 2009).

The horizontal *discretion over work* dimension distinguishes at one extreme those workers who, because of the specificity with which their work is defined, have little or no discretion as to how to perform it. For example, our assembly line operator who attaches a wheel on a car will follow a detailed, written specification of how they should perform their job. Their work discretion would be labelled low. At the other end of this dimension would be a person who had high discretion as to how to perform their work, for example, a potter, a plumber, or a doctor. Noon and Blyton's framework distinguishes four classes or types of jobs that they label as follows:

1. Specialist work: high discretion over a narrow range of work.
2. Specialized work: a narrow range of prescribed tasks.
3. Generalized work: a wide range of prescribed tasks.
4. Generalist work: high discretion over a wide range of tasks.

STOP AND THINK

Consider an organization with which you are familiar – e.g. a school, university, church, or current employer. Give one example each of *specialist*, *specialized*, *generalized*, and *generalist* work. What effect did each have on your satisfaction and motivation?

The framework can be used both to trace trends in skill changes and to compare different work organization initiatives described in empirical case studies. Noon and Blyton depict the deskilling trend with the solid arrows from high to low on the range of work dimension, and from high to low control on the discretion over work dimension. Its most extreme position labelled is (1) specialist work. The upskilling trend is shown with dotted arrows in the opposite direction with its extreme position labelled as (4) generalist work. Instead of looking for any general trends, Noon and Blyton allow any group, workplace, industry, or industrial sector to be located on their work categorization map.

Back to the future?

Instrumental orientation an attitude that sees work as an instrument to the fulfilment of other life goals.

Introjection a formerly external regulation or value that has been 'taken in' and is now enforced through internal pressures such as guilt, anxiety, or related self-esteem dynamics.

Identification the incorporation of another's thoughts, feelings, and actions into one's self-esteem, thereby transforming oneself.

Just how alienating and demotivating is Taylorism? Paul Adler (1999) offers an interesting counter-argument to this established view, claiming that Taylorism actually represents a fundamental emancipatory philosophy of job design. He reports that at the New United Motors Manufacturing, Inc. (NUMMI) auto plant in Fremont, California, which uses a classical Taylorist approach, workers show relatively high levels of motivation and job commitment (Adler, 1993a, 1993b). How can this be? Adler's argument is that his research findings reveal two fundamental flaws in the standard view that is based on two psychological assumptions. These are first, that work is only truly motivating to the extent that it resembles free play; and second, that workers have to have autonomy.

Adler states that the standard critique of Taylorism just presents motivation through extrinsic and intrinsic rewards as polar opposites, and holds that since Taylorized work lacks the potential for *intrinsic rewards*, it only leaves employees the possibility of obtaining *extrinsic rewards*. (We met these concepts in Chapter 9.) In so doing, it develops in them an **instrumental orientation** to work.

Adler draws upon the work of Richard Ryan and James Connell (1989) to argue that between the extrinsic and intrinsic polarities, there are two other, intermediate positions – **introjection** and **identification**. These are presented in Table 14.2.

Adler argues that job design at NUMMI taps into the identification motivation base. This focuses upon the internalization of company values and goals, and the means by which these are absorbed and adopted. Instead of motivating through 'free play', NUMMI employees are motivated through

Table 14.2: Four bases of motivation

Extrinsic rewards	Introjection	Identification	Intrinsic rewards
• Following rules • Avoidance of punishment	• Self- and other-approval • Avoidance of disapproval	• Self-valued goal • Personal importance	• Enjoyment • Fun
• Because I'll get into trouble if I don't • Because that's what I'm supposed to do • So the teacher won't yell at me • Because that's the rule	• Because I want the teacher to think I'm a good student • Because I'll feel bad about myself if I don't • Because I'll feel ashamed of myself if I don't • Because I want other students to think I'm smart • Because it bothers me when I don't • Because I want people to like me	• Because I want to understand the subject • Because I want to learn new things • To find out if I'm right or wrong • Because I think it's important to • Because I wouldn't want to do that (negative behaviour)	• Because it's fun • Because I enjoy it

From Adler (1999), p. 9.

- the desire for excellence, the instinct of craftsmanship, and a job well done;
- their 'psychological maturity' which recognizes the reality of the competitive situation – that they have to compete on quality and productivity with other autoworkers around the world;
- respect and trust shown to them by management that elicits reciprocal commitment.

Adler then considers the autonomy issue at the individual and team levels. Critics of Taylorism hold that the choice over work methods and pace of work is crucial for sustaining high levels of motivation and involvement. Adler argues that his research suggests it is not as important as is claimed. NUMMI's use of the Japanese form of teamworking offered little in the way of team autonomy. The teams were organized by engineers, managers, and workers; they were tightly coupled with other teams, both upstream and downstream, through just-in-time kanban systems, and with teams on other shifts. Yet workers endorsed such interdependence (low autonomy) as an effective way of managing. Adler (1999, p. 12) quotes one worker:

> The work teams at NUMMI aren't like the autonomous teams, you read about in other plants. Here we're not autonomous, because we're all tied together really tightly. But it's not like we're getting squeezed to work harder, because it's us, the workers, that are making the whole thing work – we're the ones that make the standardized work and the kaizen suggestions. We run the plant – and if it's not running right, we stop it.

Concertive control control exercised by the workers themselves who collaborate to develop the means of their own control by negotiating a consensus which shapes their own behaviour according to a set of core values such as those of the corporate vision statement.

Adler argues that when workers establish a feeling of organization-wide responsibility for the effectiveness of their work, and they come to perceive their Taylorized jobs as an effective way of accomplishing the necessary interdependent tasks, then low individual and team autonomy can coexist with high morale.

One would expect that, in contrast to traditional, hierarchically oriented, Taylorist or Fordist supervision, employees working as an autonomous or self-managing team would be less strictly supervised. James Barker (1993) found that this was often not the case. He and Tompkins and Cheney (1985) discussed the concept of **concertive control**, which is exerted not by management, but by the workers themselves. It represents a shift from overt and direct management control to a covert form of worker discipline, which is achieved by securing workers' involvement and engagement in, as well as their commitment to, their organization.

Through the discipline exerted by their team, members collaborate and develop a way to control each other. Barker labels this 'soft domination' because of the subtlety of the techniques involved. Rick Iedema and Carl Rhodes (2011) explained that such teamwork control depended on a combination of performance management techniques (staff appraisal systems) and organization culture programmes. In this way, the external values of the company become internalized within the employee, and managerial control became social control through the group. The team achieves first accommodation, then assimilation, then identification, and finally internalization. The process is described by Barker:

1. Group members have discussions, and develop a consensus over values, based on their company's 'vision statement' e.g. 'We are a principled organization that values teamwork' (Barker, 1999, p. 183).
2. This value consensus is then translated into group rules or norms of behaviour based on the agreed vision statement. Team members agree that being principled involves each one arriving at work on time, and ensuring that all the others do as well. Authority over the individual thus transfers from the company hierarchy and its formal rules, down to the team, with its socially created, informal rules.
3. Guidelines on how members are to behave are then specified (to provide a sense of stability and predictability for members).
4. These devised norms, rules, and guidelines are easily understood by new group members, who subject themselves to them.

Chimerial control a combination of management pressure exercised vertically on the individual through bureaucracy, technology, surveillance, and the manipulation of culture; and team pressure exercised horizontally through the group norms and sanctions.

What is most interesting is that, as Barker (1993, p. 433) notes, 'The teams were said to be their own masters and their own slaves'. The teams ended up doing management's work for them by dealing with their uncommitted workers by making them 'feel unworthy as a team mate' (Barker, 1993, p. 436). Iedema and Rhodes (2011) concur, stating that workers in modern organizations have been led to help management to accomplish its control over them.

When members are simultaneously exposed to the vertical pressure of management through its bureaucracy, technology, surveillance and manipulation of culture; together with horizontal pressure through the team structure, they are said to experience **chimerial control** – named after the beast of Greek mythology. From his research, Benders (2005) noted that employees tended to experience teamwork as a mixed blessing. On the one hand, they welcomed the increased freedom that it provided them with, but on the other, they expressed concerns about work intensification.

STOP AND THINK

Is concertive control a totally new form of control over employees, or does it represent a modification and updating of traditional Taylorist and Fordist ideas?

RECAP

1. *Understand how scientific management met the needs of its historical context.*
   - At the start of the twentieth century, European emigration to the United States and internal migration from rural to urban areas produced a large workforce with poor English-language skills which lacked work discipline.
   - The same period saw the establishment of large corporations, and the development of technology that permitted, for the first time, the mass manufacture of products. These factories required a large workforce.
2. *Describe the main objectives and principles of the scientific management approach.*
   - The objectives are efficiency, by increasing the output per worker and reducing deliberate 'underworking'; predictability of job performance – standardizing tasks by dividing them up into small and closely specified sub-tasks; and control by establishing discipline through hierarchical authority and introducing a system whereby all management's policy decisions can be implemented.
   - The principles are: a clear division of tasks and responsibilities between management and workers;

→

use of scientific methods to determine the best way of doing a job; scientific selection of employees; the training of the selected worker to perform the job in the way specified; and the surveillance of workers through the use of hierarchies of authority and close supervision.

3. ***Enumerate the contributions of the Gilbreths and Gantt to scientific management.***
   - Frank Gilbreth's contributions were micromotion study, the chronocyclegraph, and the 'therbligs' notation system. Lillian Gilbreth contributed fatigue study based on physiological and psychological principles.
   - Laurence Gantt supplied the 'best-known-way-at-present' approach to job design; the task-and-bonus payment scheme; and the 'Gantt chart'.
4. ***Understand how Fordism developed out of Taylorism.***
   - Ford developed the analysis of jobs; installed single-purpose machine tools to produce standardized parts; and established the mechanically paced assembly line.
   - The twin concepts of system and control underpinned his approach.
5. ***Understand the deskilling debate, and the contributions of Braverman and Ritzer.***
   - The 'Braverman thesis' holds that there is a long-run tendency for workers and their jobs to become deskilled through fragmentation, rationalization, and mechanization.
   - Some argue for the deskilling thesis, while others reject it claiming that technological developments have upskilled both workers and jobs and created new, high-skill industries.
   - The deskilling debate is often discussed in the context of Ritzer's McDonaldization process, which refers to an approach to work design based on efficiency, calculability, predictability, and control.
6. ***Provide examples of scientific management in contemporary society.***
   - Apart from fast food outlets, the process of credit-granting; semesterization and modularization of university courses; TV programmes; food packaging.

Revision

1. Taylorism has been much criticized. What are the criticisms? Which criticisms do you feel are valid and which are not? Give reasons for your assessment.
2. Have quality and flexibility requirements in modern organizations rendered Fordism redundant?
3. To what extent are performance-based pay, just-in-time inventory (stock) control, and business process re-engineering just modern-day applications of Frederick Taylor's scientific management?
4. Identify non-food examples of the McDonaldization process. Analyse them in terms of Ritzer's four key elements.

Research assignment

Visit a local fast food restaurant that uses a Taylorist/Fordist form of work organization. Observe and make notes on the behaviour of its employees ('crew members'), both those at the counter and those in the kitchen. Arrange to talk to one or two crew members – perhaps you already know someone who currently works there, or has done so in the past. Ask them about the best and worst aspects of that job. Relate their answers to the theories and research findings discussed in this chapter. Are the criticisms of McDonald's and similar organizations unfair?

Springboard

Cameron Allan, Greg Bamber and Nils Timo (2006) 'Fast-food work: are McJobs satisfying?', *Employee Relations*, 28(5), pp. 402–20. McJobs in the fast food industry are a major source of youth employment. This paper explores young people's perceptions of this industry.

Bob Carter, Andy Danford, Debra Howcroft, Helen Richardson, Andrew Smith and Phil Taylor (2011) 'All they lack is a chain: lean and the new performance management in the British civil service', *New Technology, Work and Employment*, 26(2), pp. 83–97. The authors consider the application of Taylorist and Fordist ideas in an office environment.

Anthony Gould (2010) 'Working at McDonald's: some redeeming features of McJobs', *Work, Employment and Society*, 24(4), pp. 780–802. Reviews the previous research on McJobs and provides empirical data to reconsider the positive and negative aspects of fast food jobs.

Edwin Locke (1982) 'The ideas of Frederick W. Taylor: an evaluation', *Academy of Management Review*, 7(1), pp. 14–24. This article reviews the application of scientific management ideas over the last hundred years.

OB in films

The Rebel (1961, director Robert Day), DVD track 2: 0:05:00 to 0:11:30 (7 minutes). In this film, the comedian Tony Hancock plays himself, as a London office worker who finds the routine of his job oppressive. The clip begins with a shot of the office, and ends with the manager saying to Tony 'Off you go'. As you watch this clip:

1. Identify the design principles underlying the office jobs that Tony and his (all male) colleagues are performing at United International.

2. Complete this matrix, indicating the advantages and disadvantages, to management and to employees, of designing jobs in this way:

	advantages	**disadvantages**
for management		
for employees		

3. Tony's manager diagnoses his problem and suggests some solutions. How appropriate do you think his suggestions are?

4. Is this movie out of date, because management practice and office technology have changed since the 1960s? Or can you identify jobs that you have personally had, or which you have recently observed, that are designed in the same way? What would be – or what has been – your reaction to work like this?

OB on the web

Search YouTube for 'Model T – 1936 Henry Ford Assembly Line' and '2013 Ford Focus Electric Michigan Assembly Plant' and compare the two video sequences. Both show the same type of manufacturing. Identify the differences and similarities. What changes have occurred in assembly line car production in the intervening years, and what has remained the same?

CHAPTER EXERCISES

1. The call centre experience

Objectives

1. To distinguish different forms of control within an organizational context.
2. To explain the reasons for the popularity of call centre companies.
3. To identify the problems experienced by call centre employees and how they might be addressed.

Briefing

1. Individually consider
   (a) What is meant by the term *control* within an organizational context?
   (b) In what different ways does the company that you work for control your behaviour on the job?
2. Form into groups and discuss the following questions:
   (a) What benefits do companies gain from running their call centres?
   (b) What problems does the way that work is organized in a call centre create for its employees?
   (c) How would you improve the quality of working life of call centre employees?

2. Redesigning the workplace

Objectives

1. Identify aspects of Taylorist and Fordist work organization.
2. Redesign work arrangements to improve productivity and increase employee job satisfaction.

Briefing

1. Form groups. Read the case *Bacon processing line*.
2. Which principles and practices of Taylorist and Fordist forms of work organization can you identify in the current work arrangements?
3. Management consultants have reported that these arrangements are not very efficient. It has proved impossible to balance the line effectively so that staff at each workstation are fully occupied and each machine is fully utilized. How might this process and the jobs associated with it be more effectively designed to (a) maximize output and (b) benefit the employees?

Bacon processing line

Imagine a factory in which sides of bacon (weighing about 20 kg) are cut into slices and vacuum-packed into pack sizes ranging from 500 grams to 3 kg. The small sizes are sold to supermarkets for domestic purchases and the larger packs are sold directly to hotel and catering outlets for commercial use. The bacon curing process leaves the meat wet and slippery and it has to be kept at a low temperature in order to preserve it. In practice before a side of bacon is sliced by the machine it has to be frozen in order to make it cut easily and retain its shape during the packing process. This makes the working conditions cold, damp, and unpleasant to work in. The overall process involves the slicing and packaging of bacon, and includes the following jobs and activities:

- A frozen side of bacon needs to be fed into a machine which then cuts it into slices.
- The slices need to be separated and stacked in pack quantity on a moving conveyor belt.
- The individual stacks of bacon need to be placed into a packing machine.
- The packing machine needs to be set up for the type of pack to be produced and needs to be, monitored during the packing process.
- The packed bacon needs to be weighed, priced, and labelled.
- The packs need to be checked for presentation, label accuracy, and quality.
- Individual packs of bacon need to be put into cardboard boxes ready for cold storage and despatch to customers.
- The cardboard boxes need to be labelled with the contents and customer details.
- The cardboard boxes need to be stacked onto wooden pallets and moved to the cold store for despatch to customers.

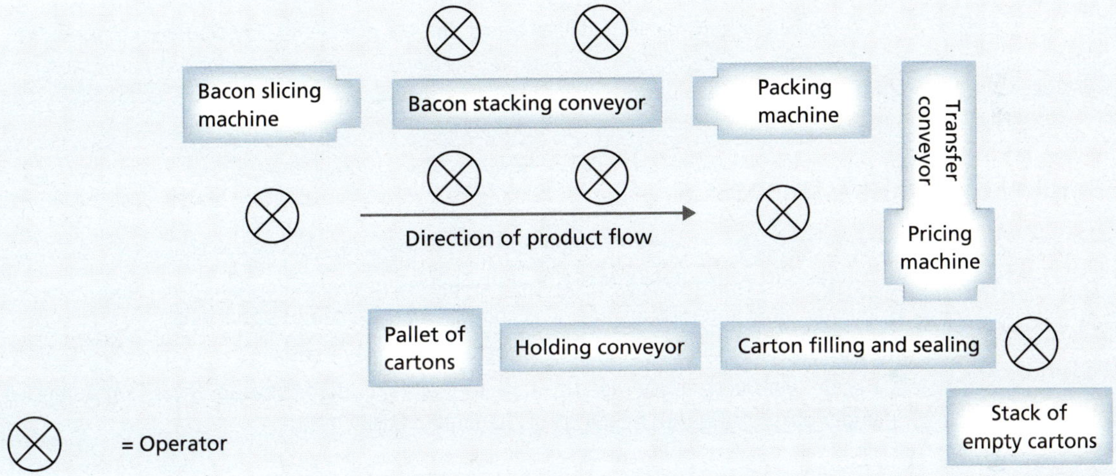

The layout diagram represents the machine layout and people workstations identified using a work-study-based job simplification exercise. The simplified tasks in this job involved:

Slicing — One person is responsible for obtaining the bacon, setting and cleaning the slicing machine, and pacing the slicing processes to keep the other workstations fully utilized. This operator could wear gloves to keep their hands warm when picking up the frozen sides of bacon and feeding them into the machine.

Stacking — Four people working on either side of a conveyor belt splitting the cut bacon into stacks of the right quantity as it passes them by. The conveyor belt speed and rate of slicing sets the pace the work for these operators. This operation was rather like separating out a specific number of pages from a sheaf of papers. It required dexterity and the ability to use the fingers and fingernails to separate out the correct number of frozen slices of bacon. It was difficult to do this wearing gloves and so the work was very cold and not the most pleasant of tasks.

Packing — One person responsible for setting the machine, placing individual stacks of bacon into it and generally ensuring a smooth operation. They would also monitor the quality of the packed product.

Pricing and boxing	One person is responsible for setting the automatic weighing and pricing machine, boxing the packs of bacon, sealing and labelling the boxes, and stacking the cartons on a pallet ready for transport to the cold store. This person would also monitor pack quality, rejecting faulty packs and stopping the line to reset the machine if necessary.
Transport	Someone else would remove loaded pallets and bring empty ones as part of a similar job for other packing stations.

In addition to these direct production activities there would be a need to keep records of output and quality. Also the group would need to ensure that the whole process worked smoothly with individuals working as a team. Using work measurement techniques the number of operators (and tasks) needed at each workstation illustrated in the diagram would be determined in order to produce the highest possible levels of output. In this case it is suggested in the diagram that a balanced line contains eight people (including one shared with other lines). However, it could be that the slicer operator is only working for 50 per cent of the time. Under these circumstances it would be common to recalculate the line speeds or design the jobs to keep worker utilization as high as possible.

Source: from Organizational Behaviour and Management, *3rd ed., Martin, J., Copyright 2005 Thomson. Reproduced by permission of Cengage Learning EMEA Ltd.*

Employability assessment

With regard to your future employment prospects:

1. Identify up to three issues from this chapter that you found significant.
2. Relate these to the competencies in the employability matrix.
3. Decide what actions you need to take to maintain and/or develop those competencies under each of the four headings of the employability matrix.

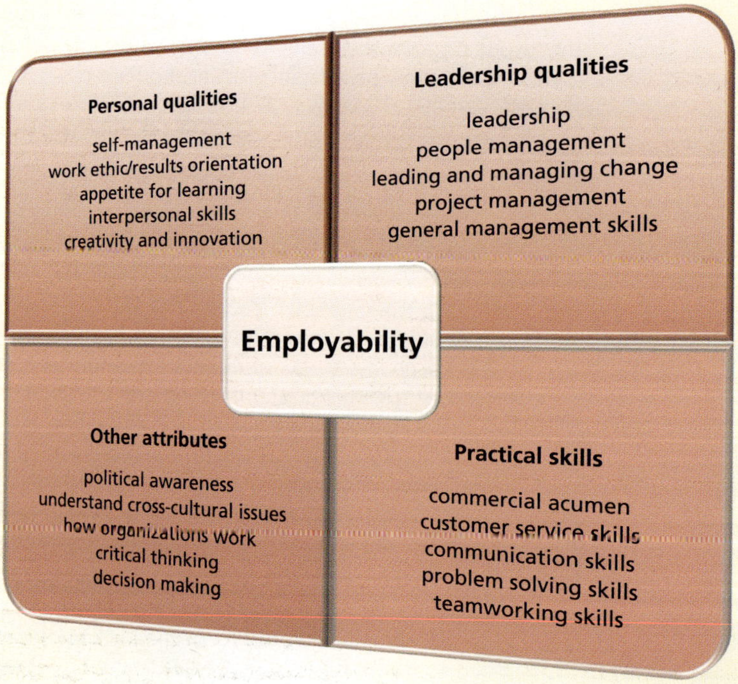

References

Ackroyd, S. and Thompson, P. (1999) *Organizational Misbehaviour*, London: Sage Publications.

Adler, P.S. (1993a) 'Time-and-motion regained', *Harvard Business Review*, 71(1), pp. 97–108.

Adler, P.S. (1993b) 'The learning bureaucracy: New United Motors Manufacturing, Inc.', in B.M. Staw and L.L. Cummings (eds), *Research in Organizational Behaviour*, Greenwich, CT: JAI Press, pp. 111–94.

Adler, P.S. (1999) 'The emancipatory significance of Taylorism', in M.P.E. Cunha and C.A. Marques (eds), *Readings in Organization Science – Organizational Change in a Changing Context*, Lisbon: Instituto Superior de Psicologia Aplicada, pp. 7–14.

Allmendinger, J., Hackman, R. and Lehman, E.V. (1994) *Life and Work in Symphony Orchestras: An Interim Report of Research Findings, Report No. 7, Cross-National Study of Symphony Orchestras*, Cambridge, MA: Harvard University.

Barker, J.R. (1993) 'Tightening the iron cage: concertive control in self-managing teams', *Administrative Science Quarterly*, 38(3), pp. 408–37.

Barker, J.R. (1999) *The Discipline of Teamwork*, London: Sage Publications.

Barley, S. (1996) *The New World of Work*, London: British-North American Committee.

Becker, G. (1964) *Human Capital*, New York: National Bureau of Economic Research.

Bell, D. (1999) *The Coming of Post-Industrial Society* (reprint of 1976 edn), New York: Basic Books.

Benders, J. (2005) 'Team working: a tale of partial participation', in B. Harley, J. Hyman and P. Thompson (eds), *Participation and Democracy at Work: Essays in Honour of Harvie Ramsey*, London: Palgrave Macmillan, pp. 55–74.

Bielefeld, M. (2009) 'Regisseure der Lüfte', *Lufthansa Magazin*, April, pp. 30–3.

Boddy, D. (2011) *Management: An Introduction* (5th edn), Harlow, Essex: Financial Times Prentice Hall.

Boje, D.M. and Winsor, R.D. (1993) 'The resurrection of Taylorism: total quality management's hidden agenda', *Journal of Organizational Change Management*, 6(4), pp. 57–70.

Braverman, H. (1974) *Labor and Monopoly Capital: The Degradation of Work in the Twentieth Century*, New York: Monthly Review Press.

Bryman, A. (2011) 'McDonaldization', in M. Tadajewski, P. Maclaran, E. Parsons and M. Parker (eds), *Key Concepts in Critical Management Studies*, London: Sage, pp. 169–73.

Buchanan, D.A. and Boddy, D. (1983) *Organizations in the Computer Age: Technological Imperatives and Strategic Change*, Aldershot: Gower.

Burawoy, M. (1979) *Manufacturing Consent*, Chicago, IL: University of Chicago Press.

Carter, B., Danford, A., Howcroft, D., Richardson, H., Smith, A. and Taylor, P. (2011) '"All they lack is a chain": lean and the new performance management in the British civil service', *New Technology, Work and Employment*, 26(2), pp. 83–97.

Chazon, D. (2009) 'Paris artists vie with false imports', BBC Online News website, 22 January.

Child, J. (1985) 'Managerial strategies, new technology and the labour process', in D. Knights, H. Willmott and D. Collinson (eds), *Job Redesign*, Aldershot: Gower, pp. 107–41.

Collier, P. and Horowitz, D. (1987) *The Fords: An American Epic*, London: Futura Collins.

Conti, R.E. and Warner, M. (1993) 'Taylorism, new technology and just-in-time systems in Japanese manufacturing', *New Technology, Work and Employment*, 8(1), pp. 31–42.

Durand, J.P. and Hatzfeld, N. (2003) *Living Labour: Life on the Line at Peugeot France*, Basingstoke: Palgrave Macmillan.

Edwards, D. (2011) *I'm Feeling Lucky: The Confessions of Google Employee Number 59*, London: Allen Lane.

Ellis, V. and Taylor, M. (2006) 'You don't know what you've got till it's gone: recontextualizing the origins, development and impact of call centres', *New Technology, Work and Employment*, 21(2), pp. 107–22.

Ellis, V. and Taylor, M. (2010) 'Banks, bailouts and bonuses: a personal account of work in Halifax Bank of Scotland during the financial crisis', *Work, Employment and Society*, 24(4), pp. 803–12.

Etzioni, A. (1986) 'The Fast-food factories: McJobs are bad for kids', *Washington Post*, 24 August.

Fincham, R. and Rhodes, P.S. (2005) *The Individual, Work and Organization* (4th edn), Oxford: Oxford University Press.

Ford, H. (with Crowther, S.) (1924) *My Life and Work*, London: William Heinemann.

Fuchs, V. (1968) *The Service Economy*, New York: Basic Books.

Fulmer, R.M. and Herbert, T.T. (1974) *Exploring the New Management*, New York: Macmillan.

Gantt, H. (1919) *Organizing for Work* New York: Harcourt, Brace and Hove.

Gartman, D. (1979) 'Origins of the assembly line and capitalist control of work at Ford', in A.S. Zimbalist (ed.), *Case Studies on the Labour Process*, London: Monthly Review Press, pp. 193–205.

Gilbreth, F.B. (1911) *Motion Study*, New York: Van Nostrand.

Gilbreth, F.B. and Gilbreth, L. (1916) *Fatigue Study*, New York: Sturgis and Walton.

Gill, C. (1985) *Work, Unemployment and the New Technology*, Cambridge: Polity Press.

Gould, A.M. (2010) 'Working at McDonald's: some redeeming features of McJobs', *Work, Employment and Society*, 24(4), pp. 780–802.

Grey, C. (2009) *A Very Short, Fairly Interesting and Reasonably Cheap Book about Studying Organizations* (2nd edn), London: Sage.

Hamel, G. and Prahalad, C.K. (1996) 'Competing in the new economy: managing out of bounds', *Strategic Management Journal*, 17(3), pp. 237–42.

Handy, C. (1984) *The Future of Work*, Oxford: Blackwell.

Iedema, R. and Rhodes, C. (2011) 'Surveillance', in M. Tadajewski, P. Maclaran, E. Parsons and M. Parker (eds), *Key Concepts in Critical Management Studies*, London: Sage, pp. 214–18.

Kanigel, R. (1997) *The One Best Way: Frederick Winslow Taylor and the Enigma of Efficiency*, London: Little, Brown.

Levine, S. and Levine, R. (1996) 'Why they are not smiling: stress and discontent in the orchestral workplace', *Harmony*, 2 (April), pp. 15–25.

Littler, C.R. (1982) *The Development of the Labour Process in Capitalist Societies*, London: Heinemann.

Littler, C. and Salaman, G. (1982) 'Bravermania and beyond: recent theories and labour process', *Sociology*, 16(2), pp. 251–69.

Noon, M. and Blyton, P. (2007) *The Realities of Work* (3rd edn), Basingstoke: Palgrave.

Pardi, T. (2007) 'Redefining the Toyota Production System: the European side of the story', *New Technology, Work and Employment*, 22(1), pp. 2–20.

Parker, M. and Slaughter, J. (1988) 'Management by stress', *Technology Review*, 91(7), pp. 36–44.

Pollard, H.R. (1974) *Developments in Management Thought*, London: Heinemann.

Quah, D.T. (1997) 'Weightless economy packs a heavy punch', *Independent on Sunday*, 18 May, p. 4.

Ray, C.A. (1986) 'Corporate culture: the last frontier of control?', *Journal of Management Studies*, 23(3), pp. 287–97.

Reich, R. (1993) *The Work of Nations*. London: Simon and Schuster.

Ritzer, G. (ed.) (2010) *McDonaldization: The Reader* (3rd edn), Thousand Oaks, CA: Pine Forge Press.

Ritzer, G. (2011) *The McDonaldization of Society: An Investigation into the Changing Character of Contemporary Social Life* (6th edn), Thousand Oaks, CA: Pine Forge Press.

Russell, B. (2009) *Smiling Down the Line: Info-Service Work in the New Economy*, Toronto: University of Toronto Press.

Ryan, R.M. and Connell, J.P. (1989) 'Perceived locus of causality and internalization', *Journal of Personality and Social Psychology*, 57(5), pp. 749–61.

Sennett, R. (2008) *The Craftsman*, New Haven, CT: Yale University Press.

Sewell, G., Barker, J.R. and Nyberg, D. (2012) 'Working under intensive surveillance: when does "measuring everything that moves" become intolerable?', *Human Relations*, 65(2), pp. 189–215.

Stewart, P., Richardson, A., Danford, A., Murphy, K., Richardson, T. and Wass, V. (2009) *We Sell Our Time No More: Workers' Struggles against Lean Production in the British Car Industry*, London: Pluto Press.

Suchman, L. (1996) 'Supporting articulation work', in Kling, R. (ed.), *Computerization and Controversy* (2nd edn), San Diego, CA: Academic Press, pp. 407–23.

Taylor, F.W. (1911) *The Principles of Scientific Management*, New York: Harper.

Taylor, P. and Bain, P. (2007) 'Reflections on call centres: a reply to Gluckmann', *Work, Employment and Society*, 21(2), pp. 349–62.

Taylor, P., Hyman, J., Mulvey, G. and Bain, P. (2002) 'Work organization, control and experience of work in call centres', *Work, Employment and Society*, 16(1), pp. 133–50.

The Economist (2010) Advertisement: 'Your Toyota is My Toyota', 29 May, p. 43.

The Economist (2012) 'Faster, faster, faster', 28 January, p. 59.

Tompkins, P.K. and Cheney, G. (1985) 'Communication and unobtrusive control in contemporary organizations', in R.D. McPhee and P.K. Tompkins (eds), *Organizational Communication: Traditional Themes and New Directions*, Beverley Hills, CA: Sage Publications.

Warhurst, C. and Thompson, P. (1998) 'Hands, hearts and minds: changing work and workers at the end of the century', in P. Thompson and C. Warhurst (eds), *Workplaces of the Future*, London: Macmillan Business, pp. 1–24.

Watts, S. (2001) *The Magic Kingdom: Walt Disney and the American Way of Life*, Boston: MA: Houghton Mifflin.

Wilson, F. (2004) *Organizational Behaviour and Work: A Critical Introduction* (2nd edn), Oxford: Oxford University Press.

Womack, J.P., Jones, D.T. and Roos, D. (1990) *The Machine that Changed the World: The Triumph of Lean Production*, New York: Macmillan.

Wooldridge, A. (2006) 'The battle for brainpower', *The Economist*, Survey of Talent Supplement, pp. 3, 4 and 6.

Zimbalist, A.S. (1979) *Case Studies on the Labour Process*, London: Monthly Review Press.

Chapter 15 Elements of structure

Key terms

organization structure
delegation
work specialization
job definition
job description
organization chart
hierarchy
span of control
line employees
staff employees
authority
responsibility
accountability
line relationship
chain of command
staff relationship
functional relationship
formal organization
informal organization
sexuality
sex
gender
role
role conflict
rules
formalization
centralization
decentralization

Learning outcomes

When you have read this chapter, you should be able to define those key terms in your own words, and you should also be able to:

1. Explain how organization structure affects human behaviour in organizations.
2. List the main elements of organization structure.
3. Relate the concept of span of control to that of organization hierarchy.
4. Identify line and staff relationships on an organization chart.
5. Distinguish between the formal and the informal organization of a company.
6. Understand the nature of sexuality and its impact on organizational behaviour.

Why study elements of structure?

People's attitudes and behaviour can be shaped as much by the structure of the organization within which they work as by the personalities that they possess and the groups and teams of which they are a part. The constraints and demands of the job, imposed through the roles that they play, can dictate their behaviour and even change their personalities. For this reason, it is impossible to explain the behaviour of people in organizations solely in terms of individual or group characteristics. Jay Lorsch described organization structure as management's formal and explicit attempts to indicate to organizational members what is expected of them. This involved the definition of individual jobs and their expected relationship to each other as indicated in organizational charts and in job descriptions. In his words, 'this was management's attempt to draw a map of whom they want to do what' (Lorsch, 1977, p. 3).

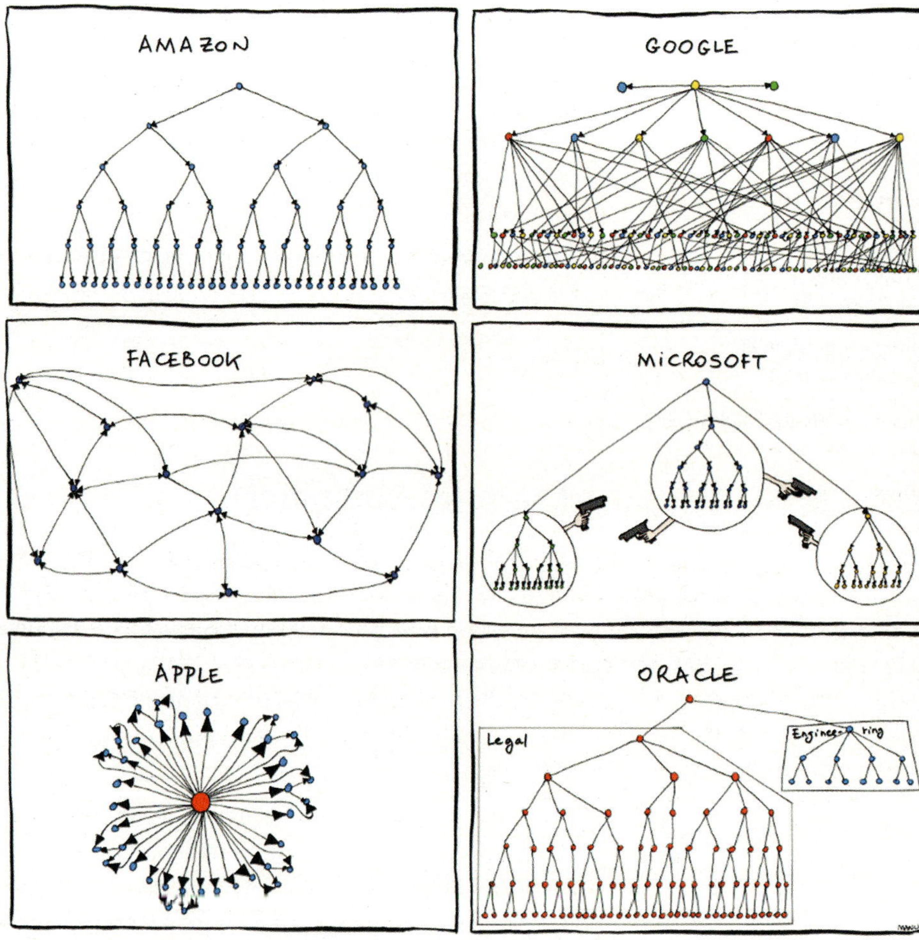

Source: Manu Cornet, www.bonkersworld.net

Alan Fox argued that explanations of human behaviour in organizations must consider structural factors (Fox, 1966). He was critical of those who insisted on explaining behaviour in organizations exclusively in terms of personalities, personal relationships, and leadership. Such explanations were highly appealing to common sense. This was because such variables were clearly visible, while the effects of structure were generally hidden. The structural approach stands in contrast to the psychologistic approach which holds that it is the internal (individual) factors that are the main determinants of human behaviour in organizations.

While corporate strategy specifies the *goals* that a company pursues, organization structure directs the *means* by which these will be achieved. John Child (2005, pp. 17–21) noted that inappropriate structure can obstruct the achievement of organizational goals by causing at least five problems:

1. Motivation and morale can fall if inappropriate delegation and spans of control lead to too little or too much responsibility being given to employees. Ill-defined roles and unclear priorities, work schedules, and performance standards all lead to staff not knowing what is expected of them.
2. Decisions may be of poor quality and will be made slowly if the company has too many hierarchical levels, if decision-makers are separated from each other, and if decision-making is over-centralized.
3. Conflict and lack of coordination – if the structure does not emphasize a single set of company-wide objectives, departmental priorities may take precedence. Conflict results from a failure to coordinate the activities of individuals, teams, and departments whose work is interdependent.
4. Changing circumstances may not be responded to imaginatively if the structure lacks people performing forecasting and planning roles; if it does not give priority to innovation and change; and if there is no top management support or adequate resources.
5. Rising costs may result if there are too many expensive bosses in tall hierarchies with narrow spans of control, and where additional staff are hired to administer excessive rules, procedures, paperwork, and targets.

STOP AND THINK

Consider the behaviour of the instructor teaching this course. Identify aspects of their behaviour that you like and do not like. Decide whether these positive and negative behaviours are influenced by that person's personality or by the organization structure within which they work.

Organizational problem? Structural solution?

Five months before visitors began flooding into the country for the 2012 London Olympics, the British Home Secretary (interior minister) announced the break-up of the UK's Border Agency (UKBA). This organization is responsible for securing the UK border at air, rail, and sea terminals, and also for immigration controls such as issuing visas. Following a scandal in 2011 concerning lapses in border security checks, an investigation was launched into security breaches. The published report placed the blame for the problems on various aspects of the UKBA's structure. Its findings highlighted a lack of clarity between the roles and responsibilities of different employees, and no shared understanding about the conditions under which different security checks could be suspended, and under whose authority. The report found that instructions to staff from senior officials and ministers had been vague, and that rules had been ignored. It catalogued deficiencies which included poor coordination, poor managerial oversight, poor record-keeping, and insufficient communication between policy-makers and policy-implementers.

The restructuring of this organization involved splitting the organization into two – the Border Force and the Border Agency. The former became a separate law-enforcement body headed by a senior police chief, while the latter ran the control operations. However, splitting policy from operations can exacerbate problems. Matt Cavanagh, a former government advisor, argued that big structural reorganizations such as this one are a tactic often used by governments trying to get through a crisis, and they may be successful. However, there are also many examples of ineffective structural reorganizations. Over the last ten years, this particular organization has changed from being the Immigration and Nationality Directorate, to the Borders and Immigration Agency, before becoming the UK Border Agency. During this period, it came to incorporate other agencies, including port staff and parts of Revenue and Customs.

While restructuring may provide each of the newly-separated units with its own tighter focus, clearer objectives, and a more rigorous law enforcement ethos, it can also reinforce the tendency for each one to operate in isolation from the other (this has been dubbed a 'silo' or 'chimney' mentality). The minister stated that the UKBA needed a whole new management culture, and was in 'better hands for the future' as a result of the new structure. However, Cavanagh argued that while structural

→

Travel Images/Alamy

change was easy for ministers to announce and for audiences to grasp, it would not necessarily improve matters. This was particularly the case if the revised structure was populated by the same people with the same incentives. The timing of change was also poor as the implementation of the structural changes coincided with staff gearing up for the operational challenge of the Olympics which involved large increases in passenger numbers and security problems. Rather than a reorganization of the structure, a better solution might have been improvements in management, and better trained and motivated staff (based on Cavanagh, 2012; Warrell, 2012).

Organization structuring

Organization structure the formal system of task and reporting relationships that control, coordinate, and motivate employees to work together to achieve organizational goals.

At the start of this text, organizations were defined as social arrangements for achieving controlled performance in pursuit of collective goals. One aspect of these 'arrangements' is the creation of a structure. The purpose of **organization structure** is, first, to divide up organizational activities and allocate them to sub-units; and second, to coordinate and control these activities so that they achieve the aims of the organization.

Because organization structure is an abstract concept, it is useful to begin by listing the seven things that it is concerned with – the elements of structure. These are shown in Table 15.1. Senior management's decisions regarding each element will have a major

Table 15.1: Elements of organization structure

Element	Concerns
1. Work specialization	Division of work tasks
2. Hierarchy	Levels of management in the organization
3. Span of control	Number of workers supervised by a single manager
4. Chain of command	Reporting relationships
5. Departmentalization	Grouping of jobs
6. Formalization	Extent of rules
7. Centralization	Location of decision-making

Delegation managers granting decision-making authority to employees at lower hierarchical levels.

impact on the employees' work satisfaction and organizational performance, either positively or negatively. A recurring theme running through these decisions is **delegation**, which refers to managers granting decision-making authority to employees at lower hierarchical levels.

1. *Work specialization*: To what degree should work tasks in an organization be subdivided into separate jobs? Should there be high specialization, or should workers do several different jobs (low specialization)? What are the implications for time, cost of training, and employee motivation?
2. *Hierarchy*: Should there be many layers or levels of management (tall hierarchy) or few (flat hierarchy)? What are the implications in terms of communication, employee motivation, and staff costs?
3. *Span of control*: How many subordinates should a single manager or supervisor be responsible for – many (wide span of control) or few (narrow span of control)?
4. *Chain of command*: To whom should a given individual or group report with respect to their work?
5. *Departmentalization*: Should jobs be grouped within departments whose staff share a common expertise (functional departmentalization); or according to the product or service they offer, the geographical area they operate in, the type of customer they serve, or some other basis?
6. *Formalization*: Should written rules, records, and procedures be used to coordinate and control the activities of different individuals and groups (high formalization) or should these be kept to the minimum (low formalization)?
7. *Centralization*: Should decisions be made at the top of the company by senior managers (centralized) or should decision-making be delegated to more junior staff lower in the organizational hierarchy (decentralized)?

Why drug dealers live with their moms

Sudhir Venkatesh and Steven Levitt investigated the working of a Chicago-based crack-cocaine-dealing organization called the Black Gangster Disciple Nation. They found that it was structured similarly to the fast food chain McDonald's – 'if you were to hold a McDonald's organizational chart and a Black Disciple org chart side by side, you could hardly tell the difference' (Levitt and Dubner, 2005, p. 87). The operation was divided into about a hundred branches (or franchises). J.T., the leader of one such franchise (gang), reported to about 20 men called (without irony) the board of directors, to whom he paid nearly 20 per cent of his revenues for the right to sell crack in a designated twelve-square-block area. The remainder of the money, he distributed as he saw fit. Three officers reported directly to J.T. – an enforcer (who ensured the gang's safety), a treasurer (who watched over the gang's liquid assets), and a runner (who transported large quantities of drugs and money to and from the supplier). Below these officers were 25–75 street-level salesmen known as foot soldiers who aspired to become officers themselves one day. At the very bottom of the hierarchy were 200 members known as the rank-and-file. These were not actually gang employees, but they did pay dues to the gang, either for protection from rival gangs or for the chance to secure a job as a foot soldier. A drug-dealing organization works like a standard capitalist enterprise. You have to be near the summit to make a lot of money. The 120 men at the top of the Black Disciples organizational pyramid were paid very well (2.2 per cent of gang members took home more than half of all the money), with the top 20 bosses netting $500,000 each per annum. The gang-leader (franchise holder) J.T. earned $66 an hour; his three officers each received $7 an hour; and the foot soldiers made $3.30 an hour – less than the US minimum wage. The authors concluded that, except for the top cats, drug dealers don't make much money, and that's why they live with their mothers (based on Levitt and Dubner, 2005; Venkatesh and Levitt, 2000; Levitt and Venkatesh, 2000).

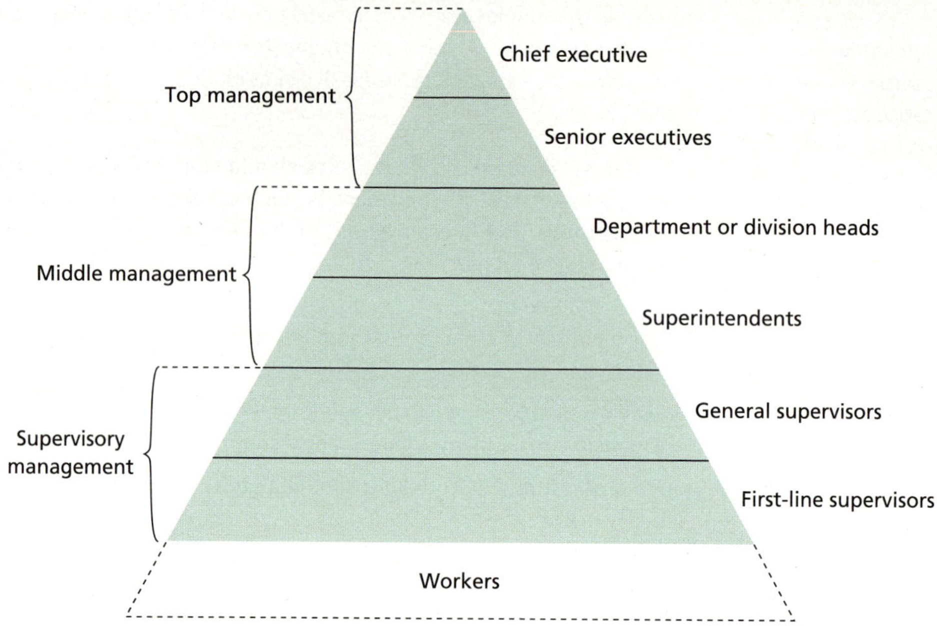

Figure 15.1: Organization structure

A popular way of depicting the structure of any large organizations is as a pyramid or triangle, as in Figure 15.1. This is only one of many possible shapes for an organization's structure. Several others will be presented later in the chapter. For the time being, we can note that the pyramidal form shows that an organization has both a vertical and a horizontal dimension. Its broad base indicates that the vast majority of employees are located at the bottom, and are responsible for manufacturing the product or providing the service (e.g. making refrigerators, selling insurance). Proponents of the formal structure claim that reporting relationships coordinate, motivate, and control employees, so that they work together better to achieve organizational goals.

In Figure 15.1, each of the six successive levels above the workers represents a layer of management. On the left-hand side of the diagram, the managerial ranks are divided into three groupings: supervisory or first-line management; middle management; and senior or top management. The diagram's right-hand side lists the commonly used job titles of managers who are members of each grouping. The layers also represent differences in status.

While most people will recognize an organization structure, they are less clear about its purpose. Robert Duncan (1979, p. 59) said: 'Organization structure is more than boxes on a chart; it is a pattern of interactions and coordination that links the technology, tasks and human components of the organization to ensure that the organization accomplishes its purpose.' For him, the purpose of a structure was twofold. First, it facilitated the flow of information within a company in order to reduce the uncertainty in decision-making that was caused by information deficiency. Second, a structure achieved effective coordination and integration of the diverse activities occurring within different departments within a firm.

Harold Leavitt (1965) has suggested that organizations can be viewed as complex systems which consist of four mutually interacting, independent classes of variables: organizational objectives, company structure, technology used, and people employed. All of these were affected by aspects of the firm's environment such as the economic, political, or social situation. The differences in organization structure can be partly accounted for by the interactions of these elements (see Figure 15.2).

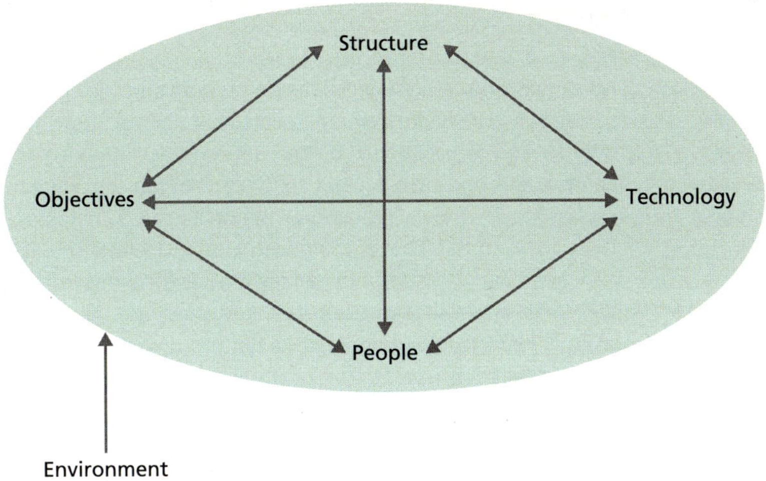

Figure 15.2: Leavitt diamond

FBI: Mission impossible?

Established in 1908, the Federal Bureau of Investigation (FBI) now has a budget of $6 billion, employs 31,000 staff, and has 56 US field offices and 50 foreign outposts. Historically, its agents have caught bank robbers, drug barons, organized crime leaders, corrupt politicians, and serial killers. The FBI was organized to solve crimes efficiently *after* they had been committed – it was reactive. After 9/11 it was required to stop crimes *before* they were committed – it had to become proactive. The new environment has meant that the FBI must change nearly everything about itself. First, its objectives have been changed. It has been mandated to take the lead in counter-terrorism and counter-intelligence, and charged with protecting Americans from terrorist attacks on US soil. To achieve this, it needs to replace its past 'shoot-from-the-hip', small-picture, strategic planning approach with a big-picture strategy involving good resource management, coordination, and teamwork. Second, its structure needs to be changed. In the past, it had a highly compartmentalized and decentralized stricture which relied on individual field officers' talents and intuition to sniff out corruption and wrongdoing. Fighting terrorism required a much more centralized approach.

Third, the FBI needs to change its people. It has doubled the number of both its linguists and intelligence analysts, and upgraded the pay of the latter. However, the bureau's cumbersome hiring and training systems are being overwhelmed processing new recruits. The integration of new analysts is increasingly a challenge. Finally, on the technology side, FBI agents have only recently all acquired the basic tools of a computer, email access, and an investigation database that was developed in 2004. Upgrading to a new $425 million system called Sentinel is proving problematic. In the future, FBI staff will have to become familiar with hostile intent systems which are currently being developed. These use 'pre-crime' technology of the type featured in Philip K. Dick's short story 'Minority report' and the film based on it.

The jury is still out on whether the bureau can achieve the necessary organizational changes being implemented by its director, Robert Mueller, so that it operates in a completely different way. A past member of the US Government Accountability Office described the challenge thus: 'You're trying to accomplish this transformation in an environment that's moving constantly. It's as if you're changing tyres on a moving car *and* you need to upgrade the vehicle you're travelling in *and* the terrain you're on is dicey and unstable' (based on Brazil, 2007, *The Economist*, 2008).

Types of jobs

Work specialization the degree to which work tasks in an organization are subdivided into separate jobs.

Job definition determining the task requirements of each job in an organization. It is the first decision in the process of organizing.

An important series of decisions on organization design relate to what types of jobs should be created. How narrow and specialized should these jobs be? How should the work be divided and what should be the appropriate content of each person's job? The detailed answers will of course depend on the type of job considered. Is it the job of a nurse, engineer, car assembly worker, teacher, or politician that is being designed? How well defined ought work tasks to be? This is the question about **work specialization**. Some argue that newly appointed staff should know exactly what their duties are in detail. They suggest that this high degree of **job definition** helps to motivate employees by letting them know exactly what is expected of them. Such detail can also assist in performance appraisal.

Specialization is a feature of knowledge, clerical, and manual jobs. After their general medical training, some doctors become paediatricians, others choose obstetrics, and so on. On the assembly line, some workers fit car tyres, while others fix on the doors. The choices concerning the extent and type of specialization depend on the criteria being used by the organization designer. These will be affected by their values, beliefs, and preferences. It may be a case of trading off efficiency of production against job satisfaction. Senior management might decide to attempt to maximize both elements. Too rigid specialization can lead to demarcation disputes. Once the elements of the job have been decided, it is possible to advertise the post.

HANDS ON CHIEF EXECUTIVE

To bring bags of presence and enormous energy to a unique global distribution operation

A package with bells on + sleigh **Far North**

This intensely private operation, which has a brand that is recognised throughout the world, has carved a unique position in a highly seasonal business. Its President and owner, who has always maintained a close personal involvement in every aspect of the operation, has decided that it's time to hand over the reins. The opportunities and challenges presented by technological change, and the potential threat of imitators, are issues which call for fresh ideas, new perspectives and, candidly, younger eyes. Ideal candidates, probably entering their second century and quite possibly retired recruitment consultants, will have the maturity which goes with white hair, the vision to penetrate the darkest night, a lightness of touch, and the leadership to direct a diminutive yet dedicated team. Skills in more than one language and sensitivity to a wide range of cultures will be essential, and experience of working with quadrupeds, especially reindeer, will help. Above all, we will be looking for the humour to overcome the intense seasonal pressures and the ability to appear to be in several places simultaneously. Please post full career details, quoting reference WE2512, up the nearest chimney, and share the joy, mystery, and magic of this special time with those you value most—with best wishes to our readers, candidates and clients, Ward Executive Limited, 4–6 George Street, Richmond-upon-Thames, Surrey TW9 1JY.

WARD EXECUTIVE
LIMITED
Executive Search & Selection

Source: from *Daily Telegraph*, Appointments, 31 December 1998.

Job title inflation

Job title inflation ('uptitling' or 'title-fluffing') is increasing. At the top of organizations, multiple senior managers now have the word 'chief' in their job title (e.g. chief executive officer; chief operations officer; chief financial officer). They are collectively known as the 'C-suite'. Recently, they have been joined by the 'chief Twitter officer' (Southwest Airlines) and the 'chief blogging officer' (Coca-Cola, Marriott Hotels). Lower down the organization structure come the presidents (vice-, assistant, and others). Their numbers have increased by 312 per cent, compared to the chiefs' increase of only 275 per cent, between 2005 and 2009. Structural factors may be responsible as the complexity of business and globalization creates 'Vice-presidents for Photocopiers – Asia Pacific'. LinkedIn, the social media website for professionals with 150 million members, calculated which job titles had experienced the greatest gains and losses. It found that the fastest-growing job title in America was 'adjunct professor' and the fastest shrinking was 'sales associate'.

Towards the bottom of the organization, title-fluffing is prevalent too. Paper boys have become 'media distribution officers'; garbage collectors are 'recycling officers'; lavatory cleaners are 'sanitation consultants'; sandwich makers at Subway are 'sandwich artists', and the receptionist is the 'director of first impressions'. Meanwhile in France, cleaning ladies have become *techniciennes de surface* (surface technicians). During economic downturns, fancy job titles can be a substitute for pay rises and bonuses. Moreover, in flatter organizations with fewer levels of hierarchy, important-sounding job titles give employees the illusion of ascending the company ladder. Additionally, managers who no longer have anyone to manage due to company downsizing can also be fobbed off with important job titles. For many employees, their job title is very important to them. It indicates their status within the company and affects their self-image and self-esteem.

Companies use fancy job titles to show that they are up with the latest fashion. The trend to be seen as environmentally responsible ('green') has created many 'chief sustainability officers' and 'green ambassadors' (BP). Company founders or senior managers also like to show that they have a sense of humour. The late Steve Jobs (Apple) called himself 'Chief Know It All'; and Jerry Yang and David Filo (the founders of Yahoo) call themselves 'Chief Yahoos'. Some of the most creative job titling can be found among IT specialists who variously style themselves chief scrum master, guru, evangelist, or ninja. Job title inflation is perhaps most prevalent in India and China, which are countries with an obsession with hierarchy, and where fancy job titles can gain you not only the admiration of friends but also a bride!

Is uptitling a problem or a small price to pay for corporate harmony? Job title inflation can create monetary inflation when people become cynical over their monikers, especially when they receive them in lieu of pay rises. Moreover, job titles cease to provide the basic information required of them on an organization chart. What exactly does a 'vision controller of multi-platform and portfolio' (the BBC) or a 'manager of futuring and innovation-based strategies' (the American Cancer Society) actually do? Perhaps it is easier to get rid of a 'chief scrum master' than an IT advisor. You need to decide whether you are a 'scholastic, end-user academic unit' or just a student (based on *The Economist*, 2010, 2012).

Some commentators believe that, far from being motivating, a high level of job definition acts to control people's behaviour and sets minimum performance standards. What is needed, they argue, is for the employee to create their own job. In practice, a detailed job definition is provided to those doing low-level manual and clerical jobs, while at more senior levels there is a greater degree of own-job-making. The physical manifestation of the choice about how much to define the job is the piece of paper on which is written the **job description**. A job description will usually contain the following information:

Job description a summary statement of what an individual should do on the job.

- the job title and the department in which the job is located;
- the job holder's position in the hierarchy;
- to whom the job holder is responsible;
- the objectives of the job;
- duties required of the job holder (regular, periodical, and optional);
- liaison with other workers, staff, supervisors, and managers;
- authority to carry out the task – the degree of freedom permitted to exercise own judgement in carrying out the job.

Organization chart a diagram outlining the positions in an organization's structure and the relationships between them.

The specialization of work activities and the consequent division of labour is a feature of all large complex organizations. Once tasks have been broken down (or 'differentiated') into sub-tasks, these are allocated to individuals in the form of jobs. Persons carrying out the jobs occupy positions in the organization's hierarchy. Particular levels of responsibility and authority are allocated to these positions. The division of labour and the relationship of one position to another is shown on the **organization chart**, which can act as a guide to explaining how the work of different people in the organization is coordinated and integrated (Chandler, 1988).

The Job Description by Bertie Ramsbottom

I trod, where fools alone may tread,
Who speak what's better left unsaid,
The day I asked my boss his view
On what I was supposed to do;
For, after two years in the task,
I thought it only right to ask,
In case I'd got it badly wrong,
Ad-hocing as I went along.

He raised his desultory eyes,
And made no effort to disguise
That, what had caused my sudden whim,
Had equally occurred to him;
And thus did we embark upon
Our classic corporate contretemps,
To separate the fact from fiction,
Bedevilling my job description.

For first he asked me to construe
A list of things I really do;
While he – he promised – would prepare
A note of what he thought they were;
And, with the two, we'd take as well
The expert view from Personnel,
And thus eliminate the doubt
On what my job was all about.

But when the boss and I conflated
The tasks we'd separately stated,
The evidence became abundant
That one of us must be redundant;
For what I stated I was doing
He claimed himself to be pursuing,
While my role, on his definition,
Was way outside my recognition.

He called in Personnel to give,
A somewhat more definitive
Reply, but they, by way of answer,
Produced some vague extravaganza,
Depicting in a web of charts,
Descriptive and prescriptive parts,
Of tasks, the boss and I agree,
Can't possibly refer to me.

So, hanging limply as I am,
In limbo on the diagram,
Suspended by a dotted line
From functions that I thought were mine,
I feel it's maybe for the best
I made my innocent request;
I hopefully await their view
On which job of the three to do!

(Windle, 1994, pp. 80–2).

Hierarchy the number of levels of authority to be found in an organization.

Let us consider the organization charts in Figures 15.3a and 15.3b, since they clarify some of the basic aspects of an organization's structure that are introduced in this chapter. These include chain of command; formal communication channels; division of labour; departmentalization; span of control; and levels of hierarchy. **Hierarchy** refers to the number of levels of authority to be found in an organization. It is a coordinating and integrating device intended to bring together the activities of individuals, groups, and departments that were previously separated by the division of labour and function. In a company that has a flat organization structure, such as that shown in Figure 15.3a, only one level of hierarchy separates the managing director at the top from the employees at the bottom. In contrast, the organization structure depicted in Figure 15.3b has four levels in between the top and the employees at the bottom.

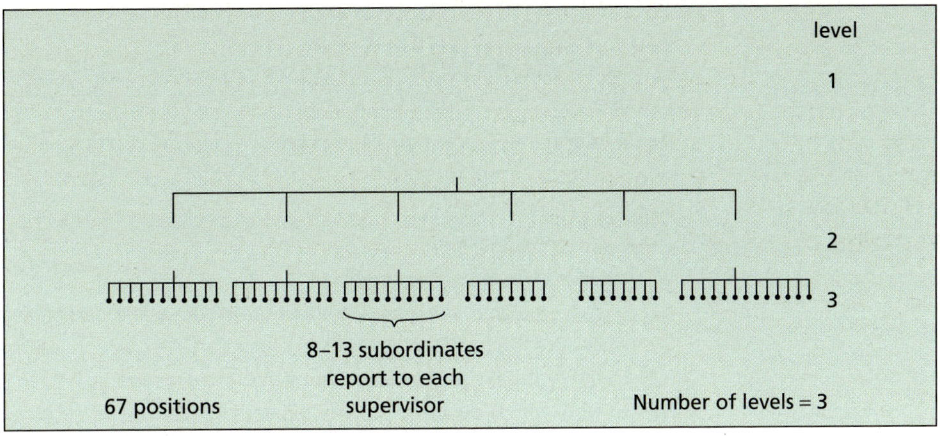

Figure 15.3a: Flat organization structure

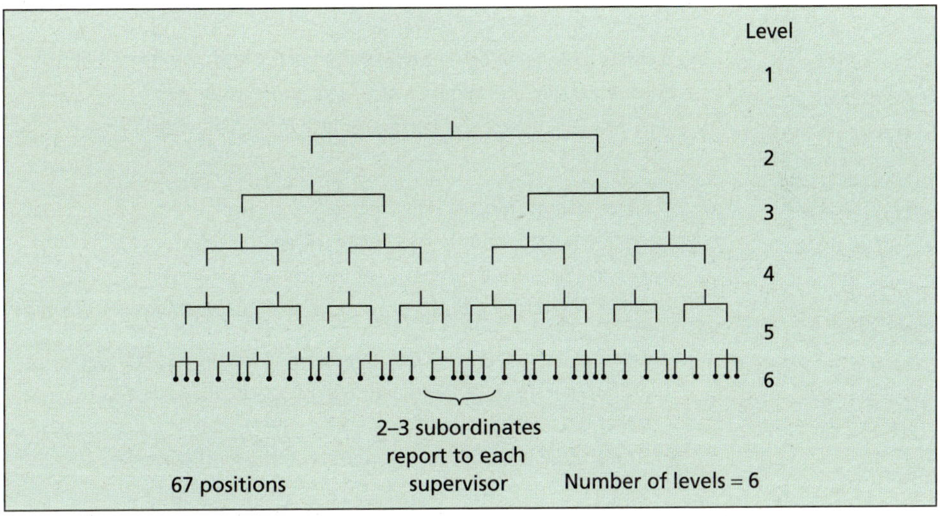

Figure 15.3b: Tall organization structure

It is useful to distinguish between organizations which have many levels in their hierarchy, such as the armed forces, the police, and the civil service (referred to as having a 'tall' hierarchy), and organizations which manage to operate with relatively few levels of hierarchy, such as small businesses (referred to as possessing a 'flat' hierarchy) and the Roman Catholic Church.

Span of control the number of subordinates who report directly to a single manager or supervisor.

Span of control refers to the number of subordinates who report to a single supervisor or manager and for whose work that person is responsible. Comparing the two organization charts in Figure 15.3, it can be seen that in the one with the flat hierarchy, there are many employees reporting to each supervisor. Hence, that person has a wide span of control. In a tall organization structure, fewer employees report to each manager and hence the span of control of each of the managers is narrow. The larger the number of subordinates reporting to one manager, the more difficult it is for her to supervise and coordinate them effectively. General Sir Iain Hamilton once said 'No one brain can effectively control more than 6 or 7 other brains.'

Job description

Job title: Logistics Manager
Department: Production Department
Responsible to: Production Director
Relationships: Head of a five-member logistics team

Main objectives:

(a) To cooperate with the sales department to ensure that orders are executed without delays.
(b) To control the inventory in order to minimize the costs and inform the production lines.
(c) To deal with all our sales representatives in order to reduce further delivery times.
(d) To work with IT department to design and produce the new software for receiving orders.

Specific duties:

Duties 40% cooperation with sales department

1. Meet every day with sales manager for the orders of the day.
2. Meet weekly with the marketing director to deal with the orders.
3. Gather daily the numbers of orders and classify them.
4. Check any delays and personally take immediate action.

Duties 30% inventory control

1. Work with production line manager and check the rate of production. In weekly meetings, decide the priorities in production of each product.
2. Personally check the capacity of the storehouse and fill in the reports for the production line.
3. Meet with employees in storehouse and resolve any problems they face.

Duties 15% sales representatives

1. Communicate with the main distributors on a weekly basis.
2. Meet once a month with the area representatives to discuss past performance.
3. Travel once a month to visit representatives in their areas.

Duties 15% development of software

1. Meet weekly with the head of the IT department to discuss the evolution of company's order-receiving software.
2. Provide to IT departments the numbers of orders.

Harold Koontz (1966) wrote that if an organization with 4,000 employees widened its span of control from 4-to-1 to 8-to-1, it could eliminate two hierarchical layers of management, which translates into nearly 800 managers. Stephen Robbins and Timothy Judge (2013) explained the simple arithmetic involved. Figure 15.4 shows an organization with 4,096 workers at level 7 – the shop floor. All the levels above this represent managerial positions. With a narrow span of control of 4-to-1, 1,346 managers are needed in levels 1 to 6. However, with a wide 8-to-1 span of control, only 585 would be required (levels 1 to 4).

The concepts of span of control and hierarchy are closely related. The wider a span of control is, the fewer levels there will be in the hierarchy. At each level, the contact between the manager and each of those reporting to him will be reduced. A supervisor responsible for eight operatives will have less contact with each operative than if she was responsible for only four. This wide span of control, with few levels of hierarchy, produces a flatter organization structure with fewer promotion steps for employees to climb. However, it is likely that the communication between the levels will be improved as there are fewer of them for any message to pass through.

With a narrow span of control of one supervisor to four workers, the daily contact between the boss and her staff will be closer. This narrower span creates vertical differentiation and

The army's span of control

The principle of chain of command ensures that each soldier knows to whom they are responsible. There can be units of different sizes for different purposes. Additionally, each man, squad, platoon, company, or regiment leader reports to his senior officer. In this way, span of control (SOC) ensures that each officer has only between two and ten soldiers reporting to him.

	Form	Commanded by one	SOC	Total soldiers
5 men	1 squad	corporal	5:1	5
2 squads	1 sergeant's squad	sergeant	2:1	10
5 sergeant's squads	1 platoon	lieutenant	5:1	50
2 platoons	1 company	captain	2:1	100
10 companies	1 regiment	colonel	10:1	1,000
10 regiments	1 brigade	general	10:1	10,000

Source: from *Bosses in British Business*, Routledge and Kegan Paul (Jervis, F.R. 1974) p. 87.

With modifications in the numbers in different units, this is the principle on which armies have been organized. The general does not have to control 10,000 men directly; he controls the ten regimental colonels, and so on. In modern armies this would be considered an excessive span of control and two or three armies would form an army group, but the principle remains. Split the task up into manageable proportions and do not have an excessive span of control so that real control is lost (Jervis, 1974, p. 87).

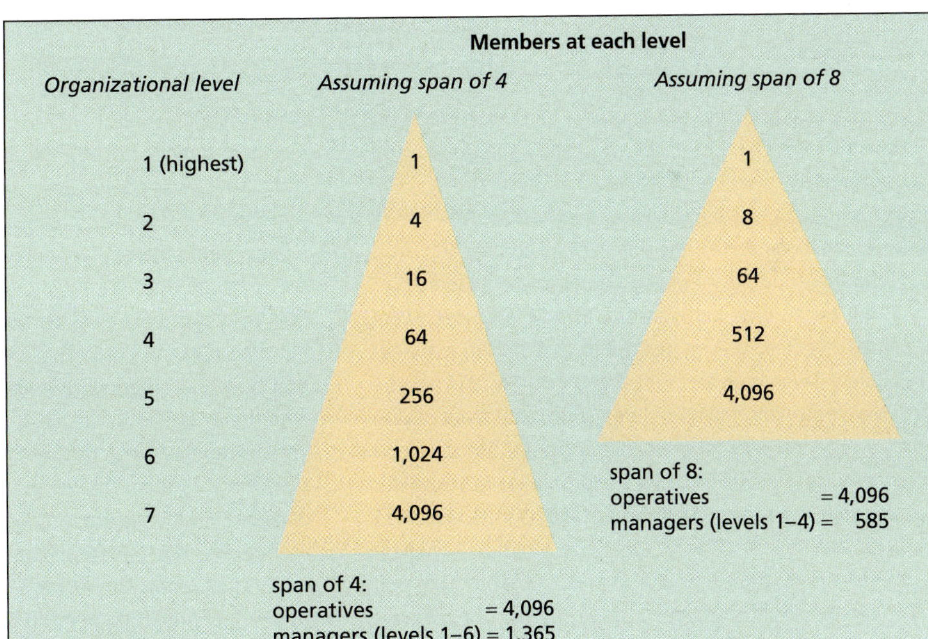

Figure 15.4: Contrasting spans of control

Source: from ROBBINS, STEPHEN P.; JUDGE, TIMOTHY A., ORGANIZATIONAL BEHAVIOR, 15th, © 2013. Printed and Electronically reproduced by permission of Pearson Education, Inc., Upper Saddle River, New Jersey.

a taller hierarchy. Although it provides more steps in a career ladder for employees to rise through, communication tends to deteriorate as the message has to go through an ever-increasing number of layers both upwards and downwards. Because resources are always limited, they restrict the decision-making process. Many factors affect the choice of a span of control, and the main ones are listed in Table 15.2.

Table 15.2: Factors determining the choice of span of control

Factors encouraging wider work spans

Similarities of tasks: The more similar the tasks carried out by subordinates are . . .

Subordinate characteristics: The more subordinates are competent, responsible, and able . . .

Interaction requirements: The lower the interaction required with subordinates . . .

Standardized procedures: The more standardized procedures there are . . .

Planning and coordination: The less planning and less coordination that is required of subordinates' work . . .

. . . the wider the span of control.

Factors encouraging narrower work spans

Geographic proximity: The more physically dispersed subordinates are . . .

New problems: The higher the frequency of new problems experienced by subordinates . . .

Knowledge gap: The greater the gap between the manager's and subordinates' expertise . . .

Task complexity: The more complex the work activities to be performed by employees are . . .

Manager's job: The greater the non-supervisory element in a manager's job . . .

. . . the narrower the span of control.

STOP AND THINK **Can a lecturer's span of control (class size) ever be too narrow or too wide? What factors determine the number of students that a single instructor can deal with in terms of teaching, assessment, and course administration? What are the effects of high and low class sizes on (a) lecturers and (b) students?**

Span of control at Google

Doug Edwards, one of Google's earliest employees, described the changes in the company's span of control as it grew.

> At most companies, the notion of an engineering head having hundreds of direct reports would be ludicrous, but because he believed that Google engineers were self-directed, Wayne just did away with the management layer between him and them. He divided the engineers into teams of three, with each team having a technical lead who was an engineer, not someone hired to manage . . . 'You could do a lot of stuff with tech leads' search quality expert Ben Gomes explained to me, 'because of the people we hired. Anywhere else having three or four hundred people report to one person would have been insane. Yet it worked reasonably well – for a while. And then at some point it didn't work' . . . all hundred and thirty engineers reported directly to Wayne. The bureaucracy was dead. There was no hierarchy. There were no in-depth performance reviews. Engineers were on their own, independent entities, connected only to the other members of their teams and tenuously tethered to PMs [product managers] to the central organization . . . With Google's expansion, the engineers found that they had outgrown the grand experiment begun with the awkward July reorg. In January 2002, Wayne announced that the company's flat structure could not scale much further. Yes, the executives had a clear line of communication to engineering, but Google intended to hire another hundred engineers that year. They couldn't all report to Wayne. The new goal would be to bring the reporting ratio down to thirty-five to one. (Edwards, 2011, pp. 226–7 and 283)

Although flat hierarchies imply a wider span of control and fewer promotion opportunities, they also force managers to delegate their work effectively if they are not to be faced with an intolerable workload. Evidence suggests that individuals with high self-actualization needs prefer flat hierarchies, while those who emphasize security needs tend to gravitate towards organizations with tall hierarchies.

At one time it was believed that the narrower the span of control was, the greater would be the level of employee productivity. However, research by Theobald and Nicholson-Crotty (2005) suggests that due to negative consequences of a narrow span, it is a moderate span of control that maximizes productivity, as shown in Figure 15.5. To recap, an organization structure performs three functions. First, it designates the formal reporting relationships, specifying both managers' spans of control and the number of hierarchical levels. Second, it groups together individuals into departments. Finally, it specifies systems within the firm, to ensure that the communication, coordination, and integration between different departments is effective.

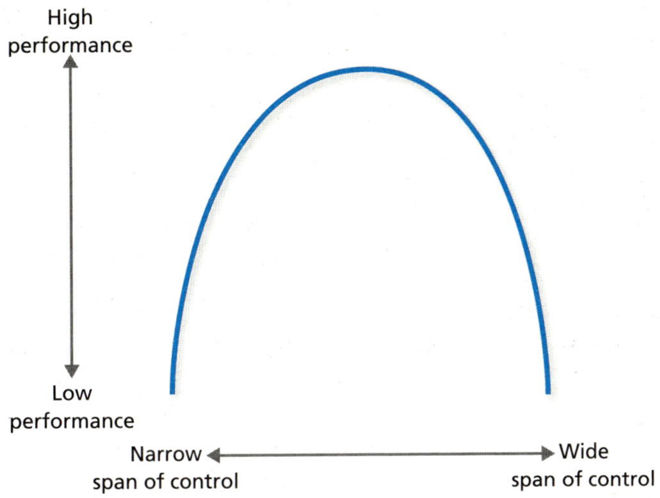

Figure 15.5: Relationship between organizational performance and span-of-control
Source: based on Theobald and Nicholson-Crotty (2005).

The graph in Figure 15.5 shows that organizational performance and span of control both increase to the point at which the supervisor or manager is unable any longer to coordinate or monitor the large number of subordinates who report to her. Companies differ, and each seeks to find the span best for it. For example, Wal-Mart sets different spans of control – narrow for store managers so as to ensure standardization, and wide for merchandizing managers at headquarters in order to implement best practices (Simons, 2005).

Line, staff, and functional relationships

Line employees workers who are directly responsible for manufacturing goods or providing a service.

Within an organization, one can distinguish two classes of workers. First, there are the **line employees**, who contribute directly to the provision of goods or services to the customer. In a motor car company, the term 'contribute directly' refers those who assemble the car (production) and those who sell the car (sales). They are considered to be the primary organizational functions. Line employees are shown on an organization chart which depicts their positions in the organization's structure, and shows the relationships between them. The line structure is the oldest and most basic framework for an organization, and all other forms are modifications of it. It is indispensable if the efforts of employees are to be coordinated. It provides channels for upward and downward communication, and links different parts of the company together with the ultimate source of authority.

Staff employees workers who occupy advisory positions and who use their specialized expertise to support the efforts of line employees.

The second class of workers are called **staff employees**. They contribute indirectly to the provision of goods or services to the customer. These individuals occupy advisory positions and use their specialized expertise to support the efforts of line employees. Staff employees work in departments such as purchasing, human resources, information technology, and legal. These are considered to be secondary organizational functions. A firm may provide line managers with advice by establishing a separate department headed by staff specialists. This is a modification of the basic line structure, and is referred to as a *line-and-staff structure*. The staff departments and the staff employees within them perform their tasks through the line structure, and not independently of it.

Within any organization structure, individuals occupying different positions will have different relationships with one another. These relationships can be labelled *line*, *staff*, and *functional*.

Authority the right to guide or direct the actions of others and extract from them responses that are appropriate to the attainment of an organization's goals.

Responsibility the obligation placed on a person who occupies a certain position in the organization structure to perform a task, function, or assignment.

Accountability the obligation of a subordinate to report back on their discharge of the duties for which they are responsible.

Line relationship a relationship in which a manager has the authority to direct the activities of those in positions below them on the same line.

Chain of command the unbroken line of authority that extends from the top of the organization to the bottom and clarifies who reports to whom.

To explain the differences between these types of relationships, it is first necessary to introduce and define the concepts of **authority**, **responsibility**, and **accountability**. You cannot be held accountable for an action unless you are first given the authority to do it. In a situation where your manager delegates authority to you, they remain responsible for your actions to senior management. Authority is vested in organizational positions, not in the individuals who occupy them. Military personnel salute the rank, not the person holding it. Authority is accepted by subordinates who comply because they believe the position holder has a legitimate right to exercise the authority. Authority flows down the vertical hierarchy of the organization, along the formal chain of command.

A **line relationship** is one in which a manager has the authority to direct the activities of those in positions below them on the same line on an organization chart. Line managers can 'tell' their subordinates on their own line what to do. Such relationships are depicted with vertical lines on the chart, and these connect positions at each hierarchical level with those above and below them. It is this set of manager–subordinate relationships that are collectively referred to as the organization's **chain of command**. Using the analogy of a river, the line relationships are the designated channels through which authority flows from its source at the top of the organizational pyramid, through the middle management ranks, down via the supervisors, to employees at the desk or on the factory floor. Thus the most junior employee has some linkage to the most senior manager. All non-managerial employees have some authority within their jobs, which may be based on custom and practice or may be formally defined in their job descriptions.

Every organization possesses line relationships if it has formally appointed leaders who have subordinates who report to them. All individuals in an organization report to a 'manager' from whom they receive instructions, help and approval. Thus in the organization chart shown in Figure 15.6 the Operations Manager (Completions) has the authority

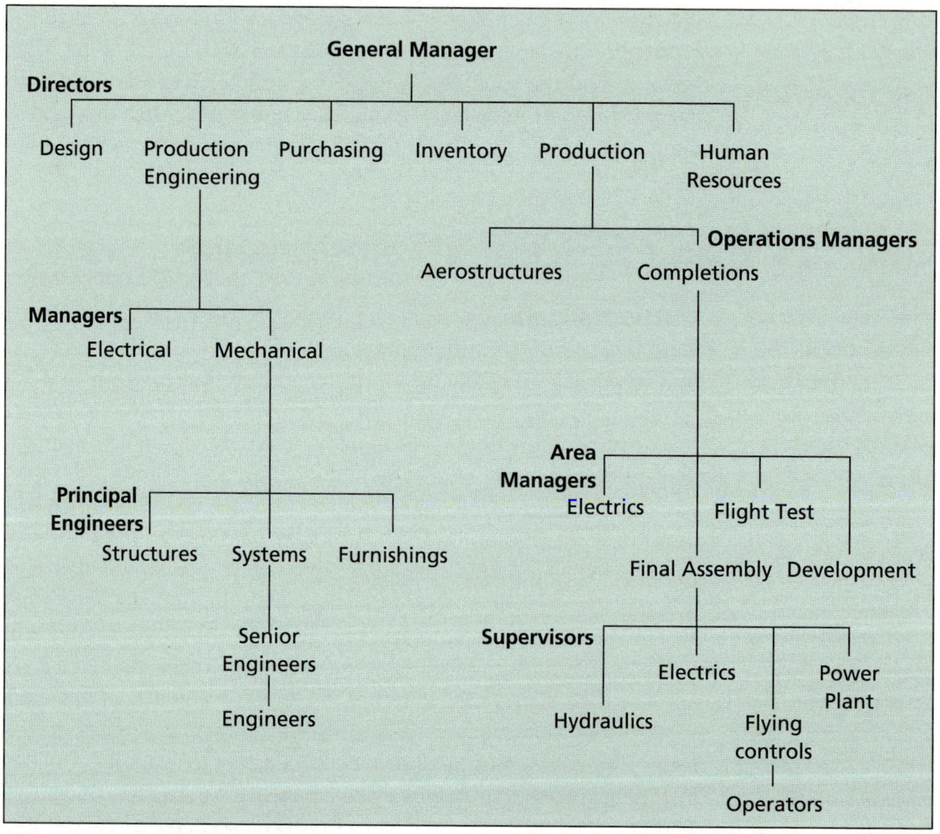

Figure 15.6: Line relationships

Source: from *Management: An Introduction*, Boddy, D. Pearson Education Limited, © Pearson Education Limited 2011.

to direct the activities of the four area managers. The Operations Manager (Completions), in turn, can be directed by the Director of Production. All the aforementioned individuals are in the same line relationship. The line relationships in a company are found within departments and functions. Line managers are responsible for everything that happens within their particular department.

Given the pyramidal nature of companies, managers located towards the top of an organization have more authority to control more resources than those below them. For this reason, lower-level managers are forced to integrate their actions with those above them, by having to ask their bosses to approve their actions. In this way, managerial control is exercised down through the organization by the *chain (or line) of command*. Figure 15.7 shows 18 'links' in the chain of command in the British Royal Navy.

Admiral of the Fleet
Admiral
Vice-Admiral
Rear-Admiral
Commodore
Captain
Commander
Lieutenant-Commander
Lieutenant
Sub-Lieutenant
Midshipman
Fleet Chief Petty Officer
Chief Petty Officer
Petty Officer
Leading Seaman
Able Seaman
Ordinary Seaman
Junior Seaman

Figure 15.7: British Royal Navy: chain of command

Source: from Royal Navy Museum website. http://www.royalnavalmuseum.org/info_sheets_nav_rankings.htm.

Staff relationship a relationship in which staff department specialists can recommend, advise, or assist line managers to implement their instructions concerning a particular issue, but have no authority to insist that they do so.

Functional relationship a relationship in which staff department specialists have the authority to insist that line managers implement their instructions concerning a particular issue.

A **staff relationship** is one in which staff department specialists provide a service to line managers. They can recommend, advise, or assist line managers to implement their instructions concerning a particular issue, but have no authority to insist that they do so. Thus they have to 'sell' their recommendations to line managers. Thus the human resources department cannot direct shop-floor workers, even when dealing with a personnel problem. It has to work with or through the line manager of the employees concerned. Staff authority is usually subordinate to line authority, and its purpose is to facilitate the activities being directed and controlled by the line managers.

A **functional relationship** is one in which staff department specialists, such as human resources, have the authority to insist that line managers implement their instructions concerning a particular issue, e.g. redundancy procedures. So, in a functional relationship, staff specialists can also 'tell' line managers what to do, but only within their prescribed area of expertise. A functional relationship is shown in Figure 15.8.

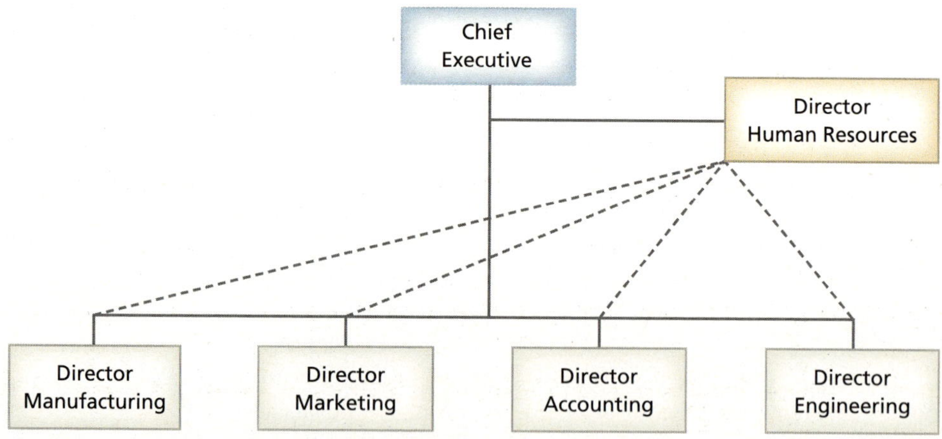

Figure 15.8: Functional relationship

The different relationships between the various positions on an organizational chart – line, staff and functional – are summarized in Figure 15.9 and depicted in Figure 15.10 using various types of lines.

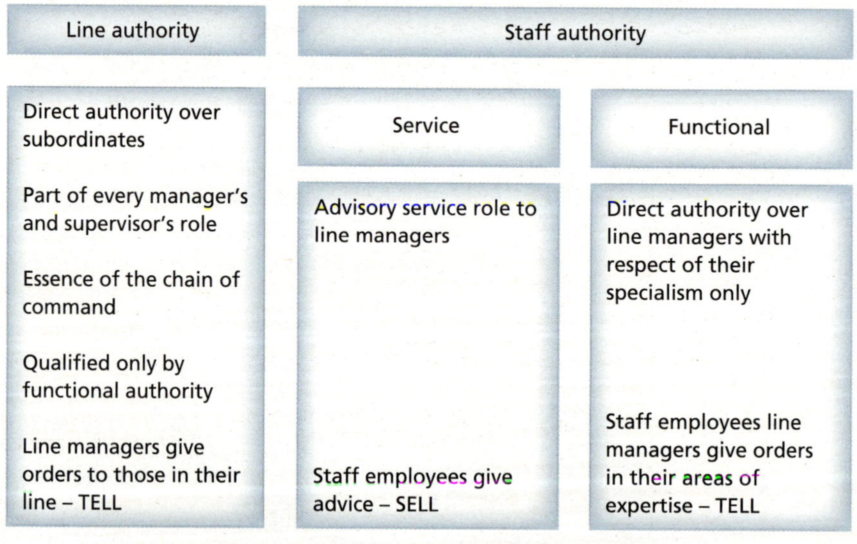

Figure 15.9: Line, staff and functional relationships of authority

Source: adapted from *Management: Theory and Practice*, Cole, G.A. and Kelley, P. © 2011 Cengage Learning EMEA. Reproduced by permission of Cengage Learning EMEA Ltd.

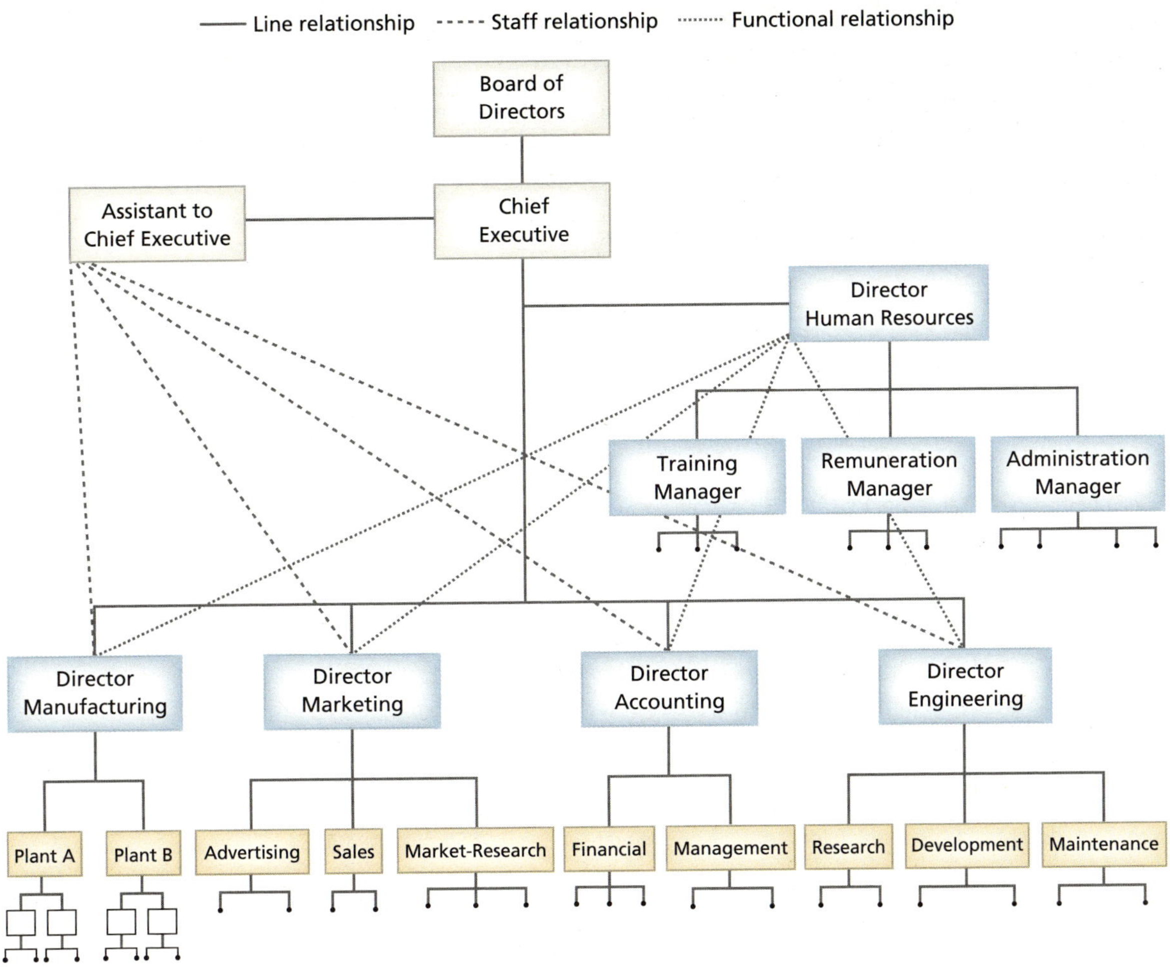

Figure 15.10: Types of relationships between positions on an organization chart

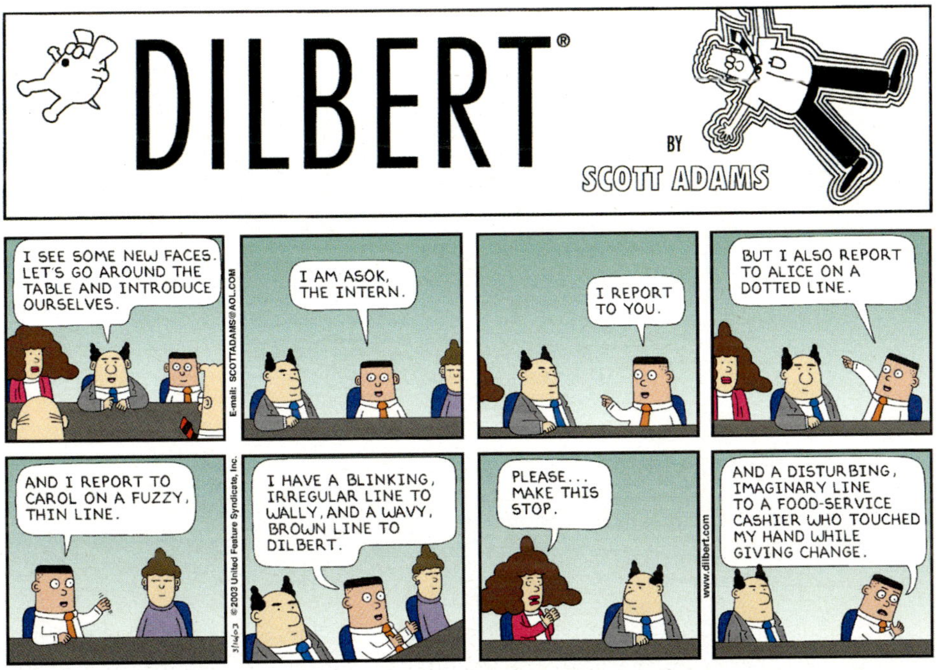

Source: DILBERT © 2003 Scott Adams. Used by permission of UNIVERSAL UCLICK.

Terrorism and organization structure

The United States Department of Homeland Security was created in 2002, and was one of the biggest mergers ever. It consolidated 22 units from 12 different departments. It has 180,000 employees, and an annual turnover of $37 billion. It is there to protect the US from terrorism and natural disasters.

When the DHS was first established, many asked if it had the appropriate organizational structure. It brought together the main functions of domestic security under one roof. Huge agencies were seized from other departments – the Immigration and Naturalization Service (39,500 employees) from Justice; the Coast Guard (43,600) from Transportation; the Customs Service (21,700) from the Treasury. Other independent entities – like the Federal Emergency Management Agency (5,100) – were gobbled up whole.

To coordinate the various functions, it was argued that having a single department with budgetary control was necessary. The powers of the various units are vested in the DHS's head (Homeland Security Secretary), in order to eliminate duplication and to enforce the adoption of common standards. He delegates authority back to the bits as he sees fit. To have folded everything into a traditional, giant department would have been logical but impractical, as the job requires specialization and expertise. To have left agencies scattered around would have been no good either. For example, if there was an attack on a nuclear power plant, one agency would distribute anti-radiation treatment if you lived within ten miles; a different one, if you lived outside that circle; a third would control the drug stockpile; and a fourth would take over if the attack also happened to be within ten miles of a nuclear weapons facility. The president saw the benefits of rationalization. In 2005, the head of the DHS announced a restructuring. Critics complained that it was 'weighed down with bureaucratic layers' and 'rife with turf warfare', and lacked 'a structure for strategic thinking'. The new head commented that 'our enemy constantly changes and adapts, so we as a department must be nimble and decisive'. The new organizational structure is shown in the organization chart for 1 February 2008. To get the last, comparable US governmental reorganization right – the establishment of the Department of Defence – took forty years and several congressional interventions (based on *The Economist*, 2002, 2005; US Department of Homeland Security website).

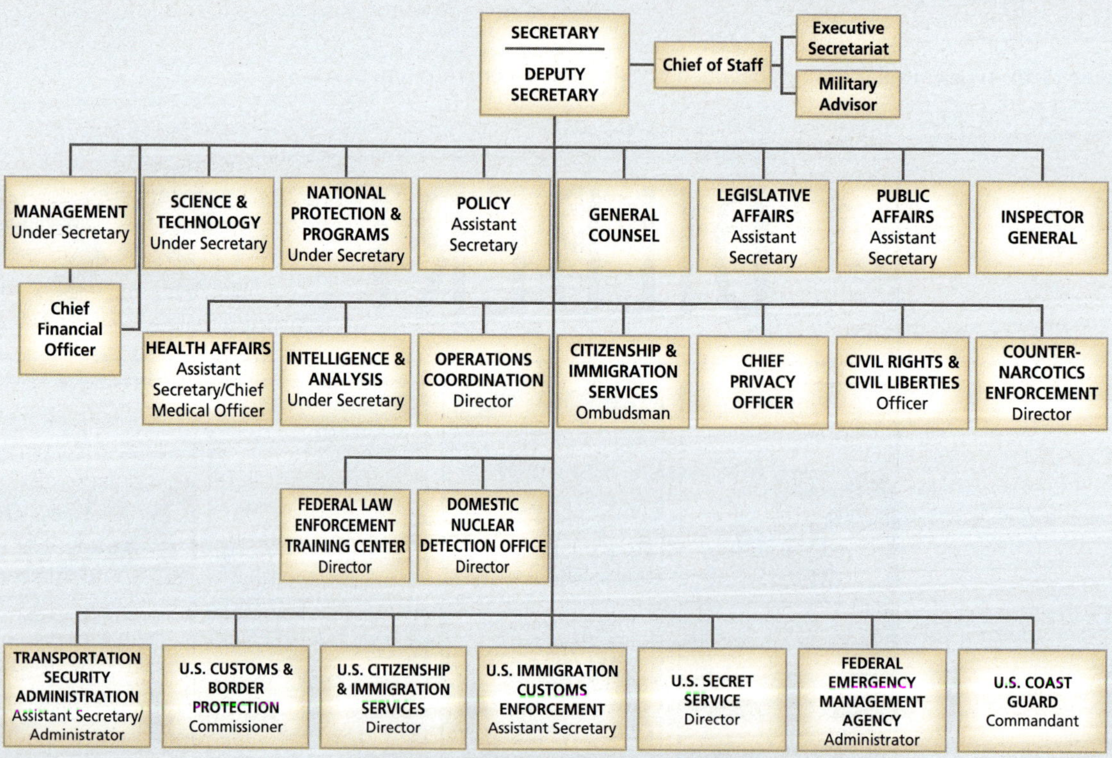

Source: http://www.dhs.gov/xabout/structure/editorial_0644.shtm, US Department of Homeland Security, Office of Multimedia, Washington, DC 20528, USA.

STOP AND THINK

Below is an organizational chart of Hogwart's School of Witchcraft and Wizardry.

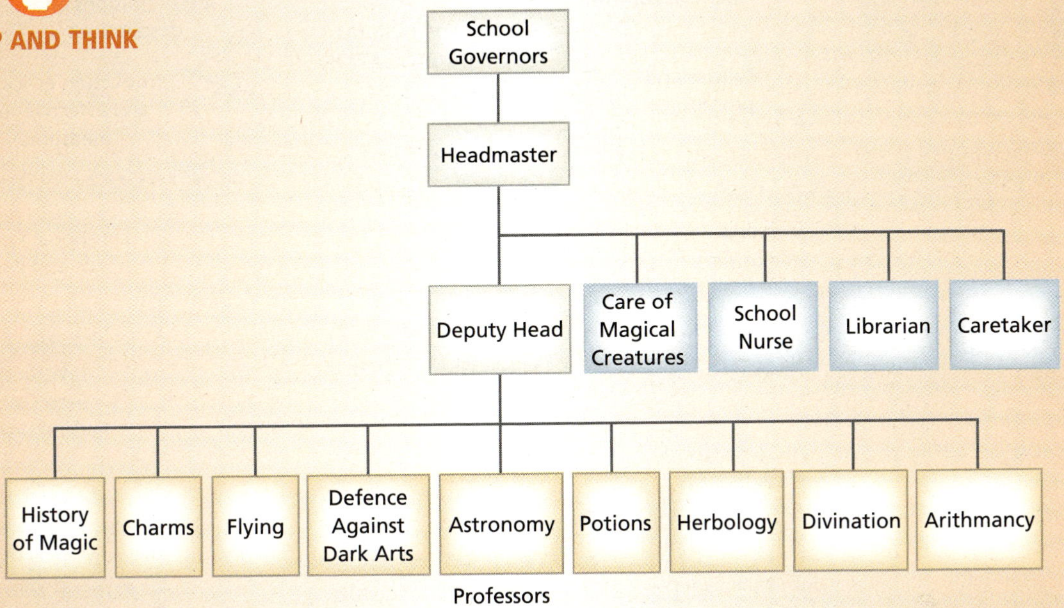

Who are the line employees and who are the staff employees? From your knowledge of the books and films (a) which aspects of organization structure are not shown in the chart? (b) how would you rate the performance of the school's professors shown in the chart? (c) how might the technology (i.e. magic) on which this organization is based, affect its structure?

Based on the Harry Potter novels by J.K. Rowling, Bloomsbury, London.

Formal organization the documented, planned relationships established by management to coordinate the activities of different employees towards the achievement of the organizational goal.

Informal organization the undocumented relationships that arise spontaneously between employees as individuals interact with one another to meet their own psychological and physical needs.

Decisions about job descriptions, organization charts, types of authority, and so on all relate to designing the **formal organization**. This refers to the documented, planned relationships established by management to coordinate the activities of different employees towards the achievement of a common goal, using the division of labour and the creation of a hierarchy of authority. These relationships between employees are all written down, and can be checked and modified, as required. However, to understand and explain the behaviour of people in organizations, it is also necessary to become familiar with the informal organization.

The **informal organization** refers to the undocumented relationships that arise spontaneously between individuals in the workplace as they interact with one another, not only to do their jobs, but also to meet their psychological and physical needs. These interactions lead to the creation of relationships between individual employees (see below) and to the development of informal groups, each with their own values and norms of behaviour, which allow people to meet their social needs (see Chapter 10). These groups are separate from those specified by the formal organization. Compared to the formal organization, the informal organization has a more transient membership, making it looser and more flexible, with interactions between individuals being more spontaneous and more emotional, resulting in their relationships being less clearly defined, and their involvement being more variable. The relationship between the formal and the informal organizations is shown in Figure 15.11. However, the informal organization created by employees can be in conflict with the formal organization established by management. Together, the two affect the human behaviours that occur within an organization. Some of the differences between the two are shown in Table 15.3.

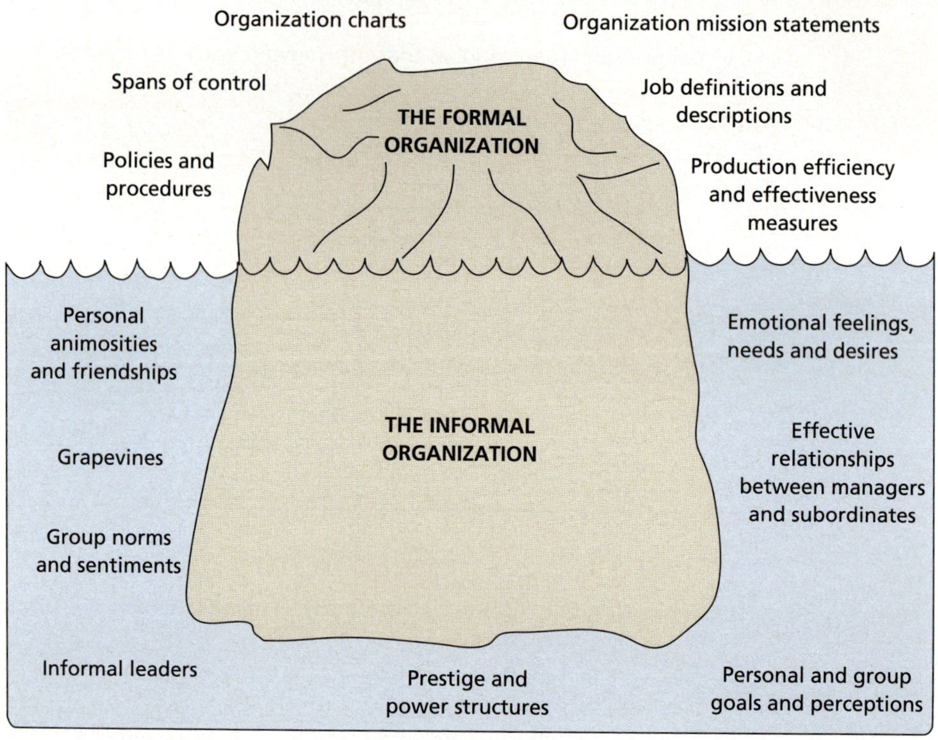

Figure 15.11: The formal and the informal organization
Source: from Lysons (1997).

Table 15.3: The formal and the informal organization compared

	Formal organization	Informal organization
A structure		
(a) origin	planned	spontaneous
(b) rationale	rational	emotional
(c) characteristics	stable	dynamic
B position terminology	job	role
C goals	profitability or service to society	member satisfaction
D influence		
(a) base	position	personality
(b) type	authority	power
(c) flow	top-down	bottom-up
E control mechanism	threat of firing or demotion	physical or social sanction (norms)
F communication		
(a) channels	formal channels	grapevine
(b) networks	well-defined, follow formal lines	poorly defined, cut across regular channels
G charting	organizational chart	sociogram
H miscellaneous		
(a) individuals included	• all individuals in work group	• only those 'acceptable'
(b) interpersonal relations	• prescribed by job description	• arise spontaneously
(c) leadership role	• assigned by organization	• result of membership
(d) basis for interaction	• functional duties or position	• personal characteristics status
(e) basis for attachment	• loyalty	• cohesiveness

Source: after GRAY, J.L./STARKE, F.A., ORGANIZATIONAL BEHAVIOR CONCEPTS AND APPLICATION, 3rd Ed, © 1984, p. 412. Reprinted and Electronically adapted by permission of Pearson Education, Inc., Upper Saddle River, New Jersey.

Temporary organization structure

Francis Dean/Rex Features

When does an informal organization become a formal organization? Protest groups such as Occupy Wall Street (OWS) fulfil the definition of an organization – a social arrangement for achieving controlled performance in pursuit of collective goals. Between September and November 2011, OWS established an encampment in Zuccotti Park in New York's financial district. Despite having no official leaders, only volunteers, this organization did have structure and rules; and it was effective in initiating similar protests against capitalism, bankers, and governments in other parts of the world, including outside St Paul's Cathedral in London. What kind of organization structure did they have?

Protesters could join 24 different working groups (identified by coloured armbands or hats) that managed day-to-day operations (e.g. internet, legal, sanitation). A general assembly met twice a day (first at 7.00 a.m.) to discuss proposals from working groups (WGs), and set short- and long-term goals. Everyone who turned up had a say, and a vote. Managing a large camp site in a city centre requires attention to mundane details. Rules had to be established concerning loud music, drugs, smoking, drinking, and toilets. There is also the problem of managing proceedings in what is, in effect, a huge debating society. The internal problem of communication of speeches was solved by 'human microphones' – participants chanting speeches, sentence by sentence. Additionally, the protesters communicated with standardized gestures, which included: both hands up, palms facing out ('yes – agreement'); both hands down, palms facing in ('no – disagree'); fingers of both hands touching to form a steeple ('request to interrupt'); and hands crossed, wrists touching ('block a proposal').

Externally oriented working groups focused on getting the message out – Tweet WG (spread news through Facebook, YouTube and Tumbir); Chat WG (through online forums and host discussions), and Stream WG (through live web video feeds of speeches and meetings). Consensus sometimes took hours and sometimes days, and detailed minutes were posted on the OWS website (based on *Bloomberg Businessweek*, 2011; *The Economist*, 2011; BBC News Online, 2011).

Sexuality and the informal organization

Sexuality the way someone is sexually attracted to another person, whether of the opposite or the same sex.

Sex the basic physiological differences between men and women.

Gender culturally specific patterns of behaviour which may be attached to either of the sexes.

In contrast to the formal organization just described, the informal organization includes personal animosities and friendships, prestige and power structures, and relationships between managers and subordinates, as well as emotional feelings, needs, and desires. **Sexuality** is an important feature of the informal organization. It has been defined as the expression of our social relations to physical, bodily desires, real or imagined, by or for others, or for oneself, together with related bodily states and experience (Hearn et al., 1989). It is useful to contrast the concept of **sex**, which refers to the basic physiological differences between men and women, with **gender**, which refers to culturally specific patterns of behaviour which may be attached to either of the sexes (Oakley, 1972). For example, who should mow the lawn? Who should change the nappies? Most people say gender when they actually mean sex.

Many of the themes of this chapter – such as jobs, hierarchy, authority, and roles – are significantly influenced by sexuality, an issue that is frequently ignored in management and organization behaviour textbooks. However, Jeff Hearn and Pauline Parkin (2001) have provided a useful overview of sexuality at work. One reason for the neglect could be because organizations treat sexuality as something that should not occur within them. A distinction is made between the public and private spheres, and sexuality is seen as belonging to the latter. The sociologist Max Weber argued that bureaucracies were based on impersonality and strict rules, with a clear division between the public sphere (which was rational and efficient) and the private sphere (which consists of a person's emotional and personal life). The suppression of sexuality was one of bureaucracy's first tasks, as sexuality was considered irrational and emotional, caused distractions, and thus interfered with the goal of efficiency (Bilimoria and Piderit, 2006).

However, sexuality is an integral part of every employee's personality and identity, and affects their interactions with other workers (Riach and Wilson, 2007). It refers to the way that a person goes about expressing themselves as a sexual being. Sexuality surrounds people in every way and in many forms. Rosemary Pringle says that it is 'alluded to in dress and self-presentation, in jokes and gossip, looks and flirtations, secret affairs and dalliances, in fantasy' (Pringle, 1989, p. 90). Various other commentators have also written that organizations are a complex of work and play; that when you enter most organizations, you are entering a world of sexuality; and that since human beings are sexual, so too will be the places where they work (Hearn, 1993; Williams et al., 1999). Moreover, sexuality is closely related to power – the first reinforces the second. Both shape, control, and maintain human interaction between employees, and therefore their behaviours. Power can be expressed through sexuality, and sexuality can be used to subordinate others to a lower status. Rosabeth Moss Kanter (1977) suggested that what may look like sex differences may in reality be power differences. Sexuality affects employees' work experiences and their job performance, as well as the organizational balance of power (Fleming, 2007).

Fiona Wilson (2004) observes that at work, sexuality refers to sex roles, sexual preference, sexual attractiveness, and notions of masculinity and femininity. According to Michel Foucault (1979), notions of masculinity and femininity are based on social meanings that have been socially and culturally constructed. These meanings therefore are not fixed, but are subject to a process of ongoing revision, through which sex is used to shape and control human relationships. Within organizations, sexuality manifests itself in issues such as sexual attractiveness, gender stereotyping, sex typing of jobs, the glass ceiling, office romances, sexual harassment, and emotional labour (see Table 15.4).

Since the 1960s, women have increasingly joined men in organizations. In Western societies, most people will spend more than a third of their adult life in the workplace, working in close proximity to one another. This, plus the social trends for later marriage and the long-hours culture, means that the boundaries between work and home have become blurred. Much courtship and mate selection now occurs at work. It is not surprising that about 30 per cent of co-workers will date at some point in their careers (Nardi, 2008). Many relationships begin (and end) in the workplace even though some companies have policies banning office romances.

Table 15.4: Issues of sexuality in organizations

Issue	Description
Sexual attractiveness	Men and women using their physical appearance to influence outcomes, e.g. decisions on appointments, promotions, pay.
Gender stereotyping	Assumption that men and women possess different personality traits, e.g. men are strong, rational, and firm; women are caring, emotional, passionate.
Sex-typing of jobs	Stereotyped attitudes towards men's and women's abilities, so that jobs are sex-typed, e.g. engineering as 'male' or nursing as 'female' jobs.
Glass ceiling	Limitation of the seniority level to which women can rise – percentage of women occupying chief executive officer positions; on boards of directors; in top leadership positions.
Office romances	Emotional, physical, or sexual involvement with another employee affecting organizational behaviour: includes daydreaming; flirting; handholding; sexual intercourse in the office.
Sexual harassment	Unwanted sexual attention that is perceived as threatening or offending; can be physical, verbal, or non-verbal.
Emotional labour	The management of feelings to create publicly observable facial and bodily displays.

Sexuality and organizational image

Sexuality is also present in the way that a company may wish to be perceived by others. Virgin Atlantic Airlines' 2009 campaign for their 25th year anniversary had the slogan 'Still Red Hot'. Their television commercial featured a male pilot as well as female cabin crew wearing glamorous and sexy red suits while walking through an airport. As they do so, mostly men ogle the group of gorgeous hostesses, and one inadvertently squirts hamburger filling over himself. The 90-second commercial caused an uproar (which perhaps it was designed to do), and complaints were sent to the Advertising Standards Authority. It was claimed that the advertisement was insulting to all women, especially those working in the aviation industry, as the all-female crew members were being promoted as the main reason for choosing the airline. The ASA responded by saying that even although some viewers might have found the representation of the women and men in the advertisement distasteful, it was unlikely to be seen as sexist towards men or women, or to reinforce those stereotypes (based on Sweney, 2009a, 2009b).

Image courtesy of The Advertising Archives

Virgin cabin crew

STOP AND THINK

Why might companies and business academics be reluctant to admit to the existence of sexuality within the workplace? What negative consequences might it have for them?

Informal relationships at Google

Google was no more immune to the lure of fraternization within the building than it was to relationships that crossed competitive lines. There were romances. There were marriages. On occasion, there were affairs . . . It's true that male-skewed tech companies sometimes devolved into frat-boy funhouses, and I never doubted Larry and Sergey's commitment to hiring technically adept women . . . 'In some parts of the world, the language of love is not Java'. Google was not one of those places. Hiring more women would not only forestall a Neanderthal culture, it would increase the odds of socialization and ultimately continuation of the species . . . we rented additional space in a facility as large as the one we already occupied. We officially called it the 'Saladoplex' because it was on Salado Road, but everyone knew it as the 'Honeyplex', because so many of our recent college grads [that] Sheryl hired, happened to be women. The outdoor patio lent itself to sunning on the warm California afternoons, and some AdWords staff members exhibited a predilection for clothing that facilitated tanning. Many a male engineer made the ten-minute walk from the Googleplex to enjoy lunch in the Saladoplex café.

Google was a company that enforced closeness more than most, from overpopulated workspaces to shared meals to all-company ski trips to constant electronic accessibility twenty-four hours a day, seven days a week. We saw a lot of one another and often became good friends – but close quarters also drove people apart. Peccadilloes and idiosyncrasies became inescapable irritants. Privacy was hard to come by, and personal hygiene took on added importance. There were undercurrents of annoyance and avoidance and sometimes overt expressions of exasperation as the pressure to perform intensified. In the midst of all that, people fell in love and out of love, formed lifelong bonds and ended their marriages. For some, Google became more of a lifestyle than an employer. My sense is that the number of these dalliances was not out of line with a normal distribution in a population the size of Google's, especially one as densely populated with energetic young overachievers. (Edwards, 2011, pp. 179–80, 182, 222 and 307)

Sexuality through informal relationships between employees in organizations can have both negative and positive aspects. The negative consequences for individuals and their fellow employees include creating jealousies; distractions from work; decreased productivity; increased errors; reduced professionalism; and exposure to sexual harassment. For the organization, the dangers include having to fire an employee, losing valuable talent, staff replacement costs, and lawsuits, as well as bad publicity. However, there are positive consequences, as a good work atmosphere can develop when informal relationships are encouraged. Rather than being a limitation on bureaucracy, sexuality can actually contribute to efficient operation. It can make work more fun and exciting for employees, thereby reducing absenteeism and late arrivals, increasing motivation and job satisfaction, and thus raising overall company performance. Some commentators have treated sexual behaviour as inappropriate, and as having nothing to do with work itself. However, they do acknowledge that sexuality is present within the workplace. Others say that informal relations are as important as formal relationships for motivating employees and making the organization function. An awareness of the effects of sexuality in the workplace provides a new perspective on organizational behaviour, and increases our ability to understand and manage it.

Home viewing

In *Erin Brockovich* (2000, director Steven Soderbergh), the eponymous character (played by Julia Roberts) is a single mother with three children, who is unemployed as the story begins. After losing a car accident personal injury claim in court, she joins her attorney's law firm as a filing clerk. She discovers a systematic cover-up of the poisoning of a town's water supply by the Pacific Gas and Electric Company. The film demonstrates the sexualization of work. Brockovich makes her sexuality explicit in the way that she dresses and behaves. She wears her long blonde hair loosely, and dresses in tight, low-cut tops, short skirts, see-through blouses, and high heels. Her sexuality and lack of self-control is shown as disrupting and threatening order in the office. Observe how she uses her sexual skills on a young male worker to obtain official documents. How does she persuade the working-class families of the town to agree to become plaintiffs in the lawsuit?

For further information about sexuality, feminine relational skills, gender stereotypes and power themes in this movie, see Bell (2008).

Roles in organizations

Role the pattern of behaviour expected by others from a person occupying a certain position in an organization hierarchy.

Roles are a central feature of every organization structure, and are specified in the organization hierarchy. All organization structuring occurs through the specification of the roles that employees are expected to play. It follows that if individuals occupying different positions in the hierarchy have mutual and complementary expectations, then the patterning and predictability of their behaviour is increased. The formal positions identified on an organization chart of a company imply the expectation of certain behaviours from any person occupying that office. This becomes the person's **role**. Roles are thus associated with positions in the organization and are involved in interactions. A single person plays many different and sometimes conflicting roles in life, both sequentially and simultaneously (e.g., mother, team leader, union official).

Subordinate swapping

The roles we play in organizations affect our behaviour. One company used role theory to resolve employee performance problems. Department managers met regularly to consider the possibility of exchanging their 'worst'-performing subordinates. These discussions were based on the assumption that poor performance was the result of the role that a person was being asked to perform in the company – that is, that there were role expectations that the person could not meet. The company philosophy was that there were no 'bad' people (individuals with poor attitude, inadequate motivation, or the wrong personality), but only individuals who were occupying roles that were unsuitable for them. The trading was a way of finding the poorly-performing employee a different and more suitable role in the organization (based on Gray and Starke, 1984, p. 124).

People's roles in organizations are ranked by status. Individuals occupying the role of manager are generally accorded more status than those occupying that of cleaner. In some companies, the ranking of roles is less obvious. John van Maanen (1991) described the rank ordering of occupations at Disneyland:

1. Disneyland Ambassadors and Tour Guides. These were the upper-class, prestigious, bilingual women in charge of ushering tourists through the park.
2. Ride operators who either performed skilled work such as live narration, or drove costly vehicles such as antique trains, horse-drawn carriages or the Monorail.
3. All the other ride operators.
4. Sweepers who kept the concrete grounds clean were designated as *proles*.

5. There was a still lower, fifth category of *sub-prole* or peasant status.
6. The 'lowest of the low' included food and concession workers, pancake ladies, peanut pushers, coke blokes, suds drivers and soda jerks.

Organizations are, to a degree, cooperative arrangements that are characterized by give-and-take, mutual adjustment, and negotiation. Their members get on with one another, often without explicit guidance, instruction, or direction. The concept of role aids our understanding of this aspect of organizational life by stressing that employees monitor and direct their own work behaviour in the light of what they know is expected of them.

STOP AND THINK It is common for people to refer to an organizational title or position (e.g. supervisor, scientist, manager) as the supervisor's role, scientist's role and manager's role, as though it were merely an established way of referring to these positions. What assumptions and problems does this use of the concept fail to appreciate?

Philip Zimbardo (b.1933)

Many of the tasks involved in any job have been learned and assimilated so well by the employee that they become accepted as being part of the person. It raises the question of whether, in behaving in a certain way, we are ourselves or just conforming to what the organization (and society) expects of us. Role relationships therefore are the field within which behaviour occurs. People's behaviour at any given moment is the result of

- their personalities;
- their perception and understanding of each other;
- their attitudes to the behavioural constraints imposed by the role relationship;
- the degree of their socialization with respect to constraints; and
- their ability to inhibit and control their behaviours.

Prison experiment

Do our attitudes, values, and self-image affect how we play roles (e.g. of a student, lecturer, doctor, or doorman) in organizations, or is it those organizational roles that determine our attitudes, values, and self-image? In a classic experiment, Philip Zimbardo created his own prison at Stanford University to answer this question. He selected 21 young men who had responded to a newspaper advertisement, interviewing them to ensure they were mature, emotionally stable, normal, intelligent North American male students from middle-class homes with no criminal record. Each volunteer was paid $15 a day to participate in a two-week study of prison life. A toss of a coin arbitrarily designated these recruits as either prisoners or guards. Hence, at the start of the study, there were no measurable differences between the two groups assigned to play the two roles (10 prisoners and 11 guards).

Those taking the role of guards had their individuality reduced by being required to wear uniforms, including silver reflector glasses which prevented eye contact. They were to be referred to as Mr Correction Officer by the prisoners, and were given symbols of their power which included clubs, whistles, handcuffs, and keys. They were given minimal instructions by Zimbardo, being required only to 'maintain law and order'. While physical violence was forbidden, they were told to make up and improvise their own formal rules to achieve the stated objective during their 8-hour, 3-man shifts.

Those assigned the role of prisoners were unexpectedly picked up at their homes by a city policeman in a squad car. Each was searched, handcuffed, fingerprinted, booked in at the Palo Alto police station, blindfolded, and then transferred to Zimbardo's 'Stanford County Prison' in the basement of the university's psychology building. Each prisoner's sense of uniqueness and prior identity was minimized. They were given smocks to wear and had nylon stocking caps on their heads to simulate

baldness. Their personal effects were removed; they had to use their ID numbers; they were housed in stark cells. All this made them appear similar to each other and indistinguishable to observers. Six days into the planned 14-day study, the researchers had to abandon the experiment. Why?

In a matter of days, even hours, a strange relationship began to develop between the prisoners and their guards. Some of the boy guards began to treat the boy prisoners as if they were despicable animals, and began to take pleasure in psychological cruelty. The prisoners in turn became servile, dehumanized robots who thought only of their individual survival, escape, and mounting hatred of the guards. About a third of the guards became tyrannical in their arbitrary use of power, and became quite inventive in developing techniques to break the spirit of the prisoners, and to make them feel worthless. Having crushed a prison rebellion, the guards escalated their aggression, and this increased the prisoners' sense of dependence, depression, and helplessness. Within 36 hours, the first 'prisoner' had to be released because of uncontrolled crying, fits of rage, disorganized thinking, and severe depression. Others begged to be paroled and nearly all were willing to forfeit their money if the guards agreed to release them.

Zimbardo attributed these changes to a number of causes. Firstly, there was the creation of a new environment within which the two groups were separated from the outside world. New attitudes were developed about this new 'mini-world', as well as what constituted appropriate behaviour within it. Secondly, within this new 'mini-world' of the prison, the participants were unable to differentiate clearly between the role that they were asked to play (prisoner or guard) and their real self. A week's experience of (temporary) imprisonment appeared to undo a lifetime of learning. Human values and self-concepts were challenged, and the pathological side of human nature was allowed to surface. The prisoners became so programmed to think of themselves as prisoners that, when their requests for parole were refused, they returned docilely to their cells, instead of feeling capable of just withdrawing from an unpleasant psychological research experiment.

Zimbardo concluded that individual behaviour is largely under the control of social and environmental forces, rather than being the result of personality traits, character, or willpower. In an organizational context such as a prison, merely assigning labels to people, and putting them in situations where such labels acquire validity and meaning, appears sufficient to elicit a certain type of behaviour. The power of the prison environment was stronger than each individual's will to resist falling into his role. Zimbardo considered the relevance of the findings of his research, conducted in the 1970s, to the behaviour of US soldiers in Abu Graib prison in Baghdad in 2004 (based on Zimbardo, 2007).

Role conflict the simultaneous existence of two or more sets of role expectations on a focal person in such a way that compliance with one makes it difficult to comply with the others.

The roles that we play are part of our self-concept, and personality theory tells us that we come to know ourselves through our interactions with others. We play different roles throughout our lives, and these require us to use different abilities, thereby adding more aspects to our self-image. Which roles we play, and how successfully we play them during our adulthood, affects our level of self-esteem. Thus the roles that we play inside and outside the organization affect both our self-image and self-esteem. In his research, Philip Zimbardo showed that people possess mental concepts of different roles, and conform to them when asked or required to do so. The woman who is both a manager and a mother may experience **role conflict** when the expectations in these two important roles pull her in opposite directions.

STOP AND THINK Identify any two roles that you currently occupy simultaneously in different social contexts, e.g. work, home, leisure. Identify a role conflict that you regularly experience as a result of such multiple role occupancy.

Changing roles: master and servant?

Sharon Bolton and Carol Boyd (2003) studied the work of airline cabin crew. In an effort to gain a competitive advantage through superior customer service, international airlines have introduced highly selective recruitment programmes for cabin crew that identify those applicants who possess the particular qualities required for the job. However, contrary to popular belief, possessing the 'right' personality is not enough. Having been selected, successful candidates undergo intensive training and culture management programmes. The airline goes to great lengths to inculcate its values into its new hires. Interestingly, customer service training takes the same amount of time as safety and emergency training, while training in areas related to the health and wellbeing of crew (e.g. dealing with violence, manual handling) is minimal or may not take place at all. The resounding message received by cabin crews is that what is most important is how they present themselves to passengers. One respondent noted that over the years, the airline industry had taught its cabin crews to be very subservient. Flight attendants, like organizational actors, are asked to assume a particular identity that helps them to perform their work role more efficiently. In their case,

Peter Jordan/Alamy

they are asked to assume the status of servant in relation to the customer who is the master.

One respondent stated that crew encountered verbal abuse on a daily basis, and that many people had no respect for them, seeing them as servants who were expected to carry their bags and place them in the overhead lockers. Another flight attendant with 21 years of experience, who had had to suffer passenger rudeness, said that 'the passenger is always right' and that passengers are fully aware of this and take advantage of the situation. They know that they can say anything they like to cabin staff, usually do, and get away with it. The airline requires the work routines to be predictable and to correspond continually to predetermined standards. Temporal and spatial constraints mean that there is little room for any variation in routine; the airline needs to be able to rely on employees to give a homogeneous role performance on every occasion.

Formalization

Rules procedures or obligations explicitly stated and written down in organization manuals.

Formalization the degree to which an organization has written rules, operating procedures, job descriptions, and organizational charts and uses formal, written communication.

A defining characteristic of every bureaucratic structure is its **rules**. From the 1930s, senior managements in large organizations increasingly adopted systems of bureaucratic (rule-governed) control. **Formalization** became widespread. This complemented the control exercised through machinery, and replaced that exercised through supervisory commands. Rules serve to regulate and control what individuals do and, to the extent that employees comply with company rules, they can ensure the predictability of human behaviour within organizations. For example, as part of the routine process of monitoring its restaurant managers, McDonald's requires 72 safety protocols to be performed daily in each of its restaurants (Robbins and Judge, 2013, p. 221). Both parties can benefit. For employees, rational and fair rules avoid managers' personal biases. This is true despite the fact that the rules are devised and policed by management, who can relax or ignore them at their discretion. Unions use rules to restrict the arbitrary power of employers, and demarcation rules protect jobs. Although rules can cause frustration to employees, they also reduce role ambiguity, and offer them high organizational identification.

Management also benefits from rules. It uses formal rules and procedures to coordinate the activities of different employees, and to establish conformity. Bureaucratic structures create job hierarchies with numerous job titles, each with its own pay rate. Elaborate formal rules (based on apparently 'objective' criteria) provide a basis for evaluating employee performance and determining rewards. For example, there are rules concerning the treatment of employees, such as those from the US Equal Employment Opportunity Commission (EEOC) relating to discrimination at work based on race, sex, age, religion, or national origin. This allows results to be traced back to the individual employee. It is all part of management's attempt to 'routinize' tasks which, together with the use of forecasting, planning, creating buffer stocks, and so on, seeks to remove the uncertainties involved in dealing with the environment. Provided that the environment is stable and unchanging, it is likely to be an effective strategy.

Source: www.callcentercomics.com

STOP AND THINK

Think of some of the rules that you have encountered in organizations to which you currently belong, or to which you used to belong. How effective are they in directing the behaviour of individuals? What problems do they cause, and what advantages do they offer, and for whom?

Centralization versus decentralization

Centralization the concentration of authority and responsibility for decision-making power in the hands of managers at the top of an organization's hierarchy.

Decentralization the dispersion of authority and responsibility for decision-making to operating units, branches, and lower-level managers.

A fundamental question faced by every chief executive is what kinds of decisions are to be made and by whom. The answer determines both the distribution of power within an organization (see Chapter 22) and the allocation of company resources. Some senior executives prefer to retain decision-making power in their hands, and thus run highly centralized organizations. **Centralization** refers to the concentration of authority and responsibility for decision-making power in the hands of managers at the top of an organization's hierarchy. Others choose to delegate their power, giving junior managers more individual autonomy and self-directed teams greater freedom, and introducing job enrichment for shop-floor workers. Thus, their organizations are much more decentralized in their structure. **Decentralization** refers to the downward dispersion of authority and responsibility for decision-making to operating units, branches and lower-level managers. New technology has facilitated this by making information easily available to all levels of employees, right down to the shop floor. The question of whether and how much to centralize or decentralize has been one of the major topics discussed in organization structuring. Each approach has its own advantages. Advantages of centralization are that

- greater uniformity in decisions is possible;
- senior managers are more aware of an organization's future plans and are more likely to make decisions in its best interests;
- fewer skilled (and highly paid) managers are required;
- greater control and cost-effectiveness in company resources are possible;
- less extensive planning and reporting procedures are required.

Advantages of decentralization are that

- lower-level decisions can be made faster;
- lower-level management problems can be dealt with quickly by junior staff;
- lower-level managers have opportunities to develop their decision-making skills;
- creativity, innovation, and flexibility are increased;
- there is increased motivation of lower-level employees, who are entrusted to make decisions rather than always following orders issued at higher level;
- an organization's workload is spread so as to allow top-level managers more time for strategic planning.

STOP AND THINK

As a shop-floor employee, would you prefer your company to be centralized or decentralized? Why?

A single organization can have a combination of both centralization and decentralization. Parts of Motorola are centralized, while other parts are not, and these change over time. Motorola's 'skunk works' are decentralized to encourage innovation, while its accountants are centralized – 'We don't want highly innovative financial accounting', said one of the company's senior managers. Centralization and decentralization also affect an organization's culture (see Chapter 4). A decentralized company which empowers its employees, and encourages and rewards creativity, creates a culture of innovation and risk-taking. However, in certain organizations, such as oil exploration platforms and nuclear power stations, it is important that employees do not make decisions on their own. Here, centralization can be used to create cultural values that reinforce safety, rule-following, obedience to authority, and the sharing of information with managers.

Motorola and Microsoft

Twenty years ago, Motorola, the co-inventor of the mobile phone, was a tightly centralized business. Three men in its headquarters at Schaumburg, Illinois (including Bob Galvin, the founder's son) were in control of almost everything that went on. As the company grew, they decided to decentralize. But by the mid 1990s the company's mobile phone business was growing so fast that the decentralization made it impossible to control. 'While the numbers are getting bigger, an organization can be falling apart', says Pat Canavan, Motorola's chief governance officer. In 1998, the company laid off 25,000 people and repatriated control back to its Schaumburg headquarters. In 2005, Microsoft had a decentralized structure consisting of seven business units. The company's senior management decided that infighting, miscommunication, and a lack of synergy between these units were causing slow product innovation. Their solution was to centralize by merging the activities of these seven groups into three divisions – Business; Platform Products and Services; and Entertainment and Devices. The effect has been to concentrate decision-making in the hands of the three division directors, and to add an additional layer of hierarchy (based on Hindle, 2006).

Arthur Bedeian and Raymond Zammuto (1991) argued that the balance between centralization and decentralization changes on an ongoing basis. It does so, in their view, in response to changes in company size, market opportunities, developments in new technology, and, not least, the quality of existing decision-making. Somewhat more cynically, Anthony Jay (1970) felt that whichever of the two is currently fashionable, it will be superseded by the other in due course. This may occur for no other reason than the incoming chief executive wishing to make a highly visible impact on his or her managers, employees, shareholders, and financial analysts.

RECAP

1. *Explain how organization structure affects human behaviour in organizations.*
   - The procedures employees are required to follow, and the rules by which they are required to abide, all control and direct their behaviour in specified directions.
   - The roles that people play, and the expectations that others have of role holders, all direct the behaviour of employees. Indeed, in the long term, these may even lead to a change in the personality of the employee.
2. *List the main elements of organization structure.*
   - The main elements include chain of command; hierarchical levels; line employees; rules; staff employees; role expectations; span of control; departmentalization; authority; and job description.
3. *Relate the concept of span of control to that of organization hierarchy.*
   - The narrower the span of control, the taller the organization hierarchy (and vice versa); and the greater the consequences for employees of having one or the other.
4. *Identify line and staff relationships on an organization chart.*
   - Line relationships are depicted vertically on a organization chart, indicating that those above possess the authority to direct the behaviours of those below.

→

- The seniors have responsibility for the work of the juniors, while the juniors are accountable for their work to their seniors.
- Staff relationships are depicted horizontally on a organization chart, indicating that those who possess specific expertise (e.g. in personnel, or in computing matters) advise those in line positions.

5. ***Distinguish between the formal and the informal organization of a company.***
   - The formal organization refers to the collection of work groups that have been consciously designed by senior management to maximize efficiency and achieve organizational goals, while the informal organization refers to the network of relationships that spontaneously establish themselves between members of the organization on the basis of their common interests and friendships.
   - The two forms consist of the same people, albeit arranged in different ways.

6. ***Understand the nature of sexuality and its impact on organizational behaviour.***
   - Sexuality refers to sex roles, sexual preferences, sexual attractiveness, and notions of masculinity and femininity in organizations.
   - Sexuality manifests itself in issues of sexual attractiveness, gender stereotyping, sex typing of jobs, the glass ceiling, the gender pay gap, work-life balance, office romances, sexual harassment, and sexual minorities.

Revision

1. Is hierarchical control an inevitable part of organization design or just a management convenience? Discuss.
2. Why do organization structures differ? Which is the best organization structure?
3. Suggest how a manager's role might be affected by the seniority of his or her position in the hierarchy, the industry sector, and organizational size.
4. What are the costs and benefits for those involved in romances at work? Should a company ignore or actively discourage romantic relationships between its employees? What can senior management do to minimize the problems associated with workplace romances?

Research assignment

Imagine that you are designing an organization structure for your new business – a café, bakery, travel agency, or similar, single shop on the high street.

1. What are the specific tasks to be accomplished by your shop's employees?
2. Draw an organization chart based on employee tasks. Each position on the chart will perform specific tasks or be responsible for particular outcomes.
3. Three years later, your business is successful, and you want to open a second shop three miles away. What challenges would you face running your business at two locations? Draw an organization chart that shows both business locations.
4. Five years later, your business has expanded to five locations in two cities in the same country. How do you keep in touch with them all? How do you coordinate and control what is going on in them? Draw an updated organization chart, and explain your rationale for it.
5. Twenty years later, you have 75 business locations in five European countries. What issues and problems do you have to deal with through organization structure? Draw an organization chart for your organization, indicating who is responsible for customer satisfaction, and explaining how information will flow through this enlarged organization.

(This assignment is adapted from Daft et al. (2010), pp. 129–30.)

Springboard

Julie Berebitsky (2012) *Sex and the Office: A History of Gender, Power and Desire*, Yale University Press, New Haven, CT. Taking a historical perspective on men and women in the workplace, the author considers the sexual tensions involved and concludes that what actually goes on between them has changed little, but what is acceptable has changed a great deal.

Robert Duncan (1979) 'What is the right organization structure?: Decision tree analysis provides the answer', *Organizational Dynamics*, 7(3), pp. 59–80. This classic article provides a structured framework with which managers can determine which type of organization structure is most suitable for their particular company.

Peter Fleming (2007) 'Sexuality, power and resistance in the workplace', *Organization Studies*, 28(2), pp. 239–56. The author considers whether the expression of sexuality in organizations represents an opportunity for employee resistance or increased management control.

Jay Galbraith (1974) 'Organization design: an information processing view', *Interfaces*, 4(3), pp. 28–36. Another classic article in which the author considers the appropriateness of various types of organization structures for different companies.

OB in films

Aliens (1986, directed by James Cameron), DVD track 14: 1:00:47 to 1:08:08 (8 minutes). The second film in this science fiction series is set in the distant future on planet LV-426. The characters include Lieutenant Gorman, the senior officer of the space marines, Sergeant Apone, Corporal Hicks, Private Hudson, and others. In addition to these military personnel, there is Burke, who represents the Weyland-Yutani Corporation which owns the facilities on the planet, and Ripley (played by Sigourney Weaver), who is employed by it. The clip begins with Ripley shouting at Gorman 'Get them out of there, do it now' and ends at the point at which Corporal Hicks says 'It's the only way to be sure. Let's do it!'. Which concepts of organizational structure introduced in this chapter are illustrated in this clip?

OB on the web

Search YouTube for Philip Zimbardo's famous psychological study 'The Stanford Prison Experiment'. Then, locate his lecture 'Philip Zimbardo: The Psychology of Evil' (www.ted.com). Zimbardo generalizes his findings into different organizational contexts. He talks about 'bad apples', 'bad barrels', and 'bad barrel-makers'. In other words, do not blame the individual, blame the organizational context (including the structure) in which the individual is operating. Use the web to find examples of inappropriate or criminal organizational behaviour e.g. in the banking industry, and write a report showing how Zimbardo's ideas may have contributed to the situations that you have discovered.

CHAPTER EXERCISES

1. Reorganizing the American Paint Company

Objective To identify problems of inappropriate organization structure and to suggest solutions.

Briefing Study the organizational chart of the American Paint Company. The company has grown over recent years without much attention being paid to its organization structure. There are now at least fifteen problems. Focus on structural issues such as job titles, hierarchical levels, span of control, and so on, identify what these problems are, and suggest how they might be solved.

American Paint Company organizational chart

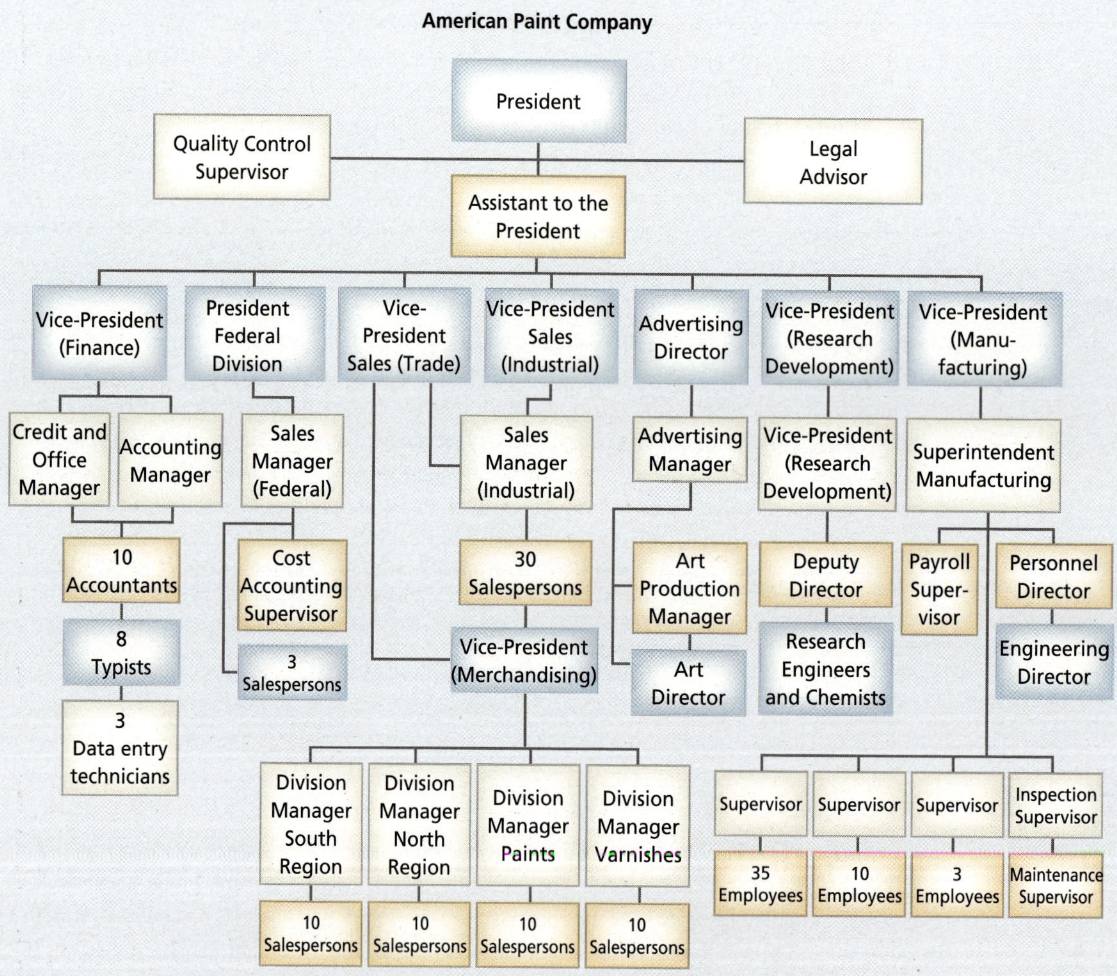

2. Human button

Objectives

1. To list the elements of organization structure.
2. To identify examples of organization structure elements.
3. To assess how structure elements contribute to achieving organizational goals.

Briefing

1. What are the main organization structure concepts/key terms? Can you define them?
2. Read the case study *Human button*, and look for examples of these.
3. What are this organization's goals? How does this organization structure operate to achieve them?

Human button

In 2012, the responsibility for the British nuclear deterrent rests with the Royal Navy. Its fleet of four ballistic submarines – the SSBNs (Ship Submersible Ballistic Nuclear) – is based at Faslane in Scotland. One of the submarines – HMS Vanguard, Victorious, Vigilant, or Vengeance – is always on patrol, undetectable, in the North Atlantic. They patrol for 90 days at a time, do not surface except in an emergency, and are not allowed any communication out of the boat. Every day, the captain is required to write a patrol report and a narration, explaining why certain things were done. Each SSBN is organized into departments, each headed by a senior officer who reports to the captain: Logistics (divided into Catering Services, Supply Chain, and Personnel); Marine Engineering; Medical; Warfare; and Weapons Engineering. Only a few of the most senior officers are allowed to know its location. Each is armed with up to 16 Trident II, D5 submarine-launched, ballistic missiles whose destructive power is equivalent to all the explosives used in the Second World War. Even if Britain was utterly destroyed in a surprise attack, that one, lone submarine will always be ready and able to strike back with overwhelming force. That is the theory of nuclear deterrence.

There is a human button communication system that triggers the retaliation procedure and has many built-in redundancy factors to anticipate problems. At one end of the communication chain is the British Prime Minster who makes the final decision. The PM's directive, detailing the target and release time, is sent from the government emergency room, somewhere below Whitehall. It is conveyed through his Chief of Defence Staff to the bunker facility at Northwood, under the Chiltern Hills in the south of England, known as 'The Hole'. Located there is Task Force 345's operations room from where the command and control of Britain's nuclear deterrent is exercised. At Northwood, the prime ministerial directive is authenticated, first by one A-list and then by one-B-list officer. The National Firing Message, as it is known, is then put into the system and goes onto the broadcast, which is continuously transmitted to the SSBN at sea. On board the submarine, the firing order is scrutinized by two officers, and checked against codes in the submarine's safe. Three keys are engaged, and the captain gives the order to fire.

What happens if the Prime Minister is killed or The Hole is destroyed in a pre-emptive nuclear attack? In anticipation of this, the PM nominates an *alternate* – that is, a decision-maker from the Cabinet, who will make a decision in their place, if required. In addition, early in each new Prime Minister's tenure, the Cabinet Secretary briefs the PM on the choices to be made from beyond the grave. Since the 1960s, each Prime Minister has written what is known as a *Letter of Last Resort*. It details what the PM's wishes are in the event of a nuclear attack on the United Kingdom. There are believed to be four options for the submarine commander: retaliate; do not retaliate; put yourself under the command of the United States or Australian Navy; or 'submarine captain to use his own judgement'. The Prime Minister makes his choice, writes the letter in longhand, and signs it personally, and a copy of it is placed in the safe of each of the four nuclear submarines. Britain is the only nuclear power that uses this letter system. When the Prime Minister demits from office, his letter of last resort is destroyed unread.

→

In a deteriorating geopolitical situation, if the submarine captain loses contact with Northwood, he first assures himself that Britain is an irradiated ruin and much of its population is dead. His orders are then to go, with his Executive Officer, to the safe in the submarine floor, remove the PM's letter of last resort, and act on its contents. However, it is not the captain who pulls the nuclear trigger. The submarine is brought up to hover position, still submerged, before firing, and the launch order is communicated by the captain to his Weapons Engineering Officer (known as 'The Weo'), who has the rank of Lieutenant Commander. It is he who pulls the trigger on the Colt 45 pistol handle whose wire runs from its butt. This allows the Weo to check other data on his control panels while holding the nuclear trigger in his hand. The trigger can only be activated if the captain turns a key on a panel in the control room. Below is the verbatim transcript of the final section of the launch procedure, as used in the practice drill. It represents the end of the firing chain which began with the Prime Minister's order. Below is the oral exchange between the commanding officer (A) and his various subordinates (B) who respond by confirming orders and asking for permission. After the sound of a click, the Weo says 'One away'. The first missile will have gone, and the end of the world will have arrived.

A: Hover command, commence hovering.
B: Commence hovering.
A: Stop engine.
B: Stop engine.
A: Ship control in condition 1SQ.
B: Condition 1SQ, Roger.
A: Weo in the missile control centre – clocks.
B: Check.
A: Come IRT.
B: Check.
A: Slow ready handover.
B: Semi-package has been shifted, we're on the active target package, in access to the safe, missile spinning up.
A: I have the system . . .

A: We are fire control. Fire control in condition 1SQ for strategic launch.
B: Fire control in condition 1SQ for strategic launch, Roger.
A: Command Weo, weapons system in condition 1SQ for strategic launch.
B: Weo requires permission to fire.
A: Supervisor Weo, initiate fire 1.

(click)

Weo: One away.

Case based on 'The human button', BBC Radio 4 programme, 2 December, 2008: Richard Knight, 'Whose hand is on the button?', 2 December, 2008, BBC website, http://news.bbc.co.uk/1/hi/uk/7758314.stm; Royal Navy website: http://royalnavy.mod.uk.

Employability assessment

With regard to your future employment prospects:

1. Identify up to three issues from this chapter that you found significant.
2. Relate these to the competencies in the employability matrix.
3. Decide what actions you need to take to maintain and/or develop those competencies under each of the four headings of the employability matrix.

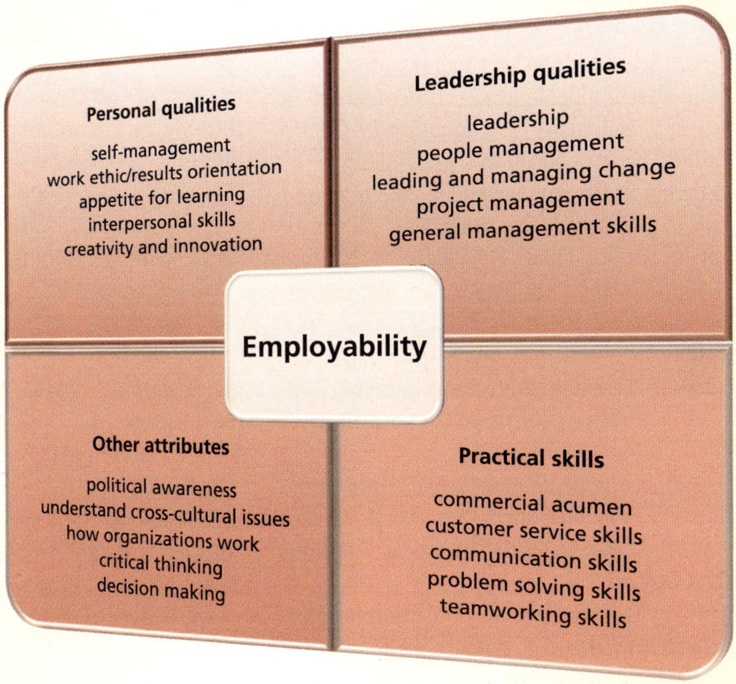

References

BBC News Online (2011) 'Occupy Wall Street: New York police clear Zuccotti Park', 15 November, http://www.bbc.co.uk/news/world-us-canada-15732661.

Bedeian, A.G. and Zammuto, R.F. (1991) *Organizations: Theory and Design*, London: Dryden Press.

Bell, E. (2008) *Reading Management and Organization in Film*, London: Palgrave Macmillan.

Bilimoria, D. and Piderit, S.K. (2006) *Handbook on Women and Business in Management*, Northampton: Edward Elgar Publishing.

Bloomberg Businessweek (2011) 'For Obama, populist peril on Wall Street', 17 October, pp. 37–8.

Boddy, D. (2011) *Management: An Introduction* (5th edn), Harlow, Essex: Financial Times Prentice Hall.

Bolton, S.C. and Boyd, C. (2003) 'Trolley dolly or skilled emotion manager: moving on from Hochschild's managed heart', *Work, Employment and Society*, 17(2), pp. 289–308.

Brazil, J.J. (2007) 'Mission impossible?', *Fast Company*, 114 (April), pp. 92–109.

Cavanagh, M. (2012) 'UK Border Agency split could deepen underlying cause of failure', *The Guardian*, 21 February.

Chandler, A.D. (1988) 'Origins of the organization chart', *Harvard Business Review*, 66(2), pp. 156–7.

Child, J. (2005) *Organization: Contemporary Principles and Practice*, Oxford: Blackwell Publishing.

Cole, G.A. and Kelly, P. (2011) *Management: Theory and Practice* (7th edn), Andover, Hants: Cengage Learning EMEA.

Daft, R.L., Murphy, J. and Willmott, H. (2010) *Organization Theory and Design*, Andover, Hants: South-Western Cengage Learning.

Duncan, R.B. (1979) 'What is the right organization structure?: Decision tree analysis provides the answer', *Organizational Dynamics*, 7(3), pp. 59–80.

Edwards, D. (2011) *I'm Feeling Lucky: The Confessions of Google Employee Number 59*, London: Allan Lane.

Fleming, P. (2007) 'Sexuality, power and resistance in the workplace', *Organization Studies*, 28(2), pp. 239–56.

Foucault, M. (1979) *Discipline and Punish*, Harmondsworth, Middlesex: Penguin Books.

Fox, A. (1966) *Industrial Sociology and Industrial Relations, Research Paper 3*, London: Royal Commission on Trade Unions and Employers' Associations.

Gray, J.L. and Starke, F.A. (1984) *Organizational Behaviour: Concepts and Applications* (3rd edn), Columbus, OH: Merrill Publishing.

Hearn, J. (1993) 'Emotive subjects: organizational men, organizational masculinities and the (de)construction of emotions', in S. Fineman (ed.), *Emotion in Organizations*, London: Sage Publications, pp. 142–66.

Hearn, J. and Parkin, P.W. (2001) *Gender, Sexuality and Violence in Organizations: The Unspoken Forces of Organization Violations*, Thousand Oaks, CA: Sage.

Hearn, J.R., Sheppard, D.L., Tancred, P. and Burrell, G. (eds) (1989) *The Sexuality of Organization*, London: Sage Publications.

Hindle, T. (2006) 'Teaming with bright ideas', *The Economist*, 21 January, The New Organization: A Survey of the Company, pp. 15–18.

Jay, A. (1970) *Management and Machiavelli*, Harmondsworth, Middlesex: Penguin Books.

Jervis, F.R. (1974) *Bosses in British Business*, London: Routledge and Kegan Paul.

Kanter, R.M. (1977) *Men and Women of the Corporation*, New York: Basic Books.

Koontz, H. (1966) 'Making theory operational: the span of management', *Journal of Management Studies*, 3(3), pp. 229–43.

Leavitt, H.J. (1965) 'Applied organizational change in industry: structural, technological and humanistic approaches', in March J.G. (ed.), *Handbook of Organizations*, Chicago: Rand McNally, pp. 1144–70.

Levitt, S.D. and Dubner, S.J. (2005) *Freakonomics*, London: Penguin Books.

Levitt, S.D. and Venkatesh, S.A. (2000) 'An economic analysis of a drug-selling gang's finances', *Quarterly Journal of Economics*, 115(3), pp. 755–89.

Lorsch, J.W. (1977) 'Organizational design: a situational perspective', *Organizational Dynamics*, 6(2), pp. 2–14.

Lysons, K. (1997) 'Organizational analysis', *British Journal of Administrative Management*, 18 (March/April) (Special Supplement).

Nardi, H. (2008) *The Greenwood Encyclopedia of Love, Courtship and Sexuality through History* (6th edn), Westport, CT: Greenwood Press.

Oakley, A. (1972) *Sex, Gender and Society*, London: Temple Smith.

Pringle, R. (1989) *Secretaries Talk: Sexuality, Power and Work*, London: Verso.

Riach, K. and Wilson, F. (2007) 'Don't screw the crew: exploring the rules of engagement in organizational romance', *British Journal of Management*, (18)1, pp. 79–92.

Robbins, S.P. and Judge, T.A. (2013) *Organizational Behaviour* (15th edn), Harlow, Essex: Pearson Education.

Simons, R. (2005) 'Designing high-performance jobs', *Harvard Business Review*, 83(7/8), pp. 54–62.

Sweney, M. (2009a) 'Virgin ad prompts complaints of sexism', http://www.guardian.co.uk/media/2009/feb/09/virgin-atlantic-ad-sexistofeom, accessed 21 April 2009.

Sweney, M. (2009b) 'Virgin ad not sexist, rules ASA', http://www.guardian.co.uk/media/2009/feb/09/virgin-atlantic-ad-notsexist-rules-asa, accessed 21 April 2009.

The Economist (2002) 'Washington's mega-merger', 23 November, pp. 51–3.

The Economist (2005) 'Imagining something much worse than London', 16 July, pp. 40–1.

The Economist (2008) 'If looks could kill', 25 October, pp. 97–8.

The Economist (2010) 'Schumpeter: too many chiefs', 26 June, p. 74.

The Economist (2011) 'Not quite together', 22 October, pp. 75–7.

The Economist (2012) 'A pixelated portrait of labour', 10 March, p. 74.

Theobald, N.A. and Nicholson-Crotty, S. (2005) 'The many faces of span of control: organization structure across multiple goals', *Administration and Society*, 36(6), pp. 648–60.

van Maanen, J. (1991) 'The smile factory: work at Disneyland', in P. Frost, L. Moore, M. Louis, C. Lundberg and J. Martin (eds), *Reframing Organizational Culture*, Newbury Park, CA: Sage Publications, pp. 31–54.

Venkatesh, S.A. and Levitt, S.D. (2000) 'The financial activities of an urban street gang', *Quarterly Journal of Economics*, 115(3), pp. 755–89.

Warrell, H. (2012) 'Break-up shows size of task ahead for May on immigration', *Financial Times*, 21 February, p. 4.

Williams, C.L., Giuffre, P.A. and Dellinger, K. (1999) 'Organizational control, sexual harassment and the pursuit of pleasure', in Annual Reviews Inc (ed.), *Annual Review of Sociology: Volume 25*, Palo Alto, CA: Annual Reviews Inc, pp. 73–93.

Wilson, F. (2004) *Organizational Behaviour and Work: A Critical Introduction* (2nd edn), Oxford: Oxford University Press.

Windle, R. (1994) *The Poetry of Business Life: An Anthology*, San Francisco, CA: Berrett-Koehler Publishers Inc.

Zimbardo, P.G. (2007) *The Lucifer Effect: How Good People Turn Evil*, London: Rider.

Chapter 16 **Organization design**

Key terms

organization design
traditional authority
charismatic authority
legitimate authority
bureaucracy
managerial activities
managerial roles
contingency approach to organization structure
technical complexity
technological interdependence
mediating technology
long-linked technology
intensive technology
task variety
task analysability
differentiation
integration
strategic choice theory
enacted environment
managerial enactment
resource dependence theory
vertical integration

Learning outcomes

When you have read this chapter, you should be able to define those key terms in your own words, and you should also be able to:

1. Distinguish between charismatic, traditional, and legitimate forms of authority.
2. State the main characteristics of a bureaucratic organization structure as specified by Max Weber.
3. Distinguish Fayol's six managerial activities and the main ideas of the classical management school.
4. Distinguish Mintzberg's ten management roles.
5. Identify the writers who comprise the early contingency approach and state their main individual contributions.
6. Discuss the strengths and weaknesses of early ideas on the design of organization structure and the practice of management.
7. Identify the influence of early organization design ideas on contemporary organizations.

Why study organization design?

Organization design senior management's process of choosing and implementing a structural configuration through which their organization seeks to accomplish their goals.

Organization design refers to senior management's process of choosing and implementing a structural configuration through which their organization seeks to accomplish their goals.

Organization design affects what they and others do, and how they spend their time. Many textbooks mention early-twentieth-century writings on organization design only briefly, before turning to explore team-based, network, virtual, and similar contemporary developments in organization structure. This chapter will demonstrate that these early ideas, far from being either out-of-date or superseded, continue to exert a pervading influence on organizational life. In addition, their source and form exercise a similar, enduring influence on modern management and organizational thinking.

Max Weber's ideas on bureaucracy were developed at the start of the twentieth century, and implemented from that time onwards. Today, the vast majority of employees in industrial societies around the world continue to work in bureaucratic organizations whose structures Weber would easily recognize. Moreover, they will continue to work under these structural arrangements for the foreseeable future. It is most likely that your own university or college is structured in this way. In contrast, at present, your chances of joining a so-called network or virtual organization are relatively slim. Little early organization design was based on systematic, empirical research. Max Weber was himself a social scientist, while his contemporary Henri Fayol was a colliery manager. Fayol and his successors developed an approach to management knowledge which was based wholly on the experiences of (mainly successful) managers. Moreover, the form it took was of principles, based on that experience. Organization structure designs conceived in the past which have been updated continue to have a significant impact today.

Max Weber and bureaucracy

Max Weber (1864–1920)

Max Weber, a German sociologist and philosopher writing at the turn of the twentieth century, was the first to address the topic of organization structure in his theory of bureaucracy. If Frederick Taylor was interested in the one best way to perform a job, Weber was interested in the one best way to structure an organization. Literally, bureaucracy means 'rule by office or by officials'. His work stemmed from his interest in power and authority. In this textbook, the term power is used to refer to the capacity of individuals to overcome resistance on the part of others, to exert their will, and to produce results consistent with their interests and objectives. Weber studied societies in history and distinguished three different types of authority – **traditional authority, charismatic authority**, and **legitimate authority** (Weber, 1947).

It is legitimate authority that concerns us here, and it carries with it 'position power' (power deriving from the position occupied within the organization). Because of the process of rationalism in modern society (the belief that the human mind can discover innate laws which govern the workings of the universe), legitimate authority has predominated. **Bureaucracy** is the form of organization structure associated with legitimate authority. The six characteristics of bureaucracy are shown in Figure 16.1.

Traditional authority the belief that the ruler has a natural right to rule, and that this right was either God-given or by descent, as with the authority of kings and queens.

Within a bureaucracy, we do what managers, civil servants, and university lecturers tell us, not because we think that they have a natural right to do so, or because they possess some divine power, but because we acknowledge that their exercise of power is legitimated and hence supported by two factors:

- the demonstrable logical relevance of their requests, directions, and instructions to us: their commands must seem rational by being justified through their relevance to the tasks of the bureaucracy and, ultimately, to its objectives;

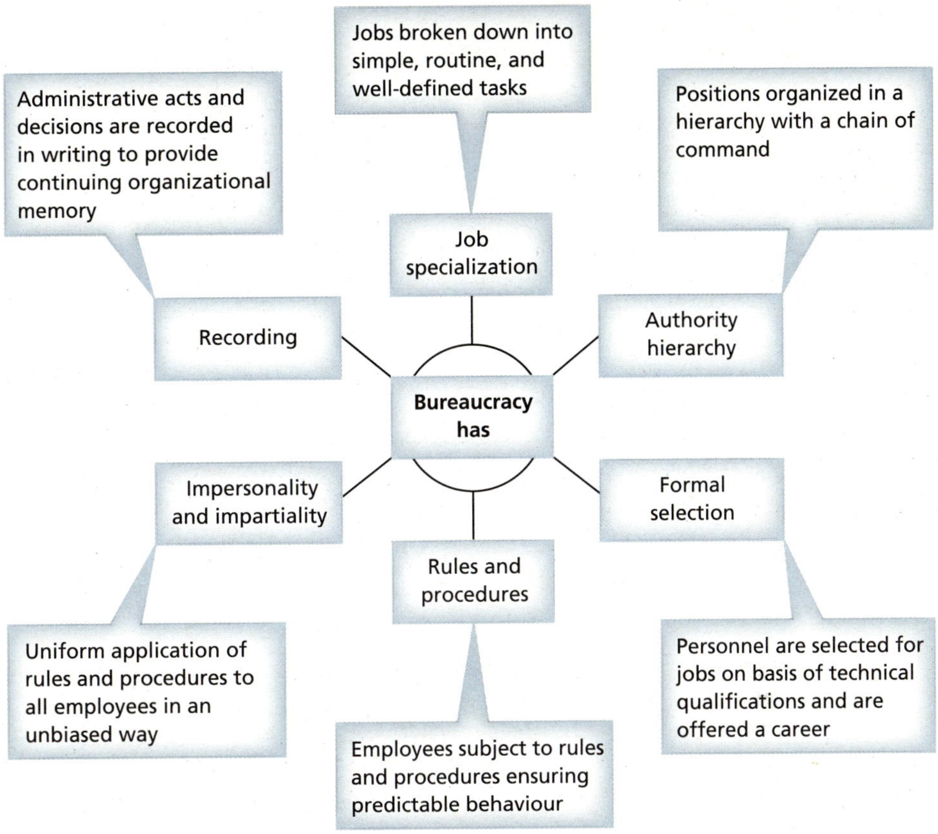

Figure 16.1: Characteristics of bureaucracy

Source: adapted from ROBBINS, STEPHEN P.; COULTER, MARY, MANAGEMENT, 10th Ed., © 2009, p. 45. Reprinted and Electronically adapted by permission of Pearson Education, Inc., Upper Saddle River, New Jersey.

Charismatic authority the belief that the ruler has some special, unique virtue, either religious or heroic, as with the authority of religious prophets, charismatic politicians, and film stars.

Legitimate authority authority based on formal, written rules that have the force of law, e.g. the authority of presidents, managers, or lecturers.

Bureaucracy legal-rational type of authority underpinning a form of organization structure that is characterized by a specialization of labour, a specific authority hierarchy, a formal set of rules, and rigid promotion and selection criteria.

- a shared belief in the norms and rules of the bureaucracy that have been arrived at rationally (not based on tradition or personal whim) and which possess a law-like character.

Weber believed that an organization based on legitimate authority would be more efficient than one based on either traditional or charismatic authority. This was because its continuity was related to formal structure and the positions within it, rather than to a particular person who might leave or die. Not every bureaucratic organization will possess all the characteristics that Weber identified. However, the more of them that it is has, the more bureaucratic it will be.

Weber used the term bureaucracy to refer to a particular type of organization structure, one in which work was divided, coordinated, and controlled. Whereas in the past authority had been based on nepotism or whim, in bureaucratic organizations it was based on rational principles. Bureaucracy for him was a form of organization that emphasized speed, precision, regulation, clarity, reliability, and efficiency. This was achieved through a fixed division of tasks, imposing detailed rules, regulations, and procedures, and monitoring through hierarchical supervision.

Many aspects of Weber's model reflected the organizational circumstances of his time. In the early twentieth century, establishing employment relationships on the basis of professional selection, and creating continuity of employment and career structures, was unusual when the methods then most commonly used were amateur, personal, and haphazard. Because they were adopted so widely, so long ago, it is difficult to believe that there was a time when organizations did not keep detailed written records (see Hall, 1963).

Dress rules at UBS and Google

Employee work wear is a key aspect of every organization's corporate image and reflects its corporate culture. Companies are therefore keen to ensure that their employees wear appropriate clothing when working alongside colleagues and meeting clients. However, how detailed the rules concerning appropriate dress in the workplace are varies considerably between companies. At one extreme, there is UBS, a Swiss bank, which issued a 42-page employee dress code to its staff. It required female staff to not wear tight, revealing shirts, ankle chains, or flashy jewellery, or to let their underwear show. Male bank employees were informed that they should not wear socks with cartoon motifs or a three-day beard on their faces. Moreover, their ties should match the bone structure of their face. Other useful advice included avoiding tight shoes, as they cause a strained smile. The new UBS dress code is an attempt aimed at improving the bank's image which suffered after it accepted Europe's biggest bailout – £37 billion – during the 2008 financial crisis. A UBS spokesperson said staff and clients had responded well to the rules which were being implemented in five offices in Switzerland. Staff appearance is important, said one financial PR consultant: 'If banks are spending money on plush carpeting and flowers in vases, then you don't want people romping around in jeans.' In contrast, Google, the search engine company, has a four-word official office dress code – 'You must wear clothes' (based on Edwards, 2011, p. 86; Jacobs, 2010; Kay, 2011; Sparkes and Salkeid, 2010).

"Miss Whitney, cancel that memo requiring that personal appearance should reflect our corporate culture."

Source: http://www.cartoonwork.com/ceos_bosses_g56-corporate_culture_p1253.html

The strength of bureaucracy lies in its standardization. Employee behaviour is controlled and made predictable. In Weber's conception, this was achieved not through time-and-motion study, but through the application of rules, regulations, and procedures. This ensures that different people in the same organization carry out their work in the same way. Bureaucratic organizations have a reasonably consistent set of goals and preferences. They devote few resources to time-consuming information searches or the analysis of current activities to check if these are meeting stated goals. Instead, they rely on rules, tradition, precedent, and standard operating procedures. Little time is spent on decision-making since decisions follow from the established routines, and few action alternatives are considered. The bureaucratic emphasis is on stability, fairness, and predictability (Pfeffer, 1981).

Weber was struck by how the bureaucratic structure of a company routinized the processes of its administration, in a way similar to how a machine routinized production. His ideas developed independently, yet they neatly complement those of Frederick Taylor. While Taylor focused on the worker on the shop floor, Weber's interest lay in a body of knowledge, administrative rules, and organization hierarchy, progressing from the top of the organization downwards. Nevertheless, Weber would have approved of the disciplining, rational conditioning, and training of workers proposed by Taylor. Different organizations can be compared in terms of the degree of their bureaucratization using the previously defined dimensions of job specialization, hierarchy, span of control, chain of command, departmentalization, formalization, and centralization.

In modern usage, the term bureaucracy has acquired a negative meaning amongst the public and the media. For example, when people come up against obstructiveness in any aspect of organizational life, they complain about there being 'too much bureaucracy' or 'too much red tape'. In response, governments and companies promise to remove or reduce it. Weber's view was in direct opposition to this. For him, bureaucracy was the most efficient form of social organization precisely because it was coldly logical and did not allow personal relations or feelings to get in the way of achieving goals. Rules and bureaucratic procedures provide a standard way of dealing with employees that avoids favouritism and personal bias. Everyone knows what the rules are and receives equal treatment. However, there is often frustration at having to follow what appear to be seemingly illogical rules, and thereby experience delays. This change in meaning has occurred because the principles of bureaucracy, originally designed to maximize efficiency, also resulted in inefficiencies. These negative aspects, costs, or 'dysfunctions' of bureaucracy were the focus of debates in organizational behaviour during the 1950s and 1960s (Merton, 1940; Gouldner, 1954; Blau, 1966). The positive and negative consequences of bureaucracy are summarized in Table 16.1.

Table 16.1: Positive and negative consequences of a bureaucracy

Characteristic	Positive consequences	Negative consequences	
		For the individual	For the organization
1. Job specialization	Produces efficient, repetitive working.	Overspecialization of employees' skills and knowledge prevents them recognizing or caring about problems not in their domain.	Inhibits job rotation and hence flexible use of personnel, and thus can reduce overall productivity.
2. Authority hierarchy	Clarifies who is in command.	Prevents employees contributing to decisions.	Allows errors to be hidden.
3. Formal selection	Most appropriate person appointed to a position and promoted.	Can restrict the psychological growth of the individual in their job.	Individuals throughout the company are promoted to their level of incompetence.
4. Recording	Creates an organization history that is not dependent on individual memory.	Employees come to see record-keeping as an end in itself rather than a means to an end.	Recorded precedents stifle attempts at company innovation. Inhibits flexibility, adaptability and responsiveness.
5. Rules and procedures	Employees know what is expected of them.	Introduces delays; stifles initiative and creativity.	Leads to individual and sub-unit goals replacing organization objectives; rules define *minimum* levels of acceptable performance.
6. Impersonality and impartiality	Fosters efficiency; reduces bias.	Dehumanizes those it purports to serve – officials prevented from responding to unique features of clients who are treated as standard cases.	Creates a climate of alienation through the firm as employees come to see themselves as small cogs in a wheel.

In contrast, there are other writers such as Harold Leavitt (2005) and Paul Du Gay (2005) who are supportive of bureaucratic organization structures, in part or in whole. They note that most large organizations of today possess many of the features of Weber's model, and that their longevity and continued existence confirm that bureaucratic firms can achieve an

Bureaucracy around the world

Every year the International Finance Corporation (part of the World Bank) compiles a report on bureaucracy (red tape) around the world. Its *Doing Business* report looks at government rules, and measures the duration and costs of standard business procedures – for example, how long it takes to register a company (one day in New Zealand; 65 days in the Congo); to register a property (one day in Portugal; 513 days in Kirbati); to obtain a construction permit (five steps in Denmark; 51 steps in Russia); to enforce a simple contract through the courts (150 days in Singapore; 1,420 days in India). In the 2012 Ease of Doing Business rankings, the top five countries were Singapore, Hong Kong, New Zealand, the United States, and Denmark; and the bottom three were Chad, the Central African Republic, and Congo-Brazzaville. The IFC shames world governments into cutting pointless rules and streamlining their processes. In the last six years, 94 per cent of the 174 economies surveyed have either simplified their processes or else implemented reforms (based on *The Economist*, 2011).

acceptable (or even exceptional) level of efficiency. In contrast, they cite example of companies which have not adopted bureaucratic features and have failed. There is a prevailing view that organizations should be structured on the basis of rationality. This means that a hierarchical structure is more likely to produce rational decisions and better control within an organization than any other structure (for example, one based upon teams).

Home viewing

Gosford Park (2001, director Robert Altman) is the story of a house party taking place in a manor house during the 1920s. The guests come from different social classes, and many bring their own servants with them. Assess which types of authority are demonstrated by the characters. Consider the roles played. How is the authority possessed by the servants 'below stairs' contingent on the status of their masters 'upstairs'? What other features of bureaucratic organization can you spot?

Insufficient bureaucracy?

Two of the most important requirements for the operation of an efficient bureaucracy are rule-following and recording. Rules and procedures within organizations are designed to make the behaviour of different employees and departments consistent and predictable. It is only when they are broken or not followed that outsiders get to hear about them. In 2007, Her Majesty's Revenue and Customs (HMRC), a government department, lost two CDs containing the (password-protected but not encrypted) personal and financial details of 25 million British households relating to child benefit payments. The data were sent by TNT courier service from the HMRC offices in Washington, Tyne and Wear, to the National Audit Office in London. The information should have been transmitted between these two institutions using the secure government intranet which had been established at the cost of tens of million of pounds. The Prime Minister commented on the problem of 'enforcing procedures'. The Poynter Report that investigated the disc loss said it was 'entirely avoidable'.

In 2008, Her Majesty's Crown Prosecution Service Inspectorate, an independent body, assessing the operation of the Crown Prosecution Service (CPS) in England and Wales, concluded that 'the majority of CPS files are not maintained in a satisfactory way'. It concluded that a third of all prosecution files had not been properly maintained. Omissions identified included the listing of defendants' bail status, requests for follow-up work, and the recording of the outcome of hearings. The inspectorate stated that court cases were being dropped because prosecutors had not been keeping up to date with their paperwork. The CPS denied that these problems regularly led to cases being abandoned. Both events illustrate the failure to conform to Weber's bureaucratic principles. In the first case, the rules and procedures principle was broken; while in the second, the recording principle was breached (based on *The Economist*, 2008; BBC Online News Channel, 2007, 2008a, 2008b; Allen, 2008).

Henri Fayol and classical management theory

Henri Fayol
(1841–1925)

Henri Fayol qualified as a mining engineer in 1860 after which he joined the Commentary-Fourchambault combine, a company in which he was to spend his entire working life. In 1866, he became manager of the Commentary collieries and in 1888, at the age of 47, he was appointed to the general manager position at a time when the financial position of the company was critical. By the time he retired in 1918, he had established financial stability in the organization. Fayol's list of managerial activities provides a definition of management. Indeed, he is credited with 'inventing' management. That is, he distinguished it as a separate activity, and defined its constituent elements. Interestingly, the word *management* is not translatable into all languages, nor does the concept exist in all cultures. Managing occurs, of course, but it is not always treated as anything special or separate.

It was in 1916, the year after Frederick Taylor died, that Fayol's book *General and Industrial Administration* was published. In it, Fayol put down in a systematic form the experience that he had gained while managing a large organization. He stressed methods rather than personalities, seeking to present the former in a coherent and relevant scheme. This formed his theory of organization. While Taylor focused on the worker on the shop floor – a bottom-up approach – Fayol began from the top of the hierarchy and moved downwards. However, like Taylor, he too believed that a manager's work could be reviewed objectively, analysed, and treated as a technical process which was subject to certain definite principles which could be taught. Fayol identified six **managerial activities** that supported the operation of every organization and needed to be performed to ensure its success. Although his list of management activities was originally developed over eighty years ago, it continues to be used to this day. It is shown in Table 16.2.

Managerial activities activities performed by managers that support the operation of every organization and need to be performed to ensure its success.

Table 16.2: Fayol's six managerial activities

1. Forecasting	Predicting what might happen in the future
2. Planning	Devising a course of action to meet that expected demand
3. Organizing	Allocating separate tasks to different departments, units, and individuals
4. Commanding	Providing direction to employees; now more commonly referred to as *directing, motivating*, or *leadership*.
5. Coordinating	Making sure that previously separated assigned tasks are integrated and that people are working well together
6. Controlling	Monitoring progress to ensure that plans are being carried out properly

The six management activities are interrelated. For example, a company management team begins by *forecasting* the demand for its product, for example, steel wire. It requires a sales forecast and will use market research to develop one. Once it is clear that there is a market for the product, the next activity, *planning*, will take place. For Fayol, planning involved 'making a programme of action to achieve an objective'. He collectively referred to the two activities of forecasting and planning as *purveyance.* Because they are so closely related, some authors and books treat them as a single management activity.

Having made the plan, the third activity to be performed is *organizing*. This involves breaking down the main task into smaller pieces, and distributing them to different people. In a company structured along functional lines (accounting, production, marketing), the organizing of people may involve creating a special, temporary project team, consisting of members from the different functions. This is the matrix structure, which will be discussed in Chapter 17.

Fayol used the word *commanding* to describe his fourth management activity. It has been defined as 'influencing others towards the accomplishment of organizational goals'. Today we would refer to it as *directing, motivating*, or *leading*. Whichever term is chosen, performing this activity involves the manager ensuring that employees give of their best. To do this,

Forecasting, planning, and organizing

© Paul Nicklen/National Geographic Society/Corbis

With a heavy clunk, the steel outer doors of the Svalbard Global Seed Vault close, shutting out the howling Arctic gale and entombing a tonne of new arrivals: 25,000 seed samples from America, Columbia, Costa Rica, Tajikistan, Armenia, and Syria. Opened in 2008, the Svalbard Vault is a backup for the world's 1,750 seed banks – the storehouses of agricultural biodiversity. The Afghani and Iraqi seed banks have already been destroyed by wars, and in 2012 the Philippines' national seed bank was destroyed by fire. Syria's bank at Aleppo is under threat. The Svalbard Vault is protected by two airlocks at the end of a tunnel sunk 160 metres into the permafrost of Norway's Arctic archipelago outside the village of Longyearbyen, one of the world's most northerly habitations. It is maintained at a constant temperature of minus 18 degrees Celsius. This is serious disaster preparedness. If its electricity were cut, the vault would take two centuries to warm to freezing point. Its concave tunnel head is designed to deflect the force of a missile strike. The facility is nicknamed the Doomsday Vault (© The Economist Newspaper Limited, London (10/03/2012)).

managers must possess knowledge both of the tasks to be done and of the people who are to do them. This management activity is mainly, although not exclusively, performed in a face-to-face situation. The fifth managerial activity, *coordinating*, involves ensuring that the various tasks previously distributed to different employees (through organizing) are being brought together and synchronized with one another. Coordination can be achieved through emails, meetings, and personal contacts between the people carrying out their unique job tasks.

The sixth and final managerial activity is *controlling*. This involves monitoring how the objectives set out in the plan are being achieved, with respect to the limitations of time and budget that were imposed. Any deviations are identified, and action taken to rectify them. It may be that the original plan will have to be amended. Although Fayol's six managerial activities have been presented as a sequence, in reality they occur simultaneously in a company. However, forecasting and planning tend to be primary. There are also loops when original plans have to be changed because certain resources are found to be unavailable (when organizing) or when cost overruns are discovered (through controlling).

Fayol's ideas are referred to as *classical management theory* (also dubbed *scientific administration*). Many commentators feel that they mirror, at the macro-organizational level, what scientific management offered at the micro-organizational level. According to classical management theory, there was one, best organization structure which would suit all organizations, irrespective of their size, technology, environment, or employees. This structure was based on the application of certain key principles which reflected the 'logic of efficiency', which stressed

- functional division of work,
- hierarchical relationships,
- bureaucratic forms of control,
- narrow supervisory span, and
- closely prescribed roles.

Airbus 380: a failure of coordination

The Airbus 380 passenger jet was unveiled in January 2005 in a grand ceremony in France. Six months later, a series of delivery delays began to be announced. Heads rolled, both at Airbus and its parent company, EADS. The immediate cause of the problem was a breakdown in the snap-together, final assembly process in Toulouse. The A380's rear fuselages are made in Hamburg, and are supposed to arrive in Toulouse with all their wiring ready to plug into the forward parts coming in from factories in north and west France.

Source: www.popularmechanics.com

Each A380 contains 500 km of wiring, weighing 580 tonnes with 100,000 electrical connections, and this is woven through its walls and floor (see diagram). When the two halves of the airplane arrived, they did not match up. The wires were too short to connect up with each other. Hamburg's failure to use the latest three-dimensional modelling software meant that nobody anticipated the effect of using lightweight aluminium wiring rather than copper. The aluminium makes the bends in the wiring looms bulkier. Worse still, engineers who scrambled to fix the problem did so in different ways. So the early aircraft all have their own, one-of-a-kind wiring systems. The greater complexity of the super-jumbo has shown up the weaknesses of Airbus's production system, and highlighted the need for a higher level of coordination (based on *The Economist*, 2006; *Fortune*, 2007).

STOP AND THINK

What are the advantages and disadvantages of having management principles based on the experience of successful managers?

Criticism of classical management theory

When considering classical management theory, it is important to locate it in its historical context. The managers of the period were dealing with larger, more complex organizations than had existed hitherto. At the beginning of the twentieth century many new companies developed. They employed vast numbers of people, had numerous plants and employed new technologies. All of this needed coordinating. With no model or experience to fall back on, those who managed these organizations had no choice but to develop their own principles and theories as to what to do to run them well. Inevitably these principles were grounded in their day-to-day experience of managing, and owed much to the models offered by military, religious, and governmental institutions. These were the only large organizations at the time. Over the years, various writers have criticized Fayol's principles (Thomas, 2003; Child, 1969; March and Simon, 1958; Peters and Waterman, 1982). Their criticisms included that he

- misleadingly proposed a single, standardized organizational model as the optimum one;
- promoted a militaristic, mechanistic organization, which stressed discipline, command, order, subordinates, and *esprit de corps*;
- overlooked the negative consequences of tight control and narrow task specialization, which can demotivate employees and hinder efficiency;
- overemphasized an organization's formal structure, while neglecting processes such as conflict management, decision-making, and communication;
- underestimated the complexity of organizations;
- based his ideas on unreliable personal knowledge, rather than systematic research evidence;
- lacked a concern with the interaction between people;
- underestimated the effects of conflict;
- underrated the capacity of individual workers to process information; and
- misunderstood how people thought.

Morgan's continuum of organization structure

Gareth Morgan (1989) presents a continuum of different organization structure designs ranging from a bureaucratic one possessing classical features at one extreme, to a flexible, organic structure at the other (see Figure 16.2). The latter possesses little task specialization, few rules, a high degree of individual responsibility and authority, and much delegated decision-making authority. He stated that a bureaucracy could probably evolve from numbers 1 to 3, and perhaps even to number 4. But for an organization to move to 5 or 6 would require a major revolution. Such a transformation would involve not only a change in an organization's structure, but also in its culture (see Chapter 4). If achieved, it would mean a loss of its bureaucratic features.

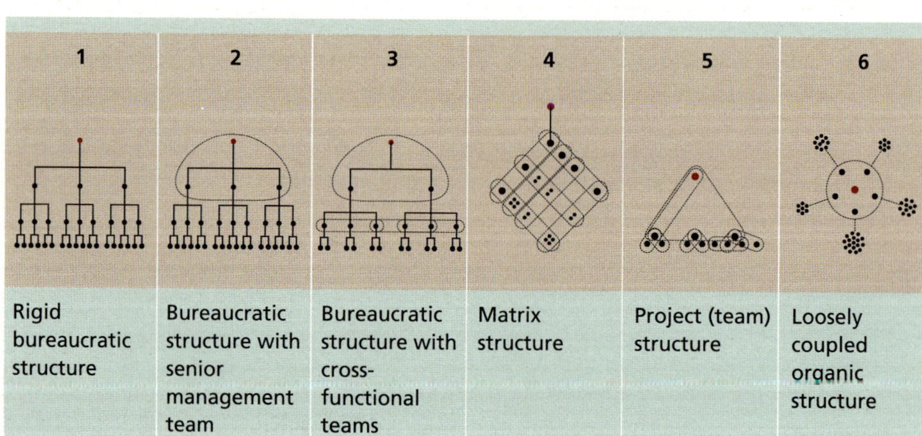

Figure 16.2: Types of organization structure
Source: from Morgan (1989, p. 66).

Rigid bureaucratic structure

This is Weber's classic bureaucratic structure. The organization operates in a very stable environment. Its structure is pyramid-shaped, and under the control of a single chief executive. Because all important principles have been codified, and every contingency is understood and has been anticipated, it is unnecessary for the executive to hold meetings.

Bureaucratic structure with senior management team

The environment is generating novel problems which cannot be anticipated, and for which responses cannot be codified. The chief executive creates a management team of departmental heads who meet regularly to deal with non-routine problems. Department heads have authority over their area of responsibility.

Bureaucratic structure with cross-functional teams

For problems requiring an interdepartmental view, a team is assembled consisting of lower-level staff from different departments. Members attend discussions as departmental representatives. They give the 'departmental view'; report back on developments to their department head; convey problems and information up to that person; and implement decisions made higher up. They operate as a less rigid bureaucracy.

Matrix structure

This is the matrix structure described in the next chapter. It attaches as much importance to projects or customer groups as to functional departments such as marketing and production. Employees report to two bosses – their departmental boss and their project boss.

Project team structure

In this design, the majority of the organization's core activities are tackled through project teams. If functional departments do exist, they play a background role. The task consists of completing a series of projects, and the vehicle for task achievement is the team. These teams are given the freedom to manage themselves within the strategic parameters defined by senior management. The organization possesses more of the features of a network of interaction than of a bureaucratic structure.

Loosely coupled organic structure

A small core of staff represent the organization and set its strategic direction. They form its 'inside' centre and sustain a network which is coupled to others, located 'outside'. They use contracting to get key operational activities performed. This network of firms is held together by its current product or service. The firm is really an open-ended system of firms, ideas, and activities. It lacks a clear organization structure and a definable boundary, making it difficult to determine what or who is inside or outside.

Persistence of bureaucracy

Why do the bureaucratic structural features described in this chapter continue to be a feature of the majority of large companies to the present day? Writers such as Leavitt and Du Gay have suggested a number of reasons to account for their continued existence.

1. *Success*: For the most part, over the last 100 years bureaucracy has worked. It has done so irrespective of technology, environment, and people, and irrespective of whether the organization has been a manufacturing, medical, educational, commercial, or military one.
2. *Large size*: Successful organizations survive and grow large, and the bureaucratic form is most efficient with large size.

3. *Natural selection favours bureaucracy*: Bureaucracy's natural features, the six identified earlier in this chapter, are inherently more efficient than any others, and thus allow the organization to compete more effectively.
4. *Static social values*: The argument is that Western values favour order and regimentation and bureaucracy is consistent with such values. People are goal-oriented and comfortable with authoritarian structures. For example, workers prefer clearly defined job responsibilities.
5. *Environmental turbulence is exaggerated*: The changes currently being experienced may be no more dynamic than those at other times in history. Management strategies can also reduce uncertainty in the environment.
6. *Emergence of professional bureaucracy*: Bureaucracy has shown its ability to adjust to the knowledge revolution, by modifying itself. The goal of standardization has been achieved in a different way among professional employees.
7. *Bureaucracy maintains control*: Bureaucracy provides a high level of standardization, coupled with centralized power, which is desired by those in command. For this reason senior managers who control large organizations favour this organization design.

Harold Leavitt (2005) believed that the bureaucratic hierarchy in modern organizations was increasing rather than declining, and that it was being helped by advances in technology. The authoritarian structures remain intact today, but are cloaked by a veil of humanism. According to Leavitt, organizational hierarchies are particularly resilient, managing to change while retaining their basic nature. They can favour one management style over others (participative, analytical, or 'hot groups'), and make that the basis of their organizational culture. They can also isolate some of their characteristics in separated sub-units (e.g. Xerox's Palo Alto Research Center) whose creation involved separating a 'hot group' from the rest of the company. They can break into smaller units; form into matrix structures; and even use technology to rid themselves of people. Despite these transmutations, the basic core of the bureaucratic organizational model remains intact.

In modern organizations, power and authority continue to lie with those at the top of the hierarchy. John Child argued that hierarchy pandered to some of the weaknesses in human nature. It 'offers some people better rewards than others, often on the basis of seniority rather than performance: it indulges people's need to feel more important than others: gives people a sense of personal progression through promotion up the ladder; legitimizes the exercises of power by some people over others' (Child, 2005, p. 394). Bureaucratic structures appeal to senior management as they centralize power in their hands, and it allows them to control those at the bottom of the hierarchy.

Henry Mintzberg's management roles

Henry Mintzberg (b.1939)

While Henri Fayol focused on managerial activities, Henry Mintzberg, a Canadian management academic, studied the different roles performed by managers. He researched how managers spent their time. His work led to a reassessment of the nature of managerial work within organizations, and a redefinition of the roles of the manager within organizational structures. Mintzberg (1973, 1975) studied chief executives in large and medium sized companies, categorizing the different behaviours associated with each of their positions, and distinguished ten **managerial roles** which he classified under the three headings of *interpersonal*, *informational*, and *decisional*, as shown in Table 16.3. Through their interpersonal roles managers acquired information; through their informational roles they determined the priority of information; and through their decisional roles they put it to use.

Mintzberg's research revealed a difference between what managers actually did and what they said they did. He showed that a manager's job was characterized by pace, interruptions, and brevity and fragmentation of tasks. In addition, managers preferred to

Table 16.3: Mintzberg's ten managerial roles

Role	Description	Examples
Interpersonal roles arise directly from a manager's formal authority and concern relations with others.		
Figurehead	Performs symbolic, representative, obligatory ceremonial, legal, and social duties.	Greets visitors; presents retirement gifts; signs contracts; takes clients to lunch; opens premises; attends annual dinners.
Leader	Creates the necessary culture and structure to motivate employees to achieve organizational goals.	Increases productivity through hiring, staffing, developing, coaching, training, and directing employees. Provides challenging assignments.
Liaison	Maintains network of contacts with those inside and outside own unit or organization who provide information and favours.	Attends staff and professional meetings; lunches with customers; meets departmental managers. Also uses email and phone.
Informational roles concern how information is used in the manager's job, where it comes from, and to whom it is communicated.		
Monitor	Scans environment for information to understand the working of own organization and its environment.	Questions subordinates and contacts; receives information from network contacts; reads business magazines; talks to customers; attends conferences.
Disseminator	Transmits information received from outsiders to the members of own organization (*internal* direction).	Makes phone calls; sends emails; writes reports; holds meetings with bosses, peers, and subordinates.
Spokesperson	Transmits information to outsiders on organization's views, policies, actions, and results (*external* direction).	Gives press conferences, media interviews, and speeches to external groups; prepares weekly status reports; conducts internal team briefings.
Decisional roles have their requirements determined by the manager's role, seniority, and availability of information.		
Entrepreneur	Searches the organization and its environment for new opportunities, and initiates planned, *voluntary* changes.	Develops new products, processes, and procedures; reorganizes departments; implements innovative employee payment systems.
Disturbance handler	Takes corrective action when organization has to react to important, *involuntary*, unexpected changes.	Intervenes to avoid a strike; deals with customer complaints; resolves personal conflicts between staff.
Resource allocator	Allocates resources to different departments by making approval decisions.	Budgets, schedules, programmes, assigns personnel, plans strategically, determines manpower load, sets targets.
Negotiator	Participates in sales or labour negotiations. Resolves inter-departmental arguments.	Negotiates merger details, supplier contracts, wage settlements, and internal disputes.

Based on Mintzberg (1973, 1975).

Managerial roles behaviours or tasks that a manager is expected to perform because of the position that he or she holds within a group or organization.

communicate face-to-face, and spent a great deal of time in meetings or in making contacts with others. Mintzberg argued that the ten roles that he identified could describe the nature of managerial work more accurately than other frameworks. The concept of role was introduced in Chapter 15. One aspect of it is that any role-holder can choose how to carry out their role. In the case of managers, they can decide how they wish to blend the ten listed roles, taking into account organizational constraints and opportunities. For Mintzberg, management is an art, rather than, as Fayol would argue, a teachable science.

Do managers make a difference?

In a British television programme entitled *Undercover Boss*, company chiefs disguised themselves and worked on the shop floor of their own companies. The climax of the programme involved the boss revealing his true identity to his co-workers. Much to his surprise (and disappointment?) his fellow co-workers often had no idea of who he was. How much difference, then, does a boss make to the performance of his or her organization? The cult of the chief executive has been promoted by business magazines who splash their photographs on the front covers, and give them all the credit for achievements to which thousands of their employees have contributed. Research by Antoinette Schoar estimated that the person at the top of a company accounted for just 5 per cent of a Fortune 500 company's performance. A survey by the Economist Intelligence Unit (2011) discovered that many bosses believed that their own words and actions were the key to motivating employees. When the same survey asked workers what they thought, most said that it was their relationship with their line manager that counted – 'people join companies but leave managers'.

Middle managers are currently unfashionable. Companies are sacking them; Lloyds banking group announced the removal of 15,000 middle managers, hoping to save £1.5 billion a year. TV shows such as *The Office* mock them. The days of the general manager 'who knew a little about lots' are over. Research by Lynda Gratton showed that knowledge workers received feedback on their performance from their peers working on the same project, and technology also helped them to monitor each other's output. So do middle managers still need to be supervised? Many firms have removed what they consider to be unnecessary layers of hierarchy. Unilever reduced the number of its levels from 36 to 6. However, middle management and bureaucracy are not synonyms. Cutting back on middle managers can be counterproductive. These individuals act as vital filters and upward communication channels, and possess crucial expertise which can impact on an organization's performance if it is removed (based on Schoar, 2011; Gratton, 2011).

Mintzberg stated that all managerial work was encompassed by these ten roles, but that the prominence of each role depends on the managerial level in the company hierarchy and the type of business. His study has provided the modern focus for all the subsequent research into debates about the nature of management. His work is most often contrasted with that of Henri Fayol.

In his most recent contribution on what managing entails, Mintzberg (2009) reviewed the research conducted into management roles over the past four decades, and developed what he calls a general model of managing, shown in Figure 16.3. This model is more elaborate than his original list of ten management roles. It presents three planes of managerial operation – information, people, and action; distinguishes between internally and externally focused roles; lists six major roles – communicating, controlling, leading, doing, linking, and dealing; and within these six, enumerates twenty-three sub-roles (Mintzberg, 2009, p. 90). To gain a fuller understanding of his current ideas, you should read his book (see Springboard).

Home viewing

Watership Down (1978, director Martin Rosen) is based on the book by Richard Adams. The amorphous group of ten rabbits are united by having to flee their home warren. They encounter several difficult and dangerous situations before finally establishing a permanent warren on Watership Down. A major theme of the story is how a shrewd, buoyant, young rabbit, Hazel, becomes transformed into the great leader, Hazel-rah. As you watch the film, make a note of which of Mintzberg's ten management roles Hazel plays, and when in the story. Decide which roles he does not play himself and which he delegates to other rabbits. Which of his behaviours shows leadership?

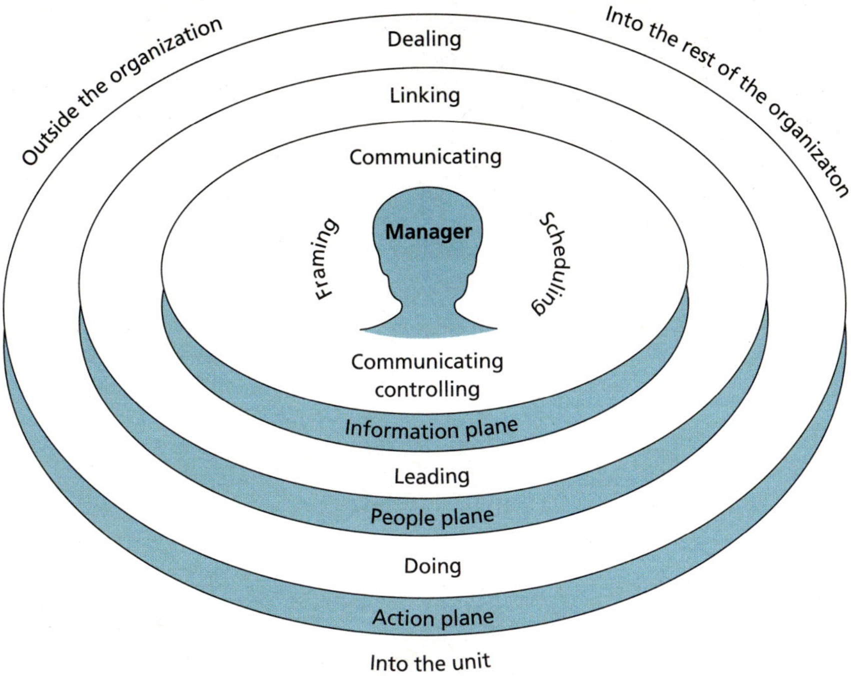

Figure 16.3: Henry Mintzberg's general model of managing
Source: Mintzberg (2009, p. 48).

Contingency approach

Contingency approach to organization structure a perspective which argues that to be effective, an organization must adjust its structure to take into account its technology, its environment, its size, and similar contextual factors.

The contingency approach to organizational behaviour asserts that the appropriate solution in any specific organizational situation depends (is *contingent* upon) the circumstances prevailing at the time. This approach has been influential in topics such as work design, leadership, and, not least, organization structuring. The **contingency approach to organization structure** argues that to be effective, an organization must adjust its structure in a manner that takes into account the type of technology it uses, the environment within which it operates, its size, and other contextual factors.

The contingency approach holds that managers need to analyse their own organization and its environment; decide and implement the most appropriate structure for the time; continually monitor the situation as it changes; and revise the structure as and when necessary. Thus organization design is an ongoing management task. Weber's bureaucratic organization structure, described earlier in this chapter, is said to be appropriate for (matches) a stable environment, while a turbulent company environment requires a more flexible organization structure. The contingency approach was a reaction to management thinking in the first half of the twentieth century which was dominated by the search for the 'one best way'. Taylor, Weber, and Fayol all recommended single, universal solutions to management problems, often in the form of laws or principles. Subsequent contributions to the contingency school came from many different researchers who studied wage payment systems, leadership styles, and job design. They sought to identify the kinds of situations in which particular organizational arrangements and management practices appeared to be most effective.

Determinism versus strategic choice

The main debate within the contingency approach to organization structuring is between two of its sub-schools – the determinists and the strategic choice thinkers. The determinists

Source: www.CartoonStock.com

assert that 'contextual' factors, such as an organization's size, ownership, technology, or environment, impose certain constraints on the choices that their managers can make about the type of structure to adopt. If the organization's structure was not adapted to its context, then opportunities would be lost, costs would rise, performance would be reduced, and the organization's existence could be threatened. They view the aforementioned variables as *determining* the organization's structure. Meanwhile, strategic writers contend that a company's structure is not predetermined in this way. Instead they say that it is always the outcome of a *choice* made by those in positions of power.

Contingency and technological determinism

Joan Woodward, James Thompson, and Charles Perrow are the leading figures in the school of *technological determinism*. They all agree that technology requires that certain tasks be performed, and that this in turn determines jobs, organization structures, and attitudes and behaviours. However, they differ both in the way in which they classify technologies and in how they conceive of the relationship been technology and organization structure.

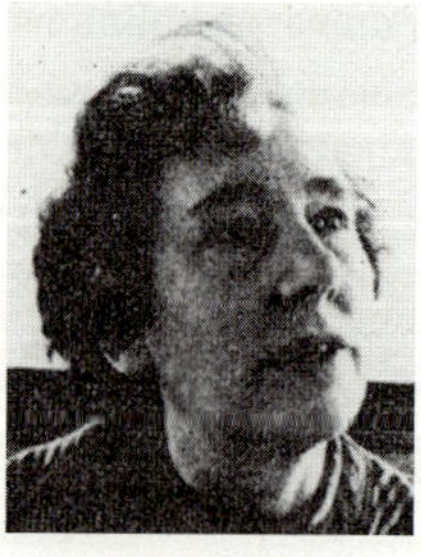

Joan Woodward (1916–1971)

Joan Woodward and technological complexity

Joan Woodward was a British academic whose work from the 1950s continues to have an impact today for at least three reasons. First, she created a typology for categorizing and describing different technologies, which gives us a 'language' with which to discuss them. Second, by discovering that no single organization structure was appropriate for all circumstances, she ended the supremacy of classical management theory, and ushered in the modern contingency approach to the design of organization structures. Third, by recognizing the impact of technology on organization design, she began a research tradition that has enhanced our understanding of the relation of new technologies to organizational forms.

Woodward studied 100 firms in south-east England. Having established their levels of performance, she correlated measures of company performance with different elements of organization structure which had been proposed by Weber, Fayol, and other writers. These elements included the number of hierarchical levels, the span of control, the level of written communication, and so on. She had expected her analysis to reveal the relationship between some of these elements of organization structure and the level of company performance, but it failed to do so. In her search for an alternative explanation, she noted that her firms used different technologies. She grouped their technologies producing a ten-step categorization based on three main types of production – unit, mass, and process. These were based on increasing **technical complexity** (1 = least complex; 10 = most complex) as shown in Figure 16.4. In unit production, one person works on a product from beginning to end, an example being a cabinetmaker producing a piece of hand-built furniture. In mass production, the technology requires each worker to make an individual contribution to a larger whole, for example, fitting a windscreen on a car assembly line. In process production, workers do not touch the product, but monitor machinery and the automated production processes, as, for example, in chemical plants and oil refineries. Technical complexity is usually related to the level of mechanization used in the production process.

Technical complexity the degree of predictability about, and control over, the final product permitted by the technology used.

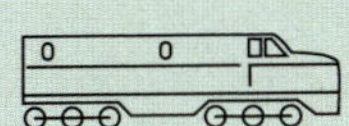

Unit production

1 Production of simple units to customers' orders

2 Production of technically complex units

3 Fabrication of large equipment in stages

4 Production of small batches

Mass production

5 Production of components in large batches subsequently assembled diversely

6 Production of large batches, assembly line type

7 Mass production

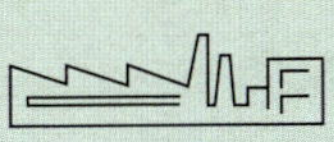

Process production

8 Process production combined with the preparation of a product for sale by large-batch or mass production methods

9 Process production of chemicals in batches

10 Continuous flow production of liquids, gases, and solid shapes

Figure 16.4: Woodward's classification of 100 British manufacturing firms according to their systems of production

Source: from Woodward (1958, p. 11).

STOP AND THINK

Woodward's classification of technologies is based on the manufacture of products. How well does it fit the provision of services? Consider services such as having your windows cleaned, buying a lottery ticket, insuring your car, or having a dental checkup. What alternative classification system would you need for these?

Woodward (1965) discovered that a firm's organization structure was indeed related to its performance, but through an important additional variable – technology. The 'best' or most appropriate organization structure, that is, the one associated with highest performance, depended (or was *contingent*) upon the type of technology employed by that firm. She introduced the concept of the 'technological imperative' – the view that technology determines an organization's structure. Specifically, she held that it was the complexity of the technology used that determined the structure.

Woodward identified differences in the technical complexity of the process of production and examined the companies' organization structures. She found that as the technology became more complex (going from type 1 through to type 10) two main things occurred. First, the length of the chain of command increased, with the number of management levels rising from an average of three to six. The proportion of managers to the total employed workforce rose, as did the proportion of indirect to direct labour. Her second major finding was that the increasing complexity of technology meant that the chief executive's span of control increased, as did that of supervisors. The span of control of first-line supervisors was highest in mass production and lowest in process production. Span of control refers to the number of subordinates supervised by one manager and represents one of the ways of coordinating the activities of different employees.

James David Thompson (1920–1973)

Woodward argued that a relationship existed between a company's economic performance and its technology. Her conclusion was that 'there was a particular form of organization most appropriate to each technical situation' (Woodward, 1965, p. 72). The reasoning underlying this conclusion is that the technology used to manufacture the product, or make available the service, places specific requirements on those who operate it. Such demands, for example, in terms of the need for controlling work or motivating staff, are likely to be reflected in the organization structure. The technology–structure link is complemented by the notion of effective performance which holds that each type of production system calls for its own characteristic organization structure.

James Thompson and technological interdependence

Technological interdependence the extent to which the work tasks performed in an organization by one department or team member affect the task performance of other departments or team members. Interdependence can be high or low.

Mediating technology technology that links independent but standardized tasks.

Long-linked technology technology that is applied to a series of programmed tasks performed in a predetermined order.

The second contributor to technological determinist perspective school was a sociologist, James Thompson (1967). He was not interested in the complexity of technologies (as was Woodward), but in the characteristic types of **technological interdependence** that each technology created. His argument was that different types of technology create different types of interdependence between individuals, teams, departments, and firms. These specify the most appropriate type of coordination required which, in turn, determines the structure needed (see Figure 16.5).

Mediating technology creates pooled interdependence

Mediating technology allows individuals, teams, and departments to operate independently of each other. Pooled task interdependence results when each department or group member makes a separate and independent contribution to the company or team performance. The individual outputs are pooled. Examples could include lecturers running their own courses, secretaries in a firm, sales representatives on the road, insurance claims units, and supermarket checkout operators. Since each individual's performance can be easily identified and evaluated, the potential for conflict between departments or individuals is low. Thus, predetermined rules, common forms, and written procedures all act to coordinate the independent contributions of different units and separate employees, while clearly defined task and role relationships integrate the functions. This produces a bureaucratic organization form in which the costs of coordination are relatively low.

Long-linked technology creates sequential task interdependence

Long-linked technology requires specific work tasks to be performed in a predetermined order. Sequential task interdependence results when one department, group, or individual

Type of technology	Form and degree of task interdependence	Main types of coordination used	Cost of coordination	Examples
Mediating	**'Pooled'** A B C D Low interdependence	*Categorization standardization* rules and procedures	low	Bank and branches University departments Baseball teams
Long-linked	**'Sequential'** A → B → C → D Medium interdependence	*Planning* scheduled meetings, committees	medium	Assembly line Fast food restaurants American football teams
Intensive	**'Reciprocal'** 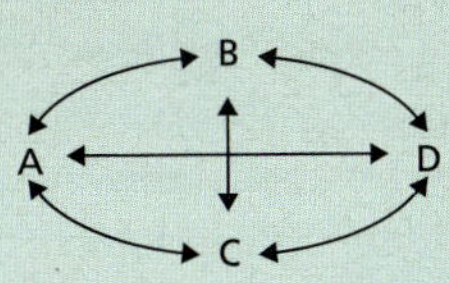 High interdependence	*Mutual adjustment* unscheduled meetings, face-to-face discussions, physical proximity, interdepartmental teams	high	Hospitals Airports Basketball teams

Figure 16.5: Thompson's typology of technology, interdependence, and coordination

employee must perform their task before the next can complete theirs. For example, in an organizational behaviour course taught by three lecturers, sequential task interdependence could mean that the first one has to complete their sessions on individual psychology before the second can teach group psychology, and only when this has been done can the third one present the material on organization structure. In a furniture factory, a cupboard has to be assembled before the handles can be attached. Sequential task interdependence means that a department's or group member's performance cannot be easily identified or evaluated, as several individuals, groups, or departments make a contribution to a single product or service.

At the company level, coordination is achieved through planning and scheduling which integrates the work of different departments. At the group level, coordination is achieved by close supervision of workers, forming work teams consisting of employees of similar levels of skills, and motivated by rewarding group rather than individual performance. The relative cost of coordination with this type of technology is medium.

Intensive technology creates reciprocal task interdependence

Intensive technology technology that is applied to tasks that are performed in no predetermined order.

Intensive technology creates reciprocal interdependence, where all the activities of all the different company departments or all of the team members are fully dependent on one another. The work output of each serves as the input for another. For example, in an organizational behaviour course which uses the group project method, a group of students can call upon different lecturers to provide them with knowledge or skill inputs to enable them to solve the project problems. Each lecturer would notice what the other had done, and would contribute accordingly. For this reason, with reciprocal task interdependence, the sequence of required operations cannot be predetermined. Thus, the mechanisms of coordination include unscheduled meetings, face-to-face contacts, project groups, task forces, and cross-departmental teams. This in turn necessitates a close physical grouping of reciprocally interdependent units, so that mutual adjustment can be accomplished quickly. Where this is impossible, then mechanisms like daily meetings, email, and teleconferencing are needed to facilitate communication. The degree of coordination required through mutual adjustment goes far beyond what is necessary for the other technologies discussed, making this the most expensive of the three.

STOP AND THINK

How do the three sports of American football, basketball, and baseball link to Thompson's three types of task interdependence?

Charles Bryce Perrow (b.1925)

Task variety the number of new and different demands that a task places on an individual or a function.

Task analysability the degree to which standardized solutions are available to solve the problems that arise.

Charles Perrow and technology and predictability

Charles Perrow (1970) is the third contributor to the technological determinist school. He saw technology's effect on organization structure as working through its impact on the predictability of providing the service or manufacturing a product. He considered two dimensions. He labelled the first **task variety**. This referred to the frequency with which unexpected events occurred in the transformation (inputs to outputs) process. Task variety would be high if many unexpected events occurred during a technological process. He termed the second dimension **task analysability**. This refers to the degree to which the unexpected problems could be solved using readily available, off-the-shelf solutions. Task analysability would be low if individuals or departments had to search around for a solution, and rely on experience, judgement, intuition, and problem-solving skills (see Figure 16.6).

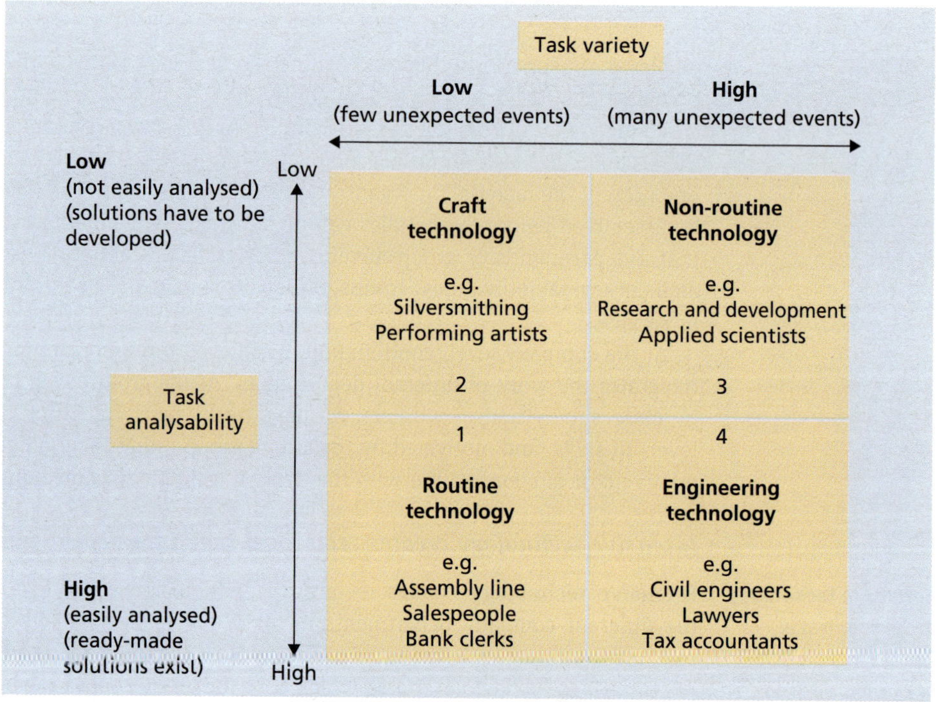

Figure 16.6: Perrow's model of technology

Source: from Perrow, Charles. *Organizational Analysis*. 1E. © 1970 Wadsworth, a part of Cengage Learning, Inc. Reproduced by permission. www.cengage.com/permissions

Types of technology

On the basis of these two dimensions, Perrow categorized technologies into four types, and discussed the effects of each one upon an organization's structure. He was particularly interested in coordination mechanisms, discretion, and the relative power of supervisors and the middle managers who supervised them.

1. *Routine technology*: In cell 1 are tasks which are simple and where variety is low (repetitive tasks). Task analysability is high (there are standard solutions available). Examples include supermarket checkout operations and fast food restaurants.
2. *Craft technology*: In cell 2 is craft technology, characterized by low task variety and low task analysability. The number of new problems encountered is small, but each requires some effort to find a solution. Examples include a plumber fitting a bath or shower, and an accountant preparing a tax return.
3. *Non-routine technology*: In cell 3 are complex and non-routine tasks, where task variability is high (with many new or different problems encountered), and task analysability is low (problems are difficult to solve). The tasks performed by research chemists, advertising agencies, high-tech product designers, and top management teams are all examples of non-routine technology.
4. *Engineering technology*: In cell 4, engineering technology is characterized by high task variety and low task analysability. Many new problems crop up, but each is relatively simple to solve. Civil engineering companies which build roads and bridges exemplify this type of technology, as do motor manufacturers producing customized cars.

When an organization's tasks and technology are routine, its structure is likely to resemble that proposed by Weber and Fayol. With a tall hierarchy, channels of authority and formal, standardized operating procedures are used to integrate the activities of individuals, groups, units, and departments. In contrast, when a firm's tasks and technology become non-routine and complex, an organization will tend to use a flatter hierarchy, more cross-functional teamworking, and greater face-to-face contact to allow individuals, groups, units, and departments to observe and mutually adjust to each other, and to engage in decision-making and problem-solving. The differences between the two structures will be manifested in the number and types of formal rules and procedures used, the degree to which decision-making is centralized, the skill levels of workers employed, the width of supervisors' span of control, and the means used for communication and coordination.

Contingency and environmental determinism

The second strand of determinism in organization structuring has been environmental. Several writers have had an interest in the relationship between a company's environment and its structure. Some of them argue that company success depends on securing a proper 'fit' or alignment between the company and its environment (see Chapter 2). For them, *environmental determinism* means that the environment determines organization structure. One prominent environmental determinist, Paul Lawrence, even said 'Tell me what your environment is and I shall tell you what your organization ought to be' (Argyris, 1972, p. 88).

The environmental determinists see the organization as being in constant interaction with its environment (see Figure 16.7). That environment consists of 'actors' or 'networks' (e.g. competitors, investors, customers). It includes the general economic situation, the market, the competitive scene, and so on. Each organization has its own unique environment. The more actors or networks that are relevant to a given company, the more complex its environment is said to be. Organizations vary in the relative degree of their *environmental complexity* (a concept we met in Chapter 2; see Duncan, 1972, 1973, 1974, 1979).

Those same actors and networks in an organization's environment can also change a great deal or remain the same. They thus differ in their degree of *environmental dynamism*. Different industries vary widely in their degree of dynamism. At one extreme of stability is the mainframe computer industry where new players must confront the barriers of an entrenched set of standards and the costs of switching are high. Here, the concepts of market segmentation, economies of scale, and pre-emptive investment are all still important. Mainframe computers are not immune to change, as the PC revolution showed, but there are periods of considerable stability. In the middle of the range, one finds businesses like

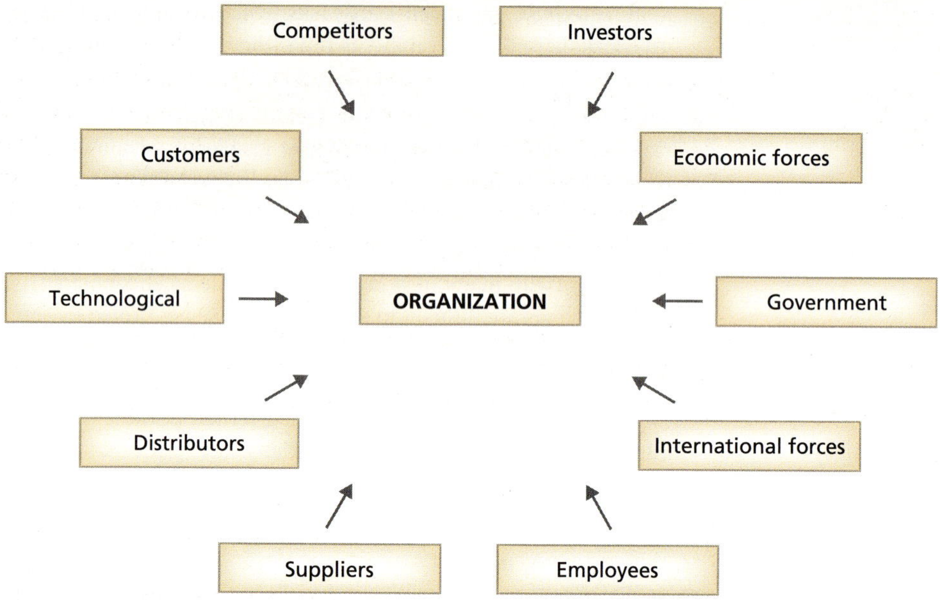

Figure 16.7: An organization depicted in its environment consisting of different actors, stakeholders, and networks

branded consumer goods. Substitution ranges from medium to high, and new entrants can replace established ones but not overnight. Survival and success depend upon capabilities and network relationships. Most industries are located in this middle ground. At the extreme of turbulence is a situation where customers can constantly and easily substitute. The environment consists of networks of players whose positions and prospects suddenly and unpredictably change. Many internet businesses are located at this end of the spectrum. For example, the popularity of the social networking website Facebook surpassed that of MySpace.

Environmental determinists argue that because a company is dependent on its environment for its sales, labour, raw materials, and so on, that environment constrains the kind of choices an organization can make about how it structures itself. As the environmental situation changes, the organization–environment relationship also changes. Hence, to be effective, a company has to structure and restructure constantly to maintain alignment (or 'fit'). The environmental determinists use the key concepts of environmental uncertainty and complexity in their explanations.

Mechanistic and organic organization structures

George McDonald Stalker (b.1925)

In the late 1950s in Britain, Tom Burns (1914–2002) and George Stalker studied the behaviour of people working in a rayon mill. Rayon is a yarn or fibre produced by forcing and drawing cellulose through minute holes. They found that this company, which was economically successful and had contented staff, was run with a management style which, according to contemporary wisdom about 'best' management practice, should have led to worker discontent and inefficiency. Some time later, the same authors studied an electronics company. It too was highly successful, but used a management style completely different from that of the rayon mill studied earlier. This contradiction gave the authors the impetus to begin a large-scale investigation to examine the relationship between management systems and organizational tasks. They were particularly interested in the way management systems changed in response to changes in the commercial and technical tasks of the firm (Burns and Stalker, 1961).

The rayon mill had a highly stable, highly structured character, which would have fitted well into Weber's bureaucratic organizational model. In contrast, the electronics firm violated many of the principles of classical management. It discouraged written communications, it defined jobs as little as possible, and the interaction between employees was on a face-to-face basis. Indeed, staff even complained about this uncertainty. Burns and Stalker gave the label *mechanistic organization structure* to the former and *organic organization structure* to the second. These represented organization structures at opposite ends of a continuum, with a mechanistic organization structure being one that possesses a high degree of task specialization, many rules, tight specification of individual responsibility and authority, and centralized decision-making, and an organic organization structure being one that possesses little task specialization, few rules, and a high degree of individual responsibility and authority, and in which decision-making is delegated (see Table 16.4). Most firms would be located somewhere in between these extremes.

Table 16.4: Characteristics of mechanistic and organic organization structures

Characteristic	Rayon mill (mechanistic)	Electronics (organic)
Specialization	High – sharp differentiation	Low – no hard boundaries, relatively few different jobs
Standardization	High – methods spelled out	Low – individuals decide own methods
Orientation of members	Means	Goals
Conflict resolution	By superior	Interaction
Pattern of authority, control, and communication	Hierarchical – based on implied contractual relation	Wide net based upon common commitment
Locus of superior competence	At top of organization	Wherever there is skill and competence
Interaction	Vertical	Lateral
Communication content	Directions, orders	Advice, information
Loyalty	To the organization	To project and group
Prestige	From the position	From personal contribution

Source: based on Litterer (1973), p. 339.

Burns and Stalker argued that neither form of organization structure was intrinsically efficient or inefficient, but that it all depended on the nature of the environment in which a firm operated. In their view, the key variables to be considered were the product market and the technology of the manufacturing process. These needed to be studied when the structure of a firm's management system was being designed. Thus, a mechanistic structure may be appropriate for an organization which uses an unchanging technology and operates in relatively stable markets. An organic structure can be more suitable for a firm that has to cope with unpredictable new tasks. Later, Rosabeth Moss Kanter (1983) relabelled these two constructs *segmentalist* and *integrative*, and argued that segmentalist systems stifled creativity, while integrative ones were more innovative.

Oticon: to organic and back again

In 1988, Oticon, a Danish manufacturer of hearing aids, was being seriously challenged by larger competitors such as Siemens and Philips. Incoming CEO Lars Kolind radically restructured ('disorganized') it, to create what he termed the 'spaghetti organization'. The company had been very bureaucratic. Vertically, it had a tall hierarchy with six levels of management. Horizontally, it was separated into divisions, and the two main ones – Electronics (product development) and International (sales) – communicated poorly with each other. Within each division, employees' work was organized around specific departments and tasks.

Kolind reorganized the work around projects instead of divisions. Project leaders (basically, anyone with a compelling idea) were appointed by a 10-person management team (the last vestige of the company's previous mechanistic structure). Project leaders competed to attract resources and recruit people to deliver results. Employees decided whether or not to join, and could only do so with the agreement of their current project leaders. The company had a hundred or so projects at any one time, so most people worked on several at once. Additionally, they needed to be multiskilled, so a software engineer had also to develop skills in marketing and aspects of production. Project owners (management team members) provided advice and support, but made few actual decisions. As a consequence, Oticon's organization structure became a fluid affair with no departments or divisions which could encourage local interests, impede communications, or make adjustments in workloads. Instead, project teams formed and re-formed as they were needed. The potential problems of this 'managed chaos' were kept at bay by the company having a clear purpose and a set of common values, which all employees knew about and subscribed to.

This allowed Oticon to dispense with the traditional features of a mechanistic structure. There were no job titles, and employees did whatever they felt was appropriate at the time. The company did not abandon physical space completely, and continued to use its headquarters building near Copenhagen, where about 150 staff were based. However, within the building there were few formal offices, only workstations with networked computers. These were often deserted as staff frequently moved around the building. Each employee had a small personal trolley for their personal belongings which they wheeled to wherever they were working that day. The building also had a conference room for teams to meet for problem-solving and brainstorming. Oticon's culture continued to value face-to-face contact, but did not dictate either its form or location. Staff members used mobile phones and email to participate in the activities of their teams while away from the office. The environment stressed motion and activity, rather than sitting at desks waiting for something to happen.

Oticon's organization structure reflected its own needs and own culture, and mixed virtual and tangible elements which allowed the maximum use of knowledge and human capital, while at the same time increasing efficiency. Over the first four years of its new, organic structure, Oticon doubled its size, and its operating profits increased by almost 1000 per cent. It had 1,200 staff in Denmark. Koland noted that 'hardware companies have organizations that look like machines: a company that produces knowledge needs an organization that looks like a brain, i.e. which looks chaotic and unhierarchical'. However, in 1996, Oticon incurred a number of unanticipated difficulties and reversed its radical restructuring. These included problems associated with coordination, employee time allocation, and the demotivating effect of managers having to intervene after projects had been approved. Additionally, management sought to align new project initiatives more closely with the company's strategic goals. The company partially abandoned its spaghetti organization, and gradually adopted a more traditional, matrix structure. The company is still characterized by considerable decentralization and delegation, but many of the key elements of the spaghetti organization have now been abandoned (based on Bjorn-Andersen and Turner, 1994; Rivard et al., 2004; Foss, 2003).

Differentiated and integrated organization structures

Differentiation the degree to which the tasks and the work of individuals, groups, and units are divided up within an organization.

During the 1960s, Paul Lawrence and Jay Lorsch (1967) built on the work of Burns and Stalker, using the concepts of *differentiation* and *integration*. First, consider **differentiation**. Differentiation refers to the process of a firm breaking itself up into sub-units, each of which concentrates on a particular part of the firm's environment. A university differentiates itself in terms of different faculties and departments. Such differentiation inevitably leads to the sub-units developing their own goals, values, norms, structures, time frames, and

Paul Roger Lawrence (b.1922)

Jay William Lorsch (b.1932)

Integration the required level to which units in an organization are linked together, and their respective degree of independence.

inter-personal relations that reflect the job that they have to do and the uncertainties with which they have to cope. Differentiation can take two forms. *Horizontal differentiation* is concerned with how work is divided up between the various company departments and who is responsible for which tasks. *Vertical differentiation* is concerned with who is given authority at the different levels of the company's hierarchy. High horizontal differentiation created many different departments, producing a flat structure as shown on an organization chart. High vertical differentiation resulted in many hierarchical levels, creating a tall structure. Lawrence and Lorsch found that effective organizations increased their level of differentiation as their environment became more uncertain. These adjustments allowed staff to respond more effectively to the specific sub-environment for which they were responsible. On the other hand, the more differentiated the sub-units became, the more their goals would diverge, and this could lead to internal conflicts.

Turning next to **integration**, this refers to coordinating the work performed in the previously divided (differentiated) departments, so as to ensure that it all contributes to accomplishing the organizational goal. Thus, for example, having divided a university into faculties, departments, and research units, there is the need to ensure that they all contribute to the goals of high-quality research, excellent teaching, and income generation. Lawrence and Lorsch found that as environmental uncertainty increased, and thus the degree of differentiation increased, so organizations had to increase the level of their integration (coordination) between different departments and their staffs, if they were to work together effectively towards the common goal. Coordination is achieved through the use of rules, policies, and procedures; goal clarification and communication; temporary task forces; permanent project teams; and liaison and integrator roles.

When environmental uncertainty is low, differentiation too is correspondingly low. Because the units share common goals and ways of achieving them, the hierarchy of authority in a company and its standard procedures are sufficient to integrate the activities of different units and individuals. However, as uncertainty increases, so too does the need for integration. While integration is expensive, using up the resources of time, money, and effort, a failure to integrate can be equally problematic, leading to conflict between departments which has to be resolved. Lawrence and Lorsch argued that the level of uncertainty in the environment that a firm has to cope with would determine the organization structure that was most appropriate for it.

STOP AND THINK

How well are the activities performed by your educational institution differentiated and integrated? Identify the problems and recommend solutions that would improve organizational performance from the student perspective.

Strategic choice

John Child (b.1940)

The debate about contemporary organization design involves a consideration of the decisions that managers make about their organizations within their environments. Thus, strategic choice and environment are central concepts. Both Tom Burns and George Stalker (1961) and Paul Lawrence and Jay Lorsch (1967) stressed the importance of an organization's environment. Their original contributions were concerned primarily with the market conditions, and took a deterministic perspective. Their critics, however, pointed to the neglect of *choice* in decisions about organization structure. John Child (1972) rectified this omission, arguing that there was no one best organization structure, and that companies could have different structures. However, he disagreed with the contention that those structures were *determined* by 'external, operational contingencies'. Instead, he stressed the part played by powerful leaders and groups, who exerted their influence to create organization structures which suited their particular values and preferences.

Strategic choice theory the view that an organization's environment, market, and technology are the result of senior management decisions.

Strategic choice theory holds that managers who control an organization make a strategic choice about what kind of structure it will have. They also manipulate the context in which their company operates, and how its performance is measured. The decisions about the number of hierarchical levels, the span of control, division of labour, and so on are ultimately based on the personal beliefs and political manoeuvrings of the senior executives who make them. Strategic choice researchers continue to focus on companies' environments, but they became interested in how senior managers make the choices that link their firms' strategies to their organization structures. These commentators have criticized the deterministic writers on a number of issues:

1. *The idea that an organization should 'fit' its environment.* That is, while there are choices about organization structure design, these will be relatively limited. Thus, for two similar companies operating in a stable environment to succeed, each would make similar choices about the shape of their organization structures. However, there are examples of companies making very different structural choices in the same circumstances and both succeeding.
2. *The idea that cause and effect are linked in a simple (linear) manner.* This ignores the fact that organizations are part of a larger, complex environmental system consisting of other organizations with which they interact. Managers can influence and shape their own company environments. The idea that organizations merely adapt to their environment is too simple a view.
3. *The assumption that the choice of organization structure is an automatic reaction to the facts presented.* Studies show that decisions are made by managers on the basis of the interpretations that they have made about the nature of their environment. The same environment can be perceived in different ways, by various managers who might implement different structures, which can be equally successful.
4. *The view that choices of organization structure are not political.* Linked to the previous point, political factors will impinge on choices about structure as much as issues of perception and interpretation.

Child suggested that organization structuring was a political process in which power and influence were used to decide on the types of jobs, levels of hierarchy, spans of control, etc. that were to be adopted and, by implication, which markets to enter and with which companies to link up. His work stimulated discussion in three main areas (Child, 1997):

- the human agents (individuals or groups) who exercise choice in the design of organizations;
- the nature of the environment within which an organization exists;
- the relationships between organizational agents (e.g. managers) and that environment.

Enacted environment the environment of an organization that exists for members by virtue of the interpretations they make of what is occurring 'outside' the organization, and the way their own actions influence or shape those occurrences.

Managerial enactment the active modification of a perceived and selected part of an organization's environment by its managers.

Figure 16.8 summarizes the different approaches to structuring organizations.

The first of the two major strategic choice perspectives was presented by Karl Weick (1979), who introduced the concept of **enacted environment**. This is the notion that organization and environment are created together (enacted) through the social interaction processes of key organizational participants – usually managers (Smircich and Stubbart, 1985; Westwood and Clegg, 2003). The environment within which managers work and make decisions does not consist of a simple set of objective conditions which are just 'given'. Here we use Tony Watson's definition of **managerial enactment**.

The environment of an organization exists for its members by virtue of the interpretations that they make of what is occurring 'outside' the organization, and the way in which their own actions influence or shape those occurrences. Watson (2002) illustrates this point with the example of a market and a product. A business organization does not go out and 'find' a market which it then satisfies in order to stay in business. Instead, its managers first strategically identify the *possibility* of a market relationship with certain would-be customers outside the organization. They then work at their product in the light of the possibilities and potentials that they envisage. Next they present the product to the would-be customers, in a way that will *persuade* them to trade with the organization, again in the light of their

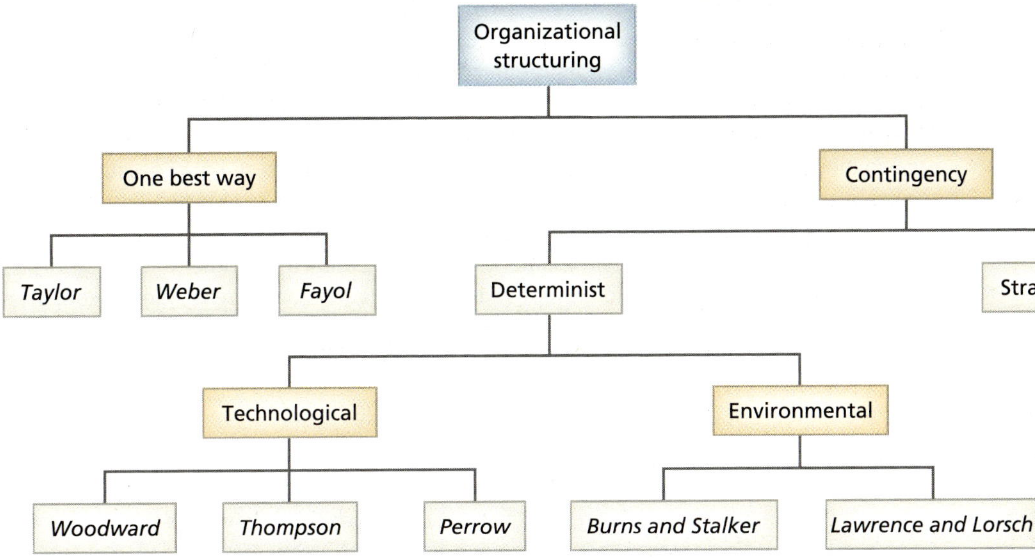

Figure 16.8: Contrasting theoretical approaches to organization structuring

interpretations of the inclinations of these potential customers. Active sense-making is central to all this.

Ian Brooks (2003) offered another example of enactment, this time from the football industry. He noted that a number of football teams are relegated annually from the higher divisions, and commented that, according to press reports, many had given up the struggle well before the end of the season. He noted that they stopped spending money on new players and prepared themselves for leaner times in lower divisions. By doing this, they increased their chances of being relegated since, without new players or the motivation to stay up, their performance remained poor, or even declined, and they were indeed relegated. When this happened, the clubs looked back and said that since they knew that they were going down, they did the sensible thing, and saved their money and energy for the following season. He asked whether these football clubs could have stayed up had they adopted a different strategy, or did they enact their environment? In Weick's view, managers *enact* their environments, rather than *reacting* to them. That is, they *create* their organization's environment, making it easier for them to understand and modify it.

Resource dependence theory theory that although organizations depend on their environments to survive, they seek to assert control over the resources they require, in order to minimize their dependence.

The second major strategic choice perspective – **resource dependence theory** – answers the question of how managers make choices. Developed by Jeffrey Pfeffer and Gerald Salancik (1978), their theory sees every organization as being at the mercy of its environment, needing resources from it in the form of employees, equipment, raw materials, knowledge, capital, and outlets for its products and services. The environment gives a firm its power, but also controls access to these resources. It thus makes the firm dependent on its environment – hence the name of the theory. The environment (in the form of customers, suppliers, competitors, government, and other stakeholders) uses its power to make demands upon the organization to provide not only desirable products and services at competitive prices, but also efficient organization structures and processes.

Pfeffer and Salancik argue that although organizations are dependent on their environments, their managers have still to achieve their chosen objectives. To do this, they need to identify the critical resources needed – defined as those without which the company cannot function. They then trace these back to their sources in their environment and identify the nature of their dependence. For practical reasons, only the most critical and scarce resources are focused on. While it is possible to distinguish and discuss a single dependency relation between an organization and an environmental element, in practice a firm will be experiencing a complex set of dependencies between itself and the various elements in its environment. When costs or risks are high, companies will team up to reduce their dependencies and risks of bankruptcy.

For example, for McDonald's fast food restaurants, having beef, buns, and cheese is critical, having plastic customer seating is not. Scarcity refers to how widely the critical resources are available in the organization's environment. Control of resources that are most critical and scarce gives environmental elements the greatest power over a company. Pfeffer and Salancik (1978) stated that the first step in applying the approach is to understand the organization's environment with respect to the criticality and scarcity of resources. The second step is for managers to find ways of reducing that dependency, eliminating it altogether, or making the others dependent on their organization. Companies use their power differences to avoid excessive dependence on their environment, in order to maintain control over required resources, and thereby reduce uncertainty and increase their autonomy.

There are a number of dependence-reduction strategies. If you are a manufacturer, you could develop long-term contracts with suppliers; have several suppliers for your crucial components; purchase part-ownership of your suppliers; establish a joint venture; or simply buy up all the resources that are critical to your company. At the start of the twentieth century, in order to secure access to the critical resources that he needed, Henry Ford bought iron mines, coal mines, rubber plantations, shipping lines, and railways. This corporate strategy, which involves acquiring related businesses that are assimilated into the purchaser's own, is called **vertical integration**. Although a popular strategy, mergers and acquisitions are only one of many kinds of relationship that one company can have with another, as it seeks to reduce its dependency on its environment.

Vertical integration a situation where one company buys another in order to make the latter's output its own input, thereby securing that source of supply through ownership.

STOP AND THINK

Select an organization that you have read about or have first-hand experience of. What are the critical resources required for its continued operation?

RECAP

1. *Distinguish between charismatic, traditional, and legitimate forms of authority.*
   - Traditional authority is based on the belief that the ruler has a natural right to rule.
   - Charismatic authority is based on the belief that the ruler has some special, unique virtue, either religious or heroic.
   - Legitimate authority is based on formal written rules which have the force of law.
2. *State the main characteristics of a bureaucratic organization structure as specified by Max Weber.*
   - Job specialization; authority hierarchy; employment and career; recording and keeping of all administrative acts and decisions; rules and procedures to which all employees are subject; and impersonality of those procedures and rules meaning that they apply to all equally.
3. *Distinguish Fayol's six managerial activities and the main ideas of the classical management school.*
   - Fayol distinguished six managerial activities: forecasting, planning, organizing, commanding, co-ordinating, and controlling.
   - The classical management school was based on the experience of managers and consultants rather than researchers.
4. *Distinguish Mintzberg's ten management roles.*
   - His ten managerial roles are figurehead, leader, liaison, monitor, disseminator, spokesperson, entrepreneur, disturbance handler, resource allocator, and negotiator.

5. ***Identify the writers who comprise the contingency approach and state their main individual contributions.***
   - Contingency writers challenged Max Weber and Henri Fayol's view that there was one best way to structure an organization.
   - They held that there was an optimum organization structure that would maximize company performance and profits, and that this structure would differ between firms.
   - Technological contingency theorists Joan Woodward, Charles Perrow, and James Thompson saw technology determining appropriate organization structure.
   - Environmental contingency theorists Tom Burns and G.M. Stalker, Paul Lawrence and Jay Lorsch saw the environment determining appropriate organization structure.
6. ***Discuss the strengths and weaknesses of early ideas on the design of organization structure and the practice of management.***
   - Bureaucracy provides a rationally designed organizational model that allows complex tasks to be performed efficiently. Persons who are best qualified to do it carry out the work. It provides safeguards against personal bias and individual favouritism.
   - However, bureaucracy creates dysfunctional consequences, with members only interested in their own jobs; following rules obsessively; and slow to respond to changes. Bureaucracies perpetuate themselves.
7. ***Identify the influence of early organization design ideas on contemporary organizations.***
   - Modern organizations continue to possess the features first described by Weber and Fayol over a century ago.
   - Early design principles have been successful; have helped large organizations to survive; reflect the static social values of many nations and cultures; are capable of withstanding environmental turbulence; and allow senior management to retain power.

Revision

1. Commentators argue that both too much and too little bureaucracy in an organization de-motivate employees and cause them stress. How can this be?
2. How does uncertainty affect the successful operation of rationally designed organization structures such as those proposed by Weber and Fayol?
3. Define and distinguish differentiation and integration. Using an example from your experience or reading, illustrate these two processes in operation, and highlight some of the problems that can be encountered.
4. Explain how technology and environment might influence the structure of an organization. Consider their effect on coordinating activities.

Research assignment

Use the internet to familiarize yourself with the Seven Wonders of the Ancient World – the Mausoleum at Halicarnassus, the Statute of Zeus at Olympia, the Temple of Artemis at Ephesus, the Hanging Gardens of Babylon, the Lighthouse of Alexandria, the Great Pyramid of Giza, and the Colossus of Rhodes. Select one of these seven. Imagine that you are living at the time that your wonder is about to be built. Decide how, given the constraints of ancient technology and science, you would construct your wonder, applying whichever of Fayol's managerial activities you consider to be appropriate. How would you plan the structure, organize the construction workers, motivate them, check quality, materials and so on? Which of Fayol's management activities would be the most difficult to apply when building your wonder? (This assignment is based on Stovall, 2010.)

Springboard

Harold Leavitt (2005) *Top Down: Why Hierarchies Are Here to Stay and How to Manage Them More Effectively*, Harvard Business School Press, Boston, MA. The subtitle exactly describes the book's content.

Henry Mintzberg (2009) *Managing*, Financial Times Prentice Hall, Harlow, Essex. The author develops his original ideas on managerial roles incorporating the research of others over the past thirty years, and presents a general model of managing.

Johan Olsen (2006) 'Maybe it is time to rediscover bureaucracy', *Journal of Public Administration Research and Theory*, 16(1), pp. 1–24. This article questions the view that bureaucracy is obsolete and undesirable, and argues that it complements more recent forms of organization structure.

Ola Vie (2011) 'Have post-bureaucratic changes occurred in managerial work?', *European Management Journal*, 28(3), pp. 182–94. The author provides an examination of changes in the work of middle and first-line managers.

OB in films

Crimson Tide (1995, director Tony Scott), DVD track 04: 0:25:00 to 0.31.33 (7 minutes). This is the story of how a global emergency provokes a power play on board a US nuclear submarine, between the battle-hardened Captain Frank Ramsay (played by Gene Hackman), who 'goes by the book', and his Executive Officer, Lieutenant Commander Ron Hunter (Denzil Washington). The captain regularly runs a weapons systems readiness test in preparation for launching nuclear missiles. The clip begins with a loudspeaker announcement saying 'Attention all hands, the fire has been contained', and ends with Ramsey saying to Hunter 'We're here to defend democracy, not to practise it'.

As you watch this clip of the weapons test, identify an example of each of Weber's six principles of bureaucracy.

Bureaucratic principle	Examples
1. Job specialization	
2. Authority hierarchy	
3. Formal selection	
4. Rules and procedures	
5. Impersonality and impartiality	
6. Recording	

OB on the web

Watch Gary Hamel's short lecture 'Passion trumps intellect' as he presents his hierarchy of human capabilities. Give examples of how, in the past, the organizations have attempted to secure the three employee capabilities at the bottom of the pyramid. Suggest how managers might redesign their company structures for the future, to encourage and obtain the three employee capabilities located at the top of Hamel's hierarchy.

CHAPTER EXERCISES

1. Debra's diary

Objectives

1. To contrast management roles with management activities.
2. To identify examples of each.

Briefing

1. Remind yourself of Mintzberg's ten management roles and Fayol's six managerial activities.
2. Form groups and nominate a spokesperson.
3. Read the case *Debra's diary* and then:
   (a) Identify one example of each of Mintzberg's ten roles played by Debra (first ten items), and of each of Fayol's managerial activities performed by her (next six items).
   (b) Do any of her tasks involve playing more than one management role or engaging in more than one managerial activity?

Debra's diary

Debra is the chief executive of a large private hospital in London. In an effort to manage her time better, she kept a diary of the tasks she performed during a couple of days.

	Mintzberg	Fayol
1. Held a meeting with all staff to inform them about the government's new requirements for the feeding and management of elderly patients.		
2. Closed the ward with the MRSA problem; instigated a 'deep clean' procedure to ensure that this outbreak within the hospital had been contained; and introduced a new hygiene management code of conduct.		
3. Had the opportunity to buy a CAT scanner at a huge discount price, if we acted immediately. I called each of the board members to get them to agree to the investment. Some were unsure, but I managed to persuade them.		
4. Went to the local radio station to represent the hospital, to be interviewed about our work and answer listeners' calls.		
5. Gave a presentation to a training course which clarified hospital goals, and stressed the importance of staff's role in achieving them.		
6. Had lunch with our local Member of Parliament and got advanced information about future trends in government healthcare policy and funding.		
7. Spent two hours surfing the web to discover how our hospital compares in terms of numbers of patients and staff, as well as facilities, with our competitors here and abroad.		
8. Acted to resolve a dispute between a doctor in charge of the X-Ray department and the union representative, concerning technicians.		
9. Finalized the budgets for all the hospital departments in line with our income and organizational objectives.		
10. Gave a speech at the Effective Healthcare Conference describing our hospital's approach to waste management.		

→

	Mintzberg	Fayol
11. Held a meeting with the different department heads to ensure nursing staff were being efficiently allocated to the different wards.		
12. Reviewed the food purchase data to ensure that all foodstuffs had been obtained in accordance with procedures laid down by the hospital, and that the quantities of food supplied by vendors had been specified.		
13. Used internet to discover illness trends among the population so as to anticipate increases and decreases for our various medical services.		
14. Devised a new 'pay for performance' compensation system which ensured that those who had exceeded their targets were appropriately rewarded.		
15. In anticipation of the upcoming annual inspection, I compiled a list of tasks to be completed then assigned these to the various senior managers.		
16. Discussed with the board of directors how the expansion of our obesity care provision would be managed over the next five years.		

2. I detest bureaucracy

Objectives

1. Understand how an organization stripped of most of Weber's bureaucratic features would operate.
2. Assess whether or not you would feel comfortable working in such an organization.

Briefing

1. Form groups. Read the case *TechTarget*.
2. Discuss:
   (a) How would you describe the organization structure of this company?
   (b) Why does it work at TechTarget?
   (c) Could this structure be applied in other organizations?
   (d) Strakosch claims that he 'detests bureaucracy' and seems to think that he has eradicated it with his 'open leave' policy. Identify Weber's six characteristics of bureaucracy (p. 541) that are likely to be applied in TechTarget.
   (e) Would you like to work at TechTarget?

TechTarget

TechTarget Inc. is an online information technology interactive media company based in Needham, Massachusetts that employs 210 staff. Founded in 1999, it became a public $100 million company in 2007, and now provides products to over 1,000 advertisers including Cisco, Dell, EMC, HP, IBM, Intel, Microsoft, and SAP. Its co-founder and Chief Executive Officer is Greg Strakosch. What is distinctive about this organization is that it has an 'open leave' policy. There are no set policies or rules concerning staff working hours or specifying sick or personal holidays. If you want to work between midnight and 6 a.m., that's OK. If you want to take a day off to take your family to the seaside, that's OK too. However, the company is not a holiday camp. TechTarget is an entirely results-oriented business. Managers set quarterly goals and timetables, and employees are measured by their contribution to the company and the results that they achieve. They are given a great deal of freedom to accomplish these but, in exchange for this flexibility, employees are expected to remain in close contact with their managers via email, cell-phone, instant messaging and laptops. The company says that it enthusiastically rewards performance with greater opportunity, compensation, and recognition. While the hours are flexible, employees can put in 50 hours in some weeks. However, at other times, staff use their time to study or to travel. The company employs 25 mothers with children under 10, who find the working arrangements ideal. The management team set high performance expectations, and have little tolerance for failure. Despite a painstaking hiring process that weeds out all but the most autonomous applicants, 7 per cent of the workforce were dismissed in the last twelve months. 'We don't carry people who underachieve', said Strakosch. Other employees have been fired for abusing the policy. The company's success is based on hiring a team of smart, self-motivated, enthusiastic, ambitious, hard-working people and giving them autonomy and flexibility while holding them accountable for their results. It is a fast-paced, stimulating work environment that fosters teamwork. Its entrepreneurial culture encourages innovation and rewards individual achievement. The company seeks to provide its employees with satisfying careers and an environment that enables them to achieve a work-life balance. Strakosch is quoted as saying 'I detest bureaucracy and silly policies'. In the middle of 2008 TechTarget was recognized as one of the best places to work by a local business journal, but at the end of the year it was planning to make 76 of its staff redundant..

Based on Saucer, 2003; Boston Business Journal, *2008a, 2008b; www.techtarget.com.*

Employability assessment

With regard to your future employment prospects:

1. Identify up to three issues from this chapter that you found significant.
2. Relate these to the competencies in the employability matrix.
3. Decide what actions you need to take to maintain and/or develop those competencies under each of the four headings of the employability matrix.

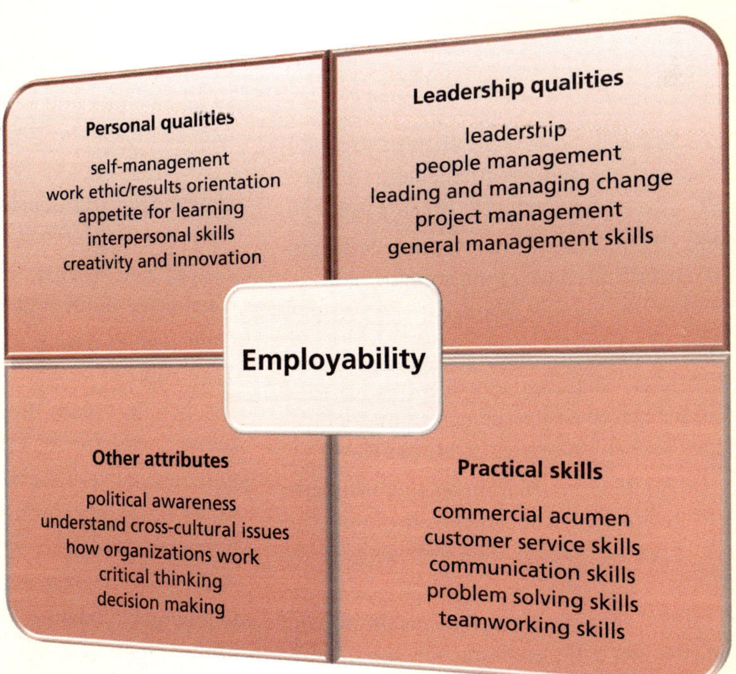

References

Allen, N. (2008) 'Court cases hampered by poor paperwork', *Daily Telegraph*, 22 May.

Argyris, C. (1972) *The Applicability of Organizational Sociology*, London: Cambridge University Press.

BBC Online News website (2007) 'Brown orders data security checks', 21 November.

BBC Online News website (2008a) 'Paperwork hampers court cases', 22 May.

BBC Online News website (2008b) 'Discs loss "entirely avoidable"', 25 June.

Bjorn-Andersen, N. and Turner, J. (1994) 'Creating the twenty-first century organization: the metamorphosis of Oticon', in R. Baskerville (ed.), *Transforming Organizations with Information Technology*, North Holland, Amsterdam: Elsevier Science, pp. 379–94.

Blau, P.M. (1966) *The Dynamics of Bureaucracy* (2nd edn), Chicago, IL: University of Chicago Press.

Boston Business Journal (2008a) 'TechTarget recognized as one of area's "Best Places to Work"', 10 June.

Boston Business Journal (2008b) 'TechTarget to cut 76 positions', 12 December.

Brooks, I. (2003) *Organizational Behaviour: Individuals, Groups and Organization* (2nd edn), Harlow, Essex: Financial Times Prentice Hall.

Burns, T. and Stalker, G.M. (1961) *The Management of Innovation*, London: Tavistock Publications.

Child, J. (1969) *British Management Thought*, London: George Allen and Unwin.

Child, J. (1972) Organizational structure, environment and performance: the role of strategic choice', *Sociology*, 6(1), pp. 1–22.

Child, J. (1997) 'Strategic choice in the analysis of action, structure, organizations and environments: retrospect and prospect', *Organization Studies*, 18(1), pp. 43–76.

Child, J. (2005) *Organization: Contemporary Principles and Practice*, Oxford: Blackwell Publishing.

Du Gay, P. (2005) *The Values of Bureaucracy*, Oxford: Oxford University Press.

Duncan, R.B. (1972) 'Characteristics of organizational environments and perceived environmental uncertainty', *Administrative Science Quarterly*, 17(3), pp. 313–27.

Duncan, R.B. (1973) 'Multiple decision making structures in adapting to environmental uncertainty: the impact on organizational effectiveness', *Human Relations*, 26(3), pp. 273–91.

Duncan, R.B. (1974) 'Modifications in decision making structures in adapting to the environment: some implications for organizational learning', *Decision Sciences*, 5(4), pp. 705–25.

Duncan, R.B. (1979) 'What is the right organization structure?: Decision tree analysis provides the answer', *Organizational Dynamics*, 7(3), pp. 59–80.

Economist Intelligence Unit (2011) *Re-engaging with Engagement: Views from the Boardroom on Employee Engagement*, London, http://www.businessresearch.eiu.com/sites/businessresearch.eiu.com/files/LON%20-%20PL%20-%20Hay%20report_WEB.pdf.

Edwards, D. (2011) *I'm Feeling Lucky: The Confessions of Google Employee Number 59*, London: Allan Lane.

Fortune (2007) 'The big picture', 155(4) (5 March), pp. 57–64.

Foss, N.J. (2003) 'Selective intervention and internal hybrids: interpreting and learning from the rise and decline of the Oticon spaghetti organization', *Organization Science*, 14(3), pp. 331–49.

Gouldner, A.W. (1954) *Patterns of Industrial Bureaucracy*, New York: Free Press.

Gratton, L. (2011) *The Shift: The Future of Work Is Already Here*, London: Collins.

Hall, R.H. (1963) 'The concept of bureaucracy: an empirical assessment', *American Journal of Sociology*, 69(1), pp. 32–40.

Jacobs, E. (2010) 'Sandy, sandy eggshell or eggy sand? What kind of khaki to wear to work?', *Financial Times*, 24 December, p. 6.

Kanter, R.M. (1983) *The Change Masters: Corporate Entrepreneurs at Work*. London: George Allen and Unwin.

Kay, J. (2011) 'A smart business dressed in principles not rules', *Financial Times*, 12 January, p. 11.

Lawrence, P.R. and Lorsch, J.W. (1967) *Organization and Environment*, Boston, MA: Addison-Wesley.

Leavitt, H.J. (2005), *Top Down: Why Hierarchies Are Here to Stay and How to Manage Them More Effectively*, Boston, MA: Harvard Business School Press.

Litterer, J.A. (1973) *The Analysis of Organizations*, Chichester: John Wiley.

March, J. and Simon, H.A. (1958) *Organizations*, New York: Wiley.

Merton, R.K. (1940) 'Bureaucratic structure and personality', *Social Forces*, 18(1/4), pp. 560–8.

Mintzberg, H. (1973) *The Nature of Managerial Work*, London: Harper Collins.

Mintzberg, H. (1975) 'The manager's job: folklore and fact', *Harvard Business Review*, 53(4), pp. 49–61.

Mintzberg, H. (2009) *Managing*, Harlow, Essex: Financial Times Prentice Hall.

Morgan, G. (1989) *Creative Organization Theory*, London: Sage Publications.

Perrow, C. (1970) *Organizational Analysis: A Sociological View*, Belmont, CA: Wadsworth.

Peters, T.J. and Waterman, R.H. (1982) *In Search of Excellence: Lessons from America's Best Run Companies*, New York: Harper and Row.

Pfeffer, J. (1981) *Power in Organizations*, London: Harper Collins.

Pfeffer, J. and Salancik, G.R. (1978) *The External Control of Organizations: A Resource Dependence Perspective*, New York: Harper and Row.

Rivard, S., Bennoit, A.A., Patry, M., Pare, G. and Smith, H.A. (2004) *Information Technology and Organizational Transformation*, Oxford: Elsevier/Butterworth-Heinemann.

Robbins, S.P. and Coulter, M. (2009) *Management*, Upper Saddle River, NJ: Pearson Education.

Saucer, P.J. (2003) 'Open door management', *Inc*, June, p. 44.

Schoar, A. (2011) 'CEO careers and style', MIT working paper, http://www.mit.edu/~aschoar/CEOCareers Style_v2.pdf.

Smircich, L. and Stubbart, C. (1985) 'Strategic management in an enacted world', *Academy of Management Review*, 10(4), pp. 724–35.

Sparkes, I. and Salkeid, L. (2010) 'No sexiness in the city: female staff ordered to wear loose-fitting skirts and flesh-coloured underwear by UBS', *MailOnline*, 16 December, www.dailymail.co.uk/news/article1338871/.

Stovall, S.A. (2010) 'Recreating the arsenal of Venice: using experiential activities to teach the history of management', *Journal of Management Education*, 34(3), pp. 458–73.

The Economist (2006) 'The airliner that fell to earth', 7 October.

The Economist (2008) 'The good, the bad and the inevitable: the electronic bureaucrat: a special report on technology and government', 16 February, pp. 6–9.

The Economist (2011) 'Pointless regulations: "It's jungle out there"', 22 October, pp. 80–1.

The Economist (2012) 'Banking against Doomsday', 10 March, p. 67.

Thomas, A.B. (2003) *Controversies in Management* (2nd edn), London: Routledge.

Thompson, J.D. (1967) *Organizations in Action*, New York: McGraw-Hill.

Watson, T.J. (2002) *Organizing and Managing Work*, Harlow, Essex: Financial Times Prentice Hall.

Weber, M. (1947) *The Theory of Social and Economic Organization* (trans. A.M. Henderson and T. Parsons), Oxford: Oxford University Press.

Weick, K.E. (1979) *The Social Psychology of Organizing*, Boston, MA: Addison-Wesley.

Westwood, R. and Clegg, S.R. (2003) 'Organization-environment', in R. Westwood and S.R. Clegg (eds), *Debating Organization*, Oxford: Blackwell, pp. 183–4.

Woodward, J. (1958) *Management and Technology*, London: HMSO.

Woodward, J. (1965) *Industrial Organization: Theory and Practice*, Oxford: Oxford University Press.

Chapter 17 Organizational architecture

Key terms

organizational architecture
departmentalization
functional structure
divisional structure
matrix structure
team-based structure
boundaryless organization
collaborative relationship structure
outsourcing
offshoring
reshoring
hollow organization structure
modular organization structure
virtual organization structure
co-opetition
strategic alliance
joint venture
user contribution system
crowdsourcing

Learning outcomes

When you have read this chapter, you should be able to define those key terms in your own words, and you should also be able to:

1. Appreciate the reason for chief executives' need to design and redesign their organization's structure.
2. Distinguish three eras of organizational design and what factors stimulated each.
3. Distinguish between functional, divisional, matrix, and team-based organization structures.
4. Distinguish between an outsourcing relationship and hollow, modular, and virtual organization structures.
5. Understand the trend towards companies' collaborative relationships with competitors and customers, and their involvement in virtual communities.

Why study organizational architecture?

The relationships between organizations and their owners, their employees, and their clients/consumers are changing rapidly. In 2012, Circle, a private company, took over the running of Hinchinbrook Hospital in Cambridgeshire, England. This was a unique moment in the history of the National Health Service (NHS) in Britain, as it was the first time that the management of an all-purpose NHS hospital had been transferred from public sector to private sector management. However, the hospital has not been privatized. The NHS retains control of the hospital's assets and staff. Circle has a ten-year contract, and can take the first £2 million of any surplus achieved. It is expected to be run like the John Lewis Partnership (a British department store owned by its employees) with staff holding a 49.9 per cent stake in the firm. The government is seeking an alternative to the traditional NHS 'command-and-control' structure. Hinchinbrook Hospital is one example of the many new structural relationships that are emerging between different groups of stakeholders (Plimmer, 2012; Neville, 2012).

Organizational architecture the framework of linked internal and external elements that an organization creates and uses to achieve the goals specified in its vision statement.

The general term given to such relationships is **organizational architecture**, which refers to the framework that an organization creates and uses to achieve the goals specified in its vision statement. It thus not only includes the internal arrangements that a firm makes to deploy its various business processes, but also considers how these may be linked with those of outsiders (other individuals, groups, and organizations) who come together with the firm to form a temporary system for their mutual benefit. The first part of this chapter will focus on internal structural arrangements, while the second part will consider external linkages.

Senior management decides on job duties, lines of authority, bases of departmentalization, and so on. They are under pressure to design structures that balance the current internal pressures and external demands in order to make their companies effective, efficient, and profitable. While a particular organization structure will not in itself ensure the achievement of a company's goals, an inappropriate structure could impede it.

Organization design refers to senior management's process of choosing and implementing a structural configuration through which their organizations seek to accomplish their goals. Chief executives actively make this choice. Whittington, Mayer and Smith (2002) note that business is too big and too complex to allow an inappropriate organization structure to interfere with creating shareholder value and ensuring long-term company survival.

Organizational structures had been a way of institutionalizing and managing stability, but now they have had to become flexible and adaptive to accommodate uncertainty in the form of discontinuous change. In the past, it was thought that an organizational arrangement whereby the company performed all its tasks internally was the best way to gain competitive advantage. Indeed, at the start of the twentieth century, Henry Ford owned railway lines, steamship companies, iron mines, and rubber plantations. A century later, however, increased competition, globalization, and technological developments have all meant that working with others has come to be seen as the best way to reduce costs and increase efficiency and productivity. Consequently, answers to the question of 'who does what' now extend beyond the organization's own boundary to encompass its partners, competitors, and customers, as well as other communities of interest.

Historically, the initial problem for management was building and maintaining large-scale production processes and the organizations that operated them. Then attention focused on coordinating and controlling these large, complex organizations and facilitating their orderly growth. Most recently, the focus has shifted onto inter-organizational relationships. Building on the work of Robert Duncan (1979), Narasimhan Anand and Richard Daft (2007) traced changes in the design of organization structures. They distinguish the three eras of organizational design shown in Table 17.1, illustrating how management thinking about organization structure changed from vertical organization to horizontal organizing, and then to boundaryless hollow, modular, virtual, and collaborative structures. In this chapter, we shall draw heavily on these authors' explanatory structure and use their framework to compare and contrast the changes that have occurred in the design of organizations.

Table 17.1: Eras of organizational design

Era 1	Era 2	Era 3			
Mid 1800s to late 1970s	1980s to mid 1990s	Mid 1990s to present			
Self-contained vertical organization structures	Self-contained horizontal organization structures	Boundaryless organization structure			
		Hollow	Modular	Virtual	Collaborative

Source: based on Anand and Daft (2007).

STOP AND THINK Think of an example of a change to the structure of an organization with which you are familiar. How has this changed the way that you and others do your work?

Era of self-contained organization structures

Departmentalization the process of grouping together activities and employees who share a common supervisor and resources, who are jointly responsible for performance, and who tend to identify and collaborate with each other.

Functional structure an organizational design that groups activities and people according to the similarities in their work, profession, expertise, goals, or resources used.

The first era identified by Anand and Daft (2007) lasted over a century, from the mid 1800s to the late 1970s. During that time, the ideal organization was held to possess the following characteristics: being self-contained; having clear boundaries between itself and its suppliers, customers, and competitors; transforming the inputs from suppliers into completed products or services; and meeting its transformation process requirements internally. Its design emphasized the need to adapt to environmental conditions, and to maximize control through reporting relationships and a vertical chain of command (Galbraith, 1973).

Anand and Daft (2007, p. 335) list the underlying design principles of a self-contained organization structure as

- grouping people into functions or departments;
- establishing reporting relationships between people and departments;
- providing systems to coordinate and integrate activities both horizontally and vertically.

A department designates a distinct area or branch of an organization over which a manager has authority for the performance of specified activities. Thus job grouping or the **departmentalization** of jobs constitutes an important aspect of organizational design. During this era, the functional, divisional, and matrix organization structures became popular. All three rely on vertical hierarchy and the chain of command.

Functional structure

A **functional structure** groups activities and people, from the bottom to the top, according to the similarities in their work, profession, expertise, goals, or resources used, e.g. production, marketing, sales, and finance (see Figure 17.1). Each functional activity is grouped into

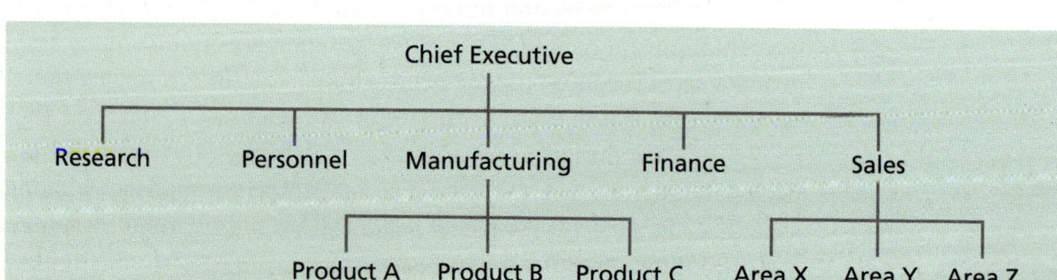

Figure 17.1: Function-based organization structure

a specific department. A university business school may group its staff into the main subject fields (finance, human behaviour; strategy and marketing and operations management).

Divisional structure

Divisional structure an organizational design that groups departments together based on the product sold, the geographical area served, or the type of customer.

A **divisional structure** splits an organization up into self-contained entities based on their organizational outputs – products or services provided, the geographical region operated in, or the customer groups served. Each division is likely to have its own functional structure replicated within it or receive functional support (e.g. marketing, human resources) from its headquarters. Each division operates as a stand-alone company, doing its own research, production, marketing, etc. (Chandler, 1962). British hospitals are increasingly divisionalized with departments such as surgery and medical diagnostics operating with functional support from departments such as finance and estates.

Product-based

A single motor company can organize around its different automotive brands. For example, Daimler's divisions include Mercedes-Benz and Smart, while BMW's include BMW and Mini. Most university business schools offer undergraduate, postgraduate, and non-graduating courses. A product- or service-based organization structure is shown in Figure 17.2.

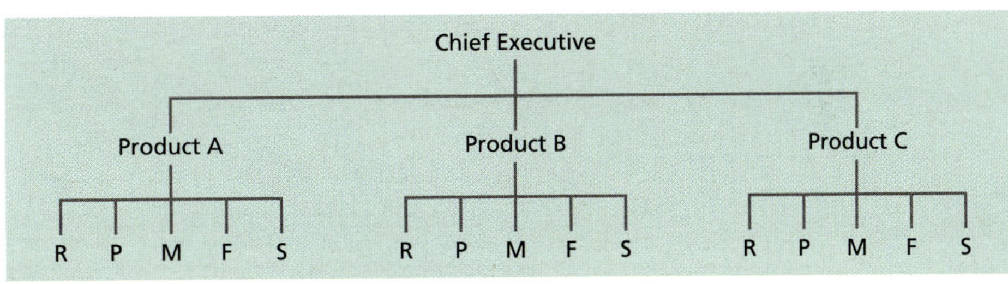

Figure 17.2: Product-based organization structure

Geography-based

Grouping on this basis is used where the product or service is provided within a limited distance. It meets customers' needs effectively and economically, and lets senior management check and control how these are provided. Hotels and supermarkets are organized in this way. A university business school may have a main campus, a city centre location, and an out-of-town, residential (hotel) facility. A geography-based (or region/location-based) organization structure is shown in Figure 17.3.

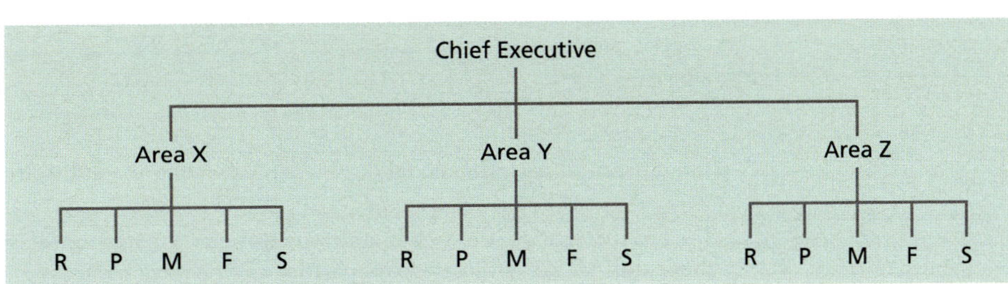

Figure 17.3: Geography-based organization structure

Customer-based

The company can be structured around its main customers or market segments. A large bank's departments may be personal, private, business, and corporate. A university business school's clients include students, companies, and research-funders. BT is divided into BT Retail (business and residential customers) and BT Wholesale (corporate customers). A customer-based organization structure is shown in Figure 17.4.

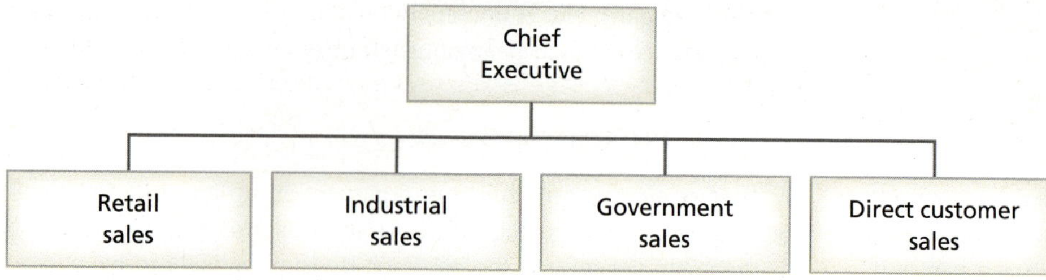

Figure 17.4: Customer-based organization structure

Matrix structure

Matrix structure an organizational design that combines two different types of structure resulting in an employee having two reporting relationships simultaneously.

A **matrix structure** combines a vertical structure with a strong horizontal overlay. The former provides downward control over the functional departments, and the latter allows inter-departmental coordination. This structure comprises employees working in temporary teams composed of employees from different functions (e.g. marketing, human resources, production) contributing to specific projects. This structure has two lines of authority. Each team member reports to two bosses – their project team manager and their functional (department) manager, e.g. the head of production. There is thus a dual, rather than a single, chain of command (Bartlett and Ghoshal, 1990; Davis and Lawrence, 1978; Lawrence and Davis, 1979). A matrix organization structure is shown in Figure 17.5.

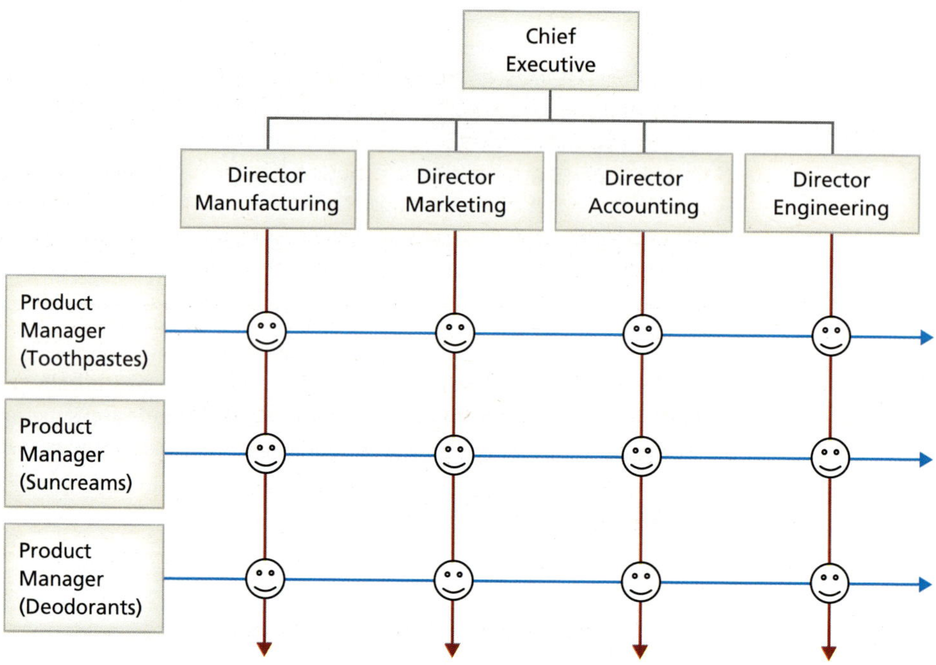

— The director of each functional department exercises line authority through the vertical chain of command.

— The product manager exercises authority through the horizontal chain of command, over those staff from the functional departments who have been assigned to work on the product.

☺ Employees at the intersections have two bosses. They report simultaneously to the director of their functional department (manufacturing, marketing, accounting, or engineering) as well as to their product manager (toothpastes, suncreams, or deodorants).

Figure 17.5: Matrix organization structure

As a student, the place that you are likely to encounter a matrix structure is on your university course or module, if it is taught by lecturers from a number of different university departments. These contributing lecturers report to two different bosses. One of these is responsible for the function, in this case, their university academic department (e.g. Accounting, Economics, Law, or Management). Their other 'boss' is the course or module coordinator responsible for the teaching, tutoring, and assessments for the module.

Philips the matrix master

Philips, a Dutch electrical giant, was one of the earliest champions of the matrix structure. After the Second World War it established both national organizations and product divisions. Philips staff are expected to have two bosses. For example, the head of its washing machine division in Italy reports to both the head of Philips in Italy, and also to the washing machine supremo in the Netherlands. Committees were used to coordinate the two lines of command that had been created, and to resolve any ensuing conflicts. By 1991, Philips was in deep financial trouble and was reviewing its structural arrangements. It had experienced problems of accountability (was the country boss or product head responsible for the profit-and-loss account?), and power plays between country heads and business bosses (consumer electronics, medical products). Bartlett and Ghoshal concluded that matrix structures led to conflict and confusion; that the proliferation of channels created informational log jams; that multiple committees and reports bogged down the organization; and that overlapping responsibilities produced turf battles and a loss of accountability. Academic commentators have described the matrix structure as one of the least successful organizational forms (based on Hindle, 2006a; Bartlett and Ghoshal, 1990).

Era of horizontal organization structures

The second era identified by Anand and Daft (2007) lasted under two decades (between the 1980s and the mid 1990s), and promoted horizontal organization structures with a team- and process-based emphasis. It developed in response to the limitations of the earlier organization structures. These included difficulties of inter-departmental coordination; the ineffectiveness of vertical authority-based reporting systems; and the opportunities offered by computers and networks to increase organizational information-processing capacity. During this time, emphasis was placed on re-shaping (eliminating) organizations' internal boundaries to improve horizontal coordination and communication. Anand and Daft (2007, p. 332) list the underlying design principles of a horizontal organization structure as

- organizing around complete workflow processes rather than tasks;
- flattening hierarchy and using teams to manage everything;
- appointing team leaders to manage internal team processes and coordinate work;
- permitting team members to interact with suppliers and customers, facilitating quick adaptation;
- providing required expertise from outside the team as required.

Team-based structure

Team-based structure an organizational design that consists entirely of project-type teams that focus on processes rather than individual jobs, coordinate their activities, and work directly with partners and customers to achieve their goals.

The above principles were predominantly implemented by means of a **team-based structure** which treats teams as organizing units of work. The company uses teams as the main way to coordinate the activities within it (Forrester and Drexler, 1999). Here, individual employees are assembled into teams in a way similar to being assigned to traditional, functional departments. In one version, the organization consists *entirely* of different teams, each of which coordinate their own activities, and works with their partners and customers, to achieve their goals. Each team member possesses a different expertise (e.g. marketing, manufacturing, finance, human resources), which contributes to the team's completion of its task or project. Team-based organizations have flattened hierarchies. This involves designing organizations around processes rather than tasks (Mohrman et al., 1997). The teams focus on processes that need to be done rather than on individual jobs. In order for the different members to coordinate their contributions successfully, they must share information effectively with each other (Cherns, 1976).

These teams are characterized by horizontal communication; shared or rotated leadership; and delegated decision-making that gives authority to junior staff to make decisions on their own. Once the goal has been achieved, the team moves onto a new project, perhaps re-forming its membership before embarking on its next task. A true team-based structure is rarely found in organizations. Where it does exist, it tends to be in smaller organizations. A team structure is very flat, as shown in Figure 17.6. A university department may use a team structure. Academic staff may be members of a multidisciplinary research team contributing to a project, funded by a research council; a teaching team responsible for delivering lectures and tutorials; and an administrative team, ensuring rooms are booked, student grades awarded, and legal requirements complied with.

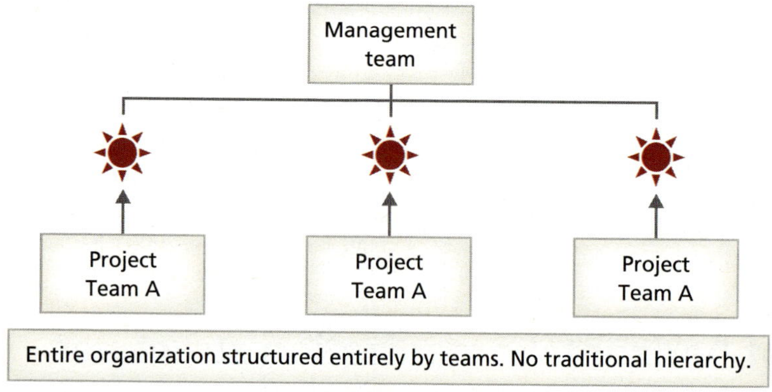

Figure 17.6: Team-based organization structure

One example of an organization with a team-based structure is Square D, a large US manufacturer of electrical equipment based in Lexington, Kentucky. In 1998, the company divided its 800 employees into 20–30 self-managed teams which were wholly responsible for their own products from start to finish. Another rare example is Whole Food Markets Inc, also in the United States, a retailer of natural foods. Each of its shops is an autonomous profit centre consisting of about ten teams. Each small, decentralized team (e.g. grocery, vegetables, bakery, prepared food) has its own team leader. It also has complete control over recruiting and selecting new employees. Using team-based hiring, after 90 days, potential hires need two-thirds of the team's support to join the staff permanently (Erickson and Gratton, 2007). The team leaders in each shop are a team; the shop leaders in each region are a team; and the company's six regional presidents are also a team (Fishman, 2007).

It is far more common for a traditional, vertically-structured company to add teams to the bottom of its hierarchy. Only lower-level employees, those who manufacture the product or provide the service, come to operate as teams rather than as individuals. When this type of work arrangement is used on a regular basis, the organization may claim to be using a team-based structure. In reality, however, all that has happened is that it has grafted a teamworking format onto the lower hierarchical levels of an existing functional or divisional structure. Its organizational chart will look like that shown in Figure 17.7.

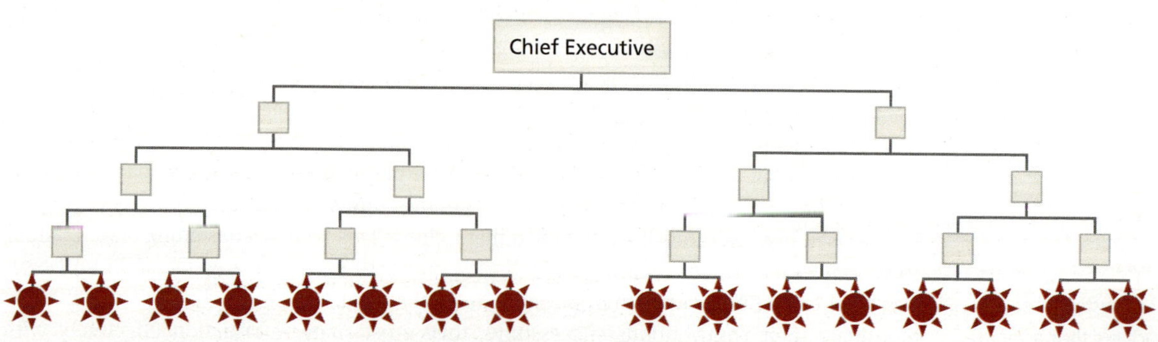

Figure 17.7: Traditional organization structure with teams at lowest level

This 'teams-at-the bottom' structure may use a *cross-functional team* approach in which a number of teams consisting of employees from various functional departments, at about the same hierarchical level, are formed to complete particular tasks. As before, the benefits of this arrangement include access to the different expertise of members, improved horizontal communication, and better inter-departmental coordination. Typical issues addressed by cross-functional teams are solving a problem, developing or launching a new product, or initiating a change programme. The development of the Ford Motor Company's Escape gas-electric hybrid sports utility vehicle involved cross-functional teamworking.

Boeing's production teams

The 787 Dreamliner is a medium sized, wide-bodied, twin-engine jet capable of carrying 210 to 330 passengers. To produce it, the company created an organization structure consisting of Life Cycle Product Teams (LCPTs) that have responsibility for the life-cycle cost of their product. Each LCPT has a team leader, an engineering leader, a manufacturing leader, a finance and business leader, and a global partner leader, and has responsibility for the design, production, and delivery of their product on schedule and on cost to the 787 programme. The LCPTs operate like companies within the bigger programme. They are of two types – vertical and horizontal.

Hanusa/AP/Press Association Images.

Final assembly of 787 aeroplane

Vertical LCPTs are responsible for the plane's structural components such as fuselage, interior, wings, propulsion, vertical tail, and landing gear. Their task is to deliver their product into final assembly where it all gets integrated with the others and built into the aeroplane. Horizontal LCPTs address matters relevant to all the different structural component teams. They are labelled systems, services, and production operations. The Systems LCPT is responsible for the architecture, testing, and the systems that go into the aeroplane. It ensures that the systems architecture for hydraulics, electrical, and other systems on the aeroplane are all integrated. The Services LCPT is responsible for obtaining the input for the structural repair manual which comes from managers in the horizontal teams. The Production Operations LCPT is responsible for putting this aeroplane together and their work begins once the final assembly of the aeroplane is initiated (based on Dodge, 2007a; 2007b).

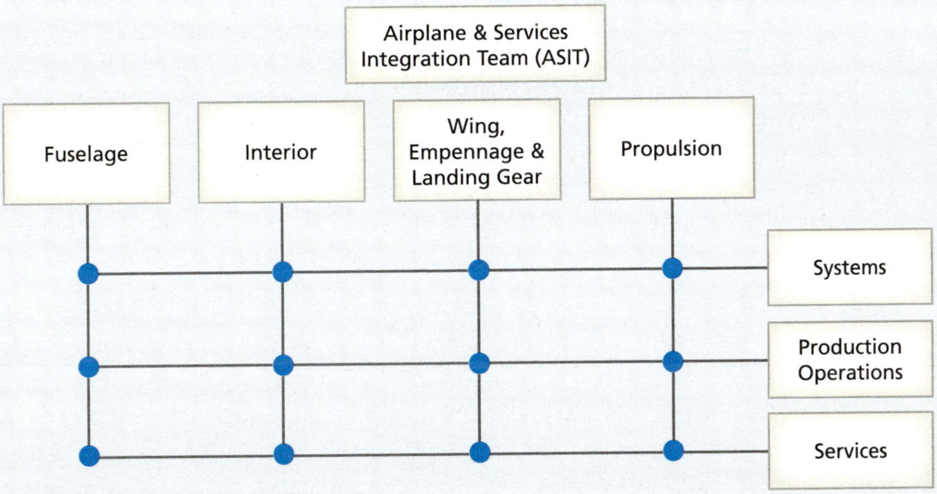

Life Cycle Product Teams (LCPTs)

Source: Boeing 787 Dreamliner Engineering Chief Describes Partners Organization, *Design News* (2007), http://www.designnews.com/article2659-Boeing_787_Dreamliner_Engineering_Chief_Describes_Partners_Organization.php. Copyrighted 2013. UBM Electronics. 98714:313BC.

There are many different structural forms that era 1 and era 2 organizations can take. To help our understanding, Christopher Mabey et al. (1998, p. 235) offered a conceptual framework based on the juxtaposition of various dimensions.

These distinguish firms with different internal structures, but all of them exist within conventional organizational boundaries. These authors' three dimensions are:

Decision-making – Organizational structures differ in terms if where decisions are made. They range from centralized (decisions made at the top) through to decentralized (power delegated for people to make decisions lower in the hierarchy).

Rules prevalence – Companies differ in terms of how many written rules, operating procedures, job descriptions, organizational charts they have, and their use of formal, written communication. This dimension is called formalization, and ranges from few rules to many rules.

Size of organization – Firms differ in size. The size dimension is usually measured in terms of the number of employees and ranges from large to small.

As summarized in Table 17.2, organizations have structures based on the main organization functions, where employees sharing common skills are placed together. This reflects Weber's bureaucracy. Then we have various divisional structures (product/service, geography, customer), selected to be most suited to a company's activities. Next there is the matrix stricture, creating cross-functional teams consisting of individuals from different departments within the company. Finally, we have a structure based entirely on teams which are given limited autonomy to complete an entire production process.

Table 17.2: Era 1 and 2 organization structures

	Decision-making	Rules	Size
Functional	highly centralized	many	large
Divisional	centralized	some	medium
Matrix	decentralize	several	intermediate
Team-based	highly decentralized	few	small

Home viewing

The film *Other People's Money* (1991, director Norman Jewison) shows how a firm's failure to react to an external threat leaves it vulnerable to a hostile takeover. New England Wire and Cable (NEWC) is an old-fashioned manufacturing company, paternalistically led for 26 years by Andrew Jorgenson (played by Gregory Peck) who values stability and predictability. However, he is unaware of the developing problems in one of his company's divisions which requires urgent re-engineering and diversification. Meanwhile, Garfield Investment Corporation (GIC), headed by Lawrence Garfield (played by Danny DeVito), looks for firms that are ripe to be taken over, and expects to make a substantial profit by liquidating NEWC. As you watch the film, consider some of the reasons that corporate restructuring takes place. How does Jorgenson's leadership and decision-making style leave his company vulnerable to a takeover?

Era of boundaryless organizations

Boundaryless organization an organization possessing permeable internal and external boundaries which give it flexibility and thus the ability to respond to change rapidly.

The third era identified by Anand and Daft (2007) began in the mid 1990s and continues to this day. It is characterized by the development of an organization architecture called the **boundaryless organization**. This concept views firms as possessing permeable boundaries, both internally and externally. The firm behaves like an organism, encouraging better integration among its functional departments and closer partnerships with outsiders, so as to facilitate the free exchange of ideas and information, in order to maximize its flexibility and be able to respond rapidly to change. The term was coined by the former chief executive of General Electric (GE) Jack Welch, who wanted to eliminate barriers inside his company, not only horizontally, between GE's different departments, but also vertically, between the different levels of GE's management hierarchy. He also sought to break down barriers outside, between his company and its customers, suppliers, and other stakeholders (Ashkenas et al., 2002).

Many organizations are adopting this approach in order to become more effective. Due to increasing costs and time pressures, companies now rarely innovate on their own. Instead, they increasingly seek partners with whom they can collaborate to share costs and speed up development. Adopting this type of organizational design involves establishing collaborative relationships with suppliers, competitors, customers, third parties, and participants in online communities. Increasingly, we are seeing examples of loosely interconnected assemblages of companies operating different types of **collaborative relationship structures** (Schilling and Steensma, 2001).

Collaborative relationship structure a structure that involves a relationship between two or more organizations, sharing their ideas, knowledge, staff, and technology for mutual benefit.

This approach has been facilitated by the opportunities created by improved communication technology (internet, mobile phones) and the rise of emerging economies (China, India), as well as by management's acceptance that an organization cannot efficiently perform alone all the tasks required to make a product or offer a service. Organizational structuring involves translating company policy into practices, duties, and functions that are allocated as specific tasks to individuals and groups. However, increasingly these individuals and groups can be located outside the company. In the last twenty years, the accent has moved from hierarchy (single chain of command) to heterarchy (multiple chains of command); from bureaucracy to adhocracy; from structures to processes; from real to virtual; and from closed to open.

Outsourcing

Outsourcing contracting with external providers to supply the organization with the processes and products that were previously supplied internally.

Underpinning all the developments in organizational structure in this era has been **outsourcing**. This describes a situation in which an organization contracts with another firm either to provide it with a business process, such as paying its staff wages (payroll), or to supply it with a component for its final product – e.g. a computer hard drive, a steering wheel, or a packaging box – which it would previously have made itself. Figure 17.8 illustrates this relationship, showing that outsourcers can supply both products and processes. Anand and Daft (2007) identified three types of organization structure used in boundaryless organizations, all of which used the outsourcing principle – hollow, modular, and virtual. To these we can add a fourth type – collaborative.

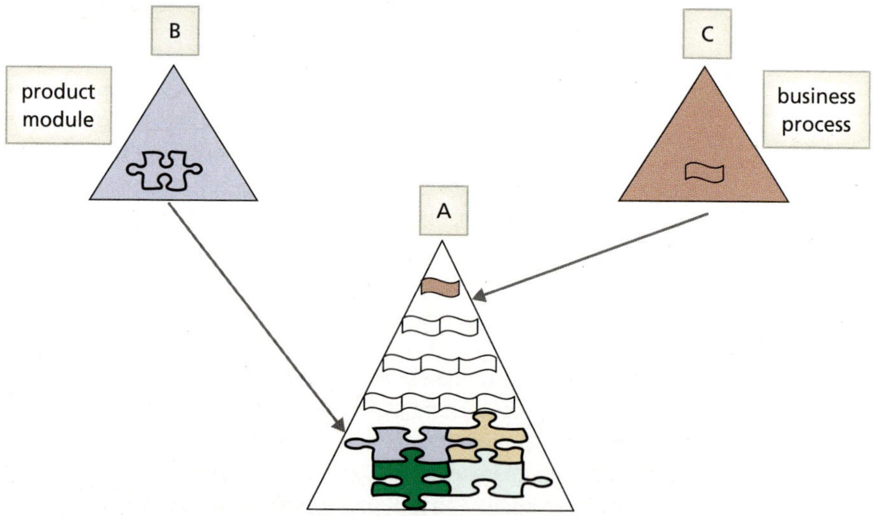

Firm B supplies Organization A with one of its product modules; Firm C provides it with one of its business processes.

Figure 17.8: Outsourcing relationship

When Henry Ford's River Rouge plant was completed in 1928, it could be seen that it had everything it needed to turn raw materials into finished cars – 100,000 workers, factory space, railway track, docks, and furnaces. Today, 'The Rouge' remains Ford's largest plant, but most of the parts are made by subcontractors, and are merely fitted together by the plant's 6,000 employees. Even the local steel mill supplying Ford is run by Severstal – a Russian company (*The Economist*, 2011). In recent decades, outsourcing has transformed global business. Companies have contracted out everything from 'mopping the floors' (providing cleaning services) to 'spotting the flaws' (in internet security software code). Even war is now outsourced. The United States military has outsourced many tasks to private security contractors such as Blackwater Worldwide in Iraq (Scahill, 2007). In Afghanistan, it had more contract workers than regular troops.

Offshoring contracting with external providers in a different country to supply the organization with the processes and products that were previously supplied internally.

Companies have used outsourcing to cut costs, to slim operations, and to concentrate on their core activities such as product development and marketing. When a business process or a product is acquired by an organization from a firm located in a different country, it is referred to as **offshoring** (Lampel and Bhaila, 2011; *The Economist*, 2007a; *The Economist*, 2008a). Nike's factory in Vietnam is an example of offshoring. It is estimated that the value of new outsourcing contracts every year in the world is $100 billion. Davis-Blake and Broschak (2009, p. 322) argued that

> Because outsourcing changes what workers do, how they do it, with whom they do it, and what they are paid for, outsourcing is as significant a change in the nature of work and organization as the industrial revolution, scientific management or the emergence of the mature bureaucratic form, each of which fundamentally affected both work and workers.

Richard Vogel/AP/Press Association Images.

Outsourcing company in Vietnam producing training shoes for Nike

Marwan Naamani AFP/Getty Images.

Blackwater Worldwide in Iraq providing security services for the US government

Outsourcing in retreat?

Outsourcing has become one of the most contentious inter-organizational arrangements. There are now signs that companies are rethinking their approach to outsourcing. American data for 2011 show a decline in outsourcing due to the economic situation, the maturity of the market (much of what can be outsourced already has), and increasing problems. Outsourcing can go wrong in many different ways. There have been legal disputes about outsourcing. EDS (an IT company) had to pay BSkyB (a media company) $469 million in damages and incurred $70m in legal fees in an outsourcing dispute. Large car companies can squeeze their smaller parts suppliers so much that the latter cut corners. Over-promising, sloppy contract writing, and injudicious sub(-sub-)contracting have all caused problems. An outsourcing problem cannot be easily corrected. When companies outsource something, they usually eliminate the department that used to do it. They become entwined with their contractors, handing over sensitive commercial information to them, and wanting them to work alongside their own staff. Extracting oneself from this relationship is difficult. It is easier to close a department than rebuild it. Sacking a contractor is no solution, as factories then grind to a halt through lack of parts. In 2011, the earthquake and tsunami in Northern Japan had a major impact on the makers of cars, construction equipment, and electronic products.

For all these reasons, companies are rethinking outsourcing and supply chain strategies and some are bringing more work back in-house, a process called **reshoring**. General Electric has added nearly half a million jobs in the US in the past two years as rapid wage growth in emerging economies, coupled with sluggish pay at home, has eroded the labour cost advantage of offshore suppliers. However, they are not jettisoning them. The business logic behind outsourcing remains compelling provided that it is done correctly.

Reshoring Returning to the home country the production and provision of products and services which had previously been outsourced to overseas suppliers.

Those tasks which are peripheral to a firm's core business are better and more cheaply done by specialists. Outsourcing is growing in emerging markets and in Europe (especially Germany and France), even if not in the United States. Large outsourcing deals are being replaced by smaller, less rigid ones; relationships are being established with several contractors, not just one; and shorter contracts are replacing longer ones (*The Economist*, 2011; Marsh, 2011; Wright, 2011, Crooks, 2012).

Hollow organization structure

Outsourcing the majority of a company's non-core *processes* such as human relations, payroll, purchasing, logistics, and security (as opposed to the production of parts) creates a **hollow organization structure**. John Child (2005, p. 180) explained that the removal of previously internally-provided processes or services 'hollows out' the organization, reducing its size and workforce, hence the name. Specialist suppliers then provide these for the company, as illustrated in Figure 17.9. Some automobile manufacturers have even outsourced the assembly of their entire vehicles (*The Economist*, 2002). This leaves the company free

Hollow organization structure an organizational design based on outsourcing an organization's non-core processes which are then supplied to it by specialist, external providers.

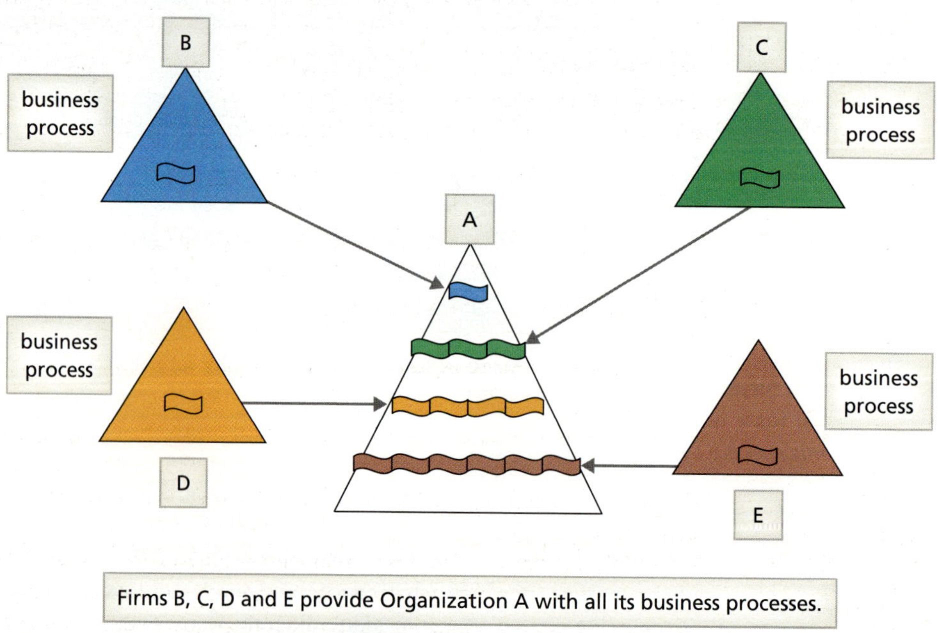

Figure 17.9: Hollow organization structure

to concentrate on those things which represent the core of their activity, those that it does best, and those which lead to more value creation – e.g. research, design, or marketing. Its remaining small number of core staff concentrate on strategic matters, including the integration of the contributions of the multiple external providers that it has created.

Anand and Daft (2007, p. 335) list the underlying design principles of a hollow organization structure as

- determining the non-core processes that are not critical to business performance, that do not create current or potential business advantage, and that are unlikely to drive growth or rejuvenation;
- harnessing market forces to get non-core processes done efficiently;
- creating an effective and flexible interface;
- aligning incentives between the organization and its outsourcing provider.

Nike, the sports goods company, considers its core competencies to be in marketing and distribution, rather than in manufacturing. In consequence, the company relies on contract manufacturers located in areas of the world with low labour costs; these produce merchandise bearing Nike's well-known swoosh logo.

Cycling into the hollow

Narasimhan Anand and Richard Daft (2007) give the example of Strida, a British company that sells lightweight, foldable bicycles, which changed its traditional, era 1 functional organization structure, to become an era 3 hollow organization. The Strida 1 was designed by Mark Sanders as a solution to traffic congestion. The authors explain how, in 2001, the company received a large order from a customer willing only to buy at a price that was below the cost of production. The chief executive decided to close the company's vertically integrated production plant in the UK and to find a Far East partner, which could make the bicycles more efficiently at lower cost. The production facilities were moved in 2001 to Ming Cycle Industrial Co. Ltd. in Taiwan, one of the world's largest bike production manufacturers. In addition, specialist contractors were engaged by Strida to develop new models, to design owners' manuals and to manage the company website. The company uses the internet to ensure effective communication between designers and manufacturers, as well as to manage accounts, materials, and documents. The previously company-owned back-end operations of warehouse management, order fulfilment, inventory control, customer service, inbound container management, and accounts generation were all transferred to a long-established vendor. The effect of the transformation for the company was reduced overhead and the ability to alter production in response to market fluctuations. The focus of the company's chief executive officer's job became managing the various relationships that now constituted the business (www.strida.com).

Modular organization structure

Modular organization structure an organizational design that involves assembling product chunks (modules) provided by internal divisions and external providers.

A **modular organization structure** is also based on outsourcing. However, unlike the hollow structure discussed earlier, in which outsourced processes such as logistics, payroll, or warehousing are supplied by outsiders, a modular structure outsources the production of *parts* of the total product. Internal and external contractors supply component parts that the company then assembles itself. A company can break down its product's design into chunks that are then manufactured by both its internal divisions and external contractors. NASA's Space Shuttle, and computer hardware and software companies, aircraft manufacturers, and household appliances firms, all organize themselves in this way. The analogy most often used is that of a Lego structure in which the different bricks are manufactured by a variety of different, external companies, and then fitted together (Schilling and Steensma, 2001). A modular organization structure is shown in Figure 17.10.

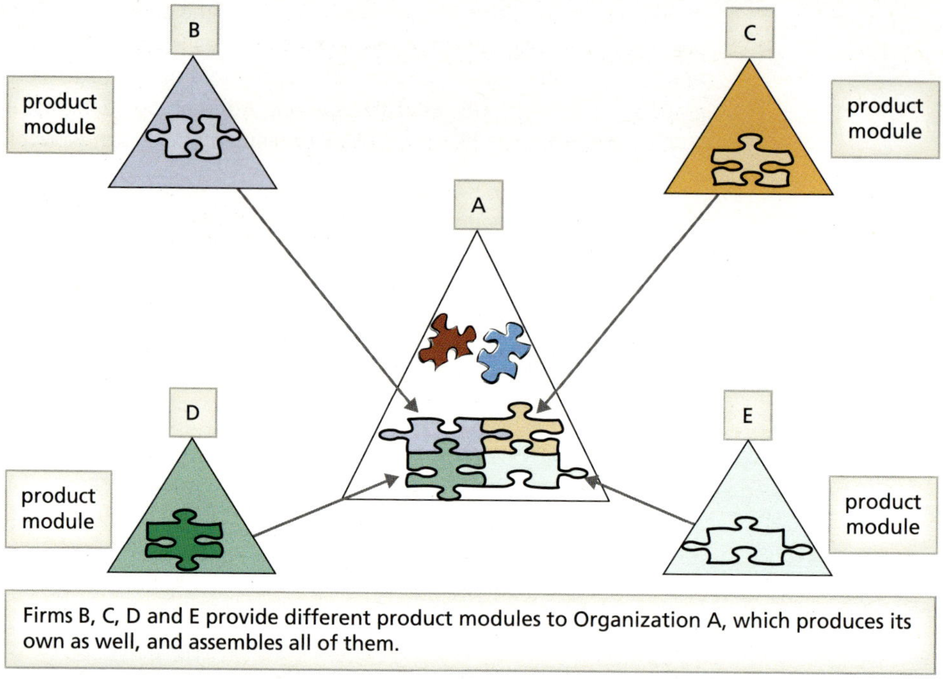

Figure 17.10: Modular organization structure

Anand and Daft (2007, p. 337) list the underlying design principles of a modular organization structure as

- breaking products into self-contained modules or chunks, capable of stand-alone manufacture;
- designing interfaces to ensure different chunks work together;
- outsourcing product chunks to external contractors who can make them more efficiently;
- ensuring that the company can assemble the chunks that are produced internally and those supplied by external providers.

This involves a single large hub-company, located at the network's centre, that outsources chunks of its production functions to external providers, except those it deems to be strategically vital and close to its core competence. Acer Computers is an example of an organization that has turned itself into a modular company. It broke itself up into modules that network together and with outside suppliers and marketers, to create multiple profit centres. It now concentrates on research, design, and branded marketing, while spinning off its manufacturing facilities into a separate company, Wistron, which focuses on competitive outsourcing (Shih et al., 2006).

Modular partners

In order to develop and manufacture its 787 Dreamliner model, Boeing Commercial Airplanes dramatically altered its usual approach, in effect creating a network organization. Boeing's assembly plants are the final stage in a long and hugely complex global supply chain. This consists of about 1,300 'tier one' suppliers, providing parts to Boeing from 5,400 factories in 40 countries. These in turn are fed by thousands of other 'tier two' suppliers which, in turn, receive parts from countless others.

This form of organizational structure did not work for Boeing. There are some forty unfinished 787 Dreamliners scattered around its Everett plant and elsewhere. They are unfinished due to a range of problems – a shortage of the fasteners that hold the plane together; faulty horizontal stabilizers from an Italian supplier; parts not fitting together; suppliers failing to deliver their components on time; and Boeing having to take over some of its subcontractors to stop them collapsing financially.

Building Boeing's 787 is a global affair

Airlines have ordered more than 600 of the 787 Dreamliners which Boeing promises will burn less fuel and cost less to maintain. Parts of the plane come from around the world.

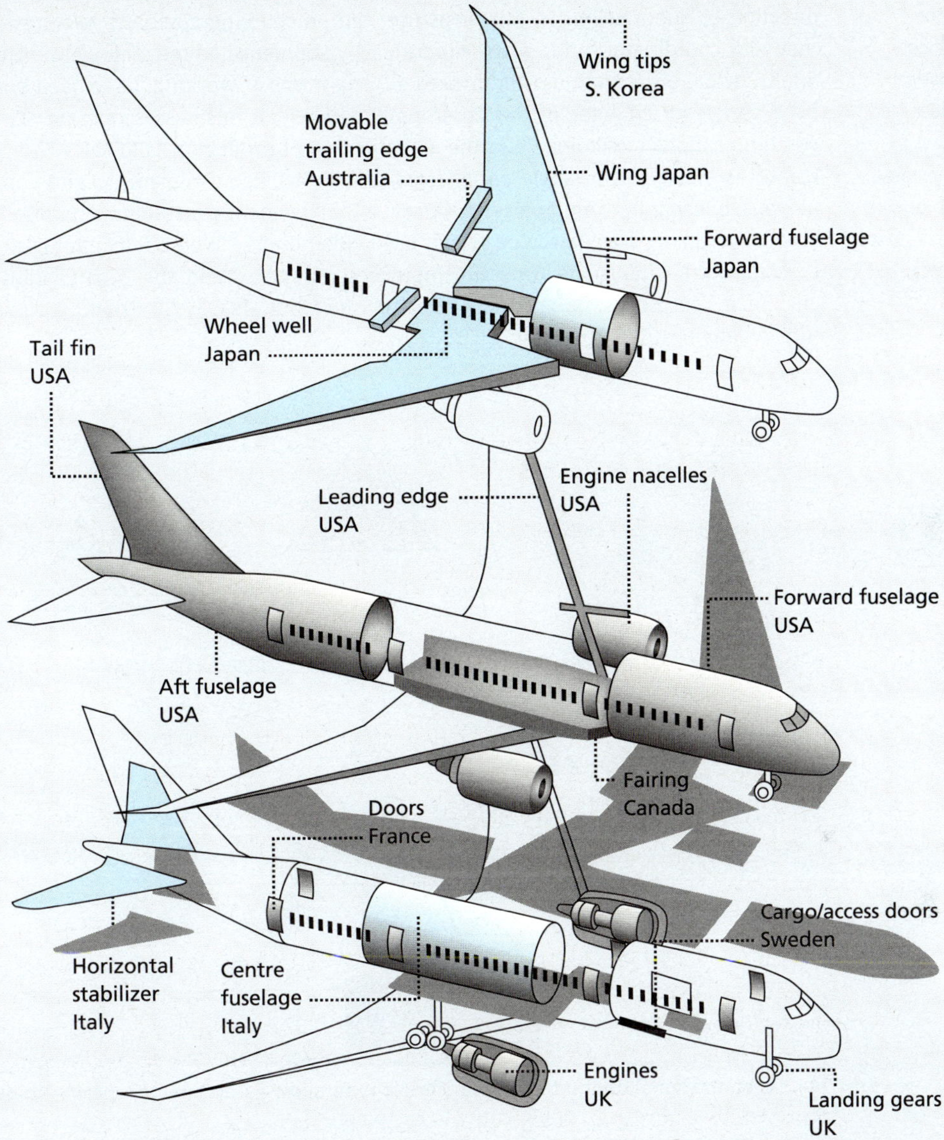

Source: Boeing/AP/Press Association Images.

Jim Albaugh, head of Boeing's commercial airliner division, admitted that too much of the Dreamliner's production had been contracted out. Some of that work has since been brought back in-house, so that the company can check it more carefully. It established a 'war room' that monitors the outside parts and raw materials, sending out 'examiners' to visit suppliers to ensure that their production meets Boeing's needs. In October 2011, the first Dreamliner, operated by ANA Airlines, made its first commercial flight from Tokyo to Hong Kong. It was three years late and billions of dollars over budget. The company is hoping to turn out ten fault-free 787s a month by early 2014. In future, companies like Boeing will need to think hard about what their core business is, and what is peripheral (based on *The Economist*, 2012a; *BusinessWeek*, 2008).

Virtual organization structure

Virtual organization structure an organizational design that uses technology to transcend the constraints of legal structures, physical conditions, place, and time, and allows a network of separate participants to present themselves to customers as a single entity.

The **virtual organization structure** consists of a temporary network of nodes (entire organizations, parts of organizations, teams, or specific individuals) linked by information technologies which flexibly coordinate their activities and combine their skills and resources in order to achieve common goals, without requiring traditional hierarchies of central direction or supervision. In this structure, the outsourcing company becomes primarily a 'network coordinator' and, when supported by sophisticated technology, a virtual organization. Virtual organizations, and indeed all new forms of working, have been brought about by a variety of changes in the environment in which businesses operate. These include communications technology and the globalization of production and sales. A virtual organization is viewed as a single entity from outside by its customers despite consisting of a network of separate companies. McKinsey, a management consultancy, reported that a new class of company was emerging which used collaborative Web 2.0 technologies intensively to connect the internal efforts of employees and to extend the organization's reach to customers, partners, and suppliers (Bughin and Chui, 2011). A virtual organization structure is shown in Figure 17.11.

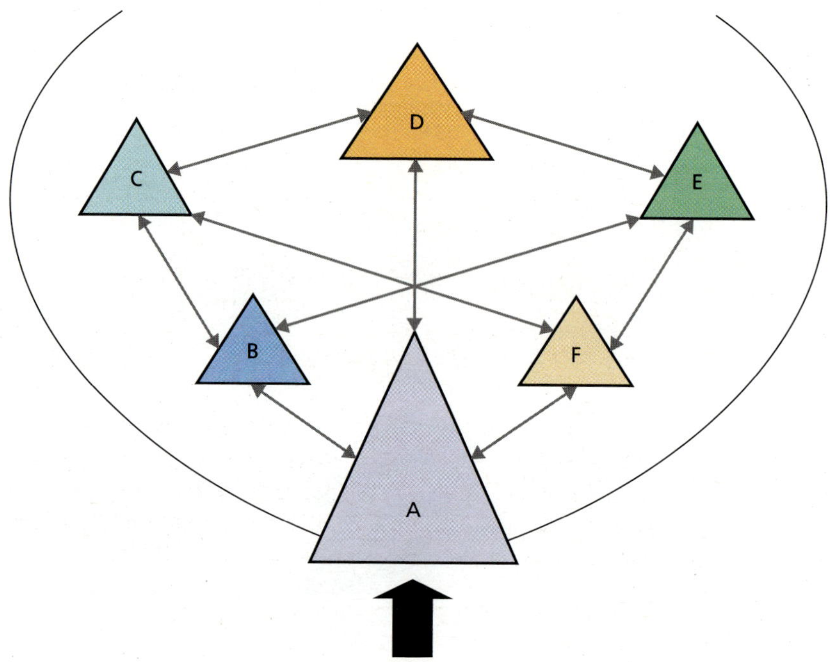

An organizational design that uses technology to allow a network of separate companies to present themselves as a single entity to customers

Figure 17.11: Virtual organization structure

Anand and Daft (2007, p. 339) list the underlying design principles of a virtual organization structure as

- creating boundaries around a temporary organization with external partners;
- using technology to link people, assets, and ideas;
- each partner contributing their domain of excellence;
- disbanding or absorbing after opportunity ends.

Many observers see virtual organizations as a panacea for many of the current organizational problems. A virtual organization has the capacity to form and re-form to deal with problems and (potentially) provide a flexibility of response to organizational needs and changing circumstances. The concept has generated considerable discussion and debate among managers, management consultants, and business commentators, although they disagree about its nature. In light of this, Warner and Witzel (2004) list the six features that nearly all virtual organizations have in common (Table 17.3).

Table 17.3: Features of virtual organizations

Feature	Description
1. Lack of physical structure	Less physical presence than conventional organizations. Fewer tangible assets such as offices or warehouses, and those possessed are physically dispersed.
2. Reliance on communication technologies	Technology is used dynamically to link people, assets, and ideas. Communication networks replace the physical structure of a conventional organization, to define it and give a shape to its activities.
3. Mobile work	Communication networks reduce the importance of where work is physically located, meaning that individuals and team members no longer have to be physically co-located to work together on a common task.
4. Hybrid forms	Short- or long-term collaboration between agencies can take various forms, called hybrids, including networks, consortia, and webs, to achieve a mutual goal.
5. Boundaryless and inclusive	Not confined to legal entities, can encompass suppliers and distributors, working with producers, and even involving customers in the production process.
6. Flexible and responsive	Can be rapidly assembled from a variety of disparate elements, to achieve a certain business goal, and then, as required, be dismantled or reconfigured.

Based on Warner and Witzel (2004), pp. 3–5.

Warner and Witzel (2004) argue that organizations should not be classified into virtual or non-virtual categories. All firms can possess some degree of virtuality, and that virtuality can take different forms. They say that every organization is a mixture of virtual and tangible elements, and they identify six dimensions along which companies can choose to organize their activities on a virtual or a tangible basis:

- nature of product
- nature of working
- relationship with suppliers
- relationship with customers
- relationship between firm's elements
- relationship between managers and employees.

A supermarket's internal operations are traditionally physical and tangible, but its links with its suppliers are virtual through its automated product reordering system. Thus the question to ask of an organization is not whether it is virtual or non-virtual, but to what degree, and in what ways, it possesses virtuality. Additionally, whatever an organization's virtual/tangible 'asset mix' may be, it can be managed in a virtual or a tangible way.

David Nadler of Mercer Delta Consulting, an organizational structure ('architecture') consultancy company, sees companies increasingly consisting of a number of strategically aligned businesses, 'linked closely where there are opportunities to create value by leveraging shared capabilities, but only loosely where the greater value lies in the undifferentiated focus' (Hindle, 2006b). This implies that close and loose relationships will coexist within and between organizations. Bob de Wit and Ron Meyer (2005) provide a taxonomy of interorganizational collaborative relationships, shown in Table 17.4. In traditional organization structures, units were either within an organization – 'densely connected' – or outside the organization – and not attached at all. In both situations, relations with external suppliers were at arm's length. Nadler argues that many of today's companies 'co-habit' – using joint ventures and strategic alliances. He says that what is inside and outside the company, previously clear, is now becoming blurred. However, when different businesses become connected to varying degrees, it causes them problems of dependency and uncertainty, which in turn create risk. What happens when a partner in a joint venture goes bankrupt? How do banks ensure that employees of companies to whom they have outsourced services do not steal their customers' PIN numbers? Commentators even suggest that companies now need an 'extended organizational form' – one shape for their external operations, and another for their in-house activities (Hindle, 2006c).

Table 17.4: Example of collaborative relationships

	Non-contractual arrangements	Contractual arrangements	Equity-based arrangements
Multilateral arrangements	• **Lobbying coalition** (e.g. European Roundtable of industrialists) • **Joint standard setting** (e.g. Linux coalition) • **Learning communities** (e.g. Strategic Management Society)	• **Research consortium** (e.g. Symbian in PDAs) • **International marketing alliance** (e.g. Star Alliance in airlines) • **Export partnership** (e.g. Netherlands Export Combination)	• **Shared payment system** (e.g. Visa) • **Construction consortium** (e.g. Eurotunnel) • **Joint reservation system** (e.g. Galileo)
Bilateral arrangements	• **Cross-selling deal** (e.g. between pharmaceutical firms) • **R&D staff exchange** (e.g. between IT firms) • **Market information sharing agreement** (e.g. between hardware and software makers)	• **Licensing agreement** (e.g. Disney and Coca-Cola) • **Co-development contract** (e.g. Disney and Pixar in movies) • **Co-branding alliance** (e.g. Coca-Cola and McDonald's)	• **New product joint venture** (e.g. Sony and Ericsson in cell phones) • **Cross-border joint venture** (e.g. DaimlerChrysler and Beijing Automotive) • **Local joint venture** (e.g. CNN Turk in Turkey)

Source: from *Strategy Synthesis: Text and Readings*, de Wit, B. and Meyer, R., Copyright 2005 International Thomson Business Press. Reproduced by permission of Cengage Learning EMEA Ltd.

Collaboration with suppliers

Morgan Witzel (2007) noted that 'Whereas collaboration used to be a matter of integrating organizations, now it is increasingly seen as a matter of integrating activities. In other words, tasks are carried out by the person or organization that is most suited to the specific issue'. While most inter-firm relationships in the early networks of the 1980s were managed by contracts, some manufacturers realized that both upstream suppliers and downstream distributors possessed technical and market knowledge that was of value to them. They thus created cross-firm relationships with their suppliers that allowed such knowledge to be to the mutual advantage of all supply chain members. Hence, discussions of organization structure and the alternatives to bureaucracy now focus increasingly on collaborative inter-organizational relationships (Miles et al., 2010). Lynda Gratton argued that the emergence of collaboration between firms was the result of four intersecting environmental, social, and technological trends (Gratton, 2007; Gratton et al., 2007; Newing, 2007):

- *rise of partnership strategies* – a change in perception away from seeing companies as competing for a piece of a finite cake (*value appropriation*), and towards their making the cake bigger (*value creation*);

- *knowledge economy* – The move towards a knowledge economy and a focus on the innovation of products and services;
- *working styles of Generation Y* – unlike the competitive post-war baby-boomer generation, Generation Y (up to 30 years) is particularly adept at, and places value upon, collaborating with others;
- *advances in collaborative technology* – companies' collaborative experiences are supported by advanced technology (videoconferencing, Skype, email, voicemail, social networks, wikis, and blogs). The current, wired-up generation of Facebook and Twitter users who are joining the commercial world prefer these ways of communicating, and this affects collaboration between businesses.

McLaren and partnerships

However successful this year's McLaren Formula 1 racing car is, it will bear little relation to next year's. Such is the pace of change in F1 engineering that 95 per cent of it will be different. The planning and design take place in McLaren's Technology Centre in Woking, England, but the ideas generated are implemented in far-flung corners of the globe. A McLaren F1 racing car contains 15,000 to 16,000 separate parts that are manufactured by 750 companies. Jonathan Neale is McLaren Racing's managing director. His job is to coordinate all this activity. 'I can just pick up the phone and say "I can't solve this problem. I need some help. I can tell you what the problem is but I don't know how to solve it" ', he says. Partnerships are the lifeblood of McLaren and its rival teams.

> A lot of this is about management process and organization. I run a high speed organization, but it's a small-to-medium enterprise of 500 people. I can't possibly expect to have the world's leading know-how in fuel lubrication, bonding and adhesive material, yet I need that to compete. So how do we get that? We plug into our partners. I have access to global research and developments in fuel lubrication.

McLaren illustrates that technological developments, speed of change and globalization mean that a single organization, however successful, can no longer 'do it all themselves'. Even the largest companies have had to develop collaborative relationships with outsiders (based on Blitz, 2007).

Collaboration with competitors

Co-opetition a form of cooperation between competing organizations which is limited to specified areas where both believe they can gain mutual benefit.

Collaboration with competitors can take the form of 'cooperative competition' which is called **co-opetition**. This occurs when two or more organizations decide that they do not possess an individual competitive advantage in a field, want to share common costs, or wish to innovate quickly but lack the necessary resources, knowledge, or skill to do so (Brandenburger and Nalebuff, 2002). An example is the cooperation between Peugeot and Toyota on shared components for a new city car for Europe. In this case, companies will save money on shared costs, while remaining fiercely competitive in other areas. For co-opetition to work, companies need to very clearly define where they are working together, and where they are competing. Co-opetition can take the legal-structural form of a strategic alliance or a joint venture.

Martin Nowak and Roger Highfield (2011) argue that the fittest do not survive merely by outrunning their rivals. The winners find ways to work together, avoid escalating conflicts, and build the trust and cooperation which allow groups to flourish. The losers are those who punish others and perish as a result. Based on Charles Darwin's evolutionary principles, they argue that humans are 'super co-operators'. As a species, humans trust each other and work together, rather than beat each other. It is cooperation and not competition that underpins innovation. Without it there can be neither construction nor complexity. Some of the world's largest industries exhibit alternating patterns of competition and cooperation. Microsoft and Intel dominate personal computing but that has not prevented them fighting about how to divide the profits. They cooperate to create value, but compete to appropriate it (Nowak and Highfield, 2011).

"No, now all of our pillaging is done electronically from a centralized office."

Source: © 11/17/2003, www.cartoonbank.com

Strategic alliances

Strategic alliance an arrangement in which two or more firms agree to cooperate to achieve specific objectives while remaining independent organizations.

A **strategic alliance** is a tight, formalized, contractual relationship with a legal element, in which firms cooperate over the medium to long term, to achieve certain commercial objectives for mutual advantage, while remaining independent entities. Each alliance partner provides their own resources, products, equipment, expertise, production facilities, and funding. In a strategic alliance, companies merge a limited part of their domain with each other, and attempt to achieve the competitive advantage that might have individually eluded them. Alliances tend to be established over a single, specific initiative, although they may be later extended to cover other activities between the participating companies (see Figure 17.12).

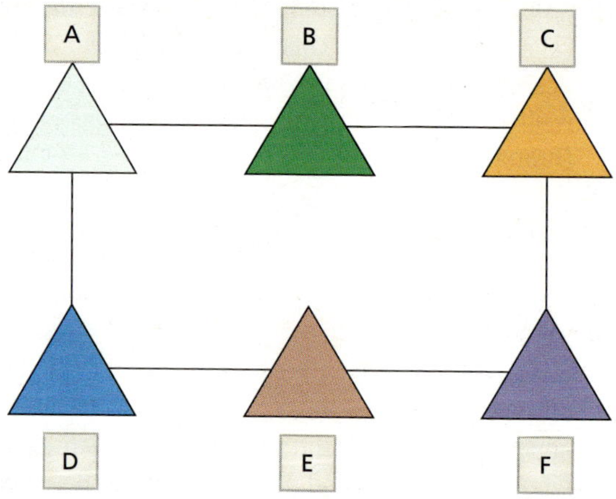

Organizations A, B, C, D, E, and F cooperate, providing resources, to achieve specific objectives while remaining independent entities.

Figure 17.12: Strategic alliance

The primary reason for alliance creation is to secure specific competencies and resources to survive and succeed in globalizing markets, particularly those in which technologies are rapidly changing. Alliances can bring about organizational learning. Rather than the partners being involved in skill substitution (one produces, while the other sells), they can learn from each other, thereby strengthening the areas in which each is weakest. However, research shows that alliances often end in disappointment for the organizations involved (Koza and Lewin, 1999).

STOP AND THINK Back in 1997, arch-rivals Microsoft and Apple entered into a five-year strategic alliance to develop Mackintosh-compatible versions of Microsoft® Office 98, Internet Explorer 4, and Java technologies. The latest edition of *Office for Mac* was recently released. What benefits do you think each of these long-time competitors saw for themselves in this alliance?

SkyTeam Alliance

Mark Lennihan/PA Photos

An airline alliance is an agreement between two or more airlines to cooperate at a substantial level.The SkyTeam Alliance is one of three mega-alliances in the international airline industry, the other two being Star Alliance and Oneworld. SkyTeam consists of fifteen airlines, including Air France, KLM, Delta Air Lines, and China Southern. Collectively, its members provide over 14,500 daily flights to 926 destinations in 173 countries. Members can offer their own customers destinations anywhere in the world without having to fly there themselves. Together, SkyTeam, Star, and One World account for 69 per cent of the world's air revenue passenger miles. Each individual airline seeks to build on its own strengths, and compensates for the others' weaknesses. Next time you are on an aeroplane, read the in-flight magazine and listen to the announcements to determine the alliance to which your particular carrier belongs. (Based on *Holland Herald* 2008, p. 68; www.staralliance.com; www.oneworld.com; www.alliance.com)

Joint venture an arrangement in which two or more companies remain independent, but establish a new organization that they jointly own and manage.

Joint ventures

Another form of co-opetition is the **joint venture** (see Figure 17.13). Competitors may wish to pool resources or collaborate to challenge other competitors. Here, two companies remain independent, but establish a new organization into which they both contribute equity and which they jointly own. They control the newly-created firm, sharing its expenses and revenues. The relationships between them are formalized, either through shareholding arrangements or by agreements specifying asset-holding and profit distribution. Airbus is a well-known company which is also a joint venture. Toyota has a number of joint venture plants with companies around the world (e.g. General Motors, Peugeot), all of which use the Toyota Production System. The joint venture is popular with Western companies operating in China, providing companies with low-cost entry into new markets. Sony Ericsson was established as a joint venture in 2001 to produce mobile phones. It combines Sony's consumer electronics expertise with Ericsson's know-how in technological communication. Both companies stopped making their own mobile phones.

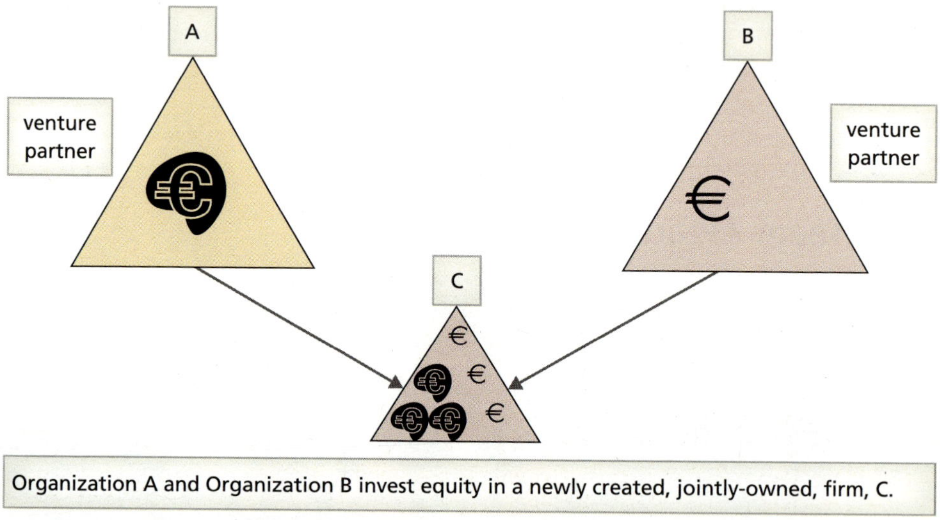

Figure 17.13: Joint venture

The odd couple

If you are on a short-haul flight, the chances are that your aircraft's engines were made by CFM International. CFM is an unusual yet durable joint venture between US-based General Electric (GE), the world's most successful conglomerate and standard bearer of raw Anglo-Saxon capitalism, and Snecma, a French firm owned by SANFRAN. CFM's engines power 71 per cent of the world's fleet of single-aisle aircraft. They can be found

Ferenc Szelepcsenyi/Alamy

in Boeing 737s, DC8s, Airbus A320s, and the AWACS. It supplied 400 commercial and military customers worldwide. These are the workhorses of aviation, and constitute the largest market for engines, much bigger than that for wide-bodied jumbos. The joint venture began in 1974 when both companies wanted to expand beyond their mostly military customers into the growing civilian business. This was dominated at the time by Pratt & Whitney, which had the best selling engine for single-aisle planes. As the technological leader, it saw no need to collaborate with anyone. Snecma decided against linking up with Rolls-Royce, after a failed collaboration on Concorde engines. That left GE, which was anxious to get close to Airbus which was founded in 1970, and was then Europe's nascent aircraft consortium.

The European home of this odd pairing is an old military airfield on the edge of the forest of Fontainebleau, outside Paris, while the American component is based within GE's aero-engine division in Cincinnati, Pennsylvania. Despite a huge disparity in size, the two firms operate their joint venture on a simple and equitable basis. In both factories, the core module of the CFM engine (a GE design originally developed for fighter aircraft) is married to a French front fan and low-pressure turbine. Each partner is responsible for the research, design, and production of its modules. Many companies set up joint ventures and other forms of collaboration, but few have one that is so central to their entire business. GE and Snecma share nothing but engine parts and sales, and they split the proceeds roughly 50–50. Jet engines may be awesomely complicated machines worth millions of dollars each, but the secret to making them successfully seems to be keep it simple (from *The Economist*, 2007b).

Collaboration with third parties

In 2008, T-Mobile, a mobile phone company owned by Germany's Deutsche Telecom, launched its new phone, the G1, made by HTC, a Taiwanese manufacturer. The device was first to be based on Google's Android software (*The Economist*, 2008b). Android is a fully 'open' operating system and Google hopes to attract third parties such as other telephone operators and handset makers to adopt Android for their smartphones. Being 'open' also means that software companies and individual developers can, free of charge, devise mobile internet services that run on the phone (Taylor and Parker, 2008; Beaumont, 2008). It promises users the ability to customize their devices, as they have done with Linux, adding features and downloading new and probably free applications. Google is hoping to make Android the dominant platform ('the Microsoft Windows') of the phone. In contrast, Apple's iPhone uses proprietary technology which enables it to keep a tight grip over what software applications are loaded onto its device and how it is used by consumers. However, Apple needs third-party developers to ensure the ongoing success of the iPhone. In mid 2008, it released its software development kit (SDK) for its iPhone and iPod Touch. The SDK tools allow these people to develop software applications that make the most of these two devices' innovative features. Apple allows developers to set their own prices for their programs, and retain 70 per cent of the sales revenue. However, Apple is in total control of the applications programs produced. It will decide which ones to approve, and these will be distributed only through its iTunes music store. Apple has to ensure that the constraints that it places on third-party developers do not drive them to competitors, and that it fosters their creativity rather than stifling it.

Collaborating with users

User contribution system a method of aggregating people's contributions or behaviours in ways that are useful to others.

At first glance, Amazon, eBay, Google, Wikipedia, YouTube, the Mozilla Foundation, and Facebook appear to have little in common. Some charge users, others are free. Some are profit-making organizations, others are not. However, they all use what are called **user contribution systems**. These are methods of aggregating people's contributions or behaviours in ways that are useful to others, and these are responsible for much of their success. The idea is not new. Firms have always used customer satisfaction surveys and focus groups to provide them with feedback to improve their products. When Maxwell House wanted to develop a new brand of instant coffee, it avoided the usual market testing approach. Instead, it approached its customers directly, obtained data from them, created a model for the 'ideal' coffee, and used this as the basis for developing the new product (Witzel, 2007). However, Scott Cook (2008) argues that what is new is that commercial companies are now developing ways in which unlimited numbers of people outside them can volunteer their time, energy, and expertise to improve things for themselves and increase profits for the company. User contribution systems are underpinned by a range of new consumer-based technologies collectively referred to as Web 2.0 (see Chapter 3).

User contribution systems can involve customers and sales prospects, as well as people with no previous connection with the company. One recent incarnation is called *unsourcing*. It involves companies setting up online communities to enable peer-to-peer support among users. Customers' problems are answered by unpaid individuals who have bought and used the same products. This is done in discussion forums set up on the company's own website or on social networks like Facebook and Twitter, and is being used by companies such as Tom Tom, Lenovo and Logitech (*The Economist*, 2012e). A user contribution structure is shown in Figure 17.14.

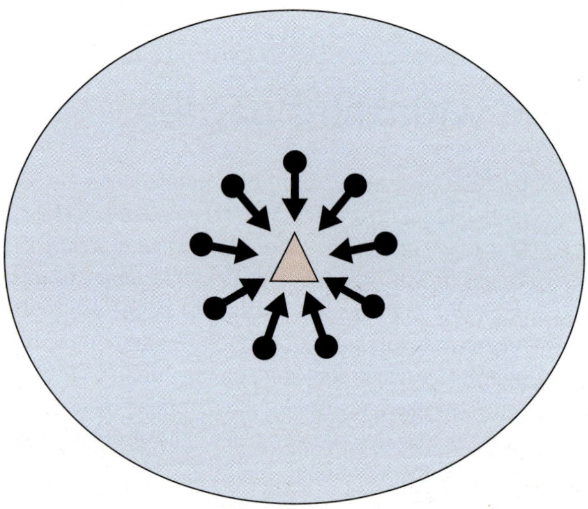

An organization uses the contributions of countless individual volunteers to help it achieve its goals.

Figure 17.14: User contribution system

The contribution of users can be active, as when they donate their work, expertise, or information; or it can be passive (and even unknowing), as in the case of behavioural data gathered from them automatically when they participate in a transaction. Wikipedia, a non-profit organization, offers a free encyclopaedia, written and frequently updated by unpaid experts in their fields; eBay makes a profit without any inventory because its customers fill its shelves. Less obviously, Google's search engine relies on the algorithmic aggregation of links created by others on websites, while its advertisement placement system depends on data from people's click behaviour.

Most user contribution systems offer no financial incentives, so what motivates individuals to contribute? Cook (2008) suggests six reasons:

- *by-product* – involuntary involvement when they provide data as a by-product of a transaction e.g. every Amazon shopper adds to its recommendation engine;

Assembling producers with users

© Toru Hanai/Reuters/Corbis

Back in 1998, LEGO released a new product – a 727-part set called *Mindstorms*. It contained a microchip that made a variety of movements possible. The product was a great success, selling 80,000 sets. However, to the company's surprise, it was being bought by adults for their own use, and not for children. Quite quickly, its users hacked the toy's code and created a variety of new applications from soda machines to blackjack dealers. The new programs spread quickly over the internet and were more sophisticated than what Lego had itself developed. Over forty guidebooks advised users how to get the most out of this LEGO set. Initially, LEGO reacted negatively, feeling that customers were misusing their products. However, after a period of confusion and inaction, the company started to listen to their product's '(ab)users' in an effort to discover what they were doing with it. Following discussions, the company decided that they were doing something interesting and important, even though it differed from LEGO's own business plan. They discovered that the product's (re)creators formed a community around the LEGO brand and shared a passion for innovation.

These users had produced physical and aesthetic add-ons to products, such as clothes for figures, and batteries for trains and cars. They had developed new play themes such as LEGO *Harry Potter* and LEGO *Life on Mars*. Indeed, some product fans even devised new building techniques using existing bricks to produce new building styles, models and colour effects. While the majority of users' improvements were incremental, leaving the basic product unchanged, just over 10 per cent were radical innovations involving new experiences and play processes. These included mosaic building – translating an image into pixels (LEGO bricks) and then assembling it digitally; strategy games such as *BrickWars* involving multi-player role-playing; *LDraw*, an open-source software program which allows users to create virtual LEGO models and scenes; and *BrickFilms*, which animators use to create short films using LEGO figures. The LEGO company now cooperates with its user community, allowing them to interact and co-create for mutual benefit. Having such an active and innovative community keeps the company focused on new products; helps it to market product innovations; and increases the chances of success as the product is devised by the consumers themselves (Kornberger, 2010, pp. 147–53).

- *practical solutions* – to obtain short-term, practical benefits, e.g. using the Del.icious.us site to organize their own website bookmarks which, when aggregated, produce an index to the web useful to others;
- *social rewards* – to gain interaction with others, to become a member of a community of common interests, e.g. Facebook;
- *reputation* – to gain recognition (e.g. receiving Amazon's badge for being a 'Top 1,000 reviewer') or the admiration of peers;
- *self-expression* – to have the opportunity to air their thoughts, opinions, or creative expression, or to gain feedback from others (e.g. millions of YouTube videos);
- *altruism* – to help others or to let the truth to be known.

Why have companies developed user contribution systems? The systems create value for businesses as a consequence of the value that they deliver to their users. User benefits include personalized purchase recommendations, obtaining hard-to-find items, reduced prices, and establishing new personal and business relationships, as well as membership of a community. Company benefits include improved products, enhancement of customer loyalty, better-served customers, more business, reduced costs, and improvements in employee performance. Harhoff and Mayrhofer (2010) gave examples of organizations establishing user communities – BMW around its series of high-powered M cars; Sun Microsystems around its operating system Solaris; and the Mozdev Group's development of its solutions-based web browser Firefox, which is coordinated by the Mozilla Foundation. Cook (2008) provides a user contribution taxonomy which is shown in Figure 17.15.

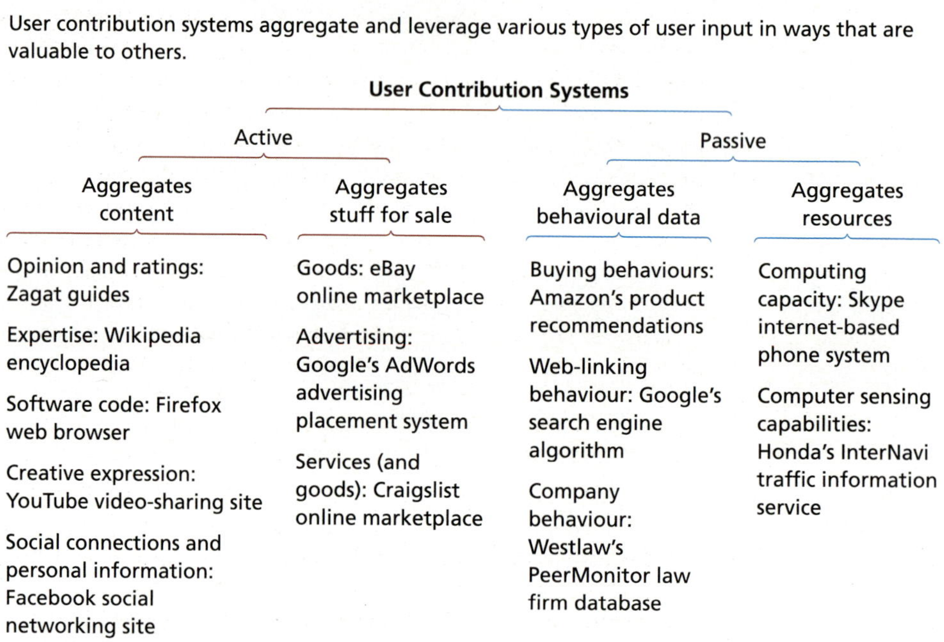

Figure 17.15: User contribution taxonomy

Source: reprinted by permission of *Harvard Business Review*. From 'The contribution revolution: Letting volunteers build your business' by Cook, S., 86(10) 2008. Copyright © 2008 by the Harvard Business School Publishing Corporation, all rights reserved.

Crowdsourcing the act of taking a task traditionally performed by a designated agent (employee or contractor) and outsourcing it to an undefined, generally large group of people, in the form of an open call for assistance.

Crowdsourcing

Crowdsourcing is a term coined by Jeff Howe in *Wired* magazine (Howe, 2006, 2009). It refers to the act of taking a task traditionally performed by an employee or a contractor and outsourcing it to an undefined, generally large group of people, in the form of an open call for assistance. BBC Radio's Traffic Unit regularly asks motorists stuck in traffic jams to call in on their mobile phones and report holdups, which it then broadcasts.

Virtual customer communities

Backplane, a tech start-up co-founded by Troy Carter, Lady Gaga's business manager, launched a web community for Lady Gaga called LittleMonsters.com (after the pop star's pet name for her fans). The aim is to create a one-stop shop where fans will be able to download her music, buy tickets for her shows, and chat to each other. 'Social ticketing' will allow them to find tickets near their friends, and start conversations beforehand with the strangers that they will be sitting next to. Initially, Little Monsters is by invitation only, and 10,000 'superfans' have been chosen from one million applicants. The data generated by the site will be used to identify and take note of the 'key influencer' fans to whom others listen. This is an attempt to create parallel virtual communities of people sharing a particular passion, an idea being evaluated by Silicon Valley venture capitalists. Backplane is exploring the possibility of creating virtual communities for mainstream brands such as Nike and ExxonMobil, to foster deeper relationships with their customers. In the latter's case, the passion is not for petrol, but for the cars it powers. The challenge is to find the key influencers (mouthy fans) and amplify their voices. Mr Carter's experience with Lady Gaga's fans suggests that what a superfan says can have a greater impact on fellow fans than a word from Lady Gaga herself (based on *The Economist*, 2012b).

Operationally, crowdsourcing involves organizations asking crowds of internet users to provide creative ideas, analyse data, supply information, help develop a new technology, carry out a design task (also known as 'community-based design' or 'distributed participatory design'), or help capture, systematize, and analyse large amounts of data. The Library of Congress asked users of Flickr, a popular photo-sharing site, to identify unknown people in its old photo collections. Clearly, this description indicates an overlap with the activities of organizations such as Wikipedia and Linux, an open-source software development project, and Firefox, an open-source web browser. However, Cook argues that crowdsourcing is not a user contribution system because the company stands between the input and the output. It sifts through people's ideas, selects those it wants, and then invests its resources as needed to develop them. A second distinguishing feature is that, while companies may receive free contributions, they are also willing to pay for them. Additionally, some contributors make a living from their contributions.

Consider the case of Quirky, a company which turns other people's ideas into products (*The Economist*, 2012c). Located in the Manhattan district of New York, it is a design studio that includes a small factory with 3D printers, a laser cutter, milling machines, a spray painting booth, and other equipment. With the help of its online community, it devises two new consumer products a week. A user submits an idea, and if enough people like it (as on Facebook), the company's product developers make a prototype. Users then review it online and contribute to its final design, as well as to its packaging, marketing, and pricing. Quirky then looks for suitable manufacturers, and sells the product through its website and retail chains (if there is sufficient demand). The Pivot Power, a $29.99 adjustable socket electrical extension lead, was invented by Jake Zien of Milwaukee, who was helped by 709 people to bring it to market. A total 200,000 have now been sold, and Mr Zien has earned £124,000 from his invention.

However, there are problems in using ideas or information supplied by community members. The firm has to check that these have not been sent to rivals, that they do not infringe patents, and that they have not been stolen. Secondly, volunteers become reluctant to contribute if they feel that someone is profiting from their hard work, hence the success of non-profit collaborations. Successful solvers in the InnoCreative network are paid between $10,000 and $100,000. A survey of marketing bosses found that 62 per cent had used crowdsourcing in some way. Obviously, getting unpaid or cheaper members of the public to do your work for you is less expensive than hiring your own staff or paying consultants (*The Economist*, 2008c). Structurally, in the case of both non-profit and commercial organizations, the organizational boundary becomes perforated, as contributions to the organizational goals come both from internal company staff and from volunteer outsiders.

The power of the crowd

Along with laboratory rats, undergraduates are popular research subjects. They are cheap and easily available. The average American university student is 4,000 times more likely to be the subject of a psychological study than the average human being. However, most undergraduates are WEIRD – Western, educated, industrialized, rich, and democratic. They are thus not representative of humanity as a whole, and drawing general conclusions about human behaviour from the results of studies of them is risky. Crowdsourcing can overcome this problem, and several firms are now using it. They include Mechanical Turk, which is run by Amazon and has half a million people (called 'Turkers') in its workforce. Most of them regard the tasks they are set as more of a hobby than a paying job, and are willing to work for $1.40 an hour. Although 40% are American, a third are Indian, and the remainder come from 100 other countries. This removes the 'W', 'I', 'R' and 'D' characteristics of research subjects. Despite Turkers being self-selecting, using them rather than undergraduates increases diversity. Crowdsourcing can allow psychologists to do easily and cheaply what was once complicated and expensive, and to do it in days rather than months or years. It offers them bargain prices, vast supply, and enormous scale. Google Scholar now counts 3,000 published papers that involve crowdsourcing experiments (from *The Economist*, 2012d).

STOP AND THINK

Are user contribution systems a good way of providing the public with the opportunity to participate and share their expertise with companies whose products and services they use? Or have companies cynically managed to persuade gullible, emotionally-challenged online users to contribute their time, creativity, and effort for free, in return for a spurious sense of participation in some sort of 'community' or a sense of 'ownership' of something?

Company applications and benefits of Web 2.0 technologies

A study of Web 2.0 technologies being used in enterprises was conducted by the management consultancy McKinsey and was reported by Jacques Bughin and Michael Chui (2011). It surveyed 3,240 executives across a range of regions, industries, and functional areas. It found that enterprises using these technologies were becoming more competitive as measured by market share gains, market leadership, and higher profit margins. Forty per cent of companies used social networking and 38 per cent used blogging. The report identified three types of organizations which had learned to benefit from Web 2.0:

- *internally networked organizations* – companies which benefited primarily within their own corporate walls, specifically in terms of greater employee cooperation between departmental silos, more project-based handling of tasks, less hierarchical information flows, and increased information sharing;
- *externally networked organizations* – companies which achieved benefits from interactions that crossed corporate boundaries, linking with customers and business partners;
- *fully networked enterprises* – those which were located much further up the learning curve and used Web 2.0 in revolutionary ways with their employees, customers, and partners.

Bughin and Chui argue that

- gaining market share from competitors resulted from technology-enabled collaboration with external stakeholders, and that this was achieved by forging closer marketing relationships with customers and involving them in customer support and marketing efforts;

- the attainment of higher profit margins resulted from creating a more agile company through decentralized decision-making – front-line staff making local decisions – and the creation of work teams consisting of both in-house employees and individuals from outside the organization;
- market leadership was achieved by using Web 2.0 to strengthen internal collaboration between employees, thereby enhancing the firm's reliance to maintain its leadership position. In contrast, market challengers would focus more on external Web 2.0 uses to win customers from industry leaders.

What mode of collaboration should a firm adopt when linking with others? Gary Pisano and Roberto Verganti (2008) suggest that senior managements should ask questions about their company's network participation and governance. First, given its corporate strategy, how open or closed does it want its network of collaborators to be? Second, who should have the power to decide which problems the network will tackle and which solutions will be adopted?

- *Participation: open or closed?*
  Collaborative networks differ in terms of participation. Totally open collaboration means that anyone can join the network (suppliers, customers, hobbyists, institutions – even competitors). The sponsor announces a problem, and requests contributions from an unlimited number of problem-solvers. It is like a throwing an open house party – you set the date and location and hope that the right people will come. Open-source software projects like Linux, Apache, and Mozilla all exemplify open collaboration networks, as does threadless.com, the T-shirt retailer. In contrast, in a closed network, a firm will tackle its problem with one or two parties, which it chooses on the basis of their possession of the required capabilities. This is like a private club which you are invited to join. Alessi, an Italian company famous for the post-modern design of its home products, invited 200 collaborators to submit designs.
- *Governance: hierarchical or flat?*
  Collaborative networks also differ in terms of governance. This relates to who gets to define the problem and choose the solution. In a hierarchical network, the 'kingpin' firm alone decides on the importance of problems, how they will be addressed, what represents an acceptable solution, and which solutions will be implemented. This allows it to control and secure a larger part of the innovation's value. In contrast, in a flat network, the different parties are equal partners and share the power to decide key issues. Such decentralized decision-making, say Pisano and Verganti, allows collaborators to share the costs, risk, and technical challenges of innovating.

Using the dimensions of participation and governance, Pisano and Verganti propose four basic modes of collaboration, shown in Figure 17.16. They label these *elite circle* (closed and hierarchical network), *innovation mall* (open and hierarchical), *innovation community* (open and flat), and *consortium* (closed and flat). These authors state that each has its own particular advantages and challenges, offers a company access to different capabilities and assets, and is suited to specific types of problems.

With respect to participation, by choosing an open network, a firm gains access to an extremely large number of problem-solvers, and thus to the possibility of obtaining a vast quantity of ideas. Moreover, it does not need to specify its contributors beforehand. The disadvantages are that it does not attract the best contributors, and that its chance of finding the best solutions from among the mountain of submissions is low. Pisano and Verganti state that open networks are most effective when participating in them is easy with the problem being divided into small, well-defined chunks that contributors can work on independently; when there is one or just a few solutions that can be clearly defined; when the proposed solutions can be evaluated at low cost; when the difference between an ideal solution and an average solution is not large; and when the chance of missing out on a greatly superior solution proposed by an elite participant is small. With a closed network, a firm receives solutions from the best contributors in a selected knowledge domain (e.g.

GOVERNANCE: Hierarchical	GOVERNANCE: Flat	PARTICIPATION
Innovation mall A place where a company can post a problem, anyone can propose solutions, and the company chooses the solutions it likes best. **Example:** *InnoCentive.com website where companies can post scientific problems.*	**Innovation community** A network where anybody can propose problems, offer solutions and decide which solutions to use. **Example:** *Linux open-source software.*	**Open**
Elite circle A select group of participants chosen by a company that also defines the problem and picks the solutions. **Example:** *Alessi's handpicked group of 200-plus design experts who develop new concepts for home products.*	**Consortium** A private group of participants that jointly select problems, decide how to conduct work, and choose solutions. **Example:** *IBM's partnerships with select companies to jointly develop semiconductor technology:*	**Closed**

Figure 17.16: Four ways to collaborate

Source: reprinted by permission of *Harvard Business Review*. From 'Which kind of collaboration is right for you?' by Pisano, G. and Verganti, R., 86(12) 2008.

software); the best partners prefer to participate in closed networks; and the chance of receiving a few suitable ideas from a small number of collaborators is high. Closed networks are most effective when a firm knows the knowledge domain from which the best solution is likely to emerge; when it can pick the best experts itself; when the problem is large and cannot be broken up into parts; and when everyone's expertise is required.

With respect to governance, hierarchical form is best when a firm possesses the capabilities and knowledge to define a problem and evaluate the submitted solutions, and when it can choose the direction to take, understands users' needs, and can first divide and then integrate outsiders' contributions. Flat forms work best when no single company possesses total capability on its own, and when all collaborators have a vested interest in how a problem is solved, and want a role in decision-making.

The dark side of new organizational forms

In a prophetic article written nearly twenty years before the boundaryless organization received media or research interest, Bart Victor and Carroll Stephens (1994) discussed the 'dark side' of the brave new world of twenty-first-century networked, information-rich, de-layered, lean, hypercompetitive organization structures. These authors discussed the 'new org form' language of empowerment, high commitment, downsizing, restructuring, and re-engineering. They observed:

1. an increase in the numbers of workers who have only temporary, part-time or short contract jobs; and noted the increases in income inequalities rather than in shared benefits.
2. the creation of jobs in virtual occupations with workers performing whatever tasks are required to achieve the work goal, instead of having a role anchored in the organization and codified in a job description.

3. new organizational forms offering roles defined by the task and the location of the worker. Time, space, and shifting group membership can become the primary definers of responsibility and accountability for the virtual wage slave.
4. traditional indicators of status becoming blurred as obligations become networked and diffused, and the rights of employees become increasingly ephemeral.
5. employees being expected to exhibit a feverish commitment to their company, and many, fearing job loss, complying despite the one-sidedness of the deal.
6. that not everyone is at ease with the free-floating demands of the hyperflexible workplace. Many people thrive on predictability and routine.
7. the periodic deskilling (based on technical progress) is replaced by the incessant demand for innovation and adaptation. The new 'learning organization' insists that everyone becomes a self-motivated, continuous learner. Those who do not are threatened with obsolescence.
8. the flat organizations forcing more demanding and intrusive interpersonal relations. Teams and networks call for new levels and kinds of cooperation. No one can escape the demand to interact or to be interactive.
9. employees' values are offered up as fodder to be transformed by management for organizational ends. The high-velocity, high-commitment, 'flash-in-the-pan' collectivities offer no ongoing relationships, no safe havens, and no personal space.

(Victor and Stephens 1994, pp. 479–82)

Victor and Stephens concluded that in the discussions of new organizational forms, there is much talk of empowering, challenging, and equalizing the advantages of the new organizational forms, but there is also much fear and loathing. They believe that the boundaryless, adaptive learning organization of the twenty-first century extracts a high price from everyone that is involved in it.

STOP AND THINK How accurate have Victor and Stephens' predictions been? What evidence from your reading, or your experience of work organizations, can you provide that either confirms or contradicts their nine fears?

RECAP

1. *Appreciate the reason for chief executives' need to design and redesign their organization's structure.*
   - Organization structure is one of the ways of achieving organizational goals.
   - An organization's structure will be changed as a result of changes in its size, strategy, technology, environment, globalization, and diversification.
2. *Distinguish three eras of organizational design and what factors stimulated each.*
   - Era 1: mid 1800s to late 1970s – self-contained organization structures.
   - Era 2: 1980s to mid 1990s – horizontal organization structures.
   - Era 3: mid 1990s to date – boundaryless organization structures (hollow, modular, virtual, and collaborative).
3. *Distinguish between functional, divisional, matrix, and team-based organization structures.*
   - A functional structure groups activities and people according to the similarities in their work, profession, expertise, goals, or resources used.
   - A divisional structure splits an organization up into self-contained entities based on their organizational outputs, geographical region operated in, or the customer groups served.
   - A matrix structure combines two different types of structure, e.g. function and product.

→

- A team-based structure consists entirely of project-type teams that coordinate their activities and work directly with partners and customers to achieve their goals.

4. *Distinguish between an outsourcing relationship and hollow, modular, and virtual organization structures.*
   - An outsourcing relationship involves contracting with external providers to supply the organization with the processes and products that were previously supplied internally.
   - A hollow organization structure is based on outsourcing an organization's non-core *processes* which are then supplied to it by specialist external providers.
   - A modular organization structure involves assembling product chunks (modules) provided by internal divisions and external providers.
   - A virtual organization structure uses technology to transcend the constraints of legal structures, physical conditions, place, and, time, and allows a network of separate participants to present themselves to customers as a single entity.

5. *Understand the trend towards companies' collaborative relationships with competitors and customers, and their involvement in virtual communities.*
   - Collaboration has become a matter of integrating activities rather than integrating organizations.
   - Factors contributing to increased collaboration include the rise of partnership strategies, the knowledge economy, the working style of generation Y, and advances in collaborative technology.
   - The increasing speed of change means that individual organizations lack the necessary resources, knowledge, or skill to respond individually so have to collaborate with others.

Revision

1. Why might Max Weber and Henri Fayol be surprised by developments in contemporary organizational design arrangements?
2. Suggest how changes in organization structuring over the last fifty years have affected what workers and managers do, and how they do it.
3. In the literature, inter-organizational collaboration is presented as the way forward. Consider the potential negative consequences of this arrangement for the companies involved and their employees and managers.
4. Why are network and virtual structures preferred by managers seeking to encourage entrepreneurship and innovation?

Research assignment

This chapter reported Warner and Witzel's (2004) view that every organization possessed a mixture of virtual and tangible elements (pp. 591–2) . They identified six dimensions along which organizations can choose to organize their activities on a virtual or a tangible basis:

- nature of product
- nature of working
- relationship with suppliers
- relationship with customers
- relationship between firm's elements
- relationship between managers and employees

Review the discussion on virtuality and organizations in this chapter. Through personal contact, gain access to two different organizations. Using the six dimensions above as a basis for discussion, interview a manager from each organization to determine its virtual/tangible elements balance. (1) Write a report on the strengths and weaknesses of the balance based on your interview findings. (2) What effects does the balance have on employees' working patterns? (3) Identify where your findings are consistent with, and where they contradict the textbook account of strengths and weaknesses of virtual forms of organization.

Springboard

Narasimhan Anand and Richard Daft (2007) 'What is the right organization design?', *Organizational Dynamics*, 36(4), pp. 329–44. The writers set developments in choices about organization structure within a historical context.

Richard Dunford, Ian Palmer, Jodie Benveniste and John Crawford (2007) 'Co-existence of "old" and "new" organizational practices: transitory phenomenon or enduring feature?', *Asia Pacific Journal of Human Resources*, 45(1), pp. 24–43. Will the 'new' organizational forms discussed in this chapter replace 'old' bureaucratic organizations?

Raymond Miles, Charles Snow, Øystein Fjeldstad, Grant Miles and Christopher Lettl (2010) 'Designing organizations to meet 21st-century opportunities and challenges', *Organizational Dynamics*, 39(2), pp. 93–103. The authors consider the factors and processes which have created and shaped the organizational structures of the past, and those that are currently shaping them in the present.

Bart Victor and Carroll Stephens (1994) 'The dark side of the new organizational forms: an editorial essay', *Organization Science*, 5(4), pp. 479–82. A prophetic article in which the authors examine the 'dark side' of the brave new world of twenty-first-century networked, information-rich, de-layered, lean, hypercompetitive, boundaryless organizations.

OB in films

In Good Company (2004, director Paul Weitz), DVD track 6: 0:19:54 to 0:28:43 (9 minutes).

In the film, Globecom International, a multinational conglomerate, buys Waterman Publishing, the parent company which owns the flagship magazine *Sports America*. Globecom appoints its own 26-year-old business school prodigy and corporate ladder climber, Carter Duryea (played by Topher Grace), to be boss. In this clip, he meets his staff for the first time. It begins with Duryea (drinking down a coffee) saying 'Yeah, just keep them coming', and ends with two seated employees talking, one of them saying 'My money's on Dan, he's prehistoric.' As you watch the clip decide:

1. What is Duryea's objective in holding this meeting with company employees?
2. How successful is he in communicating with his staff?
3. What are *Sports America* employees' concerns likely to be at this time?

OB on the web

Search YouTube for a short interview entitled 'Birdie Fanning – Virtual Organizations'. Fanning is the Chief Human Resources Officer for ISIS, a new company still in its start-up phase when this interview was recorded. She describes the benefits to the company and to its employees of being a 'virtual organization' which relies on networks, outsourcing, and partnerships. What benefits does she mention that have been discussed in this chapter? She does not mention any problems with this approach; but what might these be?

CHAPTER EXERCISES

1. University of Grantchester Business School

Objectives

1. To design alternative organization structures for a business school based on different criteria of departmentalization.
2. To assess their benefits to different stakeholders.

Briefing

1. Form groups.
2. Read the information about the University of Grantchester Business School (UGBS) below.
3. Draw alternative organizational charts for the UGBS depicting organizational structures based on the five criteria shown below. Duplicate the provision of products/services as required.
   (a) Academic subjects taught by academic staff
   (b) Products/services delivered by academic staff
   (c) Functions performed by academic staff
   (d) Geography, where the product/service is delivered
   (e) Clients who consume the product/service provided
4. Which organization structure would you prefer and why, if you were (a) a full-time undergraduate or postgraduate student; (b) an academic staff member?

Information about the University of Grantchester Business School

(a) Academic subjects taught: The UGBS's 100 academics are equally divided between the four main subject areas (equivalent to company functions): human behaviour (HB); financial management (FM); strategy and marketing (SM); and operations management (OM).

(b) Products offered: The UGBS offers the following products:

U – Undergraduate teaching – BA full-time students who fund themselves, taught on the main campus

P1 – Postgraduate teaching – MBA full-time students who fund themselves, taught on the main campus

P2 – Postgraduate teaching – MBA part-time – working managers, funded by their companies, taught in the city centre campus

T – Together, these three constitute teaching (T = U + P1 + P2);

R – Research conducted by academics funding by the research councils

D – Doctoral – supervision of conducted by doctoral (postgraduate) students who fund themselves, on the main campus

C – Consultancy – consultancy provided by academics for companies, bought by them, and provided on the companies' premises

S – Short courses – short (non-graduating) courses, taught by academics for working managers, paid for by their companies, and run on company premises.

(c) Services: The school performs three major functions: teaching, research, and consultancy.

(d) Geography: Academics can work in four locations: main campus; city centre; seaside residential facility; on the company's own premises.

(e) Customers: The school has three classes of customers: students, research council funders, and companies.

2. Team-based organizational structuring

Objectives

1. To design alternative organization structures based on different criteria of departmentalization.
2. To assess their advantages and disadvantages to different stakeholders.

Briefing

Read the case study *Saab Training Systems*, and answer the following questions:

1. Why did the functional structure not suit the company's strategy?
2. How did the team-based structure help?
3. What problems could the team-based approach create?

Saab Training Systems

In the 1990s Saab Training Systems was a high-tech company working in the defence industry. It was a fully owned subsidiary of the Swedish company Saab. In 1997 the company had 260 employees and a turnover of about £52m. It sold computer-aided equipment for military training – for example, laser-based simulators. The market was characterized by long, complicated, politicized negotiations with clients, fierce global competition, and overcapacity as defence budgets reduced as a result of the 'peace dividend'. This high degree of uncertainty and need for flexibility had forced the company to react. It shunned external alliances, which were common in the industry, and focused on exploiting its core competence in laser-based simulation. But it also needed to drastically speed up throughput times in both development and production to get new product to commercialization faster and then to shorten delivery times.

The company decided to abandon its traditional functional structure in favour of a more flexible team-based structure and a more business-process-oriented way of doing business. Before these changes the company was organized into functions (production, development, marketing, and purchasing). Each function had its own internal hierarchy. This structure created problems with cross-functional coordination and communication. In the new structure, forty teams were created that reported directly to the senior management team. Team sizes were between six and eight. If they got bigger they were split. The teams were built around the business processes. There were five *business teams* who negotiated contracts with customers and monitored contracts. Each team was responsible for one or more products and particular geographical markets. When a contract was signed it became a 'Project' to which other teams were assigned: a *delivery team* (who planned production and tested products prior to shipping); a *purchasing team* (responsible for sourcing materials and components); and an *applications team* (who adapted the company's 'standard' products to the need of particular customers). Finally, production was assigned to one of fourteen *product teams* (who were also responsible for product development). In addition to these 'front-line' teams there were central functions such as personnel and finance.

Coordination of the various teams involved in a customer's order was very important since the particular mix of teams assigned to that order was temporary. It was dissolved as soon as the order was delivered to the customer. Also, product teams were working on more than one project at any time. The responsibility for coordination of any project was shared between the business team (commercial responsibility) and delivery teams (production planning).

Source: reproduced by permission of SAGE Publications, London, Los Angeles, New Delhi and Singapore, from Mullern, T., 'Integrating team-based structure in the business process', in Pettigrew, A.M. and Fenton, E.M. (eds), *The Innovating Organisation*,

Employability assessment

With regard to your future employment prospects:

1. Identify up to three issues from this chapter that you found significant.
2. Relate these to the competencies in the employability matrix.
3. Decide what actions you need to take to maintain and/or develop those competencies under each of the four headings of the employability matrix.

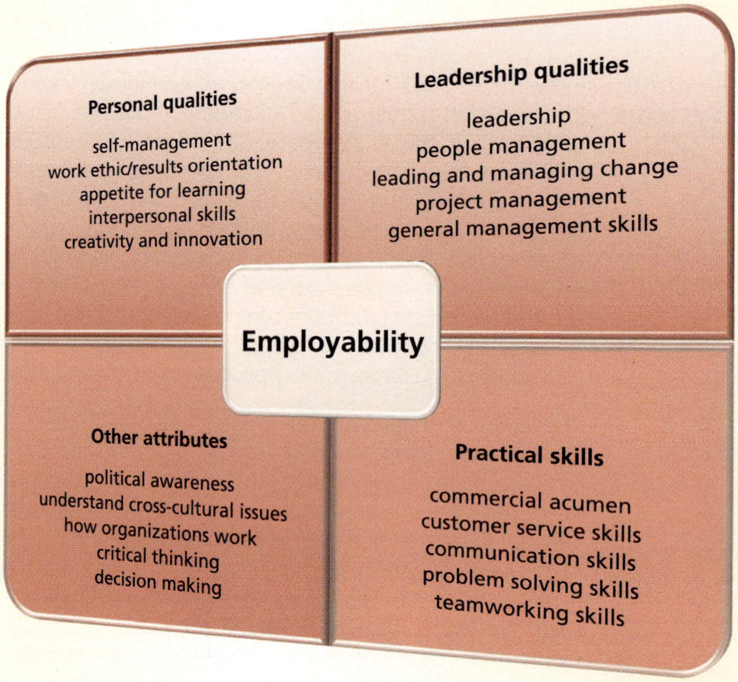

References

Anand, N. and Daft, R.L. (2007) 'What is the right organization design?', *Organizational Dynamics*, 36(4), pp. 329–44.

Ashkenas, R., Ulrich, D., Jick, T. and Kerr, S. (2002) *The Boundaryless Organization: Breaking the Chains of Organization Structure* (2nd edn), San Francisco, CA: Jossey-Bass.

Bartlett, C. and Ghoshal, S. (1990) 'Matrix management: not a structure, a frame of mind', *Harvard Business Review*, 68(4), pp. 138–45.

Beaumont, C. (2008) 'Has Apple really unlocked the toolbox?', *Daily Telegraph*, 15 March, Review section, p. 21.

Blitz, R. (2007) 'Winning formula', *Financial Times Magazine*, 11 August, pp. 22–3.

Brandenburger, A.M. and Nalebuff, B.J. (2002) *Co-opetition* (2nd edn), London: Profile Business Books.

Bughin, J. and Chui, M. (2011) 'The rise of the networked enterprise: Web 2.0 finds its payday', *McKinsey on Business Technology*, 22(Spring), pp. 6–13.

Business Week (2008) 'Globalization bites Boeing', 24 March, p. 32.

Chandler, A.D. (1962) *Strategy and Structure: Chapters in the History of American Industrial Enterprise*, Cambridge, MA: MIT Press.

Cherns, A. (1976) 'The principles of socio-technical designs', *Human Relations*, 29(8), pp. 783–92.

Child, J. (2005) *Organization: Contemporary Principles and Practice*, Oxford: Blackwell.

Cook, S. (2008) 'The contribution revolution: letting volunteers build your business', *Harvard Business Review*, 86(10), pp. 60–9.

Crooks, E. (2012) 'GE takes $1bn risk in bringing jobs home', *Financial Times*, 3 April, p. 17.

Davis, S.M. and Lawrence, P.R. (1978) 'Problems of matrix organizations', *Harvard Business Review*, 56(3), pp. 131–42.

Davis-Blake, A. and Broshack, J. (2009) 'Outsourcing and the changing nature of work', *Annual Review of Sociology*, 35, pp. 321–40.

Dodge, J. (2007a) 'Designing around the clock, and the world', *Design News*, 62, 4 June, pp. 97–100.

Dodge, J. (2007b) 'Boeing 787 Dreamliner engineering chief describes partners organization', *Design News*, 15 May.

Duncan, R.B. (1979) 'What is the right organization structure?: Decision tree analysis provides the answer', *Organizational Dynamics*, 7(3), pp. 59–80.

Erickson, T.J. and Gratton, L. (2007) 'What it means to work here', *Harvard Business Review*, 85(3), pp. 104–12.

Fishman, C. (2007) 'Total teamwork: Imagination Ltd', *Fast Company*, 19 December.

Forrester, R. and Drexler, A.B. (1999) 'A model of team-based organization performance', *Academy of Management Executive*, 13(3), pp. 36–49.

Galbraith, J. (1973) *Designing Complex Organizations*, Reading, MA: Addison-Wesley.

Gratton, L. (2007) 'Building bridges for success', *Financial Times*, 29 June, Understanding the Culture of Collaboration supplement, pp. 2–3.

Gratton, L., Voigt, A. and Erickson, T. (2007) 'Bridging fault lines in diverse teams', *Sloan Management Review*, 48(4) (Summer), pp. 22–9.

Harhoff, D. and Mayrhofer, P. (2010) 'Managing user communities and hybrid innovation processes: concepts and design implications', *Organizational Dynamics*, 39(2), pp. 137–44.

Hindle, T. (2006a) 'The matrix master', *The Economist*, 21 January, The New Organization: A Survey of the Company, p. 6.

Hindle, T. (2006b) 'Partners in wealth', *The Economist*, 21 January, The New Organization: A Survey of the Company, pp. 18–19.

Hindle, T. (2006c) 'The new organization', *The Economist*, 21 January, The New Organization: A Survey of the Company, pp. 3–5.

Howe, J. (2006) 'The rise of crowdsourcing', http://www.wired.com/wired/archive/14.06/crowds.html, accessed 7 June 2012.

Howe, J. (2009) *Crowdsourcing: Why the Power of the Crowd is Driving the Future of Business*, London: Crown Business.

Kornberger, M. (2010) *The Brand Society: How Brands Transform Management and Lifestyle*, Cambridge: Cambridge University Press.

Koza, M.P. and Lewin, A.Y. (1999) 'Putting the S-word back in alliances', *Financial Times Mastering Strategy Supplement*, 1 November, pp. 12–13.

Lampel, J. and Bhaila, A. (2011) 'Living with offshoring: The impact of offshoring on the evolution of organizational configurations', *Journal of World Business*, 46(3), pp. 346–58.

Lawrence, S. and Davis, P. (1979) *Matrix*, Reading, MA: Addison-Wesley.

Mabey, C., Salaman, G. and Storey, J. (1998) *Human Resource Management: A Strategic Introductio*, second edition, Oxford: Blackwell.

Marsh, P. (2011) 'High and dry', *Financial Times*, 13 April, p. 13

Miles, R.E., Snow, C.C., Fjeldstad, Ø.D., Miles, G. and Lettl, C. (2010) 'Designing organizations to meet 21st-century opportunities and challenges', *Organizational Dynamics*, 39(2), pp. 93–103.

Mohrman, S.A., Cohen, S.G. and Mohrman, A.M. (1997) *Designing Team-Based Organizations*, San Francisco, CA: Jossey-Bass.

Neville, S. (2012) 'NHS eyes follow John Lewis-style management experiment', *Financial Times*, 2 February, p. 2.

Newing, R. (2007) 'The great enabler: trust', *Financial Times*, 29 June, Understanding the Culture of Collaboration supplement, pp. 18–19.

Nowak, M. and Highfield, R. (2011) *Super Co-operators*, New York: Free Press.

Pisano, G. and Verganti, R. (2008) 'Which kind of collaboration is right for you?, *Harvard Business Review*, 86(12), pp. 78–86.

Plimmer, G. (2012) 'Private company to run NHS general hospital for first time', *Financial Times*, 30 January, p. 4.

Scahill, J. (2007) *Blackwater: The Rise of the World's Most Powerful Mercenary Army*, Nation Books.

Schilling, M.A. and Steensma, H.K. (2001) 'The use of modular organizational forms: an industry level analysis', *Academy of Management Journal*, 44(6), pp. 1149–1169.

Shih, S., Wang, J.T. and Yeung, A. (2006) 'Building global competiveness in a turbulent environment: Acer's journey of transformation', in W.H. Mobley and E. Weldon (eds), *Advances in Global Leadership*, Bradford: Emerald Group Publishing, pp. 201–17.

Taylor, P. and Parker, A. (2008) 'Android is set to take on smartphone market', *Financial Times*, 23 September, p. 30.

The Economist (2002) 'Incredible shrinking plants', 23 February, pp. 99–101.

The Economist (2007a) 'External affairs', 28 July, pp. 69–70.

The Economist (2007b) 'Odd couple', 5 May, pp. 71–2.

The Economist (2008a) 'Operating profit', 16 August, pp. 74–6.

The Economist (2008b) 'The un-iPhone', 27 September, p. 84.

The Economist (2008c) 'Following the crowd', 6 September, pp. 8 and 10.

The Economist (2011) 'Schumpeter: the trouble with outsourcing', 30 July, p. 62.

The Economist (2012a) 'Faster, faster, faster', 28 January, p. 59.

The Economist (2012b) 'Little monster mash', 10 March, p. 75.

The Economist (2012c) 'Collaborative manufacturing: altogether now', 21 April, Special Report: Manufacturing and Innovation, pp. 14–15.

The Economist (2012d) 'The roar of the crowd', 26 May, pp. 73–5.

The Economist (2012e) 'Outsourcing is so passé', 2 June, Technology Quarterly, pp. 7–8.

Victor, B. and Stephens, C. (1994) 'The dark side of the new organizational forms: an editorial essay', *Organization Science*, 5(4), pp. 479–82.

Warner, M. and Witzel, M. (2004) *Managing in Virtual Organizations*, London: International Thomson Business Press.

Whittington, R., Mayer, M. and Smith, A. (2002) 'Restructuring roulette', *Financial Times Mastering Leadership Supplement*, 8 November, pp. 6 and 8.

de Wit, B. and Meyer, R. (2005) *Strategy Synthesis: Text and Readings*, London: Thomson Learning.

Witzel, M. (2007) 'Types of collaboration: the right vehicle', *Financial Times*, 29 June, Understanding the Culture of Collaboration Supplement, p. 4.

Wright, R. (2011) 'After the downturn, a reformed industry copes with its first severe test', *Financial Times*, 13 April, p. 13.

Part 5 **Management processes**

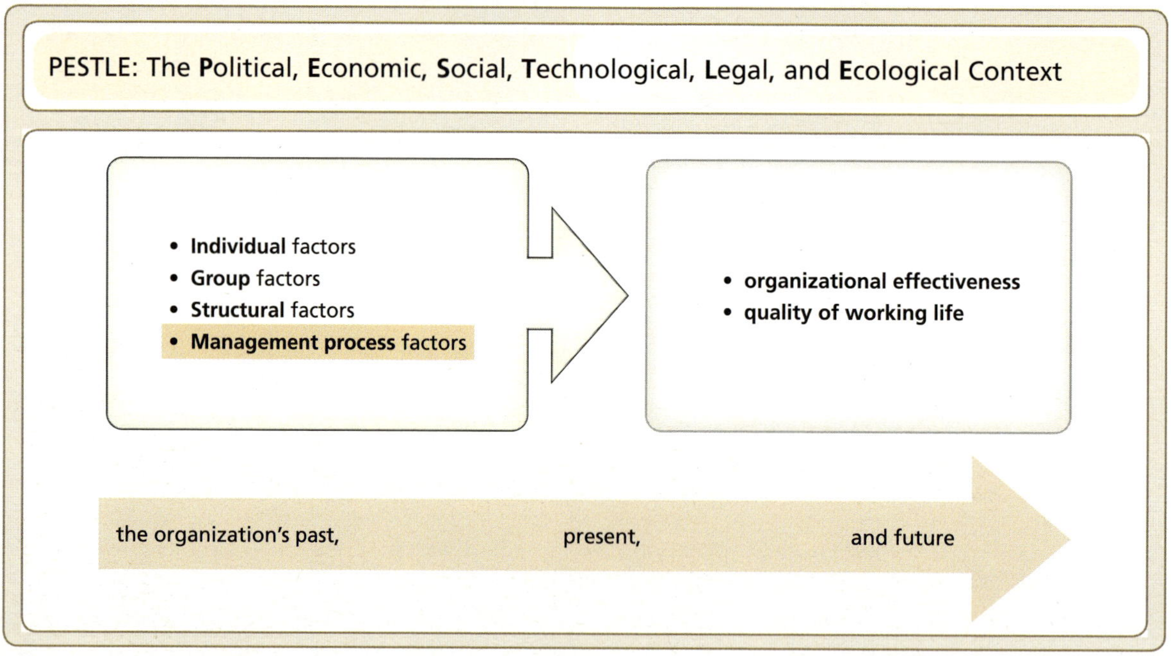

A field map of the organizational behaviour terrain

Introduction

Part 5, Management processes, explores the following five topics:

- *Organizational change*, in Chapter 18
- *Leadership*, in Chapter 19
- *Decision-making*, in Chapter 20
- *Conflict*, in Chapter 21
- *Power and politics*, in Chapter 22.

Each of these topics has an enormous impact on how employees are managed, how they experience their work environment, and how successful their organization is in achieving its goals. Each topic concerns the process of managing, which involves both managers and non-managers. Thus, the most junior of employees may be called upon to exercise leadership skills, become involved in group decision-making, and attempt to resolve a conflict between colleagues – while engaging in political behaviour in order to increase their power.

Most organizations in the twenty-first century are experiencing wrenching changes in order to respond to turbulent economic, geopolitical, and technological developments. Chapter 18 explores the nature of change, considering effective organization and management approaches along with the individual implications. This chapter concludes with an exploration of innovation processes in organizations, and what it is like to be an innovator. Chapter 19 on leadership introduces this keynote topic by covering various current perspectives and their practical implications. Chapter 20 on decision-making considers different models of decision-making, different types of decisions, different decision-makers, and different problems in decision-making.

This chapter challenges the notion that most decisions are made logically for the benefit of the organization by managers who possess the necessary information and authority. Chapter 21 on conflict considers contrasting perspectives on this challenging topic, and stresses how the way in which you perceive a situation influences what actions you will take. This chapter examines how the way a company is organized engenders conflicts which, in turn, have to be managed using conflict resolution devices. Finally, Chapter 22 addresses the abstract but critical concept of power in organizations, turning to the practice of organization politics, the latter often being defined as 'power in action'. The political perspective provides an alternative to the rational standpoint predominantly found in managerially-oriented textbooks. It challenges readers to revisit earlier chapters, to reassess their contents from this alternative viewpoint.

Invitation to see

RIA NOVOSTI/SCIENCE PHOTO LIBRARY

Industrial chemist inspecting a fermentation unit in the laboratory at Nizhpharm chemical and pharmaceutical factory in Nizhny Novgorod, Russia

1. **Decoding**: Look at this image closely. Note in as much detail as possible what messages you feel that it is trying to convey. Does it tell a story, present a point of view, support an argument, perpetuate a myth, reinforce a stereotype, challenge a stereotype?
2. **Challenging**: To what extent do you agree with the messages, stories, points of view, arguments, myths, or stereotypes in this image? Is this image open to challenge, to criticism, or to interpretation and decoding in other ways, revealing other messages?
3. **Sharing**: Compare with colleagues your interpretation of this image. Explore explanations for differences in your respective decodings.

You're the consultant: what would you do?

This manager has asked for your advice as an external management consultant, concerning problems that are going to arise with regard to a forthcoming merger:

> Our company is set to merge with a competitor in the next year and over the next few months we will be carrying out a review of our internal resources. The two companies are headquartered in different towns, with some duplication in head office functions, and in the reorganization there will undoubtedly be restructuring and redundancies. Our staff know this and are already feeling insecure: office gossip suggests that many are already looking to move on. With so many challenges ahead, the last thing we need is a talent drain, but we are unsure what messages to send out to reassure people. On the one hand we want to retain our brightest people to forge the best future for the new organization, but on the other we cannot promise a future for everybody. To add to this, we have a trade union that is clamouring for information and consultation. What actions can we take to maintain morale and treat people fairly?

From 'Troubleshooter', People Management, *13 November 2008, p. 62.*

Chapter 18 **Change**

Key terms

triggers of change
initiative decay
initiative fatigue
transformational change
coping cycle
Yerkes-Dodson law
readiness for change
resistance to change
organization development
innovation
sustaining innovations
disruptive innovations
operational innovation

Learning outcomes

When you have read this chapter, you should be able to define those key terms in your own words, and you should also be able to:

1. Explain why effective change management is important, to organizations and to individuals.
2. Identify the main types and triggers of organizational change.
3. Explain the issues that management must take into account to ensure that change is successful.
4. Understand the typical characteristics of human responses to change.
5. Understand the nature of resistance to change and approaches to overcoming it.
6. Explain the advantages and limitations of participative methods of change management.
7. Understand the significance of innovation, and the distinction between sustaining, disruptive, and operational innovations.
8. Explain the organizational properties that stimulate and stifle innovation.
9. Recognize the challenges facing creative, innovative individuals in organizations.

Why study change?

'Built-to-change' organizations

Edward E. Lawler and Christopher Worley (2009, p. 28) argue that

> To survive in a world that is changing increasingly quickly, businesses need to be able to anticipate change and to keep reconfiguring themselves. To do this, they need a built-in capacity to change continuously. Organizations that wait for an overwhelming mandate to engage in change efforts are very likely to be left behind and may struggle to survive. We believe that the only way for organizations to change rapidly enough is to design themselves so that they can adjust their strategic intents, structures and human capital deployments as a matter of routine. That means starting with a new set of core principles about what an organization should look like:

- don't assume that the future will be like the present;
- ensure no employee is more than two steps from the external environment;
- share business information with staff;
- use frequent goal-setting reviews, rather than job descriptions, to manage talent;
- stress that employment depends on willingness to accept change and learn new skills;
- encourage managers at all levels to take advantage of leadership opportunities.

It has become routine to say that 'change is a constant'. Organizations must keep changing, to keep up with global economic and geopolitical developments, competitor behaviour, changing customer demands and expectations, new legislation and regulations, new materials, new technologies – and many other surprises. Failure to change, and to change rapidly, may put an organization's survival at risk. You as an individual must also be able and willing to change. In order to 'future-proof' your career, Lynda Gratton (2011) argues that you will need to acquire new knowledge and skills every few years, allowing you to change from one job and organization to another. Failure to change as an individual will put your employability, and your career, at risk.

With so many opportunities to practise and to learn from experience, one might assume that managers have learned how to implement organizational change effectively. However, the success rate of planned change programmes is less than 40 per cent, and that estimate may be optimistic (Meaney and Wilson, 2009). With regard to major corporate transformations, two-thirds fail to achieve their objectives (Gardini et al., 2011). And Lynda Gratton argues that our education systems are not good at helping individuals to develop 'serial mastery' of new capabilities.

STOP AND THINK

How would you respond to these 'true or false' questions?

People have a natural resistance to change.	True or false?
People get bored with routine and seek out new experiences.	True or false?
Older people are more resistant to change.	True or false?

Did you answer 'true' to all three statements? These positive responses are inconsistent with each other, and contradict the evidence. For example, many people when they retire from work take up radically new activities and hobbies: painting, acting, community involvement, learning a musical instrument. We cannot have natural resistance to change and seek new experiences at the same time.

Change has never been so fast (since when?)

William Fielding Ogburn wrote this in 1922:

> That this is an age of change is an expression heard frequently today. Never before in the history of mankind have so many and so frequent changes occurred. These changes that we see taking place all about us are in that great cultural accumulation which is man's social heritage. It has already been shown that these cultural changes were in earlier times rather infrequent, but that in modern times they have been occurring faster and faster until today mankind is almost bewildered in his effort to keep adjusted to these ever increasing social changes. This rapidity of social change may be due to the increase in inventions which in turn is made possible by the accumulative nature of material culture [i.e., technology].

Triggers of change disorganizing pressures indicating that current systems, procedures, rules, organization structures, and processes are no longer effective.

Change is a constant, and it is a constant issue, for organizations, and for us as individuals. The need for organizational change is prompted by many different **triggers of change**.

External triggers for organizational change include:

- economic and trading conditions, domestic and global;
- new technology and materials;
- changes in customers' requirements and tastes;
- activities and innovations of competitors;
- mergers and acquisitions;
- legislation and government policies;
- shifts in local, national, and international politics;
- changes in social and cultural values.

Internal triggers for organizational change can include:

- new product and service design innovations;
- low performance and morale, high stress, and staff turnover;
- appointment of a new senior manager or top management team;
- inadequate skills and knowledge base, triggering training programmes;
- office and factory relocation, closer to suppliers and markets;
- recognition of problems triggering reallocation of responsibilities;
- innovations in the manufacturing process;
- new ideas about how to deliver services to customers.

Change is not simply a matter of reacting to triggers. Organizations and individuals can anticipate trends and opportunities, and be proactive as well. Susan Mohrman and Edward Lawler (2012, p. 42) argue that we need to focus on 'next practice' as well as 'best practice' because

> The major challenge for organizations today is navigating high levels of turbulence. They operate in dynamic environments, in societies where the aspirations and purposes of various stakeholders change over time. They have access to ever-increasing technological capabilities and information. A key organizational capability is the ability to adapt as context, opportunities, and challenges change.

One of the best known metaphors for change was developed by Kurt Lewin (1951), who argued for the need to *unfreeze* the current state of affairs, to *move* to a desired new state, then to *refreeze* and stabilize those changes. However, as Mohrman and Lawler suggest, refreezing is no longer an option. 'Repeat change' is the norm, and 'permanent thaw' is a better metaphor. The environment for most organizations seems likely to remain turbulent, and change will be on the management agenda for some time. The study of change, however, is paradoxical, and interesting, for several reasons:

- as the triggers and consequences of organizational change are many and complex, establishing cause and effect is difficult;
- organizational change has to be studied at different levels of analysis - individual, group, organizational, social - which are interrelated in complex ways;
- change that affects a number of different stakeholders is difficult to evaluate as there may be no agreed criteria on which to base judgements of success and failure;
- change is a process, a series of events unfolding over time, and not a static or time-bounded event, raising questions concerning the appropriate time frame for analysis.

When thinking of change, we must also be aware of what is *not* changing. It is not difficult to list features of technology, jobs, organizations, and society in the second decade of the twenty-first century that have not changed since the beginning of the twentieth. Personal transport still relies mainly on internal combustion engines running on carbohydron-based fuel. Finding employment remains a social norm and is central to most people's definition of personal identity.

Change is thus a core topic, for managers concerned with organizational performance, adaptability, and survival, and for us as individuals, concerned with our employability and our careers.

Making it happen and making it stick

The advice for managers on implementing change is relatively straightforward, with different commentators offering much the same guidance. For example, reviewing the evidence in this field, Jeffrey Pfeffer and Robert Sutton (2006) advise management to focus on four issues to ensure that, once the decision to go ahead has been taken, change happens fast and is effective:

1. *Create dissatisfaction*: As Kurt Lewin said, if people are happy with the way things are, they will be more reluctant to change. A key management task, therefore, may be to make people unhappy with the status quo.
2. *Give direction*: People need to know what they are expected to do, and why. Management must therefore be relentless in communicating the message, over and over again.
3. *Have faith*: Management must make it clear that the benefits of change will be worth the time, money, and effort, balanced with discussion of uncertainties and problems, taking new information into account.
4. *Embrace the mess*: Change is an untidy process. Despite careful planning, there will always be mistakes and setbacks. This is normal. Management must learn from and fix the problems, and not focus on who to blame.

If it is this simple, why do organizational changes fail so frequently? From his research into over 100 American companies, John Kotter (2007) argues that many make the following mistakes:

Mistakes	Nature and remedy
1. No urgency	If employees don't see the need, then they will not be motivated to change; management must create a sense of urgency.
2. No coalition	One or two people acting on their own can't drive big change; management must create a coalition with the expertise and the power to make it happen.
3. No vision	Without a picture of the future that is easy to explain and understand, a change programme becomes confusing; change needs a clear vision.
4. Poor communication	Giving people an important message once is not enough; the vision must be communicated repeatedly by management, in words and actions.
5. Obstacles not removed	Structures, design of jobs, reward and appraisal systems, and key individuals can get in the way; the obstacles must be confronted and removed.
6. No wins	Change takes time, and momentum can be lost without interim achievements to celebrate; management should create and reward short-term wins.
7. Premature victory	The job is not done when improvements appear; it is a mistake to 'declare victory' too soon, before the changes are embedded.
8. No anchoring	Change that is not seen to be beneficial will decay, and the next generation of managers may not continue the work; the change must be seen to have worked, and successors must champion the changes of their predecessors.

Source: based on Kotter (2007).

In order to be more successful with change, Kotter suggests a careful planning process, working through those eight issues more or less in sequence, and not missing or rushing any of them. This takes time. Given the rapid pace of contemporary change, perhaps many organizations try to take too many shortcuts, attempting to put change in place more quickly, but getting it wrong as a consequence.

Is change more difficult in a recession? Mary Meaney and Sarah Wilson (2009) argue that this is not necessarily the case. The same guidelines apply – clear vision, management support, good planning, employee involvement. In a recession, they argue, it is also important to balance positive and negative messages, and not to broadcast only bad news. Persuading employees of the need for change may also be more straightforward in a downturn (see box).

Another problem with change has recently emerged. The focus in the twentieth century was with making things happen, and happen faster. Despite the many pressures, there is a feeling in the twenty-first century that change really is accelerating too fast, that we need to slow things down, and perhaps keep some things the same. One problem concerns **initiative decay**, also called 'improvement evaporation', where the benefits of a change are lost as the organization moves on to deal with new priorities. Alongside the need for change, therefore, there is concern with how to *sustain* changes and improvements that are already in place (Buchanan, Fitzgerald and Ketley, 2006).

Initiative decay an organizational phenomenon where the benefits from a change initiative 'evaporate', when attention shifts to focus on other issues and priorities.

A further problem is **initiative fatigue**, as people become tired of constant demands to do things differently, work better, smarter, faster, harder. Research suggests that initiative fatigue is widespread, affecting all levels of the organization, and reducing enthusiasm for more change.

Initiative fatigue the personal exhaustion and apathy resulting from the experience of too much organizational change.

Heike Bruch and Jochen Menges (2010) argue that fast-paced change can lead to corporate burnout. In many organizations, intense market pressures encourage management to increase the number and speed of activities, raise performance goals, shorten innovation cycles, and introduce new systems and technologies. When the chief executive makes this furious pace 'the new normal', the achievements turn into chronic overloading. When people are working constantly under time pressure, with priorities frequently changing, focus is scattered, staff become tired and demotivated, and customers get confused.

Managing change in a downturn

Source: www.CartoonStock.com

Local government in England has had to cut spending dramatically while trying to maintain the same levels of services to local people. Can this be achieved by reconfiguring services in radically different ways, changing the way people work, while reducing costs? Organizational change is often hard enough, but in a downturn, employees may be demotivated and concerned about redundancy.

Sunderland City Council in the north-east of England employs 8,000 people, with two-thirds of their budget coming from central government. In 2010–11, funding fell 10 per cent, by £58 million, with more cuts to come in the following three years. At the start of 2010, the Council launched a transformation programme; could things be done differently, without losing jobs (MacLachlan, 2011)?

Unwilling to force staff to retire early or accept redeployment, the Council created an internal jobs market. This encouraged staff in areas that were shrinking to apply for jobs in expanding services, using a web-enabled assessment and employee-job matching system. This was linked to a retraining programme designed to transform the skills profile of the workforce, focusing on personality, values and potential as well as on knowledge and past experience. An employee portal was established to allow staff to create their own CVs.

Resistance to these moves came not from staff but from managers who felt that their recruitment decisions were being constrained. For staff unable to find a new role, a new unit was established called 'Switch': Staff working in transition and change. Over 200 people between roles, including managers, worked in this unit, reducing the Council's use of temporary staff on fixed-term contracts, for maternity cover, for example. The Switch team was also used to drive change, with efficiency savings projects, designing future job roles, and providing careers advice to other staff in transition.

The flexible working scheme was popular, allowing staff voluntarily to reduce their paid hours (with the option to increase them again), and to 'purchase' up to two weeks of additional annual leave by spreading the salary sacrifice over the year. A 'be your own boss' scheme offered support to employees who wanted to start their own businesses, giving them 20 days' paid leave and access to a small business adviser. The fifty staff who wanted to proceed continued working part-time for the council to give them some income security while they established their businesses. Local employers were invited to 'borrow' and to pay council staff on secondments.

An economic downturn creates uncertainty and fear. However, in these circumstances, people are often more readily convinced about the need for change. Managing change successfully in a downturn takes a combination of advance planning and imagination. In this case, the difficult financial situation itself was the trigger for implementing those innovative working practices. (Based on MacLachlan 2011.)

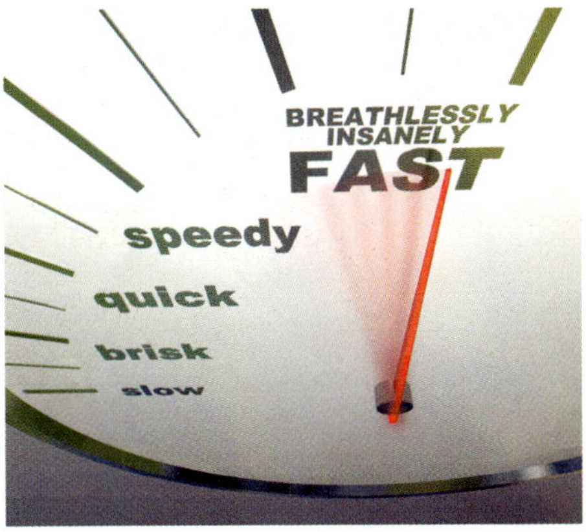

IQconcept/Shutterstock.com

Bruch and Menges call this 'the acceleration trap'. They found that in companies that were 'fully trapped', 60 per cent of employees felt that they lacked the resources to get their work done, compared with only 2 per cent who felt that way in companies that were not 'trapped'. They also (p. 83) found three typical patterns

1. *Overloading*: staff have too many activities, but not enough time or resources.
2. *Multiloading*: focus is reduced by asking employees to take on too many kinds of activities.
3. *Perpetual loading*: the organization operates close to capacity all the time, giving employees no chance to rest or retreat, but only to ask 'When is the economizing going to come to an end?'

If you answer 'yes' to five or more of these statements, then your organization may have an 'acceleration culture' (Bruch and Menges, 2010, p. 85):

- Is it hard to get important things done because too many other activities diffuse focus?
- Is there a tendency to drive the organization to the limits of its capacity?
- Does the company value hard effort over tangible results?
- Are employees made to feel guilty if they leave work early?
- Do employees talk a lot about how big their workload is?
- Are managers expected to act as role models by being involved in multiple projects?
- Is 'no' a taboo word, even for people who have already taken on too many projects?
- Is there an expectation that people must respond to emails within minutes?
- After work, do staff keep their mobile phones on because they feel they need to be reachable?

How can an organization break free from the acceleration trap? Be clear about strategy and goals. Stop less important work. Have a system that identifies more and less important initiatives. And 'declare an end to the current high-energy phase'. At one company studied by Bruch and Menges, the chief executive insisted that managers identify only three 'must-win battles', to concentrate attention and energy, instead of the 'ten top priority goals' with which they used to work.

The basic 'rules' of change implementation are simple: clear benefits, strong leadership, powerful change agents, constant communication, employee engagement, short-term wins, and making sure that change is embedded in the culture. Change implementation is complex, however, because this is a complex and untidy process, and because it is difficult to get the timing and the pacing right. Change too slowly, and the survival of the organization may be at risk. Change too quickly, and staff may be overloaded and demotivated – which could also threaten organizational performance and survival.

Transformational change

Table 18.1: Depth of organizational change

surface	**fine tuning**: focus on efficiency
↓	**restructure**: centralize, decentralize
shallow	**reallocate resources**: grow some departments, cut others
↓	**improve business planning**: symbolize a shift in thinking
penetrating	**change the leadership**: new CEO with major change remit
↓	**change the organization's definition of success**: create new goals, objectives, targets to change behaviour
deep	**change the mission, vision, values and philosophy**: symbolize a radical shift in thinking and behaviour
↓	
transformational	**paradigm shift**: change how we think, how we solve problems, how boundaries are defined, the way we do business: frame-breaking, mould-breaking, fundamental, strategic change

Transformational change large-scale change involving radical, frame-breaking, and fundamentally new ways of thinking, solving problems, and doing business.

Organizational changes vary in 'depth', from shallow to deep, as shown in Table 18.1. Faced with geopolitical, economic, demographic, sociocultural, and technological developments, most organizations seem to need deep **transformational change**. This is more difficult to implement than shallow change, as it is more costly and time-consuming, and affects larger numbers of people in more significant ways. In most organizations, many changes are likely to be under way at the same time, at different depths. We cannot argue that 'all change must be deep change'. Deep change is appropriate when dealing with 'deep problems', while fine tuning is an appropriate response to minor concerns.

Scott Keller and colleagues (2010) identify the methods that make transformational change more successful. They used information from McKinsey, a management consulting firm, whose global survey generated over 2,500 responses from executives across a range of regions, industries, specialities, and seniority. These executives identified four methods which had contributed to the success of their changes, concerning goals, structures, involvement, and leadership.

1. *Progressive change with 'stretch' targets*: One of the main themes from this study concerned the need to focus on strengths and achievements, and not just on problems. It was also important to have unambiguous measures of success, using 'stretch targets', with milestones and information systems in place to ensure that progress was constantly monitored and that problems could be addressed quickly. They also found that *progressive transformations* – going for growth, improved performance, expansion – succeeded 50 per cent more often than *defensive transformations* – reactive, seeking to cut costs.
2. *Logical programme structure*: Success was linked to breaking the change process down into specific, clearly defined initiatives, with a logical programme, which those who were involved were allowed to shape or to 'co-create'. Almost a quarter of extremely successful transformations were planned by groups of 50 or more, compared with only 6 per cent of unsuccessful change programmes. Clear roles and responsibilities, so that staff felt accountable for producing results, were also important success factors.
3. *Ownership and involvement*: Success was also associated with high levels of employee engagement and collaboration. Changes were more likely to be successful when front-line staff felt a sense of ownership of what was happening and took the initiative to drive the

changes. This meant high levels of communication and involvement at all stages of the transformation process.

4. *Exercising strong leadership*: Leadership capabilities are important (see Chapter 19), and so is the personal commitment and visible involvement of the chief executive. It helps if leaders 'role model' the desired changes, focusing on organization culture (or 'mindsets'), and developing capacity for continuous improvement. Staff thus gain new capabilities through the transformation process, and organization cultures become more receptive to further innovation and improvement.

Goals, structures, engagement, leadership – these are common themes in change management advice. However, Keller et al. also found that these tactics were more powerful when they were combined. Of the organizations which used all of these tactics, 80 per cent met their aims, compared with only 10 per cent of those organizations which had used none of these approaches. Even with defensive transformations, the chance of success using all of these tactics was 64 per cent.

As we have now seen, change management advice often comes in the form of checklists. The length of these checklists varies, but the contents seem to be broadly similar. The evidence suggests that it is important, however, to work through the whole list, rather than to pick some items and ignore others.

STOP AND THINK

If you want a high-flying, fast track career, you are unlikely to get far if you focus your energies on shallow changes. Shallow changes do not contribute much to organizational performance, and will not improve your visibility or reputation. You would be advised to work on deep changes, as long as they are successful.

What happens if all ambitious managers try to drive deep changes in the interests of progressing their careers?

Change and the individual

David Schneider and Charles Goldwasser (1998) introduced the 'classic change curve' shown in Figure 18.1. In the middle of the curve sits a 'valley of despair'. This suggests that change can mean loss and pain for those who are affected by it. Schneider and Goldwasser

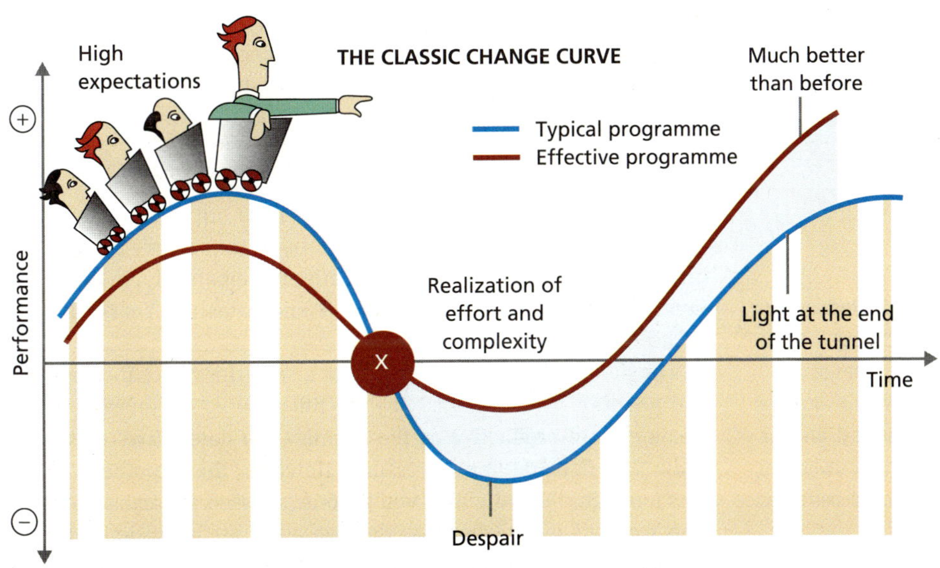

Figure 18.1: The classic change curve

Source: Schneider and Goldwasser (1998, p. 42).

also argue that this is probably inevitable in most cases of change, and that it is useful to be aware of this and to weaken the impact if possible:

> A leader of change must anticipate employees' reactions, another key factor in the process. As shown [in this diagram], these reactions occur along a 'change curve'. The blue line represents what is, unfortunately, typical. Unrealistically high expectations at the outset of a programme lead to a relatively deep 'valley of despair' when change doesn't come as quickly or easily as anticipated. Over time, employees do see a 'light at the end of the tunnel' and the change eventually produces some positive results. The red line illustrates what is possible with effective change management: a less traumatic visit to the valley and greater results as the programme reaches completion. Can you avoid the 'valley of despair' altogether? Probably not. All change programmes involve some loss. The best approach is to acknowledge that employees will mourn the loss of business as usual, much as people experience stages of grieving when trauma invades their personal lives. (Schneider and Goldwasser, 1998, p. 42)

Coping cycle the emotional response to trauma and loss, in which we experience first denial, then anger, bargaining, depression, and finally acceptance.

The change curve from Schneider and Goldwasser draws on research concerning how individuals cope with traumatic personal loss, such as the death of a close relative. Elizabeth Kübler-Ross (1969) argued that we deal with loss by moving through a series of stages, each characterized by a particular emotional response. The **coping cycle** has since been used by many others to help understand responses to major organizational changes.

The five stages in the Kübler-Ross coping cycle are defined in Table 18.2. This is an 'ideal' model. We may not all experience the same sets of responses. We may omit stages, revisit some, or pass through them more or less quickly than others. This can be a useful diagnostic tool. If we know where in the response cycle a person is, we could provide useful support.

Table 18.2: The coping cycle

Stage	Response
denial	unwillingness to confront the reality; 'this is not happening'; 'there is still hope that this will all go away'
anger	turn accusations on those apparently responsible; 'why is this happening to me?'; 'why are you doing this to me?'
bargaining	attempts to negotiate, to mitigate loss; 'what if I do it this way?'
depression	the reality of loss or transition is appreciated; 'it's hopeless, there's nothing I can do now'; 'I don't know which way to turn'
acceptance	coming to terms with and accepting the situation and its full implications; 'what are we going to do about this?'; 'how am I going to move forward?'

Yerkes-Dodson law a psychology hypothesis which states that performance increases with arousal, until we become overwhelmed, after which performance falls.

Just how much pressure can we take from organizational change? Psychology has long argued that the relationship between arousal, or sensory stimulation, on the one hand, and human performance, on the other, varies systematically, in the form of an 'inverted U' function, as shown in Figure 18.2. This is known as the **Yerkes-Dodson law**, after Robert M. Yerkes and John D. Dodson (1908).

The Yerkes-Dodson law argues that task performance increases with arousal, stimulation, and pressure. This explains why the time you spend revising for an examination seems to become more productive as the examination date draws closer. Here is the basis for the claim 'I work better under pressure'. However, this hypothesis also says that, if the pressure gets too high, the individual will become stressed and exhausted, and performance will fall. This explains why, when you delayed all of your revision until the night before, you did badly the following day.

Performance may be low if a job is repetitive and boring, so arousal is low. Performance can sometimes be improved in such settings with background music, conversation, and job

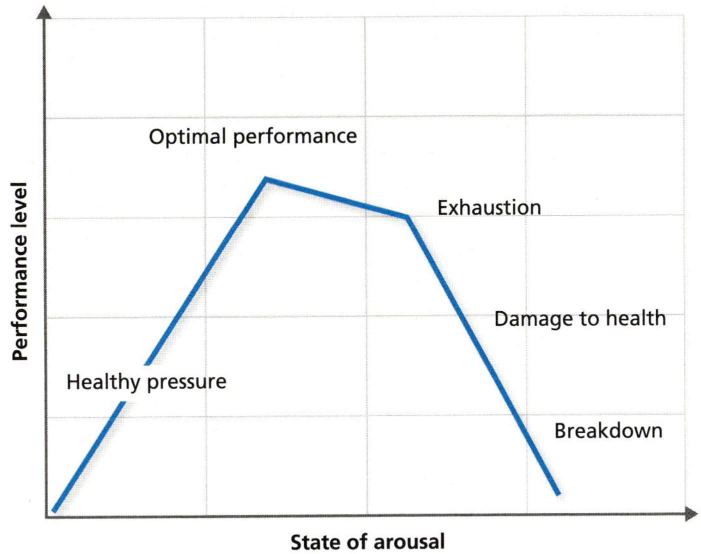

Figure 18.2: Pressure and performance – the inverted-U function

rotation. Now suppose that the job is enriched and becomes more interesting, responsible, and demanding, making more use of the individual's skills and knowledge. As the level of pressure increases, performance is likely to increase. However, a point will eventually be reached where the pressure becomes so great that it is overwhelming rather than stimulating. At this point fatigue and stress set in, and eventually ill-health and breakdown can occur if the pressure continues to escalate.

Can organizational change induce such pressure? From their survey of the management experience of change, Les Worral and Cary Cooper (2006) conclude that pressures to cut costs, intensify work, and improve performance were damaging loyalty, morale, job security, and sense of wellbeing. Factors that particularly affected wellbeing included:

- unmanageable workloads
- unrealistic objectives
- having little control over aspects of one's job
- not being involved in decisions affecting one's work
- not having enough time to do the job as well as one would like
- having little or no influence over performance targets
- ideas and suggestions not being taken into account
- working longer hours than one wanted to
- work interfering with home and personal life.

The Yerkes-Dodson law applied to work settings is summarized in Table 18.3, which plots changes in response, experience, and performance for escalating pressure levels. Deciding the optimal level of pressure is difficult, because this depends on the individual. Also, appropriate levels of stimulation depend on the difficulty of the task. If the task is easy, more stimulation can be applied. Music destroys our concentration during a chess game, but is enjoyable while backing up computer files.

How can we tell what levels of pressure people are experiencing, or when people are getting 'too close to the edge'? We can ask them, but will the answers be truthful? Fortunately, there are many proxy measures that show when people are suffering excess pressure: staff turnover, sickness rates, unexplained absences, accidents and mistakes, customer complaints, grievances. Physical appearance also changes as people become stressed, and interpersonal relationships become strained.

Table 18.3: The pressure-performance relationship explained

Pressure level	Response	Experience	Performance
very low	boredom	low levels of interest, challenge and motivation	low, acceptable
low to moderate	comfort	interest aroused, abilities used, satisfaction, motivation	moderate to high
moderate to high	stretch	challenge, learning, development, pushing the limits	high, above expectations
high to unrealistic	stress	overload, failure, poor health, dysfunctional coping behaviour	moderate to low
extreme	panic	confusion, threat, loss of self-confidence, withdrawal	low, unacceptable

Four conditions for changing mindsets

Emily Lawson and Colin Price (2010) argue that the success of change relies on persuading individuals to change their 'mindsets' – to think differently about their jobs and the way in which they work. They identify three levels of organizational change. First, desired outcomes (e.g. increased revenue) can often be achieved without changing working practices (by selling non-core assets, for example). Second, employees can be asked to change working practices in line with current thinking (finding ways to reduce waste, for example). The third level involves fundamental changes in organization culture, in collective thinking and behaviour – from reactive to proactive, hierarchical to collegial, inward-looking to externally-focused. There are four conditions for changing mindsets at level three:

> Employees will alter their mindsets only if they see the point of the change and agree with it – at least enough to give it a try. The surrounding structures (reward and recognition systems, for example) must be in tune with the new behaviour. Employees must have the skills to do what it requires. Finally, they must see people they respect modelling it actively. Each of these conditions is realized independently; together they add up to a way of changing the behaviour of people in organizations by changing attitudes about what can and should happen at work. (Lawson and Price, 2010, p. 32)

Readiness and resistance

Readiness for change a predisposition to welcome and embrace change.

Resistance to change an unwillingness or inability to accept or to discuss changes that are perceived to be damaging or threatening to the individual.

From a practical change implementation perspective, it is usually useful to ask the question: are the conditions right, or do we have to do some preliminary work before we go ahead? One approach to preparing the ground is based on the concept of **readiness for change**.

Where readiness is high, change may be straightforward. Readiness depends on understanding the need for change, knowing the direction and the goal, and having a clear plan and enough resources and capable people to implement it. Where the ingredients are in place, and readiness is high, resistance may be localized and weak. If readiness is low, implementation will be more difficult. The concept of readiness draws attention to two other issues. One is timing. Some readiness factors may strengthen naturally, on their own, with time. The second concerns deliberate action, to heighten the impatience for change, or strengthen a welcoming predisposition. Readiness factors can be managed.

Using this kind of diagnosis, it is often possible to anticipate both positive and negative responses to change, and to use that understanding to develop support, and also to address **resistance to change**.

Source: www.CartoonStock.com

Change has positive and negative aspects. On the one hand, change implies experiment and the creation of something new. On the other hand, it means discontinuity and the destruction of familiar arrangements and relationships. Despite the positive attributes, change can be resisted because it involves confrontation with the unknown, and loss of the familiar. It is widely assumed that resistance to change is natural. Many people find change both painful and frustrating.

There are many sources of resistance to change, but the main ones seem to be:

- *self-interest*: We want to protect a status quo with which we are content and which we regard as advantageous. Change may threaten to push us out of our 'comfort zone', and away from what we enjoy. We develop vested interests in organization structures and technologies. Change can mean loss of power, prestige, respect, approval, status, and security. Change can also be personally inconvenient. It may disturb relationships and other arrangements that have taken time and effort to establish. It may force an unwelcome move in location, and alter social opportunities. Perceived as well as actual threats to interests and values are thus likely to generate resistance. We may identify ourselves more closely with our functions and roles than with the organization. We have a personal stake in our specialized knowledge and skills, and may not be willing to see these made redundant or obsolete.
- *misunderstanding*: We are more likely to resist change if we do not understand the reasons behind it, or its nature and consequences. Resistance can thus be reduced by improved understanding. However, if managers have little trust in employees, information about change may be withheld or distorted. If employees distrust managers, information may not be believed. Incomplete and incorrect information creates uncertainty and rumour, which increases the perception of threat, and also raises defensiveness. The way in which change is introduced can thus be resisted, rather than the change itself.
- *different assessments*: We each differ in how we see and evaluate the costs and benefits of change. A major threat for me can be a stimulating challenge for you. Contradictory assessments are more likely to arise when communication is poor. However, those differing perceptions can lead to constructive criticism and improved proposals. Philip Atkinson (2005) thus argues that resistance is a healthy response, and that organizations need this kind of challenge which helps to redesign initiatives to strengthen support. Resistance to change is not necessarily dysfunctional, but can lead to more effective outcomes.

- *low tolerance for change*: We differ in our abilities to cope with change and uncertainty. Change that requires us to think and behave in different ways can challenge our self-concept. We each have ideas about our abilities and our strengths. One response to change may thus be self-doubt; 'can I handle this?'. Some people have a low tolerance for ambiguity and uncertainty. The anxiety and apprehension that they suffer may lead them to oppose even potentially beneficial changes.

How can resistance be managed? Different individuals and groups are likely to be affected in different ways, and are likely to react differently. To anticipate and manage these reactions, it helps to understand each stakeholder, or stakeholder group, affected by a particular change.

Stakeholder analysis is useful in planning change, and involves the following steps:

1. Draw up a list of stakeholders affected by the proposed changes.
2. Establish what each will gain or lose if the change goes ahead.
3. Use the potential benefits to strengthen support.
4. Find ways to address the concerns of those who feel they will lose out, by altering the nature of the changes, or reducing their losses in other ways.

Different stakeholders must be managed differently. Allies need to be 'kept on side', while opponents need to be converted, or perhaps discredited and marginalized. John Kotter and Leo Schlesinger (2008) identify six methods for managing resistance. The advantages and disadvantages of each of these methods are summarized in Table 18.4. These methods can of course be used in combination. While education, participation, and support are most likely to be the norm, there will be situations where negotiation, manipulation, and coercion become necessary.

Table 18.4: Methods for dealing with resistance to change

Method	Advantages	Disadvantages	Use when resistance is caused by
education and communication	increases commitment, reconciles opposing views	takes time	misunderstanding and lack of information
participation and involvement	reduces fear, uses individual skills	takes time	fear of the unknown
facilitation and support	increases awareness and understanding	takes time and can be expensive	anxiety over personal impact
negotiation and agreement	helps to reduce strong resistance	can be expensive and encourage others to strike deals	powerful stakeholders whose interests are threatened
manipulation and cooptation	quick and inexpensive	future problems from those who feel they were manipulated	powerful stakeholders who are difficult to manage
explicit and implicit coercion	quick and overpowers resistance	change agent must have power; risky if people are angered	deep disagreements and little chance of consensus

Source: based on Kotter and Schlesinger (2008).

STOP AND THINK

Faced with resistance to a desirable change, would you ever recommend manipulation and threat, or would you regard these methods as unprofessional or unethical in all circumstances?

Does it matter if some people resist a particular change? Maybe not. Peter Senge (1990) argues that 'dispositions' toward change vary on a broad continuum from commitment to compliance:

Disposition	Response to change
commitment	want change to happen and will work to make it happen; willing to create whatever structures, systems, and frameworks are necessary for it to work
enrolment	want the change to happen and will devote time and energy to making it happen within given frameworks; act within the spirit of the framework
genuine compliance	see the virtue in what is proposed, do what is asked, and think proactively about what is needed; act within the letter of the framework
formal compliance	can describe the benefits of what is proposed and are not hostile to them – do what is asked and no more; stick to the letter of the framework
grudging compliance	do not accept that there are benefits to what is proposed and do not go along with it, but do enough of what is asked not to jeopardize own position; interpret the letter of the framework
non-compliance	do not accept that there are benefits and have nothing to lose by opposing the proposition, so will not do what is asked; work outside the framework
apathy	neither support nor oppose the proposal, just serving time; don't care about the framework

Source: adapted from Senge (1990, pp. 219–20).

While it may be reassuring to have everyone fully committed to an organizational change, Senge argues that this is not necessary. Rather than attempt to persuade everyone to 'commit', it can be more useful to analyse the level of support required from each of those who are involved, and to direct management attention and energies to achieving that support.

Participation and dictatorship

Remploy is a British manufacturing company that provides employment for people with disabilities and health conditions. In 2007, the company decided that it had to cut costs by closing half of its 83 factories, while quadrupling the number of jobs that it found annually for its staff in mainstream employment. A support plan was developed, to prepare employees and to help them through the change, with leadership meetings, roadshows, face-to-face and written briefings, helplines, group sessions, and a specialist career transition company to support individual employees. Remploy funded training for trade union representatives, to help them interpret the company's business information. Union consultations led to 15 fewer closures than planned, to a voluntary redundancy scheme at the remaining factories, and to increased sales to the public sector (Jessop, 2008).

This participative approach to major organizational change has now become conventional practice, and dates from the work of Lester Coch and John French (1948) at the Harwood Manufacturing Corporation in Marion, Virginia. The company made pyjamas, and employees were complaining about frequent changes in work methods and pay rates. Absenteeism was high, efficiency was low, output was restricted deliberately, and employees were aggressive towards supervisors. Most of the grievances concerned the fact that as soon as they had learned a new job, and started to earn bonuses, they were moved to another task. This meant that they had to start learning all over again, during which time they lost the bonus.

Coch and French designed an experiment with three production groups, each with a different level of participation in changes. One group of 18 hand pressers had to accept changes imposed by the production department. A second group of 13 pyjama folders sent three representatives to discuss and approve new methods. In a third group of 15 pyjama examiners, everyone took part. The performance of the non-participating group did not improve, and hostility to management remained high. In contrast, the performance of the 'total participation' group rose to a level higher than before the experiment. Some months later, the initial non-participation group were brought together again for a new pressing job. This time, they participated fully in the changes, which resulted in a rapid increase in efficiency. This experiment confirmed that it was not the people involved but the way in which they were treated that affected resistance to or acceptance of change.

Since then, employee participation has been standard advice for managers seeking to encourage a welcoming and creative approach to change. However, participative methods have been challenged by the work of two Australian researchers, Doug Stace and Dexter Dunphy (2001). They first define the scale of change, from fine tuning to corporate transformation, as discussed earlier (see Table 18.1). They then identify four styles of change:

- **collaborative** – widespread employee participation in key decisions;
- **consultative** – limited involvement in setting goals relevant to areas of responsibility;
- **directive** – the use of authority in reaching decisions about change and the future;
- **coercive** – senior management imposing change on the organization

	Scale of change			
Style of change leadership	Fine tuning	Incremental adjustment	Modular transformation	Corporate transformation
Collaborative Consultative	**Strategy 1** Participative evolution		**Strategy 2** Charismatic transformation	
Directive Coercive	**Strategy 3** Forced evolution		**Strategy 4** Dictatorial transformation	

Figure 18.3: Scale of change and leadership style

Plotting scale of change against style of change produces the matrix in Figure 18.3. This identifies four strategies: participative evolution, charismatic transformation, forced evolution, and dictatorial transformation. Stace and Dunphy also identify four types of change leader:

- *coaches* are people-centred, inspirational communicators, and are participative;
- *captains* are systematic, task-oriented authority figures;
- *charismatics* are 'heroic' figures committed to their own dramatic and challenging vision who lead charismatic transformations;
- *commanders* are decisive, tough-minded, and forceful, and able and willing to neutralize or remove resistance and to implement dictatorial transformations.

Stace and Dunphy argue that participative strategies are time-consuming as they expose conflicting views that are difficult to reconcile. Where organizational survival depends on rapid and strategic change, dictatorial transformation is appropriate:

> Perhaps the toughest organizational change program in Australia in recent years has been the restructure of the New South Wales Police Force. The person leading that restructure and playing a classic Commander role is Police Commissioner Peter Ryan. Ryan was appointed from the United Kingdom to stamp out corruption in the force and modernize it. In his own words, he initially adopted a management style that was 'firm, hard and autocratic, and it had to be that because that is what the organization understood'. (Stace and Dunphy, 2001, p. 185)

Their approach to change implementation is summarized in Figure 18.4. This is a contingency model which recommends using an approach which fits the context. This challenges the model of participative change. Consultation can expose irreconcilable differences in view, and it takes time, which may not always be available in a rapidly changing environment.

	Incremental change strategies	**Transformative change strategies**
	Participative evolution	*Charismatic transformation*
Collaborative–consultative modes	Use when the organization needs minor adjustment to meet environmental conditions, where time is available, and where key interest groups favour change	Use when the organization needs major adjustments to meet environmental conditions, where there is little time for participation, and where there is support for radical change
	Forced evolution	*Dictatorial transformation*
Directive–coercive modes	Use when minor adjustments are required, where time is available, but where key interest groups oppose change	Use when major adjustments are necessary, where there is no time for participation, where there is no internal support for strategic change, but where this is necessary for survival

Figure 18.4: The Stace–Dunphy contingency approach to change implementation

STOP AND THINK Dictatorial transformation? Coercion? Surely these methods are more likely to generate hostility and resistance, reducing organization performance? In what circumstances – if any – do you think it is appropriate to exclude others from participating in change that affects them?

Organization development

Organization development the systematic use of applied behavioural science principles and practices to increase individual and organizational effectiveness.

Organization development (OD) approaches change with the assumption that organizational problems are due to conflict caused by poor communication and lack of understanding. OD has a toolkit based on a set of core values concerning how organizations should treat their employees. This toolkit dates from the 1960s, but economic conditions in the twenty-first century have made organizations acutely aware of the importance of employee motivation and engagement, where OD can make major contributions. OD aims to improve both organizational effectiveness and individual capabilities, through the systematic application of social and behavioural science knowledge and techniques.

Stephen Robbins and Timothy Judge (2008, p. 654) outline the OD values:

- *respect*: individuals should be treated with dignity and respect;
- *trust*: the healthy organization is characterized by trust, authenticity, and openness;
- *power equalization*: effective organizations do not emphasize hierarchical control;
- *confrontation*: problems shouldn't be hidden; they should be openly confronted;
- *participation*: those who are affected by change will be more committed to its success when the are involved in the decisions.

OD argues that 'bureaucracy is bad' and that the caring, sharing, empowering organization is a better place to work, and is financially and materially more effective. The 'bureaucracy-busting' agenda relies on the diagnosis of problems and solutions summarized in Table 18.5.

Table 18.5: Bureaucratic diseases and OD cures

Bureaucratic disease	Symptoms	OD cures
rigid functional boundaries	conflict between sections, poor communications	teambuilding, job rotation, changing structure
fixed hierarchies	frustration, boredom, narrow specialist thinking	training, job enrichment, career development
information only flows down	lack of innovation, minor problems escalate	process consultation, management development
routine jobs, tight control	boredom, absenteeism, conflict for supervisors	job enrichment, job rotation, supervisory training

One of the founders of OD, Kurt Lewin, argued, as mentioned earlier, that the process of change must pass through three stages: unfreezing, transition, and refreezing. People need to understand the need for change (unfreezing), before they will move (transition), and then changes have to be embedded (refreezing) to prevent people from reverting back to old routines. OD interventions are thus designed to help with these stages. Table 18.6 shows some common OD interventions.

Table 18.6: Common OD interventions

Intervention	Explanation	Application
action research	results from a study are used to design improvements which are the subject of further study	to solve known problems which have unclear solutions
sensitivity training	technique for improving self- and other-awareness through unstructured group discussions	to develop interpersonal skills and emotional intelligence
structure change	job rotation, job enlargement and enrichment, autonomous teams, organization restructuring	various uses – empowerment, improve information flow, signal priorities, new directions
force-field analysis	method for assessing the driving and restraining forces with respect to change	to plan actions to manage the force-field in order to facilitate the change process
process consultation	external consultant facilitates problem-solving by helping clients to develop own insights	to solve problems while developing the organization's own diagnostic capabilities
survey feedback	employee opinion survey findings are fed back to help identify actions to improve performance	to generate evidence which can help to solve leadership, culture, communications, morale, and other problems
teambuilding	various methods to identify team roles, and to rate factors influencing team effectiveness	to help team members understand their roles and improve collaboration
intergroup development	clarify the mutual expectations of groups that must work together to be effective	to improve understanding and resolve conflict between sections or functions
role negotiation	clarify the mutual expectations of individuals who must work together to be effective	to reconcile differences between two individuals and to improve collaboration and interaction

There are three criticisms of OD.

1. It ignores organizational power inequalities, claiming that conflict is due to poor communication, and not to a conflict of interests between management and employees.
2. It focuses on 'soft' attitudes and values, rather than on 'hard' operational and financial results.
3. OD interventions take time. Improved effectiveness, difficult to measure, based on intangible values, in the long run, after an expensive programme – this is not a compelling promise in a fast-moving competitive world.

However, the benefits of OD include (Warrick, 1984):

- improved productivity, morale, commitment to success;
- better understanding of organizational strengths and weaknesses;
- improved communications, problem-solving, and conflict resolution;
- creativity, openness, opportunities for personal development;
- decrease in politicking and game-playing;
- better management and teamwork, and increased adaptability;
- better ability to attract and retain quality people.

STOP AND THINK

Do current economic conditions encourage or discourage the use of OD, and why?

Why change, when you can innovate?

Is 'change' an appropriate response to a fast-paced unpredictable world? To keep ahead of the competition, organizations must encourage creativity and be innovative. In the public sector, innovation is equally necessary in order to meet rising public and political expectations with regard to service cost and quality.

Innovation the adoption of any device, system, process, programme, product, or service new to a particular organization.

Innovation is not limited to new products. Most organizations also want to create new ways to organize, to develop new and better working practices, and to provide customers, clients, or patients with innovative services. As a result, the term **innovation** is usually defined in broad terms, to mean the adoption of any device, system, process, programme, product, or service *new to that organization*. This definition means that an idea may have already been developed and applied elsewhere, but if it is 'new in this setting', then it can be regarded as an innovation *here*.

Innovation and creativity are often seen as attributes of the *individual*, and inventors are sometimes seen as mavericks. However, innovation and creativity also have *organizational* dimensions. Despite commercial pressures, some organizational norms, systems, and practices are receptive to innovation, while others encourage risk avoidance. Creative people in the wrong organization are likely to be less creative. However, ordinary people in an organization that encourages innovation and is receptive to novelty and change are more likely to become more creative in that environment.

The innovation process also has a *cultural* dimension. Manufacturing in Britain has been criticized for its lack of innovation (Porter and Ketels, 2003), which results in a prosperity and productivity gap between Britain and competitor economies such as the United States, Germany, and France. These differences are difficult to explain. Porter and Ketels argue that managers in Britain are slow to adopt new techniques, due to a combination of low investment in new technology and weak employee training policies. The individual, organizational, and national cultural influences on creativity and innovation are summarized in Figure 18.5.

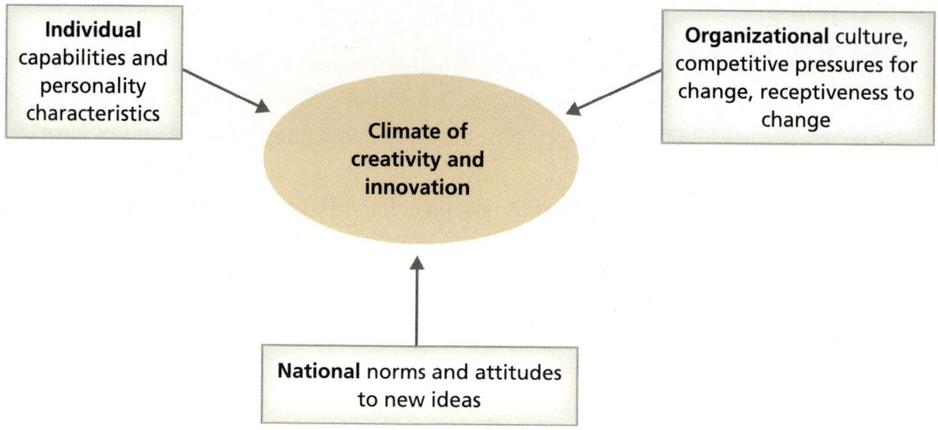

Figure 18.5: Innovation influences

Sustaining innovations innovations which make improvements to existing processes, procedures, services, and products.

Disruptive innovations innovations which involve the development of wholly new processes, procedures, services, and products.

Clayton Christensen, Richard Bohmer and John Kenagy (2000) distinguish between sustaining innovations and disruptive innovations. **Sustaining innovations** improve existing products and processes: a more efficient motor car, a mobile phone with video capability. **Disruptive innovations** introduce wholly new processes and services, such as electric cars and social networking websites. Innovations that are disruptive do not necessarily mean chaos and upheaval, as what is disrupted is often traditional ways of thinking and acting. However, truly disruptive innovations may be harder to manage, because they are riskier, and because there are no established routines for handling them.

STOP AND THINK

Identify three to five sustaining innovations that have affected you over the past year.

Identify three to five disruptive innovations that have affected you. Did you welcome these innovations because they were beneficial, or did you have cause to complain?

Operational innovation inventing entirely new ways of doing work.

Commercial companies have always focused on innovations with new technology, products, and services. Michael Hammer (2004) also advocates a focus on **operational innovation**: finding new ways to lead, organize, work, motivate, and manage.

Hammer describes a motor vehicle insurance company which introduced 'immediate response claims handling', operating 24 hours a day. This involved scheduling visits to claimants by claims adjusters who worked from mobile vans, and who would turn up within nine hours. Previously, when the adjusters were office-based, it could take over a week to inspect a damaged vehicle. Handling 10,000 claims a day, adjusters were empowered to estimate damage and write a cheque on the spot. These operational innovations led to huge cost savings, with fewer staff involved in claims handling, lower vehicle storage costs, better fraud detection, and reduction in payout costs. Customer satisfaction and loyalty also improved.

The lean production system developed by the car manufacturing company Toyota (see Chapter 3) is another example of an operational innovation which improves product quality and reduces costs by redesigning the manufacturing process, but without directly affecting the design of the product. Wal-Mart has an innovative approach to purchasing and distribution, such as the use of 'cross-docking', where goods are switched from one truck to the next at distribution centres without going into storage. The computer company Dell and its 'build to order' business model is another example of successful operational innovation.

How James Dyson, innovator, cleaned up

Getty Images

The inventor James Dyson is best known for the bagless vacuum cleaner which established his reputation, and the more recent Dyson ball. He also invented the Air Multiplier, a new type of office desk fan, and the Airblade hand dryer. In 2009–10, his company's profits were over £160 million, and his global workforce of 2,600 is expected to increase to 4,000 by 2014. His personal wealth is estimated to be over £900 million (Bowers, 2010). Is innovation easy? Here are some statistics:

Failed prototypes of Dyson's vacuum cleaner before the successful design was established	5,126
The number of times a vacuum cleaner is dropped on a hard floor in development	5,318
Hours of product testing at temperatures as low as minus 20 degrees Celsius	50,000
Number of dust mites in the average bed	10,000

Consumers see the exciting new products, but they may not see the organization that lies behind them. We see the individual inventor, but he is also part of an organization that is committed to research, design, and development. (Based on Bowers 2010.)

The best practices puzzle

Why do 'best practices' not spread more quickly? One problem with innovation is that new ideas and methods that are developed and work well in one context are often not adopted elsewhere. Known as 'the best practices puzzle', this is a long-running concern. Don Berwick (2003) notes that the treatment for scurvy, first identified in 1601, did not become standard practice in the British navy until 1865, over 260 years later. Why the delay?

The stethoscope will never be popular

That it [the stethoscope] will ever come into general use, not withstanding its value, I am extremely doubtful; because its beneficial application requires much time, and it gives a good deal of trouble both to the patient and practitioner, and because its whole hue and character is foreign, and opposed to all our habits and associations. It must be confessed that there is something ludicrous in the picture of a grave physician formally listening through a long tube applied to a patient's thorax, as if the disease within were a living being that could communicate its condition to the sense without. (John Forbes, in the preface to his translation of *De L'Auscultation Médiate ou Traité du Diagnostic des Maladies des Poumons et du Coeur* [A Treatise on the Diseases of the Chest, and on Mediate Auscultation], by R.T.H. Laënnec, T. & G. Underwood, London, 1821)

Everett Rogers (1995) argues that the probability of an innovation being adopted is increased when it is seen to have the following six properties:

1. advantageous when compared with existing practice;
2. compatible with existing practices;
3. easy to understand;
4. observable in demonstration sites;

5. testable;
6. adaptable to fit local needs.

For innovations to diffuse effectively, Rogers argues that the perceptions of adopters, and properties of the organizational context, are as important as the innovation itself. Unless you believe that an innovation will help you to improve on current methods, you are unlikely to be persuaded. New ideas have to be adapted (sometimes significantly) to fit local conditions.

Rogers also argues that the adoption of innovations follows a pattern. First, small numbers adopt, followed by 'take-off', then achieving a critical mass of adopters. Finally, the pace slackens as saturation is reached, typically short of 100 per cent (you never convince everyone). This is usually shown as an S-shaped diffusion curve. Recognizing that the shape of the curve depends on local circumstances, Rogers argues that this pattern is influenced by the five groups described in Table 18.7.

Table 18.7: From innovators to laggards

innovators	usually the first in their social grouping to adopt new approaches and behaviours, a small category of individuals who enjoy the excitement and risks of experimentation
early adopters	opinion leaders who evaluate ideas carefully, and are more sceptical and take more convincing, but take risks, help to adapt new ideas to local settings, and have effective networking skills
early majority	those who take longer to reach a decision to change, but who are still ahead of the average
late majority	even more sceptical and risk-averse; wait for most of their colleagues to adopt new ideas first
laggards	viewed negatively by others, the last to adopt new ideas, even for reasons that they believe to be rational

To infinity and beyond

© Geoff Moore/Rex Features

The animation studio Pixar gave us the movie *Toy Story*, and the cartoon character Buzz Lightyear (with his 'to infinity' catchphrase), in 1995. The company has produced two more instalments of *Toy Story* and other successful movies such as *Finding Nemo*, *Cars*, *The Incredibles*, and *Ratatouille*. How can a company be creative, and then go on being creative, especially when its president and its 'chief creative officer' are in their 60s and 50s respectively (*The Economist*, 2010)?

It helps that the two senior managers are charismatic leaders. But the company is also *organized* to be creative. Hollywood studios usually start with good ideas and then hire creative people to turn those into movies. In contrast, Pixar recruits creatives and then gets them to keep generating ideas. Pixar's 1,200 employees take collective responsibility for projects, sharing their work in progress in daily meetings to get constructive feedback. This approach is adapted from Toyota's 'lean production' method, getting constant feedback from production line workers to fix problems. The feedback from colleagues at Pixar is a further source of inspiration for creative teams. The teams are also required to conduct 'post mortems' on finished films, identifying at least five things that did not go well, as well as five that did.

Creativity depends on organization and management as well as on creative individuals. For Pixar, this involves looking to other companies and sectors for inspiration. And it means getting people to work with organization structures and a strong culture (see Chapter 4), while giving them the freedom to come up with new ideas, and to keep being creative. (Based on *The Economist* 2010.)

Diffusion of a new product or idea relies initially on innovators and early adopters, and subsequently on the pace at which the early and late majority are swayed. These are not fixed categories. An individual may be an early adopter of one idea, but a late adopter of another. To be an innovator or a laggard depends as much on the social or organizational context as on the individual. This perspective suggests two conclusions, however. First, diffusion behaviour is rarely a sudden event, but a protracted process, triggered and developed by contextual factors as well as individual perceptions and interpersonal communications. Second, there is no 'one best way' to influence people to change; interventions must consider individual needs and perceptions.

Star envy: how politics stop good ideas from spreading

Richard Walton (1975) predicted 'relatively little diffusion of potentially significant restructuring in the workplace'. He followed successful work redesign experiments from the 1960s in eight organizations, of which two were American, two Canadian, one British, two Norwegian, and one Swedish. There was little or no diffusion in seven companies, and only at Volvo (a pioneer in work redesign) was the diffusion 'truly impressive'. What went wrong?

- projects decayed through internal design inconsistencies, loss of top management support, union opposition, and premature turnover of key staff such as project leaders;
- crises encouraged a return to authoritarian management;
- experiments and their leaders became isolated from the rest of the organization;
- some pilots were seen as poor models for change elsewhere;
- resources, such as training, were often inadequate;
- vested interests preferred stability, and those whose skills were no longer required felt threatened;
- 'star envy' caused resentment when pilot sites attracted publicity, visitors, and management attention.

Walton identified two 'political' issues. First, while innovators got credit, those who later adapted their ideas got less praise, even though they too were successful (and had they failed, they probably would have lost more standing than the pioneers would have lost had they failed). Second, the leaders in innovative units had arguments with superiors and staff groups, defending their positions aggressively, and thus damaged their careers. Colleagues wanted to avoid a similar fate; 'The more successful the pioneer, the less favourable are the payoffs and the greater the risks for those who follow' (p. 21). Those barriers and deterrents explain why, although lack of diffusion undermines a demonstrator project, a successful pilot does not necessarily diffuse. Still just as relevant today as it was in 1975, Walton's advice is:

- introduce several projects at the same time;
- avoid over-exposure and 'glorification' of those projects;
- ensure that the programme is identified with top management from the start.

Killer cultures

Max McKeown (2008, 2013a, b) defines a 'high adaptability killer culture' – or HACK – as one which constantly replaces its products and services by developing better options. Creativity doesn't come from hiring the right people, but from creating the right conditions. Features that block innovation are rules and mission statements (too rigid), efficiency drives (no slack resources), and leaders who stifle ideas before their value can be demonstrated. McKeown's 'five truths about innovation' are:

1. **Even useless can be useful**. *Chindôgu* – the Japanese art of the unusual – describes inventions that solve a problem but cause so many new problems they are, in effect, useless. But we could all benefit from the *Chindôgu* philosophy because it allows us the freedom to develop new ideas.
2. **Quick fixes reveal real needs**. *Jugaad* – the Hindi word for working around – describes a quick fix necessary because of limitations of resources, including wooden cars build by carpenters and powered by water pump engines. Such quick and dirty solutions reveal real needs including, for example, that for the world's cheapest car – the new £1,200 Tata Nano developed by Indian engineers.
3. **Small differences make a big difference**. If you're like many people, you'll be looking for something BIG. After all, how can you change the world with a

→

small idea? Well, you can because often the biggest advances come from focusing on the smallest things.

4. **New ideas are made of old ideas**. People have mixed and remixed ideas to arrive at our current global society. It is to new combinations of old ideas that we must look for innovation.
5. **Power is originality's best friend**. Powerful people need ideas. And most ideas need powerful people to facilitate, legitimize, popularize, and even legislate for their adoption.

McKeown cites the following examples:

The Motorola Razr was discovered as a discarded prototype on a chance visit by a newly appointed chief executive and went on to sell over 100 million units. The first iPod prototype came from ideas developed by Tony Fadell, an engineer who had failed to find funding for the project until he arrived at Apple. The three ideas that transformed Disney were all generated by existing members of the company in the first three months of Michael Eisener's tenure as CEO. He adopted a style that was playful and bold, holding informal staff lunches to liberate creativity. He led by example, proposed off-the-wall ideas, and encouraged his team to give him the ideas that might embarrass them, that went too far. When told that a concept for standalone Disney retail stores was a small business with low margins, he answered: 'Can't a company our size try something every once in a while just because it feels right? What if it does fail? It's still not going to cost as much as one expensive movie script.'

Source: from Max Headroom, *People Management*, 14(4), pp. 28–32 (McKeown, M. 2008), the article was developed from McKeown, M. (2008), *The Truth About Innovation*, London: Prentice Hall and ideas that were then included in his subsequent publications *The Strategy Book* (2012), London: FT Prentice Hall and *Adaptability* (2012), London: Kogan Page.

Building a creative climate

Rosabeth Moss Kanter (b.1943)

Rosabeth Moss Kanter (1983; 1989) contrasts what she calls *segmentalist* organization cultures with *integrative* cultures. A segmentalist culture is preoccupied with hierarchy, compartmentalizes its decision-making, and emphasizes rules and efficiency. An integrative culture is based on teams and collaboration, adopts a holistic approach to problem-solving, has no time for history or precedent, and emphasizes results. It is not surprising to find Kanter arguing that bureaucratic, mechanistic segmentalist cultures tend to be 'innovation smothering', and that adaptable, organic, integrative cultures are stimulating to innovation.

Exploring how organizations smother and stimulate innovation, Göran Ekvall (1996; Ekvall and Ryhammar, 1999) developed the concept of *creative organization climate*. Organization climate is a combination of attitudes, feelings, and behaviours, which exists independently of the perceptions and understandings of individual members. The ten dimensions of the creative climate are summarized in Table 18.8.

In with the integrative, out with the segmentalist

I found that the entrepreneurial spirit producing innovation is associated with a particular way of approaching problems that I call 'integrative': the willingness to move beyond received wisdom, to combine ideas from unconnected sources, to embrace change as an opportunity to test limits. To see problems integratively is to see them as wholes, related to larger wholes, and thus challenging established practices – rather than walling off a piece of experience and preventing it from being touched or affected by any new experiences . . .

Such organizations reduce rancorous conflict and isolation between organizational units; create mechanisms for exchange of information and new ideas across organizational boundaries; ensure that multiple perspectives will be taken into account in decisions; and provide coherence and direction to the organization. In these team-oriented co-operative environments, innovation flourishes . . .

The contrasting style of thought is anti-change-oriented and prevents innovation. I call it 'segmentalism' because it is concerned with compartmentalizing actions, events, and problems and keeping each piece isolated from the others . . . Companies where segmentalist approaches dominate find it difficult to innovate or to handle change. (from Kanter, 1983, pp. 27–8)

Table 18.8: Dimensions of the creative organization climate

Dimension	Promoting innovation	Inhibiting innovation
1. **Challenge**	People experience challenge, joy and meaning and invest high energy.	People are alienated, indifferent, unchallenged, and apathetic.
2. **Freedom**	People make contacts, give and receive information freely, discuss problems, make decisions, take initiative.	People are passive, rule-bound, anxious to remain within their well-established boundaries.
3. **Idea support**	People listen to each other; ideas and suggestions are received in a supportive way.	Suggestions are quickly rejected with counter-arguments; usual response is to find faults and obstacles.
4. **Trust and openness**	High trust climate; ideas can be expressed without fear of reprisal or ridicule; communications are open.	Low trust climate; people are suspicious of each other, are afraid to make mistakes, and fear having their ideas stolen.
5. **Dynamism and liveliness**	New things happening all the time; new ways of thinking and problem-solving.	Slow jog with no surprises, no new projects or plans, everything as usual.
6. **Playfulness and humour**	Relaxed atmosphere with jokes and laughter; spontaneity.	Gravity and seriousness, stiff and gloomy, jokes improper.
7. **Debates**	Many voices are heard, expressing different ideas and viewpoints.	People follow an authoritarian pattern without questioning.
8. **Conflicts**	Conflict of ideas not personal; people behave in a mature manner, based on psychological insight.	Personal and emotional tensions, plots and traps, gossip and slander, climate of 'warfare'.
9. **Risk-taking**	Decisions and actions prompt and rapid; concrete experimentation is preferred to detailed analysis.	Cautious, hesitant mentality; work 'on the safe side', 'sleep on the matter', set up committees before deciding.
10. **Idea time**	Opportunities to test fresh ideas that are not part of planned work activity; these chances are exploited.	Every minute booked and specified; pressures mean that thinking outside planned routines is difficult.

STOP AND THINK

Think of an organization with which you are familiar, perhaps one where you are currently employed, or one where you have worked recently.

Assess that organization's climate on Ekvall's ten dimensions, in terms of how it promotes or inhibits innovation.

Where the organization inhibits innovation, what practical steps could management take to strengthen the creative climate, to promote innovation?

Home viewing

Inside Job (2010, director Charles Ferguson, narrated by Matt Damon) examines the global financial crisis of 2008. Over the previous decade, deregulation allowed the finance industry to take risks that older rules would have discouraged. As you watch this film, identify the various stakeholders (including academics), their competing interests, their relationships, and their efforts to conceal sensitive information. How did those competing interests, relationships, and 'information games' contribute to the crisis? The film concludes that, despite this crisis, the underlying system has remained much the same. How has the sector been able to avoid fundamental changes to financial regulation? What does this account reveal about the nature of organizational change in general?

Much commentary on this topic has a 'pro-innovation bias', assuming that 'new' must be better. But some innovations can be damaging. A good idea may not work as well as better ideas that have been sidelined. What works in one context may not work well in another. Research and experience have shown that 'best practice' is contingent, that there is no 'one best way'. In addition, groups who are advised to implement 'best practice' may be insulted by the implication that they are currently using 'worst practice'. Nevertheless, innovation is and will remain an organizational and managerial preoccupation for the foreseeable future.

To be an innovator

Being creative and innovative can be frustrating, as well as rewarding. James Dyson's bagless vacuum cleaner went through over 5,000 prototypes to get to the winning design. The development of something new often involves such a high failure rate. A lot of trial and error is necessary, to find out what works best. Despite corporate mission and values statements encouraging employees to be creative and to take risks in a 'no blame culture', management does not always look favourably on failure. In some cases, being innovative can jeopardize your job security and your career.

Rosabeth Moss Kanter's rules for stifling innovation

1. Regard a new idea from below with suspicion, because it's new, and because it's from below.
2. Insist that people who need your approval to act first go through several other levels of management to get their signatures.
3. Ask departments or individuals to challenge and criticize each other's proposals. That saves you the job of deciding; you just pick the survivor.
4. Express criticism freely, and withhold praise. That keeps people on their toes. Let them know that they can be fired at any time.
5. Treat identification of problems as signs of failure, to discourage people from letting you know when something in their area isn't working.
6. Control everything carefully. Make sure people count anything that can be counted, frequently.
7. Make decisions to reorganize or change policies in secret, and spring them on people unexpectedly. That keeps people on their toes.
8. Make sure that requests for information are fully justified, and make sure that it is not given out to managers freely. You don't want data to fall into the wrong hands.
9. Assign to lower level managers, in the name of delegation and participation, responsibility for figuring out how to cut back, lay off, move people around, or otherwise implement threatening decisions you have made. And get them to do it quickly.
10. And above all, never forget that you, the higher-ups, already know everything important about this business. (From Kanter, 2002)

Amy Edmondson (2011) argues that not all failures are bad, and they all offer opportunities for learning. She explores the reasons for failure on a spectrum ranging from blameworthy to praiseworthy, shown in Table 18.9. At one extreme, deviance, breaking the rules deliberately, is blameworthy. At the other end of the spectrum, experiments to discover whether something new will work or not are praiseworthy. Do managers recognize this spectrum, and treat employees accordingly?

> When I ask executives to consider this spectrum and then to estimate how many of the failures in their organization are truly blameworthy, their answers are usually in single digits – perhaps 2 percent to 5 percent. But when I ask how many are *treated* as blameworthy, they say (after a pause or a laugh) 70 percent to 90 percent. The unfortunate consequence is that many failures go unreported and their lessons are lost. (Edmondson, 2011, p. 50)

Table 18.9: Blameworthy and praiseworthy failures

blameworthy ↑	**deviance**	individual chooses to violate prescribed process or practice
	inattention	individual inadvertently deviates from specifications
	lack of ability	individual lacks skills, conditions, or training for the job
	process inadequacy	competent individual adheres to faulty or incomplete process
	task challenge	individual faces a task too difficult to be executed reliably
	process complexity	a complex process breaks down under novel conditions
	uncertainty	people take reasonable actions leading to undesired results
	hypothesis testing	failed experiment to see whether an idea or design will work
↓ **praiseworthy**	**exploratory testing**	experiment to expand knowledge leads to undesired result

Source: reprinted by permission of *Harvard Business Review*. Adapted from 'Strategies for learning from failure' by Edmondson, A.C., 89(4) 2011. Copyright © 2011 by the Harvard Business School Publishing Corporation; all rights reserved.

To build a learning culture, Edmondson advises promoting experimentation, not blaming individuals when organizational circumstances have contributed to failure, and analysing carefully the reasons for failures, going beyond obvious and superficial reasons. In addition, the 'messengers' who speak out with bad news, raise awkward questions or concerns, or make mistakes 'should be rewarded rather than shot'. Management should welcome the knowledge, and work out how to fix the problem. It is also necessary, she concludes, to be clear about which acts are blameworthy, and hold people accountable.

The five habits of disruptive innovators

Why are some people more innovative than others, and how do they make innovation look easy and effortless? Jeff Dyer, Hal Gregersen and Clayton Christensen (2011) argue that anyone can be innovative by using the right approach. Their research suggests that the best innovators have these five habits:

- **associating**: innovators are good at seeing connections between things that do not appear to be related, drawing ideas together from unrelated fields;
- **questioning**: innovators are always challenging what others take for granted, asking 'why is this done this way – why don't we do it differently?';
- **observing**: innovators watch the behaviour of customers, suppliers, competitors – looking for new ways of doing things;
- **experimenting**: innovators tinker with products and business models, sometimes accidentally, to see what happens and what insights emerge;
- **networking**: innovators attend conferences and other social events to pick up ideas from people with different ideas, who may face similar problems, in other fields.

Individuals can become more innovative by following this advice, and by collaborating with 'delivery-driven' colleagues. Dyer et al. argue that organizations also need to encourage these habits, stimulating employees to connect ideas, to challenge accepted practices, to watch what others are doing, to take risks and try things out, and to get out of the company to meet others.

Change is now a central organization and management issue. While participation is socially and ethically appropriate, there is a willingness to accept directive methods, accompanied by recognition of the role of organization politics in change (Butcher and Clarke, 2008). There is also recognition of the need for rapid and continual adjustment to events and trends. Change is no longer something which periodically disturbs the stable fabric, but is an ever present feature.

However, some commentators argue that change is damaging, especially when it is rapid and ongoing, and that the initiative stream should be more carefully timed and paced. The significance of context in shaping the opportunities for and directions of change is now better understood and appreciated. Finally, while change may still be relevant to improving effectiveness, the organizational capability to change rapidly and often is viewed by many as a factor contributing to competitive advantage and survival. These trends are summarized in Table 18.10.

Table 18.10: Trends in organizational change

Change in the twentieth century	Change in the twenty-first century
one theme among many	an organizational preoccupation
importance of participation and involvement	significance of political motives and actions
rational-linear model of project management	messy, untidy cocktail of reason and motive
small number of senior change agents	large number of distributed change agents
implementation method is critical	implementation must be tailored to context
changes must be frequent and fast	need to consider timing and pacing with care
focus on improvement	focus on innovation
aimed at organizational effectiveness	aimed at competitive advantage and survival

RECAP

1. *Explain why effective change management is important, to organizations and to individuals.*
    - Organizations that do not adapt to changing circumstances may see their performance deteriorate, and may go out of business.
    - The pace of organizational change means that individuals need to 'future-proof' their careers by constantly gaining new knowledge and skills.
2. *Identify the main types and triggers of organizational change.*
    - Change can be triggered by factors internal and external to the organization, and can also be proactive, anticipating trends and events.
    - Change varies in depth, from shallow fine tuning to deep transformational change.
    - The broad direction of change in most organizations is towards becoming less mechanistic and bureaucratic, and more adaptive, responsive, and organic.
3. *Explain the issues that management must take into account to ensure that change is successful.*
    - The 'basics' of change implementation include clear benefits, strong leadership, powerful change agents, constant communication, employee engagement, short-term wins, and making sure that change is embedded in the culture.
    - The timing and pacing of change are also important: too slow, and organizational survival may be at risk, but too fast, and staff may be overloaded, and demotivated by initiative fatigue.
4. *Understand the typical characteristics of human responses to change.*
    - Emotional responses to traumatic changes differ, but the typical coping cycle passes through the stages of denial, anger, bargaining, depression, and acceptance.
    - The Yerkes-Dodson law states that the initial response to pressure is improved performance,

and that increasing pressure leads to fatigue and ultimately to breakdown.

- The evidence suggests that continuous organizational changes lead to work intensification, burnout, and initiative fatigue.

5. *Understand the nature of resistance to change and approaches to overcoming it.*
   - Resistance to change has many sources, including self-interest, lack of trust and understanding, competing assessments of the outcomes, and low tolerance of change.
   - One technique for addressing possible resistance to change, as well as identifying and strengthening support for change, is stakeholder analysis.
   - The main prescribed approach for avoiding or dealing with resistance is participative management, in which those affected are involved in implementation.
   - The use of manipulation and coercion to implement change is advocated by some commentators, but the 'political' role of management in change is controversial.
6. *Explain the advantages and limitations of participative methods of change management.*
   - Participative methods can generate creative thinking and increase employee commitment to change, but this process is time-consuming.
   - Some commentators argue that rapid and major corporate transformations are more successful when implemented using a dictatorial or coercive style.
7. *Understand the significance of innovation, and the distinction between sustaining, disruptive, and operational innovations.*
   - Innovation has become a strategic imperative in order to compete and to survive.
   - Sustaining innovations are those which improve existing services and products.
   - Disruptive innovations introduce completely new services and products.
   - Operational innovations concern new ways of organizing, managing, and working.
8. *Explain the organizational properties that stimulate and stifle innovation.*
   - A creative organizational climate is one which promotes lively and challenging debate, freedom of expression, trust and openness, humour, risk-taking, and giving people time to try out new ideas – and has a high level of receptiveness to new ideas.
   - Organization properties that stifle innovation include rigid rules, suspicion of new ideas, low trust, criticism freely given, jokes seen as improper, aversion to risk, and tight time pressures.
   - Creative individuals outside creative organizational climates are likely to stop innovating; anyone in a creative climate is capable of being creative, and will be encouraged to innovate.
9. *Recognize the challenges facing creative, innovative individuals in organizations.*
   - The successful development of something new is exciting and challenging, but can involve a high rate of failure before the winning design is found.
   - Organizations vary in their tolerance for and treatment of failure; even 'praiseworthy' failures can attract blame and punishment.
   - We can become more innovative by practising the five habits of associating, questioning, observing, experimenting, and networking.

Revision

1. What are the basic rules of change implementation? Although these appear to be simple, the failure rate of organizational changes is high. Why is it so difficult to put these basic rules into practice effectively?
2. What are the main sources of resistance to organizational change, and how should resistance be managed?
3. Organizations are advised to change rapidly in order to compete to survive. What dangers come with this advice?
4. What are the main types of innovation, and how can an organization develop a climate that encourages individuals to be more creative?

Research assignment

Choose an organization that has experienced major change. Arrange to interview two managers who were involved in implementing this change. Using John Kotter's guide to corporate transformation, find out how the changes were managed. For each of the following steps, find out what was involved, how was it done, and how well it worked:

1. Establish a sense of urgency.
2. Form a guiding coalition.
3. Create a vision.
4. Communicate the vision.
5. Empower people to act on the vision.
6. Create 'short-term wins'.
7. Consolidate improvements to produce further change.
8. Embed new approaches in the organization's culture.

Finally, ask your managers for their assessment of these changes. Once you have discovered how the changes were managed, rate the organization on a 1 to 10 scale for each heading (1 = very poor; 10 = very good). A total score of 8 suggests disaster; a total score of 80 implies success. To what extent is your assessment consistent with that of the managers who you interviewed?

Now develop an action plan that answers the following questions:

1. Based on your analysis, what should management have done differently in implementing these changes?
2. What, if anything, should management do now in order to repair any damage that may have been done during the implementation of these changes?
3. What should management do differently the next time when implementing organizational change?

One final question: how useful was Kotter's model as a basis for assessing this organization's changes? How would you improve this model?

Springboard

David A. Buchanan, Louise Fitzgerald and Diane Ketley (eds) (2006) *The Sustainability and Spread of Organizational Change: Modernizing Healthcare*, Routledge, London. Explores the 'improvement evaporation effect' and 'the best practices puzzle'. Why do successful changes decay, and why are good new ideas and better working practices not adopted more rapidly?

Esther Cameron and Mike Green (2012) *Making Sense of Change Management: A Complete Guide to the Models, Tools and Techniques of Organizational Change* (3rd edn), Kogan Page, London. Offers a toolkit of frameworks, models, and perspectives for making change happen, based on theory explaining the why and how of change, illustrated with case studies.

Mee-Yan Cheung-Judge and Linda Holbeche (2011) *Organization Development: A Practitioner's Guide for OD and HR*, Kogan Page, London. Aimed at readers who want to make their organization 'change-able'. Guide to the theory and practice of OD, explaining how to create 'high performing cultures'. Explores links between HR and OD, and the role of power and politics in change.

Jonah Lehrer (2012) *Imagine: How Creativity Works*, Canongate Books, Edinburgh. Argues that creativity is a feature of our human potential which can be nurtured and encouraged, and is not limited to a few 'creative types'. Organization policies and culture are just as important, and creative thought processes can be learned, using different strategies for different creative tasks.

OB in films

Charlie's Angels (2000, director Joseph McGinty Nichols – 'McG' – 2000), DVD track 14: 0:35:57 to 0:38:10 (3 minutes). Clip begins outside the Red Star corporation headquarters; clip ends when Alex says 'Better yet, can anyone show me?'.

Alex (played by Lucy Liu) masquerading as an 'efficiency expert' leads the Angels into the Red Star corporation headquarters building, in an attempt to penetrate their security systems. As you watch this three-minute clip, paying careful attention to details, consider the following questions:

1. Is this an organization that stimulates or smothers creativity and innovation?
2. How do you know? What are the clues, visual and spoken, that support your assessment of the organization culture?

OB on the web

Go to YouTube and search for Clayton Christensen. You will find several clips where he is talking about innovation in general, and about disruptive innovation in particular. Watch two or three of these short clips. From listening to Christensen himself, what can you add to your understanding of the nature and importance of innovation – to an organization, and to you personally?

CHAPTER EXERCISES

1. Implementation planning

Objectives

1. To apply change implementation theory to a practical setting.
2. To assess the value of 'best practice' textbook advice on how to implement change effectively.

Briefing

Due to a combination of space constraints and financial issues, your department or school has been told by senior management to relocate to another building seven kilometres from your existing site within the next three months. Your management have in turn been asked to draw up a plan for managing the move, which will affect all staff (academic, technical, secretarial, administrative), all students (undergraduate, postgraduate), and all equipment (classroom aids, computing). The new building will provide more space and student facilities, but offices for academic staff are smaller, the building is on a different bus route, and car parking facilities are limited. Senior management have reassured staff that email will allow regular contact to be maintained with colleagues in other departments and schools which are not being moved.

You have been asked to help management with their planning. Your brief is as follows:

1. Conduct a stakeholder analysis, identifying how each stakeholder or stakeholder group should be approached to ensure that this move goes ahead smoothly.
2. Assess the readiness for change analysis, identifying any 'groundwork' that may have to be done to ensure the move goes ahead smoothly.
3. Determine your change implementation strategy. Is a participative approach appropriate, or is dictatorial transformation required? Justify your recommendation by pointing to the advantages and limitations of the various options you have explored.
4. With reference to the basic rules of change described in this chapter, draw up a creative and practical action plan for implementing this change effectively.

Prepare a presentation of your results to colleagues.

→

2. Force-field analysis

Objective To demonstrate the technique of force-field analysis in planning change.

Briefing Force-field analysis is a method for assessing the issues supporting and blocking movement towards a given set of desirable outcomes, called the 'target situation'. The forces can be scored, say from 1 (weak) to 10 (strong), to calculate (approximately) the balance of forces.

If the driving forces are overwhelming, then the change can go ahead without significant problems. If the resisting forces are overwhelming, then the change may have to be abandoned, or delayed until conditions have improved.

If the driving and resisting forces are more or less in balance, then the force-field analysis can be used to plan appropriate action. The extent to which the force-field is balanced is a matter of judgement. Used in a group setting, this method provides a valuable way to structure what can often be an untidy discussion covering a wide range of factors and differing perceptions.

For this analysis, your target situation is 'to double the time that I spend studying organizational behaviour'. In groups of three, complete the analysis using the following table as a guide. First identify as many driving and restraining forces as you can. Then, reach a group consensus on a score for each of those forces, from 1 (weak) to 10 (strong). Finally for this stage of the analysis, calculate the totals for each side of the force-field.

Target situation: to double the time that I spend studying organizational behaviour.

Scores	Driving forces >>>>>	<<<<< Restraining forces	Scores
	= total driving forces score	total restraining forces score =	

When you have completed this analysis, and added the scores, estimate the probability (high, medium, or low) of reaching your target situation *if the force-field stays the same*.

Now draw a practical action plan for managing the field of forces that you have identified in order to increase the probability of reaching the target situation. In devising your action plan, remember that:

1. Increasing the driving forces can often result in an increase in the resisting forces. This means that the current equilibrium does not change, but is maintained with increased tension.
2. Reducing the resisting forces is preferable as this allows movement towards the desired outcomes or target situation without increasing tension.
3. Group norms are an important force in shaping and resisting change.

Employability assessment

With regard to your future employment prospects:

1. Identify up to three issues from this chapter that you found significant.
2. Relate these to the competencies in the employability matrix.
3. Decide what actions you need to take to maintain and/or develop those competencies under each of the four headings of the employability matrix.

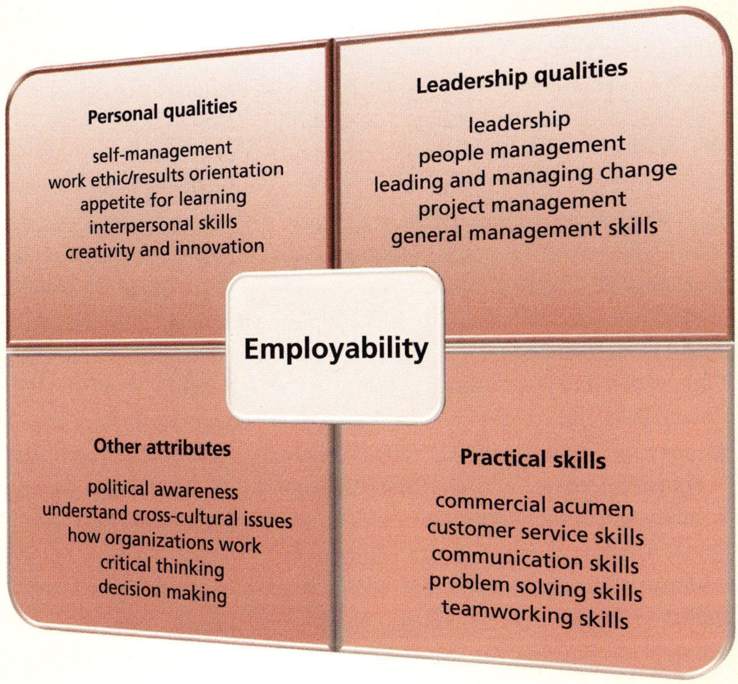

References

Atkinson, P. (2005) 'Managing resistance to change', *Management Services*, Spring, pp. 14–19.

Berwick, D.M. (2003) 'Disseminating innovations in health care', *Journal of the American Medical Association*, 289(15), pp. 1969–1975.

Bowers, M. (2010) 'Multiplier helps to double Dyson profits', *The Times*, 8 October, p. 51.

Bruch, H. and Menges, J.I. (2010) 'The acceleration trap', *Harvard Business Review*, 88(4), pp. 80–6.

Buchanan, D.A., Fitzgerald, L. and Ketley, D. (eds) (2006) *The Sustainability and Spread of Organizational Change: Modernizing Healthcare*, London: Routledge.

Butcher, D. and Clarke, M. (2008) *Smart Management: Using Politics in Organizations* (2nd edn), Houndmills, Basingstoke: Palgrave.

Christensen, C.M., Bohmer, R. and Kenagy, J. (2000) 'Will disruptive innovations cure health care?', *Harvard Business Review*, 78(5), pp. 102–12.

Coch, L. and French, J.R.P. (1948) 'Overcoming resistance to change', *Human Relations*, 1, pp. 512–32.

Dyer, J., Gregersen, H. and Christensen, C.M. (2011) *The Innovator's DNA: Mastering the Five Skills of Disruptive Innovators*, Boston, MA: Harvard Business School Press.

Edmondson, A. (2011) 'Strategies for learning from failure', *Harvard Business Review*, 89(4), pp. 48–55.

Ekvall, G. (1996) 'Organizational climate for creativity and innovation', *European Journal of Work and Organizational Psychology*, 5(1), pp. 105–23.

Ekvall, G. and Ryhammar, L. (1999) 'The creative climate: its determinants and effects at a Swedish university', *Creativity Research Journal*, 12(4), pp. 303–10.

Gardini, M., Giuliani, G. and Marricchi, M. (2011) 'Finding the right place to start change', *McKinsey Quarterly*, November, pp. 1–5.

Gratton, L. (2011) *The Shift: The future of Work Is Already Here*, London: Collins.

Hammer, M. (2004) 'Deep change: how operational innovation can transform your company', *Harvard Business Review*, 82(4), pp. 84–93.

Jessop, A. (2008) 'How I made a difference at work', *People Management*, 14(12), p. 44.

Kanter, R.M. (1983) *The Change Masters: Corporate Entrepreneurs at Work*. London: George Allen and Unwin.

Kanter, R.M. (1989) *When Giants Learn to Dance: Mastering the Challenges of Strategy, Management, and Careers in the 1990s*, London: Unwin.

Kanter, R.M. (2002) 'Creating the culture for innovation', in F. Hesselbein, M. Goldsmith and I. Somerville (eds), *Leading for Innovation and Organizing for Results*, San Francisco: Jossey-Bass, pp. 73–85.

Keller, S., Meaney, M. and Pung, C. (2010) *What Successful Transformations Share*, Chicago and London: McKinsey Quarterly Publishing.

Kotter, J.P. (2007) 'Leading change: why transformation efforts fail', *Harvard Business Review*, 85(1), pp. 96–103 (first published 1995).

Kotter, J.P. and Schlesinger, L.A. (2008) 'Choosing strategies for change', *Harvard Business Review*, 86(7/8), pp. 130–9 (first published 1979).

Kübler-Ross, E. (1969) *On Death and Dying*, Toronto: Macmillan.

Lawler, E.E. and Worley, C. (2009) 'The rebirth of change', *People Management*, 14(23), pp. 28–30.

Lawson, E. and Price, C. (2010) 'The psychology of change management', *The McKinsey Quarterly*, Special Edition: The Value in Organization, pp. 31–41.

Lewin, K. (1951) *Field Theory in Social Science: Selected Theoretical Papers by Kurt Lewin* (ed. Dorwin Cartwright), University of Michigan Research Center for Group Dynamics (UK edition published 1952).

McKeown, M. (2008) 'Max headroom', *People Management*, 14(4), pp. 28–32.

McKeown, M. (2013a) *Adaptability: The Art of Winning in an Age of Uncertainty*, London: Kogan Page.

McKeown, M. (2013b) 'High Adaptability (Killer) Cultures', *Strategic Risk Magazine*, Reading: NewsQuest Specialist Publications.

MacLachlan, R. (2011) 'A switch in time', *People Management*, July, pp. 36–9.

Meaney, M. and Wilson, S. (2009) 'Change in recession', *People Management*, 15(10), p. 62.

Mohrman, S.A. and Lawler, E.E. (2012) 'Generating knowledge that drives change', *Academy of Management Perspectives*, 26(1), pp. 41–51.

Ogburn, W.F. (1922) *Social Change: With Respect to Culture and Original Nature*, New York: B.W. Huebsch.

Pfeffer, J. and Sutton, R.I. (2006) *Hard Facts, Dangerous Half-Truths, and Total Nonsense: Profiting from Evidence-Based Management*, Boston, MA: Harvard Business School Press.

Porter, M. and Ketels, C.H.M. (2003) *UK Competitiveness: Moving to the Next Stage: Economics Paper 3*, London: Department of Trade and Industry.

Robbins, S.P. and Judge, T.A. (2008) *Organizational Behaviour* (12th edn), Upper Saddle River, NJ: Pearson/Prentice Hall.

Rogers, E. (1995) *The Diffusion of Innovation* (6th edn), New York: Free Press.

Schneider, D.M. and Goldwasser, C. (1998) 'Be a model leader of change', *Management Review*, 87(3), pp. 41–5.

Senge, P. (1990) *The Fifth Discipline: The Art and Practice of the Learning Organization*, London: Doubleday/Century Business.

Stace, D. and Dunphy, D. (2001) *Beyond the Boundaries: Leading and Re-creating the Successful Enterprise*, Sydney: McGraw-Hill.

The Economist (2010) 'Planning for the sequel', 19 June, p. 70.

Walton, R.E. (1975) 'The diffusion of new work structures: explaining why success didn't take', *Organizational Dynamics*, 3(3), pp. 3–22.

Warrick, D.D. (1984) *Managing Organization Change and Development*, New York: Science Research Associates Inc.

Worral, L. and Cooper, C. (2006) 'Short changed', *People Management*, 12(13), pp. 36–8.

Yerkes, R.M. and Dodson, J.D. (1908) 'The relationship of strength of stimulus to rapidity of habit-formation', *Journal of Comparative Neurology and Psychology*, 18(5), pp. 459–82.

Chapter 19 **Leadership**

Key terms

leadership
great man theory
consideration
initiating structure
contingency theory of leadership
structured task
unstructured task
situational leadership
new leader
superleader
transactional leader
transformational leader
distributed leadership

Learning outcomes

When you have read this chapter, you should be able to define those key terms in your own words, and you should also be able to:

1. Explain the apparent difference between the concepts of leadership and management.
2. Understand why there is little relationship between personality traits and effective leadership.
3. Understand the challenges facing women who aspire to leadership roles, and the social and business cases for 'boardroom diversity'.
4. Understand why effective leaders either adapt their style to fit the organizational and cultural context in which they operate, or find contexts which fit their personal style.
5. Explain contemporary trends in this field concerning new leadership, distributed leadership, and the argument that leaders are unnecessary.

Why study leadership?

Leading in the twenty-first century

A convergence of forces is reshaping the global economy: emerging regions, such as Africa, Brazil, China, and India, have overtaken economies in the West as engines of global growth; the pace of innovation is increasing exponentially; new technologies have created new industries, disrupted old ones, and spawned communication networks of astonishing speed; and global emergencies seem to erupt at ever-shorter intervals. Any one of these developments would have profound implications for organizations and the people who lead them. Taken together, these forces are creating a new context for leadership.

Moya Greene was appointed chief executive of the UK Royal Mail Group in 2010. Her thoughts on the personal challenges of leadership include:

> The first criterion is: do you love it? It's a seven-day-a-week job. I think that's true for anyone in these roles. If you don't love the company and the people – really love them – you can't do a job like this. I'm pretty energetic. I start at five in the morning. I don't think about it any more; the alarm goes off and I'm up. I go for a 30-minute run. I do weight training three mornings a week. I try to eat well, but not too much. I'm a big walker – that's my favourite thing. I try to get a good walk every weekend. I go on walking vacations.

Josef Ackerman retired recently from his roles as chief executive and chairman of Deutsche Bank. His thoughts on the pressures of leadership today include:

> I remember a time when after flying to Hong Kong you could take a whole day off to recover. Today, right after landing you rush to your first meeting. And maybe you already have a conference call in the car on your way into town. You are lucky if you get enough time to take a shower. And of course, with all the new information technology, you are constantly available, and the flow of information you have to manage is huge; that has added to the pressure. You are much more exposed to unforeseen shifts and negative surprises and you have to make quick decisions and respond to or anticipate market movements around the world. So you have to have a very stable psyche as well. I see more and more people these days who just burn out.

From Barton et al., 2012, pp. 4, 6, and 7.

Leadership the process of influencing the activities of an organized group in its efforts towards goal-setting and goal achievement.

Ralph M. Stogdill (1904–1978)

Leadership appears to be a critical determinant of organizational effectiveness, whether we are discussing an army, an orchestra, a hockey team, a street gang, a political party, a group of rock climbers, or a multinational corporation. It is not surprising to find, therefore, that leadership is a focus of intense research effort. This focus is a relatively recent phenomenon. Frank Heller (1997) noted that in 1896 the United States Library of Congress had not one book on leadership. The global literature on the subject is now vast.

Leadership is a controversial topic. We hear the complaint that 'we need more leadership'. However, the organizational hierarchy and formal authority that underpin leadership positions are today often challenged. We equate leadership with positions of power, influence, and status, but leadership can be seen at all levels of an organization. Leaders have job titles and working conditions which symbolize their status. But flat structures, teams, knowledge work, and virtual and networked organizational forms all weaken traditional leadership positions based on hierarchy and symbolism.

Ralph Stogdill, an influential early commentator on the topic, defined leadership as an influencing process aimed at goal achievement (Stogdill, 1950). Stogdill's definition has three components. First, it defines leadership as an *interpersonal process* in which one individual seeks to influence the behaviour of others. Second, it sets leadership in a *social context*, in which the other members of the group to be influenced are subordinates or followers. Third, it identifies a criterion for effective leadership – *goal achievement* – which is one practical objective of leadership theory and research. Most definitions of leadership share these processual, contextual, and evaluative components.

STOP AND THINK

Consider those who you would call leaders, in business, politics, sport, music, the arts. What characteristics, skills, abilities, and personality traits do they have in common?

Which of those leaders had a positive impact, and which had a negative impact? Do those whose impact was negative deserve the label of 'leader'?

Compare your list of leaders with that of colleagues.

How can the term 'leader' be applied to a diverse group of personalities whose actions have had a range of different consequences? This chapter explores six perspectives which adopt quite different views on the nature of leadership:

1. **Trait-spotting**: identifies the personality traits and related attributes of the effective leader, in order to facilitate the selection of leaders.
2. **Style-counselling**: characterizes different leadership behaviour patterns to identify effective and ineffective leadership styles, in order to improve the training and development of leaders.
3. **Context-fitting**: contingency theories argue that the leadership effectiveness depends on aspects of the organizational and cultural setting.
4. **New leadership**: 'new leaders', 'superleaders', and 'transformational leaders' are heroic, inspirational visionaries who give purpose and direction to others; their motivational role is central to strategy and effectiveness.
5. **Distributed leadership**: leadership behaviour is not confined to those with formal senior roles, but can be observed across all organizational levels.
6. **Who needs leaders?** Transformational leaders can destabilize an organization by driving too much change too quickly, causing burnout and initiative fatigue; middle managers with change implementation skills can be more effective.

Ken Parry and Alan Bryman (2006) note that these perspectives developed chronologically. Trait-spotting was popular until the 1940s when inconsistent research findings led to disillusionment, and that approach was abandoned. Style-counselling was then popular until the late 1960s, but appeared oversimplified in the face of the contingency theories which

Leaders are men with special qualities

Discussion of leadership is so often overloaded with vague but emotive ideas that one is hard put to it to nail the concept down. To cut through the panoply of such quasi-moral and unexceptionable associations as 'patriotism', 'play up and play the game', the 'never-asking-your-men-to-do-something-you-wouldn't-do-yourself' formula, 'not giving in (or up)', the 'square-jaw-frank-eyes-steadfast-gaze' formula, and the 'if. . . . you'll be a man' recipe, one comes to the simple truth that *leadership is no more than exercising such an influence upon others that they tend to act in concert towards achieving a goal which they might not have achieved so readily had they been left to their own devices.*

The ingredients which bring about this agreeable state of affairs are many and varied. At the most superficial level they are believed to include such factors as voice, stature and appearance, an impression of omniscience, trustworthiness, sincerity and bravery. At a deeper and rather more important level, leadership depends upon a proper understanding of the needs and opinions of those one hopes to lead, and the context in which the leadership occurs. It also depends on good timing. Hitler, who was neither omniscient, trustworthy nor sincere, whose stature was unremarkable and whose appearance verged on the repellent, understood these rules and exploited them to full advantage. The same may be said of many good comedians. (Dixon, 1994, pp. 214–15 (emphasis added)) dominated thinking until the early 1980s. At that point, the 'new leadership' movement emerged. Towards the close of the twentieth century, the distributed nature of leadership attracted more attention. Moving into the twenty-first century, several commentators challenged the value of leadership, observing that 'celebrity bosses' were responsible for the rapid and radical changes that caused initiative fatigue and organizational destabilization. None of these shifts in emphasis has replaced earlier accounts, and all of those perspectives can be seen in today's research, commentary, and practice.

Leadership versus management

What is the difference between leadership and management? Some commentators argue that leaders and managers make distinctly different contributions. Others argue, however, that leadership is simply one facet of a complex management role. Warren Bennis and Burt Nanus (1985) famously argued that 'managers do things right' while 'leaders do the right thing'. Leaders are thus often seen as visionaries who drive new initiatives. Managers simply seek to maintain order and stability. The leader is prophet, catalyst, mover-shaker, and strategist. The manager is technician, administrator, and problem-solver. The leader influences others to sign up to their vision, inspires them to overcome obstacles, and generates positive change. The manager establishes plans and budgets, designs and staffs the organization, monitors and controls performance, and delivers order and predictability.

This is a 'good guys, bad guys' caricature. John Kotter's (1990) contrast between leaders and managers is summarized in Table 19.1. Kotter's perspective highlights the importance of leadership and consigns management to a lesser role. Observing that this dichotomy is inaccurate and insulting, Julian Birkinshaw (2010) argues that leadership and management must be seen as complementary, as roles that the same person plays at different times, as 'two horses pulling the same cart'. Another leading commentator in this field, Henry Mintzberg (2009, pp. 8–9), also poses a fundamental challenge to the distinction between leaders and managers:

> Frankly, I don't understand what this distinction means in the everyday life of organizations. Sure, we can separate leading and managing conceptually. But can we separate them in practice? Or, more to the point, should we even try? We should be seeing managers *as* leaders, and leadership as management practised well.

Table 19.1: Leadership versus management

	Leadership functions	Management functions
Creating an agenda	*Establishes direction* vision of the future; develops strategies for change to achieve goals	*Plans and budgets* decides actions and timetables; allocates resources
Developing people	*Aligning people* communicates vision and strategy; influences creation of teams which accept validity of goals	*Organizing and staffing* decides structure and allocates staff; develops policies, procedures, and monitoring
Execution	*Motivating and inspiring* energizes people to overcome obstacles; satisfies human needs	*Controlling, problem-solving* monitors results against plan and take corrective action
Outcomes	*Produces positive and sometimes dramatic change*	*Produces order, consistency, and predictability*

Source: based on Kotter (1990).

STOP AND THINK

Mintzberg asks: Would you like to be managed by someone who can't lead? Would you like to be led by someone who can't manage?

How would you respond to those two questions?

For Mintzberg (2009), a manager's roles include framing (deciding, focusing, establishing the context in which others work) and scheduling (slicing up concerns, deciding how to allocate time). The work involved in fulfilling those roles takes place on three planes: information, people, and action (see Table 19.2). Looking at his view of the 'people' plane, leadership is one facet of the management role.

Table 19.2: The three planes of managerial work

Plane of managerial work	Management roles
Information	communicating, controlling
People	leading, linking to others
Action	getting things done, negotiating, building coalitions

Source: after Mintzberg (2009, Table 3.2).

Critical skills for effective leaders

In 2011, the consultancy company DDI surveyed over 2,500 organizations, involving over 14,000 senior managers in 52 countries (Boatman and Wellins, 2011). They asked, 'What are the most critical skills needed in the future for leadership effectiveness?' The responses were:

Critical skills	Percentage saying that they were effective in these skills
Driving and managing change	57
Identifying and developing future talent	57
Fostering creativity and innovation	50
Coaching and developing others	57
Executing organizational strategy	60
Building customer satisfaction and loyalty	65
Improving employee engagement	56

Source: republished with permission of American Society for Training and Development, adapted from It's time for a leadership (r)evolution, *Training & Development*, April, 52–8, Figure 3 Most critical skills needed in the future for leader effectiveness (Boatman, J. and Wellins, R. 2011); permission conveyed through Copyright Clearance Center, Inc.

Implementing change, talent management, and innovation were seen as leadership priorities for the next few years. Unfortunately, around half of those leaders surveyed admitted that they were not effective in those areas. The researchers conclude that the development of leaders needs to focus on the future, as the world economy recovers from recession, and that leadership development should not be seen as just another training programme, but as a strategic business priority.

Trait-spotting

For the first half of the twentieth century, researchers assumed that they could identify the personality traits and other attributes of effective leaders. It would then be possible to select individuals who possessed those markers, and to promote them to leadership positions.

The qualities of successful leaders

General intelligence, although not necessarily being very much brighter than the people they are leading.

Technical or professional knowledge and competence in their particular fields – otherwise how would leaders be respected?

Personality: leaders should be energetic and committed, maintain contact with their people, and understand their strengths and weaknesses.

The ability to inspire, although this quality may be rarer than some of the others and is perhaps the most difficult to develop.

Listening, sharing and delegating skills (and not interfering unnecessarily), because in groups of more than five people it becomes impossible to know all the necessary detail.

Self-knowledge, to understand their strengths and weaknesses, which in turn will enable them to turn to others in their group to compensate for their own biases or deficiencies. (From Cannell, 2008)

Great man theory a historical perspective which argues that the fate of societies and organizations is in the hands of powerful, idiosyncratic (male) individuals.

This search for the qualities of good leaders was influenced by **great man theory**.

Great man theory focused on political figures, arguing that leaders reach positions of influence from which they dominate and direct the lives of others by force of personality. There is no equivalent 'great woman theory'. Great men are born leaders, and emerge to take power, regardless of the social, organizational, or historical context. Research thus focused on identifying the traits of these special people. Ralph Stogdill (1948; 1974) reviewed hundreds of trait studies and compiled this typical list:

- strong drive for responsibility
- focus on completing the task
- vigour and persistence in pursuit of goals
- venturesomeness and originality in problem-solving
- drive to exercise initiative in social settings
- self-confidence
- sense of personal identity
- willingness to accept consequences of decisions and actions
- readiness to absorb interpersonal stress
- willingness to tolerate frustration and delay
- ability to influence the behaviour of others
- capacity to structure social systems to the purpose in hand.

It is difficult to challenge these qualities. Can we say that leaders should lack drive, persistence, creativity, and the ability to influence others? These are desirable qualities in many positions, however, and do not appear to be unique to leaders.

Research did not produce a consistent set of leadership traits, and as studies covered a wider range of settings, more qualities were identified. Almost eighty characteristics were reported from a review of twenty studies of leadership traits (Bird, 1940). More than half of these traits had been identified in only one study, very few appeared in four or more investigations, and only 'intelligence' was reported in at least half of the studies reviewed. In addition, many of these traits are vague. Willingness to tolerate delay? Capacity to structure social systems? Readiness to absorb stress? It is difficult to see how trait-spotting can be used in a leadership selection context, as originally intended.

Are you an alpha male or alpha female?

According to Kate Ludeman and Eddie Erlandson (2006), around 75 per cent of the world's testosterone-driven, high-achieving executives are 'alpha males'. They take charge, dominate, conquer, and make things happen. Clever and effective, they can also cause damage both to themselves and to the companies they lead. Persistence can become stubbornness. Self-confidence leads to an unwillingness to listen to others. Those strengths, in other words, can be fatal weaknesses. There are fewer alpha women, and they do less damage because they empathize rather than confront, and are less angry and impatient. There are four types of alpha leader, each with good and bad characteristics:

- **commanders**: intense, magnetic, push others hard, but ignore rules and create fear;
- **visionaries**: creative, inspiring, but ignore reality, and are closed to input;
- **strategists**: quick, analytical, but opinionated, not team players, and don't admit mistakes;
- **executors**: problem-solvers, eye for detail, get things done, overcritical micromanagers.

Organizations run by dysfunctional alphas have higher rates of illness, staff turnover, absenteeism, burnout, and early retirement (Rushe, 2006).

To find out if you have what it takes to be an alpha, score each of these items from 'strongly disagree' (zero) to 'strongly agree' (10):

- No matter what, I don't give up until I reach my goal.
- When I play a game, I like to keep score.
- I sometimes rant and rave when I don't get my way.
- My opinions and ideas are usually the best ones.
- When others don't agree, I lose my temper.
- I am accustomed to being the centre of attention.
- People have described me as a 'natural born leader'.
- I believe the end usually justifies the means.
- I only collaborate with peers when I have to.
- There are a lot of people who are just plain stupid.

Scoring

0–25	Absolute wimp; keep tissues on your desk.
26–50	Bit of a pushover.
51–75	Ambitious but afraid to wield the knife.
76–100	Congratulations, you're an alpha.

It was clear by 1950 that there was limited value in continuing to identify leadership traits, although some weak generalizations did emerge (Shaw, 1976; Fraser, 1978). Leaders do tend, on average, to score higher on measures of

- **ability** – intelligence, relevant knowledge, verbal facility;
- **sociability** – participation, cooperativeness, popularity;
- **motivation** – initiative and persistence.

The trait-spotting approach was abandoned at that time as researchers switched attention, first to leadership *styles*, and then to characteristics of *context*. However, the belief has persisted that leadership traits can be isolated, and the search for personality markers has since resumed. Paradoxically, trait-spotting is a contemporary perspective, and can be seen in many attempts to develop leadership 'competency models' (such as the 'transformational leadership' behaviours discussed later in this chapter).

Jobs for the boys?

Male and female management styles

'I just walked into my office and asked my staff if any of them would rather work for a man. Two of the women said, "Yes. If you were a man, you would be easier to manipulate." The men said nothing.' (Daisy Goodwin, television producer, 2011)

For most of the twentieth century, it was assumed that leaders had to be *men*. Leadership research was done by men whose subjects were men. Women are still poorly represented in management roles, and were largely ignored in leadership research until the 1990s. Fiona Wilson (2002) argues that we are now seeing a 'feminization of management' as flatter structures call for skills in communication, collaboration, consensus decision-making, teamwork, networking, and developing others – qualities often associated with women.

This feminization process appears to be slow in Western countries, but may be happening faster in some emerging economies. In 2011, 7 of the 14 women on *Forbes* magazine's list of self-made billionaires were Chinese. In China, 32 per cent of senior managers are female, compared with 23 per cent in America and 19 per cent in Britain. In India, 11 per cent of chief executives of large companies are female, compared with only 3 per cent of Fortune 500 chief executives in America. In Brazil, 11 per cent of chief executives and 30 per cent of senior executives are women. But even in emerging markets women with business careers face difficult problems. In the United Arab Emirates, for example, women cannot travel without a male chaperone, and it is difficult to be taken seriously in Russia where the term 'businesswoman' is synonymous with 'prostitute' (*The Economist*, 2011).

In 2010, women held only 12.5 per cent of the boardroom seats in Britain's FTSE (Financial Times Stock Exchange) top 100 companies, rising to 15 per cent in 2011 (Vinnicombe and Sealy, 2012). This growth was due to more women being appointed to non-executive director positions; women held only 6.6 per cent of executive seats; 46 per cent of FTSE 100 companies had no women on their boards. Table 19.3 shows the recent board composition of the FTSE 100 top five performers.

Table 19.3: Board composition, FTSE top five in 2011

Company	Percentage of men on board	Percentage of women on board
Diageo	55.6	44.4
Burberry	62.5	37.5
Pearson	66.7	33.3
Morrison Supermarkets	71.4	28.6
Marks & Spencer	71.4	28.6

Source: based on Vinnicombe and Sealy (2012).

In 2005, Norway passed a law requiring public companies to allocate 40 per cent of board seats to women. By 2012, the proportion of women on Norwegian company boards had gone from 10 per cent to over 40 per cent. Even private companies, exempt from the legislation, appointed female directors, and other countries now have similar regulations: Belgium, France, Italy, the Netherlands, and Spain. The national context is important. Norway has a tradition of using quotas to achieve social goals. In Britain, in contrast, there is a presumption that businesses and individuals should be free from government interference. Have Norwegian companies performed better since quotas for female board members were introduced? The evidence is mixed. One study showed that Norway had improved its position in the World Competitiveness Yearbook. A second study linked the introduction of quotas to a fall in the performance of Norwegian companies (Clegg, 2012). Other factors may play a role.

Research by the management consultancy firm McKinsey has established a positive link between the proportion of women in senior management roles and corporate performance (Devillard et al., 2012). This is due, they argue, to the different and complementary perspectives that women bring to board debates. However, and despite quotas, the proportion of women on corporate boards in Europe is still low. In France, 20 per cent of board members are women (up from 8 per cent in 2007), compared with Italy where women hold only 5 per cent of board positions. Sweden, with no quotas, has 25 per cent. Cultural and socioeconomic factors are partly responsible. Gender diversity in the workplace can be influenced by the presence or absence of support mechanisms such as childcare facilities and parental leave. Many women with initially high ambitions turn down opportunities because of family and other commitments, or because they want to stay in meaningful roles. Women are also more reluctant to promote themselves than men, and they often lack a network of sponsors to help build their reputations. Devillard et al. argue that companies themselves must act, promoting a gender diversity 'ecosystem' that combines top management commitment, development programmes, and 'collective enablers' such as supportive human resource policies (see Table 19.4).

Table 19.4: The gender diversity ecosystem

top management commitment	chief executive's priority targets for women's representation in senior positions company culture with consistent gender diversity goals
women's development programmes	networking events mentors and external coaches leadership skills development
collective enablers (human resource policies and infrastructure)	control of gender bias in recruitment, appraisal, promotion flexible working patterns encouraged not penalized facilitate remote working action to increase number of women applicants processes to retain top-performing women wishing to leave meetings scheduled only during business hours childcare facilities, in-house or external job search programmes for partners and spouses

Source: adapted from Devillard, et al. (2012, p. 9, Exhibit 4).

From their survey of 235 European companies, the McKinsey researchers found that most were taking action to improve gender diversity; 63 per cent of companies had 20 or more initiatives as part of their gender diversity programmes, such as diversity training, redesigned recruitment and promotion processes, and setting management targets for the numbers of women in senior positions. However, women accounted for more than a quarter of the top jobs in only 8 per cent of the largest companies (those with more than 10,000 employees). The researchers concluded that, while the actions that improve gender diversity are clear, gender diversity is not yet 'hardwired' in many organization cultures.

There is evidence to support the business case for boardroom diversity. Alison Konrad and Vicki Kramer (2006) found that women directors make three contributions that men are less likely to make:

1. Women broaden the discussion to include a range of stakeholders: employees, customers, community.
2. Women are persistent in getting answers to awkward questions; men don't like to admit when they don't understand.
3. Women are more collaborative, which improves communications.

However, having just one or two women on the board makes little difference. When there are three or more, they are treated just like other directors, and are less likely to be isolated or ignored. Anita Woolley and Thomas Malone (2011) studied the collective intelligence of teams. Subjects were given IQ tests, and then allocated randomly to problem-solving teams; the teams were given collective intelligence scores based on their performance. The researchers found that collective intelligence was not related to the intelligence of the individual team members. However, collective intelligence was higher in groups that included more women. How can this happen? Having smart individual members is important, but social sensitivity – a capability which on average women seem to display more strongly than men – also contributes to group performance:

> In theory, yes, the 10 smartest people could make the smartest group, but it wouldn't just be because they were the most intelligent individuals. What do you hear about great groups? Not that the members are all really smart but that they listen to each other. They share criticism constructively. They have open minds. They're not autocratic. And in our study we saw pretty clearly that groups that had smart people dominating the conversation were not very intelligent groups. (Woolley and Malone, 2011, p. 32)

However, one study challenges the view that women have a calming influence on boardroom decisions. The study tracked the fluctuating profits of Deutsche Bundesbank over sixteen years, and concluded that risk-taking *increased* when there were more female board members. Female representation seems to have changed the boardroom dynamics, increasing the variety of members with different backgrounds, values, and levels of experience, thus increasing the potential for conflict. Two other German banks, Deutsche Bank and Commerzbank, have no women directors on their boards. Of the 66 board members at Barclays, HSBC, RBS, Lloyds, and Santander banks, all of which have had recent financial problems, there are 14 women directors (Charter, 2012).

Career and family

Does career success for women mean sacrificing family life? Sylvia Ann Hewlett (2002) surveyed over 1,100 successful women in America in two age groups, 28 to 40, and 41 to 55. She defined high achievers as those earning between US$55,000 and US$65,000, and ultra-achievers as those earning more than US$100,000. For comparison, 470 men were also included in the research. Her findings showed the following percentages childless between ages 41 and 55:

	percentage childless between ages 41 and 55
high-achieving women	33
corporate women	42
high-achieving men	25
ultra-achieving men	19
ultra-achieving women	49

High- and ultra-achieving women were also less likely to be married than their male colleagues. Hewlett quotes a young professional woman:

> I know a few hard-driving women who are climbing the ladder at consulting firms, but they are single or divorced and seem pretty isolated. And I know a handful of working mothers who are trying to do the half-time thing or the two-thirds-time thing. They work reduced hours so they can see their kids, but they don't get the good projects, they don't get the bonuses, and they also get whispered about behind their backs. You know, comments like, If she's not prepared to work the client's hours, she has no business being in the profession.

Around a third of high- and ultra-achieving women worked more than 55 hours a week (thirteen hours a day including commuting), and some were occasionally working 70 hours. Hewlett argues that, for many women, 'the brutal demands of ambitious careers, the asymmetries of male-female relationships, and the difficulties of bearing children late in life conspire to crowd out the possibility of having children'.

Deborah Tannen (1995) argues that women and men acquire different linguistic styles in childhood. Girls learn to focus on rapport, while boys focus on status. Men think in hierarchical terms, and of being 'one up', like to jockey for position by putting others down, and appear confident and knowledgeable. Women can appear to lack self-confidence by concealing their certainty and expressing doubt. Those who adopt a 'masculine' style are regarded as aggressive. Reinforcing these conclusions, Deborah Rees (2004) identifies three categories of women in management:

corporate high-flyers motivated by influence and power, have pursued management careers and achieved senior roles

soloists and pioneers motivated by freedom and self-control, work on their own, or set up their own businesses

submarines as work is neither rewarding nor flexible enough, do not pursue traditional careers and direct their energies elsewhere.

Rees met many women who felt that the financial rewards of senior positions did not compensate for the lack of flexibility. Submarines were frustrated by the way in which they were discouraged from balancing their work and non-work commitments. Soloists, pioneers, and submarines said that they disliked the 'political and clubby' atmosphere at the top of male-dominated organizations, with the focus on empire building, and the absence of teamwork. For male managers, it seemed, 'winning and beating others is good', and being 'nice' to others is not seen as a valuable attribute. Despite working longer hours, soloists and pioneers expressed higher levels of satisfaction and self-fulfilment. From her research, Susan Pinker (2008) also found that many women had given up a corporate career, not because of discrimination, but because they wanted something different from life.

Source: previously appeared in *Why Women Mean Business*, Wiley, (Wittenberg-Cox, A. and Maitland, A., 2009) © Roger Beale.

The glass cliff

The debate concerning the problems facing women who aspire to leadership roles has focused on 'the glass ceiling', the invisible barrier erected by male-dominated company boards. In contrast, men's careers are helped by a 'glass escalator' which carries them to the top. Michelle Ryan and Alexander Haslam (2005, 2007) suggest that women promoted to senior roles face another set of problems. Their research found that companies are more likely to change the composition of their boards of directors when performance drops than when it is improving. Ryan and Haslam suggest that poor company performance can trigger the appointment of women to the board, on the basis that diversity leads to higher performance. They also observe that this means promoting women into positions that carry a high risk of failure. As women are a minority among senior managers, they are more visible, and their performance tends to be scrutinized more closely. The researchers conclude that women were being 'set up to fail' – placed on a 'glass cliff' – by being appointed in difficult organizational circumstances. As a consequence, their position in the company was precarious. In such cases, women may find that they are held responsible for poor performance caused by conditions that were in place before they were promoted. Thus, while women may be under-represented in senior management ranks, they may be over-represented in vulnerable senior positions.

Alice Eagly and Linda Carli (2007) argue that the 'glass ceiling' argument is misleading. They suggest that the image of the 'labyrinth' is more useful, as women face many obstacles and challenges to their careers at different stages. The difficulties do not just lie with senior roles. Male prejudice and family responsibilities are not the only problems. Women tend to have less time for socializing, and have weaker professional networks. Women need persistence and self-awareness to negotiate this labyrinth. Other remedies include changing the long-hours culture in many companies, and developing women at an early stage in their careers with challenging management assignments.

Research by the management consultancy company Ernst & Young (2012) also concludes that the concept of a 'single glass ceiling' is outdated, as women face many barriers to career progression. Their survey of 1,000 working women aged 18 to 60 identified four main barriers. First, women felt that they were always perceived as being either too young or too old. Second, lack of experience or qualifications was also seen to stand in their way. Third, many felt that becoming a mother had damaged their future career prospects. Fourth, 75 per cent said that they had few or no female role models in their organizations. Liz Bingham, Ernst & Young managing partner, said:

> The focus around gender diversity has increasingly been on representation in the boardroom and this is still very important. But the notion that there is a single glass ceiling for women, as a working concept for today's modern career, is dead. Professional working women have told us they face multiple barriers on their rise to the top.

When women were asked how their companies could remove the barriers, popular answers concerned more support when returning to work after having children, as well as support throughout their careers, and visible female role models. Those surveyed also felt that government could help by forcing companies to reveal pay differentials between male and female employees, by providing affordable childcare for working mothers, and by developing policy guidelines on flexible working.

STOP AND THINK

What other steps might women take in order to strengthen their organizational positions and achieve promotion to more senior managerial positions?

Women don't ask

An accountant, Lorna Leonard, describes her experience of being paid less than her male colleagues (Spence, 2011): 'When you find out you're earning less money just because you're a woman, it's horrible. It's genuinely gut-wrenching.' A few times, Ms Leonard confronted her employers about the disparity between her pay and that of her male colleagues. More often, she kept quiet about it. It is precisely because of this, she believes now, that women executives still earn less than most of their male counterparts. 'I think that women understate their abilities when they're putting themselves forward for jobs and pay rises', Ms Leonard says. 'Male colleagues feel comfortable about pushing themselves. They're more bullish about the salary they should command. The ladies I have coming through the door are likely to ask for less money than a man in a comparable position.'

A survey carried out by a large retail chain store company over Christmas 2005 revealed that, on average, parents in England spend about £100 more on presents for their sons than for their daughters. When asked to explain, parents said that boys asked for more items, and what they asked for was more expensive (Webb, 2006). Boys also complained more loudly if they were disappointed. The most expensive toy in the top five best-sellers for girls was the Amazing Amanda doll (£69.99), compared with the boys' Playstation Portable (£179.99).

The unwritten rule that says 'if you don't ask, you don't get' also seems to apply to adults. Research in America (Babcock and Laschever, 2003) suggests that after graduating from university, women are more likely to accept the starting salary that they are offered, while men are more likely to ask for, and to get, more. This may explain why women in Britain who work full-time are paid 18 per cent less than men, and why part-timers are paid 40 per cent less. Can this inequality be explained by the observation that women tend to leave employment to look after children? Not entirely, because the difference in salary between equally well educated men and women is 15 per cent five years after graduation, long before those women decide to start families.

Why should women be less demanding? One explanation is that men do not need to feel that they are liked by their colleagues, and are less embarrassed about complaining and asking for more money. Women, in contrast, tend to be more concerned with maintaining relationships, and assume that if they were worth a higher salary, then their boss would pay them more.

Style-counselling

Disillusionment with the traits approach meant that leadership, management, and supervisory style became a major focus for research. Attention switched from selecting leaders on the basis of personality traits, to training and developing leaders in appropriate behaviour patterns. This research tradition argues that a considerate, participative, democratic, and involving leadership style is more effective than an impersonal, autocratic, and directive style.

Two projects, known as the Michigan and Ohio studies respectively, underpinned the investigation of management style. Based mainly on a study of foremen at the International Harvester Company, the work of the Survey Research Center in Michigan in the 1940s and early 1950s (Katz et al., 1950) identified two dimensions of leadership behaviour:

1. **employee-centred behaviour**: focusing on relationships and employee needs;
2. **job-centred behaviour**: focusing on getting the job done.

This work ran concurrently with the influential studies of Edwin Fleishman and Ralph Stogdill at the Bureau of Business Research at Ohio State University (Fleishman, 1953a, 1953b; Fleishman and Harris, 1962; Stogdill, 1948; Stogdill and Coons, 1951). The Ohio results also identified two categories of leadership behaviour which they termed **consideration** and **initiating structure**. The considerate leader is relationships- and needs-oriented. The leader who structures work for subordinates is task- or job-centred.

Consideration a pattern of leadership behaviour that demonstrates sensitivity to relationships and to the social needs of employees.

Initiating structure a pattern of leadership behaviour that emphasizes performance of the work in hand and the achievement of product and service goals.

The considerate leader is interested in and listens to subordinates, allows participation in decision-making, is friendly and approachable, and supports subordinates with personal problems. The leader's behaviour indicates trust, respect, warmth, and rapport. This enhances subordinates' feelings of self-esteem and encourages the development of communications and relationships in a work group. The researchers first called this dimension 'social sensitivity'.

The leader who initiates structure decides how things are going to get done, structures tasks and assigns work, makes expectations clear, emphasizes deadlines, and expects subordinates to follow instructions. The leader's behaviour stresses production and the achievement of goals. This is the kind of emphasis that the scientific management school (see Chapter 14) encouraged, but task orientation in this perspective has a positive, motivating aspect. The researchers first called this leadership dimension 'production emphasis'.

Home viewing

Star Trek (2009, director J.J. Abrams) tells the story of how James T. Kirk (played by Chris Pine) became captain of the USS Enterprise. When the previous captain Christopher Pike is lost, the Vulcan crew member Mr Spock (Zachary Quinto) takes command, as the most senior officer on board. As you watch this movie, consider the following questions. What *leadership traits and behaviours* do Kirk and Spock each display? How would you describe the dominant *leadership style* of each of these two characters? Why do the other officers eventually accept Kirk as their commanding officer? To what extent does the *context* in which Kirk and Spock are operating influence who is more likely to be an effective leader?

Consideration and structure are independent behaviour patterns. A leader can emphasize one or both. Job satisfaction is likely to be higher, and grievances and staff turnover lower, when the leader emphasizes consideration. Task performance, on the other hand, is likely to be higher when the leader emphasizes the initiation of structure. Inconsiderate leaders typically have subordinates who complain and who are more likely to leave the organization, but can have comparatively productive work groups if they are high on initiating structure. This theory is summarized in Figure 19.1.

Consideration		Initiating structure: high	Initiating structure: low
	high	high performance few grievances low turnover	low performance few grievances low turnover
	low	high performance many grievances high turnover	low performance many grievances high turnover

Figure 19.1: The Ohio State leadership theory predictions

The work of another Michigan researcher, Rensis Likert (1961), reinforced the benefits of considerate, performance-oriented leadership. From interviews with supervisors and clerks in an American insurance company, he found that supervisors in highly productive sections were more likely to

- receive general as opposed to close supervision from their superiors;
- give general as opposed to close supervision to their subordinates;
- enjoy their responsibility and authority, and spend more time on supervision;
- be employee- rather than production-oriented.

Likert and his team identified four systems of leadership:

System 1: *Exploitative-autocratic*, in which the leader

- has no confidence and trust in subordinates;
- imposes decisions;
- never delegates;
- motivates by threat;
- has little communication and teamwork;

System 2: *Benevolent-authoritative*, in which the leader

- has superficial, condescending trust in subordinates;
- imposes decisions;
- never delegates;
- motivates by reward;
- sometimes involves subordinates in solving problems;

System 3: *Participative*, in which the leader

- has some incomplete confidence and trust in subordinates;
- listens to subordinates but controls decision-making;
- motivates by reward and some involvement;
- uses ideas and opinions of subordinates constructively;

System 4: *Democratic*, in which the leader

- has complete confidence and trust in subordinates;
- allows subordinates to make decisions for themselves;
- motivates by reward for achieving goals set by participation;
- shares ideas and opinions.

Likert concluded that effective supervisors adopted either System 3 or System 4, which he called an 'alternative organizational life style'. However, recent research by Roderick Kramer (2006) suggests that, in certain contexts, what he describes as an intimidating leadership style can be effective, too.

The great intimidators

Kramer challenges the view that managers must be nice and not tough, and should be humble and self-effacing rather than intimidating. Kramer (2006) argues that intimidation is an appropriate style when an organization has become rigid, unruly, stagnant, or drifting, or faces resistance or inertia. Abrasive leadership gets people moving. Intimidators are not bullies, but can use bullying tactics when time is short and the stakes are high: 'They are not averse to causing a ruckus, nor are they above using a few public whippings and ceremonial hangings to get attention. They're rough, loud, and in your face' (p. 90).

"In his mysterious way, God has given each of us different talents, Ridgeway. It just so happens that mine is intimidating people."

Source: © Joseph Mirachi.

Intimidators have 'political intelligence'. The socially intelligent manager focuses on using the strengths of others, through empathy and soft power, to achieve the outcomes they desire. The politically intelligent manager focuses on weaknesses and insecurities, using coercion, fear, and anxiety. Working for an intimidating leader can be a positive experience. Their sense of purpose can be inspirational, their forcefulness is a role model, and intimidators challenge others to think clearly about their objectives. Kramer quotes a journalist who said 'Don't have a reputation for being a nice guy – that won't do you any good' (p. 92). Intimidation tactics include:

Get up close and personal. Intimidators work through direct confrontation, invading your personal space, using taunts and slurs to provoke and throw you off balance.

Get angry. Called 'porcupine power', this involves the 'calculated loss of temper' (use it, don't lose it), using rage and anger to help the intimidator prevail.

Keep them guessing. Intimidators preserve an air of mystery by maintaining deliberate distance. Transparency and trust are fashionable, but intimidators keep others guessing, which makes it easier to change direction without loss of credibility.

Know it all. 'Informational intimidators' can be very intimidating. It doesn't matter whether 'the facts' are correct, as long as they are presented with total confidence at the right time.

Beverly Alimo-Metcalfe and Margaret Bradley (2008; Alimo-Metcalfe and Alban-Metcalfe, 2010) agree with Likert in arguing that a participative, engaging style improves performance. They studied 46 mental health teams involved in implementing organizational change, and found that engaging leadership increases employee motivation, job satisfaction, and commitment, while reducing stress. Each team had a designated leader, but as teams were on call around the clock, different members took the leadership role at different times. Engaging leadership had the following dimensions:

- involving stakeholders early: this helps to establish lasting relationships;
- building a collective vision: this means that the team 'owns' the work and the goals;
- no team hierarchy: leadership devolves as appropriate, even with an appointed leader;
- supportive culture: informal support from colleagues, formal support from supervision, so people can share problems, seek advice, and take risks;
- successful change management: team members are consulted about change and their views are taken into account.

Engaging with others was one of three dimensions of leadership identified in this study. *Visionary leadership* involves having clear goals, being sensitive to stakeholders' needs and interests, and inspiring employees with passion and determination. *Leadership capabilities* involves competencies such as understanding strategy, ensuring goal clarity, setting success criteria, commitment to high standards, and designing supportive systems and procedures. Of these three dimensions, engaging with others had the greatest impact on attitudes and performance, while leadership capabilities had only limited effects, as shown in Table 19.5.

Table 19.5: Which leadership dimensions have most impact?

	Leadership dimension		
	Engaging with others	**Visionary leadership**	**Leadership capabilities**
high job satisfaction	☑		☑
high motivation to achieve	☑	☑	☑
strong sense of job commitment	☑		
strong organizational commitment	☑		
high sense of fulfilment	☑	☑	
high self-esteem	☑	☑	
high self-confidence	☑		☑
low job-related stress	☑	☑	
low emotional exhaustion	☑	☑	
strong sense of team spirit	☑		
strong sense of team effectiveness	☑	☑	☑

Source: Alimo-Metcalf and Bradley (2008, table on p. 41).

This study suggests that efforts to develop leadership competencies would be better spent on developing a culture of engagement, at all levels of the organization.

Context-fitting

The Michigan and Ohio perspectives offer leaders 'one best way' to handle followers, by adopting the 'high consideration, high structure' ideal. This advice is supported by the fact that most people *like* their leaders to be considerate, even when they are performance-oriented as well. The problem, however, is that one leadership style may not be effective in all settings. Several commentators have developed frameworks showing how leadership effectiveness also depends on context.

Robert Tannenbaum and Warren Schmidt

Robert Tannenbaum (1913–2003)

Warren H. Schmidt

Departing from 'one best way', Robert Tannenbaum and Warren Schmidt (1958) considered the autocratic-democratic choice of style as a continuum, from 'boss-centred leadership' at one extreme to 'subordinate-centred leadership' at the other. This is illustrated in Figure 19.2.

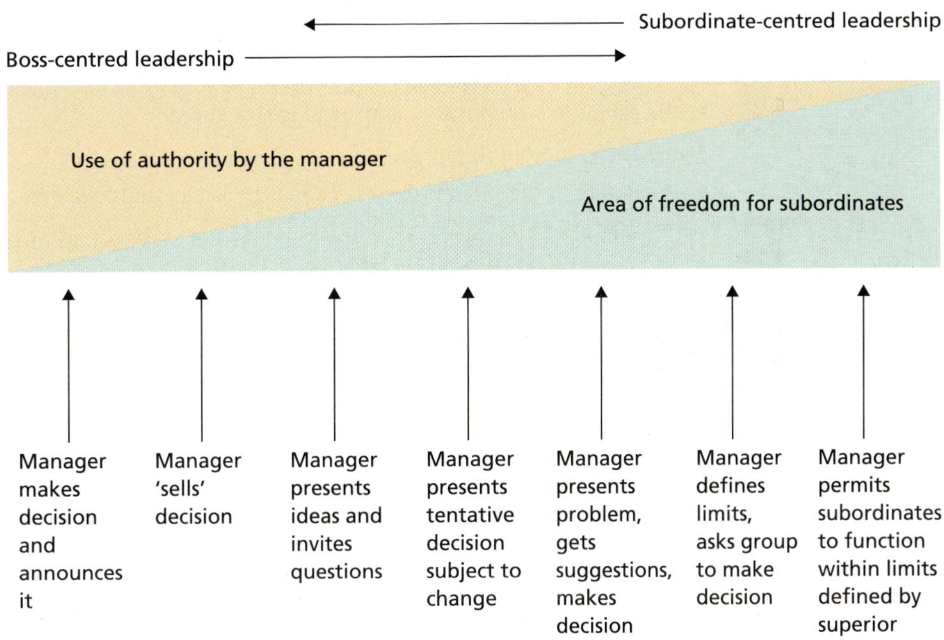

Figure 19.2: The Tannenbaum–Schmidt continuum of leadership behaviour

Source: reprinted by permission of *Harvard Business Review*. From 'How to choose a leadership pattern' by Tannenbaum, R. and Schmidt, W.H., Vol. 37, March–April reprinted in May–June, 1973, Copyright © 1958 by the Harvard Business School Publishing Corporation, all rights reserved.

The steps in this continuum are presented as alternatives for the leader. Tannenbaum and Schmidt gave their article a subtitle: 'should a manager be democratic or autocratic – or something in between?'. The answer, they suggest, depends on three sets of forces:

- **forces in the manager**: personality, values, preferences, beliefs about employee participation, confidence in subordinates;
- **forces in the subordinates**: need for independence, tolerance of ambiguity, knowledge of the problem, expectations of involvement;
- **forces in the situation**: organizational norms, size and location of work groups, effectiveness of teamworking, nature of the problem.

Contingency theory of leadership a perspective which argues that leaders must adjust their style taking into account properties of the context.

Having concentrated on 'forces in the manager', and challenged the notion of 'one best way' to lead, research now turned to consider the properties of the context in which the leader was operating. These properties included the people being led, the nature of the work they were doing, and the wider organizational setting. This perspective implies that leaders must be able to 'diagnose' the context, and then decide what behaviour will 'fit' best. As the best style is contingent on the situation, this approach is known as the **contingency theory of leadership**.

STOP AND THINK

Leadership theory seems to be consistent in arguing that a considerate, employee-centred, participative, and democratic style is more effective.

In what context would an inconsiderate, goal-centred, impersonal, and autocratic leadership style be effective? (See *OB in films* in this chapter for possible answers.)

Fred Fiedler

Frederick Edward Fiedler (b.1922)

Fred Fiedler developed one of the first contingency theories of leadership (1967; Fiedler and Chemers, 1974, 1984). From studies of basketball teams and bomber crews, he found that leadership effectiveness is influenced by three sets of factors:

- the extent to which the task in hand is structured;
- the leader's position power;
- the nature of the relationships between the leader and followers.

This argument distinguishes between a **structured task** and an **unstructured task**.

STOP AND THINK

Would you describe the task of writing an essay for your organizational behaviour instructor as a structured or as an unstructured task? Would you prefer this task to be more or less structured, and how would you advise your instructor to achieve this?

Structured task a task with clear goals, few correct or satisfactory solutions and outcomes, few ways of performing it, and clear criteria of success.

Unstructured task a task with ambiguous goals, many good solutions, many ways of achieving acceptable outcomes, and vague criteria of success.

Situational leadership® an approach to determining the most effective style of influencing, considering the direction and support a leader gives, and the readiness of followers to perform a particular task.

Fiedler identified three typical sets of conditions in which a leader might have to work:

Condition 1	Condition 2	Condition 3
highly structured task	unstructured task	unstructured task
high position power	low position power	low position power
good relationships	moderately good relationships	poor relationships

In Condition 1, task-oriented leaders get better results, because they set targets and monitor progress. Relationships-oriented leaders get poor results because they want to maintain their relationships.

In Condition 2, relationships-oriented leaders get better results, as relationships are key to exerting influence. In this case, the task-oriented leader who lacks position power gets poor results.

In Condition 3, which is highly unfavourable, task-oriented leaders once again get better results, by structuring the situation, reducing uncertainty, and ignoring resistance. The relationships-oriented leader is reluctant to pressure subordinates, avoids confrontations, and pays less attention to the task.

Fiedler's theory confirms the importance of context in determining leader effectiveness, and supports the argument that there is no one best set of leadership traits or behaviours. But can leaders change style to fit the context? Fiedler felt that most managers and supervisors have problems in changing their styles. To be effective, he argued, *leaders have to change their context* (perhaps move to another organization), to find conditions in which their preferred style was most likely to be effective.

When bossy is better

In a recent reworking of Fiedler's perspective, Stephen Sauer (2012) argues that you should base your choice of leadership style on your status. Newly appointed leaders in particular may be perceived as having low status because of their age, experience, or education. Experiments with business students showed that low-status leaders got better ratings when they took charge and told their teams what to do. Low-status leaders who adopted a participative style and asked their teams for opinions got lower ratings. Why? If team members think that their new leader has low status, asking for their input may be seen as lack of confidence and competence.

high status leaders		**low status leaders**
	most effective ↑	
participative		**directive**
powerful leaders can afford to hand authority over to subordinates		new managers need to increase their standing by appearing decisive
directive	↓ *least effective*	**participative**

Source: reprinted by permission of *Harvard Business Review*. Adapted from 'When bossy is better for rookie managers' by Sauer, S.J., 90(5) 2012. Copyright © 2012 by the Harvard Business School Publishing Corporation; all rights reserved.

Paul Hersey and Ken Blanchard

Paul Hersey

Kenneth H. Blanchard (b.1939)

Another influential contingency theory was developed by Paul Hersey and Ken Blanchard (1988). Like Fiedler, they argue that the effective leader 'must be a good diagnostician'. Unlike Fiedler, however, they believe that leaders can adapt their style to meet the demands of the situation in which they operate. Hersey and Blanchard call their approach **situational leadership®**. Their theory describes leadership behaviour on two dimensions – task behaviour and supportive behaviour.

The first dimension concerns 'task behaviour', or the amount of direction a leader gives to subordinates. This can vary from specific instructions, at one extreme, to delegation, at the other. Hersey and Blanchard identify two intermediate positions, where leaders either facilitate subordinates' decisions, or take care to explain their own.

The second dimension concerns 'supportive behaviour', or the social backup a leader gives to subordinates. This can vary from limited communication to considerable listening, facilitating, and supporting. The model thus identifies four basic leadership styles:

S1 **Telling**: High amounts of task behaviour, telling subordinates what to do, when to do it and how to do it, but with little relationship behaviour.

S2 **Selling**: High amounts of both task behaviour and relationship behaviour.

S3 **Participating**: Lots of relationship behaviour and support, but little task behaviour.

S4 **Delegating**: Not much task behaviour or relationship behaviour.

Hersey and Blanchard argue that the willingness of followers to perform a task is also a key factor. At one extreme, we have insecure subordinates, reluctant to act. At the other, we have confident and able followers. Superimpose readiness on the four leadership styles and you have a basis for selecting a style that will be effective in a particular context. The view that insecure subordinates need telling, while willing groups can be left to do the job, is consistent with other theories. The strengths of this perspective thus lie with the emphasis on contextual factors, and on the need for flexibility in leadership behaviour.

Daniel Goleman

Daniel Goleman (2000) reports research by the management consulting firm Hay McBer involving 4,000 executives from around the world. This identified six leadership styles which affect 'working atmosphere' and financial performance. The findings suggest that effective leaders use all of these styles, like an 'array of clubs in a golf pro's bag'. Each style relies on an aspect of *emotional intelligence* (see Chapter 7) which concerns skill in managing your emotions, and the emotions of others. Goleman's six styles are summarized in Table 19.6.

Table 19.6: Goleman's six leadership styles

style	in practice	in a phrase	competencies	when to use
coercive	demands compliance	'Do what I tell you'	drive to achieve, self-control	in a crisis, with problem people
authoritative	mobilizes people	'Come with me'	self-confidence, change catalyst	when new vision and direction is needed
affiliative	creates harmony	'People come first'	empathy, communication	to heal wounds, to motivate people under stress
democratic	forges consensus	'What do you think?'	collaboration, teambuilding	to build consensus, to get contributions
pacesetting	sets high standards	'Do as I do, now'	initiative, drive to achieve	to get fast results from a motivated team
coaching	develops people	'Try this'	empathy, self-awareness	to improve performance, to develop strengths

Source: based on Goleman (2000).

While coercion and pacesetting have their uses, the research showed that these styles can damage 'working atmosphere', reducing flexibility and employee commitment. The other four styles have a consistently positive impact on climate and performance. The most effective leaders, Goleman concludes, are those who have mastered four or more styles, particularly the positive styles, and who are able to switch styles to fit the situation. This is not a 'mechanical' matching of behaviour to context, as other contingency theories imply, but a flexible, sensitive, and seamless adjustment.

David Snowden and Mary Boone

David Snowden and Mary Boone (2007) also argue that leaders have to adjust their style to suit the context. Contexts vary in terms of how simple or complex they are. The *Cynefin* (pronounced ku-*nev*-in) framework identifies four types of context: simple, complicated, complex, and chaotic. Leaders can use this approach to determine how best to operate. *Cynefin* is a Welsh term that refers to the many factors in our environment. Simple and complicated contexts are ordered and predictable, and correct choices can be based on evidence. Complex and chaotic contexts are untidy and unpredictable, and decisions have to be based on emerging patterns. Effective leaders can change their styles to match the changing environment. This approach is summarized in Table 19.7.

Table 19.7: Context and leadership

Context	Characteristics	The leader's job
simple	repeating patterns, consistent events clear causal relationships; right answers known knowns fact-based management	sense, categorize, respond ensure processes are in place delegate; use best practices clear, direct communications; intensive interaction unnecessary
complicated	expert diagnosis required causal relationships discoverable; more than one right answer known unknowns fact-based management	sense, analyse, respond create panels of experts listen to conflicting advice
complex	flux and unpredictability no right answers; emergent patterns unknown unknowns many competing ideas; need for creativity and innovation pattern-based leadership	probe, sense, respond experiment, allow patterns to emerge increase interaction and communication use methods to generate ideas encourage dissent and diversity
chaotic	high turbulence no clear causal relationships, no point looking for right answers unknowables many decisions, no time to think high tension pattern-based leadership	act first, sense, respond look for what works, not for right answers immediate action to re-establish order (command and control) clear, direct communication

Being effective in one or two of these contexts is not good enough. Depending on the circumstances, a leader could be faced with all four contexts at the same time: a simple financial problem, a complicated product design issue, a complex threat from overseas competitors, and a serious accident. Snowden and Boone (2007, p. 75) conclude that 'Good leadership requires openness to change on an individual level. Truly adept leaders will know not only how to identify the context they're working in at any given time, but also how to change their behaviour and their decisions to match that context'.

Assessing contingency theories

Contingency theories argue that the most effective leadership style depends on the context. Organization structures, management skills, employee characteristics, and the nature of their tasks – all are unique. No one style of leadership is universally best. There is, however, a large body of research which suggests that a considerate, participative, or democratic style of leadership is generally more effective than a directive, autocratic style. There are two main reasons for this.

First, participative management is part of a long-term social and political trend in Western economies, which has raised expectations about personal freedom and quality of working life. These social and political values encourage resistance to manipulation by impersonal bureaucracies, and challenge the legitimacy of management decisions. Participation thus reflects democratic social and political values. Many commentators would note, however, that individual freedom, quality of working life, and genuine participation are still lacking in many organizations in different parts of the world.

Second, participative management has been encouraged by studies which have shown that this style is generally more effective, although an autocratic style can be effective in some contexts. A participative style can improve organizational effectiveness by tapping the ideas of those who have 'front-line' knowledge and experience, and by involving them in a decision-making process to which they then become committed. This approach is encouraged by the growth in numbers of knowledge workers who expect to be involved in decisions affecting their work, and whose knowledge makes them potentially valuable contributors in this respect.

People who are involved in setting standards or establishing methods are thus more likely to experience 'ownership' of such decisions, and are therefore more likely to

- accept the legitimacy of decisions reached with their help;
- accept change based on those decisions;
- trust managers who ultimately ratify and implement decisions;
- volunteer new and creative ideas and solutions.

Autocratic management stifles creativity, ignores available expertise, and smothers motivation and commitment. However, there is no doubt that autocratic management can be effective

- when time is short;
- when the leader is the most knowledgeable person;
- where those who could participate will never agree with each other on a decision - but a decision must be made.

Employee first, customer second: leadership lessons from India

Peter Cappelli and colleagues (2010a) argue that Indian companies have developed a new model of leadership, different in style and emphasis from leadership models commonly found in the West. The development of this new model dates from the early 1990s when economic reforms in India simplified the regulatory environment and exposed Indian companies to international competition. So where do the senior leaders of Indian companies today focus their energies? Their top four priorities are to be:

1. chief input for business strategy;
2. keeper of organization culture;
3. guide, teacher, and role model for employees;
4. representative of owner and investor interests.

Executives in the US and the UK would have to put short-term shareholder interests first, and not fourth, but leaders in India are more concerned with long-term investment in people:

> Far more than their Western counterparts, these leaders and their organizations take a long-term, internally focused view. They work to create a sense of social mission that is served when the business succeeds. They make aggressive investment in employee development, despite tight labour markets and widespread job-hopping. And they strive for a high level of employee engagement and openness. The higher priority these executives place on keeping the culture and guiding and teaching employees underscores their focus on human capital development. (Cappelli et al., 2010b, p. 92).

Cappelli and colleagues interviewed over 100 executives who explained the success of their companies in terms of employees' positive attitudes, which they sought to inspire in four main ways:

- *creating a sense of mission*: involvement in social issues, community services, and infrastructure; employees feel their work has an impact;
- *engagement through openness and reciprocity*: caring for employees and their families, 'employee first, customer second' policy;
- *empowering through communication*: inviting challenge and criticism, allowing employees to contribute to problem-solving, questioning traditional deference to hierarchy;
- *investing in training*: heavier investment in employee development than in Western countries (25 per cent of new hires in the US receive no training during their first two years; new hires in India typically receive at least 60 days of formal training in their first year).

The researchers argue that, while these policies are not novel, they are emphasized consistently in a coherent package which Western leaders could adapt to their own circumstances, particularly with regard to investment in training, and strengthening their social mission.

New leader an inspirational visionary, concerned with building a shared sense of purpose and mission, creating a culture in which everyone is aligned with the organization's goals and is skilled and empowered to achieve them.

Superleader a leader who is able to develop leadership capacity in others, empowering them, reducing their dependence on formal leaders, and stimulating their motivation, commitment, and creativity.

The contingency theories discussed so far have attracted some criticisms. One criticism concerns the ability of leaders to diagnose the context in which they are operating, given the vague nature of the situational variables identified by different theories. In addition, contingency theories often overlook other key dimensions of context, such as the organization culture, degree of change and levels of stress, working conditions, external economic factors, organizational design, and technology. All of these factors potentially influence the leadership process in ways not addressed by any of these theoretical accounts.

A second criticism concerns whether leaders can adapt their styles to fit the context in the ways the theories suggest. Personality may not be flexible enough. Some theorists argue that personality is inherited, inhibiting managers from being participative in some circumstances and dictatorial in others. The manager who is motivated by affiliation and who values the friendship of others may find it hard to treat employees in an impersonal and autocratic way.

A third criticism is that the expectations of other managers can influence what is 'acceptable'. There are advantages in consistency. The leader who changes style from one situation to another may not inspire confidence or trust. However, leaders should be able to adapt to their context:

1. It is now broadly accepted that leaders and managers can learn from experience to adjust their behaviour according to the circumstances.
2. Organizations are not rigid arrangements with fixed tasks and structures. With the growth in demand for flexibility, adaptability, improved quality of working life, and worker participation, leaders and managers who fail to respond will face problems.
3. The leader or manager who adapts in a flexible way to changes in circumstances may be seen as more competent than one who sticks rigidly to traditional routines.

New leadership

Transactional leader a leader who treats relationships with followers in terms of an exchange, giving followers what they want in return for what the leader desires, following prescribed tasks to pursue established goals.

Transformational leader a leader who treats relationships with followers in terms of motivation and commitment, influencing and inspiring followers to give more than mere compliance to improve organizational performance.

In the search for new ideas in the late twentieth century, the key role of heroic, powerful, visionary, charismatic leaders was recognized. Several new terms were invented to describe this role. We had the **new leader**, an inspirational figure motivating followers to higher levels of achievement. However, we also had the **superleader** who is able to 'lead others to lead themselves' (Sims and Lorenzi, 1992, p. 295). These terms clearly overlap, and are closely related to the popular and influential concept of transformational leadership.

Transformational leadership

The new leadership movement began with the work of James McGregor Burns (1978), whose study of political leaders distinguished between the **transactional leader** and the **transformational leader**. Transactional leaders see their relationships with followers in terms of trade, swaps, or bargains. Transformational leaders are charismatic individuals who inspire and motivate others to perform 'beyond contract'.

Noel Tichy and Mary Anne Devanna (1986) argue that transformational leaders have three main roles: recognizing the need for revitalization, creating a new vision, and institutionalizing change. Bernard Bass and Bruce Avolio (Bass, 1985a, 1985b; Bass and Avolio, 1990, 1994) similarly claim that transformational leadership involves 'the Four Is':

- Intellectual stimulation: encourage others to see what they are doing from new perspectives.
- Idealized influence: articulate the mission or vision of the organization.
- Individualized consideration: develop others to higher levels of ability.
- Inspirational motivation: motivate others to put organizational interests before self-interest.

Transformational chefs

Katharina Balazs (2001, 2002) argues that the *chefs de cuisine* who run the best restaurants in France are transformational leaders. The top rating of three stars in the *Guide Rouge Michelin* applies to only 30 restaurants in the world, and 22 of those are in France. Balazs interviewed these chefs and their staff, observed the preparation of meals in their kitchens, and spoke to customers, to find out how these chefs made their restaurants outstanding. The findings show that the leadership role of chefs combines two dimensions, *charismatic* and *architectural*.

Charismatic	
Visioning	providing a luxurious and extraordinary 'total dining experience' that delights customers
Empowering	giving staff a voice, showing confidence and trust, allowing staff to influence what they do, expecting high standards
Energizing	communicating vision, making staff feel part of something special, aiming for perfection, excitement, joy, passion in the work
Architectural	
Designing structure	small, organic structure with chef as 'superstar', team culture based on mutual support and collaboration
Controls	managing relationships with suppliers ('only the best is good enough'), controlling quality of the product
Rewards	offering recognition, personal growth and 'employability' in an context where pay is low, hours are long, and the work is intense

Balazs claims that a transformational leadership style works in other sectors where the starting point is an individual's creation, where implementation demands attention to detail, and where support staff are required. Those other sectors include film and theatre production, opera, fashion, and architecture.

The Transformational Leadership Questionnaire developed by Beverly Alimo-Metcalfe and John Alban-Metcalfe (2002, 2003) identifies fourteen behaviours (or competencies) in three categories:

Leading and developing others

- showing genuine concern
- empowering
- being accessible
- encouraging change

Personal qualities

- being transparent
- acting with integrity
- being decisive
- inspiring others
- resolving complex problems

Leading the organization

- networking and achieving
- focusing team effort
- building shared vision
- supporting a developmental culture
- facilitating change sensitively.

Research with public sector managers and employees suggests that these behaviours can increase job satisfaction and motivation, and reduce stress. Alimo-Metcalfe and Alban-Metcalfe also found that women were seen as more transformational than men on most of these behaviours, and were rated as better than men on being decisive, focusing effort, mentoring, managing change, inspiring others, and openness to ideas. Are these new labels a fresh development in leadership theory and practice? George Hollenbeck and colleagues (2006) argue that identifying the characteristics or competencies of transformational leaders takes us back to the 'great person' view of leadership and trait-spotting, overlooking what we know about the influence of context on leadership effectiveness.

STOP AND THINK

Considering business and political leaders with whom you are familiar, directly or through the media, which come closest to these definitions of new leader, superleader, and transformational leader?

The new, super, transformational leader looks like a 'one best way' approach. Does this vindicate trait-spotting and discredit contingency perspectives?

Distributed leadership

Distributed leadership the collective exercise of leadership behaviours, often informal and spontaneous, by staff at all levels of an organization.

Do we need visionary superheroes? Recent studies show how changes can be implemented by people at all levels of an organization. This is known as **distributed leadership**.

Leadership theory traditionally assumes that others will not act without 'strong and effective' leadership. We need leaders to generate the ideas and to provide the directions, the 'orders from above', which inspire followers, don't we? Peter Gronn (2002, 2009) contrasts this traditional idea of focused leadership, emphasizing the individual, with distributed leadership. Distributed leadership involves many people acting in concert, in formal and informal, spontaneous and intuitive roles (Bryman, 1996; Caldwell, 2005). These roles may not be permanent. Leadership functions can be shared. The leadership role can move from one person or group to another, as circumstances change. Leadership can thus involve role-sharing and turn-taking, rather than belonging to one person.

Distributed leadership is encouraged by flatter organization structures, teamwork, knowledge work, rapid developments in communication technology, and 'network' organization forms. In current turbulent economic conditions, many organizations are unstable and are evolving in novel ways. This often means creating new types of inter-organizational collaboration (see Chapter 17). The scale and complexity of these changes involve many more people, compared with change that only affects one part of an organization. These trends combine with the fashion for empowerment and engagement (see Chapter 9). Debra Meyerson (2001) highlights the importance of behind-the-scenes, 'below the radar' change leadership of middle managers. Joseph Badaracco (2002) describes a 'quiet approach to change leadership', emphasizing 'small things, careful moves, controlled and measured efforts'. In appropriate conditions, staff with motivation and capabilities can lead and implement change covertly, quietly, by stealth, just as effectively as 'celebrity bosses', but without destabilizing the organization and burning out colleagues in the process.

One of the problems with distributed leadership is that the capabilities and contributions of those who are involved may not be recognized. Sylvia Ann Hewlett and colleagues (2005) observe that members of ethnic minority groups, while holding junior posts in their organizations, often have major community leadership roles, with capabilities and talent that are neither recognized nor used by their main employer. These are the 'unsung heroes' who take personal responsibility, and risk, for driving change without always waiting patiently for others, or simply following directions.

David Buchanan and colleagues describe how complex changes to improve cancer services in a British hospital were implemented by a large number of people acting together to meet the same goals and targets, without formal change management plans, structures, or roles. Although four key people were involved at different stages, they were not senior managers, and the change process also involved 19 other individuals, and 26 managerial, administrative, and clinical groups, patients' representatives, and other organizations. Their contributions were informal and fluid, and complemented each other. The researchers note how responsibility for these changes 'migrated' around various groups and individuals. They conclude that implementing change with 'nobody in charge' can be just as effective as traditional change methods (Buchanan et al., 2007). This approach is not dependent on individuals or small teams, and survives the departure of the lone change agent.

In the distinction between leadership and management, orientation to change is a distinctive 'mark of the leader' (Zaleznik, 1977). These examples suggest that leadership is a widely distributed phenomenon. Leadership functions are best carried out by those who have the interest, knowledge, skills, and motivation to perform them effectively. This observation is reinforced by the development of self-managing teams which often have no formal leaders, or which have 'coach-facilitators' whose role is to develop team members' skills.

Leadership qualities: acting the part

It is not enough to be an innovative, visionary, strategic thinker to qualify as a leader. You also need visible qualities such as confidence, and the ability to communicate clearly (James, 2003).

1. **Get out and about.** Introduce yourself to other departments. Network until you drop. Speak up at meetings. Sit in the front row at presentations. Volunteer for high-profile tasks, such as chairing events, meeting clients, and giving presentations.
2. **Allow yourself to shine.** Deliver clear, positive, and inspirational messages with enthusiasm. Delete the whingeing, moaning, and waffling.
3. **Make a great entrance.** You have three seconds in which to make a first impression. Do not walk into the room with the stress of the journey on your face. Take a moment to compose yourself. Breathe, straighten up, relax your face. Carry your case in your left hand to leave your right hand free for greetings.
4. **Walk with confidence and energy.** Never loiter or lurk. Wear a focused expression. Always greet colleagues in passing, even if they don't respond.
5. **Listen.** Appear to have time for other people. Active listening makes you appear charming and in touch. Face the speaker with eye contact. Pace your nods to match the energy of their words. Do not speed up or it will look like you are interrupting.
6. **Mingle.** Choose your group or individual and approach them with energy. Use body language to mirror the group mood while waiting your turn to speak. Introduce issues relevant to the conversation, or ask a question. Do not sound aggressive or opinionated. If necessary, follow your comment with a quick, audible introduction.
7. **Offer a good handshake.** Avoid the 'dead fish' and the 'bone cruncher'. Firm, dry palm, look the other person in the eye, smile with your eyes as well as your mouth.
8. **Never fiddle.** Do not play with jewellery, pens, spectacles, or paper clips. This is called 'leakage', and signals anxiety which distracts the listener and can suggest incompetence.
9. **Use open gestures.** Folded arms makes you look uncomfortable and negative. Use gestures that emphasize key messages.
10. **Dress the part.** Whatever the corporate culture, always appear well groomed. Use only one or two colours at a time. Choose high contrasts for a high-status appearance. Look like a leader.

Recognition of distributed leadership does not imply a complete shift of focus away from formal, senior figures with prestige titles who continue to exercise leadership roles and functions as well. We need a 'twin track' approach in which visionary individual leaders, and a widely dispersed leadership decoupled from high office, work together. New leaders are not dictators, or charismatic figures. Their emphasis lies with the 'soft' skills of enthusing and inspiring, of coaching and facilitating.

Many commentators argue that a hostile, rapidly changing competitive climate, and pressured conditions of work, require participative, visionary and inspirational styles of leadership. An autocratic, task-oriented style encourages little more than compliance with directions. The new, transformational superleader, in contrast, encourages commitment, initiative, flexibility, and high performance. The behaviour of new leaders also seems appropriate to the motivation of knowledge workers and the development of learning organizations. The new leadership concept thus draws together the main strands of twentieth-century thinking:

The theory	The new transformational superleader
Trait-spotting	must have the right personality, appearance, attributes, voice.
Style-counselling	must be caring, inspirational and visionary, ethical, risk-taker.
Context-fitting	style is consistent with a hostile and rapidly changing environment, with the need to develop flexible organizational forms, with the need to motivate knowledge workers and develop a learning organization.

Who needs leaders?

Throughout the twentieth century, it was unquestioningly accepted that leadership was indispensable. A novel perspective emerged in the opening years of the twenty-first century, challenging the enthusiasm for charismatic, visionary, transactional superleaders. Here is a perspective which argues that some leaders are *dangerous*.

Nick Morgan (2001, p. 3) is critical of 'larger-than-life leaders and their grand strategies', arguing for 'a quieter, more evolutionary approach to change, one that relies on employee motivation instead of directives from on high'. He argues that organizations should reduce the amount of change, focus instead on incremental improvements, and 'above all lose the notion that you need heroic leaders in order to have meaningful, sustained change' (p. 2). This is consistent with views explored in Chapter 18 on organizational change, and particularly with Eric Abrahamson's (2004) approach to 'painless change' which is carefully staged and paced.

Quy Huy (2001) also dismisses the role of visionary leadership, arguing that it is middle managers who achieve the balance between change and continuity, and that radical change imposed from the top makes this difficult. Jim Collins (2001) argues that 'larger than life' leaders are not always effective, and that the most powerful senior executives display what he calls 'level 5 leadership', combining humility with persistence. We have already met Meyerson's (2001) 'tempered radicals' who operate 'below the radar', and Badaracco's (2002) 'unglamorous, not heroic, quiet approach to leadership'. It is important to pay attention to these 'non-leadership' contributions to organizational change.

Rakesh Khurana (2002, p. 62) is scathing in his assessment of transformational leaders. The popular stereotype concerns the charismatic individual who wins the confidence of investors and the business press, inspires and motivates employees, defeats overwhelming competition, and turns around dying companies. This is the white knight, the lone ranger, the heroic figure, and these images are exhilarating. Khurana offers four criticisms of such figures:

1. They 'reject limits to their scope and authority [and] rebel against all checks on their power and dismiss the norms and rules that apply to others'. In other words, they can be beyond the influence and control of other senior colleagues.
2. They rely on 'the widespread quasi-religious belief in the powers of charismatic leaders'. This belief allows them to 'exploit the irrational desires of their followers'.
3. They encourage the attribution error of understanding success in terms of the actions of prominent leaders, while overlooking 'the interplay of social, economic, and other impersonal forces that shape and constrain even the most heroic individual efforts'.
4. New chief executives often deliberately destabilize their organizations, to foster revitalization. However, this can be harmful, if not disastrous, as a number of corporate scandals in the early twenty-first century illustrated.

Vicious circles of redisorganization

This quote is taken from a 'joke' research article in a medical journal, illustrating the cynicism that many people feel about the impact of 'new leaders' (Oxman et al., 2005).

> New leaders typically take up their posts intoxicated with the prospect of transformation and radical revision. This triggers an avalanche of constant and hectic activity. Repeated redisorganizations result in exhausted managers who rush from one meeting to another with no time to step back and reflect. By the time the organization decides to saddle somebody with the blame for the resulting chaos, the leader has left to foul up some other organization. The end result is a perpetual cycle of redisorganization. While all new leaders feel compelled to redisorganize, it is nonetheless possible to distinguish among several breeds of leaders based on their canine redisorganization behaviour:
>
> *Mutts* — the most common type of leader: self-focused, with a need to piss all over everything to mark territory
>
> *Bulldogs* — well meaning, but incompetent, and dangerous when aroused
>
> *German shepherds* — bureaucratic, commonly suffer from anal retentiveness, which makes them irritable
>
> *Poodles* — ideological, focused on a specific peculiar aim derived from a specific peculiar way of looking at the world, to the exclusion of empirical evidence, practical experience, and common sense.
>
> These four breeds display, to varying degrees, the eight 'secrets of success': meet a lot, sniff a lot (yes, they can smell fear), talk a lot, listen infrequently, change a lot, delegate (particularly responsibility without authority), disappear, and move on.

Khurana thus regards the transformational leader as a 'dangerous curse'. This backlash against 'new leaders' has two interesting dimensions:

- The combined views of Morgan, Huy, Collins, Meyerson, Badaracco and Khurana take the debate back to the distinction between leadership and management. We saw that, crudely, there is a perspective which argues 'leadership is good – management is bad'. Now this argument is reversed, with the argument that leaders can be dangerously destabilizing while managers effectively drive change.
- In this approach, effective change depends on competent managers with change agency skills, and not on heroic visionaries with charismatic personalities.

Seven failures of really useless leaders

What really useless leaders do	How they do it	How to avoid the same trap
1. kill enthusiasm	micromanagement, coercion, and disrespect	try better delegation and informal feedback, plus better, easier appraisal
2. kill emotion	aggression, lack of emotional intelligence, lack of empathy, no work-life balance	publish a personal work-life balance manifesto; develop greater empathy; encourage assertiveness
3. kill explanation	partial, inconsistent communication	make communication consistent, clear, two-way
4. kill engagement	individual objectives dictated by managers; limited team goals	allow teams to set their own goals; encourage participation in decision-making
5. kill reward	rewarding the wrong things and offering the wrong sort of reward (e.g., money for someone not motivated by money)	give the right rewards to the right people at the right time; establish team rewards; give managers flexibility in rewarding staff
6. kill culture	ignoring the differences in cultures during mergers and acquisitions; punishing risk-taking while trying to introduce a culture of innovation	offer training for managers on influencing culture; allow managers to evolve their own personal mistakes policy
7. kill trust	unfair recruitment or reward decisions	offer training for managers in procedural justice and fairness; help managers to develop trust in others

Source: Moore, J. and Sonsino, S. (2007) *The Seven Failings of Really Useless Leaders*, MSL Publishing, London.

RECAP

1. *Explain the apparent difference between the concepts of leadership and management.*
   - Leaders are typically portrayed as inspiring, change-oriented visionaries.
   - Managers are typically portrayed as planners, organizers, and controllers.
   - In practice, the roles overlap, are complementary, and can be difficult to distinguish.
2. *Understand why there is little relationship between personality traits and effective leadership.*
   - Many factors besides personality traits influence leadership effectiveness.
   - It has proved difficult to establish a consensus on specific traits.
   - The characteristics of the leader's role also influence behaviour and effectiveness.
3. *Understand the challenges facing women who aspire to leadership roles, and the social and business cases for 'boardroom diversity'.*
   - Women are traditionally powerless due to discrimination and exclusion by male behaviour.
   - Women have social and interpersonal leadership qualities, improve performance by widening management discussions, and are now more likely to be promoted on merit.
   - Board gender-diversity is seen in many countries as socially desirable for equality reasons, and there is evidence suggesting that board diversity is positively linked to corporate performance.
4. *Understand why effective leaders either adapt their style to fit the organizational and cultural context in which they operate, or else find contexts which fit their personal style.*
   - Considerate behaviour reduces labour turnover and improves job satisfaction.
   - Initiating structure improves performance but reduces job satisfaction.
   - Effective leaders combine consideration with initiating structure.
   - Contingency theory argues that leaders are more or less effective depending on how structured the task is, how powerful the leader is, and how good the relationships are.
   - Situational leadership advises the manager to use telling, selling, participating, and delegating styles depending on the task, relationships, and employee readiness.
   - Some commentators argue that leaders cannot change their behaviour, and that to be effective they have to find organizational contexts that are suitable for their leadership style.
   - Most commentators argue that leaders can and should adapt their behaviour to fit the context and the culture in which they are operating.
5. *Explain contemporary trends in this field concerning new leadership, distributed leadership, and the argument that leaders are unnecessary.*
   - One trend emphasized charismatic, visionary, inspirational new leaders.
   - New leadership, superleader, and transformational leadership are close synonyms.
   - Distributed leadership can be observed at all organizational levels.
   - The new visionary leader helps to develop leadership capability in others.
   - The new leader has the right traits, and the right style, for the contemporary context, thus combining notions of trait-spotting, style-counselling, and context-fitting.
   - A more recent trend views charismatic, visionary leaders as dangerous because they can destabilize an organization; change management capabilities are more important.

Revision

1. What is the difference between leadership and management, and why is it difficult to separate these concepts in practice?
2. Why is trait-spotting such a popular theme in leadership research? What has trait-spotting told us about the personality markers of successful leaders? What are the problems with this perspective?
3. Leaders are, traditionally, men with special qualities. Why are women now more likely to be considered as effective leaders?
4. The concept of transformational leadership is popular. What advantages and drawbacks come with this leadership style?

Research assignment

Choose one of the massively multiplayer online role-playing games (MMORPGs). Examples include *World of Warcraft*, *Eve Online*, *EverQuest*, *Lineage*, and *Star Wars Galaxies*. What leadership skills are likely to be developed by players of these games? How are those skills relevant to the way that organizations operate and are managed today? Option one: reflect on and note your answers to these questions as you play one of these games yourself. Option two: observe in action and question someone that you know who plays one of these games. Prepare a report that describes how, by playing MMORPGs, you can develop skills that contribute to your employability. (This assignment is based on research by Reeves et al., 2008).

Springboard

S. Alexander Haslam, Stephen D. Reicher and Michael J. Platow (2010) *The New Psychology of Leadership: Identity, Influence and Power*, Psychology Press, New York and Hove. Argues that charisma is not an attribute of a leader, but an attribution made by followers. Successful leaders are those who can capture and champion the identity of the group to which they belong, and whose interests they advance.

Brad Jackson and Ken Parry (2011) *A Very Short, Fairly Interesting and Reasonably Cheap Book about Studying Leadership* (2nd edn), Sage Publications, London. Short, entertaining, critical, and challenging, contrasting a wide range of perspectives on leadership.

Barbara Kellerman (2004) *Bad Leadership: What It Is, How It Happens, Why It Matters*, Harvard Business School Press, Boston, MA. Argues that 'the dark side' of leadership is widespread, and develops a typology of bad leadership types: incompetent, rigid, intemperate, callous, corrupt, insular, and evil. Also illustrates how followers can encourage bad leaders.

Peninah Thomson and Tom Lloyd (2011) *Women and the New Business Leadership*, Palgrave Macmillan, London. Suggests that recent failures in corporate governance would have been less likely to happen if companies had more women on their boards of directors. Offers practical advice for developing gender-diverse boards, including cross-company mentoring.

OB in films

The Devil Wears Prada (2006, director David Frankel), DVD track 2: 0:03:20 to 0:09:47 (7 minutes). Track 2 begins with Andy coming out of the lift and heading for the office reception desk; clip ends when she is called back into the office as she is walking away.

Based on the novel by Lauren Weisberger, this movie tells the story of a naive young aspiring journalist, Andrea (Andy) Sachs (played by Anne Hathaway), who gets a job as assistant to the famous editor-in-chief of the fashion magazine *Runway*. The magazine's powerful and ruthless editor, Miranda Priestly (Meryl Streep) is a legend. In this clip, we see Andy arriving for her job interview as 'second assistant' with Miranda's 'first assistant' Emily Charlton (Emily Blunt). Miranda, however, decides to conduct the interview herself.

1. How would you describe Miranda Priestley's leadership style?
   Identify specific behaviours to support your conclusions.
2. What impact does Miranda's leadership style have on those around her?
   Identify specific employee behaviours to support your conclusions.
3. Good boss or bad boss: what is your assessment of this leadership style?
   Cite specific evidence of her impact on individual performance and organizational effectiveness to support your judgement.
4. To what extent does this leadership style apply in the real world, beyond Hollywood?
   Consider aspects of individual personality, organizational context, and industry sector in making this judgement.
5. Why do you think Miranda Priestly gave Andy the job?

OB on the web

Many individuals are described as leaders because they are *charismatic*. (We will explore referent power – the power of the charismatic personality – in Chapter 22.) We tend to think of charisma as something which some people just have, and others do not. However, can you learn how to be charismatic? Olivia Fox Cabane (2012) is an executive coach who specializes in 'high potential leadership', and who teaches charisma to executives. Search for her name on YouTube, and find her presentation on 'The science of first impressions'. Having watched her presentation, what is your assessment? Could you learn to be more charismatic? How would this contribute to your employability and to your career? For further suggestions on the tactics that you can use in order to develop your charisma, see Antonakis et al. (2012).

CHAPTER EXERCISES

1. Management and leadership

Objectives

1. To explore differences in the definition of the terms management and leadership.
2. To consider whether and how our understanding and use of these terms is changing.

Briefing

Are leadership and management different roles, or do they overlap? Look at this list of activities. Are these leadership activities, or management activities, or could they fall into both categories? Use the activities matrix (based on Gillen, 2004) to locate each of those activities depending on whether you feel they are management-oriented, leadership-oriented, or both.

Activities list

1. delegate tasks
2. plan and prioritize steps to achieve task goals
3. ensure predictability
4. coordinate effort
5. provide focus
6. monitor feelings and morale
7. follow systems and procedures
8. provide development opportunities
9. monitor progress
10. appeal to rational thinking
11. act as interface between team and others
12. motivate staff
13. inspire people
14. coordinate resources
15. give orders and instructions
16. check task completion
17. ensure effective induction
18. unleash potential
19. look 'over the horizon'
20. be a good role model
21. use analytical data to support recommendations
22. explain goals, plans, and roles
23. appeal to people's emotions
24. share a vision
25. guide progress
26. create a positive team feeling
27. monitor budgets and tasks
28. use analytical data to forecast trends
29. take risks
30. build teams

→

Activities matrix

managerially oriented	elements of management and leadership	leadership oriented

Class discussion

Consider why you placed each of those activities in those categories.

1. What makes an activity a management activity?
2. What is distinctive about leadership activities?
3. If you put some activities in the middle, why did you do that?
4. Are there any current trends and developments which encourage managers to monitor and control rather than to exercise leadership?

2. Leadership style preferences

Objectives

1. To assess your preferred leadership style.
2. To explore the diversity of style preferences across your group.

Briefing

This assessment (based on Marcic, 1992) is designed to help you assess your preferred leadership style. Complete this questionnaire honestly, in relation to your behaviour and preferences, with respect to your leadership behaviour, or in relation to how you think you would like to behave in a leadership role. Put a tick in the appropriate response column on the right depending on how accurately you feel each statement describes your behavioural preferences, using this scale:

A = Always	**B** = Often	**C** = Sometimes	**D** = Seldom	**E** = Never.

Leader behaviours	A	B	C	D	E
1. I would always act as the spokesperson for my group.	❒	❒	❒	❒	❒
2. I would allow subordinates complete freedom in their work.	❒	❒	❒	❒	❒
3. I would encourage overtime working.	❒	❒	❒	❒	❒
4. I would let subordinates use their judgement to solve problems.	❒	❒	❒	❒	❒
5. I would encourage the use of standard procedures.	❒	❒	❒	❒	❒
6. I would needle members for greater effort.	❒	❒	❒	❒	❒
7. I would stress being ahead of competing groups.	❒	❒	❒	❒	❒
8. I would let subordinates work the way they thought best.	❒	❒	❒	❒	❒
9. I would speak as representative for subordinates.	❒	❒	❒	❒	❒
10. I would be able to tolerate postponement and uncertainty.	❒	❒	❒	❒	❒
11. I would try out my ideas on subordinates.	❒	❒	❒	❒	❒
12. I would turn subordinates loose on a job and let them go at it.	❒	❒	❒	❒	❒
13. I would work hard for promotion.	❒	❒	❒	❒	❒
14. I would get swamped by details.	❒	❒	❒	❒	❒
15. I would speak for subordinates when visitors were around.	❒	❒	❒	❒	❒
16. I would be reluctant to let subordinates have freedom of action.	❒	❒	❒	❒	❒
17. I would keep the work pace moving rapidly.	❒	❒	❒	❒	❒
18. I would give some subordinates authority that I should keep.	❒	❒	❒	❒	❒
19. I would settle conflicts which occur among subordinates.	❒	❒	❒	❒	❒
20. I would let subordinates have a high degree of initiative.	❒	❒	❒	❒	❒
21. I would represent subordinates at external meetings.	❒	❒	❒	❒	❒
22. I would be willing to make changes.	❒	❒	❒	❒	❒
23. I would decide what will be done and how it will be done.	❒	❒	❒	❒	❒
24. I would trust subordinates to exercise good judgement.	❒	❒	❒	❒	❒
25. I would push for increased production.	❒	❒	❒	❒	❒
26. I would refuse to explain my actions to subordinates.	❒	❒	❒	❒	❒
27. Things usually turn out as I predict.	❒	❒	❒	❒	❒
28. I would let subordinates set their own work pace.	❒	❒	❒	❒	❒
29. I would assign subordinates to specific tasks.	❒	❒	❒	❒	❒
30. I would be able to act without consulting subordinates.	❒	❒	❒	❒	❒
31. I would ask subordinates to work harder.	❒	❒	❒	❒	❒
32. I would schedule the work that had to be done.	❒	❒	❒	❒	❒
33. I would persuade others that my ideas were to their advantage.	❒	❒	❒	❒	❒
34. I would urge subordinates to beat their previous records.	❒	❒	❒	❒	❒
35. I would expect subordinates to follow set rules and regulations.	❒	❒	❒	❒	❒

→

Scoring

Employee-centred or consideration score

You get one point if you ticked either A or a B in response to these questions:

2 ______	10 ______	22 ______
4 ______	12 ______	24 ______
6 ______	18 ______	28 ______
8 ______	20 ______	

And you get one point if you ticked either D or E in response to these questions:

14 ______ 16 ______ 26 ______ 30 ______

Total employee-centred score is: ______

Job-centred or initiating structure score

You get one point if you ticked either A or B in response to these questions:

1 ______	13 ______	25 ______	34 ______
3 ______	15 ______	27 ______	35 ______
5 ______	17 ______	29 ______	
7 ______	19 ______	31 ______	
9 ______	21 ______	32 ______	
11 ______	23 ______	33 ______	

Total job-centred score is: ______

Your two scores can be interpreted together as follows:

Employee-centred score	Job-centred score	Your leadership style
0–7	0–10	you are not involved enough with either the work or with your employees
0–7	10–20	you are autocratic, a bit of a slave-driver; you get the job done but at an emotional cost
8–15	0–10	people are happy in their work but sometimes at the expense of productivity
8–15	10–20	people enjoy working for you and are productive, naturally expending energy because they get positive reinforcement for good work

Source: from Marcic. *Organizational Behavior*, 3E. © 1992 South-Western, a part of Cengage Learning, Inc. Reproduced by permission. www.cengage.com/permissions

Employability assessment

With regard to your future employment prospects:

1. Identify up to three issues from this chapter that you found significant.
2. Relate these to the competencies in the employability matrix.
3. Decide what actions you need to take to maintain and/or develop those competencies under each of the four headings of the employability matrix.

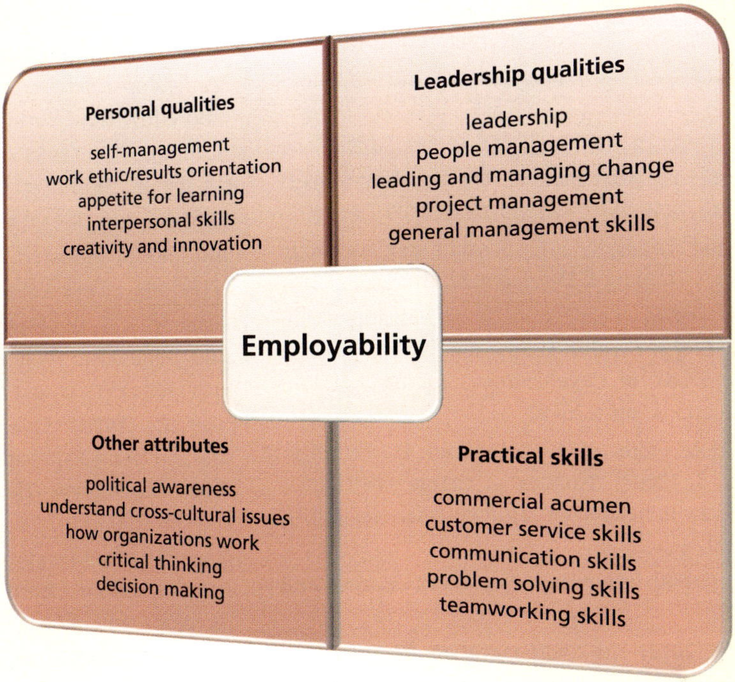

References

Abrahamson, E. (2004) *Change without Pain: How Managers Can Overcome Initiative Overload, Organizational Chaos, and Employee Burnout*, Boston, MA: Harvard Business School Press.

Alimo-Metcalfe, B. and Alban-Metcalfe, J. (2002) 'The great and the good', *People Management*, 8(11), pp. 32–4.

Alimo-Metcalfe, B. and Alban-Metcalfe, J. (2003) 'Under the influence', *People Management*, 9(5), pp. 32–5.

Alimo-Metcalfe, B. and Alban-Metcalfe, J. (2010) 'Leadership: commitment beats control', *Health Service Journal*, 22 February, p. 7.

Alimo-Metcalfe, B. and Bradley, M. (2008) 'Cast in a new light', *People Management*, 14(2), pp. 38–41.

Antonakis, J., Fenley, M. and Liechti, S. (2012) 'Learning charisma', *Harvard Business Review*, 90(6), pp. 127–30.

Babcock, L. and Laschever, S. (2003) *Women Don't Ask: Negotiation and the Gender Divide*, Princeton, NJ: Princeton University Press.

Badaracco, J.L. (2002) *Leading Quietly: An Unorthodox Guide to Doing the Right Thing*, Boston, MA: Harvard Business School Press.

Balazs, K. (2001) 'Some like it haute: leadership lessons from France's great chefs', *Organizational Dynamics*, 30(2), pp. 134–48.

Balazs, K. (2002) 'Take one entrepreneur: the recipe for success of France's great chefs', *European Management Journal*, 20(3), pp. 247–59.

Barton, D., Grant, A. and Horn, M. (2012) 'Leading in the 21st century', *McKinsey Quarterly*, June, pp. 1–17.

Bass, B.M. (1985a) *Bass and Stogdill's Handbook of Leadership: Theory, Research and Managerial Applications* (3rd edn), New York: Free Press.

Bass, B.M. (1985b) *Leadership and Performance Beyond Expectations*, New York: Free Press.

Bass, B.M. and Avolio, B.J. (1990) 'The implications of transactional and transformational leadership for individual, team and organizational development', *Research and Organizational Change and Development*, 4, pp. 321–72.

Bass, B.M. and Avolio, B.J. (1994) *Improving Organizational Effectiveness through Transformational Leadership*, Thousand Oaks, CA: Sage Publications.

Bennis, W.G. and Nanus, B. (1985) *Leaders: The Strategies for Taking Charge*, New York: Harper and Row.

Bird, C. (1940) *Social Psychology*, New York: Appleton-Century.

Birkinshaw, J. (2010) *Reinventing Management: Smarter Choices for Getting Work Done*, Chichester, West Sussex: Jossey-Bass.

Boatman, J. and Wellins, R. (2011) 'It's time for a leadership (r)evolution', *Training & Development*, April, pp. 52–8.

Bryman, A. (1996) 'Leadership in organizations', in Stewart R. Clegg, Cynthia Hardy and Walter R. Nord (eds), *Handbook of Organization Studies*, London: Sage Publications, pp. 276–92.

Buchanan, D.A., Addicott, R., Fitzgerald, L., Ferlie, E. and Baeza, J. (2007) 'Nobody in charge: distributed change agency in healthcare', *Human Relations*, 60(7), pp. 1065–90.

Burns, J.M. (1978) *Leadership*, New York: Harper and Row.

Cabane, O.F. (2012) *The Charisma Myth: How Anyone Can Master the Art and Science of Personal Magnetism*, New York: Portfolio/Penguin.

Caldwell, R. (2005) *Agency and Change: Rethinking Change Agency in Organizations*, Abingdon: Routledge.

Cannell, M. (2008) *Leadership: An Overview*. London: Chartered Institute of Personnel and Development.

Cappelli, P., Singh, H., Singh, J.V. and Useem, M. (2010a) 'The India way: lessons for the US', *Academy of Management Perspectives*, 24(2), pp. 6–24.

Cappelli, P., Singh, H., Singh, J.V. and Useem, M. (2010b) 'Leadership lessons from India', *Harvard Business Review*, 88(2), pp. 90–7.

Charter, D. (2012) 'A gentle touch in the boardroom? Don't bet on it', *The Times*, 28 March, p. 37.

Clegg, A. (2012) 'The new girls network', *People Management*, April, pp. 22–9.

Collins, J. (2001) *Good to Great: Why Some Companies Make the Leap and Others Don't*, New York: Harper Collins.

Devillard, S., Graven, W., Lawson, E., Paradise, R. and Sancier-Sultan, S. (2012) *Women Matter 2012: Making the Breakthrough*, London: McKinsey & Company.

Dixon, N.F. (1994) *On The Psychology of Military Incompetence*, London: Pimlico.

Eagly, A.H. and Carli, L.L. (2007) 'Women and the labyrinth of leadership', *Harvard Business Review*, 85(9), pp. 62–71.

Ernst & Young (2012) *The Glass Ceiling Is an Outdated Concept*, London: Ernst & Young.

Fiedler, F.E. (1967) *A Theory of Leadership Effectiveness*, New York: McGraw-Hill.

Fiedler, F.E. and Chemers, M.M. (1974) *Leadership and Effective Management*, Glenview IL: Scott, Foresman.

Fiedler, F.E. and Chemers, M.M. (1984) *Improving Leadership Effectiveness: The Leaders Match Concept* (2nd edn), New York: John Wiley.

Fleishman, E.A. (1953a) 'The description of supervisory behaviour', *Journal of Applied Psychology*, 37(1), pp. 1–6.

Fleishman, E.A. (1953b) 'The measurement of leadership attitudes in industry', *Journal of Applied Psychology*, 37(3), pp. 153–8.

Fleishman, E.A. and Harris, E.F. (1962) 'Patterns of leadership behaviour related to employee grievances and turnover', *Personnel Psychology*, 15(1), pp. 43–56.

Fraser, C. (1978) 'Small groups: structure and leadership', in Henri Tajfel and Colin Fraser (eds), *Introducing Social Psychology*, Harmondsworth: Penguin Books, pp. 176–200.

Gillen, T. (2004) *Leadership or Management: The Differences*, London: Chartered Institute of Personnel and Development.

Goleman, D. (2000) 'Leadership that gets results', *Harvard Business Review*, 78(2), pp. 78–90.

Goodwin, D. (2011) 'We're too harsh on the bitchy bosses', *The Sunday Times*, 27 March, News Review section, p. 4.

Gronn, P. (2002) 'Distributed leadership as a unit of analysis', *Leadership Quarterly*, 13(4), pp. 423–51.

Gronn, P. (2009) 'Leadership configurations', *Leadership*, 5(3), pp. 381–94.

Heller, F. (1997) 'Leadership', in Arndt Sorge and Malcolm Warner (eds), *The Handbook of Organizational Behaviour*, London: International Thomson, pp. 340–9.

Hersey, P. and Blanchard, K.H. (1988) *Management of Organizational Behavior: Utilizing Human Resources*. Englewood Cliffs, NJ: Prentice-Hall International.

Hewlett, S.A. (2002) 'Executive women and the myth of having it all', *Harvard Business Review*, 80(4), pp. 66–73.

Hewlett, S.A., Luce, C.B. and West, C. (2005) 'Leadership in your midst: tapping the hidden strengths of minority executives', *Harvard Business Review*, 83(11), pp. 74–82.

Hollenbeck, G.P., McCall Jnr, M.W. and Silzer, R.F. (2006) 'Leadership competency models', *Leadership Quarterly*, 17(4), pp. 398–413.

Huy, Q.N. (2001) 'In praise of middle managers', *Harvard Business Review*, 79(8), pp. 72–9.

James, J. (2003) 'You've got the look', *People Management*, 9(7), pp. 46–7.

Katz, D., Maccoby, N. and Morse, N.C. (1950) *Productivity, Supervision, and Morale in an Office Situation*, Ann Arbor, MI: University of Michigan Institute for Social Research.

Khurana, R. (2002) 'The curse of the superstar CEO', *Harvard Business Review*, 80(9), pp. 60–6.

Konrad, A.M. and Kramer, V.W. (2006) 'How many women do boards need?', *Harvard Business Review*, 84(12), p. 22.

Kotter, J.P. (1990) *A Force for Change: How Leadership Differs from Management*, New York: Free Press.

Kramer, R.M. (2006) 'The great intimidators', *Harvard Business Review*, 84(2), pp. 88–96.

Likert, R. (1961) *New Patterns of Management*, New York: McGraw-Hill.

Ludeman, K. and Erlandson, E. (2006) *Alpha Male Syndrome: Curb the Belligerence, Channel the Brilliance*, Boston, MA: Harvard Business School Press.

Marcic, D. (1992) *Organizational Behavior: Experiences and Cases* (3rd edn), St. Paul, MN: West Publishing.

Meyerson, D.E. (2001) *Tempered Radicals: How People Use Difference to Inspire Change at Work*, Boston, MA: Harvard Business School Press.

Mintzberg, H. (2009) *Managing*, Harlow, Essex: Financial Times Prentice Hall.

Morgan, N. (2001) 'How to overcome "change fatigue"', *Harvard Management Update*, July, pp. 1–3.

Oxman, A.D., Sackett, D.L., Chalmers, I. and Prescott, T.E. (2005) 'A surrealistic mega-analysis of redisorganization theories', *Journal of the Royal Society of Medicine*, 98(12), pp. 563–8.

Parry, K.W. and Bryman, A. (2006) 'Leadership in organizations', in Stewart R. Clegg, Cynthia Hardy, Tom Lawrence and Walter R. Nord (eds), *The Sage Handbook of Organization Studies* (2nd edn), London: Sage Publications.

Pinker, S. (2008) *The Sexual Paradox: Troubled Boys, Gifted Girls, and the Real Difference between the Sexes*, London: Atlantic Books.

Rees, D. (2004) *Women in the Boardroom: A Bird's Eye View*, London: Chartered Institute of Personnel and Development.

Reeves, B., Malone, T.W. and O'Driscoll, T. (2008) 'Leadership's online labs', *Harvard Business Review*, 86(5), pp. 58–66.

Rushe, D. (2006) 'Alpha males can make and break a business', *The Sunday Times*, 3 September, Business Section, p. 11.

Ryan, M.K. and Haslam, S.A. (2005) 'The glass cliff: evidence that women are over-represented in precarious leadership positions', *British Journal of Management*, 16(2), pp. 81–90.

Ryan, M.K. and Haslam, S.A. (2007) 'The glass cliff: exploring the dynamics surrounding the appointment of women to precarious leadership positions', *Academy of Management Review*, 32(2), pp. 549–72.

Sauer, S.J. (2012) 'When bossy is better for rookie managers', *Harvard Business Review*, 90(5), p. 30.

Shaw, M.E. (1976) *Group Dynamics* (2nd edn), New York: McGraw-Hill.

Sims, H.P. and Lorenzi, P. (1992) *The New Leadership Paradigm*, Newbury Park, CA: Sage Publications.

Snowden, D.J. and Boone, M.E. (2007) 'A leader's framework for decision making', *Harvard Business Review*, 85(11), pp. 69–76.

Sonsino, S. (2007) 'It's the fault that counts', *People Management*, 13(1), pp. 37–8.

Spence, A. (2011) 'Women climb the first rung of the ladder towards equality in pay', *The Times*, 31 August, pp. 32–3.

Stogdill, R.M. (1948) 'Personal factors associated with leadership', *Journal of Psychology*, 25, pp. 35–71.

Stogdill, R.M. (1950) 'Leadership, membership and organization', *Psychological Bulletin*, 47(1), pp. 1–14.

Stogdill, R.M. (1974) *Handbook of Leadership: A Survey of Theory and Research*, New York: Free Press.

Stogdill, R.M. and Coons, A.E. (eds) (1951) *Leader Behaviour: Its Description and Measurement, Research Monograph No. 88*, Columbus, OH: Ohio State University Bureau of Business Research.

Tannen, D. (1995) 'The power of talk: who gets heard and why', *Harvard Business Review*, 73(5), pp. 138–48.

Tannenbaum, R. and Schmidt, W.H. (1958) 'How to choose a leadership pattern', *Harvard Business Review*, 36(2), pp. 95–102 (reprinted in May–June 1973).

The Economist (2011) 'Schumpeter: the daughter also rises', 27 August, p. 60.

Tichy, N.M. and Devanna, M.A. (1986) *The Transformational Leader*, New York: Wiley.

Vinnicombe, S. and Sealy, R. (2012) *The Female FTSE Board Report 2012*, Cranfield School of Management, Cranfield.

Webb, M.S. (2006) 'Why boys get better gifts – and higher salaries', *The Sunday Times*, 1 January, Money, Section 3, p. 9.

Wilson, F. (2002) *Organizational Behaviour and Gender* (2nd edn), Aldershot: Ashgate.

Woolley, A. and Malone, T. (2011) 'What makes a team smarter? More women', *Harvard Business Review*, 89(6), pp. 32–3.

Zaleznik, A. (1977) 'Managers and leaders: are they different?', *Harvard Business Review*, 15(3), pp. 67–84.

Chapter 20 **Decision-making**

Key terms

decision-making
classical decision theory
rational model of decision-making
rationality
rational decisions
descriptive models of decision-making
behavioural theory of decision-making
bounded rationality
maximizing
satisficing
prescriptive model of decision-making
explanatory model of decision-making
heuristic
bias
certainty
risk
uncertainty
routine decisions
adaptive decisions
innovative decisions
group polarization
risky shift phenomenon
caution shift phenomenon
groupthink
brainstorming
escalation of commitment
evidence-based decision-making
decision-based evidence-making

Learning outcomes

When you have read this chapter, you should be able to define those key terms in your own words, and you should also be able to:

1. Distinguish between prescriptive, descriptive, and explanatory models of decision-making and provide an example of each.
2. Distinguish different decision conditions on the basis of risk and programmability.
3. Consider the advantages and disadvantages of group decision-making.
4. Identify the factors used to decide whether to adopt individual or group decision-making.
5. Match organizational conditions with the decision-making processes that favour them.

Why study decision-making?

Decision-making the process of making choices from among a number of alternatives.

Decision-making is the process of making a choice from among a number of alternatives. Why is the study of decision-making important? The decisions made by individual borrowers, and those made by the banks that lent them money, ultimately led to the credit crunch of 2008, the consequences of which we are still living with today. The decisions made by European governments to borrow money from the money markets in the past, and to support their banks in recent years, has had implications for the size of national debts and has contributed to the 'Euro-crisis'. The decisions of individuals, groups, organizations, and governments all affect our daily lives.

Within organizations, decisions are made at all levels, not just at the top. Both managers and non-managers make them. Herbert Simon (1957) felt that management theory should be based around the question of choice, and that decision-making was the very core of management. Henry Mintzberg (1989) concurred, stating that 'decision making is one of the most important - if not the most important - of all managerial activities, and represents one of the most common and crucial work tasks of managers'. Given the central role of decision-making within organizations, and the effect that decision outcomes have on the lives of all organization members, it is not surprising that the issue has attracted the attention of practising managers, consultants, management academics, and social science researchers. It can be analysed at a number of different levels, as Table 20.1 shows. Each level focuses on its own key issues and possesses its own theoretical perspectives. The levels however, are interrelated with one influencing and being affected by the others.

Table 20.1: Levels of decision-making

Level of analysis	Key issues	Theoretical perspectives
Individual	Limits to information-processing Personal biases	Information-processing theory Cognitive psychology
Group	Effects of group dynamics on individuals' perceptions, attitudes, and behaviours	Groupthink, group polarization, and group cohesiveness
Organizational	Effects of conflicts, power, and politics	Theories of organization conflict, power, politics, and decision-making

Classical decision theory a theory which assumes that decision-makers are objective, have complete information, and consider all possible alternatives and their consequences before selecting the optimal solution.

Rational model of decision-making a model which assumes that decision-making is and should be a rational process consisting of a sequence of steps that enhance the probability of attaining a desired outcome.

Models of decision-making

Rational models

The traditional approach to understanding individual decision making is based upon **classical decision theory** and the **rational model of decision-making**. These were originally developed in economics, and they make certain assumptions about people and how they make decisions.

The rational model of decision-making is shown in Figure 20.1. It is still popular among economics scholars in suggesting how decisions should be made. However, to understand its weaknesses, it is necessary to list its assumptions and demonstrate how they fail to match up to reality. This is done in Table 20.2.

STOP AND THINK

Think of some personal or organizational decisions that you have recently made. How many of the steps and assumptions from the rational model featured in your consideration?

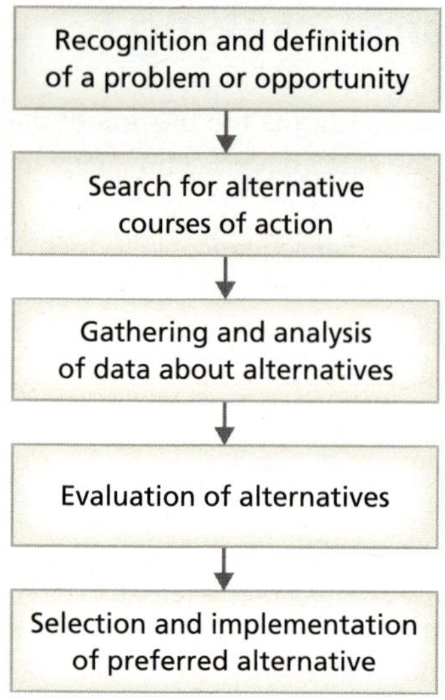

Figure 20.1: Rational model of decision-making

Rationality the use of scientific reasoning, empiricism, and positivism, along with the use of decision criteria that include evidence, logical argument, and reasoning.

Rational decisions choices based on rationality, that is, on a rational mode of thinking.

Descriptive models of decision-making models which seek to portray how individuals actually make decisions.

Behavioural theory of decision-making a theory which recognizes that bounded rationality limits the making of optimal decisions.

Bounded rationality a theory which says that individuals make decisions by constructing simplified models that extract the essential features from problems without capturing all their complexity.

Table 20.2: Rational model of decision-making: assumptions and reality

Assumption	Reality
All alternatives will be considered	Rarely possible to consider all alternatives since there are too many Some alternatives will not have occurred to the decision-maker
The consequences of each alternative will be considered	Impractical to consider all consequences Impractical to estimate many of the consequences considered Estimation process involves time and effort
Accurate information about alternatives is available at no cost	Information available is rarely accurate, often dated, and usually only partially relevant to the problem Information costs money to be generated or purchased Decisions have to be made on incomplete, insufficient, and only partly accurate information
Decision-makers are rational	Individuals lack the mental capacity to store and process all the information relevant to a decision Frequently they lack the mental ability to perform the mental calculations required

The rational view of decision-making employs the concepts of **rationality** and **rational decisions** in its discussions and prescriptions. Rationality is equated with scientific reasoning, empiricism, and positivism, and with the use of decision criteria of evidence, logical argument, and reasoning. Rational decisions are decisions which are based on rationality, that is, on a rational mode of thinking (Simon, 1986; Langley, 1989).

It is now accepted that the rational model does not provide an accurate account of how people typically make decisions. Moreover, its prescriptions for making better decisions have often been incorrect. Instead, contemporary cognitive research by psychologists has revealed the ways in which decisions are made based on heuristic models, judgements, and tacit knowledge.

Descriptive models

Descriptive models of decision-making focus on how individuals actually make decisions. Each decision made by an individual or group is affected by a number of factors, including

Richard Michael Cyert (1921–2001)

James Gardiner March (b.1928)

Herbert Alexander Simon (1916 2001)

- individual personality;
- group relationships;
- organizational power relationships and political behaviour;
- external environmental pressures;
- organization strategic considerations; and
- information availability.

The aim of these models is to examine which of these factors are the most important, and how they interrelate prior to a decision being made.

One of the earliest, and still among the most influential descriptive models, is the **behavioural theory of decision-making**. It was developed by Richard Cyert, James March, and Herbert Simon (Simon, 1960; Cyert and March, 1963; March, 1988). It is called 'behavioural' because it treats decision-making as another aspect of individual behaviour. For example, if a research study interviewed brokers who bought and sold shares in the stock market to determine what factors influenced their decisions, it would be an example of a descriptive approach to decision-making. It is also sometimes referred to as the 'administrative model' and it acknowledges that, in the real world, those who make decisions are restricted in their decision processes. Behavioural theory holds that individuals make decisions while they are operating within the limits of **bounded rationality**. Bounded rationality recognizes that

- the definition of a situation is likely to be incomplete;
- it is impossible to generate all alternatives;
- it is impossible to predict all the consequences of each alternative;
- final decisions are often influenced by personal and political factors.

The effect of personal and situational limitations is that individuals make decisions that are 'good enough' rather than 'ideal'. That is, they 'satisfice', rather than 'maximize'. When **maximizing**, decision-makers review the range of alternatives available, all at the same time, and attempt to select the very best one. However, when **satisficing**, they evaluate one option at a time in sequence, until they alight on first one that is acceptable. The option chosen will meet all the minimum requirements for the solution, but may not be the very best (optimal) choice in the situation. Once an option is found, decision-makers will look no further. The contrast between the rational decision-making described previously and the bounded rationality discussed here is shown in Table 20.3.

Maximizing a decision-making approach where all alternatives are compared and evaluated in order to find the best solution to a problem.

Satisficing a decision-making approach where the first solution that is judged to be 'good enough' (i.e. satisfactory and sufficient) is selected, and the search is then ended.

Table 20.3: Rational decision-making and bounded rationality contrasted

Rational decision-makers . . .	Bounded rationality decision-makers . . .
Recognize and define a problem or opportunity thoroughly.	Reduce the problem to something that is easily understood.
Search for a extensive set of alternative courses of action, gathering data on each.	Develop a few uncomplicated and recognizable solutions, comparable to those currently being used.
Evaluate all the alternatives at the same time.	Evaluate each alternative as it is thought of.
Select and implement the alternative with the most value *(maximize)*.	Choose the first, acceptable alternative (*satisfice*).

Based on Simon (1979) and Kahneman (2003).

STOP AND THINK

When you chose your current partner – girlfriend, boyfriend, wife, or husband – did you maximize or satisfice? Is this distinction a useful way of explaining the decision-making process?

Prescriptive models

Prescriptive model of decision-making an approach that recommends how individuals should make decisions in order to achieve a desired outcome.

Victor Harold Vroom (b.1932)

Phillip W. Yetton (b.1943)

Prescriptive models of decision-making recommend how individuals *should* behave in order to achieve a desired outcome. This makes the rational model, described earlier, also a prescriptive one. Such models often also contain specific techniques, procedures, and processes which their supporters claim will lead to more accurate and efficient decision-making. They are often based on observations of poor decision-making processes, where key steps might have been omitted or inadequately considered. They are developed and marketed by management consultants as a way of improving organization performance through improved decision-making.

One of the best known prescriptive models of decision-making was developed by Victor Vroom and Phillip Yetton (1973), later expanded by Vroom and Arthur Jago (1988). The focus is on decision-making *situations* and on seven factors, to identify the decision-making *style* that is likely to be most effective in any given situation. It focuses on *decision style*, concerning *how* a leader decides in a given decision situation, rather than *what* a leader decides. It also concentrates on *subordinate participation* – the appropriate amount of involvement of the leader's subordinates in making a decision. The model consists of three main elements:

1. Decision participation styles
2. Diagnostic questions with which to analyse decision situations
3. Decision rules to determine the appropriate decision participation style.

The model is underpinned by two key concepts – quality and acceptability. The quality of the decision relates to it achieving the aim; the cost of its implementation; and the time taken to implement it. The acceptability of the decision relates to subordinates and anyone else who either is affected by the decision or has to implement it. Leaders and managers generally select the highest-quality decision that is acceptable.

1. Decision participation styles

Five decision participation styles are identified: decide, consult individually, consult group, facilitate, and delegate. These are shown ranging along a continuum in Table 20.4. They reflect different amounts of subordinate participation in the leader's decision. Moving from left to right on the continuum,

- the leader discusses the problem or situation more with others;
- others' input changes from merely providing information to recommending solutions;
- ownership and commitment to the decision increases;
- the time needed to arrive at a decision increases.

2. Diagnostic questions with which to analyse decision situations

It was found that leaders used different decision participation styles in different situations; and all of these various styles could be equally effective, depending on the situation. The question is how to determine which style is most suitable in a given situation. To answer this, Vroom asks seven diagnostic questions to identify which decision participation style is most effective in that situation. The answers to these seven questions, in the form of 'high' (H) or 'low' (L), should determine the appropriate level of subordinate participation in the decision-making process.

1. Decision significance	How significant is this decision to the success of the project or organization? If significance is high, then the leader needs to be closely involved.
2. Importance of commitment	How important is subordinate commitment in implementing the decision? If importance is high, then leaders should involve subordinates.

Table 20.4: Participation in decision-making processes

	Leader-centred ←				→ Group-centred
Description	**(D) Decide** As leader, you feel you have the information and expertise to make the decision alone and then you either announce or 'sell' it to the group.	**(CI) Consult individually** As leader, you lack the required information or expertise. You therefore obtain this from your group members individually, either telling them the problem or not. You then make the decision alone.	**(CG) Consult group** As leader, you explain the situation and provide information to your group. Together, solutions are generated and discussed. You review these recommendations and then make the decision alone.	**(F) Facilitate** As leader, you explain the situation and provide information to your group. Acting as facilitator, you reconcile differences and negotiate a solution acceptable to everyone. The final decision is made by you and your group together.	**(D) Delegate** As leader, you explain the situation, provide information, and set the boundaries for the decision to be made. You then delegate responsibility and authority for the final decision to the group who make it themselves. You accept and implement it.
Participants	Leader	Leader and others	Leader and others	Leader and others	Leader and others
Role of participants	Leader generates and evaluates solution alone.	Individuals provide leader with skill or information.	Group generates solutions or recommendations.	Group negotiates a solution with leader.	Group generates, evaluates and makes the decision.
Who makes the decision?	Leader	Leader	Leader (perhaps reflecting group inputs)	Leader and group together	Group

Based on Vroom (2000, p. 84).

3. *Leader expertise*	What is the level of the leader's information, knowledge, or expertise in relation to the problem? If it is low, the leader should involve subordinates to obtain it.
4. *Likelihood of commitment*	If the leader were to make the decision alone, would subordinates' commitment to it be high or low? If the answer is high, then subordinate involvement is less important.
5. *Group support for goals*	What is the level of subordinate support for the team's or organization's goals with respect to this situation? If it is low, the leader should not allow the group to make the decision alone.
6. *Group expertise*	What is the level of skill and commitment that group members have in working together as a team to solve the problem? If it is high, then more responsibility for the decision can be given to them.
7. *Team competence*	What is the level of subordinates' skills and commitment in working together as a team to solve the problem? If their skill and desire to work together cooperatively is high, then more responsibility for the decision can be given to them.

3. Decision rules

The Vroom-Yetton-Jago model provides a set of decision rules in the form of a decision tree to allow the selection of the most appropriate decision-making style as shown in Figure 20.2.

<table>
<tr><th></th><th>1</th><th>2</th><th>3</th><th>4</th><th>5</th><th>6</th><th>7</th><th></th></tr>
<tr><th></th><th>Decision significance</th><th>Importance of commitment</th><th>Leader expertise</th><th>Likelihood of commitment</th><th>Group support for goals</th><th>Group expertise</th><th>Team competence</th><th></th></tr>
<tr><td></td><td>How significant is this decision to the success of the project or organization?</td><td>How important is subordinate commitment in implementing the decision?</td><td>What is the level of the leader's information, knowledge, or expertise in relation to the problem?</td><td>If the leader were to make the decision alone, would subordinates' commitment to it be high or low?</td><td>What is the level of subordinate support for the team's or organization's goals with respect to this situation?</td><td>What is the level of skill and commitment that group members have in working together as a team to solve the problem?</td><td>What is the level of subordinates' skills and commitment in working together as a team to solve the problem?</td><td></td></tr>
<tr><td rowspan="22">PROBLEM STATEMENT</td><td rowspan="18">H</td><td rowspan="13">H</td><td rowspan="5">H</td><td>H</td><td>–</td><td>–</td><td>–</td><td>Decide</td></tr>
<tr><td rowspan="4">L</td><td rowspan="3">H</td><td rowspan="2">H</td><td>H</td><td>Delegate</td></tr>
<tr><td>L</td><td rowspan="3">Consult group</td></tr>
<tr><td>L</td><td>–</td></tr>
<tr><td>L</td><td>–</td><td>–</td></tr>
<tr><td rowspan="8">L</td><td rowspan="4">H</td><td rowspan="3">H</td><td rowspan="2">H</td><td>H</td><td>Facilitate</td></tr>
<tr><td>L</td><td rowspan="3">Consult individually</td></tr>
<tr><td>L</td><td>–</td></tr>
<tr><td>L</td><td>–</td><td>–</td></tr>
<tr><td rowspan="4">L</td><td rowspan="3">H</td><td rowspan="2">H</td><td>H</td><td>Facilitate</td></tr>
<tr><td>L</td><td rowspan="3">Consult group</td></tr>
<tr><td>L</td><td>–</td></tr>
<tr><td>L</td><td>–</td><td>–</td></tr>
<tr><td rowspan="5">L</td><td>H</td><td>–</td><td>–</td><td>–</td><td>–</td><td>Decide</td></tr>
<tr><td rowspan="4">L</td><td rowspan="4">–</td><td rowspan="3">H</td><td rowspan="2">H</td><td>H</td><td>Facilitate</td></tr>
<tr><td>L</td><td rowspan="3">Consult individually</td></tr>
<tr><td>L</td><td>–</td></tr>
<tr><td>L</td><td>–</td><td>–</td></tr>
<tr><td rowspan="4">L</td><td rowspan="3">H</td><td rowspan="3">–</td><td>H</td><td>–</td><td>–</td><td>–</td><td>Decide</td></tr>
<tr><td rowspan="2">L</td><td rowspan="2">–</td><td rowspan="2">–</td><td>H</td><td>Delegate</td></tr>
<tr><td>L</td><td>Facilitate</td></tr>
<tr><td>L</td><td>–</td><td>–</td><td>–</td><td>–</td><td>–</td><td>Decide</td></tr>
</table>

Figure 20.2: Time-driven model of leadership

Source: adapted from *Organizational Dynamics*, 28(4), Vroom, V.H., Leadership and the decision making process, pp. 82–94, Copyright 2000, with permission from Elsevier.

Vroom and Yetton at the battle of Gettysburg

Jack Duncan, Kelvin La France and Peter Ginter (2003) applied the Vroom and Yetton model of decision-making to the battlefield behaviour of ten commanding generals in six major battles in the American Civil War (1861–1865) – Gettysburg, Shiloh, Antietam, Chancellorsville, Chickamauga, and Nashville. They used official war records, biographies, autobiographies, and scholarly works to reconstruct the thinking of the decision-makers. The authors did not argue that appropriate decision-making was the determining factor in the outcome of the battle. However, they felt there was an identifiable relationship between the actions that people took and the results obtained. They found that when the commanding generals on the battlefield acted consistently with the prescriptions of the Vroom and Yetton model, they were more often successful in accomplishing the goals of their campaign. Also, even though commanders favoured the autocratic (decide) decision style, the lack of information-sharing and consensus-building resulted in serious disadvantages. The authors draw three conclusions. First, in most cases, the choice of a decision-making style did matter. Second, there was a need to question the appropriateness of the universal application of the autocratic (decide) decision style in situations where information was lacking or troop support was uncertain. Third, to achieve success on the battlefield, the performance of the management functions was as vital as the exercise of leadership. The commanders had ample time to plan the battle and, in the battle itself, the time available for decision-making appeared not to be a factor.

Home viewing

Thirteen Days (2001, director Roger Donaldson) is based on the true story of the Cuban missile crisis of October 1962, a diplomatic conflict between the United States and the (then) Soviet Union which nearly triggered a nuclear war. It stars Kevin Costner who plays an aide to President John F. Kennedy. As you watch the film, apply the Vroom-Yetton-Jago decision tree model to Kennedy's problem. The quality of the decision is crucial – the wrong one could lead to war. Does Kennedy's decision style match that recommended by the model? Also notice how strategic decisions are shaped by interacting, contextual, social, emotional, temporal, and behavioural factors, as well as by the rational consideration of evidence.

Explanatory model of decision-making an approach that accounts for how individuals, groups, and organizations make decisions.

Heuristic a simple and approximate rule, guiding procedures, shortcuts, or strategies that are used to solve problems.

Bias a prejudice, predisposition, or systematic distortion caused by the application of a heuristic.

Explanatory models

An **explanatory model of decision-making** explains how a given decision was made. For example, there are studies of military fiascos which examine why generals took, or failed to take, certain actions. Often these explanations draw upon personality and leadership concepts and theories. The poor decisions made by teams have also been studied using concepts from the group level of analysis such as groupthink and group polarization. These will be examined later in this chapter. Finally, decisions such as whether to acquire or merge with another company have drawn upon the theories of conflict, power, and politics, and offer explanations at the organizational level.

The studies have highlighted the limits to rationality and introduced the concept of bounded rationality. What else might affect the individual who makes a decision? Decision-making involves choice, and choice requires both careful thought and much information. Excessive information can both overload and delay us. Many managers believe that making the right decision late is the same as making the wrong decision. Hence we speed up the process by relying on judgement shortcuts called heuristics.

The judgement **heuristics** and **biases** model represents current thinking in decision-making and represents a further step away from the rational model. The meaning of the word heuristic goes back to the Greek word 'eurisco' meaning 'I discover'. The leading authors

Daniel Kahneman (b.1934)

Amos Tversky (1937–1996)

in this field have been Daniel Kahneman and Amos Tversky (Kahneman, 2011; Kahneman and Tversky, 2000). The work of these scholars, as well as that of Robert Cialdini (2009), has highlighted certain decision biases. It revealed that heuristic-based decision-making, although faster and simpler, exposes its users to biases which are inherent in human intuition. Biases operate at the subconscious level, are virtually undetectable, and have a powerful and immediate impact on individuals' judgement. Some of the most common decision-making biases are listed in Table 20.5.

Table 20.5: Common decision-making biases

Name of bias	Description
Confirmation	searching for information that supports one's preconceived beliefs, and ignoring that which does not
Bandwagon	a belief in certain outcomes because others believe the same
Loss aversion	considering avoiding losses to be more important than acquiring gains
Representative	a predisposition of people to base their judgements of probability on the basis of things with which they are familiar
Anchor and adjustment	a predisposition to make a judgement by starting from an initial value or 'anchor', and then making adjustments from that point, before making a final decision
Availability	a predisposition to base judgements of probability on the basis of information that is readily available

Source: based on Kahneman (2011).

Decision conditions: risk and programmability

Table 20.6 distinguishes different types of environmental conditions faced by organizations and labels these 'stable equilibrium', 'bounded instability' (or chaos), and 'explosive instability'. The condition under which a decision is made affects both how it is made and its outcome. Decisions differ in terms of their degree of risk involved and their programmability. Every decision is made under conditions of certainty, risk, or uncertainty. We shall consider each in turn.

Table 20.6: Environmental and decision-making conditions

Environmental condition	Decision-making condition	Characteristics	Example
Stable equilibrium is a state in which the elements are always in, or quickly return to, a state of balance.	Certainty	Alternatives and outcomes known and fully predictable	Fixed interest rate savings accounts
Bounded instability (or chaos) is a state in which there is a mixture of order and disorder, many unpredictable events and changes, and in which an organization's behaviour has an irregular pattern.	Risk	Known alternatives with only probable outcomes predictable	Tomorrow's weather
Explosive instability is a state in which there is no order or pattern whatsover.	Uncertainty	Alternatives and outcomes poorly understood	Developing a new product

Certainty a condition in which decision-makers possess full knowledge of alternatives; there is a high probability of having these available; it is possible to calculate the costs and benefits of each alternative; and there is high predictability of outcomes.

Risk a condition in which decision-makers have a high knowledge of alternatives; know the probability of these being available; can calculate the costs and know the benefits of each alternative; and have a medium predictability of outcomes.

Uncertainty a condition in which decision-makers possess low knowledge of alternatives; there is a low probability of having these available; it is to some degree possible to calculate the costs and benefits of each alternative; and there is no predictability of outcomes.

In a situation of **certainty**, no element of chance comes between the alternative and its outcome, and all the outcomes are known in advance with 100 per cent certainty. In such circumstances, all that the individual has to do is to select the outcomes with the largest benefit. A situation of total certainty is so rare as to be virtually nonexistent. In the past, government bonds which guaranteed a fixed rate of interest over a period of time, which would be paid barring the fall of the government, represented an example of certainty. However, as the Russian government default in the late 1990s demonstrated, and the financial instability in the Eurozone shows, even government bonds carry an element of risk.

If decisions in organizations were constantly made in conditions of certainty, managers would not be needed, and junior, cheaper operatives, supplied with a rulebook, could replace them. Indeed, in conditions of certainty, a computer could quickly and accurately identify the consequences of the available options and select the outcomes with the greatest benefits. Managers are paid to make those tricky 'judgement calls' in uncertain conditions. In reality most organizational decisions are made under conditions of **risk**. Managers assess the likelihood of various outcomes occurring on the basis of their past experience, research, or other information.

Decisions made under **uncertainty** are the most difficult since the manager even lacks the information with which to estimate the likelihood of various outcomes and their associated probabilities and payoffs (March and Simon, 1958, p. 137). Conditions of uncertainty prevail in new markets, or those offering new technologies, or those aimed at new target customers. In all these cases there are no historical data from which to infer probabilities. In each case, the situation is so novel and complex that it is impossible to make comparative judgements.

STOP AND THINK

Identify three separate events in your university career or work life involving certainty, risk, and uncertainty. Consider each situation and think how it could change, or did actually change, from one condition to one of the other two.

Certainty

- from certainty to risk
- from certainty to uncertainty

Risk

- from risk to certainty
- from risk to uncertainty

Uncertainty

- from uncertainty to risk
- from uncertainty to certainty.

From Samaras (1989), p. 51.

The Eyjafjallajökull ash cloud: decision-making in uncertainty

The icecap of the Eyjafjallajökull glacier in Iceland covers a volcano that is 1,666 metres in height. The volcano crater measures between 3 and 4 km in diameter. When the magma and the ice interact, they create an ash cloud. On Wednesday, 14 April 2010, a plume of ash rose 17,000 metres into the sky. Scotland's airports, amongst the closest to Iceland, began closing that evening, and the rolling airport shutdown continued southwards on the following days down to London Heathrow and Stansted. For the next six days, the skies over the United Kingdom were quiet, as were most of those over continental Europe. When the final analysis was completed, it was found that the six-day airspace shutdown, the biggest since the Second World War, had cost the airlines £1.7 billion, and the airport operators €250 million. About 10 million people had been stranded or been unable to fly. A total of 10,000 flights had been cancelled, representing 75 per cent of European airline capacity and 30 per cent of worldwide capacity. Who made the decision to stop the planes flying and who made the decision to resume flying?

The National Air Traffic Services (NATS) took the decision to impose a zero flow rate, that is, it ceased providing a service. Following discussion with the Civil Aviation Authority (CAA), the regulator of UK airspace, NATS made the decision by following guidelines that require zero volcanic ash in the atmosphere for safe flight. The International Civil Aviation Organization manual's chapter 3.4.8 dealing with volcanic ash states that there is no current agreement as to how much ash concentration constitutes a hazard to jet aircraft engines. In view of this, it stated: 'regardless of ash concentration, AVOID, AVOID, AVOID'. The last word is repeated three times and written in capital letters. On that basis, UK airspace was shut down.

Scandinavia had been affected first. The Finnish air force sent up five of its F-18 fighter planes over Lapland, and reported significant engine damage from volcanic particles. If large numbers of commercial aircraft began encountering ash clouds and required emergency procedures or re-routing, NATS would not be able to cope. The growing number of stranded passengers was creating political problems for governments, as well as financial problems for airlines and airport operators. The last two were unconvinced about the necessity for a blanket flying ban. By the following Monday, and while UK airspace was closed, Eurocontrol (responsible for all air traffic within the European Union) announced that 55 to 60 per cent of flights in their airspace would go ahead.

The underlying area of uncertainty was the lack of any indication as to what was a safe level of ash contamination in the air. The airlines had not set a safety limit, neither had aircraft manufacturers nor aero engine manufacturers. On the following day, BA (British Airways) announced that 28 of their flights were heading into UK airspace and that it planned to land them, despite the ban. First Rolls-Royce, then Airbus and Pratt & Whitney, and then the rest, all announced new, safe limits for the operation of their engines in ash cloud conditions. So what had changed? It was the rules – the criteria of safety. If the engine manufacturers had announced their safety limits years earlier or at the beginning of the crisis and not at the end, the decisions made would have been very different. Faced with evidence and under pressure, they finally stated explicitly that there was indeed a safe level of ash contamination that did not constitute a hazard to flying. Commentators attribute their previous reluctance to a combination of commercial and safety pressures. There are levels of contamination that impact upon the useful life of an engine but which do not impair its safe operation. In the case of the Eyjafjallajökull ash cloud, the absence of any available, accepted safety standard interfered with speedy and effective decision-making (based on BBC Radio 4, 2010; *The Telegraph Online*, 2010).

Programmability of decisions

Routine decisions decisions made according to established procedures and rules.

Organization members make many different decisions every day. Some decisions are routine while others are not. **Routine decisions** are those which involve the use of pre-established organizational procedures or rules. Routine decision-makers are given considerable guidance as to what to do and how to do it through a well-established process, clearly defined goals, and the provision of information sources and decision rules. Examples of routine decisions include the reordering of stock items which have fallen to a certain level; the efficient routing of delivery vans; and the scheduling of equipment use. All these decisions tend to be repetitive and programmed, and are made by low-level employees on their own relying on predetermined courses of action.

Adaptive decisions decisions that require human judgement based on clarified criteria and are made using basic quantitative decision tools.

Innovative decisions decisions which address novel problems, lack pre-specified courses of action, and are made by senior managers.

Adaptive decisions typically require a form of judgement that no computer program, however complex, can produce. They involve a range of variables which have to be weighted and compared. Quantitative decision tools such as break-even analysis or a pay-off matrix can help to assist the manager's decision.

Finally, **innovative decisions** are made when a unique situation is confronted that has no precedent; when there are no off-the-shelf solutions; and when a novel answer has to be found. Innovative decisions are an outcome of problem-solving; they frequently deal with areas of the unknown; and company professionals or top managers typically make them. Within the organizational context, such decisions tend to be rare. Examples would include the decisions whether or not to acquire another company, to invest in a new technology, or to adopt a new marketing approach.

The differences between these types of decisions are summarized in Table 20.7.

Table 20.7: Routine, adaptive and innovative decisions

	Decision type	
	Routine ← **Adaptive** →	**Innovative**
Goals	Clear, specific	Vague
Level	Lower-level employees	Upper management
Problem	Well structured	Poorly structured
Process	Computational	Heuristic
Information	Readily available	Unavailable
Level of risk	Low	High
Involvement	Single decision-maker	Group decision
Consequences	Minor	Major
Solution basis	Decision rule and procedures	Judgement, creativity
Decision speed	Fast	Slow
Time for solution	Short	Relatively long

STOP AND THINK

Think of three very different decisions that you have recently made. How well did they fit into this routine/adaptive/innovative decision framework? What additional decision-type categories would you add?

Hormonal excess

John Coates, a Cambridge University neuroscientist and former derivatives trader, argues that hormones drive investment decisions to a far greater extent than economists or bank executives realize. When traders are on a winning streak, their testosterone levels increase by as much as five times. These spark such euphoria that they underestimate risk. Cortisol prepares humans for danger, by helping the brain retrieve important memories. Raging hormones can eventually wreck investors' ability to think rationally. This loss of judgement is exacerbated by other symptoms of stress, such as sleep deprivation. In studies, traders displayed no awareness of the rampant stress indicated by their cortisol measurements. One way to reduce the financial havoc that these hormones might wreak could be for trading houses to hire more women. Women have about 10 per cent as much testosterone as men, making them less prone to irrational exuberance. Additionally, competitive situations do not activate women's cortisol responses (© The Economist Newspaper Limited, London (24/09/2011)).

Individual and group decision-making

One of the main reasons why organizational activities are arranged around groups and teams is management's assumption that group decisions are better than individual decisions. The common-sense belief is that with many members contributing their diverse skills, knowledge, and experiences, they will make better decisions than individuals (Hill, 1982). However, experimental research data show that while the average quality of a decision made by a *group* is higher than the average quality of a decision made by an individual, the quality of work group decisions is consistently below that made by their *most capable individual* member (Rogelberg et al., 1992).

STOP AND THINK

Do you think that group decision-making is superior to individual decision-making? Why?

On the positive side, multiple individuals in a group can supply a greater range of knowledge and information to deal with more complex questions. Groups can generate more alternatives, can have a better comprehension of the problem using multiple perspectives, and can permit the specialization of labour with individuals doing those tasks for which they are best suited. The effect of this can be to improve the quality of group effort, and facilitate wider decision acceptance since more members will understand the decision better and have a feeling of ownership of it through participation. On the negative side, there are concerns that groups work more slowly; that the disagreements within them can create group conflict; and that group members may be intimidated by their group leader, creating only pseudo-involvement in decision-making. The pros and cons of group decision-making are summarized in Table 20.8.

Table 20.8: Advantages and disadvantages of group decision-making

Advantages	Disadvantages
Greater pool of knowledge: A group can bring much more information and experience to bear on a decision or problem than an individual alone.	*Personality factors*: Traits such as shyness can prevent some members offering their opinions and knowledge to the group.
Different perspectives: Individuals with varied experience and interests help the group see decision situations and problems from different angles.	*Social conformity*: Unwillingness to 'rock the boat' and pressure to conform may combine to stifle the creativity of individual contributors.
Greater comprehension: Those who personally experience the give-and-take of group discussion about alternative courses of action tend to understand the rationale behind the final decision.	*Diffusion of responsibility*: Members feel able to avoid responsibility for their actions, believing it can be shouldered by the others present.
Increased acceptance: Those who play an active role in group decision-making and problem-solving tend to view the outcomes as 'ours' rather than 'theirs'.	*Minority domination*: Sometimes the quality of group action is reduced when the group gives in to those who talk the loudest and longest.

Table 20.8: *continued*

Advantages	Disadvantages
Training ground: Less experienced members learn to cope with group dynamics by actually being involved.	*Logrolling*: Political wheeling and dealing can displace sound thinking when an individual's pet project or vested interest is at stake.
	Goal displacement: Sometimes secondary considerations such as winning an argument, making a point, or getting back at a rival displace the primary task of making a sound decision or solving a problem.
	Group brainstorming: Reduces rather than increases the quantity and quality of ideas compared to individual performance.
	'Groupthink': Sometimes cohesive 'in-groups' let the desire for unanimity override sound judgement when generating and evaluating alternative courses of action.
	Satisficing: Decisions may be made which are immediately acceptable to the group rather than the best ones.

Based on West et al. (1998) and Kreitner (1989, p. 238).

Research has revealed that whether or not a task is structured determines whether groups should or individuals are likely to perform it best (see Table 20.9). If the task to be performed is structured (has a clear, correct solution), then groups are better, although they take longer (Weber, 1984). In the case of an unstructured task (no single correct answer and creativity required), individual decision-making is to be preferred. Hence the counterintuitive finding that the performance of brainstorming groups is inferior to that of individuals.

Table 20.9: Individual and group performance compared

Factor	Individual decision-making is better when . . .	Group decision-making is better when . . .
Type of problem task	Creativity or efficiency is desired.	Diverse skills and knowledge are required.
Acceptance of decision	Acceptance is not important.	Acceptance by group members is valued.
Quality of the solution	'Best member' can be identified.	Several group members can improve the solution.
Characteristics of the individuals	Individuals cannot collaborate.	Members have experience of working together.
Decision-making climate	Climate is competitive.	Climate is supportive of group problem-solving.
Time available	Relatively little time is available.	Relatively more time is available.

Source: from *A Diagnostic Approach to Organizational Behaviour*, 4th ed., Prentice-Hall, Inc. (Gordon, J.R. 1993), p. 253.

Problems with group decision-making

Group polarization a situation in which individuals in a group begin by taking a moderate stance on an issue related to a common value and, after having discussed it, end up taking a more extreme decision than the average of members' decisions. The extremes could be more risky or more cautious.

Risky shift phenomenon the tendency of a group to make decisions that are riskier than those that individual members would have recommended.

Caution shift phenomenon the tendency of a group to make decisions that are more risk-averse than those that individual members of the group would have recommended.

It is the very strengths of a group that are also its weaknesses. The cost of bringing individuals together in one place counters the benefits of getting contributions from supposedly independent minds. Four problems will be examined here: group polarization, groupthink, brainstorming, and escalation of commitment.

Group polarization

Group polarization refers to the phenomenon that occurs when a position that is held on an issue by the majority of group members is intensified (in a given direction) as a result of discussion (Lamm, 1988). This tendency can lead to irrational and hence to ineffective group performance. Social psychologists have documented the situation in which individuals in a group begin by taking a moderate stance on an issue related to a common value and then, after having discussed it, end up taking a more extreme stance. James Stoner conducted one of the earliest of these studies in the 1950s. He found that groups of management students were willing to make decisions involving greater risks than their individual preferences. (Stoner, 1961). This phenomenon was referred to as the **risky shift**. However, the opposite can also occur, and is called the **caution shift**. Here a group can become more risk-averse than the initial average risk-averse tendencies of its individual members (Lamm and Myers, 1978; Isenberg, 1986).

Patricia Wallace (2001) believed that group polarization may be partly responsible for the extremism often found on the internet, and the apparent absence of a temperate voice. An individual might hold a relatively moderate view about an issue initially. However, after talking with others about it over the internet, they are likely to move away from the middle view towards one of the extremes. Factors that contribute to group polarization are present on the internet in abundance. First, people talk and talk endlessly. Second, members are selective about what they share with others. As talk progresses, members become increasingly reluctant to bring up items that might contradict the emerging group consensus. This creates a biased discussion where alternatives are insufficiently considered.

Hidden profiles and optimal team decision-making

Could optimal team decision-making be increased by simply getting teams to take more time to debate the issues and engage in thoughtful discussions about alternatives or is there more to it? Teams that avoid debates have shorter and more pleasant meetings, but this can result in important information not surfacing. Stefan Schultz-Hardt and his colleagues (2006) discovered how team discussions could improve decision quality by revealing an obstacle called *hidden profiles*. Hidden profiles are situations in which team members all possess some similar information about a problem needing to be solved, while also possessing unique problem-relevant information unknown to the rest of the group. For example, members of a hiring team all share the job applicants' résumés, but they divide up the tasks of reference-checking and interviewing, giving certain team members access to unique information. To make an optimal decision, the team needs its members to share the facts that are influencing each member's point of view.

In their experiment, the researchers had 135 three-person groups act as a personnel selection committee to choose between four candidates (A, B, C, and D) for a pilot's job. Although candidate C was the best fit for the job, information was manipulated to create hidden profiles, making the best fit candidates far from obvious. The committee could only reach a logical conclusion that candidate C was best if all three members shared their information. Of the 135 groups, 44 per cent made the correct decision. The researchers examined the differences between the successful and unsuccessful teams. They found that dissent was the most important success factor. Hidden profiles were most likely to be revealed in groups which expressed disagreement as to which candidate was strongest. Teams lacking dissent rarely noticed hidden profiles and typically made the wrong hiring decision. Dissent triggers more intense discussion, increases information-sharing, highlights information that is inconsistent with original opinions, and appears to lessen bias in the group decision-making process.

Groupthink

Irving Lester Janis (1918–1990)

Groupthink is a mode of thinking that occurs when the members' strivings for unanimity override their motivation to appraise realistically the alternative courses of action. One of the reasons why groups perform badly on complex, unstructured tasks is due to the dynamics of group interaction. Groups and teams can develop a high level of cohesiveness. This is generally a positive thing, but it also has negative consequences. Specifically, the desire not to disrupt the consensus can lead to a reluctance to challenge the group's thinking, which in turn results in bad decisions. Irving Janis (1982) studied a number of American foreign policy 'disasters' such as the failure to anticipate the Japanese attack on Pearl Harbor in 1941, the Bay of Pigs fiasco in 1961 when President John F. Kennedy and his administration sought to overthrow the government of Fidel Castro, and the prosecution of the Vietnam war between 1964 and 1967 by President Lyndon Johnson. Janis concluded that it was the cohesive nature of these important committees which resulted in these decisions, and which prevented contradictory views being expressed. He named this process groupthink. He listed its symptoms and how it could be prevented. These are outlined in Table 20.10.

Groupthink a mode of thinking in a cohesive in-group, in which members' strivings for unanimity override their motivation to appraise realistically the alternative courses of action.

Table 20.10: Groupthink: symptoms and prevention steps

When groups become very cohesive, there is a danger that they will become victims of their own closeness.

Symptoms	Prevention steps
1. *Illusion of invulnerability:* members display excessive optimism that past successes will continue and will shield them, and hence they tend to take extreme risks	(A) Leader encourages open expression of doubt by members
2. *Collective rationalization:* members collectively rationalize away data that disconfirm their assumptions and beliefs upon which they base their decisions	(B) Leader accepts criticism of his/her opinions
3. *Illusion of morality:* members believe that they, as moral individuals, are unlikely to make bad decisions	(C) Higher-status members offer opinions last
4. *Shared stereotypes:* members dismiss disconfirming evidence by discrediting its source (e.g. stereotyping other groups and their leaders as evil or weak)	(D) Get recommendations from a duplicate group
5. *Direct pressure:* imposition of verbal, non-verbal or other sanctions on individuals who explore deviant positions (e.g. those who express doubts or question the validity of group beliefs); perhaps use of assertive language to force compliance	(E) Periodically divide into subgroups
6. *Self-censorship:* members keep silent about misgivings about the apparent group consensus and try to minimize their doubts	(F) Members get reactions of trusted outsiders
7. *Illusion of unanimity:* members conclude that the group has reached a consensus because its most vocal members are in agreement	(G) Invite trusted outsiders to join the discussion periodically
8. *Mind-guards:* members take it upon themselves to screen out adverse, disconfirming information supplied by 'outsiders' which might endanger the group's complacency	(H) Assign someone to the role of devil's advocate
	(I) Develop scenarios of rivals' possible actions

Source: based on Janis (1982).

Source: www.CartoonStock.com

In all these different examples, groupthink led to a failure by the group to make the best decision. The group discussed a minimum number of alternatives; the courses of action favoured by the majority of the group were not re-examined from the view of hidden risks and other alternatives. The group failed to use the expert opinion that it had, and when expert opinion was evaluated, it was done with a selective bias which ignored the facts and opinions which did not support the group view.

In the groups studied by Janis, while individual doubt may have been suppressed and the illusion of group unanimity and cohesiveness maintained, the groups paid a high price in terms of effectiveness. The factors affecting group cohesiveness are listed in Table 20.11. Thus, while group cohesion can make a positive contribution to group effectiveness, it may also have negative consequences on the process of group decision-making. Group loyalty, instilled through cohesion, may act to stifle the raising and questioning of controversial issues which in turn leads to the making of poor decisions. At the heart of groupthink is the tendency for groups to seek concurrence and the illusion of unanimity. To prevent groupthink occurring, individuals who disagree with the group's evolving consensus must be willing to make their voices heard.

Table 20.11: Factors affecting group cohesiveness

Size	Smaller groups are more cohesive than larger ones, partly because their members interact more frequently.
Duration	The longer members are together, the more opportunity they have to find out about one another.
Threats	An external threat can often (although not always) serve to harden against 'the enemy'.
Isolation	Isolation leads a group to feel distinct and hence special.
Rewards	Group rewards can encourage cooperation to achieve the group goal.
Restricted entry	Difficulty of membership increases identification with the group.
Similarities	Where individuals share common goals and attitudes, they enjoy being in each other's company.

Echoing Janis's recommendation for a 'devil's advocate' role, Richard Hackman recommended including a 'deviant' in each group. This person's role was to challenge the arguments and opinions put forward by others in the group. Their task was to challenge their group's desire for too much homogeneity, which can stifle creativity, innovation, and learning. Deviants, said Hackman, are those members who stand back and say things like 'Wait a minute, why are we even doing this at all; let's look at this thing backwards; no, that's ridiculous; we've got to stop and change direction'. The deviant opens up discussions and is a source of innovation. Hackman's research revealed that teams that produced something original possessed deviants, while those which were average did not (Coutu, 2009, p. 102).

Although fewer than two dozen experimental laboratory studies have been conducted on groupthink (Turner and Pratkanis, 1998), an overview of these supports a link between the level of cohesion in the group and the occurrence of groupthink (Mullen et al., 1994). However, the strongest evidence supports the effect of directive leadership. Directive leadership is linked to less information being considered by the group; to the discouragement of dissent; to fewer solutions being found; and to more self-censorship by members (Flowers, 1977; Leana, 1985; McCauley, 1989; Moorhead and Montanari, 1986). It appears that if the group leader is strong, states their position at the start, and appears to have a strong preference for a particular outcome, the group is less likely to consider alternative information or solutions.

The space shuttle *Challenger* disaster – a case of groupthink?

On 28 January 1986, seventy-three seconds after its launch from Cape Canaveral, Florida, the space shuttle *Challenger* exploded, killing all seven members of its crew, including a civilian schoolteacher, Christa MacAuliffe. A presidential commission was established to investigate the causes of the accident. It found that the explosion was caused by an O-ring, a rubber seal that failed to do its job due to the freezing overnight temperatures at the launch pad.

NASA Images

The decision to launch was made by a group consisting of staff from Morton Thiokol, the builders of the rocket boosters, and NASA management personnel. The subsequent analysis of documents and commission testimony revealed that groupthink had increased in this group in the twenty-four hours prior to the launch. The Thiokol engineers had argued for the cancellation of the launch because, in their view, the O-rings would not withstand the pressure at the launch time temperatures. The engineers were pressed by their bosses to stifle their dissent, and their opinions were devalued. The past record of success led to overconfidence, and various pieces of information were withheld from key individuals. In consequence, the Morton Thiokol/NASA group failed to fully consider the alternatives; failed to evaluate the risks associated with their preferred course of action; used information that was biased when making their decision; and failed to work out a contingency plan. Although the physical cause of the disaster was an O-ring seal, many researchers claim that the actual cause was the flawed decision-making process that had been infected by groupthink (based on Esser and Lindoerfer, 1989; Moorhead et al., 1991).

Brainstorming

Brainstorming
a technique in which all group members are encouraged to propose ideas spontaneously, without critiquing or censoring others' ideas. The ideas so generated are not evaluated until all have been listed.

Brainstorming is usually presented as a technique to improve group decision-making. However, it can be argued that it represents a problem in group decision-making. Brainstorming asserts the superiority of a group's performance over that of an individual. Alexander F. Osborn, a principal of the New York advertising agency Batten, Barton, Durstine and Osborn, invented brainstorming in 1939. He coined the term to mean using the *brain* to *storm* a problem creatively. The technique is based on the belief that under given conditions, a group of people working together will solve a problem more creatively than if the same people worked separately as individuals. The presence of a group is said to permit members to 'bounce ideas off each other', and gives individuals the chance to throw out half-formed ideas which other group members might turn into more practical suggestions.

The purpose of the technique is to produce creative new ideas. Members of brainstorming groups are required to follow four main rules of procedure:

1. Avoid criticizing others' ideas.
2. Share even fanciful or bizarre suggestions.
3. Offer as many comments as possible.
4. Build on others' ideas to create your own.

The proponents of brainstorming argue that the flow of ideas in a group will trigger off further ideas whereas the usual evaluative framework will tend to stifle the imagination. A brainstorming group may, on occasions, perform better than an individual who applies these rules to their own thought processes. However, in a brainstorming group, when people are generating ideas, many will be talking at the same time, and this can block the thought process and eventually impede the sharing of ideas. This is called 'production blocking' (Kerr and Tindale, 2004). In contrast, if one has four individuals working alone, they can generally greatly outperform a group of four in terms of the number of ideas generated. Research has consistently shown that group brainstorming actually *inhibits* creative thinking. Taylor, Berry and Block (1958) carried out one of the earliest studies and compared the performance of brainstorming groups with 'pseudo-groups' (constructed by the experimenter from individual members' scores). They discovered that pseudo-groups were superior to brainstorming groups on criteria of idea quantity, quality and uniqueness. Over the intervening years, these original conclusions have been investigated by other researchers (Yetton and Bottger, 1982; Diehl and Stroebe, 1987; Mullen et al., 1991; Brown and Paulus, 1996, Furnham, 2000; Paulus et al., 2002; Litchfield, 2008). It may be that brainstorming is most effective with established or specially trained groups.

Electronic brainstorming

While face-to-face brainstorming has been proved to be of little value, electronic brainstorming may prove to be superior. An electronic support tool had participants sitting at their PCs, entering their ideas in one window, after which they appeared in a second window, alongside the ideas of other participants. It was found that in large groups, this support tool improved performance since it overcame the production-blocking problem, allowing individuals to glance at colleagues' contributions at any time, but did not interrupt their train of thought. The environment may have triggered disinhibition, making members feel freer to express their wildest notions without concern for negative reactions (Connelly, 1997; Cooper et al., 1998; Dennis and Valacich, 1993).

The continued use of brainstorming appears to be more related to employee commitment than to problem solution or creativity. Group members may fail to contribute to brainstorming sessions for fear of saying something foolish, because they are introverts, or because they find the process artificial, and sessions frequently end up with unremarkable solutions and ideas. However, brainstorming is a good way of gaining employee buy-in for decisions that have already been made by management.

Advocacy versus inquiry: the Bay of Pigs and the Cuban missile crisis

Garvin and Roberto (2001) distinguish between the *advocacy* approach to decision-making, which sees it as a contest involving a manager at a discrete point in time, and the *inquiry* approach, which treats it as a collaborative problem-solving process to be explicitly designed and managed.

	Advocacy	**Inquiry**
Concept of decision-making	A contest	A process
Purpose of discussion	Persuasion and lobbying	Testing and evaluation
Participants' role	Spokespeople	Critical thinkers
Patterns of behaviour	Strive to persuade others Defend your position Downplay weaknesses	Present balanced arguments Remain open to alternatives Accept constructive criticism
Minority views	Discouraged or dismissed	Cultivated and valued
Outcome	Winners and losers	Collective ownership

Source: reprinted by permission of *Harvard Business Review*. From 'What you don't know about making decisions' by Garvin, D.A. and Roberto, M.A., 79(8) 2001.

The contrast can be illustrated by two critical foreign policy decisions faced by President John F. Kennedy and his administration. During his first two years in office, Kennedy dealt with the Bay of Pigs invasion and the Cuban missile crisis. Both problems were assigned to cabinet-level task forces, and involved many of the same individuals, the same political interests, and extremely high stakes. However, the outcomes were completely different, largely because the two groups operated in different ways.

The first group, which had to decide whether to support an invasion of Cuba by a small army of US-trained Cuban exiles, worked in an advocacy mode. The outcome of its deliberations was widely considered to be an example of flawed decision-making. Shortly after taking office, President Kennedy learned of the planned attack on Cuba developed by the CIA during Eisenhower's administration. Backed by the Joint Chief of Staff, the CIA argued forcefully for the invasion. It understated the risks, and filtered the information that it presented to the president to reinforce its own position. Knowledgeable individuals from the Latin America desk were excluded from deliberations because of their likely opposition. Some members of Kennedy's own staff opposed the plan, but kept silent for fear of appearing weak in the face of the strong advocacy by the CIA. As a result, there was little debate, and the group failed to test some critical underlying assumptions – for example, whether the landing would ignite a domestic uprising against Castro, and whether the exiles could hide in the mountains if they met with strong resistance. The resulting invasion is generally considered to be one of the low points of the Cold War. About 100 lives were lost, and the remaining exiles were taken hostage. The incident was a major embarrassment to the Kennedy administration and dealt a blow to America's global standing.

After the botched invasion, Kennedy conducted a review of the foreign policy decision-making process and introduced five major changes, essentially transforming the process to one of inquiry. First, people were urged to participate in discussions as 'sceptical generalists' – that is, as disinterested critical thinkers rather than as representatives of particular departments. Second, Robert Kennedy and Theodore Sorensen were assigned the role of intellectual watchdog, and expected to pursue every possible point of contention, uncovering weaknesses and untested assumptions. Third, task forces were urged to abandon the rules of protocol, eliminating formal agendas and deference to rank. Fourth, participants were expected to split occasionally into subgroups to develop a broad range of options. Finally, President Kennedy decided to absent himself from some of the early task force meetings to avoid influencing other participants and thereby slanting the debate.

This inquiry mode of decision-making was used to great effect in October 1962, when President Kennedy learned that the Soviet Union had placed nuclear missiles on Cuban soil, despite repeated assurances from the Soviet ambassador that this would not occur. Kennedy immediately convened a high-level task force, which contained many of the same men responsible for the Bay of

→

Pigs invasion, and asked them to frame a response. The group met around the clock for two weeks, often inviting additional members to join in their deliberations to broaden their perspective. Occasionally, to encourage the free flow of ideas, they met without the president. Robert Kennedy played his new role thoughtfully, critiquing options frequently, and encouraging the group to develop additional alternatives. In particular, he urged the group to move beyond a simple go or no-go decision on a military air strike.

Ultimately, subgroups developed two positions, one favouring a blockade and the other, an air strike. These groups gathered information from a broad range of sources, viewed and interpreted the same intelligence photos, and took great care to identify and test underlying assumptions, such as whether the Tactical Air Command was indeed capable of eliminating all Soviet missiles in a surgical air strike. The subgroups exchanged position papers, critiqued each other's proposals, and came together to debate the alternatives. They presented Kennedy with both options, leaving him to make the final choice. The result was a carefully framed response, leading to a successful blockade and a peaceful resolution of the crisis (based on Garvin and Roberto, 2001).

Escalation of commitment

Escalation of commitment an increased commitment to a previously made decision, despite negative information suggesting one should do otherwise.

Escalation of commitment is the final problem in group decision-making to be considered. Have you ever waited for a lift (elevator) that did not arrive, and the longer that you waited, the less inclined you were to use the stairs instead? The concept refers to the tendency of individuals to increase their commitment to a course of action in the future, despite the evidence of negative outcomes from the past. In addition to waiting situations, this tendency has been noticed in interpersonal relations, gambling, economic investment, and policy-making.

Barry Staw (1976, 1981) first demonstrated escalation of commitment as an individual phenomenon, leading to much subsequent work on the topic (Whyte, 1986; Brockner, 1992). However, later research on group polarization and on groupthink supports Whyte's (1993) contention that groups escalate more than individuals. Risky-shift findings show us that groups make riskier decisions than individuals, and the decision to escalate in the light of past failure can be viewed as risk-seeking. From a groupthink perspective, since a majority view is sufficient to induce dissenters to conform to a decision to escalate, reliance on a group rather than on an individual to resolve an escalation dilemma is likely to increase the frequency with which escalation occurs. Figure 20.3 shows the factors that Ross and Staw (1993) identified as contributing to commitment escalation by a group or an individual. Note that although individual (psychological) variables play a part, a range of other determinants are equally, if not more important.

Task factors

The characteristics of the task itself – shooting a film, constructing a building, implementing a military tactic – are a major influence. A project like a movie or even a relationship can have had such a large amount of assets (money or emotions) previously invested in it, that it reaches the point where its abandonment would involve unacceptable financial or personal costs. The task may lack clearly defined goals, performance standards to measure those goals, or unambiguous feedback that can allow a regular check on progress. Since the benefits of a task are often delayed, decision-makers are tempted to remain with it until the end. When doing so, they tend to attribute setbacks to temporary causes that they believe can be rectified with additional expenditure.

Psychological factors

Most of these stem from the ego-involvement of decision-makers for whom the failure of the activity will threaten their self-esteem. Reinforcement traps mean that a person is reluctant to withdraw from a previously rewarding activity believing that, from past history, it can be made to succeed. Individual motivation also plays a part, especially the need for self-justification. All sorts of decision-making errors are committed as people take risks to

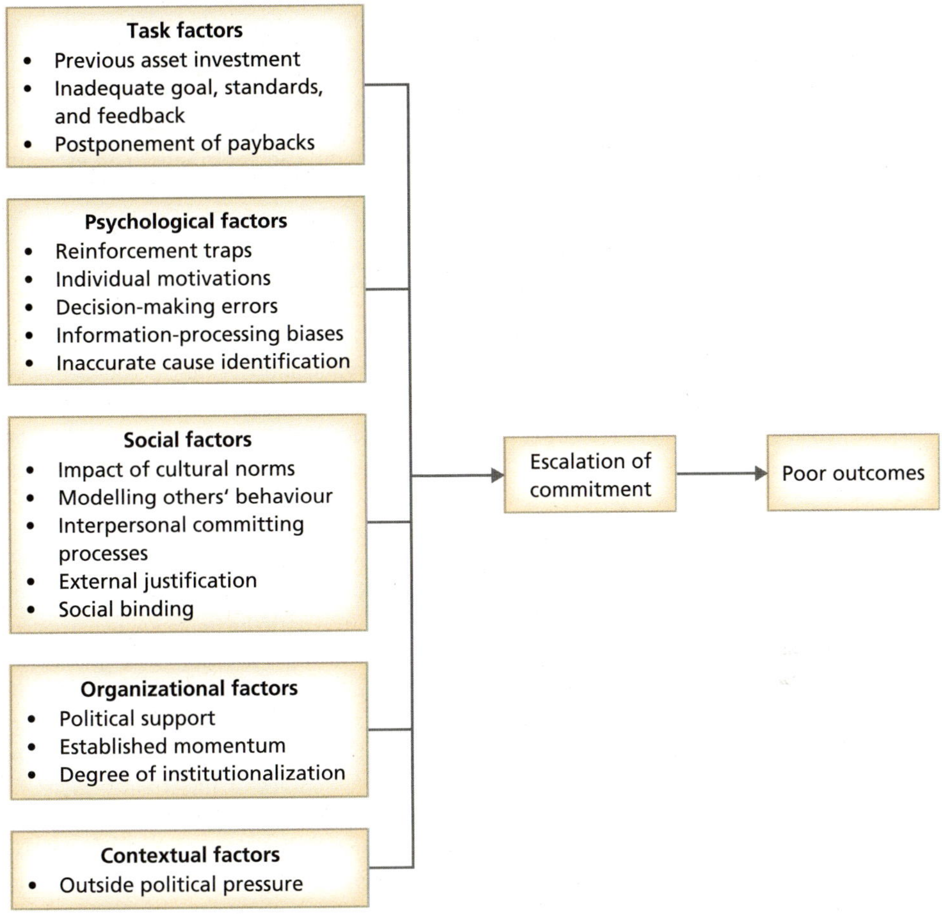

Figure 20.3: Model of escalation of commitment

Source: based on Ross and Staw (1993).

recover previously invested resources. They begin to process information in a biased way, becoming overconfident and slanting facts to suit pre-existing beliefs. Often they fail to determine the true cause of the problem by attributing negative outcomes to external rather than internal factors.

Social factors

In many countries, cultural norms favour consistent leadership (no 'U-turns') which 'triumphs in the end'. Members are likely to be put under pressure from a hostile audience to justify their actions, as well as from friendly colleagues who want to 'save face'. This need to rationalize their actions to other parties, when challenged, results in the production of renewed justifications leading, in turn, to greater commitment. Seeking direction, decision-makers are likely to make a social comparison with others, modelling their behaviour on what someone else has done in a similar situation.

Organizational factors

The idea of projects continuing because of the political support of key organizational players is well understood. Also important is the momentum towards the continuation of the task or project that is generated by the company having already recruited expert staff, invested in specialized equipment, and entered or withdrawn from certain lines of business activity. A final important variable here is how closely the project is tied to the company's values and objectives. Its degree of organizational institutionalization may be high or low.

Contextual factors

A decision taken within an organization involves forces outside its boundaries. Political, economic, societal, technological, legal, and ethical variables can all play a part. External forces that are unconnected with, but which have an interest in, the rescue or continuance of a 'permanently failing organization' can contribute to an escalation of commitment.

Organizational decision-making

The making of decisions has been examined at the level of the individual and of the group. It now remains to consider it at the organizational context. The management of any organization has two main tasks. The first is to coordinate the work activities within the organization, for example, ensuring that work is divided among departments and is completed. Its second task is to adjust to circumstances outside the organization (e.g. regulating contracts with suppliers; ensuring adherence to government regulations; responding to customers). Individuals in the organization (mainly but not exclusively managers) have to deal with the fact that rules, procedures, and precedents seldom determine what should be done in every particular case. Decisions which are 'unprogrammed' have to be made. This means that discretion has to be used, judgements have to be made, and decisions have to be implemented. This ambiguity and uncertainty provides the political context within which decision-making occurs within organizations.

Sociologists have studied how power and politics impact on the decision-making process and prevent the operation of the rational decision-making process described at the start of this chapter. Decisions in organizations involve power and conflict between individuals and groups in organizations. The more sources of uncertainty there are, the more possibility there is for individuals and groups to take up political positions. From this perspective, a particular decision is less an expression of the organization's goals, and more a reflection of the ability of a particular individual or group to impose their view or 'definition of the situation', and their solution, onto other groups.

As noted earlier, Herbert Simon criticized the rational model of decision-making, saying that it ignored the internal politics of the organization system. He and his colleagues, Richard Cyert and James March, were influential in introducing politics into the consideration of decision-making in organizations. They linked the cognitive limits to rationality with political limits. The rational model assumes that:

- decision-makers possess a consistent order of preferences:
- there is agreement among the stakeholders about the goals of the organization:
- decision rules are known and accepted by everyone.

Strategies and models

In contrast to the rational model, the bounded rationality view stresses that, for two reasons, decision-makers cannot make the types of decisions that the rational model recommends. First, there is ambiguity over which direction to take on an issue. That is, people disagree about which goals to pursue or which problems to solve. Second, there is the issue of uncertainty. This concerns the degree to which people feel certain that a given action will produce a given outcome (cause and effect).

The condition of uncertainty was examined earlier, and it was noted that extra information could reduce it. However, that same, new information could also increase ambiguity since it provided extra points over which different decision-makers could disagree. James Thompson and Arthur Tuden used the dimensions of agreement or disagreement over goals and beliefs about cause-and-effect relations as a way of distinguishing between four different situations faced by decision-makers (Thompson and Tuden, 1959; Thompson, 1967). These are shown in Figure 20.4.

Any given choice situation can be mapped on these two continua, the degree of agreement that exists between parties on the goals to be pursued, and the level of certainty that a specified outcome can be achieved through the use of a given action. Each such situation

		Consensus on goals or problem definition?	
		agree	*disagree*
Beliefs about cause-and-effect relationships	***certainty***	I Computational strategy Rational model	III Compromise strategy Political model
	uncertainty	II Judgemental strategy Incremental model	IV Inspirational strategy Garbage can model

Figure 20.4: Conditions favouring different decision-making processes
Source: based on Thompson and Tuden (1959) and Thompson (1967).

can thus be defined as falling into one of the four quadrants. The most likely form of decision-making model for each quadrant is specified.

I. Computational strategy – rational model

In this case, those concerned are clear and agreed on what outcome they desire (no ambiguity), and certain about the consequences of their actions (high certainty). For example, as demand for ice cream increases in the summer, the company introduces an extra shift. The rational model has already been considered, and may be capable of being applied in this situation since the management know the capabilities of their machines, the costs of extra manning, and the income from extra sales. The company can therefore calculate the costs and returns using a *computational strategy*.

II. Judgemental strategy – incremental model

In this case, those concerned are clear and are agreed on what outcome they desire (no ambiguity), but are uncertain about the consequences of their actions (low certainty) because information is inadequate. In the case of the ice cream makers, new equipment may need to be purchased whose performance is unknown. Charles Lindblom (1959) built on Simon's notion of bounded rationality, saying that the limited search for and evaluation of alternatives meant that those which were offered differed only slightly (i.e. incrementally) from what already existed. Hence, current judgement choices were made on the basis of past decisions. Decision-making in his view was thus remedial, concerned with 'fixing the past' by moving away from it, rather than oriented to achieving goals in the future. Decisions therefore were continually adjusted as they unfolded, and problems were continually attacked. For Lindblom, policy formulation was thus not a single event, but the outcome of countless small, often disjointed decisions, made separately, by different individuals and groups, over a period of years. He referred to the process that he described as *incrementalism* although it is more popularly referred to as the 'science of muddling through'.

III. Compromise strategy – political model

In this case, those concerned are unclear or divided as to what outcomes they desire (high ambiguity). Increasing production to manufacture a large number of extra low-profit products or a smaller volume of higher mark-up items might be equally appealing. The use of the technology provides certainty that either option can be achieved (high certainty). In this case, a compromise strategy is used.

These sorts of unprogrammed decisions are bound to be resolved, ultimately, by reasoning, judgement, influence, and politics. When faced with a question such as how strategy should be reformulated for the next five years, reasonable people will always disagree. Political behaviour is therefore an inevitable consequence of the prevalence of unprogrammed management decisions.

Many writers view an organization as a coalition of interests. Each department has its own goals, is interdependent with others, and competes for scarce resources. The task of senior management is to balance these demands and resolve any ensuing conflicts. It does so by engaging in politics, in an effort to manage or manipulate the decision-making process, to 'cut a deal'. In such circumstances, a decision is not the result of the rational decision-making process, but something that is the outcome of horse-trading, and which is acceptable to all those involved. From this perspective, individuals and groups unite their interests, propose alternatives, assess their power, join with others, negotiate, and form coalitions. In conditions of high ambiguity, decision-makers look for alternatives that can accommodate the interests of the parties involved. They are not greatly concerned with searching for information.

IV. Inspirational strategy – garbage can model

In this case, those concerned are unclear or are divided as to what outcomes they desire (high ambiguity). They are also uncertain about the consequences that their actions are likely to have (high uncertainty). When there is neither agreement on goals, nor certainty about cause-and-effect relationships, ambiguity and uncertainty prevail, and decision-making becomes random. If there is no preference between high volume / low profits and low volume / high profits, or certainty about what will happen if they do launch them, then the *inspirational strategy* is an inspired leap into the dark!

In such circumstances, Cyert and March's decision-making processes become 'uncoupled' from the decisions actually made. That is, a link ceases to exist between the problems identified and the solutions proposed or implemented. The garbage can model was developed by James March and Johan Olsen and turned the rational model on its head. Whereas both the rational and the bounded rationality models treated decisions as the outcomes of a reasoned approach of information-gathering and evaluation, the garbage can model contended that the elements that constituted decision problems were independent phenomena that came together in random ways (Cohen et al., 1972; March and Olsen, 1976; Einsiedel, 1983).

In their view, the various logical models of decision-making had failed to recognize the amount of confusion that surrounded decision-making situations. They labelled these situations *organized anarchies*. Within these, a decision 'occurred' rather than being consciously taken. Thus, decision-making involved streams of activities which served to cope with uncertainty over time. It occurred when four separate but interdependent streams fortuitously met. The four streams were:

- *Choice opportunities*: Every organization has a stream of 'occasions' at which there is an expectation of a decision, e.g. weekly staff meetings, product review meetings, government cabinet meetings.
- *Participants*: A stream of people who have an opportunity to make a choice.
- *Problems*: A stream of problems which represent matters of concern for individuals both inside and outside the organization, e.g. declining sales, need to recruit staff, or increasing hospital waiting lists.
- *Solutions*: The existence of a stream of solutions or answers, all seeking problems and questions, and all available from internal staff advisors or external consultants.

From this perspective, the choice opportunities act as the container (garbage can) for the mixture of problems, solutions, and participants that are there at the time. Because of the disorder that characterizes managerial work, preferences are rarely well ordered, they often change, and the criteria for judging the relevance of information are vague. Thus the rational model, with its logic and order, does not describe what really happens. For example, choices are made before problems are understood; solutions sometimes discover problems; and only rarely are problems resolved after choices are made. The actual decisions made are often irrelevant to the people concerned. For them, the priority may have been to blame others, pay off debts, store up favours, punish others, or position themselves in a power struggle. March and Olsen felt that

> choice situations are not simply occasions for making substantive decisions. They are also arenas in which important symbolic meanings are developed. People gain status and exhibit virtue. Problems are accorded significance. Novices are educated into the values

"My team has created a very innovative solution, but we're still looking for a problem to go with it."

Source: Copyright Randy Glasbergen, www.glasbergen.com

of the society and organization. Participation rights are certification of social legitimacy; participation performances are critical presentations of self. (1976, p. 52)

Evidence-based decision-making a situation in which a decision is made that follows directly from the evidence.

Decision-based evidence-making marshalling facts and analysis to support a decision that has already been made elsewhere in the organization.

Decision-making and evidence

Peter Tingling and Michael Brydon (2010) defined **evidence-based decision-making** as a situation in which a decision was made that followed directly from the evidence (see Figure 20.5). They contrasted it with **decision-based evidence-making** which involved marshalling facts and analysis to support a decision that had already been made elsewhere in the organization. They found that managers, when making a decision, used evidence in three different ways:

Not all decisions incorporate evidence in the same way, or intend to marshal it toward the same end. This chart shows three roles that evidence can play, depending on whether the aim is to make, inform, or support a decision.

ROLE OF EVIDENCE IN DECISION-MAKING	DESCRIPTION	ARCHETYPAL DECISION	RISKS
Make decision Evidence → Decision process → Decision	Evidence forms the basis of the decision.	Facilities location	Poor decisions due to misspecified models
Inform decision Evidence; Intuition, experience, bargaining, etc. → Decision process → Decision	Evidence is one of several inputs to the decision process.	Diagnosis, strategic planning	Mismatch between evidence and other inputs requires shift to 'make' or 'support' role
Support decision Intuition, experience, bargaining, etc. → Decision process → Decision; Evidence	Evidence is created to support a decision made using other inputs.	New product development, technology adoption	Demoralization of analysts; poor decisions due to decision biases and false consensus

Figure 20.5: The role of evidence in decision-making

Source: Tingling and Brydon (2010), p. 73. © 2010 from *MIT Sloan Management Review*/Massachusetts Institute of Technology.

- to *make* a decision – the decision arose directly from the evidence;
- to *inform* a decision – the evidence was mixed in with intuition or bargaining, to lead to a decision
- to *support* a decision – the evidence was used simply to justify a decision already made.

If decisions are allowed to trump the evidence, then decision-making is ill-informed. In the best case, a decision that contradicts the evidence is an inspired hunch based on experience, while in the worst case, it is the product of ignorant bias. Moreover, once employees know that managers are more interested in finding evidence to fit their conclusions, rather than finding out the facts, then they become demoralized and the company is infected with destructive cynicism. However, historically some companies have collected data and have successfully ignored it, while in others, the cult of data-driven decision-making leaves so little scope for personal beliefs and hunches that employees just tailor the evidence to fit pre-made decisions.

So what is to be done? Should one encourage the use of data, while leaving room for the occasional inspired decision? Tingling and Brydon offer managers four guidelines:

1. Understand the decision problem and assess the potential contribution of formal evidence to the quality of the decision-making process. For some problems (e.g. new product development), historical data is of little use and the decision is best made on instinct.
2. Use cost-benefit analysis. If the costs of obtaining evidence exceed the benefits, it may be necessary to make the decision on instinct and admit that this is what is being done.
3. Differentiate between internal and external decision audiences when engaging in decision-based evidence-making. Some evidence can have ceremonial and signalling value, but internal stakeholders (employees) are seldom fooled by decision-based evidence-making.
4. Ensure that the majority of decisions incorporate painstakingly gathered, objective evidence. If managers feel the necessity to feed manufactured evidence to internal audiences, it should be done rarely and sparingly, otherwise a disregard for evidence and analysis will become endemic throughout the organization.

RECAP

1. *Distinguish between prescriptive, descriptive, and explanatory models of decision-making and provide an example of each.*
   - Prescriptive models of decision-making recommend how individuals should behave in order to achieve a desired outcome. The original prescriptive model is the rational model, while a recent one was devised by Victor Vroom and Phillip Yetton.
   - Descriptive models of decision-making reveal how individuals actually make decisions. The behavioural theory of decision-making is the earliest and most influential descriptive model and was developed by Herbert Simon, John March and Richard Cyert.
   - Explanatory models of decision-making look at what decisions were made and aim to provide an explanation of how they occurred. The heuristics and biases model developed by Daniel Kahneman and Amos Tversky, and Irving Janis's groupthink concept, illustrate such explanations.
2. *Distinguish different decision conditions on the basis of risk and programmability.*
   - Decision conditions can be classified as those involving certainty, risk, and uncertainty.
   - Decision can be classified as routine, adaptive, and innovative.
3. *Consider the advantages and disadvantages of group decision-making.*
   - Groups offer the advantages of a greater pool of knowledge, different perspectives, greater problem comprehension, and increased acceptance of decisions.
   - Disadvantages of groups can be considered under the headings of personality factors, social conformity, diffusion of responsibility, minority domination, logrolling, goal displacement, group brainstorming, groupthink, and satisficing.

4. *Identify the factors used to decide whether to adopt individual or group decision-making.*
   - The decision whether to adopt individual or group decision-making has been made on the basis of the following factors: type of problem task, acceptance of decision; quality of the solution; characteristics of the individuals, and decision-making climate.
5. *Match organizational conditions with the decision-making processes that favour them.*
   - When there is certainty about cause and effects and there is consensus on goals or problem definition then a computational strategy involving the rational decision-making model is favoured.
   - When there is uncertainty about cause and effects, but there is consensus on goals or problem definition, then a judgemental strategy involving an incremental decision-making model is favoured.
   - When there is certainty about cause and effects, but disagreement about goals or problem definition then a compromise strategy involving a political decision-making model is favoured.
   - When there is neither certainty about cause and effects, nor agreement about goals or problem definition, then an inspirational strategy involving the garbage can model of decision-making is favoured.

Revision

1. What are the strengths and weakness of the Vroom-Jago time-driven decision-making model?
2. How does a 'satisficing' decision differ from a 'maximizing' one? Provide examples of each from your own experience. In what circumstances would one be preferable to the other?
3. 'No decision that is ever made by a manager is truly rational'. Do you agree or disagree with this statement? Support your view with arguments and examples.
4. Should decision-making by groups be avoided or encouraged by organizations?

Research assignment

Familiarize yourself with Cialdini's (2009) seven weapons of influence through extended reading. (a) Develop a set of interview questions to determine the nature of their use. (b) Interview a few managers, co-workers or friends. Explain each of the weapons, and ask them for examples of weapons being used on them, or when using them on others. (c) Use the data collected to write a report discussing the popularity of the different weapons of influence, giving examples of their use in decision making.

Springboard

Max Bazerman and Don Moore (2012) *Judgement in Managerial Decision Making* (8th edn), Wiley, New York. A comprehensive, entertaining, and interactive description of the many flaws in our decision-making processes.

Leigh Buchanan and Andrew O'Connell (2006) 'A brief history of decision making', *Harvard Business Review*, 84(1), pp. 32–41. Discusses the theories of decision-making within a historical context. The remainder of this special journal issue deals with the same topic.

Robert Cialdini (2009) *Influence: Science and Practice* (5th edn), Pearson Education, New York. Interesting and entertaining account of the biases that we experience in everyday life with suggestions on how to avoid them.

Daniel Kahneman (2011) *Thinking, Fast and Slow*, Allen Lane, London. The author contrasts what he calls System 1 and System 2 thinking, providing examples of the strengths and weaknesses of each.

OB in films

Network (1976, director Sidney Lumet), DVD track 16: 1:48:00 to 1:53:00 (5 minutes). This film is set in the US television industry. Because of his falling ratings, the Union Broadcasting System (UBS) fires its leading news anchorman Howard Beale (played by Peter Finch). Beale's on-air behaviour then becomes increasingly bizarre, after he promises to kill himself on television. Initially his ratings sky-rocket, but then they decline, affecting UBS's other programmes and its revenue. Look again at this clip, which was considered in Chapter 11, from a different point of view. It begins with the network executives assembling for a meeting, and ends with Diana saying 'let's kill the son-of-a-bitch'. The members have to make a decision.

1. What decision options do the executives have?
2. Which decision-making model is being used to make their final decision?
3. How is the decision actually made in the group in the room?
4. How might the individuals justify this decision to themselves?

OB on the web

Familiarize yourself with Kahneman's distinction between System 1 and System 2 thinking. First, search YouTube for a brief introduction to it, such as 'Daniel Kahneman "Schnelles Denken, langsames Denken" – Thinking fast and slow'. Then, watch one of his more detailed explanations, for example, 'Daniel Kahneman on the Machinery of the Mind'. Write a short report explaining the difference between his two types of thinking, providing examples of each from your own experience. Suggest why people in organizations would benefit from an understanding of the differences between these two modes of thinking.

CHAPTER EXERCISES

1. Decision types

Objectives

1. To allow you to distinguish between different types of decisions.
2. To make you aware of the requirements of each type of decision.

Briefing

The chapter defined and distinguished between routine, adaptive, and innovative types of decisions. This exercise gives you the opportunity to identify and deal with each of the three types.

1. Class divides into groups. Each group represents the executive committee of a small manufacturing company which meets regularly to review and decide upon a list of problems. The list consists of items submitted by employees for decision. This week's list of issues is shown below.
2. Each group is to sort the items on the list into three decision categories – routine, adaptive, and innovative.
3. Once all the items have been sorted into three piles, each group is to select one item from the routine pile and one item from the innovative pile, and develop an action plan for each. They should also select one adaptive decision issue, and indicate what approach might be appropriate for working on that decision.

4. After 20–30 minutes, the executive committees / small groups reassemble in a class plenary session. Each group presents *one* of the decisions that it has worked on, and describes its conclusions.
5. Class discusses:
   - Was a routine or innovative decision harder to deal with? Why?
   - Did group members and groups categorize the decision items in the same way?
   - Over which items did group members disagree?
   - How were disagreements over categorization dealt with by the group?

List of decision items

1. An assembly worker wants the committee to decide on a more equitable method for allocating scarce parking spaces.
2. A departmental manager wants a decision as to whether one of his programmers can be given a special bonus for developing a popular software item.
3. The facilities manager wants to know if part-time employees are eligible to join the company health club.
4. A division manager wants a decision on whether to open a new office in Paris, Berlin, or Moscow.
5. The cafeteria manager has asked for a decision on how to choose among suppliers of foodstuffs.
6. The marketing manager wants a decision on a new product that will not compete with other manufacturers' products but will be popular because it fills an unmet need.
7. A supervisor has asked whether overtime should be given to those who ask first or to those who have the most seniority.
8. A decision has to be made whether to emphasize desktop or laptop computers during the next quarter.
9. The research department has developed an innovative and cheap memory chip which is capable of being incorporated in many devices. It has asked what direction your committee wants to take in developing applications for this chip.
10. The board of directors has told your committee to consider whether it would be better to open company-owned retail outlets in five major cities or to franchise the outlets.

2. Choosing decision styles

Objectives

1. To introduce students to different types of decision-making styles.
2. To apply the Vroom-Yetton-Jago model of decision-making.
3. To evaluate the strengths and weaknesses of this decision-making model.

Briefing

1. Form into groups.
2. Read the scenarios as directed by your instructor.
3. Apply the Vroom-Yetton-Jago model described in the chapter, using the decision-making sheet below.
4. Agree the most appropriate decision-making style in each scenario.
5. Based on your experience of this approach, what problems would a manager encounter in trying to apply this model?

→

Scenario 1: New machines (NM)

You are a manufacturing manager in a large electronics plant. The company's management has recently installed new machines and put in a new, simplified work system. To everyone's surprise, the expected rise in productivity has not occurred. In fact, production has begun to drop off, quality has fallen, and staff turnover has increased. You do not believe that there is anything wrong with the machines. Other companies using them confirm this opinion, and representatives from the firm that built the machines report that they are operating at peak efficiency. You suspect that some parts of the new work system may be responsible for the change, but this view is not widely shared among your five immediate subordinates – four first-line supervisors, each in charge of a section, and your supply manager. They are all as concerned as you are, since it affects company profitability and thus their jobs. Each one has their own explanation based on their specialist knowledge. The drop in production has been variously attributed to poor training of the operators, lack of an adequate system of financial incentives, and poor morale. Clearly, this is an issue about which there is considerable depth of feeling among individuals and a source of potential disagreement among your subordinates. This morning you received a phone call from your divisional manager. He had just received your production figures for the last six months and was calling to express his concern. He indicated that the problem was yours to solve in any way you thought best. However, he wanted to know within a week what steps you planned to take. You share your divisional manager's concern with the situation.

Scenario 2: Sugar Substitute Research (SSR)

You are the head of a research and development (R&D) unit for a major beer company, overseeing the work of a team of scientists. They work together well, successfully contributing to different projects. One of the scientists in your unit seems to have tentatively identified a new chemical compound that has few calories but tastes more like sugar than current sugar substitutes. The company has no foreseeable need for this product, but it could be patented and licensed to manufacturers in the food industry, and be a money-earner. Since the sugar substitute discovery would require considerable time and resources to make it commercially viable, these would need to be taken away from other projects in the lab. The sugar substitute project is beyond your technical expertise, but some of the lab researchers are familiar with that field of chemistry. The amount of research needed to perfect the substitute is difficult to determine, and you do not know how much demand there would be for it. There are no rules about funding projects that would be licensed but not used by the organization. The company's R&D budget is limited, and the scientists in your work group have recently complained that they require more resources and financial support to complete their current projects. Some of these have a potential for increasing future beer sales. You believe that most researchers in the R&D unit are committed to ensuring that the company's goals are achieved.

Scenario 3: Repertory theatre (RT)

You are the director of a repertory theatre, responsible for both its artistic and financial direction. While recognizing the importance of both sets of responsibilities, your own interests and talent have led you to focus on securing the highest level of quality for the theatre's productions. Four departmental heads, responsible for administration, production, marketing, and development, report to you. Over the years, they have worked together effectively to mount numerous successful productions. Last week you received a report from an accounting firm commissioned to assess the financial health of your theatre. You were surprised to discover that the theatre's expenses were greatly exceeding its income, and shocked by the report's conclusion that unless expenses were reduced, the theatre might have to close in a year's time. You have circulated the report to your staff, and have been surprised at the variety of their reactions to it. Some dispute the report's conclusions, challenging its assumptions and methods of calculation. Others accept the findings but, shaken by its implications, are divided about what steps should be taken and when. However, what everybody is agreed on is that the theatre should not be closed.

	Question	1	2	3
		NM	SSR	RT
1. Decision significance	How significant is this decision to the success of the project or organization? If significance is high, then the leader needs to be closely involved.			
2. Importance of commitment	How important is subordinate commitment in implementing the decision? If importance is high, then leaders should involve subordinates.			
3. Leader expertise	What is the level of the leader's information, knowledge or expertise in relation to the problem? If it is low, the leader should involve subordinates to obtain it.			
4. Likelihood of commitment	If the leader were to make the decision alone, would subordinates' commitment to it be high or low? If the answer is high, then subordinate involvement is less important.			
5. Group support for goals	What is the level of subordinate support for the team's or organization's goals with respect to this situation? If it is low, the leader should not allow the group to make the decision alone.			
6. Group expertise	What is the level of group members' knowledge and expertise in relation to the problem? If it is high, then more responsibility for the decision can be given to them.			
7. Team competence	What is the level of subordinates' skills and commitment in working together as a team to solve the problem? If their skill and desire to work together cooperatively is high, then more responsibility for the decision can be given to them.			
Decision style				

Scenario 1 from Kreitner and Kinicki, 2001, p. 375; Scenario 2 from Colquitt et al., 2009, p. 482; Scenario 3 from Vroom, 2000, p. 90.

Employability assessment

With regard to your future employment prospects:

1. Identify up to three issues from this chapter that you found significant.
2. Relate these to the competencies in the employability matrix.
3. Decide what actions you need to take to maintain and/or develop those competencies under each of the four headings of the employability matrix.

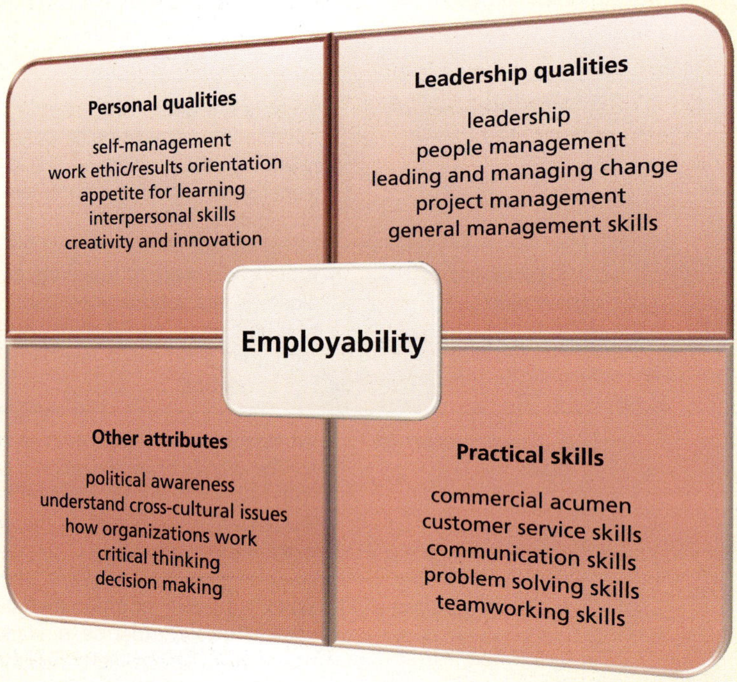

References

BBC Radio 4 (2010) 'Report: Volcano', 3 May.

Brockner, J. (1992) 'The escalation of commitment to a failing course of action: toward theoretical progress', *Academy of Management Review*, 17(1), pp. 39–61.

Brown, V. and Paulus, P.B. (1996) 'A simple dynamic model of social factors in brainstorming', *Small Group Research*, 27(1), pp. 91–114.

Cialdini, R.B. (2009) *Influence: Science and Practice* (5th edn), New York: Pearson Education.

Cohen, M.D., March, J.G. and Olsen, J.P. (1972) 'Garbage can model of organizational choice', *Administrative Science Quarterly*, 17(1), pp. 1–25.

Colquitt, J.A., LePine, J.A. and Wesson, M.J. (2009) *Organizational Behaviour: Improving Performance and Commitment in the Workplace*, London: McGraw-Hill.

Connelly, T. (1997) 'Electronic brainstorming: science meets technology in the group meeting room', in S. Kiesler (ed.), *Culture of the Internet*, Mahwah, NJ: Lawrence Erlbaum Associates, pp. 263–76.

Cooper, W.H., Gallupe, R.G., Pollard, S. and Cadsby, J. (1998) 'Some liberating effects of anonymous electronic brainstorming', *Small Group Research*, 29(2), pp. 147–78.

Coutu, D. (2009) 'Why teams don't work', *Harvard Business Review*, 87(5), pp. 99–105.

Cyert, R.M. and March, J.G. (1963) *A Behavioural Theory of the Firm*, Englewood Cliffs, NJ: Prentice Hall.

Dennis, A.R. and Valacich, J.S. (1993) 'Computer brainstorms: more heads are better than one', *Journal of Applied Psychology*, 78(4), pp. 531–7.

Diehl, M. and Stroebe, W. (1987) 'Productivity loss in brainstorming groups: towards the solution of a riddle', *Journal of Personality and Social Psychology*, 53(3), pp. 447–509.

Duncan, W.J., La France, K.G. and Ginter, P.M. (2003) 'Leadership and decision making: a retrospective application and assessment', *Journal of Leadership and Organizational Studies*, 9(4), pp. 1–20.

Einsiedel, A.A. (1983) 'Decision making and problem solving skills: the rational versus the garbage can model of decision making', *Project Management Quarterly*, 14(4), pp. 52–7.

Esser, J.K. and Lindoerfer, J.S. (1989) 'Groupthink and the space shuttle Challenger accident', *Journal of Behavioural Decision Making*, 2(3), pp. 167–77.

Flowers, M.L. (1977) 'A laboratory test of some implications of Janis's groupthink hypothesis', *Journal of Personality and Social Psychology*, 35(12), pp. 888–96.

Furnham, A. (2000) 'The brainstorming myth', *Business Strategy Review*, 11(4), pp. 21–8.

Garvin, D.A. and Roberto, M.A. (2001) 'What you don't know about making decisions', *Harvard Business Review*, 79(8), pp. 108–16.

Gordon, J. (1993) *A Diagnostic Approach to Organizational Behavior*, Boston, MA: Allyn and Bacon.

Hill, G.W. (1982) 'Group versus individual performance: are N + 1 heads better than one?', *Psychological Bulletin*, 91(3), pp. 517–39.

Isenberg, D.J. (1986) 'Group polarization: a critical review and meta-analysis', *Journal of Personality and Social Psychology*, 50(6), pp. 1141–51.

Janis, I.L. (1982) *Victims of Groupthink* (2nd edn), Boston, MA: Houghton Mifflin.

Kahneman, D. (2003) 'Maps of bounded rationality: psychology for behavioural economists', *American Economic Review*, 93(5), pp. 1449–75.

Kahneman, D. (2011) *Thinking, Fast and Slow*, London: Allen Lane.

Kahneman, D. and Tversky, A. (eds) (2000) *Choices, Values, and Frames*, Cambridge: Cambridge University Press.

Kerr, N.I. and Tindale, R.S. (2004) 'Group performance and decision making', *Annual Review of Psychology*, 55(1), pp. 623–55.

Kreitner, R. (1989) *Management* (4th edn), Boston, MA: Houghton Mifflin.

Kreitner, R. and Kinicki, A. (2001) *Organizational Behavior*, Boston: Irwin/McGraw-Hill.

Lamm, H. (1988) 'A review of our research on group polarization: eleven experiments on the effects of group discussion on risk acceptance, probability estimation and negotiation positions', *Psychological Reports*, 62(3), pp. 807–13.

Lamm, H. and Myers, D.G. (1978) 'Group induced polarization of attitudes and behaviour', in L. Berkowitz (ed.), *Advances in Experimental Social Psychology*, New York: Academic Press, Vol. 11, pp. 145–95.

Langley, A. (1989) 'In search of rationality: the purposes behind the use of formal analysis in organizations', *Administrative Science Quarterly*, 34(4), pp. 598–631.

Leana, C.R. (1985) 'A partial test of Janis's groupthink model: effects of group cohesiveness and leader behaviour on defective decision making', *Journal of Management*, 11(1), pp. 5–17.

Lindblom, C. (1959) 'The science of muddling through', *Public Administration Review*, 34(4), pp. 79–88.

Litchfield, R.C. (2008) 'Brainstorming reconsidered: a goal-based approach', *Academy of Management Review*, 33(3), pp. 649–68.

McCauley, C. (1989) 'The nature of social influence in groupthink: compliance and internationalization', *Journal of Personality and Social Psychology*, 57(2), pp. 250–60.

March, J.G. (1988) *Decisions and Organizations*, Oxford: Blackwell.

March, J.G. and Olsen, J.P. (1976) *Ambiguity and Choice in Organizations*, Oslo: Universitetsforlaget.

March, J.G. and Simon, H.A. (1958) *Organizations*, New York: Wiley.

Mintzberg, H.J. (1989) *Mintzberg on Management: Inside Our Strange World of Organizations*, New York: Free Press.

Moorhead, G. and Montanari, J.R. (1986) 'An empirical investigation of the groupthink phenomenon', *Human Relations*, 39(5), pp. 399–410.

Moorhead, G., Ference, R. and Neck, C.P. (1991) 'Group decision fiascos continue: space shuttle Challenger', *Human Relations*, 44(6), pp. 539–50.

Mullen, B., Johnson, C. and Salas, E. (1991) 'Productivity loss in brainstorming groups: a meta-analytic integration', *Basic and Applied Social Psychology*, 12(1), pp. 3–23.

Mullen, B., Anthony, T., Salas, E. and Driskell, J.E. (1994) 'Group cohesiveness and quality of decision-making: an integration of tests of the groupthink hypothesis', *Small Group Research*, 25(2), pp. 189–204.

Paulus, P.B., Dugosh, K.L., Dzindolet, M.T., Coskun, H. and Putman, V.L. (2002) 'Social and cognitive influences in group brainstorming: predicting production gains and losses', *European Review of Social Psychology*, 12, pp. 299–325.

Rogelberg, S.G., Barnes-Farrell, J.L. and Lowe, C.A. (1992) 'The stepladder technique: an alternative group structure facilitating effective group decision making', *Journal of Applied Psychology*, 77(5), pp. 337–58.

Ross, J. and Staw, B.M. (1993) 'Organizational escalation and exit: lessons from the Shoreham nuclear power plant', *Academy of Management Journal*, 36(4), pp. 701–32.

Samaras, J.T. (1989) *Management Applications: Exercises, Cases and Readings*, Englewood Cliffs, NJ: Prentice Hall.

Schultz-Hardt, S., Brodbeck, F.C., Mojzisch, A., Kerschreiter, R. and Frey, D. (2006) 'Group decision making in hidden profile situations: dissent as a facilitator for decision quality', *Journal of Personality and Social Psychology*, 91(6), pp. 1080–1093.

Simon, H. (1957) *Administrative Behaviour* (2nd edn), New York: Macmillan.

Simon, H. (1960) *The New Science of Management Decision*, New York: Harper and Row.

Simon, H.A. (1979) 'Rational decision making in business organizations', *American Economic Review*, 69(4), pp. 493–513.

Simon, H. (1986) 'Rationality in psychology and economics', *Journal of Business*, 59(4), pp. 209–24.

Staw, B.M. (1976) 'Knee deep in the big muddy: a study of escalating commitment to a chosen course of action' *Organizational Behaviour and Human Performance*, 16(1), pp. 27–44.

Staw, B.M. (1981) 'The escalation of commitment to a course of action', *Academy of Management Review*, 6(4), pp. 569–78.

Stoner, J.A.F. (1961) *A Comparison of Individual and Group Decisions Involving Risk*, Unpublished Master's degree thesis, Massachusetts Institute of Technology, Boston, MA.

Taylor, D., Berry, P.C. and Block, C.H. (1958) 'Does group participation when using brainstorming techniques facilitate or inhibit creative thinking?', *Administrative Science Quarterly*, 3(1), pp. 23–47.

The Economist (2011) 'Rogue hormones', 26 September, p. 98.

The Telegraph Online (2010) 'Iceland volcano: an eyeful of Eyjafjallajökull', 18 May.

Thompson, J.D. (1967) *Organizations in Action*, New York: McGraw-Hill.

Thompson, J. and Tuden, A. (1959) 'Strategies, structures and processes of organizational decisions', in J.D. Thompson, P.B. Hammond, R.W. Hawkes, B.H. Junker and A. Tuden (eds.), *Comparative Studies in Administration*, Pittsburgh, PA: University of Pittsburgh Press, pp. 195–216.

Tingling, P. and Brydon, M. (2010) 'Is decision-based evidence making necessarily bad?', *Sloan Management Review*, 51(4), pp. 71–6.

Turner, M.E. and Pratkanis, A.R. (1998) 'Twenty-five years of groupthink theory and research: lessons from the evaluation of theory', *Organizational Behaviour and Human Decision Processes*, 73(2–3), pp. 105–15.

Vroom, V.H. (2000) 'Leadership and the decision making process', *Organizational Dynamics*, 28(4), pp. 82–94.

Vroom, V.H. and Jago, A.G. (1988) *The New Leadership: Managing Participation in Organizations*, Englewood Cliffs, NJ: Prentice Hall.

Vroom, V.H. and Yetton, P.W. (1973) *Leadership and Decision Making*, Pittsburgh, PA: University of Pittsburgh Press.

Wallace, P. (2001) *The Psychology of the Internet*, Cambridge: Cambridge University Press.

Weber, C.E. (1984) 'Strategic thinking – dealing with uncertainty', *Long Range Planning*, 7(5), pp. 60–70.

West, M.A., Borrill, C.S. and Unsworth, K.L. (1998) 'Team effectiveness in organizations', *International Review of Industrial and Organizational Psychology*, 13, pp. 1–48.

Whyte, G. (1986) 'Escalation of commitment to a course of action: a reinterpretation', *Academy of Management Review*, 11(2), pp. 311–21.

Whyte, G. (1993) 'Escalating commitment in individual and group decision making: a prospect theory approach', *Organizational Behaviour and Human Decision Processes*, 54(3), pp. 430–55.

Yetton, P.W. and Bottger, P.C. (1982) 'Individual versus group problem solving: an empirical test of a best-member strategy', *Organizational Behaviour and Human Performance*, 29(3), pp. 307–21.

Chapter 21 **Conflict**

Key terms

conflict
frame of reference
unitarist frame of reference on conflict
pluralist frame of reference on conflict
interactionist frame of reference on conflict
functional conflict
dysfunctional conflict
conflict resolution
distributive bargaining
integrative bargaining
conflict stimulation
radical frame of reference on conflict
organizational misbehaviour
resistance
alienation
emotional labour
emotions
felt emotions
displayed emotions
emotional dissonance
surface acting
deep acting
display rules
feeling rules
expression rules
emotional harmony

Learning outcomes

When you have read this chapter, you should be able to define those key terms in your own words, and you should also be able to:

1. Distinguish between the four major frames of reference on conflict.
2. Distinguish between functional and dysfunctional conflict.
3. Explain the relationship between organizing, coordinating, and conflict.
4. List the causes of conflict in organizations.
5. Distinguish different organizational coordination devices.
6. Explain the conditions under which conflict is resolved and stimulated in organizations.
7. List Thomas's five conflict resolution approaches.
8. Distinguish between distributive and integrative bargaining.

Why study conflict?

Conflict is a fundamental force governing all aspects of life. Within an organization, conflicts can occur between individuals, groups, and departments. Conflicts are likely to concern disagreements about the conduct and goals of work, the tasks to be performed, how they should be performed, management bonuses, and workers' wages, as well as basic interpersonal conflicts. A CIPD/OPP survey (2008) revealed that the average European worker spent the equivalent of a day a month dealing with conflicts of different kinds, although this varied between countries. Employees in the Netherlands spent 0.9 hours a week on conflict-related tasks; the figure was 1.8 hours in Denmark, France, and Britain, rising to 3.3 hours in Ireland and Germany. Conflict can lead to project failure, absenteeism, and even personal attacks. Hale (2009) noted that in Britain, 99% of working days lost in 2008 were due to disputes over pay, and these accounted for 67% of all work stoppages.

Conflicts within and between organizations

Recent years have seen a number of new organizational conflicts and variants of old ones. During 2012, shareholders of several large companies including Aviva (a major insurance company) and WPP (a global advertising agency) voted against the remuneration packages for their chief executives. In the same year, doctors in the British Health Service went on a one-day strike for the first time in forty years, complaining about their government's treatment of their pension arrangements. In the same month, British and American regulatory bodies fined Barclays Bank £290 million for manipulating (possibly with other banks) the interest rate at which banks lend to each other, known as the London Interbank Offered Rate or Libor. Shortly after that, a British bank was accused of mis-selling insurance products to small and medium companies which threatened their existence, and others were being investigated. During 2009 in France, 'sequestration' or temporary kidnapping of executives came back into fashion with charges of 'hostage-taking' and 'industrial terrorism' being levelled at workers. Francois-Henri Pinault, the boss of Christie's, Printemps, and FNAC, was held for an hour while negotiating with fifty angry employees who had blocked the street; and Nicholas Polutnik, director of the Caterpillar's bulldozer plant in Grenoble, and three of his management team were forced to spend the night in their offices. The firm planned to cut 700 jobs in France. All these events have brought into sharp focus how the interests of different groups and institutions result in organizational conflict (based on Lichfield, 2009; BBC Online, 2012; *The Guardian Online*, 2012; *Financial Times*, 2012a).

Conflict a process that begins when one party perceives that another party has negatively affected, or is about to negatively affect, something that the first party cares about.

Conflict can arise from the exercise of power and politics; from particular leadership styles and decision-making processes; and from structural and cultural changes. **Conflict** is a state of mind. It has to be perceived by the parties involved. If the two or more parties concerned are not aware of a conflict, then no conflict exists. This broad definition encompasses conflicts at all different levels within an organization. Typically conflicts are based upon differences in interests and values. They occur when the interests of one party come up against the different interests of another. Parties may include shareholders, managers, departments, professionals, and groups; while conflict issues can include dividends, manager bonuses, and employee wage levels.

There has been a longstanding debate concerning whether or not conflict within organizations is harmful. Dean Tjosvold (2008) argued that conflict was an inevitable aspect of all organizations. However, if properly conducted, he believed it provided better ways of working by combining the energies of different team members who used their experience and knowledge to generate new ideas. In his view, conflict was essential to successful teamwork and organizational effectiveness. In consequence, it should be welcomed and managed appropriately. In contrast, Carsten De Dreu (2008) stated that conflict was always detrimental, and that the research that supported the beneficial aspects of workplace conflict was weak. He felt that organizations had to make efforts to manage conflict, not because it had positive effects but in order to minimize its negative consequences.

Skylab strike

NASA Images

Friday 27 December 1973 was a red-letter day in the history of industrial relations. The Apollo astronauts in Skylab 4 (the American precursor to the International Space Station) conducted the first ever day-long sit-down strike in outer space. Why did this occur? A breakdown in trust occurred at the start when ground control at Houston reprimanded the astronauts for not reporting their space sickness. Tensions mounted when, in an effort to maximize the amount of information gained, Houston minutely scheduled the astronauts' activities. The crew soon found themselves tired and behind schedule. By removing all their discretion, Houston made them into robots. It shortened their meal breaks, reduced the set-up times for experiments, and told them they were not working long or hard enough. Every day, it sent up six feet of information to the astronauts' teleprinter, containing 42 different sets of instructions. These included directions as to where to point the telescope, which scientific instruments to use, and so on, arranging their entire day for them. Astronauts normally follow such instructions to the letter.

However, the astronauts wanted Houston to provide them with only a general schedule and a 'shopping list' of things to do, so that they could decide how best to do them. Houston's view was that many jobs interfered with one another and could not be performed simultaneously. For example, one crew member rides a bicycle ergometer and shakes the space station, while another tries to film a solar flare. Other, more interesting tasks could distract the astronauts and prevent them from performing more mundane, albeit vital ones. In the Taylorist style, ground control had defined itself as the 'planners' (management) and the astronauts as the 'implementers' (workers). Eventually, the relationship between mission control and the astronauts broke down completely. The crew mutinied against mission control, turned off the communication, and refused to work for a 24-hour period, spending the time relaxing and enjoying the panoramic views. Eventually, the astronauts' workload was reduced but NASA ensured that none of them ever flew again (Weick, 1977).

STOP AND THINK

Can you provide examples from your own work experience where conflict has led to positive or negative outcomes?

Contrasting frames of reference: unitarist, pluralist, and interactionist

Frame of reference a person's perceptions and interpretations of events, which involve assumptions about reality, attitudes towards what is possible, and conventions regarding correct behaviour.

A **frame of reference** refers to the influences which structure a person's perceptions and interpretations of events. These involve assumptions about reality, attitudes towards what is possible, and conventions regarding what is correct behaviour for those involved. The adoption of differing frames of references by opposing sides can impair the effective resolution of conflicts.

For example, in a labour dispute, the unions and management will look at the industrial relations bargaining situation from completely different points of view. Management assumes that the natural state of affairs is one in which there is no inherent conflict of interest between the different individuals, groups, or collectivities that constitute the organization. It believes that managers and employees possess shared goals. From this frame of reference, cooperation is the norm, and all dissent is seen as unreasonable. Senior management cannot conceive how or why their authority might be challenged or why employees might engage in disruptive behaviour. In contrast, the union assumes differing and conflicting demands. It sees profits as something to be fought over with senior management and company shareholders. From labour's frame of reference, each party seeks legitimately to maximize its own rewards. Industrial action aims to maximize the revenues going to labour, and is explainable in these terms.

The literature distinguishes four different frames of reference on conflict, based on the distinctions made by Alan Fox. They are labelled *unitarist*, *pluralist*, *interactionist*, and *radical* (Fox, 1966). In this section, the first three will be introduced and contrasted, while the fourth, the radical, will be subjected to a more detailed analysis in its own section later. These frames are neither 'right' nor 'wrong', only different.

- The *unitarist* frame sees organizations as essentially harmonious and any conflict as bad.
- The *pluralist* frame sees organizations as a collection of groups, each with their own interests.
- The *interactionist* frame sees conflict as a positive, necessary force for effective performance.
- The *radical* frame sees conflict as an inevitable outcome of capitalism.

Moreover, academics will also adopt one of these frames when they teach the topic to their students or research it. Neither organization employees nor academics will necessarily make their chosen frame explicit, and hence students need to ask or deduce which conflict frame of reference is being used.

Pronoun test

Robert Reich described the 'pronoun test' that he used to evaluate the nature of the employment relationship in the companies that he visited as US Secretary of Labour during the first Clinton Administration, in the following way:

I'd say, 'Tell me about the company'. If the person said 'we' or 'us', I knew people were strongly attached to the organization. If they said 'they' or 'them', I knew there was less of a sense of linkage. (Rousseau, 1999)

Most of us are capable of bringing different frames of reference to bear on the situations that we face. If we analyse it this way, we reach these conclusions, but if we analyse it another way, we reach different conclusions. Some people (students, academics, managers) *may* be wedded to a particular perspective. This becomes obvious in their conversations, actions, or writings. Their chosen frame of reference on conflict will determine

- what they will notice in their environment
- how they will interpret those noticed events
- how they expect others to behave
- how they will behave themselves.

However, there is value in being able to view conflicts from a number of different standpoints, to 'switch between frames', in part, so that we can understand the viewpoints of others.

Unitarist frame of reference on conflict a perspective that regards management and employee interests as coinciding and which thus regards organizational conflict as harmful and to be avoided.

The **unitarist frame of reference on conflict** views organizations as fundamentally harmonious, cooperative structures, consisting of committed, loyal worker-management teams that promote harmony of purpose.

Stephen Ackroyd and Paul Thompson (1999) and Roger Johnston (2000) identified the key features of the unitarist frame of reference. It

- assumes a commonality of interests between an organization's workers and managers and, by implication, the company's owners (shareholders);
- accepts unquestioningly the political, economic, and social framework within which management is performed, and adopts the language, assumptions, and goals of management itself, which it supposedly seeks to study and understand;

- de-politicizes the relationships between individuals, groups, and classes within the workplace, treating conflicts and contradictions as peripheral;
- explains actual, observed instances of workplace conflict either in terms of a failure of coordination or in psychological terms (personality clash or abnormal behaviour of deviant individuals);
- applies a liberal-humanistic, individually-focused approach to conflict resolution, which is rooted in the human relations movement;
- holds that managers are capable of permanently changing the behaviour of employees in a conflict situation in an organization through the application of conflict resolution techniques;
- claims that economic, technological, and political developments of the past have now virtually eliminated non-sanctioned employee behaviour within the organization;
- moves rapidly over the consideration of causes of conflict within the workplace, in order to focus on conflict resolution techniques;
- uses communication failures between management and employees (and the interference of 'third-party agitators', normally unions) to explain workplace conflict.

Pluralist frame of reference on conflict a perspective that views organizations as consisting of different natural interest groups, each with their own potentially constructive, legitimate interests, which make conflict between them inevitable.

The **pluralist frame of reference on conflict** views organizations as a collection of many separate groups, each of which have their own legitimate interests, so that conflict between them is inevitable as each attempts to pursue its own objectives. This frame of reference therefore rejects the view that individual employees have the same interests as the management, or that an organization is one big happy family.

The pluralist frame takes a political orientation in that it sees that some of the time, the interests of the different groups will coincide, while at other times, they will clash and so cause conflict. The outbreak of conflict provides a 'relationship regulation' mechanism between the different groups. That is, it provides a clear sign to both parties as to which issues they disagree fundamentally about, and thus provides a sort of 'early warning system' of possible impending breakdown which would be to the disadvantage of all of concerned. The most common clashes may be between unions and management, but will also include differences between management functions (production versus marketing), between levels of management (senior management versus middle management), and between individual managers.

These differences do not prevent an organization from functioning, since all groups recognize that compromise and negotiation are essential if they are to achieve their goals even partially. Hence, from this perspective, the job of management becomes that of keeping the balance between potentially conflicting goals, and managing the differences between these different interest groups. This involves seeking a compromise between the different constituents such as the employees, managers, shareholders, and others, so that all these stakeholders, to varying degrees, can continue to pursue their aspirations. Underlying the pluralist view is the belief that conflict can be resolved through compromise to the benefit of all. However, it requires all parties to limit their claims to a level which is at least tolerable to the others, and which allows further collaboration to continue. A mutual survival strategy is typically agreed.

Acceptance of the pluralist frame implies that conflict is inevitable, indeed endemic. However, it does not see conflict as harmful and to be eliminated, but believes that it must be evaluated in terms of its functions and dysfunctions. For while it may reinforce the status quo, it can also assist evolutionary rather than revolutionary change, acting as a safety valve, and keep the organization responsive to internal and external changes while retaining intact its essential elements such as the organizational hierarchy and the power distribution. The inevitable conflict which results has to be managed so that organizational goals are reconciled with group interests for the benefit of mutual survival and prosperity. This ongoing internal struggle is seen as generally acting to maintain the vitality, responsiveness, and efficiency of the organization.

Interactionist frame of reference on conflict a perspective that views conflict as a positive and necessary force within organizations that is essential for their effective performance.

Functional conflict a form of conflict which supports organization goals and improves performance.

Dysfunctional conflict a form of conflict which does not support organization goals and hinders organizational performance.

The **interactionist frame of reference on conflict** views conflict as a positive force within organizations that is necessary for effective performance. It can be considered as part of the pluralist tradition. It accepts the inevitability of conflict and argues that, to be dealt with constructively, conflict has to be institutionalized within the organization through systems of collective bargaining. The interactionist frame not only accepts the inevitability of conflict, but also contains the notion that there is an optimum level of it (not too little or too much), and that the way to achieve that level is through the intervention of the manager.

The interactionist frame believes that conflict should be encouraged whenever it emerges, and stimulated if it is absent. It sees a group or a department that is too peaceful, harmonious, and cooperative as potentially apathetic and unresponsive to changing needs. It fears that extreme group cohesion can lead to groupthink (see Chapter 20), as identified by Irving Janis (1982) and Cosier and Schwenk (1990). This frame therefore encourages managers to maintain a minimum level of conflict within their organizations so to as to encourage self-criticism, change, and innovation and thereby counter apathy. However, that conflict has to be of the appropriate type. Thus, **functional conflict** supports organization goals and improves performance, but **dysfunctional conflict** hinders organizational performance.

The relationship between the two is depicted on a bell-shaped curve, as shown in Figure 21.1. If there is insufficient conflict the unit or group may not perform at its best; however, too much conflict, and its performance deteriorates. Performance improvements occur through conflict exposing weaknesses in organizational decision-making and design which prompts changes in the company.

Condition	1	2	3
Conflict level	Too little	Optimal	Too great

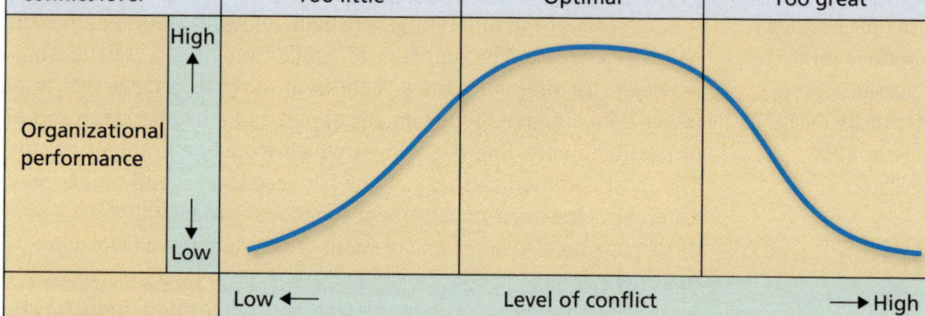

Organizational performance level	Low	High	Low
Organization's internal characteristics	• Apathy • Stagnation • Poor focus • Unmotivated • Few changes • Slow to adapt • Not integrated • Few new ideas	• Cohesive • Productive • Co-operation • Organizational goal focused • Innovative and changing • Solution searching • Creatively adapting to environment	• Chaotic • Disruptive • Distracted • Politicized • Uncooperative • Hostile to other groups
Probable impact on organization	Dysfunctional	Functional	Dysfunctional
Managerial action required	Stimulate conflict	Leave alone	Reduce conflict

Figure 21.1: Types of conflict, internal organizational characteristics, and required management actions

Source: based on Hatch (1997, p. 305) and Robbins and Judge (2013, p. 504).

Figure 21.1 is also sometimes referred to as the contingency model of conflict because it recommends that managers should increase or decrease the amount of conflict in their organizations depending (contingent) on the situation (Hatch, 1997, p. 304; Hatch with Cunliffe, 2006). Thus for example, in Condition 1 there is too little conflict, and so managers need to stimulate more. In contrast, in Condition 3, there is too much conflict and they need to reduce it. In both cases they seek to achieve an optimum level of conflict depicted in column 2. Taffinder (1998) felt that at optimal intensity, conflict produced organizational benefits which managers rarely exploited and which they even suppressed by applying conflict resolution approaches too rapidly. Amongst the benefits of functional conflict that he listed were:

- motivating energy to deal with underlying problems;
- making underlying issues explicit;
- sharpening employees' understanding of real goals and interests;
- enhancing mutual understanding between different groups of employees;
- stimulating a sense of urgency;
- discouraging engagement in avoidance behaviour;
- preventing premature and often dangerous resolution problems.

Coordination failure and conflict

The process of organizing by senior managers acts to divide up the work activities, and an outbreak of conflict can thus be seen as a symptom of management's failure to adequately coordinate these same activities later on. The coordination-conflict four-stage model organizes the diverse theoretical discussions and research findings into a framework that explains how conflict in organizations arises and how it might be managed (Figure 21.2). Such management may involve either the use of conflict resolution approaches (to reduce or eradicate conflict) or conflict stimulation approaches (to encourage and increase conflict).

Organizing

The first stage of the model consists of organizing, defined as the process of breaking up a single task and dividing it among different departments, groups, or individuals. For example, a car company allocates the work related to a new vehicle to its different subdivisions (departments, groups, and individuals) – personnel, accounting, production, sales, and research. Such functional specialization is one of many bases on which to divide the total work involved. Specialization is rational because it concentrates specialists in proper departments, avoids duplication, allows performance goals to be established, and specifies practices.

All forms of such horizontal specialization (divisions between departments) result in each sub-unit becoming concerned with its own particular part of the total objective and work process. The degree of such separation of tasks can vary, but it creates the conditions in which conflict can potentially arise. It does so because, by definition, each department, group, or individual receives a different part of the whole task to perform. This differentiates it from the other departments in six areas:

1. Goals orientation and evaluation
2. Self-image and stereotypes
3. Task interdependencies
4. Time perspective
5. Overlapping authority
6. Scarce resources.

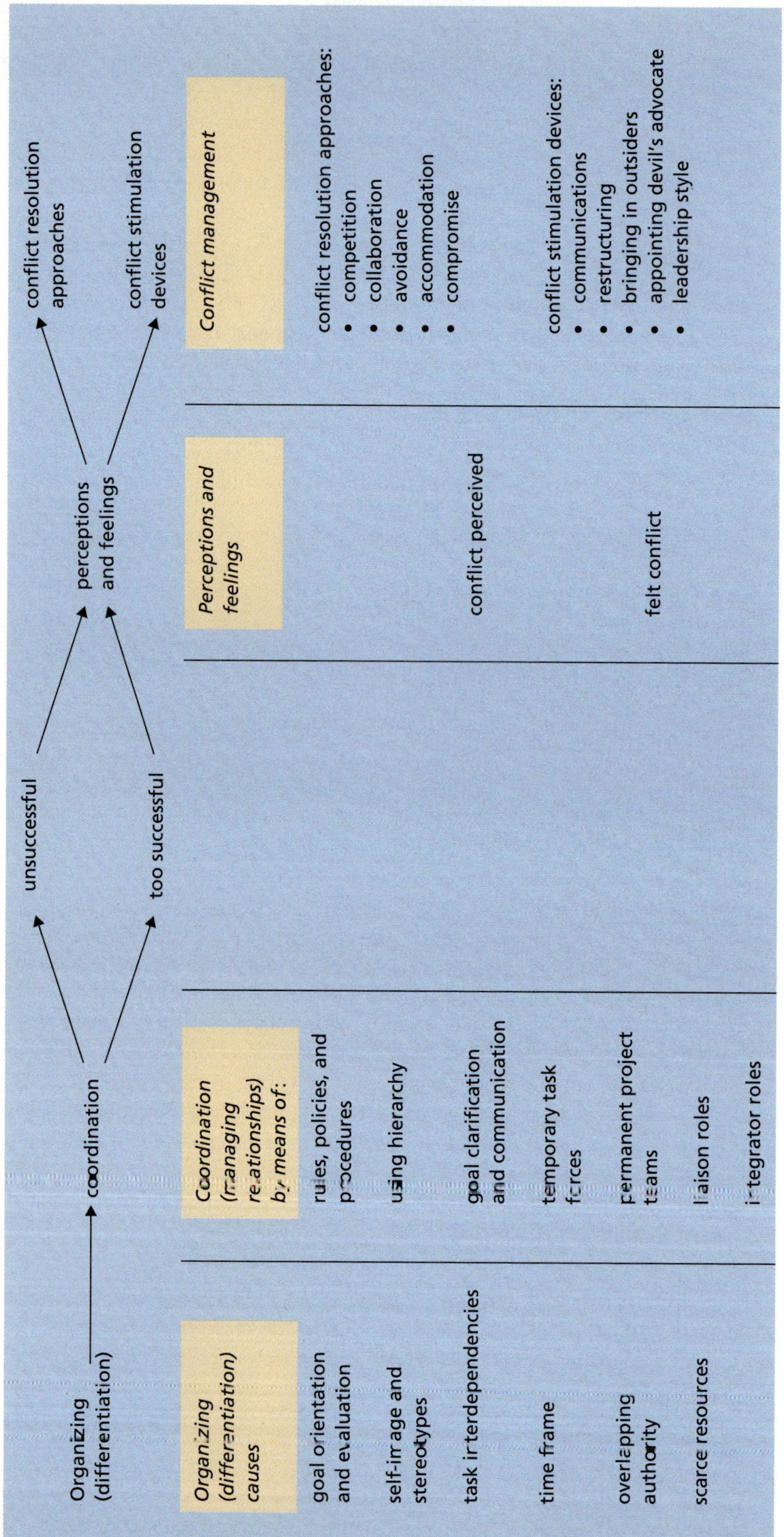

Figure 21.2: Coordination–conflict model

1. Goals orientation and evaluation

Each department is given its own goal, and its members are evaluated in terms of how well they achieve it. Ideally, the goals of different departments, groups, and individuals, although different, should be complementary, but in practice this may not be so. Moreover, the measurement process can reinforce differences. Each department's unique goals and evaluation methods lead it to have its own view about priorities, and how these are best achieved.

2. Self-image and stereotypes

Employees in each department become socialized into a particular perception of themselves and how they see the other departments in the company. A group may come to see itself as more vital to a company's operations than others, and comes to believe that it has higher status or prestige. Such an evaluation can engender an 'us-and-them' attitude. The higher-status groups may cease to adapt their behaviours to accommodate the goals of other groups, and indeed may try to achieve their objectives at the cost of others, thus creating conflict. Whenever differences between groups and departments are emphasized, stereotypes are reinforced, relations deteriorate, and conflict develops. Departments will often blame each other for problems and shortcomings (see Table 21.1).

Table 21.1: Areas of potential goal conflict between marketing and manufacturing departments

Goal conflict	***Marketing*** **operating goal is customer satisfaction**	**versus**	***Manufacturing*** **operating goal is production efficiency**
conflict area	***typical comment***		***typical comment***
1. Breadth of product line	'Our customers demand variety.'		'The product line is too broad – all we get are short, uneconomical runs.'
2. New product introduction	'New products are our lifeblood.'		'Unnecessary design changes are prohibitively expensive.'
3. Production scheduling	'We need faster response. Our lead times are too long.'		'We need realistic customer commitments that don't change like a wind direction.'
4. Physical distribution	'Why don't we ever have the right merchandise in inventory?'		'We can't afford to keep huge inventories.'
5. Quality	'Why can't we have reasonable quality at low cost?'		'Why must we always offer options that are too expensive and offer little customer utility?'

Source: reprinted by permission of *Harvard Business Review*. Adapted from 'Can marketing and manufacturing coexist?' by Shapiro, B.S., 55 (September–October) 1977. Copyright © 1977 by the Harvard Business School Publishing Corporation; all rights reserved.

3. Task interdependencies

The process of organizing results in differentiation, making individuals, groups, and departments dependent on each other to perform their own jobs satisfactorily and to achieve their own objectives. The degree of such interdependence varies. In Chapter 16, we considered James Thompson's (1967) three types of interdependence – *pooled*, *sequential*, and *reciprocal*. Groups in sequential interdependence, and, even more, those in reciprocal interdependence, required a high degree of coordination between their activities. If this was achieved, then each group would perform effectively and its members would experience satisfaction. When such coordination was absent, the result would be conflict between them. From this viewpoint, conflict results from a failure in coordination.

4. *Time perspective*

Paul Lawrence and Jay Lorsch's (1967) study found that people's perceptions of the importance accorded to different items depended on the time frame that governed their work and their goal orientations. Groups with different time perspectives find it difficult to coordinate their activities, and this can result in greater inter-group conflict. These different time frames are often incompatible, hindering communication, impeding coordination, and encouraging conflict.

5. *Overlapping authority*

Demarcation disputes have always caused difficulties, and ambiguity over responsibility or authority is one example of this. Individuals or groups may be uncertain as to who is responsible for performing which tasks or duties, and who has the authority to direct whom. Each party may claim or reject responsibility, and the result can be conflict. Groups may fight for the control of a resource, while individual managers may attempt to seize one another's authority.

6. *Scarce resources*

Once a task is allocated to an individual, group, or department, its recipient is allocated resources with which to achieve it. Since resources are finite, conflict can arise with respect to how personnel, money, space, or equipment are shared out. From a win–lose perspective, one party's gain is another's loss. For this reason, conflicts often arise at times of budget cuts, reduced promotion opportunities, and wage freezes.

STOP AND THINK

How complete is this list of conflict causes – goal orientation, self-image, interdependencies, time frame, overlapping authority, and scarce resources? Think of a conflict situation with which you have been involved in an organization. Do these causes satisfactorily account for the conflict or would you wish to add other causes?

Coordinating

If organizing involved breaking up the task into bits, then coordinating is bringing the bits together again. Coordination involves ensuring that the previously divided tasks that were allocated between different departments, groups, and individuals are brought together in the right way and at the right time. Coordination entails synchronizing the different aspects of the work process. The three general classes of coordination devices are listed in Table 21.2.

Table 21.2: Devices for coordinating relationships in organizations classified by class

Class of coordination	Description	Device
Formal direction	Written guidelines and adjudication by senior staff	• Rules, policies and procedures • Using hierarchy
Mutual adjustment	Members carrying out the work adjust to each other	• Goal clarification and communication • Temporary task force • Permanent project team
Special liaison	Specially employed coordinators use consultation and communication	• Liaison roles • Integrator roles

Source: adapted from *Managing Through Organization*, Hales, C., Copyright 1993 Routledge, Reproduced by permission of Cengage Learning EMEA Ltd.

Provided that the relationships between the differentiated departments, units, groups, or individuals are successfully coordinated, conflict will not occur. By effectively using inter-party coordination devices, a company can prevent conflict breaking out in the first place. The devices are designed to manage the relationships between the different parties so that the reasons for conflict to arise are eliminated. It is only if and when these coordination devices fail, and conflict occurs, that conflict resolution techniques will be required. Organizations use seven devices to co-ordinate their activities:

1. Rules, policies, and procedures
2. Hierarchy
3. Goal clarification and communication
4. Temporary task forces
5. Permanent project teams
6. Liaison roles
7. Integrator roles.

1. Rules, policies, and procedures

All of these specify how one party is to interact with another. For example, a standardized operating procedure will specify when additional staff can be recruited to a department. Rules and procedures reduce the need for both interaction and information flow between parties. They are most useful when inter-party activities are known in advance; when they occur frequently enough to merit establishing rules and procedures to handle them; and when there is sufficient stability to make them relevant.

2. Hierarchy

Coordination of different parties' activities is achieved efficiently, by referring any problems to a superior located higher up in the organizational hierarchy. The supervisor uses their legitimate authority, based on their position in the hierarchy, to resolve a conflict. Team members unable to agree take the problem to their mutual boss (Grant, 2002).

3. Goal clarification and communication

By specifying and communicating its goals to the others in advance, each party knows what the other is attempting to do. At the individual level this may mean clear job descriptions, while at the departmental level, it could be a statement of objectives. Parties can meet to ensure that they do not compete or interfere with the goals of others. Such discussions reduce the chances of each party misperceiving the others' intentions.

4. Temporary task forces

This involves representatives from several different departments coming together on a temporary basis, to form a task force. Once the specific problem it was created for is solved, the task force disbands, and members return to their usual duties and departments. During their membership, individuals come to understand the goals, values, attitudes, and problems of their fellow members. This helps to resolve their differences effectively, especially if more than two parties are involved.

5. Permanent project teams

For complex tasks, a project team may be established consisting of cross-functional members (e.g. from engineering, marketing, finance). This creates a matrix structure, since each individual retains a responsibility both to the project team leader and to their functional department. This solution allows coordination to occur at the team level, thus improving communication and decision-making.

6. Liaison roles

If differences remain unresolved by senior management, then a liaison role may be created. It would be used most by departments between whom the potential for conflict is the highest. The occupant of this role has to be well informed about the needs and technology of the units involved; be seen to be unbiased; and be interpersonally skilled. By holding meetings, supplying units with information, liaison personnel keep the employees in different sections in touch with each other.

7. Integrator roles

An individual or department may be dedicated to integrating the activities of several highly conflicting departments, e.g. production, sales, and research. A scientist with financial and sales experience may be recruited to occupy an integrating role. By having a 'foot in each camp', this person can assist the departments to coordinate their activities. The integrator checks that the departments' objectives complement each other, and that the output of one becomes the timely input to the other. Coordinating using liaison and integrator roles is illustrated in Figure 21.3.

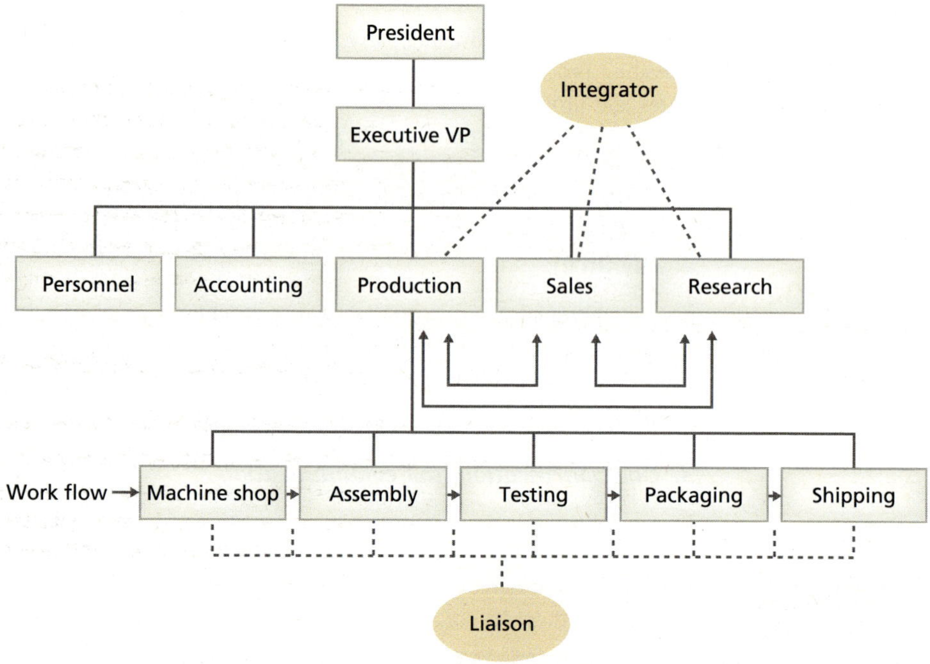

Figure 21.3: Coordinating using liaison and integrator roles

Home viewing

In the film *Twelve Angry Men* (1957, director Sidney Lumet), a jury retires to decide on the guilt or innocence of a youth from a slum background. At the outset, eleven of the twelve jurors are convinced of the boy's guilt and are keen to find him guilty without further discussion. Only one member of the jury, played by Henry Fonda, has reservations and persuades the other members to take the time to review the evidence. The film can be broken down into a series of 'conflict episodes', each of which ends with a vote (conflict reduction) or a juror's change of mind. The film illustrates many aspects of conflict. In each episode, ask yourself how the perceived and felt conflict manifest themselves in the characters' behaviour, and how does each vote become the latent conflict for the next episode? Watch Fonda's behaviour carefully. At first sight it appears that it is random. But then, you'll see a pattern. What is that pattern? Consider what types of power are possessed by the characters in the film. Finally, notice how the group's decisions are influenced by contextual, social, emotional, temporal, and behavioural factors.

Perceptions and emotions

Unsuccessful coordination need not necessarily ignite a conflict. Perception plays an important part. It is only if one party, individual, group, or department becomes aware of, or is adversely affected by, the situation, and cares about it, that latent conflict turns into perceived conflict. It occurs only when one party realizes that another is thwarting its goals. It is at this stage that the conflict issue becomes defined, and 'what it's all about' gets decided. Specifically, each party considers the origins of the conflict, why it emerged, and how the problem is being experienced with the other party. The way that the conflict is defined at this stage will determine the type of outcomes that the parties are willing to settle for in the later stages.

Not only must a party perceive a conflict, but it must also feel it. That is, it must become emotionally involved in experiencing feelings of anxiety, tension, frustration, and hostility towards the other party. The emotional dimension of conflict shapes perceptions. For example, negative emotions result in an oversimplification of issues, reductions in trust, and negative interpretations of other parties' behaviour. Positive emotions, in contrast, increase the chances of the parties taking a broader view, seeing the issue as a problem to be solved, and developing more creative solutions.

Conflict management

Within an organization, management may judge that there is too much or too little conflict.

In the case of the former, the existing coordination devices may be inadequate, thereby causing too much conflict. In such a case, the company will manage the situation by implementing **conflict resolution** approaches to reduce or eliminate the immediate conflict, before adjusting the coordination mechanism to prevent it occurring in the future. Alternatively, they may consider that the coordination devices are working too well, thereby causing complacency and apathy. In this case, they may introduce conflict stimulation approaches to increase conflict. Thus, within organizations, conflict can be managed through a combination of conflict resolution and conflict stimulation approaches.

Conflict resolution a process which has as its objective the ending of conflict between disagreeing parties.

Conflict resolution approaches

Kenneth Wayne Thomas (b.1943)

Kenneth Thomas (1976) distinguished five conflict resolution approaches based upon the two dimensions of

- how assertive or unassertive each party is in pursuing its own concerns
- how cooperative or uncooperative each is in satisfying the concerns of the other.

He labelled these *competing* (assertive and uncooperative); *avoiding* (unassertive and uncooperative); *compromising* (mid-range on both dimensions); *accommodating* (unassertive and cooperative); and *collaborating* (assertive and cooperative). They are summarized in Figure 21.4 and defined in Table 21.3.

Unless the managers are flexible and capable of switching between styles, their ability to resolve conflicts effectively will be limited. In practice, all individuals, whether managers or not, habitually use only a limited number of styles (perhaps just one) to resolve all the conflicts in which they are involved. It is not surprising that their success is limited.

STOP AND THINK Some individuals resolve conflict in one fixed way in different situations. Others change their approach to suit the circumstances. Think of a specific domestic, friendship, or organizational context that involved conflict. How did you deal with it? Did you compete, avoid, compromise, accommodate, or collaborate?

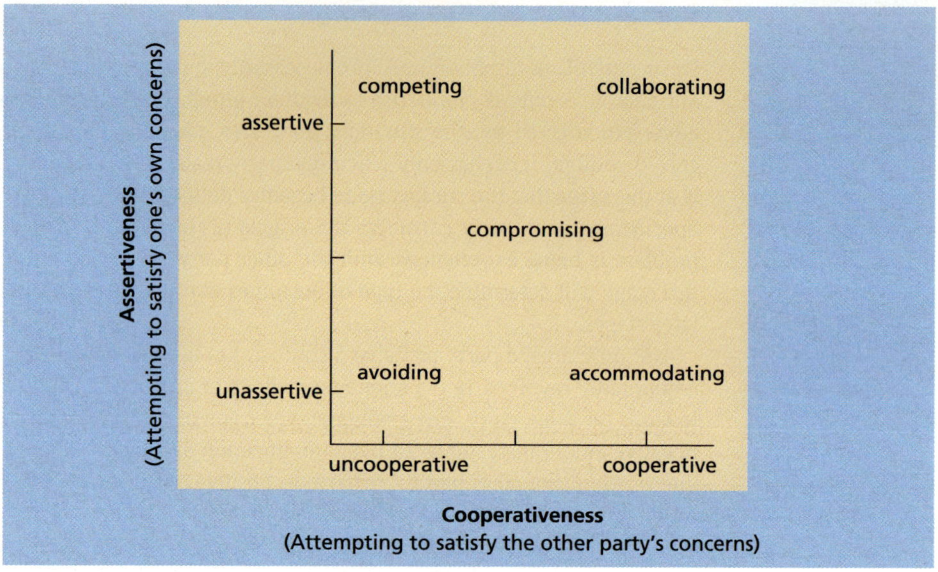

Figure 21.4: Conflict resolution approaches compared

Source: reprinted from *Organizational Behaviour and Human Performance*, Vol. 16 No. 1, T.H. Ruble and K. Thomas, Support for a two-dimensional model of conflict behaviour, p. 145, Copyright 1976, with permission from Elsevier.

Table 21.3: Conflict resolution approaches compared

Approach	Objective	Your posture	Supporting rationale	Likely outcome
1. Competing	Get your way	'I know what's right. Don't question my judgement or authority.'	It is better to risk causing a few hard feelings than to abandon the issue.	You feel vindicated, but the other party feels defeated and possibly humiliated.
2. Avoiding	Avoid having to deal with conflict	'I'm neutral on that issue. Let me think about it. That's someone else's problem.'	Disagreements are inherently bad because they create tension.	Interpersonal problems don't get resolved, causing long-term frustration manifested in a variety of ways.
3. Compromising	Reach an agreement quickly	'Let's search for a solution we can both live with so we can get on with our work.'	Prolonged conflicts distract people from their work and cause bitter feelings.	Participants go for the expedient rather than effective solutions.
4. Accommodating	Don't upset the other person	'How can I help you feel good about this? My position isn't so important that it is worth risking bad feelings between us.'	Maintaining harmonious relationships should be our top priority.	The other person is likely to take advantage.
5. Collaborating	Solve the problem together	'This is my position, what's yours? I'm committed to finding the best possible solution. What do the facts suggest?'	Each position is important though not necessarily equally valid. Emphasis should be placed on the quality of the outcome and the fairness of the decision-making process.	The problem is most likely to be resolved. Both parties are committed to the solution and satisfied that they have been treated fairly.

Source: adapted from *Developing Management Skills for Europe*, Whetton, D., Cameron, K. and Woods, M. Pearson Education Ltd © Pearson Education Ltd 2000, p. 345

National culture and conflict resolution

Research suggests that the use of conflict resolution strategies may be affected by national culture. Collectivist cultures stress the interests of the group, while individualist cultures emphasize those of individuals. Hence people in the former will be keen to maintain relationships and to promote the wellbeing of the group. They will do this by using indirect methods to resolve differences, perhaps using the intervention of third parties. In contrast, people from individualist cultures will express conflict directly and openly. Studies have shown that Japanese and Chinese negotiators, representing collectivist cultures, prefer the use of compromising and avoiding, in contrast to individualist US negotiators who use competing tactics (based on Ren and Gray, 2009; Ma, 2007).

Richard Walton and Robert McKersie's (1965) classic research into negotiation behaviour distinguished distributive bargaining strategies from integrative bargaining strategies (see Table 21.4).

Table 21.4: Bargaining strategies

Integrative bargaining **Win–win strategy**	***Distributive bargaining*** **Win–lose strategy**
1. Define the conflict as a mutual problem.	1. Define the conflict as a win–lose situation.
2. Pursue joint outcomes.	2. Pursue own group's outcomes.
3. Find creative agreements that satisfy both groups.	3. Force the other group into submission.
4. Use open, honest, and accurate communication of group's needs, goals, and proposals.	4. Use deceitful, inaccurate, and misleading communication of group's needs, goals, and proposals.
5. Avoid threats (to reduce the other's defensiveness).	5. Use threats (to force submission).
6. Communicate flexibility of position.	6. Communicate high commitment (rigidity) regarding one's position.

Source: JOHNSON & JOHNSON, JOINING TOGETHER: GROUP THEORY & GROUP SKILLS, 1st Ed., © 1975, pp. 182–3. Reprinted and Electronically adapted by permission of Pearson Education, Inc., Upper Saddle River, New Jersey.

Distributive bargaining a negotiation strategy in which a fixed sum of resources is divided up, leading to a win–lose situation between the parties.

Integrative bargaining a negotiation strategy that seeks to increase the total amount of resources, creating a win–win situation between the parties.

Distributive bargaining operates under zero-sum conditions. It seeks to divide up a fixed amount of resources, thus creating a win-lose situation. Purchasing a new car exemplifies this. The more the buyer pays, the more profit the seller makes, and vice versa. Here the pie is fixed, and the parties bargain about the share each receives. Within an organization, distributive bargaining takes place between the trade (labour) unions and management. Issues involving wages, benefits, working conditions, and related matters are seen as a conflict over limited resources.

Integrative bargaining is the type of bargaining which seeks settlements that can create a win-win solution. A union-management agreement which increases productivity and profits, and wages in line with both, would be an example of integrated bargaining because the size of the total pie is increased. Integrative bargaining is preferable to distributive bargaining because the latter makes one party a loser. It can create animosities and deepen divisions between people who have to work together on an ongoing basis.

Studies have revealed similarities between conflict resolution strategies and negotiation strategies (Savage et al., 1989; W.P. Smith, 1987). Of the five conflict resolution strategies described earlier, four (competing, avoiding, compromising, and accommodating) involve one or more of the parties sacrificing something, and would therefore be classified as distributive. David Whetton and colleagues (1996) suggested that these distributive strategies matched the natural inclination of those individuals who approached conflicts with a 'macho man', 'easy touch' or 'split the difference' style, and they thus engendered competition, exploitation, or irresponsibility. Over the last three decades, the major developers of the integrative bargaining concept have been Roger Fisher and William Ury (1981) from the Harvard Negotiating Project. Their scheme of 'principled negotiation' sets out guiding principles to apply when preparing and engaging in face-to-face negotiations. Work in this project has dealt with how negotiators should proceed if the other side does not 'play the game' (Ury, 1991; Ury and Patton, 1997).

Conflict stimulation approaches

Conflict stimulation the process of engendering conflict between parties where none existed before, or escalating the current conflict level if it is too low.

Interactionists argue that there are conditions in organizations when what is needed is more and not less conflict, i.e. **conflict stimulation** (Sternberg and Soriano, 1984; Robbins, 1974). John Kotter (1996) discussed the dangers of complacency, and the need to drive employees out of their comfort zones. Amongst the complacency-smashing and potentially conflict-stimulating techniques used by senior management were the following:

- Create a crisis by allowing a financial loss to occur or an error to blow up.
- Eliminate obvious examples of excess like corporate jet fleets and gourmet dining rooms.
- Set targets like income, productivity, and cycle times so high that they can't be reached by doing business as usual.
- Share more information about customer satisfaction and financial performance with employees.
- Insist that people speak regularly to dissatisfied customers, unhappy suppliers, and disgruntled shareholders.
- Put more honest discussions of the firm's problems in company newspapers and management speeches. Stop senior management's 'happy talk'.

Various techniques can be used to stimulate conflict where none existed before, in order to encourage different opinions and engender new thinking and problem-solving:

1. *Communications*: managers can withhold information 'to keep them guessing' or send large amounts of inconsistent information ('we're expanding'; 'we're going bust') to get people arguing. They might send ambiguous or threatening messages.
2. *Restructuring a company*: re-aligning working groups and altering rules and regulations, so as to increase or create interdependence between previously independent units. This can easily stimulate conflict, particularly if the goals of the newly interdependent departments are made incompatible, e.g. one department's objective being to minimize costs, the other's to maximize market share.
3. *Bringing in outsiders*: adding individuals to a group whose backgrounds, values, attitudes, or management styles differ from those of existing members. For example, recruiting senior executives with a career experience in automobile manufacture to manage health care organizations.
4. *Devil's advocate method*: within an organization, a person is assigned the role of critic, to stimulate critical thinking and reality testing. For example, in deciding to embark on an e-commerce strategy, one team member might be assigned the devil's advocate role to focus on its pitfalls and dangers.
5. *Dialectic method*: this method explores opposite positions called 'thesis' and' antithesis'. The outcome of the debate between the two is the 'synthesis' which, in turn, becomes the new thesis to be opened up for debate. Before deciding on a takeover, a company may establish two or more teams, give them access to the same information, and give them the task of arguing for and against the acquisition decision. The conflict of ideas throws up alternatives, which can be synthesized into a superior, final decision.
6. *Leadership style*: organizations can appoint managers who encourage non-traditional viewpoints, rather than authoritarian ones who might be inclined to suppress opposing viewpoints. Leadership style has been found to be a key element in organization change programmes, and in particular those involving changes in organization culture.

The radical frame of reference

Radical frame of reference on conflict a perspective that views organizational conflict as an inevitable consequence of exploitative employment relations in a capitalist economy.

Newspapers and human resource management magazines regularly carry accounts of company problems such as sexual harassment, racial harassment, theft and pilferage, bullying, organizational romance, sabotage, and strikes. These are all examples of human behaviour in organizations, yet the previous unitarist, pluralist, and interactionist frames of reference on conflict have difficulty in explaining such actions. Indeed, it is only the **radical frame of reference on conflict** that draws attention to such behaviour in organizations. The other conflict perspectives may recognize but then ignore them. In contrast, the radical frame sees the workplace as an arena of conflict between managers and workers, with the managers (in their role as agents of the owners) being the controllers of the means of production, and exploiting the employees. It holds that the logic of profit maximization involves managers relentlessly driving down the costs of production and controlling the manufacturing process. As conflict is an endemic property of capitalist employment relations, it cannot be resolved by any management techniques.

Organizational suicide

Yuin Schilling/PA Photos

At France Telecom, which employs 100,000 people, there has been a spate of attempted (and 24 successful) employee suicides (matching the French national average). Many of these have been explicitly prompted by troubles at work. Similar episodes have occurred in other pillars of French industry including Renault, Peugeot, and EDF. These have sparked a national debate about life in the modern corporation. One man (who survived) stabbed himself in the middle of a meeting; a women leapt from a fourth-floor office window after sending a suicidal email to her father – 'I have decided to kill myself tonight . . . I can't take the new reorganization'. The American Bureau of Labour Statistics reported that work-related suicides increased by 28 per cent between 2007 and 2008. Suicide at work may be the tip of a work-related unhappiness. In Asia, a series of suicides of employees of Foxconn, a subsidiary of Taiwan's Hon Hai Precision Industry Company ('the world's largest contract manufacturer'), has sparked protests. The company is reported to make products for some major American and Japanese electronics companies. Foxconn has 800,000 staff, half of whom live in Shenzhen in Foxconn City, across the border from Hong Kong. It has 15 multi-storey manufacturing buildings, each of which is dedicated to one customer. This is where →

its suicides have taken place. With 12 successful and 20 averted suicides in 2010 (lower than the Chinese national average), the issue of working conditions has been raised. The company is a relatively good employer paying the minimum wage, providing free food and lodging and extensive recreational activities. However, with overtime of 36 hours a week, annual staff turnover is 30 to 40 per cent. The company has now surrounded its buildings with nets, hired counsellors, and brought in Buddhist monks to pray. It has considered asking employees to sign a 'no suicide' pledge. Changes in traditional work design, dissatisfaction with the employer and with their jobs, and increased demands for both productivity improvements and employee commitment may all be suicide causes.

Changes at France Telecom have been caused by its transition from a state monopoly to a multinational company. It has shed 22,000 jobs since 2006. In a 2008 survey, the company found that two-thirds of its workers reported being 'stressed out' and another sixth reported being 'in distress'. In America, the Center for Work-Life Policy reported a slump in the proportion of employees who professed loyalty to their employers from 95 per cent to 37 per cent, and a fall in trust in them from 79 per cent to 22 per cent. In a survey by DDI, more than half of the respondents described their jobs as 'stagnant' (they had nothing interesting to do) and had little hope of promotion. People were both clinging onto their current jobs and dreaming of moving when the economy improved. The drive to improve productivity, accomplished by repeatedly measuring individuals' performance, represents another source of misery. Giant retailers use workforce management software to measure how long it takes employees to scan goods in a supermarket. The British public sector is awash with inspectorates and performance targets. Taylorism, which Charlie Chaplin lampooned in the film *Modern Times*, has spread from the industrial to the post-industrial economy, including universities. Around the world, companies are checking if their employees are smiling enough at customers. There is also a problem with employee loyalty and commitment. Some companies expect extraordinary employee dedication and time commitments to work, while others provide perks that are intended to make the office feel like a second home. However, they have no compunction about reducing their workforces at the first sign of economic trouble. Employees recognize that their employers do not feel great responsibility to protect their jobs (based on *The Economist*, 2009a, 2009b, 2010; Chrisafis, 2009).

Organizational misbehaviour anything that workers do in the workplace which management considers they should not do.

Stephen Ackroyd and Paul Thompson (1999) explain that management establishes a boundary between employee behaviour that is and is not acceptable. Employee actions are then defined as falling on one or other side of that boundary. The authors use the term **organizational misbehaviour** to refer to anything that workers do in the workplace which management considers they should not do.

Although much of the literature refers to 'conflict' in organizations, in reality, overt conflict is actually very rare. Thus, for Richard Edwards (1979) the struggle between capital and labour is the main dynamic which shapes the employment relationship. He refers to *structural antagonisms* rather than to conflict, and sees these as arising from the clash over the distribution of the surplus. Carter Goodrich (1975) wrote about the 'frontiers of control' and the notion of *resistance*. Management's attempt to exert control is met by employee resistance, and that produces clashes over interests. The notion of resistance carries with it the connotation of something intermittent (occurring regularly but not continually); changing (the frontier being pushed forward and back); and occurring below the surface. This is in contrast to conflict, with its connotations of a single, visible explosion (Jermier et al., 1994; Sagie et al., 2004).

Resistance more or less covert behaviour that counteracts and restricts management attempts to exercise power and control in the workplace.

Alienation feelings of powerlessness, meaninglessness, isolation, and self-estrangement engendered by work and organization design.

The concept of **resistance** refers to the more or less covert behaviour that counteracts and restricts management attempts to exercise power and control in the workplace. It has an application at all levels of the organizational hierarchy, from shop-floor employees developing ways of combating **alienation** through informal processes and actions; through professionals like engineers, academics, or hospital doctors resisting management directions; right up to senior management resisting the control exercised by the board of directors. It also allows a consideration of how that resistance moves to different areas within the organization, and how the parties acquire and relinquish different types of power, and gain and lose ascendancy over each other.

Noon and Blyton (2007) list five survival strategies that workers use to counter alienation, shown in Table 21.5. Noon and Blyton explain that each can be interpreted as a form of either

Table 21.5: Employee survival strategies

Survival strategy	Definition	Objectives	Examples	Interpreted as a form of consent	Interpreted as a form of resistance
Making out	Elaborate system of informal employee behaviour that regulates work processes and ensures targets are met, yet allows workers to reassert some control of their working day	Economic gain Fatigue reduction Time passing Boredom relief Social and psychological rewards Avoiding social stigma	Refuse collection staff 'totting' – searching through rubbish bins for valuables to keep or sell Shop floor workers manipulating their piece-rate payment schemes	Acts of 'game-playing' within the organization's rules which result in mutual benefit for employees and managers	Acts that undermine management control by bending the rules to satisfy the self-interest of employees
Fiddling	Illegitimately acquiring company products, services, or time for personal use	Economic gain Proving interest and excitement Expressing frustration or resentment	Stealing office supplies, inflating expense claims, personal phone calls from work, 'cyber-loafing' Supermarket staff 'grazing' – consuming crisps and sweets	'Deserved' perks that help subsidize wages and confer status on employees	Theft that affects profitability and undermines the integrity of everyone in the organization
Joking	A permitted or required interaction in which one party makes fun of the other, who in turn is required to take no offence	Maintaining social order Releasing frustration and tension Challenging authority Forging group identities Alleviating work monotony	Joke-telling Banter Playful insults Teasing (permitted disrespect) Practical jokes, initiation rituals	Forms of group regulation that preserve the status quo and provide a way of letting off steam	Challenges to management authority that undermine the status and policies of managers and make them appear foolish
Sabotage	An intentional, malicious attempt to disrupt or destroy a work process or a product	Way of expressing temporary frustration with work process, rules, managers, or any other aspect of the organization Way of asserting control over the work process	Spreading computer viruses Reporting company malpractices to the press Being intentionally rude to customers Disabling a photocopier	(a) Expressions of frustration or irresponsible behaviour (letting off steam) (b) Well-meaning actions that have unintended negative consequences	(a) Malicious acts against property and people, intended to 'get even' with the organization (b) Well-meaning actions intended to 'expose' the organization (whistleblowing)
Escaping	Removing oneself temporarily or permanently from one's work tasks	Coping with boredom	Physical withdrawal through latecoming, absenteeism, or resignation Mental withdrawal through dreaming, 'going robotic', or cynical distancing from company values	Acts of withdrawal that result in employees accepting the status quo, even though they disagree with management policy or objectives	Acts that result in withdrawal of goodwill or mental and physical effort, thereby reducing organizational performance and undermining management objectives

Source: based on Noon and Blyton (2007), p. 272.

employee consent or employee resistance by an outside observer; and that these strategies may be condoned and tolerated by management or judged to be unacceptable and punished. The authors also highlight the problem of interpreting the meaning of those engaging in these behaviours and their motivations. All this affects the nature and degree of conflict that may ensue between the workers and management.

Resistance and dissent on the internet

It was still possible for a dissatisfied middle-ranking employee who resigned from an investment bank to write an opinion piece in the *New York Times* complaining about a 'toxic' culture at the Wall Street bank where executives refereed to clients as 'muppets'. However, technological developments have radically altered the way in which employees can express resistance to their organizations. Abigail Schoneboom reviewed developments in workblogs (internet-based employee diaries), in which staff reflected critically upon their workplace experiences. These blogs offer employees the opportunity to find their voice; to form collective identities; and to express self-organized resistance in a climate where the channels for expressing disapproval are being continually closed down. Anonymous blogs sprang up in 2002 and included many from call centres with names like *Call Center Confidential* where their authors, low-level call centre employees, broadcast irreverent opinions about their work. Some of them contextualized call centre work in terms of Marx's theory of alienation, while others satirized their company's culture, poking fun at management's attempt to build a family atmosphere. Some blogs like *Non-Working Monkey* ('Je suis un singe non-travaillant') incorporated audiovisual material to communicate their message better.

Schoneboom argued that workblogs make the process of employees' creative resistance much more visible. In their blogs, workers act as vocal and resourceful critics of their own work circumstances. By critically distancing themselves from the corporate cultures in which they are immersed, employees provide themselves, through blogs, with a community in which their oppositional identity can be sustained. Meanwhile, cases of fired bloggers reveal the tension between worker misbehaviour and organizational surveillance. Changes in workblogging practices have been driven by increased searchability, by more intense workplace surveillance by companies, and by the emerging social networking technologies. Despite these challenges, workblogging continues to flourish. While dedicated office and call centre blogs may have declined, those from medical, educator and, police professions are thriving. Workbloggers have frequently faced disciplinary action from their employers. Several have achieved celebrity status, including 'Dooce', a Los Angeles-based web designer whose name subsequently became the verb for being fired for blogging ('to dooce'), and a Waterstone's employee whose firing from the bookshop chain triggered discussions about employee free speech. Fired or 'unmasked' bloggers continue to receive extensive media coverage, as in the case of the controversial 'outing' of police detective 'Nightjack'. Schoneboom concludes that those employers who are stepping up surveillance of bloggers must defend their disciplinary actions against accusations of internet McCarthyism (based on *Financial Times*, 2012b, 2012c, 2012d; Schoneboom, 2007, 2011; Ellis and Richards, 2009; Richards, 2008; Smith, 2012).

STOP AND THINK **Which of Noon and Blyton's employee survival strategies – making out, fiddling, joking, sabotage, escaping – have you personally engaged in at work? Have you observed other employees engaging in any of these behaviours?**

Edwards (1979) noted that the perpetual struggle for control in organizations is not always constant, obvious, or visible. Because employees' tactics of resistance are often covert, some knowledge of a particular organizational context is required for researchers (and indeed for managers) to become fully aware of what is going on. Resistance, as opposed to conflict, in the workplace is reflected in 'soldiering' (output restriction), pilferage, absenteeism, sabotage, vandalism, practical joking, and sexual misconduct. Ackroyd and Thompson (1999) reviewed the managerial and academic literature on the presence and absence of such misbehaviour at work, and concluded that typically such writings

- provided sanitized accounts of employee behaviour that depicted employees as invariably constructive, conforming, and dutiful;
- saw employees' behaviour as being orderly, purposeful, and directed towards the attainment of organizational (managerial) goals;
- defined 'normal' employee behaviour as that which was programmed by management (labelled 'pro-social') and which complied with managerial norms and values, and treated employees' deviations from those (management-) expected standards of behaviour as *mis*behaviour (also labelled 'counterproductive');
- assumed that when there was a lack of correspondence between management direction and the employees' response (i.e. occurrence of misbehaviour), what needed to change was the latter.

Counterproductive work behaviours, emotional exhaustion, and organizational justice

Have you noticed your co-workers regularly taking longer than permitted lunch breaks; or deliberately violating company policies and procedures? American researchers call these *counterproductive work behaviours* (CWB), while British academics refer to it as *organizational misbehaviour*. They are defined as wilful actions that may harm the organization or its employees. Such behaviours include sabotage and latecoming. Research by Mindy Krischer and her colleagues focused on two other CWBs – withdrawal (e.g. taking excessive breaks; arriving late, leaving early) and deviance (e.g. intentionally doing tasks incorrectly or working slowly). They wanted to know if such behaviours helped employees to cope with the stress that led to emotional exhaustion (the feeling of being over-extended and down) resulting from a lack of organizational justice (fairness in the allocation of rewards like pay; fairness in the way decisions are made). The researchers surveyed 295 employees in the USA assessing their perceptions of justice in their workplaces; their frequency of engagement in CWB, and their levels of emotional exhaustion.

They found that those employees who considered themselves to be in an unjust work environment experienced more emotional exhaustion. These individuals engaged in CWB so as to cope with the ensuing strain. Those who engaged in withdrawal escaped from their unpleasant situation and replenished their emotional resources. As a result, this group experienced less emotional exhaustion. With regard to employees engaging in deviance, this behaviour functioned as an emotion-focused coping mechanism which reduced emotional exhaustion by increasing employees' perceived control by 'evening the score' in the face of injustice, thereby reducing their psychological strain. The research found that when employees felt that the rewards and outcomes they received were distributed unfairly, deliberately performing work slowly or incorrectly enabled them to reduce their inputs to restore equity, thereby reducing the negative emotions associated with low distributive justice. Although usually considered harmful, withdrawal and deviance can help employees cope. They reduce employees' feelings of injustice heighten their levels of citizenship behaviour, job satisfaction, and organizational commitment. As these behaviours are signs of employees coping with perceived injustice, the researchers recommend creating grievance procedures to give staff a sense of control, and providing them with facilities to help them work off their stress (based on Krischer et al., 2010).

Conflict frames of reference: summary

In this chapter, four different frames of reference on conflict have been discussed: unitarist, pluralist, interactionist, and radical. Table 21.6 summarizes the beliefs and assumptions of each one, and suggests how conflict might be dealt with within each frame of reference.

Table 21.6: Conflict frames of reference: beliefs, assumptions, and ways of dealing with conflict

Frame of reference	Beliefs	Assumptions	How to deal with conflict
Unitarist	Organizations are fundamentally harmonious, cooperative structures.	Accepts the internal management structure. Thinks of conflict as negative.	Humanistic approach to conflict resolution. Not interested in cause of conflict. Concentrates on resolution through communication. Managers able to change behaviour.
Pluralist	Organizations are made up of diverse groups with varying needs and interests.	Conflict is inevitable. Conflict serves as a regulation mechanism between the different groups. Acts as an early warning system to provide signs that system will break down if conflict not dealt with.	Conflict does not prevent organizations from functioning. Groups recognize that compromise and negotiation are necessary if they are to achieve common goals. Manager's job is to balance conflict between various groups.
Interactionist	Conflict is a positive and necessary force and essential for effective organizational performance.	Conflict should be institutionalized through systems of collective bargaining. Optimum level of conflict; too much or too little is dysfunctional and impairs performance.	Seen as beneficial in motivating energy to deal with underlying problems. Enhancing mutual understanding of goals and interests.
Radical	Organizational conflict is an inevitable consequence of exploitative employment relations in a capitalist economy, based on Marxist critique.	Fundamental aim of capitalist enterprise is to expand capital and generate profit which is divided between managers and shareholders. Competition forces low production costs, forcing employees to earn less, which creates conflict.	Management deals with conflict by limited effects of worker resistance, walkouts, strikes, or conflict.

Source: from *The Psychology of People in Organizations*, Ashleigh, M. and Mansi, A. Pearson Education Limited © Pearson Education Limited 2012.

Emotional labour

Emotional labour the act of expressing organizationally required emotions during interactions with others at work.

Emotions intense, short-lived reactions that are linked to a specific cause and which interrupt thought processes and behaviours.

As a student, have you worked in a bar, operated a checkout in a supermarket, or waited on tables in a restaurant, dealing with people face-to-face? What emotions did you experience when dealing with your customers – anger, fear, joy, love, sadness, surprise? Did you express those feelings to them at the time; did you bite your tongue and say nothing; or did you suppress your emotions and act in the opposite way to which you felt? If you did either of the last two, then you performed **emotional labour**, which is the act of expressing organizationally required emotions during interactions with others at work. It involves expending psychological effort to keep in check both your internal emotions and your external behaviours.

Emotions are intense, short-lived reactions that are linked to a specific cause and which interrupt thought processes and behaviours. Since an emotion cannot be directly seen, it is communicated verbally and non-verbally. Thus one's 'performance' of an emotion consists of 'a complex combination of facial expression, body language, spoken words and tone of voice' (Rafaeli and Sutton, 1987, p. 33). Most work tasks involve two elements – physical labour and mental labour. The physical refers to walking, carrying, lifting, talking, and similar

Arlie Russell Hochschild (b.1940)

behaviours. The mental involves knowing, understanding, analysing, and evaluating people, things, and situations. However, there are many jobs that now require a third kind of labour – emotional. Arlie Hochschild first coined the term 'emotional labour' in her book *The Managed Heart*. In it, she discussed employees' management of their feelings to create publicly observable facial and bodily displays (Hochschild, 1983).

As a result of the increasing similarity of the offerings provided to customers by different companies in the airline, fast food, financial services, tourism, hotel, and call centre industries, some organizations have attempted to differentiate themselves from their competitors by the way that their employees deal with customers. Hochschild drew attention to the importance of social interaction in service provision. The emotional style of offering a service is now often more important than the service itself. The interactions between service providers and their customers have become the determining element in the latter's evaluation of satisfaction. In this way, the psychological aspect of service provision now takes precedence over the physical aspect (Noon and Blyton, 2007). While Hochschild (2003) was concerned that emotion was being commodified through the 'commercialization of intimate life', other writers consider the harnessing of employees' emotional energy to improve customer service as a good thing (Kinnie et al., 2000).

Historically, staff members have always been encouraged, in a general way, to provide 'service with a smile' or to 'put on a good show'. However, in recent years emotional labour has become a specific part of the employment contract and the employee's discretion concerning which feelings to show and how to show them is reduced or completely eliminated. Emotional labour occurs when employees, as part of the wage/effort bargain, are required by their bosses to display emotions which cause customers to feel and respond in particular ways. The employer thus buys not only an employee's physical and mental labour, but also their emotional labour, in return for a wage. Bolton (2000) argues that employees' private emotional systems have been appropriated by management as a renewable resource. To ensure that employees perform as required, companies use a combination of three elements:

1. **Careful applicant selection**: Choosing the appropriate employee is the first step. Disney World interviews 50,000 aspiring employees annually, and is most interested in their personality, wanting people who are enthusiastic, and who exhibit a clean and honest appearance (Henkoff, 1994; Van Maanen and Kunda, 1989). The McDonald's Corporation rejects applicants who are too poker-faced or who fail to demonstrate pleasure when describing a pleasant experience to interviewers (Slocum and Hellriegel, 2009).
2. **Employee training**: Companies run training courses for new starts whose jobs involve face-to-face or voice-to-voice interaction with customers, to develop their abilities to display appropriate emotions. Disney has overhauled its new hires orientation courses, putting less emphasis on policies and procedures, and more on emotion (Henkoff, 1994).
3. **Employee monitoring**: Organizations monitor staff interactions with customers to ensure that they display the required emotions. Ghost travellers on airlines and mystery shoppers in stores act as customers, to check staff performance. In telesales and call centres, supervisors randomly record conversations for review purposes (Taylor, 1998). Companies also use customer questionnaires to assess whether staff are eliciting the desired responses.

Emotional labour consists of five key elements. First, employees consciously manage their emotions (either inducing or suppressing them) as part of their paid work requirement. Second, they do this when interacting with others (customers and clients, as well as other staff) within the workplace. Third, they do so with the objective of creating in the recipient a particular state of mind ('I am being well treated'), a particular feeling (satisfied customer), or a particular response ('I'll use their service again'). Fourth, emotional labour should boost the self-esteem of its receiver. Finally, it is done to serve the interests of the employer (achieving organizational goals) who prescribes, supervises, and monitors the performance of that emotional labour (Taylor, 1998).

Felt emotions emotions that employees actually feel in a work situation.

In every work situation, there are the emotions that employees actually feel – **felt emotions** – and those emotions that they are required to show by management as part of their jobs –

Displayed emotions emotions that employees are required by management to show as part of their jobs.

displayed emotions. Richard Layard (2005) provides an example of the difference during an Olympic medal awards ceremony. He says that all three medallists on the rostrum display feelings of happiness and joy in front of the cameras and the crowd. In this particular 'work situation', the expressed feelings of the gold medallist and the bronze medallist are probably also their felt emotions – the former because they won, and the latter because they expected no medal at all. In contrast, the silver medallist's felt emotion may actually be disappointment due to a failure to win the gold (Medvec et al., 1995). Compare the emotional displays of the gold and bronze medal winners (centre and left respectively) with that of the silver medallist (right).

Mike Powell/Getty Images.

In our Olympic example, the silver-medallist may be experiencing a disjunction between her felt emotions and her expressed emotions. You may experience a similar situation when internally you have feelings of anger and loathing towards your customers or co-workers, but externally you display feelings of calm and interest through your facial expression, tone of voice, and content of speech. This gap between the emotions that you feel and those that you actually display is called **emotional dissonance**. It can ignite conflict in organizations when employees are unable to sustain their emotional dissonance. Their suppressed real emotions can lead to exhaustion, burnout, and aggression (Medvec et al., 1995).

Emotional dissonance the disparity between an individual's felt and displayed emotions.

Source: DILBERT © 2000 Scott Adams. Used by permission of UNIVERSAL UCLICK. All rights reserved.

Appropriate physical, mental, and emotional labour are now all required for satisfactory performance of many jobs or professions. In playing the role of a production manager, team leader or salesperson, a person may display certain emotions and suppress others. Thus, for those around that person, what you see is not necessarily how they feel. Individuals at all levels of organizations disguise their true feelings and manufacture false ones, either because it helps them to do their jobs, or because a failure to do so would be punished by management. Some typical required emotional displays are shown in Table 21.7.

Table 21.7: Examples of required emotional display

Employee	Should display emotions of
Undertaker	solemnity, sadness
Supermarket checkout assistant	friendliness
Nightclub bouncer	calm confidence
Flight attendant	happiness, reassurance
University lecturer	enthusiasm about their subject

Surface acting hiding one's felt emotions and forgoing emotional expressions in response to display rules.

Deep acting attempting to modify one's felt emotions based on display rules.

Emotional labour involves employees manipulating and 'acting out' their emotions in a way that an actor might do in the theatre. Employees come to give 'performances' during their work in front of an audience of customers. Hochschild (1983) distinguished two types of acting. **Surface acting** involves either not displaying the emotions that you do feel (emotion suppression), or displaying emotions that you do not feel (emotion simulation). In the first instance, you hide your felt emotions; in the second, you display emotions that you are not experiencing. For example, a waitress who is angry with a rude customer continues to smile, despite his rude behaviour towards her. Here, the employee complies with display rules but without internalizing emotions which they only fake. In contrast, **deep acting** is the process of attempting to modify one's felt emotions based on display rules, so that one really experiences them. By developing these inner feelings about their organizational role and the customers they serve, the employee's outward behaviour becomes automatic.

Fly and smile

Paul Doyle/Alamy.

In the photograph, an experienced flight attendant demonstrates the facial expression that she uses at work. Is she performing genuine warmth, or is it concealed irritation?

Flight attendants are under strong pressure from the airlines to show only 'positive' expressions of emotion. This is sometimes a challenge, since not all passengers are pleasant and cooperative. She and the other attendants have learned that you can say anything to a passenger as long as you smile. In the photograph, she performs the smile that she uses while dealing with unruly or inebriated passengers. The verbal content of what she says is quite negative, but as long as the attendant smiles while saying it, the passenger accepts the information without complaint. Were you correct?

The earliest studies into emotional labour were conducted on flight attendants and this occupational group continues to receive much research attention. On a flight, cabin crew will always display reassurance, even if they are afraid: 'Even though I'm an honest person, I have learned

→

not to allow my face to mirror my alarm or my fright.' Airline management sees the nature of the interaction between flight attendants and passengers as central to the latter's perceptions of service quality. Competitive pressures have stimulated managerial initiatives to manage 'natural' delivery of quality customer service during customer–attendant interactions. Taylor and Tyler found that three particular uses of body language were fundamental in establishing rapport – walking softly, making eye contact, and always smiling. Emotional labour was required when dealing with sick and nervous passengers, applying 'tender loving care' (TLC), and confronting emergency situations. Being friendly, cheerful, and helpful involves an emotional display. In organizations with a 'customer is always right' philosophy, service workers are taught to diffuse customer hostility, and in consequence end up absorbing a raft of verbal abuse during the course of a normal working day. They come to accept such verbalized customer dissatisfaction, no matter how upsetting, as 'just part of the job'. The growing incidence of both verbal and physical customer violence in Britain is likely to increase both the volume and intensity of emotional labour in service industries. The drive for competitive advantage through enhanced customer service means that an integral part of every service worker's job is to transform customer dissatisfaction into satisfaction. When management failed to invest in violence reduction strategies, exposing service workers to increasing levels of customer violence, it increasingly exploited the emotional labour of its staff. Thus there was the paradoxical situation in which cabin crew had to deploy their emotional labour (calming customers, etc.) to compensate for management's failure to remove the causes of customer abuse. However, the more success that they have in doing this, the less management feel the pressure to address the sources of customer violence (based on Hochschild, 1983; Taylor and Tyler, 2000).

Surface acting has been found to be more stressful to employees and a source of greater conflict, because it involves feigning one's true feelings (Grandey, 2003; Grandey et al., 2004). Stress tends to occur when emotional displays are prolonged; when employees are asked to take them to a level considered unacceptable; when they consider them to be inappropriate for the job; or when they are asked to maintain their emotional displays while customers are being rude or offensive.

Display rules organizational scripts concerning which feelings are appropriate in a given setting and how they should be displayed.

Feeling rules rules which dictate which feelings should be displayed in particular settings.

Expression rules rules which dictate how displayed feelings should be expressed in particular settings.

Emotional labour in an organization is governed by **display rules** (Ashforth and Humfrey, 1993; Hopfl, 2002). These are determined by management and take the form of an emotional script which specifies two types of rules. **Feeling rules** dictate which feelings should be displayed in particular settings. Your lecturer is supposed to feel enthusiastic and not bored when teaching you; a funeral director is expected to be solemn and not cheerful when dealing with a deceased person's relative; and managers are expected to be annoyed when disciplining poor performers. **Expression rules** dictate how these feelings should be expressed in particular settings. Enthusiasm by a lecturer in front of students is appropriately conveyed by tone of voice, speed of delivery, and body language. Dressing up in strange clothing and singing the lecture is usually inappropriate. Enthusiasm by a new employee at a client meeting is appropriately shown by paying attention to the person speaking, asking questions, and making comments. Applauding the speaker's contribution would be inappropriate. Expression rules are frequently specified in a verbal repertoire or script that a call centre or a restaurant employee learns during their training. Meika Loe (2002) described how waitresses at 'Bazoom' restaurant had to behave as actresses following the rules established by management and be cheerful, polite, smiling, attentive to customers, and sexy, while avoiding showing bad feelings such as sadness or anger.

While display rules are organization-specific, they can differ between cultures, creating problems for companies. The smiling rule, a key component of customer care training in the United States and Britain, is inappropriate in Muslim countries and in Japan. In Israel, smiling supermarket cashiers are perceived as inexperienced, and are therefore encouraged to look serious (Rafaeli, 1989). It is believed that the friendly, smiling greeters welcoming customers in German Wal-Mart stores contributed to that company's failure in that country; and there are other instances when companies have attempted to impose their display rules in alien cultures.

"Please pay attention as the stewardess demonstrates our new procedure for dealing with drunken passengers."

Emotions training in Japan

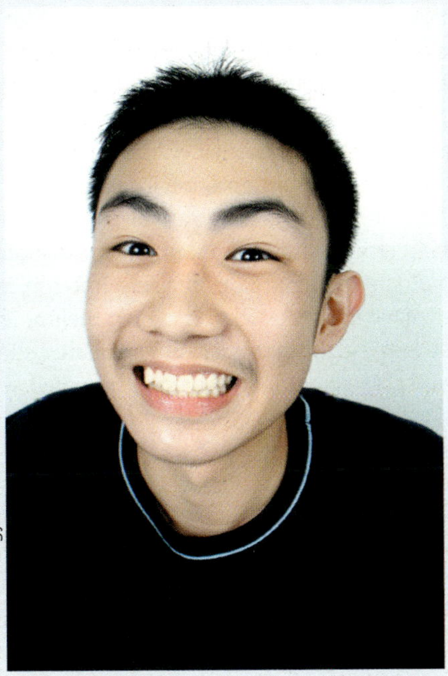

Pathathai Chungyam/Dreamstime.com.

Japanese employees who come into contact with customers are being taught to display the appropriate types of emotions. Historically, in Japanese culture, hiding one's emotions is considered a virtue because the lack of expression minimizes conflict and avoids drawing attention to the individual.

Hiroshi Leyoshi and other gas station attendants are gathered for a three-hour training session in Japan on learning how to smile. 'It's easy to say you should smile at customers' says Leyoshi, a 39-year-old gas attendant, after the seminar. 'But to be honest, it all depends on how I feel at the moment'. Leyoshi isn't the only person who has trouble smiling at customers. Tomoko Yoshi is a customer relations training expert who works at the Sheraton Hotels in Japan. He teaches hotel employees never to show inappropriate emotions or make inappropriate gestures while talking with a guest. In particular, even if the employee is upset, they are instructed never to point with their finger. Pointing is considered rude. Using one's whole hand shows more effort and is considered more polite and businesslike. Similarly, if a customer is sitting in a restaurant and the waiter raises his or her voice, it signals to the customer that the waiter wants the guest to leave and isn't welcome any longer. Yoshida also instructs hotel porters not to use their feet either to close a door or to move a guest's bags, even if the porter is upset. Why? In Japan, people believe that the ground is where they walk in shoes. When they go home, they take their shoes off because they don't want to mix the outside ground with the inside ground. Yoshikihiko Kadokawa, author of *The Power of Laughing Face*, found that even in Japan's culture, the friendliest clerks in some of Japan's biggest retail stores consistently rang up the highest sales. His research found that smiling salesclerks reported 20 per cent more sales than non-smiling ones (from Slocum and Hellriegel, 2009, p. 61).

How much of a problem is emotional labour for employees? Hochschild (1983) was concerned with the detrimental effects on employees of unacceptable levels of emotional display. Information about its effects is both limited and contradictory. It is the negative consequences that have been emphasized in the literature. For those employees who do experience emotional dissonance, creating and maintaining a separation between these two sets of feelings, at a high level, and over an extended period of time, can entail severe socio-emotional costs. These include low self-esteem, depression, and cynicism. In extreme circumstances, it may even affect their social relationships and their mental health.

Emotional harmony a match between an employee's felt emotions and their expressed emotions within the workplace.

Noon and Blyton (2007) remind us that emotional labour is a variation of what already occurs in many work contexts. For those employees who perform mundane, service jobs, smiling at customers and interacting with them in a friendly way provides meaning and pleasure, increasing their job satisfaction. There are therefore employees who engage in emotional labour who neither act (surface or deep) nor experience emotional dissonance or stress (Ashforth and Humfrey, 1993; Ashforth and Tomiuk, 2000; Lewig and Dollard, 2003). Their felt emotions and expressed emotions match, so that they experience **emotional harmony** (Mann, 1999).

The distinction between felt and displayed emotions may not be as fixed as some writers claim, partly because they are already used to performing various types of emotional scripts inside and outside work. Some research studies, such as those into the jobs of adventure guides (Sharpe, 2005), report high degrees of emotional harmony, while other research among flight attendants (Williams, 2003) revealed that the emotional labour they performed was a source of both stress *and* satisfaction for them. These types of people enjoy serving customers and obtaining a positive response from them. Many identify closely with their work roles, and thus the emotional display rules that others consider to be so onerous and stressful are, for them, wholly consistent with their personal values and identity. For these people, task performance, complete with emotional displays, is likely to enhance rather than to reduce their psychological wellbeing.

From his empirical study of banking and health employees, Wharton (1993) found no simple relationships. Whether a person who engages in emotional labour finds their job satisfying or emotionally exhausting depends on a number of variables. These include the 'fit' between an individual's personal characteristics and the requirements of their job; the level, range, and duration of the emotional labour required in the role (intense, extensive, and prolonged; or low, narrow, and brief; or some other combination); their ability to disengage ('switch off') from their job after leaving the workplace; and finally, their degree of autonomy in performing their job, with greater autonomy being associated with lower emotional exhaustion.

STOP AND THINK

Has the importance of emotional labour been overstated? Is it even a valid concept to study? We all engage in impression management all the time (see Chapter 7). We can 'put on a smile' without necessarily being happy. At what point does normal impression management become emotional labour?

RECAP

1. ***Distinguish between the four major frames of reference on conflict.***
   - The unitarist frame sees organizations as essentially harmonious and any conflict as bad.
   - The pluralist frame sees organizations as a collection of groups, each with their own interests.
   - The interactionist frame sees conflict as a positive, necessary force for effective performance.
   - The radical frame sees conflict as an inevitable outcome of capitalism.
2. ***Distinguish between functional and dysfunctional conflict.***
   - *Functional conflict* is considered by management to support organizational goals, and it improves organizational performance.
   - *Dysfunctional conflict* is considered to impede the achievement of organizational goals, and it reduces company performance.
3. ***Explain the relationship between organizing, coordinating, and conflict.***
   - Organizing concerns dividing up a large task (e.g. designing, building, and marketing a car) into sub-tasks, and assigning them to groups (e.g. design department, production department, etc.). Coordination brings those previously divided sub-tasks together to ensure that all activities are directed towards organizational goals. In the process of subdivision, departments acquire their own subordinate goals and interests, which differ from organizational ones. Conflict ensues when these divergent interests and goals clash.
4. ***List the causes of conflict in organizations.***
   - Individuals, groups, units, and departments may be in conflict with each other due to the differences in their goal orientation and evaluations, self-image and stereotypes, task interdependencies, and time perspectives, as well as overlapping authority and scarce resources.
5. ***Distinguish different organizational coordination devices.***
   - Coordination devices include rules, policies, and procedures; using hierarchy; goal clarification and communication; temporary task forces; permanent project teams; liaison roles and integrator roles.
6. ***Explain the conditions under which conflict is resolved and stimulated in organizations.***
   - Some writers contend that conflict that is dysfunctional, that is, does not achieve organizational goals, wastes time, demotivates staff, wastes resources, and generally lowers individual and hence organizational performance. In such cases it needs to be eliminated.
   - Commentators argue that conflict stimulation is necessary if employees enter 'comfort zones'; are reluctant to think in new ways; and find it easier to maintain the status quo. In rapidly changing organizational environments such behaviour not only reduces organizational success, but may endanger its very existence.
7. ***List Thomas's five conflict resolution approaches.***
   - Thomas's five conflict resolution approaches are avoidance, accommodation, compromise, collaboration, and competition.
8. ***Distinguish between distributive and integrative bargaining.***
   - Distributive bargaining refers to a negotiation situation in which a fixed sum of resources is divided up. It leads to a win–lose situation between the parties.
   - Integrative bargaining seeks to increase the total amount of resources, and it creates a win–win situation between the parties.

Revision

1. Briefly describe each of Thomas's five conflict resolution approaches and give an example of an organizational situation in which each would be most appropriate.
2. 'Since every unit and department in an organization has its own goals and interests, conflict will always be a feature of organizational life.' Consider the costs and benefits of conflict for the various organization stakeholders. Give your reasons and illustrate your points with examples.
3. Discuss some of the ways in which employees resist management actions and deal with an unsatisfying work environment.
4. Is emotional labour as great a problem as some of the literature suggests? What defensive mechanisms can employees use to cope with the emotional labour demands of their jobs?

Research assignment

Noon and Blyton (2007) and Krischer et al. (2010) describe a range of employee survival strategies and counterproductive work behaviours to be found in organizations. Familiarize yourself with examples of each of these. Reflect on your own work experience and talk to friends and relations who work or have worked in organizations. Find examples of such strategies and behaviours. For each one, answer the questions:

1. Why did the person engage in it – what was their objective?
2. What was the effect of their doing so, on themselves, their fellow workers or their organization?

Relate what you find to the theory and research on the subject.

Springboard

Jerry Greenberg (2010) *Insidious Workplace Behaviour*, Psychology Press, Hove, East Sussex. This book considers pervasive acts of counterproductive work behaviours and organizational misbehaviour directed at individual or organizational targets.

Aikaterini Koskina and Don Keithley (2010) 'Emotion in a call centre SME: a case study of positive emotional management', *European Management Journal*, 28(3), pp. 208–19. Considers the nature of emotional management in the workplace.

Emma Surman and Andrew Sturdy (2009) 'Emotion', in Philip Hancock and André Spicer (eds), *Understanding Corporate Life*, Sage, London, pp. 165–82. Provides a summary of recent research and theory on the subject of emotions in organizations.

Jeff Weiss and Jonathan Hughes (2005) 'Want collaboration?', *Harvard Business Review*, 83(3), pp. 93–101. Adopting an interactionist frame of reference on conflict, the authors argue that effective collaboration is only achieved by seeing conflict as natural and necessary, and managing it effectively.

OB in films

There Will Be Blood (2007, director Paul Thomas Anderson), DVD track 5: 01:27:00 to 01:31:00 (4 minutes). This film is set in 1898 and tells the story of a silver miner turned oil man, Daniel Plainview (played by Daniel Day-Lewis), who is engaged in a ruthless quest for wealth during Southern California's oil boom. His son, HW is badly injured in a gusher accident which leaves him profoundly deaf, and Plainview is very sensitive about this. The clip begins with Plainview and his brother Henry (Kevin J. O'Connor) going into a meeting, shaking hands, and sitting down at a table. The brothers are going to negotiate with two investors who want to buy Plainview's oil wells. The investors appear to be offering lots of money. If Plainview accepts the deal, he will be a very rich man. The clip ends with Henry and his brother walking out of the meeting.

1. Why does this negotiation session collapse into irreconcilable conflict? (Pay attention to the physical setting of the meeting, the way it is run, the nature of the conversation, the personalities involved, and the power bases of the participants).
2. How could things have been handled better, by whom?

OB on the web

Management consultants advocate using Thomas's collaboration (problem-solving) approach to resolve conflicts. Search YouTube for 'What to do when conflict happens'. It introduces the CALM model – Clarify the conflict; Address the conflict; Listen to the other side; Manage your way to resolution. Think of a current conflict that you are having with another person at work, at university, or at home, and apply the CALM model to it. Write a report describing how you implemented each step; what happened; and what you would repeat or do differently next time, if you needed to resolve a similar conflict.

CHAPTER EXERCISES

1. Organizational misbehaviour

Objectives

1. To find examples of organizational misbehaviour.
2. To suggest reasons for its occurrence in the workplace.
3. To propose management action to address it.

Briefing

1. Make a list of employee misbehaviours that you have engaged in yourself while at work, have observed others engaging in, or have read about.
2. Form into groups and discuss:
   (a) What are the causes of such organizational misbehaviour?
   (b) What options do employees have who engage in organizational misbehaviour themselves or see others doing it?
   (c) What actions can senior management take to eliminate or reduce organizational misbehaviour?

→

2. Inter-departmental conflict

Objectives

1. To practise analysing an organizational conflict situation.
2. To suggest workable solutions.

Briefing

1. Read the case below.
2. Divide into groups of 3–5, and nominate a spokesperson for each group to report its conclusions to the whole class.
3. As a group, use the coordination-conflict model and conflict resolution approaches discussed in this chapter to
   (a) identify the causes of the conflict between production and sales, and the main obstacles to resolving it;
   (b) devise an action plan for resolving the conflict that will create a good post-conflict relationship between both parties specifying (i) the appropriate conflict resolution techniques to use, and (ii) ways to design a new control and reward system to help eliminate such conflict in the future.
4. When asked by your instructor, the spokesperson will describe your group's analysis of the causes of, and solutions to, this conflict.

Case

You are the top management team of a large company that manufactures personal computers. You have been given the task of resolving the growing conflict between your production managers and sales managers. Your computers are customized to the needs of individual customers, so it is crucial that Sales provides Manufacturing with accurate information concerning each customer's specific requirements. Over the last few months, however, Production has been complaining about Sales. They say, first, that Sales provides this information too late for it to make the most efficient use of its resources; second, that Sales are increasingly making errors in describing each customer's special needs; and third, that Sales are demanding unreasonably quick product delivery times for their customers. For its part, Sales is complaining about Manufacturing's poor workmanship in the final product which has led to an increased level of customer complaints; its increasing delays in the delivery of computers to customers; and its unwillingness to respond flexibly to unexpected last-minute customer requests. The problems within your company are escalating. At the last meeting between senior production and sales managers, harsh words were spoken during a heated exchange of charges and counter charges.

Adapted from George and Jones (2005), pp. 430–1.

Employability assessment

With regard to your future employment prospects:

1. Identify up to three issues from this chapter that you found significant.
2. Relate these to the competencies in the employability matrix.
3. Decide what actions you need to take to maintain and/or develop those competencies under each of the four headings of the employability matrix

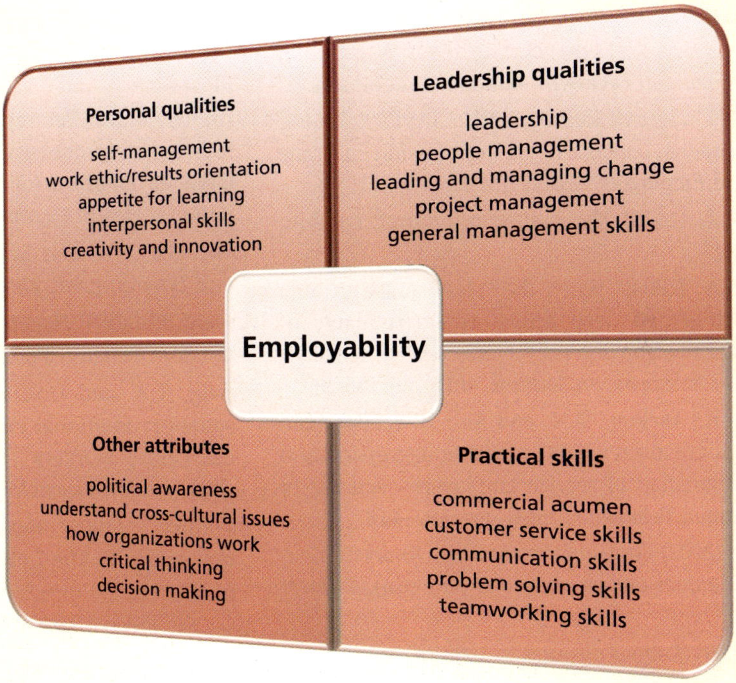

References

Ackroyd, S. and Thompson, P. (1999) *Organizational Misbehaviour*, London: Sage Publications.

Ashforth, B. and Humfrey, R. (1993) 'Emotion in the work place: a reappraisal', *Human Relations*, 48(2), pp. 97–125.

Ashforth, B.E. and Tomiuk, M. (2000) 'Emotional labour and authenticity: views from service agents', in S. Fineman (ed.), *Emotion in Organizations* (2nd edn), London, Sage, pp. 184–203.

Ashleigh, M. and Mansi, A. (2012) *The Psychology of People in Organizations*, Harlow, Essex: Pearson.

BBC Online (2012) 'Aviva boss Andrew Moss to step down', 8 May.

Bolton, S. (2000) 'Emotion here, emotion there, emotional organizations everywhere', *Critical Perspectives on Accounting*, 11(2), pp. 155–71.

Chrisafis, A. (2009) 'France: stress and worker suicides mean the future's not bright Orange', *The Guardian*, 18 September.

CIPD/OPP (2008) *Fight, Flight or Face It?*, London: Chartered Institute of Personnel and Development/OPP.

Cosier, R.A. and Schwenk, C.R. (1990) 'Agreement and thinking alike: ingredients for poor decisions', *Academy of Management Executive*, 4(1), pp. 69–74.

De Dreu, C.K.W. (2008) 'The virtue and vice of workplace conflict: food for (pessimistic) thought', *Journal of Organizational Behaviour*, 29(1), pp. 5–18.

Edwards, R.C. (1979) *Contested Terrain: The Transformation of Industry in the Twentieth Century*, London: Heinemann.

Ellis, V. and Richards, J. (2009) 'Creating, connecting and correcting: motivations and meanings of workblogging among public service workers?', in S.C. Bolton and M. Houlihan (eds), *Work Matters*, Basingstoke: Palgrave Macmillan, pp. 250–68.

Financial Times (2012a) 'Rate-rigging at Barclays was pervasive', 28 June, p. 22.

Financial Times (2012b) 'Goldman accused of "toxic" culture by departing banker', 15 March, p. 1.

Financial Times (2012c) 'The "Vampire Squid" spills its ink', 14 March, p. 15.

Financial Times (2012d) 'Silence is no longer Goldman', 14 March, p. 21.

Fisher, R. and Ury, W. (1981) *Getting to Yes: Negotiating Agreement without Giving In*, London: Hutchinson.

Fox, A. (1966) *Industrial Sociology and Industrial Relations, Research Paper 3*, London: Royal Commission on Trade Unions and Employers' Associations.

Goodrich, C.L. (1975) *The Frontier of Control*, London: Pluto Press.

Grandey, A.A. (2003) 'When the "show must go on": surface acting and deep acting as determinants of emotional exhaustion and peer-related service delivery', *Academy of Management Journal*, 46(1), pp. 86–96.

Grandey, A.A., Dickter, D.N. and Sin, H. (2004) 'The customer is not always right: customer aggression and emotion regulation of service employees', *Journal of Organizational Behaviour*, 25(3), pp. 397–418.

Grant, R.M. (2002) *Contemporary Strategy Analysis: Concepts, Techniques and Applications* (4th edn), Oxford: Blackwell.

Hale, D. (2009) 'Labour disputes in 2008', *Economic and Labour Market Review*, 3(6), pp. 26–38.

Hales, C. (1993) *Managing through Organization*, London: Routledge.

Hatch, M.J. (1997) *Organization Theory: Modern, Symbolic and Postmodern Perspectives*, Oxford: Oxford University Press.

Hatch, M.J. with Cunliffe, A.L. (2006) *Organization Theory* (2nd edn), Oxford: Oxford University Press.

Henkoff, R. (1994) 'Finding and keeping the best service workers', *Fortune*, 3 October, pp. 52–8.

Hochschild, A. (1983) *The Managed Heart*, Berkeley, CA: University of California Press.

Hochschild, A. (2003) *The Commercialization of Intimate Life*, Berkeley, Los Angeles: University of California Press.

Hopfl, H. (2002) 'Playing the part: reflections on aspects of mere performance in the customer-client relationship', *Journal of Management Studies*, 39(2), pp. 255–67.

Janis, I.L. (1982) *Victims of Groupthink* (2nd edn), Boston, MA: Houghton Mifflin.

Jermier, J.M., Knights, D. and Nord, W.R. (eds) (1994) *Resistance and Power in Organizations*, London: Routledge.

Johnson, D.W. and Johnson, F.P. (1975) *Joining Together: Group Theory and Group Skills*, Englewood Cliffs, NJ: Prentice Hall.

Johnston, R. (2000) 'Hidden capital', in J. Barry, J. Chandler, H. Clark, R. Johnston and D. Needle (eds), *Organization and Management: A Critical Text*, London: International Thomson Business Press, pp. 16–35.

Kinnie, N., Hutchinson, S. and Purcell, J. (2000) 'Fun and surveillance: the paradox of high commitment management in call centres', *International Journal of Human Resource Management*, 11(5), pp. 967–85.

Kotter, J. (1996) 'Kill complacency', *Fortune*, 5 August, pp. 122–4.

Krischer, M.M., Penney, L.M. and Hunter, E.M. (2010) 'Can counterproductive work behaviours be productive? CWB as emotion-focused coping', *Journal of Occupational Health Psychology*, 15(2), pp. 154–66.

Lawrence, P.R. and Lorsch, J.W. (1967) *Organization and Environment*, Boston, MA: Addison-Wesley.

Layard, R. (2005) *Happiness: Lessons from a New Science*, London: Penguin Books.

Lewig, K.A. and Dollard, M.F. (2003) 'Emotional dissonance: emotional exhaustion and job satisfaction in call centre workers', *European Journal of Work and Organization Psychology*, 12(4), pp. 366–92.

Lichfield, J. (2009) 'Bossnapped! (It's French for industrial action'), *The International Independent*, 2 April, p. 27.

Loe, M. (2002) 'Working for men: at the intersection of power, gender and sexuality', in C.L. Williams and A. Stein (eds), *Sexuality and Gender*, Blackwell Readers, Chapter 15.

Ma, Z. (2007) 'Chinese conflict management styles and negotiation behaviours: an empirical test', *International Journal of Cross Cultural Management*, 7(1), pp. 101–19.

Mann, S. (1999) *Hiding What We Feel, Faking What We Don't: Understanding the Role of Your Emotions at Work*, Shaftsbury: Element.

Medvec, V., Madey, S. and Gilovich, T. (1995) 'When less is more: counterfactual thinking and satisfaction among Olympic medallists', *Journal of Personality and Social Psychology*, 69(4), pp. 603–10.

Noon, M. and Blyton, P. (2007) *The Realities of Work* (3rd edn), Basingstoke: Palgrave.

Rafaeli, A. (1989) 'When cashiers meet customers: an analysis of supermarket cashiers', *Academy of Management Journal*, 32(2), pp. 245–73.

Rafaeli, A. and Sutton, R.I. (1987) 'The expression of emotion in organizational life', in L.L. Cummings and B.M. Staw (eds), *Research in Organizational Behaviour, Volume 11*, Greenwich, CT: JAI Press, pp. 1–42.

Ren, H. and Gray, B. (2009) 'Repairing relationship conflict: how violation types and culture influence the effectiveness of restoration rituals', *Academy of Management Review*, 34(1), pp. 105–26.

Richards, J. (2008) 'Because I need somewhere to vent: the expression of conflict through work blogs', *New Technology and Employment*, 23(1–2), pp. 95–110.

Robbins, S.P. (1974) *Managing Organizational Conflict: A Non-traditional Approach*, Englewood Cliffs, NJ: Prentice Hall.

Robbins, S.P. and Judge, T.A. (2013) *Organizational Behaviour* (15th edn), Harlow, Essex: Pearson Education.

Rousseau, D.M. (1999) 'Why workers still identify with organizations', *Journal of Organizational Behaviour*, 19(3), pp. 217–33.

Ruble, T.T. and Thomas, K. (1976) 'Support for a two-dimensional model of conflict behaviour', *Organizational Behaviour and Human Performance*, 16(1), pp. 143–55.

Sagie, A., Stahevsky, S. and Koslowsky, M. (2004) *Misbehaviour and Dysfunctional Attitudes in Organizations*, Basingstoke: Palgrave.

Savage, G.T., Blair, J.D. and Soreson, R.L. (1989) 'Consider both relationships and substance when negotiating strategy', *Academy of Management Executive*, 3(1), pp. 37–48.

Schoneboom, A. (2007) 'Diary of a working boy: creative resistance among anonymous workbloggers', *Ethnography*, 8(4), pp. 403–23.

Schoneboom, A. (2011) 'Workblogging in a Facebook age', *Work, Employment and Society*, 25(1), pp. 132–40.

Shapiro, B.P. (1977) 'Can marketing and manufacturing coexist?', *Harvard Business Review*, 55(5), pp. 104–14.

Sharpe, E.K. (2005) 'Going above and beyond: the emotional labour of adventure guides', *Journal of Leisure Research*, 37(1), pp. 29–50.

Slocum, J.W. and Hellriegel, D. (2009) *Principles of Organizational Behaviour* (12th edn), London: South-Western Cengage.

Smith, G. (2012) 'Why I am leaving Goldman Sachs', *The New York Times*, 14 March.

Smith, W.P. (1987) 'Conflict and negotiation: trends and emerging issues', *Journal of Applied Social Psychology*, 17(7), pp. 631–77.

Sternberg, R.J. and Soriano, L.J. (1984) 'Styles of conflict resolution', *Journal of Personality and Social Psychology*, 47(1), pp. 115–26.

Taffinder, P. (1998) 'Conflict is not always a bad thing', *Personnel Today*, 10 September.

Taylor, S. (1998) 'Emotional labour and the new workplace', in P. Thompson and C. Warhurst (eds), *Workplaces of the Future*, Basingstoke: Macmillan, pp. 84–103.

Taylor, S. and Tyler, M. (2000) 'Emotional labour and sexual difference in the airline industry', *Work, Employment and Society*, 14(1), pp. 77–95.

The Economist (2009a) 'Schumpeter: hating what you do', 10 October, p. 76.

The Economist (2009b) 'Bonjour tristesse', 10 October, p. 42.

The Economist (2010) 'Light and death', 29 May, p. 72.

The Guardian Online (2012) 'WPP boss Sir Martin Sorrell faces shareholder vote against his pay', 13 June.

Thomas, K.W. (1976) 'Conflict and conflict management', in M.D. Dunette (ed.), *Handbook of Industrial and Organizational Psychology*, Chicago, IL: Rand McNally, pp. 889–935.

Thompson, J.D. (1967) *Organizations in Action*, New York: McGraw-Hill.

Tjosvold, D. (2008) 'The conflict-positive organization: it depends on us', *Journal of Organizational Behaviour*, 29(1), pp. 19–28.

Ury, W. (1991) *Getting Past No: Negotiating with Difficult People*, New York: Bantam Books.

Ury, W. and Patton, B. (1997) *Getting to Yes: Negotiating an Agreement without Giving In* (2nd edn), London: Arrow Books.

Van Maanen, J. and Kunda, G. (1989) 'Real feelings: emotional expression and organization culture', in L.L. Cummings and B.M. Staw (eds), *Research in Organizational Behaviour*, Greenwich, CT: JAI Press, pp. 43–103.

Walton, R.E. and McKersie, R.B. (1965) *A Behavioural Theory of Labour Relations*, New York: McGraw-Hill.

Weick, K.E. (1977) 'Organizational design: organizations as self-designing systems', *Organizational Dynamics*, 6(2), pp. 30–46.

Wharton, A. (1993) 'The affective consequences of service work: managing emotions on the job', *Work and Occupations*, 20(2), pp. 205–32.

Whetton, D., Cameron, K. and Woods, M. (1996) *Effective Conflict Management*, London: Harper Collins.

Whetton, D., Cameron, K. and Woods, M. (2000) *Developing Management Skills for Europe* (2nd edn), Harlow, Essex: Financial Times Prentice Hall.

Williams, C. (2003) 'Sky service: the demands of emotional labour in the airline industry', *Gender, Work and Organization*, 10(5), pp. 513–50.

Chapter 22 **Power and politics**

Key terms

reward power
coercive power
referent power
legitimate power
expert power
strategic contingencies theory
influence
acceptance
compliance
resistance
rational model of organization
political model of organization
organization politics
need for power
Machiavellianism
locus of control
risk-seeking propensity

Learning outcomes

When you have read this chapter, you should be able to define those key terms in your own words, and you should also be able to:

1. Appreciate the importance of power and politics in organizational life.
2. Compare and contrast different perspectives on power.
3. Distinguish different bases of power.
4. Identify organizational factors which enhance the power of departments.
5. Differentiate between power tactics, influencing tactics, and influencing responses.
6. Distinguish between the rational and political models of organization.
7. Identify the characteristics of individuals most likely to engage in political behaviour.
8. Explain how women use and are affected by organization politics.

Why study power and politics?

Jeffrey Pfeffer (2010) argues:

> The effective use of power is becoming increasingly important. Yes, we have flatter organizations and more cross-functional teams than we had in the past. But getting things done in a less-hierarchical system actually requires *more* influence. And as strategies become more complicated, the importance and difficulty of effective execution increase accordingly . . . So, welcome to the real world. It may not be the world we want, but it's the world we have. You won't get far, and neither will your strategic plans, if you can't build and use power. Some of the people competing for advancement or standing in the way of your organization's agenda will bend the rules of fair play or ignore them entirely. Don't bother complaining about this or wishing things were different. Part of your job is to know how to prevail in the political battles you will face.'

"Do I really want all this power? I think I do."

Source: © 3/4/1967, www.cartoonbank.com

The popular view is that power corrupts, and that organization politics means underhand, cunning, manipulative 'dirty tricks' and backstabbing. While there may be some truth in these images, the problem is that leaders and managers who do not have power, and who are either unwilling or unable to 'play the politics' of their organizations, have difficulty in getting anything done. Inescapable features of organizational life, power and politics can be damaging, but can be also used in positive and constructive ways, to solve problems, generate consensus, and drive change.

Organizations are political systems. David Buchanan and Richard Badham (2008) note that as organization structures become flatter and hierarchical power, becomes less important, the scope for political manoeuvring increases. In other words, current trends put a premium on political skills. Power and politics are entwined.

Power can be defined as the ability to get other people to do what you want them to do, and it is often necessary to use political tactics to achieve those ends. Politics is thus called 'power in action'. Some commentators argue that management failures can often be attributed to lack of political skill (Pfeffer, 2010).

An organization's members do not always share the same values, goals, and perspectives. Disagreements over the definitions of problems, and how best to solve them, can thus be expected. Disputes of this kind are often healthy, because they expose different perspectives and issues. What happens, however, when that open sharing of views fails to produce a consensus? Sometimes, those with the best ideas win. Often, the winners are those who are better able to exercise influence 'behind the scenes', by 'playing politics'. Good ideas do not always sell themselves, and rational arguments may not be effective on their own. As the American diplomat Henry Kissinger once said,

> Before I served as a consultant to [President] Kennedy, I had believed, like most academics, that the process of decision-making was largely intellectual and all one had to do was to walk into the President's office and convince him of the correctness of one's view. This perspective, I soon realized, is as dangerously immature as it is widely held. (Pfeffer, 1992, p. 31)

Securing the city

Seen Adair/Reuters

Christopher Dickey (2009) describes how, following the terrorist attacks on the World Trade Center on 9 September 2001, the New York Police Department (NYPD) created a Counter-Terrorism Bureau (CTB). To be successful, the CTB had to be invisible to the public, who were paying for this service through taxation, and the Bureau's intelligence gathering took place elsewhere on the planet, which meant taking New York cops off the city streets. The new Real Time Crime Center at One Police Plaza in Manhattan cost US$11 million. Three years after the attacks, however, people had started to forget. To counteract the apathy, the Bureau organized impressive shows of force, deliberately turning up without warning at high-profile targets like the Empire State Building, in order to remind the public that the bad guys were still out there.

The CTB also had to work effectively with other agencies, particularly 'the three-letter guys': FBI, CIA, ATF, DEA. Relations between the FBI and the CTB were managed through a Joint Terrorism Task Force. The head of the NYPD Intelligence Division was David Cohen.

> Cohen's years at Langley and in the New York office of the CIA had taught him 'there's no such thing as information sharing, there is only information trading', as he told his colleagues at the NYPD. You go to the FBI and say, 'Tell me what you're doing', they're going to say, 'Go f*** yourself', is the way another senior official with the NYPD put it.
>
> Back channels to the CIA or other parts of the intelligence community could only take you so far. To get the stuff you needed, you had to be able to pull your weight. You had to be giving as well as getting. Otherwise you were going to be like the puny kid having sand kicked in his face by bullies. (Dickey, 2009, p. 140)

This led to an 'overseas program', with NYPD operatives working abroad in liaison positions with forces which had their own counter-terrorist units, to exchange and gather intelligence. This meant that Cohen was able to establish a power base through his own intelligence operation, and the three-letter guys had to come and ask him for information. Information sharing then became possible. The ability to understand and to use power and organization politics effectively is therefore fundamental to the success of the NYPD CTB in its efforts to detect and prevent future attacks.

Management decisions are often the result of influence, bargaining, negotiation, and jockeying for position, by individuals, and by groups who happen to share similar views on a particular issue. Leaders and managers who lack power, and who are not skilled in working with the politics of an organization, typically struggle to make things happen and to get things done. These capabilities make you more employable. After the job interviews, someone on the panel might say 'this candidate is very well qualified . . . but'. They are referring to lack of political skill: do not get caught by 'the but problem'.

An understanding of power and politics also allows us to assess the power of others, and to respond accordingly, regardless of whether we ourselves are power hungry or not. Psychologists use the term 'power tells' to describe the various signs and clues that indicate how powerful someone is – or how powerful they want to be (Collett, 2004). The power tells of dominant individuals include

- sitting and standing with legs far apart (men)
- appropriating the territory around them by placing their hands on their hips
- using open postures
- using invasive hand gestures
- smiling less, because a smile is an appeasement gesture
- establishing visual dominance by looking away from the other person while speaking, implying that they do not need to be attentive
- speaking first, and dominating the conversation thereafter
- using a lower vocal register, and speaking more slowly
- being more likely to interrupt others, and more likely to resist interruption by others.

The power tells of submissive individuals include

- modifying speech style to sound more like the person they are talking to
- more frequent hesitations, using lots of 'ums' and 'ers'
- adopting closed postures
- clasping hands, touching face and hair (self-comfort gestures)
- blushing, coughing, dry mouth, heavy breathing, heavy swallowing, increased heart rate, lip biting, rapid blinking, and sweating are 'leakage tells' which reveal stress and anxiety.

Knowledge of these tells means that we can 'read' the power signals of others. This also means that we can control our own tells so that we appear to be more (or less) powerful.

Power in organizations

Power, which we defined in Chapter 11, is a 'contested concept' because a number of competing perspectives have been developed. It is therefore useful to be able to view this concept from different angles, and to be aware of their respective strengths and limitations.

An abstract concept, power is also a difficult topic to conceptualize. The following three contrasting perspectives share some similarities. The first perspective views power as something you possess, an attribute or characteristic of the individual. The second perspective views power as a property of relationship between one individual (or group) and another. The third perspective sees power as embedded in social and organization structures.

Power as property of the individual

This perspective sees power as something that you possess, a set of resources that you accumulate. How much power do you have? Where did it come from? How can you acquire more power? Some of the main sources of power in an organization are shown in Table 22.1.

Table 22.1: Power as property

Structural sources	Individual sources
formal position, authority, allies, supporters	energy, endurance, stamina
access to and control over resources including information	ability to focus energy and avoid wasteful effort
physical and social position in the organization's communication network	sensitivity to and ability to read others
centrality of section to the business	flexibility in choice of means to achieve goals
role in resolving business-critical problems	personal toughness, willingness to engage in conflict and confrontation
degree of department unity, lack of dissent	able to play the 'subordinate' or 'team member' in order to enlist the support of others
being irreplaceable, pervasiveness of the role	

Source: based on Pfeffer (1992).

Notice that some of these sources of power relate to the position that a manager holds in the organization (structural sources; see chapter 15), while others relate to their personal attributes (individual sources).

From this perspective, as power is something you can accumulate, you can take deliberate action to strengthen both your structural and individual sources of power. Look for jobs in key departments, make friends with influential power brokers, join important networks and projects, and develop your interpersonal skills, impression management techniques, and emotional intelligence (see Chapter 7). Be aware, however, that others in the organization are also trying to accumulate power. Your own power can increase, but if you are not careful, it can also decrease.

Waiter power

A prominent American politician and ex-basketball superstar, Bill Bradley, was invited to make a speech at a political banquet (Jackson and Carter, 2000). During the meal, the waiter came round and served Bradley with a pat of butter. Bradley asked if he could have two pats of butter.

'Sorry', the waiter replied, 'Just one pat each.' 'I don't think you know who I am', Bradley responded. 'I'm Bill Bradley, Rhodes Scholar, professional basketball player, world champion, United States senator.' 'Well', the waiter said, 'Maybe you don't know who I am.' 'As a matter of fact I don't', Bradley replied. 'Who are you?'

'I'm the guy', said the waiter, 'who's in charge of the butter.'

STOP AND THINK

Given what you know about structural sources of power, can you explain why accountants tend to be more powerful and influential than human resource managers?

Symbols of organizational power

Rosabeth Moss Kanter (1979) observes that you are more powerful if you are able to

- intercede favourably on behalf of someone in trouble with the organization
- get a desirable placement for a talented subordinate
- get approval for expenditure beyond the budget
- get above-average salary increases for subordinates
- get items on the agenda at policy meetings
- get fast access to top decision-makers
- get regular, frequent access to top decision-makers
- get information about decisions and policy shifts.

Bertram Herbert Raven (b.1926)

Power as property of the relationship

John French and Bertram Raven (1958) identified five bases of power. If someone promises you promotion or money to act as they require, then they are using **reward power**. If they threaten you with demotion or redundancy, they are using **coercive power**. Where they rely on their charming personality, they are using **referent power**. If they rely on their formal organizational position to get you to comply, they are using **legitimate power**. Where they can claim better knowledge and understanding of the situation, they are using **expert power**.

Reward power the ability to exert influence based on the other's belief that the influencer has access to valued rewards which will be dispensed in return for compliance.

Coercive power the ability to exert influence based on the other's belief that the influencer can administer unwelcome penalties or sanctions.

Referent power the ability to exert influence based on the other's belief that the influencer has desirable abilities and personality traits that can and should be copied.

Legitimate power the ability to exert influence based on the other's belief that the influencer has authority to issue orders which they in turn have an obligation to accept.

Expert power the ability to exert influence based on the other's belief that the influencer has superior knowledge relevant to the situation and the task.

Referent power is also known as charisma (in German, *Ausstrahlung*, force of personality). Legitimate power is also called position power, relying on formal organizational role and title. Perception is a more important driver of our behaviour than 'reality' (see Chapter 8). An individual may have access to rewards or possess expertise, but others will be less willing to comply if they do not believe that the individual has those resources (even if they do). Similarly, a person may lack reward capacity or expertise, but will gain compliance from others because they are able to persuade them that they do have these. An individual can thus manipulate others' perceptions to gain compliance. Because two parties and their perceptions are involved, this perspective treats power as a *relational* construct, and not as solely the personal property of an individual.

"Can everyone clearly fear me?"

Source: © Michael Shaw/The New Yorker Collection/www.cartoonbank.com

STOP AND THINK

While each of these power bases can be useful in influencing others to do what you want them to do, they can have other consequences as well. For example, if your manager uses coercive power to get you to carry out a particular task, what longer-term effects might this have? If your team leader uses expert power over the other team members, what consequences might this have, other than compliance with their immediate instructions?

Managers, of course, can use several different power bases, in different combinations, at different times, depending on the context, and the target of their influence attempts. The American gangster Al Capone is reputed to have said 'You can get a lot more done with a kind word and a gun than with a kind word alone' (McCarty, 2004). Managers typically work with a range of different groups, and while particular power bases may be appropriate in some settings, other methods will be required in different circumstances. Traditionally, managers have relied on legitimate and coercive power, which have over time become less acceptable – and less effective. In the twenty-first century, expert and referent power are more appropriate, in most circumstances. However, an individual's power also depends on whatever resources are available to them at any given time. Minorities, for example, are often able to influence policies and decisions that concern them by pointing to their *lack* of power and influence, thus generating sympathy, which in turn leads to the decision that they want. The list of power bases extends well beyond that of French and Raven, and is potentially infinite.

Reward power only works if those who are being influenced actually want the rewards that are on offer. Rewards that are desirable for one person may not influence another. The use of those power bases must be tailored to the situation, and to those whose behaviour one wants to influence. Allan Cohen and David Bradford (1991) identify eight types of reward which they call *organizational currencies*, and which can be used to persuade others to comply with your requests. These are summarized in Table 22.2.

Table 22.2: Organizational currencies

Currencies	Examples
resources	lending or giving money, staff, or space
information	sharing technical or organizational knowledge
advancement	assigning a task that will lead to promotion
recognition	acknowledging another's efforts and achievements
network, contacts	providing opportunities to link with others
personal support	giving personal and emotional support
assistance	helping with projects
cooperation	responding rapidly to requests, approving a project

Source: based on Cohen and Bradford (1989, 1991).

Expert power on the rostrum

Toscanini

Shortly before the concert was about to begin, the great conductor, Arturo Toscanini, was approached by a distraught member of the orchestra who reported that one of the keys on his instrument was broken. He did not know how he would be able to play in the concert. Toscanini thought for a moment, and replied, 'All is well. That note is never played in tonight's performance.' (Greenberg and Baron, 2007, p. 473).

Power as a property of social and organizational structures

This perspective explores how power controls our behaviour through less obvious means. Power is woven into the fabric of our organizations and society at large. We take for granted many things, such as the social and organization structures in which we find ourselves, the system of rules that we normally follow, and the day-to-day 'natural order'. All of these routine, 'normal' features of our surroundings influence our behaviour in subtle ways, and we rarely challenge them, simply because they are routine. It can be difficult to challenge 'the way things are' without appearing to be odd or extreme. So, we tend not to challenge hierarchical structures or power and income differentials, because these are 'normal' features of our organizations and of society as a whole.

Power that is *embedded* in social and organizational structures may be less visible (unless you pay attention), but can be just as powerful in controlling behaviour as more visible sources (such as Al Capone's gun). However, it is in the interests of those who can manipulate and exploit the unequal distribution of power and wealth that we do not challenge 'the way things are'.

When power is embedded in this way, expertly woven into the fabric of the organization, we simply accept it, in the same way that we accept that offices have desks, and bosses have bigger offices. We accept the structure of the organization – job description, operating rules and policies, performance targets, equipment, and how we will be rewarded.

Embedded controls

Don Hellriegel and John Slocum (1978) identify six control strategies that organizations can use to exercise power over individuals in ways that are not immediately obvious:

Control through structure: Large organizations give employees job descriptions, setting out tasks and responsibilities. These can be detailed and specific, or broad and vague. Job descriptions also specify communication flows and the location of decision-making responsibility.

Control through policies and rules: Written policies and rules guide actions, structure relationships, set standards, define acceptable behaviour, and establish performance levels.

Control through recruitment and training: Organizations rarely want staff to behave in variable, idiosyncratic, and random ways. To achieve predictability, they select stable, reliable individuals, who are then trained how to behave.

Control through rewards and punishments: Employees receive extrinsic rewards in the form of money and fringe benefits such as company cars and free meals. Intrinsic rewards include satisfying work, personal responsibility, and autonomy. Offering to provide or withdraw these rewards gains employees' compliance.

Control through budgets: Individuals and organizational units can be given financial and other resource targets in order to guide their performance. These targets may concern, for example, revenue, costs, machine utilization, or sales volume, and often have a time frame attached (e.g. revenue per month).

Control through technology: This can include both material technology (tools, equipment) and social technology (standard working procedures). Various forms of electronic surveillance have been available for some time.

STOP AND THINK

Consider your next organizational behaviour assignment. Have you been given a specified maximum word limit, a submission date, and a warning about plagiarism? How do those instructions influence your behaviour as a student?

In most organizations, different sections or units have different levels of power. Why should this be the case? Groups or departments that are responsible for dealing with the issues that are key to the organization's performance and survival, or solving urgent problems, or dealing with a crisis, tend to be more powerful than those parts of the organization that are less critical. In one organization, at one period, research and development may be critical in terms of developing new products and getting ahead of the competition. In a recession, when consumer spending is low, marketing and sales may be more important. The finance function in most organizations is always a high priority, and they tend to have high levels of power and influence over key decisions.

Strategic contingencies theory a perspective which argues that the most powerful individuals and departments are those best able to deal effectively with the issues that are most critical to the organization's survival and performance.

This is known as the **strategic contingencies theory** of organizational power (Hickson et al., 1971; Salancik and Pfeffer, 1977; Mintzberg, 1983). Strategic contingencies are events that must take place if the organization is to survive and succeed. If your department handles these contingencies, then it will have more power and influence. A department's ability to deal with strategic contingencies depends on five factors: dependency creation, financial resources, centrality of activities, non-substitutability, and ability to reduce uncertainty. These five factors overlap, and the more of them a department possesses, the greater the power that it will exert in the organization.

Dependency creation

A department is powerful if other units and departments depend on it for materials, information, resources, and advice. The receiving department is always in an inferior power position. The number and strength of these dependencies are also important.

Financial resources

A department's ability to control financial resources increases power. Money can be converted into many other different resources that are valued by others. Because of the power-enhancing value of financial resources, departments in all organizations compete with others for new projects or tasks which have new (and preferably large) budgets attached to them.

Centrality of activities

Centrality refers to the degree to which a department's activities are critical to achieving the organization's goals. The more central a department is, the more powerful it is likely to be. Low-centrality departments such as training, payroll management, human resources, and advertising can be outsourced without jeopardizing the organization's performance.

Non-substitutability

A department is likely to be more powerful where its work cannot easily be done by another department, either within or outside the organization. Individuals and sections increase their power by handling more specialized work that requires high levels of skill and knowledge.

Uncertainty reduction

Those with the ability to reduce uncertainty can gain significant reputations and positions of influence, by providing clear definitions of problems and solutions, thus restoring an otherwise confused situation.

Your personal strategic contingencies

'Once you have chosen the right department three things matter more than anything else. The first is the ability to "manage upwards". This means turning yourself into a supplicant: Barack Obama asked about a third of his fellow senators for help when he first arrived in the institution. It also means mastering the art of flattery: Jennifer Chatman, of the University of California, Berkeley, conducted experiments in which she tried to find a point at which flattery became ineffective. It turned out there wasn't one. The second is the ability to network. One of the quickest ways to the top is to turn yourself into a "node" by starting an organization or forging a link between separate parts of a company. The third, more admirable, quality is loyalty: Booz Allen, a consultancy, calculates that four out of every five CEO appointments go to insiders. Those insiders last almost two years longer in their jobs than outsiders.' (© The Economist Newspaper Limited, London (11/09/2010)

STOP AND THINK

Does the pursuit of power interfere with or contribute to an organization's performance? Explain your answer.

Three faces of power

Steven Lukes (b.1941)

Stephen Lukes (2005) argues that power may be visible and self-evident, or subtle and covert, or institutionalized, as we have seen, in organizational structures. Power, for Lukes, thus has three faces:

- First, power that is exercised to secure a decision in situations where there is observable conflict or disagreement.
- Second, power that is exercised to keep issues off the decision-making agenda, so that potential conflicts or disagreements are precluded, and are therefore unobservable.
- Third, institutionalized power defines reality for others, by indicating what is 'normal' and to be 'taken for granted'. If norms and meanings become internalized by an organization's members, they will then act in accordance with those norms, as defined by senior management, even if these work against their 'real' interests.

The first face of power is the most obvious, and concerns a clash of interests between those making a decision and those who are likely to be affected by that decision. This face focuses on the *observable behaviours* that influence the form or content of a decision. For example, in the army, a sergeant threatens to put a private on a charge unless he completes his assigned task before midnight. The sergeant's words and actions, and their effect on the soldier's behaviours, can be observed.

The second face of power concerns the manipulation of issues. The interests of certain groups can be excluded from a bargaining or decision-making arena: 'sorry, that topic does not fall within the remit of this committee'. The focus here is thus on the non-observable behaviour involved in keeping issues on or off an agenda. You may know that, if you bring a particular issue to a particular management group, you will not be thanked for raising that problem – so you keep quiet about it, even though there is no pressure on you to do this. This is also known as *nondecision making* (Bachrach and Baratz, 1963), which those with power can use to avoid conflict with and resistance to their plans. This form of power prevents controversial issues from ever reaching the public domain, so discussion is prevented, and no decisions are taken. With the first face of power, at least you know what you are up against. With this second face of power, you are not invited to the conversation.

The third face of power involves shaping others' perceptions, cognitions, and preferences, so that they accept their current situation, because they cannot see an alternative. Acceptance may be perceived as natural, unchangeable, or divinely ordained, and also as beneficial, and can lead us to act against our objective interests. So we come to understand that maximizing profit through reducing waste and cutting costs are fundamental, unchallengeable features of reality (even though such actions may make working conditions more unpleasant or difficult). In this way, 'the powerful' define reality for 'the powerless', whose interests and grievances are obscured and silenced. Paradoxically, this face of power is characterized by harmony, as power is not exposed in public, those subjected to it are unaware of its presence and influence, and overt conflict is avoided.

Another distinguishing feature of institutionalized power is that it cannot be linked readily with the actions of any one particular individual. This contrasts with the first face of power where we can observe individuals influencing a decision. And it may be seen with the second face of power, in the 'behind the scenes' manoeuvres of particular individuals who want to prevent the open discussion of controversial issues. But if you can control the actions of others indirectly by getting them to accept particular norms and assumptions, in other words to 'internalize' those values and beliefs, not only is challenge stifled, but it is difficult to point to individuals who may be to blame for doing the stifling. Institutional power sustains the dominance of the powerful by reducing the ability of the powerless to complain. This can be achieved quite simply: 'I'm afraid that my role does not give me responsibility for solving problems like that'; 'This committee does not deal with those issues.'

Disciplinary power

Michel Foucault (1926–1984)

Michel Foucault, a French philosopher and historian, provides yet another perspective on power. His thinking relates to Lukes's third 'institutional' face of power focusing on the ways in which management remains dominant by defining reality and normality in ways that reduce the likelihood of challenge or resistance. Foucault (1979, p. 93) observed that 'power is everywhere, not because it embraces everything, but because it comes from everywhere'. The related concepts of *bio-power* and *disciplinary power* are central to understanding Foucault's thinking.

Bio-power

Bio-power is another term for power that operates by establishing what is normal or abnormal, socially acceptable or deviant, in thought and behaviour. Bio-power is targeted at society as a whole, and is achieved through a variety of *discursive practices*: talk, writing, debate, argument, representation. The media play a major role in sustaining and altering what we conceive as socially normal. Bio-power exercises its control over us by 'constituting the normal' and operates through our individual cognition and understanding. If you accept without challenge 'the way things are', the way a situation is currently represented, 'the constitution of the normal' as Foucault puts it, then bio-power takes on a self-disciplining role with regard to your thinking and behaving:

> As you walk onto the street, you realize just how late it is. You can't believe that you have been at work for so long. You should be used to this by now. Most days you spend twelve hours in the office, with only a fading tourist photograph of an Indian village to remind you of what it was like to be free. There isn't anyone holding a gun to your head, is there? But long hours have their drawbacks. Even though you might want a family, you know that is impossible. Anyway, you have made your decision. You're out to achieve big things, and this requires a few small sacrifices. (Fleming and Spicer, 2007, p. 19)

There is no manager or supervisor telling you what to do or how to behave. Sets of procedures, instructions, and controls are applied by individuals to themselves in pursuit of goals that they have been persuaded are their own, but which are maintained by self-interested elites. These 'technologies of the self'(Rose, 1989) mean that, rather than having individuals' behaviour regulated through external systems of monitoring and control (supervisors, technology, appraisal systems), these controls get inside the 'hearts and minds' of organization members, and work through self-regulation.

STOP AND THINK

How is bio-power influencing your behaviour? Which goals do you accept as your own, but which have actually been 'given' to you by your university and/or its staff? In your work, current or past, which procedures and instructions have you accepted without criticism, and to which have you conformed without challenge? If you did decide to challenge those goals, procedures, and instructions, how would you do that, and how would you estimate your chances of success in getting any of them changed?

Disciplinary power

Disciplinary power targets individuals and groups and works through the construction of social and organizational routines. Through this lens, Foucault sees power as a set of techniques, the effects of which are achieved through what he calls *disciplinary practices*. These practices include the tools of surveillance and assessment that are used to control and regiment individuals, rendering them docile and compliant. The tools, or mechanisms, that achieve compliance include (Hiley, 1987, p. 351)

- the allocation of physical space in offices or factories, which establishes homogeneity and uniformity, individual and collective identity, ranks people according to status, and fixes their position in the network of social relations;
- the standardization of individual behaviour through timetables, regimentation, work standards, and repetitive activities;
- the 'composition of forces', where individuals become parts of larger units, such as cross-functional teams, or production lines;
- the creation of job ladders and career systems which, through their future promises of promotion and reward, encourage compliance with the organization's demands.

We do not normally consider office layouts, timetables, career ladders, or work assignments to be manifestations of power. However, these normal features of organizational life help to shape and discipline our daily activities and interpersonal relationships, controlling us, and guaranteeing our compliance with social and organizational norms and expectations. It is precisely because they are 'micro techniques', so small, so unobtrusive, and so embedded in the organization's structure and processes, that they are hardly noticed. Foucault's concept of power is thus different from traditional concepts, as the contrasts shown in Table 22.3 indicate (Buchanan and Badham, 2008, p. 296).

Table 22.3: Foucault and traditional concepts of power

Traditional concepts of power	Foucault's concepts of power
Power is possessed, accumulated, vested in the individual.	Power is pervasive, a totality, reflected in concrete practices.
Power is in the hands of social and organizational elites; resistance is futile.	Power is found in the micro-physics of everyday social life; power depends on resistance.
We are subject to the domination of those who are more powerful than us.	We construct our own web of power by accepting current definitions of normality.
Power is destructive: it denies, represses, prevents, corrupts.	Power is productive: it contributes to social order, which is flexible and shifting.
Power is episodic, visible, observable in action, deployed intermittently, absent except when exercised.	Power is present in its absence, discreet, operating through taken-for-granted daily routines and ways of living.
Knowledge of power sources and relationships is emancipatory, helping us to overcome domination.	Knowledge maintains and extends the web of power, creating further opportunities for domination.

Source: from Buchanan, D.A. and Badham, R.J., *Power, Politics, and Organizational Change: Winning the Turf Game*, Copyright (© Sage Publications 2008).

STOP AND THINK

How are disciplinary practices affecting your behaviour? Identify examples of practices to which you have been subjected, either in your educational institution or at work, which have shaped your routine daily activities and social interactions. So what? Is this a problem (discuss)?

Foucault argues that we are trapped in a 'field of force relations', a web of power which we help to create, and which we are always re-creating. We are thus creators of that web of power, and prisoners within it. At an organizational level, disciplinary practices condition employees' thought processes, leading them to treat taken-for-granted processes, such as performance-based pay, as 'natural' and beyond question. This 'force field', however, is neither stable nor inevitable. Challenge may be difficult, but is not impossible. As a consequence, this force field changes as points of resistance are encountered, networks of alliances change, fissures open up, old coalitions break up, and new ones are formed. Foucault also points out that resistance (by employees to management demands, for example) only demonstrates and reinforces the need for such disciplinary measures.

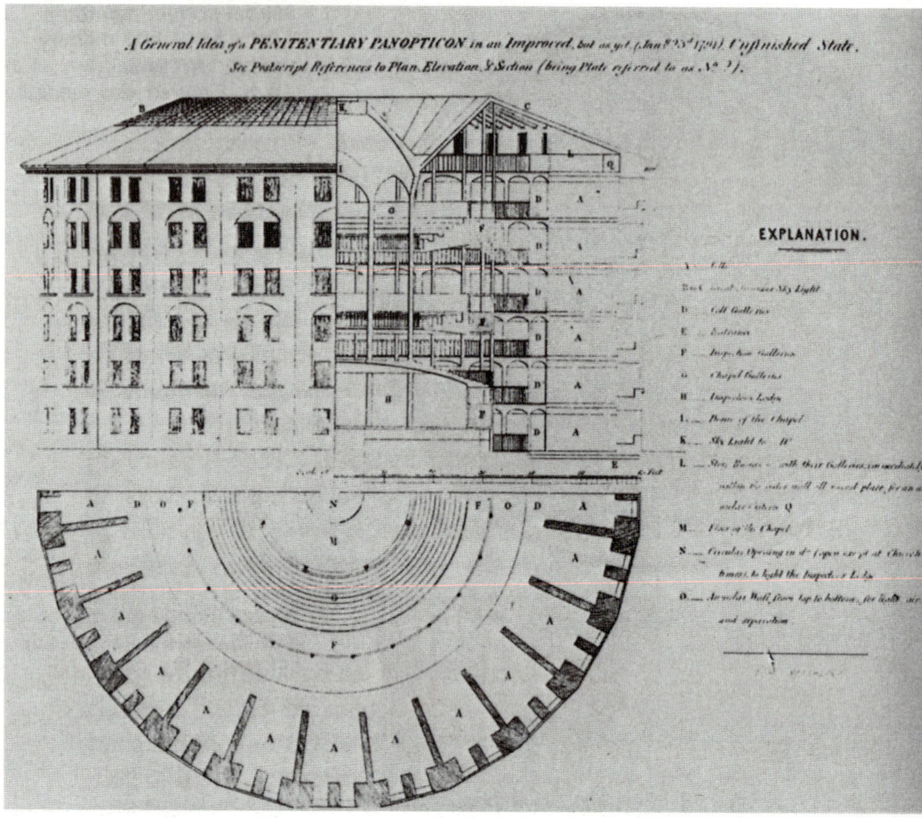

Bentham's Panopticon

Foucault uses the metaphor of the *panopticon* for his image of disciplinary power. This is a circular prison designed by the eighteenth-century philosopher Jeremy Bentham, allowing all the prison inmates to be observed, in their cells, by one observer who cannot be seen by the prisoners. The prisoners cannot avoid this constant surveillance, but they do not know when they are being observed. They must therefore behave at all times *as if* they are being watched. They thus monitor themselves. As McAuley et al. (2007, p. 263) argue, 'we are not necessarily compelled to act as we do by some external agency. Instead, through society's disciplines of schools, hospitals, prisons and the military, we have internalized [power] to become self-governed or "normalized".'

The new golden rule: the person with the gold gets to make the rules

Jeffrey Pfeffer (2010) argues that, to make things happen in an organization, you need to have power, which he defines as 'the ability to have things your way'. He offers the following suggestions:

1. Mete out resources. 'The new golden rule: the person with the gold gets to make the rules.' Use discretionary control over resources – money, equipment, space, information – to build power, do favours, generate reciprocity.
2. Shape behaviour through rewards and punishments. Reward those who help, punish those who get in the way. Rewards can be substantive or symbolic.

3. Advance on many fronts. Faced with obstacles on one front, shift to another. Be persistent.
4. Make the first move. Surprise moves catch opponents off guard.
5. Co-opt antagonists. Win over opponents by making them part of your team, giving them a stake.
6. Remove rivals – nicely if possible. Show them the door gracefully – achieve 'strategic outplacement'. Help them to move; they may even be grateful.
7. Don't draw unnecessary fire. Live to fight another day; do not challenge or criticize in ways that will rebound on you or create unnecessary opposition.
8. Use the personal touch. Meet people in person, or call them; return calls promptly, flatter, build personal ties – and this includes staffers, assistants, secretaries – the gatekeepers to the power brokers.
9. Persist. Wear the opposition down. Stay in the game.
10. Make important relationships work – no matter what. Your feelings, or others' feelings about you, don't matter. Resentments, jealousies, anger – put those aside or they will prevent you from getting the job done.
11. Make your vision compelling. 'It's easier to exercise power when you are aligned with a compelling, socially valuable objective' (p. 92). Your opponents will have problems challenging that agenda.

Power and influence

Influence the process of affecting someone else's attitudes, beliefs, or behaviours, without using coercion or formal position, such that the other person believes that they are acting in their own best interests.

How can we use power to get others to do what we want? Remember that power is defined as exerting one's will and overcoming resistance in order to produce the results that we desire. Those over whom power is exercised may be aware of this, and resentful. However, it is also possible to achieve the desired end results in such a way that those affected are not aware, and only occasionally resentful, and may even be grateful. Andrzej Huczynski (2004) defines **influence** as one person's ability to affect another's attitudes, beliefs, or behaviours. Influence can be achieved without force or 'pulling rank'. When this is successful, the person who is influenced often believes that they have not been pressured or forced into doing something, but that they are acting in their own best interests.

We use influence tactics to persuade others to do what we want them to do, sometimes against their judgement and preferences. This topic has attracted a lot of research interest, and we will consider two influential perspectives. One is based on the work of Kipnis et al. (1984), who identified eight categories of influence tactic: assertiveness, ingratiation, rational appeal, sanctions, exchange, upward appeal, blocking, and coalition (see Table 22.4). Kipnis et al. note that managers do not exercise influence for self-interest and enjoyment, but in order to promote new ideas, encourage others to work more effectively, or introduce new working practices, for example.

From their study of American, Australian, and British managers, Kipnis et al. (1984) identified four types of manager based on their patterns of use of these tactics:

- *Bystanders* rarely use any of these influence tactics, have low organizational power, have limited personal and organizational objectives, and are frequently dissatisfied.
- *Shotguns* use all of these influence tactics all the time, have unfulfilled goals, and are inexperienced in their job.
- *Captives* use one or two 'favourite' tactics, habitually, and with limited effectiveness.
- *Tacticians* use rational appeal frequently, make average use of other tactics, tend to achieve their objectives, have high organizational power, and are usually satisfied.

Discussing what he calls 'the science of getting what you ask for', Robert Cialdini (2008) identifies six principles of influence by observing the 'compliance professionals' who persuade other people for a living: salespeople, fund-raisers, advertisers, political lobbyists, cult recruiters, confidence tricksters. He shows how compliance professionals exploit the socialized responses that we automatically make to familiar cues (see *OB on the web* at the end of this chapter). Anyone can learn these techniques.

Table 22.4: Influence tactics

Assertiveness	Order the person to do it. Point out that the rules demand it. Keep reminding them about what is required.
Ingratiation	Make the request politely and humbly. Act in a friendly way and be complimentary before asking. Sympathize with any hardships they may face.
Rational appeal	Write a detailed justification. Present relevant information in support. Explain the reasoning behind your request.
Sanctions	Threaten to get them fired. Threaten to block their promotion. Threaten them with a poor performance evaluation.
Exchange	Offer an exchange of favours – mutual backscratching. Remind them of favours you have provided them in the past.
Upward appeal	Get higher level management to intervene in your support. Send the person to speak to your boss.
Blocking	Threaten to stop working with the person. Ignore the person and stop being friendly. Withhold collaboration until they do what you want.
Coalition	Get the support of colleagues to support your request. Make the request at a formal meeting where others will support you.

Source: based on Kipris et al. (1984).

1. **Reciprocity**: we are more likely to comply with a request from someone who has previously given us a gift, favour, or concession.

   We have a socially trained sense of obligation, to give 'something in return', even when the gift is unsolicited. Survey researchers include small payments to increase questionnaire response rates; restaurant staff increase tips by giving customers sweets with their bills.

2. **Social proof**: we are more likely to comply with a request, or to adopt a behaviour, which is consistent with what similar others are thinking or doing.

   If other people think something is correct, then we tend to agree. If others are doing something (e.g. driving fast on a stretch of road), then we feel justified in doing the same. Bartenders 'salt' their jar of tips to indicate that tipping is 'appropriate'. Church ushers use the same method, and evangelical preachers use 'ringers' who are briefed to 'spontaneously' come forward at predetermined moments during the service.

3. **Commitment/consistency**: we are more likely to comply with a request which leads to actions consistent with our previous acts and commitments.

   Consistency is linked to intellect, rationality, honesty, and integrity, and tends to be valued; we like to appear to be consistent. If we can get you to commit to something (meeting me for a cup of coffee), then it will be easier to persuade you to behave in ways that are consistent with that prior commitment (joining me for dinner tonight).

4. **Friendship/liking**: we are more likely to comply with requests from friends, or from others who we like.

   Charities recruit volunteers to collect donations in their local area. Compliance professionals, as strangers, however, have to find ways to get us to like them. Attractive individuals are generally more persuasive, and we are more easily influenced by those who are similar to us in some way – opinions, background, lifestyle, personality, dress. In one study, a survey response rate was doubled by giving the person sending the questionnaire a name similar to that of the respondent: Bob Gregar and Cindy Johanson sent survey questionnaires to Robert Greer and Cynthia Johnson.

5. **Scarcity**: we are more likely to comply with requests that will lead to the acquisition of opportunities that are scarce.

   Opportunities tend to be more highly valued when they are less available, and items that are difficult to possess are 'better' than items that can be easily acquired, including information. Customers are told that products, services, or membership opportunities are in short supply and will not last long, or 'offer available for one week only – Hurry, buy now.'

6. **Authority**: we are more likely to comply with requests from those in positions of legitimate authority.

   Position power can be persuasive. The title 'doctor' often commands blind obedience to dangerous instructions, such as administering an unsafe level of a drug. People are more likely follow instructions from a security guard in uniform, and an expensive business suit has a similar effect.

Gary Yukl (2005) reviewed numerous studies of how people influence their managers, co-workers and subordinates, and assessed the effectiveness of tactics. Some of his results are outlined in Tables 22.5 and 22.6.

Table 22.5: Influencing tactics – most effective

Tactic	Description	Examples
Rational persuasion	Present factual evidence and logical argument to support your request, making a challenge difficult.	'As you can see from the cost comparison, the second tender is 20% lower, and completion is earlier.'
Consultation	Allow the target to decide how to implement your request.	'I need you to work 20 hours of overtime in the next month, but you decide when.'
Inspirational appeal	Appeal to the target's values, ideals, or aspirations to elicit an emotional or attitudinal reaction.	'It's not about extra hours without overtime pay, it's about improving the health of the nation!'
Collaboration	Make it easy for the target to agree to your request by providing resources or removing barriers.	'If you agree to lead the team, I'll give you administrative support, and reallocate your other tasks.'

Source: based on Yukl (2005).

Table 22.6: Influencing tactics – least effective

Tactic	Description	Examples
Pressure	Make strident verbal statements and regularly remind the target of your request.	'As I said yesterday, it's vital that your presentation tomorrow is of the highest standard.'
Coalitions	Mobilize others to support you, and thereby strengthen your request.	'Claire and Peter are also affected, and that's why we would like you to change, too.'
Upward appeals	Seek assistance from someone senior to your target, either through the use of their authority or as mediator.	'Since I can't persuade you, let's meet with our boss to see what they think about this.'
Legitimating	Base a request on your own authority, organization rules, or the express/implied support of superiors.	'As project lead, I'm asking you to postpone your holiday until the job is done, which is company policy.'

Source: based on Yukl (2005).

Acceptance agreeing with and becoming committed to an influencing request both attitudinally and behaviourally.

Compliance reluctant, superficial, public, and transitory change in behaviour in response to an influencing request, which is not accompanied by attitudinal change.

We tend to respond to influence attempts in one of three main ways: acceptance, compliance, or resistance. **Acceptance** means agreement to the request which will be carried out enthusiastically, with commitment, and with a high probability that it will be fulfilled successfully. In this case, the target's behaviour and attitude both change. **Compliance**

Resistance rejecting an influencing request by means of a direct refusal, making excuses, stalling, or making an argument against, indicating neither behavioural nor attitudinal change.

involves reluctance to do what the influencer is asking. The response is apathetic and unenthusiastic, involving minimal effort, and further prodding may be required in order to meet minimum requirements. In this case, the target's behaviour changes, but not their attitude. **Resistance** involves rejection of the request, with steps to avoid having to do what is asked, such as excuses, or a direct refusal. In other words, neither behaviour nor attitude change in this situation.

STOP AND THINK Think of a situation, at home, school, university, or work, when someone tried to influence you. Give examples of where your response was acceptance, compliance, and resistance.

Organizations: rational or political?

Are organizations *rational* or *political*? Assessing the role of power and politics depends on whether or not one considers organizations to be political systems in the first place. Table 22.7 contrasts the dimensions of the rational model of organization with the political model (Pfeffer, 1992). These models have different implications for our understanding of how people in organizations think and behave.

Table 22.7: Rational and political models of organization

Organization characteristic	Rational model	Political model
goals and preferences	consistent among members	inconsistent, pluralistic
power and control	centralized	decentralized, shifting coalitions
decision processes	orderly, logical, rational	disputed, push and pull of interests
rules and norms	optimization	conflict is legitimate
information	extensive, systematic, accurate	ambiguous, used strategically
beliefs about cause and effect	known, understood	many views and disagreements
decisions	based on maximizing outcomes	result of interest group bargains
ideology	efficiency and effectiveness	struggle, conflict, winners, losers

Source: based on Pfeffer (1981, p. 31).

Rational model of organization a perspective that holds that organizational goals are clear; objectives are defined, alternatives are identified, and choices are made on the basis of reason and logic.

The rational model of organization is based on *rationalism* (the theory that reason is the foundation of certainty in knowledge) and *rationality* (the use of scientific reasoning, empiricism, and positivism, along with the use of decision criteria that include evidence, logical argument, and reasoning). Rational actions are undertaken on the basis of reason; a person adopts the same actions in the same circumstances, and choices are made objectively, on valid knowledge rather than on intuition. The beliefs of the **rational model of organization** are contrasted with those of the political model on eight organization characteristics. At the heart of the rational model is the view that employees possess goals that conform to, and are compatible with, the goals of other organization members. Individuals are considered to share a collective purpose that can be called the 'organizational goal'. All the remaining features of the model assume the existence of this overarching goal.

The rational model of organization assumes that people's behaviour is not random or accidental, but is instead directed towards achievement of the organizational goal. Rationalists argue that when making a choice, the decision-maker is guided by the norm of optimization, that is, seeking the most favourable outcome for a particular end. In this process, various available alternatives are uncovered, their likely consequences are assessed, and the risks of each are considered. Finally, the course of action which best meets the organizational goal is chosen.

Rationalists argue that this is the best way to make choices on issues such as the introduction of new technology, work organization, distribution of rewards, organization structure, and so on. However, rational writers are not only *prescriptive*, saying how, in their view, things should be done, but also claim to be *descriptive* – that is, to describe how decisions are actually made in organizations.

STOP AND THINK

Suggest reasons to account for the popularity of the rationalist view of organizations, among managers, management consultants, management academics, and politicians.

Political model of organization a perspective that holds that organizations are made up of groups that have separate interests, goals, and values, and in which power and influence are needed in order to reach decisions.

The **political model of organization** is based on different assumptions. James March (1962) was one of the first modern writers to note that the rationalist model did not take into account the different interests and objectives of an organization's members. He described organizations as *political coalitions*.

The political model holds that, normally, there is no overarching goal to which all members of the organization subscribe. The behaviour of individuals and groups can be explained with reference to their own particular goals. Those with the most power will be more successful in furthering their interests and achieving their goals.

Researchers studying how decisions are made in organizations have discovered a general absence of the use of reason, consistency, empirical data, or means–end sequencing that was supposed to characterize rational decision-making. In the place of consensus they have found conflict, and discovered decisions being made on the basis of bargaining and compromise (Allison, 1971). In the place of organization-wide consensus on goals, they have found individuals, groups, units, and departments with their own local objectives, in conflict with the aims of others, resolving issues through negotiation and the use of power.

The political model thus appears to be a better representation of organizational reality. The point of departure for this perspective concerns the absence of an overarching goal to which all of an organization's members can subscribe. A rationalist may want to complain about this messy and conflict-ridden view. However, competing perspectives, differences in viewpoint, and conflicting ways of defining and understanding problems can all contribute in healthy and productive ways to creative problem-solving. It would be dull if everyone thought the same way and were in agreement all the time. Conflict and disagreement can generate the energy for change and development.

The constructivist view of politics (see Chapter 1) argues that it is individual perception which determines judgement. Table 22.8 illustrates how behaviours can be described or labelled depending on the observer's perception (Krell et al., 1987).

STOP AND THINK

Suggest reasons that might account for the relative unpopularity of the political model of organization among managers, management consultants, management academics, and politicians.

From your own experience of organizations of different kinds, which of these two models, rational or political, provides better explanations for the behaviour of their members?

The rational and political models take different views of the nature of organizations and the behaviour of their members. As with the nature/nurture debate concerning personality, there is evidence and argument to support both the rational and political views, and each can be seen as partial. Perhaps it is more appropriate to see these two models as 'different ways of seeing' organizational behaviour.

Table 22.8: Politics in the eye of the beholder

Political viewpoint	Rational viewpoint
blaming others	allocating responsibility
kissing up	developing good working relationships
apple polishing	demonstrating loyalty
passing the buck	delegating authority
covering your rear	documenting decisions
creating conflict	encouraging change and innovation
forming coalitions	facilitating teamwork
whistleblowing	improving efficiency
scheming	planning ahead
overachieving	being competent and capable
ambitious	career-minded
opportunistic	astute
cunning	pragmatic
arrogant	confident
perfectionist	attentive to detail

Source: based on Krell et al. (1987) in ROBBINS, STEPHEN P.; JUDGE, TIMOTHY A., ORGANIZATIONAL BEHAVIOR, 12th Ed., © 2007, p. 483. Reprinted and Electronically adapted by permission of Pearson Education, Inc., Upper Saddle River, New Jersey.

Organization politics

Gerald R. Ferris (b.1951)

Organization politics the ability to understand others at work, and to use that knowledge to influence others to act in ways that enhance one's personal and/or organizational objectives.

Political skill has been defined as

> an interpersonal style construct that combines social astuteness with the ability to relate well, and otherwise demonstrate situationally appropriate behaviour in a disarmingly charming and engaging manner that inspires confidence, trust, sincerity, and genuineness. We suggest that people high in political skill not only know precisely what to do in different social situations at work, but they know exactly how to do it in a sincere manner that disguises any potentially manipulative motives and renders the influence attempt successful. (Gerald Ferris et al., 2000, pp. 30–1)

The study of **organization politics** is the study of who gets what, when, and how. Engaging in political behaviour, or performing political acts, involves activities designed to acquire, develop, retain, and use power. The main categories of political tactics used by managers are summarized in Table 22.9 (Buchanan and Badham, 2008). Political tactics are more likely to be used when

- decisions are unstructured and complex;
- there are no clear decision rules;
- there is uncertainty; and
- the members of the organization are in competition with each other.

Why does political behaviour arise in the first place? Jean-Francois Chanlat (1997) identified four sets of factors driving political behaviour: personal, decisional, structural, and organizational change.

STOP AND THINK 'One of the main problems with political behaviour in organizations is that most people lack the necessary skills to engage effectively.' Do you agree or disagree, and why?

Table 22.9: Political tactics

image building	we all know people who didn't get the job because they didn't look the part – appearance is a credibility issue; support for the right causes, adherence to group norms, self-confident manner
information games	withholding information to make others look foolish, bending the truth, white lies, massaging information, timed release, overwhelming others with complex technical details
scapegoating	ensure that someone else is blamed, this is the fault of another department, or external factors, or my predecessor, or trading conditions, or a particular individual; avoid personal blame
alliances	doing secret deals with influential others to form a critical mass, a coalition, to win support for and to progress your proposals
networking	friends in influential positions, 'wine and dine' them to get your initiatives onto the senior management agenda, improve your visibility, gather information
compromise	give in, all right, you win this time, I won't put up a fight and embarrass you in public – if you will back me next time
rule games	refuse requests because the have not followed correct procedures or are contrary to company policy; accept similar requests from allies on the grounds of 'special circumstances'
positioning	choose and move to roles that make you visible and appear successful; withdraw from failing projects; locate yourself appropriately in the building, sit in the 'right' place at meetings
issue selling	package, present, and promote your plans and ideas in ways that make them more appealing to your target audiences
dirty tricks	keep dirt files for blackmail, spy on others, discredit and undermine competitors, spreading false rumours, corridor whispers

Source: adapted from Buchanan, D.A. and Badham, R.J., *Power, Politics, and Organizational Change: Winning the Turf Game*, Copyright (© Sage Publications 2008).

Personal drivers

Organizations hire individuals who possess ambition, drive, creativity, and ideas of their own. Thus recruitment, appraisal, training, and promotion policies all directly encourage political behaviour. For example, staff selection methods seek to identify candidates who possess the personality traits related to a willingness to use power and engage in political behaviour. These are the *need for power*, *Machiavellianism*, *internal locus of control*, and *risk-seeking propensity* (House, 1988).

Need for power

Need for power (nPow): the desire to make an impact on others, change people or events, and make a difference in life.

David McClelland (1961) developed the theory that three types of need in particular are culturally acquired, or learned. These are the **need for power** (*n*Pow), the need for achievement (*n*Ach), and the need for affiliation (*n*Aff). Some of us have a strong motive or need to influence and lead others, and are thus more likely to engage in political behaviour. Since a desire to control others and events, and thus to have an impact on what is going on, is often associated with effective management, it is not surprising that selectors look for this trait in candidates for managerial jobs (McClelland and Boyatzis, 1982).

McClelland and colleagues (McClelland and Burnham, 1995; McClelland et al., 1976) distinguish between 'institutional managers' and 'personal power managers'. The latter seek personal gain at the expense of others and 'are not disciplined enough to be good institution builders' (McClelland and Burnham, 1995, p. 130): they 'exercise their power impulsively. They are more often rude to other people, they drink too much, they try to exploit others sexually, and they collect symbols of personal prestige such as fancy cars or big offices.'

Institutional managers, in contrast, combine power motivation with self-control, and represent 'the socialized face of power' (McClelland and Burnham, 1995, p. 129):

> [T]he good manager's power motivation is not oriented towards personal aggrandizement but toward the institution that he or she serves. [They] are more institution minded; they tend to get elected to more offices, to control their drinking, and have a desire to serve others.

Good 'institutional' managers have the following profile:

- they feel responsible for developing the organizations to which they belong;
- they believe in the importance of centralized authority;
- they enjoy the discipline of work, and getting things done in an orderly way;
- they are willing to sacrifice self-interest for organizational welfare;
- they have a keen sense of justice, concerning reward for hard effort.

In other words, good managers use power in the interests of the organization, rather than in pursuit of self-interest. The use of power can therefore be acceptable, as long as it is subject to discipline, control, and inhibition. However, this viewpoint argues that institution building and personal career enhancement can be pursued at the same time.

Niccolò Machiavelli (1469–1527)

Machiavellianism

Machiavellianism a personality trait or style of behaviour towards others which is characterized by (1) the use of guile and deceit in interpersonal relations, (2) a cynical view of the nature of other people, and (3) a lack of concern with conventional morality.

Machiavellianism is another trait which those who tend to engage in organization politics are likely to possess. Niccolò Machiavelli was a sixteenth-century Florentine philosopher and statesman who wrote a set of guidelines for rulers (and princes in particular) to use in order to secure and hold on to power. These were published in *The Prince*, and suggested that the primary method for achieving power was the manipulation of others (Machiavelli, 1514). Since then, Machiavelli's name has come to be associated with opportunism and deceit in interpersonal relations. We speak about someone's Machiavellian behaviour, or describe them as being Machiavellian.

Richard Christie and Florence Geis (1970) produced a famous study of Machiavellian personality characteristics. Those who score highly on their Machiavellian test – 'High Machs' – tend to agree with statements such as

- The best way to handle people is to tell them what they want to hear.
- Anyone who completely trusts anyone else is asking for trouble.
- Never tell anyone the real reason you did something unless it is useful to do so.

'Low Machs' tend to disagree with those statements. High Machs prefer to be feared rather than to be liked. They manipulate others using their persuasive skills, especially in face-to-face contact. They initiate and control interactions, are prepared to use deceit, engage in ethically questionable behaviour, and believe that the means justifies the desired end.

Internal locus of control

Locus of control an individual's generalized belief about internal control (self-control) versus external control (control by the situation or by others).

A third personality trait that encourages political behaviour concerns an individual's **locus of control**. Some people believe that what happens to them in life is under their own control; they are said to have an *internal* locus of control. Others believe that their life situation is under the control of fate or other people; they are described as having an *external* locus of control (Rotter, 1966). It is the 'internals', who believe that they control what happens to them, who tend to use more political behaviour than 'externals'. Internals are more likely to expect that their political tactics will be effective, and are also less likely to be influenced by others.

Risk-seeking propensity

Risk-seeking propensity the willingness of an individual to choose options that entail risk.

A final personality trait that is likely to determine whether a person engages in political behaviour is their **risk-seeking propensity**. Engaging in political behaviour is not risk-free, and there are negative as well as positive outcomes for those who do it. They could be demoted, passed over for promotion, or given low performance assessments. Some people are naturally risk-averse, while others are risk-seekers (Sitkin and Pablo, 1992; Madison et al., 1980). Risk-seekers are more willing to engage in political behaviour. For those who are risk-averse, the negative consequences of a failed influencing attempt outweigh the possible benefits of a successful outcome.

The need for power, Machiavellianism, internal locus of control, and risk-seeking propensity: these personality characteristics are associated with a strong desire for career advancement. All organizations have a proportion of ambitious individuals who compete with each other, arguing and lobbying for their personal ideas, innovations, and projects. However, traditional organizational structures are hierarchical, and there are fewer positions available at each higher level. Those who are ambitious, therefore, are in constant competition to secure those desirable, but scarce, senior posts.

Decisional drivers

The extent to which politics enters the decision-making process depends on the type of decisions. Decisions vary; some are structured, and others are unstructured. Structured decisions are programmable, and can be resolved using clear decision rules. Routine decisions, such as how much stock to order, are structured. Normally, if a decision is structured or programmed, and if there is no opposition to what a manager wants to do, then it will be less necessary to use politics.

The problem is, the number of management decisions that can be based simply on information, calculation, and logic is small. Unstructured decisions also depend on judgement, experience, intuition, preference, values, and 'gut feel'. Unstructured or unprogrammable decisions are more common, and virtually all senior management decisions are unstructured to some degree. Examples include:

- Should we seek to maximize profitability in the short term, or develop our medium-term market share instead?
- Should we develop our human resource management function, or outsource this to a specialist management services organization?
- Should we develop our technical expertise in that sector, or buy another company that already possesses this capability?

Home viewing

The film *Contact* (1997, director Robert Zemeckis) is about Dr Eleanor (Ellie) Arroway (played by Jodie Foster). It recounts humankind's first contact with alien life. The whole endeavour of searching for extra-terrestrial life is fraught with personal, scientific, economic, political, and ethical uncertainties. While she may be an excellent scientist, Ellie is not a particularly good organizational politician. As you watch the film, answer the following questions. What organizational political mistakes does Ellie make? What organizational political skills does Dr David Drumlin display? What mistakes does Ellie make in the President's advisory committee meeting? What tactics does Drumlin use to maintain his controlling position? What advice would you give Ellie if she wanted to become a more effective organizational politician?

With unstructured decisions, one can expect different managers, with their own past experiences, opinions, values, and preferences, to disagree. This debate is natural and valuable. Put another way, 'When two people always agree, one of them is unnecessary' (Pfeffer and Sutton, 2006, p. 31). Since information, calculation, and logic cannot help to reach an unstructured decision, what strategies are left? In these kinds of situations, those involved are more likely to use political tactics to gain the support of others, and to deflect resistance when necessary, in order to win the debate and ensure that their preferred course of action is endorsed. The success or failure of rivals can of course have an impact on an individual's reputation and career progress, as well as on the status of their section or occupational group.

In other words, political behaviour is a direct consequence of the numerical superiority of unstructured over structured decisions, which explains its predominance in the higher levels of organizations, where such decisions tend to be made most frequently. Political behaviour is also encouraged by the tendency of informed and interested parties to disagree with each other, partly on the interpretation of information, and partly because they hold differing beliefs, values, and preferences.

Structural drivers

Jeffrey Pfeffer (b.1946)

Organization structures tend to be based on departments which, naturally, compete with each other. Jeffrey Pfeffer (1992) describes just how these structures produce the conditions that encourage political behaviour (see Figure 22.1 – let's follow the numbering). The starting point is that functions tend to be differentiated between sections, units, or departments, such as purchasing, production, marketing, finance, and sales (1). This degree of specialization can increase efficiency and reduce costs. However, it can also be divisive, because those different sections each have their own goals and priorities, which are unlikely to be consistent with the goals and priorities of other sections (2). Marketing and sales want to maximize revenue while finance and production want to minimize costs. In addition, those departments require different sets of information, leading them each to view the world through the lens of their own function's perspective. (Remember that staff tend to be recruited into a department, rather than into an organization.) Differentiation thus encourages different beliefs about how things should be done (3). We may agree on a goal, but disagree on how to get there. Then we have the differing personalities and backgrounds of those who work in those different departments, affecting how they see their unit's goals, and also their assumptions about how those goals should be pursued (4).

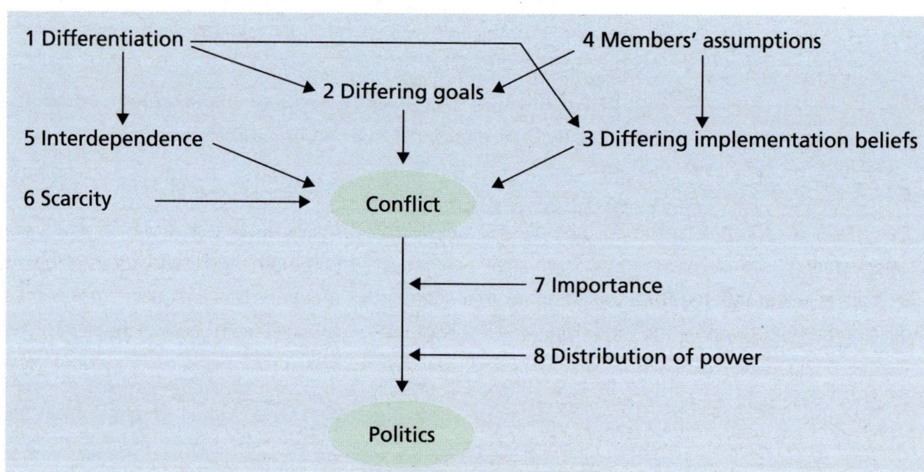

Figure 22.1: Structural drivers of political behaviour

Source: reuse of figure, p. 69 'Structural conditions producing the power . . .' from POWER IN ORGANIZATIONS by JEFFREY PFEFFER. Copyright © 1981 by Jeffrey Pfeffer (1992). Reprinted by permission of HarperCollins Publishers.

Differentiation also creates *interdependence* between roles and departments (5). It thus ties groups and individuals together, making each concerned with what the other does and gets in terms of resources. Scarce resources are the most valuable. Labelling a resource as *scarce* produces a vigorous action to obtain it, and greater dissatisfaction with its apparent unavailability (6). Scarcity is more likely to arise in relation to recruitment, promotions and transfers, pay, budget allocations, facilities and equipment, delegation of authority, interdepartmental coordination, personnel policies, disciplinary penalties, appraisals, and grievances and complaints.

This combination of factors can produce conflict, and is more likely to result in the use of power and politics if two further conditions are met; these relate to the importance of the issues, and how widely power is distributed across the organization. Engaging in political behaviour requires time and effort, and is more likely to be reserved for the more important issues (7). Bargaining, the creation of coalitions, and the use of other political tactics become more important when power is widely dispersed, rather than being concentrated at the top (8). As a result, political behaviour in our organizations is an almost inevitable consequence of structural differentiation.

Organizational change drivers

Organizational change – especially major or strategic change (see Chapter 18) – creates more unstructured decisions, particularly with regard to the direction and purpose of change, and also how the goals of change should best be achieved. The scope for political behaviour during periods of major change is therefore high. Change also generates uncertainty, and those who have the appropriate political knowledge and skill can exploit that uncertainty to their advantage, to influence decisions in their preferred direction, and to position themselves favourably in the new structure.

These four sets of drivers – personal, decisional, structural, and organizational change – present a powerful combination. Political behaviour in organizational settings is a naturally occurring phenomenon, and is highly resistant to management attempts to stifle or eradicate it.

Women and organization politics

Carly Fiorina was the first female chief executive of a Fortune 20 company, Hewlett-Packard. In her autobiography, she says that 'Life isn't always fair, and is different for men than for women' (Fiorina, 2006, p. 70). Women suffer from sex role stereotyping that associates management with masculinity: 'think manager – think male', and women's abilities are consequently underestimated.

Not till the lady leaves

Carly Fiorina (2006) tells the following story about her early career:

You've just graduated from the company management development programme for 'high flying' university graduates, and you've been assigned to your first role, as a sales team member, in a successful division which provides government communications services. Your boss is not welcoming, and gives you a stack of paperwork which you are still reading at the end of the week. Talking to your new colleagues, you discover that your boss is having an affair with a colleague in another department, so he doesn't have much time for you. Marie, the only other woman on the team, is prepared to offer advice. David manages one of the team's largest clients, servicing a large national communications network. You are assigned to 'co-manage' this client with him. David thinks this is a bad idea. Two of the client's regional (male) managers, who decide on major purchases, are planning a visit. You ask if you can join them, and David agrees. However, the day before the meeting, David explains that you will not be able to join them after all, because the clients have specifically requested that they meet at their 'favourite restaurant'. You are confused, until Marie explains that this is a strip club, with table dancing during dinner. You know when and where they are meeting, and you are embarrassed and anxious.

Your options are:

1. This is just one meeting. It doesn't matter. Don't go.
2. Express outrage and insist that they hold the meeting somewhere else.
3. Tell David that you're coming anyway and that you'll meet them there.

Which option would you choose, and why? Fiorina's answer is at the end of the chapter.

Women are as likely to experience and to use organization politics as are men. However, there appear to be subtle differences between the sexes. Table 22.10 summarizes the evidence contrasting traditional female and male stereotypes with regard to attitudes to organization politics. That evidence is the source of the cliché that 'men are bad but bold, and women are wonderful but weak'. It is important to recognize that these are predispositions, broad patterns, and general tendencies, and must be treated with caution. Differences between the sexes must not be confused with individual differences.

Table 22.10: Traditional gender stereotypes in approach to organization politics

Wonderful but weak female stereotype	Bad but bold male stereotype
Politically innocent, naive	Politically aware, skilled
Organizational power is difficult to acquire	Organizational power is readily acquired
Use passive or 'soft' influence tactics such as coalition forming	Use aggressive or 'hard' influence tactics such as threats and assertiveness
Use formal systems to get information	Use informal systems to get information
Uncomfortable with self-promoting behaviour	Self-promotion taken for granted
Career depends on doing a good job	Career depends on self-promotion

Source: adapted from Buchanan, D.A. and Badham, R.J., *Power, Politics, and Organizational Change: Winning the Turf Game*, Copyright (© Sage Publications 2008).

In developing their summary, Buchanan and Badham (2008) emphasize that much of the research evidence in this area is dated. Social norms and attitudes change rapidly, and these stereotypes may therefore be less applicable in contemporary organizations.

There is evidence, however, suggesting that women may not use political tactics to the same degree, or in the same manner, as their male colleagues. This may be one explanation for the lack of women in senior management roles. Women have been shown to be less successful in acquiring organizational power (Mann, 1995), and are often more likely to suffer 'political skill deficiency' (Perrewé and Nelson, 2004). As political skill is more important at senior organizational levels, women can struggle in the competition to secure those top jobs, or struggle once they are in those positions. It is possible that women lack confidence and perceived competence in their ability to play organization politics (Arroba and James, 1988).

Source: www.joyoftech.com

Reviewing the evidence on influence tactics, Ferris et al. (2002, p. 103) found that

- women tend to use fewer influence tactics than men;
- the tactics most used by women tend to be consistent with female stereotypes;
- organizational norms reward those who use traditional 'masculine' influence tactics;
- women who use 'male' tactics may attract organizational rewards (promotion, pay rises) but may receive less social support from colleagues.

Studies by Singh et al. (2002) into the use of impression management tactics (see Chapter 7) found that networking, ingratiation, and self-promotion were used more often by men than by women. The differences between male and female managers were greater at junior levels. Those female managers who used impression management techniques reported that they had begun to do this after noticing that men with equivalent experience and qualifications were being preferred for promotion.

How can we explain these apparent differences in the ways in which women and men approach organization politics? There are individual, social, and structural explanations.

Individual explanations

Personality

Variations in attitudes and behaviours may be attributable to innate personality traits and predispositions. Some psychologists argue that these are genetically acquired, while others believe that socialization, in the form of upbringing and cultural norms, have a major impact on personality (see Chapter 6). Research has suggested that women are socialized to be more passive and accommodating than men. For example, Deborah Tannen (1995) argues that boys and girls acquire different linguistic and relational styles in childhood (boys are expected to be more competitive), which subsequently influence their working styles and career prospects.

Awareness

Women may not be aware of, or may prefer to deny, the role of organization politics. Sandi Mann (1995) argues that women can be politically naive, adopting 'innocent' behaviours at work, putting their faith in rationality and fairness. They believe that they can mobilize the resources that they need through formal channels, and secure promotion by working hard without the need to influence others. From this standpoint, politics interferes with the process of getting the job done, and those who think this way are less likely to use informal relationships, friends, or favours in order to achieve their goals.

Preference

Singh et al. (2002) found that, despite apparent gender differences, women understood as well as men the need to 'read' the organization and 'play the game' in order to become more visible and increase their promotion chances. However, women reported that they were uncomfortable in having to behave in a self-promoting manner, and that networking was not a natural female behaviour. Women in that study thus knew 'the rules of the game', but some chose deliberately not to play.

Authenticity

Women who seek or acquire a senior management position have the option of employing the 'take charge', 'dominant male' leadership stereotype. Alice Eagly (2005) noted that women who moderated their display of femininity, and who modelled confident, authoritative, masculine behaviours, were more likely to feel that they were inauthentic, unnatural, and play-acting.

Motivation

A study of General Electric's 135,000 professional workers found that voluntary turnover among female staff was 8 per cent compared to 6.5 per cent among men. Also, 26 per cent of professional women who were not yet in senior posts said that they did not want those jobs. Of the 108 women who had appeared in the Fortune 500 lists of the most powerful women, at least 20 had left their prestige positions, most of them by their own volition. Apparently, it is not that women cannot get the top jobs, but they may be choosing not to. The General Electric study also found that women did not greet promotions to senior roles eagerly. Some did not actively seek promotion; some declined promotion outright; others replied to the invitation, out of modesty, with the question, 'Are you sure?' The American politician Hillary Clinton suggested that many women pushed less strongly for promotion than men, not because they were reining in their ambition, but because they did not hang their egos on the next rung of the corporate ladder. Some women reject the offer of greater power because they are unwilling to make personal sacrifices, while others demand more satisfaction in their lives than men do (Sellers, 2003).

Social explanations

Women can copy the male leadership stereotype: aggressive, competitive, intense. It appears that certain behaviours are seen as being reserved for men, and that 'tough female managers are often labelled with epithets such as *battle axe*, *dragon lady*, *bitch* and *bully broad*':

> If a leadership role requires a highly authoritative or competitive behaviour that is perceived as masculine, the mere fact that a woman occupies the role can yield disapproval . . . [T]he more confidently a woman conveys those values, the less effective she may become because of her challenge to traditional gender norms and her overturning of the expected gender hierarchy. (Eagly, 2005, p. 464)

Structural explanations

Work experience

Women can be rendered 'structurally powerless' by being limited to routine, low-profile jobs, and by having restricted access to line management roles early in their careers. Women face discrimination in what are often secretive promotion decisions, in organizations that are typically characterized by 'old boys networks' and unequal power distribution (Oakley, 2000).

You can't be a good girl and get on

Exploring why there are so few women in senior positions in business and politics, Eleanor Mills (2011) observes:

> Men are good at helping each other through informal networks (drawing on them for contacts, advice, jobs etc), while women, even successful ones, often lack such support. They need it if they are to match their numbers and talent with their achievement . . . While men push themselves forward, women who are just as qualified hang back. Over and over again I heard women say how they had assumed – erroneously – that by being quietly excellent at their job, hitting their targets, working away in their bunker, they would be recognized and succeed.
>
> How do women break through into the male world of power? At one conference I chaired a panel of successful women who had done just that. What, I asked, were the 'hinge moments' when, against the odds, they had moved onwards and upwards? The answer was simple: courage.
>
> The stories they told were all about being brave, even when they were terrified and quaking inside. One super-tough former City trader described how her

working life became impossible because she was not invited to a crucial morning meeting. She fretted and dithered and thought about quitting but then, feeling so terrified she thought she might vomit, she just turned up at the meeting without being asked. No one said anything, so from then on she attended every one.

A woman must be bold and brazen; she must hustle, use humour, blow her own trumpet and know her own value if she is to succeed . . . Yet these qualities are the antithesis of those associated with being a 'good girl' – to most women they don't come naturally. Until we throw off the shackles of being good girls and awaiting our turn, modestly playing by the rules and hoping to be asked and recognized, women will continue to languish in business and politics.

Source: © *Mills*/The Sunday Timers/*News International Trading Ltd, 27 November 2011.*

Work practices

A male-dominated organization culture encourages long working hours. This prevents women with family responsibilities from participating in breakfast meetings or evening drinks. Women are also excluded from informal male gatherings, at the golf club, for example, and the locker room at the gym. Exploring the low proportion of women in senior positions, Barsh and Yee (2011) found that women often turn down promotion in order to stay in a role from which they derive a sense of meaning, and thus avoid the 'energy-draining meetings and corporate politics at the next echelon' (p. 4). Women are also confronted by negative institutional mindsets: 'everybody "knows" you can't put a woman in that job'. The 'always on 24/7 executive lifestyle with travel' is the ultimate barrier, disrupting work-life balance. Barsh and Yee found that increasing numbers of men disliked this, too.

In conclusion, therefore, there are several explanations for women's apparent reluctance to use organization politics. This reluctance may in turn help to explain why there are relatively few women in senior management roles. Alice Eagly and Linda Carli (2007) argue that women have to navigate a 'labyrinth' of obstacles on their way to the top, and that possible solutions lie with

- increasing awareness of prejudice concerning women in leadership roles;
- changing the 'long hours' culture;
- reducing the subjectivity in performance evaluations;
- ensuring a critical mass of women in executive positions, to avoid 'tokenism';
- preparing women for line management with demanding assignments;
- implementing family-friendly human resource practices.

Eagly and Carli also suggest that women may need help in order to grow their 'social capital' – a valuable network of professional colleagues. Women tend not to invest time in networking due to family responsibilities, and because they may not see this as important. Organizations can help by providing supportive mentoring relationships and links to powerful networks.

One study found that 80 per cent of senior and middle managers in Britain had received no training or skills development in organization politics (Buchanan, 2008). While women who are concerned with developing their management careers may benefit from developing and using political skills, this advice clearly applies to anyone who is trying to change things in an organization and to get promoted.

RECAP

1. *Appreciate the importance of power and politics in organizational life.*
   - Whether real or perceived, greater turbulence in the context of organizations has created increased fluidity, uncertainty, ambiguity, and discontinuity, providing the ideal conditions in which power and politics can be exercised.
2. *Compare and contrast different perspectives on power.*
   - Power can be considered from the 'power-as-property', 'faces of power', and 'disciplinary power' viewpoints.
   - The 'power-as-property' viewpoint offers three perspectives, seeing power as a property of individuals, as a property of relationships, and as an embedded property of structures.
   - The 'faces of power' viewpoint offers three dimensions, seeing power as overt and observable; as covert and unobservable; and as internalized by employees.
   - Disciplinary power reduces subordinates' ability to dissent by creating and managing meanings for them.
3. *Distinguish different bases of power.*
   - The five bases of power are reward, coercion, referent, legitimate, and expert.
4. *Identify organizational factors which enhance the power of departments.*
   - Factors enhancing the power of departments are dependency creation, financial resources, centrality of activities, non-substitutability, and uncertainty reduction.
5. *Differentiate between power tactics, influencing tactics, and influencing responses.*
   - Power tactics can be classified under the headings of image building, selective information, scapegoating, formal alliances, networking, compromise, and rule manipulation, as well as covert 'dirty tricks' methods.
   - Influencing tactics include rational persuasion, consultation, inspirational appeal, collaboration, ingratiation, exchange, personal appeal, apprising, pressure, and coalitions.
   - Influencing responses are engagement, compliance, and resistance.
6. *Distinguish between the rational and political models of organization.*
   - The rational model of organizations sees behaviour in organizations as guided by clear goals and choices made on the basis of reason.
   - The political model of organization sees no such logical behaviour, but sees organizations made up of groups possessing their own interests, goals, and values, and in which power and influence are needed in order to reach decisions.
7. *Identify the characteristics of individuals most likely to engage in political behaviour.*
   - Persons most likely to engage in political behaviour have a high need for power (n*Pow*), a high Mach score, an internal locus of control, and risk-seeking propensity.
8. *Explain how women use and are affected by organization politics.*
   - Sex role stereotyping associates management with masculinity, leading to a systematic underestimation of women's abilities.
   - Women appear to use power, influencing, and impression management tactics differently from men.
   - Differences between men and women in organizations can be explained under the three headings of individual, social, and structural.

Revision

1. How can someone low in the organizational hierarchy obtain more power?
2. Discuss the costs and benefits to an organization of its employees engaging in political behaviour.
3. 'Power is most potent when it appears to be absent.' What does this statement mean? Do you agree with it? Give reasons and examples to support your view.
4. Why are some departments, units, or groups in organizations more powerful than others?

Research assignment

Read the literature on the difference between rational and political decision-making. Interview three managers from the same or different organizations, ideally at junior, middle, and senior manager levels. First, ask each one to give you a specific example of 'workplace politics in action'. Second, make three copies of the scoresheet from Chapter exercise 2 below. Third, ask each manager to rank each type of decision according to the extent that they believe politics plays a part in it in their organization (1 = most political; 11 = least political). They should enter their ranking in column 3. Finally, ask them what makes a decision 'political' in their organization.

Springboard

David A. Buchanan and Richard Badham (2008) *Power, Politics, and Organizational Change: Winning the Turf Game* (2nd edn), Sage, London. Updated edition considers the use of power and politics particularly in the role of change agent.

Lois P. Frankel (2004) *Nice Girls Don't Get the Corner Office: 101 Unconscious Mistakes Women Make that Sabotage Their Careers*, Warner Business Books, New York. This is about 'playing the game', and the kinds of mistakes that women make which slow their promotion. Frankel also argues that 'if you don't play, you can't win'.

Jeffrey Pfeffer (2010) *Power: Why Some People Have It – and Others Don't*, Harper Business, New York and London. An honest practical exploration of the skills involved in acquiring, holding on to, and using power to progress one's career – getting noticed by the right people, building networks, overcoming opposition, and building a reputation for getting things done.

Jonathan Powell (2010) *The New Machiavelli: How to Wield Power in the Modern World*, The Bodley Head, London. Powell was Chief of Staff to the UK government of Tony Blair from 1994 to 2007. He explains the internal politics of government, relating this perspective to organizations in general, with lessons for anyone with access to the levers of power who wants to change things.

OB in films

Dirty Rotten Scoundrels (1988, director Frank Oz), DVD track 2: 0:07:42 to 0:10:55 (4 minutes). Freddy Benson (played by Steve Martin) is a conman working on the French Riviera. This clip begins with a shot of Zurich railway station platform and ends with Benson's 'Thank you'. Benson persuades a woman on a train, a complete stranger, to buy him a meal. How does he achieve this?

1. What impression management techniques does he use?
2. What influencing tactics does he employ?

OB on the web

Search YouTube for *Robert Cialdini, The 6 Principles of Influence*, which we discussed earlier in this chapter. Watch him explain his six influencing techniques in person. Cialdini argues that these techniques are ethically acceptable, when they are a natural part of the influence situation. However, these techniques can be abused when conditions surrounding their use are fabricated to suit the influencer's purpose. In what kinds of situations do you think the use of these influencing techniques is unethical and inappropriate?

CHAPTER EXERCISES

1. Power in a changing environment

Objectives

1. To introduce different types of power.
2. To explore the PESTLE change drivers in the environment which impact on the power of employees.
3. To understand how power in organizations is gained and lost as a result of these environment changes.

Briefing

1. Form groups and nominate a spokesperson. Read the description *Your organization*.
2. Read each of the *Five environmental change scenarios* in order. For each one, decide:
   (a) Which environment change driver is affecting your organization in this scenario?
   (b) What types of activities are likely to increase / become more important in the company, as a result?
   (c) Which five company employees' power bases will *increase* most in the light of this changed environmental condition?
   (d) Why did you select these persons?

   Each scenario is separate from the others. Make any reasonable assumptions as you discuss the matter.
3. Each group's spokesperson presents and justifies their conclusions to the entire class.

Your organization

Your medium-sized company manufactures portable, petrol-driven, electric power generators that are sold to domestic and office customers, often for use in emergencies. It has the following employees:

Advertising expert (m)	Charted accountant (m)
Chief financial offer (f)	General manager (m)
Operations manager (f)	Marketing manager (f)
Industrial engineer (m)	Computer programmer (f)
Product designer (m)	Industrial chemist (m)
Public relations expert (m)	In-house legal advisor (m)
Company trainer (m)	Human resource manager (f)

(m = male; f = female)

Five environmental change scenarios

1. The existing small batch production of generators will be replaced by a state-of-the-art, automated assembly line.
2. New laws about engine and factory emissions are being passed by the European Parliament.
3. Sales are greatly reduced, and the industrial sector seems to be shrinking.
4. The company is planning to go international in the next year or two.
5. The Equality Commission is pressing companies to establish better male/female balance in senior posts and is threatening to 'name-and-shame' companies.

Source: adapted from Barbuto, J.E., Power and the changing environment, in Journal of Management Education, *24(2), pp. 288–96, Copyright © 2000, OBTS Teaching Society for Management Educators, reprinted by permission of SAGE Publications.*

2. Politics in decision-making

Objectives

1. To contrast perceptions about the use of politics in decision-making.
2. To predict when and where politics will be used in organizations.
3. To contrast political with rational decision-making processes.

Briefing

1. Individually, using the worksheet, rank each of the eleven organizational decisions (a to k) in terms of the extent to which you think politics play a part. Rank the most political decision as '1' and the least political as '11'. Enter your ranking in the first column on your worksheet – 'Individual ranking'.
2. Form groups of four to seven members. Rank the eleven items again, this time as a group. Use consensus to reach agreement, that is, listen to each person's ideas and rationale before deciding. Do not vote, bargain, average, or toss a coin. Base your decision on the logical arguments made by group members rather than your personal preference. Enter your rankings in the second column on the scoresheet – 'Team ranking'.
3. After all teams have finished, your instructor will read out the rankings produced by a survey of managers which indicates the frequency with which they believe that politics plays a part in each type of decision. As these are read out, enter them in column 3 on the scoresheet – 'Manager ranking'.
4. Still in your groups:
   (a) Compare the individual rankings (column 1) of group members. On which decisions did group members' perceptions differ significantly? Why might that be?
   (b) Compare your group ranking (column 2) with the manager ranking (column 3). On which decisions did group and managers' perceptions differ significantly? Why might that be?

Scoresheet

To what extent do you believe politics plays a part in the decision?

(1 = most political; 11 = least political)

Decision	**1**	**2**	**3**
	Individual ranking	**Team ranking**	**Manager ranking**
a. Management promotions and transfers			
b. Entry-level hiring			
c. Amount of pay			
d. Annual budgets			
e. Allocation of facilities, equipment, offices			
f. Delegation of authority among managers			
g. Inter-departmental coordination			
h. Specification of personnel policies			
i. Penalties for disciplinary infractions			
j. Performance appraisals			
k. Grievances and complaints			

→

5. In plenary, answer the questions as directed by your instructor:
   (a) What distinguishes the most political decision items (ranked 1–4 in column 3) from the least political (ranked 8–11)?
   (b) In what circumstances might a rational decision process be used in making a decision, and when would a political process be used?
   (c) Research suggests that that political behaviour occurs more frequently at higher rather than lower levels in organizations. Why should this be so?
   (d) How would you:
      (i) apply rationality to those decisions currently possessing a large political element?
      (ii) politicize decisions currently made using rational processes?
   (e) How would you advise a manager who felt that politics was bad for the organization and should be avoided at all costs?

Based on Daft and Sharfman (1990), pp. 339–41.

Employability assessment

With regard to your future employment prospects:

1. Identify up to three issues from this chapter that you found significant.
2. Relate these to the competencies in the employability matrix.
3. Decide what actions you need to take to maintain and/or develop those competencies under each of the four headings of the employability matrix.

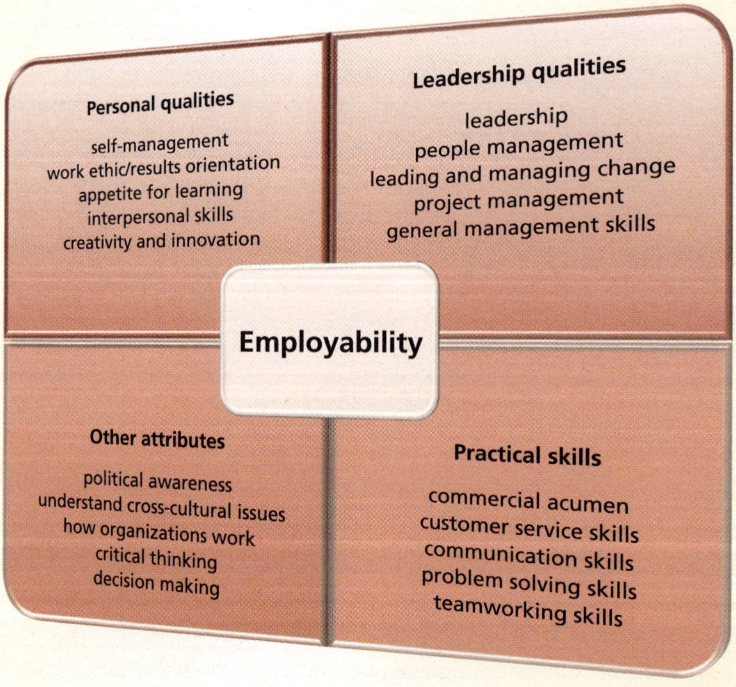

Not till the lady leaves: the answer

Fiorina chose option 3. She wore a conservative business suit, and carried a briefcase. At the 'restaurant', in order to reach the client group, she had to walk in front of the stage, where about a dozen women were performing. She tried to sound relaxed and knowledgeable, ignoring the show, while David continued drinking and asking the women to come and dance on their table. All of the women who approached their table said 'Sorry gentlemen. Not till the lady leaves.' The meeting lasted several hours. The client's business was secured. Fiorina concludes:

After a few hours, having made my point, I left them all there. They heaved a sigh of relief, I'm sure, but the next day in the office, the balance of power had shifted perceptibly. I had shown David that I would not be intimidated, even if I was terrified. I truly cared about doing my job even when it meant working in difficult circumstances. Having tried to diminish me, David was himself diminished. He was embarrassed. And Bill [one of the other team members] decided that he would take me under his wing and help me succeed. We cannot always choose the hurdles we must overcome, but we can choose how we overcome them. (Fiorina, 2006, p. 31)

References

Allison, G.T. (1971) *The Essence of Decision: Explaining the Cuban Missile Crisis*, Boston, MA: Little, Brown.

Arroba, T. and James, K. (1988) 'Are politics palatable to women managers? How women can make wise moves at work', *Women in Management Review*, 3(3), pp. 123–30.

Bachrach, P. and Baratz, M.S. (1963) 'Decisions and nondecisions: an analytical framework', *American Political Science Review*, 57(3), pp. 641–51.

Barsh, J. and Yee, L. (2011) *Unlocking the Full Potential of Women in the US Economy*, New York: McKinsey & Company.

Buchanan, D.A. (2008) 'You stab my back, I'll stab yours: management experience and perceptions of organization politics', *British Journal of Management*, 19(1), pp. 49–64.

Buchanan, D.A. and Badham, R. (2008) *Power, Politics, and Organizational Change: Winning the Turf Game* (2nd edn), London: Sage Publications.

Chanlat, J.-F. (1997) 'Conflict and politics', in A. Sorge and M. Warner (eds), *IEBM Handbook of Organizational Behavior*, London: International Thomson, pp. 472–80.

Christie, R. and Geiss, F.L. (1970) *Studies in Machiavellianism*, New York: Academic Press.

Cialdini, R.B. (2008) *Influence: Science and Practice* (5th edn), Boston, MA: Allyn and Bacon.

Cohen, A.R. and Bradford, D.L. (1991) *Influence without Authority*, New York: Wiley.

Collett, P. (2004) 'Show and tell', *People Management*, 10(8), pp. 34–5.

Dickey, C. (2009) *Securing the City: Inside America's Best Counterterror Force – The NYPD*, New York: Simon and Schuster.

Eagly, A.H. (2005) 'Achieving relational authenticity in leadership: does gender matter?', *The Leadership Quarterly*, 16, pp. 459–74.

Eagly, A.H. and Carli, L.L. (2007) 'Women and the labyrinth of leadership', *Harvard Business Review*, 85(9), pp. 62–71.

Ferris, G.R., Perrewé, P.L., Anthony, W.P. and Gilmore, D.C. (2000) 'Political skill at work', *Organizational Dynamics*, 28(4), pp. 25–37.

Ferris, G.R., Hochwarter, W.A., Douglas, C., Blass, F.R., Kolodinsky, R.W. and Treadway, D.C. (2002) 'Social influence processes in organizations and human resource systems', *Research in Personnel and Human Resources Management*, 21, pp. 65–127.

Fiorina, C. (2006) *Tough Choices: A Memoir*, London and Boston: Nicholas Brealey Publishing.

Fleming, P. and Spicer, A. (2007) *Contesting the Corporation: Struggle, Power and Resistance in Organizations*, Cambridge: Cambridge University Press.

Foucault, M. (1979) *Discipline and Punish*, Harmondsworth, Middlesex: Penguin Books.

French, J.R.P. and Raven, B.H. (1958) 'The bases of social power', in D. Cartwright (ed.), *Studies in Social Power*, Ann Arbor, MI: Institute for Social Research, University of Michigan Press, pp. 150–67.

Greenberg, J. and Baron, R.A. (2007) *Behaviour in Organizations* (9th edn), Englewood Cliffs, NJ: Pearson/Prentice Hall.

Hellriegel, D. and Slocum, J.W. (1978) *Management: Contingency Approaches*, Reading, MA: Addison-Wesley.

Hickson, D.J., Hinings, C.R., Lee, C.A., Schneck, R.E. and Pennings, J.M. (1971) 'A strategic contingencies theory of intra-organizational power', *Administrative Science Quarterly*, 16(2), pp. 216–29.

Hiley, D.R. (1987) 'Power and values in corporate life', *Journal of Business Ethics*, 6(5), pp. 343–53.

House, R.J. (1988) 'Power and personality in complex organizations', in B.M. Staw and L.L. Cummings (eds), *Research in Organizational Behaviour: Volume 10*. Greenwich, CT: JAI Press, pp. 305–57.

Huczynski, A.A. (2004) *Influencing Within Organizations* (2nd edn), London: Routledge.

Jackson, N. and Carter, P. (2000) *Rethinking Organizational Behaviour*, Harlow, Essex: Financial Times Prentice Hall.

Kanter, R.M. (1979) 'Power failure in management circuits', *Harvard Business Review*, 57(4), pp. 65–75.

Kipnis, D., Schmidt, S.M., Swaffin-Smith, C. and Wilkinson, I. (1984) 'Patterns of managerial influence: shotgun managers, tacticians, and bystanders', *Organizational Dynamics*, 12(3), pp. 58–67.

Krell, T.C., Mendenhall, M.E. and Sendry, J. (1987) 'Doing research in the conceptual morass of organizational politics', paper presented at the Western Academy of Management Conference, Hollywood.

Lukes, S. (2005) *Power: A Radical View* (2nd edn), London: Macmillan.

McAuley, J., Duberley, J. and Johnson, P. (2007) *Organization Theory: Challenges and Perspectives*, Harlow, Essex: Financial Times Prentice Hall.

McCarty, J. (2004) *Bullets Over Hollywood: The American Gangster Picture from the Silents to 'The Sopranos'*, Cambridge, MA: Da Capo Press.

McClelland, D.C. (1961) *The Achieving Society*, Princeton, NJ: Van Nostrand Reinhold.

McClelland, D.C. and Boyatzis, R.E. (1982) 'Leadership motive pattern and long term success in management', *Journal of Applied Psychology*, 67(6), pp. 737–43.

McClelland, D.C. and Burnham, D.H. (1995) 'Power is the great motivator', *Harvard Business Review*, 73(1), pp. 126–39 (first published 1976).

McClelland, D.C., Atkinson, J.W., Clark, R.A. and Lowell, E.L. (1976) *The Achievement Motive* (2nd edn), New York: Irvington.

Machiavelli, N. (1514) *The Prince* (trans. George Bull London: Penguin Books, 1961).

Madison, D.L., Allen, R.W., Porter, L.W. and Mayes, B.T. (1980) 'Organizational politics: an exploration of managers' perceptions', *Human Relations*, 33(2), pp. 79–100.

Mann, S. (1995) 'Politics and power in organizations: why women lose out', *Leadership and Organization Development Journal*, 16(2), pp. 9–15.

March, J.G. (1962) 'The business firm as a political coalition', *Journal of Politics*, 24(4), pp. 662–78.

Mills, E. (2011), 'You can't be a good girl and get on in this world', *The Sunday Times News Review* section, 27 November, p. 4.

Mintzberg, H. (1983) *Power in and around Organizations*, Englewood Cliffs, NJ: Prentice Hall.

Oakley, J. (2000) 'Gender-based barriers to senior management promotions: understanding the scarcity of female CEOs', *Journal of Business Ethics*, 27(4), pp. 323–34.

Perrewé, P.L. and Nelson, D.L. (2004) 'Gender and career success: the facilitative role of political skill', *Organizational Dynamics*, 33(4), pp. 366–78.

Pfeffer, J. (1992) *Managing with Power: Politics and Influence in Organizations*, Boston, MA: Harvard Business School Press.

Pfeffer, J. (2010) 'Power play', *Harvard Business Review*, 88(7/8), pp. 84–92.

Pfeffer, J. and Sutton, R.I. (2006) *Hard Facts, Dangerous Half-Truths, and Total Nonsense: Profiting from Evidence-Based Management*, Boston, MA: Harvard Business School Press.

Rose, N. (1989) *Governing the Soul*, London: Routledge.

Rotter, J.B. (1966) 'Generalized expectations for internal versus external control of reinforcement', *Psychological Monographs*, 80(609; whole issue), pp. 1–28.

Salancik, G.R. and Pfeffer, J. (1977) 'Who gets power – and how they hold on to it: a strategic contingency model of power', *Organizational Dynamics*, 5(3), pp. 2–21.

Sellers, P. (2003) 'Power: do women really want it?', *Fortune*, 13 October, pp. 58–65.

Singh, V., Kumra, S. and Vinnicombe, S. (2002) 'Gender and impression management: playing the promotion game', *Journal of Business Ethics*, 37(1), pp. 77–89.

Sitkin, S.B. and Pablo, A.L. (1992) 'Reconceptualizing the determinants of risk behaviour', *Academy of Management Review*, 17(1), pp. 9–38.

Tannen, D. (1995) 'The power of talk: who gets heard and why', *Harvard Business Review*, 73(5), pp. 138–48.

The Economist (2010) 'The will to power', 11 September, p. 68.

Yukl, G. (2005) *Leadership in Organizations* (6th edn), Thousand Oaks, CA: Prentice Hall.

Glossary

Acceptance: agreeing with and becoming committed to an influencing request both attitudinally and behaviourally. (Chapter 22)

Accountability: the obligation of a subordinate to report back on their discharge of the duties for which they are responsible. (Chapter 15)

Action team: a team that executes brief performances that are repeated under new conditions. Its members are technically specialized, and need to coordinate their individual contributions with each other. (Chapter 13)

Activities: in Homans's theory, the physical movements and verbal and non-verbal behaviours engaged in by group members. (Chapter 10)

Adaptive decisions: decisions that require human judgement based on clarified criteria and are made using basic quantitative decision tools. (Chapter 20)

Additive task: a task whose accomplishment depends on the sum of all group members' efforts. (Chapter 10)

Advice team: a team created by management to provide the latter with information for its own decision-making. (Chapter 13)

Aggregate: a collection of unrelated people who happen to be in close physical proximity for a short period of time. (Chapter 10)

Alienation: feelings of powerlessness, meaninglessness, isolation, and self-estrangement engendered by work and organization design. (Chapter 21)

Asynchronous communication: communication that occurs when participants start a discussion topic (or thread) and post replies to each other, and when, after delays, individuals read to catch up with the discussion. It is similar to a dialogue conducted by post. (Chapter 11)

Attribution: the process by which we make sense of our environment through our perceptions of causality. (Chapter 8)

Authority: the right to guide or direct the actions of others and extract from them responses that are appropriate to the attainment of an organization's goals. (Chapter 15)

Autonomous work group or team: a group or team allocated to a significant segment of the workflow, with discretion over how their work will be carried out. (Chapter 3)

Balanced scorecard: an approach to defining organizational effectiveness using a combination of quantitative and qualitative measures to assess performance. (Chapter 1)

Basic assumptions: invisible, preconscious, unspoken, 'taken-for-granted' understandings held by individuals within an organization concerning human behaviour, the nature of reality, and the organization's relationship to its environment. (Chapter 4)

Behaviour modification: a technique for encouraging desired behaviours and discouraging unwanted behaviours using operant conditioning. (Chapter 5)

Behavioural modelling: learning how to act by observing and copying the behaviour of others. (Chapter 5)

Behavioural self-management: a technique for changing one's own behaviour by systematically manipulating cues, cognitive processes, and contingent consequences. (Chapter 5)

Behavioural theory of decision-making: a theory which recognizes that bounded rationality limits the making of optimal decisions. (Chapter 20)

Behaviourist psychology: a perspective which argues that what we learn are chains of muscle movements, and that mental processes are not observable, and are not valid issues for study. (Chapter 5)

Bias: a prejudice, predisposition, or systematic distortion caused by the application of a heuristic. (Chapter 20)

Big five: trait clusters that appear consistently to capture main personality traits: Openness, Conscientiousness, Extraversion, Agreeableness, and Neuroticism. (Chapter 6)

Boreout: boredom, demotivation, and lack of energy and enthusiasm caused by uninteresting, unchallenging, and monotonous work. (Chapter 9)

Boundaryless organization: an organization possessing permeable internal and external boundaries which give it flexibility and thus the ability to respond to change rapidly. (Chapter 17)

Bounded rationality: a theory which says that individuals make decisions by constructing simplified models that extract the essential features from problems without capturing all their complexity. (Chapter 20)

Brainstorming: a technique in which all group members are encouraged to propose ideas spontaneously, without critiquing or censoring others' ideas. The ideas so generated are not evaluated until all have been listed. (Chapter 20)

Bureaucracy: legal-rational type of authority underpinning a form of organization structure that is characterized by a specialization of labour, a specific authority hierarchy, a formal set of rules, and rigid promotion and selection criteria. (Chapter 16)

Caution shift phenomenon: the tendency of a group to make decisions that are more risk-averse than those that individual members of the group would have recommended. (Chapter 20)

Centralization: the concentration of authority and responsibility for decision-making power in the hands of managers at the top of an organization's hierarchy. (Chapter 15)

Certainty: a condition in which decision-makers possess full knowledge of alternatives; there is a high probability of having these available; it is possible to calculate the costs and benefits of each alternative; and there is high predictability of outcomes. (Chapter 20)

Chain of command: the unbroken line of authority that extends from the top of the organization to the bottom and clarifies who reports to whom. (Chapter 15)

Characteristics of mass production: mechanical pacing of work, no choice of tools or methods, repetitiveness, minute subdivision of product, minimum skill requirements, and surface mental attention. (Chapter 3)

Charismatic authority: the belief that the ruler has some special, unique virtue, either religious or heroic, as with the authority of religious prophets, charismatic politicians, and film stars. (Chapter 16)

Chimerial control: a combination of management pressure exercised vertically on the individual through bureaucracy, technology, surveillance, and the manipulation of culture; and team pressure exercised horizontally through the group norms and sanctions. (Chapter 14)

Chronotype: a cluster of personality traits that can affect whether someone is more active and performs better in the morning or in the evening. (Chapter 6)

Classical decision theory: a theory which assumes that decision-makers are objective, have complete information, and consider all possible alternatives and their consequences before selecting the optimal solution. (Chapter 20)

Coding: the stage in the interpersonal communication process in which the transmitter chooses how to express a message for transmission to someone else. (Chapter 7)

Coercive power: the ability to exert influence based on the other's belief that the influencer can administer unwelcome penalties or sanctions. (Chapter 22)

Cognitive psychology: a perspective which argues that what we learn are mental structures, and that mental processes can be studied by inference, although they cannot be observed directly. (Chapter 5)

Collaborative relationship structure: a structure that involves a relationship between two or more organizations, sharing their ideas, knowledge, staff, and technology for mutual benefit. (Chapter 17)

Communication climate: the prevailing atmosphere in an organization – *open* or *closed* – in which ideas and information are exchanged. (Chapter 7)

Communication network analysis: a technique that uses direct observation to determine the source, direction, and quantity of oral communication between congregated members of a group. (Chapter 11)

Communication pattern analysis: a technique that uses analysis of documents, data, and voicemail transmission to determine the source, direction, and quantity of oral and written communication between the dispersed members of a group. (Chapter 11)

Communication pattern chart: indicates the source, direction, and quantity of oral and written communication between the dispersed members of a group. (Chapter 11)

Communication process: the transmission of information, and the exchange of meaning, between at least two people. (Chapter 7)

Communigram: a chart that indicates the source, direction, and quantity of oral communication between the members during a group meeting. (Chapter 11)

Compensatory effects: processes that delay or deflect employment replacement effects, and which lead to the creation of new products and services, and new jobs. (Chapter 3)

Compliance: reluctant, superficial, public, and transitory change in behaviour in response to an influencing request, which is not accompanied by attitudinal change. (Chapter 22)

Compliance (in the context of a group): a majority's influence over a minority. (Chapter 12)

Concertive control: control exercised by the workers themselves who collaborate to develop the means of their own control by negotiating a consensus which shapes their own behaviour according to a set of core values such as those of the corporate vision statement. (Chapter 14)

Concurrent feedback: information which arrives during our behaviour and which can be used to control behaviour as it unfolds. (Chapter 5)

Conflict: a process that begins when one party perceives that another party has negatively affected, or is about to negatively affect, something that the first party cares about. (Chapter 21)

Conflict resolution: a process which has as its objective the ending of conflict between disagreeing parties. (Chapter 21)

Conflict stimulation: the process of engendering conflict between parties where none existed before, or escalating the current conflict level if it is too low. (Chapter 21)

Conformity: a change in an individual's belief or behaviour in response to real or imagined group pressure. (Chapter 12)

Conjunctive task: a task whose accomplishment depends on the performance of the group's least talented member. (Chapter 10)

Consideration: a pattern of leadership behaviour that demonstrates sensitivity to relationships and to the social needs of employees. (Chapter 19)

Constructivism: a perspective which argues that our social and organizational worlds have no ultimate objective truth or reality, but are instead determined by our shared experiences, meanings, and interpretations. (Chapter 1)

Contingency approach to organization structure: a perspective which argues that to be effective, an organization must adjust its structure to take into account its technology, its environment, its size, and similar contextual factors. (Chapter 16)

Contingency theory of leadership: a perspective which argues that leaders must adjust their style taking into account properties of the context. (Chapter 19)

Controlled performance: setting standards, measuring performance, comparing actual with standard, and taking corrective action if necessary. (Chapter 1)

Conversion: a minority's influence over a majority. (Chapter 12)

Co-opetition: a form of cooperation between competing organizations which is limited to specified areas where both believe they can gain mutual benefit. (Chapter 17)

Coping cycle: the emotional response to trauma and loss, in which we experience first denial, then anger, bargaining, depression, and finally acceptance. (Chapter 18)

Corporate social responsibility: the view that organizations should act ethically, in ways that contribute to economic development, the environment, quality of working life, local communities, and the wider society. (Chapter 2)

Cross-functional team: employees from different functional departments who meet as a team to complete a particular task. (Chapter 13)

Crowdsourcing: the act of taking a task traditionally performed by a designated agent (employee or contractor) and outsourcing it to an undefined, generally large group of people, in the form of an open call for assistance. (Chapter 17)

Cybernetic analogy: an explanation of the learning process based on the components and operation of a feedback control system. (Chapter 5)

Decentralization: the downward dispersion of authority and responsibility for decision-making to operating units, branches, and lower-level managers. (Chapter 15)

Decision-based evidence-making: marshalling facts and analysis to support a decision that has already been made elsewhere in the organization. (Chapter 20)

Decision-making: the process of making choices from among a number of alternatives. (Chapter 20)

Decoding: the stage in the interpersonal communication process in which the recipient interprets a message transmitted to them by someone else. (Chapter 7)

Deep acting: attempting to modify one's felt emotions based on display rules. (Chapter 21)

Deindividuation: an increased state of anonymity that loosens normal constraints on individuals' behaviour, reducing their sense of responsibility, and leading to an increase in impulsive and antisocial acts. (Chapter 12)

Delayed feedback: information which is received after a task is completed, and which can be used to influence future performance. (Chapter 5)

Delegation: managers granting decision-making authority to employees at lower hierarchical levels. (Chapter 15)

Departmentalization: the process of grouping together activities and employees who share a common supervisor and resources, who are jointly responsible for performance, and who tend to identify and collaborate with each other. (Chapter 17)

Descriptive models of decision-making: models which seek to portray how individuals actually make decisions. (Chapter 20)

Differentiation: the degree to which the tasks and the work of individuals, groups, and units are divided up within an organization. (Chapter 16)

Differentiation perspective on culture: a perspective which sees organizations as consisting of subcultures, each with its own characteristics, which differ from those of its neighbours. (Chapter 4)

Discretionary behaviour: freedom to decide how work is going to be performed; discretionary behaviour can be positive, such as putting in extra time and effort, or it can be negative, such as withholding information and cooperation. (Chapter 1)

Disjunctive task: a task whose accomplishment depends on the performance of the group's most talented member. (Chapter 10)

Display rules: organizational scripts concerning which feelings are appropriate in a given setting and how they should be displayed. (Chapter 21)

Displayed emotions: emotions that employees are required by management to show as part of their jobs. (Chapter 21)

Disruptive innovations: innovations which involve the development of wholly new processes, procedures, services, and products. (Chapter 18)

Distributive bargaining: a negotiation strategy in which a fixed sum of resources is divided up, leading to a win–lose situation between the parties. (Chapter 21)

Distributed leadership: the collective exercise of leadership behaviours, often informal and spontaneous, by staff at all levels of an organization. (Chapter 19)

Divisional structure: an organizational design that groups departments together based on the product sold, the geographical area served, or the type of customer. (Chapter 17)

Double-loop learning: the ability to challenge and to redefine the assumptions underlying performance standards and to improve performance. (Chapter 5)

Drive: an innate, biological determinant of behaviour, activated by deprivation. (Chapter 9)

Dysfunctional conflict: a form of conflict which does not support organization goals and hinders organizational performance. (Chapter 21)

Emotional dissonance: the disparity between an individual's felt and displayed emotions. (Chapter 21)

Emotional harmony: a match between an employee's felt emotions and their expressed emotions within the workplace. (Chapter 21)

Emotional intelligence: the ability to identify, integrate, understand, and reflectively manage one's own and other people's feelings. (Chapter 7)

Emotional labour: the act of expressing organizationally required emotions during interactions with others at work. (Chapter 21)

Emotions: intense, short-lived reactions that are linked to a specific cause and which interrupt thought processes and behaviours. (Chapter 21)

Employment cycle: the sequence of stages through which all employees pass in each working position they hold, from recruitment and selection to termination. (Chapter 1)

Empowerment: organizational arrangements that give employees more autonomy, discretion, and decision-making responsibility. (Chapter 9)

Enacted environment: the environment of an organization that exists for members by virtue of the interpretations they make of what is occurring 'outside' the organization, and the way their own actions influence or shape those occurrences. (Chapter 16)

Encounter stage of socialization: the period during which the new recruit learns about organizational expectations. (Chapter 4)

Engagement: the extent to which people enjoy and believe in what they do, and feel valued for doing it. (Chapter 9)

Environment: issues, trends, and events outside the boundaries of the organization, which influence internal decisions and behaviours. (Chapter 2)

Environmental complexity: the range of external factors relevant to the activities of the organization; the more factors, the higher the complexity. (Chapter 2)

Environmental determinism: the argument that internal organizational responses are primarily determined by external environmental factors. (Chapter 2)

Environmental dynamism: the pace of change in relevant factors external to the organization; the greater the pace of change, the more dynamic the environment. (Chapter 2)

Environmental scanning: techniques for identifying and predicting the impact of external trends and developments on the internal functioning of an organization. (Chapter 2)

Environmental uncertainty: the degree of unpredictable turbulence and change in the political, economic, social, technological, legal, and ecological context in which an organization operates. (Chapter 2)

Equity theory: a process theory of motivation which argues that perception of unfairness leads to tension, which motivates the individual to resolve that unfairness. (Chapter 9)

Escalation of commitment: an increased commitment to a previously made decision, despite negative information suggesting one should do otherwise. (Chapter 20)

Ethical stance: the extent to which an organization exceeds its legal minimum obligations to its stakeholders and to society at large. (Chapter 2)

Ethics: the moral principles, values, and rules that govern our decisions and actions with respect to what is right and wrong, good and bad. (Chapter 2)

Evidence-based decision-making: a situation in which a decision is made that follows directly from the evidence. (Chapter 20)

Evidence-based management: systematically using the best available research evidence to inform decisions about how to manage people and organizations. (Chapter 1)

Expectancy: the perceived probability that effort will result in good performance; measured on a scale from 0 (no chance) to 1 (certainty). (Chapter 9)

Expectancy theory: a process theory which argues that individual motivation depends on the *valence* of outcomes, the *expectancy* that effort will lead to good performance, and the *instrumentality* of performance in producing valued outcomes. (Chapter 9)

Expert power: the ability to exert influence based on the other's belief that the influencer has superior knowledge relevant to the situation and the task. (Chapter 22)

Explanatory model of decision-making: an approach that accounts for how individuals, groups, and organizations make decisions. (Chapter 20)

Explicit knowledge: knowledge and understanding which is codified, clearly articulated, and available to anyone. (Chapter 5)

Expression rules: rules which dictate how displayed feelings should be expressed in particular settings. (Chapter 21)

External adaptation: the process through which employees adjust to changing environmental circumstances to attain organizational goals. (Chapter 4)

External work team differentiation: the degree to which a work team stands out from its organizational context, in terms of its membership, temporal scope, and territory. (Chapter 13)

External work team integration: the degree to which a work team is linked with the larger organization of which it is a part. (Chapter 13)

Extinction: the attempt to eliminate undesirable behaviours by attaching no consequences, positive or negative, such as indifference and silence. (Chapter 5)

Extreme job: a job that involves a working week of 60 hours or more, with high earnings, combined with additional performance pressures. (Chapter 9)

Extrinsic feedback: information which comes from our environment, such as the visual and aural information needed to drive a car. (Chapter 5)

Extrinsic rewards: valued outcomes or benefits provided by others, such as promotion, pay increases, a bigger office desk, praise, and recognition. (Chapter 9)

Feedback: information about the outcomes of our behaviour. (Chapter 5)

Feedback (in the process of interpersonal communication): processes through which the transmitter of a message detects whether and how that message has been received and decoded. (Chapter 7)

Feeling rules: rules which dictate which feelings should be displayed in particular settings. (Chapter 21)

Felt emotions: emotions that employees actually feel in a work situation. (Chapter 21)

Fordism: a form of work design that applies scientific management principles to workers' jobs; the installation of single-purpose machine tools to manufacture standardized parts; and the introduction of the mechanized assembly line. (Chapter 14)

Formal group: a group that has been consciously created by management to accomplish a defined task that contributes to the organization's goal. (Chapter 10)

Formal organization: the documented, planned relationships established by management to coordinate the activities of different employees towards the achievement of the organizational goal. (Chapter 15)

Formal status: the collection of rights and obligations associated with a position, as distinct from the person who may occupy that position. (Chapter 11)

Formalization: the degree to which an organization has written rules, operating procedures, job descriptions, and organizational charts and uses formal, written communication. (Chapter 15)

Fragmentation (or conflict) perspective on culture: a perspective which regards culture as consisting of an incompletely shared set of elements that are loosely structured, constantly changing, and generally in conflict. (Chapter 4)

Frame of reference: a person's perceptions and interpretations of events, which involve assumptions about reality, attitudes towards what is possible, and conventions regarding correct behaviour. (Chapter 21)

Free rider: a member who obtains benefits from team membership without bearing a proportional share of the costs for generating that benefit. (Chapter 12)

Functional conflict: a form of conflict which supports organization goals and improves performance. (Chapter 21)

Functional relationship: a relationship in which staff department specialists have the authority to insist that line managers implement their instructions concerning a particular issue. (Chapter 15)

Functional structure: an organizational design that groups activities and people according to the similarities in their work, profession, expertise, goals, or resources used. (Chapter 17)

Fundamental attribution error: the tendency to emphasize explanations of the behaviour of others based on their personality or disposition, and to overlook the influence of wider social and contextual influences. (Chapter 1)

Gender: culturally specific patterns of behaviour which may be attached to either of the sexes. (Chapter 15)

Generalized other: what we think other people expect of us, in terms of our attitudes, values, beliefs, and behaviour. (Chapter 6)

Global virtual team: a team that is nationally, geographically, and culturally diverse and which communicates almost exclusively through electronic media. (Chapter 11)

Globalization: the intensification of world-wide social and business relationships which link localities in such a way that local conditions are shaped by distant events. (Chapter 2)

Goal orientation: the motivation to achieve goals – aggressive masculinity versus passive femininity. (Chapter 4)

Goal-setting theory: a process theory of motivation which argues that work motivation is influenced by goal difficulty, goal specificity, and knowledge of results. (Chapter 9)

Great man theory: a historical perspective which argues that the fate of societies and organizations is in the hands of powerful, idiosyncratic (male) individuals. (Chapter 19)

Group: two or more people, in face-to-face interaction, each aware of their group membership and interdependence, as they strive to achieve their goals. (Chapter 10)

Group cohesion: the number and strength of mutual positive attitudes between individual group members. (Chapter 12)

Group dynamics: the forces operating within groups that affect their performance and their members' satisfaction. (Chapter 10)

Group norm: an expected mode of behaviour or belief that is established either formally or informally by a group. (Chapter 12)

Group polarization: a situation in which individuals in a group begin by taking a moderate stance on an issue related to a common value and, after having discussed it, end up taking a more extreme decision than the average of members' decisions. The extremes could be more risky or more cautious. (Chapter 20)

Group process: the patterns of interactions between the members of a group. (Chapter 11)

Group sanction: a punishment or a reward given by members to others in the group in the process of enforcing group norms. (Chapter 12)

Group self-organization: the tendency of groups to form interests, develop autonomy, and establish identities. (Chapter 10)

Group socialization: the process whereby members learn the values, symbols, and expected behaviours of the group to which they belong. (Chapter 12)

Group structure: the relatively stable pattern of relationships among different group members. (Chapter 11)

Groupthink: a mode of thinking in a cohesive in-group, in which members' strivings for unanimity override their motivation to appraise realistically the alternative courses of action. (Chapter 20)

Growth need strength: a measure of the readiness and capability of an individual to respond positively to job enrichment. (Chapter 9)

Habituation: the decrease in our perceptual response to stimuli once they have become familiar. (Chapter 8)

Halo effect: a judgement based on a single striking characteristic, such as an aspect of dress, speech, posture, or nationality. (Chapter 8)

Hawthorne effect: the tendency of people being observed to behave differently than they otherwise would. (Chapter 10)

Heuristic: a simple and approximate rule, guiding procedures, shortcuts, or strategies that are used to solve problems. (Chapter 20)

Hierarchy: the number of levels of authority to be found in an organization. (Chapter 15)

High context culture: a culture whose members rely heavily on a range of social and non-verbal clues when communicating with others and interpreting their messages. (Chapter 7)

High performance work system: a form of organization that operates at levels of excellence far beyond those of comparable systems. (Chapter 9)

Hollow organization structure: an organizational design based on outsourcing an organization's non-core processes which are then supplied to it by specialist, external providers. (Chapter 17)

Human relations approach: a school of management thought which emphasizes the importance of social processes at work. (Chapter 10)

Human resource management: the function responsible for establishing integrated personnel policies to support organization strategy. (Chapter 1)

Hygiene factors: aspects of work which remove dissatisfaction, but do not contribute to motivation and performance, including pay, company policy, supervision, status, security, and physical working conditions. (Chapter 9)

Identification: the incorporation of another's thoughts, feelings, and actions into one's self-esteem, thereby transforming oneself. (Chapter 14)

Idiographic: an approach to the study of personality emphasizing the uniqueness of the individual, rejecting the assumption that we can all be measured on the same dimensions. (Chapter 6)

Impression management: the processes through which we control the image or impression that others have of us. (Chapter 7)

Influence: the process of affecting someone else's attitudes, beliefs, or behaviours, without using coercion or formal position, such that the other person believes that they are acting in their own best interests. (Chapter 22)

Informal group: a collection of individuals who become a group when they develop interdependencies, influence one another's behaviour, and contribute to mutual need satisfaction. (Chapter 10)

Informal organization: the undocumented relationships that arise spontaneously between employees as individuals interact with one another to meet their own psychological and physical needs. (Chapter 15)

Initiating structure: a pattern of leadership behaviour that emphasizes performance of the work in hand and the achievement of product and service goals. (Chapter 19)

Initiative and incentive system: a form of job design in which management gives workers a task to perform and provides them with the financial incentive to complete it, but then leaves them to use their own initiative as to how they will perform it. (Chapter 14)

Initiative decay: an organizational phenomenon where the benefits from a change initiative 'evaporate', when attention shifts to focus on other issues and priorities. (Chapter 18)

Initiative fatigue: the personal exhaustion and apathy resulting from the experience of too much organizational change. (Chapter 18)

Inner work life theory: a process theory of motivation which argues that our behaviour and performance at work are influenced by the interplay of our perceptions, emotions, and motives. (Chapter 9)

Innovation: the adoption of any device, system, process, programme, product, or service new to a particular organization. (Chapter 18)

Innovative decisions: decisions which address novel problems, lack pre-specified courses of action, and are made by senior managers. (Chapter 20)

Instrumental orientation: an attitude that sees work as an instrument to the fulfilment of other life goals. (Chapter 14)

Instrumentality: the perceived probability that good performance will lead to valued rewards; measured on a scale from 0 (no chance) to 1 (certainty). (Chapter 9)

Integration: the required level to which units in an organization are linked together, and their respective degree of independence. (Chapter 16)

Integration (or unitary) perspective on culture: a perspective which regards culture as monolithic, characterized by consistency, organization-wide consensus, and clarity. (Chapter 4)

Integrative bargaining: a negotiation strategy that seeks to increase the total amount of resources, creating a win–win situation between the parties. (Chapter 21)

Intensive technology: technology that is applied to tasks that are performed in no predetermined order. (Chapter 16)

Interaction Process Analysis: a technique used to categorize the content of speech. (Chapter 11)

Interactionist frame of reference on conflict: a perspective that views conflict as a positive and necessary force within organizations that is essential for their effective performance. (Chapter 21)

Interactions: in Homans's theory, the two-way communications between group members. (Chapter 10)

Intermittent reinforcement: a procedure in which a reward is provided only occasionally following correct responses, and not for every correct response. (Chapter 5)

Internal integration: the process through which employees adjust to each other, work together, and perceive themselves as a collective entity. (Chapter 4)

Internal work team differentiation: the degree to which a team's members possess different skills and knowledge that contributes towards the achievement of the team's objective. (Chapter 13)

Intrinsic feedback: information which comes from within, from the muscles, joints, skin, and other mechanisms such as that which controls balance. (Chapter 5)

Intrinsic rewards: valued outcomes or benefits which come from the individual, such as feelings of satisfaction, competence, self-esteem, and accomplishment. (Chapter 9)

Introjection: a formerly external regulation or value that has been 'taken in' and is now enforced through internal pressures such as guilt, anxiety, or related self-esteem dynamics. (Chapter 14)

Japanese teamworking: use of scientific management principles of minimum manning, multi-tasking, multi-machine operation, pre-defined work operations, repetitive short-cycle work, powerful first line supervisors, and a conventional managerial hierarchy. (Chapter 13)

Job definition: determining the task requirements of each job in an organization. It is the first decision in the process of organizing. (Chapter 15)

Job description: a summary statement of what an individual should do on the job. (Chapter 15)

Job diagnostic survey: a questionnaire which assesses the degree of skill variety, task identity, task significance, autonomy, and feedback in jobs. (Chapter 9)

Job enlargement: a work design method in which tasks are combined to widen the scope of a job. (Chapter 3)

Job enrichment: a technique for broadening the experience of work to enhance employee need satisfaction and to improve motivation and performance. (Chapter 9)

Job rotation: a work design method in which employees are switched from task to task at regular intervals. (Chapter 3)

Joint venture: an arrangement in which two or more companies remain independent, but establish a new organization that they jointly own and manage. (Chapter 17)

Just-in-time system: a system of managing inventory (stock) in which items are delivered when they are needed in the production process, instead of being stored by the manufacturer. (Chapter 13)

Kaizen: Japanese term for 'continuous improvement' which refers to an element within total quality management in which employees are given responsibility, within limits, to suggest incremental changes to their work practices. (Chapter 13)

Knowledge management: the conversion of individual tacit knowledge into explicit knowledge so that it can be shared with others in the organization. (Chapter 5)

Leadership: the process of influencing the activities of an organized group in its efforts toward goal-setting and goal achievement. (Chapter 19)

Lean production: a manufacturing method which combines machine-pacing, work standardization, just-in-time materials flow, continuous improvement, problem-solving teams, and powerful supervision. (Chapter 3)

Learning: the process of acquiring knowledge through experience which leads to a lasting change in behaviour. (Chapter 5)

Learning organization: an organizational form that enables individual learning to create valued outcomes, such as innovation, efficiency, environmental alignment, and competitive advantage. (Chapter 5)

Legitimate authority: authority based on formal, written rules that have the force of law, e.g. the authority of presidents, managers, or lecturers. (Chapter 16)

Legitimate power: the ability to exert influence based on the other's belief that the influencer has authority to issue orders which they in turn have an obligation to accept. (Chapter 22)

Line employees: workers who are directly responsible for manufacturing goods or providing a service. (Chapter 15)

Line relationship: a relationship in which a manager has the authority to direct the activities of those in positions below them on the same line. (Chapter 15)

Locus of control: an individual's generalized belief about internal control (self-control) versus external control (control by the situation or by others). (Chapter 22)

Long-linked technology: technology that is applied to a series of programmed tasks performed in a predetermined order. (Chapter 16)

Low context culture: a culture whose members focus on the written and spoken word when communicating with others and interpreting their messages. (Chapter 7)

McDonaldization: a form of work design aimed at achieving efficiency, calculability, predictability, and control through non-human technology, to enhance organizational objectives by limiting employee discretion and creativity. (Chapter 14)

Machiavellianism: a personality trait or style of behaviour towards others which is characterized by (1) the use of guile and deceit in interpersonal relations, (2) a cynical view of the nature of other people, and (3) a lack of concern with conventional morality. (Chapter 22)

Maintenance activity: in Interaction Process Analysis, an oral input, made by a group member, that reduces conflict, maximizes cohesion, and maintains relationships within a group. (Chapter 11)

Managerial activities: activities performed by managers that support the operation of every organization and need to be performed to ensure its success. (Chapter 16)

Managerial enactment: the active modification of a perceived and selected part of an organization's environment by its managers. (Chapter 16)

Managerial roles: behaviours or tasks that a manager is expected to perform because of the position that he or she holds within a group or organization. (Chapter 16)

Mass production: a form of work design that includes mechanical pacing of work, no choice of tools or methods, repetitiveness, minute subdivision of product, minimum skill requirements, and surface mental attention. (Chapter 14)

Material technology: tools, machinery, and equipment that can be seen, touched, and heard. (Chapter 3)

Matrix structure: an organizational design that combines two different types of structure resulting in an employee having two reporting relationships simultaneously. (Chapter 17)

Maximizing: a decision-making approach where all alternatives are compared and evaluated in order to find the best solution to a problem. (Chapter 20)

Mechanistic organization structure: an organization structure that possesses a high degree of task specialization, many rules, tight specification of individual responsibility and authority, and centralized decision-making. (Chapter 4)

Mediating technology: technology that links independent but standardized tasks. (Chapter 16)

Metamorphosis stage of socialization: the period in which the new employee adjusts to their organization's values, attitudes, motives, norms, and required behaviours. (Chapter 4)

Modular organization structure: an organizational design that involves assembling product chunks (modules) provided by internal divisions and external providers. (Chapter 17)

Motivating potential score: an indicator of how motivating a job is likely to be for an individual, considering skill variety, task identity, task significance, autonomy, and feedback. (Chapter 9)

Motivation: the cognitive decision-making process through which goal-directed behaviour is initiated, energized, directed, and maintained. (Chapter 9)

Motivator factors: aspects of work which lead to high levels of satisfaction, motivation, and performance, including achievement, recognition, responsibility, advancement, growth, and the work itself. (Chapter 9)

Motive: a socially acquired need activated by a desire for fulfilment. (Chapter 9)

Need for achievement: (*n*Ach) a concern with meeting standards of excellence, the desire to be successful in competition, and the motivation to excel. (Chapter 6)

Need for power: (*n*Pow) the desire to make an impact on others, change people or events, and make a difference in life. (Chapter 22)

Negative reinforcement: the attempt to encourage desirable behaviours by withdrawing negative consequences when the desired behaviour occurs. (Chapter 5)

New leader: an inspirational visionary, concerned with building a shared sense of purpose and mission, creating a culture in which everyone is aligned with the organization's goals and is skilled and empowered to achieve them. (Chapter 19)

Noise: factors outside the communication process which interfere with or distract attention from the transmission and reception of the intended meaning. (Chapter 7)

Nomothetic: an approach to the study of personality emphasizing the identification of traits, and the systematic relationships between different aspects of personality. (Chapter 6)

Nonstandard work: employment that does not involve a fixed schedule at the same physical location for an extended time. (Chapter 3)

Non-verbal communication: the process of coding meaning through behaviours such as facial expressions, limb gestures, and body postures. (Chapter 7)

Obedience: a situation in which an individual changes their behaviour in response to direct command from another. (Chapter 12)

Offshoring: contracting with external providers in a different country to supply the organization with the processes and products that were previously supplied internally. (Chapter 17)

Open system: a system that interacts, in a purposive way, with its external environment in order to survive. (Chapter 3)

Operational definition: the method used to measure the incidence of a variable in practice. (Chapter 1)

Operational innovation: inventing entirely new ways of doing work. (Chapter 18)

Organic organization structure: an organization structure that possesses little task specialization, few rules, and a high degree of individual responsibility and authority, and in which decision-making is delegated. (Chapter 4)

Organization: a social arrangement for achieving controlled performance in pursuit of collective goals. (Chapter 1)

Organization chart: a diagram outlining the positions in an organization's structure and the relationships between them. (Chapter 15)

Organization design: senior management's process of choosing and implementing a structural configuration through which their organization seeks to accomplish their goals. (Chapter 16)

Organization development: the systematic use of applied behavioural science principles and practices to increase individual and organizational effectiveness. (Chapter 18)

Organization politics: the ability to understand others at work, and to use that knowledge to influence others to act in ways that enhance one's personal and/or organizational objectives. (Chapter 22)

Organization structure: the formal system of task and reporting relationships that control, coordinate, and motivate employees to work together to achieve organizational goals. (Chapter 15)

Organizational architecture: the framework of linked internal and external elements that an organization creates and uses to achieve the goals specified in its vision statement. (Chapter 17)

Organizational behaviour: the study of the structure and management of organizations, their environments, and the actions and interactions of their individual members and groups. (Chapter 1)

Organizational choice: the argument that work design is not determined by technology, and that the technical system does not determine the social system. (Chapter 3)

Organizational culture: the shared values, beliefs, and norms which influence the way employees think, feel, and act towards others inside and outside the organization. (Chapter 4)

Organizational dilemma: how to reconcile inconsistency between individual needs and aspirations on the one hand, and the collective purpose of the organization on the other. (Chapter 1)

Organizational effectiveness: a multi-dimensional concept defined differently by different stakeholders, including a range of quantitative and qualitative measures. (Chapter 1)

Organizational misbehaviour: anything that workers do in the workplace which management considers they should not do. (Chapter 21)

Organizational socialization: the process through which an employee's pattern of behaviour, values, attitudes, and motives is influenced to conform to that of the organization. (Chapter 4)

Organizational values: the accumulated beliefs held about how work should be done and situations dealt with, that guide employee behaviour. (Chapter 4)

Outsourcing: contracting with external providers to supply the organization with the processes and products that were previously supplied internally. (Chapter 17)

Pavlovian conditioning: a technique for associating an established response or behaviour with a new stimulus. (Chapter 5)

Perception: the dynamic psychological process responsible for attending to, organizing, and interpreting sensory data. (Chapter 8)

Perceptual filters: individual characteristics, predispositions, and preoccupations that interfere with the effective transmission and receipt of messages. (Chapter 7)

Perceptual organization: the process through which incoming stimuli are organized or patterned in systematic and meaningful ways. (Chapter 8)

Perceptual set: an individual's predisposition to respond to people and events in a particular manner. (Chapter 8)

Perceptual threshold: a boundary point, either side of which our senses respectively will or will not be able to detect stimuli such as sound, light, or touch. (Chapter 8)

Perceptual world: the individual's personal internal image, map, or picture of their social, physical, and organizational environment. (Chapter 8)

Peripheral norms: socially defined standards relating to behaviour and beliefs that are important but not crucial to a group's objective and survival. (Chapter 12)

Personality: the psychological qualities that influence an individual's characteristic behaviour patterns, in a stable and distinctive manner. (Chapter 6)

PESTLE analysis: an environmental scanning tool identifying Political, Economic, Social, Technological, Legal, and Ecological factors that affect an organization. (Chapter 2)

Pivotal norms: socially defined standards relating to behaviour and beliefs that are central to a group's objective and survival. (Chapter 12)

Pluralist frame of reference on conflict: a perspective that views organizations as consisting of different natural interest groups, each with their own potentially constructive, legitimate interests, which make conflict between them inevitable. (Chapter 21)

Political model of organization: a perspective that holds that organizations are made up of groups that have separate interests, goals, and values, and in which power and influence are needed in order to reach decisions. (Chapter 22)

Positive reinforcement: the attempt to encourage desirable behaviours by introducing positive consequences when the desired behaviour occurs. (Chapter 5)

Positivism: a perspective which assumes that the world can be understood in terms of causal relationships between observable and measurable variables and that these relationships can be studied objectively using controlled experiments. (Chapter 1)

Post-modern organization: a networked, information-rich, de-layered, downsized, boundaryless, high-commitment organization employing highly skilled, well-paid autonomous knowledge workers. (Chapter 2)

Power: the capacity of individuals to overcome resistance on the part of others, to exert their will, and to produce results consistent with their interests and objectives. (Chapter 11)

Power orientation: the appropriateness of power/ authority within organizations – respect versus tolerance. (Chapter 4)

Power tells: non-verbal signals that indicate to others how important and dominant someone is, or how powerful they would like us to *think* they are. (Chapter 7)

Pre-arrival stage of socialization: the period of learning in the process that occurs before an applicant joins an organization. (Chapter 4)

Predictive validity: the extent to which assessment scores accurately predict behaviours such as job performance. (Chapter 6)

Prescriptive model of decision-making: an approach that recommends how individuals should make decisions in order to achieve a desired outcome. (Chapter 20)

Process theory: an approach to explaining organizational behaviour based on narratives which show how many factors, combining and interacting over time in a particular context, are likely to produce the outcomes of interest. (Chapter 1)

Production team: a stable number of individuals who share production goals, and who perform specific roles which are supported by a set of incentives and sanctions. (Chapter 13)

Project team: a collection of employees from different work areas in an organization brought together to accomplish a specific task within a finite time. (Chapter 13)

Projective test: an assessment based on abstract or ambiguous images, which the subject is asked to interpret by projecting their feelings, preoccupations, and motives into their responses. (Chapter 6)

Provisional selves: from observing others, the experiments that we make with the ways in which we act and interact in new organizational roles. (Chapter 5)

Psychometrics: the systematic testing, measurement, and assessment of intelligence, aptitudes, and personality. (Chapter 6)

Punishment: the attempt to discourage undesirable behaviours through the application of negative consequences, or by withholding a positive consequence, following the undesirable behaviour. (Chapter 5)

Quality circle: shop-floor employees from the same department, who meet for a few hours each week to discuss ways of improving their work environment. (Chapter 13)

Quality of working life: an individual's overall assessment of satisfaction with their job, working conditions, pay, colleagues, management style, organization culture, work-life balance, and training, development, and career opportunities. (Chapter 1)

Radical frame of reference on conflict: a perspective that views organizational conflict as an inevitable consequence of exploitative employment relations in a capitalist economy. (Chapter 21)

Rational decisions: choices based on rationality, that is, on a rational mode of thinking. (Chapter 20)

Rational model of decision-making: a model which assumes that decision-making is and should be a rational process consisting of a sequence of steps that enhance the probability of attaining a desired outcome. (Chapter 20)

Rational model of organization: a perspective that holds that organizational goals are clear; objectives are defined, alternatives are identified, and choices are made on the basis of reason and logic. (Chapter 22)

Rationalism: the theory that reason is the foundation of certainty in knowledge. (Chapter 14)

Rationality: the use of scientific reasoning, empiricism, and positivism, along with the use of decision criteria that include evidence, logical argument, and reasoning. (Chapter 20)

Readiness for change: a predisposition to welcome and embrace change. (Chapter 18)

Referent power: the ability to exert influence based on the other's belief that the influencer has desirable abilities and personality traits that can and should be copied. (Chapter 22)

Reliability: the degree to which an assessment delivers consistent results when repeated. (Chapter 6)

Replacement effects: processes through which intelligent machines substitute for people at work, leading to unemployment. (Chapter 3)

Reshoring: Returning to the home country the production and provision of products and services which had previously been outsourced to overseas suppliers. (Chapter 17)

Resistance (in conflict): more or less covert behaviour that counteracts and restricts management attempts to exercise power and control in the workplace. (Chapter 21)

Resistance (in influencing): rejecting an influencing request by means of a direct refusal, making excuses, stalling, or making an argument against, indicating neither behavioural nor attitudinal change. (Chapter 22)

Resistance to change: an unwillingness or inability to accept or to discuss changes that are perceived to be damaging or threatening to the individual. (Chapter 18)

Resource dependence theory: theory that although organizations depend on their environments to survive, they seek to assert control over the resources they require, in order to minimize their dependence. (Chapter 16)

Responsibility: the obligation placed on a person who occupies a certain position in the organization structure to perform a task, function, or assignment. (Chapter 15)

Reward power: the ability to exert influence based on the other's belief that the influencer has access to valued rewards which will be dispensed in return for compliance. (Chapter 22)

Risk: a condition in which decision-makers have a high knowledge of alternatives; know the probability of these being available; can calculate the costs and know the benefits of each alternative; and have a medium predictability of outcomes. (Chapter 20)

Risk-seeking propensity: the willingness of an individual to choose options that entail risk. (Chapter 22)

Risky shift phenomenon: the tendency of a group to make decisions that are riskier than those that individual members of the group would have recommended. (Chapter 20)

Role: the pattern of behaviour expected by others from a person occupying a certain position in an organization hierarchy. (Chapter 15)

Role conflict: the simultaneous existence of two or more sets of role expectations on a focal person in such a way that compliance with one makes it difficult to comply with the others. (Chapter 15)

Role modelling: a form of socialization in which an individual learns by example, copying the behaviour of established organization members. (Chapter 4)

Routine decisions: decisions made according to established procedures and rules. (Chapter 20)

Rules: procedures or obligations explicitly stated and written down in organization manuals (Chapter 15).

Satisficing: a decision-making approach where the first solution that is judged to be 'good enough' (i.e. satisfactory and sufficient) is selected, and the search is then ended. (Chapter 20)

Scenario planning: the imaginative development of one or more likely pictures of the dimensions and characteristics of the future for an organization. (Chapter 2)

Schedule of reinforcement: the pattern and frequency of rewards contingent on the display of desirable behaviour. (Chapter 5)

Scientific management: a form of job design which stresses short, repetitive work cycles; detailed, prescribed task sequences; a separation of task conception from task execution; and motivation based on economic rewards. (Chapter 14)

Selective attention: the ability, often exercised unconsciously, to choose from the stream of sensory data, to concentrate on particular elements, and to ignore others. (Chapter 8)

Self-actualization: the desire for personal fulfilment, to develop one's potential, to become everything that one is capable of becoming. (Chapter 9)

Self-categorization: perceiving ourselves as sharing the same social identity as other category members, and behaving in ways consistent with that category stereotype. (Chapter 12)

Self-concept: the set of perceptions that we have about ourselves. (Chapter 6)

Self-esteem: that part of the self which is concerned with how we evaluate ourselves. (Chapter 12)

Self-fulfilling prophecy: a prediction that becomes true simply because someone expects it to happen. (Chapter 8)

Sentiments: in Homans's theory, the feelings, attitudes, and beliefs held by group members towards others. (Chapter 10)

Sex: the basic physiological differences between men and women. (Chapter 15)

Sexuality: the way someone is sexually attracted to another person, whether of the opposite or the same sex. (Chapter 15)

Shaping: the selective reinforcement of chosen behaviours in a manner that progressively establishes a desired behaviour pattern. (Chapter 5)

Shared frame of reference: assumptions held in common by group members, which shape their thinking, decisions, actions, and interactions, while being constantly defined and reinforced through those interactions. (Chapter 12)

Single-loop learning: the ability to use feedback to make continuous adjustments and adaptations, to maintain performance at a predetermined standard. (Chapter 5)

Situational leadership: an approach to determining the most effective style of influencing, considering the direction and support a leader gives, and the readiness of followers to perform a particular task. (Chapter 19)

Skinnerian conditioning: a technique for associating a response or a behaviour with its consequence. (Chapter 5)

Social categorization: classifying the people we meet on the basis of how similar to or different from the way that we see ourselves they are. (Chapter 12)

Social compensation: persons increasing their effort, and working harder, when in a group. (Chapter 12)

Social facilitation: the effect of the presence of other people reducing an individual's performance. (Chapter 12)

Social identity: that part of the self-concept which comes from our membership of groups and which contributes to our self-esteem. (Chapter 12)

Social influence: the process whereby attitudes and behaviours are changed by the real or implied presence of others. (Chapter 12)

Social inhibition: the effect of the presence of other people reducing an individual's performance. (Chapter 12)

Social intelligence: the ability to understand the thoughts and feelings of others and to manage our relationships accordingly. (Chapter 7)

Social loafing: the tendency for individuals to exert less effort when working as part of a group than when working alone. (Chapter 12)

Social orientation: the relative importance of the interests of the individual versus the interest of the group – individualism versus collectivism. (Chapter 4)

Social representations: the beliefs, ideas, and values about objects, people, and events that are constructed by current group members, and which are transmitted to its new members. (Chapter 12)

Social role: the set of expectations that others hold of an occupant of a position. (Chapter 11)

Social status: the relative ranking that a person holds and the value of that person as measured by a group. (Chapter 11)

Social technology: the methods which order the behaviour and relationships of people in systematic, purposive ways through structures of coordination, control, motivation, and reward. (Chapter 3)

Socialization: the process through which individual behaviours, values, attitudes, and motives are influenced to conform with those seen as desirable in a given social or organizational setting. (Chapter 5)

Sociogram: a chart which shows the liking (social attraction) relationships between individual members of a group. (Chapter 11)

Sociometry: the study of interpersonal feelings and relationships within groups. (Chapter 11)

Socio-technical system: system which has both a material technology (machinery, equipment) and a social organization (job specifications, management structure). (Chapter 3)

Span of control: the number of subordinates who report directly to a single manager or supervisor. (Chapter 15)

Staff employees: workers who occupy advisory positions and who use their specialized expertise to support the efforts of line employees. (Chapter 15)

Staff relationship: a relationship in which staff department specialists can recommend, advise, or assist line managers to implement their instructions concerning a particular issue, but have no authority to insist that they do so. (Chapter 15)

Stakeholder: anyone who is concerned with how an organization operates, and who will be affected by its decisions and actions. (Chapter 2)

Stereotype: a category or personality type to which we allocate people on the basis of their membership of some known group. (Chapter 8)

Strategic alliance: an arrangement in which two or more firms agree to cooperate to achieve specific objectives while remaining independent organizations. (Chapter 17)

Strategic choice: the ability of an organization to decide on the environment, or environments – that is, sectors, and parts of the world – in which it will operate. (Chapter 2)

Strategic choice theory: the view that an organization's environment, market, and technology are the result of senior management decisions. (Chapter 16)

Strategic contingencies theory: a perspective which argues that the most powerful individuals and departments are those best able to deal effectively with the issues that are most critical to the organization's survival and performance. (Chapter 22)

Strong culture: a culture in which an organization's core values are widely shared among employees and intensely held by them, and which guides their behaviour. (Chapter 4)

Structured task: a task with clear goals, few correct or satisfactory solutions and outcomes, few ways of performing it, and clear criteria of success. (Chapter 19)

Superleader: a leader who is able to develop leadership capacity in others, empowering them, reducing their dependence on formal leaders, and stimulating their motivation, commitment, and creativity. (Chapter 19)

Surface acting: hiding one's felt emotions and forgoing emotional expressions in response to display rules. (Chapter 21)

Surface manifestations of organizational culture: culture's most accessible forms, which are visible and audible behaviour patterns and objects. (Chapter 4)

Sustaining innovations: innovations which make improvements to existing processes, procedures, services, and products. (Chapter 18)

Synchronous communication: communication that occurs when people are online at the same time, engaging in a real-time conversation with others, somewhat similar to normal face-to-face discussions. (Chapter 11)

Synergy: the positive or negative result of the interaction of two or more components, producing an outcome that is different from the sum of the individual components. (Chapter 12)

System: something that functions through the interdependence of its component parts. (Chapter 3)

Systematic soldiering: the conscious and deliberate restriction of output by operators. (Chapter 14)

Tacit knowledge: knowledge and understanding specific to the individual, derived from experience, and difficult to codify and to communicate to others. (Chapter 5)

Task activity: in Interaction Process Analysis, an oral input, made by a group member, that contributes directly to the group's work task. (Chapter 11)

Task analysability: the degree to which standardized solutions are available to solve the problems that arise. (Chapter 16)

Task variety: the number of new and different demands that a task places on an individual or a function. (Chapter 16)

Team: a group whose members share a common goal that they pursue collaboratively and who can only succeed or fail collectively. (Chapter 13)

Team autonomy: the extent to which a team experiences freedom, independence, and discretion in decisions relating to the performance of its tasks. (Chapter 13)

Team-based structure: an organizational design that consists entirely of project-type teams that focus on processes rather than individual jobs, coordinate their activities, and work directly with partners and customers to achieve their goals. (Chapter 17)

Team performance: a measure of how well a team achieves its task, and meets the needs and expectations of management, customers, and shareholders. (Chapter 13)

Team player: a person who works willingly in cooperation with others for the benefit of the whole team. (Chapter 11)

Team role: an individual's tendency to behave in preferred ways which contribute to, and interrelate with, other members within a team. (Chapter 11)

Team viability: a measure of how well a team meets the needs and expectations of its members. (Chapter 13)

Technical complexity: the degree of predictability about, and control over, the final product permitted by the technology used. (Chapter 16)

Technological determinism: the argument that technology explains the nature of jobs, work groupings, hierarchy, skills, values, and attitudes in organizations. (Chapter 3)

Technological interdependence: the extent to which the work tasks performed in an organization by one department or team member affect the task performance of other departments or team members. Interdependence can be high or low. (Chapter 16)

Thematic apperception test: an assessment in which the individual is shown ambiguous pictures and is asked to create stories of what may be happening in them. (Chapter 6)

Time-and-motion studies: measurement and recording techniques used to make work operations more efficient. (Chapter 14)

Time orientation: the time outlook on work and life – short-term versus long-term. (Chapter 4)

Total quality management: a philosophy of management that is driven by customer needs and expectations, and which is committed to continuous improvement. (Chapter 13)

Total rewards: All aspects of work that are valued by employees, including recognition, development opportunities, organization culture, and attractive work environment, as well as pay and other financial benefits. (Chapter 9)

Traditional authority: the belief that the ruler has a natural right to rule, and that this right was either God-given or by descent, as with the authority of kings and queens. (Chapter 16)

Trait: a relatively stable quality or attribute of an individual's personality, influencing behaviour in a particular direction. (Chapter 6)

Transactional leader: a leader who treats relationships with followers in terms of an exchange, giving followers what they want in return for what the leader desires, following prescribed tasks to pursue established goals. (Chapter 19)

Transformational change: large-scale change involving radical, frame-breaking, and fundamentally new ways of thinking, solving problems, and doing business. (Chapter 18)

Transformational leader: a leader who treats relationships with followers in terms of motivation and commitment, influencing and inspiring followers to give more than mere compliance to improve organizational performance. (Chapter 19)

Triggers of change: disorganizing pressures indicating that current systems, procedures, rules, organization structures, and processes are no longer effective. (Chapter 18)

Type: a descriptive label for a distinct pattern of personality characteristics, such as introvert, extravert, or neurotic. (Chapter 6)

Type A personality: a combination of emotions and behaviours characterized by ambition, hostility, impatience, and a sense of constant time pressure. (Chapter 6)

Type B personality: a combination of emotions and behaviours characterized by relaxation, low focus on achievement, and ability to take time to enjoy leisure. (Chapter 6)

Uncertainty: a condition in which decision-makers possess low knowledge of alternatives; there is a low probability of having these available; it is to some degree possible to calculate the costs and benefits of each alternative; and there is no predictability of outcomes. (Chapter 20)

Uncertainty orientation: the emotional response to uncertainty and change – acceptance versus avoidance. (Chapter 4)

Unconditional positive regard: unqualified, non-judgemental approval and respect for the traits and behaviours of the other person (a term used in counselling). (Chapter 6)

Unitarist frame of reference on conflict: a perspective that regards management and employee interests as coinciding and which thus regards organizational conflict as harmful and to be avoided. (Chapter 21)

Unstructured task: a task with ambiguous goals, many good solutions, many ways of achieving acceptable outcomes, and vague criteria of success. (Chapter 19)

User contribution system: a method of aggregating people's contributions or behaviours in ways that are useful to others. (Chapter 17)

Valence: the perceived value or preference that an individual has for a particular outcome; can be positive, negative, or neutral. (Chapter 9)

Variance theory: an approach to explaining organizational behaviour based on universal relationships between independent and dependent variables which can be defined and measured precisely. (Chapter 1)

Vertical integration: a situation where one company buys another in order to make the latter's output its own input, thereby securing that source of supply through ownership. (Chapter 16)

Vertical loading factors: methods for enriching work and improving motivation, by removing controls and increasing accountability, and by providing feedback, new tasks, natural work units, special assignments, and additional authority. (Chapter 9)

Virtual organization structure: an organizational design that uses technology to transcend the constraints of legal structures, physical conditions, place, and time, and allows a network of separate participants to present themselves to customers as a single entity. (Chapter 17)

Virtual team: a team that relies on technology-mediated communication, while crossing boundaries of geography, time, culture, and organization, to accomplish an interdependent task. (Chapter 11)

Weak culture: a culture in which there is little agreement among employees about their organization's core values, the way things are supposed to be, or what is expected of them. (Chapter 4)

Web 2.0 technologies: internet-based information systems that allow high levels of user interaction, such as blogs, wikis (collaborative databases), and social networking. (Chapter 3)

Work specialization: the degree to which work tasks in an organization are subdivided into separate jobs. (Chapter 15)

Yerkes-Dodson law: a psychology hypothesis which states that performance increases with arousal, until we become overwhelmed, after which performance falls. (Chapter 18)

Name Index

Subject Index